# Festival Fever

**The Ultimate Guide to Musical Celebrations in the Northeast™**

James R. Campbell

Maine
New Hampshire
Vermont
Massachusetts
Rhode Island
Connecticut
New York
New York City

**FESTPRESS™**

GLEN RIDGE • NEW JERSEY

# FestPress™

## P. O. BOX 147 • GLEN RIDGE, NJ 07028

**Festival Fever: The Ultimate Guide to Musical Celebrations in the Northeast** (and all its derivations), and FestPress are trademarks of James R. Campbell

Printed in the United States of America
First Printing 1995

Library of Congress Catalog Card Number: 95-090446

International Standard Book Number: 0-9647309-9-5

# Dedication

To the memory of my grandparents, John and Doris Campbell. Their shared love of traveling and entertaining throughout 65 years of marriage is reborn in this book. May the circle be unbroken...

# Acknowledgement

Compiling a printed resource of this scale could not be accomplished without significant contributions from a great many individuals. It would be impossible to attempt to name them all without serious omissions; therefore, I wish to acknowledge at least the following few for their invaluable participation on my behalf:

- To the 99 festival promoters I interviewed who gave of themselves so freely and candidly. They helped make this book a much richer celebration of their efforts than if I had relied on my field observations alone.

- To my two magazine publishers, Lydia Hutchinson and Steve Spence, respectively, for taking a chance on this novice-in-print, thus greatly enhancing credibility to my interview requests.

- To my friends and family for their unstinting encouragement; and especially to my terrific parents, James and Mary, for continually volunteering whatever I seemed to need, but was afraid, or unaware, to ask for. Their generous assistance sped this book to market months ahead of when I might have been able to do so by myself.

- Most of all, to my dearest wife, Ulana, for her truly unconditional support. To make a long story short, she believed in this venture before anyone else, then strove daily to make it her own. This book simply would not have appeared without her sustaining presence. If you profit from its contents in any fashion, you can thank her equally, if not considerably more so. *Lublu muya kohana!*

Copy edited by Mary Campbell.

Research assisted by Mary Campbell, Ulana Campbell, and Mary Campbell Bates.

Interviews transcribed by Nationwide Reporting Coverage, New York, NY.

Cover designed by Melinda Beck, Brooklyn, NY.

Book design and database consulting by Bill Caemmerer for microManagement Systems, Inc., New York, NY.

Book printed by Cushing-Malloy, Inc., Ann Arbor, MI.

Front cover photographs: Yvonne Ronin of Loup Garou at the Crawfish Boil in the Mountains; unidentified dancers at the Crawfish Boil; unidentified marchers at the Lowell Folk Festival.

Back cover photographs: Tiger Okoshi of Tiger's Baku at the Boston Globe Jazz Festival; unidentified marchers at the West Indian-American Day Carnival Parade.

Photographs processed by Duggal Color Projects, Inc., New York, NY.

All photographs by James R. Campbell.

# Sources

Whenever I come across a festival listing, I create a file folder for the information. As you can imagine, these folders are so stuffed with multiple cross-references that it would be impractical, if not impossible, to list them all. Where there's been merely one source for a given festival, however, I usually make a corresponding note on my computer database. Here's a list of these particular sources:

- Bangor Daily News, Beachcomber, Berkshire Magazine, Berkshires Guide, Bluegrass Unlimited, Blues Revue Quarterly, Boston Globe, Boston Herald, Boston Magazine, Boston Phoenix, Bravo, Brazilian Times, Buffalo News, Cajun News, Calendar for New Music, Casco Bay Weekly, Catskill Country, Chariho Times, Columbia Daily Spectator, Connecticut Magazine, Country Fever, Cowboy Beat, Dance Gypsy, Democrat and Chronicle, Dirty Linen, Down Beat, El Diario, Evening Observer, Everybody's Caribbean Magazine, Face Magazine, Fairfield County Advocate, Fast Folk Musical Magazine, Folkfare, Freetime, Frogbelly Local, Good Times, Hartford Advocate, Hartford Courant, Hartford Planet, Highlight In Percussion, Hudson Valley, Irish Echo, Irish Times, Island Ear, Ithaca Times, Jazziz, JazzTimes, Jewish Week, Kittery Magazine, Latino Village Press, Love Express, Maine Sunday Telegram, Manhattan Spirit, Metroland, Mixx Magazine, Music Festival News, New England Folk Almanac, New England Jazz News, New England Performer, New Haven Advocate, New York Amsterdam News, New York Daily News, New York Newsday, New York Times, Newsday, NYPress, Old Rhode Island, Old Time Herald, Providence Sunday Journal, Rhythm Music Monthly, Rolling Stone, Routes, Score, Sing Out!, Singing News, South East Connecticut Guide, Southern Maine Coastal Beacon, Springfield Advocate, Springfield Sunday Republican, Syracuse New Times, The Newpaper, The Sextant, The Source, The Weekly, Times Herald-Record, Traditional MusicLine, Upstate New York Guide, Valley Advocate, Vermont News Guide, Vermont Times, Village Voice, Wall Street Journal, Woodstock Times, York County Coast Star.

Many thanks...

# Contents

*Jason and Neon Frontier, CMJ Music Marathon.*

# Introduction

1. **Festival Fever** — Its Unique "Breadth-Plus-Depth" Overload .....1

2. "What Is a Festival?" — Towards a First-Time Industry Definition .....3

3. Notes on Festival Attendance and Equipment .....6

# Maine

1. Sugarloaf's Cool Runnings: .....11

    SUGARLOAF SKI-A-PALOOZA/COLLEGE WEEKS; **SUGARLOAF REGGAE SKI BASH** (Early April); SUGARLOAF MOUNTAIN BLUES FESTIVAL; SUGARLOAF COUNTRY MUSIC FESTIVAL.

2. Downeast's Coastal Roots, July: .....14

    BLUE HILL POPS; **WERU 89.9 FM FULL CIRCLE SUMMER FAIR** (Early July); DOWNEAST DULCIMER AND FOLK HARP FESTIVAL; SCHOONER DAYS; NATIVE AMERICAN FESTIVAL; NORTH ATLANTIC BLUES FESTIVAL; **LEFT BANK CAFE COUNTRY BLUES FESTIVAL** (Middle July).

3. Portland's Variety Party: .....19

    OLD PORT FESTIVAL; **DEERING OAKS FAMILY FESTIVAL** (Middle July to Late July).

4. Thomas Point Beach's Acoustic Roots, August: .....22

    **MAINE ARTS FESTIVAL** (Early August); MAINE HIGHLAND GAMES; THOMAS POINT BEACH BLUEGRASS FESTIVAL; NEW YEAR'S EVE PORTLAND.

5. Maine Festival Listings .....25

# New Hampshire

1. Portsmouth's Waterfront Jazz: .....49

    MARKET SQUARE DAY; **PORTSMOUTH JAZZ FESTIVAL** (Late June); WHITE MOUNTAINS JAZZ AND BLUES CRAFTSFESTIVAL; FIRST NIGHT PORTSMOUTH.

2. New Hampshire Festival Listings .....53

# Vermont

1. Burlington's Jazz Blast: .....67

    DISCOVER JAZZ FESTIVAL (Early June to Middle June); PICO MOUNTAIN JAZZ FESTIVAL.

2. Vermont's Funky Freebies: .....70

    BEN AND JERRY'S ONE WORLD, ONE HEART FESTIVAL (Late June); VERMONT REGGAE FESTIVAL.

3. Burlington's Folk Traditions: .....74

    UNIVERSITY OF VERMONT LANE SERIES/49TH PARALLEL MUSIC FESTIVAL; FAMILIES OUTDOOR FESTIVAL; CHAMPLAIN VALLEY FESTIVAL (Early August); FIRST NIGHT BURLINGTON.

4. Vermont Festival Listings .....79

# Massachusetts

1. Harper's Blues Ferry: .....95

    BOSTON BLUES FESTIVAL (Late January to Late February); BATTLE OF THE BLUES BANDS (Late June to Early July); CITY OF PRESIDENTS BLUES FESTIVAL.

2. Songstreet's Singer-Songwriters: .....98

    SONGSTREET FESTIVAL OF FUNNY SONGWRITERS; SONGSTREET FOLK AND BLUEGRASS FESTIVAL; HARVARD WINTER FOLK FESTIVAL (Early March); SONGSTREET FESTIVAL OF WOMEN SONGWRITERS; SONGSTREET FOLK-ROCK FESTIVALS; SONGSTREET CAJUN-BLUEGRASS FESTIVAL.

3. Boston's Radio Rocks, I: .....101

    BOSTON PHOENIX/WFNX BEST MUSIC POLL CELEBRATION (Late March); WFNX BIRTHDAY PARTY.

4. Northampton's College Rock: .....104

    LOUD MUSIC FESTIVAL (Early April).

5. New England's Folk Traditions: .....106

    RALPH PAGE LEGACY WEEKEND; NEW ENGLAND FOLK FESTIVAL (Late April); STRATHSPEY AND REEL SOCIETY OF NEW HAMPSHIRE'S FALL CONCERT GALA.

6. Boston's Radio Rocks, II: .....109

    WBCN ROCK 'N' ROLL RUMBLE (Early May to Late May); WBCN ROCK OF BOSTON CONCERT.

7. Boston's Radio Rocks, III: .....112

KISS CONCERT (Early June).

8. Boston's Jazz Edge: .....117

BOSTON GLOBE JAZZ FESTIVAL (Middle June).

9. Boston's Celtic Galas: .....121

BOSTON SCOTTISH FIDDLE RALLY; IRISH CULTURAL CENTER'S FESTIVAL (Middle June); CELTIC FESTIVAL AT THE HATCH SHELL; GAELIC ROOTS: THE MUSIC, SONG AND DANCE OF IRELAND (Early October).

10. Northampton's College World-Beat: .....124

BRIGHT MOMENTS FESTIVAL (Middle July to Late July).

11a. Lowell's Ethnic Folk Traditions: .....126

PRAISE AND HARMONY; LATIN AMERICAN FESTIVAL; BOARDING HOUSE PARK CONCERT SERIES KICKOFF; LOWELL FOLK FESTIVAL (Late July); SUMMERTIME BLUES WEEKEND; JOHNSTOWN FOLK FESTIVAL; BANJO AND FIDDLE CONTESTS; LOWELL FAMILY FIRST NIGHT.

11b. Booking the LOWELL FOLK FESTIVAL:
A Conversation With Joe Wilson .....130

12. Tanglewood's Classical Alternatives: .....133

TANGLEWOOD FESTIVAL OF CONTEMPORARY MUSIC; TANGLEWOOD JAZZ FESTIVAL (Early September).

13. Cambridge's Variety Party: .....136

CAMBRIDGE INTERNATIONAL FAIR; CAMBRIDGE RIVER FESTIVAL (Middle September).

14. Boston's Arts Extravaganza, New Year's Eve: .....139

FIRST NIGHT BOSTON (Late December).

15. Massachusetts Festival Listings .....143

# Rhode Island

1.  Escoheag's Reggae Ranch:                              .....199

    NEW ENGLAND REGGAE FESTIVAL (Late July).

2.  Newport's Classic Revivals:                           .....201

    NEWPORT RHYTHM AND BLUES FESTIVAL; BEN AND JERRY'S NEWPORT FOLK
    FESTIVAL (Early August); JVC JAZZ FESTIVAL/NEWPORT.

3.  Escoheag's Mardi Gras Ranch:                          .....206

    CAJUN AND ZYDECO MARDI GRAS BALL; BIG EASY BASH; CAJUN AND
    BLUEGRASS MUSIC-DANCE-FOOD FESTIVAL (Early September).

4.  Providence's Variety Party:                           .....210

    EARTH DAY CONCERT; RHODE ISLAND INDIAN COUNCIL POW-WOW: "TEMPLE
    TO MUSIC"; PROVIDENCE WATERFRONT FESTIVAL/WATERFRONT JAZZ FESTIVAL
    (Middle September).

5.  Rhode Island Festival Listings                        .....213

# Connecticut

1.  Hartford's Local Showcases:                           .....227

    HARTFORD ADVOCATE'S BEST OF THE LOCAL MUSIC BASH (Late May);
    HONEY, HIDE THE BANJO, IT'S THE FOLK NEXT DOOR.

2.  Strawberry Park's Bluegrass:                          .....231

    STRAWBERRY PARK BLUEGRASS FESTIVAL (Early June); STRAWBERRY PARK
    COUNTRY WESTERN JAMBOREE.

3.  Mystic Seaport's Chanteymen:                          .....234

    LOBSTERFEST; SEA MUSIC FESTIVAL (Middle June); TASTE OF HISTORY;
    CHOWDERFEST; COMMUNITY CAROL SING.

4.  Woodstock's Roots-Beat:                               .....237

    BLUEGRASS FESTIVAL; DIFFERENT TASTES OUTDOOR CRAWFISH AND ALLIGATOR
    FEAST; MAD MURPHY'S CAJUN, ZYDECO MUSIC AND ART FAIR (Middle
    June); GREAT AMERICAN BLUES FESTIVAL; EARTH JAM.

5.  Connecticut's Country Radio Fair:                     .....241

    GREAT AMERICAN MUSIC FEST (Late June); EASTERN STATES EXPOSITION —
    THE BIG E!.

6.   Norwalk's Jazz Picnic:                                          .....243

     AFTERNOON OF JAZZ (Late June).

7.   Woodbury's World-Beat:                                          .....246

     ALTERNATIVE SKATEBOARD FESTIVAL; REGGAE FESTIVAL; WORLD MUSIC
     FESTIVAL (Middle July); SOUTHERN FRIED FESTIVAL.

8.   Hartland's Singer-Songwriters:                                  .....249

     HARTLAND FOLK FESTIVAL (Middle July).

9.   Hartford's Jazz, I:                                             .....252

     RAW JAZZ FESTIVAL (Late July).

10.  Hartford's Jazz, II:                                            .....255

     GREATER HARTFORD FESTIVAL OF JAZZ FUNDRAISER; WEST INDIAN
     INDEPENDENCE CELEBRATION WEEK/HARTFORD MEGA! WEEKEND; GREATER
     HARTFORD FESTIVAL OF JAZZ/HARTFORD MEGA! WEEKEND (Late July to
     Early August).

11.  Connecticut Festival Listings                                   .....259

# New York

1.   Artist Sightings, I — Oscar Brand:                              .....295

     NASSAU COMMUNITY COLLEGE FOLK FESTIVAL (Late March);
     INTERNATIONAL JEWISH ARTS FESTIVAL OF LONG ISLAND.

2.   Fox Hollow's Folk Traditions:                                   .....298

     OLD SONGS SAMPLER CONCERT; GOTTAGETGON FOLK FESTIVAL (Late May);
     OLD SONGS FESTIVAL OF TRADITIONAL MUSIC AND DANCE (Late June); FOX
     HOLLOW REUNION FOLK CONCERT.

3.   Stanfordville's Fais-Do-Do:                                     .....303

     STANFORDVILLE MUSIC AND DANCE FESTIVAL (Late May and Late August);
     WOODSTOCK/NEW PALTZ ARTS AND CRAFTS FAIR.

4a.  Syracuse's Jazz and Blues Shuttles:                             .....306

     SYRACUSE AREA MUSIC AWARDS [SAMMIES]; SYRACUSE JAZZ FEST (Middle
     June); NEW YORK STATE BUDWEISER BLUES FESTIVAL (Late July).

4b.  Promoting the SYRACUSE JAZZ FEST:
     A Conversation with Frank Malfitano                             .....313

# New York

5.  Artist Sightings, II — Pete Seeger:                    .....317

    PEOPLE'S MUSIC NETWORK; SHADFEST; STRAWBERRY FESTIVAL; **CLEARWATER'S GREAT HUDSON RIVER REVIVAL** (Middle June); NEW YORK CITY CLEARWATER FESTIVAL; CLEARWATER FESTIVAL; HARVEST MOON FESTIVAL; CLEARWATER PUMPKIN SAIL.

6.  Huntington's Variety Party:                            ....324

    FOLK MUSIC SOCIETY OF HUNTINGTON MEMBERS CONCERT; **SUMMERSCAPE SUMMER ARTS FESTIVAL** (Late June to Late August); FOLK MUSIC SOCIETY OF HUNTINGTON SUMMER FESTIVAL.

7.  Chautauqua's Variety Party:                            .....327

    CHAUTAUQUA SUMMER MUSIC PROGRAM (Late June to Late August).

8.  Saratoga's Jazz Bash:                                  .....331

    NEWPORT JAZZ FESTIVAL/SARATOGA (Early July).

9.  Ithaca's New Old-Time Scene, I:                        .....335

    WILLIAM SMITH AND HOBART COLLEGES FOLK FEST; ITHACA FESTIVAL; **GREAT BLUE HERON MUSIC FESTIVAL** (Early July); **FINGERLAKES GRASSROOTS FESTIVAL OF MUSIC AND DANCE** (Middle July to Late July).

10. Catskills' Irish Traditions:                           .....343

    PINES SCOTTISH WEEKENDS; PINES NUMBER ONE IRISH WEEKENDS; **FLEADH: OLD MUSIC OF IRELAND FESTIVAL** (Early July); GALA ALL-STAR IRISH CRUISE; LEEDS IRISH FESTIVAL; IRISH MUSIC PARTY OF THE YEAR.

11. Ithaca's New Old-Time Scene, II:                       .....347

    LILAC FESTIVAL; **CORN HILL FESTIVAL/FIDDLER'S FAIR** (Early July to Middle July); BILLY LABEEF'S BASTILLE DAY, BARBEQUE, AND ROCK AND ROLL RODEO.

12. Hillsdale's Acoustic Roots Spectaculars:               .....351

    **WINTERHAWK BLUEGRASS FAMILY FESTIVAL** (Middle July); **FALCON RIDGE FOLK FESTIVAL** (Late July).

13. Hunter Mountain's Country Marathon:                    .....359

    AMERICAN PATRIOT FESTIVAL; **COUNTRY MUSIC FESTIVALS** (Middle July to Late July and Early August to Middle August); ROCKSTALGIA; INTERNATIONAL CELTIC FESTIVAL; MOUNTAIN EAGLE INDIAN FESTIVAL; CELTIC FAIR.

14. Gold Coast Jazz:                                       .....364

    RIVERHEAD JAZZ FESTIVAL; **LONG ISLAND JAZZ FESTIVAL** (Late July); ISLIP JAZZ FESTIVAL (Late August).

15. Ithaca's New Old-Time Scene, III: .....371

ROONEY MOUNTAIN BLUEGRASS FESTIVAL (Late July to Early August); MIDDLESEX MUSIC FESTIVAL.

16. Artist Sightings, III — Paul Simon: .....374

GREAT MIRACLE PRAYER FESTIVAL; RAINFOREST BENEFIT CONCERT; BACK AT THE RANCH FESTIVAL (Early August).

17. Western New York's End-of-Summer, I — Modern Christian: .....380

PRAISE; KINGDOM BOUND (Late August); NIAGARA: THE STUDENT AND ADULT LEADERSHIP CONFERENCE ON EVANGELISM.

18. Western New York's End-of-Summer, II — Acoustic Roots: .....385

BUFFALO IRISH FESTIVAL (Late August); BLUEGRASS FESTIVAL; TURTLE HILL MUSIC FESTIVAL; MECK MUSIC FESTIVAL; FINGERLAKES DIXIELAND JAZZ FESTIVAL; BUFFALO BEER FEST.

19. Schenectady's Blues Variety Party: .....388

BLUES BAR-B-QUE; PARK JAM; LAKE GEORGE JAZZ WEEKEND; TAKIN' IT TO THE STREETS: THE ELECTRIC CITY MUSIC CELEBRATION (Middle September).

20. New York Festival Listings .....393

# New York City

1. Greenwich Village's Singer-Songwriters: .....483

FAST FOLK REVUE (Late January); FURNALD FOLK FEST; GREENWICH VILLAGE FOLK FESTIVAL (Early October); SHELTER: THE NEW YORK SINGER-SONGWRITER FESTIVAL.

2. Manhattan's New Music Scene: .....491

BANG ON A CAN FESTIVAL (Middle March to Early May); ROULETTE CONCERT SERIES/LE SALON ROULETTE; EXPERIMENTAL INTERMEDIA FESTIVAL WITH NO FANCY NAME; ROULETTE CONCERT SERIES/MIXOLOGY FESTIVAL (Late April to Early May); AMERICAN FESTIVAL OF MICROTONAL MUSIC (Middle September to Early November); EXPERIMENTAL INTERMEDIA FOUR COUNTRY FESTIVAL.

3a. Mahattan's Cabaret Scene: .....499

BACK STAGE BISTRO AWARDS; HEARTS AND VOICES WINTER BENEFIT SERIES (Middle March to Late April); MANHATTAN ASSOCIATION OF CABARETS AND CLUBS AWARDS; HEARTS AND VOICES IN CONCERT; GRAND NIGHTS FOR SINGING; CABARET SYMPOSIUM; CABARET CONVENTION (Middle October to Late October); TEDDYCARE.

# New York City

3b.  Advising CABARET CONVENTION Artists:
A Conversation with Donald Smith ..... 508

4.  Symphony Space's Variety Party: ..... 512

GOSPEL CELEBRATION; MARDI GRAS CELEBRATION; WALL TO WALL (Late March); NEW YORK WINTER BLUES FESTIVAL (Late March); WORLD OF PERCUSSION; CAJUN/ZYDECO JAMBOREE AND HALLOWEEN DANCE.

5.  College Rock Get-Togethers: ..... 520

INDEPENDENT MUSIC FEST (Late March to Early April); NEW MUSIC NIGHTS/NEW MUSIC SEMINAR (Middle July to Late July); CMJ MUSIC MARATHON AND MUSICFEST (Early September); WDRE MODERN ROCK FEST; WDRE ACOUSTIC CHRISTMAS.

6.  Classic Acappella: ..... 527

UNITED IN GROUP HARMONY BLACK HISTORY MONTH CELEBRATION; RONNIE I.'S HARMONY HAPPENING WEEKEND; HARMONY SWEEPSTAKES A CAPPELLA FESTIVAL/N. Y. REGIONAL (Early April); UNITED IN GROUP HARMONY HALL OF FAME AWARDS CEREMONY (Early April); RICHARD NADER'S ROCK AND ROLL REVIVAL SPECTACULARS; DICK FOX'S DOO-WOPP EXTRAVAGANZAS.

7.  Downtown Jazz, I: ..... 533

BROOKLYN BEAT MEETS THE BLACK ROCK COALITION; P. S. 122 NEW MUSIC SERIES (Early April); FIRE WALL TOTAL ARTS FESTIVAL (Middle June to Late June); JIMI HENDRIX BIRTHDAY PARTY.

8.  Jazz Get-Togethers: ..... 537

INTERNATIONAL ASSOCIATION OF JAZZ EDUCATORS CONVENTION; NEW YORK BRASS CONFERENCE FOR SCHOLARSHIPS (Early April); JAZZTIMES CONVENTION (Middle November).

9.  Gospel Choir Get-Togethers: ..... 544

MCDONALD'S GOSPELFEST (Early April to Middle June); QUEENS COLLEGE CULTURAL HERITAGE "GREAT GOSPEL" COMPETITION; GOSPEL MUSIC WORKSHOP OF AMERICA/NEW YORK STATE CHAPTER CONVENTION (Middle June); GOSPEL MUSIC WORKSHOP OF AMERICA NATIONAL CONVENTION (Early August to Middle August).

10.  Lincoln Center's Variety Party: ..... 550

CARNEGIE HALL FOLK FESTIVAL (Middle April to Late April); MIDSUMMER NIGHT SWING (Late June to Late July); SERIOUS FUN!; LINCOLN CENTER OUT-OF-DOORS/ROOTS OF AMERICAN MUSIC FESTIVAL (Early August to Late August).

11.   Manhattan's African American Scene:                          .....557

BLACK EXPO U. S. A. (Middle May); HARLEM WEEK/HARLEM DAY (Early August to Middle August); KWANZAA HOLIDAY EXPO.

12.   Manhattan's Ska Scene:                                        .....561

ROCK AGAINST RACISM CONCERT; OI!/SKAMPILATION (Late May); SKAVOOVEE; SKARMAGEDDON.

13.   Queens' Irish Scene:                                          .....565

IRISH-AMERICAN FESTIVAL AND HERITAGE FEIS (Late May); GATEWAY TO THE NATIONS POW WOW; ROCKAWAY IRISH FESTIVAL (Late July); AFRICAN CARIBBEAN LATINO AMERICAN FESTIVAL; NYC BLUEGRASS BAND AND BANJO CONTEST/GATEWAY MUSIC FESTIVAL/CITY GARDENERS' HARVEST FESTIVAL; GREAT IRISH FAIR (Early September to Middle September); ROCKAWAY MUSIC AND ARTS COUNCIL FALL FESTIVAL; GATEWAY SUKKOS FESTIVAL.

14.   New York City's Ethnic Dance Traditions:              .....570

NEW YORK ETHNIC MUSIC AND DANCE FESTIVAL (Late May); BRONX ETHNIC MUSIC AND DANCE FESTIVAL (Middle June); QUEENS FESTIVAL/NATIONS IN NEIGHBORHOODS MULTICULTURAL DANCE PARTY (Middle June); NEW YORK COUNTRY MUSIC FESTIVAL; BROOKLYN ETHNIC MUSIC AND DANCE FESTIVAL (Late October).

15.   Downtown Jazz, II:                                            .....575

JULIUS WATKINS FRENCH HORN FESTIVAL; CORNER STORE SYNDICATE NEW JAZZ FESTIVAL; SUN RA FESTIVAL; BROOKLYN WOODSTOCK (Early June); KNITTING FACTORY'S "WHAT IS JAZZ?" FESTIVAL (Middle June to Early July); KNITTING FACTORY AT MERKIN HALL.

16a.  Central Park's Variety Party:                                 .....581

CENTRAL PARK SUMMERSTAGE (Middle June to Early August).

16b.  Outreach at CENTRAL PARK SUMMERSTAGE:
      A Conversation with Erica Ruben                               .....585

17.   Bronx's Irish Traditions:                                     .....588

IRISH TRADITIONAL DANCE FESTIVAL; IRISH TRADITIONAL MUSIC AND DANCE FESTIVAL (Middle June).

18.   Brooklyn's Variety Party:                                     .....591

WELCOME BACK TO BROOKLYN; NEW YORK CITY'S GOSPEL FESTIVAL; CELEBRATE BROOKLYN PERFORMING ARTS FESTIVAL (Late June to Early September); MIDWOOD CONCERTS AT SEASIDE/MARTIN LUTHER KING JR. CONCERT SERIES (Middle July to Late August); AFRICA MONDO FESTIVAL; BROOKLYN'S SUMMER GOSPELFEST!; NEW YORK BEER FEST.

# New York City

19. Uptown Jazz: .....596

JVC Jazz Festival/Bryant Park Jazz Festival (Late June to Early July); JVC Jazz Festival/Newport; QE2: Newport Jazz Festival at Sea.

20. Brooklyn's African American Scene: .....602

African Street Festival (Late June to Early July).

21. Classic Jazz, I: .....606

Lyrics and Lyricists/The New Breed; Folksongs Plus; Lyrics and Lyricists/Boys Night Out; Jazz in July (Late July).

22. Classic Jazz, II: .....610

Classical Jazz at Lincoln Center (Early August).

23. Lower Manhattan's Carnival: .....615

Mother's Day Caribbean All-Stars Festival; Tribute to African Diaspora Women; Carnival in New York (Early August); Uprise and Shine Youth Concert; Expressions International Festival; Chango Celebration.

24. August Jazz Freebies: .....620

Westchester Community College Jazz Festival; Riverside Park Arts Festival (Early August to Late August); Charlie Parker Jazz Festival (Late August).

25. Queens' Gospel Radio Picnic: .....625

Save our Park/WWRL Radiothon; Southeast Queens' Youth Sports and Spring Festival/Juneteenth; WWRL Family Day Picnic and Festival (Middle August); Northeast Native American Association Pow Wow; WWRL Gospel Explosion.

26. Brooklyn's Carnival: .....628

New York Trini-Jam Fest; New York Reggae Summer Beach Party (Late August); West Indian-American Day Carnival and Parade (Early September).

27. Midtown Manhattan's Carnival: .....633

Concierto Del Amor; Festival De Los Soneros; Columbia Te Canta; Brazilian National Independence Day Street Festival (Early September); New York Salsa Festival (Early September); Combinacion Perfecta.

28. Queens for a Day: .....638

WIGSTOCK (Early September); VILLAGE HALLOWEEN PARADE/ALL SOULS'
HALLOWEEN BALL.

29. Manhattan's Seasonal Jazz Spirits: .....640

BEACONS IN JAZZ; ALL NITE SOUL (Early October); BENDING TOWARDS THE
LIGHT...A JAZZ NATIVITY (Early December).

30. New York City Travel Tips .....644

31. New York City Festival Listings .....649

32. Varied Sites Festival Listings .....737

# Index

I.    Festival Names in Chronogical Order .....743

II.   Festival Names in Alphabetical Order .....772

III.  Festival Cities in Alphabetical Order .....800

IV.   Festival Names by Primary Genre .....828

# Introduction

*"God bless America, yeh man,"* West Indian-American Carnival Day and Parade.

however, I've substituted a summary top-ten list for novices on how to best survive your trip.)

- **See Also** — "for further reading," as they say, annotated cross-referencing to other related festivals, either by the same promoter, of the same genre, on the same weekend, and/or occupying the same site or proximity.

Why this format? It corresponds in rough measure to how I sell my friends to attend top festivals I've already been to and loved.

For instance: I caught the generally-acknowledged world's best festival, the NEW ORLEANS JAZZ AND HERITAGE FESTIVAL, twice by the time I hit graduate school in '84. I was a bug on the subject, incessantly goading my classmates to make the roadtrip down to The Big Easy come the last weekend in April. They had a vague image of a Dixieland tourist trap, so I had to paint the picture of "JAZZFEST" in all its exotic funky soulfulness:

- Translating foreign words like "bon temps," "zydeco," and "jambalaya";

- Getting them hyped on certain local artists they'd never heard of ("Beausoleil? Isn't that what the bride tosses out to the single women?");

- Reassuring them I had ways to deal with 300,000-plus revelers charging town;

- Plotting suitable off-day diversions for less musically-inclined spouses.

All my prodding finally bore fruit in '87, and the resulting pilgrimage created half-a-dozen instant converts-for-life. Now they and scores of others bug me! "Hey, Jim, ya' goin' to 'JAZZFEST' this year?!" "...Ya' goin' to 'ESCOHEAG'?!" "...Goin' to 'WINTERHAWK'?!" "...To 'FINGERLAKES'?!" "...'JAMBOREE'?!" And so forth as I reap the fruits of being their festival pied piper. **Festival Fever** will be one-stop shopping for them and merely a formal presentation of what I've been doing informally for over a decade.

The key words here, and throughout this entire depth element, are "first-person account."

My lone published competitor in the field of festival previews gives a page or two apiece to 156 festivals nationwide of which 120 relate to classical music and opera. That leaves just 36 festivals for the entire spectrum of pop-music for the whole country! It's clear from the avalanche of grievous omissions that the author simply doesn't know the festival market for pop music nor, from the frequent mislabellings, even pop music generally. Labelling "JAZZFEST" a "Jazz/Ragtime/Dixieland" festival? Does 1992's The Neville Brothers, Hugh Masakela, Sounds of Blackness, Rickie Lee Jones, Huey Lewis, Bobby Womack, Jimmy Buffett, Al Green, Johnny Winter, Blues Traveler, Sister Carol, and a second line of high-powered Louisiana luminaries sound like a ragtime band to you? 'Didn't think so!

All it would've taken is five minutes in the flesh watching main-stage monitors blasting pigeons off poles to gain a more accurate reading.

Not knowing the totality of pop music's no crime in starting out. Hey, there were many of my 43 genres and sub-genres in which I wasn't previously conversant! However, I bought their respective CDs by the hundreds, subscribed to their magazines by the dozens, talked to their insiders, caught their concerts, and, above all, made the treks to their festivals — over 300 such visits during one frantic two-year stretch. (In fact, I've already got the field research done for my next two regional editions, Mid-Atlantic and North Central.)

Being on hand has yielded far deeper and juicier reading than my competitor's, I believe, but it's also presented you with one current, insightful and consistent point-of-view you can rely upon. No phone-ins and committees here! I don't claim to be an expert on all genres, nor that you'll always agree with my observations or opinions. But once you get a feel for where I'm coming from, you'll be able to plot your own itinerary, accordingly, and with confidence.

The bottom line is **Festival Fever**'s unique "breadth-plus-depth" overload — as informed by first person accounts — is much more than merely "Complete"; for the pop music lover, it's **The Ultimate Guide to Musical Celebrations in the Northeast**! "Yeah, you right," as they say down "N' Awlins" way.

# Festival Fever — Its Unique "Breadth-Plus-Depth" Overload

Welcome to **Festival Fever: The Ultimate Guide to Musical Celebrations in the Northeast**™! For even the festival-savvy, I predict this book — the first of eight regional editions planning to cover the country — will truly open eyes. **Festival Fever**'s the only one of its kind to bring the vast, heretofore-hidden world of pop music festivals to life. This is a hefty package, setting the standard for all who dare to follow, but I assume the true pop-music lover would not have it any other way. As the motto goes of New York City's Lone Star Cafe: "Too much ain't never enough!"

I've been having a debate with one of my friends in the ad game who insists the word, "Complete," is a more appropriate suffix for **Festival Fever**. To me, "Complete" would do well merely to describe the trailblazing breadth element of this book; that is, the festival listings found at the back of each state's respective section. (Those in the music "biz," feel free to skip right ahead to what you need.) There you encounter an astonishing 1439 events across 43 musical genres and sub-genres. By contrast, my lone published competitor in the field of multiple-genre listings presents 1,200 festivals — for all of North America! **Festival Fever** boasts superior numbers within just seven states!

Not only do you see more extensive coverage than currently listed elsewhere for many genres, but you also witness the first gathering of any kind for a host of other genres:

- Modern Rock; Classic Rock; Alternative Rock; Hard Rock; Modern Country; Alternative Country; Modern R&B; Acappella and Doo-Wop; Irish; Jewish; Native American; Modern Latin; Traditional Latin; Brazilian and South American; Reggae, Ska and Caribbean; Avant-Garde and New Music; Cabaret; Drum Corps and Marching Bands, etc.

Moreover, among the concluding indices you find summary lists where these, or any genres, predominate. You'll never have any difficulty again in following your favorite musical style wherever it might appear here all throughout the year!

So, that's **Festival Fever**'s breadth; let's talk about its depth! All these listings can be intimidating — how do you know which festivals to gamble your hard-earned weekends on? Well, to help you get started on what may well become a lifestyle, **Festival Fever** presents no fewer than 83 chapters highlighting 121 top festivals of the Northeast region, along with their 174 ancillary events, for a grand total of 295 festivals given priority coverage.

Most chapters portray their lead festival(s) in depth as follows:

- **Introduction** — background, context and characteristic strengths, including an extensive interview with its promoter;

- **Festival Preview** — my first person account of a past festival to give you an opinionated sense of what it looked like, what it felt like, and what you might expect from a visit;

- **Artist Mini-Reviews** — taking the first person account a bit further with brief reviews of representative performances (promoters may also comment);

- **Attendance Tips** — for those festivals requiring a little advance strategy, advice on how to avoid pitfalls and gain the most from your visit;

- **Travel Tips** — what other sights in the area their promoter suggests catching on off-days or evenings for a fully-rounded festival weekend (For New York City,

# "What Is a Festival?" — Towards a First-Time Industry Definition

The breadth of **Festival Fever**'s listings stems from two sources:

The first source is dogged research. After all, festivals are what economists would describe as an "imperfect market." There's no single place for this data, so you've often got to roll up your sleeves within local markets and dig. And dig, and dig. My listings originally derive from hundreds of incidental cross-references far too numerous to cite.

The second source is an expanded and, I believe, enlightened definition of what I consider to be a festival.

Again, this "imperfect market" suffers for lack of any credible criteria. The few I've seen fail inspection badly. I guess it's just not a priority for those compilers working primarily for music magazines, since few festivals draw national audiences (something **Festival Fever** seeks to start changing!) and would be prospects for national advertising. Without enough festival ad dollars flowing in, perhaps compilers don't bother with rigorous standards or pursuit, especially over those festivals that appear, at first, beyond their respective genre myopias. Instead, they likely print whatever gets sent to them. Who knows?

It takes an admitted fanatic like myself to do the excavating, plus wrestle with objective standards of what's in and what's out. I've struggled long and hard to achieve a sieve wide enough to let through all those festivals that truly belong, yet tight enough to exclude others that may call themselves "festivals" but conform more to a singular concert experience. Herewith, towards a first-time industry definition.

I consider the root festival experience to be a marriage of two basic features, "quality music in quantity." And, sifting through thousands of festival lineups, I'd break this pairing down in numerical terms as follows:

- Four acts or more per day, preferably with at least one of the acts being a national or regional headliner.

To me, that's the root festival experience — all the rest is gravy, much like location, decor, ambience, service, wine lists and such are to a restaurant's food. The best restaurants will have "all that," as the slang goes, but their food is the bottom line. Subtract from that and you've got nothing but a bar. Same deal with "four acts or more per day..." for festivals. Subtract from that and you've got nothing but a concert with festival dressing.

However, my definition doesn't end there. There are many top musical events, like New York City's JVC JAZZ FESTIVAL, which are organized more into compact concert series formats that strain to meet this "four acts or more day..." criteria. Nevertheless, every true pop-music lover knows the best ones provide the root festival experience over a given intensive period. So what to do? For these concert series formats, I propose a third basic feature, "density," and would break this feature down in numerical terms as follows:

- One act or more per day for three or more consecutive days with at least one act being a national or regional headliner.

To me, that's a worthy weekend; the root festival experience, if you will.

We're still not done, though. Part of the root festival experience depends on a fourth basic feature, "context." Three acts per day wouldn't raise a pulse in Manhattan, but might be big stuff in the far reaches of Maine. Assuming "quality" is there, those from beyond may be musically well-justified in making the trek. Therefore, I've reserved my compiler's perogative for those events which may fall short in "quantity," but otherwise provide the root festival experience for their unlikely locales.

Also, I believe all festivals must be relatively unique to their locales, or "context," and not available anytime or most everywhere else. Otherwise, what's the point in making a special trip on a particular weekend to a particular locale when most any weekend or other locales will do as nicely? To me, festivals are indigenous to their times and places.

Let's now use this sieve on those events I don't consider festivals, regardless of their titles:

- Weekly concert series.

These events generally suffer their "quantity" and "context" features for festival interest. I don't care how marvelous their settings may be, the standard twin bill of most weekly concert series is an inadequate reason to travel when you can catch comparable, if not identical, pairings in your own home market. Sorry.

However, some weekly concert series annually juice their fare in parts, such as Providence's Convergence series does with its season finale, the multi-stage PROVIDENCE WATERFRONT FESTIVAL/WATERFRONT JAZZ FESTIVAL. Accordingly, you'll find the latter in **Festival Fever**.

- Regular schedules of amphitheaters, concert halls or clubs.

These events, too, fall down on their "quantity" and "context" features for festival interest. Invariably, their lineups are built up from touring twin bills that make their way around the country and which you can catch exactly the same most everywhere else. A few venues do book uniquely in festival quantities, such as the nightly lineups of New York City's CBGBs, which run upwards of seven acts rarely seen elsewhere in similar combinations. Still, there's nothing unique in "context" from one night to the other to merit a special visit — just stop by for whichever acts you choose whenever you're in town, as with most clubs, concert halls or amphitheaters.

However, some venues will spice their regular bookings with indigenous happenings, such as Massachusetts' Great Woods Performing Arts Center does in hosting the annual KISS CONCERT extravaganza. Accordingly, you'll find the latter in **Festival Fever**.

- Packaged festival tours, plus other intermittent or erratic events.

Ditto for packaged festival tours, such as Lollapalooza, which touched down in 22 cities last year. Also, I find these events overwhelmingly to be "one-shots." Even those exceptions surviving a few years still vary wildly as to which sites and dates they'll occupy.

Now you'll find listings in **Festival Fever** that do move around from year to year, like the GOSPEL MUSIC WORKSHOP OF AMERICA NATIONAL CONVENTION does. However, this choir confab has run on the same dates like clockwork for nearly three decades. I'm not saying Lollapalooza and the rest need that kind of longevity to be included here, just enough so I can be reasonably sure of their tour bookings over, say, the expected three-year tenure of this edition prior to revision. Predictability for planning festival trips far in advance is the issue. Fair?

- Instrumental workshops or camps.

These events boast high "quality," but usually require steep all-inclusive fees for their students, which effectively exclude non-musician listeners of ordinary means like myself. Also the faculty recitals I'd be inclined to catch are normally limited to fewer than one per day, thus straining their "density" feature for festival interest.

However, there are some instrumental workshops, such as those at West Virginia's Augusta Heritage Center, which make festival-caliber events (Thursday nights in this case) open to the public at affordable prices. Accordingly, you'll find the latter in **Festival Fever**.

- Dance workshops or camps.

Ditto for dance workshops and camps that often even suffer their "quality" features for nondancing listeners, as well. However, there are some dance workshops, such as Lincoln Center's MIDSUMMER NIGHT'S SWING, which make festival caliber events (five nights a week in this case) open to the public at affordable prices. Accordingly, you'll find the latter in **Festival Fever**.

- Festivals solely featuring pedestrian local acts.

I've lost track of how many local acts I've seen at festivals go on to record label deals and begin touring nationally. Still there's a big difference between these quality aspirants and bar bands, cover bands, wedding bands, and the like. Listings will designate, to the best of my knowledge, the caliber of performers: "national," "regional" and/or "local." Those festivals presenting solely pedestrian local acts will be excluded from **Festival Fever**. What's the point in traveling to see wedding bands, unless you're planning a reception?

Sounds harsh, narrow? Quite the opposite! This is a greatly-expanded and, in my opinion, enlightened definition of festivals, one that lets a whole slew of previously-unconsidered celebrations pass through my musical sieve: arts festivals, crafts festivals, food festivals, wine festivals, balloon festivals, harvest festivals, ethnic festivals, all kinds of community festivals, fairs, benefits, awards shows, talent contests, showcases, conferences, expos — the works!

You're probably thinking, "Music at a wine festival?" Well, check out 1993's bill from the two-day MID-ATLANTIC WINE FESTIVAL in Annapolis, Maryland, for a good 20,000 imbibers: The Fabulous Thunderbirds, (the late) Danny Gatton, The Greenberry Woods, disappear fear, Deanna Bogart, Duende, The Angie Miller Band, Kiss Tyler and The Rivers, and Mama Jama. (Pop quiz: name four "locals" here who subsequently went on to record-label deals.)

Meanwhile here's 1992's lineup for Baltimore's three-day arts/crafts/food explosion, ARTSCAPE, enjoyed by one million revelers that very same weekend: Gladys Knight, Tammy Wynette, Monty Alexander, The Cris Cain Band, The Stanley Jordan Trio, C. J. Chenier and The Red-Hot Louisiana Band, The Five Blind Boys of Alabama featuring Clarence Fountain, Diane Schuur, plus 28 classy local acts across nearly as many genres. (One, The New St. George, subsequently got signed.) Not bad, huh?

**Festival Fever** boasts hundreds of these festivals which have never seen the light of day in any music magazine, nor anywhere else quote-unquote music festivals are listed! Pop music lovers, feast your eyes, your ears, and most of the rest of you, too — a brave new world awaits your weekends!

~     ~     ~

# Notes on Festival Attendance and Equipment

The beauty of festivals is that, at a minimum, you can always pick yourself and your family up and go! "Boom...just like that," as the Robert Ellis Orrall song goes. Of course, there are a few wise precautions to take for your attendance, especially if you're traveling some distance:

- Contact festivals in advance.

Extraordinary festivals may sell out their seats months ahead, though **Attendance Tips** will help alert you to any possibilities I'm aware of. Get to know your local TicketMaster outlet, just in case.

For ordinary festivals, two advance contacts are recommended: (1) one or two months ahead, especially if there are any "early-bird" purchase discounts available; (2) the week of your trip to reconfirm. This double check is helpful because, although the overwhelming majority of festivals are reliably-run, they all are subject to last minute changes or cancellations. Accordingly, **Festival Fever** is not responsible for this, or any other, inconvenience which may result from any listing found therein.

(I've only been "skunked" twice — once at the hands of an unnamed, but not un-shamed, Indianapolis blues promoter. This joker sent me a schedule five weeks ahead, yet cancelled his festival one week later without bothering to alert his mailing list. Not verifying the week prior cost me a 15-hour drive there, plus the same going back! Never again.)

Ask for a festival flyer or brochure to be mailed to you. Most such literature will answer a majority of your pertinent questions right there. Pay attention to any restrictions cited: food, alcohol, bottles, coolers, re-entry, flash cameras, recorders, children, pets, motorcycles, camping, fires, etc. You don't want to plan your whole weekend around something, only to be forced to check it at the gates.

- Secure lodgings in advance.

Ditto for lodgings. Ask the festival, the local tourism and convention bureau, or your travel agent if there are any packaged rates available. These typically offer you the best deals, as well as the surest guarantees of availability. You'll also enjoy the camaraderie of fellow festival patrons, and possibly of any festival musicians put up there for the night. Late night jams are not uncommon.

Otherwise, simply consult your travel guides. I recommend the following for getting started:

- **Mobil Travel Guides** (Prentice Hall) — useful for rating lodgings and restaurants, though prices always seem out-dated.

- **AAA Regional Tourbooks** (American Automobile Association) — a cross-check of the above with more current prices. (Their modest yearly membership also gains you lodging discounts, a free, reliable and honest 24-hour towing service — quite handy for those out-of-the-way festival locales — as well as free street maps upon request. Recommended for festival travelers!)

- **Stephen Birnbaum Travel Guides** (HarperPerennial) — seemingly the hippest of the mainstream travel guides.

- **Let's Go Travel Guides** (St. Martin's Press) — Harvard-compiled budget guides for the young of heart and wallet.

Campers will want to add a campground directory to this list, while those upscale travelers might consider the **America's Wonderful Little Hotels and Inns** series (St. Martin's Press) by Sandra Soule.

I warn you to steer clear of bed-and-breakfasts, youth hostels, or other "amateur" lodgings. You may encounter curfews and restrictions, written or unwritten, which conflict with your festival hours. (One unnamed, but not un-shamed, B&B owner in Lafayette, Louisiana, even cancelled our reservation on the spot despite pre-payment for late arrival because my wife and I sought to check in after the Festival Internationale de Louisiana ended. Apparently, this clown's normal bedtime was 9:00 p.m., and she went ballistic at having to stay up an extra hour. We were forced to drive around for four hours in the rain before finding the last hotel room in Baton Rouge! Never again.)

For an unsolicited endorsement, I really like Marriott Courtyards. Each has spacious suites, exercise rooms and nice breakfast buffets without all the full-service nonsense I'm never around for anyway. This helps keep their rates reasonable for such luxury. Econolodges make decent budget alternatives.

• Gather entertainment listings and street maps.

These are invaluable tools to help you supplement your festival weekends. This is America, presumably you speak the language, so why deny yourself anything you're accustomed to in your own home market? If there's also a hot movie, concert, restaurant, club, happening or attraction in town that weekend, why not check it out? Entertainment listings and street maps tell you what else to do and how to get there pronto! You'll feel like a native, even where you're not.

So that's attendance; let's talk about equipment. Again, the beauty of festivals is, at a minimum, you can always just pick yourself and your family up and go! You may even choose to visit your first one "unarmed" just to see how others are prepared. Campers, backpackers and beach-goers, obviously, will have a leg-up on the rest, though nobody's got anything over on the fanatics of New York's NEWPORT JAZZ FESTIVAL/SARATOGA. These guys wheel in every creature comfort you could possibly think of, short of mobile homes. Whew!

I'm more Spartan. Here's my festival attendance kit tried-and-true in all conditions; adopt what you will.

• High-seat folding chair, plus a beach blanket for sunbathing.

A precious few festivals, like Long Island's BACK AT THE RANCH MUSIC FESTIVAL, reserve seating exclusively for low-seat beach slings. Bring these to most others, however, and all you'll see is the back of the head of the person in front of you. High seating rules! Get yourself an inexpensive high-seating, light-weight folding beach chair or patio chair, one that has thick, smooth vinyl tubing or slats for comfort. (I've a hard polyurethane deal from IKEA I'm sitting on now as I type this — steep at $50, but solid and versatile.) Those woven mesh ones feel scratchy after awhile, and their aluminum tubes just under your hamstrings soon begin to hurt.

You can leave your director chairs at home — too heavy — as well as your folding beach chaises. The latter are too cumbersome and seat you too low. If you wanna' sunbathe, simply fold up a beach blanket within your folded chair. It's light, compact and you can lay it out beside your chair or way in the back if you need a supine breather.

• Layered clothing.

Even the most tropical summer day in the woods can turn goose-pimply cold in the evening. So forget your fashion statements — dress comfortably and practically in layers. I wear swim trunks under baggy shorts, then pack sweat pants and rain pants in my backpack. Same deal with my top layers, though if I'm headed north for an off-season over-nighter, like Michigan's WHEATLAND MUSIC FESTIVAL in Middle September, I'll throw in a wool sweater or down vest, too. Also changes of tops — a must for dancers.

It's expensive, but I swear by GoreTex, a waterproof fabric supplied to a host of rain wear manufacturers. It breathes, unlike those plastic or vinyl jobs, which can leave you wetter on the inside from perspiration than on the outside from precipitation.

- Multiple footwear.

Just a half-hour's cloudburst can turn any field into muck. I bring multiple footwear: flip-flops or sandals (those new athletic kinds by Teva and others are great — expensive, but comfy and sturdy); sneakers (the footwear of choice for 95% of festival cruising); and waterproof boots, which I'll leave in my car. Dancers will also want their trusty hard-soles for sliding and gliding.

- Ear plugs.

A lifesaver for rock festivals, most indoor festivals and many outdoor festivals, as well. I prefer the foam kind (they're rated for decibel reduction on the package) and would be near deaf without 'em. Parents: ear plugs are especially advised for your children's more sensitive hearing, since you can't always guard where they'll roam.

- Sun protection.

It's amazing how much thinner the ozone's gotten since I was a kid! I bring 15-rated sun-block, lipblock, sun glasses, a bandana and a brim'd cap. It's not always "tres chic," but my straw Stetson does give me the most protection from sun (and also from rain). If you do get fried, a thin, light-colored long-sleeved top can come in handy to keep it from getting any worse.

- Hand-held cooler, plus a master cooler for the car.

There's nothing more pathetic at festivals than seeing two guys straining to haul some massive cooler from the parking lot just so their group can have all their food and drink right before them at all times. You don't have to get a hernia! Most festivals permit re-entry, so leave the big bruiser in the trunk where the ice'll keep longer and just get everyone their own compact hand-held coolers.

Mine holds a six-pack, a lunch and a snack. If I run out, I can return to my car to reload, although I usually buy my dinner on-site to support the cause. Aside from country and bluegrass festivals, where food is lamentably caloric and bland (corn dogs and funnel cakes, anyone?), most festivals provide healthy, tasty fare, even gourmet deluxe in places. What more do you need?

- Options.

My festival attendance kit, above, fits lightly in two hands, yet covers nearly all contingencies. There are further options if you so choose.

For big parties and those who simply must have their battleship ice chests, an industrial hand-truck or wagon might spare somebody's back. Binoculars are useful, though mine are bulky and I keep forgetting 'em. Photography and recording buffs, you know your own equipment requirements; I suggest bringing extra film and Ziplock Baggies to keep your electronics water-proof. Ziplocks do well, furthermore, for festival programs or other rain-sensitive valuables.

I've almost never had a problem with bugs, but worriers could pack some insect repellent. Backpackers seem to prefer Avon's Skin-So-Soft, ironically maintaining bug-fighting citronella within its conditioner. More pertinent is a modest first-aid kit, plus something to keep the sun from baking your car interior for when you return, like windshield screens or seat cushions. You can bring your various musical instruments for late-night and parking lot jams, but not for accompanying the stage musicians from your seat, thank you very much!

Forget about too much reading material; you'll never get to it. Light reading and magazines work best. Also the sun-averse should be mindful of any umbrellas, tents or small cabanas they bring. It's super rude to have them blocking people's view, so set them up on the periphery, please. (By the way, the better bluegrass festivals do a great job in erecting shaded seating for the elderly, immobile and sun allergic.) For frisbees and such — the periphery, too. Spare cash is smart for the food, crafts and merchandise you'll encounter, while a pocket flashlight is ace for finding your way back in the dark.

Ah, there's no feeling quite like the afterglow of a great festival when you flit from lantern jam to campfire singalong, soaking in the sweet sounds of communal music at its most welcoming, joyous and free-spirited. It's a high not unlike scaling a tall peak.

Unfortunately for some, capturing this feeling requires overnight camping, which may not be their cup of tea. (Select jazz and bluegrass promoters have been producing indoor festivals at hotels and resorts, but these laudable affairs are still a long way from predominating.) Still, I can't tell you how many of my former camping antagonists have sucked it up to "festival all night," so to speak, and have even come to enjoy camping — somewhat.

The right equipment helps, especially during camping's ultimate nemesis: RAIN. The good news is you don't need all that much to travel securely and comfortably, and most gear you'll purchase finds other uses in the household. Start slowly. See how others are equipped at a festival or two before plotting your purchases.

Here's my festival camping kit. It's bare bones, I know, but unlike for a weekend in the wilderness, I find festivals just don't require any more of my backpacking stuff. Instead, these few items fit nicely within a box I keep in my car trunk, so I can load up my cooler Thursday nights, change my clothes in the restroom Fridays after work, and split!

• A two-person backpacking tent with ground tarp and seam sealant.

Avoid those hideous gaggles of poles, stakes and ropes made to sleep half of Hartford and taking all afternoon to erect! I own a nice, tight $100 version made by Eureka, though you can spend far less. It sets up in under five minutes (a huge plus if you arrive in the dark or in heavy weather) and folds into a small duffle. You'll also need a plastic or vinyl ground tarp, but cut it slightly smaller than the outline of your tent's bottom. This'll prevent rain from catching and weeping in underneath. Make sure, as well, to waterproof all the stitching with seam sealant.

• A three-season sleeping bag and foam mattress.

You're not scaling Everest, so a three-season model will do fine. Most of the better brands note their recommended degree ranges on the packing. Mine's a good generic costing $100, but you can spend far less. Couples should ask for "male-female" zippers to connect 'em into one big sleeping bag. My ol' three-quarter-length Thermarest air mattresses have gotten expensive lately, so I recommend buying one of that manufacturer's full-length foam Ridgerests for about $20 instead; two Ridgerests if you're a sensitive sleeper. Pack a pillow, too.

• Options.

...And that's it! As for options, see what you see around the grounds. I'd start with a Coleman lantern, maybe followed by one of those screened rooms, not so much for the screen to ward off bugs, but more for the vinyl or plastic roof to ward off rain. It aids sociability during such inclement times.

This list should get you started on what could range from a pleasant weekend diversion to an addictive lifestyle of uninhibited, year-round, musical indulgence. Good luck wherever you venture "imbibing the festival vibe!"

~      ~      ~

# Maine

*Mother and daughter, WERU 89.9 FM Full Circle Summer Fair.*

# Sugarloaf's Cool Runnings

SUGARLOAF SKI-A-PALOOZA/COLLEGE WEEKS, Kingfield, ME
> Early January to Middle January
> Alternative and College Rock

**SUGARLOAF REGGAE SKI BASH**, Kingfield, ME
> Early April
> Reggae, Ska and Caribbean
> ***Attended***

SUGARLOAF MOUNTAIN BLUES FESTIVAL, Kingfield, ME
> Middle April
> Blues and Traditional R&B

SUGARLOAF COUNTRY MUSIC FESTIVAL, Kingfield, ME
> Late July and Late August
> Modern Country

**Introduction**

It's spring skiing, when the resorts compete for diehards squeezing out their last few runs. Chip Carey, Vice President of Marketing at Sugarloaf and creator of its year-round music program, calls it "value season" with a friendly, Maine-flavored chuckle "when you need to drive business during the off-peak and entice somebody to come this far."

Back in '88 Carey was having a brainstorming session with a travel group, Jamaican Holidays, about an open weekend in April when he suggested, "Why don't we have a reggae festival? Let's put something together."

The result was not merely successful, it was a smash!

"Boom! It just took off," Carey recalls. "I couldn't believe it. All we did the first year was put reggae music in the Widowmaker Lounge, and we had lines outside — people waiting to get in all night." He immediately moved the music to the larger King Pine Room downstairs to handle the overflow. Carey also scheduled another concert the following week with The Beaver Brown Band "to build on that momentum."

This follow-up concert has since blossomed into a winter series of 24 dates with national and regional acts (e.g., Asleep at the Wheel, Peter Wolf, Eddie Money, Belly, Southside Johnny, Bim Skala Bim, Warren Zevon), plus a summer weekend festival of national country acts. "It all started from this reggae thing moving from the Widowmaker to the King Pine Room," exclaims Carey. "That's where the concert series started from...and it's the reason we have the country one, too."

It's also brought more and more reggae-thirsty skiers every year. The SUGARLOAF REGGAE SKI BASH is now up to four venues (including the outdoor patio in the base camp during the afternoon when the weather permits), and four days plus music from noon to midnight on Saturday. Irie! Carey's proud to point out, "Our biggest day at Sugarloaf — this is in April, which is amazing — is the reggae festival. [In '92] it set the single-day attendance record, plus the two-day attendance record of over 7,000 people.

"For us," Carey exclaims, "that's the epitome that we're doing people right."

**Festival Review** The drive to see the SUGARLOAF REGGAE SKI BASH was worth it, all by itself. My brother, Rich, and I enjoyed a dreamy, two-hour-plus jaunt from Portland where the view alternated between pastoral, snow-laden farms, State Troopers setting speed traps, and tacky road sings. My favorite? "Live Bait: Shiners, Suckers, Smelts and Ice" (there's gotta be a country song in there somewhere). The last half hour is a particular treat as the rugged, silvery Carrabasset Valley recalls Wyoming in miniature.

Heeding 3,000-foot drops and a 70-inch base still in place, Rich took off for some runs, while I settled in for a rasta afternoon, all warm and snug in Sugarloaf's sunny atriums. The music wasn't bad, mostly recruits from Boston's still-thriving, roots-reggae community. I liked The I-Tones' three-part harmonies and their "culture/roots" stylings, plus locals, The Danny Tribesman, in their cover of Dylan's "I Shall Be Released."

However, the closing act in the Widowmaker Lounge, Winston Grennan, bowled me over.

**Artist Mini-Review** <u>Winston Grennan and The Ska-Rocks Band</u>: You may not have heard the name of this Baltimore-based drummer, but I promise you've heard his sound.

Grennan is credited with pioneering the "one-drop" beat, which serves as the bedrock of reggae rhythms, while an original member of Toots and The Maytals back in the early sixties. When Paul Simon needed that beat on "Mother and Child Reunion," which introduced reggae to America in the early seventies, he called in Grennan. Grennan is also the drummer in Jimmy Cliff's movie, "The Harder They Come." He's been a top session and touring drummer for over 30 years and has backed an incredible array of rock, R&B, jazz and reggae greats.

Needless to say, Grennan can play.

His kit fronts a five-piece band, and he handles the lead vocals in fine style with an appealing combination of croon and rasp. His set, composed entirely of originals (Grennan has over 400 compositions to his credit), departed from expected in two manners. First, his lyrics are interesting, real, spiritual — not spliff-headed party stuff. I was moved by his impassioned history of black struggle in "King James Version," for example.

Second, Grennan's music was enticingly sinuous and unpredictable — Caribbean collages, in effect. His drumming was a clinic, showcasing a virtual history of rasta rhythms by mixing and matching several per song. Nothing flashy (save for an occasional wrist flip at one of the high hats stacked high behind him), just perfect fills, transitions, and accents with one power-house solo at the end. A special revelation, though, is his ska technique that is so lithe and smooth it nearly stole my breath away.

By the time he was done, even those wearing ski boots were clunking on the dance floor!

Carey promised me that "Winston's going to come back in a much bigger way next year." Good. If Grennan's a regular at the SUGARLOAF REGGAE SKI BASH, then I'm a regular, too!

**Travel Tip** Sugarloaf's got more than enough shopping, dining and activities to keep even non-skiers occupied all weekend. With 22 places to eat on site, Carey feels the resort's own Seasons Restaurant gets unjustly overlooked. Nevertheless, he cites another local eatery, One Stanley Avenue, as serving "the most consistently good cuisine in the state." Finally, he recommends summertime visitors check out Houston Brook Falls as "a place to get away and see a beautiful waterfall and a nice, clean swimming hole."

**See Also** For someone who started out in public relations, Carey is amassing an impressive festival-promotion resume. His SUGARLOAF SKI-A-PALOOZA / COLLEGE WEEKS boasts a strong array of Boston-based college-rock acts, usually one per day, Tuesdays through Thursdays, over the first two weeks in January. The SUGARLOAF COUNTRY MUSIC FESTIVAL is actually two bashes — one day in late July and one weekend in late August — with both featuring an impressive roster of intelligent-but-kickin' country headliners.

Things are going so well that Carey is planning two more additions to his April offerings: one featuring regional country acts, the other regional blues acts. The latter, called the SUGARLOAF MOUNTAIN BLUES FESTIVAL, is set to debut in '95. Carey's also fielded a proposal from promoter folk-singer Bruce Pratt (HARTLAND FOLK FESTIVAL, East Hartland, CT — see chapter) regarding a summer folk festival.

Given this veritable avalanche of musical happenings, you better put 1-800-THE-LOAF on your festival Rolodex.

~ ~ ~

*Winston Grennan and The Ska-Rocks Band, Sugarloaf Reggae Ski Bash.*

# Downeast's Coastal Roots, July

BLUE HILL POPS, Blue Hill, ME
Early July
Variety, General

**WERU 89.9 FM FULL CIRCLE SUMMER FAIR**, Union, ME
Early July
Variety, General
***Attended***

DOWNEAST DULCIMER AND FOLK HARP FESTIVAL, Bar Harbor, ME
Early July to Middle July
Traditional Folk

SCHOONER DAYS, Rockland, ME
Early July to Middle July
Variety, General

NATIVE AMERICAN FESTIVAL, Bar Harbor, ME
Early July
Native American

NORTH ATLANTIC BLUES FESTIVAL, Rockland, ME
Early July
Blues and Traditional R&B

**LEFT BANK CAFE COUNTRY BLUES FESTIVAL**, Blue Hill, ME
Middle July
Blues and Traditional R&B

**Introduction**  O. K., follow me through all these "downeast" festival connections.

First, there's the Peter Paul and Mary connection, or rather, the Noel Stookey connection. He's "Paul" in the legendary pop/folk trio. I read somewhere how the group's initial manager had come up with this catchy quasi-religious monicker, "Peter, Paul and Mary." He had a "Peter," Peter Yarrow; he had a "Mary," Mary Travers. But he didn't have a "Paul," so Stookey took on the first name, professionally, as well as the matching goatee.

Anyway, Stookey makes his home in the bucolic artists' community of Blue Hill, perched before a gentle harbor along Maine's exquisite coastline. "Downeast" is how the natives refer to this particular stretch, which runs roughly from Boothbay Harbor to the famed resort town of Bar Harbor. Along one of Blue Hill's back roads, Stookey owns an office building within which he rents space to a much-beloved community radio station, WERU 89.9 FM.

True, there are any number of wealthy potenial donors residing within WERU's domain. Yet it's still a relatively sparse, rural population that the nonprofit community station serves, thus further exacerbating the onerous enough difficulty of soliciting funds to keep their airwaves humming. To make ends meet, on the Sunday of every July 4th weekend, WERU holds its annual fundraiser, the **WERU 89.9 FM FULL CIRCLE SUMMER FAIR** ['FULL CIRCLE'], which also serves to showcase the profuse local arts and crafts scene as well as to pay back the community and station volunteers for their support.

In a parallel development, every year Peter, Paul and Mary rotate amongst themselves to select a benefit for the group to perform, gratis. It was Stookey's turn in '93, and he gave the nod to WERU. The trio booked themselves into that year's 'FULL CIRCLE', drawing fans from all over and effectively putting the station and its local music sampler on the regional map.

In '94, 'FULL CIRCLE's normal site, the Blue Hill Fairgrounds, underwent restoration during the summer. WERU needed a temporary replacement, so it settled on the Union Fairgrounds about 90 minutes' drive southwest at the outer reaches of its served market. However, things went so well with the fairgrounds site, the day's weather and the festival attendance that WERU now thinks of extending their limited run there into a permanent engagement. So much for that Blue Hill connection.

But wait!

Nestled just off the side of another Blue Hill back road sits WERU's live-music counterpart and one of the very, very coolest venues on the planet. We're talking about the just as beloved Left Bank Cafe and Bakery. (Its stationery proclaims it "A Home Away From Home," and it truly is! My wife and I couldn't stay out of the place during our recent vacation nearby.) Run by a graying, bearded, former counter-culture educator, Arnold Greenberg, the Left Bank's added a cozy performance wing in recent years. There, just below the wafting fragrance of croissants and sticky buns, performs an incredible lineup of stars drawn from the cream of the folk crop plus jazz, blues, world-music and otherwise. On any given week last summer you could've thrilled to the likes of Anita O'Day, Tony Trischka, Cheryl Wheeler, Inca Son, Mose Allison, John Jackson, or Iris Dement — joined by no more than 100 lucky comrades at a time.

In '94 Greenberg had been ruminating on how well his acoustic blues bookings had gone and how some of these "heritage" artists in their 60s, 70s and 80s wouldn't be around forever. Seeing a gap in the market, he scheduled a full week of acoustic blues, starting Monday, July 11, that paired older artists like Nat Reese, Honeyboy Edwards and Etta Baker with younger champions like Paul Geremia, Lonnie Pitchford and Roy Bookbinder. He'd have a twin or triple bill at night, preceded by two sets of afternoon workshops. With only a few small ads in the national blues press, Greenberg sold out all nine days to devotees flying in from as far away as Germany. His **LEFT BANK CAFE COUNTRY BLUES FESTIVAL** ['COUNTRY BLUES'] went so well that he's planning to make it an annual. Great!

Now for the blues connection. If you'd been driving up for your first 'COUNTRY BLUES' concert that Monday, you could've stopped off the day before in Rockland, a stone's throw from 'FULL CIRCLE's adopted site. There, on the Rockland Public Landing commenced the first **NORTH ATLANTIC BLUES FESTIVAL** (wrapping up the three-day-long **SCHOONER DAYS**), featuring a charged lineup of stars, electric and electrifying. Of the day's nine acts, fully seven were national or regional headliners, topped off by the James Cotton Band. Let's hope this cool clambake becomes a yearly attraction.

Which brings us to the Bar Harbor connection, or the second-weekend-in-July connection, if you will. If you'd been driving down, instead of up, to Monday's 'COUNTRY BLUES' show, you could've stopped off in Bar Harbor that prior weekend for two festivals: the three-day **DOWNEAST DULCIMER AND FOLK HARP FESTIVAL** [DOWNEAST DULCIMER'] and the one-day **NATIVE AMERICAN FESTIVAL**. They're both run steadily by several more beloved organizations.

**DOWNEAST DULCIMER'** is sponsored by a delightful musical instrument shop, Song of the Sea, which is owned by Edward and Anne Damm. It hosts a full afternoon's worth of workshops, song-sharing and handmade instrument-trading at Agramont Park off the Town Pier; then an evening concert at Congregational Church for the first 250 who arrive. That's on Saturday; other activities keep the attending folk instrumentalists occupied Friday and Sunday.

The **NATIVE AMERICAN'** is brought forth by the 75-year-old Abbe Museum and the year-old Maine Indian Basketmakers Alliance at the College of the Atlantic. These two groups unite to celebrate the native cultures of four local tribes — the Maliseet, the Micmac, the Passamaquoddy, and the Penobscot. Their primary focus is an extensive crafts vending across nearly 10 categories, but there's also a full day's agenda of native dancing, drumming, singing, storytelling, ceremonies, food, and demonstrations of all kinds. That's on Sunday.

Both festivals appear to be classy, intimate affairs — as if you needed any further excuse to visit this glorious corner of heaven-on-earth. So go ahead. Choose your music from the menu above, and dial up your lodging reservations for either, or both, of the first two weeks of July. Your own "downeast" festival connection awaits you!

**Festival Review I**  Mainers often joke that their state has two seasons: winter and 4th of July. The joke might soon work as well by substituting 'FULL CIRCLE' for July 4th! After a decade of preparation (plus considerable advocacy from Stookey), WERU hit the airwaves in '88. Its 'FULL CIRCLE' proceeded on Independence Day weekend the next year and, likewise, has become something of a mini-institution in these parts.

Perhaps 'FULL CIRCLE's main attraction is its relaxed communion among all segments who populate the area's coastal and inland regions, from wealthy travelers (Bangor author, Stephen King, was spied among last year's patrons) to sustenance farmers, loggers and fishermen. Native "old-timers" freely intermingle with those "from away," contributing to the willfully unpretentious vibe that pervades.

There's an excellent gathering of, roughly, 200 local crafters. What's for sale under the paddock eaves is appealingly artsy/funky but also very affordable — an unusual combination among the top shows I've attended. The food fare from over 20 vendors follows suit, with two of the more renowned being Gardiner's A1 Diner and Portland's Uncle Billy's Barbeque. (You haven't lived until you've bitten into the latter's "pulled pork" sandwich slathered in its unique neon-green "Creole mayonnaise.") There's also an active Children's Area, which holds a throng of young tikes in squealing thrall all day long.

Finally, there's the music. Live sounds float down from five locations: Main Stage, Music in the Park, Drum Village (now called Rhythm Section), Fiddler's Field, and Contradance Barn. The first three sites yield performances continuously; the latter two intermittently. Now, I won't kid you. It's all local talent donating their services to entertain the milling 6,000. Aside from Peter, Paul and Mary's 1993 appearance, there's nobody yet resembling a national or regional headliner on 'FULL CIRCLE's bill. But that doesn't mean there aren't pleasant discoveries to be had.

I felt '94's opening vocal duo of <u>Paul Anderson and Lei Garofalo</u> were promising. She had a soulful style that projected well, while the two fielded good harmonies together. <u>Bruce Pratt</u>, a longtime troubadour and festival promoter (see HARTLAND FOLK FESTIVAL, East Hartland, CT, Mid Jul.) who'd just relocated to his fishing camp upstate, then held court with his usual humorous banter, rolling fingerpicking and folk/blues standards. Moreover, Pratt debuted two strong originals: "Driving Through The Delta," a sentimental account of his recent family vacation, and "The End Of The Earth," a harrowing confession by a disappointed small-town woman. Both lyrics hooked my ear firmly.

The vendors stole my attention for our remaining stay, though I did escape for another solid act. Led by the artful, passionate soloing of its trumpeter, Mike Mitchell, <u>The Belle Island Quintet</u> did credit to such jazz covers as Wayne Shorter's "Blue Nile" and Tad Dameron's "Good Bait," as well as Mitchell's own pensive compositions.

Credit Dave Pizcz for the bill. This likeable carpenter hailing from Chicopee, Massachusetts, who serves WERU as volunteer DJ and jazz playlist coordinator, also coordinated 'FULL CIRCLE's eclectic musical stages. "You see, I was trying to reflect what it is we do as a station," Pizcz explains:

- "We do have a heavy folk stretch, but we also play reggae, and salsa, and jazz, and alternative rock and roll. There's an R&B show on now and a gospel show on Sunday morning. There are various mixtures. I tried to make it like doing an eclectic radio show: 'How would I mix it up?' We try to provide the best of the area musicians for the people, for the musicians to play to a decent crowd ('cause a lot of the rooms around here are pretty small), and to make it as broad as possible."

Jazz is Pizcz' personal favorite: "I think it's great music and under-appreciated, perhaps. I love to get it out in public." For that reason, he's happy to see The Belle Island Quintet freed from their more customary supper club engagements. "People don't necessarily want you to be stretching out and just blowing at a dinner situation. It was a chance for them to really get up and play," Pizcz remarks, adding, "yeah, they were good; they were really good. And by the end, they played a samba for the last number, and people were dancing!"

Still, five stages gives Pizcz plenty of room to play to his diverse audiences. "I like the concept of having a lot of stuff going on at once," he exclaims, "because not everybody wants to sit and listen to jazz, necessarily. So they can go and contradance if they see fit, or sit and listen to a singer."

Piszcz reflects on this varied programming philosophy of WERU and its annual "Independance":

- "We are sort of working somewhat outside of the so-called normal radio idea, which is to target your audience, define what they want to hear, and just pound it out, you know? We're doing something different. We're saying, 'If you can't find what you want elsewhere, well, we're the one. We'll play it and stuff.' To my mind, it should be a broad mix of music. You've got a lotta' different musical tastes out in the community there.

  "Tell people they should come and see it for themselves. It doesn't cost too much, and they'll see a whole day's worth of musicians. They'll see the spirit of community at work in many ways here, 'cause it wouldn't happen without a lot of volunteers, it just wouldn't. It wouldn't be financially viable, but there's such an energy that you get when everybody's pitching in towards the same cause. I was glad to see people dancing at the stage and smilin'. I was glad to see having a good sound system and throwing it down the best they could.

  "That, to me, was worth it."

**Artist Mini-Review**

<u>Zulu Leprechans</u>. "In some ways they were, perhaps, the most interesting outfit there," Piszcz explains, "because the lead instrument was an electrified dulcimer; then they had a bass and percussion with various African drums and stuff. They would do things, like, start out with 'Greensleeves,' turn it into 'The Other' by the 'Dead and play that for a while. So they had a very fresh approach to the music, I thought, and the crowd really enjoyed them."

~　　~　　~

**Festival Review II**

If WERU spins eclectic over the air, Arnold Greenberg's Left Bank Cafe and Bakery does it fresh in the flesh most weekends throughout the year. Unlike far too many of his "folk-Nazi" brethren, Greenberg is one folk club owner who's not afraid of other pop genres — namely, jazz, blues and C&W — nor of artists who've achieved some measure of commercial success. The result is a near-perfect spectrum of respected names and emerging acts occupying one of the homiest, friendliest and tastiest (literally, for three meals a day) spaces you'll ever encounter.

Perhaps when I've more of a budget in future editions, I'll pay to reprint the whole of Maureen Farr's interview with Greenberg — "'Everyone who comes to my door is Godsent': a conversation with Arnold Greenberg of the Left Bank Cafe" — which appeared in a recent issue of local entertainment weekly, *Preview!* It's a genuinely inspiring tale of a regular Joe who's followed his heart, soul and conscience to actively address many of his immediate societal concerns. This ex-high school dropout went on to found an alternative high school in his native Philadelphia, a homesteading school, and school programs in "Backyard Self-Suffiency" involving edible landscapes, before founding the Bakery here in '88.

Greenberg's self-publishing a book of his essays, **Adventures on Arnold's Island**, which details many of his educational philosophies, including one especially pertinent one on "homesteading for the 21st century." Farr quotes his interest in seeing:

- "...People living more in their homes; having a more home-centered life; home schooling; having a home business...using computers and technology, as opposed to now where the home is the place where people keep their possession, and pass in the night, and very little interaction takes place. I consider this a homestead. I live and work in my home. It's a bakery, a cafe — an extreme example of a home industry. There's a lot of things that people can do in their homes.

"In the long run, it will make people more willing to go out to cafes and to socialize. Now people travel to work and so forth. They drive some distance and they spend so much time out on the road that when they're home, they want to stay home."

Greenberg discusses making his home in Blue Hill and extending it toward the musicians he invites to perform, effectively making the cafe feel like "coming home" for them. This, in turn, creates a home-like environment for musically-interested families from the area, as well as those others who travel half the country to come here.

This homesteading interest also drove Greenberg's creation of 'COUNTRY BLUES' in '94. He sought to preserve the art of blues "elders" in the intimate "back porch" scale where their music is usually passed down. Greenberg gives me an example:

- "Like when Etta Baker played here. She's not really an entertainer; she's a great player, and it was just like she was sitting in her living room. She might as well have been sitting on her couch playing for neighbors. And that's exactly the feeling I wanted. I captured that. Big festivals lose their intimacy. That's not to say they're not good in their own right, but that's not what I want.

"The other thing about this blues festival is that people who have been to other festivals said that our [daytime] workshop was a real workshop. ...They said it was more instructional. They said that most workshops are mini-concerts; this was not a mini-concert. These were actually small — eight-to-ten people with each workshop — and they could really ask questions and look at what was being done. Many said it was the most satisfying workshop they'd ever been to."

I wasn't able to query Greenberg further about his beliefs in home and hearth. The phone kept interrupting, as did a fresh batch of rye breads he needed to attend to. However, here's an apt comment Farr captured of Greenberg's:

- "For me, there is no greater joy than making people happy. It makes me happy. When I see the house full, and people singing and laughing, I really feel in some way that it's healing. I didn't plan it that way, but it's nice when it happens. Having people singing and laughing is really uplifting.

"It's not escapism because the music here is not mainstream pop radio. It's serious and heartfelt, and people walk away with something rich. So I really feel good about that. It transcends just pure entertainment."

**See Also** You want more festival connections? More, you say?! Well, the day prior to 'FULL CIRCLE' there's the BLUE HILL POPS, which boasts a four-act show. Last year, it even had the Atlantic Clarion Steel Band, which graced 'FULL CIRCLE' the year before that.

At 'FULL CIRCLE's former site, the Blue Hill Fairgrounds, there's the BLUE HILL FAIR over Labor Day weekend. Calling itself "a down-to-earth country fair," it usually features two or three national C&W acts spread over its five days. Last year this meant The Forester Sisters followed by Waylon Jennings.

Finally, WERU lends a musical hand to another local gathering, Belfast's one-day SANKOFA FESTIVAL in Middle August, by hosting two music stages of continuous ethnic and world-beat locals to supplement the street fair's dancers, performance artists and poets.

Which brings the "downeast" festival connections 'FULL CIRCLE'!

~ ~ ~

# Portland's Variety Party

OLD PORT FESTIVAL, Portland, ME
   Early June
   Variety, General
   ***Attended***

DEERING OAKS FAMILY FESTIVAL, Portland, ME
   Middle July to Late July
   Variety, General
   ***Attended***

Portland has always been one of my favorite weekend destinations, even before my brother, Rich, **Introduction** moved there in the early '90s. It's got a real appealing character — historic-seaport-meets-Small-Town-USA — populated by a mix of wholesome artsy/outdoorsy types and classic curmudgeons ("The road doesn't go anywhere, it stays right here," as an old salt might reply to your request for directions).

Portland's a perfect staging ground for great day trips: the jagged coastline stretches out to Canada; the rugged mountains are just a few hours' drive; and Outlet Madness Central is right up the road in Freeport (home of L. L. Bean's Factory Store, open "24/7/365," as the slang goes). In town there's also plenty to do. Start the day with Green Mountain Coffee and end it with a Geary's Ale.

If your travelin' mates still need a nudge, however, you can bait the hook with two events: the OLD PORT FESTIVAL and the DEERING OAKS FAMILY FESTIVAL, both run Keith Citrine for Portland's Chamber of Commerce. The former features one day of mostly local acts on eight stages throughout the Old Port District. The latter is more of a family affair — over the hill and by the bay — hosting national and local acts on three stages, but over all but Monday of an entire week.

"I've always said that music builds community."

That's how the Director, Keith Citrine, summarizes his mission in improving the quantity and quality of the music lineup for the DEERING OAKS FAMILY FESTIVAL, which he produces for the Chamber of Commerce of the Greater Portland Region. The site, Deering Oaks Park, offers a picturesque pond under a nice canopy of trees where neighbors can enjoy a pleasant stroll.

Typical "family festivals" seem to target the children, what with petting zoos, bright lights, cotton candy, carnival rides, mimes, magicians, and the like. Amidst these warm fuzzies, good music often gets the cold shoulder.

Last year, however, Citrine booked four fine national acts spead across the evenings, plus a busy undercard of local acts throughout the entire six days. His full slate had you sneaking musical treats all day long, while kids romped gleefully among the copious attractions.

Citrine has two motivations on his mind. First, he straightens the fedora of a community leader and gently explains, "When I look at these events I see such a wide variety of people from different socio-economic backgrounds there enjoying the music, having a common thread between them. That's what makes it all worthwhile for me."

But then he slips on the baseball cap of being a former concert promoter for 10 years and happily lets you know, "The musical part is something I have a real personal interest in and put a lot of energy into. I have a very eclectic appreciation for music."

Citrine sports a particular ear for rising stars (encouraging me, for example, to put the word out among "bright, fresh talent" interested in performing here to submit their demo tapes and press kits to the Chamber). "What we try to do with many of these acts is hit them right before they go big time," he explains, citing Davis Daniel and Suzy Bogguss as two of his C&W coups within recent years. "We caught Hal Ketcham right before his first record hit it big," Citrine recalls of another. "The next thing I knew, his records were all over the stores. We wouldn't be able to hire him now."

Citrine's favorite memory, however, was non-musical:

- "There were two friends of mine who were going to get married. I talked them into getting married on stage with Martha Reeves and The Vandellas. It was wonderful. The park was packed Friday night. Martha Reeves played 'The Wedding Song.' The couple had a ceremony; Martha caught the bouquet. We had it timed between my assistant, a relay across the pond, and the guy who controlled the switches — all with walkie-talkies — that when they said, 'You may kiss the bride,' and the couple's lips touched, the fireworks went off over the duck pond.

"I kept telling the couple, 'You're going to have to hold that kiss for a long time!'"

A lifetime, perhaps, as befits a true family festival.

**Festival Review**  'Twas a dreary, rainy opening Tuesday, brightened only by lights of the carnival rides. Fortunately, the DEERING OAKS FAMILY FESTIVAL has a number of Food Court vendors serving tasty barbeque to warm our innards, and a tent to shield some fairly spirited reggae by locals, Rockin' Vibrations. The rain subsided by dusk, however, and a dense mist lent the proper swampy ambience for bayou refugees, Terrance Simien and The Mallet Playboys.

**Artist Mini-Review**  <u>Terrance Simien and The Mallet Playboys</u>: Thanks to routing dates I was lucky enough to catch Simien three times that week in three states. It felt like being a Grateful Dead groupie — all I needed was a beat-up VW bus and some useless trinkets to hawk in the parking lot before shows.

You may recall Simien from his cameo in the film, "The Big Easy." That portrayal was somewhat inaccurate. First, you rarely have enough room at Tipitina's, as did Dennis Quaid and Ellen Barkin, for an uninterrupted waltz. Second, Simien and pals rarely dip the tempo below hyperdrive. Since that film appearance, the band has been a mainstay on the festival circuit — landing over two hundred dates per year, despite only recently having a disc to recommend them. As you can imagine from that much work, Simien's band was tight as a drum and had their showmanship skills in full force.

What I enjoy about Simien's zydeco is its exotic flavoring. You could hear it on his second number, a rippin' "Zydeco la Pas a Lait," which has an African feel, and on "Zydeco on the Bayou," which features a calypso beat. Congas galore! Simien also displayed a nice Aaron-Neville-inspired yodel on an extended ballad, "Don't Call Me Anymore."

The audience was surprisingly sedate, at first, considering how many Acadian immigrants live in the area. (In nearby Biddeford there may be more French spoken than English.) Simien is not one to accept a placid crowd, however. In quick succession, he:

- Implores all his soloists with a round, malleable face beaming 100 watts of fun;

- Dances about the stage in bare feet, flailing his hair and stretching his button accordion to improbable lengths;

- Pulls children up on stage to create an small army of washboard players;

- Drags his percussion section out into the crowd to create a conga line.

By the time his set ended with an extended "Iko Iko," Simien had everybody standing, and the whole dance floor full and rockin' — a wonderful send-off into the evening's chilly dampness.

**Travel Tip**  Citrine recommends Portland generally. "It's a delightful, delightful town," he exclaims. "It has everything you'd want in a city, yet it's small, comfortable and on the ocean." He advises checking out the revived local music scene, particularly the recently-restored State Theater ("A hidden gem...it's beautiful."). Los Lobos just christened it with a concert. Other new venues on Citrine's list include Dos Locos for blues and the recently re-opened Raoul's Roadside Attraction for most everything else.

The Old Port district is worth a trip in itself. It's a tight 20-block warren of 19th-century brick **See Also**
buildings right up from Portland's wharfs. Perfect for strolls, day or night, it entices with the most
number of tastefully retro-fitted clubs, clam bars, boutiques, pool halls, and cafes this side of
Saratoga, NY.

Citrine's crew takes over this historic cluster one day per year for the OLD PORT FESTIVAL,
packing an extraordinary amount of music into one afternoon for a good 60,000 revelers. Figure
an average of four acts per stage on eight different performing areas. The lineup is comprised of
an eclectic assortment of local heroes, but a few always stand out, often on the folk side. A recent
bill featured singer-songwriter Catie Curtis, a Portland native who's now touring nationally to
raves (her excellent self-produced disc, "From Years to Hours," has already sold 10,000 copies off
her coffeehouse gigs). The Boneheads are an alternative rock band making waves regionally, while
Citrine advises keeping an eye on Don Campbell as another potential up-and-comer.

"The festival's really becoming an urban arts festival," Citrine notes of it's expanding
offerings, including plans for a dance stage. The momentum has built sufficiently that he plans to
develop two more such events for the Chamber that feature music, one being a brewer's festival.
Call ahead for current listings.

~     ~     ~

# Thomas Point Beach's Acoustic Roots, August

**MAINE ARTS FESTIVAL**, Brunswick, ME
Early August
Variety, Folk and International
***Attended***

**MAINE HIGHLAND GAMES**, Brunswick, ME
Middle August
Scottish

**THOMAS POINT BEACH BLUEGRASS FESTIVAL**, Brunswick, ME
Early September
Bluegrass

**NEW YEAR'S PORTLAND**, Portland, ME
Late December
Variety, General
***Attended***

**Introduction** All three festivals share the same site, Thomas Point Beach Campground, which easily rates within my top-ten among Northeast festivals for scenery. You reach it at the end of a frost-heaved country road that runs past some of those charmingly-eccentric Maine farm houses, which have enough additions to make their rambling compounds look like accordions.

It occupies an intimate spit within an inlet that looks out upon reedy marshes, gently-lapping waves, and evergreen-wooded shores dotted by a bungalow or two. The grounds are equal parts shaded groves, open fields, and rustic shelters and boast a pond, a beach, and a view. Its effect is superbly tranquil and relaxing.

As Burl Hash, Director of the **MAINE ARTS FESTIVAL**, says succinctly, "When you're here, you know you're in Maine."

**Festival Review** Madonna's personal trainer once described her body as a "pocket Venus" or minor masterpiece. I'm no Madonna fan, but I've always admired that phrase and felt it applied perfectly to the **MAINE ARTS FESTIVAL**. Like Madonna's wardrobe, this extraordinary fine-arts cornucopia literally bursts at its seams. It's folksy, but first-rate — competitive in breadth and depth with any of the other fine-arts extravaganzas I've attended all across the country.

Maine Arts, Inc., a Portland-based nonprofit, presents such a complete offering of quality arts and crafts, comestibles, inflatables, sculpture installations, cultural demonstrations, performance arts, and children's' activities that it almost makes five stages of excellent music take a back seat. All state-based vendors, too! Behind the wheel of every skidder hurtling down a Maine blacktop, maybe there's a trained artisan who's turning out simply beautiful work.

That's not to say the music deserved the back seat. Quite the contrary!

Hash previously ran the underdog **CELEBRATE BROOKLYN PERFORMING ARTS FESTIVAL** within New York City's melting-pot borough of Brooklyn (see chapter), so you can count on two things, musically: strong ethnic offerings and genuine surprises, despite a limited budget. In fact, I kept being unexpectedly seduced into the performing tents while browsing the incredible crafts, or admiring the peaceful cove through the sculpture garden. Even though I knew Hash was tick-ing off musical categories to satisfy various constituencies, it didn't feel pigeon-holed. Rather, a full range of great sounds in close settings is the pervading vibe.

"I always go for quality, and not just name value," Hash states of his programming choices. "I'm a place where you can plug in a talented artist who's not well-known. That's the kind of programming I like to do. After four years now, I feel like I've begun to develop an audience that trusts the music's going to be different, interesting and quality."

Hash cites help he received from a local 100,000-watt C&W station in selecting Sunday's headliner for '92. "Hey, we can't afford all those 'hot shots' who get $20,000," he queried, "but who's down in Nashville who's an 'up-and-comer,' yet a seasoned artist, who's really going to make a difference?" The station recommended Mac McAnally.

Slide guitarist Sonny Landreth was a similar programming coup in '93. "People were coming up to me," Hash recalls, "saying, 'Wow! That guy was incredible! Where'd you find that guy?'"

Music has been less the primary achievement for Hash, however, than simply moving the 17-year-old festival, founded by the late Maine humorist, Marshall Dodge, back to it's origins near Bowdoin College. "The audience and the press recognized that the MAINE ARTS FESTIVAL had come home again to the best site it's ever had," he notes. "It had regained a really substantive focus on Maine arts and Maine culture — celebrating Maine creativity across the board.

"We turned the corner [in '93] in terms of getting new audiences out," Hash adds. "We had four days of absolutely perfect weather. We refined the site plan and had no sound-bleed problem whatsoever. We've re-scheduled the event so it's not so frenetic. There's more time for contemplative things and participatory things.

"We're feelin' good!"

**Artist Mini-Reviews**

Mac McAnally: Nashville scares me. Here's a guy known primarily as a songwriter (e.g., Restless Heart, Sawyer Brown, Jimmy Buffett, Andy Childs), yet he picked the guitar perfectly, sung handsomely, and carried himself well on stage, despite a drizzling rain. It makes you wonder how many other triple threats are hiding out down there under publishing contracts.

McAnally's songs are flawlessly-crafted country pop, frequently funny, and done solo. His topics cover a lot of interesting ground, although he seems to prefer statements of home and hearth. In that regard, I don't think his work would be at all out of place on the Christian Country charts, a la Paul Overstreet. I enjoyed his "Simple Life," about "...trying to lead a simple life in a difficult time." Aren't we all! Nice guy, too, with an enjoyably self-deprecating demeanor.

Cris Williamson and Tret Fure: Williamson takes the exact opposite approach of fellow women's artist, Holly Near, and to much better effect. Whereas Near cheerfully glides through a dizzying procession of lefty social concerns, as in a politically-correct cabaret, Williamson focuses on one topic at a time in a warmer, more personal and more meaningful way. Her humorous introductions inform solid songs, like "Holding On," without preaching or scolding. I was quite taken with Williamson here and at BEN & JERRY'S NEWPORT FOLK FESTIVAL the day before (Newport, RI — see chapter), and recommend her appeal to anyone.

Allan McHale and The Old-Time Radio Gang: Straight-ahead, home-grown, old-timey music. McHale is an ingratiating showmen who runs through the standards with flair. The real treat is his accordion player who contributes French-Canadian overtones to enliven the repertoire. Old-fashioned country fun!

Inca Son: There are many Peruvian groups playing good stuff on the streets of New York City, but these guys from Boston are better by far. Their costumes are extraordinary (they could've placed themselves in the juried crafts exhibit and won!); their tunes were authentic, elaborate, rhythmic and subtle; their violinist's playing lends an unusual, classy touch. The crowd loved their mini-symphonies as much as I did.

Pura Fe-Soni: Pura Fe is the name of a Cherokee/Turscaroran singer-songwriter; Soni is her Aztec/Mayan harmony partner. They were joined by two Native American drummers, Kevin Tarrant and Randy Whitehead, and together put on a simply entrancing show. Much of their material is traditional from their respective tribes, but there is also modern songwriting in folk and blues vernaculars. All of it possesses a searing emotion and transcendent spirituality that kept me riveted to my seat.

Key was the otherworldly harmonies and pulsing rhythms of the two singers. Both women can also solo effectively to match their poignant lyrics. "Tucson On My Mind," "Necklace of Broken Hearts," and "Love Call" all resonated within the heart. I left immediately afterward because I didn't want anything else to intrude upon this exceptional listening experience.

**Travel Tip**    Hash recommends a two-to-three-day stay, including Portland ("...which offers a lot, culturally, all within walking distance), Freeport ("...where you can shop in the morning, then visit us in the afternoon"), and a drive along the coast ("...down Route 24, there's some spectacular Maine coast-line").

**See Also**    The MAINE HIGHLAND GAMES there the following weekend features the usual assortment of Scottish activities, including a piping competition. Next, the THOMAS POINT BEACH BLUEGRASS FESTIVAL on Labor Day weekend hosts one of the best traditional-bluegrass lineups in New England, equally balanced between national and local acts.

Finally, if you want another taste of Hash's musical stew, you might pay a visit to the NEW YEAR'S PORTLAND his organization coordinates. I made the trek, oh, about a good five or six years ago and like with the best party-hearties, I can't remember much about it other than having a blast cruising clubs, chatting locals, pounding brews, and dodging snow sprinkles. Good music, good people, good times, good town.

~    ~    ~

# Maine Festival Listings

**Caveat**

Although the vast majority are festivals are reliable and predictable, all are subject to last-minute changes or cancellations. Accordingly, FESTPRESS is not responsible for any festival listing information that follows. Readers are well advised to contact festivals at least twice before preparing a festival vist: (a) once at least one or two months ahead of time; and (b) once more during the week of your visit for confirmation. Ask for a festival flyer or brochure to be mailed to you. Festival promoters usually are willing to comply, and the resulting literature may answer any questions you still have.

**Key Codes**

## Restrictions:

| | | | | | |
|---|---|---|---|---|---|
| • Food and drink... | 1; | • Cameras... | 6; | • Motorcycles... | 11; |
| • Alcohol... | 2; | • Audio recording... | 7; | • Re-entry... | 12; |
| • Cans... | 3; | • Video recording... | 8; | • Other restrictions... | 13. |
| • Bottles... | 4; | • Children... | 9; | | |
| • Coolers... | 5; | • Pets... | 10; | | |

## Secondary Genre[s]:

| | | | |
|---|---|---|---|
| • Variety, General... | VRGL; | • Bluegrass... | BLGS; |
| • Variety, Jazz & Blues... | VRJB; | • Modern Folk... | MFOL; |
| • Variety, Country & Bluegrass | VRCB; | • Traditional Folk... | TFOL; |
| • Variety, Folk & International | VRFI; | • Fiddle and Banjo Events... | FDDL; |
| • Modern Jazz... | MJAZ; | • Maritime... | MARI; |
| • Traditional Jazz & Ragtime... | TJAZ; | • Cajun and Zydeco... | ZYDC; |
| • Alternative Jazz... | AJAZ; | • Irish... | IRSH; |
| • Modern Rock and Pop... | MRCK; | • Jewish... | JWSH; |
| • Classic Rock and Oldies... | CRCK; | • Native American... | NATV; |
| • Alternative & College Rock | ARCK; | • Scottish... | SCOT; |
| • Hard Rock & Heavy Metal | HRCK; | • Modern Latin... | MLAT; |
| • Rap... | RAP; | • Traditional Latin... | TLAT; |
| • Modern R&B... | MR&B; | • African American... | AFRM; |
| • Blues and Traditional R&B... | TR&B; | • African... | AFRC; |
| • Acappella and Doo Wop... | ACAP; | • Brazilian & So. American... | BRZL; |
| • Modern Christian... | CHRS; | • Reggae, Ska & Caribbean... | RGGE; |
| • Black Gospel... | BGOS; | • Avant Garde & New Music... | AVNT; |
| • Southern & Bluegrass Gospel | SGOS; | • Cabaret... | CBRT; |
| • Traditional Gospel & Sings... | TGOS; | • Gay and Lesbian... | GYLS; |
| • Modern Country... | MC&W; | • Drum Corps & March. Bands | DRUM; |
| • Traditional Country... | TC&W; | • Fairs... | FAIR; |
| • Alt. Country & Rockabilly | AC&W; | • Other Genres... | OTHR. |

**Note**

Wherever "**Help!**" appears readers are invited to answer the proceeding questions and/or provide updates. New festival listings that meet the criteria of this book certainly are welcome too! Please mail any current festival information you obtain — especially flyers or brochures — to FESTPRESS, P. O. Box 147, Glen Ridge, NJ 07028. *Thanks!*

### SUGARLOAF SKI-A-PALOOZA/COLLEGE WEEKS, Kingfield, ME
Early Jan. to Middle Jan.
Alternative and College Rock

Three nights midweek for two weeks; one act per night. **Days:** 6. **Site:** indoor. Sugarloaf/USA Ski Resort. **Acts:** national acts, regional acts. **Sample series lineup:** Day One: Belly; Day Two: Cliffs of Donneen; Day Three: O Positive. **Contact:** Sugarloaf/USA, RR 1, Box 5000, Kingfield, ME 04947-9799, 800-THE LOAF.

### PRIDE OF MAINE FIDDLING FESTIVAL, Caribou, ME
Early Feb.
Fiddle and Banjo Events

"A must" - Casco Bay Weekly. See other dates and sites. **Days:** 1. **Site:** indoor. Caribou Performing Arts Center, Sweden Street. **Admission:** paid. **Daily entry:** under $10. **Discounts:** student discounts. **Secondary genre[s]:** TC&W, BLGS, TFOL, IRSH, OTHR. **Acts:** regional acts. **Sample day's lineup:** Ben Guillemette, Tim Farrell, Ellen Gawler, The Old Grey Goose. **Contact:** Caribou Performing Arts Center, Sweden Street, Caribou, ME, 207-493-4278.

### PRIDE OF MAINE FIDDLING FESTIVAL, Machias, ME
Middle Feb.
Fiddle and Banjo Events

"A must" - Casco Bay Weekly. See other dates and sites. **Days:** 2. **Site:** indoor. University of Maine at Machias, Performing Arts Center, 9 O'Brien Avenue. **Admission:** paid. **Daily entry:** under $10. **Discounts:** student discounts. **Secondary genre[s]:** TC&W, BLGS, TFOL, IRSH, OTHR. **Acts:** regional acts. **Sample day's lineup:** Ben Guillemette, Tim Farrell, Ellen Gawler, The Old Grey Goose. **Contact:** University of Maine at Machias, Performing Arts Center, 9 O'Brien Avenue, Machias, ME, 207-255-3313 x213.

### DOWN EAST COUNTRY DANCE FESTIVAL, South Portland, ME
Middle Mar.
Traditional Folk

Since 1990. "NEFFA-like" -- The Dance Gypsy. **Days:** 2. **Site:** indoor. Memorial Middle School. **Admission:** paid. **Daily entry:** under $10, $10 to $24. **Discounts:** multiple event or day passes. **Acts:** local acts. **Sample lineup:** Swallowtail, Dave Kaynor and The Greenfield Dance Band, Lisa Greenleaf and Anything Can Happen, Ted Sanella, others. **Contact:** Down East Country Dance Festival, RFD 1, Box 302, Belgrade, ME 04917, 207-495-2331 **or:** Down East Country Dance Festival, 128 Dresden Avenue, Gardiner, ME 04345.

### RIVER TREE ARTS COUNTRY JAMBOREE, Kennebunk, ME
Middle Mar.
Traditional Country

See other dates and sites. **Help!** One time only? **Days:** 1. **Site:** indoor. Kennebunk High School. **Admission:** paid. **Daily entry:** under $10. **Discounts:** other discounts. **Acts:** regional acts, local acts. **Sample day's lineup:** Gene Hooper Family Show, Little Betty Cody and Denny Breau, Amanda Morton, Alan MacHale and The Old-Time Radio Gang. **Contact:** River Tree Arts, P. O. Box 1056, Kennebunk, ME 04046, 207-985-4343.

BLISTERED FINGERS HELPING HANDS OF BLUEGRASS, Brunswick, ME
Late Mar. to Early Apr.
Bluegrass

Benefits infirm members of bluegrass community. See other dates and sites. **Days:** 2. **Site:** indoor. Atrium Motel, Cooks Corner. **Admission:** paid. **Daily entry:** $10 to $24. **Discounts:** multiple event or day passes, advance purchase discounts. **Restrictions:** 13. **Secondary genre[s]:** SGOS, TC&W. **Acts:** regional acts, local acts. **Sample day's lineup:** Blistered Fingers, White Mountain Bluegrass, Jimmy Cox and Maine Grass, Morse Brothers, Stonewall Bluegrass, Prindhall Family, Oakhurst Boys, Bluegrass Supply Co, Kendall Morse, others. **Contact:** Blistered Fingers Helping Hands of Bluegrass, RFD 1, Box 7560, Waterville, ME 04901, 207-873-6539.


SUGARLOAF REGGAE SKI BASH, Kingfield, ME
Early Apr.
Reggae, Ska and Caribbean

**Days:** 3. **Hours per day:** 13. **Site:** outdoor and indoor. Sugarloaf/USA Ski Resort. **Acts:** regional acts, local acts. **Sample day's lineup:** Winston Grennan and The Ska-Rocks Band, The Danny Tribesman, The I-Tones, Irration. **Contact:** Sugarloaf/USA, RR 1, Box 5000, Kingfield, ME 04947-9799, 800-THE-LOAF.


SUGARLOAF MOUNTAIN BLUES FESTIVAL, Kingfield, ME
Middle Apr.
Blues and Traditional R&B

**Help!** A sample lineup? **Days:** 1. **Hours per day:** 13. **Site:** outdoor and indoor. Sugarloaf/USA Ski Resort. **Acts:** regional acts, local acts. **Contact:** Sugarloaf/USA, RR 1, Box 5000, Kingfield, ME 04947-9799, 800-THE-LOAF.


FIDDLEHEAD FESTIVAL, Unity, ME
Middle May
Bluegrass

**Help!** A sample lineup? **Days:** 1. **Hours per day:** 4. **Site:** indoor. Cafeteria of Unity College, Quaker Hill Road. **Admission:** paid. **Daily entry:** under $10. **Acts:** local acts. **Contact:** Unity College, HC 78, Box 1, Unity, ME 04988, 207-948-3131.


PRIDE OF MAINE FIDDLING FESTIVAL, Waldo, ME
Middle May
Fiddle and Banjo Events

"Top fiddlers of differing styles...back[ed] by a hot band. Always a sell-out." -- Program. See other sites and dates. **Days:** 1. **Site:** indoor. Waldo Theatre. **Admission:** paid. **Daily entry:** under $10, $10 to $24. **Discounts:** children's discounts, advance purchase discounts. **Secondary genre[s]:** BLGS, TFOL, IRSH, OTHR. **Acts:** regional acts, local acts. **Sample day's lineup:** Ben and Dan Guilemette, J. Walter Snipe, Smokey McKeen. **Contact:** Waldo Theatre, 916 Main Street, P. O. Box 587, Waldoboro, ME 04572-0587, 207-832-6060.

HEBRON PINES BLUEGRASS FESTIVAL, Hebron, ME
        Late May
        Bluegrass

Since 1990. See other dates. **Days:** 3. **Hours per day:** 7. **Site:** outdoor. Hebron Pines Campground, Route 124. **Admission:** paid. **Daily entry:** under $10, $10 to $24. **Discounts:** multiple event or day passes, advance purchase discounts. **Acts:** regional acts, local acts. **Sample day's lineup:** Bob Paisley and The Southern Grass, Cedar Ridge, Back to Basics, Hobbs and Partners, Dyer Switch, Backroads, Brian Jiguere, Good Clean Fun, Eddy Poirier and The Bluegrass 4. **Contact:** Hebron Pines Campground, RR 1, Box 1955, Hebron, ME 04238, 207-966-2179/2909.

KALEIDOSCOPE FAMILY ARTS FESTIVAl, Augusta, ME
        Early Jun.
        Variety, General

**Days:** 1. **Hours per day:** 7. **Site:** outdoor. University of Maine at Augusta. **Secondary genre[s]:** MJAZ, MRCK, MFOL, TFOL, IRSH, OTHR. **Acts:** local acts. **Sample day's lineup:** Rugburn, UMA Jazz-on-Tour Band, Barbara Truex, Schleigho, Willow Wind with Tim Dean, Martin Swinger's Jug Band, others. **Contact:** Forum-A, University of Maine at Augusta, 46 University Drive, Augusta, ME 04330-9410, 207-621-3209.

OLD PORT FESTIVAL, Portland, ME
        Early Jun.
        Variety, General

Since 1973. **Days:** 1. **Hours per day:** 8. **Site:** outdoor. 8 stages in Old Port district. **Admission:** free. **Secondary genre[s]:** MJAZ, TJAZ, MRCK, CRCK, ARCK, TR&B, MC&W, BLGS, MFOL, TFOL, RGGE. **Acts:** regional acts, local acts. **Sample day's lineup:** Catie Curtis, Lazy Mercedes, Anni Clark, Lisa Gallant, Slaid Cleaves, Denise and Brad, Peter Galway, Don Campbell, Brenda Moore, Stan Moeller and T. S. Baker, Pyschovsky, Broken Men, Boneheads, Port City Allstars, Streamliner, Jim Ciampi, Papa Loves Mambo, Bellamy Jazz Band, A Cappella Fellas, Sandy River Ramblers, Thomas Hoffman, Midnite Rider, Sleeper. **Contact:** Chamber of Commerce of the Greater Portland Region, 145 Middle Street, Portland, ME 04101, 207-772-2811 **or:** Citrine Resources, 1 Dana Street, Portland, ME 04101, 207-780-8242. .

FESTIVAL OF TRADITIONAL SEA MUSIC, Bath, ME
        Early Jun.
        Maritime

Since 1990. "Sea Shanties and Sailors' Songs from the Great Age of Sail" -- Program. Modeled after Mystic Seaport's Sea Music Festival. No festival in 1993, but Robert Webb, Curator, anticipates resuming it in some form in 1994. **Days:** 2. **Hours per day:** 9. **Site:** outdoor and indoor. Maine Maritime Museum and Shipyard. **Admission:** free and paid. **Daily entry:** under $10, $10 to $24. **Discounts:** student discounts, group sale discounts. **Acts:** regional acts, local acts. **Sample day's lineup:** Forebitter, Bob Webb, Stan Hugill, John Townley, Tony Davis, Ellen Cohn, Felicia Dale, Will Pint, Dick Swain, Jerry Bryant, Tom Goux, Tom Lewis. **Contact:** Maine Maritime Museum and Shipyard, 243 Washington Street, Bath, ME 04530, 207-443-1316.

ARCADY MUSIC FESTIVAL/RAGTIME EVENING BENEFIT, Bangor, ME
        Early Jun.
        Traditional Jazz and Ragtime

Since 1993. Part of a classical music series, the Arcady Music Festival, held in multiple cities. "The [ragtime] evening sold out, with back orders." -- Emily Bean, Event Chairperson. **Days:** 2. **Hours per day:** 5. **Site:** indoor. Theological Seminary. **Admission:** paid. **Daily entry:** $10 to $24. **Discounts:** advance purchase discounts. **Acts:** local acts. **Sample day's lineup:** Masanobu Ikemiya and The Arcady Ragtime Orchestra, Dr. Maynard Beech, others. **Contact:** Arcady Music Society, P. O. Box 780, Bar Harbor, ME 04609, 207-288-3151/942-0214.

## FAMILY FUN FAIR, Portland, ME
Middle Jun.
Variety, General

Since 1993. **Days:** 1. **Hours per day:** 4. **Site:** outdoor. 331 Veranda Street. **Admission:** free. **Secondary genre[s]:** TJAZ, TFOL, MARI. **Acts:** national acts, local acts. **Sample day's lineup:** Schooner Fare, State Street Jazz Band, others. **Contact:** Martin's Point Health Care Center, 331 Veranda Street, Portland, ME, 207-774-5801.

## BACK COVE FAMILY DAY, Portland, ME
Middle Jun.
Variety, General

Since 1987. **Days:** 1. **Hours per day:** 5. **Site:** outdoor. Payson Park, Baxter Boulevard and Back Cove. **Admission:** free. **Secondary genre[s]:** TJAZ, MFOL. **Acts:** local acts. **Sample Day's Lineup:** Hoose Family, Port City Allstars, Next Voice. **Contact:** Portland Recreation, 389 Congress Street, Portland, ME, 207-874-8793.

## HAPPY HORSESHOE BLUE GRASS FESTIVAL, North New Portland, ME
Middle Jun.
Bluegrass

Since 1985. Focal point of a summer-long program of Saturday-night C&W shows. **Days:** 2. **Site:** outdoor. **Acts:** regional acts, local acts. **Sample day's lineup:** Shady Creek, Sandy River Ramblers, others. **Contact:** Happy Horseshoe Blue Grass Festival, HCR 68, Box 258, Anson, ME 04958, 207-635-2965.

## BLISTERED FINGERS FAMILY BLUEGRASS MUSIC FESTIVAL, Sidney, ME
Middle Jun.
Bluegrass

Since 1991. "Off-stage field pickin' 24 hours a day!" -- Program. See other dates and sites. **Days:** 4. **Hours per day:** 15. **Site:** outdoor. Silver Spur Riding Club. **Admission:** paid. **Daily entry:** $10 to $24. **Discounts:** multiple event or day passes, advance purchase discounts. **Restrictions:** 13. **Secondary genre[s]:** SGOS, TC&W. **Acts:** national acts, regional acts, local acts. **Sample day's lineup:** Rhonda Vincent and The Sally Mountain Show, Bill Mounce and The Outlaws, The Cox Family, Bluegrass Supply Co., Stonewall Bluegrass, River Bottom Band, Yodelin' Slim Clark, Herb Applin and The Berkshire Mountain Boys, Bear Bridge Band, Blistered Fingers. **Contact:** Blistered Fingers Family Bluegrass Music Festival, RFD 1, Box 7560, Waterville ME, 04901, 207-873-6539.

## FIDDLING COMPETITION AND CONTRA DANCE, Damariscotta, ME
Middle Jun.
Fiddle and Banjo Events

Since 1993. "It went great! We'd like to do it again." -- Office Manager. **Help!** One time only? **Days:** 1. **Site:** indoor. Round Top Center for the Arts. **Secondary genre[s]:** BLGS, TFOL. **Acts:** local acts. **Sample day's lineup:** Greg Boardman and Friends. **Contact:** Round Top Center for the Arts, Box 1316, Damariscotta, ME 04543, 207-563-1507.

KATAHDIN FAMILY BLUEGRASS MUSIC FESTIVAL, Medway, ME
> Late Jun.
> Bluegrass

Since 1992. "Off-stage field pickin' 24 hours a day" -- Program. **Days:** 3. **Hours per day:** 14. **Site:** outdoor. East Branch Sno Rovers Club. **Admission:** paid. **Daily entry:** $10 to $24. **Discounts:** multiple event or day passes, advance purchase discounts. **Restrictions:** 13. **Secondary genre[s]:** SGOS, TC&W. **Acts:** regional acts, local acts. **Sample day's lineup:** Smokey Greene and The Boys, Eddy Poirer and Bluegrass, Blistered Fingers, Yodelin' Slim Clark, Bluegrass Supply Co., Jimmy Cox and The Maine Grass, New Shade of Blue, Misty Mountain Revue, Poirer Family, Windy Ridge. **Contact:** Katahdin Regional Tourism Council, P. O. Box 502, East Millinocket, ME 04430, 207-746-5410.

LAKERMESSE FRANCO-AMERICAINE FESTIVAL, Biddeford, ME
> Late Jun.
> Variety, General

Since 1983. "As the weekend progresses, enjoy the memories that are awakened in you as you smell the boudin, taste the tourtiere and listen to the traditional French music." -- Robert R. Provencher, Festival President. **Days:** 3. **Hours per day:** 10. **Site:** outdoor and indoor. **Admission:** free and paid. **Daily entry:** under $10. **Secondary genre[s]:** MJAZ, TJAZ, CRCK, MC&W, MFOL, OTHR. **Acts:** local acts. **Sample day's lineup:** Bushwack, Dick Coffin, Canadien Revival, La Famille Gagne, C'est si Bon, Bellamy Jazz Band, Annick Gagnon, Easy Money, Cheyenne, Silver Dollar Band, Lucie Therrien, Glenn Jenks, Roger and Ray, Saco River Rats, Touch and Go, Mario Sevigny, Cool Shade of Blue, Spectrum. **Audio merchandise:** "Acadien Music of the St. John Valley" (Northeast Archives of Folklore and Oral History, Dept. of Anthropology, South Stevens Hall, University of Maine, Orono, ME 04469). **Contact:** Biddeford-Saco Chamber of Commerce and Industry, 170 Main Street, Biddeford, ME 04005-2597, 207-282-1567 **or:** La Kermesse Franco-Americaine de Biddeford, Inc., P. O. Box 289, Biddeford, ME 04005-0289, 207-283-2826.

BLUES FESTIVAL, North Yarmouth, ME
> Late Jun.
> Blues and Traditional R&B

Since 1990. **Days:** 1. **Hours per day:** 7. **Site:** indoor. Westcustogo Grange Hall. **Admission:** paid. **Daily entry:** under $10. **Secondary genre[s]:** ACAP, BGOS. **Acts:** regional acts, local acts. **Sample day's lineup:** BBQ Blues Boys, The Streetwalkers, Men of Faith, Shirley Lewis. **Contact:** Southern Maine Blues Society, P. O. Box 4703, Portland, ME 04112, 207-865-3455/627-7284.

PORTLAND WATERFRONT FESTIVAL, Portland, ME
> Late Jun.
> Modern Folk

**Days:** 1. **Hours per day:** 7. **Site:** outdoor. Portland Fish Pier. **Admission:** free. **Secondary genre[s]:** MARI. **Acts:** national acts, regional acts, local acts. **Sample day's lineup:** Devonsquare, Lazy Mercedes, Brownie and Julie, others. **Contact:** Portland Waterfront District, Two Portland Fish Pier, Portland, ME 04101, 207-773-1613.

STRAWBERRY FESTIVAL, South Berwick, ME
> Late Jun.
> Variety, General

Since 1976. **Days:** 2. **Hours per day:** 12. **Site:** outdoor and indoor. Various locations downtown. **Admission:** free and paid. **Daily entry:** under $10, $10 to $24. **Discounts:** advance purchase discounts. **Secondary genre[s]:** TJAZ, CRCK, ACAP, MC&W, OTHR. **Acts:** local acts. **Sample day's lineup:** Nightwind, Time Travelers, Women of Note, Tim Samples. **Contact:** Strawberry Festival, 14 Alder Drive, South Berwick, ME 03908, 207-384-5515.

GREAT WHATEVER WEEK AND RACE, Augusta, ME
Late Jun. to Early Jul.
Variety, General

Huge affair with over 50 events, including the featured "fun race" down the Kennebec River on the final day. "The river thrives! Our Kennebec stage is set for a tremendous celebration of our environment, our quality of life in the valley." -- Kennebec Valley Chamber of Commerce. **Help!** A sample lineup? **Days:** 10. **Hours per day:** 17. **Site:** outdoor and indoor. **Admission:** Free. **Secondary genre[s]:** ACAP, MC&W, OTHR. **Acts:** local acts. **Sample series lineup:** Day One: "Evening of A Cappella Singing"; Day Two: "True Country/GMC Truck Country Showdown" with The Silver Dollar Band; Day Three: "Whatever Week Rock Festival." **Contact:** Kennebec Valley Chamber of Commerce, 1 University Drive, P. O. Box E, Augusta, ME 04332-0192, 207-623-4559/622-4255.

GRAND RIVIERE FESTIVAL, Van Buren, ME
Late Jun. to Middle Aug.
Variety, General

**Days:** 3. **Site:** outdoor. **Admission:** free and paid. **Daily entry:** under $10. **Discounts: Secondary genre[s]:** MFOL, NATV, AFRC, OTHR. **Acts:** local acts. **Sample day's lineup:** Ida Roy, Don Cyr, Maliseet Indians. **Contact:** Van Buren Chamber of Commerce, 65 Main Street, Van Buren, ME, 207-868-5059.

WINDJAMMER DAYS, Boothbay Harbor, ME
Late Jun.
Variety, General

Since 1963. Celebrating Boothbay Harbor's proud history as a seaport for sailing schooners, called "windjammers." "A three-day, power-packed, family entertainment and vacation event." -- Gail Clarke, Executive Director. **Days:** 2. **Hours per day:** 12. **Site:** outdoor. Various locations downtown. **Admission:** free. **Secondary genre[s]:** TJAZ, MRCK, TR&B, MFOL, MARI, SCOT, AVNT. **Acts:** regional acts, local acts. **Sample series lineup:** Day One: Heavy Metal Horns, Arlo West; Day Two: Atlantic Clarion Steel Drum Band, Finger Twisters; Day Three: Northern Caledonia Pipe Band, Royal River Philharmonic Jazz Band, others. **Contact:** Windjammer Days, Box 356, Boothbay Harbor, ME 04538, 207-633-2353.

ACADIAN FESTIVAL CELEBRATION, Madawaska, ME
Late Jun. to Early Jul.
Variety, Folk and International

Since 1978. "Though we have lost our lovely Acadia, never will we forget her." -- Program. "Let the good times roll!" -- St. John Valley Times. **Days:** 6. **Hours per day:** 16. **Site:** outdoor and indoor. Main Street, Bicentennial Park, Knights of Columbus Hall, Multi-Purpose Building. **Secondary genre[s]:** CRCK, ZYDC, OTHR. **Acts:** national acts, regional acts, local acts. **Sample day's lineup:** Beausoleil, Acadian Singers from Fort Kent, C'est Si Bon Band, others. **Audio merchandise:** "Acadien Music of the St. John Valley" (Northeast Archives of Folklore and Oral History, Dept. of Anthropology, South Stevens Hall, University of Maine, Orono, ME 04469). **Contact:** Madawaska Chamber of Commerce, P. O. Box 387, Madawaska, ME 04756, 207-728-7000.

OLD HOME WEEK AND INDEPENDENCE DAY, Eastport, ME
    Late Jun. to Early Jul.
    Variety, General

"The town goes from 2,000 people to 10-to-20,000. It's a great reunion week both for residents and for visitors." -- Valerie Maziani, Festival President. **Days:** 3. **Site:** outdoor. **Admission:** free. **Secondary genre[s]:** TJAZ, ACAP, TGOS, TC&W, MFOL, SCOT, RGGE. **Acts:** regional acts, local acts. **Sample day's lineup:** Roger Asselin Band, Barbara Smith, Sunrise Serenaders, Shead High School Band, Allan MacHale and The Old-Time Radio Gang, Gene Hooper and Family, Jimmy Simmonds and The Orange River Jazz Band, Adams Family, Kiwanis All Steel Band, others. **Contact:** Eastport Chamber of Commerce, P. O. Box 254, Eastport, ME 04631-0254, 207-853-4644.

BATH HERITAGE DAYS, Bath, ME
    Early Jul.
    Variety, General

**Days:** 4. **Hours per day:** 12. **Site:** outdoor. **Admission:** free and paid. **Daily entry:** $10 to $24. **Secondary genre[s]:** TJAZ, CRCK, ARCK, MC&W, MFOL, TFOL, OTHR. **Acts:** national acts, regional acts, local acts. **Sample day's lineup:** Rob Eberhard-Young, The Killer Greens, Steve Gurlack, Keith Perry, Scott Link, Blue Hill Brass Quintet, Open Mind, Krazy Knave, In The Pocket, On The Street, Glenshane, Blue Chips Trio, Devonsquare, Rapture of the Deep, Hot Cherry Pie. **Contact:** Bath Area Chamber of Commerce, 45 Front Street, Bath, ME 04530, 207-443-9751.

BLUE HILL POPS, Blue Hill, ME
    Early Jul.
    Variety, General

Since 1991. **Days:** 1. **Site:** indoor. George Stevens Academy. **Admission:** paid. **Daily entry:** $10 to $24. **Discounts:** group sale discounts. **Secondary genre[s]:** TFOL, RGGE, OTHR. **Acts:** local acts. **Sample day's lineup:** Atlantic Clarion Steel Band, Bagaduce Chroal Singers, Kneisel Hall Faculty Ensemble, Blue Hill Brass Quintet, Oakum Bay String Band. **Contact:** George Stevens Academy, Green's Hill, Blue Hill, ME 04614, 207-374-5121.

**WERU 89.9FM** FULL CIRCLE SUMMER FAIR, Union, ME
    Early Jul.
    Variety, General

Since 1990. **Days:** 1. **Hours per day:** 8. **Site:** outdoor and indoor. Union Fairgrounds, Route 17. **Admission:** paid. **Daily entry:** under $10, $10 to $24. **Discounts: Secondary genre[s]:** MJAZ, ARCK, TR&B, ACAP, BLGS, MFOL, TFOL, MARI, IRSH, AFRC. **Acts:** regional acts, local acts. **Sample day's lineup:** Paul Anderson and Lei Garofalo, Bruce Pratt, Bar Scott, Killer Greens, Positive Fuzz, Belle Isle Quintet, Zulu Leprechans, Streetwalkers, Liberty Balalaika Orchestra, Bowen Swerzy and Hawk Henries, Spindrift, Abbe Anderson, Chord On Blue, Frank Gotwals, Many Land Dance Band, Pixie Lauer and Diana Hansen, Solstice, Miriam Brody, The Pajamen, Joel and Robin Mann, Topaz Weis, Huddled Masses/Bar Harbor Folk Orchestra, Karl's Dance Band. **Contact:** WERU 89.9FM, The Hen House, Blue Hill Falls, ME 04615, 207-374-2313/2314.

NEW VINEYARD MOUNTAINS BLUEGRASS FESTIVAl, North Anson, ME
    Early Jul.
    Bluegrass

Since 1989. "Picnic with family and friends beneath the boughs of majestic pines in this beautiful 150 acre area while enjoying the best in bluegrass entertainment." -- Program. **Days:** 2. .**Admission:** paid. **Daily entry:** $10 to $24. **Discounts:** multiple event or day passes, advance purchase discounts, group sale discounts. **Restrictions:** 13. **Acts:** local acts. **Sample day's lineup:** Bluegrass Supply Co., plus talent contests in 15 categories. **Contact:** Owens Farms Bluegrass Co., 2013 Channel Road, Pylesville, MD 21132, 410-836-0528/452-5828.

## COOR'S LITE MUSIC FESTIVAL, Brewer, ME
   Early Jul.
   Modern Rock and Pop

Since 1987. **Days:** 1. **Hours per day:** 12. **Site:** outdoor. Doyle Field. **Admission:** paid. **Daily entry:** under $10. **Secondary genre[s]:** CRCK, MC&W. **Acts:** local acts. **Sample day's lineup:** The Dogs, Mr. Know-It-All, Unfinished Business, Shy Boy, Dakota. **Contact:** F. A. Productions, 428 Wilson Street, Brewer, ME 04412, 207-843-6096.

## ROCK 'N' ROLL BAR-B-Q, Old Orchard Beach, ME
   Early Jul.
   Classic Rock and Oldies

"The beach rocks again! Be there!" -- Advertisement. **Help!** One time only? **Days:** 1. **Site:** outdoor. Maine Entertainment Center at the Ballpark. **Admission:** paid. **Daily entry:** $10 to $24. **Discounts:** group sale discounts. **Secondary genre[s]:** TR&B. **Acts:** national acts. **Sample day's lineup:** Southside Johnny and The Asbury Jukes, Clarence Clemmons and The Red Bank Rockers, Magic Dick and "J"Erome Geils Bluestime. **Contact:** Ballpark Productions, Inc., P. O. Box F, Old Orchard Beach, ME 04064, 207-934-1124.

## THOMASTON INDEPENDENCE DAY CELEBRATION, Thomaston, ME
   Early Jul.
   Variety, General

**Site:** outdoor. Harbor Park Public Landing. **Secondary genre[s]:** MJAZ, TR&B. **Acts:** local acts. **Sample day's lineup:** Blind Albert Band, Mid-Coast Community Band, Lincolnville Town Band, others. **Contact:** Rockland-Thomaston Area Chamber of Commerce, P. O. Box 508, Rockland, ME 04841, 207-596-0376.

## BREAKNECK MOUNTAIN BLUEGRASS FESTIVAL, Crawford, ME
   Early Jul.
   Bluegrass

Since 1985. "The music was great, the location pleasant...and the people really friendly. Maine was beautiful..." -- Peter V. Kuykendal, Bluegrass Unlimited. **Days:** 3. **Hours per day:** 12. **Site:** outdoor. Kennedy Homestead, a 100-acre farm. **Admission:** paid. **Daily entry:** under $10, $10 to $24. **Discounts:** multiple event or day passes, advance purchase discounts. **Restrictions:** 10, 13. **Secondary genre[s]:** SGOS, TC&W. **Acts:** regional acts, local acts. **Sample day's lineup:** Close to Home, Bluegrass Supply Co., Fred Pike, Sam Tidwell and The Kennebec Valley Boys, Sandy River Ramblers, Sassygrass, Out of Hand, Fogg Brothers, Jimmy Cox and Maine Grass, Evergreen, Yodelin' Slim Clark. **Contact:** Breakneck Mountain Productions, Inc., RFD 1, Box 1210, Harmony, ME 04942, 207-277-3733/454-2950.

## DOWNEAST DULCIMER AND HARP FESTIVAL, Bar Harbor, ME
   Early Jul.
   Traditional Folk

**Days:** 3. **Hours per day:** 8. **Site:** outdoor and indoor. Daytime workshops at Agamont Park (Town Pier); evening concerts at Congregational Church (Mount Desert Street). **Admission:** free and paid. **Daily entry:** under $10. **Secondary genre[s]:** IRSH. **Acts:** regional acts, local acts. **Sample day's lineup:** Aubrey Atwater, Sam Moffatt, Kim Robertson, Jerry and Nancy Bell, Kasha Breau. **Contact:** Song of the Sea, 47 West Street, Bar Harbor, ME 04609, 207-288-5653.

FESTIVAL DE LA BASTILLE, Augusta, ME
> Early Jul.
> Variety, Folk and International

Since 1984. Big blowout celebrating a range of French music. **Days:** 3. **Hours per day:** 15. **Site:** outdoor and indoor. Le Club Calumet field, Old Belgrave Road. **Admission:** free and paid. **Daily entry:** under $10. **Secondary genre[s]:** MFOL, ZYDC, OTHR, **Acts:** national acts, regional acts, local acts. **Sample day's lineup:** Basin Brothers Cajun Band, C'est Si Bon Band with Therese "Dube" Desbiens, Denis Cote, Gagne Family, Breton Twins, Josee Vachon, Jean-Paul Poulain, The Psaltery, Lucie Therrien Duo. **Contact:** Festival de la Bastille, P. O. Box 47, North Leeds, ME 04263, 207-524-3252 **or:** Festival de la Bastille, P. O. Box 110, Augusta, ME 04330, 207-623-8211. .

SCHOONER DAYS, Rockland, ME
> Early Jul.
> Variety, General

"We pride ourselves on quality music and try to get a good mixture to keep people entertained. Schooner Fare has been an annual fixture for seven years." -- Festival Manager. **Days:** 3. **Site:** outdoor. Multiple locations. **Admission:** free and paid. **Daily entry:** under $10. **Secondary genre[s]:** MJAZ, TJAZ, MC&W, BLGS, TFOL, MARI, SCOT. **Acts:** national acts, local acts. **Sample day's lineup:** Schooner Fare, Woods Tea Co., The Morgans, Pine Ridge Boys, Dick Curliss, Stan Catell and Down East Jazz. **Contact:** Rockland-Thomaston Area Chamber of Commerce, P. O. Box 508, Rockland, ME 04841, 207-596-0376.

SEASIDE FESTIVAL, Kittery, ME
> Early Jul.
> Variety, General

Since 1983. "We are pleased to bring together local artisans, food concessions, entertainers, clowns, costume characters and sensational fireworks!" -- Program. **Days:** 1. **Hours per day:** 12. **Site:** outdoor. Fort Foster Park. **Secondary genre[s]:** CRCK, ACAP, MFOL, OTHR. **Acts:** local acts. **Sample day's lineup:** Shades of Harmony, Merseyside Quartet, Tony Vance and Finesse, Gene Stamell, The Harbor Belles, Wayne Read, Janine. **Contact:** Kittery Recreation Department, P. O. Box 808, Cole Street, Kittery, ME 03904, 207-439-3800.

ROTARY OYSTER FESTIVAL, Damariscotta, ME
> Early Jul. to Middle Jul.
> Variety, General

"We don't repeat acts -- we've had Allan McHale and Schooner Fare in past years -- but we have a good time." -- Howard Hebb, President. **Days:** 3. **Hours per day:** 15. **Site:** outdoor. Downtown municipal parking lot. **Admission:** free. **Secondary genre[s]:** TC&W, MFOL, TFOL, MARI, OTHR. **Acts:** national acts, local acts. **Sample series lineup:** Day One: Anderson-Gram, Zingo Zango Generic Jug Band, German Oktoberfest Blaz Band; Day Two: Pete Collins; Day Three: Rick Adam, Robin Mello, Bath Municipal Band. **Contact:** Damariscotta Rotary Club, P. O. Box 565, Damariscotta, ME 04543, 207-882-6583.

CELEBRATE GORHAM, Gorham, ME
> Early Jul.
> Variety, General

**Days:** 1. **Hours per day:** 12. **Site:** outdoor and indoor. Narragansett School, 300 Main Street. **Secondary genre[s]:** TFOL. **Acts:** local acts. **Sample day's lineup:** Bellamy Jazz Band, Fanfare Band, Pard and The Countrymen. **Contact:** Gorham Arts Council, P. O. Box 126, Gorham, ME 04038, 207-839-4849.

NATIVE AMERICAN FESTIVAL, Bar Harbor, ME
> Early Jul.
> Native American

Since 1989. **Days:** 1. **Hours per day:** 6. **Site:** outdoor. College of the Atlantic, Route 3. **Admission:** free. **Contact:** Abbe Musuem, P. O. Box 286, Bar Harbor, ME 04609, 207-288-3519.


NORTH ATLANTIC BLUES FESTIVAL, Rockland, ME
> Early Jul.
> Blues and Traditional R&B

Since 1994. **Days:** 1. **Site:** outdoor. Rockland Public Landing. **Admission:** paid. **Daily entry:** $10 to $24. **Discounts:** advance purchase discounts. **Restrictions:** 5, 10. **Secondary genre[s]:** CRCK. **Acts:** national acts, regional acts, local acts. **Sample day's lineup:** James Cotton Band, Eddie Kirkland and The Energy Band, Magic Dick/"J"erome Geils Bluestime, Tony Lynn Washington Band, Little Anthony and The Locomotives, Carey Bell Blues Band, Heavy Metal Horns, The Blues Flames, Susan Tedeschi. **Contact:** North Atlantic Blues Festival, P. O. Box 1522, Scarborough, ME 04070, 207-883-1774.


MOTAHKMIKUK INDIAN DAY CELEBRATION, Princeton, ME
> Middle Jul. to Middle Jul.
> Native American

Since 1985. **Days:** 3. **Site:** outdoor. .**Acts:** local acts. **Contact:** Motahkmikuk Indian Day Committee, P. O. Box 301, Princeton, ME 04668, 207-796-5118/2301 x15.


MAINE POTATO BLOSSOM FESTIVAL/CROWN OF MAINE BALLOON FESTIVAL, Fort Fairfield, ME
> Early Jul. to Middle Jul.
> Variety, General

Since 1948. **Days:** 8. **Hours per day:** 15. **Site:** outdoor and indoor. **Secondary genre[s]:** ACAP, SGOS, BLGS, SCOT, OTHR. **Acts:** local acts. **Sample day's lineup:** Wild Ginger, Family Castonguay, Portland Brass Quartet, Crash Alley, Atlantic Clarion Steel Band. **Contact:** Fort Fairfield Chamber of Commerce, 121 Main Street, Fort Fairfield, ME, 207-472-3802.


LEFT BANK CAFE COUNTRY BLUES FESTIVAL, Blue Hill, ME
> Middle Jul.
> Blues and Traditional R&B

Since 1994. **Days:** 7. **Hours per day:** 6. **Site:** indoor. Left Bank Bakery and Cafe. **Admission:** paid. **Daily entry:** $10 to $24 **Discounts:** multiple event or day passes. **Acts:** national acts. **Sample day's lineup:** Howard Armstrong, Nat Reese, Paul Geremia. **Audio merchandise:** "Live at the Left Bank, Vol. One" (self-produced and distributed). **Contact:** Left Bank Bakery and Cafe, P. O. Box 981, Blue Hill, ME 04614, 207-374-2201.


BELFAST BAY FESTIVAL, Belfast, ME
> Middle Jul.
> Variety, General

Since 1948. **Days:** 5. **Hours per day:** 10. **Site:** outdoor. Belfast City Park. **Admission:** free. **Secondary genre[s]:** MJAZ, TJAZ, MC&W, TC&W, BLGS, TFOL, SCOT, OTHR. **Acts:** regional acts, local acts. **Sample day's line-up:** Billy Chinook and The Asbury Dukes Horns, Blue Hill Bras Quintet, River City Harmonizers, Acadian Pipes and Drums, others. **Contact:** Belfast Area Chamber of Commerce, 31 Front Street, Belfast, ME 04915, 207-338-5900 **or:** Belfast Days Festival, P. O. Box 37, Belfast, ME 04915, 207-338-4910.

### YARMOUTH CLAM FESTIVAL, Yarmouth, ME
Middle Jul.
Variety, General

Since 1966. "It's a hot time in the old clam town tonight!" -- Program. "...One of those annual Maine events that nobody ought to pass up." -- Casco Bay Weekly. **Days:** 3. **Hours per day:** 16. **Site:** outdoor. **Admission:** free. **Secondary genre[s]:** MJAZ, TJAZ, CRCK, ACAP, BGOS, TGOS, MC&W, BLGS, MFOL, TFOL, MARI, BRZL, OTHR. **Acts:** national acts, local acts. **Sample day's lineup:** Devonsquare, Royal River Philharmonic Jazz Band, Fogg Brothers, Electric Quintet, Renegades, Doc's Banjo Band, Pacto Andino, Ellen and The Sea Slugs, Downeasters Barbershop Chorus and Quartet. **Contact:** Yarmouth Chamber of Commerce, U. S. Route 1, Yarmouth, ME, 207-846-3984.

### CELEBRATION OF THE ARTS, Kennebunk, ME
Middle Jul. to Late Jul.
Modern Folk

See other dates and sites. **Days:** 8. **Site:** outdoor. Franciscan Monastery. **Secondary genre[s]:** TR&B, OTHR. **Acts:** local acts. **Sample series lineup:** Day One: Steven Bracciotti; Day Two: Ed Roseman; Day Three: Spider John Koerner. **Contact:** River Tree Arts, P. O. Box 1056, Kennebunkpor,t ME 04046, 207-985-4343.

### MOLLYOCKETT DAY, Bethel, ME
Middle Jul.
Variety, General

Since 1950. Honoring the legendary healing and storytelling gifts of 18th-Century Pequawket Indian princess, Mollyockett. **Days:** 2. **Hours per day:** 13. **Site:** outdoor. Bethel Common. **Admission:** free. **Secondary genre[s]:** CRCK, FDDL. **Acts:** local acts. **Sample day's lineup:** Brandon Moore and The Flat Road Riders, plus fiddlers' contest. **Contact:** Bethel Chamber of Commerce, P. O. Box 439, Bethel, ME 04217, 207-824-2282.

### OLD HALLOWELL DAY, Hallowell, ME
Middle Jul.
Variety, General

Since 1968. Historic riverside town, part bohemian, part antique center, sees its poulation swell to ten times its size for a two-day bash. "You can see whatever you want [on multiple stages], from heavy metal to folk. It ranges from a rockin' good time to All-American family entertainment!" -- Pat Gilbert, City Manager. **Days:** 2. **Hours per day:** 12. **Site:** outdoor and indoor. **Admission:** free. **Secondary genre[s]:** ARCK, HRCK, MC&W, BLGS, MFOL, TFOL, OTHR. **Acts:** local acts. **Sample day's lineup:** Bellamy Jazz Band, Fat Alice, The Danny Tribesmen, Eight to the Bar, Trillium, School Street Band, Benny Rheel, others. **Contact:** Town of Hallowell, 1 Winthrop Street, Hallowell, ME 04347, 207-623-4021.

### RICHMOND DAYS, Richmond, ME
Middle Jul. to Late Jul.
Variety, General

Since 1969. **Days:** 8. **Hours per day:** 14. **Site:** outdoor. **Secondary genre[s]:** CRCK, MC&W, OTHR. **Acts:** local acts. **Sample series lineup:** Day One: Dawn Renee and The Lonesome Dove Band; Day Two: Flashback, Sugar and Spice. **Contact:** Richmond Town Office, Gardiner Street, Richmond, ME, 207-737-8602/8613.

## RANGELEY'S OLD-TIME FIDDLERS' CONTEST, Rangeley, ME
Middle Jul.

Fiddle and Banjo Events

Since 1981. "A real family kind of thing in a very pleasant spot -- on a big lawn in front of a flower pond in beautiful Rangeley" -- Priscilla St. Louis, Festival Promoter. **Days:** 1. **Hours per day:** 3. **Site:** outdoor, Rangeley Inn. **Admission:** paid. **Daily entry:** under $10. **Acts:** local acts. **Contact:** Rangeley Friends of the Arts, Star Route, Box HC32-1060, Rangeley, ME 04970, 207-864-5571/5200.

## DEERING OAKS FAMILY FESTIVAL, Portland, ME
Middle Jul. to Late Jul.

Variety, General

Since 1982. **Days:** 7. **Hours per day:** 12. **Site:** outdoor. Deering Oaks Park, corner of State Street and Park Avenue. **Admission:** free. **Secondary genre[s]:** MJAZ, TJAZ, CRCK, MC&W, BLGS, MFOL, TFOL, MARI, ZYDC, RGGE, OTHR. **Acts:** national acts, local acts. **Sample day's lineup:** Davis Daniel, Silver Dollar Band, Wicked Good Band, Big Chief and The Continentals, Broken Men, Rick Charette and The Bubblegum Band. **Contact:** Chamber of Commerce of the Greater Portland Region, 145 Middle Street, Portland, ME 04101, 207-772-2811 **or:** Citrine Resources, 1 Dana Street, Portland, ME 04101, 207-780-8242. .

## CENTRAL MAINE EGG FESTIVAL, Pittsfield, ME
Middle Jul. to Late Jul.

Variety, General

"Eggscovering the Americas [honoring Christopher Columbus]." -- Program. **Days:** 7. **Hours per day:** 16. **Site:** outdoor. Manson Park. **Admission:** free. **Secondary genre[s]:** MC&W, TC&W, TFOL. **Acts:** local acts. **Sample day's lineup:** Loose Change, Davis Family Band, Bob Elston and The Road Rangers, Doug Goodwin and Country Swing. **Contact:** Central Maine Egg Festival, P. O. Box 82, Pittsfield, ME 04967, 207-487-5416.

## YORK DAYS, York, ME
Late Jul. to Early Aug.

Variety, General

Since 1982. **Days:** 10. **Site:** outdoor. .**Secondary genre[s]:** TC&W, BLGS, OTHR. **Acts:** local acts. **Sample day's lineup:** Mike Preston, Fifth of Brass, Yankee Strummers Banjo Band, others. **Contact:** York Chamber of Commerce, 226 York Street, York, ME, 207-363-4422.

## SUGARLOAF COUNTRY MUSIC FESTIVAL, Kingfield, ME
Late Jul. and Late Aug.

Modern Country

Since 1993. **Days:** 3. **Hours per day:** 8. **Site:** outdoor. Sugarloaf/USA Ski Resort. **Admission:** paid. **Daily entry:** $10 to $24, $25 to $49. **Acts:** national acts, local acts. **Sample day's lineup:** Emmylou Harris, Waylon Jennings, Jerry Jeff Walker, two local bands. **Contact:** Sugarloaf/USA, Box 5000, Kingfield, ME 04947, 800-THE-LOAF.

## GAMPER FESTIVAL OF CONTEMPORARY MUSIC, Brunswick, ME
Late Jul.

Avant Garde and New Music

Presents works of living composers. **Help!** Does anyone have a sample program? **Days:** 4. **Site:** indoor, Kresge Auditorium, Bowdoin College. **Admission:** paid. **Daily entry:** under $10. **Contact:** Music Department, Bowdoin College, Brunswick, ME, 207-725-3322/3895.

BAR HARBOR FESTIVAL/NEW COMPOSERS CONCERT, Bar Harbor, ME
Late Jul.
Avant Garde and New Music

Since 1984. Part of a classical music series, the Bar Harbor Festival. **Site:** indoor. Bar Harbor Congregational Church. **Admission:** paid. **Daily entry:** under $10, $10 to $24. **Discounts:** student discounts. **Sample day's lineup**: Duo Sequenza performs works of Conkey, Zaimont, Harbison. **Contact:** Bar Harbor Music Festival, Rodick Building, 59 Cottage Street, Bar Harbor, ME 04609, 207-288-5744.


BANGOR STATE FAIR, Bangor, ME
Late Jul. to Early Aug.
Fairs

Since 1849. **Days:** 10. **Hours per day:** 12. **Site:** outdoor and indoor. Bass Park Complex, Buck and Main Streets; Bangor Auditorium, 100 Dutton Street. **Admission:** paid. **Daily entry:** under $10. **Secondary genre[s]:** CRCK, MC&W, TC&W, BLGS, MFOL. **Acts:** national acts, regional acts, local acts. **Sample series lineup:** Day One: Tracy Lawrence; Day Two: Mark Collie, David Mallett, Northern Lights; Day Three: Allan McHale and The Old-Time Radio Gang. **Contact:** Bass Park Complex, 100 Dutton Street, Bangor, ME 04401, 207-942-9000.


HOMECOMING, Grand Isle, ME
Late Jul. to Early Aug.
Variety, General

**Days:** 3. **Hours per day:** 14. **Site:** outdoor and indoor. .**Admission:** free and paid. **Secondary genre[s]:** OTHR. **Acts:** local acts. **Sample series lineup:** Day One: Jerry Thibeault Band; Days Two, Three: "Variety Shows." **Contact:** Homecoming, P. O. Box 1993, Grand Isle, ME, 207-492-3771.


INTERNATIONAL FESTIVAL, Calais, ME
Late Jul. to Early Aug.
Variety, General

Since 1974. "Over the past twenty years, the festival has grown from a small local event to an international celebration that draws performers and tourists from all areas of the U. S. and Canada." -- Program. **Days:** 9. **Site:** outdoor. **Admission:** free and paid. **Daily entry:** under $10, $10 to $24. **Secondary genre[s]:** SGOS, TGOS, MC&W, TC&W, BLGS, MFOL, OTHR. **Acts:** national acts, regional acts, local acts. **Sample series lineup:** Day One: "Annual International Blues Concert," featuring Luther "Guitar Jr." Johnson, International Choir Festival; Day Two: "Summersong" with local folk and country musicians; Day Three: "Festival of Praise," "Gospel Concert." **Contact:** International Festival, Box 175, Calais, ME 04619, 207-454-3216.


EAST BENTON FIDDLERS' CONVENTION AND CONTEST, East Benton, ME
Late Jul.
Fiddle and Banjo Events

Since 1973. "Five finalists compete in the Maine Fiddling Contest. First prize: $500." -- Program. **Days:** 1. **Hours per day:** 8. **Site:** outdoor. Littlefield Farm. **Admission:** paid. **Daily entry:** under $10. **Restrictions:** 4, 10. **Secondary genre[s]:** TC&W, BLGS, TFOL. **Acts:** local acts. **Sample day's lineup:** Yodeling Slim Clark, Scott Markee, Vaughn Meader and Friends, Country Choir, Sopers Old Time Band, East Benton Jug Band. **Contact:** East Benton Fiddlers' Convention and Contest, Box 215, Clinton, ME 04927, 207-453-2017.

## H. O. M. E. Craft and Farm Fair, Orland, ME
Early Aug.
Variety, General

**Days:** 1. **Hours per day:** 12. **Site:** outdoor. Route 1. **Admission:** paid. **Daily entry:** under $10. **Secondary genre[s]:** MRCK, MC&W, AFRC. **Acts:** local acts. **Sample day's lineup:** Rick Kelly, Elzadia Parsons, Marie Dow, Linwood Stover, Numazahake, Bucksport Band, Scott Carter, Willie and Bunnie Furge, Grey Maxim, Helen Shaw, Phil Kelly and Ruby G., Bonnie and Peter Tucker, Patrick Coombs. **Contact:** H. O. M. E., Inc., P. O. Box 10, Orland, ME 04472, 207-469-7961.

## Maine Lobster Festival, Rockland, ME
Early Aug.
Variety, General

"Join King Neptune and His Court for Pageantry, Parades, Lobster, Fun-Filled Events and More...Great Entertainment Throughout the Festival" -- Flyer. **Help!** A sample lineup? **Days:** 4. **Site:** outdoor. Harbor Park. **Contact:** Maine Lobster Festival, P. O. Box 552, Rockland, ME 04841, 207-596-0376/594-5199.

## Summer in the Parks, Portland, ME
Early Aug. Middle Aug.
Variety, General

**Days:** 7. **Hours per day:** 2. **Site:** outdoor. **Admission:** free **Secondary genre[s]:** MFOL. **Acts:** national acts, local acts. **Sample series lineup:** Day One: Devonsquare; Day Two: Jazz Workshop Orchestra; Day Three: Lisa Gallant, Darien Brahms. **Contact:** Portland Recreation, 389 Congress Street, Portland, ME, 207-874-8793.

## Maine Festival of the Arts, Brunswick, ME
Early Aug.
Variety, Folk and International

Since 1976. **Days:** 4. **Hours per day:** 8. **Site:** outdoor. Thomas Point Beach. **Admission:** paid. **Daily entry:** $10 to $24. **Discounts: Restrictions:** 1, 10. **Secondary genre[s]:** MJAZ, RAP, TR&B, ACAP, BGOS, MC&W, TC&W, BLGS, MFOL, TFOL, NATV, BRZL, RGGE, OTHR. **Acts:** national acts, regional acts, local acts. **Sample day's lineup:** Boukman Eksperyans, Five Blind Boys of Alabama, Devonsquare, Greg Boardman, Ellen Gawler, Kaity Newell, Krakow Youth Jazz Ensemble, Sandy River Ramblers, The Huddled Masses, Pura Fe-Soni, 2 Fresh 2B Hype, Rick Charette and The Bubblegum Band, Super Bennett's Super Kids' Show, Monica Grabin, Robin Mello, People of the Dawn, Samaki Ensemble Portland, Wasyl Moros, Lorraine Ouellette Group, Downeast Fiddlers, Crooked Stovepipe Band, Bar-B-Q Blues Boys, A Cappella Fellas, Anni Clark, J. C. High Eagle, Soul Fire Odyssey, New Depression Review. **Audio merchandise:** "Traditional Music of Maine" (Northeast Archives of Folklore and Oral History, Dept. of Anthropology, South Stevens Hall, University of Maine, Orono, ME 04469). **Contact:** Maine Arts, Inc., 582 Congress Street, Portland, ME 04101, 207-772-9012.

## Sweet Chariot Music Festival and Schooner Gam, Swans Island, ME
Early Aug.
Variety, Folk and International

**Days:** 3. **Site:** indoor. Swans Island: Oddfellows Hall; Rockport: Rockport Opera House. **Admission:** paid. **Daily entry:** under $10. **Discounts:** multiple event or day passes. **Restrictions:** 1. **Secondary genre[s]:** TFOL, MARI. **Acts:** local acts. **Sample day's lineup:** David Dodson, Doug Day, Jenny Armstrong, Dean Stevens, Bob Lucas, Eric Kilburn, Denny Williams, Any Monday, Chloe Manor, Suzanna and Georgia Armstrong-Park. **Contact:** Sweet Chariot Music Festival, Box 57, Atlantic, ME 04608, 207-526-4443/374-5400.

KNIGHTS OF COLUMBUS FESTIVAL DE JOIE, Lewiston, ME
Early Aug.
Variety, Folk and International

**Days:** 3. **Hours per day:** 14. **Site:** indoor. Central Maine Civic Center, Birch Street. **Admission:** paid. **Daily entry:** under $10. **Discounts:** multiple event or day passes. **Secondary genre[s]:** OTHR. **Acts:** regional acts, local acts. **Sample day's lineup:** Les Souers Boivins, C'est Si Bon, La Famille LeBlanc, La Famille Gagne, Josee Vachon, Herve Gendreau et sa Troupe, Les Jumeau Breton, Lorraine Oullette et sa Troupe, others. **Contact:** Knights of Columbus #106, 150 East Avenue, Lewiston, ME, 207-782-9265.

FAT TIRE POLO TOURNAMENT AND MUSIC BASH, Farmington, ME
Early Aug.
Variety, General

"Battle of the bands to follow tournament" -- Listing. **Help!** One time only? **Days:** 1. **Site:** outdoor. Troll Valley Ski Resort and Fitness Center, Red Schoolhouse Road. **Acts:** local acts. **Contact:** Troll Valley Ski Resort and Fitness Center, Red Schoolhouse Road, Farmington, ME, 207-778-3656.

SKOWHEGAN STATE FAIR, Skowhegan, ME
Middle Aug.
Fairs

Since 1818. **Days:** 10. **Hours per day:** 14. **Site:** outdoor. **Admission:** paid. **Daily entry:** under $10. **Secondary genre[s]:** MJAZ, CRCK, MC&W. **Acts:** national acts, local acts. **Sample series lineup:** Day One: "True Value/GMC Truck Country Showdown" with Tom Wopat; Day Two: Four Lads, New Chordettes; Day Three: Bill Anderson. **Contact:** Skowhegan Chamber of Commerce, P. O. Box 326, Skowhegan, ME 04976, 207-474-3621.

TITCOM MOUNTAIN FIDDLING AND BLUEGRASS FESTIVAL, Farmington, ME
Middle Aug.
Fiddle and Banjo Events

Since 1993. "It's getting bigger and bigger every year." -- Evelyn Ferrari. **Help!** A sample lineup? **Days:** 1. **Hours per day:** 6. **Site:** outdoor and indoor. Titcomb Mountain Ski Area Base Lodge. **Secondary genre[s]:** BLGS. **Acts:** local acts. **Contact:** Farmington Ski Club, 107 Perham Street, Farmington ME 04938, 207-778-2117/2621or: Farmington Ski Club, c/o Heritage Printing, Farmington, ME 04938, 207-718-3581/2901. .

PASSAMAQUODDY TRADITIONAL INDIAN FESTIVAL, Perry, ME
Middle Aug.
Native American

Since 1966. "...You owe it to yourself to join the Passamaquoddys for three days of celebration...Try the moosemeat stew, hullcorn soup, fry bread, venison steak, fish chowder and assorted seafood dishes." -- Portland Monthly. **Days:** 3. **Site:** outdoor. Pleasant Point Reservation, Route 190. **Audio merchandise:** "Songs of the Passamaquoddy" (Northeast Archives of Folklore and Oral History, Dept. of Anthropology, South Stevens Hall, University of Maine, Orono, ME 04469). **Contact:** Pleasant Point Reservation, P. O. Box 343, Community Building, Perry, ME 04667, 207-854-4644/2551.

SUDBURY CANADA DAYS, Bethel, ME
Middle Aug.
Traditional Gospel and Sings

Since 1980. **Days:** 4. **Site:** outdoor and indoor. **Secondary genre[s]:** OTHR. **Acts:** local acts. **Contact:** Bethel Historical Society, Moses Mason House, Bethel, ME 04217, 207-824-2908.

## BUTTERMILK HILL OLD TIME MUSIC SHOW, Belgrade Lakes, ME
### Middle Aug.
### Traditional Country

Since 1975. **Days:** 1. **Hours per day:** 8. **Site:** outdoor. Gawler Farm. **Admission:** paid. **Secondary genre[s]:** TC&W, BLGS, TFOL, IRSH, OTHR. **Acts:** local acts. **Sample day's lineup:** Carter and Katy Newell, Old Grey Goose, The Troubadors, Elliot and Louise Osborne, Ben and Dan Guilimette, Brian Jones and Susan Boyce, Michael Looney, Rick and Jackie Davis, The Evergreens, Timmy Farnell, The Family Band. **Audio merchandise:** "Pioneers of Maine Country Music" (Northeast Archives of Folklore and Oral History, Dept. of Anthropology, South Stevens Hall, University of Maine, Orono, ME 04469). **Contact:** Buttermilk Hill Old Time Music Show, Gawler Farm, Belgrade Lakes, ME, 207-495-2928.

## OXFORD COUNTY BLUEGRASS FESTIVAL, Norway/Oxford, ME
### Middle Aug.
### Bluegrass

Since 1986. "Pickin' in the hills." -- Program. **Days:** 3. **Hours per day:** 12. **Site:** outdoor. Oxford County Fairgrounds. **Admission:** paid. **Daily entry:** under $10, $10 to $24. **Discounts:** multiple event or day passes, advance purchase discounts. **Restrictions:** 13. **Secondary genre[s]:** SGOS, TC&W. **Acts:** national acts, regional acts, local acts. **Sample day's lineup:** Carl Story and The Rambling Mountaineers, Smokey Greene and The Boys, White Mountain Bluegrass, Blistered Fingers, Berkshire Mountain, Southern Rail, Stonewall Bluegrass, Pine Tree Bluegrass Boys. **Contact:** Oxford County Fair Association, RFD 1, Box 1912, South Paris ME, 04281, 207-743-2905.

## MAINE HIGHLAND GAMES, Brunswick, ME
### Middle Aug.
### Scottish

Since 1979. "Thrill to the skirl of bagpipes!" -- Program. **Days:** 1. **Site:** outdoor and indoor. Thomas Point Beach. **Admission:** paid. **Daily entry:** under $10. **Discounts:** advance purchase discounts. **Acts:** local acts. **Sample day's lineup:** Carl Peterson, pipe bands, piping competitions. **Contact:** St. Andrew's Society of Maine, P. O. Drawer 2810, Augusta, ME 04338, 207-549-7451.

## SANKOFA STREET FESTIVAL, Belfast, ME
### Middle Aug.
### Variety, General

"A community celebration of people and their art" -- Program. **Days:** 1. **Hours per day:** 6. **Site:** outdoor, Church Street. **Admission:** free. **Secondary genre[s]:** ACAP, MFOL, NATV, AFRC, BRZL, RGGE, OTHR. **Acts:** regional acts, local acts. **Sample day's lineup:** Celebration Dancers and Drummers, Leslie Stern and Loren Murray, Negro Gato, Carol Dowd, Arthur Hall, Benny and Denise Rheel, Tony Finney, Antonio Rocca, Patty Luchetti, John Jenkins. **Contact:** Community Multicultural Arts Project, P. O. Box 47, Belfast, ME 04915, 207-338-5380 **or:** Belfast Dance Studio, P. O. Box 114, 55 High Street, Belfast, ME 04915, 207-338-6410. .

## SPRING POINT FESTIVAL, South Portland, ME
### Middle Aug.
### Variety, General

Since 1982. **Days:** 1. **Hours per day:** 6. **Site:** outdoor. Southern Maine Technical College. **Admission:** free. **Secondary genre[s]:** CRCK, ARCK, OTHR. **Acts:** local acts. **Sample day's lineup:** Rick Charette and The Bubblegum Band, Swinging Heart, Boneheads, Scott Hooper and Elvis Tribute, Phil Huff, Mr. and Mrs. Fish, John Alexander, others. **Contact:** Southern Maine Technical College, Fort Road, South Portland, ME 04106, 207-767-9500.

### DOWN EAST JAZZ FESTIVAL, Camden, ME
　　Late Aug.
　　Traditional Jazz and Ragtime

Since 1977. "...Four outstanding [traditional] jazz bands from the New England area." -- Program. **Days:** 1. **Hours per day:** 10. **Site:** outdoor and indoor. Samoset Resort Inn (cabaret), Camden Opera House (concert), Gilbert's Publick House and Camden Harbour Inn (pub crawl), piers and a flatbed truck. **Admission:** free and paid. **Secondary genre[s]:** MJAZ. **Acts:** national acts, local acts. **Sample day's lineup:** Stan Catell and Down East Jazz, Paradise City Jazz Band, Noel Kaletsky-Scott Philbrick Quintet with Muriel Havenstein, Jazz Workshop Orchestra. **Contact:** Down East Jazz Society, P. O. Box 202, Camden, ME 04841, 207-596-7874.

### NEW ENGLAND SALTY DOG BLUEGRASS FESTIVAL, Cambridge, ME
　　Late Aug.
　　Bluegrass

**Days:** 3. **Hours per day:** 12. **Site:** outdoor. **Admission:** paid. **Daily entry:** under $10, $10 to $24. **Discounts:** multiple event or day passes, advance purchase discounts. **Restrictions:** 10, 11, 13. **Secondary genre[s]:** SGOS, TC&W. **Acts:** regional acts, local acts. **Sample day's lineup:** Smokey Greene and The Boys, Kennebec Valley Boys, Berkshire Mountain Boys, Timmy Farrell, Sandy River Ramblers, Yodelin' Slim Clark, Bluegrass Supply Co. **Contact:** Pike Family Productions, RFD 1, Box 548, Cambridge, ME 04923, 207-277-5624.

### CIRCLE OF SOUND BENEFIT CONCERT, Bath, ME
　　Late Aug.
　　Modern Folk

**Help!** One time only? **Days:** 1. **Site:** indoor. Center for the Arts. **Admission:** paid. **Daily entry:** under $10, $10 to $24. **Discounts:** advance purchase discounts. **Acts:** local acts. **Sample day's lineup:** Glenshane, Driftwood, Abby Chapman, Reel Folk, Dick Dufresne, Marie Dufresne, Mark McNeil. **Contact:** The Chocolate Church, 804 Washington Street, Bath, ME, 207-729-3185.

### THOMAS POINT BEACH BLUEGRASS FESTIVAL, Brunswick, ME
　　Early Sep.
　　Bluegrass

Since 1978. **Days:** 3. **Hours per day:** 12. **Site:** outdoor. Thomas Point Beach. **Admission:** paid. **Daily entry:** $10 to $24. **Discounts:** multiple event or day passes, advance purchase discounts. **Restrictions:** 11, 13. **Secondary genre[s]:** SGOS, TC&W. **Acts:** national acts, regional acts, local acts. **Sample day's lineup:** Raymond Fairchild and The Maggie Mountain Boys, Bluegrass Patriots, Johnson Mountain Boys, Lorne Buck and The Flatland Mountaineers, IIIrd Tyme Out, Bill Harrell and The Virginians, Bluegrass Supply Co., Redwing, White Mountain Bluegrass. **Contact:** Thomas Point Beach Bluegrass, Meadow Road, Box 5419, Brunswick, ME 04011, 207-725-6009.

### MAINE HEALING ARTS FESTIVAL, Freedom, ME
　　Early Sep.
　　Modern Folk

Since 1980. "Now going into its twelfth year, the Festival has evolved from its New Age countercultural roots into a family-oriented event that provides childcare and special programs for teens...Spread out over a lush 300 acres, Hidden Valley offers an abundance of facilities for creating the perfect Holistic Health vacation" -- Earth Star. 'We encourage love, light, sharing, common sense and healing." -- Program. **Days:** 4. **Hours per day:** 15. **Site:** outdoor and indoor. Hidden Valley Camp. **Restrictions:** 10, 13. **Secondary genre[s]:** OTHR. **Acts:** regional acts, local acts. **Sample lineup:** Guy Frigon, Sarah Benson, Vivian Ytterhus, Laraaji Nadananda, Persis Ensor, Gwyn Peterdi. **Contact:** Healing Arts Festival, Route 1, Box 569, Buckfield, ME 04220, 207-336-2065.

OLD TIME COUNTRY MUSIC FESTIVAL, Hebron, ME
Early Sep.
Traditional Country

See other dates. **Days:** 1. **Hours per day:** 4. **Site:** outdoor. Hebron Pines Campground, Route 124. **Admission:** paid. **Daily entry:** under $10. **Acts:** local acts. **Sample day's lineup:** Allan McHale and The Old-Time Radio Gang, Jovial John Edgerton, Jack Thurlow, Black Mountain Band. **Audio merchandise:** "Pioneers of Maine Country Music" (Northeast Archives of Folklore and Oral History, Dept. of Anthropology, South Stevens Hall, University of Maine, Orono, ME 04469). **Contact:** Hebron Pines Campground, RR 1, Box 1955, Hebron, ME 04238, 207-966-2179/2909.

RIVER TREE ARTS FIDDLE CONTEST AND OLD TIME COUNTRY MUSIC SHOW, Kennebunk, ME
Early Sep.
Fiddle and Banjo Events

Since 1989. "It's time to get down." -- Casco Bay Weekly. See other events and sites. **Days:** 1. **Site:** indoor, Kennebunk Town Hall. **Admission:** paid. **Daily entry:** under $10. **Discounts:** advance purchase discounts. **Secondary genre[s]:** TC&W. **Acts:** regional acts, local acts. **Sample day's lineup:** 15 fiddlers, including Juan Fiestas and Lisa Schneckenberger, plus Allan McHale and The Old-Time Radio Gang. **Audio merchandise:** "Pioneers of Maine Country Music" (Northeast Archives of Folklore and Oral History, Dept. of Anthropology, South Stevens Hall, University of Maine, Orono, ME 04469). **Contact:** River Tree Arts, P. O. Box 1056, 56 Portland Road, Kennebunkport, ME 04046, 207-985-4343.

SALMON SUNDAY, Eastport, ME
Middle Sep.
Variety, General

**Days:** 1. **Site:** indoor. La Sardinia Loca Restaurant. **Secondary genre[s]:** CRCK, BLGS, MFOL, SCOT. **Acts:** local acts. **Contact:** Eastport Chamber of Commerce, P. O. Box 254, Eastport, ME 04631, 207-853-4644.

NATIVE AMERICAN APPRECIATION DAY, Cumberland, ME
Middle Sep.
Native American

"Tribal nations throughout New England and eastern Canada host a cultural exchange with Indians and non-Indians." -- Casco Bay Weekly. **Days:** 2. **Site:** outdoor. Cumberland County Fairgrounds. **Acts:** regional acts, local acts. **Contact:** Native American Appreciation Day, P. O. Box 280, East Lebanon, ME 04027, 207-339-9520.

ROCKPORT FOLK FESTIVAL, Rockport, ME
Middle Sep.
Modern Folk

Since 1972. "The 'leaf-peepers' don't come until early October, the weather is still warm and the crowds are light. You'll really enjoy the restored Opera House where the evening concert is held." -- Festival Volunteer. **Days:** 2. **Site:** indoor. Rockport Opera House (evening concert); Rockport Elementary School (daytime work-shops, etc.). **Admission:** free and paid. **Daily entry:** under $10. **Discounts:** multiple event or day passes. **Secondary genre[s]:** TFOL, MARI, IRSH. **Acts:** national acts, regional acts, local acts. **Sample day's lineup:** Gordon Bok, Short Sisters, Chavin. **Contact:** Rockport Folk Festival, P. O. Box 25, Rockport, ME 04856, 207-236-3632.

DUKE ELLINGTON FESTIVAL, Portland, ME
> Middle Sep.
> Variety, General

Part of a superb series, "Big Sounds From All Over," presenting various world beat, folk, jazz and blues concerts. Themes and dates vary, so call for current schedules. **Help!** One time only? **Days:** 2. **Site:** indoor, Portland Performing Arts Center. **Admission:** paid. **Daily entry:** $10 to $24. **Discounts:** multiple event or day passes, advance purchase discounts. **Secondary genre[s]:** MJAZ, MC&W, BLGS, MFOL, TFOL, OTHR. **Acts:** national acts, local acts. **Sample day's lineup:** Bellamy Jazz Band, Fogg Brothers, Al Hawkes String Fusion, Penumbra Trio, Portland Brass Quintet, Brad Terry and Tony Gaboury, Knots and Crosses, Chris Moore, Maine Clarinet Choir, Don Doane's Trombone Quartet, Al Gardiner Middle Eastern Ensemble, Old Grey Goose, Pine Tones, Mark Polishook and Scott Reeves, Red Light Revue, USM Jazz Band. **Contact:** Portland Performing Arts, 25A Forest Avenue, Portland, ME 04101, 207-774-0465.

MAINE INVITATIONAL COUNTRY MUSIC SEMI-FINALS SHOW, West Buxton, ME
> Middle Sep. to Late Sep.
> Modern Country

State-wide band competition. Top two winners per category drawn from 5 district invitationals compete. Winners go on to finals in Early Nov. **Days:** 7. **Site:** indoor. The Roost, Chicopee Road. **Acts:** local acts. **Contact:** Down East Country Music Association, RR 3, Box 1845, Wells, ME 04090, 207-646-7118.

OLD TIME COUNTRY JAMBOREE, Waterville, ME
> Middle Sep.
> Traditional Country

**Help!** One time only? **Days:** 1. **Hours per day:** 3. **Site:** indoor. Waterville Opera House. **Admission:** paid. **Acts:** local acts. **Sample day's lineup:** Allan McHale and The Old-Time Radio Gang, Al Hawkes Country Trio, Gene Hooper Family Show, Yodeling Mike Preston, others. **Audio merchandise:** "Pioneers of Maine Country Music" (Northeast Archives of Folklore and Oral History, Dept. of Anthropology, South Stevens Hall, University of Maine, Orono, ME 04469). **Contact:** Waterville Opera House, Waterville, ME, 207-873-5381.

COMMON GROUND COUNTRY FAIR, Windsor, ME
> Late Sep.
> Traditional Folk

"Song swap Friday...fiddle contest Saturday...daytime workshops Sunday...lots of good acoustic music all three days." -- Listing. **Help!** Does anybody have a sample lineup? **Days:** 3. **Site:** outdoor and indoor. **Acts:** local acts. **Contact:** Maine Organic Farmers and Gardeners Association, P. O. Box 2176, Augusta, ME 04330, 207-622-3118.

SCOTTISH PERFORMING ARTS WEEKEND AND WORKSHOP, Bar Harbor, ME
> Middle Oct.
> Scottish

Since 1990. **Help!** A sample lineup? **Days:** 2. **Site:** indoor. St. Savior's Church, Mount Desert Street. **Contact:** Scottish Performing Arts Weekend and Workshop, HCR 62, Box 267A, Mount Desert Island, ME 04660-9615, 207-244-7193.

## BLUE HILL FESTIVAL OF MUSIC/SINGER-SONGWRITER MARATHON, Blue Hill, ME
Late Oct.
Variety, General

In addition to two classical concerts held elsewhere, the Left Bank Cafe will also host a jazz concert featuring three Maine acts, plus a "Singer-Songwriter Marathon" of locals from noon 'til whenever. **Days:** 2. **Site:** indoor. Left Bank Bakery and Cafe. **Admission:** paid. **Daily entry:** $10 to $24. **Discounts:** multiple event or day passes. **Secondary genre[s]:** MJAZ, MFOL, OTHR. **Acts:** local acts. **Sample day's lineup:** University of Maine at Augusta's "Jazz-on-Tour" featuring Don Stratton, The Tom Hoffman Ensemble, Rebecca Wing Ensemble. **Audio merchandise:** "Live at the Left Bank, Vol. One" (self-produced and distributed). **Contact:** Left Bank Bakery and Cafe, Blue Hill, ME 04614, 207-374-2201.


## FALL MUSICFEST, Portland, ME
Late Oct. to Early Nov.
Variety, General

"University of Southern Maine's...MusicFest will present more than 100 faculty, students and alumni in 41 performances of classical, jazz and folk music." -- Casco Bay Weekly. **Help!** A sample lineup? **Days:** 5. **Site:** indoor. Portland City Hall Auditorium, Portland High School Auditorium, University of Southern Maine, various clubs. **Admission:** free and paid. **Daily entry:** under $10. **Secondary genre[s]:** MJAZ, MFOL, OTHR. **Acts:** local acts. **Contact:** University of Southern Maine, Music Dept., 96 Falmouth Road, Portland, ME, 207-780-5265/5256.


## MAINE INVITATIONAL COUNTRY MUSIC FINALS SHOW, West Buxton, ME
Early Nov.
Modern Country

State-wide band competition. Winners go on to New England regional finals in Mid Feb. **Days:** 1. **Site:** indoor. The Roost, Chicopee Road. **Acts:** local acts. **Contact:** Down East Country Music Association, RR 3, Box 1845, Wells, ME 04090, 207-646-7118.


## NEW YEAR'S EVE PORTLAND, Portland, ME
Late Dec.
Variety, General

"City-wide non-alcoholic celebration featuring music, dance, family entertainment." **Days:** 1. **Site:** indoor. Multiple clubs downtown. **Admission:** paid. **Daily entry:** $10 to $24 **Secondary genre[s]:** ARCK, TR&B, TFOL, OTHR. **Acts:** local acts. **Sample day's lineup:** Boneheads, Killer Greens, Don Roy, Mandala Folk Dance Ensemble, others. **Contact:** Maine Arts, Inc., 582 Congress Street, Portland, ME 04101, 207-772-9012.

# R. I. P., M. I. A. Festival Listings

**Caveat** The following festivals are either confirmed or suspected to be discontinued (i.e., R. I. P.); or have not responded to various information requests (i.e., M. I. A.). Since all festivals are subject to last-minute changes or reinstatement, however, FESTPRESS is not responsible for any festival listing information that follows. Readers are encouraged to notify FESTPRESS of any status changes they uncover.

SPRING FESTIVAL, Orland, ME
> Late May

Discontinued in 1993. See other dates. **Days:** 2. **Hours per day:** 7. **Site:** outdoor. **Contact:** H. O. M. E., P. O. Box 10, Orland, ME, 207-469-7961.

MAINE MASTERS FIDDLE CONTEST, Augusta, ME
> Aug.
> Fiddle and Banjo Events

**Help!** Does anyone know the status of this event, or the whereabouts of its promoters? **Site:** indoor. Augusta Civic Center. **Contact:** Northeast Productions, Box 199, Alfred, ME 04001, 207-793-8374/8020.

FAMILY FESTIVAL, Bridgton, ME
> Late Aug.
> Modern Folk

"Cancelled in 1993. Possibly in 1994." -- Office. **Days:** 2. **Site:** outdoor. Shawnee Peak Ski Area. **Acts:** national acts, local acts. **Sample day's lineup:** Devonsquare, local bands. **Contact:** Family Festival, Shawnee Peak Ski Area, Bridgton, ME, 207-647-3472.

BLUEGRASS JAMBOREE, Unity, ME
> Early Sep.
> Bluegrass

Since 1990. Discontinued in 1993 due to scheduling conflicts. Substituted an excellent pop music series, instead. **Hours per day:** 5. **Site:** indoor. Unity College. **Acts:** local acts. **Contact:** Unity College, HC 78, Box 1, Unity, ME 04988, 207-948-3131.

~     ~     ~

*Bruce Pratt, WERU 89.9 FM Full Circle Summer Fair.*

# New Hampshire

*Betty Silberman, Shirim Klezmer Orchestra, Portsmouth Jazz Festival.*

# Portsmouth's Waterfront Jazz

MARKET SQUARE DAY, Portsmouth, NH
> Early June to Middle June
> Variety, General

PORTSMOUTH JAZZ FESTIVAL, Portsmouth, NH
> Late June
> Modern Jazz
> ***Attended***

WHITE MOUNTAINS JAZZ AND BLUES CRAFTSFESTIVAL, North Conway, NH
> Early September
> Variety, Jazz and Blues

FIRST NIGHT PORTSMOUTH, Portsmouth, NH
> Late December
> Variety, Folk and International

**Introduction**

Portsmouth, like the PORTSMOUTH JAZZ FESTIVAL, is a genuine sleeper. It might not be the first destination that comes to mind when conceiving a weekend trip to New England, but I've really come to enjoy its welcoming and picturesque qualities — the strolling, the browsing, the seafood, the scenery, the architecture.

Portsmouth oozes history. It has retained its overall scale and detail over the centuries such that you can imagine yourself in the shoes of its original Colonial dwellers as you stalk the bricks and cobblestones. In particular, the Strawberry Banke district — a 10-acre, 42-house, "neighborhood museum" first settled in 1630 — kept what my aesthetics professor would have commended as "not just the historic houses, but the historic spaces in-between." (Very Zen, no?)

The whole town reminds me of a suburban version of Boston's Old North End with the same pocket squares, petite feel and spare, Yankee ornamentation. Likewise, the sea beckons nearby. If you ever, ever run out of boutiques and restaurants (fat chance), there's Kittery's outlet malls across the river, while the rugged White Mountains lie just a few hours' drive north.

**Festival Review**

"The PORTSMOUTH JAZZ FESTIVAL is really a secret," confides Richard Smith who has been booking the talent through his CERAS agency since the festival's inception in '82. "But anyone like yourself who would attend would really have a good time."

Here's a recap of the sort of pleasant surprises he's referring to.

Surprise No. 1: its duration. I'll contradict the various directories and let you know this event extends for four days, not just one. True, the main focus is Sunday's outdoor affair, but there are also three evenings of club bookings: two acts on Thursday; nine on Friday; eleven on Saturday. Varied genres, too. I didn't recognize all the names, but a few ringers stood out:

- Bill Staines is a well-regarded folk singer-songwriter who records on independent labels and tours nationally;

- T. J. Wheeler is a local blues hero, just beginning to book national dates, who recently won a prestigious W. C. Handy Award for his successful "Blues Into Schools" program.

Certainly, these two beckon a pub crawl to check out the other local performers.

Surprise No. 2: its primary site (due to move one street north to Harbor Place in '94). The organizers, the Seacoast Council on Tourism, managed to find the one back alley I hadn't yet explored, Ceres Street. It's a narrow plank of road fronting the Piscataqua River and surrounded by basement-level shops. They set up two stages that were timed to alternate and provide continuous music all day. When one set ended, the manageably-sized crowd would shift to the next already-sound-checked stage like a deck full of tipsy sailors on the high seas. This lent professional pacing to an otherwise relaxed, comfortable, charismatic ambiance.

Surprise No. 3: its variety. Eight acts, seven different flavors of jazz, including big band swing, klezmer, vocalese, R&B, straight-ahead, and Dixieland. There was even a jazz tap trio! "I think [variety] is the key to making it interesting where the majority of people can stay there for the whole day," Smith explains. "In order to keep people's attention, it's important to give them a full spectrum."

Smith mixes it up between years, as well. "The beauty of this festival," he continues, "is that every year it's different. The only thing that's the same every year is that there's a variety of jazz." Smith credits Dick and Tommy Gallant (whose Allstars opened the '93 affair) at the outset for "setting this direction that's been one of the best focuses, or visions, I've had to work with."

Which brings me to Surprise, No. 4: its regional stars. "We've always had strong regional talent," Smith states. "The people associated with the festival are always searching out artists that may have been with it a long time but were never really in the spotlight. A lot of these people, hopefully, will go on and get national, or international, acclaim."

Smith fondly recalls a number of performances from such up-and-comers, including Tiger Okoshi's Baku ("He's blown people away."), Uno Mundo (formerly Do'Ah), Mike Metheney, Randy Roos, and Jelly Belly, among others. His favorite memory, though, was from one of Clark Terry's pupils, jazz harmonica whiz, William Galison: "With the boats going up and down behind him on the river, he had one of those rare, magic moments where everything came together. It was exciting to see him capture the festival that day."

A similar act on '93's bill included Cercie Miller. Smith raves:

- "She's a great saxophone player from Boston with a lot of charisma. Portsmouth loves her. She's been playing here for about 15 years. She used to be in Patty Larkin's band. Those two were really tight. When Larkin was playing rock and roll, Miller was the sax player and they'd have a ball. It was really fun to see and hear."

(Maybe a reunion's in order here for a future year, eh Richard?)

"The greatest rewards of doing the festival," Smith relates, "are getting phone calls afterward saying how excited they were about an individual artist, like Galison or Miller." Yeah, like mine about Bruce Katz!

**Artist Mini-Review** Bruce Katz Band. My wife and I caught part of pianist Bruce Katz's set (Smith called it "unbelievable") before having to dash off to AN AFTERNOON OF JAZZ in Norwalk, CT, later that afternoon (see chapter). For a few tunes, at least, we were treated to a synthesis that many have recently tried (from John Zorn to Wynton Marsalis), but few have really nailed — mixing high-jazz stylings within low-down American genres, such as blues, soul and funk.

A graduate of the prestigious New England Conservatory (where he studied under pianist Geri Allen), Katz clearly possesses avant chops. He dazzles with unpredictable, high-energy runs punctuated with edges, swoops and stops-on-a-dime that nevertheless compliment his overall schemes.

Katz's advantage, however, is that he's close in touch with his roots, frequently sitting in with blues aces, such as Ronnie Earl, Mighty Sam McLain, and Johnny Adams during their Boston gigs. He calls upon his alter-ego in composing infectiously rollicking tunes where you can study his playing, or "chair-dance," or both.

"Crescent Crawl" begins with a N' Awlins funk, then cuts into a walking blues before returning. "Boomer's Thing," with Katz taking an uptempo turn on organ, pays homage to soul/jazz master, Jimmy Smith. Brain food you can boogie to. We hated to have to go, both for his act, as well as for the festival in general.

Smith considers Portsmouth a great town for everyone — families or singles, old or young — but        **Travel Tip**
reserves extra praise for its dining. "You cannot go to a bad restaurant here," he exclaims. "It's fantastic! It's tough to go hungry in this town."

If you like Smith's booking touch, you'll also enjoy two more New Hampshire events where he        **See Also**
has a musical hand:

- The WHITE MOUNTAINS JAZZ AND BLUES CraftsFestival on Labor Day weekend,
  which he produces and features four acts similar to the JAZZ FESTIVAL's funkiest;

- FIRST NIGHT PORTSMOUTH, a folk music-oriented outburst on New Year's Eve
  which he co-founded.

Finally, Smith's sponsoring organization, Pro Portsmouth, Inc., kicks off its summer
series, the Prescott Park Arts Festival, with one huge blowout the second Saturday in June. It's
called MARKET SQUARE DAY and it really takes over the whole town. To entertain its 100,000 patrons
there are no fewer than eight performing areas boasting local acts to accompany 300 vendors, kids'
activities, a road race, a sail regatta, exhibits, displays, auctions — the whole nine yards!

~        ~        ~

*Mad hatter, Portsmouth Jazz Festival.*

# New Hampshire Festival Listings

**Caveat**

Although the vast majority are festivals are reliable and predictable, all are subject to last-minute changes or cancellations. Accordingly, FESTPRESS is not responsible for any festival listing information that follows. Readers are well advised to contact festivals at least twice before preparing a festival vist: (a) once at least one or two months ahead of time; and (b) once more during the week of your visit for confirmation. Ask for a festival flyer or brochure to be mailed to you. Festival promoters usually are willing to comply, and the resulting literature may answer any questions you still have.

## Key Codes

Restrictions:

| | | | | | |
|---|---|---|---|---|---|
| • Food and drink... | 1; | • Cameras... | 6; | • Motorcycles... | 11; |
| • Alcohol... | 2; | • Audio recording... | 7; | • Re-entry... | 12; |
| • Cans... | 3; | • Video recording... | 8; | • Other restrictions... | 13. |
| • Bottles... | 4; | • Children... | 9; | | |
| • Coolers... | 5; | • Pets... | 10; | | |

Secondary Genre[s]:

| | | | |
|---|---|---|---|
| • Variety, General... | VRGL; | • Bluegrass... | BLGS; |
| • Variety, Jazz & Blues... | VRJB; | • Modern Folk... | MFOL; |
| • Variety, Country & Bluegrass | VRCB; | • Traditional Folk... | TFOL; |
| • Variety, Folk & International | VRFI; | • Fiddle and Banjo Events... | FDDL; |
| • Modern Jazz... | MJAZ; | • Maritime... | MARI; |
| • Traditional Jazz & Ragtime... | TJAZ; | • Cajun and Zydeco... | ZYDC; |
| • Alternative Jazz... | AJAZ; | • Irish... | IRSH; |
| • Modern Rock and Pop... | MRCK; | • Jewish... | JWSH; |
| • Classic Rock and Oldies... | CRCK; | • Native American... | NATV; |
| • Alternative & College Rock | ARCK; | • Scottish... | SCOT; |
| • Hard Rock & Heavy Metal | HRCK; | • Modern Latin... | MLAT; |
| • Rap... | RAP; | • Traditional Latin... | TLAT; |
| • Modern R&B... | MR&B; | • African American... | AFRM; |
| • Blues and Traditional R&B... | TR&B; | • African... | AFRC; |
| • Acappella and Doo Wop... | ACAP; | • Brazilian & So. American... | BRZL; |
| • Modern Christian... | CHRS; | • Reggae, Ska & Caribbean... | RGGE; |
| • Black Gospel... | BGOS; | • Avant Garde & New Music... | AVNT; |
| • Southern & Bluegrass Gospel | SGOS; | • Cabaret... | CBRT; |
| • Traditional Gospel & Sings... | TGOS; | • Gay and Lesbian... | GYLS; |
| • Modern Country... | MC&W; | • Drum Corps & March. Bands | DRUM; |
| • Traditional Country... | TC&W; | • Fairs... | FAIR; |
| • Alt. Country & Rockabilly... | AC&W; | • Other Genres... | OTHR. |

**Note**

Wherever "**Help!**" appears readers are invited to answer the proceeding questions and/or provide updates. New festival listings that meet the criteria of this book certainly are welcome too! Please mail any current festival information you obtain — especially flyers or brochures — to FESTPRESS, P. O. Box 147, Glen Ridge, NJ 07028. *Thanks!*

### RALPH PAGE LEGACY WEEKEND, Durham, NH
    Early Jan.
    Traditional Folk

Since 1988. "Come and enjoy a weekend of dancing, workshops for callers and musicians, traditional and contemporary contras and squares. The Ralph Page legacy continues!" -- Program. **Days:** 3. **Hours per day:** 10. **Site:** indoor. University of New Hampshire. **Admission:** paid. **Daily entry:** $10 to $24, $25 to $49. **Discounts:** multiple event or day passes. **Acts:** local acts. **Sample lineup:** Fred Breunig, Susan Conger, Fresh Fish, George Hodgson, Dave Kaynor, Bob McQuillen, Ted Sannella, Storm in the Tea, Steve Zakon. **Contact:** New England Folk Festival Association, 21A Prospect Street, Portsmouth, NH 03801, 617-354-1340 **or:** New England Folk Festival Association, 1950 Massachusetts Avenue, Cambridge, MA 02140, .

### SEACOAST AFRICAN-AMERICAN HERITAGE FESTIVAL, Portsmouth, NH
    Early Feb. to Late Feb.
    African American

Since 1984. Celebrating Black History Month. "A community-wide, multi-organizational event" -- T. J. Wheeler. **Help!** A sample lineup? **Site:** indoor. Multiple locations. **Secondary genre[s]:** TR&B. **Acts:** local acts. **Contact:** Blues Bank Collective, 9 Towle Farm Road, Hampton Falls, NH 03844, 603-929-0654.

### SEACOAST MUSIC AWARDS, Portsmouth, NH
    Early Feb.
    Variety, General

**Days:** 1. **Site:** indoor. Portsmouth Music Hall, 28 Chesnut Street. **Admission:** paid. **Secondary genre[s]:** MJAZ, ARCK, TR&B, MFOL. **Acts:** local acts. **Sample day's lineup:** Gravity, Truffle, Carrie Coltrane, T. J. Wheeler, plus a dozen others. **Contact:** Portsmouth Music Hall, 26 Chesnut Street, Portsmouth, NH 603-436-2400.

### COUNTRYFEST, Laconia, NH
    Early Mar.
    Modern Country

Since 1993. **Days:** 2. **Site:** indoor. Gunstock Ski Resort. **Acts:** local acts. **Sample day's lineup:** Pony Express, Silver Dollar Band, others. **Contact:** Gunstock Ski Resort, P. O. Box 1307, Laconia, NH 03247, 603-293-4341.

### CLARK TERRY/UNIVERSITY OF NEW HAMPSHIRE JAZZ FESTIVAL, Durham, NH
    Middle Mar.
    Modern Jazz

**Days:** 2. **Site:** indoor. University of New Hampshire. **Acts:** national acts. **Sample day's lineup:** Clark Terry, Red Holloway, Jon Hendricks, Alan Dawson, others. **Contact:** Department of Music, University of New Hampshire, Durham, NH 03824, 603-862-2404.

### NEW ENGLAND BLUES CONFERENCE, Portsmouth, NH
    Late Apr.
    Blues and Traditional R&B

Since 1992. "Last year's conference was attended by a mix of journalists, blues society members, club owners, record company people, musicians, fans, etc....When everyone's all talked out, there will be live music, more schmoozing and a sit-down dinner." -- Lucille's BluesLetter. **Days:** 2. **Hours per day:** 12. **Site:** indoor. Rosa's Restaurant, 80 State Street. **Admission:** paid. **Daily entry:** $10 to $24, $25 to $49. **Acts:** national acts, local acts. **Sample day's lineup:** Muddy Waters Tribute Band, T. J. Wheeler and The Smokers, others. **Contact:** Blues Bank Collective, 9 Towle Farm Road, Hampton Falls, NH 03844, 603-929-0654.

CONTEMPORARY MUSIC FESTIVAL, Concord, NH
> Early May
> Avant Garde and New Music

Concord Community Music School commissions a new work each year to be performed by their best students. Faculty perform a recital the night before. **Days:** 2. **Site:** indoor. Concord Community Music School, 23 Wall Street. **Admission:** paid. **Daily entry:** under $10. **Discounts:** student discounts. **Acts:** local acts. **Sample day's lineup:** Works by Ives, Oboe Lee, Copland and Aldridge performed by Laurel Browne, Mirela Chisbora, Peggo Hortsman Hodes, Leslie Moye, Bozena O'Brien, Peggy Senter, Patricia Shands, Kathryn Southworth. **Contact:** Concord Community Music School, 23 Wall Street, Concord, NH 03301, 603-228-1196.

INTERNATIONAL FESTIVAL, Manchester, NH
> Early May
> Variety, Folk and International

Since 1983. "We expect 30 different ethnic groups to participate in the largest event of its kind in New Hampshire. Have a great time touring the world!" -- Program. **Days:** 2. **Hours per day:** 8. **Site:** indoor. JFK Coliseum. **Admission:** paid. **Daily entry:** under $10. **Secondary genre[s]:** IRSH, NATV, TLAT, OTHR. **Acts:** local acts. **Sample day's lineup:** Pat Heffernan, New Hampshire Association of Asian Indians, Latin American Center Singers and Dancers, Siriporn, Chomchay Khotpanya, Jasmin Shah, Georgia Gancarz, Josee Vachon, others. **Contact:** Manchester Consolidated Services, 102 North Main Street, Manchester, NH 03102, 603-668-8600.

DARTMOUTH FESTIVAL OF NEW MUSICS, Hanover, NH
> Middle May
> Avant Garde and New Music

Since 1984. **Days:** 1. **Site:** indoor. Hopkins Center, Dartmouth College. **Admission:** paid. **Daily entry:** under $10. **Sample day's lineup:** Works by Coffey, Berkley, Wolff, Ray, Polansky, Moravec, Shabazz and Umezaki performed by Rebecca McCallum, Shameen Abbassy, Chrsitopher Bahng, Tom Medlioranza, Kelly Horsted, John Kelley, Paul Moravec, Renata Bratt, Lee Ray, Laura Markowitz, Devin Hurd, Alex Ogle, Kojiro Umezaki, Hafiz Shabazz. **Contact:** Hopkins Center, Dartmouth College, 6041 Lower Level, Wilson Hall, Hanover, NH 03755, 603-646-2422.

NEW HAMPSHIRE'S LILAC TIME FESTIVAL, Lisbon, NH
> Late May
> Variety, General

Music varies with annual festival theme. **Days:** 3. **Site:** outdoor. **Secondary genre[s]:** MJAZ, MC&W. **Acts:** local acts. **Sample day's lineup:** Dick Curless, plus 5 other bands for festival's C&W theme. **Contact:** New Hampshire's Lilac Time Festival, RFD 1, Landaff, NH 03585, 603-838-6336.

MARKET SQUARE DAY, Portsmouth, NH
> Early Jun. to Middle Jun.
> Variety, General

Since 1978. "Promoting and celebrating Portsmouth's artists, its culture, its unique maritime and architectural history, and its thriving business community...The finest arts and cultural festival in the region." -- Program. **Days:** 3. **Hours per day:** 8. **Site:** outdoor. Multiple locations downtown. **Admission:** free. **Secondary genre[s]:** MJAZ, CRCK, ACAP, MFOL, TFOL, IRSH. **Acts:** national acts, regional acts, local acts. **Sample day's lineup:** The Makem Brothers with Brian Sullivan, Ryan and Co., Stan Moeller and T. S. Baker, White Noise, Slaid Cleaves, Robert Loechler, Brenda Curry, Nightlifes, Vicious Circle, Doc Johnson Blues Band, Douglas Clegg with Joyce Anderson, Beach Cowboys, Merseyside, Memorial Bridge Allstars, Umbrellahead, Busy Little Kitchen, VocalEase, Buddy and The Shephers, Larry and Leona, Curtis Coleman, The Hots Shots, Good Vintage. **Contact:** Pro Portsmouth, Inc., 226 State Street, P. O. Box 1008, Portsmouth, NH 03802, 603-431-5388.

### NEW HAMPSHIRE WOMEN'S MUSIC FESTIVAL, Northfield, NH
Middle Jun.
Modern Folk

Since 1994. "Everyone welcome" -- Flyer. **Days:** 1. **Hours per day:** 7. **Site:** outdoor. Highlands Ski Area, Bean Hill Road. **Admission:** paid. **Daily entry:** under $10, $10 to $24, $25 to $49. **Discounts:** advance purchase discounts. **Restrictions:** 2. **Secondary genre[s]:** ACAP. **Acts:** regional acts, local acts. **Sample day's lineup:** Cosy Sheridan, Kathy Lowe, Ladies Choice, Crystal and The Cleavage, Susie Burke and Betty Davis, Nancy DelGuidice, Lucie Therrien, Yagottawanna, Heidi Batchelder, Purly Gates, Monica Nagle, Songweavers. **Contact:** New Hampshire Feminist Connection, P. O. Box 311, Concord, NH 03302-0311, 603-225-3501.

### NEW ENGLAND BLUEGRASS FESTIVAL, Laconia, NH
Middle Jun.
Bluegrass

Since 1992. Benefits the Belknap County 4-H Association and the Belmont Fire Dept. **Days:** 2. **Hours per day:** 11. **Site:** outdoor. Belknap County Fairgrounds, Mile Hill Road. **Admission:** paid. **Daily entry:** $10 to $24. **Discounts:** advance purchase discounts. **Acts:** national acts, local acts. **Sample day's lineup:** The Osborne Brothers, The New Blue Velvet Band, The Bluegrass Connection, Iron Skillet, Granite Grass. **Contact:** New England Bluegrass Festival, 50 Buzzell Hill Road, Weare, NH 03281, 603-529-4197/627-7227.

### SOMERSWORTH INTERNATIONAL CHILDREN'S FESTIVAL, Somersworth, NH
Middle Jun.
Variety, General

Since 1981. Five music stages: 2 children's; 2 international; 1 teen's. **Days:** 1. **Hours per day:** 6. **Site:** outdoor. Multiple locations downtown. **Admission:** free. **Secondary genre[s]:** TJAZ, CRCK, MC&W, MFOL, AFRC, RGGE, GYLS, OTHR. **Acts:** national acts, regional acts, local acts. **Sample day's lineup:** Western Aires, New Horizons, Ben Guilmette, Tri City Storm Cadets, World Beat, Airborne, Caribbean for Kids, Julie and Brownie, Joan Robb, Motion, Garrison Players, Blue Hill Kickers, Groove Child, plus "national recording artist." **Contact:** Somersworth International Children's Festival, P. O. Box 255, Somersworth, NH 03878, 603-692-5869.

### HIGH HOPES HOT AIR BALLOON FESTIVAL, Milford, NH
Middle Jun.
Variety, General

"Musicians donate their time...45-minute sets throughout the day...many acts" -- Judy Chappell. **Help!** A sample lineup? **Days:** 2. **Hours per day:** 8. **Site:** outdoor. Old Wilton Road, Perry Field. **Admission:** free. **Acts:** local acts. **Contact:** High Hopes Foundation Center, Amherst Chapter, P. O. Box 326, Amherst, NH 03031, 603-639-6804/673-7005.

### JAZZ SHOWCASE, Portsmouth, NH
Late Jun.
Modern Jazz

Since 1994. **Days:** 1. **Site:** indoor. Press Room, 77 Daniel Street. **Admission:** paid. **Daily entry:** under $10. **Acts:** local acts. **Sample day's lineup:** Paul Jobin, Lauren Wool, Alan Chase. **Contact:** Jazz Showcase, 235 West Road, #10, Portsmouth, NH 03801, 603-436-7678.

## PORTSMOUTH JAZZ FESTIVAL, Portsmouth, NH
> Late Jun.
> Variety, Jazz and Blues

Since 1983. **Days:** 4. **Hours per day:** 8. **Site:** outdoor and indoor. Harbor Place, plus 11 different clubs. **Admission:** free and paid. **Daily entry:** $10 to $24. **Discounts:** advance purchase discounts. **Secondary genre[s]:** MJAZ, TJAZ, AJAZ, ACAP, MFOL, ZYDC, JWSH, CBRT. **Acts:** national acts, regional acts, local acts. **Sample day's lineup:** Ed Shaughnessy with The Seacoast Big Band, Cercie Miller Quartet, Hedgehog Stompers, VocalEase, Bruce Katz Band, Shirim-Klezmer Orchestra, Tommy Gallant and The Allstars with Donna Byrne, Ben Baldwin and The Big Note, Carrie Coltrane, The Moonbeams, others. **Contact:** Seacoast Council on Tourism, 235 West Road, #10, Portsmouth, NH 03801, 603-436-7678 **or:** CREA, P. O. Box 4585, Portsmouth, NH 03802, 603-436-8596.

## CLASSIC ROCK FESTIVAL, Plymouth, NH
> Late Jun.
> Classic Rock and Oldies

**Help!** One time only? **Days:** 10. **Site:** outdoor. State Fairgrounds, Fairgrounds Road. **Admission:** paid. **Acts:** national acts. **Sample day's lineup:** John Kay and Steppenwolf, Georgia Satellites, Ray Sawyer and Dr. Hook, Mitch Ryder and The Detroit Wheels, Molly Hatchet, Iron Butterfly, Rare Earth. **Contact:** State Fairgrounds, Fairgrounds Road, Plymouth, NH 603-626-5000.

## FIDDLER'S CONTEST, Lincoln, NH
> Late Jun.
> Fiddle and Banjo Events

See other dates. **Days:** 1. **Site:** indoor and outdoor. Governor Adams Lodge, Loon Mountain Ski Resort. **Contact:** Loon Mountain Ski Resort, Kancamagus Highway, Lincoln, NH 03251, 603-745-6281.

## STARK OLD TIME FIDDLERS' CONTEST, Stark, NH
> Late Jun.
> Fiddle and Banjo Events

Since 1974. "What started out to be a one-time event mezmerized the listeners and organizers. The unique scenery and family theme has made the event the most popular in the North Country." -- Program. **Days:** 1. **Hours per day:** 8. **Site:** outdoor. Whitcomb's Field. **Admission:** paid. **Contact:** Stark Old Time Fiddlers' Contest, RFD 1, Box 359, Stark, NH 03582, 603-636-1325/1613.

## ALL AMERICANFEST, Lincoln, NH
> Early Jul.
> Variety, Country and Bluegrass

Since 1995. See other dates. **Days:** 2. **Site:** outdoor and indoor. Loon MountainPark, Kancamagus Highway. **Admission:** paid. **Daily entry:** under $10. **Secondary genre[s]:** MC&W, TC&W, BLGS. **Acts:** regional acts, local acts. **Sample day's lineup:** Stonewall Bluegrass Band, Sweet, Hot and Sassy, others. **Contact:** Loon Mountain Ski Resort, Kancamagus Highway, Lincoln, NH 03251, 603-745-6281.

### AMERICAN PIT MASTERS BAR-B-Q ROUND-UP, Manchester, NH
Early Jul.
Variety, General

Since 1993. "A festival for the heart and soul -- and especially the stomach." -- New Hampshire Sunday News. See other dates and sites. **Days:** 4. **Hours per day:** 12. **Site:** outdoor. Riverfront Park. **Admission:** paid. **Daily entry:** under $10. **Secondary genre[s]:** CRCK, ARCK, TR&B, MC&W, MFOL, FDDL. **Acts:** national acts, regional acts, local acts. **Sample day's lineup:** The Band, Lori Sargent, T. H. and The Wreckage, The Bristols, Bruce Marshall, Hypnotic Clambake, Mr. Stones Country. **Contact:** Conventures, Inc., 250 Summer Street, Boston, MA 02210, 617-439-7700.

### TWIN MOUNTAIN COUNTRY WESTERN JAMBOREE, Bretton Woods, NH
Early Jul.
Modern Country

**Help!** A sample lineup? **Days:** 1. **Site:** outdoor. Bretton Woods Ski Area. **Secondary genre[s]:** TC&W. **Acts:** local acts. **Sample day's lineup:** N. H. Country Musicians Association. **Contact:** Twin Mountain Country Western Jamboree, Bretton Woods Ski Area, Bretton Woods, NH 800-245-8946.

### STREET FAIR, Keene, NH
Middle Jul.
Variety, General

**Days:** 3. **Site:** outdoor. Main Street. **Secondary genre[s]:** MJAZ, MFOL, AFRC, OTHR. **Acts:** local acts. **Sample day's lineup:** Slam Bone Drummers, Afro-Jazz Dance, AKA, Larry Heath, Cheshiremen. **Contact:** Keene Chamber of Commerce, 8 Central Square, Keene, NH 03431, 603-352-1303.

### GILMANTON BLUEGRASS FESTIVAL, Gilmanton, NH
Middle Jul.
Bluegrass

Since 1991. Benefits Restoration Project of Smith Meeting House, a "really nice" 17th-century grounds where the festival is held. **Days:** 1. **Hours per day:** 9. **Site:** outdoor. Smith Meeting House. **Admission:** paid. **Daily entry:** $10 to $24. **Acts:** regional acts, local acts. **Sample day's lineup:** Dyer Switch, Banjo Dan and The Mid-Nite Plowboys, Wild Branch, White Mountain Bluegrass, Blistered Fingers. **Contact:** Gilmanton Bluegrass Festival, 4 Park Street, Suite 100, Concord, NH 03301, 603-224-3690.

### HAYSEED MUSIC FEST, Franconia, NH
Middle Jul.
Bluegrass

**Days:** 2. **Site:** outdoor. Dow Field. **Admission:** paid. **Daily entry:** under $10. **Secondary genre[s]:** MC&W, TC&W. **Acts:** local acts. **Sample day's lineup:** Backporch String Band, Tri-State Bluegrass Band, Day Break, Strawberry Farm Band, Silver Dollar String Band. **Contact:** Franconia Chamber of Commerce, Box 516, Franconia, NH 03580, 603-823-5344/5640.

### NATIVE AMERICAN SHOW, Littleton, NH
Middle Jul.
Native American

"Gathering of Native Americans" -- Listing. **Days:** 3. **Contact:** Littleton Town Office, 1 Union Street, Littleton, NH 03561, 603-444-3996.

## Waterville Valley Summer Music Festival, Waterville Valley, NH
Middle Jul. to Early Sep.
Variety, General

Weekly concert series in resort setting, but several dates feature festival-like multiple bills, including a Town Square Irish Festival. **Days:** 7. **Site:** indoor. Pavillion, Town Square, Waterville Valley Ski Resort. **Admission:** paid. **Daily entry:** $10 to $24. **Secondary genre[s]:** TR&B, MC&W, MFOL, TFOL, MARI, IRSH. **Acts:** national acts. **Sample day's lineup:** Pousette-Dart Band, the story, Jonathon Edwards. **Contact:** Waterville Valley Festival, P. O. Box 464, Waterville Valley, ME 03215, 800-468-2553.

## Hanover Street-Fest, Hanover, NH
Middle Jul.
Variety, General

Since 1980. **Days:** 1. **Hours per day:** 7. **Site:** outdoor. Main, Allen and Lebanon Streets. **Secondary genre[s]:** TFOL, AFRC. **Acts:** local acts. **Sample day's lineup:** North Country Chordsmen, African Drumming, Upper Valley Community Band, others. **Contact:** Hanover Chamber of Commerce, 37 South Main Street, Hanover, NH 03755, 603-643-3115.

## Loon MountainPark BrewFest, Lincoln, NH
Late Jul.
Alternative and College Rock

Since 1995. See other dates. **Days:** 2. **Site:** outdoor and indoor. Loon MountainPark, Kancamagus Highway. **Admission:** paid. **Daily entry:** under $10. **Acts:** local acts. **Sample day's lineup:** Smokin' Toad, Nobody's Fault, others. **Contact:** Loon Mountain Ski Resort, Kancamagus Highway, Lincoln, NH 03251, 603-745-6281.

## Pemi Valley Bluegrass Festival, Campton, NH
Early Aug.
Bluegrass

Since 1993. "Natural ampitheater, plus grassy, groomed grounds of AAA-rated campground in the scenic White Mountains. Country dance Saturday night; Sunday gospel; field pickin' 24 hours." -- Program. **Days:** 3. **Hours per day:** 14. **Site:** outdoor. Branch Brook Campground. **Admission:** paid. **Daily entry:** under $10, $10 to $24. **Discounts:** multiple event or day passes, advance purchase discounts. **Restrictions:** 13. **Secondary genre[s]:** SGOS, TC&W, BLGS, **Acts:** national acts, regional acts, local acts. **Sample day's lineup:** Front Range, Dry Branch Fire Squad, Cornerstone, Smokey Greene and The Boys, Southern Rail, Traver Hollow, Back to Basics, Gibson Brothers, Ed Poirier and The Bluegrass 4. **Contact:** Pemi Valley Productions, P. O. Box 658, Campton, NH 03223, 603-726-3471.

## Loon MountainPark IrishFest, Lincoln, NH
Early Aug.
Irish

Since 1995. See other dates. **Days:** 2. **Site:** outdoor and indoor. Loon MountainPark, Kancamagus Highway. **Admission:** paid. **Daily entry:** under $10. **Acts:** local acts. **Sample day's lineup:** Unicorn, others. **Contact:** Loon Mountain Ski Resort, Kancamagus Highway, Lincoln, NH 03251, 603-745-6281.

MUSICFEST, Exeter, NH
Early Aug.
Variety, General

Since 1990. "It could be the Seacoast's best live music smorgasbord this year..." -- The Beachcomber. **Days:** 1. **Hours per day:** 6. **Site:** outdoor. Swasey Parkway. **Admission:** free. **Secondary genre[s]:** MJAZ, MFOL. **Acts:** regional acts, local acts. **Sample day's lineup:** T. J. Wheeler and The Smokers, The Has-Beens, Steve Brennan and Meg Daley, plus a guitar competition. **Contact:** Exeter Music, 135 Water Street, Exeter, NH 03833, 603-772-5440.

LOON MOUNTAINPARK CAJUNFEST, Lincoln, NH
Middle Aug.
Cajun and Zydeco

Since 1995. See other dates. **Days:** 2. **Site:** outdoor and indoor. Loon MountainPark, Kancamagus Highway. **Admission:** paid. **Daily entry:** under $10. **Acts:** local acts. **Sample day's lineup:** Ryan Thompson and The Crawdad Wranglers, others. **Contact:** Loon Mountain Ski Resort, Kancamagus Highway, Lincoln, NH 03251, 603-745-6281.

ARTS JUBILEE/COUNTRY IN THE VALLEY, North Conway, NH
Late Aug.
Modern Country

Part of Arts Jubilee, a season-long performing-arts series. **Help!** One time only? **Days:** 1. **Site:** outdoor. Schouler Park. **Admission:** free. **Acts:** local acts. **Sample day's lineup:** Tequila Sunrise, Katie Belle, Bill Madison. **Contact:** Arts Jubilee, P. O. Box 647, North Conway, NH 03860, 603-356-9393.

PRESCOTT PARKS ARTS FESTIVAL/CELEBRATION OF JAZZ, Portsmouth, NH
Late Aug.
Traditional Jazz and Ragtime

Since 1993. Part of the Prescott Park Arts Festival, a summer-long performing arts series. "Come on down and swing!" -- Program. **Days:** 1. **Site:** outdoor. Prescott Park. **Admission:** free. **Secondary genre[s]:** MJAZ. **Acts:** local acts. **Sample day's lineup:** Ben Baldwin and The Big Note, Mike Hashem's Dixieland, The Swingsters, Pam Pryor and Chuck Chaplin, Louise Rogers Quartet, Allan Chase Quartet. **Contact:** Prescott Park Arts Festival, P. O. Box 4370, Portsmouth, NH 03802-4370, 603-436-2848.

WHITE MOUNTAIN JAZZ AND BLUES CRAFTSFESTIVAL, Bartlett, NH
Early Sep.
Variety, Jazz and Blues

Since 1992. "The League of New Hampshire Craftsmen will [also] offer a crafts show featuring 40 juried artists. A 100-foot tent will be spilling over." -- Program. **Days:** 1. **Site:** outdoor. Fields of Attitash. **Admission:** paid. **Daily entry:** $10 to $24. **Discounts:** advance purchase discounts. **Restrictions:** 5. **Secondary genre[s]:** MJAZ, TR&B. **Acts:** national acts, regional acts. **Sample day's lineup:** Tiger's Baku, The Holmes Brothers, Heavy Metal Horns, Rebecca Parris. **Contact:** White Mountain Jazz and Blues CraftsFestival, P. O. Box 530, North Conway, NH 03860, 603-356-6862/5701.

BLUES FESTIVAL, Portsmouth, NH
>       Early Sep.
>       Blues and Traditional R&B

Since 1994. "We try to address some social issues and take some risks -- that's what a nonprofit blues society is all about." -- T. J. Wheeler. **Days:** 3. **Site:** outdoor and indoor. Portsmouth Harbor Place (Sat.); plus pub crawls. **Admission:** paid. **Acts:** national acts, regional acts, local acts. **Sample lineup:** Tommy Ridgley, Mighty Sam McLain, Paul Geremia, Pinetop Perkins, T. J. Wheeler and The Smokers, Shirley Lewis, Paul Rishell, Doc Johnson Blues Band, Charlie Archer, Tony Lynn Washington, others. **Contact:** Blues Bank Collective, 9 Towle Farm Road, Hampton Falls, NH 03844, 603-929-0654.


LABOR DAY WEEKEND MUSIC FESTIVAL, Conway, NH
>       Early Sep.
>       Modern Folk

"For musicians, singers, dancers and music lovers of all ages." -- Program. **Days:** 4. **Site:** indoor. New Hampshire World Fellowship Center, NH Route 16. **Acts:** local acts. **Sample day's lineup:** Douglas Clegg, Patricia Shih, Danny Harper, Taylor Whiteside. **Contact:** World Fellowship, P. O. Box 2280, Conway, NH 03818, 603-447-2280.


RIVERFEST: MANCHESTER CELEBRATING ITSELF, Manchester, NH
>       Early Sep. to Middle Sep.
>       Variety, General

**Days:** 3. **Hours per day:** 15. **Site:** outdoor. Arms Park. **Admission:** free and paid. **Daily entry:** under $10. **Secondary genre[s]:** CRCK, MC&W, OTHR. **Acts:** national acts, local acts. **Sample day's lineup:** Peter Wolf, McBride and The Ride, Pony Express. **Contact:** WGIR-FM, P. O. Box 101, Manchester, NH 03105, 603-625-6915.


SEAFOOD FESTIVAL AND SIDEWALK SALE DAYS, Hampton Beach, NH
>       Middle Sep.
>       Variety, General

Since 1990. **Days:** 2. **Hours per day:** 9. **Site:** outdoor. Ashworth Avenue and Ocean Boulevard on the boardwalk. **Secondary genre[s]:** CRCK, MC&W, MFOL, IRSH. **Acts:** local acts. **Sample day's lineup:** The Maldens, The Falcons, Dr. Humble and The Super Bees, Bluehemia, Ray DeMarco's Street Level Swing, Recycled Folk, Mike Hashem's Dixeland Strollers, Duo Bueno, Larry Garland Quintet, Skip Tilley with Sweet Boy, The Unlimited Blues Band with K. T. Faith and K-Wreck, Solstice, Wayne. **Contact:** Hampton Beach Area Chamber of Commerce, P. O. Box 790, 836 Lafayette Road, Hampton Beach, NH 03842, 603-926-8718.


NEW HAMPSHIRE HIGHLAND GAMES, Lincoln, NH
>       Middle Sep.
>       Scottish

Since 1976. **Days:** 4. **Site:** outdoor and indoor. Loon Mountain Recreation Center. **Admission:** paid. **Daily entry:** under $10, $10 to $24. **Acts:** national acts, regional acts, local acts. **Sample day's lineup:** Strathspey and Reel Society of New Hampshire, Sue Richards, The Brigadoons, Carl Peterson, Guest Band, Alasdair Fraser, Robin Ellis's SCD Band. **Contact:** New Hampshire Highland Games, P. O. Box 130, Cambridge, MA 02238-0130, 617-661-5899/864-8945 **or:** North Woodstock/Lincoln Chamber of Commerce, P. O. Box 358, Lincoln, NH 03251, 603-745-6621.

### FOLK SONG SOCIETY OF GREATER BOSTON FALL GETAWAY WEEKEND, Hillsboro, NH
Middle Sep.
Traditional Folk

"Song swap, dance, workshops, teaching sessions, mini concerts, swimming, sauna, tennis, canoeing, hiking...Everyone is welcome and you don't have to be a performer to participate and enjoy" -- Program. **Help!** A sample lineup? **Days:** 3. **Site:** outdoor and indoor. Camp Interlocken. **Admission:** paid. **Daily entry:** $50 and over. **Secondary genre[s]:** MFOL. **Acts:** local acts. **Contact:** Folk Song Society of Greater Boston, P. O. Box 492, Somerville, MA 02143, 617-623-1806.

### STAR HAMPSHIRE TRADITIONAL MUSIC/DANCE RETREAT, Portsmouth, NH
Late Sep.
Variety, Folk and International

**Days:** 3. **Site:** indoor. Star Island. **Admission:** paid. **Secondary genre[s]:** TFOL, ZYDC, IRSH, SCOT, OTHR. **Acts:** local acts. **Sample lineup:** Mary DeRosiers, Nat Hewitt, Ruth Richards, Jane Orzechowski, Deanna Stiles, Bob McQuillen. **Contact:** Star Hampshire Traditional Music/Dance Retreat, 21A Prospect Street, Portsmouth, NH 03801, 603-436-8372.

### STRATHSPEY AND REEL SOCIETY OF NEW HAMPSHIRE'S SCOTTISH GALA CONCERT, Concord, NH
Late Nov.
Scottish

Since 1990. **Days:** 1. **Site:** indoor. Concord Auditorium. **Acts:** local acts. **Sample day's lineup:** Brian Yates and Ensemble, Anthony Moretti Tufts, Rod Stradling, Barley Court, William Tobin, Viveka Fox. **Contact:** Strathspey and Reel Society of New Hampshire, 102 Little Pond Road, Concord, NH 03301, 603-225-6546.

### CHRISTMAS REVELS, Hanover, NH
Middle Dec.
Traditional Folk

"A Celebration of the Winter Solstice: traditional and ritual dances, processionals, carols and drama." -- Program. See other sites and dates. **Days:** 3. **Site:** indoor. Hopkins Center, Dartmouth College. **Acts:** local acts. **Sample day's lineup:** Solstice Singers, Revels Children, Featherstonehaugh Mummers, Heritage Brass Ensemble, Coldwinters Musik, Old Bells of Branston, others. **Audio merchandise:** "The Christmas Revels"; "Seasons for Singing"; "Blow, Ye Winds in the Morning" (all on Revels Records). **Contact:** Revels North, Box 415, Hanover, NH 03755, 603-646-2422.

### FIRST NIGHT KEENE, Keene, NH
Late Dec.
Variety, Folk and International

"Celebrate the New Year with family and friends....Performances, demonstrations, visual displays and hands-on arts events will provide something for everyone!" -- Program. **Days:** 1. **Hours per day:** 8. **Site:** indoor, 31 venues. **Admission:** paid. **Daily entry:** under $10. **Discounts:** multiple event or day passes, advance purchase discounts. **Restrictions:** 2. **Secondary genre[s]:** MJAZ, TC&W, BLGS, MFOL, TFOL, IRSH, SCOT, CBRT, OTHR. **Acts:** national acts, local acts. **Sample day's lineup:** Livingston Taylor, Peter Tavalin, Kimberly Consort, Bob Cuniff Orchestra, Keene Chorale, Edita, Carl Peterson, St. Andrews Ladies Pipe Band, Purly Gates Trio, Pati and Ken Cloutier, Keene High Jazz Band, Tom and Elizabeth Martin, Patty Carpenter, Amidon Family, Jazz Express, Harvey Reid, Kenny LaRoche, Tapper and Bridges, Grassroots Players, Apple Hill Chamber Players, Northeast Winds, The Flextones, The MacArthur Family, Mimi Kates, Indian Summer, Close Enough, Stonewall Bluegrass, Texas Round-Up, others. **Contact:** Grand Monadnock Arts Council, P. O. Box 835, Keene, NH 603-357-3906.

FIRST NIGHT NEW HAMPSHIRE, Concord, NH
> Late Dec.
> Variety, Folk and International

"Swing upon a star." -- Program. **Days:** 1. **Hours per day:** 8. **Site:** indoor, 26 venues. **Admission:** paid. **Daily entry:** under $10. **Discounts:** multiple event or day passes, advance purchase discounts. **Restrictions:** 2. **Secondary genre[s]:** MJAZ, CRCK, ACAP, MC&W, MFOL, TFOL, IRSH, NATV, OTHR. **Acts:** national acts, regional acts, local acts. **Sample day's lineup:** Devonsquare, T. J. Wheeler and The Smokers, Blackwater Band, Ring Around the Moon, The Cronetones, Lowe Profiles, Steve Schuch, Paul Hubert, Skip Gorman and Buffalo Hump, Femme M'amie, Home for Dinner, Bob Leslie, Curt Bessette, Tom Pirrozzoli, Tommy Gallant and The Allstars, Carolyn Parrott, Mary Lou Philbin, New Hampshire Philharmonic String Quatete, Stan Moeller and T. S. Baker, The Turning Pointe, Richard Lederer and Kathy Lowe, R. P. Hale, Wellspring, Canciones, Sweet River, CCMS Woodwind Ensemble, Bob Leslie, Danihel and Sheppard, Peggosus, Cosy Sheridan, CCMS Jazz and Vocal Ensemble, Douglas Clegg, Goodmorrow Consort, Authentic Forgery, Purly Gates Trio, Suzuki Strings, Medicine Story, Colburn and Stuart, Song Weavers, Elizabeth and Lydia Reed, Brownie and Thompson, High Jinks, Lucie Therrien, Corno-Copia, Philomel. **Contact:** First Night New Hampshire, P. O. Box 96, Concord, NH 03302-0096, 603-224-1411.


FIRST NIGHT PORTSMOUTH, Portsmouth, NH
> Late Dec.
> Variety, Folk and International

**Days:** 1. **Hours per day:** 7. **Site:** outdoor and indoor, 30 venues. **Admission:** paid. **Daily entry:** under $10. **Discounts:** multiple event or day passes, advance purchase discounts. **Restrictions:** 2. **Secondary genre[s]:** MJAZ, ACAP, BLGS, MFOL, TFOL, IRSH, NATV, SCOT, OTHR. **Acts:** regional acts, local acts. **Sample day's lineup:** Lui Collins, Cosy Sheridan, VocalEase, The Maldens, Harbroside Harmony, The King and The Memphis Mafia, Memorial Bridge Allatars, Rick Watson and Jerry Short, Hampshire Brass, Lucie Therrien, Paul Hubert, Mostly Baroque, White Noise, Harbor Belles, Salt Water Tuffies, Yagottawanna, Uno Mundo, Medicine Story, Sarah Bauhan, Strafford County Wind Symphony, Amare Cantare, Consortium for Early Music, Just Bob and Marla. **Contact:** Pro Portsmouth, Inc., 161 Court Street, P. O. Box 1008, Portsmouth, NH 03802-1008, 603-431-5388.

# R. I. P., M. I. A. Festival Listings

**Caveat** The following festivals are either confirmed or suspected to be discontinued (i.e., R. I. P.); or have not responded to various information requests (i.e., M. I. A.). Since all festivals are subject to last-minute changes or reinstatement, however, FestPress is not responsible for any festival listing information that follows. Readers are encouraged to notify FestPress of any status changes they uncover.

CELTIC FESTIVAL, Nashua, NH
> Late Mar.
> Irish

**Help!** Does anyone know the status of this event, its contacts, or a sample lineup? **Days:** 1. **Site:** indoor, Church of the Good Shepherd, 214 Main Street. **Contact:** Institute of Celtic Studies East, 214 Main Street, Nashua, NH 617-524-4386.

JAMBOREE AT JIMMY'S SEAFOOD, Concord, NH
> Middle May
> Modern Country

Benefits the Arthritis Foundation. **Help!** One-time only? **Days:** 1. **Hours per day:** 6. **Site:** indoor. Jimmy's Seafood Restaurant, 4 Dover Road (Loudon Road). **Admission:** paid. **Daily entry:** under $10. **Acts:** local acts. **Sample day's lineup:** Backroom Band, Shannon Smith and The Country Caravan, Linda Jean and Her Gamblers, Cellar Brothers, Gary Stewart and The Silver Spurs, Straight Tequila Naiades. **Contact:** Jimmy's Seafood Restaurant, 4 Dover Road, Concord, NH 03301, 603-224-5515.

FATHER'S DAY COUNTRY AND WESTERN JAMBOREE, Epsom, NH
> Middle Jun.
> Modern Country

Since 1993. One time only. **Days:** 1. **Site:** outdoor. Circle 9 Ranch. **Admission:** paid. **Daily entry:** under $10 **Discounts:** advance purchase discounts. **Contact:** 603-736-9656.

FOLK JAM/NEW HAMPSHIRE ACOUSTIC GUITAR AND BANJO CONTEST, Portsmouth, NH
> Middle Aug.
> Modern Folk

Since 1986. Part of the Prescott Parks Arts Festival, a summer-long performing-arts series. The afternoon contest, traditionally combined with a multiple bill of national folk acts at night, was cancelled in 1993. Hopefully, local grumblings will restore the event. **Days:** 1. **Hours per day:** 8. **Site:** outdoor. Prescott Park. **Acts:** national acts, local acts. **Sample day's lineup:** Richie Havens, Livingston Taylor, Dave Van Ronk. **Contact:** Prescott Park Arts, P. O. Box 4370, Portsmouth, NH 03802, 603-436-2848.

HERITAGE MUSIC FESTIVAL, Rochester, NH
> Middle Aug.
> Variety, General

Since 1982. Discontinued in 1993. **Days:** 1. **Site:** outdoor, Rochester Common. **Admission:** paid. **Daily entry:** under $10. **Secondary genre[s]:** MC&W, TC&W, BLGS, MFOL, OTHR. **Acts:** local acts. **Sample lineup:** Salmon Falls River Friends of Music Present (Jackie Vanderzanden, Bill Simpson, Craig Werth), Three Dollar Bill, Cold River String Band, Bill Cormier and The Dixieland Dads, Carmen and The Country Drifters, Earth Ecos, Tom Pirozzoli, Rabbit in a Log, Joe Pomerleau and Friends. **Contact:** Arts Rochester, P. O. Box 451, Rochester, NH 03867, 603-335-1018 **or:** City of Rochester, 31 Wakefield Street, Rochester NH 03867, 603-332-1167. .


GREAT BAY FOLKLIFE FESTIVAL AND DANCE WEEKEND, Newmarket, NH
> Middle Aug.
> Variety, Country and Bluegrass

Since 1990. Cancelled in 1992. **Days:** 3. **Hours per day:** 14. **Site:** outdoor and indoor, Landroche Fields, Newmarket High School. **Secondary genre[s]:** TC&W, BLGS, MFOL, TFOL, ZYDC, IRSH, SCOT. **Acts:** national acts, regional acts, local acts. **Sample lineup:** Crawdad Wranglers, Main Brace, Magnolia, Mary Desrosiers, Harvey Reid, T. J. Wheeler and The Smokers, Dudley Laufman, Doug Clegg, Swing Pirates, Open to Suggestion, Maple Sugar Band, Lamprey River Band, Cuckoo's Nest, Strathspey and Reel Society, Lorraine Lee and Bennett Hammond, Sammie Haynes, Cormac McCarthy, others. **Contact:** Great Bay Folklife Festival, 4 Elm Street, Portsmouth, NH 0385703801, 603-659-2658 **or:** Great Bay Folklife Festival, P. O. Box 1452, Portsmouth, NH 03857, 603-942-7604. .


ATTITASH RODEO WITH BANJO AND FIDDLE CONTEST, Bartlett, NH
> Late Aug.
> Fiddle and Banjo Events

Since 1992. Contest held in conjunction with the rodeo was one time only. However, Director, Nancy Clark, wants to program more music events at Attitash, separately. Promoters, sponsors, any takers? **Days:** 1. **Hours per day:** 6. **Site:** outdoor, Attitash Mountain Ski Resort. **Contact:** Attitash Ski Resort, P. O. Box 308, Bartlett, NH 03812, 603-374-2368 **or:** Clegg Yolk Music, 328 Concord Stage Road, Weare, NH 03281, 603-529-1051.

~     ~     ~

# Vermont

*Marquee, Discover Jazz Festival.*

# Burlington's Jazz Blast

**DISCOVER JAZZ FESTIVAL**, Burlington, VT
> Early June to Mid June
> Variety, Jazz and Blues
> ***Attended***

**PICO MOUNTAIN JAZZ FESTIVAL**, Sherburne, VT
> Late July
> Modern Jazz

Festival Director Jimmy Swift is recapping some of his booking highlights for the wonderfully **Introduction** funky DISCOVER JAZZ FESTIVAL [DISCOVER JAZZ']. In addition to Manny Oquendo and Libre, plus Jerry Gonzalez and The Fort Apache Band, he cites ska-music legends, The Skatalites. A ska band at a jazz festival? A stretch, you say? Swift counters:

- "Actually, The Skatalites were the perfect group because they embody the history of jazz; because that's where they started, in Jamaica, listening to jazz on the radio. They wanted to play [Count] Basie, [Duke] Ellington, and Charlie Parker, but in order to accommodate the commercial club scene, they had to give it a dance beat. That's how ska was born!

  "They are a legitimate artistic connection to the roots, and you have players in their late sixties who have been doing it since '62, playing this music. But, at the same time, a 16-year-old kid can go down there, or a 25-year-old, or whoever, and just have a ball and say, 'Hey, this band is fantastic,' not even thinking about jazz or the tradition.

  "For us it's perfect because it's a band that works in Burlington and that's really where our programming comes from — what's really going to work in Burlington. And if it doesn't boogie, you know, it's got less of a chance. So about half of our program is always going to be something that really moves right along."

Of course, the other half is quite sophisticated, thank you, and keeps you glued to your seat. Whereas Swift comes from the R&B club circuit, his partner, Artistic Director of the Flynn Theater for the Performing Arts, Phillip Bither, arrives via "Brooklyn Academy of Music" aesthetics. Bither contributes leading jazz lights along the lines of The David Murray Quartet, The Joe Henderson Quartet, and The Kenny Burrell Trio — to name three headliners from the reverse side of '94's bill.

Ironically, DISCOVER JAZZ' began in '84 as a mainstream jazz music festival with conservative leanings. "The ticket sales were pretty abysmal," Swift recalls:

- "So I was hired as a Music Coordinator, along with a new Director [Bither], and the first thing I said was, 'We've got to get the most popular band in the area to play,' which is the Unknown Blues Band. We sold, like, three thousand tickets to that event at five bucks a pop and there is money flowing in. We also did Dizzy Gillespie, who was not really that hot at the time, but it sold out. And I said, 'Let's also get Roomful of Blues!' And we went for Sun Ra and The Arkestra because I know they had done well on a club date two years prior that I had worked on that my partner actually produced.

  "Again, it was a little bit adventuresome [with] some major jazz, but definitely some stuff you could dance to, and the Burlington audiences could relate to. Right away, we had great sales."

If this funky/classy musical mix reminds you of the ever glorious NEW ORLEANS JAZZ AND HERITAGE FESTIVAL (see New Orleans, LA, Late April to Early May), you'd be half-right in placing the main events most influencing Swift and Bither. In fact, Swift pays his annual visit there to scout out potential soul shouters and boogie bands. The other one is the FESTIVAL INTERNATIONAL DE JAZZ DE MONTREAL (see Montreal, Quebec, Late June to Early July), which DISCOVER JAZZ' emulates in form by virtually taking over its town, filling seemingly every block to bursting with impromptu performances, and creating venues where none exist during the regular year. The result is a complete community happening supported by the entire populace in a full court press to present Burlington at its best and most accessible. (Eat your hearts out New York City festival promoters.)

Normally, such bounty comes at the expense of intimacy. Not so here, as Swift relates: "Three years ago there was somebody who worked at the [FESTIVAL INTERNATIONAL'] who said, 'We have one of the best festivals in the world, but your festival is special because it's intimate. You can get right up close and meet the musicians. You've got an intimacy and a proximity to the musicians that's special.'"

DISCOVER JAZZ's proximity is best achieved in its two dance parties that feature blues and world-beat musics, respectively: Thursday night at Champlain Mill and Saturday night at the Waterfront Tent. Swift often programs unusual pairings there, exhorting the musicians to try different things. The last thing he wants is "the same old concert," much preferring the jam session to the stock set.

"The spirit of the thing," Swift explains, "is that David Murray can fly in from London on no hours' sleep, play his gig, and then go up and jam for two hours with the local band (which he did), and then go party with them at a hotel room 'till the wee hours. You just can't plan on that stuff. You can set the stage and put the musicians on it, but you just can't plan for all the other stuff that's going to happen — all the connections and the spirit of the music that's going to come alive."

**Festival Review**   If you learned about DISCOVER JAZZ' through the mail, you'd never know this much of Swift's "stuff" goes on all six days. All the festival brochure lists is the headliners, merely hinting at the remaining profusion of local acts.

Take the Friday I drove up in '94:

- It began at noon with three high school jazz ensembles at the Church Street Marketplace; followed there at 3:00 p.m. by a "Friday Block Party" with The Swingin' Vermont Big Band;

- Jamie Masefield played ragtime/jazz banjo all afternoon on a series of three bus tours called, "Jazz on the Bus," alternating with The Jalapeno Brothers;

- The club gigs started with a 4:00 p.m. happy hour featuring Style A's Trio, and continued past midnight with 13 more acts, each at a different venue.

- Joe Henderson did an hour-long "Meet the Artist" from 5:00 to 6:00 p.m. preceding his 8:00 p.m. main-stage show at the Flynn Theater, an art deco masterpiece with its hush of burgundy mohair and plush carpet; its glow from wrought iron chandeliers 40 feet up; and its shimmering red velvet curtains tied up with gold brocade.

- The "newest and hippest" nightclub, 242 Main, hosted the Willem Sellenraad Trio, plus the Full-Metal Revolutionary Jazz Ensemble at 8:00 p.m., while 10:00 p.m. began an All-Star Jam Session" in City Hall's stately chambers — an energetic 11-year tradition!

There were no street buskers that night, but there might've well as been, since music seemed to follow me everywhere I wandered in the crisp mountain air.

Venues were comfortably attended while spirits ran high! For Henderson's show, the collegiate-looking crowd (students, alumni, faculty, and staff, it appeared) applauded everything — the opener, the announcer, the announcer's announcer, the mere fact of their own presence making the night a success. Their vibe was clearly one of contagious appreciation and celebration, while sacrificing nothing in the way of sophisticated attention.

<u>The Joe Henderson Quartet</u>. I don't know if tenor-sax ace Henderson caught this euphoric vibe **Artist** going on — he's all business on stage — but he sure dug into a fascinating set. I pictured my days **Mini-Reviews** in film-making class, and imagined a master editor chopping up a reel of celluloid, then putting it back together in a different order, frame by thoughtfully-placed frame, in which each image re-invented the original, but in such a way as not to lose its continuity or feeling.

Whereas Henderson awed with long, fluid lines that seemed to stretch on forever without losing their imagination, guitarist John Scofield took a different tact. He deconstructed the changes more in block form, relying on jump cuts to make transitions from one brief, angular sequence to the next. The two played off each other beautifully all night long for a contrast that was challenging, absorbing and satisfying — one of my performance highlights of the year!

Swift: "We knew [Henderson] was a solid home-run across the board."

<u>George Petit and The Desired Effect</u>. Local guitarist, Petit, opened and lead his quartet through three tunes: "There Will Never be Another You," plus two originals. His solos appeared reasonably adept at first but then degenerated into all these unnecessary, cutsey, popular quotes as if he'd spent too much time playing bars and weddings. Here was one place, I felt, where an audience didn't need to be so obviously wooed. Chris Peterson on tenor sax took a strong, straightforward approach and was rewarded with the biggest applause among the group's four soloists.

Oh, and did I mention how marvelous Burlington is for a long weekend rendezvous? Picture a **Travel Tip** pocket San Francisco with incredible sunset panoramas reflecting the Adirondacks' bumpy silhouette off Lake Champlain's glittering expanse. And, like Key West, the friendly townsfolk stroll down 19th century walkways to the piers every clear dusk just to bask in the flaming beauty.

Here's how Swift describes the appeal: "What's selling the festival is definitely two parts, the vacation experience, as well as the music. It's an incomparable setting with views — mountain and lake. [Burlington's] a jewel of a city. And the intimate scale is another thing that people talk about, the fact that there is a real warm and homey feeling without crowding."

Just down the road at the Pico Mountain Ski Resort is the PICO MOUNTAIN JAZZ FESTIVAL, which **See Also** occupies the fourth weekend in July. It features far less quantity than DISCOVER JAZZ' — only three acts per day for two days — but definitely comparable quality, albeit of a more conservative nature. Its first year in '92 was an artistic success, but not a financial one, causing a one-year hiatus while its organizers sought a corporate sponsor. Happily, it returned in '94, thus giving jazz fans two good excuses to head northward.

~ ~ ~

# Vermont's Funky Freebies

**BEN AND JERRY'S ONE WORLD, ONE HEART FESTIVAL,** Warren, VT
Late June
Variety, General
***Attended***

**VERMONT REGGAE FESTIVAL,** Johnson, VT
Middle July
Reggae, Ska and Caribbean

**Introduction** Ben Cohen and Jerry Greenfield, respective founders of Ben and Jerry's Ice Cream [B&J], are my kind of guys — business role models, if you will. Why? 'Cause they walk it like they talk it and that's no scoop! Want an example? Despite steering their ice cream and frozen yogurt empire to annual sales of over $100 million, both partners take out salaries of just $100,000 each in deference to their modest life styles, stockholder assurance, and employee morale (vs. others like Michael Eisner, who plundered Disney's coffers last year for an astonishing $230 million in executive compensation!). You could say that they've funded a series of the coolest festivals in the country right out of their own pockets.

Ben, the one with the red beard, summarizes his corporate philosophy of "caring capitalism" in their newsletter, *Chunk Mail*, "Business has the responsibility to give back to the community." Where big business usually gives lip service to such tenets (witness the continuing orgy of relatively unnecessary layoffs to fatten profits and spike stock prices), B&J's has declared a "Social Mission" and designates 7.5% of pre-tax profits to "innovative ways to improve the quality of life of a broad community — local, national and international." Their efforts at recycling, environmental preservation, "green" investing, universal healthcare, community development, and a host of other issues, while not always successful, have nonetheless gained them favorable coverage in publications ranging from *Rolling Stone* to the *Wall Street Journal*.

I admire how the two leaders have learned lessons from their hippie days, in selecting causes that don't polarize left against right but pay heed to an over-reaching "right thing to do" for both groups.

A good example is their "Social Action Area" agenda for '93's BEN AND JERRY'S ONE WORLD, ONE HEART FESTIVALS: "the health and well-being of America's children." On the left, various feminist organizations have consistently dropped the ball on day care and other family concerns in favor of such male-antagonistic causes as date rape. On the right, the "family-values" crowd in corporate America have failed to maintain inflation-adjusted salaries for the middle and working classes sufficient to allow one parent to stay at home. They've also fought such issues as parental leave and universal health care. Thanks partly to both camps, child-rearing has suffered to the point where recent studies have ranked the U. S. near-bottom among developed nations across most child-welfare indices.

Go to a free (!!) B&J fest, however, and there's no partisan proselytizing. Rather, they just lay out the facts on children's needs and invite your participation. Last year you could buy a postcard for a quarter and address it to your congressperson or representative. They didn't tell you what to say, or to whom to say it. Needed more info.? They laid out scads of pamphlets and had representatives on hand from half-a-dozen child-advocacy organizations, including the Children's Defense Fund. Your reward? A free B&J Peace Pop. Afterwards, you could maintain your involvement by registering to vote or by joining their Call for Kids Campaign (1-800-BJ-KIDS-1).

Naturally, B&J also hosted a bonanza-land of children's activities creative enough to seduce the parents ("Hey, move over kid and let me paint a Brown Bag Crown!"). Games, races, arts, crafts, face-painting, the ubiquitous Ben & Jerry's Traveling Bus Show, Bread and Puppet

Theater, and an incredible hand-carved carousel I couldn't stop marveling at — all spelled great fun for kids but not at the entertainment expense of entire families who seemed to predominate among the day's early revelers.

Which brings us to the credo of the other partner, Jerry: "If it's not fun, why do it?" Indeed, fun defines the eclectic musical experience as a wide swath of music genres, and ethnic cultures are represented by name artists chosen to make you smile, sing or dance — all while pondering your social action. Check out Saturday's bill at the inaugural Vermont bash: Buckwheat Zydeco, NRBQ, John Prine, Paul Winter, Christine Lavin, Unknown Blues Band, Don Rose. No old scolds here, even among the folkies!

It all falls to B&J's bubbly, high-octane Special Projects Manager, Evy Dworetzky, who's able to pull off as many as five major festivals in a year (helped by Festival Productions, Inc.), plus every other B&J activity with just four people! Her modest events department typically controls three-fourths of B&J's annual marketing budget with a single day's production costs running upwards of $300,000.

"We're able to do that because we have in-house staff," Dworetzky exhales in a rare moment of rest:

- "We have in-house public relations; we have an in-house art department; we have in-house festival events whereas so many companies stick their logo onto somebody else's event. I think that there's a real different feel for that. We create events that we think are worthwhile or beneficial. We say people come for the music but leave hopefully becoming a little more educated on either the recycling aspects or association with the Children's Defense Fund.

  "I think that so much of what we're seeing is that maybe the social ills that are happening are a result of our inability to take care of our own children. The whole health-care issue, I mean, that's shocking! [It] can stem from birth, whereas if you have proper treatment as an infant with immunization and things like that, all those things relate to later on in life. It was quite funny, this is our third year working with the Children's Defense Fund, but then it became very politically-correct when the Clintons were elected. [laughs] We're thrilled that it's becoming more of a national priority, and we will continue this year in our focus on the Children's Defense Fund."

Dworetzky credits her co-workers ("an incredibly talented bunch of people"), reserving special praise for the art department who lends B&J events their characteristically funky look and feel:

- "We actually work really hard at it. After one of our festivals, we have postings at all of our locations because our employees work the festivals, so they're the eyes and ears. The person that's selling t-shirts is not just somebody that's 'temp-ing' for the day, they're somebody that's possibly working in our freezer, or somebody that works as a tour guide, or somebody that works in our retail shop, so they can hear the comments right from the festival-goers. And we can use that to focus on the feedback. We had 17 pages of feedback from last year's Vermont festival, [and] we look back on that and what type of things we can improve for this year."

Of course leadership steers the B&J bus. "The thing is they both personally attend every festival," Dworetzky describes of her two bosses, "they're not stuck behind cages. People see them out there at Newport (BEN AND JERRY'S NEWPORT FOLK FESTIVAL, Newport, RI — see chapter) dancing, or sitting on the blanket with their families, or talking to customers. The same thing at every one of our festivals in Vermont or Chicago — they're out there, and they're accessible. People talk to them. I think that's a big difference."

Dworetzky's accumulated a slew of musical memories in her three years' stewardship of Vermont's family gathering/stockholder celebration (B&J's annual stockholders' meeting also occurs onsite the same weekend):

- "Arlo Guthrie I thought was awesome last year. He did a really hot show. And Buddy Guy gettin' off stage and goin' into that sand pit... He grabbed a little kid and let him play his guitar. [laughs] I think kinda' hearin' some of The Band songs like 'The Weight' and stuff like that...

"I think about Rockin' Dopsie — now he's passed away, [but] we were fortunate to have Dopsie senior [with] Dopsie junior doin' splits and comin' up on stage with The Fabulous Thunderbirds. That's a lot of fun stuff when they start playin' together. And Shawn Colvin, I mean, how do you follow Rockin' Dopsie, [but] Shawn Colvin gets up there acoustically and gets a standing ovation after them. Nobody moved! She was just fantastic."

Her most treasured memory, though, was more in passing:

- "The first year we did the festivals I was so, so nervous. 'I mean, is anybody gonna come to your birthday party?' At the end of the first day, I was kinda' like, 'Wow,' and just check-ing out when people were getting on the busses and some man who was obviously not very well-off came up to me and said, 'I want to tell you that I have three kids and I've never been able to bring my kids to see live music before. They just can't believe how great this is.'

"To me, that just about brought tears to my eyes."

**Festival Review**    When you drive up Vermont way, you'll notice bumper stickers everywhere in reference to a neighboring ski resort: "Ski Mad River Glen...if you can!" Well, my wife and I took Mad River Glen virtually on two wheels as we completed a festival race that began that morning in New York City and included the delightfully-homey OLD SONGS FESTIVAL' (Altamont, NY — see chapter) and the wonderfully celebratory NEWPORT JAZZ FESTIVAL/SARATOGA (Saratoga Springs, NY — see chap-ter). Yet, it was worth it just for the scene before us as we squealed to a halt in the parking lot grav-el at the Sugarbush Ski Resort: a sea of heads bopping in hyperdrive to Little Feat's rollicking "Cajun Girl."

Call it a party in progress — one best captured with a telephoto lense to compress the acres of dancing, happy faces silhouetted against the damp, green hillside and leafy trees. Pan 180 degrees and you'd gaze over the Green Mountains and ridge after forested ridge all the way to New Hampshire and beyond. To borrow a phrase from the old bluegrass standard, "Sittin' on top of the world!"

We got there too late for the day's acts, so here are my notes on the BEN AND JERRY'S ONE WORLD, ONE HEART FESTIVAL that took place earlier that year in New York City's Central Park. My pages are still dusted from the infield dirt that got stirred up head-high by 150,000 dancing Gothamites. Prior to The Band's set, the threat of rain chased us away but not before my friends and I tasted a thoroughly groovin' afternoon.

**Artist Mini-Reviews**    <u>Eddie Palmieri and his Orchestra</u>. Every time I see Palmieri's band I come away more impressed. His genius truly transcends genre, as his extraordinarily complex and sinuous "salsa symphonies" sacrifice nothing in terms of party-down dance-ability. Palmieri revealed himself to be a quintu-ple threat: arranger/composer, pianist, trumpeter, timbale banger, and singer. He even cheerled a roaring "Quanto Cosa" with handclaps while his three gifted percussionists took turns outdoing eachother. People were still assembling for his opening set, but Latin dancers rimmed the crowd with their trademark boogying, kinda' like walking in place while gyrating south of the waistline equator.

<u>Women of the Calabash</u>. Charming acappella harmonies, gentle choreography, and color-ful costumes illustrated this affecting three-piece African trio. They delivered a nice mix of world-beat styles, including African, Calypso, and N' Awlins ("Big Chief"), all augmented by shaker and gourd rattles. Big smiles, but too soft to maintain Palmieri's brash momentum. They would've been better, I imagine, as the opening act, or on a side stage. Dworetzky attempted to land the incendiary Malathini and The Mahotella Queens, but couldn't coordinate routing. 'Win some...

<u>Peter Blegvad</u>. No such problem with this folkie as his driving rhythms and emphatic, Dylan-inflected vocals brought the crowd back to life. His brief four-song set connected via eco-

nomical, yet provocative, writing on "Northern Lights," "I'm the Last Man," "I Fell in Love with Karen" and what he described as "a cheerful little ditty about drowning in love," entitled "Swim." Creative, engaging, tuneful.

Steel Pulse. I have few notes on "The Pulse" because I was too busy dancing along with everyone else. These reggae stars bounced and jumped through an unending medley of hits pegged somewhere between roots-rockin' and dancehall — all put forth smoothly, powerfully, and soulfully. They deftly turned changes on a dime while turning up the tempos in irresistible waves. The band climaxed this universal boogie blast with an extended take of "Sensemilla." Sensational!

"I'll have to tell you a funny story, because no one believes this is true," Dworetzky confides of her dealings:

- "I'm a personal lover of reggae music, and at our first festival we had Toots and The Maytals, which was definitely a lot of fun. I mean, he's a legend. But with Steel Pulse, their message is very strong and I think a lot of people maybe don't pay attention to that. The band actually, really believes things. I had never seen them live before, but I loved their music and liked what they stood for. So I called their manager over in England and we kinda' played phone tag a little bit. He was like, "Central Park? A free show?" [laughs] And he was really up for it!

  "We did this whole thing on a verbal agreement! A lot of times it's not a business where you can do that. I would say, frequently, there's not a lot of ethics in this business, but he was a wonderful person, incredibly professional, and easy to deal with. [He] bent over backwards to be accommodating, and I would love to have Steel Pulse on any show I could do. As I said, I can't give them a high enough recommendation."

**Attendance Tip**

We came too late to witness it, but Northern Lights (who played earlier in the day) had to be greeted three miles down the road to receive their escort past the line of waiting cars. In other words, get there plenty early to beat the traffic on the narrow, winding mountain road. Also, even though the festival is free, you'll want to bring some change for the parking fee plus the excellent crafts and food vendors.

**See Also**

In recent years B&J has also produced ONE WORLD, ONE HEART blowouts throughout the summer in Chicago, San Francisco, and Los Angeles. These particular events (plus New York City's) took a breather in '94 as B&J introduced a new product line using more traditional means of advertising. However, Dworetzky recommends calling the festival hotline (1-800-BJ-FESTS) just in case future marketing plans call for their return, as well as to keep tabs on the continuing BEN AND JERRY'S NEWPORT FOLK FESTIVAL. More work for her, ah, but more fun for us!

Meanwhile, you can keep that funky Vermont vibe alive the very next month as the VERMONT REGGAE FESTIVAL takes over the Johnson Mud Bog about a half hour's drive southeast of Burlington. It's also free, though there are parking and camping charges, and it has a good 30,000 jammin' to the all-day sounds of at least three national headliners plus another six acts or so drawn from throughout the region's thriving scene. Picture every possible accompaniment from fireworks to, as *Reggae Report* described, "a 200-foot Reggae Ski Kite and sky divers for Jah who trailed red, green, and gold streamers as they descended." It's been a summertime institution since '86 and is eagerly awaited by its loyal collegiate and family crowd. As they say, "Big up!"

~ ~ ~

# Burlington's Folk Traditions

UNIVERSITY OF VERMONT LANE SERIES/49TH PARALLEL MUSIC FESTIVAL, Burlington, VT
> Late January
> Avant Garde and New Music

FAMILIES OUTDOOR FESTIVAL, Ferrisburgh, VT
> Middle July
> Variety, Folk and International

**CHAMPLAIN VALLEY FESTIVAL**, Burlington, VT
> Early August
> Variety, Folk and International
> ***Attended***

FIRST NIGHT BURLINGTON, Burlington, VT
> Late December
> Variety, Folk and International

**Introduction**  How's that Gil Scott Heron song go? "...And we almost lost Detroit." Well the same could be said of the Champlain Valley, or rather, the delightful folk music potpourri which thankfully still bears its name, the CHAMPLAIN VALLEY FESTIVAL [CHAMPLAIN'].

The troubles began in '93. For eight years prior, the CHAMPLAIN' had commanded Kingsland Bay State Park a few miles south in Ferrisburgh — a parkland site idyllic in itself, not even considering the exquisite panorama peeking through its trees of Lake Champlain and the Adirondack Mountains reflected in the placid ripples. "Ooh-aah's" abounded from nearly every patron I ever spoke to about the place.

Kingsland Bay's suited more for pastoral picnicking, however, than for hosting 10 stages of continuous performing and dancing that evolved over time. Space rentals rose under this kind of encroachment while facility abilities (i.e., parking, electrical, shuttles, etc.) remained static, prompting the '93 CHAMPLAIN' to move to the still-being-developed Waterfront Park in Burlington.

Three chief difficulties arose.

First, this downtown setting proved a bit off-putting to many devotees. A typical letter from Kelly and Barry King, as published in the festival's remarkably open quarterly publication, *Champlain Folk*, expressed the prevailing sentiments:

- "...I think the delight so many performers have in coming has a lot to do with the magical feeling that Kingsland Bay becomes a world apart for that weekend... I hate to see the weekend at Kingsland Bay taken away from those who see it as a reward and/or respite for having supported folk music here, there, and everywhere around the area..."

Local folkies were further alienated by the CHAMPLAIN' choosing to allow Vermont Public Radio to broadcast live from the grounds, despite this station's having recently terminated a popular local show, Mark Hauser's "Rural Rhythms."

Second, volunteer burn-out began to take its toll. The CHAMPLAIN' had grown into a year-round nonprofit, producing weekly concerts, contradances, workshops and what-have-you; their late CHAMPLAIN VALLEY MIDWINTER FEST being one example. Unfortunately, this continuous whirl-wind appeared to have stretched human resources too thin. In the Spring '93 issue of *Champlain Folk*, Executive Director Mark Sustic complained of insufficient replacement candidates for near-ly every major volunteer role, including his own. Whew! This drastic plea may explain the numerous production gaffs transpiring several months later.

Irish Echo's Earle Hitchner complained of a "claustrophobic feeling" to '93's Champlain' site-prep, as well as one opening set suffering "bad sound, bad physical setting, no chairs [for the performers] and two separate lobbings of pinecones from behind the stage by some mischievous kids." *Dirty Linen*'s Steve Winick seconded those notes, as well as fewer stages open for fewer hours, hard-to-find and wrongly-titled workshops, plus an overall "poor organization evident this year." Since the folk-music press normally takes a "matador-style" approach in waving its own through positive reviews no matter what, you can well imagine these incidents, plus others unmentioned, being genuinely egregious.

Third, the new listeners expected from among the bustling proximity didn't materialize. In fact, gate sales of about 2,000 were approximately half of their projected requirements. Accordingly, the '93 Champlain' experienced a $20,000 short-fall, not impossible to surmount, but neither a breeze in a small market such as this. It was almost painful to read the desperation in Sustic's fundraising letters that finally raised the deficit in the months that followed and fore-shadowed his shortly passing the baton from sheer exhaustion.

When I finally tracked down a contact for an interview I found that all these travails may have been for the good. I discovered the '94 Champlain' had been partially adopted by the University of Vermont and presented within its Lane Series by the Division of Continuing Education. I learned that the school's "beautiful and historic Redstone campus" now afforded a "Saturday night Contra Dance" right there (instead of miles away as had been in the past), plus every other amenity, including "rooms available at the site" — another first for the festival.

I never did obtain a sample day's lineup (though the advance materials in years past had never contained one either to my continual consternation). However, the new festival flyer promised many of the same musical features that augured past Champlain's, including strong Quebecois, Celtic and Native American offerings, participatory dancing galore, and a sampling of other folk "traddies" drawn from across the regional scenes.

Most importantly, I encountered Rick Davis, a model of calm, openness, and confidence vs. what I'd suffered from transitional principals all winter long.

"I am the Assistant Director of the University of Vermont Lane Series," explains Davis. Though he'd done mostly classical music and theater offerings, traditional folk music snuck onto his plate in the form of touring artists with the "bigger" names, like Doc Watson, being presented at the marvelous Flynn Theater; the "smaller," such as a John Renbourn/Robin Williamson pairing, reserved for the university's recital hall.

"As I began doing that and became more involved in the local arts community," Davis continues:

- "I encountered Mark Sustic who, of course, is the driving force behind the Champlain'. Mark and I got along real well and we cooperated to present several different events, both shared-risk and also events where I just facilitated their use of campus spaces. Everything was going great.

  "During this time Mark was beginning to talk about [not] having the organization be a stand-alone, you know, with great relationships with all of the other presenters in the area, but really out there on its own. He was beginning to look for a major sponsor to get in there with him. I was pretty interested in that.

  "When Mark decided this year to take a sabbatical from the Champlain', I went to the festival board with a proposal that Lane Series and the festival co-present this year. Over the course of negotiations with other people at the university and with the festival board, that agreement was modified so that, at this point, I'm serving as sort of coordinator of the Champlain'. The model that we're using is that of an executive on loan to the United Way; that my services to the Champlain' are sort of the university's donation. There is no shared risk; there is no university financial involvement in the festival. It's all still hanging on the organization's head rather than the university's. The university is helping with the space. There's no rental fees for the space; there's just fees for services, like police.

"I'm working basically full time on the CHAMPLAIN'," notes Davis on his creative management solution, not unlike many of the other civic collaborations that routinely take place in this progressive small city (DISCOVER JAZZ FESTIVAL — see chapter).

Davis details the advantages afforded by the CHAMPLAIN's new home: stunning lake and mountain views; an air-conditioned 300-seat recital hall; a collection of available instruments, including pianos; warm-up spaces for musicians; "a great area" for festival merchandising; and an "historic ballroom with a wood bar, windows on three sides, and a stage so the dance maniacs can go absolutely haywire." Of course, dust free lawns, copious parking, affordable and proximate housing, ingress and egress, proximity to town while being segregated from street traffic, etc. are also mentioned.

Sounds to me like an improvement, I suggest, not only over Waterfront Park, but possibly upon Kingland Bay as well.

"I think I'm going to say yes," Davis affirms. "The people who went to Ferrisburgh are going to remind us how beautiful it was right on the lake and so on, and they're right. The only way this could be improved is if there was a nice little pond right behind it, or if somehow it was down on the lake, as well as up on the hill. [However,] Ferrisburgh had a great deal of isolation. And I think for festivals that's both a real positive thing in the sense of this feeling of community and a very negative thing in the sense that if you don't already have some commitment in the music, you ain't gonna' go there."

Davis then explains how the '94 CHAMPLAIN's been programmed and priced to entice the curious as well as the committed:

- "I think for the noncommitted, people at this point are so accustomed to short sound bites and short time commitments; I think people plan their lives in quarter hours now, rather than days. So we found that last year even a one-day commitment was too much for most people. We've broken it up. We're doing separate tickets for the daytime events and the evening concerts. For the people who have that commitment, they're going to be there for the weekend, or two days, or whatever, and the pricing is set up to make that reasonable for them.

  "For our noncommitted types, the daytime prices are not much more than they'd pay to go to a craft show, so they can reasonably take a family for a couple of hours to the CHAMPLAIN'. If they're having a good time they'll stay longer and not pay any more until they get into the evening concert. If they're having a great time, they'll pay a little bit more and stay for that, but at least there's that option for everybody of going for that brief period of time at a reasonable charge.

  "In a sense, as an administrator, I'm looking at it as a reasonable alternative to going to a movie downtown."

Damn reasonable, in my opinion. 'Looks like Sustic gets a much-needed breather, the Board obtains a fresh, able replacement who's nevertheless faithful to their aims, and their CHAMPLAIN' gains a fully-featured facility attractive to novices and old-timers, alike.

"What I wanted to say about the festival, if I could sort of put a coat on it," Davis summarizes, "is that Mark's original vision of a festival celebrating the tradition present in this valley has not changed. I'm overjoyed to go to a little festival in Montreal and have people come up to me in French accents, you know, 'Your festival is our festival, too.' And to be getting call after call, and letter after letter from all areas of Eastern Canada, saying, 'We want to come to the CHAMPLAIN', send information.'

"We've tried hard not to change that," Davis assures.

**Festival Review**  Davis readily concedes the '93 CHAMPLAIN' overreached, both in presenting a week's worth of free lead-in concerts around town that really didn't convince sufficient newcomers to buy tickets, and in booking such national acts as The McGarrigle Sisters, Norman and Nancy Blake, The Horseflies and Tish Hinojosa that it really couldn't afford. Davis sought to steer '94's version back toward the lone weekend accumulation of regional heroes — ethnic, traditional folk, participatory dance — that distinguished Sustic's earlier purvey.

With only one day to spend in '92, I kinda' got suckered by the vagueness of the brochures into one of those pre-fest affairs in Burlington — this one Thursday on a parkland bluff overlooking the glorious sunset view. It turned out to be just four acts — three of 'em local and one flown in a day early from Ireland. Unfortunately, the Celtic duo was delayed in their flight connections, leaving the three locals to carry the evening. My impression? "Eh." (In fact, I could see why this kind of middling pre-sampling strategy would come up short the following year; you need some firepower to attract the noncommitted into sticking around for the weekend.)

Absent the Irish headliners, I didn't think my experience was representative of what you'd experience from a weekend visit; therefore, here are a few of Davis' highlights from recent years, instead.

"My own interest tends to be a little more blues-related and blues have not been a strength of this **Artist** festival," Davis notes:  **Mini-Reviews**

- "Annie Cohen has been here and will be back this year. Paul Geremia was here last year. This year we're also going to have John B. Holman. He was an N. E. A. National Heritage Fellow several years back. He's a 60-or-so-year-old gentleman from Durham, North Carolina [and] just a great Piedmont blues player. I am really excited about having John D. up here. We're also going to have Etta Baker. She's unbelievable. I'm half her age and probably have half of her energy and none of the talent.

    "Locally, Steve Gillette and Cindy Mangsen [are] just fantastic talents as far as I'm concerned. Anne Dodson from Maine, also. She's out there on the circuit. Other highlights, other people that just blew me away? Actually, last year being able to have Rhythm In Shoes here was really nice. There was a cooperation with the Flynn Theater where they were in residency for a week and a half, I believe."

I prompt Davis about one Board leader and frequent festival performer, Bob Yellin, who's also one of the founding members of the Greenbriar Boys. He responds:

- "We're having this Greenbriar Boys reunion this year. John Herald will be here. Jody Stecher will be here (he played with them for several years). [Ralph] Rinzler is not going to be here. He's way too ill at this point; he's very sick... It'll be three members of the original Greenbriar Boys. They'll be doing classic Greenbriar Boys repertoire: Monroes' and Stanleys' and originals. They were one of the seminal folk revival groups and they are strictly bluegrass. These are the sons of Bill Monroe, but they went to college and half of them are Jewish. So in that sense they are a true folk-revival group, as opposed to the Osbornes."

I also ask Davis about Tish Hinojosa from '93's bill. He replies:

- "I don't think people really knew Tish, and, as it turned out, she had exactly 20 minutes of stage time all weekend. That was our biggest problem last year — that and the ticket prices for the casual listener — was that there were so many great artists that relatively few of them got a lot of stage time. And the evening concerts particularly were overloaded. So Tish, who did not do any workshop, did 20 minutes onstage one evening, and that was the end of it...

    "I would say that the emotional response [for her] was as great as any performer received all weekend, and it was seriously considered to bring her back this season. The only reason we didn't is that we kind of made a decision to concentrate a little bit more on traditional and local traditions, sort of a little bit more of our core than reaching out to the 'Southwest and country-flavor' thing. With The Greenbriar Boys and the folks from Appalachia, I think we have a strong showing of different American traditions."

Davis seconds my viewpoint that Burlington is a visual treat second to none in the region. He con- **Travel Tip** tributes such travel benefits as: "clean air; great accessibility; reasonable proximity to major urban centers, but way away from them; great proximity to other recreational opportunities from the lakes to the mountains; and yet, in the middle of all of this, an incredibly viable cultural community — incredibly active! We seem to have replaced the summer SHAKESPEARE FESTIVAL with a baseball team," he chuckles, "but some people feel that's an improvement."

**See Also** Though the 'MIDWINTER FEST has passed on, you can catch another "snowsplash" of the local folk scene at the community-run FIRST NIGHT BURLINGTON. This alcohol-free family celebration is one of the largest of its 20-plus brethren occurring throughout New England on New Year's Eve. Look for at least 200 performances by about 75 artists at nearly 30 locations all about town. Doubtlessly magical.

As for the two principals, above, you can also sample their programming wares other times throughout the year: Davis's at the UNIVERSITY OF VERMONT LANE SERIES/49TH PARALLEL MUSIC FESTIVAL, and Sustic's at the FAMILIES OUTDOOR FESTIVAL back at Kingsland Bay State Park. Enjoy!

~     ~     ~

# Vermont Festival Listings

**Caveat**

Although the vast majority are festivals are reliable and predictable, all are subject to last-minute changes or cancellations. Accordingly, FESTPRESS is not responsible for any festival listing information that follows. Readers are well advised to contact festivals at least twice before preparing a festival vist: (a) once at least one or two months ahead of time; and (b) once more during the week of your visit for confirmation. Ask for a festival flyer or brochure to be mailed to you. Festival promoters usually are willing to comply, and the resulting literature may answer any questions you still have.

**Key Codes**

## Restrictions:

| | | | | | |
|---|---|---|---|---|---|
| • Food and drink... | 1; | • Cameras... | 6; | • Motorcycles... | 11; |
| • Alcohol... | 2; | • Audio recording... | 7; | • Re-entry... | 12; |
| • Cans... | 3; | • Video recording... | 8; | • Other restrictions... | 13. |
| • Bottles... | 4; | • Children... | 9; | | |
| • Coolers... | 5; | • Pets... | 10; | | |

## Secondary Genre[s]:

| | | | |
|---|---|---|---|
| • Variety, General... | VRGL; | • Bluegrass... | BLGS; |
| • Variety, Jazz & Blues... | VRJB; | • Modern Folk... | MFOL; |
| • Variety, Country & Bluegrass | VRCB; | • Traditional Folk... | TFOL; |
| • Variety, Folk & International | VRFI; | • Fiddle and Banjo Events... | FDDL; |
| • Modern Jazz... | MJAZ; | • Maritime... | MARI; |
| • Traditional Jazz & Ragtime... | TJAZ; | • Cajun and Zydeco... | ZYDC; |
| • Alternative Jazz... | AJAZ; | • Irish... | IRSH; |
| • Modern Rock and Pop... | MRCK; | • Jewish... | JWSH; |
| • Classic Rock and Oldies... | CRCK; | • Native American... | NATV; |
| • Alternative & College Rock | ARCK; | • Scottish... | SCOT; |
| • Hard Rock & Heavy Metal | HRCK; | • Modern Latin... | MLAT; |
| • Rap... | RAP; | • Traditional Latin... | TLAT; |
| • Modern R&B... | MR&B; | • African American... | AFRM; |
| • Blues and Traditional R&B... | TR&B; | • African... | AFRC; |
| • Acappella and Doo Wop... | ACAP; | • Brazilian & So. American... | BRZL; |
| • Modern Christian... | CHRS; | • Reggae, Ska & Caribbean... | RGGE; |
| • Black Gospel... | BGOS; | • Avant Garde & New Music... | AVNT; |
| • Southern & Bluegrass Gospel | SGOS; | • Cabaret... | CBRT; |
| • Traditional Gospel & Sings... | TGOS; | • Gay and Lesbian... | GYLS; |
| • Modern Country... | MC&W; | • Drum Corps & March. Bands | DRUM; |
| • Traditional Country... | TC&W; | • Fairs... | FAIR; |
| • Alt.  Country & Rockabilly | AC&W; | • Other Genres... | OTHR. |

**Note**

Wherever "Help!" appears readers are invited to answer the proceeding questions and/or provide updates. New festival listings that meet the criteria of this book certainly are welcome too! Please mail any current festival information you obtain — especially flyers or brochures — to FESTPRESS, P. O. Box 147, Glen Ridge, NJ 07028. *Thanks!*

### UNIVERSITY OF VERMONT LANE SERIES/49TH PARALLEL MUSIC FESTIVAL, Burlington, VT
Late Jan.
Avant Garde and New Music

Since 1995. Part of a 40-year-old classical/folk music series, the Lane Series, running from Mid Oct. to Early May. **Days:** 1. **Site:** indoor. University of Vermont Recital Hall. **Admission:** paid. **Daily entry:** $10 to $24. **Acts:** national acts. **Sample day's lineup:** Michael Arnowitt, others perform works of Maxwell Davies, Schoenberg, Webern, Jaeger. **Contact:** University of Vermont Lane Series, 30 South Park Drive, Colchester, VT 05446-2501, 802-656-4455.

### CABIN FEVER FOLKLIFE FESTIVAL, Middlebury, VT
Early Apr.
Modern Folk

Since 1987. **Days:** 1. **Hours per day:** 10. **Site:** indoor. Middlebury Municipal Building. **Admission:** free. **Daily entry:** under $10. **Secondary genre[s]:** TR&B, TC&W, BLGS, IRSH, NATV, OTHR. **Acts:** local acts. **Sample day's lineup:** Dorothy Rice, Alli Lubin, Jeter LePont, Patti Casey and Bob Gagnon, Blue Jay Stone, Woodchuck's Revenge, Mandolinquints, Dave Keller, Dana Robinson, Horace Williams, Mary Ann Samuels. **Contact:** Cabin Fever Folklife Fest, 158 Adams Street, Rutland, VT 05701, 802-425-3415.

### VERMONT MAPLE FESTIVAL/FIDDLER'S VARIETY SHOW, St. Albans, VT
Late Apr.
Fiddle and Banjo Events

Since 1968. Part of the Vermont Maple Festival. "We are proud of our Vermont maple syrup and maple products, and invite your participation in this annual statewide celebration." -- Program. **Help!** A sample lineup? **Days:** 3. **Hours per day:** 16. **Site:** outdoor and indoor. **Admission:** free and paid. **Daily entry:** $10 to $24, under $10. **Secondary genre[s]:** BLGS, TFOL. **Acts:** local acts. **Other merchandise:** Vermont Maple Festival Cookbook, "Sugarhouse Treats" (self-published and distributed). **Contact:** Vermont Maple Festival Council, Inc., P. O. Box 255, St. Albans, VT 05478, 802-524-5800.

### ABENAKI FESTIVAL DAYS, Rutland/Burlington, VT
Late Apr. to Early May
Native American

**Days:** 3. **Site:** indoor. Crossroads Arts Council, 5 Court Street, Rutland; Flynn Theater, 153 Main Street, Burlington. **Admission:** free and paid **Daily entry:** under $10. **Contact:** Crossroads Arts Council, 5 Court Street, Rutland, VT 05701, 802-775-5413.

### IRISH CULTURAL DAY, Burlington, VT
Early May
Irish

See other dates. **Days:** 1. **Hours per day:** 4. **Site:** outdoor and indoor. Ethan Allen Homestead. **Acts:** local acts. **Sample day's lineup:** Robert Resnick, Marty Morrissey, Puccine. **Contact:** Ethan Allen Homestead Trust, P. O. Box 1141, Burlington, VT 05401-1141, 802-865-4556.

### RAVEN WIND POW-WOW, Evansville, VT
Middle May
Native American

Since 1994. See other dates and sites. **Days:** 3. **Site:** outdoor. Auction Barn Field. **Admission:** paid. **Daily entry:** under $10. **Contact:** Kowasuck of North America Grand Council, Territorial Headquarters, RFD 2, Box 530A, Newport, VT 05855, 802-334-5306.

## BENNINGTON FOLK FESTIVAL, Bennington, VT
Middle May
Modern Folk

Since 1995. "The Music of America's Heartland." -- Brochure. **Days:** 2. **Site:** indoor. Old Castle Theater. **Admission:** paid. **Daily entry:** $10 to $24. **Discounts:** multiple event or day passes. **Secondary genre[s]:** TFOL, IRSH. **Acts:** national acts, regional acts, local acts. **Sample day's lineup:** Priscilla Herdman, Steve Gillette and Cindy Mangsen, New Breman Town Musicians. **Contact:** Bennington Center for the Arts, P. O. Box 260, Bennington, VT 05201, 802-447-1267 **or:** Old Castle Theater, P. O. Box 1555, Bennington, VT 05201, 802-447-0564 .

## LAMPLIGHT SERVICE AND HYMN SING, North Danville, VT
Late May to Late Aug.
Traditional Gospel and Sings

Since 1832. Last Sunday of month. **Days:** 4. **Site:** indoor. Old North Church. **Contact:** Old Home Day Lamplight Service and Hymn Sing, RFD 2, Box 165, St. Johnsbury, VT 05819, 802-748-9350.

## LAKE CHAMPLAIN BALLOON FESTIVAL, Essex Junction, VT
Early Jun.
Variety, General

Since 1989. "New England's largest balloon festival...an exciting family weekend" -- Press Release. **Days:** 3. **Hours per day:** 14. **Site:** outdoor. Champlain Valley Exposition. **Admission:** paid. **Daily entry:** under $10. **Secondary genre[s]:** CRCK, BLGS, MFOL, OTHR. **Acts:** national acts, regional acts, local acts. **Sample day's lineup:** "Beatlemania," Burlington Taiko Drummers, Rick Charette and The Bubblegum Band, Jon Gailmor, Banjo Dan and The Mid-Nite Plowboys, others. **Contact:** Lake Champlain Balloon Festival, P. O. Box 83, Underhill Center, VT 05490, 802-899-2993.

## VERMONT DAIRY FESTIVAL, Enosburg Falls, VT
Early Jun.
Variety, General

"It takes over the whole village!" -- Dennis Kale. **Days:** 3. **Site:** outdoor. **Secondary genre[s]:** CRCK, MC&W, BLGS, GYLS. **Acts:** local acts. **Sample Series Lineup:** Day One: Hidden Drive Band; Day Two: Randle Twins, plus marching bands; Day Three: Southbound. **Contact:** Enosburg Falls Lions Club, RD 1, East Fairfield, VT 05448, 802-827-4451/933-2513.

## DISCOVER JAZZ FESTIVAL, Burlington, VT
Early Jun. to Middle Jun.
Variety, Jazz and Blues

Since 1984. **Days:** 6. **Hours per day:** 12. **Site:** outdoor and indoor. Multiple locations downtown. **Admission:** free and paid. **Daily entry:** under $10, $10 to $24. **Discounts:** advance purchase discounts. **Secondary genre[s]:** MJAZ, TJAZ, AJAZ, TR&B, BGOS, MLAT, AFRC, BRZL, RGGE, OTHR. **Acts:** national acts, regional acts, local acts. **Sample day's lineup:** Manny Oquendo and Libre, David Murray Quartet, Pure Pressure, Onion River Jazz Band, Hannibal and Agosti, Sam Armstrong Trio, Downtown Quartet, New England Exploratory Orchestra, Cuba Jazz Project, New Nile Orchestra, Bob Neese, Andrei Kondakov/Steve Blair Quartet, Ellen Powell and Co., Belisbeha, No Walls, Freefall, Panashe, Bob Gagnon Trio, Alex Betz Trio, Professor Fairbanks, Martin Guigui, George Petit and The Desired Effect, William Sellenraad Trio, Champlain Valley Union High School Jazz Ensemble. **Contact:** Discover Jazz Festival, 153 Main Street, Burlington, VT 05401, 802-863-7992/658-9300.

RATTLING BROOK BLUEGRASS FESTIVAL, Belvidere, VT
>Middle Jun.
>Bluegrass

Since 1985. "It's a good time. Bluegrass people are the best you'd ever meet." -- Larry Brown. **Days:** 1. **Hours per day:** 9. **Site:** outdoor. Recreational Field, Route 109. **Admission:** paid. **Daily entry:** $10 to $24. **Acts:** regional acts, local acts. **Sample day's lineup:** Southern Rail, Breakaway, Cardigan Mountain Tradition, Gibson Brothers, Wild Branch, Lost Posse, Three Easy Pieces. **Contact:** Belvidere Community Club, RR 1, Box 1062, Belvidere, VT 05492, 802-644-2498/8924.

QUECHEE HOT AIR BALLOON FESTIVAL, Quechee, VT
>Middle Jun.
>Variety, General

Since 1980. **Days:** 3. **Hours per day:** 11. **Site:** outdoor and indoor. **Admission:** free and paid. **Secondary genre[s]:** MJAZ, CRCK, ACAP, BLGS, MFOL, TFOL, OTHR. **Acts:** national acts, local acts. **Sample day's lineup:** Bill Staines, Cardigan Mountain Tradition, Mary DeRoschers, Northern Spy, David Graf, Opera Etc., The AC&S. **Contact:** Quechee Chamber of Commerce, Main Street, Quechee, VT 802-295-7900.

GREEN MOUNTAIN CHEW CHEW/VERMONT FOOD FEST, Burlington, VT
>Late Jun.
>Variety, General

Since 1986. "The festival spotlights over 75 area restaurants and Vermont food producers in a three-day, family-oriented festival of flavor and will bring an estimated 60,000 foraging people to the seven-acre, lakeside park." -- The World. **Days:** 3. **Hours per day:** 12. **Site:** outdoor. Waterfront Park, College Street. **Admission:** free. **Secondary genre[s]:** TJAZ, CRCK, TR&B, MC&W, TC&W, BLGS, MFOL, TFOL. **Acts:** national acts, regional acts, local acts. **Sample day's lineup:** Carolyn Hester, Barry and Holly Tashian, Steve Gillette and Cindy Mangsen, Derek and Hazel Sarjeant, The Style A's, The Unknown Blues Band feauring Joe Burrell. **Contact:** Airflyte Productions, 216 Battery Street, Burlington, VT 05401, 802-864-6674.

RUTLAND REGION ETHNIC FESTIVAL, Rutland, VT
>Late Jun.
>Variety, Folk and International

Since 1992. "It's great to have an ethnic festival like this to see where people come from....The food was wonderful, and so was Habiz Shabazz's band. We hope to have them back." -- Patty Garber, Festival Director. **Days:** 1. **Hours per day:** 8. **Site:** outdoor. Downtown Rutland Parking Deck. **Admission:** free. **Secondary genre[s]:** AFRC, OTHR. **Acts:** regional acts, local acts. **Sample day's lineup:** Fortaleza, Middlebury Russian Choir, Bay State Polka Band, Hafiz Shabazz and The Bala Bala Ryhthm Band. **Contact:** Rutland Partnership, 103 Wales Street, Rutland, VT 802-773-9380.

BEN AND JERRY'S ONE WORLD, ONE HEART FESTIVAL, Warren, VT
>Late Jun.
>Variety, General

Since 1990. **Days:** 2. **Hours per day:** 8. **Site:** outdoor. Sugarbush Ski Resort. **Admission:** free. **Secondary genre[s]:** AJAZ, CRCK, TR&B, MC&W, BLGS, MFOL, ZYDC, IRSH, AFRC, RGGE. **Acts:** national acts, regional acts, local acts. **Sample day's lineup:** The Band, Buddy Guy, Bela Fleck and The Flecktones, Tish Hinojosa, Women of the Calabash, Unknown Blues Band, Don White. **Contact:** Ben and Jerry's, Route 100, Box 240, Waterbury, VT 05676, 800-BJ-FESTS.

## VERMONT LESBIAN GAY BISEXUAL PRIDE DAY, Burlington, VT
Late Jun.
Gay and Lesbian

Since 1984. "Proud, not cowed." -- Program. **Days:** 1. **Hours per day:** 13. **Site:** outdoor and indoor. **Secondary genre[s]:** ARCK, ACAP, MFOL, AFRC, CBRT. **Acts:** local acts. **Sample day's lineup:** Kwanzaa Percussion Ensemble, John Calvi, Queen City Cabaret, Lisa McCormick, Virginia and The Wolves, The Fabulous Flirtations, Steph Pappas, Diane Horstmyer. **Contact:** Pride, P. O. Box 1572, Burlington, VT 05402, 802-655-6312.

## BURLINGTON INDEPENDENCE DAY WATERFRONT CELEBRATION, Burlington, VT
Early Jul.
Variety, General

**Days:** 1. **Hours per day:** 12. **Site:** outdoor. Waterfront Park. **Admission:** free. **Secondary genre[s]:** TR&B, MC&W, TFOL. **Acts:** local acts. **Sample day's lineup:** Big Joe Burrell and The Unknown Blues Band, Rick Norcross and The Nashfull Ramblers, Blue Streak, Plan B, Tom "T-Bone" Stankus. **Contact:** Burlington Parks and Recreation Department, 216 Leddy Park Road, Burlington, VT 802-241-3655 **or:** WEZF 93FM, 1500 Hedgeman Avenue, Colchester, VT 802-655-0093. .

## MOUNTAIN JAM, Killington, VT
Early Jul.
Alternative and College Rock

Since 1993. **Days:** 1. **Admission:** paid. **Daily entry:** under $10. **Discounts:** advance purchase discounts. **Restrictions:** 3, 4. **Acts:** regional acts, local acts. **Sample day's lineup:** Valentine Smith, Paul Collins Band, Steve Ellis, Sandra Wright Band, Martin Guigui Band, Red Reddington/Huge Members, Gypsy Reel, Guy Burlage Band, Moondogs, Mother Pluckers. **Contact:** WEBK 105.3 FM, Killington Road, Killington, VT 802-422-3156.

## BASIN BLUEGRASS FESTIVAL, Brandon, VT
Early Jul.
Bluegrass

Since 1995. **Days:** 3. **Site:** outdoor. Basin Road, off Route 73. **Secondary genre[s]:** SGOS, TC&W, BLGS. **Acts:** regional acts, local acts. **Sample day's lineup:** Blistered Fingers, Grass Creek, Misty Mountain Review, Cedar Ridge, Smokey Greene and The Boys, Al and Kathy Bain, Cold Country Bluegrass, Andy Pawlenko and The Smoky Hollow Boys. **Contact:** Basin Bluegrass Festival, RR 2, Box 2042, Brandon, VT 05733, 802-247-6738/8260.

## WAREBROOK CONTEMPORARY MUSIC FESTIVAL, Irasburg, VT
Early Jul.
Avant Garde and New Music

Since 1991. "Present[ing] an entertaining and suprisingly accessible mixture of 20th century classics, along with thought-provoking works on the cutting edge of new music." -- Brochure. **Days:** 3. **Hours per day:** 10. **Site:** indoor. Multiple locations in Coventry, Newport and Johnson. **Admission:** free and paid. **Daily entry:** under $10. **Discounts:** student discounts. **Acts:** national acts, regional acts, local acts. **Sample day's lineup:** Michael Arnowitt, Emmanuel Feldman, Pascal Feldman, Julie Hanson, Sandra Helbert, Paul Kirby, Judson Scott, Anthony Tommasini, Marshall Urban, Arcadian Winds, Artaria Quartet, EOS Ensemble, Made in the Shade, Matt Doherty perform works by Babbitt, Carter, Wheeler, McAllister, Doncaster. **Contact:** Warebrook Contemporary Music Festival, RFD 1, Box 38, Irasburg, VT 05845, 802-754-6631.

MIDSUMMER FESTIVAL OF VERMONT ART AND MUSIC, Montpelier, VT
    Early Jul.
    Variety, Folk and International

Since 1982. "...Recalls the midsummer traditions and gives it new life through our own community summer rituals." -- Program. **Days:** 2. **Hours per day:** 13. **Site:** outdoor. **Admission:** Paid. **Daily entry:** under $10. **Discounts:** advance purchase discounts. **Restrictions:** 4, 10. **Secondary genre[s]:** MJAZ, TGOS, BLGS, MFOL, TFOL, IRSH, TLAT, AFRC, CBRT, OTHR. **Acts:** national acts, local acts. **Sample day's lineup:** Kanda Bongo Man, Chatty's Revenge, Dick McCormack, Vermont Philharmonic, Edwards/Farnham Ensemble, Stretch 'n' the Limits, Kairos Duo, Bartholdy Ensemble, Cadenza, Matthew Witten and Linda Gionti, Banjo Dan and The Mid-Nite Plowboys, Sheefra, Saltash Serenaders, Kevin Parry, Jeter LePont, Jazz Hooligans, Los Carajos, Diane Ziegler and Geoffrey Cary Sather, So-Called Jazz Kwintet, Woods Tea Company, Gideon Fueudman, Bob Yellin and The Joint Chiefs of Bluegrass, Jon Gailmor, Village Harmony, The Brother Brothers. **Contact:** Onion River Arts Council, 43 State Street, Montpelier, VT 05602, 802-229-9408.

FAMILIES OUTDOOR FESTIVAL, Ferrisburgh, VT
    Middle Jul.
    Variety, Folk and International

**Help!** A sample lineup? **Days:** 1. **Hours per day:** 6. **Site:** outdoor. Kingsland Bay State Park. **Acts:** local acts. **Contact:** Families Outdoor Festival, c/o Champlain Valley Festival, 202 Main Street, Burlington, VT 05401, 802-241-3651/656-7717.

MIDDLEBURY SUMMER FESTIVAL-ON-THE-GREEN, Middlebury, VT
    Middle Jul.
    Variety, Folk and International

Since 1979. **Days:** 7. **Hours per day:** 10. **Site:** outdoor. Town Green. **Admission:** free. **Secondary genre[s]:** MC&W, BLGS, MFOL, TFOL, ZYDC, OTHR. **Acts:** national acts, regional acts, local acts. **Sample day's lineup:** Danielle Martineau and Rockabayou, Mike Dever and Lausanne Allen, Gary Dulabaum. **Contact:** Middlebury Summer Festival-on-the-Green, P. O. Box 451, Middlebury, VT 05753, 802-388-2727.

SOUTHERN VERMONT HIGHLAND GAMES, Mount Snow, VT
    Middle Jul.
    Scottish

Since 1994. **Days:** 2. **Site:** outdoor and indoor. Mount Snow Ski Resort. **Admission:** paid. **Contact:** Southern Vermont Highland Games, 617-661-5899.

CELEBRATE VERMONT ARTS AND CRAFTS SHOW, Rochester, VT
    Middle Jul.
    Variety, General

Since 1992. **Days:** 1. **Hours per day:** 6. **Site:** outdoor. "One the Park." **Acts:** local acts. **Sample day's lineup:** Nightcrawlers, Seth Parker and Friends, McIntyre Brothers, plus open mic. **Contact:** Celebrate Vermont Arts and Crafts Show, P. O. Box 251, Rochester, VT 05767, 802-767-4610.

VERMONT REGGAE FEST, Johnson, VT
    Middle Jul.
    Reggae, Ska and Caribbean

Since 1986. **Days:** 1. **Hours per day:** 11. **Site:** outdoor. Johnson Arena, Route 15. **Admission:** free. **Acts:** national acts, regional acts, local acts. **Sample day's lineup:** Pato Banton, Culture, Joe Higgs, Big Youth, Awareness Art Ensemble, One Tribe, New Nile Orchestra, Chatty's Revenge, others. **Contact:** Committee for Vermont Reggae Fest, P. O. Box 1558, Burlington, VT 05402, 802-862-3092.

## AQUAFEST, Newport, VT
### Middle Jul.
### Variety, General

"A little bit of everything, from C&W to Top 40, on a waterfront of a lake 32 miles long. A real nice place on the beach; a real nice event." -- Festival Volunteer. **Days:** 3. **Site:** outdoor. Provty Beach. **Admission:** paid. **Secondary genre[s]:** MC&W. **Acts:** regional acts, local acts. **Sample day's lineup:** Hot Tub Coronas, Signature, Chrome Cowboys, Silver Eagles. **Contact:** Greater Newport Area Chamber of Commerce, The Causeway, Newport, VT 05855, 802-334-8417.

## PICO MOUNTAIN JAZZ FESTIVAL, Sherburne, VT
### Late Jul.
### Modern Jazz

Since 1992. **Days:** 2. **Site:** outdoor and indoor. Pico Mountain Ski and Summer Resort. **Daily entry:** $10 to $24. **Discounts:** multiple event or day passes. **Acts:** national acts, local acts. **Sample day's lineup:** Billy Taylor Trio, Turtle Island String Quartet, Marble City Swing Band. **Contact:** GEMS Productions, R. R. 2, Box 7412, Mendon VT 05701, 802-773-4854or: Pico Mountain Ski and Summer Resort, Sherburne Pass, Rutland, VT 05701, 802-775-4346. .

## CRACKERBARREL FIDDLERS CONTEST, Newbury, VT
### Late Jul.
### Fiddle and Banjo Events

Since 1970. Occurs Friday night, preceeding a crafts bazaar and "Irish Music Event," featuring one band, the following day. **Days:** 1. **Site:** outdoor. Common, Route 5. **Secondary genre[s]:** TC&W, BLGS, TFOL. **Acts:** local acts. **Contact:** Fiddlers Contest, P. O. Box 36, Newbury, VT 05051, 802-866-5518.

## OLE TIME FIDDLERS CONTEST, Hardwick, VT
### Late Jul.
### Fiddle Contests and Events

Since 1982. "Offering a fantastic day of excellent music and fun for the entire family!" -- Program. **Days:** 1. **Admission:** paid. **Daily entry:** under $10. **Contact:** Sanville Realty, Main Street, Hardwick, VT 802-472-6425.

## VERMONT WOMEN'S CELEBRATION, Burlington, VT
### Late Jul.
### Modern Folk

Since 1993. **Help!** One time only? **Days:** 1. **Hours per day:** 8. **Site:** outdoor. Waterfront Park. **Admission:** paid. **Daily entry:** under $10. **Acts:** regional acts, local acts. **Sample day's lineup:** Jayne Bernasconi, Jaime Morton, Virginia and The Wolves, Rachel Bissex, Lisa Savio, Catie Curtis, Anne Weiss, Mary McKenzie, Ellen Powell, Jody Albright, others. **Contact:** One Take Productions, P. O. Box 3283, Burlington, VT 05402, 802-864-0123.

## HARMONY RIDGE BRASS CENTER SUMMER FESTIVAL, Poultney, VT
### Early Aug.
### Variety, General

Workshop with top-flight instructors, called "Fellows," who give concerts throughout the week and lead a multi-stage production of participants the final day. "Our whole mission is [fostering] solo brass performance at the orchestral level." -- Ginger Culpepper. **Days:** 5. **Site:** indoor. Green Mountain College. **Secondary genre[s]:** TJAZ, OTHR. **Acts:** national acts, local acts. **Sample lineup:** New York Philharmonic, Canadian Brass, Sam Pilafian's Travelin' Light, others. **Contact:** Harmony Ridge Brass Center, 9 Sanders Avenue, White River Junction, VT , 802-295-6916 **or:** Harmony Ridge Brass Center, P. O. Box 573, East Poultney, VT 05741, 802-287-9171.

CHAMPLAIN VALLEY FESTIVAL, Burlington, VT
> Early Aug.
> Variety, Folk and International

Since 1984. **Days:** 3. **Site:** outdoor and indoor. University of Vermont "at the historic Pine Grove." **Admission:** paid. **Daily entry:** $10 to $24, under $10. **Discounts:** multiple event or day passes, other discounts. **Restrictions:** 2. **Secondary genre[s]:** TR&B, BGOS, TGOS, TC&W, AC&W, BLGS, MFOL, TFOL, MARI, ZYDC, IRSH, JWSH, NATV, SCOT, TLAT, AFRC, OTHR. **Acts:** national acts, regional acts, local acts. **Sample lineup:** Cathy Barton and Dave Para, Sara Grey, Skip Gorman and Ron Kane, Paul Geremia, Bob Yellin and The Joint Chiefs of Bluegrass, Liz Carroll, Billy McComiskey and Daithi Sproule, Tony DeMarco and Linda Hickman, Billy Jackson and Tony Cuffe, Mark Roberts and Sandol Astrausky, Ella Jenkins, Horseflies, Farm and Wilderness Stringband, Rhythm in Shoes, Wild Asparagus, Jane Sapp, Jarvelan Pikkupelimannit, Serge Desaunay, Shasmaqam, Jothi Raghavan, Kevin Locke, Jeanne Brink, Norman and Nancy Blake, Mike Seeger, Ralph Blizard, Phil Jamison and Gordy Hiners, Jody Stecher and Kate Brislin, Dan Berggren, Bill Smith, Benoit Bourque and Friends, La Bottine Souriante, Gabriel and Richard Labbe, Denis Lanctot, Tom Hodgson and Gilles Losier, Conrad Pelletier, Denis Pepin, Bayley Hazen Singers, Village Harmony, Jeter LePont, Dick McCormack, Tish Hinohosa, Kate and Anna McGarrigle. **Audio merchandise:** "Champlain Valley Festival Sampler 1988-1989" (Straight Arrow Recordings). **Contact:** Champlain Valley Festival, 202 Main Street, Burlington, VT 05401, 802-656-7717.

NATIONAL FIFE AND DRUM MUSTER, Waterbury, VT
> Early Aug.
> Drum Corp and Marching Bands

**Days:** 1. **Site:** outdoor. Recreation Park. **Acts:** national acts, regional acts, local acts. **Contact:** National Fife and Drum Muster, Covey Road, Cambridge, VT 802-899-3165.

GREEN MOUNTAIN DULCIMER DAZE AND RENDEZVOUS, West Dover, VT
> Middle Aug.
> Modern Folk

**Days:** 3. **Hours per day:** 12. **Site:** outdoor and indoor. Mount Snow Base Lodge. **Secondary genre[s]:** FDDL. **Acts:** national acts, local acts. **Sample day's lineup:** Bennett Hammond and Lorraine Lee, Margaret McArthur, Sue Carpenter, others. **Contact:** Folk Craft Music Store, North Main Street, P. O. Box 1572, Wilmington, VT 05363, 802-464-7450/5569.

BENNINGTON BATTLE DAY WEEKEND, Bennington, VT
> Middle Aug.
> Drum Corps and Marching Bands

Barbeque on Friday; drum and bugle corps competition on Saturday; parade on Sunday. **Days:** 3. **Site:** outdoor. **Acts:** local acts. **Contact:** Bennington Chamber of Commerce, Veteran's Memorial Drive, Bennington, VT 05201, 802-447-3311.

HOT COUNTRY MUSIC FESTIVAL, Burlington, VT
> Middle Aug.
> Modern Country

Since 1992. **Days:** 2. **Hours per day:** 11. **Site:** outdoor. Waterfront Park. **Admission:** free. **Acts:** local acts. **Sample Series Lineup:** Day One: Chrome Cowboys, Rick Norcross and The Nashfull Ramblers. **Contact:** 98.9 WOKO, P. O. Box 4489, Burlington VT 05406, 802-862-9890/864-6674.

## COORS COUNTRY CHILI FEST, Stratton Mountain, VT
> Late Aug.
> Modern Country

Switched to national blues acts in 1994? **Days:** 3. **Site:** outdoor. .**Admission:** Paid **Daily entry:** $10 to $24$25 to $49 **Secondary genre[s]:** BLGS, **Acts:** national acts, local acts. **Sample day's lineup:** Clinton Gregory, Appalusia, Chris Harrington and The Country Directors, Natalie Cote Band, others. **Contact:** Stratton Resort Area Association, RR 1, Box 145, Stratton Mountain, VT 05155-9406, 802-297-2200.

## NATIVE AMERICAN ABENAKI POW-WOW, Evansville, VT
> Late Aug.
> Native American

Since 1993. See other sites and dates. **Days:** 3. **Site:** outdoor. Auction Barn Field. **Admission:** paid. **Daily entry:** under $10. **Restrictions:** 2. **Contact:** Kowasuck of North America, Grand Council, Territorial Headquarters, RFD 2, Box 530A, Newport, VT 05855, 802-334-5306.

## NORTH AMERICAN NORTHUMBRIAN PIPER'S CONVENTION, North Hero, VT
> Late Aug.
> Scottish

Since 1985. "...This sleepy, little town's peace and quiet is replaced with the drone and squeal of large numbers of roving, happy bagpipers... Even for a non-piper like myself, this evening was very enjoyable and quite an education in the complexity and variety of the bagpipe in all its forms." -- Lahri Bond, Dirty Linen. **Days:** 3. **Site:** outdoor and indoor. **Secondary genre[s]:** IRSH, OTHR. **Acts:** national acts, regional acts, local acts. **Sample lineup:** Richard Butler, Colin Ross, Lance Robson, Gordon Mooney, Hamish Moore, David Moore, Sam Grier, Jean Christophe Maillard, Gerry O'Sullivan, Ray Sloan, Ad Vielle Que Pourra, Michael MacHarg, Patric O'Riordan, Brian MacCandless, Mike MacNintich, Tom Childs, Ian MacHarg, Bruce Childress, Bill Thomas, Quebecois Traditional Musicians, Tatyana Subrinska, Steve Jones, David Papazian, Ralph Thompson, others. **Contact:** North American Northumbrian Piper's Convention, P. O. Box 130, Rouses Point, NY 12979, 514-674-8772.

## QUECHEE SCOTTISH FESTIVAL, Quechee, VT
> Late Aug.
> Scottish

Since 1973. "We urge you to stroll throughout the festival grounds and try to see a bit of everything." -- Program. **Help!** A sample lineup? **Days:** 1. **Hours per day:** 7. **Site:** outdoor. Quechee Polo Field. **Admission:** paid. **Daily entry:** under $10. **Contact:** St. Andrew's Society of Vermont, 19 Brigham Hill Lane, Essex Junction, VT 05452, 802-879-7679/295-5351.

## CHAMPLAIN VALLEY EXPOSITION, Essex Junction, VT
> Late Aug. to Early Sep.
> Fairs

**Days:** 8. **Site:** outdoor. Fairgrounds, 105 Pearl Street. **Admission:** paid. **Daily entry:** under $10. **Secondary genre[s]:** MC&W. **Acts:** national acts. **Sample series lineup:** Day One: Vince Gill; Day Two: Reba McEntire; Day Three: Alan Jackson. **Contact:** Champlain Valley Exposition, P. O. Box 209, 105 Pearl Street, Essex Junction, VT 05453-5404, 802-878-5545.

CHANDLER'S NEW WORLD FESTIVAL, Randolph, VT
        Early Sep.
        Variety, Folk and International

**Help!** One time only? **Days:** 2. **Hours per day:** 4. **Site:** indoor. Chandler Music Hall, Main Street. **Admission:** paid. **Secondary genre[s]:** MFOL, IRSH, OTHR. **Acts:** national acts, local acts. **Sample day's lineup:** Livingston Taylor, others. **Contact:** Chandler's Music Hall, Main Street, Randolph, VT 802-728-9133.


VERMONT STATE FAIR, Rutland, VT
        Early Sep. to Middle Sep.
        Fairs

Since 1845. "Of course, you're going!" -- Program. **Days:** 10. **Hours per day:** 12. **Site:** outdoor. **Admission:** free and paid. **Daily entry:** under $10. **Discounts:** multiple event or day passes. **Restrictions:** 13. **Secondary genre[s]:** TGOS, MC&W, TC&W. **Acts:** national acts, local acts. **Sample series lineup:** Day One: Ronnie Milsap, One-Man Band, Milk Duds, Schottler Family Singers; Day Two: John Conlee, Williams and Ree, Dave and Sugar; Day Three: Couriers, Robbie Hiner, Skyword Gospel Singers. **Contact:** Vermont State Fair Office, 175 South Main Street, Rutland, VT 05701, 802-775-5200.


VERMONT BREWERS FESTIVAL, Various, VT
        Middle Sep.
        Modern Country

**Days:** 2. **Hours per day:** 6. **Site:** outdoor. **Admission:** paid. **Daily entry:** under $10. **Secondary genre[s]:** TR&B, BLGS. **Acts:** local acts. **Sample day's lineup:** The Jalapeno Brothers, Rick Norcross and The Nashfull Ramblers, Jamie Lee and The Rattlers, Albert Otis Blues Band. **Contact:** 98.9 WOKO, P. O. Box 4489, Burlington VT 05406, 802-658-1230.


SHELBURNE FARMS HARVEST FESTIVAL, Shelburne, VT
        Middle Sep.
        Variety, Folk and International

Since 1981. Two stages fronting a turn-of-the-century barn on a beautiful lakeside with gorgeous mountain views. "A traditional festival of mixed arts, celebrating the way things used to be." -- Judy Candido, Director. **Days:** 1. **Hours per day:** 7. **Site:** outdoor. Shelburne Farms, 102 Harbor Road. **Admission:** paid. **Daily entry:** under $10. **Secondary genre[s]:** TGOS, BLGS, MFOL, TFOL, SCOT. **Acts:** regional acts, local acts. **Sample day's lineup:** Banjo Dan and The Mid-Nite Plowboys, Peter and Karen Sutherland, John Gailmor, Margaret MacArthur, Well-Digger Boys, Highland Weavers, Mac Parker, Tim Jennings and Leanne Ponder, Gary Dulabaum, Bayley-Hazen Singers, Pipes and Drums of St. Andrews, Mandolinquints, Bill Shontz and The Green Up Band, others. **Contact:** Shelburne Farms Resources, 102 Harbor Road, Shelburne, VT 05482, 802-985-8686.


AUTUMNFEST, Middlebury, VT
        Middle Sep.
        Variety, General

**Days:** 1. **Hours per day:** 9. **Site:** indoor. Middelbury College Center for the Arts. **Admission:** free. **Secondary genre[s]:** MJAZ, TJAZ, TFOL, RGGE, OTHR. **Acts:** local acts. **Sample day's lineup:** Mary Hogan Band, Vergennes City Band, US Airforce Colonial Brass Band, Pandemonium, Childers Jazz Band, Tibetan Institute of Performing Arts, Bobolinks, The Dig Quartet, AC&S, Dick Forman and Jazz Northeast, Susan Rule and Dorothy Robson, David Marcum and Pamela McClain, Beth Kaiser, Chelsea Dippel, Su Lain Tan and Emory Fanning, Jessica Roemischer, Vermont Youth Orchestra. **Contact:** United Way of Addison County, P. O. Box 555, Middlebury, VT 05753, 802-388-7189.

## BANJO CONTEST, Craftsbury, VT
### Middle Sep.
### Fiddle and Banjo Events

Since 1968. **Days:** 1. **Site:** outdoor. Williams Field, North Wolcott Road. **Admission:** paid. **Daily entry:** under $10. **Secondary genre[s]:** TC&W, BLGS, TFOL. **Acts:** local acts. **Contact:** United Church of Craftsbury, South Main Street, Box 24, Craftsbury, VT 05826, 802-586-2835.


## SUGARBUSH BREWERS FESTIVAL, Warren, VT
### Middle Sep.
### Variety, General

Since 1992. "Good beer and a good time -- a lot of fun!" -- John Atkinson. **Days:** 2. **Hours per day:** 6. **Site:** outdoors. Sugarbush Ski Resort. **Admission:** paid. **Daily entry:** under $10. **Discounts:** student discounts. **Secondary genre[s]:** CRCK, TR&B, MFOL. **Acts:** local acts. **Sample day's lineup:** Bridgewater Brothers, Isaacson Brothers, Martin Guigui Band. **Contact:** Sugarbush Ski Resort, Sugarbush Access Road, Warren, VT 05674, 800-53SUGAR.


## NATIONAL TRADITIONAL OLD TIME FIDDLERS' AND STEP DANCING CONTEST, Barre, VT
### Late Sep.
### Fiddle and Banjo Events

Since 1968. "Hear and enjoy 'Old-Time Fiddling' at its best, and become involved with the true meaning of music that played so important a role in our American heritage." -- Program. **Days:** 2. **Hours per day:** 12. **Site:** indoor. Barre Municipal Auditorium. **Admission:** paid. **Daily entry:** under $10. **Discounts:** multiple event or day passes. **Secondary genre[s]:** TC&W, BLGS, TFOL. **Contact:** Northeast Fiddlers Association, 293 Colchester Road, Essex Junction, VT 05452, 802-434-4515 **or:** Northeast Fiddlers Association, 77 Ferguson Avenue, Burlington, VT 05401, .


## VERMONT APPLE FESTIVAL AND CRAFTS SHOW, Springfield, VT
### Middle Oct.
### Variety, Folk and International

Since 1985. **Days:** 2. **Hours per day:** 7. **Site:** indoor.. **Secondary genre[s]:** TC&W, BLGS, TFOL, IRSH, BRZL. **Acts:** regional acts, local acts. **Sample day's lineup:** Banjo Dan and The Mid-Nite Plowboys, Gyspy Reel, Mark Weinstein, Purly Gates, Jericho Road, Almost in Tune Stringband, Alli Lubin Trio, others. **Contact:** Springfield Chamber of Commerce, 55 Clinton Street, Springfield, VT 05156, 802-885-2779 **or:** Vermont Apple Festival and Crafts Show, 75 Parker Hill Road, Rockingham, VT 05101, 802-463-4702. .


## FRENCH HERITAGE FESTIVAL, Barre, VT
### Late Oct.
### Variety, Folk and International

Since 1987. **Days:** 1. **Site:** indoor. Spaulding High School. **Admission:** paid. **Daily entry:** under $10, $10 to $24. **Secondary genre[s]:** OTHR. **Acts:** regional acts, local acts. **Sample day's lineup:** Collette Fournier, Benoit Bourque, Michel Parent, Hommage Aux Aine, Les Petit Savages, Jeter LePont. **Contact:** Franglais Enterprises, RD 3, Box 4290, Middlesex, VT 05602, 802-229-4668.


## BATTLE OF THE BANDS, Burlington, VT
### Early Nov.
### Alternative and College Rock

"Four nights, seven bands a night...It's gonna' be great!" -- Club Toast employee. Previously held at Flynn Theater. **Help!** A sample lineup? **Days:** 4. **Site:** indoor. Club Toast, 165 Church Street. **Admission:** paid. **Acts:** local acts. **Contact:** Club Toast, 165 Church Street, Burlington, VT 05401, 802-660-2088.

FIRST NIGHT BURLINGTON, Burlington, VT
> Late Dec.
> Variety, Folk and International

Since 1983. "Your presence with us is the gift that brings First Night to life, for without you, we would have no celebration. ...Whatever you choose to see and do, it will be worth every special moment." -- Program. **Days:** 1. **Hours per day:** 10. **Site:** indoor, 17 venues. **Admission:** paid. **Daily entry:** under $10. **Discounts:** advance purchase discounts, group sale discounts. **Restrictions:** 2. **Secondary genre[s]:** MJAZ, ACAP, MC&W, BLGS, MFOL, TFOL, IRSH, JWSH, SCOT, OTHR. **Acts:** regional acts, local acts. **Sample day's line-up:** Michael Arnowitt, Banjo Dan and The Mid-Nite Plowboys, Bayley-Hazen Singers, Rachel Bissex, Blues for Breakfast Allstars, Bonneau and Schuster, Shane Brodie, Burlington Taiko Drummers, Tim Caira, Casey and Gagnon, Champlain Echoes, Cold Country Bluegrass, Constitution Brass Quintet, Craftsbury Chamber Players, Joan Crane, The Doppler Duo, Downtown Quartet, Jon Gailmor, Steve Gilette and Cindy Mangsen, Daniel Hecht, Highland Weavers, Karelian Folk Music and Dance, Susan Keniston, Lambsbread, Penny Lang, Tom MacKenzie, Mixed Company, Nisht Geferlach Klezmer Band, Rick Norcross and The Nashfull Ramblers, Onion River Jazz Band, Panache, Ellen Powell Duo, Dana Robinson, Larry Rudiger, Sheefra, So-Called Jazz Kwintet, Marian Tanau, Mark Trifilio, UVM Saxophone Quartet, Vermont Jazz Ensemble, Vermont Symphony Orchestra, Barbara Wells, Denise Whittier, Woods Tea Company, Diane Ziegler. **Contact:** First Night Burlington, Inc., 191 College Street, Burlington, VT 05401, 802-863-6005.

FIRST NIGHT RUTLAND, Rutland, VT
> Late Dec.
> Variety, Folk and International

**Days:** 1. **Hours per day:** 8. **Site:** indoor, 18 locations. **Admission:** paid. **Daily entry:** under $10. **Discounts:** advance purchase discounts. **Restrictions:** 2. **Secondary genre[s]:** CRCK, MR&B, TR&B, MC&W, BLGS, MFOL, IRSH, AFRC, OTHR. **Acts:** local acts. **Sample day's lineup:** D'Moja, Wayne Devaul, First Republic Brass, Gollum's Brigade, Lakes Region Youth Orchestra, Spencer Lewis, Dick McCormack, New Bremen Town Musicians, Sal and The Salutes, Silvertones, Tradewinds, Vacancies, Bruce White, Wild Branch, Woodland Woodwinds, Woods Tea Company, Bob Yellin and The Joint Chiefs of Bluegrass. **Contact:** First Night Rutland, P. O. Box 97, Rutland, VT 05072, 802-747-9090.

FIRST NIGHT ST. JOHNSBURY, St. Johnsbury, VT
> Late Dec.
> Variety, Folk and International

Since 1993. "First Night is a magical time to be in St. Johnsbury and you are a part of this magic...for without you we would have no celebration. Come join the fun!" -- Kathy Goslant, Project Director. **Days:** 1. **Hours per day:** 7. **Site:** outdoor and indoor, 15 locations. **Admission:** paid. **Daily entry:** under $10. **Discounts:** advance purchase discounts. **Restrictions:** 2. **Secondary genre[s]:** CRCK, TR&B, ACAP, MC&W, MFOL, OTHR. **Acts:** regional acts, local acts. **Sample day's lineup:** Albert Otis Band, The Bel-Aires, Big Band, Burke Brass Quintet, Champlain Echoes Chorus, Christopher's Pocket, Maple Leaf Seven Dixieland Band, Hilltones, Hired Help, Jeter le Pont, Just in Time, Kevin K, Ken Langer, Kathy Lowe, Noel and Friends, Sue Persson, Pumpkin Hill Singers, Karla Boone and Michelle Authier, Donald Mullally, South Church Handbell Ringers and Bells of Joy, Lucie Therrien, Through the Opera Glass, Twilight Jazz Group, Williams, Abetti and Anderson. **Contact:** Community Partnership, NVRH Hospital Drive, St. Johnsbury, VT 05819, 802-748-4561.

# R. I. P., M. I. A. Festival Listings

The following festivals are either confirmed or suspected to be discontinued (i.e., R. I. P.); or have **Caveat** not responded to various information requests (i.e., M. I. A.). Since all festivals are subject to last-minute changes or reinstatement, however, FestPress is not responsible for any festival listing information that follows. Readers are encouraged to notify FestPress of any status changes they uncover.


CHAMPLAIN VALLEY MIDWINTER FEST, Burlington, VT
> Middle Jan.
> Traditional Folk

Discontinued after 1993. **Days:** 3. **Site:** indoor. Multiple locations. **Admission:** paid. **Contact:** Champlain Valley Midwinter Fest, Box 163, Fairfax, VT 05454, 802-849-6968.


MUSKEG MUSIC SUMMER FEST, Norwich, VT
> Jun.
> Traditional Folk

"Unfortunately, we won't be having a festival [in 1993] because of low organizational energy. We've had a series of poorly-attended, though excellent, events. Maybe next year!" -- Ruth Sylvester. **Acts:** local acts. **Contact:** Muskeg Music, P. O. Box 212, Lebanon, NH 03766, 802-649-1164.


STRATTON 50S/60S REVIVAL, Stratton Mountain, VT
> Early Jul.
> Classic Rock and Oldies

Discontinued in 1991. **Days:** 4. **Site:** outdoor. **Admission:** paid. **Acts:** national acts. **Sample day's lineup:** Beatlemania. **Contact:** Stratton Resort Area Association, Village Square, P. O. Box 501, Stratton Mountain, VT 05155, 802-297-0100.


FOLK HARP CONFERENCE, Burlington, VT
> Early Jul.
> Variety, Folk and International

One time only. **Days:** 6. **Site:** outdoor and indoor, 4 venues, including the Flynn Theater **Admission:** paid. **Secondary genre[s]:** MJAZ, TR&B, TFOL, IRSH, TLAT, OTHR. **Acts:** national acts, regional acts, local acts. **Sample day's lineup:** Elisabeth von Trapp, Tina Tourin, Big Joe Burrell and The Unknown Blues Band, Murillas and Quiceno, Vida. **Contact:** Folk Harp Conference, P. O. Box 134, Jericho Center, VT 05465, 802-899-2457.


STRATTON FOLK FESTIVAL, Stratton Mountain, VT
> Middle Jul. to Late Jul.
> Modern Folk

Discontinued in 1991. **Days:** 3. **Site:** outdoor. **Admission:** paid. **Acts:** national acts, local acts. **Sample day's lineup:** "Tribute to Harry Chapin." **Contact:** Stratton Resort Area Association, Village Square, P. O. Box 501, Stratton Mountain, VT 05155, 802-297-0100.

STRATTON JAZZ FESTIVAL, Stratton Mountain, VT
Late Jul.
Modern Jazz

Discontinued in 1991. **Days:** 3. **Site:** outdoor. **Admission:** paid. **Acts:** national acts, local acts. **Sample day's lineup:** Lionel Hampton. **Contact:** Stratton Resort Area Association, Village Square, P. O. Box 501, Stratton Mountain, VT 05155, 802-297-0100.

VALLEY SINGER-SONGWRITER FESTIVAL, Dummerston, VT
Early Aug.
Modern Folk

One time only. **Days:** 1. **Hours per day:** 7. **Site:** outdoor. Maple Valley Ski Area. **Admission:** paid. **Acts:** national acts, local acts. **Sample day's lineup:** Richie Havens, Dress Left, Sunk In The Funk, Stockwell Brothers, Robin Zegge, Lisa McCormick and Intelligent Life, Herschler Brothers, Andrew Robinson, Peter Miles. **Contact:** Maple Valley Ski Area, Route 30, Dummerston, VT 802-254-6083.

SUGARBUSH FOLK FESTIVAL, Warren, VT
Middle Aug.
Variety, Folk and International

Discontinued in 1991. **Days:** 3. **Hours per day:** 12. **Site:** outdoor. Warren Ski Resort. **Admission:** paid. **Daily entry:** $10 to $24. **Discounts:** multiple event or day passes, advance purchase discounts, **Secondary genre[s]:** MJAZ, CRCK, BLGS, MFOL, TFOL, ZYDC. **Acts:** national acts, regional acts, local acts. **Sample day's lineup:** The Band, Shawn Colvin, Chubby Carrier and The Bayou Swamp Band, David Wilcox, Lisa Smith, Richard Meyers, Brook Williams, Barbara Kessler, Lydia Adams-Davis, Cliff Eberhardt, Happy Traum, Steve Charney, others. **Contact:** BEWI Productions, Inc., 80 Eighth Avenue, Suite 1102, New York, NY 10011, 212-242-6582.

~    ~    ~

*Groovin', Ben and Jerry's One World, One Heart Festival.*

# Massachusetts

*Cell, Loud Music Festival.*

# Harper's Blues Ferry

**BOSTON BLUES FESTIVAL**, Allston, MA
> Late January to Late February
> Blues and Traditional R&B
> ***Attended***

**BATTLE OF THE BLUES BANDS**, Allston, MA
> Late June to Early July
> Blues and Traditional R&B
> ***Attended***

**CITY OF PRESIDENTS BLUES FESTIVAL**, Quincy, MA
> Early July
> Blues and Traditional R&B

If Cliff and Norm from TV's "Cheers" were a bit younger, a bit crazier, and into hearing the blues **Introduction** instead of just living them, they'd likely be hanging out at Harper's Ferry.

Unlike the actual "Cheers" bar, which occupies a basement in the patrician Beacon Hill district (and has actually become one of Boston's biggest tourist attractions), Harper's resides among the plebes in Allston — a blue-collar enclave at the juncture of four college communities: Kenmore Square (Boston U.), Cambridge (Harvard U.), Brookline (Northeastern U.), and Chestnut Hill (Boston College). This neon-lit intersection of Brighton and Harvard Avenues hosts factory workers meeting frat brothers for weekend bouts of elbow-bending.

The fair-sized tavern's got a nice finish — exposed brick, soft lights and light-stained wood stools, counter and trim — all covered by a curved ceiling, which suggests, perhaps, an old airplane hanger. There's also a pool table and darts' stalls closer to the storefront window. Upon closer inspection you'll notice there are no sharp edges. That's because hard-drinking Bostonians routinely get early starts to beat early closing times, and the plank floors are built to handle any burliness that might bubble up around midnight or so.

Even Carla and Diane would agree, it's a proper place for the blues.

Some blues artists really rise to the occasions created by these kinds of fired-up fans. I enjoyed Texas guitarist Lonnie Mack's hour-long set headlining the BIG EASY BASH a few summers back (Escoheag, RI — see chapter), but my friend, Brian, couldn't stop yakking about Mack's incendiary three-hour blowout the night before at Harper's. If there was such a thing as a blues sing-along, that's what Mack was leading by night's end — to x-rated lyrics!

Harper's Ferry generally features local bands spiced by touring national acts, such as Mack. Twice a year, however, they raise their sights for a pair of extended events: the BOSTON BLUES FESTIVAL and the BATTLE OF THE BLUES BANDS launched in 1985 and 1987, respectively.

For Charlie Able, Harper's driving force and co-founder of the Boston Blues Society, both events are a tribute to Boston's copious musician pool: "I once had an act cancel on me. This was due to a breakdown with a vehicle at 8:30 at night. They were due to set up at 8:00 and go onstage at 9:00. I had another band there performing at 10:30, and I did not lose one step as far as the quality of the act! In order to pull that off, you absolutely have to have a tremendous wealth of musicians in this city."

It all began in 1985 when one of Able's softball buddies took over a "men's bar," in the vernacular, and was floundering with C&W music. He implored Able to take it over, but Able insisted on switching the format to blues and R&B. Able recalls his motivations:

- "In the early '70s, I went to see the embryonic stage of Roomful of Blues at the Inman Square Men's Bar, the old Zircon's, the Tam, also the Speakeasy. I used to go to see blues acts at all of those places. Blues was the backbone of the music revolution of the early-and-late-'60s, as we all know, and it is the nucleus of all American music. At that point in time, I had no idea this was the case; I just knew what I liked.

  "I had been frequenting those places to listen to R&B and blues — always to a cramped and packed situation did I go! Never was there a place where I could go and feel comfortable and sit down and just move around. I was a fairly claustrophobic guy, so when I saw this chance, I just jumped at it. I said, 'I know it's going to work.'"

The festival started humbly that first year — just a few groups on a Thursday night in February. Able termed it the "Allston Blues Festival" and had one of his better turnouts. He's repeated it annually as the BOSTON BLUES FESTIVAL, building it up by adding a night or two every year. "From a small blues festival of three local acts on one night," Able exclaims, "we have turned it into 11 nights covering almost the whole month of February featuring 10 national acts and one local act, and that local act happens to be Evil Gal... I think it's very credible that we can support all of these acts with the audience that we have here in Boston."

As national acts began to dominate the bill, Able sought another way to spotlight his local acts. Thus began the BATTLE OF THE BLUES BANDS two years later staged over the July 4th weekend. Perhaps the crowning glory of this hotly-contested affair came when 1992's winner, the aforementioned Evil Gal, went onto the National Amateur Blues Band Competition in Memphis, TN, later that summer. Not only did they win "Best Band," but their guitarist also won the Albert King Award as "Best Promising Blues Guitarist." Their success proved instrumental in landing them a subsequent label deal with Rounder Records.

This is just one payback for Able's commitment to an aspiring, local blues scene. Other recognition for Harper's includes recent awards as "Best Blues Club" by *Rolling Stone*, the *Boston Globe*, and *Boston Magazine*.

"We could never have continued to do what we're doing if it weren't for the local musicians. I can't say enough about them, simply because there's no way you can run a club on national acts," Able expresses. "We're grassroots, but we're ingrained grassroots. There are people who would stand behind us through thick and thin. I wouldn't give those folks up for anything."

**Festival Review** Budweiser was sponsoring the BOSTON BLUES FESTIVAL and seemed to be getting their money's worth. In the fine Boston tradition, the crowd (which ranged from bankers to bikers) was poundin' 'em back early and often. They decorated the stage, the floor, and every nook and cranny with enough empty bottles to stage Bud Bowls into the next century.

Bud reciprocated by distributing T-shirts, staging a drawing for a weekend trip for two to Manny's Car Wash (a blues bastion in New York City), and parading a pair of young lovelies known as "Bud Label Girls." Indeed, their skimpy dresses looked as if they'd been shrink-wrapped upon them like on a six-pack. I raced over from the excellent HARVARD WINTER FOLK FESTIVAL (Cambridge, MA — see chapter) held earlier that night to catch the last set from A. C. Reed and The Sparkplugs who were busy igniting the already-Bud-lit crowd.

**Artist Mini-Review** A. C. Reed and The Spark Plugs. Reed, longtime sax man for Buddy Guy/Junior Wells, among others, looked like a million bucks with a satin strip down the side of his gray slacks, which were held up by an enormous WWF-style belt emblazoned with rhinestones and a gold buckle shouting "A. C." He also wore a white shirt with its collar spread-eagled, plus black Ray Bans perched precariously on his shaved temples. He topped it all off with a black leather biker's cap. Star time!

Reed had clearly ingratiated himself with the audience and took time to share animated, demonstrative reminiscences of toughing it out on his way up. A more printable sample: "Rock and roll is bullshit! It's what we had to play to get paid back in 1957. The blues is the good stuff.

"Dig!," he shouted before sliding into the lugubrious grooves of a grinding, "Shake, Rattle and Roll."

Reed's five-piece band (Reed on sax/vocals, plus twin guitars, bass and drums) served up basic, Chicago-style blues, but were best on mid-tempos where the rhythm section locked in rock-solid and soulful. Reed's vocals were surprisingly strong, considering he's spent over 50 years singing in smoky bars like this. He benefitted, too, from good harmonies by the band. "Goin' Down the Road," "Even the Blues are Killing Me," "I Believe I'm Travelin' On" — all sounded great. He had me drumming on my steering wheel nearly the whole drive back to New York.

If Reed and his 'Plugs — out-of-towners, mind you — were this successful in working the crowd, you imagine how such Hub natives as Ronnie Earl, Luther "Guitar Jr." Johnson, Mighty Sam McLain, and Duke Robillard fared other nights of the festival. Well worth a roadtrip to find out.

**Travel Tip**

"There's a place in Brookline on Harvard Street called The Village Fish," notes Able. "It's about two miles from my club, and it has the most spectacular fish. They cook the fish right — you name the dish, whatever dish you order. It's an open cooking area where everybody sees their meal being prepared, and the food is absolutely terrific! That's where I'd send them if they want fish."

**See Also**

If you're in town for the finals of the BATTLE OF THE BLUES BANDS, why not stay over one week for the CITY OF PRESIDENTS BLUES FESTIVAL in nearby suburban Quincy? This other showcase of the best in Boston blues takes place outdoors at Veteran's Memorial Stadium, and represents the efforts of another determined blues club owner, Joe Hajjar, of Quincy's The Yard Rock. Between his place and Able's, this gives you at least two venues for post-fest reverie.

~     ~     ~

# Songstreet's Singer-Songwriters

SONGSTREET FESTIVAL OF FUNNY SONGWRITERS, Somerville, MA
> Middle January
> Modern Folk

SONGSTREET FOLK AND BLUEGRASS FESTIVAL, Cambridge, MA
> Early Febuary
> Variety, Folk and International

**HARVARD WINTER FOLK FESTIVAL**, Cambridge, MA
> Early March
> Modern Folk
> ***Attended***

SONGSTREET FESTIVAL OF WOMEN SONGWRITERS, Somerville, MA
> Middle March
> Modern Folk

SONGSTREET FOLK-ROCK FESTIVALS, Somerville, MA
> Middle March and Middle November
> Modern Folk
> ***Attended***

SONGSTREET CAJUN-BLUEGRASS, Somerville, MA
> Early April
> Variety, Folk and International

**Introduction**  "It was like David and Goliath," recounts Rick Lammachia, Founder of Songstreet Productions, about its third HARVARD WINTER FOLK FESTIVAL in 1992. "We moved it from a venue of 150 to 1,200, selling it out... against all odds, against all predictions. It was a shocker, kind of like the Mets winning the '69 World Series."

You can't help but feel his pride in pulling off the improbable, although savvy bettors might've placed their money with the doubters. After all, Lammachia had no real experience. He had been a security guard for Harvard's library system and was merely seeking to pay back the school's student-run charity, Phillips Brooks House, for their help in organizing his union. His first "Folk Festival Fundraiser" two years prior — actually, just a pair of Lammachia's musician friends, Elmer Hawks and Peter Keane — was staged in a Harvard dorm room before 50 curious onlookers.

Furthermore, he was attempting a lineup limited to four "local folk" musicians with either of the words in that quoted couplet, not to mention both combined, foreboding a likely commercial defeat. Lammachia not only packed Cambridge's Sanders Theater but became emboldened enough to take on other unlikely pairings.

First up, the folk/bluegrass connection. Doesn't ring a bell for you either? Well, there are so few festivals in the Northeast with this combination that I don't even have this category in my book. Lammachia landed a bill of The Seldom Scene, Jonathon Edwards, Northern Lights, and Melissa Ferrick, however, to debut his fledgling organization in January, 1993.

"The SONGSTREET FOLK AND BLUEGRASS FESTIVAL had never before been quite phrased that way," Lammachia recalls. "[It] was also the first major bluegrass concert in Boston in two years, and it sold out." Sometimes sounding more like a music-awed bystander in his breathless, Boston-flavored speech, he adds, "It was a great show, too."

More naysaying, more successes:

- Re the Songstreet Women Songwriters' Festival: "Again, this was one of those concerts where they said, 'You're kidding! You can't fill up Somerville Theater with six local women!' We came close to selling out. That's a 900-seat venue, and we had 850 there. People were just blown away; they can't wait to come back."

- Re the Songstreet Concert of Grammy Winners, pairing Alison Krauss and Union Station with Don Henry plus locals, Southern Rail: "When we booked that show six months before, people said, 'Alison's not that big a draw; you're going to have to package her carefully. I don't think you have a show there.' Her popularity really developed over the summer (partly because I worked my butt off promoting it), but the timing was incredible. She just exploded. Her show sold out five days in advance....[and] got three standing ovations."

I'll assure you that not everything Lammachia's put on has sold out. He cancelled a Songstreet Flying Fish Festival after two years because its mixed genres didn't draw sufficiently. Two other themes — Songstreet Women in Harmony plus a Songstreet Country and Bluegrass Family Christmas Concert — are being reconstituted after qualified results. Also the Harvard Summer Folk Festival is on hiatus until a suitable site can be permanently arranged.

Yet Lammachia's winners have left his year-old company with a stable roster of six "unique indoor mini-festivals" which are making waves on the Boston scene. A recent feature in the *Boston Globe* placed Songstreet Productions alongside such established folk-music promoters as Revolutionary Acts [see New Women's Voices, Cambridge, MA, Early February] and Folktree Concertmakers [see Folktree Jamboree, Boston, MA, Middle October].

He's pleased to be counted among such "great company" but seems more focused on spotting tomorrow's stars, usually by scouting out the various coffeehouses, clubs, and festivals about town. Twenty-six of the 31 artists he presented in 1993 were home-grown sightings. Two of the five out-of-towners — "disappear fear" and Carrie Newcomer — were discovered in local shows as well.

Lammachia describes Boston folk duo, "the story," as a characteristic find:

- "I look for a Songstreet type of artist — someone who's stretching the music, who's got some kind of dynamic quality, some kind of interesting quality, something that makes them unique. You put four or five of them together, and it makes for a great show! My biggest satisfaction is to take somebody who's good and develop them, put them in a concert hall, as opposed to a coffeehouse, and see them make that leap.

  "We've gotten a great response from the fans. They like the idea of a mini-festival format where they can come to a show and in one evening see four or five of the best up-and-coming acts in the area — folk, folk-rock, bluegrass or whatever — even a couple who are from out of the area. They like that; it's exciting. It lasts a little bit longer than usual, but it's not something that takes place every week.

  "Most of the people feel it's a bargain. One of the letters I got says, 'Thanks for making great concerts available at an affordable price.' That really sums up the attitude, I think, of most of our fans. The last show we did we got a standing ovation. That's not unusual."

We've talked about rising stars, creative themes, and affordable prices but not about a key **Festival** Songstreet asset: the two, pre-war auditoriums it rents. The Somerville Theater, with it's decora- **Review** tive flourishes and cartoonish stenciling in candy colors, looks like it could stage Laurel and Hardy's "March of the Tin Soldiers." Roasting popcorn fumes followed me up to the balcony where I took my antique wooden folding seat with its leather bottom.

Whereas that venue is petite, charming, and neighborly, the Sanders Theater on Harvard's campus is grand. It occupies the back end of a Romanesque-revival fortress. Passing through an imposing hallway that lacks only suits of armor to complete its Medieval decor, I felt like I had stepped into Wagner's Hall of the Valkyries — a roughly semi-spherical, historical shape all wrapped in burnished wood. It boasts a towering ceiling suspending an omnivorous chandelier plus buttresses, banisters, pillars, panels, moldings, murals, stencils, and scrolls. Pews gather around on two stories.

These exalted-but-informal surroundings doubtless inspired the five acts (with two openers: Barbara Kessler and Harvard Din and Tonics) for 1993's HARVARD WINTER FOLK FESTIVAL. Lammachia confirms, "We had a couple of members from the [Boston Music Awards] committee there at that show. It was no coincidence that a few days later four of the artists were nominated right off that bill, and one of them won!"

**Artist Mini-Reviews**   Carrie Newcomer. Newcomer first seemed a near-parody of her native Indiana: baggy denim dress and jacket cloaking a humble, homespun persona. Her corn-fed image quickly gave way, however, to reveal real talent.

Newcomer served up five compelling tunes that communicated effectively across a range of topics, emotions, and genres. Accompanied by The Dorkestra's Jeff Barries bowing an acoustic bass, she also sang them in a warm, dynamic manner. A nostalgic "Angel on My Shoulder," an anthemic "Hold On," and a bluesy tongue-in-cheek "My Mama Said It's True" all captured the crowd's delight.

Catie Curtis. I noted Curtis from a two-song showcase at the FALCON RIDGE FOLK FESTIVAL earlier in the year (Hillsdale, NY — see chapter) and was even more impressed by her full set. My notes on the performing style of this ex-social worker read, "direct, solid, confident." She delivers very well-crafted, interesting, and catchy songs in an attractive voice: half breathy folksiness; half country tear. Although she scores with local references and social concerns, I feel she's best when emotions inhabit her topics, such as the mournful dread of her opener, "Minefields." A real highlight.

Ellis Paul. That year's Boston Music Awards winner in the folk category was easily the evening's most original artist — so much so that I'll have to hear him again to get a handle on his style. Paul's an ex-social worker, too, but his lyrics have more of street edge than Curtis's, as in his macabre poetry about a teenage cocaine dealer, "Angel." He was joined by Stu Ferguson on electric guitar and Laurie Goldsmith on congas, who tastefully amplified his messages.

Despite a nasal singing technique, Paul gained extraordinary projection and color. He put himself so fully into every song, I could picture him in his long, blond hair fronting some English rock band. Different, charismatic, and well worth a closer listen.

**Attendance Tip**   Since Songstreet concerts have been selling out, Lammachia recommends out-of-towners calling ahead for tickets and such. Driving directions within the Cambridge/Somerville labyrinth are particularly valuable. "Get a subway map," advises Lammachia, "because it's probably easier to get around by the T than by driving. Driving around here is no picnic if you're not used to it."

**Travel Tip**   "A great afternoon," Lammachia says, "would be to go to the Omni Center at the Boston Museum of Science. It's high-tech movies. The film only lasts an hour, but it's an incredible video as well as an emotional experience. They tend to be very informative as well." He would also visit a local coffeehouse on the off-night, possibly The Nameless, plus any number of good-but-inexpensive restaurants in the squares before their respective shows.

**See Also**   The remaining Songstreet events listed in the heading are all self-explanatory. Since their dates are not especially set in stone, call ahead. You may even find a new theme on the schedule!

~     ~     ~

# Boston's Radio Rocks, I

**BOSTON PHOENIX/WFNX BEST MUSIC POLL CELEBRATION**, Boston, MA
> Late March
> Alternative and College Rock
> ***Attended***

**WFNX BIRTHDAY PARTY**, Boston, MA
> Early November
> Alternative and College Rock

I had just about given up on music awards shows. Too often the big names who are promised on **Introduction** the marquee don't show or don't play. If they do play, it's only for one song, usually to taped backing. Maybe they're taped, too. The ticket prices are usually steep, with the best seats being "comp'ed" for the media. With all the private parties going on, you feel like the brown shoes at a black-tie affair.

All told, you're lucky to get 45 minutes of actual music after suffering through the inevitable commentaries, cameos, presentations, set changes, and other intrusions that stretch the proceedings out for hours!

However, the **BOSTON PHOENIX/WFNX BEST MUSIC POLL CELEBRATION** rotated my attitude on awards shows 180 degrees! WFNX 101.7 FM, Boston's lone alternative-rock station, has turned theirs into one of the fullest such events in the country — a veritable Lollapalooza for the local scene. Consider that it stretches out over two full days, including:

- Two days of seminars (including a demo derby) for music-career hopefuls, all broadcast live on WFNX;

- A showcase night at the Paradise club with five local bands;

- A club night on Landsdowne Street with four large venues and 17 bands — national and local acts;

- An awards show/concert at the Orpheum Theater with full sets from four bands — again, national and local acts.

Want a taste of the lineup? Try 1993's Pornos for Pyros, Belly, Social Distortion, Gin Blossoms, Helmet, School of Fish, Therapy?, Black 47, Grant Lee Buffalo, Seka, and 16 more. If every name doesn't yet ring a bell, just wait a few years. The 1991 fall bash featured two then-unknowns, Nirvana and Smashing Pumpkins, jamming together on the same stage.

This kind of exposure for future stars is what WFNX strives for. According to their engaging, uptempo Marketing Director, Jenny Markowitz:

- "Most of our national bands that play are up-and-coming 'baby' bands that nobody really wants to see, but six months later they become somebody like The Gin Blossoms. They played here and all of a sudden they're huge. Plus, we want to give the local bands some exposure that they wouldn't necessarily have unless they're at this kind of event. We bring 3,000 people over to Landsdowne Street and 2,500 over to the Orpheum. There's a lot of people who may not necessarily be exposed to these bands, so we like to give the younger bands a chance."

More than once over the event's five-year tenure, these younger bands have played one year in the clubs as "locals" then returned the next year to the Orpheum as "nationals." Markowitz lists Belly and The Mighty Mighty Bosstones as two recent examples.

Given this track record for star-catching, you can understand why the Orpheum show sells out two weeks ahead, while Landsdowne Street transforms into one long line of party people waiting for the four clubs to open. Get there too late and you could get shut out.

Markowitz cites the anticipated crush of 6,000, among other reasons, for their scheduling strategy:

- Re Landsdowne Street: "We have had some crowding problems [in the past], so when we figure out the lineup this year, we'll try and put bands that people are going to like together, so that...there's a headliner at the same time in every club. People won't be disappointed if they don't get into one or the other."

- Re the Orpheum: "Most of our listeners are 18-to-34. They've gotta' get up the next day and go to work. We do try and have some of the [national] acts earlier and try to get the whole event in by 1:00 a.m. ...For the most par, people have seen who they want to see."

The whole affair is a charity benefit with proceeds going to either AIDS action or homelessness. In some cases this helps in recruiting participants the station could otherwise not afford. "The Porno for Pyros show," recalls Markowitz, "was the only free festival show that they did that year."

It was also gratifying to Markowitz that MTV recognized their efforts by sending a crew to film excerpts for their annual year-in-rock retrospective:

- "That was huge for us. We're an alternative station with not a lot of money. We've been in the typical alternative land for 10 years. Now it's becoming the way of the future, but it wasn't for a long time. We don't have a big marketing budget, so there was never this big push for press. But, I gotta' tell ya', I made a call, told [MTV] the bands, and they said, 'O. K., we'll be up.' I was so surprised!

"I really enjoy the whole party atmosphere," Markowitz interjects, noting that her personal highlight was getting to share a glass of Farrell's favorite wine with him after his set. "I like to see people having a good time. We get tons and tons of response from it. People just love it."

**Festival Review**  Seminars. I didn't quite catch my seminar quota — one good contact, marketing idea, band, and disc — but at just $5 admission, plus a free lunch, it was tough to complain. I simply retreated to my other objective as your basic music fan: to learn more about how the industry works. Since Boston has proven such fertile ground over the years, WFNX was able to draw a high caliber of participants who directed themselves to the young-ish audience with little condescension. After all, they could be fishing for the next Lemonheads.

I got the most out of the demo derby where a panel of six pros critiqued tapes randomly drawn out of a box. Young artists in the audience got on-the-spot assessments that were fairly kind and encouraging (too kind in a few instances). The lesson was, in effect, "you never know." One of the label reps described how he passed on Arrested Development's first demo tape because he felt it too raw, too rough. Had he kept the contact alive for their second tape, containing the song that got them signed by another label, he could've been sitting on a million-seller.

Talent Showcase. Tuesday night's affair suffered from two of the five bands having to withdraw. One absentee who would've definitely made the evening worthwhile was Stranger Than Pretty — a promising hard-rock power trio featuring strong vocals from their female bassist. I caught a bit of their set at the LOUD MUSIC FESTIVAL in Northampton, MA, the week prior (see chapter) and was looking forward to confirming my impression. Alas, none of the other bands captured my attention, but one out of five would've been a fair percentage for this sort of thing.

Awards Show/Concert. The next night at the Orpheum, however, it was four out of four — one of the best nights of music I heard all year.

Interestingly, the bands enjoyed one common thread — that of reaching back into the past for inspiration. New York's Black 47 mixed rock and rap with traditional Irish instrumentation. Boston's The Mighty Mighty Bosstones did the same, but for ska. Boston's Belly offered a strong nod in the direction of Joni Mitchell, while L. A.'s Social Distortion updated the rockabilly-rebel stance for the '90s.

The Orpheum helped carry through this retro theme. Shoe-horned into an alley off Boston Common, its filigreed facade gave way to a cavernous ex-movie palace decked out with extravagant fittings and finishings. Fortunately, it had been neglected just enough to lend comfort and a proper sense of decadence for the highly-charged crowd.

<u>Black 47</u>. I'm not a complete convert yet. They need to replace their drum machine with a live drummer who would help their rhythms and horn charts breathe. Their strength, however, lies in the boyish charisma of red-headed lead singer, Larry Kirwin. His writing is full of personality, humorous scenarios, and impassioned working-class politics. Doubtless there were many in this Irish-heavy crowd who could relate to his antagonisms. A spirited kickoff, well-received. **Artist Mini-Reviews**

<u>The Mighty Mighty Bosstones</u>. Picture about a dozen nerdy-looking whites and blacks in English prep-school attire rocking the house with caffeinated ska rave-ups. Gang-ska! Their lead singer/rapper was a show all unto himself, as he worked his hometown cheering section like a maestro, tossing the mic out for choruses, tossing himself out to be caught by a sea of hands, trading caps, and dragging half of them up on stage for a final group rant. It was tough to catch the lyrics amidst his gravel-throated shouts and impulsive stage antics, but no matter. One fan complained, but he barked back, "If you could hear me, you wouldn't want to stay!"

<u>Belly</u>. Captivating, entrancing. Their sound combined muscular drum patterns, playfully funky bass lines, and shimmering guitar swirls to support the girlish vocals of singer/rhythm guitarist Tonya Donnelly. Dressed for tea in a wispy print skirt, she was a bit self-conscious at being the lone female lead on the bill (joking that she felt like "the meat in a testosterone sandwich"). Yet she held her own, delivering songs that balanced wistful emotions with urgent purposes. Donnelly saved her best tune for last, when the band allowed a rapid harmony duet between her and the bassist to shine through the mix.

<u>Social Distortion</u>. The lead-singer/guitarist certainly had the greaser looks and the moves down pat: his pompadour slicked up into a high-top fade; a sleeveless ribbed T-shirt exposing an upper torso slathered with tattoos; black wool chinos held up by black suspenders; and black lizard-skin cowboy boots. He wouldn't just take a solo, he'd strut to the lip of the stage, take a drag on his cigarette, and rip off fuzzy, fiery lines with a sneer. Attitude!

Their rockabilly-goes-metal was smoother than I expected, though, perhaps because his voice is lighter and higher than the average metal-meister, and requires classier settings. I liked it, and so did the two drunks next to me who kept chanting, "Social D.! Social D.!" I had to leave early to drive back to New York but not before enjoying them take it full circle with a nasty take on Johnny Cash's "Ring of Fire."

Unfortunately, you'll have to choose between the awards show/concert and the club night, which take place simultaneously. Tickets for the former are available through Ticketmaster about four weeks in advance. Get your's early. For club night you'll need to stand on line well before the doors open at 7:00 p.m. Dress warmly. Markowitz advises choosing the one club whose lineup you'd most prefer, since you may not be able to hop to another. **Attendance Tip**

If you want to make it an alternative-rock week to remember, consider hooking up with the Loud Music Festival (Northampton, MA — see chapter), which takes place three days later. Your spring breaks, as well as your hearing ability, will never be the same! **See Also**

WFNX does it all over again in the fall for the WFNX Birthday Celebration. No Orpheum show, but three bands jam on an outdoor stage on Landsdowne Street, while a dozen others play the clubs indoors. Look for a similarly enticing mix of national and local acts.

~     ~     ~

# Northampton's College Rock

**LOUD MUSIC FESTIVAL**, Northampton, MA
Early April
Alternative and College Rock
***Attended***

**Introduction**    "The town of Northampton had gained some notoriety in the past couple of years as being sort of a hotbed of new music," says LOUD MUSIC FESTIVAL Promoter Bill Troper who lists such local launchings as Dinosaur Jr., Sebadoah, Buffalo Tom, and The Pixies. "We've known it all along. We've been partying here for a number of years. We've known what a rockin' town it is."

Actually, Northampton has other reputations as well.

It's renown for its five neighboring colleges, including two of the venerable "seven sisters," Smith and Mount Holyoke. These schools help attract numerous young sub-cultures, one of which earned Northampton the sobriquet, "Lesbianville U. S. A.," in a recent *Time* cover story. Fans of roots music have been making pilgrimages for 15 years to one of the most prominent venues in New England, The Iron Horse Cafe. Troper also claims, "People drive up from New Haven and all over to shop and eat at the restaurants — it's really quite a culture town."

Quite a charming town, too — a remarkably-preserved slice of Norman Rockwell's New England as tidy Victorian storefronts guard over treed squares, iron railings, brick walkways, and other period features. Even if there weren't so many book shops, record shops, boutiques, cafes, coffeehouses, and other alcoves for browsing and grazing, you'd still be tempted to stroll lazily about Northampton's tightly-gathered streets. That goes for everybody who visits, whether they're New York yuppies or neo-dread hippies.

"That's the thing," adds Troper, "the town's very conducive for a festival like this. You can walk from Pearl Street to The Iron Horse in four minutes. When there's a festival like that in New York City, it's, like, one show's at the Knitting Factory, the next one's up on 26th Street — you have to take a cab."

The two New York City festivals Troper refers to, the CMJ MUSIC MARATHON and NEW MUSIC NIGHTS (see chapter), are pretty much those he's modelled the LOUD MUSIC FESTIVAL after. Even though the music shares a common thread of being loud (and proud of it), the emphasis is not upon metal, but more upon variety. Among 1993's 36 bands, this ranged from the "thrash-grass" of Austin's Killbilly, the Celtic rock of Northampton's own Big, Bad Bullocks, aggro surf stylings from San Francisco's Hypnolovewheel, retro-seventies grunge from New York's Cell, and the brooding noise pop of Boston's Swirlies. Troper struggles for an encompassing definition before settling on a combination of "loud guitar rock," "new rock," and "alternative rock."

Spurred on by a October, 1992 article in *Billboard*, which posed Northampton as the next possible Seattle, Troper joined up with a local record label, Jama Disc, run by Radius Management. "It dawned on us," recalls Troper, "to maybe capitalize on some of the notoriety the town had been getting as far as [being] a rock-and-roll town. We had the idea in early January [and] we pulled it together." Just two months later they had actually accomplished their self-described "rock-and-roll Mardi Gras," which boasted a hospitality suite where 300 insiders were lavishly wined and dined, consuming 10 kegs of beer in two days.

Unfortunately, the costs of it all were higher than anticipated, while a decision to sell only $20 weekend passes kept some cash-strapped day travelers at home. Caught in the financial squeeze, Radius Management broke up, and it appeared 1993's affair would end up as nothing more than a fond memory.

Troper was fortunate, however, to land professional support from two of the local club owners, Mal Thursday of the Bay State Cabaret and Jordy Herold who had just sold The Iron Horse for seven figures. With them handling the booking and budgeting, Troper anticipates 1994 bringing stronger lineups ("an order of magnitude stronger"), breaking even, national press, and his ultimate ambition, a sponsor for 1995 and beyond. There will be individual day passes sold for a program that's now grown to encompass Friday through Sunday evenings plus Saturday afternoon.

"At this point," Troper explains three months before the kickoff, "setting the whole thing up is going so much smoother. Jordy, Mal, and I are having fun with it. It's gonna' work great; we're all enthusiastic.... The thing is definitely gonna' shine on for years!"

**Festival Review**

It never fails. Just as with CMJ and NEW MUSIC NIGHTS (see above), the acts I target never turn out to be the "buzz bands" championed by press and insiders. A small part of the reason is I'm more inclined toward roots music; the larger part is I guess I'm becoming an old fart. (Sigh!)

Linda Wood, previewing 1993's lineup for the *Valley Advocate*, pointed her readers toward The Swirlies, Hypnolovewheel and Cell. She also quoted Bex Zumbruski, of Northampton's Main Street Records, in his recommendations of Versus and Love Child. Troper, himself, was very pleased afterward by sets from Big, Bad Bullocks, The Lunachicks, Madder Rose, No Safety, and Culture Shock.

Of course, my picks were different. I wanted to hear Morphine, reconstituted from ex-members of Treat Her Right, but I arrived Friday night just as their kickoff set was concluding. I also would've loved to stay until Saturday for Killbilly's set, since they'd been forced to cancel their appearance at the NASSAU COMMUNITY COLLEGE FOLK FESTIVAL earlier in the week (Garden City, NY — see chapter). Others I recognized, such as Spring House and The Lyres, were booked Saturday, too. (This year, Troper is scheduling the "larger-drawing bands" for Friday and Sunday to encourage attendees to stay the weekend.)

Instead, I wandered the clubs with an open mind and ears stuffed safely with my trusted foam plugs. I endured three "misses" — Dam Builders, Hypnolovewheel, and Gobblehoof — but also enjoyed two hits. Be forewarned, though, of my self-acknowledged "fogey factor."

**Artist Mini-Reviews**

Stranger Than Pretty: A basic hard-rock power trio from Boston with a difference — the sharp, soulful vocals of it's singer/rhythm guitarist. The lead guitarist and drummer thrashed and bombed in a controlled fury, but steered clear of burying the singer's emotive strengths in the rubble. Worth a closer listen.

Cell: This four-piece band from New York City beamed their grunge-rock back a few decades. Describing themselves as "Black Sabbath on 'ludes," they employed seventies-style power chords to achieve a certain tunefulness lacking among the other "wall-of-noise" bands. Like Smashing Pumpkins, they staged their attacks in waves that sucked you into the riptides before pounding you at the crests. Their varied tempos and somewhat more spacious arrangements also helped the raspy lead singer to get his message through to where I could actually follow it. Cell might be throw-backs to a degree, but they also projected themselves forward and distinct from the pack.

**Travel Tip**

"Five or six really intense book stores...four phenomenal record stores...a zillion excellent restaurants...and an incredible arboretum at Smith College," notes Troper of daytime diversions in the area. His picks for a bite include The Haymarket Cafe plus Fiorentino's for pastry. He also recommends the art museum at Smith plus free ice-skating at the indoor rinks of UMass/Amherst on Saturday evenings and Sunday afternoons. Above all, Troper warns travelers, "Rest up and be prepared to jam!"

**See Also**

Earlier the same week in Boston is the outstanding two-day blowout, the WFNX/BOSTON PHOENIX BEST MUSIC POLL CELEBRATION (see chapter). Combine both alternative-rock festivals for a spring break to remember. Your ears will ring for the rest of the semester.

~     ~     ~

# New England's Folk-Dance Traditions

RALPH PAGE LEGACY WEEKEND, Durham, NH
   Early January
   Traditional Folk

NEW ENGLAND FOLK FESTIVAL, Natick, MA
   Late April
   Variety, Folk and International
   ***Attended***

STRATHSPEY AND REEL SOCIETY OF NEW HAMPSHIRE'S FALL CONCERT GALA, Concord, NH
   Late November
   Scottish

**Introduction**  Fifty years! That's the anniversary the New England Folk Festival Association [NEFFA] will be celebrating in 1994. While this fondly-revered rendezvous of folk-dance enthusiasts may not be the very, very oldest event on my list, it's definitely up there. Surprisingly, it's never received any national coverage of the sort regularly enjoyed by other landmark events, such as the GALAX OLD FIDDLERS' CONVENTION (see Galax, VA, Middle August) or Bill Monroe's BEAN BLOSSOM BLUEGRASS FESTIVAL (see Bean Blossom, IN, Middle June). 'Sounds like it would've made a good assignment for TV's recently retired Charles Kurault!

**NEFFA** (how both the association and its event are referred to — pronounce it phonetically, like NAFTA) started a year in advance to solicit oral histories, stories, reminiscences, and memorabilia for transcription and display. Judging from the loyalty of the many **NEFFA** heads I've encountered on the festival circuit, the finished exhibit, planned ceremonies, and scheduled performances should be wonderful — a thick cross cut from the folk-revival tree growing throughout the 20th century.

Now you might be afraid that such a lengthy tenure suggests there'd be a dated feeling to **NEFFA**, or a stuffy atmosphere at their event.

I wouldn't call the festival dated at all — timeless is a better description — but its atmosphere is positively loose, swinging, and bursting with activities and camaraderie. Dancers are amiable creatures to begin with, well-accustomed to asking strangers to partner. If you're ambulatory and loitering by any of the dance halls, you can expect propositions all day — to dance, that is. Or possibly to sing along, or jam within one of the many informal gatherings in the courtyard, the halls, the classrooms, and everywhere else on the grounds. Instrumental notes, plus the pitter-patter of dancers' feet, stream through every crevice.

Sylvia Miskoe, the bright, chipper 50th Anniversary Chair, sums it up better than I ever could: "**NEFFA** is friendly; it's cheap; the food is fantastic; it's all under one roof and there's something for everybody. It's a three-day, music-and-dance orgasm!" I second that in spades!

**Festival Review**  Natick High School, **NEFFA**'s epicenter, resides just west of a quiet, modest tree-lined town in the western suburbs of Boston. It's the only high school I know of with its own small lake and bathing beach, nicely framed with scrub pines and oaks.

You get a sense of the comparatively massive scale of **NEFFA** (typical dance festivals usually draw in the 100's) by the lines of cars parked on both sides of the streets blocks before you get there. If you don't arrive early, make sure your dancing shoes are comfortable for the short commute. Also pack a parka or sweater and at least one change of clothes for the walk back through the chilly night air.

The '60s-style architecture of the school seems incongruous for a folk-roots affair, but it's quantity that counts at **NEFFA**. The building can handle a performance guide that stretches 22 pages in the program booklet in tiny 8-point print!

There are 10 sites for activities: two big halls for dances, an auditorium for dance performances, and separate classrooms for jamming, singing, playing, demonstrations, seminars, family concerts, and music workshops. There's also the courtyard that alternates no fewer than 19 "Morris, Sword and Rapper Teams" with impromptu music performances. These are traditional harvest dance troops usually wearing colorful ethnic costumes with ribbons and bells — picture Balky from TV's "Perfect Strangers." My performing highlight of the festival occured here in the courtyard when Rhode-Island-based Cajun band, Magnolia, came up after its dance set, sat down, and traded tunes for a good hour or two.

It's all balanced, as Miskoe explains: "50% for contra and square dancing; 50% for everything else." "Everything else" ranges from "Polish Pivot Polkas" to a "Bones Workshop" to "Songs of the Whalers" to an "Irish Music Jam Session." **NEFFA**'s intent is to have you sample their smorgasbord and experience new musical tastes. Miskoe recounts that attendees typically write, "I came here because of the Sacred Harp Singing and learned how to dance," or vice-versa. Mission accomplished.

Miskoe's own involvement began as a young woman:

- "As a kid, I always liked to dance. There was a local square dance, and my family used to go to it once a week. I was kind of an awkward, socially-unattractive person, but I could dance, so I always had a partner.

  "Then I got interested in playing the accordion and was invited to play at **NEFFA** as part of the Stage Orchestra. I was just thrilled! I didn't realize they just went down and picked everybody who played an instrument. But still, it was a wonderful feeling to be able to sit there in the background and play with all these other people who were older and sharing their music and their knowledge."

Even today, Miskoe remarks, "Sitting up there on Saturday night with 40 other musicians, like Bob McQuillen on piano and Vince O'Donnell fiddling, is a trip to heaven."

**Artist Mini-Reviews**

Forget about mini-reviews here — I was too busy dancing and dashing from one performance to another. However, those folk-festival frequenters looking at "50 years' history" and expecting a roster of musical heavy-hitters should be cautioned. The only recorded name I recognized beforehand from among over 200 acts was guitarist Bennett Hammond who conducted a workshop, "Slick Tricks for Fingerpickers."

Part of the reason, Miskoe points out, "is nobody at **NEFFA** gets paid. We do get a lot of inquiries from artists of different kinds and when they find out they wouldn't get paid, and they're only allotted 45-to-60 minutes, they hang up." Of course, that works to the festival's advantage, too — only those who really want to come, do. Miskoe explains that **NEFFA** has to turn away many musicians every year.

The main reason, though, is that the primary focus of **NEFFA** is dancing. The musicians come out of the copious, if generally unrecorded and non-professional, folk-dance-band scene from all across the country. There are excellent individual players who'll give solo concerts and workshops aplenty (Miskoe cites McQuillen, O'Donnell, Charlie Pilser and Cal Howard among many others). However, they're there mainly to support the dancing as they flit from one backing group to another. Solid ensemble work rules the roost!

Musicians will experience no shortage of playing partners at all different levels of expertise. Dancers will find every imaginable genre available, as well as dances graded in three levels: "beginner, experienced, and mixed." Listeners will also profit from codes that cite "teaching, no teaching, group participation, entertainment, presentation, and/or family event." Even kids will encounter beacoups playmates in this family-oriented affair.

If you get overwhelmed, simply wander over to the cafeteria for a tasty snack, or to the excellent concessions and crafts exhibits. Bring extra cash for sampling the wares, Miskoe advises.

**See Also** NEFFA also runs the RALPH PAGE LEGACY WEEKEND, which Miskoe describes as "a very nice weekend devoted exclusively to New England squares and contras, with workshops on playing and calling." Furthermore, Miskoe's personal playing interest, the STRATHSPEY AND REEL SOCIETY OF NEW HAMPSHIRE, puts on its annual FALL CONCERT GALA the Saturday after Thanksgiving.

~　　~　　~

*Stage Orchestra, New England Folk Festival.*

# Boston's Radio Rocks, II

**WBCN Rock 'n' Roll Rumble**, Boston, MA
> Early May to Late May
> Hard Rock and Heavy Metal
> ***Attended***

**WBCN Rock of Boston Concert**, Boston, MA
> Late October
> Modern Rock, Pop and Top 40

There aren't many annual rock-and-roll events that predate MTV, which may explain why the **Introduction** cable network, founded in 1980, makes yearly pilgrimages to **WBCN's Rock 'n' Roll Rumble**.

The "Rumble," as it's known locally, has been facing off the best 24 of Boston's young hopefuls each year since 1979. Stipulations include no major-label record contracts in-hand or in-process plus no past participants. WBCN does invite reconstituted bands, though. Droll blues-hounds, Treat Her Right, competed in 1987, but broke up after two well-received albums. Some members re-formed as Morphine and entered 1992's affair.

A list of past **Rumble** winners includes major-label signings Seka ('91), Heretix ('88), and 'Til Tuesday ('83). A more impressive roster, however, would include non-winning bands. This isn't my scene, either geographically or musically, yet even I recognize these runners-up:

- '92: Letters to Cleo, Morphine, Swinging Steaks, Concussion Ensemble;

- '91: Cliffs of Dooneen, Uncle Betty, Dam Builders;

- '89: Blake Babies, Blood Oranges;

- '88: Bim Skala Bim, Incredible Casuals, Lemonheads, Raindogs, Tribe, Dharma Bums, Think Tree;

- '87: Treat Her Right;

- '85: Scruffy the Cat, O-Positive;

- '83: The Del Fuegos.

You're looking at 10 signings that I know of plus some local heroes who may have deserved to join them. Of course, there are a host of others who faded into oblivion sporting names like Rash of Stabbings, Left Nut, Smegma and The Nuns, Jerry's Kids, Judy's Tiny Head, and my favorite, Hell Toupee.

It's enough to get a laugh out of the otherwise low-key **Rumble** Coordinator and Local Music Director for WBCN 101.4 FM, Albert O, who rues that "90% of our past participants aren't even around anymore." But this also serves tribute to the keen ear of Albert, his co-captain, Bill Abbate, and other members of the **Rumble** braintrust from WBCN who are willing to take chances on promising bands just getting started.

Albert has been handling the overnight chores at WBCN for over a decade and listens to every local tape sent to the station. He goes so far as to field calls from local bands after 10 p.m. on Monday nights. Back in 1988 Albert saw potential in The Lemonheads even though he claims, "They were terrible back then; they'd be the first to tell you, too." He had them compete in that year's **Rumble**, which Albert feels may have been their best-stocked ever.

"We don't get too much of that anymore," Albert explains, "because the bands get snatched up a lot faster. It was much more regionalistic back then. Now a band can make a splash and go overseas. A band like Buffalo Tom has never been in the RUMBLE because they were huge overseas before they could even draw a fly in Boston." Albert cites Barrance Whitfeld and The Savages, The Pixies, Throwing Muses, and Juliana Hatfield as other area followers of that route.

Another RUMBLE trend Albert notes has been toward heavy-metal/hard-rock/grunge styles: "There's been a lot of that and they tend to be a lot more immediate. The judges tend to respond to that sort of thing. I would say [1994] will probably be one of the more diverse years we've had in a long time, but the last two to three years have leaned heavily in that direction."

Regardless of their styles, contestants have plenty of motivation to impress the judges. First, there are eight prize packages loaded with goodies. The Grand Prize in 1993 included 54 hours of studio time, 10 hours of engineering time, press coverage in five publications, a photo session, all kinds of rentals, gift certificates at seven clubs, tapes and services, T-shirt printing, and more. All participants also get write-ups in a nice printed program and are featured on WBCN's "Boston Emissions" program, aired Sunday nights.

Second, the judges, themselves, represent potential media and label contacts. Albert mentions Timothy White, Editor of *Billboard*, as a perennial. "More and more we're trying to get A&R people from across the U. S., " says Albert. "Most of them don't want to come in, though, on the preliminary nights. They all want to come in on the semi-final nights. [laughs] When you're flying in from L. A...."

All this exposure doesn't always go Albert's way. He continues to hold a torch for 1992's challenger, Concussion Ensemble. "I can't believe they're not signed or something," he rues, "they're just an amazing band."

Still, Albert's rewards are more intrinsic:

- "If only one or two people come up to me and say they had a good time and discovered something they wouldn't have otherwise seen, that's the point of the whole thing. You know? The prizes are secondary; we try and play them down even though they are there and they are pretty huge. It's essentially a showcase for people who couldn't otherwise go out and see these bands."

**Festival Review** Great to be back at the Paradise, a narrow, modern sculpted space on Commonwealth Avenue near the Boston University campus. It's figured prominently in the Boston scene over the years (hosting the celebrated early appearances of Steve Earle in the mid-'80s, for example) and has been a recent home to the RUMBLE after the latter's years of roving.

This particular preliminary showdown coincided with the last broadcast of TV's "Cheers." Traffic was backed up on the freeways for miles as well-wishers congregated to bid the cast farewell and bask in the media attention. Doubtless this accounted for a straggling crowd, that began to swell with biker-jacket types after the fireworks were over.

I cited the various runners-up above because their roots-rocking orientation is more to my taste. Hard-core isn't quite my scene. Yet if Wagner's Ring Cycle were being recast for head-banging, the angry women of Malachite would be perfect for the orchestra pit.

**Artist Mini-Review** Malachite. The words "gothic death-metal" are somehow inadequate to describe the booming assault of these mean mistreaters on your ears and sensibilities. Unlike the previous bands of this night, these four members are very controlled in their purpose of delivering raging doom and seething hatred. No wasted movements, just growling vocals straight out of "The Exorcist" plus pounding, pounding, pounding on guitars, bass, and drums. Whew!

My friend, Kem, calls it "music for ethnic cleansing," while I term it "soundtrack to a serial murder." Their third number, "Take Me to the Serpent's Den," induced an asthma attack in me and drove us both reeling onto the street. Needless to say, the crowd loved 'em, which made me feel especially old at that very moment. I forgot to ask Albert how they fared, or was I afraid to find out? I'll let you and Rod Serling be the judges in this episode of "The Twilight Zone."

"Pace yourself," advises Albert. "There are six nights of preliminaries with four bands each night. Don't run yourself into the ground the first two nights; you've still got four more to go." I'd bring earplugs to the early rounds as well.

**Attendance Tip**

The Middle East in Cambridge's Central Square is where Albert would first bring his out-of-town guests: "It's a melting pot. Not only do you get good food, but if you were to stick around later at night, there's great bands and stuff like that. It's the place to be." Other options include the various prize- donating clubs, not to mention the Paradise, itself.

**Travel Tip**

Every Halloween Friday WBCN sells out the 14,000-seat Boston Garden for it's annual WBCN ROCK OF BOSTON CONCERT. Their lineup ranges from mainstream to alternative, boasting a hearty Boston flavor. The lineup from 1993 included local heroes Peter Wolf, Extreme, and The Mighty Mighty Bosstones, along with Joe Satriani, Ian Moore and The Crash Test Dummies. Albert considered 1992's a particular highlight as both The Spin Doctors and Phish were caught "on their way up." Tickets go on sale via Ticketmaster four weeks ahead.

**See Also**

~     ~     ~

# Boston's Radio Rocks, III

**KISS-108 FM Concert**, Mansfield. MA
Early June
Modern Rock, Pop and Top 40
***Attended***

**Introduction**  There are going to be quite a few surprises in this book. I'll even give you one. Out-of-towners might not know that Brooklyn's WEST INDIAN-AMERICAN DAY CARNIVAL AND PARADE (see chapter) stretches out over five full days and draws a good 2.5 million to its Labor Day finale. I doubt, though, that such a Caribbean celebration will come as a complete shock, only that it occurs on such a massive and prolonged scale.

But I'm convinced that the mere existence of something like the **KISS-108 FM CONCERT** [KISS'] will blow peoples' minds! We're talking a veritable pop WOODSTOCK' here, rolled up into a single day, then rolled out onto a single stage. If can't imagine the mercenary rock-music industry providing this kind of entertainment value more than once every quarter century then check out 1994's lineup order, which commenced at noon and concluded by 11:00 p.m. And remember, it's just one stage:

- Funky Poets, Juliet Roberts, Salt-n-Pepa, Joshua Kadison, US3, Zhane, Crash Test Dummies, Kenny G., Jon Secada, The Puppies, Ovis, Richard Marx, Tony Toni Tone, Robin S., Color Me Badd, Gabrielle, Booker T. and The MGs, Aaron Neville, Jack Mack and The Heart Attack, Peter Wolf, Rosco Martinez, Meat Loaf, All-4-One, Fem-2-Fem, Luther Vandross, Tavares/Shannon/K. Sledge, The Village People, Tevin Campbell, Z. Z. Top.

A fluke, you say? O. K., then set your sights on 1993's bill, in alphabetical order:

- After 7, The Bee Gee's, Boy Krazy, Cameo, Neneh Cherry, Classic Example, George Clinton and The P-Funk All Stars, Erin Cruise, Chris Cuevas, Terence Trent D'Arby, Sonia Dada, Duran Duran, Expose, Hi-Five, Inner Circle, Chris Isaak, Jeremy Jordan, Jordy, Jack Mack and The Heart Attack, Mitch Malloy, Wendy Moten, Jeffrey Osborne, PM Dawn, Shanice, Shannon, Silk, Patty Smyth, Snow, Keith Sweat, SWV, Tecnotronic, Tony Terry, Barry White and The Love Unlimited Orchestra, Tene Williams, Peter Wolf.

Whew! Kinda' puts LOLLAPALOOZA in a little perspective, doesn't it?

Now, here's the most mind-blowing feature of all — that the **KISS'** has happened uninterrupted for 15 straight years! This impressive longevity occurs in a rock music genre where the average tenure of its benefit shows is precisely one. As in one year, over-and-out.

So once you tally up the quantity of **KISS**'s acts, their popularity and their eclectic range, then factor in the word "annual," well you just have to make like Mike Myers' Wayne Campbell movie character, bow down, and proclaim repeatedly, "I'm not worthy! I'm not worthy!"

"It's quite a spectacle," admits Mark Kroninger, Marketing Director of **KISS**'s sponsor, KISS-108 FM. "[But] when it really, really comes right down to who the driving force behind the show is, it's [station owner] Rich Balsbaugh. He's basically the man who gets the acts, along with our Program Director, Steve Rivers. Those guys, literally, start the day after the **KISS**' putting the feelers out. ...It's the one time of the year where all the favors kinda' get pulled, you know?"

Balsbaugh bought the Boston-based pop station in 1979 and set to work on the first **KISS**' immediately afterward. "That was back in the real disco heyday," Kroninger says of Balsbaugh's efforts to book and fill a downtown club called Metro (now Avalon). He chuckles at Balsbaugh's oft-told tale how "he was out in the street basically begging people to come in to the radio station's concert for free just so we would have the house packed." Apparently, Balsbaugh's hawking worked, and the event grew, moving to the Boston Garden before landing outdoors at the Great Woods amphitheater in 1988.

During this time Balsbaugh's crew guided KISS-108 FM to a leading position on Boston's radio dial. Kroninger recites that the station is number two overall in the Boston market among ages 12-plus, number one on the FM band, and number one in the prized 18-to-34 demographic. Now the latter stat might come as a surprise to those who picture Top 40 — "contemporary hit radio," as Kroninger relays the standard format description — as being exclusively for teeny-bopping gum chompers. Kroninger describes the more typical listener profile as a woman in her mid-to-late 20s: "That's where our real bread-and-butter is."

This spread, in terms of ages, sexes and races, helps explain the programmatic sweep of the **KISS'**, along with the exquisite contrasts that often result. A real treat for me is comparing future rock-and-roll Hall of Famers, like Aaron Neville and Z. Z. Top, with such young lions as Crash Test Dummies and Salt-n-Pepa. Live, no less!

Kroninger crows that the **KISS'** has an extraordinary track record for predicting future stars (citing, for example, Whitney Houston on 1987's bash), but cautions:

- "You gotta' get the classics because our legacy is not just Top 40 radio. I mean, we've cultivated this image in the market where there's a slight idiosyncrasy to us; where you'll hear stuff on KISS that you might not expect sometimes. And now the Top 40 scene's getting so diverse almost that I kinda' like it myself 'cause I kinda' like that type of sound. You hear Pearl Jam next to Whitney Houston.

"I think what one of the real selling points on this thing is the diversity of it," says Kroninger, sequeway-ing to the festival:

- "It's almost funny when you look down the lineup of this thing sometimes because the acts you'll see side-by-side, you almost wouldn't think it would work. Who are these guys marketing to? It's evolved to be that people come to it for the diversity. I mean, where else are you gonna' see Z. Z. Top, Luther Vandross and Tom Jones on the same stage on the same date? It's funny, there's so much of something for everybody [laughs]. It's almost trite to say that."

Perhaps, but true!

Here are three other unique qualities which the **KISS'** flaunts in abundance:

- It's one of the very, very few venues for two festival dispossessed genres: alternative rockers and young modern R&B singers.

The station gets kudos for presenting either genre on a festival stage, not to mention both together.

- It lets you see which aspiring artists have got the real goods and which others are mere products of today's studio and video technology.

The two modern R&B singers calling themselves <u>Zhane</u>, for example, clearly owed everything to their producers. They couldn't coordinate their nasal whines into a consistent harmony, nor did they exhibit any dynamics, modulation, interpretation, improvisation, or charisma. Take away their two taped tracks, and these young women had basically nothing to offer but their looks.

By contrast, the jazz/rap band who preceded them, <u>US3</u>, had it all "going on!" "Phat" beats, sharp horn charts, sprightly tempo changes, deft solos, active stage manners — these young guys took a distracted early afternoon crowd and had them instantly up-and-dancing as one! I particularly enjoyed their second number, which alternated a Jimmy Smith organ funk with a ska rave-up overlaid by a dub vocal.

"Yeah, they were good," Kroninger agrees of US3, "and when you go down through who's been here in the past and stuff, it's those people who did pull it off who you might still see around, whereas you always get your one-hit wonders who have been here and gone, and it's, 'Where are they residing now?' [laughs] Most of the acts are pretty well received, I think. The ones who don't have that strong staying power are generally the ones who are on for a song or two."

- It also lets you see how artists employ their entertainment skills within relatively brief sets, and what really makes budding stars, stars.

Given an average of 20 minutes each (longer for biggies, shorter for rookies), young pop singers like Jon Secada did like I might've done. He came out smoking, reaching peak intensity from his first footstep, then raising the stakes by tearing his shirt off and tearing into three other-wise-middling R&B anthems. This display naturally revved his many female fans, and I could see Secada as a real contender for the '90s, assuming some decent material comes his way.

However, Richard Marx took a subtler tact afterward to equal effect. This young pop singer started out with slow tempos, taking time to debut two new songs, relay many anecdotes, tell self-deprecating jokes, and build an extensive rapport. This drew the milling crowd into his engaging personality and primed them for his closing hit, a rousing "It Don't Mean Nothing," which he handed over for them to complete acappella. Smart! I hadn't expected much from Marx, but I now understand why he's kept himself so on the "shed" circuit.

To keep the crowd continuously charged, **KISS'** spikes the early and intermediate slots with surprise headliners, often announced just the day or two beforehand. "A lot of times, these acts also have other shows later that day," Kroninger explains:

- "Like, we had Duran Duran the year before last, and they were doin' the MTV Movie Awards, which gets taped that weekend. It seems to coincide with our show every year, and so there's always a few people who're going off to perform on that. We got them in as the opening act. But then by doing that and promoting that fact, we were able to get the seats filled up much better than we had the year prior when it wasn't as heavily loaded at the front of the show. So it serves our interest to try and balance it out.

"You'd be surprised," he continues, repeating this chapter's mantra:

- "There are a lot of people who go there who're, like, moms with grown-up kids and stuff, and these people aren't gonna' be out to 11:30 or 12:00 for baby reasons and all that stuff. So it gives them an opportunity to take part in it because it's kinda' one of those events that has become, like, 'Did you go?'; that everybody wants to be at. There's so much press that comes out before and after it generating so much excitement that it allows them to go and stay for six hours and see, basically, as good of a lineup as anyone who goes for any por-tion of the day sees."

That certainly describes my **KISS'** experience. My wife and I were en route to a Maine weekend and could only stay for four hours, but got more than our money's worth. We even sat next to a middle-aged mom chaperoning her two pre-teens who brought along her knitting nee-dles to keep herself occupied. Her kids didn't mind, since the MTV live remote came right up to our last row and put 'em both on the tube! 'Guess they'll have something to crow about back in class.

"We manage, actually, to grow it every year," Kroninger adds, as if we need any further excuse to return.

- "Each year we try and outdo ourselves. That's one of the things where I think how we got to such an incredible, lengthy lineup is we kept trying to outdo ourselves to make this thing bigger by adding more people every year than you can possibly imagine could be packed into one show.

"I think that has something to do with it, the success, the longevity and just, really, Rich Balsbaugh's commitment to this. I mean, it's his baby he lives for. And it's a whole week-end-long event as far as the station goes. It's a one-day show, basically, but we have all the record guys in for the whole weekend, and the acts, and we have a private pre-party and post-party. You know, I think he loves it. This is his one most shining moment of the year, so he likes to keep it going and do everything; pull out all the stops and make it just a first-class event."

Hallelujah, what a beautiful day! The brilliant sunshine doubtless inspired the mostly twenty-something revelers to doff their shirts — the men, that is. New Englanders there definitely had their own look. Guys: close-cropped hair, white baseball caps with their college insignia over a perfectly-rolled brim, an anonymous T-shirt or Oxford shirt, baggy shorts, low socks, chunky sneakers and one piece of jewelry. No goatees or tattoos, yet. Girls: exactly the same, save for bigger hair and daintier sneakers. All-in-all, **KISS'** drew a clean-cut crowd caught between whoopin' their faves and scoping the opposite sex.

**Festival Review**

I've already covered some of the attention-grabbers from my stint, above, but I did want to mention the Crash Test Dummies, as well.

**Artist Mini-Reviews**

<u>Crash Test Dummies</u>. These guys were new to me, but I found their sound original and compelling. The five-piece band played mostly acoustic and was led by a charismatic vocalist whose unusually arch, droll baritone recalled Iggy Pop or Frank Zappa swallowing their syllables. Still, he projected well and delivered good tunes with interesting lyrics — deliberate, thoughtful, affirming. The crowd reacted to their presumed hit, "Mmm-mmm" (I think I got this chorus line right), but I also enjoyed "Someday" and "If I Could Meet The Artists." I suppose I'll pop down to the store and pick up their disc for a closer listen!

Kroninger's always too busy orchestrating **KISS'**s incredible backstage whirlwind for any music-viewing himself, but he did recall one particular highlight:

- "1989. <u>Cher</u>! Big show! Our Program Director at that time, Sonny Joe White, knew her personally and convinced her to come out. It was the first time she'd performed live in, like, years! That was really somethin' because she was like a nervous, nervous wreck. She just had not performed on stage for so long — she was just kind of riding high on hits on the radio — and she just did not know how she was gonna' be received. That was really cool."

Cher's triumphant return capped such a gaudy lineup that nobody even bothered complaining when Rod Stewart, who was on the premises, had to cancel his night's closer due to "throat problems." Now, there's a party!

**Attendance Tip**

Copping the **KISS'** tickets requires quick reflexes. The reserved pavilion seats are typically gone in a matter of hours, while the lawn seats disappear after a few days. You'll need to stay on top of Ticketmaster for the opening sale date, which usually precedes the show by roughly five weeks.

Tickets aren't cheap, mind you, but a portion of the proceeds goes for a good cause. Each year, the **KISS'** contributes $50,000 to the Genesis Fund, a charity devoted to "the specialized care and treatment of New England children born with birth defects, genetic diseases and mental retardation." Balsbaugh's on their Board, so you know the funds are being properly channeled and applied.

~ ~ ~

*Rockin' Dopsie and The Zydeco Twisters meet The Sunshine Skiffle Band, Lowell Folk Festival.*

# Boston's Jazz Edge

**BOSTON GLOBE JAZZ FESTIVAL**, Boston, MA
Middle June
Modern Jazz
***Attended***

This is the one with the attitude! Of all the leading jazz festivals George Wein's Festival **Introduction**
Productions, Inc. [FPI] handles, the BOSTON GLOBE JAZZ FESTIVAL stands tallest in featuring cutting-edge artists — sufficiently so that I'm tempted to move its classification one notch leftward into the realm of alternative jazz. And that's a compliment!

It may not have quite the budget of its other FPI contemporaries, such as New York City's JVC JAZZ FESTIVAL (see chapter), but programmers use that to their advantage. When the New York City fest wanted a Latin night last year, for example, they thumbed their well-worn Rolodex for the legendary Tito Puente and paired him up with vocal hero Celia Cruz. 'Hard to complain about seeing the exuberant Puente and his wonderful band — yet again — but check out these Latin artists from recent Boston bashes: Willie Colon and Legal Alien, Danilo Perez Quintet, Jerry Gonzalez and The Fort Apache Band, Eddie Palmieri and his Orchestra, Mario Bauza and his Orchestra, Milton Cardona, plus all those up-and-comers who comprised the late Dizzy Gillespie's United Nations Orchestra. And these were just the national acts! The local Latin stars had plenty to offer in their own right. Many were programmed for free-wheeling dances, moreover, not at stuffy concert halls.

Three parties merit applause for letting out the leash. First, the city's daily newspaper, the *Boston Globe*, has sponsored the festival for the past 27 years specifically to showcase the Boston scene. That means presenting Boston artists to all parts of Boston, not just at a few downtown sites. Last year there was not a single repeat venue as 19 paid and free concerts were staged from one end of town to the other. (Talk about a producer's nightmare!)

Second, Boston's jazz scene, which the 'Globe covers, hasn't yet gotten the nationwide recognition it deserves. However, it is exceptionally strong and surprisingly diverse, even on the ethnic side as Boston's strong Latin, Caribbean, and Brazilian communities have produced many fine musicians with plenty of events to work. Its top-rated music schools sharpen the edge by recruiting leading, often-experimental practitioners the world over to teach at places like the Berklee College of Music, the New England Conservatory and the Boston Conservatory. (Harvard, M. I. T., Northeastern, and several others also maintain jazz posts.) Once there, instructors such as Ricky Ford find a welcoming audience among Boston's liberal listeners while taking advantage of the nation's closest international airport to Europe where they land a majority of their big-paying gigs. Students also keep in touch as they go on to "bigger and better" — witness such home-taught talent as Geoff Keezer, Christian McBride and Joshua Redman being brought back for last year's BOSTON GLOBE JAZZ FESTIVAL.

Third, FPI gets a special pat-on-the-back for smoothly accommodating the publication's wishes, for booking national artists that broaden and compliment the local flow (two good examples from 1993's bill involved Chicago's Ed Wilkerson Jr. and 8 Bold Souls, as well as Austrian-born, Berklee-trained guitar whiz Wolfgang Muthspiel), and for not letting the programming drift far afield to where audiences are alienated, or where diminished attendance jeopardizes the event's finances.

Kudos to all for one of my very favorite jazz festivals!

Dan Melnick is the FPI producer who's inherited 1994's affair in what must seem like a dream come true. This is the 26-year-old's first hand on the reigns after four years assisting with other FPI affairs across the world. Needless to say, Melnick is pumped for the task. "It's an amazing,

amazing thing and I've been very lucky," he exclaims, "but it is very frantic and very insane and very demanding at the same time:

- "One of the beauties about Boston that I've come to learn in the last few months is that because the *'Globe* is so open to allowing us to do what we like to do, it's a very open situation for a producer, a very giving situation. ...It's saying to us, 'Give us everything you got and be interesting and be diverse and take a chance because it's free and it's small stages and it's all over the city.' And it's great, it's been so much fun! It's given me the opportunity to really do some things that I've wanted to do for the last few years that I just haven't had the chance to do. I'm very grateful for that."

One example involves moving the festival's centerpiece, a three-act maxi-concert kicking off the week, from Boston Common to the Hatch Shell on the Charles River — just a few blocks walk from the "Cheers" bar. Another was expanding the delightful solo concert site I attended last year at the rim of Jamaica Pond into a three-act mini-festival to close the show.

As for individual artists, here's a few Melnick is psyched to showcase:

- Re: <u>Joe Lovano/Tom Harrell</u>. "Lovano has been for years an absolutely brilliant force on the scene and finally we, as a company, are starting to book him as a leader. He's going to be in Newport (JVC NEWPORT JAZZ FESTIVAL, Newport, RI — see chapter) this year, and he's also working at Saratoga (NEWPORT JAZZ FESTIVAL/SARATOGA, Saratoga Springs, NY — see chapter) this year for us, too. And I think that it's time. Joe is a Berklee alum. As a matter of fact, last month he was on the cover of *Berklee Today*. He's got a helluva' following up in Boston; he's a monster.

  "And Tom Harrell, he's a musician's musician and he's one of the most lyrical and melodic and beautiful trumpet players out there. And I felt very, very strongly about booking Tom as a leader because he is the perennial side man. He's led some brilliant bands in the clubs and his records are fantastic, and I really wanted him to lead his own group — I didn't want him to be Joe's guest as he was at [New York City's Village Vanguard] last month.

  "I called the agent, who happens to represent both bands, and I said, 'I want the package, and this is what I can afford, and I want you to make this work.' And he did! I feel very, very lucky about that, and I really have a lot of confidence that that show will do some incredible business. I think it's going to be a great critical show up there for the press and the media, and for the scene, I think its gonna' be great."

- Re: <u>Wayne Naus</u>. "The opening act on the Hatch concert is going to be a guy named Wayne Naus, who has a brilliant, smokin' Latin-jazz band. He is a professor at Berklee. It's the first time he has ever played on the festival, but I gave him this opening slot, which is a very, very important position, because he's got this band, and it's absolutely insane. I mean, they're just fantastic!

  "I went to Boston about a month ago to do some business up there and stayed at a friend's apartment. I was looking through his CD collection and Wayne's CD was there, and I said, 'Geez, what's this?' And he said, 'Oh man, this guy's amazing. He plays every month at so-and-so' — some small club. I put the CD on and whammo, he's got this eight-piece band, three horns up front, he's a trumpet player, and it was brilliant. I called him and I said, 'Man, this CD is smokin'!' He said, 'Oh, great, I got this band, you know, and we never get to play." (He tours Europe where he makes his money.) I said, 'Well, I've got a slot available for you, and I really want you to do this date." He was available, and we made a deal, and there it is. He is very happy and excited and I am, too, 'cause I think its gonna' start off the festival with a bang!"

- Re: <u>Mili Bermejo</u>. "We're gonna close the festival this year on Saturday afternoon with a mini-festival at Jamaica Pond. I've booked three bands there, and one of them is Mili Bermejo. She is a Boston vocalist, but she's from Mexico, and she is a Latin-jazz vocalist who sings in English and Spanish. She's got a helluva' band, and she's a really beautiful singer. So I kinda' book-ended the festival with two outdoor, free festivals and tried to have Latin jazz on both of them."

This whole discussion of the festival's Latin programming sprung from my complimenting their customary Latin dance party. Melnick confesses his current difficulties with performance fees, airline costs, artist routing, and site-selection, all which cast doubt on the dance party's return for 1994. He offers Naus and Bermejo as his Latin alternatives.

"One of the major, major factors in our planning and our business, and something that I've learned from George [Wein]," Melnick confides, "is to be wise with the money so that you can continue to do what you're doing — not sacrificing artistic value of the shows or what you want to present — but just being smart. And this is one of the situations with this Latin program where it might be more beneficial to the [financial] health of the festival to pass on the show this year."

Otherwise, Melnick considers a real treat of his first producer's experience as getting to know Boston's prolific jazz milieu:

- "You can say everything you want to know about jazz being in New York, but the scene up there in Boston is pretty heavy. I have about 30 or 40 CDs and tapes that I've gotten from all these unbelievable musicians that I'd never heard of before. That's great for me because the more I learn about the music and the more musicians I get to know about, the better it is for me, and the more that I can do.

"I think the personal highlight for me [is] that I have been given the opportunity to do something that George used to do early in his career, himself, as an individual. When you read the heading on the festival, it says 'Produced by George Wein,' it doesn't say 'Festival Productions.' For me, that's an honor... The fact that George has seen in me the confidence to take this on, something that he quote-unquote, produces, is very special. If the festival is successful I'll be even happier.

"The history is there and the future is right in front of us," Melnick concludes, "and we're just trying to just continue the tradition of the festival and to be as current and as challenging as possible. One of my goals is to just continue to bring a first-class event to a first-class city!"

**Festival Review**

Tuesday afternoon's free concert at Jamaica Pond is a perfect illustration of the BOSTON GLOBE JAZZ FESTIVAL's embracing its neighborhoods and bringing the music to the people. The location is equivalent to an outer borough of New York City, say Queens, with this particular strip buffering the working classes of Roxbury from the upper classes of Brookline. New Yorkers can similarly picture Queens' namesake, Jamaica Estates.

However unlikely this destination might be considered for world-class music, it did offer pretty, Watteau-like visuals of grassy hills dipping down to wispy willows and the reservoir beyond. A perfectly relaxed and pastoral vibe. Half the laid-back crowd seemed to be neighborhood families of all races and incomes interspersed with serious jazz heads (you can always spot 'em by their festival t-shirts), while the other half looked like joggers and bikers captivated by the music sufficiently to interrupt their workouts 'round the pond paths. With a brisk breeze pushing dappled clouds, all eyes were on the Tiger.

**Artist Mini-Review**

Tiger's Baku. For trumpeter Tiger Okoshi, this was like coming full circle. First, his near-annual appearance here always represents something of a homecoming to where he's resided since graduating from Berklee in 1975 (Okoshi being more likely to be gigging abroad). Second, he was debuting his new album, "That Was Then, This Was Now" which paid homage to his original inspiration, Louis Armstrong, whom Okoshi witnessed during a 1961 concert in his native Japan. Okoshi was 11 at the time, in case you're wondering.

Okoshi fronted an electrified four-piece band consisting of keyboards, guitar, bass, and drums. They were amply capable of a broad range of styles from kickin' funk to pretty ballads to smooth fusion to straight-ahead. Okoshi amused with his self-deprecating stage banter in fractured English, much like that wacky Asian cook on cable TV. His opening tune, "Fruit of the Root," referred to musical heritage, he explained, not the underwear.

I especially enjoyed Okoshi's tributes and interpretations of Armstrong tunes, including a silky "Never." The highlight was his entrancing cover of "St. Louis Blues," which Okoshi recreated in spirit to what he noted was Armstrong's original version as a tango, a la Jelly Roll Morton. A wonderful concept given a strong treatment as Okoshi kept the composition segue-ing into supple swing time for his solos. My notes simply read, "Yeah!" — sentiments echoed loudly by the hometown crowd.

**Travel Tip**  "One of the most special things to do in Boston is go to Fenway [Park, home of the Boston Red Sox]," Melnick suggests, "because it's just such an amazing place. On the street right behind the Green Monster [i.e, west side] at the corner, there's an excellent brew pub. It's a restaurant, like a burger joint, but they make like 8-to-10 different home-made brews every day. I was there about a month ago. The food is really good and the beer is fantastic, just delicious. Boston is known for their home-made brews."

Otherwise, I recommend taking in all the nooks and crannies of the city the festival will expose you to during the day and after the concerts, to patronize the various participants in the "Globe Jazz Festival Week at the Clubs." Music tourism at its finest!

~　　~　　~

# Boston's Celtic Galas

BOSTON SCOTTISH FIDDLE RALLY, Cambridge, MA
> Middle April
> Scottish

IRISH CULTURAL CENTER'S FESTIVAL, North Easton, MA
> Middle June
> Irish
> ***Attended***

CELTIC FESTIVAL AT THE HATCH SHELL, Boston, MA
> Early September
> Scottish

GAELIC ROOTS: THE MUSIC, SONG AND DANCE OF IRELAND, Chestnut Hill, MA
> Early October
> Irish

**Introduction**

Irish expatriate Oscar Wilde once punned, "Nothing exceeds like excess." He must have imagined the IRISH CULTURAL CENTER'S FESTIVAL (formerly, A GALA IRISH CELEBRATION) held on the grassy, dewy fields of Stonehill College out in the leafy Southern suburbs of Boston.

In cooking up his cultural stew, Founder and Chairman Edward Barron likes to build the base with traditional Irish musicians whom he labels, "the heart and soul of the festival." These acts might include the likes of Cape Breton fiddler Natalie MacMaster, New York City ensemble Cherish the Ladies, and local heros, fiddler Seamus Connolly or harpist Aine Minogue.

Then Barron spikes the broth with major names such as folk vets, The Clancy Brothers...

- Plus Irish-American rock groups from the alternative scenes of Boston and New York such as rowdy Black 47 and the U2-ish Cliffs of Dooneen...

- Plus commercial "show-bands" straight out of a Catskills wedding such as Joe Glynn and Irish Mist...

- Plus a plethora of activities, such as rugby games, step-dancing, film screenings, story telling and a "Dublin Horse Jumping Show"...

- Plus a 300-foot street market, carnival rides, a beer garden, exhibit tents, a tea house, a food emporium, and Heaven knows what else.

Plus, plus, plus! The result? Something truly savory for everybody — 40,000 revelers in all, from ages 8-to-80 — in one of the most fun-loving events I graced upon all year!

Remarkably, Barron describes his prior musical background as "none whatsoever — I had never even been to a festival before." With 325,000 Irish-Americans living within a 20-minute drive of the site, though, he felt he had a compelling market to serve.

Barron recounts in his delightful lilt how he visited three Irish festivals to prepare: Tewksbury, MA (see IRISH FESTIVAL IN THE PARK, Middle July); Bethlehem, PA (see CHEVROLET CELTIC CLASSIC, Late September); and the biggest of them all in Milwaukee, WI (see MILWAUKEE IRISH FESTIVAL, Late August). He and fellow members of the Irish Cultural Center then sat down and designed their dream event from scratch.

"When we conceived the idea of a festival," Barron explains:

- "A lot of people told us that [Irish] festivals aren't working anymore... But the reason they're not making it is they're not offering the quality product. People today, I think, are very conscious of, 'Is there some depth to the festival?' They want to be able to walk somewhere else and get educated and what have you. They're not interested in drinking festivals. Even though we sell a lot of drink, we don't make that a priority."

What Barron does make as priorities are two-fold. First, there's a multiplicity of experience. For example, you can study historical exhibits with themes like "Avenue of the Presidents," or "Ireland's Contribution to Industrial America." Or, you can also walk across the way to the Tea House for a sip and some scones and enjoy a more hands-on experience of daily Irish culture. Ditto for the concession tents, the children's activities, the dancing options, and such. Barron's even working on importing traditional buskers from abroad to stroll between the tents.

Second, there's a multiplicity of audiences being served. Barron lists six distinct segments he caters to (one being a growing Scottish contingent), including the most overlooked constituency in family festivals: teens and twenties.

Barron shrewdly schedules rock bands Friday night expressly for "the kids," as he calls them, then watches their restless spirits taking in other traditional offerings. "If you ask one of those Irish kids to a show band in the show-band tent," Barron chuckles, "they will laugh at you! When you actually go into the show-band tent on Friday or Saturday night, those are the ones dancing and having a blast. It kind of educates them to that extent."

Things are going so well on the pop/rock side, Barron is negotiating with Van Morrison, The Cranberries, and others for 1994 to supplement his range of traditional acts. Barron laughs: "The older folks say, 'Who's Van Morrison,' but they'll find out when they try to park, and all the spaces are taken up.

"In regards to doing the festival," Barron concludes, "we're only limited by our imagination. We're open for anything at all that's going to give it the [inclusive] spirit we want to achieve. People get entertainment with an education and a part of their heritage, you see? It's all tied up in one."

**Festival Review I**   Up 48 hours straight, bleary-eyed from having driven over 2,000 miles between four other festivals that weekend, I staggered into the last few hours of the IRISH CULTURAL CENTER'S FESTIVAL Saturday night wanting nothing more than a warm bed. The whole scene was so festive, however, that I left fully revived and satisfied.

The huge fields were lit up like a Christmas tree. Lights streamed out from underneath an endless walkway of tents for crafts, food, brew, exhibits and, above all, dancing — lending a warm, inviting feeling for exploring and imbibing. The whole backside of the site was right out of fantasy land, with neon-lit carnival rides for the children, plus a main stage decorated like a Disney castle. Rows of plastics chairs were thoughtfully provided, but most of us were too busy sampling things to sit still.

I would've pictured kitschy show bands as more for my aunts and uncles. Just as Barron said, however, teens crowded the dance floor and gleefully whirled each other around in what were, no doubt, just-learned ceilidh steps. It was fascinating to see this unlikely segment grab hold of a traditional activity and make it their own, just like the bluegrass fans in Escoheag, RI, gone mad about Cajun dancing.

Same deal with The Clancy Brothers as teens out-numbered retirees maybe three-to-one.

**Artist Mini-Review**   <u>The Clancy Brothers</u>. On the folk side, I feel The Clancy Brothers have not yet been given their proper due in inaugurating the "Great Folk Scare" in the 60's. True, families like the Weavers, the Seegers, the Carters, and the Watsons had kept the flame alive for decades, but the Clancys helped pioneer the club scene in New York City, making it possible for a young Bob Dylan to migrate there and earn a living. It was no accident that backstage at the recent Dylan Tribute Concert everyone was joining the Clancys in Irish songs.

On the ethnic side, it would've been impossible to grow up Irish-American in the early '60s and not know every tune of theirs by heart. If my father didn't have one of their scratchy LPs on the hi-fi, then my mother did. Their irresistible hooks buried themselves deep in the subconscious — if you couldn't recall the lyrics off hand, all you needed was a chorus and you'd find the words spilling from you as if drawn out by a divining rod.

That's exactly what happened Saturday night to me and about 10,000 others from all age groups. The four — brothers Paddy, Bobby and Liam, with nephew Robbie O'Connell — led what amounted to a 60-minute singalong. Some songs, like "The Irish Rover," were unabashedly sentimental and simple enough for toddlers. Others, like "Whiskey You're the Devil," well, what can you say about a pub standard. Liam Clancy peppered his ingratiating stage banter with tippling references, emphasizing that their fall festival cruiseliner, the S. S. Norway, had 13 bars and how he intended to have a drink in every one of them! This brought roars from the surprising number of fairly-buzzed college kids crashed out on the straw before the stage.

They intermingled infectious rhythms, melodies and harmonies, accessible verses, amusing narratives, generous spirits, twinkling winks, and choruses so solid you could hop aboard and ride them like one of those Dublin ponies on display. That's how the Clancys capped the evening, putting on a virtual clinic in entertaining that any performer would've profited from.

~     ~     ~

**GAELIC ROOTS: THE MUSIC, SONG AND DANCE OF IRELAND**, presented by Boston College's Irish Studies Program and Music Department under the guiding hand of master-fiddler Seamus Connolly, is about one-tenth the size of the **IRISH CULTURAL CENTER'S FESTIVAL** and hones in on traditional music exclusively. It emphasizes an outpouring of quality players across three traditional Celtic styles — Irish, Scottish, and Cape Breton — in workshops, in concerts, or in dance sessions and ceilidhs. Earle Hitchner, covering the 1993 festival for the *Irish Echo*, cited the breadth of outstanding performances as well as the "laser-direct and unshakable communication" between artists and the attentive crowd. **[Festival Review II]**

When I've got more of a budget in future editions, I'll pay to reprint the whole of Hitchner's glowing review. For now, here are excerpts of what he had to say about the following artists: **[Artist Mini-Reviews]**

- American fiddle prodigy, Eileen Ivers: "great confidence and maturity...her bowhand work is second to none";

- Button accordionist James Keane: "hard-driving and exhilarating";

- Uilleann pipers Robbie Hannan, Jerry O'Sullivan, Paddy Keenan and Matty Connolly: "in top trim...cutting loose brilliantly";

- Cape Breton fiddle ace, Natalie MacMaster: "first rate";

- Tin whistler and ex-Chieftain, Sean Potts: "jubilant...high spirits."

Kitchner lauded the educational workshops and lectures in particular, summarizing the day as "pure magic, never to be forgotten by those lucky enough to attend."

The Irish Cultural Center also helps subsidize a fine concert on Labor Day, the **CELTIC FESTIVAL AT THE HATCH SHELL**, which is produced by the Boston Scottish Fiddle Club with assistance from Boston's MetroParks. Like **GAELIC ROOTS**, you'll enjoy a mix of Irish, Scottish and Cape-Breton musical styles from some of the better players in New England, including several up-and-comers. **[See Also]**

While we're talking about the Boston Scottish Fiddle Club, you won't want to miss their **BOSTON SCOTTISH FIDDLE RALLY** in the Cambridge area, consisting of a master concert, two days of workshops, and a dance. It's a spirited way to pass a cold April weekend!

~     ~     ~

# Northampton's College World-Beat

BRIGHT MOMENTS FESTIVAL, Amherst, MA
Middle July to Late July
Variety, Jazz and Blues
***Attended***

**Introduction** The Fine Arts Center, planted amidst the concrete blocks and grassy expanses of the University of Massachusetts at Amherst (U/Mass), has been so far out in front of "multi-culturalism" that most jazz festivals are only now catching up.

Their BRIGHT MOMENTS FESTIVAL has been presenting summer concerts in a jazz/world-beat vein since 1979. For every concert that featured mainstream jazz artists such as U/Mass Adjunct Professor, drummer Max Roach or U/Mass Ph. D., pianist Billy Taylor, they'd put on another the prior week spotlighting a Latin artist (e.g., percussionist Tito Puente); then a third the following week with an African artist (e.g., trumpeter Hugh Masakela) — thus completing the circle on the African-American/Hispanic aspect of jazz music.

Yvonne Mendez, Managing Director of this cheery, homey affair, summarizes their long-standing mission to "present works by people of color and really look at jazz as a growing musical form."

Of course, there are other, more practical, considerations. "There really wasn't any programming happening [here] in the summer," Mendez continues. "There was a need for some kind of event that would cater more to students, graduate students, and married students with families. BRIGHT MOMENTS is really geared for families."

What she doesn't say, though, is that the festival is also great for dancing. Weather permitting, the concerts are held outside. There, on a broad lawn by a pond rimmed with vendors, folks are encouraged to get up and boogie if the spirit moves them. Indeed, Mendez evaluates successful bookings in terms of spontaneous dance combustions: "Pancho Sanchez was fantastic! We got a really, really good response. The group was great; the audience loved it. He had a mix of music that really had people dancing." ("Dancing," see?)

Mendez credits an enlightened programming committee that sorts among its many submissions to arrive at themes and selections for its two world-beat concerts. The remaining concert features associate faculty members and advanced students from the school's two-week Jazz in July Workshop in Improvisation. In 1992 this workshop aggregation included Taylor, Roach, Sheila Jordan, and members of the Jazz All Stars — Ted Dunbar, Charles Ellison, Jeff Holmes, Don Stratton, Frederick Tillis — plus two separate student groups calling themselves "Jazz in July Express I and II."

**Festival Review** The workshop concert was the one I caught on a drizzly day that forced the affair indoors to an auditorium. Spirits remained sunny as the umber tones of the carpet, the fabric seats, the wooden stage, the attractive backdrop design (a portrait of John Coltrane, undoubtedly blowing a solo on one of his signature tunes, "Bright Moments"), and the funky T-shirts helped project an especially comfortable feeling.

**Artist Mini-Reviews** Sheila Jordan. An inside joke of mine would be to include jazz vocalist Sheila Jordan on my own list of Talent Deserving Wider Recognition. That's because she's virtually owned the same-titled category appearing annually in *Down Beat*, winning their Critic's Poll nine times over 25 years. However, the recent wave of layoffs in the advertising industry, which cost her a long-time day job as a receptionist, helped push her into the spotlight as a full-time artist. The day is hopefully coming soon where you won't be saying, "This singer's great, who is she?"

Jordan, sporting her trademark page-boy haircut, looked regal in a floor-length purple velour dress. My notes on her unique vocal style read, "poetry in motion," though you could picture her sound as what pop-singer Rickie Lee Jones might sound like with 30 years' experience interacting with the best jazz players in the country.

She handled a wide range of genres with ease: sorta' bop ("Bottom Out Oriole"), quasi-samba (Tom Harrell's "Sail Away"), light swing ("If I Had You"), and vocalese ("Where You At"). Each selection contained challenging lyrics that Jordan enunciated clearly, regardless of whatever liberties her phrasing took. Her highlight, though, was on her most lyrically-simplistic cover, "Inchworm," where she lent the children's tune a poignant, atonal drama. I'd describe how she intercut "Walking My Baby Back Home," but it wouldn't work — you just had to be there.

<u>Max Roach</u>. Drumming legend Max Roach looked sharp: blue blazer over a white turtle-neck with houndstooth slacks and black-and-white wing tips. He brought a dignity and purpose-fulness to his drum kit at first, but then relaxed later with some funny asides (sample: kidding the band on introducing Coleman Hawkin's "Mountain Out" — "Be careful, 'cause the drummer up here thinks he's tricky."). His set only consisted of four or five numbers but left you exhausted from his subtle virtuosity.

The highlight was his closer, a solo on nothing more than his kick snare and stool.

Five months before at the Spectacor Presidential Jazz Festival (see Philadelphia, PA, Middle February), Roach closed his set similarly, but walked off without a word. This time, in befitting a familiar academic setting, he explained how his inspiration, Philly Joe Jones, topped off a 12-hour tribute of drummers to Gene Krupa in New York's Central Park during the Newport Jazz Festival many years back (JVC Jazz Festival, New York, NY — see chapter). Roach cited Jones's influence in creating the vocabulary of swing beats while drumming with the Count Basie Band — in essence, laying down the foundation for the dominant genre in jazz prior to bebop. Jones was considered the authority among that day's community of great drummers.

By bringing it down to this baseline — an understated solo on just the kick snare — then Jones, now Roach, was able to articulate a virtual history of jazz drumming, after which nobody had anything left to say. It was a fitting cap to a spell-binding clinic as Roach walked off to a sus-tained, standing ovation. History repeats!

**Travel Tip**

The concerts occur on consecutive weeks, midweek, so you'd have to stretch to make a mini-vaca-tion out of it. Not to worry, says Mendez, who recommends just coming for the day: "It's a big event. It's not just the music, it's really the atmosphere of being outside amidst the crafts and food and dancing."

**See Also**

If you enjoy this mix of jazz and world beat and are targeting New England for your travel plans, you should also investigate the Discover Jazz Festival in Burlington, VT, the prior month (see chapter). It's run by different promoters, but offers more of the same high quality acts in an equal-ly delightful small-town environment.

~     ~     ~

# Lowell's Ethnic Folk Traditions

PRAISE AND HARMONY, Lowell, MA
    Middle June
    Black Gospel

LATIN AMERICAN FESTIVAL, Lowell, MA
    Late June
    Traditional Latin

BOARDING HOUSE PARK CONCERT SERIES KICKOFF, Lowell, MA
    Early July
    Variety, Folk and International

**LOWELL FOLK FESTIVAL**, Lowell, MA
    Late July
    Variety, Folk and International
    ***Attended***

SUMMERTIME BLUES WEEKEND, Lowell, MA
    Middle August
    Blues and Traditional R&B

JOHNSTOWN FOLK FESTIVAL, Johnstown, PA
    Early September
    Variety, Folk and International
    ***Attended***

BANJO AND FIDDLE CONTESTS, Lowell, MA
    Middle September
    Fiddle and Banjo Events

LOWELL FAMILY FIRST NIGHT, Lowell, MA
    Late December
    Modern Folk

**Introduction**  Lowell is an extraordinary place for history and architecture buffs. While many historic enclaves retain their residential or mercantile quaintness, Lowell celebrates a long timeline of blue collar work. It's been a mill town since the early days of the industrial revolution in the 1820's. Textile barons with names like Lowell and Cabot ("...where the Lowells talk only to Cabots and Cabots talk only to God") diverted water power from the adjoining Merrimack Falls to create an imposing warren of canals and factories.

There's water racing past you on all different levels, lending a sense of near vertigo as you make your way through a labyrinth of brick archways, granite curbs, and cobblestone streets. Monolithic red factory walls, punctuated with rows of framed windows, dominate the scene. The closest effect I can recall is spinning around before the towering sandstone cliffs of New Mexico's Canyon de Chelle.

Lowell native and former U. S. Senator, Paul Tsongas, prompted a restoration drive in the late '70s which led to much of this unique property being preserved and maintained by the U. S. Government as as the Lowell National Historic Park. Where once sat a monument to industrial decay, now boasts an emerging community of condo conversions, offices, shops, and hotels.

The Federal Park Service had its NATIONAL FOLK FESTIVAL touch down for a three-year stint from 1987 to 1989, but the Lowell park staff extended it on their own to keep the economic-development momentum going. The LOWELL FOLK FESTIVAL now draws 200,000 people each year for a free ethnic-folk frolic on six stages. Things are going so well, they've launched a summer-long concert series at its Boarding House Park, which contains all the other festival events listed above within its weekly schedule.

All told, they promise a hot time in the old mill town tonight!

"You're seeing a commitment to traditional music," explains Audrey Ambrosino, Public Information Officer for the Lowell National Historic Park and member of the talent selection committee for the LOWELL FOLK FESTIVAL. "The Northeast really lends itself to that kind of thing. It's where a lot of ethnic groups have settled, made their homes, and practiced their crafts or music — and still do to a great extent. It's not that difficult to find real quality performers, and real quality presentation, as well." **Festival Review**

Ambrosino's not kidding!

I spent two full days here, thanks to my car breaking down in the parking lot, yet did not experience a bad act. Most every performer shined, whether it was one of the usual folk headliners, or some local act unknown to anyone but their family and friends. I even saw several ethnic genres in a whole new light: Polish, Greek, Cape-Verdean, Cape-Breton — hey, their musics were fun, not just questions to $500 answers on TV's "Jeopardy."

Of course, I was usually finger-popping with one hand while holding some edible delight in the other. The rows of food booths, comprising a virtual encyclopedia of ethnic delicacies, were situated right in the middle of downtown Lowell amidst the five main stages. You couldn't help but be tempted as you wandered past from one act to the next. Budget an extra five pounds for the weekend, I'd say.

"The food is certainly not to be missed," Ambrosino confirms with a devilish chuckle, but cites her favorite feature as the street parade:

- "In 1993 we had an all-girl band from New Orleans [The Pinettes Brass Band], basically high school girls, but boy could they play! We start in Boston's Fanueil Hall. The band gathers up people in Boston parading through town before taking the train to Lowell and parading through the streets here. They just played their hearts out; the community really responded. They probably weren't the most experienced, or the best, band in New Orleans for sure, but the spirit and the energy and the music were there. And the community was there. It really represented what the festival was all about.

  "Then there are these real quiet moments which are also special. We had a Native-American dancer who was very quiet, very petite. Her movements were absolutely graceful, very intricate. She captured the band as much as the brass band did, but in a different way — another part of people's spirit and emotion. That's the beauty of this festival; there's something to capture all of your moods and interests.

"The festival is looked at by the folk-festival community as one to learn from in terms of how we program and how we pull off the logistics," Ambrosino claims:

- "It's earned a lot of respect in the festival community. That adds a level of respect to the event and the city hosting the event. [Our greatest compliment, however] is hearing people who have never been to Lowell talk about what a great city Lowell is and how great the people of Lowell are in hosting it, just being so friendly. At the same time, it's hearing from the people of Lowell — their pride that the festival is here and that those other people come in.

"I like to think of it," reflects Ambrosino, "as the City of Lowell opening it's doors to all types of people, all communities and people interested in having a good time... It's sort of a welcoming weekend to see what Lowell has to offer."

**Artist Mini-Reviews**

<u>Algiers Brass Band</u>. There were all kinds of good-timin' performances in 1992 (e.g., Sunshine Skiffle Band, Walt Solek's polkas delivered in a clown suit, Cape-Verdean Norberto Tavares and Tropical Power, etc.), but none was as much fun as the Algiers Brass Band's street parade Saturday evening. Several hundred revelers, many boasting New Orleans "JAZZFEST" shirts, immediately fell into some genuine second-lining. Led by trumpeter, Ruddy Thibodeaux, the band boogied for blocks to "Didn't He Ramble" and other standards before depositing us in the South Common for the nighttime concert.

<u>Los Pleneros del Batey</u>. This Philadelphia-based troupe of 14 were a wonderful discovery. They specialize in an acoustic-string-driven folk music from the mountains of Puerto Rico called "plena," or "jibaro," although they'd also toss in some examples of the more African-percussion-influenced "bomba" music from the coast.

Each male member was clad in matching white slacks, red shirts, white kerchiefs, and white straw hats. There was a lone female dancer in a flowing purple skirt, and she and her male partner illustrated each song with a demonstration. Employing big smiles, joyous movements, colorful costumes, informative introductions, and irresistible rhythms they rounded up half of JFK Civic Plaza, Sunday afternoon, into a swirling, cheering conga line for their closer, "Don't Bury My Clothes."

<u>Charles Brown</u>. Brown was probably the festival's chief headliner, although, if Bonnie Raitt hadn't rescued him for her 1990 tour, he'd likely have remained a footnote in the history of R&B. Rock and roll bands in the 1950's followed Louis Jordan, but R&B singers such as Ray Charles were more inspired by Brown's classy vocal stylings and uptown keyboard tinklings.

Brown certainly looked the part in a black dinner jacket, gold vest, and black velvet cap faintly twinkling with tiny rhinestones. His four-piece band looked sharp, too, in their black tuxedos and French cuffs with onyx links. Ooo-ah. Smooth cocktail jazz/swing (e.g., "Turn Me Loose"), supported by impeccable drumming, comprised his early set Saturday night. Soon, though, Brown delved into a medley of down-and-dirty blues from his 1940's heyday that had me groovin': "I'm Drinkin'," "Dad Gum Whiskey," and "After My Baby Has Gone."

<u>Laurie Lewis and Grant Street</u>. Bluegrass bands frustrate me. Put 'em front of a big crowd where I can finally tout their virtues to nonbelievers, and they choke. Put 'em in the close confines, however, and they come back to life. That was the story of West Coast fiddle-wizard Laurie Lewis and her progressive quartet of pickers and singers called Grant Street. Their set list Saturday night before 10,000 was herky-jerky and tentative — you don't do a bunch of ballads when people want to party!

The next day's gig in the cozy horseshoe of JFK Civic Plaza was a whole different story. Lewis' tunes flowed well from one to the next, building a nice momentum. Her selections, originals and covers, were interesting and well-introduced by her amusing, personable confessionals. She gave her whole band (including guitar-ace "Mahavishnu" Peter McLaughlin, as she tagged him) plenty of space to shine before ending with an uptempo "Diamond Joe." Redeemed.

<u>The Rankin Family</u>. The *Boston Herald* described them that year as "dazzling." The *Boston Globe* called them "charming." The *Lowell Sun* cited their "crowd-pleasing debut [featuring] spine-tingling harmonies." Get the picture? I felt the Nova-Scotia-based Rankin Family were the hit of 1992's bash. Not bad for a seven-piece band that had only been playing professionally for three years.

This attractive gaggle of fresh-faced twenty-somethings were led by the guitar/vocals of John Morris plus the fiddle/vocals of brother, Jimmy, with the three sisters, Heather, Cookie, and Raylene alternating lead and harmony vocals. Two others supplied the rhythm. Their sound was an acoustic mix of Irish standards and traditional country originals — "The Chieftains meet The McCarters" — that was crisp, accessible, and captivating. "The Fisherman's Song" and "Fare Thee Well Love" were followed by a sweetly-rousing version of "Marie's Wedding" that finished with the three lasses step-dancing in unison. A winning mix!

Ambrosino recommends a variety of day trips to other historical attractions, including **Travel Tip**
Minuteman National Park, Walden Pond and Old Sturbridge Village. She also says, "We're so
close to Boston that, in terms of nightlife, you can certainly hop in your car and be there in 30 minutes for a play, a restaurant, or what have you."

PRAISE AND HARMONY, the LATIN AMERICAN FESTIVAL, the BOARDING HOUSE PARK CONCERT SERIES **See Also**
KICKOFF, the SUMMERTIME BLUES WEEKEND, and the BANJO AND FIDDLE CONTESTS are all part of the
summer-long concert series at Boarding House Park. The first four events feature multiple acts per
day programmed by outside groups, but you can find out more information by calling the Lowell
National Historic Park. The latter contests are put on by the park, although they plan to present
them on an every-other-year basis beginning in 1995.

The NATIONAL FOLK FESTIVAL left Johnstown, PA, in 1992 before heading off to its next
three-year engagement in Chattanooga, TN, from 1993 to 1995. Johnstown's organizers decided,
like Lowell's, to maintain it as the JOHNSTOWN FOLK FESTIVAL. Mosey over there Labor Day weekend for similar ethnic-folk offerings on multiple stages.

Finally, the LOWELL FAMILY FIRST NIGHT began in 1993, though I've no word on whether it's
maintained ongoing. One key performer from that year's affair was Scott Alarik, Publisher of the
*New England Folk Almanac* and folk critic for the *Boston Globe*. Wherever he's involved, look for a
flock of fine New England folkies to follow.

~     ~     ~

# Booking The LOWELL FOLK FESTIVAL: A Conversation With Joe Wilson.

*Speaking with Joe Wilson, who coordinates talent booking for the NATIONAL FOLK FESTIVAL among his many other activities in the music business, is like wading into a warm bath or pulling up a chair to watch an Appalachian sunset off a front porch. He has this wonderfully warm and fatherly quality to his speech that seems to invite a lengthy chat. Picture a backwoods Raymond Burr drawing equally long pauses but with a sense of humor.*

*Wilson's talent has been to derive procedures that have procured the best among traditional folk genres — future stars as well as amateur keepers-of-the-flame unknown to virtually anyone but their next of kin. He strives for quality and balance within limited budgets and seeks to serve up something for everybody. Proof of the pudding is that the LOWELL FOLK FESTIVAL draws 200,000 of all ages and denominations for such otherwise obscure musics as Chinese dulcimer, South Carolina chanteys, Cape-Verdean merengue, Puerto-Rican plena, French-Canadian fiddling, and the like.*

*Here's how Wilson, who chairs Lowell's talent screening committee, describes the process. (Aspiring promoters, as well as interested music fans, take note.)*

- "What happens is that there's 15 to 20 people who serve on a Program Committee. They're all from Lowell. There's a variety of people: the editor of the newspaper, representatives of ethnic organizations, someone from the Lowell National Historic Park, people from the City of Lowell.

  "What I am is Chairman of the committee. I get one vote like everybody else. We get about 1,100 suggestions per year. You try to be as fair as you can, and you go through and take out the things that obviously don't fall in your bailiwick. Everybody that plays guitar thinks that they're in folk, and that's all right. They've got a place, but it might not be your place. You just try to sort out what stays in.

  "Then you sit down and set yourself goals about what you intend to do with a particular year. We don't have themes so much as to try and look around and see what would be interesting to do that we've not done — to do some things that are New England and some that are local. We figure that the whole country, and even the world, is our business to talk about. Sometimes we don't listen more than 30 seconds and don't talk about it at all, but just vote and that's that.

  "Nobody gets into an advocacy role on behalf of a particular group. My friends come up like everyone else's. Because they're my friends doesn't give them any credit from that bunch of wolves [laughs].

  "I've had the pleasure, the honor, the whatever, of being able to sit down and book entire festivals all by myself. Big festivals, too, with major budgets! I've been doing this for 30 years, and it's very humbling to find out that what comes out of this process in Lowell is better than what I'd do on my own. That cuts you down to size!

- "I think to become a headliner takes a little bit of luck and a lot of hard work, and so forth. The truth is that it's easy to get arrogant about your taste and think you've heard all the good stuff, especially when you've been tooling around as long as I have. But it's humbling to sit down and encounter the array of talent that we do in hearing all those recordings and video tapes and plowing through it. A lot of it's predictable, and a lot of it's as bad as you think it would be. But in every stack there's something that'll haul you up short and make you realize you don't know as damn much as you thought you did.

"I was listening to a tape here just last week by Eddie Pennington — guitar player, thumb picker, like [Merle] Travis. We had found him at a little festival we had organized at Mammoth Cave in Kentucky. 'Never had a record then. He's got one now — self-produced. He's one of the best God-damned guitar players in the country! He's amazing. [Citing his tour, Masters of the Steel String Guitar] I know a pile of super guitar players, but Eddie is a world-class guitar player. And an undertaker — he can plant you or cover you with the guitar [laughs].

- "There comes a time [in festival programming] when everybody says, 'I've seen that.' That's a subtle problem that tends to creep up on people. They have a really nice little festival, and everybody loves it. So they have it again, and everybody loves it. And they have it a third year. There comes a time, though, when it's time again for the festival and everybody says, 'Ooh, I've seen that.' That's fatal. You're dead then.

"For that reason we're not much on repeating. We seldom repeat an artist. In fact, if they're real good, after two or three years, four even, they might make it back. We have a little repeating, but people who come to the Lowell festival in 1994 won't see the 1993 festival.

"We did [Wayne Toups and Zydecajun] again, and that's great. Wayne I've known and dealt with a lot of different places. They just loved Wayne. They indeed brought him back. He's also been back in the concert series [at Boarding House Park]. But if I had repeated Wayne at every festival since he was first there, which was first, I think in 1988, I'd have a problem at this point, and Wayne would have a problem. As it is, Wayne has a damn good audience in Lowell.

- "We have enormous participation from about 40 ethnic organizations that have food there. You can gain five pounds just walking down a Lowell street that weekend. I think we've skinned everyone on food [laughs].

"We do it, not with commercial vendors, but with clubs and organizations. They get to keep all the money. They do it for fundraising, so it puts a lot of money back into the community. That's good for the community. All the hotels sell out. Anybody who does any business does a lot of business when we're around.

"I don't think that's the reason why people do festivals, though. I think that Lowell, which is a mill town, really had a depression when the mills started closing down in the early part of this century. The industry shut-down effected areas of the Midwest which we call 'the rust belt' now. There was a pre 'rust belt' [here] in these mill closings. Along with the economic depression, there was a depression of the spirit. Lowell became a place that was depressed, where there were difficulties.

"Lowell has changed — the park, the fixing up. It came roaring back. It's had its ups and downs. The computer industry roared there for a while; it's in a slack period now. But the city's in much better shape than it was 25 years ago.

"It's easy to get people from Chicago or Miami to the Lowell National Historic Park. You put up some brochures and people go around and they see this. They have no bias against Lowell. It's hard as hell, though, to get people who live in [nearby] Woburn to come over, or Bostonians or Cambridge people to come up. But the folk fest has got them coming up and doing 200,000 people.

- [Citing Los Pleneros del Batey] "Actually, we met them doing honest-to-God field work for the Johnstown festival. We got a little money from Pennsylvania sources to go out and do some looking around. Some 'walking-around money,' as they'd call it in the political world here in Maryland.

"You know, field work's amazing if you do some of it and have any ear. Taking time to go about things systematically seems to be one of the most important things, I tell you. That's true of our committee in Lowell, and it's true of field work. If you go about your situation of choosing talent systematically, you come up with a far better festival than a dozen buffs who sit around the table and harbor favorites — even if they're well-informed buffs like you and me. It's again humbling to set some folks out. They don't know as much as you and I, but they come back with a Los Pleneros del Batey.

For people who want to draw their circle a little bigger [in terms of scouting out ethnic music], it's a great time to be in this country!"

~     ~     ~

*Norberto Tavares and Tropical Power, Lowell Folk Festival.*

# Tanglewood's Classical Alternatives

TANGLEWOOD FESTIVAL OF CONTEMPORARY MUSIC, Lenox, MA
> Late July to Late August
> Avant Garde and New Music

**TANGLEWOOD JAZZ FESTIVAL**, Lenox, MA
> Early September
> Modern Jazz
> ***Attended***

Ah, Tanglewood — hallowed ground amidst the gently hilly and settled terrain of the Berkshire **Introduction** Mountains in Western Massachusetts.

The minute you pass through its turnstiles, you'll feel like you've just stepped into a Maxfield Parrish mural, or a Louis Tiffany stained-glass window. That lawn! Those trees! That view! It's time to dust off the wicker hamper you got as a wedding gift and have your local gourmet shop pack it for a Tanglewood picnic under the stars with that special someone.

The site, itself, is a former estate donated to the Boston Symphony Orchestra [BSO] back in 1936. Most orchestras retreat to their pastoral summer digs for, well, a retreat. The BSO has been coming here for nearly 50 years — but to work! In fact, the entire organization, staff and all, relocates to this self-owned-and-operated facility for two full months.

The BSO has stood out in using Tanglewood summers to build the genre in America: introducing new works; re-examining the classical repertoire; and educating generations of the finest students in its famous Tanglewood Music School, which claims "no less than 20% of the members of the major orchestras in this country" among its graduates. No fluff stuff. The lengthy tenure here of the late Leonard Bernstein's is a legendary example of their round-the-calendar workaholism.

Manager Daniel Gustin credits Tanglewood's unique proximity, roughly equidistant to two major markets, Boston and New York: "There is this tradition in the Berkshires of a more sophisticated kind of urban sensibility in a way that only a cross-section of New York or Boston (or Chicago) audiences could support for classical music. We're very lucky in order to be able to take advantage of that. For a summer festival, I think location is 50% of the deal."

Perhaps the rest of the deal is being open to happy accidents. Take the TANGLEWOOD JAZZ FESTIVAL, **Festival** a three-day affair whose genesis Gustin attributes to jazz trumpeter Wynton Marsalis: **Review**

- "Wynton was a student at Tanglewood. He was here for a summer, playing in the orchestra, when he was 17. He came in and played all this classical stuff. He did a little jazz on the side, but he was basically a classical performer.

  "One year, seven or eight years ago, the BSO was playing Friday night and Sunday, so we had an opening Saturday night. As an experiment — which we'd never done before at Tanglewood — we invited Wynton and his septet to play a concert in the Music Shed. It sold out; it was a great concert. So, we said to ourselves, 'Hmm, we should do more of this!'"

"More of this" evolved into a Labor Day-weekend institution that will expand in 1994 to four nights and two sites: the 5,000-seat Music Shed with its 5,000-seat lawn plus a brand-new 1,200-seat Music Hall for more intimate performances. Gustin regrets that this one-weekend format "ghetto-izes" jazz at Tanglewood (he'd like to see it interspersed among their classical programming, more like with Marsalis's first concert, or the TANGLEWOOD FESTIVAL OF CONTEMPORARY MUSIC), but sighs, "That's what festivals do anyway."

In addition to the commercial benefits of extending Tanglewood's season and expanding its audience, however, Gustin is quick to underscore artistic imperatives driving Tanglewood's commitment to jazz:

- "Institutions like the BSO or Lincoln Center [CLASSICAL JAZZ AT LINCOLN CENTER, Manhattan, NYC — see chapter] get into jazz programming because jazz is recognized as an important, indigenous American music. As an art form, if I can use that term, it is in many ways comparable to the so-called classical music tradition. It's something, which as Americans, we can all be proud.

  "Wynton, in parallel, has developed this classical idea of jazz in terms of looking back to the important historical figures in jazz and doing the proper kind of obeisance to them — recognizing their importance as American artists and all that, as opposed to [merely] entertainers. I'm thinking of Louis Armstrong, in particular. You know, Wynton's been so articulate about Armstrong's revolutionary things and the great artistry he brought to jazz, versus 'Satchmo,' the entertainer, which he kind of became later in his life."

The appeal of Tanglewood's jazz festival, in my opinion, is their openness toward this type of artistic exploration. Yes, they'll program acts with the conservative "seal-of-approval" for classical audiences. But they'll also feature Marsalis's recent concern, perhaps an extended Charles Mingus composition conducted by noted scholar/composer Gunther Shuller, as Gustin recalls one year, plus two programs of lesser-known talent during the weekend afternoons. They'll comfort you, but they'll challenge you, too.

Frequently, their young challengers are TMS alumni. Gustin relates how "[pianist/singer] Harry Connick, Jr., [trumpeter] Marlon Jordan, [guitarist] John Pizzarelli, and many others have come up through our side, the classical side, and that's healthy. That's really healthy."

**Artist Mini-Reviews**

<u>Modern Jazz Quartet</u>. Gustin described the MJQ's delicate chamber jazz as exactly the sort of act the smaller Music Hall was designed for. Even from my perch in the last row of the cavernous Music Shed on Friday night, however, I could still appreciate the charismatic underpining of Percy Heath's bass. His sensual blues-with-a-feeling provided an effective counterpoint to the more narrative approaches of the two lead soloists, Milt Jackson's cat-like vibes and the moody piano of their Musical Director, John Lewis.

Lewis never lost his "inside" quality during their set, but Jackson frequently dropped down to join Heath in some delicious vamps. I especially enjoyed a four-song segment midway through: "Blues in A Minor," Gershwin's "Summertime" and "I Loves You Porgy," and Basie's "Not Enough". The crowd loved a Charlie Parker composition, "Confirmation," that followed — indeed it was the group's lone uptempo — but I was well-satisfied with the bluesy medley that came before.

<u>Ray Charles</u>. Charles is the perfect booking for a classical series like Tanglewood's, or for anywhere else on the high-toned performing arts circuit where he has become a ubiquitous presence. Few other artists draw from as many constituencies — R&B, blues, jazz, rock, pop, even C&W (for those with memories of his breakthroughs in that genre back in the sixties). Few others can provide Charles's unique combination of entertainment, charm, artistry, humor, emotion, and house-rockin' — all with the proper class for this type of crowd. And who else comes with five backup singers named after himself. Move over Vanna White, the Raelets are comin' to town!

My notes are filled with adjectives like "strong, earthy, soulful, unpredictable," as Charles brought new life to tunes I thought I already knew. "I'm Busted" achieved a topical poignancy, if not for this gentry, then certainly for me. "Georgia" received a particularly sanctified treatment, with Charles engaging in a vocal/piano riffing off his own licks. "On the Mississippi" got more of the same.

I had to scoot back to New York City midway through his set, but not before thrilling to a tortured "How Long Has This Been Going On." Charles exhibited spine-chilling range on this slow-blues version, going from falsetto wails to bass growls to spoken pleading, doing whatever it took to make you feel the remorseful betrayal of the lyrics deep down in your gut. Uh-hunh!

"Two places," recommends Gustin. "One is the Norman Rockwell Museum in Stockbridge; the   **Travel Tip**
other would be the Hancock Shaker Village in Hancock. Both of these places are museums, but it's
fascinating stuff, and it's just different enough from going to a concert that it provides a nice contrast."

The 20th Century gets its due from the TANGLEWOOD FESTIVAL OF CONTEMPORARY MUSIC. This "fes-   **See Also**
tival within a festival" runs concurrent with the regular programming but is concentrated over
two, week-long "clusters." You'll enjoy a heady combination of new-music activists, established
mainstream stars, and advanced students take on a full spectrum of modern pieces, including
works by Tanglewood's resident composers. The Bang-On-a-Can Allstars (BANG ON A CAN
FESTIVAL, Manhattan, NYC — see chapter) will open 1994's series, for example. Well-advised, not
just for classical music buffs with open minds, but for any progressive-music fan with open ears.

~     ~     ~

# Cambridge's Variety Party

CAMBRIDGE INTERNATIONAL FAIR, Cambridge, MA
   Middle June
   Variety, Folk and International

CAMBRIDGE RIVER FESTIVAL, Cambridge, MA
   Middle September
   Variety, General
   ***Attended***

**Introduction** When you talk of all-bohemian capitals of America, you'd have to include Cambridge right up there with Greenwich Village and Haight-Ashbury. It helped launch "The Great Folk Scare" in the '60s and remains the most prolific scene for folk-music performance in the country. If singer-songwriters are not playing at one of a zillion coffeehouses like Passim's (into its fourth decade), they're busking in Harvard Square, one of the most vibrant public spaces in the nation. That's where Tracy Chapman was discovered.

Cambridge possesses a dramatic range of cultures and income classes. You can go from poor to patrician to middle class to yuppie to working class, all within a mile or so. Yet, despite having one of the densest urban populations in the U. S., it never loses its human scale and inviting livability. Boutiques, cafes, and especially book stores abound.

Being home to two of the world's leading universities, Harvard and MIT, along with leading architecture, high-tech., software, and bio-tech. companies, Cambridge enjoys a never-ending stream of free-thinkers, many of whom choose to live in the community. They help make the area particularly fertile ground for the arts.

Don't take my word, however. Listen to Lindsay MacCoy, a spokesperson for the Cambridge Arts Council, who gently swells when upon her favorite topic:

- "Cambridge is not just any neighborhood, Cambridge is very special. Cambridge is such an incredibly rich, active community. There is so much going on in Cambridge that we really have hired, for the most part, Cambridge performing groups — not because we're trying to give the work to local people, but because they're the best. In hiring local people, we're getting world-class talent."

**Festival Review** The CAMBRIDGE RIVER FESTIVAL, which MacCoy produces for the Council, is your best bet to witness what she's talking about.

The event has had its ups and downs since the first fest took place in '77. It was even forced into hiatus in '91 due to funding cuts ("Massachusetts Miracle" gone belly-up, and all that). A partnership with Continental Cablevision helped restore its financial base, while switching the date from the second Saturday in June to the second Saturday in September in '92 has brought good weather and greater attention.

There is no "Cambridge River," of course. Rather, the festival occupies the grassy banks of the Charles River toward the Western end of town. Sycamore trees shade two music stages, a gospel tent, a frisbee field, a food alley, a children's stage, and a crafts cage. MacCoy expressed '94's plans for a large tent to house the crafts plus a third stage for dance performance. There may even be a gradual return to the festival's glory days in featuring some preliminary events all across town during the week leading up.

The theme in '93 was "Food for the Body; Food for the Soul," as attendees were invited to bring food donations for the Cambridge Food Pantry Network.

The vibe was unpretentious and down-right neighborly. It didn't feel like 75,000 people but more like a big lawn party of folks you'd like to hang out with or ask onto the dance floor for some free-spirited boogie. Funky personalities were everywhere — the collegiate, the arty, the ethnic, and the urbane — all mixing and mingling. According to MacCoy, "There've been several long-term relationships that've come out of people meeting each other at the River Festival; it's got that reputation."

"People seemed to feel that the music this year was the highest quality ever," MacCoy exclaimed of the day's primary social facilitator. "I attribute that to the fact that, for the first time, we had this jury of professional radio DJ's do the talent selection. You didn't have any bias from one person's own preferences. The three DJ's we had all represented different types of music: rock, Caribbean and jazz."

Oddly, they picked a lineup that didn't differ dramatically from 1992's. No problem, because solid acts prevailed both years. I recognized these two local legends from my own Boston days in the mid-'80s: longtime Merle Haggard devotee, John Lincoln Wright, plus '50s R&B maestro, Little Joe Cook. The only roots name missing was rockabilly veteran, Sleepy LaBeef (no doubt, a past booking). The jazz side was amply represented by the Bruce Katz Band. Folk, worldbeat, Cajun, blues, gospel — even a harmonica orchestra — were also presented in what was one of the better gatherings of diverse, local talent in this book.

I didn't get the full dose during my visit (being at the end of one of my patented mad dashes to three festivals across three states in one day), but I did get to enjoy the last half-set from Stan Strickland and Ascension, with Wanetta Jackson guesting on vocals. They purveyed a nice bit of jazz, Latin, African, and Brazilian with steady "riddims" and lots of personality — great for dancing.

A cinematographer could have had a field day with this finale, pulling the lens back, back, back: first the warm patterns of afternoon sun dappling through dancing legs; then the sailgliders lazily drawing white lines into the river's dark ripples; and finally the electric blue swath above the Cambridge skyline encompassing all.

**Artist Mini-Reviews**

MacCoy notes that while she loves all the acts selected, she'd be most tempted to hire Strickland if she could afford to put on that kind of a party for herself. Here's what she had to say about a few others on the bill.

Bruce Katz Band. MacCoy: "He went over real well. He's enormously popular. [The talent selection committee] was really thrilled to see he was one of the applicants among the 150 proposals we received. In fact, Eric Jackson of WGBH-FM had someone else on as a guest artist on his show and Bruce Katz was playing back-up. He got incredible numbers of phone calls about the back-up musician."

The Jane Gang. This seven-piece band, led by singer Jane Goldman, describes their western-swing/jazz hybrid as "Hank Williams meets McCoy Tyner." MacCoy: "They went over really well, too. I'd say they're a little avant-garde. Jane, herself, is a very fine visual artist as well as being a musician and a singer. It's upbeat; it can be a little jazzy. I know Joe Mulholland plays piano with her group quite a lot, and he's a very well-known jazz pianist in the area. Bob Nesky, the bassist, is also a big jazz name."

John Lincoln Wright and The Sour Mash Boys. Wright, a salty C&W traditionalist, records for Cambridge-based Rounder Records. MacCoy: "John Lincoln Wright is great! The group that was supposed to be coming after him got delayed for about 40 minutes, and he played right through it. He just stayed on stage and everybody loved it."

Little Joe Cook and The Thrillers. Cook had a top-ten R&B hit, "Peanuts," nearly forty years ago, and plays every week in his own Cantab Lounge on nearby Massachusetts Avenue. MacCoy: "He's great; he's a real star! We had him at another event last April where we were sort of doing re-creations of the great black performing artists. We had Joe Cook there as himself doing the '50s, and he was just a true professional."

**Attendance Tip**

"Parking is tough," admits MacCoy. "There are some city parking lots which are 25 cents an hour, but it's hard to find spaces. What I really suggest, and do myself, is to park at, say, Sullivan Station — they have huge parking lots there — then take the T [Boston's rail system]. The T is very easy and efficient."

**Travel Tip**  MacCoy's a fan of Boston's museum scene: the Museum of Science, the Boston Aquarium, the Museum of Fine Arts, the Isabella Stewart Gardner Museum, etc. Check your local guide book. For day trips she recommends the historic sites in Salem, Plymouth, Lexington, or Concord.

**See Also**  The Cambridge Arts Council maintains the second Saturday in June for their CAMBRIDGE INTERNATIONAL FAIR, begun in '91. The action occurs inland throughout Central Square in eleven performing areas. Each stage is organized around an ethnic theme. Acts vary among dance troupes, musical groups, and workshop presenters. As their program describes, it's "a day filled with discoveries!"

*Copley Square, First Night Boston.*

# Boston's Arts Extravaganza,
# New Year's Eve

**FIRST NIGHT BOSTON**, Boston, MA
Late December
Variety, Folk and International
***Attended***

Across the river from the offices of FIRST NIGHT BOSTON and its International Alliance of First **Introduction**
Night Celebrations sits another venerable institution, Harvard Business School, which has set the
standard in business education with its case-study method. Well, one of their adjunct professors
should hustle right over and write up a case on FIRST NIGHT BOSTON's extraordinary success — a
textbook example of nonprofit marketing.

Consider that FIRST NIGHT BOSTON:

- Found the common thread among two generally-besieged and often mutually-
  exclusive "services" — [a] high-quality arts awareness across all media, and [b]
  accessible, affordable, alcohol-free, family entertainment (being especially ahead
  of the curve on the alcohol-free aspect);

- Identified the one day of the year, New Year's Eve, which presented the greatest
  need, as well as the greatest opportunity, for it's unique pairing — effectively
  carving out what has become a proprietary niche in stark contrast to the night's
  customarily expensive, boozy shenanigans;

- Systematically enlisted strong constituencies sharing a common interest — artists,
  institutions, churches, government, the press;

- And, when demand exploded like midnight fireworks over Boston Common,
  replicated their formula throughout the country.

Move over McDonald's, FIRST NIGHT, Inc. is headed to your town!

FIRST NIGHTS have spread to 118 markets throughout the U. S. and Canada entertaining an
estimated 2.5 million sober revelers — likely the largest, single-day turnout for any such festival
in North America (ahead of even Brooklyn's WEST INDIAN-AMERICAN DAY PARADE & CARNIVAL on
Labor Day). In 18 years FIRST NIGHTS have earned a dizzying array of awards and promise to
become one of those rare institutions actually capable of changing the attitudes and behavior of a
segment of society at a given place and time. Marketing students, take note.

Of course, FIRST NIGHT BOSTON's President and Founder, Zeren Earls, whose warm and measured
speech still enjoys the coloring of her native Turkey, pooh-poohs such heady praise as well as all
this marketing jargon. "We didn't even use the word 'marketing,'" she explains, "but it made common sense that if you were going to create a community-wide celebration, you needed that broad-
based attraction of support."

Earls paints the FIRST NIGHT picture more in terms of her own dual role as a former art
teacher on one hand and family woman on the other. Artistic quality for families and communities is her leitmotif:

- "The people who started this event are serious artists. What happens is, if you look at most
  so-called 'family' or 'community' festivals and who's behind it, they are marketing people,
  civic people, event people. Usually, their art background is negligible, if there is anything

there at all. FIRST NIGHT BOSTON had been conceived by artists and has been directed by artists all along. The quality you see at FIRST NIGHT BOSTON, I will take responsibility for it. I make sure that we have the variety, the diversity, the richness, the rich palette of the arts, no matter how esoteric they may be.

"Just because it's families or kids, we don't need to undermine what they can appreciate. FIRST NIGHT opens doors. It opens people up to creations they don't ordinarily experience. People return home with a spirit of appreciation and discovery. You don't have to have an art background to appreciate good music.

"I suppose what this event has done is that it's not often arts and community come together, because when you say 'community,' people's expectations are not about art, it's more fun and entertainment. You have a few clowns, lots of food... Or, if something is clearly called an 'arts festival,' it's highbrow and not everyone goes. We have been able to close that gap and to bring the best of the arts to the people on the street and not just as entertainment. While they're entertained, there is depth in what we offer them, and they seem to respond to it."

Quality aside, the quantities of FIRST NIGHT BOSTON offerings alone are impressive: nearly 70 acts covering over 30 music genres plus over 100 groups representing over 30 artistic mediums — all at close to 90 sites attended by 700,000 cheery, bundled troopers. Other FIRST NIGHTS are smaller in scale, naturally, although "smaller" applies more to their attendance than to their extensive programming. FIRST NIGHT BOSTON benefits from its tenure and its market size, but time is swelling the crowds elsewhere, especially on the West Coast where FIRST NIGHTS are rapidly taking hold.

Remarkably, this expanding empire began from nothing more than a simple house party among artist friends. Earles relates the inspiring tale of FIRST NIGHT BOSTON's origins:

- "Because of our art involvement [Earles' husband is a musician], all our friends are artists of one kind or another. Prior to [1976] we would get together in each other's homes, not necessarily for a drinking party, but just to do something creative (the most creative we got was making our own hats). There was no life in town. In fact, I remember going on New Year's Eve to a friend's house — the streets were bleak! There was no street life at all in Boston or Cambridge or anywhere nearby.

"After a few years of this kind of thing, we literally sat down at one of the artist's homes, Claire Wainwright's, [who] invited us over to specifically talk about what could be done on New Year's Eve. These were all very creative people just [sitting] around her dining room table. It was a small group. We took turns going around coming up with ideas of the possibilities of the city becoming the nucleus for a communal coming-together, a public celebration, people re-discovering the city, what they have left behind... [We discussed] the churches opening, becoming hosts to the community, like open houses.

"And, of course, since this was a group of artists, one of the major goals, or incentives, was to develop audiences for the work they do. Whether you are a musician or a visual artist, your visibility is really limited to selling tickets, or gallery openings. There is not this reaching-out to the people who might really appreciate your work...

"All of this was discussed at that table. We left that meeting with a great deal of excitement and enthusiasm, and took it beyond a small group talking about it.

"There were a lot of skeptics because of the weather in Boston, and New Year's Eve not being a tradition for cultural activities, etc. But there were sufficient believers, like the churches, [who] were very willing to open their doors and see what happens... The Mayor was very receptive — that was the Bicentennial year of the city — and he felt this would be a good finale to the year-long variety of celebrations that had taken place in Boston. We got the support of the *Boston Globe*. The publisher felt this was great; it would get the drinking people off the streets. Everybody had a reason, an angle, why they felt this was a good idea to give a try. Of course, the artistic community was most excited about it — that didn't take any work to convince them.

"So we literally got it going. The first year we had 16 sites, most of them churches, and all close to the Boston Common. The outdoor life was pretty much limited to what happened on the Boston Common, and we ended the event with fireworks.

"The first year we didn't think, we didn't conceive of repeating any programs because we didn't know who would turn up. Well, to our surprise, within five minutes of opening the doors, every site was filled. We were running around looking for papers to put up signs saying, 'House Full.' A lot of people would come to see their friends — some got in and some couldn't. That was an indication to us that our small group of people were not the only ones looking for something different than your traditional revelry on New Year's Eve. There was a need there."

FIRST NIGHT BOSTON has since evolved a structure comfortable enough to let Earls leave her original post this year exclusively to promote her growing FIRST NIGHT network. These duties include fielding referrals, consulting and development, attending regional meetings, and hosting an annual conference every April. When advising interested cities Earls emphasizes, "That this is not just one person's booking engagement; this is not an agent's sitting around. If that was the case, I could develop a program in a week... It's about involving the community. The more participation, the better it is, so that they feel invested in it."

On the home front, Earls assures that new artists will continue to comprise one-third of FIRST NIGHT BOSTON's lineup. Although the screening committees, assisted by music industry professionals, are not adverse to national acts (Tom Paxton was invited in 1993), the focus remains local.

"We benefit from all the talent that's right here," Earls notes, "and it's really a joy to see them grow up and become famous." Citing local folk duo, "the story," as an example, she adds:

- "Before they had big-time agents, they were always FIRST NIGHT BOSTON participants playing small venues and people appreciated them. So I've seen these two wonderful, down-to-earth young people really grow and become professional [to] where now we're talking to their agent in Chicago. That's what's happening at FIRST NIGHT BOSTON.

"When you attend FIRST NIGHT BOSTON, you get a quick sense of the spirit of Boston through its arts and culture, the dynamic quality of what the music world is here. I think you can quickly get the pulse between jazz and folk music and classical music. I've been very proud of developing that aspect."

**Festival Review**

Nineteen ninety-three expired with a bitterly cold "last night," which only seemed to heighten the festivity. Blue lights beamed through elaborate ice sculptures as the streets around Copley Square teemed with red-cheeked families in garish ski parkas. Hundreds "ooh'd" and "aah'd" in front of one magnificent example, an expansive tribute to whales, which spanned half the width of the grounds before the ornate Trinity Church. Hundreds more, who obtained their red cheeks through more artificial means, were bleating into red plastic horns, shouting, "Happy freakin' New Year!" Fortunately, both groups con-celebrated peaceably.

My wife and I got a late start for FIRST NIGHT BOSTON, much to our regret. We both agreed there were more than enough attractions, especially on the fine arts side, to justify a full 10-to-12 hours, interrupted by a few leisurely meals. Even if we didn't fulfill our wish list from the program book, we would've wanted to wander more amidst the excitement.

Still, there was time to rotate from the Berklee Performance Center to the Hynes Convention Center and back again. The cavernous Convention Center was hosting very active "Participatory Dances" on three floors with brisk rhythms from the showy Zafem Haitian Band, spirited whirling courtesy of the Scottish Fiddle Club, and eclectic dance instruction via DJ's from the MASSABA. The narrow Performance Center was packing its green fabric seats for alternating shows of juggling, opera, alternative jazz, and alternative roots music. Here's the alternative jazz act:

**Artist Mini-Review**  Either/Orchestra. This ten-piece band really seemed to be having too much fun (I wonder if they were Berklee School of Music grads returning to their home auditorium?). They wore funky shirts and hats, bantered self-deprecatingly with the crowd, and teased each other to death. Once, when the trumpeter overextended his solo, the drummer casually tip-toed over and stage-whispered in his ear, "Play a little longer."

Their original compositions — brusk, angular, wiry — were markedly more serious. I preferred the two tunes that bookended their set: [a] a chunky cover of "Caravan," given an Arab/Rai tinge; and [b] a soulful tribute to Miles Davis, "Miles Away." The latter began with funky organ chords and shakers, then let moody horn charts build toward a bright, driving, tuneful chorus. The piece concluded in near-cacophony, but entertained along the way by juxtaposing the catchy with the avant-garde — just like the band itself.

**Attendance Tip**  "I would say not to leave their planning to the last minute," counsels Earls. She notes that program books are available in advance, and that events are "clustered" so attendees don't have to troop all across town to gain variety. Bluegrass fans should know that such concerts historically have been the toughest ticket — schedule your itinerary to get there early. We both advise taking Boston's rail system, the T, since all the pedestrian and car traffic clogs the roads downtown. And, of course, you should bundle up, including long johns, hats, gloves and boots.

"We have so much going on out-of-doors," Earls concludes, "that...even though you may be a music fan, do take in some of the outdoor wonder of the event."

**See Also**  If you're seeking the FIRST NIGHT BOSTON experience, but on a more-intimate scale, take your pick from among the **Festival Listings** at the back of each state's section. All authentic versions will contain the trademarked words, "FIRST NIGHT," and take place, of course, on New Year's Eve.

~     ~     ~

# Massachusetts Festival Listings

**Caveat**

Although the vast majority are festivals are reliable and predictable, all are subject to last-minute changes or cancellations. Accordingly, FESTPRESS is not responsible for any festival listing information that follows. Readers are well advised to contact festivals at least twice before preparing a festival vist: (a) once at least one or two months ahead of time; and (b) once more during the week of your visit for confirmation. Ask for a festival flyer or brochure to be mailed to you. Festival promoters usually are willing to comply, and the resulting literature may answer any questions you still have.

## Restrictions:

| | | | | | |
|---|---|---|---|---|---|
| • Food and drink... | 1; | • Cameras... | 6; | • Motorcycles... | 11; |
| • Alcohol... | 2; | • Audio recording... | 7; | • Re-entry... | 12; |
| • Cans... | 3; | • Video recording... | 8; | • Other restrictions... | 13. |
| • Bottles... | 4; | • Children... | 9; | | |
| • Coolers... | 5; | • Pets... | 10; | | |

## Secondary Genre[s]:

| | | | |
|---|---|---|---|
| • Variety, General... | VRGL; | • Bluegrass... | BLGS; |
| • Variety, Jazz & Blues... | VRJB; | • Modern Folk... | MFOL; |
| • Variety, Country & Bluegrass | VRCB; | • Traditional Folk... | TFOL; |
| • Variety, Folk & International | VRFI; | • Fiddle and Banjo Events... | FDDL; |
| • Modern Jazz... | MJAZ; | • Maritime... | MARI; |
| • Traditional Jazz & Ragtime... | TJAZ; | • Cajun and Zydeco... | ZYDC; |
| • Alternative Jazz... | AJAZ; | • Irish... | IRSH; |
| • Modern Rock and Pop... | MRCK; | • Jewish... | JWSH; |
| • Classic Rock and Oldies... | CRCK; | • Native American... | NATV; |
| • Alternative & College Rock | ARCK; | • Scottish... | SCOT; |
| • Hard Rock & Heavy Metal | HRCK; | • Modern Latin... | MLAT; |
| • Rap... | RAP; | • Traditional Latin... | TLAT; |
| • Modern R&B... | MR&B; | • African American... | AFRM; |
| • Blues and Traditional R&B... | TR&B; | • African... | AFRC; |
| • Acappella and Doo Wop... | ACAP; | • Brazilian & So. American... | BRZL; |
| • Modern Christian... | CHRS; | • Reggae, Ska & Caribbean... | RGGE; |
| • Black Gospel... | BGOS; | • Avant Garde & New Music... | AVNT; |
| • Southern & Bluegrass Gospel | SGOS; | • Cabaret... | CBRT; |
| • Traditional Gospel & Sings... | TGOS; | • Gay and Lesbian... | GYLS; |
| • Modern Country... | MC&W; | • Drum Corps & March. Bands | DRUM; |
| • Traditional Country... | TC&W; | • Fairs... | FAIR; |
| • Alt. Country & Rockabilly... | AC&W; | • Other Genres... | OTHR. |

**Note**

Wherever "**Help!**" appears readers are invited to answer the proceeding questions and/or provide updates. New festival listings that meet the criteria of this book certainly are welcome too! Please mail any current festival information you obtain — especially flyers or brochures — to FESTPRESS, P. O. Box 147, Glen Ridge, NJ 07028. *Thanks!*

## CMAC's A Joyful Noise, Cambridge, MA
Middle Jan.
Black Gospel

Since 1988. Tribute to Dr. Martin Luther King Jr. "Gospel has a common joyfulness, something with rhythm and harmony that's energetic, positive and uplifting." -- Dr. Donnell Patterson. See other dates and sites. **Days:** 1. **Site:** indoor. Sanders Theater, Harvard University. **Admission:** paid. **Daily entry:** under $10, $10 to $24. **Acts:** local acts. **Sample day's lineup:** Ruth Hamilton with Vivian Taylor, Maynard School Chorus of Cambridge, The New Temple Singers of St. Paul A. M. E. Church, The Community Chorus, Freda Battle and Family. **Contact:** Cambridge Multicultural Arts Center, 41 Second Street, Cambridge, MA 02141, 617-577-1400 **or:** GNE Studio, 675 Massachusetts Avenue, Cambridge, MA 02139, 617-661-6007. .

## Songstreet Festival of Funny Songwriters, Somerville, MA
Middle Jan.
Modern Folk

Since 1993. **Days:** 1. **Site:** indoor. Somerville Theater, Davis Square. **Admission:** paid. **Daily entry:** $10 to $24. **Discounts:** student discounts, advance purchase discounts. **Acts:** regional acts, local acts. **Sample day's lineup:** Nancy Tucker, Jim Infantino, Don White, Cosy Sheridan, Michael Duffy. **Contact:** Songstreet Productions, P. O. Box 85, Somerville, MA 02143, 617-628-3390.

## Papsaquoho Pow-Wow, Braintree, MA
Middle Jan.
Native American

See other dates and sites. **Days:** 1. **Site:** indoor. Thayer Academy. **Acts:** local acts. **Contact:** Massachusetts Center for Native American Awareness, Inc., P. O. Box 5885, Boston, MA 02115-5885, 617-884-4227.

## New Women's Voices, Cambridge, MA
Late Jan.
Modern Folk

Since 1993. "A showcase of some of the country's best new women performers." -- Advertisement. **Days:** 1. **Hours per day:** 4. **Site:** indoor. Sanders Theater, Harvard University. **Admission:** paid. **Daily entry:** $10 to $24. **Acts:** national acts, local acts. **Sample day's lineup:** Susan Werner, Carrie Newcomer, Meryn Cadell, Jann Arden. **Contact:** Revolutionary Acts, P. O. Box 606, Cambridge, MA 02238, 617-661-1252.

## Boston Blues Festival, Allston, MA
Late Jan. to Late Feb.
Blues and Traditional R&B

Since 1986. **Days:** 14. **Hours per day:** 5. **Site:** indoor. Harper's Ferry, 158 Brighton Avenue. **Admission:** paid. **Acts:** national acts, regional acts, local acts. **Sample series lineup:** Day One: Roomful of Blues, Rick Russell and The Cadillac Horns; Day Two: Luther "Guitar Jr." Johnson, "Monster" Mike Welch; Day Three: Mighty Sam McLain, Ernie Williams and The Wildcats. **Audio merchandise:** "Boston Blues Blast, Vols. I, II" (Tone Cool). **Contact:** Boston Blues Society, 158 Brighton Avenue, Allston, MA 02134, 617-254-7380.

## BLACK HISTORY MONTH, Boston, MA
Early Feb. to Late Feb.
African American

Co-sponsored by the Boston African-American National Historic Site and the Museum of Afro-American History. **Days:** 4. **Hours per day:** 3. **Site:** indoor. African Meeting House, 46 Joy Street. **Secondary genre[s]:** TR&B, BGOS, OTHR. **Acts:** national acts, local acts. **Sample series lineup:** Day One: George Russell Jr. Trio; Day Two: Johnny "Clyde" Copeland; Day Three: Abyssinian Baptist Choir, Peoples Baptist Church Choir, Twelfth Baptist Churches Choir. **Contact:** Boston African-American National Historic Site, 46 Joy Street, Boston, MA 02114, 617-742-5415.

## ANTHONY SPINAZZOLA GALA FESTIVAL OF FOOD AND WINE, Boston, MA
Early Feb.
Variety, General

Since 1986. "Enjoy New England's premier culinary event, sampling the fare of more than 70 of the region's finest restaurants and leading wineries for the annual, elegant evening of dining, wine-tasting and outstanding entertainment." -- Listing. **Days:** 1. **Site:** indoor. World Trade Center. **Secondary genre[s]:** MJAZ, TR&B, RGGE. **Acts:** local acts. **Sample day's lineup:** White Heat Swing Orchestra, Monster Mike Welch, Jimmy and Donnie Demers, Paul Broadnax Trio, Wendy John and The Culture Jam. **Contact:** Anthony Spinazzola Gala, 5 Cabot Place, Stoughton, MA 02072, 617-344-4413/439-5088.

## SONGSTREET FOLK AND BLUEGRASS FEST, Cambridge, MA
Early Feb.
Variety, Folk and International

Since 1992. **Days:** 1. **Site:** indoor. Sanders Theater, Harvard University. **Admission:** paid. **Daily entry:** $10 to $24. **Discounts:** student discounts, advance purchase discounts. **Secondary genre[s]:** BLGS, MFOL. **Acts:** national acts, regional acts. **Sample day's lineup:** The Seldom Scene, Jonathon Edwards, Northern Lights, Melissa Ferrick. **Contact:** Songstreet Productions, P. O. Box 85, Somerville, MA 02143, 617-628-3390.

## NORTHEAST INDOOR BLUE GRASS FESTIVAL, Boxborough, MA
Early Feb. to Middle Feb.
Bluegrass

Since 1994. "Why not turn those mid-winter blues into mid-winter bluegrass? [We're] bringing together some of the hottest names in bluegrass music all under one roof -- and the key word here is roof!" -- Program. **Days:** 3. **Hours per day:** 12. **Site:** indoor. Boxborough Host Hotel and Conference Center, off I-495. **Admission:** paid. **Daily entry:** $10 to $24, $25 to $49, $50 and over. **Discounts:** multiple event or day passes, advance purchase discounts. **Acts:** national acts, regional acts, local acts. **Sample day's lineup:** Peter Rowan and The Panama Red Riders, Nashville Bluegrass Band, Del McCoury Band, Amy Galatin and Stillwaters, Grassroots, Way Station, Band Contest Winner. **Contact:** Northeast Indoor Blue Grass Festival, 106 Connecticut Boulevard, East Hartford, CT 06108, 508-263-8701.

## FOLK SONG SOCIETY OF GREATER BOSTON'S MEMBER'S CONCERT, Watertown, MA
Middle Feb.
Traditional Folk

See other dates and sites. **Days:** 1. **Site:** indoor. First Parish Church, 35 Church Street. **Admission:** paid. **Daily entry:** under $10. **Secondary genre[s]:** MFOL. **Acts:** local acts. **Sample day's lineup:** Two for the Show, Fool's Errand, Dr. Joe, Paul Beck, Sydelle Pearl, Will Whiteley, Izzy Doveburd, Pamela Roberts. **Contact:** Folk Song Society of Greater Boston, Inc., P. O. Box 492, Somerville, MA 02143, 617-623-1806.

BOSTON FESTIVAL: A CARNIVAL OF CULTURES, Boston, MA
> Middle Feb. to Late Feb.
> Variety, General

Since 1991. "Showcases Boston's cultural and artistic diversity...[including] A Celebration of Difference, a two-day musical series of local and national headliners..." -- Listing. Discontinued for 1994, but scheduled to resume in 1995. **Help!** A sample lineup? **Days:** 11. **Site:** outdoor and indoor. **Acts:** national acts, local acts. **Contact:** Boston Festival: A Carnival of Cultures, 4 Walnut Avenue, Cambridge, MA 02140, 617-497-5909/742-7077.


BRAZILIAN FESTIVAL OF THE ARTS, Somerville, MA
> Middle Feb.
> Brazilian and South American

Since 1992. **Help!** The status of this event? **Days:** 2. **Hours per day:** 5. **Site:** indoor. Holiday Inn, 30 Washington Street. **Admission:** paid. **Daily entry:** $10 to $24. **Acts:** local acts. **Sample day's lineup:** Hermanes Abreu, Tereza Ines Group, Som Brasil, Blue Jeans, others. **Contact:** Brazilian Festival of the Arts, 117 Austin Street, Somerville, MA 02145, 617-426-8600.


MULTICULTURAL FESTIVAL, Roxbury, MA
> Late Feb.
> Variety, General

See other dates. **Days:** 1. **Hours per day:** 8. **Site:** indoor. Roxbury Community College, 1234 Columbus Avenue. **Admission:** free. **Secondary genre[s]:** TR&B, BGOS, TLAT. **Acts:** local acts. **Sample day's lineup:** Little Joe Cook and The Thrillers, Holy Tabernacle Gospel Choir, Grupo Folklorico Latino, others. **Contact:** Vinfen Corp., 28 Travis Street, Allston, MA 02134, 617-254-7300.


HARVARD WINTER FOLK FESTIVAL, Cambridge, MA
> Early Mar.
> Modern Folk

Since 1990. **Days:** 1. **Site:** indoor. Sanders Theater, Harvard University. **Admission:** paid. **Daily entry:** $10 to $24. **Discounts:** student discounts, advance purchase discounts. **Acts:** national acts, local acts. **Sample day's lineup:** Greg Greenway, Ellis Paul, Peter Keane, Carrie Newcomer, Eileen McGann, Jay Mankita. **Contact:** Songstreet Productions, P. O. Box 85, Somerville, MA 02143, 617-628-3390.


UMASS JAZZ FESTIVAL, North Dartmouth, MA
> Early Mar.
> Modern Jazz

**Days:** 4. **Site:** indoor. UMass/North Dartmouth, Campus Center. **Acts:** national acts, local acts. **Sample day's lineup:** John Scofield Quartet, plus various college ensembles. **Contact:** Music Department, UMass, North Dartmouth, MA 02747, 508-999-8570/8568/8586.


BERKLEE COLLEGE OF MUSIC HIGH SCHOOL JAZZ FESTIVAL, Boston, MA
> Early Mar.
> Modern Jazz

Since 1969. **Days:** 1. **Site:** indoor. Berklee College of Music, 1140 Boylston Street. **Acts:** local acts. **Contact:** Berklee College of Music, 1140 Boylston Street, Boston, MA 02215, 617-266-1400.

## GLOUCESTER FOLKLIFE FESTIVAL, Gloucester, MA
Early Mar.
Variety, Folk and International

**Days:** 1. **Hours per day:** 7. **Site:** indoor. O'Mally School. **Admission:** paid. **Daily entry:** under $10. **Secondary genre[s]:** TJAZ, ACAP, MFOL, MARI, SCOT, AFRC, OTHR. **Acts:** local acts. **Sample day's lineup:** The Hounds, Cape Ann Finnish Singers, Amaranth, Beverly Johnson, Greg Morrow, Chick Marston, Jazz One, Hazel Maerotomi, others. **Contact:** Gloucester Folklife Festival, Box 95, Gloucester, MA 01931, 508-283-9181.

## CMAC's GALA BENEFIT, Cambridge, MA
Middle Mar.
African American

Since 1992. "Experiencing cabin fever? Get set to embark on an exhilirating evening of fun and fellowship" -- Program. See other dates and sites. **Days:** 1. **Hours per day:** 4. **Site:** indoor. Royal Sonesta Hotel. **Admission:** paid. **Daily entry:** $25 to $49. **Secondary genre[s]:** MJAZ, ACAP, MLAT, AFRC, OTHR. **Acts:** local acts. **Sample day's lineup:** Stan Strickland Group, Jorge Arce and Humano, D-VA, Vocal Summit, others. **Contact:** Cambridge Multicultural Arts Center, 41 Second Street, East Cambridge, MA 02141, 617-577-1400.

## HARPOON'S ST. PATRICK'S DAY BASH, Boston, MA
Middle Mar.
Irish

Since 1988. "The Harpoon Brew Crew brings out a new, seasonal beer to the general drinking public...[and] likes to throw a party that focuses on the beer. Large amounts of beer are consumed while having a great time." -- Program. See other dates. **Days:** 1. **Hours per day:** 9. **Site:** outdoor and indoor. Massachusetts Bay Brewing Co., 306 Northern Avenue. **Admission:** paid. **Daily entry:** under $10. **Acts:** regional acts, local acts. **Sample day's lineup:** Glenshane, Skip Healey, The Emeralds, The Bards. **Contact:** Massachusetts Bay Brewing Co., 306 Northern Avenue, Boston, MA 02210, 617-951-4099/574-9551.

## SONGSTREET FESTIVAL OF WOMEN SONGWRITERS, Somerville, MA
Middle Mar.
Modern Folk

Since 1993. **Days:** 1. **Site:** indoor. Somerville Theater, Davis Square. **Admission:** paid. **Daily entry:** under $10, $10 to $24. **Discounts:** student discounts, advance purchase discounts. **Acts:** local acts. **Sample day's lineup:** Laurie Sargent, Catie Curtis, Dianne Ziegler, Les Sampou, Maria Sangiolo, The Nields, Wendy Beckerman. **Contact:** Songstreet Productions, P. O. Box 85, Somerville, MA 02143, 617-628-3390.

## HOT, HOT TROPICS, Boston, MA
Late Mar.
Variety, General

"The benefit bash line-up of the week, if not the decade." -- Boston Phoenix. Dates vary between Mar. and Dec., so call ahead. **Days:** 1. **Site:** indoor. Avalon, 7 Landsdowne Street. **Admission:** paid. **Daily entry:** $50 and over. **Secondary genre[s]:** MRCK, CRCK, MR&B. **Acts:** national acts, local acts. **Sample day's lineup:** Buster Poindexter, Lesley Gore, Eartha Kitt, CeCe Peniston. **Contact:** Fenway Community Health Center, 7 Havalind Street, Boston, MA 02115, 617-247-CARE.

### BOSTON PHOENIX/WFNX BEST MUSIC POLL CELEBRATION, Boston, MA
Late Mar.
Alternative and College Rock

Since 1989. **Days:** 2. **Hours per day:** 13. **Site:** indoor. The Paradise, Avalon, Axis, Venus de Milo, Bill's Bar and Lounge, Orpheum Theater, others. **Admission:** paid. **Daily entry:** $10 to $24. **Discounts:** multiple event or day passes. **Acts:** national acts, local acts. **Sample day's lineup:** Social Distortion, Belly, The Mighty Mighty Bosstones, Black 47, Pornos for Pyros, School of Fish, Helmet, 808 State, Supreme Love Gods, Therapy?, Grant Lee Buffalo, Gin Blossoms, The God Machine, Best Kissers in the World, Robyn Hitchcock, Star Club, Seka, Sidewalk Gallery, City This, Mighty Joe Young, 32-20s. **Contact:** WFNX 101.7 FM, 25 Exchange Street, Lynn, MA 01901, 617-595-6200 x31.

### LOUD MUSIC FESTIVAL, Northampton, MA
Early Apr.
Alternative and College Rock

Since 1993. **Days:** 3. **Hours per day:** 12. **Site:** indoor. Pearl Street, Hotel Northampton, Iron Horse Cafe, Bay State Cabaret. **Admission:** paid. **Daily entry:** $10 to $24. **Secondary genre[s]:** HRCK, IRSH. **Acts:** national acts, regional acts, local acts. **Sample day's lineup:** Killybilly, Vestrymen, Cul De Sac, No Safety, Smack Dab, Madder Rose, Nisi Period, Crack Sex, Big Bad Bullocks, Piss Factory, Angry Johnny, Foo, Supreme Dicks, Green Magnet School, Lyres, Spring House, Trojan Ponies, Lunachicks, Oat Pearl, Eyelid, Wombat, Mr. Cranky, PSD, Cheetahs, Rent Party. **Contact:** Loud Music Festival, 227 Chestnut Hill Road, Montague, MA 01351, 413-367-0350/9404.

### SONGSTREET CAJUN-BLUEGRASS FESTIVAL, Somerville, MA
Early Apr.
Variety, Folk and International

Since 1995. **Days:** 1. **Site:** indoor. Somerville Theater, Davis Square. **Admission:** paid. **Daily entry:** $10 to $24. **Secondary genre[s]:** TC&W, BLGS, ZYDC. **Acts:** national acts, regional acts, local acts. **Sample day's lineup:** Claire Lynch, The Heartbeats, Boogaloo Swamis, Bluegrass Supply Co. **Contact:** Songstreet Productions, P. O. Box 85, Somerville, MA 02143, 617-628-3390.

### WORLD FAIR AT BOSTON UNIVERSITY, Boston, MA
Early Apr. to Middle Apr.
Variety, Folk and International

Since 1983. Celebration of culture and diversity put on by 30 student clubs and 15-20 community organizations. **Help!** A sample lineup? **Site:** outdoor and indoor. Various locations on, and off, campus. **Admission:** free and paid. **Daily entry:** under $10, $10 to $24. **Discounts:** student discounts, advance purchase discounts. **Secondary genre[s]:** TLAT, AFRM, AFRC, RGGE, CBRT, OTHR **Acts:** local acts. **Contact:** Boston University, International Students and Scholars Office, 19 Deerfield Street, Boston MA, 02215, 617-353-3565/3581.

### AMERICAN INDIAN DAY AT THE CHILDREN'S MUSEUM, Boston, MA
Early Apr.
Native American

Since 1981. "The museum-wide celebration of Native Americans features food, crafts, music and dancing representative of Native tribes throughout the Americas." -- Listing. **Days:** 1. **Site:** indoor. Children's Museum, 300 Congress Street. **Contact:** Children's Museum, 300 Congress Street, Boston, MA 02210, 617-426-6500.

## PEPSI BOSTON MUSIC AWARDS, Boston, MA

Early Apr.
Variety, General

Since 1987. **Days:** 1. **Site:** indoor. Wang Center. **Admission:** paid. **Daily entry:** $25 to $49, $50 and over. **Secondary genre[s]:** ARCK, HRCK, RAP, MR&B, TR&B, MC&W, BLGS, MFOL, ZYDC, MLAT, RGGE. **Acts:** national acts, regional acts, local acts. **Sample day's lineup:** Aimee Mann, Concussion Ensemble, Ronnie Earl and The Broadcasters, the story, Ellis Paul, Chris Harford, many others. **Contact:** Boston Music Awards, 216 Tremont Street, Suite 806, Boston, MA 02116, 617-338-3144.

## NATIVE AMERICAN DAY AT THE FORUM, Framingham, MA

Early Apr.
Native American

See other dates and sites. **Days:** 1. **Hours per day:** 9. **Site:** indoor. Framingham State College, 100 State Street. **Contact:** Massachusetts Center for Native American Awareness, Inc., P. O. Box 5885, Boston, MA 02114-5885, 617-884-4227.

## SONGSTREET FOLK-ROCK FESTIVAL, Somerville, MA

Early Apr.
Modern Folk

Since 1993. **Days:** 1. **Site:** indoor. Somerville Theater, Davis Square. **Admission:** paid. **Daily entry:** $10 to $24. **Discounts:** student discounts, advance purchase discounts. **Acts:** national acts, regional acts, local acts. **Sample day's lineup:** Greg Greenway Band, disappear fear, Catie Curtis, The Burns Sisters. **Contact:** Songstreet Productions, P. O. Box 85, Somerville, MA 02143, 617-628-3390.

## SCOTTISH FIDDLE RALLY, Somerville, MA

Middle Apr.
Scottish

Since 1985. "The music is rhythmically insistent. The songs start out moderately and mount in speed and excitement... No, it's not rock and roll, it's Scottish fiddle music -- some of the finest examples of which you can hear [here]." -- Boston Phoenix. **Days:** 3. **Site:** indoor. Concert: Somerville Theater, Davis Square; workshops: Cambridge Center for Adult Education, 42 & 56 Brattle Street; celidh: Canadian-American Club, 202 Arlington Street, Watertown. **Admission:** free and paid. **Daily entry:** $10 to $24, under $10 **Acts:** national acts, local acts. **Sample day's lineup:** Aly Bain, Jerry Holland, John Cokely, Hillel Jason, Lawrence Scott, Boston Scottish Fiddle Club, others. **Audio merchandise:** "Scottish Fiddle Rally, Vols, 1, 2, 3" (self-produced and distributed). **Contact:** Boston Scottish Fiddle Club, P. O. Box 823, North Cambridge, MA 02140, 508-922-8595.

## WBOS-FM EARTH DAY CONCERT AND FESTIVAL, Boston, MA

Late Apr.
Variety, General

Kick-off to a summer-long weekly music series, "Music Festival For The Earth," featuring national acts. **Days:** 1. **Site:** outdoor. MDC Hatch Shell. **Admission:** free. **Secondary genre[s]:** MRCK, CRCK, MFOL, OTHR. **Acts:** national acts, regional acts, local acts. **Sample day's lineup:** Roger McGuinn, Richie Havens, Jeffrey Gaines, Orleans, The Waltons, The Williams Bros., Karen Farr, others. **Contact:** WBOS-FM, 1200 Soldier's Field Road, Boston, MA 02134, 617-787-0929/254-9267.

NEW ENGLAND FOLK FESTIVAL, Natick, MA
> Late Apr.
> Variety, Folk and International

Since 1945. **Days:** 3. **Hours per day:** 13.5. **Site:** outdoor and indoor. Natick High School, Campus Drive off Pond Street. **Admission:** paid. **Daily entry:** under $10. **Discounts:** student discounts, multiple event or day passes. **Secondary genre[s]:** TJAZ, TR&B, ACAP, TGOS, TC&W, BLGS, MFOL, TFOL, MARI, ZYDC, IRSH, JWSH, NATV, SCOT, TLAT, AFRC, OTHR. **Acts:** regional acts, local acts. **Sample day's lineup:** Tony Parkes, Yankee Ingenuity, Vince O'Donnell, Festival Orchestra, Dick Tracy, Mary Devlin, Brad Foster, Walter Lenk and Sarah Gregory Smith, Lisa Greenleaf and Tony Saletan, Nasty Habits, Marilyn Richards, MIT Folk Dance Club, Beth Parkes, Rum and Onions, Andrea Majewska, Anthony Moretti Tufts, Strathspey and Rell Society of NH, Ted Sanella, Planetary Socks, Susan Roth Rose, Uncle Gizmo, Carol Kopp, Yonina Gordon, Rumpetroll, Gammaldansbandet, Ira Gessell, Froggie on the Carport, Andrea Adder, Evelyn Murray, White Cockade, Susie Petrov, Local Hero, Mel Meer, Becky States, Toby Weinberg, Magnolia, Rick Mohr, Susan Kevra, Lynn Baumeister and Lisa Tamres, Robin Rogers-Browne, Brad Foster, Pleasure of the Town, Flying Tomatoes, Different Village, Steve Zakon, Fresh Fish, Linda Leslie, Sound Bight, Dudley Laufman, Jacqueline Gilman and Bob McQuillen, Reel Nutmeg, Carol Ormand, Jump at the Sun, Judith Stames-Hamilton, Cambridge Folk Orchestra, Salmon Run Cloggers, Hanny Budnick, AJDE Folk Dance Band, Judy Anscombe, Peter Barnes, Steve Brown, Ted Crane, Silvia Cornell and Friends, Becky Tracy, Jonathon Finger, Sol Weber, Boston Scottish Fiddle Club, Agbekor Drum and Dance, Rick Avery and Judy Greenhill, Robin Spaar, Tom Smith, Daisy Nell and David Coffin, Andy Woolf, Victor Cockburn, Annie Patterson, Peter Blood, Jackson Gillman, Ginnie Ely, Gail Rundlett, The Beans, Folk Song Soc. of Greater Boston, Brad Hurley and Chris Abel, Catherine Crowe, Andy Davis, Deanna Stiles, Allan Block and Ken Sweeney, Helen Bonchek Schneyer, Jeff Warner, Bridget Fitzgerald, Dick Swain, Mystic Seaport Chanteymen, Bob Walser, Pam Weeks, Larry Kaplan, Allen Hopkins, Bennett Hammond, Drew Smith and Friends, Kasha Breau, Kathy Westra and Friends, Rozmarin, Sonja Savig, The Patons, Walker Street, others. **Contact:** New England Folk Festival Association, 1950 Massachusetts Avenue, Cambridge, MA 02140, 617-354-1340.

EARTH DAY POW-WOW, Leominster, MA
> Late Apr.
> Native American

See other dates and sites. **Days:** 1. **Hours per day:** 5. **Site:** indoor. Sears Town Mall. **Contact:** Massachusetts Center for Native American Awareness, Inc., P. O. Box 5885, Boston, MA 02114-5885, 617-884-4227.

KENMORE SQUARE RITES OF SPRING CHARITY ROCKFEST, Boston, MA
> Late Apr.
> Alternative and College Rock

**Days:** 1. **Site:** outdoor. Kenmore Square, Commonwealth Avenue. **Admission:** free. **Acts:** local acts. **Sample day's lineup:** Thumper, The Turbulent Daughters, Powerman 5000, The Fighting Cocks, T. H. and The Wreckage, Rapt Rascals and The Sorority House, Horns. **Contact:** Kenmore Square Association, 510 Commonwealth Avenue, Boston, MA 617-262-6246.

STUDENTS FOR STUDENTS/HUMAN RIGHTS FESTIVAL, Boston, MA
> Late Apr.
> Alternative and College Rock

Since 1989. **Days:** 1. **Hours per day:** 6. **Site:** outdoor and indoor. Faneuil Hall Marketplace. **Admission:** free. **Acts:** regional acts, local acts. **Sample day's lineup:** Swinging Steaks, Letters to Cleo, Lava Beat, Cosmos Factor. **Contact:** Amnesty International, 58 Day Street, Somerville, MA 02144, 617-623-0202.

## SHEEP SHEARING FESTIVAL, Waltham, MA
Late Apr.
Traditional Folk

Since 1988. **Days:** 1. **Hours per day:** 6. **Site:** outdoor and indoor. Gore Place, 52 Gore Street. **Admission:** paid. **Daily entry:** under $10. **Restrictions:** 10. **Secondary genre[s]:** MARI, IRSH. **Acts:** regional acts, local acts. **Sample day's lineup:** Joe Cormier, Gail Rundlett, others. **Contact:** Gore Place, 52 Gore Street, Waltham, MA 02154, 617-894-2798.

## ARTS FIRST: A HARVARD/RADCLIFFE CELEBRATION, Cambridge, MA
Late Apr. to Middle May
Variety, General

Since 1993. "The goal of this festival is to celebrate students in the arts and to galvanzie the arts community at Harvard and Radcliffe. [It] comprises some 85 student performances and events, a film festival, and 16 exhibitions." -- Program. **Days:** 3. **Hours per day:** 12. **Site:** outdoor and indoor. 26 locations around the two adjoining campuses. **Admission:** free and paid. **Daily entry:** under $10. **Discounts:** student discounts. **Secondary genre[s]:** MJAZ, ARCK, ACAP, MFOL, SCOT, AFRC, AVNT, CBRT, OTHR. **Acts:** local acts. **Contact:** Office for the Arts at Harvard and Radcliffe, Harvard Information Center, 1350 Massachusetts Avenue, Cambridge, MA 617-495-8676.

## BLACKSMITH HOUSE DULCIMER FESTIVAL, Cambridge, MA
Late Apr. to Early May
Traditional Folk

See other dates. **Days:** 3. **Hours per day:** 13. **Site:** indoor. Blacksmith House, 56 Brattle Street, Harvard Square. **Admission:** paid. **Daily entry:** under $10, $10 to $24, $25 to $49. **Discounts:** multiple event or day passes. **Secondary genre[s]:** IRSH, OTHR. **Acts:** regional acts, local acts. **Sample day's lineup:** Aubrey Atwater, Bob Wey, Roasamond Campbell, Lorraine Lee-Hammond, Sally McKnight, Gail Rundlett, Debbie Suran, Pam Weeks, Zhentian Zhang, Sam Rizzetta, others. **Contact:** Cambridge Center for Adult Education, 42 Brattle Street, P. O. Box 9113, Cambridge, MA 02238-9113, 617-547-6789.

## HARVARD SQUARE'S MAY FAIR, Cambridge, MA
Early May
Variety, General

Since 1984. **Days:** 1. **Hours per day:** 6. **Site:** outdoor. JFK and Brattle Streets. **Admission:** free. **Secondary genre[s]:** ARCK, TR&B, TFOL, RGGE. **Acts:** local acts. **Sample day's lineup:** Inca Son, Nightcrawlers, Premiers, Branches Steel Orchestra, Harbor Lights Jam Troup, Southern Hammered Dulcimers, Leonard Solomon Bellowphone. **Contact:** Harvard Square Business Association, 18 Brattle Street, Cambridge, MA 617-491-3434.

## WBCN ROCK 'N' ROLL RUMBLE, Boston, MA
Early May to Late May
Hard Rock and Heavy Metal

Since 1979. **Days:** 9. **Hours per day:** 5. **Site:** indoor. The Paradise Rock Club, 1277 Commonwealth Avenue. **Admission:** paid. **Daily entry:** under $10. **Secondary genre[s]:** ARCK. **Acts:** local acts. **Sample day's lineup:** Augusta Furnace, Sidewalk Gallery, Mercy Beat, Malachite. **Contact:** WBCN 104.1 FM, 1265 Boylston Street, Boston, MA 02215, 617-536-8000/266-1111 x239.

BOSTON BREWER'S FESTIVAL, Boston, MA
Middle May
Blues and Traditional R&B

Since 1993. "The East Coast's Premier Beer-Tasting Event. Taste as many beers as you want... over 150 great beers, 50 micro breweries, home-brew exhibits. It's entertainment with a head on it!" -- Advertisement. **Days:** 1. **Hours per day:** 8. **Site:** indoor. World Trade Center, Northern Avenue. **Admission:** paid. **Daily entry:** $10 to $24. **Secondary genre[s]:** ARCK. **Acts:** regional acts, local acts. **Sample day's lineup:** Heavy Metal Horns, Madhouse, Mighty Sam McLain, Monster Mike Welch. **Contact:** Beacon Kendall Entertainment, 238 Broadway, Cambridge, MA 02139, 617-547-6311.

WGBH "T" PARTY, Boston, MA
Middle May
Variety, General

"Ride the 'T' and hear great music!" -- Advertisement. **Days:** 1. **Hours per day:** 5. **Site:** outdoor and indoor. 6 subway stops. **Admission:** free. **Secondary genre[s]:** MJAZ, ARCK, ACAP, AC&W, MFOL, ZYDC, AFRC, BRZL, RGGE, OTHR. **Acts:** national acts, regional acts, local acts. **Sample day's lineup:** Janice Allen, Jorge Arce, Boogaloo Swamis, Boston Basketeers of New England Conservatory, Brasilierinho, Cosmos Factor, Courage Brothers, Emotional Rollercoaster, Gus, Jane Hayes Quartet, Sally Rogers and Howie Bursen, Ibrahima Camara, Inca Son, Eula Lawrence and Plus Three, Metro Steel Orchestra, Jane Miller Band, Myanna, Ron Reed and Sunsteel, Sonabo, Stan Strickland and Syd Smart, Livingston Taylor, Whiz Bang Deal Band. **Contact:** WGBH Special Events Department, 125 Western Avenue, Boston, MA 02134, 617-492-2777.

SIGONOMEG POW-WOW, Middleboro, MA
Middle May
Native American

See other dates and sites. **Days:** 2. **Site:** outdoor. Pratt Farm, Route 105. **Contact:** Massachusetts Center for Native American Awareness, Inc., P. O. Box 5885, Boston, MA 02114-5885, 617-884-4227.

ACOUSTIC UNDERGROUND CONCERTS AND CD RELEASE PARTIES, Varies, MA
Middle May
Modern Folk

Celebrating release of live recordings made during month-long, singer/songwriter competition held the prior fall. See other dates and sites. **Days:** 3. **Site:** indoor. Boston: The Paradise, 967 Commonwealth Avenue. Westborough: Old Vienna Kaffeehaus, 22 South Street. Northampton: Iron Horse Cafe, 20 Center Street. **Admission:** paid. **Acts:** regional acts, local acts. **Sample day's lineup:** Catie Curtis, Ellis Paul, Flathead, Wendy Sobel and Kathy Phipps, Dave Crossland, Vox One, Jim Infantino, Laurie Geltman Band, Don White, Barbara Kessler, McDonnel/Tane, Liz Brahm. **Contact:** The Acoustic Underground, 491 Riverside Avenue, Box 8, Medford, MA 02155, 617-254-1050 **or:** Entertainment Concepts, 173 Brighton Avenue, Brighton, MA 02134, 617-327-6470. .

BOSTON KITE FESTIVAL, Boston, MA
Middle May
Modern R&B

Since 1969. See other dates and sites. **Days:** 1. **Site:** outdoor. William Devine Golf Course, Franklin Park. **Admission:** free. **Secondary genre[s]:** RGGE. **Acts:** national acts, local acts. **Sample day's lineup:** Tene Williams, Chen Cey, Savage, Here and Now. **Contact:** Boston Parks and Recreation Department, 1010 Massachusetts Avenue, Boston, MA 02118, 617-635-4505.

ART NEWBURY STREET, Boston, MA
> Middle May
> Variety, General

"Stroll Boston's elegant 8-block street and enjoy 30 gallery open-houses and special exhibits." -- Listing. See other dates. **Days:** 1. **Hours per day:** 4. **Site:** outdoor and indoor. Newbury Street. **Secondary genre[s]:** MJAZ, AFRC, OTHR. **Acts:** local acts. **Sample day's lineup:** Tom Pollard Trio, Elliot Gibbons, Herbs Heard, Cora Connection, Saltre Bigelow Trio, Eastwood String Orchestra. **Contact:** Newbury Street League, 158 Newbury Street, Boston, MA 02116, 617-267-7961.

MAKE-A-WISH-FOUNDATION COUNTRY JAMBOREE, Ipswich, MA
> Middle May
> Modern Country

**Help!** One time only? **Days:** 1. **Hours per day:** 8. **Site:** indoor. Majestic Dragon Restaurant and Lounge, Route 1. **Admission:** paid. **Daily entry:** under $10. **Acts:** local acts. **Sample day's lineup:** Blue River Band, Johnny Russell, Country Fever, Cat Ballou, Lee Blais. **Contact:** Majestic Restaurant and Lounge, Route 1, Ipswich, MA 01938, 508-356-0706.

HOMEFOLKS CONCERT, Boston, MA
> Late May
> Modern Folk

Benefits the Massachusetts Coalition for the Homeless. **Days:** 1. **Site:** indoor. Paulist Church Center, 5 Park Street. **Admission:** paid. **Daily entry:** under $10, $10 to $24. **Discounts:** advance purchase discounts. **Acts:** regional acts, local acts. **Sample day's lineup:** Catie Curtis, Patty Griffith, Martin Sexton, Diane Ziegler. **Contact:** Homefolks, 15 St. Mark's Road, Boston, MA 02124, 617-825-1184.

FOLK FESTIVAL/FLEA MARKET AND CRAFT SHOW, Braintree, MA
> Late May
> Traditional Folk

Continuous music outdoors by day, "Singer/Songwriter Showcase Concert" indoors by night. See other dates and sites. **Help!** A sample lineup? **Days:** 1. **Hours per day:** 14. **Site:** outdoor and indoor. All Souls Unitarian Universalist Church, Elm and Church Streets. **Admission:** free and paid. **Daily entry:** Under $10. **Contact:** Folk Song Society of Greater Boston, P. O. Box 492, Somerville MA 02143, 617-298-8533.

INDIAN RANCH COUNTRY MUSIC FESTIVAL AND CHICKEN BARBEQUE, Webster, MA
> Late May
> Modern Country

"Good food. Lots of music." -- Program. See other dates. **Help!** A sample lineup? **Days:** 1. **Site:** outdoor. Indian Ranch, Route 16. **Admission:** paid. **Daily entry:** under $10, $10 to $24. **Acts:** local acts. **Contact:** Indian Ranch, P. O. Box 1157, 275 Main Street, Webster, MA 01570, 508-943-3871/2936/4159.

STREET PERFORMERS FESTIVAL, Boston, MA
> Late May
> Variety, General

"This extravaganza of talent...takes to the streets of Faneuil Hall Marketplace for a weekend of continuous entertainment....March gaily in the Kazoo Parade, or simply sit back and enjoy the entertainment." -- Listing. **Help!** A sample lineup? **Days:** 3. **Site:** outdoor. Faneuil Hall Marketplace. **Admission:** free. **Acts:** local acts. **Contact:** Street Performers Festival, Faneuil Hall Marketplace, Inc., Boston, MA 02109-1616, 617-523-1300.

### SALEM SEAPORT FESTIVAL, Salem, MA
Late May
Variety, Folk and International

See other dates and sites. **Days:** 3. **Hours per day:** 9. **Site:** outdoor and indoor. Salem Maritime National Historic Site and Pickering Wharf. **Admission:** free. **Secondary genre[s]:** TR&B, BLGS, MARI, IRSH, TLAT, RGGE, OTHR. **Acts:** local acts. **Sample day's lineup:** Angel Gould, Zhentian Zang, Gerdes Fluerant, Ethnographico Portugal des Pequeninos, Howie Tarnower, Fantasia, Silas Hubbard and The Hot Ribs. **Contact:** Salem Maritime National Historic Site, 178 Derby Street, Salem, MA 01970, 508-744-432 3**or:** Waterfront Festivals, Ltd., 4 Greenleaf Woods Drive, Suite 302, Portsmouth, NH 03801, 207-439-2021.

### PLANTING MOON POW-WOW, Topsfield, MA
Late May
Native American

**Days:** 3. **Hours per day:** 7. **Site:** outdoor. Topsfield Fairgrounds. **Admission:** paid **Daily entry:** under $10. **Contact:** Massachusetts Center for Native Americans, P. O. Box 5885, Boston, MA 02114, 617-884-4227.

### INDIAN POW WOW, Charlemont, MA
Late May to Late Sep.
Native American

Approximately 7 times per year at same site. "Traditional-style, the way it's supposed to be done." -- Festival Volunteer. **Days:** 18. **Site:** outdoor. Indian Plaza, Route 2. **Contact:** Indian Plaza, Route 2, Charlemont, MA 01339, 413-339-4096.

### BLUEGRASS FESTIVAL, Washington, MA
Late May
Variety, Country and Bluegrass

Modest, but long-running, festival on lawn at 22-room inn. See other dates. **Days:** 1. **Site:** outdoor. Bucksteep Manor, Washington Mountain Road. **Secondary genre[s]:** MC&W, BLGS. **Acts:** regional acts, local acts. **Sample day's lineup:** Southern Rail, Sassygrass, Way Out West, Dooley-Austin. **Contact:** Bucksteep Manor, Washington Mountain Road, Washington, MA 01223, 413-623-5535.

### MARITIME MUSIC FESTIVAL, Salem, MA
Late May
Maritime

See other dates. **Help!** A sample lineup? **Days:** 1. **Hours per day:** 4. **Site:** indoor. Peabody and Essex Museum. **Admission:** free and paid. **Daily entry:** under $10, $10 to $24. **Acts:** regional acts, local acts. **Contact:** Peabody and Essex Museum, East India Square, Salem, MA 508-745-1876.

### COUNTRY MUSIC FESTIVAL TO BENEFIT AMERICAN HEART ASSOCIATION, Webster, MA
Late May
Modern Country

Since 1977. See other dates. **Days:** 1. **Hours per day:** 8. **Site:** outdoor. Indian Ranch, Route 16. **Admission:** paid. **Daily entry:** under $10. **Acts:** regional acts, local acts. **Sample day's lineup:** John Penny Band, Sleepy LaBeef, John Lincoln Wright and The Sour Mash Boys, Liz Boardo and Borderline, John Hicks and Revolution, Bobby Carlson and Silver Saddle, Bobby Sheppard Band, County Line, Marilyn and The Monroe Brothers, Heartbreak City, Jackie lee Williams Band, Nash Sisters, Johnny White, Mike Preston, Cheyenne. **Contact:** Indian Ranch, Box 1157, 275 Main Street, Webster, MA 01570, 508-943-3871/2936/4159.

## AMERICAN PIT MASTERS BAR-B-Q ROUND-UP, Boston, MA
Early Jun.
Variety, General

"Come taste the excitement as Bar-B-Q Masters from Texas to Canada offer up their award-winning smokehouse meats and seafoods." -- Advertisement. See other dates and sites. **Days:** 4. **Hours per day:** 11. **Site:** outdoor. Boston Fan Pier, Northern Avenue. **Admission:** paid. **Daily entry:** under $10. **Secondary genre[s]:** CRCK, ARCK, TR&B, BGOS, MC&W, MFOL, FDDL, RGGE. **Acts:** national acts, regional acts, local acts. **Sample day's lineup:** Bo Diddley and The Debbie Hastings Band, Toni Lynn Washington Band, Miss Xanna Don't, Letters to Cleo, The Bristols. **Contact:** Conventures, Inc., 250 Summer Street, Boston, MA 02210, 617-439-7700.

## BOSTON FESTIVAL OF BANDS, Boston, MA
Early Jun.
Drum Corp and Marching Bands

Since 1988. **Help!** A sample lineup? **Days:** 1. **Hours per day:** 8. **Site:** outdoor. Fanueil Hall. **Admission:** free. **Secondary genre[s]:** OTHR. **Acts:** regional acts. **Contact:** Metropolitan Wind Symphony, 62 Mossdale Road, Jamaica Plain, MA 617-983-1370.

## TASTE OF CHICOPEE, Chicopee, MA
Early Jun.
Variety, General

Since 1990. "Serving up for your pleasure." -- Advertisement. **Days:** 3. **Hours per day:** 12. **Site:** outdoor. Chicopee Center, Exchange and Perkins Streets. **Secondary genre[s]:** MRCK, CRCK, MC&W, IRSH. **Acts:** local acts. **Sample day's lineup:** Ray Guillemette, Jay Murphy Irish Band, The Goatropers, Strawberry Jam Band, Friends, The Entertainers. **Contact:** Mayor's Office, 17 Springfield Street, Chicopee, MA 01013, 413-594-4711 x203.

## LA FESTA, North Adams, MA
Early Jun. to Late Jun.
Variety, General

"Northern Berkshire's Community Festival!" -- Program. **Days:** 7. **Hours per day:** 10. **Site:** outdoor and indoor. Multiple locations. **Admission:** paid. **Daily entry:** under $10, $10 to $24. **Discounts: Secondary genre[s]:** TJAZ, CRCK, TR&B, MC&W, IRSH, JWSH, SCOT, OTHR. **Acts:** national acts, regional acts, local acts. **Sample series lineup:** Day One: Robin Lee, Deirdre Reilly; Day Two: Sammy Kaye Big Band; Day Three: Shirley Lewis. **Contact:** La Festa, P. O. Box 1704, North Adams, MA 01247, 413-663-6998/3604.

## KISS-108 FM CONCERT, Mansfield, MA
Early Jun.
Modern Rock and Pop

Since 1980. **Days:** 1. **Hours per day:** 12. **Site:** outdoor. Great Woods Center for the Performing Arts. **Admission:** paid. **Daily entry:** $25 to $49, $50 and over. **Restrictions:** 1, 6, 7, 8. **Secondary genre[s]:** CRCK, ARCK, RAP, MR&B, TR&B, RGGE. **Acts:** national acts, regional acts, local acts. **Sample day's lineup:** After 7, Barry White and The Love Unlimited Orchestra, The Bee Gee's, Boy Krazy, Cameo, Chris Isaak, Classic Example, Chris Cuevas, Duran Duran, Erin Cruise, Expose, George Clinton and The P-Funk All Stars, Hi-Five, Inner Circle, Jack Mack and The Heart Attack, Jeremy Jordan, Jeffrey Osborne, Jordy, Keith Sweat, Mitch Malloy, Nenh Cherry, Patty Smyth, Peter Wolf, PM Dawn, Shanice, Shannon, Silk, Snow, Sonia Dada, SWV, Technotronic, Tene Williams, Terence Trent D'Arby, Tony Terry, Wendy Moten. **Contact:** Great Woods Center for the Performing Arts, P. O. Box 810, Mansfield, MA 02048, 508-339-2333 **or:** WXKS-FM, 99 Revere Beach Parkway, P. O. Box 128, Medford, MA 02155, 617-396-1430.

JAMAICA PLAIN FOLK FESTIVAL, Jamaica Plain, MA
> Early Jun.
> Variety, Folk and International

**Days:** 1. **Site:** indoor. First Unitarian Church, 6 Eliot Street. **Admission:** paid. **Daily entry:** $10 to $24. **Discounts:** advance purchase discounts. **Secondary genre[s]:** MFOL. **Acts:** local acts. **Sample day's lineup:** Linda Waterfall, Fortaleza, David Dodson, Tom Pirozzoli. **Contact:** Volcano Records, P. O. Box 368, Boston, MA 02134, 617-783-4244/445-7998.

HYANNIS HARBOR FESTIVAL, Hyannis, MA
> Early Jun.
> Variety, General

Since 1982. **Days:** 2. **Hours per day:** 8. **Site:** outdoor. Bismore Park, Ocean Street. **Admission:** free. **Secondary genre[s]:** MJAZ, MFOL. **Acts:** local acts. **Sample day's lineup:** All Star Jazz Band, The Natives, Gene Burque Group, Troy Williams Group, Rosemary Small. **Contact:** Hyannis Area Chamber of Commerce, 319 Barnstable Road, Hyannis, MA 02601, 508-775-2201.

POW-WOW, Rutland, MA
> Early Jun.
> Native American

"Public is cordially invited" -- Program. See other sites and dates. **Days:** 2. **Site:** outdoor. Memorial Field, Rutland Center, Routes 56 and 122A. **Restrictions:** 2. **Contact:** Worcester Inter-Tribal Indian Center, 196 Highland Street, Worcester, MA 01609, 508-754-3300.

NATIVE AMERICAN INTERTRIBAL FESTIVAL/CAPE HERITAGE, Mashpee, MA
> Early Jun.
> Native American

Pow Wow in conjunction with Cape Heritage. See other dates and sites. **Days:** 1. **Hours per day:** 5. **Site:** outdoor. Mashpee Commons, Routes 151 and 28. **Admission:** free. **Contact:** Massachusetts Center for Native American Awareness, Inc., P. O. Box 5885, Boston, MA 02114-5885, 617-884-4227.

HARPOON'S BREWSTOCK, Boston, MA
> Late Jun.
> Alternative and College Rock

Since 1988. "Over 20 of this country's best, small regional breweries!" -- Advertisement. See other dates. **Days:** 3. **Hours per day:** 9. **Site:** outdoor and indoor. Massachusetts Bay Brewing Co., 306 Northern Avenue. **Admission:** paid. **Daily entry:** under $10. **Secondary genre[s]:** HRCK, RGGE, OTHR. **Acts:** local acts. **Sample day's lineup:** Hot Like Fire, Heretix, The Oberlander Boys, Sub Terranians, Happy Bunny, Natives, The Candles, Royal Ramblers. **Contact:** Massachusetts Bay Brewing Co., 306 Northern Avenue, Boston, MA 02210, 617-951-4099/574-9551.

RIVERFEST, Buckland, MA
> Middle Jun.
> Variety, General

**Days:** 1. **Site:** outdoor. Nepco Park. **Secondary genre[s]:** TJAZ, TFOL, OTHR. **Acts:** local acts. **Sample day's lineup:** Lee Ross, Riverfront Jump, Suzy Robbins, Peter Blank and Peter Michaline, Becky Ashiton. **Contact:** Shelburne Falls Area Business Assoication, P. O. Box, Shelburne Falls, MA 01370, 413-625-8179.

## Rock 'n Roll Block Party, Holyoke, MA
Middle Jun.
Modern Rock and Pop

Since 1994. **Days:** 1. **Site:** indoor. Holiday Inn. **Admission:** paid. **Daily entry:** under $10. **Restrictions:** 5. **Acts:** local acts. **Sample day's lineup:** Urban Decay, Hooker Crook, Bombastics, Love Junkyard, The Sighs, Dim Wolfgang, PRS 7. **Contact:** Holiday Inn, 245 Whiting Farms Road, Holyoke, MA 01040, 413-534-3311 x570.

## Irish Cultural Center's Festival, North Easton, MA
Middle Jun.
Irish

Since 1991. **Days:** 3. **Hours per day:** 14. **Site:** outdoor. Stonehill College. **Admission:** paid. **Daily entry:** $10 to $24. **Discounts:** multiple event or day passes. **Secondary genre[s]:** ARCK, SCOT. **Acts:** national acts, regional acts, local acts. **Sample day's lineup:** Cherish The Ladies, The Clancy Brothers, Sharon Shannon Band, Johnny McEvoy, Sean Potts, Paddy Reilly, Aoife Clancy, Seamus Connolly, Christine Harrison, Joe Glynn and Irish Mist, Alfie O'Shea, Pipe Band Parade, Mary McGonigle, Black Velvet Band, Fintan Stanley, Silver Spears, Paddy Keenan, David O'Doherty, Len Graham and John Campbell, others. **Contact:** Irish Cultural Center, 1895 Centre Street, Suite 7, West Roxbury, MA 02132, 617-323-3399/8005.

## Cambridge International Fair, Cambridge, MA
Middle Jun.
Variety, Folk and International

Since 1991. Launches "Summer in the City" -- a series of concerts and cultural events culminating in Cambridge River Festival. On hiatus in 1993, but planned again for 1994. **Days:** 1. **Hours per day:** 7. **Site:** outdoor. University Park, Sydney Street and Massachusetts Avenue. **Secondary genre[s]:** ACAP, BLGS, TFOL, FDDL, ZYDC, IRSH, TLAT, AFRC, RGGE, OTHR. **Acts:** local acts. **Sample day's lineup:** Humano, Diversity, Camara Samba School, Suzuki Institute Violinists, Horace Faith, Jorge Arce, Alejandro Rivera and Michael Hayes, Fortaleza, Sandy's Music, The Red Hots, Nymah Kumah, Won In Heart, Lionel Charles, James Greenfield, Jaffar, Stone Montgomery, Panorama Steel Band, Sally McKnight, Christos Govetas and Beth Cohen, Jerry Robichaud and Ed Boudreau, Allen Combs, Capoeira Camara, others. **Contact:** Cambridge Arts Council, 57 Inman Street, Cambridge, MA 02139, 617-349-4394/4380.

## Cambridge Public Library Jazz Festival, Cambridge, MA
Middle Jun.
Modern Jazz

Since 1986. **Days:** 1. **Hours per day:** 3. **Site:** indoor. Cambridge Public Library, 449 Broadway. **Admission:** free. **Acts:** local acts. **Sample day's lineup:** Matt Johnson, Jayne Hayes Quartet, Collective Experience. **Contact:** Cambridge Public Library, 449 Broadway, Cambridge, MA 617-349-4040.

## Boston Waterfront Festival, Boston, MA
Middle Jun.
Variety, Folk and International

See other dates and sites. **Help!** One time only? **Days:** 2. **Hours per day:** 9. **Site:** outdoor. Christopher Columbus Park, Commercial Street. **Admission:** free. **Secondary genre[s]:** TR&B, BLGS, MARI, IRSH, TLAT, RGGE, OTHR. **Acts:** local acts. **Sample day's lineup:** Angel Gould, Zhentian Zang, Gerdes Fluerant, Ethnographico Portugal des Pequeninos, Howie Tarnower, Fantasia, Silas Hubbard and The Hot Ribs. **Contact:** Waterfront Festivals, Ltd., 4 Greenleaf Woods Drive, Suite 302, Portsmouth, NH 03801, 617-262-1414.

FALL RIVER FESTIVAL, Fall River, MA
        Middle Jun.
        Variety, General

Since 1982. **Days:** 2. **Hours per day:** 11. **Site:** outdoor and indoor. Fall River Heritage State Park, 200 Davol Street West. **Secondary genre[s]:** MJAZ, CRCK, TR&B, ACAP, MFOL, CBRT, OTHR. **Acts:** local acts. **Sample day's lineup:** Charlie Quintal and the Talk of the Town, Heritage State Park Singers, All Horn'd Up, Shot in the Dark, Deppin, Bigelow and Moran Jazz Trio, Durfee High School Band. **Contact:** Fall River Office of Economic Development, One Government Center, Fall River, MA 02722, 508-675-1497.

PRIDEFEST, Boston, MA
        Middle Jun.
        Gay and Lesbian

Gay Pride Breakfast; Gay Pride Parade; Gay Pride Rally and Festival; Street Dances. **Help!** A sample lineup? **Days:** 2. **Site:** outdoor and indoor. The Cyclorama, Copley Square to Boston Common, Chandler and Canal Streets, The Castle. **Admission:** free. **Acts:** national acts, local acts. **Contact:** Pridefest , c/o Share Systems, 58 Day, Somerville, MA 617-623-4500 x317.

WOLLOMONUPPOAG INDIAN COUNCIL INTER-TRIBAL POW WOW, Attleboro, MA
        Middle Jul.
        Native American

"Walk the Earth softly." -- John Running Deer. **Days:** 1. **Hours per day:** 8. **Site:** outdoor. LaSalette Shrine Festival Field, Route 118. **Admission:** free. **Restrictions:** 2. **Acts:** local acts. **Sample day's lineup:** Roaming Buffalo Singers, others. **Contact:** Wollomonuppoag Indian Council Inter-Tribal Pow Wow, 40 Laurel Lane, Raynham, MA 02767-1914, 508-822-5061.

**BOSTON GLOBE JAZZ FESTIVAL**, Boston, MA
        Middle Jun.
        Modern Jazz

Since 1967. **Days:** 7. **Hours per day:** 12. **Site:** outdoor and indoor, 19 locations around town. **Admission:** free and paid. **Daily entry:** under $10, $10 to $24. **Secondary genre[s]:** AJAZ, TR&B, MLAT, AFRC, BRZL. **Acts:** national acts, regional acts, local acts. **Sample day's lineup:** Ray Charles, Bobby Watson and Horizon, Wolfgang Muthspiel Trio with Tom Harrell, Ivo Perlman. **Contact:** Festival Productions, Inc., 311 West 74th Street, New York, NY 10023, 617-523-404 7**or:** Public Affairs Department, Boston Globe, Boston, MA 02107, 617-929-2649. .

RACE UNITY DAY, Boston, MA
        Middle Jun.
        African American

"Race Unity Day was inaugurated in 1957 by the National Spiritual Assembly of the Baha'is of the U. S. to promote racial harmony and understanding throughout the nation." -- Program. **Days:** 1. **Hours per day:** 6. **Site:** outdoor. Boston Common Bandstand. **Secondary genre[s]:** MJAZ, ARCK, RAP, MR&B, MFOL, NATV, MLAT, OTHR. **Acts:** local acts. **Sample day's lineup:** Urban Nation, Jabbering Trout, The Latin Boyz, Kauzze-In-Affecck, Tim Seibles, Aixa Sobin, Robin Chandler, John Licata Sextet, Patricia Smith, Gang Peace Rappers, The Elders, Licia Sky, Franco Esile, Kim Tallbear, Talking to Animals. **Contact:** Boston Bahai Center, 495 Columbus Avenue, Boston, MA 02118, 617-266-2928 **or:** Boston Bahai Center, 100 Chestnut Avenue, Apt. 2, Jamaica Plain, MA 02130, 617-262-4672.

## PETER PAN TASTE OF SPRINGFIELD, Springfield, MA
Middle Jun.
Variety, General

Since 1984. "The area's largest outdoor smorgasbord and Massachusetts' oldest 'Taste'" -- Press release. **Days:** 5. **Hours per day:** 11. **Site:** outdoor. Court Square. **Admission:** free. **Secondary genre[s]:** MJAZ, TJAZ, MRCK, CRCK, MC&W, GYLS. **Acts:** local acts. **Sample day's lineup:** Crescents, Radiators, Northeast 40, others. **Contact:** Spirit of Springfield, Inc., 101 State Street, Suite 220, Springfield, MA 01103-2006, 413-733-3800.

## MIDSUMMER REVELS, Lincoln, MA
Middle Jun. .
Traditional Folk

Since 1990. See other dates and sites. **Days:** 2. **Site:** outdoor. DeCordova Museum Amphitheater. **Admission:** paid. **Daily entry:** under $10, $10 to $24, $25 to $49. **Discounts: Secondary genre[s]:** MARI. **Acts:** national acts, local acts. **Sample day's lineup:** Revels Chorus, David Coffin, Daisy Nell, Louis Killen. **Audio merchandise:** "The Christmas Revels"; "Seasons for Singing"; "Blow, Ye Winds in the Morning" (all on Revels Records). **Contact:** Revels, Inc., One Kendall Square, Building 600, Cambridge, MA 02139-1562, 617-621-0505.

## BOSTON POPS, Boston, MA
Middle Jun. to Early Jul.
Variety, General

**Days:** 16. **Site:** indoors. Symphony Hall. **Admission:** paid. **Daily entry:** $10 to $24, $25 to $49. **Secondary genre[s]:** TJAZ, BGOS, IRSH, SCOT, TLAT. **Acts:** national acts, regional acts, local acts. **Sample series lineup:** Day One: Grant Llewellyn conducts music from Ireland, Scotland and Wales; Day Two: Gisele Ben-Dor conducts an "Hispanic Fiesta"; Day Three: "Gospel Night." **Contact:** Boston Pops, 301 Massachusetts Avenue, Boston, MA 617-266-2378.

## SUMMERFEST, Great Barrington, MA
Middle Jun.
Variety, General

Over 30 different performers in all [on multiple stages]...a huge range of music" -- Penny Halley. **Days:** 1. **Hours per day:** 4. **Site:** outdoor. Main Street. **Secondary genre[s]:** MJAZ, TJAZ, CRCK, MFOL, TFOL, AFRC, OTHR. **Acts:** regional acts, local acts. **Sample day's lineup:** Xavier, Little Big Band, East Creek String Band, Big Wa Scratch Band, Amarillas Trio, Friendship Chorale, Ugambo Drums, others. **Contact:** Summerfest, P. O. Box 428, Great Barrington, MA 01230, 413-528-4786/229-0230.

## BOSTON BOOK FAIR, Boston, MA
Middle Jun.
Modern Jazz

Since 1992. 'To highlight the city's rich literary tradition and to encourage reading among schoolchildren...Great food and fun for all!" -- Program. See other dates and sites. **Days:** 2. **Hours per day:** 10. **Site:** outdoor. Copley Square Park, between Boylston Street and St. James Avenue. **Admission:** free. **Secondary genre[s]:** TR&B, RGGE. **Acts:** local acts. **Sample day's lineup:** Boston Jazz Orchestra, Mark Adamy and The RealTime Band, Robert Blackhorse. **Contact:** Boston Parks and Recreation Department, 1010 Massachusetts Avenue, Boston, MA 02118, 617-635-4505.

OAK BLUFFS HARBOR DAY, Oak Bluffs, MA
> Middle Jun.
> Variety, General

Since 1992. "The Victorian seaside resort on Martha's Vineyard." -- Program. **Days:** 1. **Hours per day:** 8. **Site:** outdoor. Oak Bluffs Harbor. **Admission:** free. **Secondary genre[s]:** MJAZ, TR&B, ACAP, MARI, RGGE. **Acts:** local acts. **Sample day's lineup:** Maynard Silva, Bettlebung Steel Band, Entrain, Vineyard Sounds, Mark Lovewell. **Contact:** Oak Bluffs Association, P. O. Box 1521, Oak Bluffs, MA 02557, 508-693-4986.

PRAISE AND HARMONY, Lowell, MA
> Middle Jun.
> Black Gospel

"A festival of religious and gospel music featuring nine different individuals and groups." -- Program. **Help!** A sample lineup? **Days:** 1. **Hours per day:** 6. **Site:** outdoor. Boarding House Park, French and John Streets. **Admission:** free. **Acts:** local acts. **Contact:** UMass Lowell, Center for the Arts, One University Avenue, Lowell, MA 01824, 508-459-1000.

POW-WOW, Sterling, MA
> Late Jun.
> Native American

"Public is cordially invited." -- Program. See other sites and dates. **Days:** 2. **Site:** outdoor. Sterling Springs Campground, Pratt Junction Road. **Admission:** paid. **Daily entry:** under $10. **Restrictions:** 2. **Contact:** Worcester Inter-Tribal Center, 196 Highland Center, Worcester MA 01609, 508-754-3300.

FUN SUMMER CONCERTS, Wellfleet, MA
> Late Jun.
> Alternative and College Rock

**Help!** One time only? **Days:** 3. The Beachcomer. **Admission:** paid. **Daily entry:** under $10. **Acts:** local acts. **Sample day's lineup:** Mark Erodi's Lounge, Explotion, Miles Dethmuffin, Betty Please, Scarce, Flying Nuns, Lester Bangs, Philth Shack. **Contact:** The Beachcomer, P. O. Box 1409, Wellfleet, MA 02667, 508-349-6055.

AMESBURY DAYS FESTIVAL, Amesbury, MA
> Late Jun. to Early Jul.
> Variety, General

Since 1974. "We hire about a dozen bands and have them play everywhere in town throughout the week, culminating in a July 4th concert before about 20,000." -- Scott Ackerly. **Help!** A sample lineup? **Days:** 11. **Site:** outdoor and indoor. **Secondary genre[s]:** MFO. **Acts:** national acts, regional acts, local acts. **Sample lineup:** Livingston Taylor, Devonsquare, Aztec Two-Step, Anderson-Graham, Sleepy LaBeef, others. **Contact:** Amesbury Chamber of Commerce, 41 Main Street, Amesbury, MA 01913, 508-388-3178.

NEWBURYPORT YANKEE HOMECOMING, Newburyport, MA
> Late Jun. to Early Jul.
> Modern Folk

**Days:** 9. **Hours per day:** 9. **Site:** outdoor. Waterfront Park. **Admission:** Free **Acts:** regional acts, local acts. **Sample day's lineup:** Kenny Girard, Kristina Olsen, Cosy Sheridan, Stan Moeller and T. S. Baker, Ed Gearhart, others. **Contact:** Newburyport Yankee Homecoming, 77 Bromfield Street, Newburyport, MA 01950, 508-465-2853.

## JOE VAL MEMORIAL BLUEGRASS FESTIVAL, Waltham, MA
Late Jun.
Bluegrass

Since 1986. "Celebrating the musical legacy of the late Joe Val, legendary mandolin player, tenor singer and bluegrass-band leader" -- Program. **Days:** 1. **Hours per day:** 6. **Site:** outdoor. Bentley College, Forest Street. **Admission:** free. **Secondary genre[s]:** TC&W. **Acts:** regional acts, local acts. **Sample day's lineup:** Southern Rail, Sassy Grass, Willow Creek, Bear Acker with Billings Gap, Slow Grass, Salamander Crossing, The Country Masters, Gerry Robichaud and Joe Cormier, John Lincoln Wright, Kevin Lynch, Herb Applin, others. **Contact:** Boston Bluegrass Union, 8 Cypress Road, #1, Brighton, MA 02135, 617-782-2251 **or:** Watch City Arts, 230 Lowell Street, Waltham, MA 02154, 617-647-1055/1075.

## PICKIN' IN THE PINES BLUEGRASS DAY, Northampton, MA
Late Jun.
Bluegrass

Since 1977. "There is a family atmosphere here and it is an enjoyable day for all." -- Program. **Days:** 1. **Hours per day:** 8. **Site:** outdoor. Pines Theater, Look Park, Route 9. **Admission:** paid. **Daily entry:** under $10. **Secondary genre[s]:** TC&W. **Acts:** regional acts, local acts. **Sample day's lineup:** Smokey Greene and The Boys, Southern Rail, Maple Ridge, Herb Applin and The Berkshire Mountain Boys, Bear Acker and Billings Gap. **Contact:** Starrflower Productions, P. O. Box 56, Cushman, MA 01002, 413-584-5457/549-6640.

## CHILIFEST, Boston, MA
Middle Jun.
Variety, General

Since 1991. Benefits Horizons for Youth. See other dates and sites. **Days:** 1. **Hours per day:** 6. **Site:** outdoor. Marine Industrial Park, 600 Summer Street. **Admission:** pai. **Daily entry:** under $10. **Secondary genre[s]:** CRCK, ARCK, TR&B, RGGE. **Acts:** local acts. **Sample day's lineup:** Errol Strength and The Conscious Reggae Band, Vision Thing, Mark Adamy and The Real Time Band, The Touch, Crisis of Faith, Sub Terranean. **Contact:** Horizons for Youth, Inc., 121 Lakeview Street, Sharon, MA 02067, 617-828-7550.

## MASSACHUSETTS HIGHLAND GAMES, Waltham, MA
Late Jun.
Scottish

**Days:** 1. **Hours per day:** 9. **Site:** outdoor. **Admission:** paid. **Daily entry:** under $10. **Secondary genre[s]:** IRSH. **Acts:** local acts. **Contact:** Massachusetts Highland Games Committee, P. O. Box 2316, Cambridge, MA 02238, 617-491-1236/661-9167.

## PAN-AFRICAN CULTURAL FESTIVAL, Boston, MA
Late Jun.
African

See other dates. **Help!** A sample lineup? **Days:** 1. **Site:** outdoor. City Hall Plaza. **Admission:** free. **Secondary genre[s]:** AFRM, AFRC. **Contact:** Boston City Hall, One City Hall Plaza, Real Property Dept., Room 811, Boston, MA 02201, 617-635-3593/325-1204.

## WBCS BOSTON COUNTRY SUNDAY, Mansfield, MA
Late Jun.
Modern Country

Since 1994. **Days:** 1. **Site:** outdoor. Great Woods Performing Arts Center. **Admission:** paid. **Daily entry:** $10 to $24. **Acts:** national acts. **Sample day's lineup:** Travis Tritt, Trisha Yearwood, Joe Diffie, Lee Roy Parnell. **Contact:** WBCS, 330 Stuart Street, Boston, MA 617-542-0241.

### YANKEE MUSIC FESTIVAL BIG BAND JAZZ INVITATIONAL, Salem, MA
    Late Jun.
    Modern Jazz

**Days:** 1. **Hours per day:** 4. **Site:** outdoor. East India Square. **Admission:** free. **Acts:** local acts. **Sample day's lineup:** U. S. Air Force Amassadors Jazz Band, U. S. Navy Jazz Ensemble, Daniel Ian Smith Big Band, others. **Contact:** Peabody Essex Museum, East India Square, Salem, MA 01970, 508-745-9500.

### PLYMOUTH SUMMER BLASTOFF, Plymouth, MA
    Late Jun.
    Variety, General

"America's official start to summer." -- Program. **Days:** 2. **Hours per day:** 8. **Site:** outdoor and indoor. Water Street, Brewster Gardens, North Street, Court Street, Cordage Park, Maritime Museum, Town Pier, Plimouth Plantation. **Admission:** free. **Secondary genre[s]:** TR&B, MFOL, MARI. **Acts:** national acts, local acts. **Sample day's lineup:** Livingston Taylor, D. D. and The Road Kings, Night Owls, Usual Suspects, Penny Merriment Victorian Singers, others. **Contact:** Plymouth Area Chamber of Commerce, 91 Samoset Street, Plymouth, MA 02360, 508-830-1620/746-3377.

### CAMBRIDGE STREET PERFORMER'S FESTIVAL, Cambridge, MA
    Late Jun.
    Variety, Folk and International

**Days:** 1. **Hours per day:** 5. **Site:** outdoor. Harvard Square, Brattle Street. **Admission:** free. **Secondary genre[s]:** MFOL. **Acts:** local acts. **Sample day's lineup:** Stephen Baird, Elliot Gibbons, Peter Sosna, Fortaleza, Kevin McNamara, Ken Zemach, others. **Contact:** Folk Arts Network, P. O. Box 867, Cambridge, MA 02238, 617-522-3407.

### MARBLEHEAD FESTIVAL OF THE ARTS, Marblehead, MA
    Late Jun. to Early Jul.
    Variety, Folk and International

"Massachusetts' largest community-based arts festival." -- Program. **Days:** 4. **Hours per day:** 7. **Site:** outdoor and indoor. Fort Sewall, Crocker Park, Abbot Hall, Unitarian Universalist Church. **Admission:** free and paid. **Daily entry:** $25 to $49. **Discounts:** advance purchase discounts, **Secondary genre[s]:** MJAZ, CRCK, BGOS, MC&W, TFOL, TLAT, OTHR. **Acts:** regional acts, local acts. **Sample day's lineup:** John Lincoln Wright and The Sour Mash Boys, Ron Murray and Vueol, Valery Asaturov, Stephen Baird, New England, The Hounds. **Contact:** Marblehead Festival of the Arts, Inc., P. O. Box 331, Marblehead, MA 01945, 617-639-ARTS.

### BOSTON HARBORFEST, Boston, MA
    Late Jun.
    Variety, General

Since 1982. This enormous celebration encompassing the entire city seems strangely light on music, according to my materials. **Days:** 6. **Hours per day:** 10. **Site:** outdoor and indoor. Multiple locations. **Admission:** free and paid. **Secondary genre[s]:** MJAZ, TFOL. **Acts:** local acts. **Sample day's lineup:** Doris Justice, Richard Elliot, Dixie Jazz Kings, Mike Hashem's Dixieland Strollers. **Contact:** Boston Harborfest, 45 School Street, Boston, MA 02108, 617-227-1528.

## BATTLE OF THE BLUES BANDS, Allston, MA
Late Jun. to Early Jul.
Blues and Traditional R&B

Since 1987. **Days:** 11. **Hours per day:** 5. **Site:** indoor. Harper's Ferry, 158 Brighton Avenue. **Admission:** paid. **Acts:** regional acts, local acts. **Sample day's lineup:** Swanky Moes, Evil Gal, Hammerheads, Little Jimmy and The Homewreckers, Loaded Dice. **Audio merchandise:** "Boston Blues Blast, Vols. I, II" (Tone Cool). **Contact:** Boston Blues Society, 158 Brighton Avenue, Allston, MA 02134, 617-254-7380.

## BOARDING HOUSE PARK CONCERT SERIES KICKOFF, Lowell, MA
Early Jul.
Variety, Folk and International

Since 1987. **Help!** A sample lineup? **Days:** 2. **Hours per day:** 6. **Site:** outdoor. Boarding House Park, French and John Streets. **Admission:** free. **Acts:** local acts. **Contact:** UMass Lowell, Center for the Arts, One University Avenue, Lowell, MA 01824, 508-459-1000.

## YOUR HOMETOWN AMERICA PARADE, Pittsfield, MA
Early Jul.
Drum Corps and Marching Bands

Since 1977. "Between 25 and 35 [marching band] units are expected to be in the final lineup on parade day. With 110,000 spectators expected and millions of TV viewers around the world -- it's an American tradition you won't want to miss!" -- Program. **Help!** A sample lineup? **Days:** 2. **Site:** outdoor. **Admission:** free. **Acts:** national acts, regional acts, local acts. **Contact:** Your Hometown America Parade, P. O. Box 621, Pittsfield, MA 01202, 413-499-3861.

## MASHPEE WAMPANOAG POWWOW, Mashpee, MA
Early Jul.
Native American

"A celebration of local Indian culture." -- Listing. **Days:** 3. **Site:** outdoor. Ballfield, off Route 130. **Contact:** Wampanoag Indian Museum, Route 130, Mashpe,e MA 508-477-0208/1536.

## CAPE VERDEAN FESTIVAL, Boston, MA
Early Jul.
Modern Latin

See other dates. **Help!** A sample lineup? **Days:** 1. **Site:** outdoor. City Hall Plaza. **Admission:** free. **Contact:** Boston City Hall, One City Hall Plaza, Real Property Dept., Room 811, Boston, MA 02201, 617-635-3593/3140.

## MONSON'S SUMMERFEST, Monson, MA
Early Jul.
Variety, General

**Days:** 1. **Hours per day:** 11. **Site:** outdoor. Dan Grieves Park, Main Street. **Admission:** free. **Secondary genre[s]:** CRCK, TR&B, MC&W. **Acts:** local acts. **Sample day's lineup:** Debbie Weyl Band, Salamander Crossing, Ray Manson Band, Dave Foster and The Shaboo All-Stars. **Contact:** Monson's Summerfest, 6 Belmont Avenue, Monson, MA 01057, 413-267-9385.

### BLANDFORD MOUNTAIN BLUEGRASS FESTIVAL, Blandford, MA
Early Jul.
Bluegrass

**Days:** 2. **Site:** outdoor. Blandford Ski Area, Route 20. **Acts:** regional acts, local acts. **Sample day's lineup:** Alice's Homemande Jam, Bear Bridge Band, Old Cold Tater, Bear Acker/Billings Gap, Burnt Hills Bluegrass, Thunder Mountain Bluegrass, Blandford Fiddlers, Southern Rail. **Contact:** Blandford Mountain Bluegrass Festival, 5 Woronoco Avenue, Westfield, MA 01085, 413-568-2845/562-3111.

### PUERTO RICAN CULTURAL FESTIVAL, Springfield, MA
Early Jul. to Middle Jul.
Modern Latin

"An opportunity to travel with a very limited budget." -- Marcel Mangual. **Help!** A sample lineup? **Days:** 4. **Hours per day:** 8. **Site:** outdoor. Gerena Community School, Birnie Avenue and Plainfield Street. **Admission:** paid. **Daily entry:** under $10. **Secondary genre[s]:** TLAT. **Contact:** Puerto Rican Cultural Center, 200 Birnie Avenue, Springfield, MA 413-731-5141 **or:** Puerto Rican Cultural Center, 2345 Main Street, Springfield, MA 413-737-7450. .

### CITY OF PRESIDENTS BLUES FESTIVAL, Quincy, MA
Early Jul.
Blues and Traditional R&B

Since 1992. "Keeping the blues alive." -- Advertisement. **Days:** 1. **Hours per day:** 8. **Site:** outdoor. Veterans Memorial Stadium, Hancock Street. **Admission:** paid. **Daily entry:** under $10, $10 to $24. **Restrictions:** 1, 5. **Acts:** national acts, regional acts, local acts. **Sample day's lineup:** Ronnie Earl and The Broadcasters, Luther "Guitar Jr." Johnson, James Montgomery Band, Paul Rishell and Little Annie Raines, Clutch Grabwell and The Leadfoot Horns, John Putnam and Used Blues, The Radio Kings, The Susan Tedechi Band, Madeline Hall and The Rhythm Hounds, Steve Murphy and The Yardrockers. **Contact:** The Yard Rock, 132 East Howard, Quincy, MA 617-472-9383/847-0929.

### LATIN AMERICAN FESTIVAL, Lowell, MA
Early Jul.
Traditional Latin

Since 1987. **Days:** 1. **Hours per day:** 6. **Site:** outdoor. Boarding House Park, French and John Streets. **Admission:** free. **Acts:** regional acts, local acts. **Sample day's lineup:** Los Pleneros del Coco, Inca Son, Jorge Arce Group, Mariachi Guadalajara, Milie Bermejo, Jose Rivera Y Su Grupo Lowell, Grupo Folklorico Ecuatoriano. **Contact:** UMass Lowell, Center for the Arts, One University Avenue, Lowell, MA 01824, 508-459-1000.

### WHALING CITY FESTIVAL, New Bedford, MA
Early Jul. to Middle Jul.
Variety, General

**Days:** 3. **Hours per day:** 12. **Site:** outdoor. Buttonwood Park, Rockdale Avenue. **Secondary genre[s]:** MJAZ, CRCK, ARCK, TR&B, BGOS, MC&W, MFOL, MLAT. **Acts:** national acts, local acts. **Sample day's lineup:** "WFHN-'FUN 107' Special National Act," plus New Orleans Connection, Mill City Rockers, Over and Under, Split Decision, 4-Play, Robert Black and The Poor Boyz, Mike Leveques, Rebecca Paris, Suburban Blues, No Limit, One Night Stand, East Bay Jazz Band. **Contact:** Whaling City Festival, 222 Union Street, Room 302, New Bedford, MA 02740, 508-996-3348.

OXFAM AMERICA WORLDFEST, Boston, MA
> Early Jul. to Middle Jul.
> Variety, Folk and International

"Oxfam America works in parnership with people around the world fighting hunger." -- Program. **Help!** One time only? **Days:** 2. **Hours per day:** 7. **Site:** outdoor. Boston Common. **Admission:** free. **Secondary genre[s]:** BGOS, TFOL, NATV, TLAT, AFRC, RGGE, OTHR. **Acts:** national acts, local acts. **Sample day's lineup:** Lucky Dube, Fortaleza, Somaly Hay, Mixashawn, PENC, Jane Sapp. **Contact:** Oxfam America, 26 West Street, Boston, MA 02111, 617-482-1211.

BRIGHT MOMENTS FESTIVAL, Amherst, MA
> Middle Jul. to Late Jul.
> Variety, Jazz and Blues

Since 1979. **Days:** 3. **Hours per day:** 4. **Site:** outdoor. UMass/Amherst. **Admission:** paid. **Daily entry:** under $10. **Secondary genre[s]:** MJAZ, MLAT, TLAT, AFRM, AFRC, RGGE. **Acts:** national acts, regional acts, local acts. **Sample day's lineup:** Billy Taylor, Max Roach, Sheila Jordan, The Jazz All Stars, Jazz In July Express I and II. **Contact:** New World Theater, Fine Arts Center, 15 Curry Hicks, UMass/Amherst, Amherst, MA 01003, 413-545-3671/4161.

TOWWAKEESWUSH POW-WOW, Marshfield, MA
> Middle Jun.
> Native American

**Days:** 2. **Hours per day:** 7. **Site:** outdoor. Marshfield Fairgrounds. **Admission:** paid. **Daily entry:** under $10. **Contact:** Massachusetts Center for Native Americans, P. O. Box 5885, Boston, MA 02114, 617-884-4227.

UPCOUNTRY HOT AIR BALLOON FAIR, Greenfield, MA
> Middle Jul.
> Modern Folk

Since 1987. **Days:** 2. **Hours per day:** 6. **Site:** outdoor. Greenfield Community College. **Admission:** paid. **Daily entry:** under $10. **Discounts:** advance purchase discounts. **Secondary genre[s]:** MC&W, TC&W, BLGS. **Acts:** national acts, local acts. **Sample day's lineup:** Blue Streak, Robert Earl Keen Jr., Jonathon Edwards, Cheryl Wheeler, Cox Family. **Contact:** Franklin County Chamber of Commerce, P. O. Box 790A, Greenfield, MA 01302, 413-773-5463.

IRISH FESTIVAL IN THE PARK, Tewksbury, MA
> Middle Jul.
> Irish

"Bring the family" -- Program. **Days:** 3. **Hours per day:** 12. **Site:** outdoor. State Field, Livingston Street, off Route 38. **Admission:** paid. **Daily entry:** under $10. **Acts:** local acts. **Sample day's lineup:** Silver Spears, Wild Rovers, Fintan Stanley, Boston Irish, others. **Contact:** Billerica Irish-American Social Club, Inc., Middlesex Turnpike, Billerica, MA 508-663-3900.

MULTICULTURAL FAMILY FESTIVAL, Roxbury, MA
> Middle Jul.
> Variety, Folk and International

Since 1990. "Featuring music, food and fun from many areas of the world, the festival is organized with a different theme each year." -- Newsletter. See other dates. **Days:** 1. **Hours per day:** 4. **Site:** outdoor. Roxbury Community College, 1234 Columbus Avenue. **Admission:** free. **Secondary genre[s]:** NATV, TLAT, RGGE. **Acts:** local acts. **Sample day's lineup:** Inca Son, Wampanoag Singers and Dancers, Humano. **Contact:** Community Change, Inc., 14 Beacon Street, Room 602, Boston, MA 02108, 617-523-0555.

PROVINCETOWN WATERFRONT FESTIVAL, Provincetown, MA
> Middle Jul. to Late Jul.
> Variety, Folk and International

Since 1994. See other dates and sites. **Days:** 2. **Hours per day:** 9. **Site:** outdoor. **Admission:** free. **Secondary genre[s]:** TR&B, BLGS, MARI, IRSH, TLAT, RGGE, OTHR. **Acts:** local acts. **Sample day's lineup:** Angel Gould, Zhentian Zang, Gerdes Fluerant, Ethnographico Portugal des Pequeninos, Howie Tarnower, Fantasia, Silas Hubbard and The Hot Ribs. **Contact:** Waterfront Festivals, Ltd., 4 Greenleaf Woods Drive, Suite 302, Portsmouth, NH 03801, 207-439-2021.

PUERTO RICAN FESTIVAL, Boston, MA
> Late Jul.
> Modern Latin

Since 1968. **Help!** A sample lineup? **Days:** 5. **Site:** outdoor. Rotch Park, South End. **Contact:** Mayor's Office of Neighborhood Services, 1 City Hall Plaza, Room 708, Boston, MA 02201, 617-635-3911/3485.

GLASGOW LANDS SCOTTISH FESTIVAL, Blandford, MA
> Late Jul.
> Scottish

**Help!** A sample lineup? **Days:** 1. **Hours per day:** 8. **Site:** outdoor. Blandford Fair Grounds, North Street. **Admission:** paid. **Daily entry:** under $10. **Secondary genre[s]:** IRSH. **Acts:** local acts. **Contact:** White Church Restoration Committee, P. O. Box 65, Blandford, MA 01008, 413-848-2052.

WPVQ MUSIC DAY, Greenfield, MA
> Late Jul.
> Modern Country

**Days:** 1. **Site:** outdoor. **Acts:** national acts, local acts. **Sample day's lineup:** David Ball, others. **Contact:** WPVQ Music Day, 424 State Road, Whately, MA 413-665-0939.

GREAT NEW ENGLAND BREWERS' FESTIVAL, Northampton, MA
> Late Jul.
> Variety, General

Since 1993. "Featuring over 50 outstanding draft ales and lagers from regional microbreweries and brew pubs..." -- Advertisement. Proceeds benefit Northampton Center for the Arts and WFCR-FM. **Days:** 2. **Hours per day:** 8. **Site:** outdoor. Quality Hotel, I-91 and Route 5. **Admission:** paid. **Daily entry:** under $10. **Secondary genre[s]:** TJAZ, MRCK, MR&B, TR&B, AC&W, BLGS. **Acts:** regional acts, local acts. **Sample day's lineup:** The Swinging Steaks, Motion, Happy Bunny, Al and Declan, Four Piece Suit, The Natives, Planet Be, Random House of Soul, Search Party, The Candles. **Contact:** Northampton Brewery, 11 Brewster Court, Northampton, MA 413-584-9903.

### LOWELL FOLK FESTIVAL, Lowell, MA
    Middle Jul.
    Variety, Folk and International

Since 1987. **Days:** 3. **Hours per day:** 11. **Site:** outdoor. Lowell National Historical Park. **Admission:** free **Secondary genre[s]:** TR&B, ACAP, BGOS, TC&W, BLGS, TFOL, MARI, ZYDC, IRSH, SCOT, MLAT, TLAT, OTHR. **Acts:** national acts, regional acts, local acts. **Sample day's lineup:** Charles Brown, Capoeira Camara, New England Pentecostal Crusade Choir, Jock Coen and Friends, Menhaden Chanteymen, Los Pleneros del Batey, Rockin' Dopsie and The Zydeco Tiwsters, The Rankin Family, Laurie Lewis and Grant Street, The Makredes Ensemble, Walt Solek, Algiers Brass Band, Sunshine Skiffle Band, Tony Ellis, Cliff Haslam, Norberto Tavares and Tropical Power, Eddie Pennington, Norman Kennedy, Ben Guillemete and Friends, Zhentian Zhang. **Audio merchandise:** "1990 Lowell Folk Festival: Folk Music Sampler" (Lowell Festival Committee, P. O. Box 217, Lowell, MA 01844), plus four other cassettes in series. **Contact:** Lowell National Historical Park, 246 Market Street, Lowell, MA 01852, 508-459-1000/970-5000.

### QUABOAG SCOTTISH FESTIVAL, Warren, MA
    Late Jul.
    Scottish

**Days:** 1. **Hours per day:** 8. **Site:** outdoor and indoor. Quaboag Regional High School, Old West Brookfield Road. **Admission:** paid. **Daily entry:** under $10. **Acts:** local acts. **Contact:** Quaboag Scottish Festival Committee, P. O. Box 981, West Brookfield, MA 01585, 508-867-0203 **or:** Quaboag Scottish Festival Committee, 49 Bell Street, North Brookfield, MA 01535, .

### NATIVE AMERICAN FAIR AND POW WOW, Grafton, MA
    Late Jul.
    Native American

**Days:** 1. **Hours per day:** 6. **Site:** outdoor. Hassanamisco Reservation, Brigham Hill Road. **Admission:** paid. **Contact:** Native American Fair and Pow Wow, 81 Washburn Street, Northboro, MA 01532, 508-393-2080/839-7394.

### ... FESTIVAL, Foxboro, MA

...k-off, too. **Days:** 1. **Admission:** paid. **Site:** outdoor. Foxboro Stadium. **Daily** ...onal acts. **Sample day's lineup:** The Mavericks, Wynonna, Neil McCoy, Hal ...CLB, 800 Boylston Avenue, Boston, MA 617-375-2100.

### ... ...ford, MA

... outdoor. Middlesex 4-H County Fairgrounds. **Admission:** paid. **Daily entry:** ...etts Center for Native Americans, P. O. Box 5885, Boston, MA 02114, 617-884-

ARTBEAT, Somerville, MA
> Late Jul.
> Variety, Folk and International

Since 1987. **Days:** 1. **Site:** outdoor. Davis Square. **Secondary genre[s]:** MJAZ, JWSH, TLAT. **Acts:** local acts. **Sample day's lineup:** Jorge Arce and Humano, Klezmer Conservatory Band, Stan Strickland and Ascension. **Contact:** Somerville Arts Council, Somerville City Hall, 50 Evergreen Avenue, Somerville, MA 02145, 617-625-6600.

TANGLEWOOD FESTIVAL OF CONTEMPORARY MUSIC, Lenox, MA
> Late Jul. to Late Aug.
> Avant Garde and New Music

Since 1983. **Days:** 8. **Site:** indoor. Theater-Concert Hall, Tanglewood Music Center, West Street. **Admission:** paid. **Daily entry:** under $10, $10 to $24. **Discounts:** advance purchase discounts. **Acts:** national acts, regional acts, local acts. **Sample day's lineup:** Cynthia Richards Lewis, Timothy Mount, Tanglewood Chorale, Neil Farrell, Dennis Helmrich, Margo Garrett performing works by Lang, Stockhausen, Henze, Rorem, Perle, Dallapiccola. **Contact:** Tanglewood Music Center, West Street, Lenox, MA 01240, 413-637-1666/1940 **or:** Boston Symphony Orchestra, Symphony Hall, Boston MA 02115, 617-638-9231. .

BOSTON JAZZ SOCIETY BARBEQUE AND FESTIVAL, Milton, MA
> Early Aug.
> Modern Jazz

Since 1977. "Honoring jazz musicians and their music....Proceeds to benefit the Boston Jazz Society Scholarship Fund." -- Program. **Days:** 1. **Hours per day:** 6. **Site:** outdoor. Curry College, Blue Hill Avenue. **Admission:** paid. **Daily entry:** under $10, $10 to $24. **Discounts:** advance purchase discounts. **Restrictions:** 7, 8. **Acts:** national acts, local acts. **Sample day's lineup:** Roy Haynes Quartet, Eula Lawrence, Juan Cruz Urquiza Quintet. **Contact:** Boston Jazz Society, Inc., P. O. Box 178, Boston, MA 02134, 617-445-2811/254-3991.

AMERICAN INDIAN HONOR-THE-EARTH POW WOW, Northampton, MA
> Early Aug.
> Native American

**Days:** 2. **Site:** outdoor. County Fairgrounds. **Admission:** paid. **Daily entry:** under $10. **Contact:** American Indian Honor-the-Earth Pow Wow, 741 Bay Road, Amherst, MA 01002, 413-253-7788.

TAM O'SHANTER SCOTTISH HIGHLAND GAMES AND FESTIVAL, Easton, MA
> Early Aug.
> Scottish

Since 1984. **Days:** 1. **Hours per day:** 8. **Site:** outdoor. Stonehill College, Route 138. **Admission:** paid. **Daily entry:** under $10. **Discounts:** student discounts. **Secondary genre[s]:** IRSH. **Acts:** local acts. **Sample day's lineup:** Carl Peterson, Christina Harrison, Larry Reynolds Irish Band, Jack Brown, Odd Couples, others. **Contact:** Tam O'Shanter Scottish Highland Games and Festival, 32 Walnut Street, West Bridgewater, MA 02379, 508-584-7116.

NATIVE AMERICAN AWARENESS POW-WOW, Peabody, MA
> Early Aug.
> Native American

Since 1991. See other dates and sites. **Days:** 2. **Hours per day:** 7. **Site:** outdoor. Higgins Field, King Street. **Admission:** paid. **Daily entry:** under $10. **Contact:** Massachusetts Center for Native Americans, P. O. Box 5885, Boston, MA 02114, 617-884-4227.

## TASTE OF THE SOUTH SHORE, Quincy, MA
Early Aug.
Variety, General

Since 1992. See other dates and sites. **Days:** 2. **Hours per day:** 8. **Site:** outdoor. Hancock Street, downtown. **Admission:** free. **Secondary genre[s]:** CRCK, ARCK, HRCK, RAP, TR&B. **Acts:** national acts, local acts. **Sample day's lineup:** WXKS (KISS-FM) to supply national headliner, plus Crisis of Faith, Ed'e, Rockhouse Rebels, Carreira, Brian Stratton with The Infractions. **Contact:** Horizons for Youth, Inc., 121 Lakeview Street, Sharon, MA 02067, 617-828-7550.

## DOMINICAN FESTIVAL, Boston, MA
Early Aug.
Modern Latin

**Help!** A sample lineup? **Days:** 1. **Site:** outdoor. Rotch Park, South End. **Contact:** Mayor's Office of Neighborhood Services, 1 City Hall Plaza, Room 708, Boston, MA 02201, 617-635-3911/3485.

## TASTE OF NORTHAMPTON, Northampton, MA
Middle Aug.
Variety, General

Since 1991. "The Taste' reflects much of what is best about Northampton -- [43] wonderfully-diverse restaurants, superb entertainment and a community spirit that is supported by local businesses and is second to none." -- Susan Wiggin, Laura Davenport, Promotion Committee. **Days:** 4. **Hours per day:** 10. **Site:** outdoor. Armory Street parking lot. **Admission:** free. **Secondary genre[s]:** MJAZ, ARCK, TR&B, BGOS, MC&W, BLGS, MFOL, RGGE, OTHR. **Acts:** local acts. **Sample day's lineup:** The Marion Groves Group, The Rude Girls, The Sax Maniacs, Jamie Rivera Caribbean Sounds, The Equalites. **Contact:** Greater Northampton Chamber of Commerce, 62 State Street, Northampton, MA 01060, 413-584-1900.

## HYANNIS SEAPORT FESTIVAL, Hyannis, MA
Middle Aug.
Modern Folk

Since 1993. See other sites and dates. **Days:** 4. **Hours per day:** 10. **Site:** outdoor. Town Green. **Secondary genre[s]:** CRCK, AC&W. **Acts:** national acts, regional acts, local acts. **Sample day's lineup:** Roger McGuinn, Ellis Paul, Martin Sexton, Andrea Bensmiller. **Contact:** Conventures, Inc., 250 Summer Street, Boston, MA 02210, 617-330-1992.

## MASSACHUSETTS ROCK AND REGGAE FOR THE HOMELESS, Great Barrington, MA
Middle Aug.
Reggae, Ska and Caribbean

Since 1991. "It's getting bigger and bigger with an excellent lineup." -- Susan Coker, Butternut Basin. Benefits the Massachusetts Coalition for the Homeless. **Days:** 1. **Hours per day:** 7. **Site:** outdoor. Butternut Basin Ski Area, Route 23. **Admission:** paid. **Daily entry:** $10 to $24. **Secondary genre[s]:** ARCK, BLGS. **Acts:** national acts, regional acts, local acts. **Sample day's lineup:** Bim Skala Bim, Acoustic Junction, The Danny Tucker Band, I-N-I, The Equalites, The Pearls. **Contact:** Massachusetts Rock and Reggae for the Homeless, Butternut Basin Ski Area, Route 23, Great Barrington, MA 01230, 413-274-6584/229-8787 x205.

FALL RIVER CELEBRATES AMERICA , Fall River, MA
   Middle Aug.
   Variety, General

Since 1987. "Though the [Statue of Liberty] stands in New York Harbor, what she stands for are those things which make our city great...the strength of will, spirit of acceptance and international diversity of Fall River and its people." -- Program. **Days:** 3. **Hours per day:** 11. **Site:** outdoor. Fall River Heritage State Park, Battleship Cove, Fall River Line Pier -- all at junction of Route 79 and I-195 (Braga Bridge). **Secondary genre[s]:** MJAZ, TR&B, MC&W, BLGS, MFOL, ZYDC, NATV, SCOT, TLAT, RGGE, OTHR. **Acts:** regional acts, local acts. **Sample day's lineup:** Northern Lights, Humano, Funky White Honkies, Magnolia, Heritage State Park Singers, King Ludwig's Bavarian Band, Mid-East Ensemble, Crayz, others. **Contact:** Fall River Area Chamber of Commerce and Industry, P. O. Box 1871, Fall River, MA 02722, 508-676-8226.


SUMMERTIME BLUES WEEKEND, Lowell, MA
   Middle Aug.
   Blues and Traditional R&B

**Days:** 2. **Site:** outdoor. Boarding House Park, French and John Streets. **Admission:** free. **Acts:** national acts, regional acts. **Sample series lineup:** Day One: Shirley Lewis; Day Two: Otis Clay and Chicago Fire. **Contact:** UMass Lowell, Center for the Arts, One University Avenue, Lowell, MA 01824, 508-459-1000.


PRECISION AND PAGEANTRY DRUM AND BUGLE CORPS COMPETITION, Pittsfield, MA
   Middle Aug.
   Drum Corps and Marching Bands

"Top drums corps compete; jazz, popular, classical and Broadway songs are performed." -- Listing. **Days:** 1. **Site:** outdoor. Wahconah Park Stadium. **Acts:** national acts, regional acts, local acts. **Sample day's lineup:** Phantom Regiment, Madison Scouts, Velvet Knights, Troopers, Spirit of Georgia, Carolina Crown, Spartans, Cardinals. **Contact:** Your Hometown America Parade, 306 Pittsfield Road, Lenox, MA 413-637-8270/499-3861.


CARLOS FEST, Brookline, MA
   Middle Aug.
   Alternative and College Rock

Since 1993. **Days:** 1. **Site:** indoor. The Tam, 1648 Beacon Street. **Acts:** local acts. **Sample day's lineup:** Michael Beatty, Hollywood Squares, Made in the Shade, Stone Soup Poets, Goddess Dancing. **Contact:** Carlos Fest, c/o The Tam, 1648 Brookline Avenue, Brookline, MA 617-277-0982.


HARVEY ROBBINS' ROYALTY OF ROCK 'N ROLL/CAPE COD MELODY TENT, Hyannis, MA
   Middle Aug.
   Classic Rock and Oldies

Part of a summer "shed" schedule. **Days:** 1. **Site:** indoors. Cape Cod Melody Tent, West Main Street. **Admission:** paid. **Daily entry:** $10 to $24. **Acts:** national acts, local acts. **Sample day's lineup:** Lesley Gore, The Shangra-La's, The Coasters, Frankie Ford, The Drifters, Caesar Valentino. **Contact:** Cape Cod Melody Tent, West Main Street, Hyannis, MA 617-383-1400.

GLOUCESTER WATERFRONT FESTIVAL, Gloucester, MA
>	Middle Aug.
>	Variety, Folk and International

See other dates and sites. **Days:** 2. **Hours per day:** 9. **Site:** outdoor. Stacey Boulevard. **Admission:** free. **Secondary genre[s]:** TR&B, BLGS, MARI, IRSH, TLAT, RGGE, OTHR. **Acts:** local acts. **Sample day's lineup:** Angel Gould, Zhentian Zang, Gerdes Fluerant, Ethnographico Portugal des Pequeninos, Howie Tarnower, Fantasia, Silas Hubbard and The Hot Ribs. **Contact:** Waterfront Festivals, Ltd., 4 Greenleaf Woods Drive, Suite 302, Portsmouth, NH 03801, 508-283-1601.

MARTHA'S VINEYARD AGRICULTURAL FAIR FIDDLE CONTEST: A FESTIVAL OF
TRADITIONAL MUSIC, Vineyard Haven, MA
>	Middle Aug. to Late Aug.
>	Fiddle and Banjo Events

"Fun! Music! Dancing! Fame! Fortune! Foolery!" -- Program. **Days:** 3. **Secondary genre[s]:** TC&W, TFOL. **Acts:** local acts. **Contact:** Martha's Vineyard Agricultural Society/Country Dance Society, P. O. Box 4495, Vineyard Haven, MA 02568, 508-627-7405.

BOSTON SEAPORT FESTIVAL, Charlestown, MA
>	Middle Aug. to Late Aug.
>	Variety, General

"A seafood festival featuring delicious selections from Boston's finest restaurants, the Fleet tour of classic sailing vessels and children's entertainment..." -- Advertisement. See other dates and sites. **Days:** 4. **Hours per day:** 12. **Site:** outdoor. Charlestown Navy Yard. **Admission:** free. **Secondary genre[s]:** CRCK, ARCK, TR&B, AC&W, MFOL, TFOL, RGGE. **Acts:** national acts, regional acts, local acts. **Sample day's lineup:** Chris Smither, Joan Osborne, Susan Werner, Greg Greenway, The Revels. **Contact:** Conventures, Inc., 250 Summer Street, Boston, MA 02210, 617-439-7700/787-0929.

CARIBBEAN CARNIVAL, Boston, MA
>	Middle Aug. to Late Aug.
>	Reggae, Ska and Caribbean

"The largest summer festival in New England, the Caribbean Carnival...concludes with a parade complete with steel bands, floats, and the crowning of the Carnival King and Queen." -- Listing. **Help!** A sample lineup? **Days:** 5. **Site:** indoors. Prince Hall; outdoors: Franklin Park. **Admission:** free and paid. **Acts:** local acts. **Contact:** Caribbean Carnival, 1537 Blue Hill Avenue, Mattapan, MA 02126, 617-534-5832.

GREAT YANKEE RIB COOK-OFF, Boston, MA
>	Late Aug.
>	Variety, General

Since 1992. **Days:** 3. **Hours per day:** 12. **Site:** outdoor. City Hall Plaza. **Admission:** paid. **Daily entry:** under $10. **Secondary genre[s]:** CRCK, TR&B. **Acts:** national acts, regional acts, local acts. **Sample lineup:** Buster Poindexter and His Banshees of Blue, Lesley Gore, Heavy Metal Horns, others. **Contact:** Great Yankee Rib Cook-Off, 1 Beacon Street, Suite 1320, Boston, MA 02108, 617-742-7077/267-4343.

WESTERN NEW ENGLAND BLUEGRASS AND OLD-TIME CHAMPIONSHIPS AND STEAK FRY, Sheffield, MA
> Late Aug.
> Fiddle and Banjo Events

**Days:** 1. **Site:** outdoor. Berkshire School, Route 41. **Admission:** paid. **Daily entry:** under $10. **Secondary genre[s]:** TC&W, BLGS. **Acts:** local acts. **Contact:** Western New England Bluegrass and Old-Time Championships, P. O. Box 594, Great Barrington, MA 01230, 413-528-2553.

MALDEN IRISH FESTIVAL, Malden, MA
> Late Aug.
> Irish

Donations to WEET 590 Fund to Support the Homeless. **Days:** 1. **Hours per day:** 9. **Site:** outdoor. Pleasant Street. **Admission:** paid. **Daily entry:** under $10. **Acts:** local acts. **Sample day's lineup:** Silversprears, Patsy Whalen and Pat Dunlea, Brogue, Red Branch Knights, Kevin Barry Bagpipers, others. **Contact:** My Honey Fitz, 142 Pleasant Street, Malden, MA 02148, 617-324-0111.

NEWSOUND FESTIVAL, Merrimac, MA
> Early Sep.
> Modern Christian

Part of a series of eight concerts per year, including one held each quarter. **Days:** 1. **Acts:** national acts, regional acts, local acts. **Sample day's lineup:** News Boys, Vigilantes, Michael Stein, others. **Contact:** Newsound Festival, P. O. Box 197, Merrimac, MA 01860, 508-346-4577.

TANGLEWOOD JAZZ FESTIVAL, Lenox, MA
> Early Sep.
> Modern Jazz

Since 1987. **Days:** 4. **Hours per day:** 7. **Site:** outdoor and indoor. Tanglewood Music Center, West Street. **Admission:** free and paid. **Daily entry:** $10 to $24, $25 to $49. **Secondary genre[s]:** TJAZ. **Acts:** national acts. **Sample series lineup:** Day One: The Manhattan Transfer, Abbey Lincoln; Day Two: Joshua Redman Quartet, Ahmad Jamal Trio; Day Three: Marcus Roberts, Dave Brubeck, Shirley Horn Quartet. **Contact:** Tanglewood Music Center, West Street, Lenox, MA 01240, 413-637-1666/1940 **or:** Boston Symphony Orchestra, Symphony Hall, Boston, MA 02115, 617-638-9231. .

BLANDFORD FAIR OLD TIME FIDDLE CONTEST, Blandford, MA
> Early Sep.
> Fiddle and Banjo Events

**Days:** 1. **Site:** outdoor. Fairgrounds. **Secondary genre[s]:** TC&W, BLGS, TFOL. **Acts:** local acts. **Contact:** Blandford Fair Old Time Fiddle Contest, P. O. Box 3, Blandford, MA 01008, 413-848-2177.

NEWBURYPORT WATERFRONT FESTIVAL, Newburyport, MA
> Early Sep.
> Variety, Folk and International

See other dates and sites. **Days:** 3. **Hours per day:** 9. **Site:** outdoor. Plum Island Fairgrounds. **Admission:** free. **Secondary genre[s]:** TR&B, BLGS, MFOL, MARI, IRSH, TLAT, RGGE, OTHR. **Acts:** local acts. **Sample day's lineup:** Angel Gould, Zhentian Zang, Gerdes Fluerant, Ethnographico Portugal des Pequeninos, Howie Tarnower, Fantasia, Silas Hubbard and The Hot Ribs. **Contact:** Waterfront Festivals, Ltd., 4 Greenleaf Woods Drive, Suite 302, Portsmouth, NH 03801, 617-262-1414.

CELTIC FESTIVAL AT THE HATCH SHELL, Boston, MA
        Early Sep.
        Scottish

Since 1988. **Days:** 1. **Hours per day:** 3. **Site:** outdoor. Hatch Shell, Charles River Esplanade. **Admission:** free **Secondary genre[s]:** IRSH. **Acts:** national acts, regional acts, local acts. **Sample day's lineup:** Comhaltas Ceoltoiri Eireann, Ed Pearlman, Laura Scott, Bridget Fitzgerald, Fourin A Fiere, Joe Cormier, Iain Massie, Skip Healey, Tony Cuffe and Billy Jackson, Paddy Keenan, Boston Scottish Fiddle Club, others. **Audio merchandise:** "Scottish Fiddle Rally, Vols. 1, 2, 3" (Boston Scottish Fiddle Club). **Contact:** Boston Scottish Fiddle Club, P. O. Box 823, North Cambridge, MA 02140, 508-922-8595.

REGGAE FESTIVAL, Washington, MA
        Early Sep.
        Reggae, Ska and Caribbean

Modest, but long-running, festival on lawn at 22-room inn. See other dates. **Days:** 1. **Site:** outdoor. Bucksteep Manor, Washington Mountain Road. **Acts:** national acts, local acts. **Sample day's lineup:** Inner Circle, Loose Caboose, Dread-I. **Contact:** Bucksteep Manor, Washington Mountain Road, Washington, MA 01223, 413-623-5535.

SOBER IN THE SUN LABOR DAY WEEKEND EXPERIENCE, Spencer, MA
        Early Sep.
        Modern Folk

Since 1989. "Alcohol and drug-free weekend of live music, camping and workshops...Health and recovery workshops all weekend. Meetings around the clock." -- Program. **Days:** 4. **Site:** outdoor. Camp Spencer, off Route 31. **Admission:** paid. **Daily entry:** $10 to $24. **Discounts:** advance purchase discounts. **Restrictions:** 2, 7, 8. **Secondary genre[s]:** TR&B, ZYDC, OTHR. **Acts:** regional acts, local acts. **Sample day's lineup:** Michael Brown, Steve Key, Revin Kevin and The Accelerators, Vance Gilbert, Midnight Snack, Aztec Two-Step, Shirley Lewis, Allard/McCollum Band, Peter Piper, Rachel Bissex, Michael Barrett, Dewet Burns, Chuck and Mud, Jim Henry, Jan Luby, Rob Lytle, Bill MacMillan, Don White, Rae Linda Woade, Carl Kamp, Kathleen Corcoran. **Contact:** Word of Mouth Productions, P. O. Box 585, Fiskdale, MA 01518, 508-792-2876/892-1307.

BREAD AND ROSES LABOR DAY HERITAGE HERITAGE FESTIVAL, Lawrence, MA
        Early Sep.
        Variety, Folk and International

Since 1985. "Offers a multi-ethnic, multi-stage day of music, art and much, much more and celebrates the achievements of Lawrence's workers, past and present, while commemorating the 1912 'Bread and Roses' strike." -- Program. **Days:** 1. **Hours per day:** 8. **Site:** outdoor. Lawrence Heritage State Park and Pemberton Park. **Admission:** free. **Secondary genre[s]:** TR&B, MFOL, TFOL, ZYDC, JWSH, NATV, SCOT, TLAT, AFRC, OTHR. **Acts:** national acts, regional acts, local acts. **Sample day's lineup:** Judy Collins, Tony Bird, Crawdad Wranglers, Fred Small, Fortaleza, MA 01843's, Hiep Lam, Orlow Family, Comite Noviembre, Strathspey and Reel Society of New Hampshire, Tatiana and Koliu, Mixashawn, Rosalie Gerut, Cathy Winter, Stephen Baird, Kim Wallach, Jonathon Stevens, Jeanine Schiavoni, The Poodles, Les Sampou, Martha Leader, Sherli Sherwood. **Contact:** Bread and Roses Heritage Committee, Inc., P. O. Box 1137, Lawrence, MA 01842-1137, 508-682-1863.

DeCordova Labor Day Jazz Festival, Lincoln, MA
>    Early Sep.
>    Modern Jazz

Since 1989. "A spirited finale to our summer-long musical celebration...Gather among the shady pine trees, contemporary sculpture and beautiful vistas that characterize DeCordova's parklands." -- Program. **Site:** outdoor. DeCordova Museum Ampitheater, 51 Sandy Pond Road. **Admission:** paid. **Daily entry:** $10 to $24. **Discounts:** advance purchase discounts. **Secondary genre[s]:** MLAT. **Acts:** local acts. **Sample day's lineup:** Boston Jazz Orchestra, Mili Bermejo Quartet Nuevo, Schwendener and Farquharson. **Contact:** DeCordova Concerts, P. O. Box 9101, Lincoln, MA 01773-9101, 617-259-8355.

New England Country Jamboree, Webster, MA
>    Middle Sep.
>    Modern Country

See other dates. **Help!** A sample lineup? **Days:** 1. **Site:** outdoor. Indian Ranch, Route 16. **Admission:** paid **Daily entry:** under $10, $10 to $24. **Acts:** local acts. **Contact:** Indian Ranch, P. O. Box 1157, 275 Main Street, Webster, MA 01570, 508-943-3871/2936/4159.

Lowell Riverfest, Lowell, MA
>    Early Sep. to Middle Sep.
>    Variety, General

"Fun for the entire family...on the banks of the Merrimack River." -- Advertisement. **Days:** 5. **Hours per day:** 12. **Site:** outdoor. Regatta Field, Route 113. **Admission:** paid. **Daily entry:** under $10. **Discounts:** multiple event or day passes. **Secondary genre[s]:** ARCK, MR&B, MC&W. **Acts:** national acts, regional acts. **Sample series lineup:** Day One: McBride and The Ride; Day Two: Tribe; Day Three: Peter Wolf. **Contact:** Lowell-Lexington-Concord Convention and Visitors Bureau, 18 Palmer Street, Suite 200, Lowell, MA 01852-1818, 508-458-2650.

Banjo and Fiddle Contest, Lowell, MA
>    Middle Sep.
>    Fiddle and Banjo Events

Since 1980. May switch to every-other-year schedule, beginning in 1995. **Days:** 1. **Site:** outdoor. Boarding House Park, French and John Streets. **Admission:** free. **Secondary genre[s]:** BLGS, TFOL. **Acts:** local acts. **Contact:** UMass Lowell, Center for the Arts, One University Avenue, Lowell, MA 01824, 508-459-1000.

Pedal Steel Guitar Anniversary Bash, Lee, MA
>    Early Sep.
>    Modern Country

Since 1982. "Afternoon is filled with excitement...we try to utilize every moment." -- William Hankey. Dates vary, so call ahead. **Help!** A sample lineup? **Days:** 1. **Hours per day:** 9. **Site:** indoor. VFW Hall, Route 102. **Secondary genre[s]:** TC&W. **Acts:** national acts, local acts. **Contact:** Pedal Steel Guitar Anniversary Bash, 121 Calumet Street, Pittsfield, MA 01201, 413-442-5198.

Chief Red Blanket Memorial Pow-Wow, Haverill, MA
>    Early Sep. to Middle Sep.
>    Native American

See other dates and sites. **Days:** 2. **Site:** outdoor. Plug Pond, Mill Street. **Acts:** local acts. **Contact:** Massachusetts Center for Native American Awareness, Inc., P. O. Box 5885, Boston, MA 02115-5885, 617-884-4227.

## MARTHA'S VINEYARD SINGER-SONGWRITERS' RETREAT, Vineyard Haven, MA
Early Sep. to Middle Sep.
Modern Folk

Since 1992. Folksinger Christine Lavin recruits up to 50 of her performing friends and associates for workshops, songswaps and such, including intimate live sets recorded in the evenings. **Help!** Open to the public? **Days:** 2. **Site:** indoor. Wintertide Coffeehouse. **Acts:** national acts, regional acts, local acts. **Sample day's lineup:** Christine Lavin, Laurie Geltman, Martin Sexton, Ellis Paul, Greg Greenway, Russell Hallac, Peggy Tileston, many others. **Audio merchandise:** "Big Times in a Small Town" (Rounder). **Contact:** Wintertide Coffeehouse, 5 Corners, Vineyard Haven, MA 508-693-8830.


## BOURNE SCALLOP FEST, Buzzards Bay, MA
Early Sep. to Middle Sep.
Variety, General

Since 1970. "The Scallop Fest is a blast!" -- Program. **Days:** 3. **Hours per day:** 11. **Site:** outdoor. Buzzards Bay Park, Main Street. **Admission:** free. **Restrictions:** 2. **Secondary genre[s]:** MJAZ, MC&W, MFOL. **Acts:** regional acts, local acts. **Sample day's lineup:** John Lincoln Wright and The Sour Mash Boys, Jon Frattasio, John Salerno Trio, Ruth Weaver. **Contact:** Cape Cod Canal Region Chamber of Commerce, 70 Main Street, Buzzards Bay, MA 02532, 508-759-3122.


## CAMBRIDGE RIVER FESTIVAL, Cambridge, MA
Middle Sep.
Variety, General

Since 1977. **Days:** 1. **Hours per day:** 7. **Site:** outdoor. Charles River banks along Memorial Drive from JFK to Western Avenues. **Admission:** free. **Secondary genre[s]:** MJAZ, TR&B, BGOS, MC&W, MFOL, ZYDC, MLAT, AFRC, OTHR. **Acts:** regional acts, local acts. **Sample day's lineup:** United Voices for Christ, The Persuaded Ensemble, Gordon Michaels, Joyful, Patricia Dance, Bruce Katz Band, Little Joe Cook and The Thrillers, Lourdes Pita and Friends, Silas Hubbard Jr. and The Hot Ribs, The Jane Gang, Kevin Connolly, Stan Strickland and Ascension with Wanetta Jackson, Samba Camara, John Lincoln Wright and The Sour Mash Boys, Master Ibrahima Camara, Mili Bermejo, Semenya McCord, Carolyn Ritt, Valerie Stephens, Jon Voigt, Herb King, Krew De Roux. **Contact:** Cambridge Arts Council, 57 Inman Street, Cambridge, MA 02139, 617-349-4394/4380.


## DAY AT THE LAKE, Worcester, MA
Middle Sep.
Variety, General

**Days:** 1. **Hours per day:** 6. **Site:** outdoor. Quinsigamond State Park, Lake Avenue North. **Admission:** paid. **Daily entry:** under $10. **Discounts:** advance purchase discounts. **Secondary genre[s]:** TR&B, MFOL. **Acts:** regional acts, local acts. **Sample day's lineup:** Shirley Lewis, She's Busy, Don White, Walter and Valerie Crockett, Little Ronnie and The Sloan Sharks, Chuck and Mud with The Hole in The Dam Band, Walter and Valerie Crockett. **Contact:** Regatta Point Community Sailing, Lake Avenue North, Worcester, MA 508-757-2140/845-0071.


## SEPTEMBERFEST, Groton, MA
Middle Sep.
Variety, Folk and International

**Days:** 1. **Site:** outdoor and indoor. Groton Center for the Arts. **Secondary genre[s]:** TR&B, MFOL, TFOL, IRSH. **Acts:** local acts. **Sample day's lineup:** Late August, Les Sampou, others. **Contact:** Groton Center for the Arts, P. O. Box 105, Groton, MA 01450, 508-448-3001/5453.

NIPMUCK POW WOW, Oxford, MA
Middle Sep.
Native American

**Days:** 2. **Hours per day:** 7. **Site:** outdoor. Greenbriar Park, Route 12. **Admission:** paid. **Daily entry:** under $10. **Contact:** Nipmuck Indian Council of Chaubunagungamaug, 20 Singletary Avenue, Sutton, MA 01590, 508-865-9828/248-7544.

FALL FESTIVAL, Attleboro Falls, MA
Middle Sep.
Variety, General

**Days:** 1. **Hours per day:** 6. **Site:** outdoor. Mason Field. **Admission:** paid. **Daily entry:** under $10. **Secondary genre[s]:** TJAZ, TC&W, BLGS. **Acts:** local acts. **Sample day's lineup:** Tarbox Ramblers, Parson's Plunkers, Doc and The Northettes, Bill Davis, Jim Burke and The Dixie All Stars. **Contact:** North Attleboro/Plainville Chamber of Commerce, P. O. Box 1071, North Attleboro, MA 02761, 508-695-6011.

EASTERN STATES EXPOSITION -- THE BIG E!, West Springfield, MA
Middle Sep. to Late Sep.
Fairs

Since 1921. "New England's Great State Fair! Jam in the fun! Preserve the memories!" -- Program. **Days:** 12. **Hours per day:** 12. **Site:** outdoor and indoor. The Big E, 1305 Memorial Avenue, off Route 147. **Admission:** paid. **Daily entry:** under $10. **Discounts:** multiple event or day passes, group sale discounts. **Restrictions:** 10. **Secondary genre[s]:** CRCK, ACAP, MC&W, OTHR. **Acts:** national acts, local acts. **Sample day's lineup:** The Everly Brothers, Darryl and Don Ellis, Little Anthony and The Imperials, Southern Reign, Robin Lee, Stratton Mountain Boys, Reggie's Red Hot Feet Warmers. **Contact:** The Big E, P. O. Box 419, West Springfield, MA 01090, 413-787-0271/737-BIG E.

CODMAN FARM FESTIVAL, Lincoln, MA
Middle Sep.
Variety, Folk and International

Musical theme varies. **Days:** 1. **Site:** outdoor. Codman Community Farm, Codman Road. **Secondary genre[s]:** TJAZ, TR&B, BLGS, TFOL, IRSH. **Acts:** local acts. **Sample day's lineup:** Pine Hill Ramblers, Yankee Division, Stephen Baird, others. **Contact:** Codman Community Farm, P. O. Box 285, Lincoln, MA 01773, 617-259-0378.

GLOUCESTER SEAFOOD FESTIVAL, Gloucester, MA
Middle Sep.
Variety, General

Since 1994. "It was a big success...Everything is free but the food." -- Connie Condon. **Days:** 3. **Hours per day:** 11. **Site:** outdoor. **Admission:** free. **Secondary genre[s]:** TR&B, ACAP, MC&W, BLGS, TFOL, OTHR. **Acts:** local acts. **Sample day's lineup:** Old Cold Tater, Megawatts Blues, Sweet Mercy, Walker Creek, The Younger Gang, others. **Contact:** Cape Ann Chamber of Commerce, 33 Commercial Street, Gloucester, MA 01930, 800-321-0133.

## GREAT AWAKENING FEST, Granby, MA
### Middle Sep.
### Southern and Bluegrass Gospel

**Days:** 1. **Hours per day:** 10. **Admission:** paid. **Secondary genre[s]:** BLGS. **Acts:** regional acts, local acts. **Sample day's lineup:** Southern Rail, Steve Taylor, Michael Kelly Blanchard, Fortress, The Messengers, John Barron, Fellowship, Green Point Gospel. **Contact:** Great Awakening Ministries, Inc., 151 Taylor Street, Granby, MA 01033, 413-476-FEST.

## NORTHEAST SQUEEZE-IN, Washington, MA
### Middle Sep.
### Traditional Folk

Since 1990. "Informal workshops and jam sessions, Saturday evening dance and concert, and opportunities to buy, sell and trade instruments. For accordion, concertina and other 'squeeze-box' players and fans." -- Folkfare. **Help!** A sample lineup? **Days:** 3. **Site:** outdoor and indoor. Bucksteep Manor, Washington Mountain Road. **Admission:** paid. **Daily entry:** $10 to $24, $25 to $49, $50 and over. **Secondary genre[s]:** ZYDC,. **Contact:** The Button Box, 9 East Pleasant Street, Amherst, MA 01002, 413-549-0171.

## BUD ROCKS THE BLOCK PARTY, Lowell, MA
### Middle Sep.
### Alternative and College Rock

Since 1989. "Welcome back UMass./Lowell! Come and rock the block with us!" -- Advertisement. **Days:** 1. **Hours per day:** 4. **Site:** indoor. The Safe, 160 Merrimack Street. **Admission:** paid. **Daily entry:** $10 to $24. **Acts:** local acts. **Sample day's lineup:** O Positive, Deliriants, Childhood. **Contact:** The Safe, 160 Merrimack Street, Lowell, MA 508-937-9998.

## CHOWDERFEST, Charlestown, MA
### Middle Sep.
### Variety, General

Since 1982. See other dates and sites. **Days:** 1. **Hours per day:** 6. **Site:** outdoor. Charlestown Navy Yard, Pier 5. **Admission:** free. **Secondary genre[s]:** ARCK, HRCK, TR&B, MFOL, AFRC, RGGE. **Acts:** regional acts, local acts. **Sample day's lineup:** Vision Thing, The Search Party, Ellis Paul, Rockhouse Rebels, Courage Brothers, Errol Strength and The Conscious Reggae Band. **Contact:** Horizons for Youth, Inc., 121 Lakeview Street, Sharon, MA 02067, 617-828-7550.

## JOHN PENNY LIVER FOUNDATION JAMBOREE, Webster, MA
### Middle Sep.
### Modern Country

See other dates. **Days:** 1. **Hours per day:** 8. **Site:** outdoor. Indian Ranch, Route 16. **Admission:** paid. **Daily entry:** under $10. **Secondary genre[s]: Acts:** regional acts, local acts. **Sample day's lineup:** John Penny band, Sleepy LaBeef, John Lincoln Wright and The Sour Mash Boys, Liz Boardo and Borderline, John Hicks and Revolution, Bobby Carlson and Silver Saddle, Bobby Sheppard Band, County Line, Marilyn and The Monroe Brothers, Heartbreak City, Jackie lee Williams Band, Nash Sisters, Johnny White, Mike Preston, Cheyenne. **Contact:** Indian Ranch, Box 1157, 275 Main Street, Webster, MA 01570, 508-943-3871/2936/4159.

### ART NEWBURY STREET, Boston, MA
Middle Sep.
Variety, General

"Stroll Boston's elegant eight-block street and enjoy 30 gallery open-houses and special exhibits." -- Listing. See other dates. **Days:** 1. **Hours per day:** 4. **Site:** outdoor and indoor. Newbury Street. **Secondary genre[s]:** MJAZ, AFRC, OTHR. **Acts:** local acts. **Sample day's lineup:** Tom Pollard Trio, Elliot Gibbons, Herbs Heard, Cora Connection, Saltre Bigelow Trio, Eastwood String Orchestra. **Contact:** Newbury Street League, 158 Newbury Street, Boston, MA 02116, 617-267-7961.

### FOLK HERITAGE FESTIVAL, Lexington, MA
Middle Sep.
Traditional Folk

"This year's event will be a salute to the Wild West." -- 1993 Program. See other dates. **Days:** 1. **Hours per day:** 5. **Site:** outdoor. Museum of Our National Heritage, 33 Marrett Road. **Admission:** paid. **Daily entry:** under $10. **Secondary genre[s]:** TC&W. **Acts:** local acts. **Sample day's lineup:** John Penny Band, Nash Sisters, others. **Contact:** Museum of Our National Heritage, P. O. Box 519, Lexington, MA 02173, 617-861-6559/862-6541.

### EISTEDDFOD FESTIVAL OF TRADITIONAL MUSIC AND DANCE, North Dartmouth, MA
Late Sep.
Traditional Folk

Since 1972. See other dates. **Days:** 3. **Hours per day:** 12. **Site:** indoor. UMass/Dartmouth, Old Westport Road. **Admission:** paid. **Secondary genre[s]:** TR&B, TGOS, TC&W, BLGS, MARI, IRSH, AFRC, OTHR. **Acts:** national acts, regional acts, local acts. **Sample day's lineup:** Bryan Bowers, Dry Branch Fire Squad, Sally Rogers and Howie Bursen, Bridget Fitzgerald, Dick Holdstock and Allan McLeod, Betty and Norman McDonald, Dick Swain, Laura Travis, Larry Unger, Sarah Bauhan, Lorraine Hammond, Cesar Villalobos, others. **Contact:** UMass/Dartmouth, Old Westport Road, North Dartmouth, MA 02747-2300, 508-999-8546.

### AUTUMN HILLS DULCIMER FESTIVAL, Great Barrington, MA
Late Sep.
Traditional Folk

Since 1984. "...A magnificent blend of historic buildings and modern facilities." -- Program. **Days:** 3. **Hours per day:** 14. **Site:** outdoor and indoor. Eisnor Camp and Conference Center, Brookside Road. **Admission:** paid. **Daily entry:** under $10, $10 to $24, $24 to $49, $50 and over. **Restrictions:** 10. **Secondary genre[s]:** IRSH. **Acts:** national acts, regional acts, local acts. **Sample day's lineup:** Dan Duggan, Helicon, Lois Hornbostel, Susan Trump, Kendra Ward and Bob Bence, Mountain Laurel, others. **Contact:** Folkcraft Instruments, P. O. Box 807, Winsted, CT 06098, 203-379-9858.

### COUNTRY FEST, Webster, MA
Middle Sep.
Modern Country

See other dates. **Days:** 1. **Hours per day:** 8. **Site:** outdoor. Indian Ranch, Route 16. **Admission:** paid. **Daily entry:** under $10. **Acts:** regional acts, local acts. **Sample day's lineup:** John Penny Band, Sleepy LaBeef, John Lincoln Wright and The Sour Mash Boys, Liz Boardo and Borderline, John Hicks and Revolution, Bobby Carlson and Silver Saddle, Bobby Sheppard Band, County Line, Marilyn and The Monroe Brothers, Heartbreak City, Jackie Lee Williams Band, Nash Sisters, Johnny White, Mike Preston, Cheyenne. **Contact:** Indian Ranch, Box 1157, 275 Main Street, Webster, MA 01570, 508-943-3871/2936/4159.

M. C. M. A. A. Awards Show, Randolph, MA
> Late Sep.
> Modern Country

They also host four-hour Jamborees the third Sunday of each month at various area clubs to raise money for the annual show. Typical lineups consist of local C&W acts: Robin Right, John Hadaupis and Unity, Jane Melcher, The Nash Sisters, others. **Days:** 1. **Site:** indoor. Lombardo's, Route 28. **Acts:** regional acts, local acts. **Sample day's lineup:** John Lincoln Wright and The Sour Mash Boys, Michael Leery and Midnight Rodeo, The Jimmy Allen Band, McGregor Maegee, Sigy, Tommy Hambridge. **Contact:** Massachusetts Country Music Awards Association, P. O. Box 2066, Abington, MA 02351, 617-335-2411.

John Coltrane Memorial Concert, Boston, MA
> Early Oct.
> Modern Jazz

Since 1980. "Organized in tribute to the musical genius and the spiritual message of Coltrane." -- New England Jazz News. **Days:** 1. **Site:** indoor. Blackman Auditorium, Northeastern University, 360 Huntington Avenue. **Admission:** paid. **Daily entry:** $10 to $24. **Discounts:** student discounts. **Acts:** national acts, local acts. **Sample day's lineup:** Karnau Adilifu, Diego Urcola, Leonard Brown, Bill Pierce, Vincent Davis, Giovanni Hidalgo, Santi Debriano, Keith Gibson, Syd Smart, Tim Ingles, Bill Lowe, Danilo Perez, Frank Wilkins, Stan Strickland, Gary Valente. **Contact:** Northeastern University, Department of Music, 360 Huntington Avenue, Boston, MA 02115, 617-373-2247/2440.

Boston International Festival, Dorcester, MA
> Late Oct. to Late Nov.
> Variety, Folk and International

"75 regional ethnic communities will be on hand at this year's larger site to present an exciting exhibition of art, music, dance, crafts, food and fashion in a unique and ambitious collaboration." -- Program. **Days:** 6. **Hours per day:** 8. **Site:** indoor. Bayside Exposition Center. **Admission:** paid. **Daily entry:** under $10. **Secondary genre[s]:** ZYDC, IRSH, JWSH, SCOT, TLAT, AFRC. **Acts:** local acts. **Sample day's lineup:** Karishima, Ramon y Badiana, Ballet Folklorico, El Arte Flamenco, Smooth Rhythm, Starnbarndet, Fusion Venezuela, PAMAS, GBC Folk Dancers, Grupo Maya, Srijan Dance Co., Mystic Vibes, Gurjar, Haitian Combite, Miners Silkersian, Cora Connection, Campbell Highlanders, Latvian Folk Dancers, SA Greek Dancers, Lancy lee, Fortaleza, Hartford Sangerbund, Sumaj Chasquis, Rocirdi D'Italia, Madeirense, Lietuviu Tautiniu, Karmen Zayas, Uh Cum Frum, Kaleo O Kalua, Mandrivka, Krakowiak Dancers, Estrellas Tropicales, Matices Peruanos, Cache, Sayat Nova, Taranga, Tatiana Sarbinska, Ramsiah Hassan, Dudley Orchestra, Aloha Lani, Jonathon Young, Jack Lawrence, Mia Pem, Joan Hantman, Mark Sherling, Pratibha Shah, Joel Breazeaale, Pung Mul Pae, Brasileirinho, Naida Sintas, Karen Gottier, Santiagi Paredes, Jorge Arce, Saengerchor Bsoton, Patrick Lacroix, Gleisser Allen, Diversity, Elisabeth Stone, Aaron Yacubian, Celia Ayala, Ale Noise. **Contact:** Boston International Festival, 405 Waltham Street, Suite 200, Lexington, MA 02173, 617-861-9729.

Acoustic Underground: Boston's National Acoustic Music Showcase, Boston, MA
> Early Oct. to Early Nov.
> Modern Folk

Since 1991. Performing-songwriter competition. "New judging categories, thousands of dollars in top prizes, top industry exposure, annual CD compilation and much, much more!" -- Advertisement. See other dates and sites. **Days:** 9. **Site:** indoor. Preliminary rounds at different clubs in Boston area; finals at Berklee Performance Center, Massachusetts Avenue. **Admission:** paid. **Acts:** regional acts, local acts. **Sample day's lineup:** Catie Curtis, Ellis Paul, Flathead, Wendy Sobel and Kathy Phipps, Dave Crossland, Vox One, Jim Infantino, Laurie Geltman Band, Don White, Barbara Kessler, McDonnel/Tane, Liz Brahm. **Contact:** The Acoustic Underground, 491 Riverside Avenue, Box 8, Medford, MA 02155, 617-254-1050 **or:** Entertainment Concepts, 173 Brighton Avenue, Brighton, MA 02134, 617-327-6470/391-4159.

### GAELIC ROOTS: THE MUSIC, SONG AND DANCE OF IRELAND, Chestnut Hill, MA
Early Oct.
Irish

Since 1993. **Days:** 3. **Hours per day:** 9. **Site:** indoor. Gasson Hall, Boston College. **Admission:** paid. **Daily entry:** $10 to $24, $25 to $49. **Discounts:** multiple event or day passes. **Secondary genre[s]:** SCOT. **Acts:** national acts, regional acts, local acts. **Sample day's lineup:** Natalie MacMaster, Liz Carroll, Eileen Ivers, Seamus Connolly, Roger Burridge, Jerry O'Sullivan, Paddy Keenan, Robbie Hannan, Matty Connolly, Patrick Hutchinson, Robbie O'Connell, Tony Cuffe, Josephine McNanara Gillman, John McGann, Zan McLeod, James Keane, Sean Potts, Jimmy Noonan, Billy Jackson, Tracy Dares, Fourin A Feire. **Audio merchandise:** "My Love Is In America: The Boston College Irish Fiddle Festival" (Green Linnett). **Contact:** Boston College Irish Studies Program, Carney Building, Room 439, Chestnut Hill, MA 02167-3806, 617-552-3716/4843.

### MIX 98.5 FALL FEST, Boston, MA
Early Oct.
Variety, General

Co-produced by Boston Parks and Recreation. See other dates and sites. **Days:** 2. **Hours per day:** 9. **Site:** outdoor. Parade Ground, Parkman Bandstand, Tremont Street. **Secondary genre[s]:** MJAZ, ARCK, MR&B, TR&B, MFOL, JWSH, RGGE, CBRT. **Acts:** national acts, regional acts, local acts. **Sample day's lineup:** Aaron Neville, Laurie Sargent Band, Jennifer Trynin Band, Oleta Adams, Cliffs of Dooneen, Rockers International, Laura Branigan, Matt Sevier, Greg Greenway, Jeff Arundel, Forever Plaid, Timothy J., Shirim Klezmer Orchestra, Monster Mike Welch, Made in the Shade. **Contact:** Avery-Gold Productions, 711 Atlantic Avenue, 4th Floor, Boston, MA 02111, 617-338-3144.

### WHALING CITY JAZZ FESTIVAL, New Bedford, MA
Early Oct.
Modern Jazz

**Help!** One time only? **Days:** 1. **Hours per day:** 7. **Site:** indoor. United Portugese Fisherman's Club, 639 Orchard Street. **Secondary genre[s]:** MLAT. **Acts:** regional acts, local acts. **Sample day's lineup:** Rebecca Paris, John Allmark Jazz Orchestra, Stan Strickland and Ascension. **Contact:** Whaling City Jazz Festival, c/o United Portugese Fisherman's Club, 639 Orchard Street, New Bedford MA 508-636-3955/991-4849.

### WESTPORT HARVEST FESTIVAL, Westport, MA
Early Oct. to Middle Oct.
Variety, General

**Help!** A sample lineup? **Days:** 3. **Hours per day:** 7. **Site:** outdoor and indoor. Westport High School, 19 Main Road. **Admission:** free. **Secondary genre[s]:** MC&W, MFOL, ZYDC, NATV. **Acts:** local acts. **Contact:** Westport Harvest Festival, 110C Pettey Lane, Westport, MA 508-636-4695.

### IRISH VARIETY SHOW, Braintree, MA
Middle Oct.
Irish

Since 1984. **Days:** 1. **Site:** indoor. Archbishop Williams High School. **Admission:** paid. **Daily entry:** $10 to $24. **Acts:** local acts. **Sample day's lineup:** Rita MacDonald, Dick McManus and His Irish Showband with Richie Travers and Dr. Michael Fitzpatrick, Roderick Thomson, Rev. John E. McLaughlin, others. **Contact:** Patricians of St. Patrick's Church, 10 Magazine Street, Roxbury, MA 02119, 617-445-7645.

CHILIFEST, Charlestown, MA
> Middle Oct.
> Variety, General

Since 1991. See other dates and sites. **Days:** 1. **Hours per day:** 6. **Site:** outdoor. Charlestown Navy Yard, Pier 5. **Admission:** free. **Secondary genre[s]:** CRCK, ARCK, TR&B, RGGE. **Acts:** local acts. **Sample day's lineup:** Errol Strength and The Conscious reggae Band, Vision Thing, Mark Adamy and The Real Time Band, The Touch, Crisis of Faith, Sub Terranean. **Contact:** Horizons for Youth, Inc., 121 Lakeview Street, Sharon, MA 02067, 617-828-7550.


IRISH MUSIC FESTIVAL, Boston, MA
> Middle Oct.
> Irish

Since 1993. "Benefits the youth programs supported by Boston Ireland Ventures, a grassroots charitable group involved in employment and investment in troubled areas of Ireland." -- Irish Echo. **Days:** 1. **Site:** indoor. Green Dragon Tavern, Marshall and Union Streets. **Admission:** paid. **Daily entry:** $10 to $24. **Secondary genre[s]:** ARCK. **Acts:** local acts. **Sample day's lineup:** Davey Arthur, Anton McAuley, Noel Barrett, Setena Shay Walker, Liam Tiernan, Alan Loughnane, Larry Reynolds, Jim Noonan and Friends, Dante's Grin, City This, Double Barrell. **Contact:** Green Dragon Tavern, 11 Marshall Street, Boston, MA 617-247-4112.


FOLKTREE JAMBOREE, Boston, MA
> Late Oct.
> Modern Folk

**Days:** 3. **Site:** indoor. Symphony Hall. **Admission:** paid. **Daily entry:** $10 to $24. **Secondary genre[s]:** MC&W, **Acts:** national acts. **Sample series lineup:** Day One: Nanci Griffith, Jerry Jeff Walker; Day Two: Nanci Griffith, Jonathon Edwards; Day Three: Nanci Griffith, Livingston Taylor. **Contact:** FolkTree Concertmakers, P. O. Box 313, Arlington, MA 02174, 617-641-1010.


WBCN ROCK OF BOSTON CONCERT, Boston, MA
> Late Oct.
> Modern Rock and Pop

**Days:** 1. **Site:** indoor. Boston Garden, 150 Causeway Street. **Admission:** paid. **Daily entry:** $10 to $24. **Secondary genre[s]:** ARCK. **Acts:** national acts, regional acts. **Sample day's lineup:** Peter Wolf, Extreme, Joe Satriani, Ian Moore, Crash Test Dummies, The Mighty Mighty Bosstones. **Contact:** WBCN 104.1 FM, 1265 Boylston Street, Boston, MA 02215, 617-536-8000/227-3200.


WFNX BIRTHDAY PARTY, Boston, MA
> Early Nov.
> Alternative and College Rock

**Days:** 1. **Site:** outdoor and indoor. Landsdowne Street, plus multiple club locations. **Admission:** free and paid. **Daily entry:** $10 to $24. **Discounts:** multiple event or day passes. **Acts:** national acts, local acts. **Sample day's lineup:** Social Distortion, Belly, The Mighty Mighty Bosstones, Black 47, Pornos for Pyros, School of Fish, Helmet, 808 State, Supreme Love Gods, Therapy?, Grant Lee Buffalo, Gin Blossoms, The God Machine, Best Kissers in the World, Robyn Hitchcock, Star Club, Seka, Sidewalk Gallery, City This, Mighty Joe Young, 32-20s. **Contact:** WFNX 101.7 FM, 25 Exchange Street, Lynn, MA 01901, 617-595-6200 x31.

### CMAC's BOSTON RHYTHM, Cambridge, MA
Early Nov.
African American

Since 1993. "Don't miss Boston's first annual rhythm festival featuring master dancers and drummers from Africa, Brazil, the Caribbean and the Americas." -- Program. See other dates and sites. **Days:** 1. **Site:** indoor. Kresge Auditorium, Massachusetts Institute of Technology. **Admission:** paid. **Daily entry:** $10 to $24. **Secondary genre[s]:** NATV, MLAT, AFRM, AFRC. **Acts:** local acts. **Sample day's lineup:** Capoeira Camara, Art of Black Dance and Music, Earth Drum Council, Afro-Latin Pop Ensemble, Ibrahima Camara. **Contact:** MIT's Office of the Arts and World Music, 720 Massachusetts Avenue, Cambridge MA 02139, 617-876-9240 **or:** Cambridge Multicultural Arts Center, 41 Second Street, Cambridge MA 02141, 617-577-1400/1403.

### PHIL OCHS SONG NIGHT, Cambridge, MA
Early Nov.
Modern Folk

"Proceeds to benefit The Nameless Coffeehouse, WUMB and other area radio folk funding." -- Folkfare. **Help!** One time only? **Days:** 1. **Site:** indoor. Firsh Parish, Massachusetts Avenue and Church Street. **Admission:** paid. **Daily entry:** under $10, $10 to $24. **Discounts:** student discounts, advance purchase discounts. **Acts:** regional acts, local acts. **Sample day's lineup:** Kim and Reggie Harris, Magpie, Pat Humphries, Nancy Tucker, Betty and The baby Boomers, Jay Makita and Lori Gross, Eric Kilburn, Laura Berkson, Dennis Pearne and Elastic Wasteband, Joyce Katzberg, Nancy Snyder, Charles S. Montroll, Siouxie D. **Contact:** Phil Ochs Song Night c/o First Parish, Massachusetts Avenue and Church Street, Cambridge, MA 617-491-8973.

### BLACKSMITH HOUSE FOLK FESTIVAL/FOLK ARTS CONFERENCE, Cambridge, MA
Middle Nov.
Modern Folk

Folk Arts Network's Folk Arts Conference for New England producers and artists features more than 30 presenters. See other dates. **Days:** 3. **Hours per day:** 14. **Site:** indoor. Blacksmith House, 56 Brattle Street, Harvard Square. **Admission:** paid. **Daily entry:** under $10, $10 to $24, $50 and over. **Discounts:** multiple event or day passes. **Secondary genre[s]:** TFOL, MARI. **Acts:** national acts, regional acts, local acts. **Sample series lineup:** Day One: Vance Gilbert; Day Two: Gordon Bok; Day Three: Lorraine and Bennett Hammond, Victor Cockburn. **Contact:** Cambridge Center for Adult Education, 42 Brattle Street, P. O. Box 9113, Cambridge, MA 02238-9113, 617-547-6789.

### NATIONAL NATIVE AMERICAN HERITAGE DAY POW-WOW, Concord, MA
Middle Nov.
Native American

**Days:** 1. **Hours per day:** 7. **Site:** indoor. Sandborn Middle School. **Admission:** paid. **Daily entry:** under $10. **Contact:** Massachusetts Center for Native Americans, P. O. Box 5885, Boston, MA 02114, 617-884-4227.

### SONGSTREET FOLK-ROCK FESTIVAL, Somerville, MA
Middle Nov.
Modern Folk

Since 1993. **Days:** 1. **Site:** indoor. Somerville Theater, Davis Square. **Admission:** paid. **Daily entry:** $10 to $24. **Discounts:** student discounts, advance purchase discounts. **Acts:** national acts, regional acts, local acts. **Sample day's lineup:** The Nields, disappear fear, Laurie Sargent, Kathy Phillips and Wendy Sobel. **Contact:** Songstreet Productions, P. O. Box 85, Somerville, MA 02143, 617-628-3390.

## CMAC's FALL BENEFIT, Cambridge, MA
Middle Nov.
African American

"If blues makes you smile, if scat's where it's at, or if gospel makes you shout hallelujah! -- you'll have a fabulous time at our tribute to African music..." -- Program. See other dates and sites. **Days:** 1. **Hours per day:** 4. **Site:** indoor. House of Blues. **Admission:** paid. **Daily entry:** $25 to $49. **Secondary genre[s]:** MJAZ, TR&B, ACAP, BGOS. **Acts:** local acts. **Sample day's lineup:** Gordon Michaels, Valerie Stephens, Herb King, Patricia Dance, Greg Jackson, Linda Brown, James McDaniels, others. **Contact:** Cambridge Multicultural Arts Center, 41 Second Street, East Cambridge, MA 02141, 617-577-1400 **or:** GNE Studio, 675 Massachusetts Avenue, Cambridge MA 02139, 617-661-6007.

## FESTIVAL OF LIGHT AND SONG, Jamaica Plain, MA
Middle Dec.
Modern Folk

"Make your MidWinter merrier!" -- Program. Site varies, so call ahead. Also known as "Songs for the Longest Night" and "Brightest Night." **Days:** 2. **Site:** indoor. Jamaica Plain Arts Center. **Admission:** paid. **Acts:** local acts. **Sample day's lineup:** Anabel and Wild Rose, Koleda, The Belfana Players, The Light and Song Chorus. **Contact:** Light and Song, Inc., P. O. Box 27, Cambridge, MA 02140, 617-232-6760 **or:** Light and Song, Inc., 258 Harvard Street, Suite 116, Brookline, MA 02146, 617-232-5880. .

## IRISH AND CAPE BRETON CHRISTMAS CONCERT AND CEILI, Chestnut Hill, MA
Middle Dec.
Irish

Since 1993. **Help!** One time only? **Days:** 1. **Hours per day:** 4. **Site:** indoor. Gasson Hall, Boston College. **Admission:** paid. **Daily entry:** under $10, $25 to $49. **Discounts:** student discounts, multiple event or day passes. **Secondary genre[s]:** SCOT. **Acts:** national acts, regional acts, local acts. **Sample day's lineup:** Joe Cormier, Connie MacGillavray, Ronnie Hache, John Whelan, Gabriel Donoghue, Deirdre Goulding, Boston College Singers. **Contact:** Boston College Irish Studies Program, Carney Building, Room 439, Chestnut Hill, MA 02167-3806, 617-552-3716/4843.

## CHRISTMAS REVELS, Cambridge, MA
Middle Dec. to Late Dec.
Traditional Folk

Since 1970. "A Celebration of the Winter Solstice: traditional and ritual dances, processionals, carols and drama." -- Program. See other dates and sites. **Days:** 10. **Site:** indoor. Sanders Theater, Harvard University. **Admission:** paid. **Daily entry:** under $10, $10 to $24, $25 to $49. **Secondary genre[s]:** OTHR. **Acts:** local acts. **Sample day's lineup:** Karelian Folk Ensemble, Mountain Horn Trio, Karin Brennesink and Sigbjorn Rua, Boston Spelemannslag, Fjord Gutene, Cambridge Symphonic Brass Ensemble. **Audio merchandise:** "The Christmas Revels"; "Seasons for Singing"; "Blow, Ye Winds in the Morning" (all on Revels Records). **Contact:** Revels, Inc., One Kendall Square, Building 600, Cambridge, MA 02139-1562, 617-621-0505.

**FIRST NIGHT BOSTON**, Boston, MA
    Late Dec.
    Variety, Folk and International

Since 1976. **Days:** 1. **Hours per day:** 12. **Site:** outdoor and indoor, 83 locations. **Admission:** paid. **Daily entry:** $10 to $24. **Restrictions:** 2. **Secondary genre[s]:** MJAZ, AJAZ, TR&B, ACAP, BGOS, MC&W, BLGS, MFOL, TFOL, FDDL, IRSH, JWSH, NATV, SCOT, MLAT, TLAT, AFRC, RGGE, AVNT, CBRT, OTHR. **Acts:** national acts, regional acts, local acts. **Sample day's lineup:** Ninots Transition Brass Band, Stephen Baird, Calmet Quintet, Flying Tomatoes, Fred MacArthur, Mother Church Chimers, Opera-to-Go, Youth Pro Musica, Batucada Belles, Caribbean Carnival Band Leaders Association, Geometric Progression Band, Hot Tamale Brass Band, Middlesez County Fif and Drum Corps, St. Andrew's Ladies Pipe Band, Samba Camara, Tony Barrie Marching Band, Wakeby Lake Singers, Wampanoag Dancers and Drummers, American Guild of Organists, American Music Ensemble, American Vocal Arts Quintet, Leslie Amper and Randall Hodgkinson, Beacon Brass Quintet, Boston Baroque, Boston Conservatory Chamber Ensemble, Boston Saxophone Quartet, Dou Maresienne, Friends of Dr. Burney, Tom Handel, Handel and Hayden Society, Andrew Paul Holman, Raymond Jackson, Janus Opera Company, Kammerton, Frederick Moyer, Old South Brass, Renaissonics, Ashmont Hill Chamber Music, Boston Cecilia, Gary Lee Nelson, Alain Mallet Group, Mili Bermejo and Dan Greenspan with Mick Goldrick, Boston Baked Blues, Either/Orchestra, Human Feel, Jane Miller Group, John Licata/George Garzone Quintet, Lisa Thorson Trio, Macey's Parade, Silas Hubbard Jr. and The Hot Ribs, Spirit Jazz, Vox One, Acousticity, Boston Village Gamelan, Brasileirinho, Clarence Thompson Sr. and The New Spirits, Cora Connection, Fortaleza, Rosalie Gerut and Friends, Hypnotic Clambake, John Lincoln Wright and The Sour Mash Boys, Cindy Kallet, Ellen Epstein and Michael Cicone, Libana, Mariachi Guadalajara, Tom Paxton, RESQ, Southern Rail, the story, Women Inc. Chorus, Boston Scottish Fiddle Club, Roaring Jelly, Metro Steel Orchestra, Zafem Haitian Band, Black Jokers, Roberto Rios, Six Bagatelles, Caleb Sampson with Ken Field, Capoiera Camara, Toby Mountain, Dar Williams, Michael Zerphy and Rodney Miller, ALDA's Verbal Jazz from Dorchester, Alloy Orchestra, Brother Blue. **Contact:** First Night, Inc., 20 Park Plaza, Suite 927, Boston, MA 02116, 617-562-5094/542-1399.

**FIRST NIGHT BROCKTON**, Brockton, MA
    Late Dec.
    Variety, Folk and International

Since 1992. **Days:** 1. **Site:** outdoor and indoor. **Admission:** paid. **Daily entry:** under $10. **Discounts:** advance purchase discounts. **Restrictions:** 2. **Secondary genre[s]:** MJAZ, CRCK, RAP, MR&B, TR&B, MC&W, MFOL, TFOL, MLAT, RGGE, CBRT, OTHR. **Acts:** regional acts, local acts. **Sample day's lineup:** Ralph Rontando Duo, Catie Curtis, David Andrews, Michael Welch, Goodtime Ragtime Vaudeville Revival, Me, Myself and I, Stephen Baird, Roxule, Professor Paddy Whack's One-Man Band, Dave Neiman, Kerrie Powers, Brooks Williams, Smoov Wit Da Ruffness, Alias Brown Band, Silver Reed Quartet, Lee Yunits, Sumaj Chasquis, Branches Steel Band, Shaun England Trio, New Orleans Dixieland Band, Hank Reynolds and Uncharted Territory, Christ Church Choir, Bill Shontz Green Up Family Show, Vathena Chea, Sonido Sensacional, Close Quarters, Prime Time Jazz Rock Ensemble, Silver Wings, Jubilate Chorale, World Premier, Lori Inglis Band, Mystic Vibes, Jimbo Wilson and The Cranberry Junction Band, Darryl Hill, Lydon and DiRusso, Aileen Alicia Ford, Merry Foxworth and Nancy Fitton, Sidekicks, Take Two, Heff and Riffer, Vance Gilbert. **Contact:** Brockton Jaycees, 372 Hillberg Avenue, Brockton, MA 02401, 508-583-2072 x61.

**FIRST NIGHT CHATHAM**, Chatham, MA
    Late Dec.
    Variety, Folk and International

**Help!** A sample lineup? **Days:** 1. **Site:** indoor. **Admission:** paid. **Daily entry:** under $10. **Discounts:** advance purchase discounts. **Restrictions:** 2. **Acts:** local acts. **Contact:** First Night Chatham, Box 80, Chatham, MA 02633, 508-945-2019.

FIRST NIGHT IN HYANNIS, Falmouth, MA
    Late Dec.
    Variety, Folk and International

**Help!** A sample lineup? **Days:** 1. **Site:** indoor. Falmouth Village. **Admission:** paid. **Daily entry:** under $10 **Discounts:** advance purchase discounts. **Restrictions:** 2. **Acts:** local acts. **Contact:** First Night in Hyannis, P. O. Box 662, Marston Mills, MA 02648, 508-790-ARTS/420-0204.

FIRST NIGHT NEW BEDFORD, New Bedford, MA
    Late Dec.
    Variety, Folk and International

**Help!** A sample lineup? **Days:** 1. **Site:** indoor. **Admission:** paid **Daily entry:** under $10. **Discounts:** advance purchase discounts. **Restrictions:** 2. **Acts:** local acts. **Contact:** First Night New Bedford, 47 Seventh Street, New Bedford, MA 02740, 508-979-1427 **or:** First Night New Bedford, 772 Purchase Street, New Bedford, MA 02740, 508-999-2166. .

FIRST NIGHT NEWBURYPORT, Newburyport, MA
    Late Dec.
    Variety, Folk and International

**Days:** 1. **Hours per day:** 6. **Site:** indoor, 23 locations. **Admission:** paid. **Daily entry:** under $10. **Restrictions:** 2. **Secondary genre[s]:** MJAZ, TR&B, MC&W, MFOL, TFOL, IRSH, AFRC, OTHR. **Acts:** regional acts, local acts. **Sample day's lineup:** Victorian Chamber Players, Mr. Kevin, Kristina Olsen and Jonathon Tynes, Newbury Chroal Scoiety, Atwater-Donnelly, Misty Martin, John Battis Swing Band, Cosmos Factor, Dixieland Strollers, Midnight Snack, Tom O'Carroll, Infinities, d'Vent Classique, Renee Randall Blues Band, Lynn Taylor and Dakota, Sherlie Sheerwood, Apollo Consortium, Quintessential Brass Quintet, Late August, Brandon Lapere, Roger Ebacher, Emily Corbato, Tenley Oldack and Friends, Carol Amaya. **Contact:** Newburyport Community Teen Center, P. O. Box 663, Newburyport, MA 01950, 508-463-0477.

FIRST NIGHT NORTHAMPTON, Northampton, MA
    Late Dec.
    Variety, Folk and International

Since 1985. **Days:** 1. **Hours per day:** 10. **Site:** indoor, 11 locations downtown. **Admission:** paid. **Daily entry:** under $10, $10 to $24. **Discounts:** advance purchase discounts. **Restrictions:** 2. **Secondary genre[s]:** MJAZ, TR&B, MC&W, BLGS, MFOL, TFOL, TLAT, CBRT, OTHR. **Acts:** local acts. **Sample day's lineup:** Kimsa, Roger Tincknell, Roger Salloom and The Stragglers, The Workin' Band, The Sundogs, Craig Eastman and Jim Henry, Arcadia Players, Young at Heart Chorus, Judy Polan, Paul Kaplan, Henry Cory, Erika Wheeler, Bernice Lewis, Justina and Joyce, Herschler Brothers, Bill Waaagh Scratch Band, Andy Jaffe Trio, Montenia, Andrei Ryabov, Marion Groves, Helene Criscio and Susan Burris, Quetzal, Herman Hampton, Susan Gillan and Into the Blue, Debbie Weyl Band, Art Steele Band, Dress Left, Straight from the Heart, Michael Robinson, Patty Carpenter, Joan Robb, Tim Van Egmond, Bernice Lewis, Oye Productions. **Contact:** Northampton Center for the Arts, Old School Commons, 17 New South Street, Northampton, MA 01060, 413-584-7327.

FIRST NIGHT PITTSFIELD, Pittsfield, MA
    Late Dec.
    Variety, Folk and International

Since 1992. "The first night, the best night." -- Program. **Days:** 1. **Hours per day:** 5. **Site:** outdoor and indoor, 19 locations. **Admission:** paid. **Daily entry:** under $10. **Discounts:** advance purchase discounts. **Restrictions:** 2. **Secondary genre[s]:** MJAZ, CRCK, TR&B, ACAP, BGOS, MC&W, BLGS, MFOL, TFOL, MLAT, OTHR. **Acts:** regional acts, local acts. **Sample day's lineup:** Jake Larkin Band, Lynn Rossini Jazz Trio, The Big Waagh Scratch Band, Angels Without Wings, Second Congregational Gospel Choir, Judy Lundseth, Mike Haynes, Doo Wah Days, The Sweet Tarts, The Bear Bridge Band, Joe Ancora, Carl Uhrig, Gideon Freudman, Dusty Miller Band, Tambora, Blue Rose, Sage City Six, Level One Latin Jazz Fusion Band, David Grover's Gang, Champagne Jam Dance Band, The Berkshire Hillsmen, George Morrell Trio, F. M. Reception Dance Band, Castaways Big Band, Eagles Band, The Poncherellos, Joanne Spies, Wish, Absinthe Dance Band, Leon Savage Band, Allusions, Rick and Nancy Powers, Dawn Fulvi, Pittsfield High School Choir, Vikki True, Chapel Hill Band, Wintergreen, N. U. D. E., Berkshire Country. **Contact:** Lichtenstein Center for the Arts, 28 Renne Avenue, Pittsfield, MA 01201, 413-499-9348.

FIRST NIGHT QUINCY, Quincy, MA
    Late Dec.
    Variety, Folk and International

Since 1992. 'The city's first New Year's Eve celebration Thursday night was by all accounts a booming success, from the glittery parade at the start to the final bang of fireworks at midnight." -- Patriot Ledger. **Days:** 1. **Hours per day:** 8. **Site:** outdoor and indoor, 23 locations. **Admission:** paid. **Daily entry:** under $10. **Restrictions:** 2. **Secondary genre[s]:** MJAZ, CRCK, TR&B, TGOS, MC&W, TC&W, BLGS, MFOL, IRSH, AFRC, RGGE, CBRT, OTHR. **Acts:** national acts, regional acts, local acts. **Sample day's lineup:** Robin Lane, D. C. Hall's New Concert and Quadrille Band, Lois Van Dam, Wollaston Glee Club, City of Presidents String Quartet, Bradway Cabaret, Iveria, Rita O'Shea, Eniko Konye and The Herman Johnson Jazz Quartet, Terry Sinskie Jazz Trio, Peter Kolson, Twisters, Guy Van Duser and Billy Novak, Hot Like Fire, Orin Star and Friends, Rex Tariler, Back Bay Rhythm Makers, PAMAS, Pater Jae, New Liberty Jazz Band, Mike Blake and Mike Sullivan, Sandy Kiefer, Les Sampou, Peter Keane, Dewey Burns, Rick Tarquinio, La Femme, Elizabeth Smith, Carol Shepardson, Branches Caribbean Steel Band, Widdershin, Billy Walsh, Hiro Hinshuku, Wildest Dreams, Blue Suede Boppers, Teka and Paris. **Contact:** City Hall, 1305 Hancock Street, Quincy, MA 02169, 617-376-1000/471-1493.

FIRST NIGHT WORCESTER, Worcester, MA
    Late Dec.
    Variety, Folk and International

Since 1982. "We have this once-a-year opportunity, not only to begin the year with high-minded resolutions, but to do it in concert with others who share the same devotion to community and a passion for the arts." -- Jonathon Finklestein, President. **Days:** 1. **Hours per day:** 8. **Site:** outdoor and indoor, 21 locations. **Admission:** paid. **Daily entry:** under $10. **Discounts:** advance purchase discounts. **Restrictions:** 2. **Secondary genre[s]:** MJAZ, ARCK, TR&B, MC&W, BLGS, MFOL, MARI, IRSH, NATV, AFRC, RGGE, OTHR. **Acts:** national acts, regional acts, local acts. **Sample day's lineup:** Abbott Chamber Players, Bolu Fatunmise and The Roots of African Percussion, Chuck and Mud, Paul Clemente, Eddie Bee, Flubber, Flat Stanley, Gloucester Hornpipe and Clog Society, Greendale Retired Men's Club Chorus, Emil Haddad and Dick Odgren, Bill Harley, Jah Spirit Reggae, The Joeys, Jolly Kopperschmidts German Band, Milestones Big Band, Aine Minogue, Mixashawn, Bill Morrissey, Kristina Olsen, Prudence and The Plowboys, The Psaltery, The Rhythm Rockers, Salisbury Singers, Slo-Grass, Cecilia Smith Quartet, Trumpet and Organ Duo, Interplanetary Big Band of Worcester, Worcester Community Gospel Choir. **Contact:** First Night Worcester, P. O. Box 351, Worcester, MA 01614, 508-799-4909.

LOWELL FAMILY FIRST NIGHT, Lowell, MA
    Late Dec.
    Modern Folk

**Days:** 1. **Hours per day:** 6. **Site:** outdoor and indoor, Lowell National Historical Park. **Secondary genre[s]:** TFOL. **Acts:** local acts. **Sample day's lineup:** Alex Demas, Scott Alarik, Leonard Solomon, others. **Contact:** Lowell National Historical Park, 246 Market Street, Lowell, MA 01852, 508-459-1000/970-5000.

OPENING NIGHT, Salem, Salem, MA
    Late Dec.
    Variety, Folk and International

"Celebration of the arts, a family affair throughout downtown Salem. Music, dance and theater." Chamber of Commerce. **Help!** A sample lineup? **Days:** 1. **Admission:** paid. **Daily entry:** under $10. **Restrictions:** 2. **Contact:** Salem Chamber of Commerce, 32 Derby Square, Salem, MA 01970, 508-744-0004.

# R. I. P., M. I. A. Festival Listings

**Caveat** The following festivals are either confirmed or suspected to be discotinued (i.e., R. I. P.); or have not responded to various information requests (i.e., M. I. A.). Since all festivals are subject to last-minute changes or reinstatement, however, FESTPRESS is not responsible for any festival listing information that follows. Readers are encouraged to notify FESTPRESS of any status changes they uncover.

### BEAT-THE-WINTER-BLUES MUSIC FESTIVAL, Waltham, MA
Middle Jan.
Variety, General

**Help!** One time only? **Days:** 1. **Site:** indoor. Luthier's Workshop, 99 Moody Street. **Admission:** paid. **Daily entry:** under $10. **Secondary genre[s]:** BLGS, TFOL, **Acts:** local acts. **Sample day's lineup:** Willow Creek Bluegrass Band, Lourdes, The Whiz Bang Deal, Mare Streetpeople. **Contact:** Luthier's Workshop, 99 Moody Street, Waltham, MA 617-489-1921/894-4292.

### BLACK HISTORY MONTH EXTRAVAGANZA, Roxbury, MA
Middle Feb.
African American

**Help!** One time only? **Days:** 1. **Hours per day:** 4. **Site:** indoor. Dillway-Thomas House, 183 Roxbury Street. **Secondary genre[s]:** MJAZ, TR&B, ACAP, **Acts:** local acts. **Sample day's lineup:** Powerhouse, Three as One, Sister Matara, Thad D. Tinsley Jr., others. **Contact:** Bernice's Sweet Shop, 62 Warren Street, Boston, MA 617-445-9446.

### N. E. C./THOMAS A. DORSEY GOSPEL JUBILEE, Boston, MA
Middle Feb.
Black Gospel

**Help!** One time only? **Days:** 2. .**Acts:** local acts. **Sample day's lineup:** Soloists from New England Conservatory, George Russell Trio, Semenya McCord, others. **Contact:** Jordan Hall, 30 Gainsborough Street, Boston, MA 617-536-2412.

### NIGHT OF NEW FOLK, Cambridge, MA
Early Mar.
Modern Folk

Since 1993. One-time only. **Days:** 1. **Site:** indoor. Paine Hall, Harvard University. **Admission:** paid **Daily entry:** $10 to $24 **Acts:** regional acts, local acts. **Sample day's lineup:** Ellis Paul, Catie Curtis, Jon Svetsky, Raymond Gonzalez and Amy Malkoff, Diane Ziegler. **Contact:** Born to Choose , c/o Paine Hall, Harvard University, Cambridge, MA 617-556-8800.

WOMEN'S SINGING TRADITIONS FROM NEW ENGLAND, Lexington, MA
> Middle Mar.
> Variety, Folk and International

See other dates. **Help!** One time only? **Days:** 1. **Site:** outdoor. Museum of Our National Heritage, 33 Marrett Road. **Admission:** paid **Daily entry:** $10 to $24 **Discounts:** advance purchase discounts, **Secondary genre[s]:** IRSH, AFRM, AFRC, OTHR **Acts:** local acts. **Sample day's lineup:** Bridget Fitzgerald, Vergie Kelley, Tatiana Sarbinska, Ana Vinagre, Sophia Bilides, Josee Vachon. **Contact:** Museum of Our National Heritage, P. O. Box 519, Lexington, MA 02173, 617-861-6559/862-6541.

CELTIC HARP FESTIVAL, Chestnut Hill, MA
> Early Apr.
> Irish

Since 1990. In 1993, it became Gaelic Roots and moved to Early Oct. **Days:** 3. **Hours per day:** 14. **Site:** indoor. Gasson Hall, Boston College. **Admission:** paid **Daily entry:** $10 to $24, $25 to $49 **Discounts:** multiple event or day passes, **Secondary genre[s]:** SCOT, **Acts:** regional acts, local acts. **Sample day's lineup:** Maire Ni Chathasaigh, Triantan, Others. **Contact:** Boston College Irish Studies Program, Carney Building, Room 439, Chestnut Hill, MA 02167-3806, 617-552-3716/4843.

JAZZ AND BLUES, Northampton, MA
> Early Apr. to Middle Apr.
> Variety, Jazz and Blues

"Kick off Iron Horse's 15th Year of Jazz" -- Advertisement. **Help!** One time only? **Days:** 7. **Site:** indoor. Springfield Symphony Hall, Iron Horse Cafe, Academy of Music. **Admission:** paid **Daily entry:** $10 to $24 **Discounts:** advance purchase discounts, **Secondary genre[s]:** MJAZ, MR&B, TR&B, ZYDC, MLAT, AFRC, **Acts:** national acts, local acts. **Sample day's lineup:** Chaka Kahn, Philip Bailey, Gerald Albright, Bobby Lyle, Keiko Matsui, Hugh Masakela. **Contact:** Iron Horse Music Hall, 20 Center Street, Northampton, MA 01060, 413-586-8686.

NORTH SHORE SPRING FEST, Salem, MA
> Middle Apr.
> Reggae, Ska and Caribbean

**Help!** One time only? **Days:** 3. **Site:** indoor. Club Oasis at Bleachers, 143 Washington Street. **Acts:** local acts. **Sample day's lineup:** Free "I", Oral, Skiffy, Mr. B, Rockers International. **Contact:** Club Oasis at Bleachers, 143 Washington Street, Salem, MA, 508-867-6393.

BOSTON SPRING CELTIC FESTIVAL, Boston, MA
> Late Apr.
> Irish

Since 1993. The first and last. Unfortunately, a lot of people came to this ambitious event dressed as empty chairs. Having it the same weekend as NEFFA couldn't have helped. **Days:** 3. **Hours per day:** 14. **Site:** indoor. World Trade Center. **Admission:** paid **Daily entry:** $10 to $24 **Secondary genre[s]:** SCOT, **Acts:** national acts, local acts. **Sample day's lineup:** Barley Bree, Ronnie Browne, Gerry Timlin, Alexander Brothers, Seamus Kennedy, Carolyn Hannan, Celtic Pride, Liam Tiernan and Johnny Cunningham, Anne MacCall and Davey MacPherson, others. **Contact:** Boston Spring Celtic Festival, 15 Broad Street, Suite 225, Boston, MA 02109, 617-973-5850.

MOBIUS'S PARTY UNIVERSE, Boston, MA
> Late Apr.
> Reggae, Ska and Caribbean

"Enter a new dementia." -- Advertisement. **Help!** One time only? **Days:** 1. **Hours per day:** 4. **Site:** indoor. Mobius, 348 Congress Street. **Admission:** paid **Daily entry:** $10 to $24 **Discounts:** advance purchase discounts, **Secondary genre[s]:** ARCK, **Acts:** local acts. **Sample day's lineup:** Hi-Hats, Steady Earnest, Made in the Shade, Raquib Hassan Ensemble. **Contact:** Mobius, 348 Congress Street, Boston, MA 02210, 617-542-7416.


EARTH DAY SOUND ACTION CONCERT, Foxboro, MA
Late Apr.
> Modern Rock and Pop

Since 1990. Minneapolis-based Concerts for the Environment discontinued it's annual rock affair here in 1993 after bouts with bad weather. Stadium organziers would like to have it back, however, so stay tuned. **Days:** 1. **Hours per day:** 9. **Site:** outdoor. Foxboro Stadium. **Secondary genre[s]:** ARCK, **Acts:** national acts, . **Sample day's lineup:** Steve Miller Band, Midnight Oil, The Kinks, Fishbone, The Violent Femmes, others. **Contact:** Earth Day Sound Action Concert, Foxboro Stadium, Foxboro MA 508-543-0350.


SONGSTREET FLYING FISH FESTIVAL, Cambridge, MA
> Early May
> Variety, Folk and International

Since 1992. Successful artistically, but not financially. Discontinued after 1993. **Days:** 1. **Site:** indoor. Sanders Theater, Harvard University. **Admission:** paid **Daily entry:** $10 to $24 **Discounts:** student discounts, advance purchase discounts, **Secondary genre[s]:** BLGS, MFOL, TLAT, **Acts:** national acts, regional acts, local acts. **Sample day's lineup:** Tom Paxton, Fred Small, Northern Lights, Flor de Cana. **Contact:** Songstreet Productions, P. O. Box 85, Somerville, MA 02143, 617-628-3390.


BOSTON SONGOS ONSTAGE, Cambridge, MA
> Middle May
> Modern Folk

Since 1991. "Our motto: That's the way the Songos." Fast Folk-inspired annual review of weekly songwriter's-exchange participants. **Help!** The status of this event, or the whereabouts of its promoters? **Site:** indoor. Old Cambridge Baptist Church, 1171 Massachusetts Avenue. **Admission:** paid **Daily entry:** Under $10 **Discounts:** advance purchase discounts, **Acts:** local acts. **Sample day's lineup:** Liz Brahm, Geoffrey Cary Sather, Steve Brennan, Paul Rogoshewski, Jenny Burtis, Max Pokrivchak, Phyllis Copanna, Jan Luby, Elizabeth Connolly, Jim Infantino, Meg Daly, Paul Hatem, Deb Galiga, Laurie Goldsmith, David Goldfinger, Geoff Bartley. **Contact:** Circle Productions, P. O. Box 1364, Arlington, MA 02174, 617-648-8318.


SONGSTREET NEW RISING ARTISTS FESTIVAL, Somerville, MA
> Late May
> Modern Folk

Since 1993. One time only. First Congregational Church, 95 College Avenue. **Admission:** paid **Daily entry:** $10 to $24 **Acts:** local acts. **Sample day's lineup:** Jon Svetsky, Jim Infantino, Kathy Phipps, Marie Sangiolo, Laurie Goldsmith and The Rodeo Kids, Nancy Lee Snyder. **Contact:** Songstreet Productions, P. O. Box 85, Somerville, MA 02143, 617-628-3390.

## BOSTON'S GRANDEST CABARET, Boston, MA
> Late May
> Cabaret

Benefit for Living with Aids Theater Project. **Help!** The status of this event, or the whereabouts of its promoters? **Days:** 1. **Site:** indoor. Roxy, 279 Tremont Street. **Admission:** paid **Daily entry:** $10 to $24 **Secondary genre[s]:** MJAZ, **Acts:** local acts. **Sample Day's Lineup:** Mae Arnette, Rebecca Paris, Sandy Martin, Neicy Boswell, Lisa Thorson, Peter DiMuro-Performance Associates, others. **Contact:** Living with Aids Theater Project , c/o Roxy, 279 Tremont Street, Boston, MA 617-277-7699.


## JAMAICA PLAIN WORLD'S FAIR, Jamaica Plain, MA
> Early Jun.
> Variety, Folk and International

Since 1988. Cancelled in '95. Resumption uncertain. **Days:** 1. **Hours per day:** 6. **Site:** outdoor. Centre Street. **Admission:** free. **Contact:** Pleasant Realty, Jamaica Plain, MA 02130, 617-522-4600.


## CAPE COD INTERNATIONAL FESTIVAL, West Barnstable, MA
> Early Jun.
> Variety, Folk and International

Discontinued in 1993. **Days:** 1. **Hours per day:** 12. **Site:** indoor. Cape Cod Community College, Route 132. **Admission:** paid **Contact:** Cape Cod Community College, Route 132, West Barnstable MA 508-362-8050.


## CELEBRATE BACK BAY, Boston, MA
> Middle Jun.
> Variety, General

Discontinued in 1993. **Days:** 3. **Site:** outdoor. Copley Square Park, Boylston and Dartmouth Streets. **Secondary genre[s]:** MJAZ, ARCK, **Acts:** local acts. **Contact:** Back Bay Association, 224 Clarendon Street, Boston, MA 02116, 617-266-1992.


## ENTERTAINMENT SHOWCASE, Danvers, MA
> Middle Jun.
> Variety, General

"A festival of music by talented entertainers from the North Shore." -- Listing. Discontinued in 1992. **Days:** 1. **Hours per day:** 8. **Site:** indoor. King's Grant Inn, Route 128, exit 21. **Admission:** paid **Acts:** local acts. **Contact:** King's Grant Inn, Route 128, Danvers, MA 508-921-4990.


## HOWLIN' AT THE MOON: A BLUES REVIEW, Salisbury, MA
> Middle Jun.
> Blues and Traditional R&B

Benefits The Strongest Link AIDS Services. **Help!** One time only? **Days:** 1. **Site:** indoor. The Beach Club. **Admission:** paid **Daily entry:** $10 to $24 **Discounts:** advance purchase discounts, **Acts:** national acts, local acts. **Sample day's lineup:** Ronnie Earl and The Broadcasters, Rick Russell Band with The Cadillac Horns, Afternoon Blues Coalition, others. **Contact:** Howlin' at the Moon: A Blues Review, The Beach Club, Salisbury, MA 508-346-8106.

## USTRUST GREAT WOODS FOLK FESTIVAL, Mansfield, MA
### Modern Folk

Since 1989. Presented several of the best single-day/same-stage lineups I'd ever witnessed, but inadequate attendance over the years forced its cancellation. "A superb folk festival without enough folks," one review-er lamented. Discontinued in 1991. **Days:** 2. **Hours per day:** 10. **Site:** outdoor. Great Woods Center for the Performing Arts. **Admission:** paid **Daily entry:** $10 to $24 **Discounts:** multiple event or day passes, advance purchase discounts, **Restrictions:** 1, 6, 7, 8, **Secondary genre[s]:** TR&B, ACAP, MC&W, BLGS, ZYDC, IRSH, AFRC, **Acts:** national acts, regional acts, local acts. **Sample day's lineup:** Rickie Lee Jones, Lyle Lovett, Leo Kottke, Joe Ely, Malathini and The Mahotella Queens, Wayne Toups and Zydecajun, Tony Rice Unit, The Bobs, Norman Blake and Tony Rice, Stephen Baird, Wright Brothers, Sally Rogers, Cephas and Wiggins, Bill Morrissey. **Contact:** Great Woods Center for the Performing Arts, P. O. Box 810, Mansfield, MA 02048, 508-339-2333.

## ROCK A BLUE MOON IN JUNE, Boston, MA
### Middle Jun.
### Blues and Traditional R&B

Since 1993. "Promoting racial harmony through educational outreach by discovering and applying the social, spiritual and artistic legacy of the blues." -- Advertisement. **Help!** One time only? **Days:** 1. **Hours per day:** 6. **Site:** indoor. Avalon, 15 Lansdowne Street. **Admission:** paid **Daily entry:** $25 to $49, $50 and over **Acts:** national acts, local acts. **Sample day's lineup:** Lonnie Mack, Tinsley Ellis, Monster Mike Welch, Sticky Mike and The Jam. **Contact:** Massachusetts House of Blues Foundations, Inc., P. O. Box 381303, Cambridge, MA 02238, 617-497-0270/0277.

## UPHAMS CORNER MULTICULTURAL FESTIVAL, Dorchester, MA
### Late Jun.
### Variety, Folk and International

Since 1993. **Days:** 1. **Hours per day:** 6. **Site:** indoor. Strand Theater, 543 Columbia Road. **Admission:** free **Acts:** local acts. **Sample day's lineup:** Son Moreno, La Tour, Jeff Danger, others. **Contact:** Strand Theater, 543 Columbia Road, Dorchester, MA 617-282-8000/5230.

## USTRUST GREAT WOODS JAZZ FESTIVAL, Mansfield, MA
### Late Jun.
### Modern Jazz

Discontinued in 1991. **Days:** 1. **Hours per day:** 10. **Site:** outdoor. Great Woods Center for the Performing Arts. **Admission:** free and paid **Daily entry:** $10 to $24 **Discounts:** advance purchase discounts, **Restrictions:** 1, 6, 7, 8, **Acts:** national acts, local acts. **Sample day's lineup:** Wynton Marsalis, Dianne Schuur, Roy Hargrove, Christopher Hollyday, Marlon Jordan, Marcus Roberts, Mark Whitfield, Dewy Redman Quartet, Jimmy Giuffre, Paul Bley, Gary Peacock, Human Feel. **Contact:** Great Woods Center for the Performing Arts, P. O. Box 810, Mansfield, MA 02048, 508-339-2333.

## HARVARD SUMMER FOLK FESTIVAL, Cambridge, MA
### Middle Jul.
### Modern Folk

Site difficulties forced this event's cancellation for 1993, but it may re-surface elsewhere in the future. **Days:** 1. **Hours per day:** 7. **Site:** outdoor. Harvard University Yard. **Admission:** paid **Daily entry:** $10 to $24, under $10 **Restrictions:** 5, **Acts:** national acts, regional acts, local acts. **Sample day's lineup:** Tom Rush, Cheryl Wheeler, David Buskin, Peter Keane, Catie Curtis, Ellen Cross, Dr. Joe, Atwater-Donnelly, Jake Kensinger and Ellen Schmidt, Jericho Rose and Nancy Lee Snyder. **Contact:** Cambridge Discovery, Inc., P. O. Box 1987, Cambridge, MA 02238, 617-495-1573/628-3390.

## KINDRED HEARTS: A CELEBRATION OF WOMEN AND MUSIC, Lowell, MA
Middle Jun.
Modern Folk

Benefit for Greater Lowell Rape Crisis Center. Discontinued in 1993, but may resume in 1994, possibly at a later date so as not to compete with Lowell's copious summer schedule. **Days:** 1. **Hours per day:** 6. **Site:** outdoor. Sampus Pavilion, Lowell Heritage State Park, Pawtucket Boulevard. **Admission:** free **Acts:** regional acts, local acts. **Sample day's lineup:** Aubrey Atwater, Les Sampou, others. **Contact:** Kindred Hearts: A Celebration of Women and Music , 381-100 Hildreth Street, Lowell, MA 01850, 508-459-9943/452-7721.

## ONE WORLD ROOTS FESTIVAL, Boston, MA
Middle Jul.
Reggae, Ska and Caribbean

Since 1993. **Help!** One time only? **Days:** 1. **Site:** indoor. Roxy, 279 Tremont. **Admission:** paid **Daily entry:** $10 to $24 **Acts:** national acts, local acts. **Sample day's lineup:** Lucky Dube, Ras Michael and The Sons of Negus, The Itals, Kolo Mboka. **Contact:** One World Roots Festival, c/o Roxy, 279 Tremont, Boston, MA 02116, 617-227-7699.

## FOLKTREE'S BLUEGRASS HEAVEN, Lincoln, MA
Middle Jul.
Bluegrass

Discontinued in 1990. **Days:** 1. **Hours per day:** 12. **Site:** outdoor. DeCordova Museum Ampitheater, Sandy Pond Road. **Admission:** paid **Daily entry:** $10 to $24 **Acts:** national acts. **Sample day's lineup:** Bill Monroe, Doc Watson, The Seldom Scene, John Hartford, David Bromberg. **Contact:** FolkTree Concertmakers, P. O. Box 313, Arlington, MA 02174, 617-641-1010.

## INTERNATIONAL SEAPORT FESTIVAL, Boston, MA
Middle Jul.
Variety, Folk and International

Since 1992. Discontinued in 1994, perhaps to return. **Days:** 3. **Site:** indoor. World Trade Center, 164 Northern Avenue. **Contact:** World Trade Center, 164 Northern Avenue, Boston, MA 02210, 617-439-5198.

## HIGHLAND ALL DAY JAZZ FESTIVAL, Newton, MA
Middle Jul.
Modern Jazz

**Help!** The status of this event? **Days:** 1. **Hours per day:** 5. **Site:** indoor. Laventhal-Sidman Community Center, 333 Nahanton Street. **Admission:** paid **Daily entry:** $10 to $24. **Contact:** Highland Jazz, Inc., P. O. Box 37, Newton Highlands, MA 02161, 617-965-4424.

## SIT 'N BULL'S BARBEQUE/MUSIC FESTIVAL, Northboro, MA
Middle Jul.
Blues and Traditional R&B

Since 1992. Discontinued in 1993, perhaps to return. **Days:** 1. **Site:** outdoor. Northboro Fish and Game, Bear Hill Road. **Admission:** paid **Daily entry:** under $10, $10 to $24 **Discounts:** advance purchase discounts, **Acts:** national acts, regional acts, local acts. **Sample day's lineup:** Drivin' Sideways, Barrence Whitfield and The Savages, James Montgomery Band, Allen Estes Band. **Contact:** Sit 'n Bull Pub, 163 Main Street, Maynard, MA 01754, 508-897-7232.

HYANNIS STREET FESTIVAL, Hyannis, MA
> Late Jul. to Early Aug.
> Variety, General

Since 1977. Discontinued in 1992. **Days:** 1. **Hours per day:** 13. **Site:** outdoor. Main Street. **Contact:** Hyannis Street Festival, Main Street, Hyannis, MA 508-775-2201.


BEAVERBROOK BLUEGRASS FESTIVAL, Pepperell, MA
> Early Aug.
> Bluegrass

**Help!** The status of this event, or the whereabout of its promoters? **Site:** outdoor. Harvard Sportsmen's Club. **Acts:** regional acts, local acts. **Contact:** Beaverbrook Bluegrass Festival, 20 Pleasant Street, Pepperell, MA 01463, 508-433-8184.


FOLKTREE'S SUMMERFEST, Lincoln, MA
> Early Aug.
> Modern Country

Discontinued in 1990. **Days:** 1. **Hours per day:** 12. **Site:** outdoor. DeCordova Museum Ampitheater, Sandy Pond Road. **Admission:** paid **Daily entry:** $10 to $24 **Secondary genre[s]:** MFOL, **Acts:** national acts, . **Sample day's lineup:** Emmylou Harris, The O'Kanes, Don Mclean, Cris Williamson, Tom Paxton. **Contact:** FolkTree Concertmakers, P. O. Box 313, Arlington, MA 02174, 617-641-1010.


WAMPANOAG SUMMER MUSIC FESTIVAL, Gay Head, MA
> Early Aug.
> Modern Folk

Since 1992. Benefits Wampanoag tribe of Gay Head (Martha's Vineyard), plus the River Fund which subsidizes hospice work. Discontinued in 1993, but may be revived. **Days:** 1. **Hours per day:** 7. **Site:** outdoor. Aquinah Park. **Secondary genre[s]:** MJAZ, CRCK, NATV, **Acts:** national acts, local acts. **Sample day's lineup:** Arlo Guthrie, Kate Taylor, Bill Lee, Arlen Roth, Tommy Hambridge, Johnny Hoy and Bluefish. **Contact:** Gay Head Chamber of Commerce, RR 1, Box 137, Gay Head, MA 02535, 508-693-0085/645-9265.


SISTERS IN THE SPIRIT, North Dartmouth, MA
> Middle Aug.
> Modern Jazz

"An evening of cabaret and dance performances by New England women performers..." -- Listing. **Help!** One time only? **Days:** 1. **Site:** indoor. Hawthorne Country Club, 970 Tucker Road. **Admission:** paid **Daily entry:** $10 to $24 **Acts:** regional acts, local acts. **Sample day's lineup:** Cercie Miller, Semenya McCord, Valerie Stephens, Mili Bermejo and Dan Greenspan. **Contact:** Sisters in the Spirit, Hawthorne Country Club, 970 Tucker Road, North Dartmouth, MA 508-999-3255.


NEW ALCHEMY BENEFIT FOLK FESTIVAL, Falmouth, MA
> Late Aug.
> Modern Folk

Since 1990. Discontinued in 1991. **Days:** 1. **Hours per day:** 7. **Site:** outdoor. Barnstable County Fairgrounds, Route 151. **Admission:** paid **Daily entry:** $10 to $24, under $10 **Secondary genre[s]:** BLGS, **Acts:** national acts, regional acts, local acts. **Sample day's lineup:** Rory Block, John Gorka, Bill Morrissey, Lui Collins, Patty Larkin, Northern Lights, Barbara Kessler. **Contact:** New Alchemy Institute, 237 Hatchville Road, East Falmouth, MA 02536, 508-564-6301.

## USTRUST GREAT WOODS BLUES FESTIVAL, Mansfield, MA
Late Aug.
Blues and Traditional R&B

Discontinued in 1991, alas! **Days:** 1. **Hours per day:** 10. **Site:** outdoor. Great Woods Center for the Performing Arts. **Admission:** paid **Daily entry:** $10 to $24 **Restrictions:** 1, 6, 7, 8, **Secondary genre[s]: Acts:** national acts. **Sample day's lineup:** Robert Cray, Los Lobos, Koko Taylor, Danny Gatton, Ronnie Earl and Sugar Ray with The Broadcasters. **Contact:** Great Woods Center for the Performing Arts, P. O. Box 810, Mansfield, MA 02048, 508-339-2333.

## BIG GIG: THE ULTIMATE NO BOZOS JAM, Mansfield, MA
Late Aug.
Hard Rock and Heavy Metal

Since 1992. "Featuring 80 of New England's hottest bands. Plus: art show, leather and lace show, temporary tattoos, heavy metal karaoke, velcro toss, big hair competition, emergency broadcast network, midway rides, games, WBCN Rock Stop, palm reader and much more!" -- Advertisement. **Help!** Discontinued in 1994? **Days:** 1. **Hours per day:** 11. **Site:** outdoor. Great Woods Center for the Performing Arts. **Admission:** paid **Daily entry:** under $10 **Discounts:** advance purchase discounts, **Restrictions:** 1, 6, 7, 8, 13, **Secondary genre[s]:** ARCK, **Acts:** local acts. **Sample Day's Lineup:** Flesh, I-Mok, 3 Steps Out, Jodee Frawlee Band, Crash of Rhinos, Wicked Witch, Restless Souls, Witch Bonnie, Joystick Joe, Stump, Motherlode, Jon Finn Group, Blazing Angels, Slave to Seduction, Iron Suasage, Paris, Contagious, Abby Normal, Mystery Jones, Gypsy Child, Jagged Edge, Krucix, Hollywood East, Love Life and Fury, 6 Gun City, No Way Out, Live Wire, Rain, Trip Wire, Tin Pan Alley, Boa, Candy Striper Death Orgy, Jealous Dogs, Sly Boyz, Fighting Cocks, Jumper Freefall, Sinister Kane, The Verdict, Creative Force, Forty Thieves, One-Eyed Jake, Play Rough Gracie, Touch 2 Much, Taurus, Alliance, Steadfast, Rated R, Reason Enough, Open Perception, Flash Addict, Highway Child, Woopie Cats, Bab Blood, The Tears, Eye to Eye, She's So Loud, Cartoon Factory, Twisted Roots, Tripp Hammer, Cobolt 60, Arcturus, Atunga, Electrichicka, Love Pollution, Mood Crush, Heavy Metal Tap Dancer. **Contact:** Don Law Presents, P. O. Box 810, Mansfield, MA 02048, 508-339-2333 **or:** Rochefort and Associates, 20 Park Plaza, Suite 632, Boston, MA 02116, 617-482-5822. .

## INTERNATIONAL MUSIC FESTIVAL: THE WORLD OF MUSIC OF WESTERN MASS., Lowell, MA
Late Aug.
Variety, Folk and International

**Help!** One time only? **Days:** 1. **Site:** outdoor. Boarding House Park, French and John Streets. **Admission:** free **Acts:** local acts. **Sample day's lineup:** "Six acts of varying ethnic heritages." **Contact:** UMass Lowell, Center for the Arts, One University Avenue, Lowell, MA 01824, 508-459-1000.

## BENEFIT CONCERT, Adams, MA
Early Sep. Modern Country

Since 1992. "Proceeds to help area youth programs." -- Berkshires Week. **Help!** The status of this event, or the whereabouts of its promoters? **Days:** 1. **Site:** outdoor. Renfrew Field, Route 8. **Admission:** paid **Acts:** national acts, local acts. **Sample day's lineup:** Charlie Daniels Band, Berkshire Country, Whirlwind, Journey's End. **Contact:** 413-743-3438.

## FOLKTREE FESTIVAL, Lincoln, MA
Early Sep.
Modern Folk

Since 1985. Discontinued in 1990. **Days:** 1. **Hours per day:** 12. **Site:** outdoor. DeCordova Museum Ampitheater, Sandy Pond Road. **Admission:** paid **Daily entry:** $10 to $24 **Secondary genre[s]:** ZYDC, **Acts:** national acts. **Sample day's lineup:** Tom Rush, Livingston Taylor, Cris Williamson, Jesse Winchester, Beausoleil. **Contact:** FolkTree Concertmakers, P. O. Box 313, Arlington, MA 02174, 617-641-1010.

BRAZILIAN INDEPENDENCE DAY CELEBRATION, Cambridge, MA
> Early Sep.
> Brazilian and South American

**Help!** The status of this event, or the whereabouts of its promoters? **Days:** 1. **Site:** outdoor. **Acts:** national acts, local acts. **Sample day's lineup:** Elba Ramalho, others. **Contact:** Brazil Tropical Productions.


CONCERT FOR WALDEN WOODS, Foxboro, MA
> Early Sep.
> Modern Rock and Pop

Since 1991. "Walden Woods, for all intents and purposes, is the cradle or the birthplace of the modern ecological movement." -- Don Henley, Hartford Courant. **Help!** The status of this event? **Days:** 1. **Site:** outdoor. Foxboro Stadium. **Admission:** paid **Daily entry:** $25 to $49, $50 and over **Acts:** national acts. **Sample day's lineup:** Don Henley, Elton John, Sting, Melissa Etheridge, Aerosmith, Jimmy Buffett. **Contact:** Foxboro Stadium, Foxboro, MA 508-543-0350.


CAMBRIDGE IRISH FESTIVAL, Cambridge, MA
> Middle Sep.
> Irish

Since 1992. Cancelled in 1993 due to funding cuts, but planned to resume in 1994. **Help!** A sample lineup? **Days:** 1. **Site:** outdoor. Canal Park, behind Cambridgeside Galleria Mall. **Contact:** Irish Immigration Center, 18 Tremont Street, Suite 207, Boston, MA 02108, 617-367-1126.


ASSABET RIVER BLUES FESTIVAL, Northboro, MA
> Middle Sep.
> Blues and Traditional R&B

Since 1990. Skipped in 1992 and 1993 as promoter sought sponsorship, but rejected companies attempts to "plaster their name everywhere." Re-forming as nonprofit and seeking funding to resume in 1994. **Help!** The status of this event? **Days:** 1. **Hours per day:** 7. **Site:** outdoor. Northboro Fish and Game Reservation, Barefoot Road. **Admission:** paid **Daily entry:** $10 to $24 **Discounts:** advance purchase discounts, **Contact:** Assabet River Blues Festival, Northboro Fish and Game Reservation, Barefoot Road, Northboro, MA 508-853-5030.


RIVERBANK FAMILY FOLK FESTIVAL, Concord, MA
> Middle Sep.
> Modern Folk

Since 1990. Discontinued in 1994. **Days:** 1. **Hours per day:** 6. **Site:** outdoor. Damonmill Square, Route 62 West. **Admission:** paid **Daily entry:** under $10 **Acts:** national acts, regional acts, local acts. **Sample day's lineup:** Livingston Taylor, Cheryl Wheeler, Cormac McCarthy, Don Henry, Ellis Paul, Fred Small, David Mallett, Brooks Williams, Les Sampou. **Contact:** Walden 1120 AM, Damonmill Square, Concord, MA 01742, 508-371-3200.


BOSTON SONGWRITERS COLLABORATIVE ANNIVERSARY CONCERT, Newton, MA
> Early Oct.
> Modern Folk

"A fantastic experience last year [1992]; we may do it again this year" -- Bob Weiser, Watch City Arts. **Help!** One time only? **Days:** 1. Eliot Church, 474 Center Street. **Admission:** paid **Daily entry:** under $10 **Discounts:** advance purchase discounts, **Acts:** regional acts, local acts. **Sample Day's Lineup:** Eric Kilburn, Catie Curtis, Rick Goldin, Ben Tousley, Marcia Taylor, Bob Blue, Sue Kranz, Jill Stein, Joanne Olshansky, Peri Smilow, Cindy Mapes. **Contact:** Watch City Arts, 230 Lowell Street, Waltham, MA 02154, 617-647-1075.

CELTIC HARMONY, Brockton, MA
> Late Oct.
> Irish

**Help!** One time only? **Days:** 1. **Site:** indoor. Fine Arts Center, Massasoit Community College. **Secondary genre[s]:** SCOT, **Acts:** national acts, local acts. **Sample day's lineup:** Natalie MacMaster, John Whelan, Peter Barnes, Jacqueline Schwab, Jeanne Morrill, Tony Cuffe. **Contact:** Fine Arts Center, Massasoit Community College, One Massasoit Boulevard, Brockton, MA 02402, 508-586-6578.

~    ~    ~

*Circlin', Cambridge River Festival.*

# Rhode Island

*The Band, Ben and Jerry's Newport Folk Festival.*

# Escoheag's Reggae Ranch

New England Reggae Festival, Escoheag, RI
Late July
Reggae, Ska and Caribbean
***Attended***

**Introduction**

"So far, everyone's amazed at how well-organized it has been," exclaims Lon Plynton, who has presented the New England Reggae Festival annually since 1990. "Everybody expects reggae bands, you know, 'Reggae, oh my gosh, this is gonna' be...'"

He laughs without finishing the sentence, but his implication is all too clear. The very next month, in fact, I was victimized by the Budweiser Charity Reggae Fest fiasco in Bridgeport, CT, which publicized 12 hours a day of big-name acts, yet had delivered nothing more than an hour-long sound check from anonymous locals by the time I bailed out at 9:00 p.m. Plynton's contrasting gift to reggae fans from Maine to Maryland has been to create an Island vibe but not on "Island time." His inviting affair runs every year as promised and pretty much as scheduled.

Even when past lineups have been threatened, Plynton's cool head has prevailed. Take the year vocalist Human Rights [HR] was in a snit. He recalls:

- "He had his different problems as far as him relating to his management and all that. That year, it was a big, big upset, but I was able to talk to the management, talk to everybody screaming. The business was concluded in three seconds. HR performed. He brought Al Anderson from The Wailers up on stage and he did a phenomenal set! That was a great moment; everybody was so happy over that."

  "The next year, some people came back and said, 'I saw HR's band at the Vermont Reggae Festival [Johnson, VT — see chapter], but I didn't see HR.' I said, 'Oh, that could've been us!'"

Plynton chuckles with relief.

Of course, his party is more than just the closing sets. Being a musician, himself (playing in the locally-based Mystic Jammers), Plynton knows the best reggae bands throughout the region to fill up the two-day-long bill. Being a vendor, too (hawking gifts from his own Caribbean shop in Providence), he supports a full palette of high-quality arts, crafts, and cuisine on site. Plynton also takes special pride in the event's family features. "The children's activities have been really good every year," he says. "They do little games, things to keep the kids occupied, so that the parents can have a little time to run around themselves!"

If you've ever been to the Stepping Stone Ranch, site of the glorious Cajun and Bluegrass Music-Food-Dance Festival and Big Easy Bash (see chapter), you know it's a welcoming place to do the kind of running around he speaks of: rustic, but full-featured; cozy, but not cramped. The Ranch even offers horseback riding, as it always does when not hosting music. It actually inspired Plynton's festival in the first place, as he and some friends were invited by a mutual buddy, sound engineer Paul Brown, to inspect the site. Plynton remembers, "It was such a nice place that we figured we'd get everybody together."

Buoyed by longtime reggae supporters around Providence, Plyton's been able to expand that first year's informal gathering of roots rockers into an annual institution encompassing ska, dance hall, soca, and world beat. This branching-out has contributed a number of memorable performances. Plynton cites a pair:

- Arrow: "No one knew Arrow. A lot of people didn't know anything about soca... Who is this guy, Arrow? Everybody was waiting around. Then Arrow burst on the scene, and everybody jumped up and started dancing for the rest of the night!"

- Winston Grennan and The Ska-Rocks Band: "Last year, he had them eating out of his hand. When he gets into the vibe, and he gets into his 'fatherly' sort of image, you know, talking to the crowd as if [they're] little children as he teaches them... There was a long line of people [for signing] autographs afterwards. Winston Grennan's definitely great. You get him on those good nights..."

Plynton's greatest satisfaction, though, has been seeing a regular audience congregate from afar:

- "I've noticed a lot of people now meet [here]. They plan, 'Oh, I'll see you at the reggae festival!' ...They make friends at the festival and they want to meet them again the next year. It's a way for people from different far parts of the region to meet.

"So far, everything's gone on time, all the bands have gotten here. No big row, no big blast. Our whole thing is more low-key, more aimed toward having a good regional event. However, the greatest compliments we get are the people who say they're gonna' come back every year. ...They're looking for a good festival and our festival's always been a very homey sort of thing. The Rhode Island countryside is so beautiful.

"Everybody's just said that it's well-organized," Plynton proudly re-iterates, "and they come back every year."

**Festival Review** Plynton has good things to say about all the prior years' headliners for the NEW ENGLAND REGGAE FESTIVAL, including Israel Vibrations, Sister Carol, The Itals, Inner Circle, and others. He also commends past regional bookings such as Igina, Ras Junior, Bolu Fatunmise, Errol Strength and The Conscious Reggae Band, The Tribulations, Bobemba U. S. A, Babatundi, etc.

The area scene these reggae bands spring from is so entrenched that one middle-aged guy I talked to was doing his doctoral dissertation on the topic. Notebook in hand, he stood out among the easy-goin' crowd of goateed collegiates and rastafari families basking in the "bright, bright, sun-shiny day." I had to quickly scoot up to the LOWELL FOLK FESTIVAL (Lowell, MA — see chapter), but was able to catch one regional act, Wilson Blue.

**Artist Mini-Review** Wilson Blue: Resplendent in a loose-fitting cotton suit of purple, gold and green tie-dye, Blue managed to coax a surprisingly full, funky and danceable sound from his mere four-piece band. Virtually all tunes were uptempo, including covers of Harry Belafonte's "Camelia Brown," John Holt's "The Tide is High," Jimmy Cliff's "The Harder They Come," and a Bob Marley medley. O.K., so the set-list wasn't cutting edge, but he did put his quick, syncopated signature on nearly everything, and delivered it with personality and presence. Blue got the mid-day off to a groove.

Plynton: "Wilson Blue, he's a real professional. He started on the north coast [doing] hotels and that sort of scene. He's always a lot of energy — a big party band."

**Travel Tip** "I would say they should visit Narraganset or Mitunic Beaches — the nearby beaches," suggests Plynton, "or the hot night scene in either Newport or Providence." If it's Providence, he recommends an African restaurant, Cecilia's, on Friendship Street. By the way, his own store, The Lion's Eye, is on Brook Street.

~     ~     ~

# Newport's Classic Revivals

NEWPORT RHYTHM AND BLUES FESTIVAL, Newport, RI
> Late July
> Blues and Traditional R&B

BEN AND JERRY'S NEWPORT FOLK FESTIVAL, Newport, RI
> Early August
> Modern Folk
> ***Attended***

JVC JAZZ FESTIVAL/NEWPORT, Newport, RI
> Middle August
> Modern Jazz
> ***Attended***

**Introduction**

"It's a real burden for me," sighs Bob Jones, good naturedly. This gravely-voiced Senior Vice-President of Festival Productions, Inc. [FPI] and Director of BEN AND JERRY'S NEWPORT FOLK FESTIVAL is relaying his annual dilemma in selecting from among reams of deserving applicants to support the event's impressive headliners. He flashes me the prior month's 47 submissions which include some recognizably solid performers.

"I think people don't understand," Jones relates. "My burdens are brought on by working on the old festivals, the tradition of the old festivals, and coming up to that mark. Sure, I gotta' have enough people in the door to pay for the bills and so forth, but the other burden that rests on my head wants to fulfill the things that we did in the '50s and '60s."

The original NEWPORT FOLK FESTIVAL he speaks of had a remarkable impact on the music world, considering it's relatively spotty reign. It was the first folk festival I'm aware of that boasted major names; it was extraordinarily eclectic; and it scored a long series of artistic triumphs in rediscovering traditional legends of all different stripes and presenting them alongside up-and-coming superstars. Sometimes, this crossover mix backfired — notoriously when a young Bob Dylan debuted his electrified sound in '65 and was promptly booed off the stage by folk purists.

According to Jones, the first affair commenced in '57 as a partnership between festival icon, George Wein, who'd launched the NEWPORT JAZZ FESTIVAL three years earlier (JVC JAZZ FESTIVAL, New York, NY — see chapter), and Dylan's manager, Albert Grossman. "It stopped in '60 because of problems with the jazz festival," Jones recounts. "Then in '62, it came back under a board of directors under the foundation structure [with] the 'old guard': Jean Ritchie, Oscar Brand, Pete Seeger, etc. It went on until '69. There was no festival in '70. There was one planned in '71, but it didn't happen because of the influence of the jazz festival [referring to that year's riots]. The city wouldn't give us a permit."

Jones joined Wein's crew to work the folk festival from '63 through '65: "In '65, George said, 'What do you do the other part of the year?' I said, 'Not much.' George said, 'Wanna' work with some jazz people?' So, I said, 'Sure!' And he said, 'You're gonna' take Dave Brubeck to Europe.'"

That gig led Jones to a thirty-year career with FPI that included helping to build what is universally considered the world's best music festival, the NEW ORLEANS JAZZ AND HERITAGE FESTIVAL (see New Orleans, LA, Late April to Early May), celebrating it's 25th anniversary in '94. (Jones: "If you take the folk festival in the '60s and the jazz festival in the '60s, and you put 'em together, you end up in New Orleans. The concept of jazz artists and folk artists, a melange of people back and forth, was basically what we did in New Orleans.") When FPI jumpstarted the folk festival in '85 after it's 15-year hiatus, Jones was the natural candidate to take charge.

"My only concern in this case as a producer is the undercard," Jones continues:

- "I have to really devote a lot of energy to the undercard and whether or not I have the correct undercard to push them in the direction that they're not apt to go into — the pop side. Because of the general space and time allocation at the festival, I sometimes, probably, in my own mind, fall short. You would remember that in the early folk festivals the same thing was done. I mean, we had Peter, Paul and Mary and Mississippi John Hurt — from one to the other — but we also had four days, four nights, workshops, a lot of room to play with..."

On the contrary, I've always been amazed how well Jones has overcome his limitations in recent years, considering he has fewer than 10 supporting slots to play with each year. The contrasts and comparisons (even collaborations on special occasions) between these artists is almost always enlightening. Different musical cultures, from Cajun to Haitian, take their place among traditional and contemporary folk stars, including several acts from the pop side. Indeed, it's the bringing of folk and pop worlds together, both older and younger, which makes Jones's efforts so uniquely successful in cross-fertilizing audiences.

A particular crossover success was on 1993's bill, which featured "Four Voices in Harmony" with Joan Baez, Mary Chapin Carpenter, and Indigo Girls. "There was a perfect example," Jones notes. "George sat on the stage the whole time saying, 'This is what the festival is all about,' which is true. It was great!"

Interestingly, these crossover angles were not immediately apparent to Jones, as the event's resumption largely spotlighted major folk names from the '60s, such as Baez. That year was a surprise smash, selling 8,000 tickets. "The next year, we didn't get any 'name' kind of artists," Jones recalls, "[nor] any that made us move into this kind of crossover thing." Net result: only 4,000 attendees. FPI also struggled with the third-world/infant-formula controversy surrounding it's then-sponsor, Nestle's, and began fishing around for a corporate substitute.

Jones remembers:

- "Don Sidney, who worked for us at one point, said, 'Look, give me a few days, I'm going to go up and see this person I know up at this ice cream company in Vermont.' Don walked into the office of the advertising director of Ben & Jerry's [Alan Kaufman] and said, 'Look, would you be interested in sponsoring the Newport Folk Festival?' And [Kaufman] said, 'What are the dates?' And that was the end of the conversation!" [laughs]

  "So, [Kaufman] was a big, big folk music fan. He was incredibly interested in younger singer-songwriters, very dedicated to them, and he really pushed me in that direction. I was aware of them, but Alan was a really strong influence, saying, 'You've got listen to these younger people!'"

The mainstage bill from '89, for example, featured Jones's "old guard": Pete Seeger, John Prine, Leon Redbone, The Clancy Brothers, Theodore Bikel, Odetta, Randy Newman, etc. But the early-morning songwriters' workshop introduced Kaufman's "younger people": David Massengill, Ashley Cleveland, Bill Morrissey, Rod MacDonald, Northern Lights, Christine Lavin, Frank Tedesso, and Chris Smither. By '90 the roles had reversed, as veterans Baez, Ry Cooder/David Lindley and Richard Thompson anchored a mainstage lineup consisting largely of the prior year's songwriters, plus such up-and-comers as Indigo Girls, Michelle Shocked, Luka Bloom, and Robert Earl Keen, Jr. Thus, Newport's current folk/pop crossover was set.

"I felt that the contemporary side was really amiss," Jones explains:

- "On the old folk festival, there was a Sunday afternoon concert basically produced by Peter Yarrow and Jim Rooney in the later years... and they really presented the contemporary side of what was happening in the folk scene in those days: Joni Mitchell, Van Morrison, James Taylor. So, I started fashioning the event more and more like that — pushed that element. Hopefully, we've made a niche that we can stick with and stay with. And we have enough people like Suzanne [Vega] who, I guess, either see the value of it, or that we pay them enough and make them comfortable so they can play."

Jones points out how making artists comfortable backstage (and on stage via a solid sound crew) is key to having the various connections click:

- "Within our staff we try to foster that activity. We make it possible. We really dedicate a lot of effort to making sure the artists are comfortable there. The artist is pleased to be there, the artist knows what's gonna' go on with other artists; they know where they're all gonna' be staying.

  "Essentially, I think the notion of festivals also creates more of an aura of this kind of activity, as well. It's this festival concept where people get together and can come and hear anybody else. When John Hiatt was here — he was playing Northampton or something [the day before] — I remember his person saying, 'Well, we've got to get here real early because John wants to see so-and-so, I mean, there's always somebody to see at Newport.' ...This interplay of other artists that goes on backstage is very important to making the whole feeling of what goes on, as far as we're concerned.

  "Again, I think that's part of the way we see artists. Getting back to the festival structure, the undercard, we don't use the 'headline' kind of notion [where], when people headline financially, they take a huge percentage and the other artists are low on the list. We've never done that. The group or person that opens is as important to us as the guy who closes, in one sense. We treat them as equals. We know that the artist who generally closes is more important for other reasons — we pay them more for one thing — but basically, they're treated in the same way. And I think that's another reason why people like to come to our event."

Jones has tinkered with various ways to expand the undercard, but not yet to his satisfaction. Some of his frustrations included: (a) having workshop tents on the rear grounds one year buffeted by main-stage sound-bleed and gusty bay breezes; (b) seeing early-morning workshops outside the entry gate another year suffering from milling distractions; (c) experiencing late-night concerts in Newport's hotels last year failing to maintain the folksy ambience valued by daytime attendees.

"Theoretically, the fort is going to be upgraded to the point where we can eventually put something inside," Jones assures:

- "Then we could really do something because I could change slightly the position of the main stage so that I still play to the bulk of the audience. I could also put a large tent up inside the fort that seats, like, 600 or 700 people. Then, I can put up a secondary stage, and now I've got it! You can put many more people on [the secondary stage] than you could put on the main stage, because you wouldn't want some people to sustain themselves for 50-to-55 minute sets; you'd put on people for 30-to-35 minutes [instead].

  "The real hope is that we'll be able to expand it — that's the real vision."

Stay tuned, although Jones would be just as likely to program more of his first love, bluegrass. "Yeah, lots of bluegrass," he chuckles, pointing out that "we were the first ones to bring Bill Monroe, The Dillards...the crossover bluegrass people." The re-incarnated festival has also had it's share of discoveries. According to Jones, "The first time I brought Alison [Krauss and Union Station], nobody knew who the hell she was. Mary Chapin [Carpenter's] first year, too. She opened, or she comes on early, and she was unbelievable."

As for Jones's own most-memorable B&J moments, he cites two:

- Ry Cooder: "When Ry Cooder came back his first year. He came on a fluke, because somebody cancelled. He came over early to set up his gear, and I remember he started playing his slide guitar and all of the crafts people just flocked over. They couldn't actually believe it. He was a legend and he never played [around] too much."

- Arlo Guthrie: "And I guess the first year when Arlo played. It was the Sunday of the first year. He was kind of mumbling, walking around on the stage, and I said, 'Do you wanna' be introduced?' He said, 'No,' then he said, 'Do you think I should do that? Do you think I should do this tune?' And I said, 'I dunno.'" It didn't occur to me what he was saying.

"Suddenly, it dawned on me that the first time he ever played in Newport, he sang 'Alice's Restaurant.' He played it in a workshop, and then we put him on at night 'cause he did this incredible song. We, like, added him on. It dawned on me what he was talking about, and I looked at him and said, 'Absolutely, you should do that!' And he walked out on the stage playing the riff which everybody knew — no introduction, nothing — and suddenly people realized that he was next and that he was in the middle of a chorus of the tune.

"People went crazy!"

**Festival Review** You'll go crazy over the festival site — easily among the top-ten most scenic in the country. The stage occupies the base wall of a Civil-War-era fort within Fort Adams State Park. The Spartan grounds quickly fan out toward an isthmus jutting into Newport harbor. You'll enjoy unobstructed views of the stage, with its majestic backdrop, while behind you lies little more than interloping boats, gunmetal water, cerulean sky, and miles and miles of Narraganset Bay.

And that's just where the concert takes place! Getting there is no less scenic, as you troll through the self-described "America's First Resort," a picturesque cuddling of New England farms, Colonial clapboards, Victorian spindles, bustling wharfside boutiques, and restaurants plus the 70-room "cottages" of Gilded-Age aristocracy. The Bouvier homestead (i.e., Jacqueline Bouvier Kennedy Onassis) is not too far from the entry gates.

Of course, trying to sneak down narrow alleyways and cowpaths in an already-crowded resort mecca at the height of summer with thousands of fellow folk-music pilgrims spells traffic headaches. I've spent a good hour or more creeping the few miles through town before and after the day's show. Although Jones promises better signage for alternate routes, you're best advised either to: (a) get there way early; (b) take the boat shuttle from the Newport Convention Center; (c) ride a bicycle there; (d) write the Chamber of Commerce for a township street map to plot a route as far opposite the prevailing trend as possible.

The '92 affair was dogged by rain on Sunday, but my wife and I enjoyed a simply glorious Saturday of great music, sunshine, cheers and smiles. She had the presence of mind to wear a bathing suit underneath her clothes, and joined hundreds of others in refreshing dips into the gentle surf.

Here are notes on the day's acts:

**Artist Mini-Reviews** Pat Donohue. An exceptionally facile guitarist, Donohue also displayed some energetic vocals, including scat singing on Duke Ellington's "It Don't Mean A Thing If It Ain't Got That Swing." Mostly, he finger-picked away on Blind Blake blues tunes and his own spunky "Pig Iron."

Yomo Toro. Making his first return to the festival since '66, this Puerto Rican string legend was actually the act I most eagerly anticipated. Playing a 10-string "cuatro," which delivered an exotic tone midway between a guitar and a harpsichord, Toro dazzled with elaborate lines which ranged freely among Latin styles — jibaro, merengue, flamenco. He also strummed mightily for percussive effect and playfully interspersed recognizable cuts from such cheezy pop tunes as "Mexican Hat Dance" and "Tequila."

David Wilcox. This handsome young singer-songwriter was introduced to squeals from the crowd and accommodated his female fans with several "sensitive-new-age-guy" ruminations on love, such as "Language of the Heart" about a one-night-stand role-reversal (he fell in love; she didn't). I enjoyed the strong imagery of his bluesy "Like A Needle Against the Rain," plus a pair of driving road songs, "That Old American Dream" and "She Rides In The Eye Of The Hurricane." I also liked his unusual guitar strumming and the husky timbre and lithe grace notes of his vocals.

Patty Larkin. A Vanessa Redgrave lookalike, this Cape-Cod based singer-songwriter is a real treat: charismatic humor; fluid vocals and guitar work; strong song concepts exhibiting wide range, real feelings and a natural voice. No phony conceits. I especially enjoyed the seductive rhythms carrying both her whimsical romance, "Tango," as well as her environmental caution, "Metal Drums," and could picture her sophisticated stylings captivating next weekend's jazz crowd.

Cris Williamson. Mature, warm, sincere, accessible — Williamson presented "women's music" that transcended the genre and encouraged the entire audience with it's heartfelt relevancy. Varying between acappella tunes and accompanying herself on guitar and piano, she never evangelized or generalized. Rather, she personalized. "Sisters of Mercy" expressively bespoke struggling to find yourself in a hostile world, while "I'm Leaving In The Morning" launched such a journey with "a suitcase full of sorrow." Even her topical numbers, including an ironically liberating ode to the sad, last run of the Nez Pierce tribe, "Good Day Today," delivered a genuine individual perspective.

The Band. Once these grizzled vets found the groove a few tunes into their set, they rocked the house! Even fellow Canadian Bruce Cochburn, who'd played the set before, couldn't resist and jumped onstage to jam along on "The Weight" and "Caledonia," the latter done as a bluesy shuffle. In fact, most every number got unusually funky treatments with several topped off by the rough, soulful vocals of bassist Rick Danko. I liked Danko's mournful wailing on J. J. Cale's "Crazy Mama" in counterpoint to the unexpectedly chunky rhythm, while his passionate singing infused the driving marchbeat of their closing anthem, "The Shape I'm In."

Shawn Colvin. Marches are also Colvin's most effective tempos. They allow her sinewy guitar to drive the beat, while her willowy vocal phrasings can dart amidst and soar above. Unfortunately for Colvin (a replacement for the ailing Michelle Shocked), there was only one new tune which afforded this sympathetic pace — "On the Block." The rest of her set charted visibly still uncomfortable territory (at one point Colvin self-consciously stumbled through an intro., then begged the crowd's indulgence for working out her new material on stage). Still, two older songs, "Shotgun Down The Avalanche" and "Diamond In The Rough," both moody inner landscapes with striking imagery and catchy motifs, brought out her best and earned roars from the faithful.

Suzanne Vega. What a nice surprise! Vega exhibited a charming stage manner that engaged the audience and helped bring her artful material to life. She explained the genesis of mostly familiar songs (as well as a few new numbers) with forthrightness and humor, ingratiating a set that flowed and communicated smoothly. Going solo brought clarity to the subtleties of her lyrics, which contained more mythic narratives than I expected. I liked the way she served up "She's Gone," "As A Child," and "David's Song" prior to wrapping up with her MTV hit, "Luka," to everyone's delight. A perfect cap to a perfect day!

**Travel Tip** Scoring weekend lodgings in town is no less difficult than negotiating the traffic, and most hotels will require a full weekend's guarantee. Public campgrounds are at even more of a premium, with the nearest one in Narraganset awarding minimum five-day reservations by mail only. Jones recommends saving money by going the B&B route in nearby towns, or the hotel route in places like Fall River and Seekonk, MA.

Oh, and look for Rhode Island's own jumpin' jivers, Roomful of Blues, to be playing some Newport club that Friday night.

**See Also** Although it's of different genres, FPI's own JVC JAZZ FESTIVAL/NEWPORT (JVC JAZZ FESTIVAL, New York, NY — see chapter) at the same site the following weekend just begs taking the whole week off. Block Island, anyone? Otherwise, you can enjoy a somewhat funkier modern-folk mix at BEN AND JERRY'S ONE-WORLD, ONE-HEART FESTIVAL (Warren, VT — see chapter). Mountain views and miles of smiles await you.

Finally, FPI appears to have gotten its long-awaited NEWPORT RHYTHM AND BLUES FESTIVAL off the ground for '95 (it had been announced for '94, but was withdrawn). Picture the boogie stew of the NEW ORLEANS "JAZZFEST" and you've got a good view of the lineup — halfway between the two FPI festivals it immediately preceeds. "Book 'em, Dano," as TV's Jack Lord might say for my festival vacation plans!

~   ~   ~

# Escoheag's Mardi Gras Ranch

CAJUN AND ZYDECO MARDI GRAS BALL, Providence, RI
Middle February
Cajun and Zydeco
***Attended***

BIG EASY BASH, Escoheag, RI
Late July
Variety, General
***Attended***

**CAJUN AND BLUEGRASS MUSIC-DANCE-FOOD FESTIVAL**, Escoheag, RI
Early September
Variety, General
***Attended***

**Introduction**   W. C. Fields once quipped, "A woman drove me to drink, and I never stopped to thank her." I guess I can similarly blame/thank the CAJUN AND BLUEGRASS MUSIC-DANCE-FOOD FESTIVAL for launching me on my mad fest quest.

"Bartender, another round as I tell the tale..."

I was an impressionable twenty-something from Long Island, residing briefly in Southern Mississippi in '81 and '82, when I first stumbled across zydeco music. Mind you, this was the driving, blues-based, electric-powered zydeco, as played by French-speaking African-Americans — not yet the more rustic, swirly, acoustic Cajun rhythms performed by white descendants of exiled French-Canadians. Zydeco's funky, up-beatin', feet-tappin' proved irresistible, but I always assumed it was more-or-less confined to the Gulf Coast, aside from the occasional club tour. Festival "bon temps" were a way of life for blacks and whites alike in swamp country, I'd heard, but they weren't indulged elsewhere, were they?

Fast-forward six years to a daytrip to Newport, RI. That morning, I spied a tiny listing in the local newspaper for a "CAJUN AND BLUEGRASS FESTIVAL" in Escoheag. "Yeah, right," I muttered to my road buddy, Kem, "Cajun music in Rhode Island? Probably sucks." Since we were all "mansioned-out" at Newport, however, we took a lark on the 45-minute drive.

We got as far as the main gate of the festival before a traffic guard turned us around: "No parking left, guys, it's all taken." As we sat to plot our next move, I couldn't help but be impressed by the waves of happy campers washing across the tree-shaded, two-lane blacktop separating Oak Embers RV Park on the left from the sprawling Stepping Stone Ranch on the right. Everyone was smiling, everyone was bouncing.

Then I heard it — those infectious zydeco beats! — bouncing up over the roof into the sun-spangled air. The next set had just started and pedestrians quickly streamed toward the entry gate, many swinging each other in what I would later learn as Cajun two-steppin'. I leaned toward Kem and nodded, "Make a note for next year!"

Well, I made it back in '88 and promptly had the curtains part for me on several music genres:

- Zydeco: I'd already experienced zydeco bands playing all night long in New Orleans bars, but never outdoors into the wee hours for packed floors of dance-aholics. Close call, but this environment seemed to bring out their best.

- Cajun: I'd never really appreciated Cajun music before, since it's acoustic mid-tempos are not conducive to stand-alone rock-and-roll dancing. However, Escoheag furnished the missing link — couples dancing — by providing free lessons for beginners on up. No partner? No worries, as each dance area was rimmed with willing participants. A host of other heretofore-bland genres, such as swing, country and tango, all began to make perfect sense!

- Bluegrass: An ol' college chum had dragged me a decade ago to see bluegrass legends Bill Monroe and Ralph Stanley, all the while coaching me on the "high-lonesome" of Appalachian soul. His enthusiasm never overcame my resistance. Here, though, were young, progressive, dynamic bands I could immediately relate to — Hot Rize, The Tony Rice Unit, Northern Lights, Peter Rowan, Laurie Lewis — dishing out blazing licks, heartfelt singing, winning harmonies, and relevant songs, all served up with a generous garnish of humor. When the Austin Lounge Lizards finally covered a Pink Floyd tune, I knew I could say "no" no longer.

Up until now, I had only experienced the NEW ORLEANS JAZZ AND HERITAGE FESTIVAL (see Late April to Early May) in all it's massive bounty. Now I'd found a similarly professional celebration, intimate-yet-still-bountiful, but with other features besides. The CAJUN AND BLUEGRASS 'FESTIVAL:

- Offers camping on site, which lets you casually carry on into the morning dew and savor the festival spirit for as long as you wanted — just like the no-closing policies of New Orleans bars, except outdoors. Cheap and convenient too! No hassles with flights, hotels, traffic, parking, lines, bus rides, or where to eat or party afterward.

- Features a shaded grove behind the parking lot that hosts, not just workshops, but superb, intimate sets by various, main-stage acts. You can huddle, oh, just ten feet away as Hugh and Katy Moffat alternate exquisite duets with The Whitstein Brothers under the heading of "Family Harmony." Or, hear that charming Cajun jester, D. L. Menard, leading a round of tributes to his idol, Hank Williams, in which he sings chillingly-accurate renditions of long-lost songs he heard Williams do on Louisiana radio shows back in the war years.

- Has not one, but three dance floors: a platform to the right of stage, a huge wedding tent over by the food booths, and a big ol' barn up the hill. Even if you aren't into taking a spin, you can still revel in the sight of live music accompanied by a veritable stage show spinning right past your eyes.

- By rubbing shoulders with the same people all weekend (especially those kind folks who take pity on your first dance fumblings), helps you to accumulate all the Cajun-music pals your address book can handle, many of whom you'll later see on the festival circuit.

Finally, I felt as if I'd discovered the "fais do do" lifestyle of bayou lore just a four-hour-drive north of New York City! Were there others? I started to subscribe to magazines — first one, then several, now over 60. I began to pick up flyers and keep files. I'd ask my ever-growing circle of Escoheag acquaintances, and they'd ask me, "Hey, did you hear C. J. Chenier's gonna be at such-and-such with so-and-so? Wanna' ride?" (You laugh, but watch it happen to you!)

When I got laid off from my corporate job and my outplacement counselor asked me what I wanted to do next, I knew there was one unfulfilled need that burned bright — a travel guide to these events within a day's drive for my festival friends and music fanatics everywhere. Then my compulsion really kicked into overdrive with three years of 100-hour weeks at double speed to visit 300-plus festivals and accumulate thousands of listings. But here it is, the first installment!

Often, throughout, I've wondered if W. C. Fields was Cajun.

I stopped back to the CAJUN AND BLUEGRASS 'FESTIVAL in '93 for the expressed purpose of sharpening my recollections for a **Festival Review** and making notes for **Artist Mini-Reviews**. Forget it! Within five minutes, I fell in with old friends and couldn't stop until the fat lady sang — a blur of fun, just like always. Same deal with the delightful CAJUN AND BLUEGRASS MARDI GRAS BALL, whose costume contest yields some outrageous entries. Picture an ornately-decorated, gold-painted, Egyptian head, 10' high by 5' wide, gracefully bobbing to a Beausoleil beat.

Instead, I thought I'd share a conversation with Chuck Wentworth.

His Lagniappe Productions is contracted by the events' founder, Franklin Zawacki and Cajun Music Ltd., to run two summer festivals: the fourteen-year old CAJUN AND BLUEGRASS 'FESTIVAL and the four-year old BIG EASY BASH. Wentworth also produces the two-year-old 'MARDI GRAS BALL on his own, as well as approximately 20 dances and concerts during the off-season at the Holy Ghost Brotherhood Hall in Providence. Wentworth is a Research Associate at the University of Rhode Island, assisting students with practical applications of aquaculture. When not doing this or promoting his winter music series, he serves as the Folk Music Director for WRIU-FM where he hosts his own show, "Traditions of Folk."

"To me, that's the key to everything I do," Wentworth explains. "That weekly radio show keeps me in tune with what's going on in music, and gives me a chance to really get out there and play some things and gage people's reactions on what's good and what they like. Mostly, I play what I like."

Here's a few examples Wentworth relays of how this radio connection helps his festivals work so well:

- "I don't know how many other promoters do this, but I talk to these musicians and I tell them exactly what I want. I've spent many hours... [laughs]

  "We first brought Nathan [Williams and The Zydeco Cha-Chas] up and he had never played anywhere outside of Louisiana. These guys were as raw as could be. It was funny, because they had no clue how to play to an audience outside of Richard's Club, or El Sido's. So I sat down with the guys in the van for half an hour, and Nathan kept sayin', 'Talk to 'em, talk to 'em, tell 'em what you want.' You know, that's what I had to do.

  "It was the same thing with C. J. [Chenier and The Red-Hot Louisiana Band]. Originally, C. J. was into this thing that most zydeco bands are into where the band comes out and they do a couple of numbers, blues numbers, and then they call up the leader of the band. I said, 'Look, C. J., you've got one hour and five minutes on stage. The whole day is built up so you are going to close this day out, so the energy's here. Man, don't blow it! Don't have this down time of, you know, a couple of songs where people lose interest. You come out and hit 'em hard!'

  "Again, it all goes back to my radio training where I try to put a show together on stage like I would build a radio set; where you put the pieces together and build slowly until you can end on a high note. And it's trying to get that idea across to the musicians... I don't shy away from these guys whoever they are. I tell them, 'Look we're paying for you guys to play, this is what I want, this is what I expect.'"

- "We made a conscious decision years ago, I think it was year 10, where I decided that bands would play once per day on the main stage. Prior to that, bands were going for two 45-minute sets. On the surface it looked like more music because you had a listing of maybe 18 or 19 different sets during the day. But when I started totaling up the amount of actual music and the amount of time spent on set changes, I found by giving people just one longer shot on stage, we ended up with close to 45 minutes of more music.

  "So sometimes we're forced, because we don't have that available spot on the main stage, to do a mini-concert, or something like that, in the grove.

  "What I'd rather do with the grove is mix genres, just find situations where I can throw Cajun, bluegrass, old-timey people together in one setting [to] see what comes out of that. I really put a lot of thought and time into those workshops. I spend a lot of time all winter once I finalize the lineup... After that, I have a grid that I set up where I look where I can start moving different performers when they're not on the main stage, and try to look for combinations when people are free.

  "Like I say, I can use a lot of my background from radio because I know what people have done in the past and what interesting things that they've recorded, and just try and use that to come up with different things each year."

- "[The dance lessons] just came out of the patrons themselves. The thing I had pushed for real early to build our mailing list was to have a questionnaire. I especially wanted the feedback to go along with that, to find out specifically what people didn't like about the festival, and to have an avenue for them to express their opinions. I think the biggest thing was they had asked for dance lessons.

"The one thing I've really tried to do is to just keep an ear open for what people are looking for.... I know immediately after a festival if there's been a problem somewhere.

"For instance, I think it was about the sixth or seventh year, we must have gotten 300 to 400 complaints about the conditions of the port-a-johns. You can go around the festival and not see these things. They can be right in front of your nose! But I got that feedback, so we fired that company and brought in a new one. The next year, no problem. But every year it's something. One year people complained bitterly about the parking situation, so we knew that was the priority to focus in on for the next year. Because, that's how you're going to lose a festival, if you don't respond immediately to where people's concerns are."

Wentworth's personal highlight? "The first time we brought Dewey Balfa back to Rhode Island," he recalls of the fiddler's first return since introducing Cajun music to mass audiences at the Newport Folk Festival 20 years prior [BEN AND JERRY'S NEWPORT FOLK FESTIVAL, Newport, RI — see chapter]:

- "The crowd brought him back out for five encores. He was unbelievable! I was on stage MC-ing that night, and the energy just about knocked me over. Queen Ida was waiting up in the barn to play a dance, and nobody would leave the stage area. They would not leave! They were just legitimately on their feet for five encores. They were in awe of him, rightly so."

Finally, does Wentworth ever abandon his onstage trademark — a stern Yankee countenance? "When it's over," he laughs, "I smile."

**Attendance Tip**

"Bring the kids," encourages Wentworth. "If you're single, come prepared to have a great time. Don't be inhibited! You'll see people out there dancing — some of them can dance real well — but don't let that deter you, just get out there and have fun. There are no rules as far as that goes. We just encourage people to come out and kind of have a New England Mardi Gras celebration!"

**See Also**

The BIG EASY BASH was spun off in '90 to spotlight the Cajun/zydeco side plus integrate conjunto, blues, rock, alternative country, and whatever else. Wentworth's disappointed it hasn't done as well as he'd like, financially. Artistically, though, we both agree it's been terrific. The crowds are also lighter than on the packed Labor Day blow-out, so there's more room to dance and get to know people. "To me, that's the one I always look forward to the most," Wentworth confesses. "I get more of a chance to stretch out and bring in a lot of the music that I love."

Wentworth's own CAJUN AND ZYDECO MARDI GRAS BALL was an unexpected smash it's first year out in '93 — a full house in costume regalia swinging to one of the best sets I've ever heard from Beausoleil. Scheduling problems the following year pushed it back a week and up into the spanking-new Rhode Island Convention Center. Wentworth assures, "It's a great facility, so I think we'll be able to do it up right there as well."

~     ~     ~

# Providence's Variety Party

EARTH DAY CONCERT, Providence, RI
 Late April
 Variety, General

RHODE ISLAND INDIAN COUNCIL POW-WOW: "TEMPLE TO MUSIC," Providence, RI
 Early July
 Native American

PROVIDENCE WATERFRONT FESTIVAL/WATERFRONT JAZZ FESTIVAL, Providence, RI
 Middle Sepember
 Variety, General
 ***Attended***

**Introduction** Borrowing from the Doublemint Gum ad on TV, "It's two, two, two fests in one."

We're talking both halves of the combined PROVIDENCE WATERFRONT FESTIVAL/WATERFRONT JAZZ FESTIVAL. The former (referred to as "WATERFRONT") is the self-described "whale of a weekend" that draws 100,000 people to Roger Williams Park for three days the week after Labor Day. Picture a loose, lanky blow-out spread out on six simultaneous stages, each with an expansive water view.

The latter (called "JAZZFEST") has finally found a home within the former as a "festival-within-a-festival," so to speak. It's held on Sunday on the main stage at the southeast corner of the park and is accessible via an additional, but modest, admission fee. JAZZFEST is strictly jazz, mind you, while WATERFRONT offers nearly everything else. JAZZFEST also features a national headliner, whereas WATERFRONT concentrates exclusively on the copious music scene shared between Providence and Boston.

Want more?

Festival Director Bob Rizzo, who's been handling the programming chores for the Providence Parks Department for 18 years, also schedules a performing-arts series at Roger Williams Park, called CONVERGENCE. This series, which runs from Early July through Late August, provides an umbrella for other festival events at the park, such as the RHODE ISLAND INDIAN COUNCIL POW-WOW: "TEMPLE TO MUSIC." Furthermore, Rizzo expects his Public Programming Department to end up handling the annual EARTH DAY CONCERT, previously run by outside environmental groups.

Still more? Well, consider that Rizzo's department originally co-founded a gamut of ethnic festivals that, as the program states, "are now conducted solely by the communities they were created to celebrate." These celebrations occur throughout the city and include the LATIN AMERICAN FESTIVAL and the CAPE VERDEAN FESTIVAL. Plus, Rizzo advised in the creation of an impressive FIRST NIGHT PROVIDENCE (see Late December), along with a passel of other events.

It all adds up to a pretty big bubble of musical fun. Rizzo's crew basically makes sure there's something going on somewhere in Providence most every summer weekend. Their musical efforts help sweeten the offer to witness one of the most attractive, ongoing waterfront and community revivals this side of Baltimore.

**Festival Review** Rizzo is a performance artist by trade, but don't hold that against him. He's a regular guy you could see yourself with, throwing down a brew or two. In his generous laugh he's the first to poke fun at his avocation, describing his own efforts as "strange and bizarre theater."

Yet his relaxed persona doesn't sacrifice a strategic mind for planning big events, or a keen ear for the best of Providence's music scene. Here's how Rizzo describes his repositioning the

PROVIDENCE WATERFRONT FESTIVAL/WATERFRONT JAZZ FESTIVAL in '93 after it's eight-year tenure under prior organizers:

- "WATERFRONT got started after they began rehab-ing along the waterfront. There was a group of businessmen who got together and thought, 'Let's do some big public event that'll get people and show them what's down there,' because the land was really neglected....[They] put together the first couple of festivals. Then that expanded. There's another nonprofit called, Keep Providence Beautiful, which started doing the Pasta Challenge [a food festival which continues to run simultaneously] during that period of time, and it just grew and grew.

  "Unfortunately, what happened was as it grew, the message got really confused. So, when we ended up taking it over, we changed the format and the message behind it... We went back and added the boats, the tall ships, the sailboat races and that kind of stuff and swung it back towards an environmental water theme — it being a water festival, they had gotten to the point where there was nothing water-related! We took it and turned it into a viable waterfront festival and found that was really key to sponsorship."

The water aspects Rizzo refers to include a "Whaling Wall" mural by Wyland, harbor tours (c/o Narraganset Bay Commission), river tours (c/o Blackstone Valley Tourism Council), a "Speed Circle" sailboating demonstration (c/o Sailing World Magazine), a "Save the Bay Cup" sailing competition for college and high-school teams, along with all kinds of boats and ships tied to docks for your inspection. The environmental aspects were presented under a pair of tents exhibiting "Expo-Earth" conservation activities in one and "Sea-Life" ecological and economic impacts in the other.

Once past these offerings (plus children's activities, dancing, storytelling, strolling entertainers, arts, crafts and food), Rizzo quickly hones in on his primary interest — programming as broad a spectrum of local musicians as funds permit. "Eclectic," Rizzo laughs, "that's my trademark, actually. I try to be as diverse as possible because there's so much talent out there."

Three generally-overlooked constituencies benefit in particular from Rizzo's acumen.

The first are Providence's various ethnic groups. "We tried to make sure the quality was there," Rizzo explains:

- "If we brought in somebody who was going to be doing Cape Verdean music, we tried to find the best Cape Verdean performer we could. Same thing with the African performers. We tried to find the highest quality we could because one of the things I'm really concerned about is when you start doing multi-cultural programming, you've got to be real careful that the quality is there. Because, if you present the stuff and you don't present a good act, people get really turned off to it, big time!"

The second are under-25's:

- "[At family festivals], that's an audience that's always forgotten. A lot of that, I think, is because people are afraid of how the crowd's going to react. But, we've been doing [rock and roll music] for about six-to-eight years and have never had any problem. The kids really appreciate that they don't have to pay to get in. Plus, it's always done around non-alcohol kind of venues. It just works out perfectly."

The third are local jazz fans (with Rizzo describing the JVC JAZZ FESTIVAL in Newport, Middle August as "more for out-of-state visitors"). For the previous three years, Rizzo and local promoter Sal Corio tried to maintain different permutations of the PROVIDENCE JAZZ FESTIVAL, finally being undone by bad weather and Corio's mounting losses. Rizzo recalls: "Rather than let the thing die, I had an opportunity to try another approach, which was to take an event I already knew was going to draw 100,000 people, tag the jazz thing on, and see what happens. By doing that, it was easier to sell the sponsorship."

In Rizzo's words, drawing these three segments helped make '93's joint affair "extremely successful...probably one of the most successful versions of the festival. Because of the programming, people really just had a good time. We got a much more diverse audience than they'd ever gotten."

Rizzo's personal highlight?

- "Riding around in the golf cart over the 18 acres of the festival grounds and listening to all the mix of music because we had all these stages running simultaneously...being able to be at points where the music did blend, [but] where it wasn't overpowered, and feel all that diversity. That's kind of the experience I was having."

"Then just seeing all these regular folks experiencing all this stuff and realizing that they had probably never seen an African dancer; they had never listened to Cape Verdean music. And just realizing that's what programming was supposed to be doing."

**Artist Mini-Reviews**    <u>Atwater-Donnelly</u>: This wife-and-husband team (Aubrey and Elwood, respectively) cover traditional Celtic and English tunes in handsome harmony. Atwater also sings her own folk originals, which address social and personal issues in an appealingly plainspoken way.

Rizzo: "I thought they would fit that particular stage, there by the tall ships and the whole bit. 'Kind of gave it a sea deal [laughs]. What I tried to do there was put different talent in that was more on the quiet side but had real different range. They were really well-received; people loved them."

<u>Bolu Fatunmise</u>: Bolu [called by his first name] leads a terrific 12-piece, African-drumming/dancing troupe garbed in wonderfully-exotic printed caftans. Their style showcases the sinuous and percolating rhythm structures of their heritage with Nigerian/Yoruban "talking drums."

Rizzo: "He's great; he's a lot of fun. He actually did a lot of composing for King Sunny Ade. We got lucky in that he lives here in Providence, and I try to use him whenever I can. He can definitely stand some wider recognition, and he'll tell you the same thing [laughs]."

<u>Fat City</u>: This popular, local R&B band has fewer horn players than Providence-based Roomful of Blues, plus a broader entertainment style, but fans of one will certainly enjoy the other.

Rizzo: "It seems like they've been around forever, probably as long as Roomful' has. They're always well-received. They did fine; people loved them."

<u>Louise Taylor</u>: One of the few out-of-towners, Vermont-based Taylor, is a performing songwriter known for her sensual vocals and rhythmic guitar style strongly reminiscent of Shawn Colvin's or Patty Larkin's.

Rizzo: "I was really surprised. People who normally are jaded by that type of music ended up buying her CD by the end of the day [laughs]. She's wonderful; she really is riveting. She did a great, great job for me."

<u>Tribe</u>: This alternative-rock band was a co-finalist in the legendary WBCN ROCK 'N' ROLL RUMBLE of '88 (Boston, MA — see chapter).

Rizzo: "Tribe I really enjoyed; they really put on a great show... I've got photographs of the audience pressed as close to the stage as they possibly could get [laughs]. It was pretty mind-boggling — not what I had expected. People were just up on their feet, right there in their face, and they just were right back. It was great!"

**Attendance Tip**    Rizzo advises using the shuttle busses. "They're free, [and] they leave out of the center of town where there's plenty of parking. That really helps us in the long run. Come early and plan to stay for the whole day. Expect the unexpected!"

**Travel Tip**    Roger Williams Park sits at the foot of a charming hill that houses Brown University, Rhode Island School of Design [RISD], and one of the most concentrated collections of Colonial architecture in the country — a perfect place for leisurely strolls. Rizzo lauds the RISD museum, "which just added a brand-new $2 million wing for their contemporary art collection, which is really wonderful." Rizzo also cites a new arts center being built in downtown Providence on Empire Street, as well as Providence's "world-class zoo."

As Rizzo remarks of the festival proximity, "It hasn't gotten touristy, yet... In that whole neighborhood there's all sorts of galleries opening up, all sorts of coffeehouses. It's a neat place, it really is."

# Rhode Island Festival Listings

**Caveat**

Although the vast majority are festivals are reliable and predictable, all are subject to last-minute changes or cancellations. Accordingly, FESTPRESS is not responsible for any festival listing information that follows. Readers are well advised to contact festivals at least twice before preparing a festival vist: (a) once at least one or two months ahead of time; and (b) once more during the week of your visit for confirmation. Ask for a festival flyer or brochure to be mailed to you. Festival promoters usually are willing to comply, and the resulting literature may answer any questions you still have.

Restrictions:

| | | | | | |
|---|---|---|---|---|---|
| • Food and drink... | 1; | • Cameras... | 6; | • Motorcycles... | 11; |
| • Alcohol... | 2; | • Audio recording... | 7; | • Re-entry... | 12; |
| • Cans... | 3; | • Video recording... | 8; | • Other restrictions... | 13. |
| • Bottles... | 4; | • Children... | 9; | | |
| • Coolers... | 5; | • Pets... | 10; | | |

Secondary Genre[s]:

| | | | |
|---|---|---|---|
| • Variety, General... | VRGL; | • Bluegrass... | BLGS; |
| • Variety, Jazz & Blues... | VRJB; | • Modern Folk... | MFOL; |
| • Variety, Country & Bluegrass | VRCB; | • Traditional Folk... | TFOL; |
| • Variety, Folk & International | VRFI; | • Fiddle and Banjo Events... | FDDL; |
| • Modern Jazz... | MJAZ; | • Maritime... | MARI; |
| • Traditional Jazz & Ragtime... | TJAZ; | • Cajun and Zydeco... | ZYDC; |
| • Alternative Jazz... | AJAZ; | • Irish... | IRSH; |
| • Modern Rock and Pop... | MRCK; | • Jewish... | JWSH; |
| • Classic Rock and Oldies... | CRCK; | • Native American... | NATV; |
| • Alternative & College Rock | ARCK; | • Scottish... | SCOT; |
| • Hard Rock & Heavy Metal | HRCK; | • Modern Latin... | MLAT; |
| • Rap... | RAP; | • Traditional Latin... | TLAT; |
| • Modern R&B... | MR&B; | • African American... | AFRM; |
| • Blues and Traditional R&B... | TR&B; | • African... | AFRC; |
| • Acappella and Doo Wop... | ACAP; | • Brazilian & So. American... | BRZL; |
| • Modern Christian... | CHRS; | • Reggae, Ska & Caribbean... | RGGE; |
| • Black Gospel... | BGOS; | • Avant Garde & New Music... | AVNT; |
| • Southern & Bluegrass Gospel | SGOS; | • Cabaret... | CBRT; |
| • Traditional Gospel & Sings... | TGOS; | • Gay and Lesbian... | GYLS; |
| • Modern Country... | MC&W; | • Drum Corps & March. Bands | DRUM; |
| • Traditional Country... | TC&W; | • Fairs... | FAIR; |
| • Alt.  Country & Rockabilly... | AC&W; | • Other Genres... | OTHR. |

**Note**

Wherever "**Help!**" appears readers are invited to answer the proceeding questions and/or provide updates. New festival listings that meet the criteria of this book certainly are welcome too! Please mail any current festival information you obtain — especially flyers or brochures — to FESTPRESS, P. O. Box 147, Glen Ridge, NJ 07028. *Thanks!*

### NEWPORT WINTER FESTIVAL, Newport, RI
    Late Jan. to Early Feb.
    Variety, General

"Alive with sparkle and excitement, the Winter Festival offers a unique winter experience combining food, music, and entertainment, with fun for all ages." -- Program. **Days:** 10. **Hours per day:** 15. **Site:** outdoor and indoor. Multiple locations. **Admission:** paid. **Daily entry:** under $10. **Secondary genre[s]:** MJAZ, CRCK, MFOL, OTHR **Acts:** national acts, local acts. **Sample day's lineup:** "Beatlemania," Mac Churucala Quartet with Billy Weston. **Contact:** Newport County Convention and Visitors Bureau, 23 America's Cup Avenue, Newport, RI 02840, 800-326-6030.

### CAJUN AND ZYDECO MARDI GRAS BALL, Cranston, RI
    Middle Feb.
    Cajun and Zydeco

Since 1993. **Days:** 1. **Hours per day:** 5. **Site:** indoor. Rhodes-on-the-Pawtuxet, 60 Rhodes Place. **Admission:** paid. **Daily entry:** $10 to $24, $25 to $49. **Discounts:** advance purchase discounts, **Acts:** national acts, local acts. **Sample day's lineup:** C. J. Chenier and The Red-Hot Louisiana Band, Steve Riley and The Mamou Playboys, Magnolia. **Contact:** Lagniappe Productions, 255 Holly Road, Wakefield, RI 02879, 401-783-3926.

### MARDI GRAS CELEBRATION, Woonsocket, RI
    Late Feb.
    Cajun and Zydeco

Since 1995. Revived a local tradition, dormant 20 years, when Woonsocket was a leading Northern Mardi Gras site owing to its significant French-Canadian population. "Turned out to be huge!" -- Jack Lawhead. **Days:** 1. **Site:** indoor. Embassy Club, Elk's Club, St. Joseph's Veteran's Hall. **Admission:** paid. **Secondary genre[s]:** MJAZ, OTHR **Acts:** national acts, regional acts, local acts. **Sample day's lineup:** Tommy Dorsey Orchestra, Basin Brothers Cajun Band, others. **Contact:** Mardi Gras Celebration, P. O. Box 425, Slaterville RI 02876, 401-769-0699.

### WOMEN'S VOICES, Providence, RI
    Early Mar.
    Modern Folk

Benefits Dorcas Place Parent Literacy Center. **Days:** 1. **Site:** indoor. Lincoln School, Butler and Orchard Streets. **Admission:** paid. **Daily entry:** $10 to $24. **Discounts:** advance purchase discounts, **Acts:** regional acts, local acts. **Sample day's lineup:** Tish Adams, Aubrey Atwater, Laura Berkson, Sparky Davis, R. I. Feminist Chorus. **Contact:** Women's Voices, P. O. Box 204, Hope RI 02831, 401-826-3522/273-8866.

### EARTH DAY CELEBRATION, Providence, RI
    Late Apr.
    Variety, General

**Help!** A sample lineup? **Days:** 1. **Hours per day:** 6. **Site:** outdoor. Roger Williams Park, Elmwood Avenue. **Contact:** Providence Parks Department, Dalrymple Boat House, Elmwood Avenue, Providence, RI 02905, 401-785-9450 x244.

## MARITIME ARTS FESTIVAL, Newport, RI
> Middle May
> Variety, General

See other dates. **Days:** 3. **Hours per day:** 9. **Site:** outdoor and indoor. Multiple locations. **Admission:** paid. **Daily entry:** under $10, $10 to $24, $25 to $49. **Discounts: Secondary genre[s]:** TFOL, MARI, IRSH, RGGE, GYLS, OTHR **Acts:** local acts. **Sample day's lineup:** Mickey Scotia, 4th Street String Band, Ger Campbell and Company, plus performance of Gilbert and Sullivan's "HMS Pinafore." **Contact:** Maritime Arts Festival, P. O. Box 60, Newport RI, 02840, 401-849-2243 **or:** Newport Cultural Commission, City Hall, 43 Broadway, Newport, RI 02840, 401-847-1996. .

## NATIVE AMERICAN DAYS, Westerly, RI
> Late May
> Native American

See other sites and dates. **Days:** 1. **Hours per day:** 6. **Site:** outdoor. Elder John Crandall Wildlife Refuge and Nature Reserve, 104-105 Pound Road. **Contact:** Naragansett Indian Tribe, P. O. Box 268, Charlestown, RI 401-364-1100/322-7590.

## SUMMER ARTS FEST CHAIR FAIR, West Kingston, RI
> Early Jun.
> Variety, General

**Days:** 2. **Site:** outdoor and indoor. South County Center for the Arts, off Route 138. **Secondary genre[s]:** TJAZ, MR&B, ACAP, MFOL, IRSH, OTHR **Acts:** local acts. **Sample Day's Lineup:** Laura Berkson, Wakefield Child Guitar Ensemble, Dixie Angels, John Campbell, others. **Contact:** South County Center for the Arts, 3501 Kingstown Road, West Kingston, RI 02892, 401-782-1018.

## SCHWEPES CHOWDER COOK-OFF, Newport, RI
> Middle Jun.
> Variety, General

Since 1982. "Spicy or mild, clear broth or creamy texture, this festival has every kind of chowder you can imagine." -- Program. **Days:** 1. **Hours per day:** 7. **Site:** outdoor. Newport Yachting Center, 4 Commercial Wharf. **Admission:** paid. **Daily entry:** under $10. **Discounts: Secondary genre[s]:** MJAZ, TJAZ, CRCK, RAP, TR&B, MC&W, OTHR **Acts:** national acts, local acts. **Sample day's lineup:** The Cowsills, Northeast Navy Show Band, Newport Saxophone Quartet, Jackie Henderson's Hip Hop Jam Session, Nightlife Orchestra, others. **Contact:** Newport Yachting Center, America's Cup Avenue, P. O. Box 550, Newport, RI 02840, 401-846-1600.

## HARLEM RENAISSANCE GARDEN PARTY, Cranston, RI
> Middle Jun.
> Modern Jazz

"Pack a picnic basket" -- Listing. **Days:** 1. **Site:** outdoor and indoor. Rhodes-on-the-Pawtuxet, 60 Rhodes Place. **Admission:** paid. **Daily entry:** $25 to $49. **Secondary genre[s]:** AFRM, AFRC, **Acts:** national acts, local acts. **Sample day's lineup:** Marlena Shaw, Hank Crawford, Leland Brown. **Contact:** Langston Hughes Center for the Arts and Education, 1 Hilton Street, Providence RI 02905, 401-454-5422.

COUNTRY MUSIC SHOWS, Escoheag, RI
>    Middle Jun. to Early Aug.
>    Modern Country

Dates vary, so call ahead. **Days:** 3. **Site:** outdoor. Stepping Stone Ranch, Route 165. **Admission:** paid. **Daily entry:** $10 to $24. **Discounts: Acts:** regional acts, local acts. **Sample day's lineup:** Dick Curless, Tricia Elliott, Charlie Carson, John Penny Band. **Contact:** Stepping Stone Ranch, Escoheag Hill Road, West Greenwich, RI 401-397-3725.

PEQUOT AND NARRAGANSETT INDIAN NATIONS POW WOW, Westerly, RI
>    Middle Jun. to Late Jun.
>    Native American

See other sites and dates. **Days:** 2. **Hours per day:** 6. **Site:** outdoor. Elder John Crandall Wildlife Refuge and Nature Reserve, 104-105 Pound Road. **Contact:** Naragansett Indian Tribe, P. O. Box 268, Charlestown, RI 401-364-1100/322-7590.

BIG EASY BASH, Escoheag, RI
>    Late Jun.
>    Variety, General

Since 1990. **Days:** 2. **Hours per day:** 12. **Site:** outdoor and indoor. Stepping Stone Ranch, Route 165. **Admission:** paid. **Daily entry:** $10 to $24. **Discounts:** multiple event or day passes, advance purchase discounts, **Restrictions:** 3, 5, 7, 8, 10, 13, **Secondary genre[s]:** TR&B, BGOS, AC&W, MFOL, ZYDC, **Acts:** national acts, regional acts, local acts. **Sample day's lineup:** D. L. Menard and The Lousiana Aces, Nathan and The Zydeco Cha-Chas, John Mooney and Bluesiana, Steve Riley and The Mamou Playboys, Big Sandy and The Fly-Rite Boys, Voodoo Rhythm Kings, Zydeco Zombies. **Contact:** Cajun Music, 151 Althea Street, Providence, RI 02907-2801, 401-351-6312.

AMERICAN PIT MASTERS BAR-B-Q ROUNDUP, Providence, RI
>    Late Jun.
>    Variety, General

See other dates and sites. **Days:** 3. **Hours per day:** 11. **Site:** outdoor. **Admission:** paid. **Daily entry:** under $10. **Secondary genre[s]:** CRCK, ARCK, TR&B, MC&W, FDDL, **Acts:** national acts, regional acts, local acts. **Sample day's lineup:** Bo Diddley, Young Neal and The Vipers, Bruce Marshall, Letters to Cleo, Big Nazo Band, plus fiddlers contest. **Contact:** Conventures, Inc., 250 Summer Street, Boston, MA 02210, 617-330-1992.

CAPE VERDEAN HERITAGE FESTIVAL, Providence, RI
>    Early Jul.
>    Modern Latin

See other dates and sites. **Days:** 1. **Site:** outdoor. Roger Williams Park. **Secondary genre[s]:** TLAT, **Acts:** local acts. **Sample day's lineup:** Norberto Tavares and Tropical Power, others. **Contact:** Rhode Island Heritage Commission, 150 Benefit Street, Providence, RI 02903-1209, 401-277-2669.

LUPO'S BIRTHDAY PARTY, Providence, RI
>    Early Jul.
>    Alternative and College Rock

Since 1994. **Help!** One time only? **Days:** 1. **Site:** indoor. Lupo's Heartbreak Hotel, 239 Westminster Street. **Admission:** paid. **Daily entry:** under $10. **Secondary genre[s]:** AC&W, **Acts:** national acts, regional acts, local acts. **Sample day's lineup:** Velvet Crush with Mitch Easter, Medicine Ball, Boss Fuel, Blood Oranges, Delta Clutch, Star Darts. **Contact:** Lupo's Heartbreak Hotel, 239 Westminster Street, Providence, RI 401-272-LUPO.

## New England Reggae Festival, Escoheag, RI
Late Jul.
Reggae, Ska and Caribbean

Since 1990. **Days:** 2. **Hours per day:** 14. **Site:** outdoor. Stepping Stone Ranch, Route 165. **Admission:** paid. **Daily entry:** $10 to $24. **Discounts:** multiple event or day passes, advance purchase discounts, **Secondary genre[s]:** AFRC, **Acts:** national acts, regional acts, local acts. **Sample day's lineup:** The Itals, Inner Circle, Mighty Charge, Bankie Banks, Motion, Wilson Blue, UHF, New Horizon, Tribulation, Bolu and The Roots of African Percussion, Igina, Ras Junior, others. **Contact:** Lion's Eye, 163 Brook Street, Providence, RI 02906, 401-331-7910.

## Barbershop Quartet Benefit Concert, Block Island, RI
Late Jul.
A Cappella and Doo Wop

Since 1965. **Days:** 1. **Hours per day:** 4. **Site:** indoor. Block Island School Gym, High Street. **Acts:** local acts. **Sample day's lineup:** Naragansett Bay Chorus, others. **Contact:** Barbershop Quartet Benefit Concert, Block Island Chamber of Commerce, Block Island, RI 401-466-2982.

## Newport Rhythm and Blues Festival, Newport, RI
Late Jul.
Blues and Traditional R&B

Since 1995. Announced for 1994, but cancelled. Re-announced for 1995. **Days:** 1. **Hours per day:** 7. **Site:** outdoor. Fort Adams State Park. **Admission:** paid. **Daily entry:** $10 to $24, $25 to $49. **Discounts:** multiple event or day passes, advance purchase discounts, **Restrictions:** 4, **Secondary genre[s]:** MRCK, BGOS, **Acts:** national acts, regional acts. **Sample day's lineup:** Charles Brown, Ruth Brown, Bonnie Raitt, Steve Cropper, Clarence Carter, Allen Toussaint and His Orchestra, Irma Thomas, Narada Michael Walden, Clarence Fountain and The Blind Boys of Alabama. **Contact:** Festival Productions, Inc., 311 West 74th Street, New York NY, 10023, 212-496-9000.

## East Providence Heritage Festival, East Providence, RI
Late Jul.
Variety, General

Since 1982. Also programs a smaller City Arts Festival in Early Aug. **Days:** 3. **Hours per day:** 8. **Site:** outdoor. Pierce Memorial Field and Stadium, Mercer Street. **Secondary genre[s]:** TJAZ, CRCK, BGOS, MC&W, TLAT, AFRC, **Acts:** national acts, regional acts, local acts. **Sample day's lineup:** Freddy Canon, The Coasters, The Five Satins, The Classics, Master Ibrahima Camara, New Liberty Jazz Band, Rhythm Machine, Gary Krinski. **Contact:** Heritage Days, City Hall, 145 Taunton Avenue, East Providence, RI 02914, 401-434-3311 x289.

## Rhode Island Indian Council Pow Wow: Temple to Music, Providence, RI
Late Jul. to Early Aug.
Native American

**Days:** 2. **Hours per day:** 8. **Site:** outdoor. Roger Williams Park, Elmwood Avenue. **Contact:** Providence Parks Department, Dalrymple Boat House, Elmwood Avenue, Providence, RI 02905, 401-785-9450 x244.

CHARLESTOWN CHAMBER OF COMMERCE SEAFOOD FESTIVAL, Charlestown, RI
Early Aug.
Variety, General

Since 1985. "The area's best seafood!" -- Program. **Days:** 1. **Hours per day:** 10. **Site:** outdoor. Ninigret Park. **Secondary genre[s]:** TJAZ, CRCK, MC&W, **Acts:** local acts. **Sample day's lineup:** Eight to the Bar, Moonlighters, Bay State Stompers, Hillwilliams, Surfside Eight, others. **Contact:** Charlestown Chamber of Commerce, P. O. Box 633, Charlestown, RI 02813, 401-364-4031.


CUMBERLANDFEST, Cumberland, RI
Early Aug.
Variety, General

**Days:** 5. **Hours per day:** 11. **Site:** outdoor. Diamond Hill State Park, Route 114, Diamond Hill Road. **Secondary genre[s]:** MJAZ, MRCK, CRCK, TR&B, MC&W, MFOL, IRSH, OTHR **Acts:** national acts, local acts. **Sample day's lineup:** James Montgomery Band, Murphy's Law, Funk Monks, Jasper James, Debra Mann Trio, Pat Mollica. **Contact:** Cumberlandfest, Diamond Hill State Park, Route 114, Cumberland, RI 401-658-0248.


AMERICAN INDIAN FEDERATION OF RHODE ISLAND POW WOW, Escoheag, RI
Early Aug.
Native American

Since 1934. **Days:** 2. **Hours per day:** 7. **Site:** outdoor. Stepping Stone Ranch, Route 165. **Contact:** American Indian Federation of Rhode Island Pow Wow, 21 Richard Street, Smithfield, RI 401-231-9280.


**BEN AND JERRY'S NEWPORT FOLK FESTIVAL**, Newport, RI
Early Aug.
Modern Folk

Since 1985. **Days:** 2. **Hours per day:** 7. **Site:** outdoor. Fort Adams State Park. **Admission:** paid. **Daily entry:** $10 to $24, $25 to $49. **Discounts:** multiple event or day passes, advance purchase discounts, **Restrictions:** 4, **Secondary genre[s]:** MRCK, CRCK, TR&B, BGOS, AC&W, BLGS, ZYDC, IRSH, MLAT, OTHR **Acts:** national acts, regional acts. **Sample day's lineup:** Indigo Girls, Richard Thompson, Fairport Convention, The Mighty Clouds of Joy, the story, The Williams Brothers, Ellis Paul, Richard Shindell, Dar Williams. **Audio merchandise:** "Ben and Jerry's Newport Folk Festival Mementos"; "Ben and Jerry's Newport Folk Festival '88 Live" (both Alcazar); "Turn of the Decade: Ben and Jerry's Newport Folk Festival" (Red House), plus numerous live recordings of the former Newport Folk Festival (Vanguard). **Contact:** Ben and Jerry's Newport Folk Festival, P. O. Box 1221, 670 Thames Street, Newpor,t RI 02840, 401-847-3700 **or:** Festival Productions, Inc., 311 West 74th Street, New York, NY 10023, 212-496-9000.


JVC JAZZ FESTIVAL/NEWPORT, Newport, RI
Middle Aug.
Modern Jazz

Since 1981. **Days:** 3. **Hours per day:** 7. **Site:** outdoor. Friday: Newport Casino, 194 Bellevue Avenue; Saturday and Sunday: Fort Adams State Park. **Admission:** paid. **Daily entry:** $10 to $24, $25 to $49, $50 and over. **Discounts:** multiple event or day passes, advance purchase discounts, **Restrictions:** 4, **Secondary genre[s]:** TJAZ, TR&B, **Acts:** national acts, regional acts. **Sample day's lineup:** David Sanborn, Dave Brubeck, Buddy Guy, Terrence Blanchard with Jeannie Bryson, The Dirty Dozen Brass Band, Rachelle Ferrell. **Audio merchandise:** "Duke Ellington Live!"; "Count Basie at Newport" (both on Verve), plus numerous live recordings on various labels (Omega, Bluebird, etc.). **Contact:** JVC Jazz Festival/Newport, P. O. Box 605, 670 Thames Street, Newport, RI 02840, 401-847-3700 **or:** Festival Productions, Inc., 311 West 74th Street, New York, NY 10023, 212-496-9000.

## WASHINGTON COUNTY FAIR, Richmond, RI
    Middle Aug.
    Fairs

Since 1967. "Summer's best entertainment value!" -- Advertisement. **Days:** 5. **Hours per day:** 14. **Site:** outdoor. Washington County Fairgrounds, Route 112. **Admission:** paid. **Daily entry:** under $10. **Secondary genre[s]:** MC&W, **Acts:** national acts. **Sample Series Lineup:** Day One: Holly Dunn, Davis Daniel; Day Two; Trisha Yearwood; Day Three: McBride and The Ride. **Contact:** Washington County Fairgrounds, Route 112, Richmond, RI 401-539-7042.

## POW WOW, Charlestown, RI
    Middle Aug.
    Native American

Since 1688. See other sites and dates. **Days:** 2. **Site:** outdoor. Location varies. **Contact:** Naragansett Indian Tribe, P. O. Box 268, Charlestown, RI 401-364-1100.

## SHAKE-A-LEG BENEFIT CONCERT, Newport, RI
    Middle Aug.
    Alternative and College Rock

"Organizers jokingly called it Parapalooza, a benefit for Shake-a-Leg, an outfit in Newport, RI, that provides therapy to those with physical disabilities." -- Rolling Stone. Status iffy, tho'. May revert to single act. **Days:** 1. **Site:** outdoor. Fort Adams State Park. **Admission:** paid. **Acts:** national acts. **Sample day's lineup:** Buffalo Tom, Belly, Billy Bragg, Natalie Merchant. **Contact:** Shake-a-Leg, P. O. Box 1002, Newport, RI 02840, 401-849-8898.

## SCITUATE MUSIC FEST, Scituate, RI
    Middle Aug.
    Variety, General

Since 1993. Benefits Scituate Jr./Sr. High. See other sites and dates. **Site:** outdoor. Broad Oak Farm. **Admission:** paid. **Secondary genre[s]:** MJAZ, MC&W, MFOL, **Acts:** local acts. **Sample day's lineup:** Moonlighters, Tanya, Atwater-Donnelly, others. **Contact:** Scituate Music Fest, 342 Old Plainfield Pike, Scituate, RI 02825, 401-647-3473/0057.

## BLUES BASH FOR HOMELESS PEOPLE, Smithfield, RI
    Late Aug.
    Blues and Traditional R&B

Since 1991. "If you're not here, you're not there yet." -- Advertisement. Also hosts a Rock and Roll Pig Roast with five bands earlier in the month. **Days:** 1. **Hours per day:** 13. **Site:** outdoor and indoor. Sandbag Johnny's, 325 Farnum Pike. **Admission:** paid. **Daily entry:** under $10. **Acts:** regional acts, local acts. **Sample day's lineup:** Young Neal and The Vipers, R. I. Blues Mafia, Little Anthony and The Locomotives, Little El feat. Karen Cappelli, Ted Stevens Band, Paul Murphy, Eight to the Bar, others. **Contact:** Sandbag Johnny's, 325 Farnum Pike, Smithfield, RI 401-231-5151.

## DOMINICAN FESTIVAL, Providence, RI
    Late Aug.
    Modern Latin

Since 1988. Formerly the Latin American Fest held in Early Jun. Past festivals featured 8-to-9 bands; 1995's may host just 1-to-2 due to financial difficulties. Call for current lineups. **Help!** Does anyone have a contact address or sample lineup? **Site:** outdoor. multiple locations. **Acts:** national acts, local acts. **Contact:** Dominican Festival, 401-941-1993.

CHOPMIST HILL INN SUMMER FESTIVAL, North Scituate, RI
    Late Aug.
    Variety, Country and Bluegrass

**Help!** One time only? **Days:** 1. **Hours per day:** 6. **Site:** outdoor. Chopmist Hill Inn, Route 102. **Admission:** paid. **Daily entry:** $10 to $24. **Secondary genre[s]:** MC&W, BLGS, MFOL, **Acts:** national acts, local acts. **Sample day's lineup:** Northern Lights, Jonathon Edwards, Frankie O'Rourke and The Full Circle Band, Lori Lacaille and Electric Rodeo, others. **Contact:** Chopmist Hill Inn, Route 102, North Scituate, RI 401-647-2388.

CAJUN AND BLUEGRASS MUSIC-DANCE-FOOD FESTIVAL, Escoheag, RI
    Early Sep.
    Variety, General

Since 1980. **Days:** 3. **Hours per day:** 13. **Site:** outdoor and indoor. Stepping Stone Ranch, Route 165. **Admission:** paid. **Daily entry:** $10 to $24, $25 to $49. **Discounts:** multiple event or day passes, advance purchase discounts, **Restrictions:** 3, 5, 7, 8, 10, 13, **Secondary genre[s]:** AC&W, BLGS, ZYDC, **Acts:** national acts, regional acts, local acts. **Sample day's lineup:** C. J. Chenier and The Red-Hot Louisiana Band, Tim and Mollie O'Brien, Steve Riley and The Mamou Playboys, California, Ranch Romance, Basin Brothers Cajun Band, Balfa Toujours, Stoney Lonesome, Joe Simien and Lisa Haley, Southern Rail, others. **Contact:** Cajun Music, 151 Althea Street, Providence, RI 02907-2801, 401-351-6312.

LABOR AND ETHNIC HERITAGE FESTIVAL, Pawtucket, RI
    Early Sep.
    Variety, Folk and International

**Days:** 1. **Hours per day:** 6. **Site:** outdoor. Slater Mill Historic Site. **Admission:** free. **Secondary genre[s]:** BLGS, TFOL, MARI, NATV, MLAT, TLAT, AFRM, AFRC, **Acts:** national acts, regional acts, local acts. **Sample day's lineup:** Grupo Folclorico Madeirense, Northern Lights, Mixashawn, World Out, Jorge Arce and Humano, Babema USA, Anne Feeney, Luci Murphy and Steve Jones, Tom Juravich, Wickford Express, Patricia Shih, Sarah Pirtle. **Contact:** Institute for Labor Studies, 99 Bald Hill Road, Cranston, RI 02920, 401-463-9900.

NATIVE AMERICAN DAYS, Westerly, RI
    Early Sep.
    Native American

See other sites and dates. **Days:** 3. **Hours per day:** 6. **Site:** outdoor. Elder John Crandall Wildlife Refuge and Nature Reserve, 104-105 Pound Road. **Contact:** Naragansett Indian Tribe, P. O. Box 268, Charlestown, RI 401-364-1100/322-7590.

PROVIDENCE WATERFRONT FESTIVAL/WATERFRONT JAZZ FESTIVAL, Providence, RI
    Middle Sep.
    Variety, General

Since 1985. **Days:** 2. **Hours per day:** 6. **Site:** outdoor. India Point Park. **Admission:** paid. **Daily entry:** under $10, $10 to $24. **Secondary genre[s]:** MJAZ, TJAZ, ARCK, TR&B, BLGS, MFOL, TFOL, IRSH, MLAT, AFRC, BRZL, OTHR **Acts:** national acts, regional acts, local acts. **Sample day's lineup:** Richard Elliott, Roland Vasquez, Dan Moretti, Midtown Jazz, Pa Koua Vang, Atwater-Donnelly, Fuzek-Rossoni, Julie Garnett, Sparky Davis, Len Cabral, Smoking Jackets, Neo 90's Dance Band, Burning Flames of Antigua, Big Nazo Band, Funky White Honkies, Prescription Horns, The Senders, Steve Smith and The Nakeds, 2nd Avenue, Eight to the Bar, others. **Contact:** Providence Parks Department, Dalrymple Boat House, Elmwood Avenue, Providence, RI 02905, 401-785-9450 x244.

IRISH FALL FESTIVAL, Lincoln, RI
   Middle Sep.
   Irish

Since 1985. Previously hosted three regional bands in cramped college setting, yet plans to add a "big draw" (Black 47? Cherish the Ladies?) to fill 1995's larger outdoor/indoor site. Call for current lineups. **Days:** 1. **Hours per day:** 9. **Site:** indoor. Lincoln Greyhound Park, Louisquisset Pike. **Admission:** paid. **Daily entry:** under $10. **Acts:** regional acts, local acts. **Sample day's lineup:** Paddy Noonan, Fintan Stanley, John Connors and The Irish Express, others. **Contact:** Ireland's "32" Society, 68 Ash Street, Lincoln, RI 02865, 401-725-5163.

RHODE ISLAND'S HERITAGE DAY, Providence, RI
   Middle Sep.
   Variety, Folk and International

Since 1978. "30 ethnic cultures celebrate their heritage with song, food, dance and entertainment." -- Listing. See other dates and sites. **Days:** 1. **Hours per day:** 7. **Site:** outdoor. State House lawn, Smith Street. **Admission:** free. **Secondary genre[s]:** MC&W, MARI, IRSH, NATV, TLAT, AFRM, AFRC, BRZL, OTHR **Acts:** local acts. **Sample day's lineup:** O. K. Corral, Bolu and The Roots of African Percussion, Fraidy Cats, Hiawatha Brown, Pandango, others. **Contact:** Rhode Island Heritage Commission, 150 Benefit Street, Providence, RI 02903-1209, 401-277-2669.

SETTLERS' DAY, Lincoln, RI
   Late Sep.
   Traditional Folk

Since 1993. Also hosts a French Farmer's Market featuring three regional acts (e.g., Maine French Fiddlers) the prior weekend in Woonsocket. **Days:** 2. **Site:** outdoor and indoor. Manville Sportsman's Club, Sayles Hill Road. **Secondary genre[s]:** TC&W, FDDL, IRSH, SCOT, **Acts:** local acts. **Sample day's lineup:** South County Rounders, Wickford Express, Wind Harp, Fiddle Dee Dee, plus "old fiddlers." **Contact:** Settlers' Day, P. O. Box 425, Slaterville RI 02876, 401-769-0699.

TASTE OF RHODE ISLAND, Newport, RI
   Late Sep.
   Variety, General

Since 1989. "Appetizer-sized portions of Rhode Island's best cuisine for sale by 40 area restaurants..." -- Program. **Days:** 2. **Hours per day:** 10. **Site:** outdoor. Newport Yachting Center, 4 Commerical Wharf. **Admission:** paid. **Daily entry:** under $10. **Secondary genre[s]:** MJAZ, TJAZ, CRCK, RAP, TR&B, MC&W, OTHR **Acts:** national acts, local acts. **Sample day's lineup:** The Cowsills, Northeast Navy Show Band, Newport Saxophone Quartet, Jackie Henderson's Hip Hop Jam Session, Nightlife Orchestra, others. **Contact:** Newport Yachting Center, America's Cup Avenue, P. O. Box 550, Newport, RI 02840, 401-846-1600.

SWAMP YANKEE DAYS, Charlestown, RI
   Late Sep.
   Variety, Country and Bluegrass

"A great time." -- Jim Calhoun. **Days:** 2. **Hours per day:** 9. **Site:** outdoor. Ninigret Park. **Secondary genre[s]:** MC&W, BLGS, **Acts:** local acts. **Sample day's lineup:** Swamp Yankees, Back Stage Pass, The Tailfins. **Contact:** Chariho Rotary Club, P. O. Box 543, Hope Valley, RI 02832, 401-596-3040.

Pow Wow, Charlestown, RI
    Early Oct.
    Native American

See other sites and dates. **Days:** 2. **Site:** outdoor. location varies. **Contact:** Naragansett Indian Tribe, P. O. Box 268, Charlestown, RI 401-364-1100.

Norman Bird Sanctuary Harvest Fair, Middletown, RI
    Early Oct.
    Variety, Folk and International

Since 1975. "The traditional fair lives on." -- Program. **Days:** 2. **Hours per day:** 7. **Site:** outdoor. Norman Bird Sanctuary, Aquidneck Island, 583 Third Beach Road. **Admission:** paid. **Daily entry:** under $10. **Secondary genre[s]:** MC&W, TC&W, MFOL, TFOL, IRSH, **Acts:** regional acts, local acts. **Sample day's lineup:** Mark Swab and Joe Fontaine, Wild Again, Sparky Davis, Atwater and Donnelly, 4th Street String Band, others. **Contact:** Norman Bird Sanctuary, 583 Third Beach Road, Middletown, RI 02840, 401-846-2577.

Autumnfest, Woonsocket, RI
    Early Oct.
    Variety, General

Since 1980. **Days:** 3. **Hours per day:** 12. **Site:** outdoor. WWII Veteran's Memorial Park, Social Street. **Secondary genre[s]:** MRCK, CRCK, BGOS, MC&W, OTHR **Acts:** national acts, regional acts, local acts. **Sample day's lineup:** Danny and The Juniors, continuous acts on two stages, plus a parade with 25 bands and 20 floats. **Contact:** Autumnfest, P. O. Box 574, Woonsocket, RI 02895, 401-334-1000/765-6110.

Scituate Arts Festival, North Scituate, RI
    Early Oct.
    Variety, General

Since 1968. "Over 200 artists, craftsmen and antique dealers." -- Listing. See other sites and dates. **Site:** outdoor. Village Green, Route 116. **Secondary genre[s]:** MJAZ, MC&W, MFOL, **Acts:** local acts. **Sample day's lineup:** Moonlighters, Tanya, Atwater-Donnelly, others. **Contact:** Scituate Art Festival, 342 Old Plainfield Pike, Scituate, RI 02825, 401-647-3473/0057.

Bowen's Wharf Waterfront Seafood Festival, Newport, RI
    Middle Oct.
    Variety, General

Since 1990. See other dates. **Days:** 2. **Hours per day:** 8. **Site:** outdoor and indoor. Bowen's Wharf. **Admission:** paid. **Daily entry:** under $10, $25 to $49. **Discounts: Secondary genre[s]:** MJAZ, MRCK, MFOL, TFOL, RGGE, **Acts:** local acts. **Sample day's lineup:** Barb Schloff, 4th Street String Band, Dark Horse, Ellen Fleming, Leslie Henry, Skampground, others. **Contact:** Maritime Arts Festival, P. O. Box 60, Newport, RI 02840, 401-849-2243 **or:** Newport Cultural Commission, City Hall, 43 Broadway, Newport, RI 02840, 401-847-1996. .

FIRST NIGHT PROVIDENCE, Providence, RI
> Late Dec.
> Variety, Folk and International

Since 1986. "Once again the streets and performance halls of our capital city welcome a cast of thousands for an evening of alcohol-free New year's Eve entertainment!" -- Program. **Days:** 1. **Hours per day:** 13. **Site:** outdoor and indoor. 40 locations. **Admission:** paid. **Daily entry:** under $10. **Discounts:** advance purchase discounts, group sale discounts, **Restrictions:** 2. **Secondary genre[s]:** MJAZ, TJAZ, MRCK, MR&B, TR&B, ACAP, BGOS, MC&W, BLGS, MFOL, TFOL, IRSH, SCOT, MLAT, RGGE, AVNT, CBRT, **Acts:** regional acts, local acts. **Sample day's lineup:** Manny Silvia, Edgewood Ensemble, Gerard LeDoux and Joy Williams, L-Shaped Room, Paula Feldman, Eric Armour, Bill Hall and Northwinds Bluegrass, Bolu and The Roots of African Percussion, Capital Hill Singers, Prudence and The Plowboys, Joe Macy Band, Todd Taylor, Crwydryn, Diana Smirnov, Dixie Allstars, Martin Grosswendt, Joyce Katzberg, Foster Fling, Good Friends, Georgia Concert Choir and Orchestra, Heart of Gold Vaudeville, High Rollers, Dan Moretti and Friends, Joe Parillo Ensemble, John Worsley's Swingtime, Keith Michael Johnson, Lincoln Pratt, Little Rest Chorus, Marilyn Meardon and Fiddle Dee Dee, Mark Levitt's Blue Bug Radio Cabaret, Mill City Rockers, Mount Pleasant High School Dionysiac Players, Narragansett Bay Chorus, Neo 90's Dance Band, Northern Lights, O. K. Corale, Parson's Plunkers, Pendragon, Penny Loafers, Pink Tuxedo, Praise Unlimited Choir, RI Youth Jazz Ensemble, Roberts and Astrausky, Ron Reid and Sun Steel, Sauterie, Tish Adams and Paul Odeh, Tony y Sus Tipicos, Young Neal and The Vipers. **Contact:** First Night, 10 Dorrance Street, Suite 1205, Providence, RI 02903, 401-521-1166.


OPENING NIGHT, Newport, RI
> Late Dec.
> Variety, Folk and International

"City-wide celebration of the arts." -- Listing. **Help!** A sample lineup? **Days:** 1. **Site:** outdoor and indoor. multiple locations. **Admission:** paid **Daily entry:** under $10. **Acts:** local acts. **Contact:** Newport County Convention and Visitors Bureau, 23 America's Cup Avenue, Newport, RI 02840, 800-326-6030.

# R. I. P., M. I. A. Festival Listings

**Caveat**  The following festivals are either confirmed or suspected to be discontinued (i.e., R. I. P.); or have not responded to various information requests (i.e., M. I. A.). Since all festivals are subject to last-minute changes or reinstatements, however, FestPress is not responsible for any festival listing information that follows. Readers are encouraged to notify FestPress of any status changes they uncover.

CLARENCE "GATEMOUTH" BROWN'S AMERICAN MUSIC FEST, Escoheag, RI
Middle Jun.
Blues and Traditional R&B

"Wonderful for years, but more than a family could handle." -- John O'Neill. Dormant since 1991; seeking sponsorship. **Days:** 2. **Site:** outdoor. Stepping Stone Ranch, Route 165. **Admission:** paid. **Secondary genre[s]:** MRCK, CRCK, ARCK, AC&W, **Acts:** national acts, regional acts, local acts. **Sample day's lineup:** Clarence "Gatemouth" Brown and Gate's Express, Young Neal and The Vipers, Magneatos, Sugar Ray and The Bluetones, Hans Thessink, Renee Brown, Jack Smith and Rockabilly Planet, Duke Robillard Band. **Contact:** Gate's Family of Fans, P. O. Box 963, Manchester, CT 06040, 203-649-2534.

PROVIDENCE JAZZ FESTIVAL, Providence, RI
Middle Jul.
Modern Jazz

Discontinued in 1992. See Providence Waterfront Festival/Waterfront Jazz Festival. **Days:** 2. .**Acts:** national acts, regional acts, local acts. **Contact:** Stage Door Productions, Inc., 400 Resevoir Avenue, Suite 3K, Providence, RI 02907, 401-781-5070/785-2916.

NEWPORT SUMMER FEST, Escoheag, RI
Late Jul. to Early Aug.
Reggae, Ska and Caribbean

Since 1993. "Multicultural waterfront festival for the whole family." -- Advertisement. See other date and site. **Help!** One time only? **Days:** 2. **Hours per day:** 9. **Site:** outdoor. Newport Yachting Center. **Admission:** paid. **Daily entry:** under $10. **Discounts:** multiple event or day passes, **Secondary genre[s]:** MR&B, ZYDC, MLAT, AFRC, OTHR **Acts:** local acts. **Sample day's lineup:** One Track, Ron Reid and Sun Steel, Eyes of a Blue Dog, Neo 90's Dance Band. **Contact:** Full Circle Productions, 839 Newport Avenue, Cambridge, MA 800-THE-FEST.

WORLDBEAT FEST, Escoheag, RI
Late Aug.
Reggae, Ska and Caribbean

Since 1993. "Hotter than July." -- Advertisement. See other date and site. **Help!** One time only? **Days:** 2. **Hours per day:** 12. **Site:** outdoor. Stepping Stone Ranch, Route 165. **Admission:** paid. **Daily entry:** $10 to $24. **Discounts:** multiple event or day passes, advance purchase discounts, **Secondary genre[s]:** MR&B, ZYDC, MLAT, AFRC, OTHR **Acts:** local acts. **Sample day's lineup:** One Track, Sun Steel, Eyes of a Blue Dog, Neo 90's Band. **Contact:** Full Circle Productions, 839 Newport Avenue, Cambridge, MA 800-THE-FEST.

"IT'S A THING CALLED LOVE" EXTRAVAGANZA, Escoheag, RI
> Late Aug.
> Variety, General

Benefits Rhode Island's homeless families. **Help!** One time only? **Days:** 2. **Site:** outdoor. Stepping Stone Ranch, Route 165. **Admission:** paid. **Daily entry:** $10 to $24. **Discounts:** multiple event or day passes, advance purchase discounts, **Restrictions:** 3, 4, 10, **Secondary genre[s]:** CRCK, TC&W, **Acts:** national acts, local acts. **Contact:** Project Independence, Inc., 936 Smithfield Avenue, Lincoln, RI 02865, 800-726-8716.


FAMILY MUSIC FEST, Charlestown, RI
> Late Aug.
> Variety, General

Since 1985. One time only. See other dates. **Days:** 1. **Hours per day:** 10. **Site:** outdoor. Ninigret Park. **Admission:** paid. **Secondary genre[s]:** CRCK, TR&B, **Acts:** national acts, local acts. **Sample day's lineup:** Three Dog Night, Roomful of Blues, others. **Contact:** Charlestown Chamber of Commerce, P. O. Box 633, Charlestown, RI 02813, 401-364-4031.


MAIN STREET BLOCK PARTY, Woonsocket, RI
> Middle Nov.
> Variety, Jazz and Blues

Cancelled in 1995 due to road construction. **Days:** 1. **Site:** outdoor. Main Street. **Secondary genre[s]:** MRCK, ZYDC, **Contact:** The Call, 75 Main Street, P. O. Box A, Woonsocket, RI 02895, 401-762-3000/767-8562.

~ ~ ~

# Connecticut

*Joe Cormier, Sea Music Festival.*

# Hartford's Local Showcases

**HARTFORD ADVOCATE'S BEST OF THE LOCAL MUSIC BASH**, Hartford, CT
Late May
Variety, General
***Attended***

**HONEY, HIDE THE BANJO, IT'S THE FOLK NEXT DOOR**, West Hartford, CT
Early June
Modern Folk

God bless alternative weeklies! No knock on the dailies, most of whom do a fairly credible job **Introduction** with their local listings, but typically it's the weeklies who've got their fingers pressed firmest to the pulse of local music.

Take Jayne Keedle. Not only does she actively champion original bands in her weekly column for the *Hartford Advocate*, but she conducts an annual poll of the best local acts, plus organizes a virtual festival to showcase the year's winners. In just three years she's steered the HARTFORD ADVOCATE'S BEST OF THE LOCAL MUSIC BASH to where it's outgrown the biggest club in Connecticut and hopefully is headed outdoors to the spacious greenery of Bushnell Park in downtown Hartford.

She's talking multiple stages amidst rows of refreshment booths manned by area restaurants and micro-breweries. She's working to get national A&R people to check out the artists. Inspired by a similar showcase of regional folk artists (HONEY, HIDE THE BANJO, IT'S THE FOLK NEXT DOOR), which is recorded live by Hartford's WWUH-FM for a commercial disc, she's thinking about a CD compilation.

Keedle's success in Hartford has even inspired the other five weeklies of the New Mass Media group — the *New Haven Advocate* [CT] , the *Springfield Advocate* [MA], the *Valley Advocate* [Northampton, MA] , the *Fairfield County Weekly* [CT] , and the *Westchester County Weekly* [NY] — to launch their own bashes.

How's that for a local music advocate, no pun intended!

The delightfully personable Keedle, in her cheery English accent, describes her modus operandi:

- "We originally got the idea from [another alternative weekly] the *Dallas Observer*, which does a best-of-the-bands thing. It's a poll. They all have their readers write in and vote.... We saw that and thought it was a good idea.

  "What I usually do, because I don't want to be the sole arbiter of taste, is call around around to anyone who would have a connection to local music. I call college radio stations, high school radio stations, other publications, writers, and try to get people into different genres. In the past, I called booking agents; I do that less. I stay away from people who have a vested interest in the bands... I cover all kinds of music, so I know enough about all of the genres to be able to tell if I'm getting bogus [nominations] or not.

  "The idea of getting nominations is to give the bands exposure so that the names get out there, and also to avoid, where possible, it just being a popularity contest where the band with the largest mailing list wins."

- "We do it on an off-night (usually middle-of-the-week) because the bands are free; because we don't know who won until we've tallied up all the ballots; and [because] we'd like to have the party as soon after as we can.

"The bands don't get paid for this.... We rent equipment so they have basic drum sets and stuff that they can share as much as possible to make it easy for switchover, otherwise it becomes a great roadie show. That's all you see is a whole bunch of people swapping mics, and then you see a band for 10 minutes, and then you see another half hour of dead time.

"It wasn't in headlining order. Basically, we dove from quiet to loud... I keep it to sort of the things that'll appeal to the crowd, like the folk crowd. The jazz crowd tends to be an early crowd, so I put them on first. We start with acoustic, and we move up. Then, sort of towards the end of the night, you end up with your later crowd, which would be hip-hop [and] heavy metal. I mean, that crowd doesn't think about leaving the house 'till 10! So I try to schedule so that each band will get the largest audience, and the audience that they're likely to get. I don't think you can start off the evening with a really, really loud death-metal band [laughs].

"It's also logistically easier to start with an acoustic [act], and move up as the gear gets more involved.

"The idea behind it is to expose as many people as possible to as many different styles of music as possible, and to mix 'em all up! ...The clubs were chosen because they had multiple stages, which meant that you could stagger the bands so that they overlapped. The first year we had reggae and folk and Cajun outside on the patio, and then, upstairs, we had some of the more popular, more basic rock and roll and R&B — the kind of stuff that appeals to a wide variety of people. Downstairs, the club was kind of underground, and we had more of the alternative music down there.

"What was nice about it was that people could go from upstairs to downstairs. You got together a crowd that you would never see in the same room — ever!

"We felt strongly that we wanted it in one place, and all on the same night. Some of the other *Advocates* tried it on separate nights, and some places tried it in different clubs. And you kind of disperse the crowd, and you don't mix the crowd up at all. You'll have, like, the quiet night, where there'll all be folk and acoustic and country and what-have-you. And then you'll have the loud rock/metal night, and those two crowds never meet. You end up with a low turnout for one and a high turnout for the other.

"Now, there's a problem with it, because we've really outgrown all the clubs. We hit The Sting this past year ['93], because it's the biggest club in the state. We had wanted to mix it up as much as possible, but a lot of people really preferred having two stages... The year before, literally, I was hearing zydeco downstairs and came upstairs and heard swing. And you could literally just bounce up and down the stairs and you'd be in different worlds. It was lots of fun!"

• "We invite the media, and often they come cover it, which means that, in lots of cases, it's the only time that a [daily] paper like the *Hartford Courant* will really do anything with local music.

"It's good for the bands because they all get a write-up [in that week's *Hartford Advocate*], and it's a good thing for them to put on their bio... They get lots of club bookings as a result of it, because the clubs like to book and say 'Winner of...Best of...' Usually there's some momentum to be ridden with that.

"It usually doesn't cost the paper anything at all because it's basically advertising space, and, frankly, we get a lot of advertising out of it. So the paper usually makes money on the issue. The clubs like it because we can guarantee we'll fill the club, because we hype it so long, and we get radio hype as well. The clubs are looking at free advertising, and they make a mint every year on liquor sales.

"I just like how the people say they had a great time there. That's the idea of it — it's a big party! I really like to hear when people come up to me and say, 'You know, I would never had heard that group, and I would never have gone to see them play, [but] I really liked them and I'll go see them again.' Or people coming up and saying, 'I didn't even know that genre of music existed!'

"That's really the best thing!"

I cruised into The Sting, a rock-and-roll barn smack in the middle of a suburban strip mall right off I-84, not knowing what to expect. The only two names I recognized beforehand were an Indigo Girls-style folk trio, The Nields, and the Grateful Dead-inspired Max Creek, longtime regulars at NYC's neo-hippie hangout, Wetlands. While I can't say that any band knocked me out that night (aside, perhaps, from the New England Jazz Ensemble), neither did any make me cringe. I found the quality reasonably and uniformly high — a compliment, considering how diverse the bill was.

**Festival Review**

Keedle and crew presented 14 acts that night from 5:30 p.m. to 12:30 a.m. pretty much on schedule — a miracle! Here's what we thought about a few of the evening's winners:

New England Jazz Ensemble: This sophisticated-yet-smokin' 14-piece big band — probably the most talented act of the night — featured interesting compositions by three of their members that didn't sacrifice steady, pulsing rhythms.

**Artist Mini-Reviews**

Keedle: "They've been playing jazz festivals in Europe, and they're sort of a regional act in that they have members come from all over. They'll drive two hours to go play, because where else can you play original big band music? Nowhere! Most of them are working musicians who just got fed up doing Glenn Miller every day."

The Nields: The bill's biggest buzz act, The Nields, are quickly developing a crossover folk following up and down the "Bo-Wash" corridor. Spunky stage presence, nice harmonies, and intriguing, passionate songs were mitigated by somewhat-grating lead vocals. I liked the psychedelic, "This Happens Again and Again," and the propulsive lament, "Julia." Worth a closer listen.

Frogboy: An interesting mix of staccato funk/core with razor-sharp breaks, punctuated by the lead singer's raspy raps, Frogboy was angry, charismatic and unique. Appealingly odd was their raw, twisted cover of "Eye of the Tiger."

Keedle: "I liked Frogboy. Their guitarist actually flew out to L. A. to audition for the Red Hot Chili Peppers."

Zydeco Zombies: They're not the very best local zydeco outfit I've heard (I'd nod more toward Loup Garou, Philly Gumbo or Robin Lacy and DeZydeco) but they're sure headed in the right direction. No limp-wristed beats here.

Keedle: "They rock, they really do. They're really a good-time party band; they really are super. They've got great senses of humor — a lot of energy on stage."

Max Creek: These tight '70s revivalists segued fluidly from one groove to another for their entire 30-minute set. They're possibly the perfect backing band in search of a lead focus, either vocally or instrumentally, but I could've floated on their syncopated lines all night, including their funky re-working of the ol' Peter, Paul and Mary chestnut, "There's a Big Boat Up the River."

Keedle recommends the Hartford Brewery along with the local restaurant scene:

**Travel Tip**

- "Max on Main is really great, a very upwardly-mobile sort of restaurant. Capricorn's is good as well, sort of your 'chic bistro.' A safe bet is Spencer's. In the summer it's got an outdoor patio; inside it's like a very traditional English kind of place. They have a restaurant in back and a discoteque downstairs, also a billiards room. For one-stop shopping...

"All of our theaters are really good. Real Art Ways (RAW JAZZ FESTIVAL — see chapter), that's cutting-edge art. That's where all the performance art comes to town. [laughs] You may not like it, but I guarantee you won't see it anywhere else in the area."

**See Also**   Three days later you can take in a strong sampling of rising singer-songwriters from Connecticut and points beyond. HONEY, HIDE THE BANJO, IT'S THE FOLK NEXT DOOR is a 12-hour benefit for college radio station WWUH-FM with an unusual twist — it's recorded live for a compilation CD. Just 225 seats are available at the University of Hartford's Harry Jack Gray Center to witness over 40 artists each doing 10-minute sets. Your $20 ticket to evening show has, in recent years, included the price of the CD, which is faithfully mailed to you several months later.

Folk Program Director Ed McKeon and local folk-singer Bruce Pratt (HARTLAND FOLK FESTIVAL, East Hartland, CT — see chapter) got the idea in '92, then watched as 2,000 CDs were sold, garnering rave reviews from the press, airplay across the country, and exposure for a rising generation of folk hopefuls. The whole process was repeated the next year and looks to become an annual institution. By the way, you can refer to it simply as 'THE FOLK NEXT DOOR.

~     ~     ~

# Strawberry Park's Bluegrass

**STRAWBERRY PARK BLUEGRASS FESTIVAL**, Preston, CT
> Early June
> Bluegrass
> ***Attended***

**STRAWBERRY PARK COUNTRY WESTERN JAMBOREE**, Preston, CT
> Late September
> Modern Country

**Introduction**

If the connection between classical music and bluegrass music seems unfamiliar to you, if not bloody unlikely, imagine how it must have first sounded to Buck Biber, now producer of one of New England's better bluegrass festivals, the **STRAWBERRY PARK BLUEGRASS FESTIVAL**.

Originally, the gentlemanly Biber had been trained in classical and jazz piano at Hartford's Hart School of Music. Needing summertime income to sustain his concert playing, he purchased some woodland in Southeastern Connecticut with plans to develop a private campground. "I was looking for something that wouldn't take too much of my time," Biber laughs ruefully, since his current efforts span 12 months a year, 12 hours a day. Patches of wild strawberries on site lent the name to his venture, which opened in '74.

Biber quickly built up the recreational aspects of his facilities. The physical plant now includes three swimming pools, a sauna and whirlpool spas, an arcade and adult rec center, a dance pavilion, a baby animal barn, horseback riding corrals and trails, basketball, volleyball and shuffleboard courts plus all kinds of yard games. Yet he also wanted to create a social atmosphere by instituting a series of weekend activities for the regulars. Some worked, some didn't, but Biber's willingness to experiment made him a ripe target for the suggestion of....yes, you guessed it, a bluegrass festival.

Biber recounts his conversion from bluegrass novice to devoted presenter via his first festival in '78:

- "From my musical background I have some friends who played in different styles. They had formed a bluegrass band, but I was totally unfamiliar with the music. When they first started talking to me about bluegrass music, 'bluegrass' meant horses in Kentucky. I literally didn't know it!

  "They said, 'Well, you should have a festival.' I didn't know what they were talking about, but I knew them for many years. I said, 'You guys gotta' tell me a little bit about this.' So we talked about it in the fall and the winter, and we talked all about bluegrass festivals, but at that point, honestly, I still couldn't identify the music. We were kinda' looking at it as a recreational project for the campground, because we knew there were people interested in bluegrass. The first time I was really exposed to bluegrass music was at my own bluegrass festival! [laughs]

  "The first time, I just liked it — it was fun! We had mostly local groups, plus one or two better-known groups. These people helped us plan our first festival because, obviously, we had no idea of what we were doing. We just built the stage (they told us to get an ace of a stage). But after we finished, and I thought about this, I said, 'This is something I really want to do.'"

  "Now I've become, I don't know, a hard-line, died-in-the-wool, true-blue, bluegrass music fan. This is somebody who grew up basically analyzing Bach and Schubert and playing Chopin! But I love the music and because of the way I was exposed to it, I have a theory

— that bluegrass needs a long-time exposure for people who didn't grow up with it. It shares a commonality with jazz, not in any musical sense, but in how it grows on people. When a lot of people hear jazz the first time, it leaves them cold. It's almost an acquired taste — you gotta' be exposed to it and exposed to it and exposed to it. Then, some things will start to grip you.

"I remember — it must have been the third or fourth festival, and I don't even remember which group was performing (it might have been the Dry Branch Fire Squad) — just a song about somebody's mother and father. Now I just didn't hear anything like that in any other genre that I'd ever heard. You don't hear that in Top 40; you don't hear that in pop. This was just a heartfelt song about a son and his mother and father — nothing else — no heavy-duty angst, no feelings of resentment, just pure love for somebody's parents. Just very simple, unashamed sentiment — that's one of the great strengths of bluegrass, and it's one that will grow on you if anybody gives it an honest chance.

"From a commercial aspect, the differences between that and C&W are just enormous in that a top bluegrass performer cannot command a small fraction of what a C&W performer can get. And I think that's unfortunate for bluegrass because C&W grew out of this music. All they did was electrify the guitars and add a drum, maybe a few other things, but this was the original country music! This is where it came from — there's a lot of history.

"I think it's always gonna' be here. I'd love to see it grow faster, but it's not the kind of thing you throw on 5,000 radio stations or on TV. Yet, it's something that's a very important part of our heritage. I think it's fantastic! If I pick up a bluegrass station somewhere now on the radio, I want to listen to it. Of course, it's a unique thrill when you're listening to someone who's at your own festival.

"I tell ya', we're gonna' keep doing this. We don't make a heck of a lot of money on it, after everything's said and done. We cover our expenses and we do a few other things, but I just love doing it. As long as we continue to do things, we're just going to keep doing bluegrass."

**Festival Review** The STRAWBERRY PARK BLUEGRASS FESTIVAL has three main draws. First, the campground itself is a treat — a relaxing mini-resort drenched in soothing greenery. It would invite a good getaway, even without the lure of a festival.

Second, the stage area is par excellence by bluegrass standards. Biber honored the insistent requests of his early musical participants and constructed a modern steel-reinforced shed worthy of a chamber orchestra. (There was even theatrical lighting above and fabric sound baffles behind the band.) It sits at the base of a sloping grove, lending it the same woodsy ambience as the amphitheater at Bill Monroe's BEAN BLOSSOM BLUEGRASS FESTIVALS (see Bean Blossom, IN, Late May to Late September).

Finally, and most importantly, the lineup balances a strong mix of national, regional, and local acts as well as various bluegrass styles. You won't be frozen out if your tastes lean to either side, traditional or progressive. "I've never heard a group here that I thought would be so progressive, or so extreme, that it should turn anybody off," claims Biber.

Biber cites numerous highlights over the years, including Alison Krauss and Del McCoury, but his two favorite headlining acts have been The Johnson Mountain Boys and The Seldom Scene. "In my judgement, musically, both of those groups reached impressively high levels," remarks Biber. "Going to the other extreme, there's a young band we had at the festival for the first time last year, and I think they're terrific. Their name is Cornerstone [and] we really liked these kids."

I made the scene on a drizzly Sunday afternoon, missing my buddies, Northern Lights, who had played the day before. (Biber on Northern Lights: "I think they're in a niche of their own, and I like the things they do. They excite people — people really enjoy listening to them.")

Another regional act, Southern Rail, did a variety of Monroe-inspired tunes (including Monroe's own "Tennessee Blues"), although I was most taken with their earnest original, "I'm a Little Man." One of my true highlights from a past festival, Paul Adkins and The Borderline Band, struggled to overcome the absence of their dobro player who had just left the band four days prior. They admitted on stage not achieving the solid artistry of the sort I so fondly remembered, alas.

The day was rounded out by two traditionalists, The Warrior River Boys and The Boys from Indiana. Here are my notes on one act, Dry Branch Fire Squad, before the rain closed my notebook.

Dry Branch Fire Squad. God bless vocalist/mandolinist Ron Thomason and his four-piece crew. **Artist Mini-**
They always grab the opening slot on Sunday morning to do their specialty gospel set — a **Review**
Herculean gesture of generosity considering all the performers were most likely up jamming near-
ly to daybreak.

Their second set featured more secular material — old chestnuts mixed with an occasional original, instrumental, or gospel number. Thomason broke ranks midway to introduce a
provocative solo-banjo ode to the plight of pregnant teenagers, "Teenage Lovers to Unwed
Mothers" ("Unwed fathers can't be bothered and run like water in a mountain stream"). Poignant
sentiments with an all-too-real currency, effectively sung in Thomason's high-lonesome tear.

Yet rarely will he stay serious. (Sample quip: "The difference between a banjo and a trampoline is that you take your shoes off to jump on a trampoline.") A man who looks something like
a grown-up Opie from TV's "Mayberry RFD," but with the sly wit of Judge Harry T. Stone from
TV's "Night Court," Thomason is one of the great monologue-givers in music today. Garrison
Keillor has nothing on Thomason's wacky, homespun excursions that affectionately poke fun at
hillbilly habits along the way to hearteningly wise conclusions. Somebody ought to put this
Kentucky-based English teacher/horse breeder on syndicated radio — and soon!

Among nearby attractions, Biber cites the Fox Woods High Stakes Bingo and Casino, Mystic **Travel Tip**
Seaport, plus ocean beaches and rural apple farms. However, Strawberry Park offers the entire
family "the whole package," as Biber explains, "and people feel warm and comfortable here.
We're out in the country and it's nice and quiet."

Biber's crew also puts on a COUNTRY WESTERN JAMBOREE weekend in late September, although **See Also**
strictly with New England acts so far. It's smaller than the bluegrass festival, according to Biber,
but it's proven successful, and he likewise seeks to "build it up."

~     ~     ~

# Mystic Seaport's Chanteymen

LOBSTERFEST, Mystic, CT
    Late May
    Maritime

SEA MUSIC FESTIVAL, Mystic, CT
    Middle June
    Maritime
    ***Attended***

TASTE OF HISTORY, Mystic, CT
    Early August
    Maritime

CHOWDERFEST, Mystic, CT
    Early October
    Maritime

COMMUNITY CAROL SING, Mystic, CT
    Middle December
    Traditional Gospel and Sings

**Introduction**    O. K., admit it. When I say, "sea chanteys," does a parody first spring to mind? Something like the crusty sea captain who frequently drags his peg leg onto TV's "The Simpsons?" You know, the old salt who's always muttering, "Arrrgh!" Well...same here.

Imagine my surprise, then, when I snuck into the Mystic Seaport Museum's SEA MUSIC FESTIVAL (the world's longest-running maritime festival) and found songs real enough to slap me in the face like brisk sea spray.

Actually, I wasn't surprised that the event was so well-produced and presented. Anyone who's ever visited this highly-popular tourist attraction knows that it preserves an authentic 19th-century shipbuilding village to the same standards as Colonial Williamsburg's. It stood to reason that a maritime music festival here would receive the same study, care, and sparkle. I was surprised, though, that the material still communicated relevantly through the film of history.

These were the workaday words of lower-classes escaping the oppressive bowels of peasant/industrial Europe. (After all, if you were not the eldest son to inherit the family farm in a country such as Ireland, how many occupations were realistically open to you? Soldier, priest, beggar, or criminal were pretty much your other choices.) They spoke in many cultures — the original world-beat music. They spoke in the communal rhythms of manual labor with a raw economy that could teach today's songwriters a thing or two.

Tales of cruelty, homesickness, morality, fatigue, giddyness, boredom, comradeship, dissipation — all came to life in simple, tuneful ways. Call it an oral history, if you will, of ordinary working men whose voices are infrequently and/or unconvincingly presented by modern musicians.

Geoff Kaufman is the festival's friendly Coordinator and one of the six resident "Mystic Seaport Chanteymen." (You missed him when TV's "Good Morning America" filmed the other five hoisting a sail to the acappella rhythm of a chantey, but that gives you the general picture of his job.) I asked him about the work element in these songs, and their currency, referring to one heart-wrenching account he sung of an Irishman's slaving aboard an American-bound "packet ship":

"I'm delighted that you did pick up on that element of it because we certainly feel that strongly," Kaufman remarks:

- "The chanteys, work songs, per-se, grew out of the desperation of sailors under the duress of extreme physical hardship in that period when sail became very, very competitive. The packet ships you talked about were the ones that developed a reputation for driving these men to their limits because they were trying to get goods across the Atlantic in competition.

  "It's interesting when you mention work in that we all work crazy hours these days, but the work that we do, most of us, is not physical labor — it's mental, it's high-pressure, it's intellectual. We've lost that sense of rhythm very important for people, I think. It's something that can be internalized and give your life structure, and it may be one of the reasons that our culture is a little bit at loose ends and fraying around the edges. [laughs]

  "Part of what I'm trying to get at is that for all of those people involved in the endeavor of the Great Age of Sail, there was something bigger than them, and that was the sea. The sea had the ability to snatch a ship at a moment's notice. Going around Cape Horn, there were times when the sea would lift up the stern of a ship and drive it under. In four minutes, it was gone!

  "So that kind of power of something clearly larger than yourself is something that we don't have a great impression of these days. We really are in a position to be pretty egotistical because things are so easy in some ways for us, nowadays."

Kaufman's own musical voyage into chantey singing began in New York City during the mid-'70s. His Irish vocal quartet, "Stout," decided to work up a sea-music repertoire in order to participate in OpSail '76. The group remained together in this vein long enough to be invited to the Mystic Seaport Museum's first festival in '80. Kaufman's performed at every one since, joining the museum staff permanently in '84.

For him, planning the festival these days is not strictly about historical preservation but also about keeping the spirit of the sea alive — it's stories, it's emotions, it's inspirations. Kaufman points to contemporary maritime songwriters such as Larry Kaplan, Cindy Kallick, and Jerry Bryant, whose modern narratives he feels rank with the best of current folksongs. In his words, "The power of the sea and it's effect on human imagination runs throughout all this material, and it's still alive for people."

Working for this renowned an institution has given Kaufman the high profile to seek out the best maritime performers the world over. Indeed, he describes how an increasing share of his budget is going toward recruiting artists with foreign traditions, notably France, Holland, and Russia. (Between the foreigners and the preservationists, Kaufman promises you'll witness unusual musical instruments rarely heard at music festivals, including a virtual museum of concertinas.)

Kaufman prides his festival lineup on two features: (a) a high standard of "performers who have knowledge and a serious interest in the history"; and (b) "an incredible sense of camaraderie among the performers." A good example of both was when legendary Irish folk-singer, Tommy Makem, joined the bill in 1990. Kaufman explains:

- "Here's someone who really stands above the rest of the roster of people in terms of recognition to the public and, yet, he walked around all weekend in a sort of a glowing daze because he was having such a good time. He said that to me he just had never really experienced a festival that was so relaxed and so friendly. He sorted blended in with everybody else — not being a superstar, but just kinda goin' along and havin' a good time.

  "There are also other people, like Gordon Bok, who have more recognition than most of the people we bring in and, yet, they come and they're content to just be one of the crowd because that's the way this festival works."

**Festival**   "Blending in" — that's the true glory of the SEA MUSIC FESTIVAL, other than the pretty panorama
**Review**   of historic buildings mirrored in Mystic's pocket harbor.

There is continuous music both Saturday and Sunday afternoons at seven different locations on the grounds plus evening concerts Friday and Saturday nights, as well as a Saturday
Night Country Dance. But it's programmed in indigenous settings: aboard one of three tall ships,
under a tree upon the village green, behind the pulpit within the tiny chapel, and in other nooks
and crannies.

You drift on by and feel as if you're a regular 19th-century townsperson building ships for
the Greenman family, singing to relieve the strain and make the day go by. There's a remarkable
spontaneity and intimacy as rarely are you more than a few heads away from the music — a photography buff's delight!

Songs aside, my favorite set the day I visited was with Cape Breton fiddle master, Joe
Cormier, who led a 90-minute "Tribute to Canada."

**Artist**   Joe Cormier and Band. Cormier was an instrumental delight. His dexterous bow and beautiful
**Mini-Review**   tone seemed to just reach out into the brisk salt air and shanghai passerbys underneath the small,
waterside pavilion.

Cormier anchored two partners who switched around on mandolin, guitar, and electric
bass. Together they played a series of medleys — reels, jigs, strathspeys — which possessed a rich,
almost hypnotic quality about them. I kept thinking of the melodic and rhythmic progressions of
Cajun music, to which Cormier's traditional Cape Breton stylings are historically related. This was
similarly infectious music to tap your feet to, music to sway to, music to give your tensions away
to.

Kaufman: "Now there's a maritime culture in which, when people were on shore, by gum,
they were going to dance! Wonderful fiddling tradition. Cormier's neat!"

**Travel Tip**   Between the festival and the museum's grounds, buildings, tall ships, demonstrations, exhibits,
and shops, you've got a full day and then some. Add in the other area attractions, including
Mystic Marinelife Aquarium, Maple Breeze Action Park, and Fox Woods High Stakes Bingo and
Casino, and you've got a good, long weekend.

Be forewarned, however, that summertime lodgings book up way ahead. Sixty percent of
the festival's 10,000 attendees are from out-of-state, according to Kaufman. If you're coming in on
the fly and need a place to stay, your best best is to head toward Providence, RI. For local lodging
information and more, write: Mystic Chamber of Commerce, P. O. Box 143, Mystic, CT 06355

**See Also**   Kaufman's resident chanteymen are busy at the museum most every weekend, all year long. If
you can't make the SEA MUSIC FESTIVAL, but prefer having a festival environment in which to enjoy
their music, the museum presents other events, too. Its summer season generally kicks off with the
LOBSTERFEST, Memorial Day Weekend, and concludes with the CHOWDERFEST on the first weekend
in October. Eat up and enjoy!

~     ~     ~

# Woodstock's Roots-Beat

BLUEGRASS FESTIVAL, Woodstock, CT
> Late May
> Bluegrass

DIFFERENT TASTES OUTDOOR CRAWFISH AND ALLIGATOR FEAST, Hartford, CT
> Early June
> Cajun and Zydeco

**MAD MURPHY'S CAJUN, ZYDECO MUSIC AND ART FAIR**, Woodstock, CT
> Middle June
> Cajun and Zydeco
> ***Attended***

GREAT AMERICAN BLUES FESTIVAL, Woodstock, CT
> Middle July
> Blues and Traditional R&B

EARTH JAM, Woodstock, CT
> Middle August
> Alternative and College Rock

**Introduction**

I came across notice for '93's inaugural season of festivals at the Woodstock Valley Ski Lodge in Northeastern Connecticut while making a pit stop on an isolated stretch of I-84. There, on a dark wood-paneled wall of the rest area right above the water fountain, was taped a handsomely-designed white poster advertising "A glorious day of art, music, dancing & fun!"

Two aspects of the poster startled my road-weary eyes. First, it enticed me with everything a festival freak would desire: six, out-of-the-ordinary acts from all across North America, plus "dance instruction every other hour, hiking, volleyball, food, crafts" — the whole nine yards, as they'd say up in these woods.

Second, that it made it to the rest-area wall at all. State tourism departments are not usually festival-friendly. The *1994 Connecticut Vacation Guide* contains a "Special Events" calendar, for example, but with absolutely no contact information. That's like publishing movie listings without the theaters — how do they expect you to attend if you don't know who to call for locations, directions, times, lineups, prices, etc.?

For Steve McKay, the events' founder and manager of Hartford's Municipal Cafe, it was just one more obstacle to overcome in his own resourceful way. In this case, he'd worked at that particular stop right after college and managed to get the maintenance guys to put the poster up. Since taking over the affectionately-nicknamed "Muni" in '90, he's been able to employ a right-minded ethic, born of an upbringing by missionary school teachers, to turn many such negatives into positives.

Here's how McKay, who grew up in Woodstock after being born in Turkey, describes his unlikely journey from rest-area worker to festival promoter:

- "My parents had this [restaurant] in Hartford, which my uncle had originally started. They started a lease with another Turkish group and it fell to pieces. They lost a lot of goodwill and money. At the very end, my dad asked me if I'd like to come in and take over the night business and try to straighten it up.

"They had just started in a very half-assed way to do live music. There was no real format; the scheduling was very erratic. The [previous] manager left a little calendar book that had bands crossed out. To be quite truthful, I probably had seen in my entire life maybe six concerts. I didn't know anything — Zydeco Zombies, Cajun music — I didn't have a clue! I knew what I liked, though, and I always liked a more earth-toned style of music. I didn't like heavy-metal; I liked folk, bluegrass — more of the roots.

"So I called up the bands (they had been making guarantees here), and I said, 'Listen, I can't make those guarantees to you, but I'd be willing to work as hard, or harder than you are, to make these shows work.'

"We began to develop a reputation for doing good music and on a cooperative level with the bands. Very often it's an antagonistic relationship that club owners and bands have. It's 'us-and-them,' and both sides tend to try and screw the other for all they're worth in gettin' the one gig. In ours, we worked almost in a communal way, ending up doing three bands [for example] that were all friends together. The whole thing really evolved in a very positive direction.

"Our reputation for dealing professionally and honestly with bands began to grow. All of a sudden we're getting tapes from [places like] DC. As you know, when you get a little bit of a reputation, people from all over the country start coming to you, instead of the other way around. After we worked with a couple of big agencies, even some bigger acts were coming in at lower than their lowest guarantees but were walking away with more money than they would've asked for originally.

"I said, 'If we're going to be a music club in Hartford, we want to be the best'. So we declared ourselves the biggest and the best before we were. And it worked! [laughs] We backed it up with product, with talented acts — not the regular four house bands every week. We took the chances that it took to back up our claim."

- "Now the thing at the [Woodstock Valley Ski Lodge] started out as a little bit of a fluke. As a teenager I taught skiing up there. An old Hungarian chicken farmer built that place from the land there with his bare hands — and he's still around! He puts me to shame whenever we work on something. He's about 70 years old; his name is Josef Kemper."

"Joe called up about a year and a half ago and asked, 'Stephen, would you like the ski lodge?' I knew it hadn't been skied on for a couple of years, and I knew my uncle, David McKay, about 11 years prior had done a big bluegrass festival there — a very successful one. I said, 'Well, I don't have any money. The restaurant here in Hartford is my parents' and I take a salary from that."

"He said, 'That's not what I'm concerned about.' His wife had died of cancer. He never had any kids. It was more of almost bequeathing it to me; that we had similar visions for the land, not to put [up] condos. So he gave me an unbelievably generous arrangement on leasing the property — it was just about a gift. That's how it began.

"We began putting together a schedule fairly quickly... During the winter, we did some indoor Cajun things to let the local people see what we were doing. We [also] had some folk music inside [the lodge], just breaking the rooms in, getting the logistics worked out.

"Starting out the summer we did five major concerts, and we ended up probably a little better than breaking even. But, to me, the real success was that it was the first year out [and] the weather was fantastic for every show. Nobody had ever heard of the Woodstock Valley Lodge before last year. It was a new name, a new venue, and everything else that went down, and it went down extremely well. Not one arrest, no fights.

"[The festivals] ended up being extremely fun, community-oriented events. It was very positive entertainment — just good, clean fun."

The one thing the poster neglected to mention was the beautiful grounds, probably because
McKay and crew were still struggling to construct it just hours before the first Mad Murphy's
Cajun, Zydeco Music and Art Fair. You reached it via back roads that McKay had thoughtfully
marked with road signs at each turn. Up a wooded hill, into a grassy parking lot, and there y'at.

**Festival Review**

McKay sets the scene:

- "The site blows people's minds...When [you] walk around the corner from that lodge, all
  you see is a wall of trees when you come out of your car. You come through that little tun-
  nel, and it's almost like a chapel — that lodge there. You walk around the corner, [and] it's
  like standing on the edge of a cloud because you're at the top. It's very unusual for ski area
  to be located there on top of a mountain.

  "What I like is that people could go sit on the side of the slope that wasn't even facing the
  music. They could hike. It was not just standing in an asphalt parking lot looking at a shell,
  [being] completely focused."

Indeed, the vibe was thoroughly pastoral, a peaceable kingdom of Cajun dance fans —
from hippies to yuppies to families — all enjoying the expansive view, the warm sunshine, the
syncopated beat, the plywood dance floor, and the spicy jambayalya. One even practiced tai chi
while looking out over the hilltops. The cook's T-shirt said it best, "God is Cajun."

I managed to catch a bit of ex-Basin Brother and button-accordion player, Danny Collet and The
Swamp Cats, in all his woolly, gyrating glory. McKay and I had differing reasons for failing to
trumpet Collet's set; mine involved Collet's nasal squeak of a voice, which only a Cajun mother
could've loved. Instead, here are McKay's comments on several of the other acts who contributed
to the festivities:

**Artist Mini-Reviews**

Zydeco Zombies: "The first time they ever played was here at our restaurant. Ken
Karpowitz, the squeezebox player, used to be a polkaman... When they started, it sounded like
polka-zydeco; it was hilarious. To see these guys grow is really fantastic."

Darren and The Swamp Stompers: "They were very good. Darren had played fiddle with
File for quite a while. He moved up here to marry a gal that he had met on the road. He's a luthier, a real nice guy to deal with."

Danielle Martineau and Rockabayou: "I would do anything for those guys... She's played
with some very heavy acts over in Europe, and [she's] an extraordinarily high-caliber person, as
well as a great musician. They're really exciting stuff...

"She works very hard on the technical end. I think she's one of the more technical players
around. She's [also] an extremely sincere player — the crowd really appreciates that. During that
time her parents were very ill, [but] she came down here. In spite of that, she put out, I mean, she
made the show, she made it all happen. Fortunately, things worked out well with her folks."

Terrance Simien and The Mallet Playboys: "I think we got Terrance at a fair price because
he was treated fairly here at our club [when] we had him here before... He's on fire! Those guys
he has with him — it's like a circus, just so entertaining."

Woodstock is just a stone's throw from the Southbridge area, which McKay lauds for Sturbridge
Village, as well as for the copious shopping and dining about. He recommends reserving a camp-
ground site nearby and exploring the proximity: "To go to Woodstock is like going to New
Hampshire, but it's only an hour outside of Hartford."

**Travel Tip**

McKay is committed to instituting all four festivals on an annual basis — the other three being the
Bluegrass Festival, the Great American Blues Festival and the Earth Jam. He's also considering
developing a deluxe campground on the site, which would afford extending the music over full
weekends.

**See Also**

Of the three events, McKay exclaims, "Earth Jam was my favorite musical event of my
life. That was really, really neat! Acoustic Junction are a really fantastic, kind of Rocky
Mountain/bluegrass/rock band — young guys, extraordinarily talented. It was just the perfect,
perfect night."

You should also know that 1995 witnessed McKay's "Muni" playing host to the DIFFERENT TASTES OUTDOOR CRAWFISH AND ALLIGATOR FEAST , which had previously been run by others at other sites. Its flyer boasted "one ton of Louisiana crawfish," as if you needed another excuse to "pass a good time!"

~     ~     ~

*Twirlin', Mad Murphy's Cajun, Zydeco Music and Art Fair.*

# Connecticut's Country Radio Fair

GREAT AMERICAN MUSIC FEST, Goshen, CT
    Late June
    Modern Country
    ***Attended***

EASTERN STATES EXPOSITION — THE BIG E!, West Springfield, MA
    Middle September to Late September
    State and County Fair

**Introduction**

The GREAT AMERICAN MUSIC FEST may be the biggest single-day bash of country music northeast of Maryland. It draws over 30,000 people and features six straight hours of major names — despite taking place in a region long considered "the heart of darkness" within the C&W industry.

"For the last umpteen years they've been saying that," exclaims Steve Peters, energetic marketing guru for WWYZ-FM Country 92.5. "Since we came to be country [switching formats in '89], I think we've been dispelling that with some speed and some fervor, proving a lot of people wrong that you can't play country music in New England and be successful."

Partly by seizing upon the same demographic changes that have pushed musically-disenfranchised baby-boomers toward C&W, but more through dogged hard work and marketing prowess, Peters has helped guide his station to a leading share among adults ages 25 to 54 within their three Connecticut markets.

The number of promotional techniques the marketing department employs could fill up the rest of this chapter, including Peters jokes, "our official Country 92.5 breath mints — keep your breath fresh and smile clean!" None's been bigger, however, than the station's decision in '90 to host their first festival.

"It was really a listener-appreciation party," remarks Peters. "That's how it unfolded. We wanted to say 'thank you' to the community for supporting our station so whole-heartedly. What we thought we'd do is bring the stars and the talent they hear on the radio to them live, in-person, at a very reasonable price. The first year it was free."

Peters laughs at what happened:

- "We printed up lots of tickets and gave them out at sponsors' locations. The first year over 50,000 people showed up! We had to stop giving out the tickets when we realized that there wasn't going to be a percentage that wasn't going to be used. I was looking when we were doing the free-ticket giveaways and was saying that these people aren't standing in line for an hour to get these tickets just to throw them away!

"We backed up traffic 12 miles in each direction," Peters recalled of his premonition confirmed on festival day.

Peters and crew have since scaled it back to what the site can more comfortably accommodate by charging a nominal fee (typically under $10) and requiring that all tickets be purchased in advance at one of their sponsors' locales. No tickets are sold at the gate.

Peters contends the station's costs are not recouped financially. Rather its rewards are intangibles such as local media coverage, publicity in the C&W trades, artist recognition and, of course, listener appreciation. "The listeners love it," assures Peters, "It really does make us look good in front of their eyes."

**Festival Review**  Country 92.5's audience could've stepped out of Shepler's catalog. I couldn't believe how much Western wear was being worn. Elaborate outfits, too! Good thing all the tattoos helped me confirm where I was — in New England, not New Mexico. If you come without the requisite accoutrements, though, no worries as there is a huge hall of merchants hawking their Western wares. Once clad, you can roll down a festive food alley, stock up on barbeque, and settle down for a great day of music.

**Artist Mini-Reviews**  I have to give the station credit; they covered all the bases in plotting the bill the year my wife and I attended.

First, they had a promising singer-songwriter and New England native, Teresa, open up. Peters notes:

- "Teresa's a very talented young woman. She's opened the fest every year with the national anthem. She's got a recording contract now in Nashville [Warner Bros./Nashville] and asked if we could have her do a couple of her newest songs. It worked out well, and she had local fans that came in. It helped keep that family feeling to the event."

They followed with a solo instrumentalist, fiddler/guitarist Mark O'Connor, who was his usual amazing self — elevating rural vernacular nearly into the avant garde with his characteristic intensity. A band set, however, might've captured the crowd's attention better.

Next up, an established singer-songwriter, Michael Johnson, who handled himself well facing down a packed infield with nothing but a guitar. No hat, even. I became involved chatting with a guy wearing a "Galax Old Fiddler's Convention" shirt but did get to enjoy Johnson caress his own "Drops of Water," one of my favorite Judds covers. A treat.

Great Plains, the day's choice for "new band," followed. They were in the midst of one of their first tours, yet got the milling crowd to stop and take notice. Even I could follow their sweetly-driving "In a Perfect World," despite sitting back in Deep Space 9. Their sound combined spare country stylings, hard-rock rhythms, and fine harmonies. No excesses, just whatever was needed to put the song over. Great Plains also got my kudos for being personable between numbers.

My wife and I then had to dash off to another event (WORLD MUSIC FESTIVAL, Woodbury, CT — see chapter), but Peters filled me in on the day's highlight that we missed, headliners Clint Black and Wynonna: "They just loved Wynonna, no question about it. Black also put on an outstanding performance — they were on their feet. The culmination of the day was great! Clint and Wynonna just did a number one bang-up job!"

**Attendance Tip**  If you want to attend, here are some cautions. First, you'll need to buy your tickets beforehand. Call the station four weeks ahead to learn the ticket prices and purchase locations. Out-of-staters can write the radio station at least four-to-six weeks in advance for tickets. Peters requests your sending a SASE containing a money order or certified check (no personal checks, please).

Second, there's no re-entry, which eliminates setting your chairs up early, then tailgating it back in the parking lot. Pack a cooler, or bring sufficient cash to munch throughout the day. There's also no video screen; late-comers may want to bring binoculars. Finally, there's no shade or rain cover. Bring sunblock, plus a longsleeve garment and cap for protection from the sun or any sudden chill. Peters has thousands of ponchos available if it rains (station logo-ed, of course).

**See Also**  Country 92.5 actively supports every event in the area which books country music. Unfortunately, my area files are littered with fly-by-night affairs which came and went, taking their national C&W headliners with them.

However, the EASTERN STATES EXPOSITION, also known as THE BIG E! after the site formerly shared by the GREAT AMERICAN MUSIC FEST, has stayed the course. It's a huge regional fair for all of New England. Accordingly, it presents one of the most prolific lineups you'll find among state fairs, featuring as many as four different headliners per day. Big C&W names predominate, as you'd expect, letting you wrap up the summer season with Country 92.5 tighter than a bolo knot.

~     ~     ~

# Norwalk's Jazz Picnic

**AFTERNOON OF JAZZ**, Norwalk, CT
> Late June
> Modern Jazz
> ***Attended***

Everybody always talks "NEWPORT, NEWPORT, NEWPORT" among premier jazz festivals, citing its **Introduction** long tenure, deluxe setting, VIP patrons, big-name sponsors, and top-drawer talent (JVC JAZZ FESTIVAL/NEWPORT, Newport, RI — see chapter). No knock against "NEWPORT," but let's talk "NORWALK," too.

An **AFTERNOON OF JAZZ** ["NORWALK"] kicked off back in '63, ten years after NEWPORT but still decades before most other events of its kind. Its chief host was the late Jackie Robinson, the legendary Hall-of-Famer, who was the first to break the color barrier in major-league baseball. He and his wife, Rachel, were eager to support the emerging Civil Rights movement and sought to create a benefit fundraiser for such causes as the NAACP, the SCLC, Operation Breadbasket, and others. They deputized jazz piano master, Billy Taylor, as Music Director to help corral leading jazz names to perform. Sitting amidst the crowd in that historic first year were the late Rev. Martin Luther King Jr., Roy Wilkins and Rev. Jesse Jackson.

In '71, two years after her husband's passing, Rachel Robinson incorporated their charitable activities as the Jackie Robinson Foundation. Two years after that her foundation became the sole beneficiary of the annual Sunday concert — an occasion celebrated on stage by such stars as the late Dizzy Gillespie, Max Roach, Herbie Mann, the late Sarah Vaughan, Ella Fitzgerald, Carmen McRae, Gerry Mulligan, Dave Brubeck, Joe Williams, and Taylor. Not bad, huh?

The foundation has since designated its proceeds for college scholarships. Last year 115 Jackie Robinson Scholars were supported on 51 campuses in 21 states. (In a nice touch, current recipients are introduced on stage and mingle with their benefactors in the crowd as they sell raffle tickets.) Making these impressive gifts possible are an "A-list" of corporate contributors, including Anheuser-Busch, Coca-Cola, The Equitable, Pepsico, Woolworth's, Xerox, Perkin-Elmer, and Ryder Truck Rental.

In '85 the foundation undertook a cultural pilgrimage to Senegal, bringing 25 musicians and 400 patrons for a week of sold-out concerts in Dakar's National Theater. In '86 it occupied its present concert site in Norwalk's Cranbury Park. These lushly-landscaped estate grounds, which house a stone mansion backing the stage, invoke "ooh-ahhs" just as readily as Newport's Casino.

When you attend this wonderful eight-hour affair, your MC's will include radio personalities from the two top-rated jazz stations in the country: the noncommercial WBGO-FM Jazz 88 in Newark, NJ, and the commercial CD-101.9 in New York City. Accordingly, the lineup will balance various straight-ahead styles with current crossover trends. And there's the main element that distinguishes NORWALK from NEWPORT — NORWALK generally mates the jazz and R&B worlds closer together. Some examples from recent years:

- <u>New talent</u>: Stacie Precia follows Santita Jackson ;

- <u>Rising stars</u>: Nnenna Freelon follows Marion Meadows;

- <u>Young lions</u>: Wynton Marsalis follows Take 6;

- <u>Prime time</u>: Gerry Mulligan follows Jon Lucien;

- <u>Classic jazz</u>: Lionel Hampton follows Joe Williams.

In one day NORWALK lets you connect the dots between these two timelines of African-American music from the current generation back 50 years to Hampton's era when jazz was barely segregated from R&B, either artistically or commercially. Spice the musical broth with other jazz seasonings, including a leading Latin artist or two, and you have a fluidly varied lineup that's even more amazing when considering every performer is playing for free!

NORWALK's producer, the gracious Robin Bell, is first taken aback by my noting her jazz/R&B linkup, but mulls it over and agrees. "I think it's a fair statement to say that in recent years we certainly have reached out to more R&B performers and have given them a venue." However, she sees her mission more in terms of presenting the totality of jazz in historical terms — what's happening now and what's still happening from back then:

- "We like to take pride in [that] we're cross-generational. People who had never heard Lionel Hampton strike one vibe have now heard him, love him, and come back every year saying, 'God, I hope Lionel's gonna be here again!' And it's wonderful! The parents say, 'Wow, I couldn't get you to listen to one of his albums at home, but here is live and in front of you and you're going crazy!' We like to being able to introduce the classic jazz artists to these younger kids.

  "Certainly there's a place for 'all of the above' because there was once a time when jazz first started that your traditional jazz artists would listen to a Louis Armstrong and say, 'What is this syncopated stuff that he's playing? That's not jazz; this is jazz!' Or listen to a Miles Davis, even before his 'Bitches' Brew' album, and argue.

  "But when the last chapter is written on jazz (which I'm sure won't be for many generations to come), I think we're going to find that jazz [has been] a revolutionary kind of music — and I mean that in a 'revolving' sense. That's part of its charm, if you like. It's a good thing that it's always evolving, that it's always changing, and that there's always room for the classics in jazz."

Bell came to jazz through her father who played with Duke Ellington for many years and went on to get a Ph.D. in the subject of jazz as a classical art form. One legendary NORWALK appearance by Ellington's band gained young Bell access to backstage where she got to meet Joe Williams. Since taking over the producer's reigns in '81, one of the first calls Bell makes each year is to Williams. "If he is available," she exclaims, "he is there! He does it because he believes in the foundation, the work that it does in providing scholarships for students across the country... He's just a great performer."

A lineup ranging from Freelon to Williams, support from record companies and corporations, PSAs from 32 radio stations across six states, and the efforts of 200 volunteers help create what seems less like a concert than one huge reunion for 7,000 family members of all ages. Indeed, Bell cites "one family who says they have their family reunion every year here. It's like 30 of them who come without fail — they get their area, and they're there!"

Bell reciprocates the artists' generosity by putting them on a virtual pedestal and catering to their every need while on site. Her checklist would prove instructive to any festival promoter:

- "We have our staff of volunteers there to unload, get all their equipment up, get them into their dressing rooms. If they want to do a quick run-through, we have a rehearsal room where they can do that. We have an all-day luncheon buffet. We make sure [that] if they have family or friends traveling with them, we take care of them. We have a tent for the performers so they can have their own private area. If they want to be interviewed by the press, we make it happen. If they don't, we make sure it doesn't happen.

  "Whether you're a side man or the main talent, it doesn't matter to us, we give you the same VIP treatment. If you need an ironing board and iron, [laughs] we not only have that, we have someone who's happy to iron your suit for you. We just sort of cover the whole gamut for them.

  "So when you have a musician who comes to our jazz concert, has played their heart and soul out, has not been paid a dime for their efforts and says to me, 'Robin, this is the best festival I've been to; count me in next year,' you know they're talking about the respect that the musician is given," Bell remarks, "because we certainly do respect our jazz artists in every possible way."

And their R&B artists, too.

My wife and I dashed down from the PORTSMOUTH JAZZ FESTIVAL (Portsmouth, NH — see chapter) **Festival** earlier in the afternoon just in time to catch an absolute happening — the last half-set from <u>Lionel</u> **Review** <u>Hampton and his Big Band</u>.

The joint was jumpin' as what remained of the well-dressed gathering of black middle-class families revelled in the sensational showmanship and unrelenting rhythms of Hampton's huge crew. Just as Bell described, most of those dancing before the stage were twenty-somethings who just wouldn't let Hampton quit. He reciprocated by carrying on his encore, "Flying Home," for what seemed like forever, directing his horn section to strut back and forth across the stage like in film clips I've seen of Jimmy Lunceford's band. "Rhythm is my business!"

As we gloried in Hampton's closing grooves amidst the richness of the scene, I was immediately transported back to the big-band heyday. Hearing it live, loud, and hot — not on scratchy recordings, but by real masters in the flesh — made it instantly clear to me how jazz was capable of boogying ballrooms of up to 5,000 war-era jitterbuggers at a clip. It's irresistible dance music — a point I hope some "classic jazz" mothballers don't forget!

On-site parking's at a premium, so plan to be there early if you have special requirements. **Attendance** Otherwise, there are shuttle buses from the lots at nearby Perkin-Elmer Corp., as well as from the **Tip** local train station. Klondike Sound assures excellent acoustics throughout the spacious main lawn, but those coveting stage-front should join the cue beginning around 8:30 a.m. Bring the family, pack a picnic, and lay way, way back.

"I would plan to stay for the weekend," offers Bell. "Norwalk has so much to offer as a city." She **Travel Tip** lists township beaches, parks, restaurants, the aquarium, and the entire South Norwalk waterside as worthy family diversions.

~　　~　　~

# Woodbury's World-Beat

ALTERNATIVE SKATEBOARD FESTIVAL, Woodbury, CT
    Late May
    Alternative and College Rock

REGGAE FESTIVAL, Woodbury, CT
    Late June
    Reggae, Ska and Caribbean

**WORLD MUSIC FESTIVAL**, Woodbury, CT
    Middle July
    Reggae, Ska and Caribbean
    ***Attended***

SOUTHERN FRIED FESTIVAL, Woodbury, CT
    Middle August
    Blues and Traditional R&B

**Introduction**  Promoter of the WORLD MUSIC FESTIVAL, Rod Taylor, was in the mood of another Rod — Rodney Dangerfield, that is. "No respect!" Perhaps I caught him on an off-moment as the falling January snow brought this owner of the Woodbury Ski Area plenty of skiiers, but also an unending stream of distractions. He'd also just finished a four-week court battle with the township to expand his summer festival schedule, running late May through middle August, from once-a-month to once-every-two-weeks, and was awaiting a decision.

Despite his legal hassles, Taylor's resolve remained unshaken: "It's because I love the music and I love what I do. If you feel you're right, just like Bob Marley said, 'Stand up for your rights!' I feel we need a fair share and it's not fair."

It's a shame because few others have done as much to maintain New England's reputation as a reggae hotbed over the past two decades. Taylor's been producing concerts at this site since '72, and reggae and world-beat shows since '77. Probably, he was among the first in the U. S. to combine the two genres. Taylor's personally responsible for the American debuts of a number of name acts, including Aswad, Culture, Majek Fashek, and King Sunny Ade. Concert videos from his self-produced series of 25 tapes, stretching back to '86, have been broadcast worldwide.

Taylor's influence even extends modestly into the rock world. As he claims:

- "I brought music in here that nobody else did. I brought in Blues Traveler, Spin Doctors, Phish, and all these other 'Grateful-Dead' bands who are big now, huge. When they played here, they were nobody. So I kinda' feel like I'm the place to come to expose new bands. There's something about the people who come here who are very instrumental in pushing, or starting, a new vibe or new type of music... I'm kinda' like a showcase here for rising stars, and I feel like I've been a big part of it.

"One of these days," he sighs, "they'll give the promoter more credit."

Taylor's voyage into the warm waters of reggae music evolved, interestingly enough, from being on the U. S. Olympic Ski Team from '67 through '71. "I've been involved with different cultures from all over the world through ski racing," he notes, explaining how he always had an international contingent for parties he'd throw that would number up to 1,000 guests at a clip.

Upon retiring from active competition, he purchased the Woodbury Ski Area in '72, and began producing various concerts on site during the summer. Five years later his then-girlfriend, "a kinda' hip California type," as Taylor describes her, suggested reggae music.

"Reggae," Taylor replied, "You know, black music? In Woodbury, CT? What, are you nuts! Who the hell's gonna' come out in the country, here?" Yet he said he'd always loved reggae — the beat, the dancing, the culture, the unity and religious aspects — and soon relented.

The first time, Taylor recalls:

- "I got all the West-Indian community in Hartford involved. I got anybody I could think of who knew anything about reggae and asked them, 'Hey, I want to do this big festival and would they help me out?' Basically, I gave [away] all the tickets for free...trying to be the nice guy, the ambassador. I was amazed how many people helped me out in the early days. Unfortunately, it rained, but [for] the rain date it was incredible. I had more people than I had on any of my other concerts. I've been doing it ever since.

"People liked coming here because they felt so secure, and they felt like everybody, black and white together, was [enjoying] such an easy, great, friendly atmosphere."

Among his many highlights, Taylor cites four shows in particular:

- Aswad's first U. S. appearance [in '86], joined by Burning Spear and another act;

- Culture's first U. S. appearance, joined by Third World, Pato Banton, The Killer Bees, and Arriva Posse;

- Reuniting Israel Vibrations, together with The Wailers and Yellowman;

- King Sunny Ade's first U. S. appearance [in '87], joined by Max Creek and another band.

About Ade, he marvels, "Nobody had ever heard of [him], but I'll never forget, he had a 35-to-40-piece band here with dancers. I mean, oh, it was just an incredible show!"

It all harkens Taylor back to "that Olympic feeling," as he calls it, although it seems he has to leave town to experience much appreciation: "It's the greatest when I go to Jamaica and people come and say, 'You're that promoter from Connecticut, aren't you? You're an amazing man; those shows are the best. I wait every year for those videos — you come up with the greatest ideas!' They just can't believe I do it.

"I always get many, many compliments down there," Taylor glows, "and they make me feel really, really good."

**Festival Review**

Forget about reggae music, Woodbury appears an unlikely place even for a ski area. You reach the rather-homey slopes by passing through a Colonial village right out of a Norman Rockwell illustration, and following a rocky brook up a modest hill. A state trooper directs you to a parking lot, you cross back over the two-lane blacktop and you're there — "reggae central" on the steep, grassy slopes.

The crowd for the WORLD MUSIC FESTIVAL was an interesting mix of funky young neo-hippies, middle-aged ex-hippies, and a fair smattering of just-plain-folks. There were even a few West Indians. My wife and I parked ourselves down beside just such a well-dressed family who occupied their blankets like a pride of lions contentedly surveying their cultural domain. Frisbees flew, footballs threw, and volleyballs did what volleyballs do, although our attention was drawn more to one Jamaican vendor who dexterously wielded a machete to serve up fresh milk from a hacked coconut, plus a slice of sugar cane to stir it up. Jah rastafari!

We settled down in the sun-drenched day to bask in the headlining set of African reggae star, Lucky Dube.

**Artist Mini-Review**

Lucky Dube. Dube thanked the welcoming crowd for making him "feel like a natural man" before proceeding into a lengthy show — remarkable, since the late-day sun was beating directly into his face and cooking the enclosed wooden stage like a Jamaican hot pot.

Dube and crew proved irresistible. Within three-to-four songs they had the base of the slope filled with dancing dervishes whirling up dust. "Groove it and they will come." The band's heavy, edgy beat and tasteful synth licks, along with Dube's smooth, but impassioned, vocals, extended the perfect invitation to party. If you weren't sure how to join in, you could follow the separate choreographies of either his backup singers on the left, or the horn section on the right. The singers were especially animated on "We're Here to Serve," while the horns dropped into intricately-flailing zombie steps on an extended "Frankenstein."

Like so many before him on this very stage, Dube simply served notice that a rising star was born. Catch his fire if he comes nearby you.

**Attendance Tip** Taylor has very rough camping on site, although you may prefer to take him up on his offer of half-price specials at area hotels. Call him for reservations and, who knows, you'll likely be staying at the same place as the musicians! In '92, fans got to hang out afterward with the national "World Beat Tour": Jimmy Cliff, Burning Spear, Majek Fashek, Zulu Spear, and others.

**Travel Tip** "Woodbury is famous all over the world for antiques," Taylor explains, "but it's also famous for all their restaurants. There's got to be 30 restaurants in town."

About Woodbury, itself, Taylor lauds its small-town historic character as well as the recreational opportunities: "We have tennis courts here, fishing, bungee-jumping, a skateboard park, bicycling, hiking trails — all kinds of things. It's a great place to just get away."

**See Also** The other three festivals listed in the heading above are all part of the summer series Taylor is fighting his town fathers to expand. Themes vary, so call ahead for current schedules, "mon."

~     ~     ~

# Hartland's Singer-Songwriters

**HARTLAND FOLK FESTIVAL**, East Hartland, CT
   Middle July
   Modern Folk
   ***Attended***

O. K. folks, pop quiz:

Introduction

- What was the best song on Lacy J. Dalton's comeback album, *Survivor*? Guy Clark's "Old Friends" (of course, the Paul Simon cover is awfully strong, too).

- What was the best number on Vince Gill's breakthrough disc, *When I Call Your Name*? Guy Clark's "Rita Ballou" (although I'm also partial to several of Gill's originals there).

- What was the best tune on Foster and Lloyd's influential debut, *Faster and Llouder*? The one co-written with Guy Clark, "Fair Shake."

And so on...

You get the picture, by now, about the songwriting prowess of Guy Clark. Yet rarely do you find this craggy-voiced dean of the Austin scene, and mentor to Lyle Lovett and Rodney Crowell among others, booked into modern folk festivals up this-a-way. Clark's headlining appearances at the '91 and '92 lineups of the HARTLAND FOLK FESTIVAL should help clue you into its iconoclastic organizer, folk-singer Bruce Pratt, and what makes his unassuming showcase one of the tops around.

"I see a difference in this festival in that we really try and focus on the music," Pratt explains. "I hope it's the most laid-back in terms of atmosphere, and the most charged in terms of performance, that people get to go to in a year."

Pratt also has a hand in several other folk projects, including HONEY HIDE THE BANJO, IT'S THE FOLK NEXT DOOR (Hartford, CT — see chapter), and a winter concert series at nearby Roaring Brook Nature Center. His programming interests are two-fold: (a) to promote quality, typically at the expense of quantity; and (b) to develop new audiences for folk music, often among the country crowd where artists like Clark are more commonly associated. The two concerns are related, he believes, in that if you're taking the time to recruit new listeners, you'd better give 'em your best shot when they get there. If this means flying in the face of folk-community back-scratching and political-correctness, well, that's too damn bad!

Here's how the refreshingly outspoken Pratt utilizes bookings like Clark's to bait converts:

- "I knew Guy Clark was a pro and a great songwriter and a good guy to hang out with. I said to him, 'Man, I really wanted you here because I wanted the people who listen to the radio to hear you. They'll play more of you if you're comin' and I want people to see the connection between what you do with what these other guys do. The connection is there!'

  "He said, 'Oh hell, it's just all music.' I said, 'Yeah, but Guy, there are people who will drive down the road listenin' to commercial country music stations in Connecticut and they occasionally get a little Guy Clark, or they get a cover of a song you've written. I want them to start goin' to coffee houses, not just line dances, because I want to expand that part of the audience. I wanna get those people in.'

  "So I got free advertising, PSA's, on some commercial stations, because I went to them and said, 'C'mon, I got f___in' Guy Clark, don't tell me your audience doesn't know about this.' And they'd say, 'Well, I don't know how many really know him, but geez, on Saturday night when we get away from the format, you know, maybe we could play 'Home Grown Tomatoes,' or 'Desperadoes Waiting for a Train,' or 'L. A. Freeway,' or somethin' like that.' And I'd say, 'Good, do it!'

"Fred Koller [in '89 and '90] was my other sort-of outlaw from the folk thing, because I knew that people were gonna' say, 'Oh, I know that song! He wrote that?' I also knew that Fred would get up there with his incredible vocal style (which I happen to think is wonderful) and would do stuff that nobody was expecting. When he did 'Little Green Buttons,' the *Hartford Courant* reporter who was there [made that] the lead for his article. I knew when he did that, the next year there would be people coming to my festival who had never gone to a folk music festival before because they were afraid it was going to be 'little brown ducks swimming in the water.'

"...The reason The Nields are opening and closing this year is because they're the only Connecticut-based group that's bringin' in hundreds and hundreds of new people. I love doin' shows with them, because I know there are gonna' be people there who have never heard of me, yet live within 10 miles of where I've spent most of my life [laughs].

"And that's why I got a guy like Guy. He was up until six in the mornin' on my deck listen' to everybody's songs. That was his second year here... Guy told me that he liked HARTLAND' better than any festival he'd ever played for one reason. He said, 'This is all about songs! It's all about people havin' a good time [and] there ain't one snotty sonuvabitch here!'"

**Festival Review** Talk about a one-horse town! East Hartland is little more than a pretty postcard of rural New England — one road, a few churches, a few houses, and the East Hartland Volunteer Fire Department which has served as the beneficiary since the HARTLAND FOLK FESTIVAL's inception in '87.

Oh, and there's a tiny swatch of green grass off the town square which might've otherwise held a bake sale, or a flea market, or a clam bake, or some other fundraiser. Instead, it's been hosting a powerhouse lineup of singer-songwriters for its relaxed gathering of a thousand townsfolks or so.

Credit Pratt who called upon his fishing buddy, folk-singer Greg Brown, to headline the first event. That one turned a profit, thanks to the all-volunteer crew of 30, and has averaged a $7,000 contribution ever since.

I was on a tear that also had me in Philadelphia and Baltimore that same day in '92 and couldn't stay for Pratt's big guns. I was able to take in the first few acts, however, including a bright, young (and tall) talent, Ellen Cross. Pratt thinks highly of this Boston-based folk-singer, managed by Passim's Bob Donlan, and cites another opening cameo to ponder:

* "The second year we had Shawn Colvin open up the show and [John] Gorka showed up. He was getting ready to pay, and I said, 'Nahh, John, come on in for chrissake; you don't have to pay.' He said, 'Can I go up and sing a couple with Shawn?' And I said, 'Yeah, sure!'" [laughs] And that's the way the festival opened that morning! People didn't know at that time really who either of them were, but I'd seen them and said, 'Well, they're good; they're gonna' be goin' somewhere.'"

Moral? Get there early! Also bring a blanket and some sunscreen and don't be surprised if the performers hang out beside you during the day. (Pratt says, "If I find my performers not mingling with the crowd, I ask them what's wrong with them!") Then soak up one good song after another.

**Artist Mini-Review** Ellen Cross. A gangly brunette wearing a purple tank top and cut-offs, Cross connected with the assembling few through her appealingly shy demeanor and full-ranging talents. Vocally, she alternated plainspoken vocals with a near-belting expressiveness. Lyrically, her songs combined introspective moods and interior conversations but in an unforced, natural manner. My favorite among her five originals is "So Long Ago," which utilizes jazzy guitar chords to contrast the first promising words of a relationship with it's currently deteriorating status. Fresh, accessible, promising!

Pratt: "People came up to me and said, 'Who was that tall girl from Boston; she was really good.' She's just one of those [examples] where they don't have to be known, they just have to be good."

"If they're comin' up on Friday and plannin' on spendin' the night somewhere, they should definitely go to the Mark Twain house in Hartford," Pratt offers. "It's one of the greatest guided tours I've ever been on." **Travel Tip**

Pratt also points his weekend travelers southeast to the Mystic Village coastal area or northwest to Massachusetts' Berkshire mountains. When Greg Brown's on the bill, however, Pratt leads him the next day to "some of the premier fly fishing in all of New England located right down the road on the Farmington River." One-day licenses are available for you anglers.

Connecticut may have more "family" folk festivals than any other state in the country. **See Also** (HARTLAND's had the word "family" in it's title before Pratt tired of receiving droves of demo tapes from whom he describes as "bad children's performers.") Their lineups may not be as high-powered as HARTLAND's, but most offer up their charms in equally intimate and picturesque surroundings. Check **Connecticut Festival Listings**.

~     ~     ~

# Hartford's Jazz, I

**RAW JAZZ FESTIVAL**, West Hartford, CT
Late July
Alternative Jazz
***Attended***

**Introduction** "You missed something special," crows Wil K. Wilkins, who directs the **RAW JAZZ FESTIVAL** for Real Art Ways [RAW], a longtime alternative-arts presenter. He's been scolding me for splitting before the headlining set of fiery avant-guitarist Sonny Sharrock (since passed away, sad to say), who apparently tore up the postage stamp-sized park hidden amidst an ethnic enclave in West Hartford.

"Sonny's stuff was just phenomenal; one of the best concerts I've ever seen in my life," Wilkins carries on. "He really got into the whole neighborhood setting — the kids in the swings, everybody playing ball. He really got into it and was just groovin'. It was really great!"

To get that kind of a rise out of the ordinarily droll, urbane Wilkins is noteworthy. Since moving up from New York City four years ago to help run RAW, Wilkins has presided over emerging artists from a variety of progressive mediums: performance art, film and video, visual arts, public installations, and spoken word. He's seen it all on the outskirts.

Yet Wilkins' praise of Sharrock is unequivocal and could best illustrate his organization's non-commercial mission:

- "It's interesting because Sonny does this stuff that's very lyrical — you could almost listen to it and think, 'Wow, it's just kinda' mainstream or middle-of-the-road or something.' Then he'll just rip the sound out of his guitar, you know? He's amazing. He's at a point where he's integrated so many different sounds and effects into his style that he's really unclassifiable."

RAW began in '75 as a living and working space for artists, gradually transforming itself into a presenter of artistic disciplines, which Wilkins describes as "new, innovative, experimental." One such discipline has been avant-garde/new music from both classical and jazz camps. RAW hosted the roving NEW MUSIC AMERICA (see Varied Sites, VAR, Early October) in '84, to name one of its new music bookings.

"Particularly in the early years you'd see people like Phillip Glass, Terry Reilly, and Steve Reich performing to audiences of, like, 30 people in an upstairs loft in Hartford," Wilkins relates. "Also there's been a commitment to free jazz. If you look at people like Reggie Workman, Henry Threadgill, David Murray, Oliver Lake — all these people back in the late '70s/early '80s — they were all performing here."

Since '79 RAW has showcased these jazz lights in its annual mini-festival weekend — two main acts per afternoon. Its past festival names have included RAW AUGUST JAZZ and the ORNETTE COLEMAN FESTIVAL. Dates have changed from August to its current fourth weekend in July. Sites have moved from the original RAW loft, to the State House lawn, to its present Day Playground across the street from the two converted mills that house RAW and the *Hartford Advocate*, respectively. The festival was cancelled in '92 when it's annual funding source inexplicably passed it by.

"That sent me into a certain level of rage that I actually still have not recovered from," deadpans Wilkins. "[However], I think quality is the common thread that holds it all together, and a certain amount of daring, appreciating the fact that people can listen to music which isn't necessarily what they would hear on their radio, and appreciate it."

Wilkins credits such characteristic early bookings as Don Byron, Brandon Ross, Ed Blackwell, John Zorn, Ed Harris, Zena Parkins, Steve Coleman, Walt Dickerson, Ellen Christie, and Thomas Chapin for the longevity, not just of the jazz festival, but of RAW in general:

- "The fact that RAW was able to continue [from it's early NEA and CETA funding days] was not just a matter of luck. There's historically been some really daring programming by RAW that has paid off in the long run. If they had been presenting middle-of-the-road artists who nobody really cared about, they wouldn't exist right now. Instead, they've been presenting cutting-edge artists who nobody really cared about [chuckles], but it looked better in retrospect. It looked like you were taking a chance."

A multi-instrumentalist on the side, Wilkins considers himself "more of a cultural agitator... I've always been involved at sort of the juncture of art and social work, or something like that. I've always been interested in how art in various ways can help people communicate with each other."

These interests led him to a one-year stopover at New York City's eclectic, multi-cultural CENTRAL PARK SUMMERSTAGE [see chapter], from which he's taken programming cues:

- "One of the things that 'SUMMERSTAGE does quite well is that there's a diversity of programming and they mix things up real well — you're never sure exactly what you're going to get there, but you know it's going to be good. The two acts that you might have on the same day aren't necessarily similar to each other [but] there's some relationship.

  "I'm not really sure what makes something jazz and what doesn't. I think some of the most interesting music being made today is stuff that really doesn't fit into that pat classification of 'Oh, this is jazz; this is rock.' Young composers growing up today, they're all influenced by rock and roll and have been for years. That comes out often in people's music, and that's what makes it interesting — that change, you know, the fact you're not playing things necessarily the way people have played them in the past."

The **RAW JAZZ FESTIVAL**'s unlikely, informal, intimate setting presents Wilkins with the perfect laboratory for his experiments in cross-pollinating genres and audiences.

- "To be in a working-class neighborhood puts a very special light on everything we do. It's easier to be a snob when you're in a neighborhood where nobody lives. But when people live around you, and you're part of the community, I think that it's incumbent upon you to participate in a way that's respectful of the people who live around there. It's been very positive to be in this neighborhood."

**Festival Review**

O. K., O. K., so I had to scoot back to New York City and miss Sonny Sharrock's set at West Hartford's **RAW JAZZ FESTIVAL**. At least I managed a few of the guitar-driven excursions of Marc Ribot and Quartet in one of the closest, humblest festival environments I've experienced.

Day Playground was a tiny wedge of shaded blacktop, about a half-block wide. You could lean back on your plastic padded chair and see-saw from kids swinging on your left, world-class avant-jazz in the middle, and kids shooting hoops on your right. Talk about local flavor, the playing didn't stop the entire time! This easy scene drew a laid-back mix of intent jazz heads from all over plus curious passers-by. Sodas for a buck and parking for three were the only optional charges I witnessed for this especially interesting afternoon.

**Artist Mini-Review**

<u>Marc Ribot and Quartet</u>. Unlike compatriot guitarist Bill Frisell, who's identified by his trademark slippery sound, Ribot seems to re-invent himself for every gig. He performs around New York City's downtown scene with various assemblages depending upon how angry/experimental/ethnic he wants to play. This one split the middle with his longtime aggro pounders, drummer Jim Pugliese and percussionist Christine Bard, balancing the more lyrical Sebastian Steinberg on bass and Chris Wood on guitar.

Everything about Ribot bespeaks calm conflict. He sported a haircut that was close-cropped, but unkempt; a purple silk shirt, but with the tail out; and gray designer chinos, but over black Converse. His restless compositions and solo lines wavered from otherwordly prettiness to edgy nastiness, typically within the same piece. Fortunately, his set exhibits sufficient respect for jazz tradition to sidestep the unrelenting honk-and-screech which can plague this kind of experimentation.

Ribot began with an avant riff on Albert Ayler's child-like "Bells" before segueing into a tangled, tortured spin on Gershwin's "Summertime," featuring his own hilariously bent vocal.

After some faux Jetsons noodling, he cut in a snippet of Hendrix's "The Wind Cries Mary," before traveling onto staccato blasts of industrial dislocation. A soft guitar solo then gave way to a dysfunctional drum breakdown that climaxed in a raging anthem, "Human Sacrifice."

Whew!

I kept imagining Ribot's crew opening for Smashing Pumpkins, Soundgarden, or another of the more progressive grunge-rock bands. I don't know if it'll ever happen, but this would be the perfect venue for it. Hey possible sponsors, any takers?

**Attendance Tip** "Arrive early," suggests Wilkins. "Bring a blanket, bring something to eat, and bring something for me."

**Travel Tip** "It's a terrible hardship, but we're the most interesting thing in Hartford," Wilkins sighs, tongue-in-cheek. "No offense to all my colleagues." He does suggest two clubs, 8/80 and City's Edge, for hanging out plus the Mark Twain House for daytime cavorting with the ghost of the famed author. The immediate neighborhood offers a variety of unpretentious ethnic eateries, according to Wilkins, while a country drive through northwestern Connecticut can lead you to what he anticipates will be "an exquisite restaurant opening up just outside of Northampton, MA, called The Squire's Smoke and Game Club."

**See Also** The weekend after the **RAW JAZZ FESTIVAL** offers the combined GREATER HARTFORD FESTIVAL OF JAZZ/HARTFORD MEGA! WEEKEND (see chapter) — a great bookend for weekday sightseeing.

~ ~ ~

# Hartford's Jazz, II

GREATER HARTFORD FESTIVAL OF JAZZ FUNDRAISER, Hartford, CT
> Middle February
> Modern Jazz

WEST INDIAN INDEPENDENCE CELEBRATION WEEK/HARTFORD MEGA! WEEKEND,
Hartford, CT
> Late July to Early August
> Reggae, Ska and Caribbean

**GREATER HARTFORD FESTIVAL OF JAZZ/HARTFORD MEGA! WEEKEND**, Hartford, CT
> Late July to Early August
> Modern Jazz
> ***Attended***

I caught a few moments with Paul Brown, Artistic Director of the GREATER HARTFORD FESTIVAL OF **Introduction**
JAZZ and a wonderfully genial spokesman for the genre, just before he was to meet with a
Japanese concert promoter. Brown, a jazz bassist who's played with Walter Bishop, John Hicks,
John Stubblefield, Johnny Coles, Bill Hardman, Junior Cook, and many others, explained to me
how leading American jazz musicians now make up to 80% of their annual income from touring
Japan.

"You know, you're never famous in your own hometown; you're just one of the boys,"
Brown muses:

- "There's never been a great respect for jazz in this country, [but] go to the Orient, man, I
  tell ya', I never play to an empty house. I don't care where it is, when it is, what the weather is, the place is packed! They've got records over there in Japan that I forgot about. I'm
  not a Ron Carter, but in Japan they know me from all the records I'm on — you can't buy
  'em here anymore."

Fortunately, Brown's never given up on his adopted hometown. Since '67 he's recruited
the finest from among his many musician friends to perform at his MONDAY NIGHT JAZZ SERIES in
downtown Hartford's expansive Bushnell Park.

In '92 Brown helped team up with the "powers-that-be" from various local government
and civic organizations and whipped up a three-day jazz feast for the last weekend in July. The
city responded by wrapping an entire extravaganza, HARTFORD MEGA! WEEKEND, around the
event. Starting early Wednesday morning, there's a continuing procession of cultural, musical and
family events stretching through to late Sunday evening. Brown's ongoing concert series even
extends the festivities until Monday night.

The music genres of HARTFORD MEGA! WEEKEND run the gamut — daytime concerts
around town feature polka, marching band, folk dance, and something called "Vegas-style."
There's also a two-day "Family Folk Festival" at Elizabeth Park plus a one-day "West Indian
Festival" at the Main Street Market that wraps up the WEST INDIAN INDEPENDENCE CELEBRATION
WEEK.

Brown's modern jazz reigns supreme, however. He organizes each night's offerings
around a theme. Here are samples from 1993:

- Friday: big band (McCoy Tyner Big Band, Collective Expression) and local dixieland (Dixie 4 + 1);

- <u>Saturday</u>: Latin jazz (Arturo Sandoval Quintet, Hilton Ruiz Sextet) and locals (Jimmy Green Quartet, Artists Collective Youth Jazz Orchestra, Greater Hartford Academy of Performing Arts Jazz Ensemble, Hall High Quintet);

- <u>Sunday</u>: "N'Awlins" funk (Dirty Dozen Brass Band, Bruce Katz Band) and local gospel (Selena and The Voices of Joy, Celebration Community Choir);

- <u>Monday</u>: small groups, national (Jimmy Heath Combo with Slide Hampton and Winard Harper) and local (Kitty Kathryn with the late Bobby Buster).

"This gives all the areas a chance to be exposed," offers Brown:

- "It gives the local musicians that are playing in that theme a chance to perform with some biggies, their idols. They have their idols and I talk with them and see who they'd like to have up here. I try to get them to come up so they can perform on the same stand with them. It helps to bring the people out, and it helps to get the money. Sometimes, you run into a foundation that likes a certain thing and they'll support a certain kind of music."

If you sniff at the prospect of locals sharing the stage with national headliners, Brown proudly cites such Hartford graduates as The Harper Brothers, Wallace Roney, Sue Terry, Thomas Chapin, and Ricky Ford who were all first exposed on Bushnell Park stages. He boasts that festival-goers are "going to see the very best to offer in this music, absolutely the best! And they'll always see some great local talent that aren't recorded but are really worth seeing and hearing."

Brown's got a special handle on this local pipeline from teaching jazz performance and history at the Greater Hartford Academy of Performing Arts for many years. Indeed, his Monday night concerts sprang from another teaching gig at the long-since-closed Garden Area Neighborhood Center.

Brown recalls:

- "I got married in New York and it wasn't happening for [my wife]. Somebody got killed in front of our door, and I said, 'I'm out of here!' Her parents lived in Glastonbury, so we just moved up here. I was trying to stay off the road and I started teaching at the University of Hartford. Max Roach and Jackie McLean and I and Archie Shepp had a group up here years ago called 'The Jazz Professors." Max was teaching up here [at UMass/Amherst], and Jackie had just started [at the U. of Hartford]. The festival just kind of mushroomed out of all that stuff.

"I stayed [at the U. of Hartford] a while, but then an organization in town hired me in a social-work status. After going out in the community, I found there was a need for kids to learn instruments. I started doing this in a storefront. When guys like Clifford Jordan would come through town, or Harold Vick, or Thad Jones — all the guys I worked with before I moved out of New York — they'd stop over and see me. Sometimes, we'd have a little session and the local guys started coming..."

"One day, I think it was Donald Byrd, he stayed with me all day, and we were just playing. He was helping me with my kids. Bobby Head was there that day, too — you know, the guy who wrote 'Sonny' — he was in town and stopped over. In fact, he stayed with me that week.

"They were all hanging out at the Center with me [when] somebody came in from City Hall and said, 'Why don't you take this out in the Park?' We thought about it and started talkin' to the guys. I said, 'Man, you're going to be in town with so-and-so. You do this concert out there and I'll get you some money, a little extra bread.' It went from that."

Of course, Brown underscored the word "little" as part of that financial phrase, explaining how he's been able to field fantastic lineups largely on the strength of his relationships and the musicians' willingness to support these community efforts. It's still run on a shoestring. One of Brown's favorite anecdotes stemmed from just such a desire to sacrifice on the part of one long-time series participant, the late Charles Mingus:

- "Mingus said one time he'd come here any time for me; anybody else has got to pay him! He'd always use my bass when he came here, too. I remember the first time he used it. He picked up my instrument — listen, Mingus was a big man and I had a very expensive instrument back then — he picked it up with one hand and kind of turned it around like a cello. He said, 'The strings are too low. 'Gotta let 'em up.' I was looking at him. Then he said, 'Don't worry, I ain't gonna' hurt it.' I said, 'Mingus, I don't care. Play it, man! This instrument will never sound that good again when I'm playing it.'

- "Anytime he'd come in town, he'd call me. If I had a gig, I'd say, 'Shucks, 'can't play this gig, Mingus needs my bass.' He was a beautiful cat, man — I loved him as a person. Just having people like that willing to give up some bigger money elsewhere to help make this happen is significant."

Just as significant for Brown is the impact the festival is having in promoting the city, countering negative stereotypes that sprouted from Hartford's recent economic downturn. "What this has done has made the area come alive. I live here! I don't want to see Hartford have a bad rep.," he exclaims:

- "I think the arts are one thing that brings people together. You don't think about the other problems that people usually find in one another when the arts are there. People are enjoying stuff like that, and it really stops a lot of one-on-one problems. You go to an art exhibit and people are looking at the art, they don't care who's rubbing elbows. You're looking at a band and thousands of people are sitting there together, eating and listening to the music."

Brown points out that in 27 years of concerts he's never experienced one incident. Instead, he trumpets the family-orientation of concerts:

- "I'm on the air a lot during that period and I encourage people to bring their kids. You'd be surprised. I've had mothers come up to me and tell me, 'My dad brought me here when I was like 6 or 7, and now I'm bringing my kids here.' And it happens every year, it just cracks me up!"

**Festival Review**

Bushnell Park is an extraordinary urban space: a wide, lush sheet of grass flanked by ancient trees, rimmed by glass skyscrapers and backed by the gleaming, gold dome of the state capitol. It's Hartford's Central Park but without New York hassling your contemplation. "Cool quiet and time to think." I casually spread my blanket and nibbled my picnic dinner amidst the few thousand families who congregated for their Monday-night ritual of first-rate jazz for free.

After a fine opening set by a local combo, with the late Bobby Buster tinkling a soul-jazz organ behind vocalist Kitty Kathryn, The Jimmy Heath Combo took the stage:

**Artist Mini-Review**

The Jimmy Heath Combo: Don't you know that Brown had a pair of aces up his sleeve: longtime friend, Slide Hampton, on trombone plus local hero, Winard Harper, on drums. He rounded out the quintet with guitar and bass.

Heath on sax — all smiles in a knitted scull cap — clearly enjoyed the mellow setting, attentive audience and friendly interplay on stage. He took special delight in the inventive staccatos of young Winard's drumming, once doing a quick jump between breaks in appreciation.

Neither Heath nor Hampton indulged in "hot licks." Rather, they strung together seemingly endless lines that articulated the flow in handsome manners. Heath tended to climax in anthem notes after blowing smooth and full, while Hampton's playing — a revelation to me for it's incredible facility — leaned toward funk-flavored finishes. I could've listened to them groove together the whole balmy night!

**Travel Tip**

"See the town," advises Brown. "Come in, spend the day, maybe the day before. There are a lot of nice things going on, especially during the summer." Brown's area picks include the Mark Twain House ("very interesting") and the Gilette Castle ("really something to see"). For dining, he recommends Bloomfield's The Fishmarket — "Man, if you want some seafood really cooked well, that's my favorite watering hole."

**See Also**  Brown also hosts an annual GREATER HARTFORD FESTIVAL OF JAZZ FUNDRAISER deep in the heart of winter. Come summertime, though, and his **GREATER HARTFORD FESTIVAL OF JAZZ** sits in the middle of three solid weeks of Hartford jazz. The previous weekend there's the RAW JAZZ FESTIVAL in West Hartford (see chapter), while the outstanding GREAT CONNECTICUT TRADITIONAL JAZZ FESTIVAL in nearby East Haddam occurs the following weekend. Jazz styles aplenty!

~     ~     ~

*The Jimmy Heath Combo with Slide Hampton, Greater Hartford Festival of Jazz.*

# Connecticut Festival Listings

**Caveat**

Although the vast majority are festivals are reliable and predictable, all are subject to last-minute changes or cancellations. Accordingly, FESTPRESS is not responsible for any festival listing information that follows. Readers are well advised to contact festivals at least twice before preparing a festival vist: (a) once at least one or two months ahead of time; and (b) once more during the week of your visit for confirmation. Ask for a festival flyer or brochure to be mailed to you. Festival promoters usually are willing to comply, and the resulting literature may answer any questions you still have.

Restrictions:

| | | | | | |
|---|---|---|---|---|---|
| • Food and drink... | 1; | • Cameras... | 6; | • Motorcycles... | 11; |
| • Alcohol... | 2; | • Audio recording... | 7; | • Re-entry... | 12; |
| • Cans... | 3; | • Video recording... | 8; | • Other restrictions... | 13. |
| • Bottles... | 4; | • Children... | 9; | | |
| • Coolers... | 5; | • Pets... | 10; | | |

Secondary Genre[s]:

| | | | |
|---|---|---|---|
| • Variety, General... | VRGL; | • Bluegrass... | BLGS; |
| • Variety, Jazz & Blues... | VRJB; | • Modern Folk... | MFOL; |
| • Variety, Country & Bluegrass | VRCB; | • Traditional Folk... | TFOL; |
| • Variety, Folk & International | VRFI; | • Fiddle and Banjo Events... | FDDL; |
| • Modern Jazz... | MJAZ; | • Maritime... | MARI; |
| • Traditional Jazz & Ragtime... | TJAZ; | • Cajun and Zydeco... | ZYDC; |
| • Alternative Jazz... | AJAZ; | • Irish... | IRSH; |
| • Modern Rock and Pop... | MRCK; | • Jewish... | JWSH; |
| • Classic Rock and Oldies... | CRCK; | • Native American... | NATV; |
| • Alternative & College Rock | ARCK; | • Scottish... | SCOT; |
| • Hard Rock & Heavy Metal | HRCK; | • Modern Latin... | MLAT; |
| • Rap... | RAP; | • Traditional Latin... | TLAT; |
| • Modern R&B... | MR&B; | • African American... | AFRM; |
| • Blues and Traditional R&B... | TR&B; | • African... | AFRC; |
| • Acappella and Doo Wop... | ACAP; | • Brazilian & So. American... | BRZL; |
| • Modern Christian... | CHRS; | • Reggae, Ska & Caribbean... | RGGE; |
| • Black Gospel... | BGOS; | • Avant Garde & New Music... | AVNT; |
| • Southern & Bluegrass Gospel | SGOS; | • Cabaret... | CBRT; |
| • Traditional Gospel & Sings... | TGOS; | • Gay and Lesbian... | GYLS; |
| • Modern Country... | MC&W; | • Drum Corps & March. Bands | DRUM; |
| • Traditional Country... | TC&W; | • Fairs... | FAIR; |
| • Alt. Country & Rockabilly... | AC&W; | • Other Genres... | OTHR. |

**Note**

Wherever "Help!" appears readers are invited to answer the proceeding questions and/or provide updates. New festival listings that meet the criteria of this book certainly are welcome too! Please mail any current festival information you obtain — especially flyers or brochures — to FESTPRESS, P. O. Box 147, Glen Ridge, NJ 07028. *Thanks!*

KISS 95.7 ANNIVERSARY BIRTHDAY JAM, Hartford, CT
> Early Jan.
> Modern Rock and Pop

Since 1986. Benefits The AIDS Service Organizations of Greater Hartford. May move to fall date. **Days:** 1. **Site:** indoor. Hartford Civic Center. **Admission:** paid. **Daily entry:** $10 to $24. **Secondary genre[s]:** ARCK, **Acts:** national acts. **Sample day's lineup:** Duran Duran, Ru Paul, Weird Al Yankovic, James. **Contact:** WKSS-FM, 10 Columbus Boulevard, Hartford, CT 203-249-9577.


REGGAEFESTS, New Haven, CT
> Early Jan.
> Reggae, Ska and Caribbean

Approximately four times per year. Call for current dates. **Days:** 4. **Site:** indoor. Toad's Place, 300 York Street. **Admission:** paid. **Daily entry:** under $10. **Acts:** local acts. **Sample day's lineup:** Cool Runnings, Affinity, Reggae Culture. **Contact:** Toad's Place, 300 York Street, New Haven, CT 06511, 203-624-TOAD/772-4089.


GOSPEL FESTIVAL, Hartford, CT
> Middle Feb.
> Black Gospel

"Hallelujah!" -- Brochure. See other dates. **Days:** 1. **Site:** indoor. Charter Oak Cultural Center, 21 Charter Oak Avenue. **Admission:** paid. **Daily entry:** $10 to $24. **Acts:** regional acts, local acts. **Sample day's lineup:** Charley Storey and His All-Stars, True Light Gospel Singers, Inspirational Gospel Singers of Hartford with Jerry Latimer, Golden Voices of New Haven. **Contact:** Charter Oak Cultural Center, 21 Charter Oak Avenue, Hartford, CT 06106, 203-249-1207.


GREATER HARTFORD FESTIVAL OF JAZZ FUNDRAISER, Hartford, CT
> Middle Feb.
> Modern Jazz

Since 1991. **Days:** 1. **Site:** indoor. Sheraton Hotel, downtown. **Admission:** paid. **Daily entry:** $25 to $49. **Secondary genre[s]:** TR&B, **Acts:** national acts, regional acts, local acts. **Sample day's lineup:** Shirley Scott, Johnny Coles Trio, Allen Dawson, Paul Brown. **Contact:** Greater Hartford Festival of Jazz, 250 Constitution Plaza, Hartford, CT 06103, 203-525-4451 x236 **or:** Greater Hartford Festival of Jazz, 195 North Beacon Street, Hartford, CT 06105, 203-233-5105. .


JAZZ EXPOS, New Haven, CT
> Late Feb.
> Modern Jazz

Approximately four times per year. Also programs a two-act "New Orleans Jazz Festival" of traditional jazz and blues on Fat Tuesday. Call for current dates. **Days:** 4. **Site:** indoor. Toad's Place, 300 York Street. **Admission:** paid. **Daily entry:** under $10. **Acts:** local acts. **Sample day's lineup:** Collectively Speaking, Magic, Funkzilla, Mike Coppolla. **Contact:** Toad's Place, 300 York Street, New Haven, CT 06511, 203-624-TOAD/772-4089.


BLACK EXPO, New Haven, CT
> Middle Mar.
> African American

"Black to the future." Khalid Lum, New Haven Advocate. **Help!** A sample lineup? **Days:** 1. **Site:** indoor. New Haven Veterans Memorial Coliseum. **Secondary genre[s]:** RAP, BGOS, OTHR **Acts:** local acts. **Contact:** Elm City Nation, c/o New Haven Veterans Memorial Coliseum, 275 South Orange St., New Haven, CT 203-786-5970/772-4200.

## CONNECTICUT HISTORICAL SOCIETY'S INTERNATIONAL SPRING FESTIVAL, Hartford, CT
Early Apr.
Variety, Folk and International

**Help!** A sample lineup? **Days:** 1. **Site:** indoor. 1 Elizabeth Street. **Secondary genre[s]:** IRSH, SCOT, TLAT, BRZL, OTHR. **Acts:** local acts. **Sample day's lineup:** 5 acts. **Contact:** Connecticut Historical Society, 1 Elizabeth Street, Hartford, CT, 203-236-5621 **or:** Irish American Historical Society, 143 Haverford Street, Hamden, CT 06517, 203-248-6050.

## OLDE TYME FIDDLERS CONCERT, Sterling, CT
Middle Apr.
Fiddle and Banjo Events

**Help!** A sample lineup? **Days:** 1. **Site:** indoor. Ekonk Grange Hall, Route 49. **Admission:** paid. **Daily entry:** under $10. **Secondary genre[s]:** TFOL, **Acts:** local acts. **Contact:** Ekonk Grange Hall, Route 49, Sterling, CT 203-564-2401.

## COUNTRY JAMBOREES, New Haven, CT
Late Apr.
Modern Country

Approximately twice per year. Call for current dates. **Days:** 2. **Site:** indoor. Toad's Place, 300 York Street. **Admission:** paid. **Daily entry:** under $10. **Acts:** local acts. **Sample day's lineup:** Ray T. and The Triple T Band, Knee Deep, Gunsmoke. **Contact:** Toad's Place, 300 York Street, New Haven, CT 06511, 203-624-TOAD/772-4089.

## NUTMEG BLUEGRASS GET-TOGETHER, Burlington, CT
Middle May
Bluegrass

Since 1993. "Field picking encouraged!" -- Flyer. See other dates and sites. **Days:** 1. **Hours per day:** 7. **Site:** outdoor and indoor. Bristol Swedish Social Club, South Main Street. **Admission:** paid. **Daily entry:** under $10, $10 to $24. **Discounts:** multiple event or day passes, advance purchase discounts, **Acts:** national acts, local acts. **Sample day's lineup:** Traver Hollow, Grassroots, Shady Creek, Northern Bound, The Flatlanders. **Contact:** Connecticut River Valley Bluegrass Association, P. O. Box 246, Middlefield, CT 06455, 203-347-5007/237-3966.

## LEGENDS OF FOLK MUSIC, Westport, CT
Middle May
Modern Folk

Since 1994. See other dates. **Help!** One time only? **Days:** 1. **Site:** indoor. Westport Country Playhouse, 25 Powers Court. **Admission:** paid. **Daily entry:** $10 to $24. **Discounts:** advance purchase discounts, **Secondary genre[s]:** TR&B, **Acts:** national acts, regional acts, local acts. **Sample day's lineup:** Ramblin' Jack Elliott, Dave Van Ronk, Paul Geremia, Eric Von Schmidt, Bruce Pratt, Linda Clifford, Harvey Brooks, Gordon Titcomb. **Contact:** Sally's Place, 190 Main Street, Westport, CT 203-454-0303.

JAMBALAYA ON THE RIVER: SPRING RIVERBOAT FESTIVAL, Hartford, CT
Middle May to Late May
Cajun and Zydeco

Music cruises. May be switching to once-weekly format. **Days:** 9. **Hours per day:** 3. **Site:** outdoor. Harbor Park. **Admission:** paid. **Daily entry:** $25 to $49. **Secondary genre[s]:** CRCK, TR&B, **Acts:** national acts, regional acts, local acts. **Sample Series Lineup:** Day One: Magneatos; Day Two: Sleepy LaBeef, Zydeco Zombies; Day Three: Boozoo Chavis, Larry Willey and The Blues Talkers. **Contact:** Deep River Navigation Company, P. O. Box 382, River Street, Hartford, CT 06417, 203-526-4954.

TASTE OF SUMMER, Middletown, CT
Middle May
Modern Rock and Pop

"Red, White, Blue and Hot!" -- Advertisement. Club presents periodic multi-act "parties" throughout the summer on their outdoor "floating stage." Also hosts Springfest. **Help!** One time only? **Days:** 1. **Site:** outdoor. America's Cup, 80 Harbor Drive. **Admission:** paid. **Daily entry:** $10 to $24. **Acts:** local acts. **Sample day's lineup:** All the Voices, Savage Brothers Band, Dave and Charlie, Infinity, Bates Motel, Sean and Jamie Duo. **Contact:** America's Cup, 80 Harbor Drive, Middletown, CT 203-347-9999.

ALTERNATIVE SKATEBOARD FESTIVAL, Woodbury, CT
Late May
Alternative and College Rock

**Days:** 1. **Hours per day:** 7. **Site:** outdoor. Woodbury Ski Area, Route 47. **Admission:** paid. **Daily entry:** $10 to $24. **Discounts:** advance purchase discounts, **Acts:** national acts, local acts. **Sample day's lineup:** God Street Wine, Solar Circus, The Other Half, others. **Other merchandise:** 25 VHS recordings of past festivals -- all genres -- available via promoter. **Contact:** Woodbury Ski Area, Route 47, Woodbury, CT 06798, 203-263-2203.

HONEY, HIDE THE BANJO! IT'S THE FOLK NEXT DOOR, West Hartford, CT
Late May
Modern Folk

Since 1992. **Days:** 1. **Hours per day:** 12. **Site:** indoor. University of Hartford -- Wilde Auditorium and Harry Gray Center Courtyard -- 200 Bloomfield Avenue. **Admission:** paid. **Daily entry:** $10 to $24. **Restrictions:** 5, 10, **Secondary genre[s]:** TR&B, BGOS, AC&W, BLGS, TFOL, MARI, ZYDC, **Acts:** national acts, regional acts, local acts. **Sample day's lineup:** Amy Gallatin, Please and Thank You Band, Pete Lehndorf, Stan Sullivan, Paul Howard Band, Donna Martin, Dar Williams, Michael Blake, Don Sinetti, 5 Chinese Brothers, Gospel All Stars, Bruce Pratt, Dave Druillard, Zydeco Zombies, The Nields, Barbara Kessler, Jack Hardy, Eric Von Schmidt, Lui Collins, Grassroots, Delta Boogie, Dewey burns, Patrick McGinley, Joel Blumert, Storyville, Steven Nystrup, J. P. Jones, Dan Gardella, Robin Lawlor, Tangled Up In Blue, David Paton, McDonnell-Tane, Smith-Jones, Hugh Blumenfeld, Mark DeLorenzo, Jim Mercik, Marian Heyman, Ebin-Rose, Little City String Band, Gina Gunn, Old Paint, Ellen Cross, Catie Curtis. **Audio merchandise:** "The Folk Next Door"; "Honey, Hide the Banjo! It's the Folk Next Door Again..."; "Hoot: The Folk Next Door" (all on Uh-Oh Records). **Contact:** WWUH-FM, University of Hartford, West Hartford, CT 06117, 203-768-4703.

BLUE SKY MUSIC FEST, Wallingford, CT
Late May
Modern Folk

See other dates. **Help!** One time only? **Days:** 1. **Site:** outdoor. Oakdale Theater, 96 South Turnpike Road. **Acts:** local acts. **Sample day's lineup:** Colossal Olive, McDonnell-Tane, others. **Contact:** Oakdale Theater, 96 South Turnpike Road, Wallingford, CT 06492, 203-269-8721/265-1501.

## HARTFORD ADVOCATE'S BEST OF THE BANDS BASH, New Britain, CT
Late May
Variety, General

Since 1990. **Days:** 1. **Hours per day:** 7. **Site:** indoor. The Sting, 677 West Main Street. **Secondary genre[s]:** MJAZ, MRCK, CRCK, ARCK, HRCK, RAP, MR&B, TR&B, MC&W, MFOL, ZYDC, OTHR **Acts:** regional acts, local acts. **Sample day's lineup:** New England Jazz Ensemble, The Nields, Borderline, Eight to the Bar, Frogboy, Zydeco Zombies, Max Creek, Word of Mouth, Mr. Right, Crank, D-Law and The Bounty Hunters, Liquid Circus, Run 21, Physical Graffiti. **Contact:** Hartford Advocate, 100 Constitution Plaza, Hartford, CT 06103, 203-548-9300.

## SPRING FOLK MUSIC WEEKEND, Falls Village, CT
Late May
Traditional Folk

See other dates and sites. **Days:** 4. **Site:** outdoor and indoor. Camp Isabella Freedman. **Admission:** paid. **Daily entry:** $50 and over. **Discounts:** other discounts. **Acts:** local acts. **Sample day's lineup:** John Krumm, Helen Schneyer, Newton Street Irregulars, Joanne Davis, Bob Malenky, Ed Roffman. **Contact:** New York Pinewoods Folk Music Club, 31 West 95th Street, New York, NY 10025, 212-666-9605 **or:** New York Pinewoods Folk Music Club, 19 Dongan Place, #3B, New York, NY 10040, 212-942-2847.

## BLUEGRASS FESTIVAL, Woodstock, CT
Late May
Bluegrass

Since 1994. **Help!** A sample lineup? **Days:** 1. **Hours per day:** 9. **Site:** outdoor. Woodstock Valley Lodge, 73A Bungay Hill Road. **Admission:** paid. **Daily entry:** under $10. **Discounts:** advance purchase discounts, **Contact:** Municipal Cafe, 485 Main Street, Hartford, CT 06103, 203-527-5044/974-1040.

## LOBSTER FEST, Mystic, CT
Late May
Maritime

**Days:** 3. **Hours per day:** 12. **Site:** outdoor and indoor. Mystic Seaport Museum, 50 Greenmanville Avenue. **Admission:** paid. **Daily entry:** under $10, $10 to $24. **Secondary genre[s]:** OTHR **Acts:** local acts. **Sample lineup:** Mystic Seaport Chanteymen, others. **Audio merchandise:** "Sea Chanteys and Forecastle Songs at Mystic Seaport" (Folkways). **Contact:** Mystic Seaport Museum, P. O. Box 6000, Mystic, CT 06355-0990, 203-572-0711/5350.

## FAIR HAVEN FESTIVAL, New Haven, CT
Early Jun.
Variety, General

"All kinds of music!" -- Pat Albee. **Days:** 2. **Hours per day:** 12. **Site:** outdoor. Quinnipiac River Park, South Front Street. **Secondary genre[s]:** MRCK, CRCK, TR&B, MLAT, **Acts:** local acts. **Sample day's lineup:** Gary and The Moodswingers, Doc Merlin Blues Band, Latin Power, The Shags, The Starlighters, James Velvet. **Contact:** Chenley Company, Grand Avenue, New Haven, CT 203-467-7719/7425.

**STRAWBERRY PARK BLUEGRASS FESTIVAL**, Preston, CT
> Early Jun.
> Bluegrass

Since 1978. **Days:** 3. **Hours per day:** 11. **Site:** outdoor. Strawberry Park Campground, Route 165 East. **Admission:** paid. **Daily entry:** $10 to $24, $25 to $49. **Discounts:** multiple event or day passes, **Acts:** national acts, regional acts, local acts. **Sample day's lineup:** Alison Krauss and Union Station, The Cox Family, Dry Branch Fire Squad, Warrior River Boys, Old Cold Tater, Breakaway, Cornerstone. **Contact:** Strawberry Park Campground, P. O. Box 830, Norwich, CT 06360, 203-886-1944.

**DIFFERENT TASTES OUTDOOR CRAWFISH AND ALLIGATOR FEAST**, Hartford, CT
> Early Jun.
> Cajun and Zydeco

Since 1992. **Days:** 1. **Site:** outdoor and indoor. The Municipal Cafe, 485 Main Street. **Secondary genre[s]:** TR&B, **Acts:** national acts, regional acts, local acts. **Sample day's lineup:** Zydeco Zombies, Larry Willy and The Blues Talkers, Blues Benders, Furnest and The Thunders. **Contact:** The Municipal Cafe, 485 Main Street, Hartford, CT 06103, 203-527-5044/232-5332.

**CITY FEST ARTS JUBILEE**, Middletown, CT
> Early Jun.
> Variety, General

**Days:** 1. **Hours per day:** 6. **Site:** outdoor. South Green, Main Street. **Secondary genre[s]:** MJAZ, MRCK, ACAP, TFOL, IRSH, OTHR. **Acts:** local acts. **Sample day's lineup:** Michael Cleary Band, Conscious Monkey, United Voices Chorale, Kitchen Ceili, Connecticut Youth Jazz Workshop, Dadon Dawadolma, Valley Street Chrous, Little City String Band, Middletown Stage Band. **Contact:** City of Middletown Commission on the Arts, 245 DeKoven Drive, P. O. Box 1300, Middletown, CT 06457-1300, 203-344-3520.

**BLOOMFIELD FESTIVAL**, Bloomfield, CT
> Early Jun.
> Variety, General

**Days:** 1. **Hours per day:** 7. **Site:** outdoor. Bloomfield Park/School Complex, 330 Park Avenue. **Secondary genre[s]:** MRCK, RGGE, OTHR. **Acts:** local acts. **Sample day's lineup:** Tony Harring and Touch, Island Riddims, others. **Contact:** Bloomfield Parks and Recreation Department, 330 Park Avenue, Bloomfield, CT 06002, 203-243-2923.

**RIVERSPLASH**, Simsbury, CT
> Early Jun.
> Variety, General

**Days:** 1. **Hours per day:** 9. **Site:** outdoor. Drake Hill Bridges area, Route 10. **Secondary genre[s]:** MJAZ, TR&B, MC&W, GYLS, OTHR. **Acts:** local acts. **Sample day's lineup:** Blues Blasters, Coherent Melodic Improvisation, Wild Horses, Cactus Rose with Robin Barnes, Pro Musica, Bill Hildebrandt, others. **Contact:** Farmington River Watershed Association, 749 Hopmeadow Street, Simsbury, CT 06070, 203-658-4442.

STERLING PARK CAMPGROUND BLUEGRASS FESTIVAL, Sterling, CT
Early Jun. to Middle Jun.
Bluegrass

See other dates. **Days:** 3. **Hours per day:** 10. **Site:** outdoor. Sterling Park Campground, 177 Gibson Hill Road. **Admission:** paid. **Daily entry:** under $10, $10 to $24. **Discounts:** multiple event or day passes, **Acts:** local acts. **Sample day's lineup:** Traver Hollow, Grass Roots, Northern Bound, Fred Pike and Sam Tidwell, Kennebec Valley Boys, Dyer Switch, Amy Gallatin and Still Waters, Sweet Meadow Boys. **Contact:** Sterling Park Campground, 177 Gibson Hill Road, Sterling, CT 06377, 203-564-8777.


TASTE OF HARTFORD, Hartford, CT
Early Jun. to Middle Jun.
Variety, General

"A festival of good taste!" -- Flyer. **Days:** 4. **Hours per day:** 9. **Site:** outdoor. Costitution Plaza, Main Street Market. **Secondary genre[s]:** MJAZ, TJAZ, MRCK, CRCK, BGOS, MC&W, TFOL, MLAT, BRZL, RGGE, OTHR. **Acts:** local acts. **Sample day's lineup:** Espada, People of Goodwill, Locomotion, Cuba Libre, C-Jammers band, Quetzal, Connecticut Opera Express, Mount Olive Baptist Church Gospel Choir. **Contact:** Greater Hartford Convention and Visitors Bureau, 1 Civic Center Plaza, Hartford, CT 06103, 800-446-7811.


MAIN STREET U. S. A., New Britain, CT
Early Jun.
Variety, General

Since 1976. **Days:** 1. **Hours per day:** 8. **Site:** outdoor. Central Park vicinity. **Admission:** free. **Secondary genre[s]:** MJAZ, CRCK, RAP, TR&B, BGOS, MC&W, SCOT, MLAT, TLAT, OTHR. **Acts:** local acts. **Sample day's lineup:** La Dynamica Orquestra, John Jesky Band, Tim Meyers and The Possee, Jazz Explorers, Steve Davis, Don Deplama and Selena, Tiny Joe, Fast Leslie, Brothers Proclaim Truth, Jeff Miller, Desert Skies, Son Del Barrio, Tight Brown Suit, others. **Contact:** Main Street U. S. A., Inc., P. O. Box 517, New Britain. CT 06050, 203-223-3586/229-1665.


CITIBANK TASTE OF STAMFORD, Stamford, CT
Early Jun. to Middle Jun.
Variety, General

Benefits Leukemia Society of America. **Days:** 2. **Site:** outdoor. Veteran's Park. **Secondary genre[s]:** MJAZ, MFOL, **Acts:** national acts, regional acts, local acts. **Sample day's lineup:** Aztec Two-Step, Robert James and The James Daniel Orchestra, Joyce DiCamillo Trio. **Contact:** Leukemia Society of America, 102 King's Highway East, Fairfield, CT 06430, 203-579-1628/359-4761.


BRASS VALLEY ETHNIC MUSIC FESTIVAL, Waterbury, CT
Middle Jun.
Variety, Folk and International

**Days:** 1. **Hours per day:** 9. **Site:** outdoor. Library Park. **Secondary genre[s]:** IRSH, MLAT, RGGE, OTHR. **Acts:** local acts. **Sample day's lineup:** Gina Braziliera, ONYX, Bristol Senior Center Band, Dancing Shamrocks, New Generations Band, Pablo Ortega and The Mongues, The Gondoliers, La Optima, others. **Contact:** Mattatuck Museum, 144 West Main Street, Waterbury, CT 06702, 203-753-0381.

### MAD MURPHY'S CAJUN, ZYDECO MUSIC AND ART FESTIVAL, East Haddam, CT
Middle Jun.
Cajun and Zydeco

Since 1993. **Days:** 1. **Hours per day:** 9. **Site:** outdoor and indoor. Sunrise Resort, Moodus. **Admission:** paid. **Daily entry:** $10 to $24. **Discounts:** advance purchase discounts, **Secondary genre[s]:** TR&B, **Acts:** national acts, regional acts, local acts. **Sample day's lineup:** Bruce Daigrepont Cajun Band, Danielle Martineau and Rockabayou, Zydeco Zombies, Darren and The Swamp Stompers, Washboard Slim and The Blue Lights. **Contact:** Municipal Cafe, 485 Main Street, Hartford, CT 06103, 203-527-5044/873-8681.

### MANCHESTER ASSOCIATION OF PIPE BANDS FESTIVAL, Manchester, CT
Middle Jun.
Scottish

See other dates. **Site:** outdoor. Manchester Community Technical College, 60 Bidwell Street. **Admission:** free. **Restrictions:** 10, **Secondary genre[s]:** IRSH, **Acts:** local acts. **Sample day's lineup:** Manchester Pipe Band, St. Patrick's Pipe Band, Highlanders of The Sphinx Temple, Stewart Highlanders. **Contact:** St. Patrick's Pipe Band, 96 Dartmouth Road, Manchester, CT 06040, 203-647-8811.

### CELEBRATE! WEST HARTFORD, West Hartford, CT
Middle Jun.
Variety, General

Since 1987. **Days:** 2. **Hours per day:** 8. **Site:** outdoor. Town Hall, South Main Street. **Secondary genre[s]:** MJAZ, TR&B, MC&W, **Acts:** local acts. **Sample day's lineup:** Ray T and The Triple T Country Band, Wild Horse, Satin Star, Street Temperature, Word of Mouth. **Contact:** Celebrate! West Hartford, Town Hall Common, West Hartford, CT 06107, 203-523-3159.

### SEA MUSIC FESTIVAL, Mystic, CT
Middle Jun.
Maritime

Since 1980. **Days:** 3. **Hours per day:** 12. **Site:** outdoor and indoor. Mystic Seaport Museum, 50 Greenmanville Avenue; St. Patrick's Church (Saturday night Contra Dance); Seamen's Inne (Saturday Pub night). **Admission:** paid. **Daily entry:** under $10, $10 to $24. **Secondary genre[s]:** TFOL, IRSH, SCOT, OTHR. **Acts:** national acts, regional acts, local acts. **Sample lineup:** Ancient Mariners, Jerry Bryant, Julie and Josee Carle, Daisy Nell and David Coffin, Ellen Cohn, Michel Colleu, Joe Cormier, Clary Croft, Mary Malloy and Stuart Frank, Tom Goux and Jacek Sulanowski, Cliff Haslam, Shanty Jack, Larry Kaplan, Louis Killen, Sherry Mortimer, Mystic Seaport Chanteymen, David Parry, Dick Swain, John Townley, Bob Walser, Bob Webb, Catherine Perrier and John Wright, Marek Siurawski. **Audio merchandise:** "Sea Chanteys and Forecastle Songs at Mystic Seaport" (Folkways). **Contact:** Mystic Seaport Museum, P. O. Box 6000, Mystic, CT 06355-0990, 203-572-0711/5350.

### TASTE OF FAIRFIELD, Fairfield, CT
Middle Jun.
Variety, General

Since 1987. **Days:** 3. **Hours per day:** 10. **Site:** outdoor. Burr Homestead, 639 Old Post Road. **Admission:** paid. **Daily entry:** under $10. **Secondary genre[s]:** MJAZ, MRCK, MR&B, TR&B, **Acts:** local acts. **Sample day's lineup:** Jay Rowe Band, YRB, Satin Star, Michael Cleary Band, Brian Torff Jazz, Blue In The Face, others. **Contact:** Burr Homestead, 639 Old Post Road, Fairfield, CT 203-366-7551.

## OLD HOME DAY, Middlefield, CT
   Middle Jun.
   Variety, General

**Days:** 1. **Hours per day:** 12. **Site:** outdoor. Peckham Field, Main Street. **Secondary genre[s]:** TJAZ, MRCK, IRSH, OTHR. **Acts:** local acts. **Sample day's lineup:** Ringrose Band, Endless Journey, Bill Benson, Middletown Stage Band. **Contact:** Old Home Day, Town Hall, 393 Jackson Hill Road, Middlefield, CT 203-349-7114/347-3460.

## LOCAL BANDS ON THE DOWNTOWN GREEN, New Haven, CT
   Middle Jun. to Late Aug.
   Alternative and College Rock

All-day concerts of local rock acts with occasional national headliners. From three to ten events per summer. Promoters: Steve Rogers (see below), WPLR's Dennis Nardella (see other dates), Andrea Kaplan. **Help!** A sample lineup? **Days:** 10. **Hours per day:** 8. **Site:** outdoor. Town Green; Lighthouse Point Park. **Admission:** free. **Secondary genre[s]:** MRCK, HRCK, TR&B, **Acts:** local acts. **Contact:** 203-288-6400.

## PINK TENT FESTIVAL OF THE ARTS, Stamford, CT
   Middle Jun.
   Variety, General

**Days:** 3. **Site:** outdoor. Mill River Park, Mill River and West Broad Streets. **Secondary genre[s]:** MRCK, BGOS, MC&W, OTHR. **Acts:** local acts. **Sample day's lineup:** Bob Sterling and Southern Cookin', Slim Sterling, Jan and Dale Melikan, others. **Contact:** Pink Tent Festival of the Arts, P. O. Box 4628, Stamford, CT 06907, 203-352-3386.

## FAIRFIELD COUNTY IRISH FESTIVAL, Fairfield, CT
   Middle Jun.
   Irish

Since 1988. "All attractions under tents." -- Advertisement. **Days:** 3. **Hours per day:** 11. **Site:** outdoor. Roger Ludlowe Field, Unquowa Road. **Admission:** paid. **Daily entry:** under $10. **Discounts:** multiple event or day passes, **Acts:** national acts, regional acts, local acts. **Sample day's lineup:** The Clancy Brothers with Robbie O'Connell, Cherish The Ladies, Kips Bay Ceili Band, Paddy Noonan Showband, Celtic Cross, Music In The Glen, Gerry Finlay and the Cara Band, Once Removed, Give Liam A Shout, Mike O'Brien, Morrison's Visa, Greenbriar Ceili Band, Clan Na Gael Players, others. **Contact:** Gaelic American Club, 74 Beach Road, Fairfield, CT 06430, 203-259-9300.

## BLUES BLOCKBUSTERS, New Haven, CT
   Middle Jun.
   Blues and Traditional R&B

Approximately seven times per year. Call for current dates. **Days:** 7. **Site:** indoor. Toad's Place, 300 York Street. **Admission:** paid. **Daily entry:** under $10. **Acts:** local acts. **Sample day's lineup:** Shaboo All-Stars, Rebel Montez, Triple Threat, Chris Tolfield and The Blues Benders. **Contact:** Toad's Place, 300 York Street, New Haven, CT 06511, 203-624-TOAD/772-4089.

## WEST FEST/TASTE OF WESTVILLE, Westville, CT
   Middle Jun.
   Variety, General

**Days:** 1. **Hours per day:** 6. **Site:** outdoor. Library Green. **Secondary genre[s]:** TJAZ, OTHR **Acts:** local acts. **Sample day's lineup:** Faye and The Funky All Stars, Morgan Scott, Tom Hughes, others. **Contact:** Chavoya's Restaurant, 883 Whalley Avenue, New Haven, CT 203-389-4730.

MOTHER OF WATERS, Rocky Hill, CT
Middle Jun.
Native American

**Help!** Does anyone have a contact address? **Days:** 2. **Hours per day:** 11. **Site:** outdoor. Ferry Park, Route 160. **Contact:** Mother of Waters, Ferry Park, Route 160, Rocky Hill, CT 203-258-2772.

BARNUM FESTIVAL/GOSPEL FESTIVAL, Bridgeport, CT
Middle Jun.
Black Gospel

Since 1960. "Hear the sounds of several popular local Gospel choirs. The program will have you dancing in the aisles!" -- Flyer. Part of Barnum Festival, a month-long city celebration. See other dates and sites. **Help!** A sample lineup? **Days:** 1. **Site:** indoor. Mount Airy Baptist Church. **Admission:** free. **Daily entry:** $10 to $24. **Acts:** local acts. **Contact:** Barnum Festival, Bridgeport Holiday Inn, 1070 Main Street, Bridgeport, CT 06604, 203-367-8495.

SUMMER SERIES, Westport, CT
Middle Jun. to Middle Aug.
Variety, General

See other dates. **Days:** 62. **Site:** outdoor. Levitt Pavilion for the Performing Arts, Jesup Road. **Admission:** free. **Secondary genre[s]:** MJAZ, TJAZ, CRCK, ARCK, TR&B, AC&W, MFOL, ZYDC, CBRT, GYLS, OTHR. **Acts:** national acts, regional acts, local acts. **Sample series lineup:** Day One: Barry and Holly Tashian; Day Two: Hugh Blumenfeld; Day Three: Zydeco Zombies. **Contact:** Levitt Pavilion for the Performing Arts, Town Hall, Westport, CT 06880, 203-226-7600.

RED CROSS WATERFRONT FESTIVAL, Greenwich, CT
Middle Jun.
Variety, General

**Days:** 2. **Hours per day:** 7. **Site:** outdoor. Roger Sherman Baldwin Park, Arch Street. **Admission:** paid. **Daily entry:** under $10. **Secondary genre[s]:** MJAZ, CRCK, MC&W, OTHR **Acts:** national acts, regional acts, local acts. **Sample day's lineup:** Marshall Tucker Band, Chris Brubeck and His Jazz Allstars, Joyce DiCamillo Trio, Darryl Tooks, Annie and The Natural Wonder Band, Alvin and The Chipmonks, others. **Contact:** Red Cross Waterfront Festival, 231 East Putnam Road, Greenwich, CT 06830, 203-869-8444.

LOUISIANA COOKIN' AND CAJUN MUSIC FESTIVAL, Norwich, CT
Late Jun.
Cajun and Zydeco

Part of Norwich Rose Arts Festival, a two-week community celebration. Chef Paul Prudhomme was special guest in 1994. **Days:** 2. **Hours per day:** 13. **Site:** outdoor. Chelsea Parade Grounds. **Admission:** paid. **Daily entry:** $10 to $24. **Discounts:** multiple event or day passes, **Secondary genre[s]:** TJAZ, TR&B, MC&W, **Acts:** national acts, local acts. **Sample day's lineup:** Al Hirt, Doug Kershaw, Heritage Hall Jazz Band, Dr. John, Chubby Carrier and The Bayou Swamp Band, basin Brothers Cajun Band, Nathan and The Zydeco Cha-Cha's, The Pinballs. **Contact:** Foxwoods Casino, P. O. Box 410, Ledyard, CT 06339, 203-885-3352 x4063 **or:** Jerry Kravat Entertainment, 205 Lexington Avenue, Lobby Suite, New York, NY 10016, 212-686-2200.

## STRAWBERRY MOON POW-WOW, Somers, CT
Late Jun.
Native American

Since 1987. See other dates and sites. **Days:** 2. **Hours per day:** 10. **Site:** outdoor. Four Town Fairgrounds, Egypt Road. **Admission:** paid. **Discounts:** group sale discounts, **Contact:** Connecticut River Pow-Wow Society, 244 East Street, Stafford, CT 06075, 203-684-6984.

## HOT STEAMED MUSIC FESTIVAL, Essex, CT
Late Jun.
Traditional Jazz and Ragtime

"Don't miss this marvelous experience!" -- Advertisement. **Days:** 3. **Hours per day:** 12. **Site:** outdoor and indoor. Valley Railroad. **Admission:** paid. **Daily entry:** $10 to $24. **Discounts:** multiple event or day passes, **Secondary genre[s]:** TGOS, **Acts:** regional acts, local acts. **Sample day's lineup:** Happy Feet Dance Orchestra, Big Easy Jazz Band, Dr. Jazz and The Dixie Hotshots, New Traditional Jazz Band, Blue Horizon Jazz Band, Eight to The Bar, University of Maine Youth Jazz Band. **Contact:** Hot Steamed Music Festival, P. O. Box 293, Essex, CT 06426-0293, 203-630-3016/767-0103.

## REGGAE FESTIVAL, Woodbury, CT
Late Jun.
Reggae, Ska and Caribbean

Since 1977. **Days:** 1. **Hours per day:** 7. **Site:** outdoor. Woodbury Ski Area, Route 47. **Admission:** paid. **Daily entry:** $10 to $24. **Discounts:** advance purchase discounts, **Acts:** national acts, local acts. **Sample day's lineup:** Lucky Dube, Majek Fashek and Bankie Banx, Zulu Spear, Dread I, Affinity. **Other merchandise:** 25 VHS recordings of past festivals -- all genres -- available via promoter. **Contact:** Woodbury Ski Area, Route 47, Woodbury, CT 06798, 203-263-2203.

## CONNECTICUT IRISH FESTIVAL, New Haven, CT
Late Jun.
Irish

**Days:** 2. **Hours per day:** 9. **Site:** outdoor. North Haven Fairgrounds, Washington Avenue, Route 5. **Admission:** paid. **Daily entry:** under $10. **Discounts:** advance purchase discounts, **Restrictions:** 2. **Acts:** local acts. **Sample day's lineup:** Johnny McEvoy, New York Showband and Tommy Flynn, O'Hagen Family Irish Showband, Gaelic Highland Bagpipe Band, Comhaltas Ceoltoiri Eirann, Boys of Wexford, Tipperary Knights, Mark James Band, Music In The Glen, Paul Pender, Dan Ringrose, Fiddler's Green, Tommy Ryder, Morrison Visa. **Contact:** Irish American Community Center, Venice Place, East Haven, CT 203-469-3080/237-9127.

## GREAT AMERICAN MUSIC FEST, Goshen, CT
Late Jun.
Modern Country

Since 1990. **Days:** 2. **Hours per day:** 6. **Site:** outdoor. Goshen Fairgrounds. **Admission:** paid. **Daily entry:** under $10. **Restrictions:** 12, **Acts:** national acts, local acts. **Sample day's lineup:** Clint Black, Wynonna, Michael Johnson, Great Plains, Mark O'Connor, Teresa. **Contact:** WWYZ-FM Country 92.5, 151 New Park Avenue, Hartford, CT 06106, 203-247-1102.

**AFTERNOON OF JAZZ**, Norwalk, CT
> Late Jun.
> Modern Jazz

Since 1963. **Days:** 1. **Hours per day:** 8. **Site:** outdoor. Gallagher Estate, Cranbury Park. **Admission:** paid.**Daily entry:** $25 to $49. **Discounts:** advance purchase discounts, **Secondary genre[s]:** MR&B, MLAT, **Acts:** national acts, local acts. **Sample day's lineup:** Gerald Albright, Black/Note, Bobby Rodriguez, Joyce DiCamillo Trio, Lala Hathaway, Phyllis Hyman, Gerry Mulligan, Max Roach, Billy Taylor Trio. **Contact:** Jackie Robinson Foundation, 3 West 35th Street, 11th Floor, New York, NY 10001, 212-290-8600.

**BARNUM FESTIVAL/CHAMPIONS ON PARADE**, Bridgeport, CT
> Late Jun.
> Drum Corps and Marching Bands

Since 1960. "One of the most popular Barnum Festival events is back! Come watch six popular drum corps compete." -- Flyer. Part of Barnum Festival, a month-long city celebration. See other dates and sites. **Days:** 1. **Site:** outdoor. Kennedy Stadium. **Admission:** paid. **Daily entry:** under $10, $10 to $24. **Acts:** national acts, regional acts, local acts. **Sample day's lineup:** USMC Drum and Bugle Corps, Ancient Mariners, plus six contestants. **Contact:** Barnum Festival, Bridgeport Holiday Inn, 1070 Main Street, Bridgeport, CT 06604, 203-367-8495.

**BLUES AT THE IVES**, Danbury, CT
> Late Jun.
> Blues and Traditional R&B

See other dates. **Days:** 1. **Site:** outdoor. Charles Ives Center for the Arts. **Admission:** paid. **Daily entry:** $10 to $24, $25 to $49. **Acts:** national acts. **Sample day's lineup:** John Mayal and The Bluesbreakers, John Campbell, Albert Collins and The Icebreakers. **Contact:** Charles Ives Center for the Arts, P. O. Box 2957, Danbur,y CT 06813, 203-797-4002.

**LAKE WANGUMBAUG FOLK FESTIVAL**, Coventry, CT
> Late Jun.
> Modern Folk

**Days:** 1. **Hours per day:** 5. **Site:** outdoor. Patriot's Park, Lake Street. **Admission:** free. **Restrictions:** 10, **Acts:** national acts, regional acts, local acts. **Sample day's lineup:** Aztec Two-Step, Adrienne Jones and Ed Smith, Atwater-Donnelly, Bruce Pratt, Hugh Blumenfeld. **Contact:** Coventry Arts Commission, Coventry Town Hall, Main Street, Coventry, CT 203-742-7723.

**TRUMBULL DAY**, Trumbull, CT
> Late Jun.
> Variety, General

Since 1962. "Generations of family fun." -- Brochure. **Days:** 1. **Hours per day:** 12. **Site:** outdoor. Hillcrest Junior High School, Daniels Farm and Stroebel Roads. **Admission:** paid. **Daily entry:** under $10. **Secondary genre[s]:** MJAZ, TJAZ, MRCK, CRCK, MC&W, MFOL, TFOL, **Acts:** local acts. **Sample day's lineup:** Don Cooper, Frank Porto Orchestra, Westport Community Band, Jay Stollman and The Black Rock Allstars, Nightbreeze, The Nifty 50's Band, Ray T and the Triple T Band, Center Street Band, The Issuemen, others. **Contact:** Trumbull Day Commission, Trumbull Town Hall, Trumbull, CT 06611, 203-452-5000 **or:** Lee Salzberg and Associates, 37 Partridge Lane, Trumbull, CT 06611, 203-377-2858.

## 4TH OF JULY CELEBRATION, Enfield, CT
Early Jul.
Variety, General

**Days:** 3. **Hours per day:** 11. **Site:** outdoor. Enfield Town Green, Enfield Street. **Admission:** free. **Secondary genre[s]:** MJAZ, MRCK, CRCK, MC&W, **Acts:** regional acts, local acts. **Sample series lineup:** Day One: The Savage Brothers, RTM; Day Two: M-Town Review, Prism; Day Three: Tirebiters, Nifty 50's Band. **Contact:** 4th of July Celebration Committee, P. O. Box 3203, Enfield, CT 06082, 203-763-2590.

## MINERAL SPRINGS FOOT STOMP'N FESTIVAL, Stafford Springs, CT
Late Jun. to Early Jul.
Bluegrass

"Come and enjoy." -- Flyer. See other dates. **Days:** 3. **Hours per day:** 14. **Site:** outdoor and indoor. Mineral Springs Campground, 135 Leonard Road. **Admission:** paid. **Daily entry:** under $10, $10 to $24. **Discounts:** multiple event or day passes, group sale discounts, **Acts:** regional acts, local acts. **Sample day's lineup:** Southern Rail, Traver Hollow, Amy Gallatin and Still Waters, Bear Bridge Band, Stonewall Bluegrass, Gary Ferguson Band, Case Brothers, Grassroots, Flatlanders. **Contact:** Mineral Springs Foot Stomp'n Festival, 48 Village Hill Road, Willington, CT 06076, 203-684-2993/9647.

## RIVERFEST, Hartford, CT
Early Jul.
Variety, General

Since 1981. "We're back on the river with spectacular fireworks and great music on 4 stages!" -- Advertisement. **Days:** 1. **Hours per day:** 4. **Site:** outdoor. 5 locations. **Secondary genre[s]:** MRCK, CRCK, ARCK, MC&W, OTHR. **Acts:** national acts, local acts. **Sample day's lineup:** Wild Horse, Abbey Road, Adrian Legg, Hartford Symphony Orchestra, others. **Contact:** Riverfront Recapture, 1 Hartford Square West, Suite 104, West Hartford, CT 06106-1984, 203-293-0131.

## BATTLE OF THE BANDS, Westport, CT
Early Jul. to Middle Aug.
Modern Rock and Pop

Two rounds, plus "Winner's Concert" -- each about three weeks apart. See other dates. **Help!** A sample line-up? **Days:** 3. **Site:** outdoor. Levitt Pavilion for the Performing Arts, Jesup Road. **Admission:** free. **Restrictions:** 2. **Acts:** local acts. **Contact:** Levitt Pavilion for the Performing Arts, Town Hall, Westport CT 06880, 203-226-7600.

## FUNKFEST, New Haven, CT
Early Jul.
Modern R&B

See other dates. **Help!** One time only? **Days:** 1. **Site:** indoor. Toad's Place, 300 York Street. **Admission:** paid. **Daily entry:** under $10. **Acts:** local acts. **Sample day's lineup:** Boogie Chillun, Clarke Brothers, Rearview, TNT Band. **Contact:** Toad's Place, 300 York Street, New Haven, CT 06511, 203-624-TOAD/772-4089.

## ROUND HILL SCOTTISH GAMES, Norwalk, CT
Early Jul.
Scottish

Since 1923. **Days:** 1. **Hours per day:** 9. **Site:** outdoor. Cranbury Park. **Contact:** Round Hill Scottish Games, 43 Hoyt Street, Darien, CT 06820, 203-854-7806.

WPLR JULY 4TH CELEBRATION, New Haven, CT
        Early Jul.
        Alternative and College Rock

See other dates. **Days:** 1. **Hours per day:** 7. **Site:** outdoor. Lighthouse Point Park. **Acts:** national acts, local acts. **Sample day's lineup:** The Skeletons, Secret Smile, Rival, others. **Contact:** WPLR-FM, 1191 Dix Well Avenue, Hamden, CT 06514, 203-488-5062.


SUBFEST, Groton, CT
        Early Jul.
        Variety, General

"Connecticut's Family Festival." -- Flyer. **Days:** 3. **Hours per day:** 14. **Site:** outdoor. Naval Submarine Base. **Secondary genre[s]:** CRCK, MC&W, **Acts:** national acts, regional acts, local acts. **Sample series lineup:** Day One: Lee Greenwood; Day Two: Nik and The Nice Guys; Day Three; Frankie Valli and The Four Seasons. **Contact:** Marketing Department, Naval Submarine Base, Groton, CT 203-449-4904/3011.


NEW HAVEN JAZZ FESTIVAL, New Haven, CT
        Early Jul. to Late Jul.
        Modern Jazz

Since 1979. **Days:** 5. **Site:** outdoor. New Haven Green. **Admission:** free. **Secondary genre[s]:** MLAT, **Acts:** national acts, local acts. **Sample series lineup:** Day One: Stanley Turrentine, Addison Thompson Quartet; Day Two: Bob Berg, Jay Hoggard; Day Three: Roland Vasquez, Giacomo Gates and Trio. **Contact:** City of New Haven, 95 Orange Street, New Haven, CT 06510, 203-787-2788/7821.


SUMMER CELEBRATION, Dayville, CT
        Early Jul.
        Variety, General

Since 1983. **Days:** 1. **Hours per day:** 11. **Site:** outdoor. Owen Bell Park, Hartford Pike. **Secondary genre[s]:** TJAZ, MC&W, MFOL, **Acts:** local acts. **Sample day's lineup:** Sleepy Maggie, Wayne and John Springland, Dixieland Sounds, others. **Contact:** Dayville Parks and Recreation Department, Dayville, CT 203-779-3503.


GLOBAL BLUES FEST, Norwalk, CT
        Early Jul.
        Blues and Traditional R&B

Since 1994. "The Globe. You are here." -- Advertisement. **Days:** 1. **Site:** indoor. Globe Theater, 71 Wall Street. **Admission:** paid. **Daily entry:** $10 to $24. **Acts:** national acts, local acts. **Sample day's lineup:** James Cotton, J. Geils and Magic Dick, Shaboo Allstars. **Contact:** Globe Theater, 71 Wall Street, Norwalk, CT 203-866-2999.


NEW LONDON SAIL FESTIVAL/CONNECTICUT MARITIME FESTIVAL, New London, CT
        Early Jul. to Middle Jul.
        Variety, General

**Days:** 3. .**Secondary genre[s]:** MJAZ, TJAZ, MRCK, CRCK, TR&B, TFOL, GYLS, **Acts:** local acts. **Sample day's lineup:** Little Sister and The Fat Cats, 102nd U. S. Army Field Band, Vic Elci Orchestra, Busman's Holiday, Red Hot and Blue, Bob Norman, Johnny and The East Coast Rockers. **Contact:** City of New London Marine Commerce and Development Committee, 111 Union Street, New London, CT 06320, 203-443-8331.

## CONNECTICUT CONVENTION OF THE SACRED HARP, Middletown, CT
Early Jul. to Middle Jul.
Traditional Gospel and Sings

Since 1984. "A shape-note singing gala...Singers of all parts and expertise -- including beginners -- are welcome." -- Flyer. **Days:** 2. **Hours per day:** 7. **Site:** indoor. World Music Hall, Wesleyan University, Wyllys Avenue. **Contact:** Connecticut Valley Harmony, RD 2, Box 8, South Main Street, Terryville, CT 06786, 203-583-0841/347-3003.

## HIGH RIDGE FOLK FESTIVAL, Stamford, CT
Early Jul. to Middle Jul.
Traditional Folk

"A festival of traditional American music workshops and concerts held in a beautiful natural setting." -- Advertisement. **Days:** 2. **Hours per day:** 6. **Site:** outdoor and indoor. workshops: Stamford Museum and Nature Center, 39 Scofieldtown Road; concerts: Turn of River School, 117 Vine Street. **Admission:** paid. **Daily entry:** $10 to $24. **Secondary genre[s]:** TJAZ, TR&B, MARI, **Acts:** regional acts, local acts. **Sample day's lineup:** Smith Street Society Jazz Band, Easton Banjo Society, Washboard Slim and The Blue Lights, Jamie Watson, Joan Crane, Dave Sear, Elijah Wald, Sandy and Caroline Paton. **Contact:** Stamford Museum and Nature Center, 39 Scofieldtown Road, Stamford, CT 06903, 203-322-1646.

## WXCT FAMILY FESTIVAL, New Haven, CT
Middle Jul.
Modern Latin

**Days:** 1. **Hours per day:** 8. **Site:** outdoor. East Rock Summit, off English Drive. **Acts:** national acts, local acts. **Sample day's lineup:** El Gran Combo Y Su Combo Show, Johnny Ventura, Los Hermanos Ventura, five other bands. **Contact:** WXCT, 473 Denslow Hill Road, Hamden, CT 06514, 203-288-8282 **or:** WXCT, P. O. Box 121, Ardsley, NY 10502.

## HARTLAND FOLK FESTIVAL, East Hartland, CT
Middle Jul.
Modern Folk

Since 1987. **Days:** 1. **Hours per day:** 10. **Site:** outdoor. Berg Field, Route 20. **Admission:** paid. **Daily entry:** $10 to $24. **Discounts:** advance purchase discounts, **Secondary genre[s]:** MC&W, BLGS, TFOL, MARI, **Acts:** national acts, regional acts, local acts. **Sample day's lineup:** Greg Brown, Dave Mallett, Cormac McCarthy, Kate McDonnell, Bruce Pratt, Nancy Tucker, Erica Wheeler, Mustard's Retreat, The Strange Rangers, Cosy Sheridan, Steve Nystrup, Stan Sullivan, Amy Gallatin and Still Waters, others. **Contact:** Hartland Folk Festival, P. O. Box 308, Hartland, CT 06027, 203-653-5577/5885 **or:** Hartland Folk Festival, RR 1, Box 85, East Holden, ME 04424.

## ROXBURY PICKIN' N FIDDLIN' CONTEST, Roxbury, CT
Middle Jul.
Fiddle and Banjo Events

**Days:** 1. **Hours per day:** 7. **Site:** outdoor. corner of Routes 67 and 199. **Secondary genre[s]:** TC&W, BLGS, TFOL, **Acts:** local acts. **Contact:** Roxbury Pickin' N Fiddlin' Contest, 60 East Woods Road, Roxbury, CT 06783, 203-354-3588.

AFRO-LATIN-CARIBBEAN FESTIVAL, Waterbury, CT
Middle Jul.
African American

**Help!** A sample lineup? **Days:** 3. **Site:** outdoor. Liberty Park, Grand Street. **Secondary genre[s]:** MLAT, RGGE, **Acts:** local acts. **Contact:** New Opportunities for Waterbury, 232 North Elm Street, Waterbury, CT 203-575-9799.

GREAT AMERICAN BLUES FESTIVAL, Woodstock, CT
Middle Jul.
Blues and Traditional R&B

Since 1993. **Days:** 1. **Hours per day:** 9. **Site:** outdoor. Woodstock Valley Lodge, 73A Bungay Hill Road. **Admission:** paid. **Daily entry:** $10 to $24. **Discounts:** advance purchase discounts, **Acts:** national acts, local acts. **Sample day's lineup:** Johnny "Clyde" Copeland, Ronnie Earl and The Broadcasters, D. Smith Blues Project, Rhythm Rockers. **Contact:** Municipal Cafe, 485 Main Street, Hartford, CT 06103, 203-527-5044/974-1040.

WORLD MUSIC FESTIVAL, Woodbury, CT
Middle Jul.
Reggae, Ska and Caribbean

**Days:** 1. **Hours per day:** 7. **Site:** outdoor. Woodbury Ski Area, Route 47. **Admission:** paid. **Daily entry:** $10 to $24. **Discounts:** advance purchase discounts, **Secondary genre[s]:** AFRC, **Acts:** national acts, local acts. **Sample day's lineup:** Youssou N'Dour, Culture, Worl-A-Girl, Dub Mystic. **Other merchandise:** 25 VHS recordings of past festivals -- all genres -- available via promoter. **Contact:** Woodbury Ski Area, Route 47, Woodbury, CT 06798, 203-263-2203.

DEEP RIVER ANCIENT FIFE AND DRUM CORPS MUSTER AND PARADE, Deep River, CT
Middle Jul.
Drum Corps and Marching Bands

"The oldest and largest event of its kind...[with well over] 60 fife and drum corps." -- Listing. **Days:** 2. **Site:** outdoor. Devitts Field, Main Street. **Contact:** Deep River Ancient Fife and Drum Corps Muster and Parade, P. O. Box 274, Westbrook, CT 06498, 203-399-6665.

STAMFORD A. O. H. FEIS, Stamford, CT
Middle Jul.
Irish

Since 1969. **Days:** 1. **Hours per day:** 8. **Site:** outdoor and indoor. Trinity Catholic High School, 926 Newfield Avenue. **Restrictions:** 8, **Acts:** local acts. **Contact:** Stamford A. O. H. Feis, 76 Treat Avenue, Stamford, CT 06906, 203-325-3172/967-9774.

SUMMER SIZZLER, East Hartford, CT
Middle Jul.
Classic Rock and Oldies

See other dates. **Help!** One time only?**Days:** 1. **Site:** outdoor and indoor. 125 Riverside Drive Restaurant and Lounge, 125 Riverside Drive. **Secondary genre[s]:** MRCK, TR&B, **Acts:** regional acts, local acts. **Sample day's lineup:** Young Neal and The Vipers, Motown Review, Bates Motel, Infinity, Dave and Charlie. **Contact:** 125 Riverside Drive Restaurant and Lounge, 125 Riverside Drive, East Hartford, CT 203-569-3003.

## ROCK 'N' BLUES AIDS BENEFIT, East Hartford, CT
      Late Jul.
      Blues and Traditional R&B

See other dates. **Help!** One time only? **Days:** 1. **Site:** outdoor and indoor. 125 Riverside Drive Restaurant and Lounge, 125 Riverside Drive. **Admission:** paid. **Daily entry:** under $10. **Discounts:** advance purchase discounts, **Secondary genre[s]:** MRCK, **Acts:** local acts. **Sample day's lineup:** Savage Brothers Band, The Hornets, Sunburn Band, The Lamoreaux Brothers, Tiny Joe Eleaser, The Stingrays, Burt Teague and Word Of Mouth, Jesse "Wild Bil" Austin and His Big Blues Band. **Contact:** 125 Riverside Drive Restaurant and Lounge, 125 Riverside Drive, East Hartford, CT 203-569-3003.

## FOLK MUSIC SHOWCASE, Westport, CT
      Late Jul.
      Modern Folk

See other dates. **Help!** A sample lineup? **Days:** 1. **Site:** outdoor. Levitt Pavilion for the Performing Arts, Jesup Road. **Admission:** free. **Restrictions:** 2. **Contact:** Levitt Pavilion for the Performing Arts, Town Hall, Westport, CT 06880, 203-226-7600.

## BASH: BRADLEY AIRPORT SUMMER HAPPENING, Windsor Locks, CT
      Late Jul.
      Modern Country

"A fun-packed day for the whole family!" -- Flyer. Benefits Paul Newman's Hole in the Wall Gang Camp. **Days:** 1. **Hours per day:** 9. **Site:** outdoor. airport grounds, Route 75. **Admission:** paid. **Daily entry:** under $10. **Secondary genre[s]:** CRCK, **Acts:** local acts. **Sample day's lineup:** Wild Horse, Borderline, Cactus Rose, AKA. **Contact:** Bradley Boosters, 24 King Spring Road, Windsor Locks, CT 06096, 203-627-9338.

## R. A. W. JAZZ FESTIVAL, Hartford, CT
      Late Jul.
      Alternative Jazz

Since 1980. **Days:** 2. **Site:** outdoor. Day Playground, Arbor Street. **Admission:** free. **Acts:** national acts. **Sample series lineup:** Day One: Marc Ribot Quartet, Sonny Sharrock's Highlife; Day Two: Either/Orchestra, Trevor Watts Moire Music Drum Orchestra. **Contact:** Real Art Ways, 56 Arbor Street, Hartford, CT 06106-1402, 203-232-1006.

## ROCKFEST, East Hartford, CT
      Late Jul.
      Modern Rock and Pop

See other dates. **Help!** One time only? **Days:** 1. **Site:** outdoor and indoor. 125 Riverside Drive Restaurant and Lounge, 125 Riverside Drive. **Admission:** paid. **Daily entry:** under $10. **Discounts:** advance purchase discounts, **Secondary genre[s]:** CRCK, ARCK, TR&B, **Acts:** local acts. **Sample day's lineup:** Burt Teague and Word Of Mouth, Physical Graffiti, Thunderroad, Michael Cleary, Society's Children, Primal Scream, Pete Gounda, Jeff Pichell, Puss N' Boots, Doug Jones, Dewey Burns, Naked Truth, Pat McGinley. **Contact:** 125 Riverside Drive Restaurant and Lounge, 125 Riverside Drive, East Hartford, CT 203-569-3003.

CONNECTICUT AGRICULTURAL FAIR, Goshen, CT
> Late Jul.
> Fairs

Since 1968. See other dates. **Days:** 3. **Hours per day:** 10. **Site:** outdoor. Goshen Fairgrounds, Route 63. **Admission:** paid. **Daily entry:** under $10. **Secondary genre[s]:** SGOS, MC&W, BLGS, **Acts:** national acts, regional acts, local acts. **Sample day's lineup:** Cheryl Cormier, Bristol Old Tyme Fiddlers, Bolton Notch, New Vintage Quartet. **Contact:** Connecticut Agricultural Fair, P. O. Box 63, Winchester Center, CT 06094, 203-379-2527.

GREATER HARTFORD IRISH FESTIVAL, Glastonbury, CT
> Late Jul.
> Irish

Since 1984. **Days:** 3. **Hours per day:** 8. **Site:** outdoor and indoor. Irish American Home, 132 Commerce Street. **Admission:** paid. **Daily entry:** under $10. **Discounts:** advance purchase discounts, **Restrictions:** 5, 10, **Acts:** regional acts, local acts. **Sample day's lineup:** Comhaltas Coeltoire Eireann, The Savage Brothers, Marie McVicer, New York Showband feat. Tommy Flynn, Johnny Murphy and The Clubmen, Joe Glynn and The Irish Mist, Larry Reynolds, Fergus Keane and Boston's Comhaltas, Music In The Glen. **Contact:** Greater Hartford Irish Festival, 24 Fairfax Avenue, West Hartford, CT 06119, 203-633-9691/644-9572.

### GREATER HARTFORD FESTIVAL OF JAZZ/HARTFORD MEGA! WEEKEND, Hartford, CT
> Late Jul. to Early Aug.
> Variety, General

Since 1992. **Days:** 6. **Hours per day:** 14. **Site:** outdoor and indoor. Bushnell Park (Festival of Jazz); multiple locations (Mega Weekend). **Admission:** free. **Secondary genre[s]:** MJAZ, TJAZ, TR&B, BGOS, MFOL, MLAT, RGGE, GYLS, OTHR **Acts:** national acts, regional acts, local acts. **Sample day's lineup:** Arturo Sandoval Quintet, Jimmy Green Quartet, Hilton Ruiz Sextet, Artist Collective Youth Jazz Orchestra, Greater Hartford Academy of Performing Arts Jazz Ensemble, Hall High Quintet. **Contact:** Greater Hartford Festival of Jazz, 250 Constitution Plaza, Hartford, CT 06103, 203-525-4451 x236 **or:** Greater Hartford Festival of Jazz, 195 North Beacon Street, Hartford, CT 06105, 203-233-5105. .

WORLD MUSIC FEST, Groton, CT
> Late Jul.
> Variety, Folk and International

Since 1994. "All activities are under tents." -- Flyer. **Days:** 2. **Site:** outdoor. Burrows Field, Route 1. **Admission:** paid. **Daily entry:** $10 to $24. **Discounts:** advance purchase discounts, **Secondary genre[s]:** CRCK, TR&B, BGOS, ZYDC, IRSH, MLAT, TLAT, AFRC, BRZL, RGGE, OTHR **Acts:** national acts, regional acts, local acts. **Sample day's lineup:** Bo Diddley, Los Pleneros Del Coco, Ibrahima Master Camara, Samite Of Uganda, New Alborada, Sirius Coyote. **Contact:** Groton Community Events Committee, 45 Fort Hill Road, Groton, CT 06340, 203-441-6776/6777.

POSITIVELY POMFRET DAY, Putnam, CT
> Late Jul.
> Variety, Folk and International

**Help!** A sample lineup? **Days:** 1. **Hours per day:** 10. **Site:** outdoor. Community School, Route 101. **Admission:** free. **Secondary genre[s]:** TJAZ, TR&B, MFOL, AFRC, **Acts:** local acts. **Sample day's lineup:** 5 acts. **Contact:** Positively Pomfret Day, 146 Fay Road, Pomfret Center, CT 06259, 203-974-1202/3098.

## ROCK AND ROLL HALL OF FAME REVUE, Danbury, CT

Late Jul.

Classic Rock and Oldies

See other dates. **Days:** 1. **Site:** outdoor. Charles Ives Center for the Arts. **Admission:** paid. **Daily entry:** $10 to $24, $25 to $49. **Acts:** national acts, local acts. **Sample day's lineup:** The Drifters, The Marvelettes, The Coasters, Clark Eno and Friends. **Contact:** Charles Ives Center for the Arts, P. O. Box 2957, Danbury, CT 06813, 203-797-4002.

## CONNECTICUT FAMILY FOLK FESTIVAL, Hartford, CT

Late Jul. to Early Aug.

Traditional Folk

Also program a winter-long coffeehouse series. **Days:** 2. **Hours per day:** 9. **Site:** outdoor. Elizabeth Park, Prospect and Asylum Avenues. **Admission:** free. **Secondary genre[s]:** TR&B, TC&W, BLGS, MFOL, **Acts:** national acts, local acts. **Sample day's lineup:** Guy Van Duser, Bill Staines, Little City String Band, Tequila. **Contact:** The Sounding Board, 14 Southwood Road, Cromwell, CT 06416-1632, 203-632-7547.

## WEST INDIAN INDEPENDENCE CELEBRATION WEEK/HARTFORD MEGA! WEEKEND, Hartford, CT

Early Aug.

Reggae, Ska and Caribbean

Since 1978. Concludes with a Carnival-Parade and Anniversary Ball on Saturday. **Help!** A sample lineup? **Days:** 7. **Hours per day:** 11. **Site:** outdoor and indoor. Bushnell Park, Main Street Market, elsewhere. **Admission:** free and paid. **Contact:** West Indian Foundation, Inc., P. O. Box 320394 Blue Hill Station, Hartford, CT 061320-0394, 203-241-0379.

## SoNo ARTS CELEBRATION, South Norwalk, CT

Early Aug.

Variety, General

Since 1977. **Help!** A sample lineup? **Days:** 3. **Hours per day:** 14. **Site:** outdoor. Washington and South Main Streets. **Admission:** free. **Secondary genre[s]:** MJAZ, TR&B, MFOL, MLAT, AFRC, RGGE, OTHR **Acts:** national acts, regional acts, local acts. **Sample day's lineup:** Michael Hill's Blues Mob, others on four stages. **Contact:** SoNo Arts Committee, P. O. Box 600, South Norwalk, CT 06856, 203-866-7916/857-0404.

## GREAT CONNECTICUT TRADITIONAL JAZZ FESTIVAL, East Haddam, CT

Early Aug.

Traditional Jazz and Ragtime

"Pray for sunshine." -- Brochure. **Days:** 3. **Hours per day:** 13. **Site:** outdoor and indoor. Sunrise Resort, Route 151, Moodus. **Admission:** paid. **Daily entry:** $10 to $24. **Discounts:** student discounts, multiple event or day passes, advance purchase discounts, group sale discounts, **Secondary genre[s]:** TGOS, **Acts:** national acts, regional acts, local acts. **Sample day's lineup:** Budapest Ragtime Band, Blue Street Jazz Band, Igor's Jazz Cowboys, Orphan Newsboys, Paramount Jazz Band, paris Washboard, Rent Party Revellers, South Frisco Jazz Band, Bill's 98, Connecticut Jazz Festival Band, Galvanized Jazz Band, Hot Cat Jazz Band, Nutmeg Foxtro-Jazz orchestra, Squabble Hill Backyard Jazz Band. **Contact:** T. G. C. T. J. F., 1032 Chapel Street, New Haven, CT 06510, 203-495-6096 **or:** T. G. C. T. J. F., Goodspeed Marketplace, 9 Main Street, P. O. Box 273, East Haddam, CT 06423, .

TASTE OF HISTORY, Mystic, CT
>Early Aug.
>Maritime

**Days:** 3. **Hours per day:** 12. **Site:** outdoor and indoor. Mystic Seaport Museum, 50 Greenmanville Avenue. **Admission:** paid. **Daily entry:** under $10, $10 to $24. **Secondary genre[s]:** OTHR **Acts:** local acts. **Sample lineup:** Mystic Seaport Chanteymen, others. **Audio merchandise:** "Sea Chanteys and Forecastle Songs at Mystic Seaport" (Folkways). **Contact:** Mystic Seaport Museum, P. O. Box 6000, Mystic, CT 06355-0990, 203-572-0711/5350.

KENT SUMMER DAYS, Kent, CT
>Early Aug.
>Variety, General

**Help!** A sample lineup? **Days:** 3. **Site:** outdoor. Main Street. **Admission:** free. **Secondary genre[s]:** MC&W, MFOL, OTHR. **Acts:** local acts. **Contact:** Kent Chamber of Commerce, P. O. Box 124, Kent, CT 06757, 203-927-1463/1691.

VERANO EXPLOSIVO FESTIVAL, West Hartford, CT
>Early Aug.
>Modern Latin

Since 1992. Fun is the only goal." -- Helen Ubinas, Hartford Courant. **Days:** 1. **Hours per day:** 9. **Site:** outdoor. Parking lot of Calixto Custom Furniture, 485 New Park Avenue. **Restrictions:** 2. **Acts:** local acts. **Sample Day's Lineup:** Juan Merengue and La Ciencia Latina, Orchestra Melodia, La Del Leon Band, Rey Gonzalez and La Versatil, Maria Reyes and Magica Blanca, others. **Contact:** Chanel 13, 886 Maple Avenue, Hartford, CT 06114, 203-956-1303 **or:** Calixto Custom Furniture, 485 New Park Avenue, West Hartford, CT.

CONNECTICUT RIVER VALLEY BLUEGRASS FESTIVAL, East Haddam, CT
>Middle Aug.
>Bluegrass

Since 1989. "Great music, good friends, great fun." -- Flyer. See other dates and sites. **Days:** 3. **Site:** outdoor and indoor. Sunrise Resort, Route 151, Moodus. **Admission:** paid. **Daily entry:** under $10, $10 to $24. **Discounts:** multiple event or day passes, advance purchase discounts, **Acts:** national acts, regional acts, local acts. **Sample lineup:** Del McCoury Band, Paul Adkins and Borderline, Warrior River Boys, Traver Hollow, Grassroots, Cornerstone, Risky Business, Tobacco Valley Bluegrass, Bluegrass Tradition, Bear Bridge, Blistered Fingers, Chestnut Mountain. **Contact:** Connecticut River Valley Bluegrass Association, P. O. Box 246, Middlefield, CT 06455, 203-347-5007/267-4087.

IRISH NIGHT, Manchester, CT
>Middle Aug.
>Irish

See other dates. **Days:** 1. **Site:** outdoor. Manchester Community Technical College, 60 Bidwell Street. **Admission:** free. **Restrictions:** 10, **Acts:** local acts. **Sample day's lineup:** St. Patrick's Pipe Band, others. **Contact:** St. Patrick's Pipe Band, 96 Dartmouth Road, Manchester, CT 06040, 203-647-8811.

## SUMMERTIME STREET FESTIVAL, New Haven, CT
Middle Aug.
Variety, General

Since 1990. Coincides with the Volvo International Tennis Tournament. **Days:** 9. **Hours per day:** 9. **Site:** outdoor. Chapel Street, between College and Park Streets. **Secondary genre[s]:** MJAZ, TJAZ, ARCK, MR&B, ACAP, BGOS, MC&W, MFOL, MLAT, TLAT, OTHR. **Acts:** regional acts, local acts. **Sample lineup:** Norman Evans, Val Ramos, Mighty Purple, Common Ground, Pat Dorn, Sweeter Than Wine, The Nields, Espada, Gravel Pit, TNT Jazz Band, The Undertones, Jane Gang, Boogie Chillun', New England Brass Quintet, John Thomas, Elm City Banjo Society, Bells of Joy, many, many others. **Contact:** Greater New Haven Convention and Visitors Bureau, 1 Long Wharf Drive, New Haven, CT 06511, 203-777-8550.

## MORRIS BLUEGRASS FESTIVAL, Morris, CT
Middle Aug.
Fiddle and Banjo Events

Since 1981. Contests in guitar, mandolin, trick and fancy fiddle, bluegrass, Old Time banjo, Dobro/slide guitar; also "Battle of the Bluegrass Bands." "A wonderful festival...on the green, near the pond...very family-oriented...our judges swear it's the best in Connecticut." -- Volunteer. **Days:** 1. **Hours per day:** 8. **Site:** outdoor. Morris Memorial Park, Routes 109, 61. **Admission:** paid. **Daily entry:** under $10. **Secondary genre[s]:** TC&W, BLGS, TFOL, **Acts:** local acts. **Contact:** Scholarship Fund of Morris, P. O. Box 312, Morris, CT 06763, 203-567-0270/5547/4278.

## DURACELL JAZZ FESTIVAL, Danbury, CT
Middle Aug.
Modern Jazz

See other dates. **Days:** 2. **Site:** outdoor. Charles Ives Center for the Arts. **Admission:** paid. **Daily entry:** $10 to $24, $25 to $49. **Secondary genre[s]:** TR&B, MLAT, **Acts:** national acts. **Sample day's lineup:** George Benson, Dave Brubeck, Rachelle Ferrell, Marvin Stamm. **Contact:** Charles Ives Center for the Arts, P. O. Box 2957, Danbury, CT 06813, 203-797-4002.

## NEWCOMERS OF COUNTRY, Wallingford, CT
Middle Aug.
Modern Country

See other dates. **Help!** One time only? **Days:** 1. **Site:** outdoor. Oakdale Theater, 96 South Turnpike Road. **Acts:** national acts. **Sample day's lineup:** Tracy Lawrence, Stacy Dean Campbell, Martina McBride, Dixiana. **Contact:** Oakdale Theater, 96 South Turnpike Road, Wallingford, CT 06492, 203-265-1501/269-8721.

## LOBSTERFEST/CELEBRATE CANTON, Canton, CT
Middle Aug.
Modern Country

"Just a lot of fun...people have a blast." -- Volunteer. Benefits Canton Volunteer Fire Dept. **Days:** 3. **Site:** outdoor. Canton Springs Road. **Secondary genre[s]:** MFOL, **Acts:** local acts. **Sample day's lineup:** O. K. Chorale, two other bands. **Contact:** Canton Volunteer Fire Dept., Canton Springs Road, Canton, CT 203-693-8120.

CABARET SYMPOSIUM, Waterford, CT
    Middle Aug. to Late Aug.
    Cabaret

Since 1992. "Blend of boot camp and group therapy...for 35 'cabaret fellows' hoping to follow in the fresh foot-prints of Michael Feinstein, Karen Akers and Andrea Marcovicci." -- Joanne Kaufman, Wall Street Journal. Four evening concerts open to the public: (a) Celebrity Performance; (b) Composer's Performance; (c) Master Teacher's Performance; (d) Cabaret Fellows Performance. Ticket prices vary for each. **Help!** A sample lineup? **Site:** indoor. Eugene O'Neill Theater Center, Waterford Beach Park. **Admission:** paid. **Daily entry:** $10 to $24, $25 to $49 **Acts:** national acts, regional acts, local acts. **Contact:** Eugene O'Neill Theater Center, 305 Great Neck Road, Waterford, CT 06385, 203-443-5378.

EARTH JAM, Woodstock, CT
    Middle Aug.
    Alternative and College Rock

Since 1994. **Days:** 1. **Hours per day:** 9. **Site:** outdoor. Woodstock Valley Lodge, 73A Bungay Hill Road. **Admission:** paid. **Daily entry:** under $10. **Discounts:** advance purchase discounts, **Acts:** national acts, local acts. **Sample day's lineup:** Acoustic Junction, Shockra, Band Du Jour. **Contact:** Municipal Cafe, 485 Main Street, Hartford, CT 06103, 203-527-5044/974-1040.

SOUTHERN FRIED FESTIVAL, Woodbury, CT
    Middle Aug.
    Blues and Traditional R&B

**Days:** 1. **Hours per day:** 7. **Site:** outdoor. Woodbury Ski Area, Route 47. **Admission:** paid. **Daily entry:** $10 to $24. **Discounts:** advance purchase discounts, **Secondary genre[s]:** ARCK, **Acts:** national acts, local acts. **Sample day's lineup:** Magic Dick/J. Geils "Blues Time," This Is It, Skankin' Pickle, Ashes of The Red Heffer. **Other merchandise:** 25 VHS recordings of past festivals -- all genres -- available via promoter. **Contact:** Woodbury Ski Area, Route 47, Woodbury, CT 06798, 203-263-2203.

QUINNEHUKQUT RENDEZVOUS AND NATIVE AMERICAN FESTIVAL, Haddam, CT
    Middle Aug. to Late Aug.
    Native American

**Days:** 3. **Site:** outdoor. Haddam Meadows State Park. **Contact:** Quinnehukqut Tendezvous and Native American Festival, c/o Haddam Meadows State Park, Haddam, CT 203-282-1404.

MUSIC FEST, Danielson, CT
    Late Aug.
    Modern Folk

Since 1989. **Days:** 1. **Hours per day:** 4. **Site:** outdoor. Quinebaug Valley Community Technical College, Rogers Ampitheater, 742 Upper Maple Street. **Admission:** paid. **Daily entry:** under $10. **Secondary genre[s]:** TFOL, **Acts:** regional acts, local acts. **Sample day's lineup:** Margo Hennebach, Don Baker and Tom Sullivan, Sleepy Maggie, Jay Swan, Jim Halloran, Dave Drouillard, Springwater, Hugh Blumenfeld, Adrienne Jones, Mug Tomany and Carol Rosetti. **Contact:** State of Connecticut Department of Mental Retardation, 670 Main Street, Willimantic, CT 06226, 203-456-6411/928-3052.

## TASTE BUDS FESTIVAL, Hartford, CT
　　　Late Aug.
　　　Variety, General

See other dates. **Days:** 2. **Site:** outdoor. Bushnell Park. **Admission:** free. **Secondary genre[s]:** MRCK, MC&W, MFOL, **Acts:** national acts. **Sample series lineup:** Day One: Nicolette Larson; Day Two: Kenny Rankin, Orleans. **Contact:** Hartford Restaurant Association, 221 Main Street, Hartford, CT 06106, 203-525-8200.

## WESTBROOK DRUM CORPS MUSTER, Westbrook, CT
　　　Late Aug.
　　　Drum Corps and Marching Bands

"45-50 fife and drum corps perform." -- Listing. **Days:** 2. **Site:** outdoor. Ted Lane Field. **Contact:** Westbrook Drum Corps Muster , P. O. Box 274, Westbrook, CT 06498, 203-399-6436.

## CONNECTICUT RIVER POW-WOW, Farmington, CT
　　　Late Aug.
　　　Native American

Since 1985. See other dates and sites. **Days:** 3. **Hours per day:** 8. **Site:** outdoor. Polo Grounds, Town Farm Road. **Admission:** paid. **Daily entry:** under $10. **Discounts:** group sale discounts, **Acts:** national acts, local acts. **Sample day's lineup:** Zuni Pueblo Singers, Fernando Callicion, others. **Contact:** Connecticut River Pow-Wow Society, 244 East Street, Stafford, CT 06075, 203-684-6984.

## HAFOS: FESTIVAL HISPANO-AMERICANO DE STAMFORD, Stamford, CT
　　　Late Aug.
　　　Traditional Latin

The festival will be a...celebration of Hispanic-American traditions and culture, and offers the community arts and crafts exhibitions, ethnic foods, folk music and dance, entertainment, games and a lot more in a friendly atmosphere." -- Press release. **Help!** One time only? **Days:** 3. **Hours per day:** 12. **Site:** outdoor and indoor. Anthony Truglia Theater, 307 Atlantic Street (Friday night), Lathon Wider Community Center, 137 Henry Street. **Admission:** paid. **Daily entry:** under $10. **Secondary genre[s]:** MLAT, **Acts:** national acts, local acts. **Sample day's lineup:** Conjunto Charey, Conjunto Galaxy, La Sociedad, Orquestra Libron, Orquesta Libre, others. **Contact:** Lathon Wider Community Center, 137 Henry Street, Stamford, CT 203-324-2204.

## HARBOR DAY, Norwich, CT
　　　Late Aug.
　　　Variety, General

**Days:** 1. **Hours per day:** 12. **Site:** outdoor. Howard T. Brown Memorial Park. **Admission:** free. **Secondary genre[s]:** TR&B, ACAP, MC&W, TFOL, NATV, **Acts:** regional acts, local acts. **Sample day's lineup:** Shaboo All-Stars, Melaena, County Line, Ramblin' Dan Stevens, Rose City Chorus, others. **Contact:** Harbor Day, c/o Norwich Chamber of Commerce, Norwich, CT 06360, 203-886-1463 **or:** Harbor Day, c/o Eastern Savings and Loan, 257 Main Street, Norwich, CT 06360, 203-889-7381 x245.

ELI WHITNEY FOLK FESTIVAL, New Haven, CT
> Early Sep.
> Modern Folk

Since 1990. Benefits CT Fund for the Environment, Farmington Canal Rail-to-Trail Association. Caps a summer-long coffeehouse series at the Eli Whitney Barn. **Days:** 1. **Site:** outdoor. Edgerton Park, Whitney Avenue at Cliff Street. **Admission:** paid. **Daily entry:** $10 to $24. **Discounts:** advance purchase discounts, **Secondary genre[s]:** MC&W, BLGS, ZYDC, **Acts:** national acts, regional acts, local acts. **Sample day's lineup:** Emmylou Harris and The Nash Ramblers, Northern Lights, Zydeco Zombies. **Contact:** Connecticut Fund for the Environment, 1032 Chapel Street, New Haven, CT 06510, 203-248-6582.

WPLR LABOR DAY CELEBRATION, New Haven, CT
> Early Sep.
> Alternative and College Rock

See other dates. **Days:** 1. **Hours per day:** 7. **Site:** outdoor. Lighthouse Point Park. **Acts:** national acts, local acts. **Sample day's lineup:** The Skeletons, Secret Smile, Rival, others. **Contact:** WPLR-FM, 1191 Dix Well Avenue, Hamden, CT 06514, 203-488-5062.

SOUTHBURY JAZZ FESTIVAL, Southbury, CT
> Early Sep.
> Traditional Jazz and Ragtime

**Help!** A festival contact? **Days:** 1. **Site:** outdoor. Heritage Village Green. **Admission:** free. **Acts:** regional acts, local acts. **Sample day's lineup:** Charisma, Eastern Standard Time Quartet, Giacomo Gates, Funky Butt Jazz Band, Andy Nichols Orchestra. **Contact:** Southbury Town Hall, 501 Main Street South, Southbury, CT 203-262-0600.

WELCOME BACK TO SCHOOL SHOW: THE BEGINNING OF THE END, New Haven, CT
> Early Sep.
> Alternative and College Rock

See other dates. **Days:** 1. **Site:** indoor. Toad's Place, 300 York Street. **Admission:** paid. **Daily entry:** under $10. **Acts:** local acts. **Sample day's lineup:** Sweetwater, Micah Anderson and Ice Bucket, Bad Bob. **Contact:** Toad's Place, 300 York Street, New Haven, CT 06511, 203-624-TOAD/772-4089.

SIMSBURY SEPTEMBERFEST, Simsbury, CT
> Early Sep.
> Variety, General

Since 1989. 'Simsbury pulls out all the stops." -- Connecticut Magazine. **Days:** 3. **Hours per day:** 11. **Site:** outdoor. Iron Horse Boulevard. **Secondary genre[s]:** CRCK, TR&B, MC&W, **Acts:** regional acts, local acts. **Sample day's lineup:** Max Creek, Eight to the Bar, Wild Horse, others. **Contact:** Simsbury Chamber of Commerce, P. O. Box 224, Simsbury, CT 06070, 203-651-7307.

OYSTER FESTIVAL, South Norwalk, CT
> Early Sep. to Middle Sep.
> Variety, General

Since 1978. "Top 100 events in America." -- American Bus Association. **Days:** 3. **Hours per day:** 13. **Site:** outdoor. Veteran's Park, Seaview Avenue. **Admission:** paid. **Daily entry:** under $10. **Discounts:** student discounts, **Secondary genre[s]:** MJAZ, TJAZ, MRCK, CRCK, MR&B, TR&B, MC&W, MFOL, IRSH, MLAT, GYLS, **Acts:** national acts, local acts. **Sample day's lineup:** Fast Idle, Charlie Saunders, U. S. Army Volunteers, The Turtles, Festival Jazz All-Stars, The Drifters, Fred Roos, Jay Stollman and The All-Stars, Tor and The Newcomers, Yankee Maids, Bob Riccio Quintet, Hot Wired, Funkestra, John Nolan. **Contact:** Norwalk Seaport Association, 132 Water Street, South Norwalk, CT 06854, 203-838-9444.

TASTE OF CONNECTICUT FOOD FESTIVAL, Mystic, CT
> Early Sep. to Middle Sep.
> Variety, General

Benefits the Mystic Community Center. **Days:** 3. **Hours per day:** 11. **Site:** outdoor. Cottrell Street. **Secondary genre[s]:** TJAZ, SCOT, OTHR. **Acts:** local acts. **Sample day's lineup:** Mystic Highland Pipe Band, Strawberry Rhubarb Dixie Jamboree, others. **Contact:** Mystic Chamber of Commerce, Bank Square, Mystic, CT 06355, 203-536-8550.

APPLE VALLEY FAMILY FOLK FESTIVAL, Southington, CT
> Middle Sep.
> Modern Folk

Since 1992. "More than a festival..." -- Brochure. **Days:** 1. **Hours per day:** 6. **Site:** outdoor. YMCA Sloper outdoor Center, 100 East Street. **Admission:** paid. **Daily entry:** $10 to $24. **Discounts:** student discounts, advance purchase discounts, other discounts **Restrictions:** 10, **Secondary genre[s]:** TR&B, ZYDC, **Acts:** national acts, regional acts, local acts. **Sample day's lineup:** Rod MacDonald, Alligator Farmhouse, Hugh Blumenfeld, Dave Drouillard, Steve Gillette and Cindy Mangsen, Donna Martin, The Nields, Bruce Pratt, Stan Sullivan, Zydeco Zombies. **Contact:** Apple Valley Family Folk Festival, Southington YMCA, 29 High Street, Southington, CT 06489, 203-628-5597/5789621-2038 **or:** Red Jacket Music, P. O. Box 607, Southington, CT 06489, 203-621-2038. .

TASTE OF GREATER DANBURY, Danbury, CT
> Middle Sep.
> Variety, General

Since 1987. "Relax, indulge yourself, enjoy all the entertainment, visit the nonprofit tables and learn what's available in the greater Danbury Community." -- Program. **Days:** 1. **Hours per day:** 7. **Site:** outdoor. CityCenter, Ives Street. **Admission:** free. **Secondary genre[s]:** TJAZ, MC&W, BLGS, AFRC, RGGE, GYLS, **Acts:** local acts. **Sample day's lineup:** GDYMA Youth Band, World Oyama, TBone, Caribbean Cruisers, Tennessee Connection, J & B Band, Poetic Justice, Eadton Banjo Society, Danbury Drum Corps. **Contact:** Taste of Greater Danbury Board, City Center Danbury, 7 National Place, Danbury, CT 06810, 203-792-1711/790-6970.

STERLING PARK CAMPGROUND BLUEGRASS FESTIVAL, Sterling, CT
> Middle Sep.
> Bluegrass

See other dates. **Days:** 2. **Hours per day:** 10. **Site:** outdoor. Sterling Park Campground, 177 Gibson Hill Road. **Admission:** paid. **Daily entry:** under $10, $10 to $24. **Discounts:** multiple event or day passes, **Secondary genre[s]:** SGOS, BLGS, **Acts:** local acts. **Sample day's lineup:** Traver Hollow, Grass Roots, Blistered Fingers, Shady Creek, East Wind. **Contact:** Sterling Park Campground, 177 Gibson Hill Road, Sterling, CT 06377, 203-564-8777.

SCHEMITZUN: FEAST OF GREEN CORN, Hartford, CT
> Middle Sep.
> Native American

Since 1992. "This week's powwow, which instantly vaulted the tribe into the major leagues of Indian dance competition, drew about 1,200 American Indian performers from all across North America, some attracted by the $200,00 offered by the Pequots -- by far the richest purse on the competitive powwow circuit -- others invited by the tribe to come and share their traditional ways and skills, all expenses paid." -- Kirk Johnson, New York Times. **Days:** 4. **Site:** indoor. Hartford Civic Center. **Admission:** paid. **Daily entry:** under $10 . **Acts:** national acts, regional acts, local acts. **Sample lineup:** Wahpe Kute, Rose Hill, Elk's Whistle, Cozad's, Black Lodge, Stoney Park, Eyabay, Whitefish Bay, Blackstone, Sioux Assiniboine, Fly In Eagle, Pipestone Creek, Northern Wind, White Fish Jr.'s, Youngblood, Yellow Hammer, Cedar Tree, Red Bull, Sun Eagle, Eagle Whistle, Mandaree, Grey Eyes, Wisconsin Dells, M. G. M., White Eagle, Cathedral Lake, Pigeon Lake, T-6, The Boyz, Charlie Hill, Buddy Big Mountain, Trudie Lamb Richmond, Laughing Woman and Eagle Wing, Mixashawn, Joanne Shenandoah, Shingoose, Floyd Westerman, others. **Contact:** Schemitzun Committee, P. O. Box 3161, Mashantucket, CT 06339-3160, 800-203-CORN.

HOUSATONIC DULCIMER CELEBRATION, New Milford, CT
> Middle Sep.
> Traditional Folk

**Help!** A sample lineup? **Days:** 3. .**Secondary genre[s]:** TC&W, **Contact:** Housatonic Dulcimer Celebration, P. O. Box 518, Sherman, CT 06784, 203-567-8262.

BARBERSHOP HARMONY DAY, Mystic, CT
> Middle Sep.
> A Cappella and Doo Wop

**Help!** A sample lineup? **Days:** 1. **Hours per day:** 6. **Site:** outdoor and indoor. Olde Mystick Village. **Acts:** regional acts, local acts. **Contact:** Barbershop Harmony Day, Olde Mystick Village, Mystic, CT 06355, 203-536-4941.

HARTFORD JAZZ SOCIETY RIVERBOAT CRUISE, Middletown, CT
> Middle Sep.
> Modern Jazz

Since 1961. "Keeping jazz alive." -- Flyer. Note: advance ticket sales only. Bring picnic baskets. **Days:** 1. **Hours per day:** 7. **Site:** outdoor. departs Harbor Park Dock. **Admission:** paid. **Daily entry:** $25 to $49. **Restrictions:** 10, **Secondary genre[s]:** TR&B, **Acts:** national acts, regional acts, local acts. **Sample day's lineup:** The Bill Doggett Band, The Nat Reeves/Mark Johnston Group, Mark Templeton, Mark Johnson. **Contact:** Hartford Jazz Society, Inc., 116 Cottage Grove Road, Suite 204, Bloomfield, CT 06002, 203-242-6688/2942.

TRUMBULL ARTS FESTIVAL, Trumbull, CT
> Middle Sep.
> Variety, Folk and International

Since 1979. **Days:** 1. **Hours per day:** 7. **Site:** outdoor. Town Hall Green. **Secondary genre[s]:** CRCK, MFOL, ZYDC, SCOT, TLAT, BRZL, **Acts:** regional acts, local acts. **Sample day's lineup:** Sandy and Caroline Patton, Sirius Coyote, Bayou Midnight, John Redgate, Phil Rosenthal, Johnny Prytko and The Good Times Band, others. **Contact:** Trumbull Arts Commission, Trumbull Town Hall, Trumbull, CT 06611, 203-452-5065.

DURHAM AGRICULTURAL FAIR, Durham, CT
        Late Sep.
        Fairs

Since 1920. **Days:** 3. **Hours per day:** 13. **Site:** outdoor. Routes 17, 68. **Admission:** paid. **Daily entry:** under $10. **Secondary genre[s]:** MC&W, **Acts:** national acts, local acts. **Sample series lineup:** Day One: Roger Miller, "local acts all day long"; Day Two: The Bellamy Brothers, others; Day Three: John Conlee, others. **Contact:** Durham Agricultural Fair, P. O. Box 225, Durham, CT 06422, 203-349-9495/9479.

NEW ENGLAND RAGTIME FESTIVAL, East Lyme, CT
        Late Sep.
        Traditional Jazz and Ragtime

Since 1993. "A weekend of ragtime music, entertainment and presentations ensures that your stay will be fun-filled...One listen and you'll be hooked!" -- Brochure. **Days:** 3. **Hours per day:** 14. **Site:** indoor. St. Agnes Hall, East Lyme High School, East Lyme Community Center, Connecticut Yankee Inn. **Admission:** paid. **Daily entry:** under $10, $10 to $24. **Discounts:** multiple event or day passes, **Acts:** national acts, regional acts, local acts. **Sample lineup:** Glenn Jenks, Mathew Davidson, Sue Keller, Jeff Barnhart, Douglas Henderson, Marge Burgess, Ross Petot, Mark Lutton, Galen Wilkes, others. **Contact:** New England Ragtime Festival, P. O. Box 568, Niantic, CT 06537, 818-994-3420.

WESTPORT BLUES FESTIVAL, Westport, CT
        Late Sep.
        Blues and Traditional R&B

Since 1993. "Happy blues: Westport to host one hell of a blues festival." -- Jim Motavelli, The Weekly. See other dates. **Days:** 2. **Hours per day:** 9. **Site:** indoor. Westport Country Playhouse, 25 Powers Court. **Admission:** paid. **Daily entry:** $10 to $24. **Discounts:** advance purchase discounts, **Secondary genre[s]:** MFOL, **Acts:** national acts, regional acts, local acts. **Sample lineup:** Mark Naftalin, Debbie Davies, Danny Kortchmar, Harvey Brooks, Sonny Rhodes, Bob Griffin, Jesse "Wild Bill" Austin, Chance Brown, Blue In Your Face, Washboard Slim and The Blue Lights, Gary and The Moodswingers, Sonny Jr. and Code Blue, Triple Threat, Paul Geremia, Eric Von Schmidt, others. **Contact:** Westport Country Playhouse, 25 Powers Court, Westport, CT 203-454-0303.

STRAWBERRY PARK COUNTRY WESTERN JAMBOREE, Preston, CT
        Late Sep.
        Modern Country

Since 1979. **Days:** 3. **Hours per day:** 11. **Site:** outdoor. Strawberry Park Campground, Route 165 East. **Admission:** paid. **Daily entry:** $10 to $24, $25 to $49. **Discounts:** multiple event or day passes, **Acts:** regional acts, local acts. **Sample day's lineup:** Liz Bordeau and Borderline, Robin Brown's 5 and 10 Band, Gin Mill Band, two other bands. **Contact:** Strawberry Park Campground, P. O. Box 830, Norwich, CT 06360, 203-886-1944.

EAGLE WING PRESS POWWOW, Watertown, CT
        Late Sep.
        Native American

**Help!** Still ongoing? **Days:** 2. **Hours per day:** 8. **Site:** outdoor. Black Rock State Park, Route 6. **Admission:** paid. **Daily entry:** under $10. **Contact:** Eagle Wing Press, 257 Southbury Road, Roxbury CT 203-355-7050.

## Roots and Fruits Fiddle and Dance Festival, Hartford, CT
Early Oct.
Traditional Folk

Since 1992. "Participants experience both the roots of present practice and the fruits of the 400-year evolution today...A great event!" -- Newsletter. See other dates. **Days:** 1. **Hours per day:** 9. **Site:** indoor. Charter Oak Cultural Center, 21 Charter Oak Avenue. **Secondary genre[s]:** FDDL, IRSH, SCOT, **Acts:** national acts, local acts. **Sample day's lineup:** Reel Nutmeg, American Music Theater Group, Bristol Old Tyme Fiddlers, Oak Roots Band, Ellen Cohn, Stacy Phillips, Stanley Scott, Paul Woodiel, others. **Contact:** Charter Oak Cultural Center, 21 Charter Oak Avenue, Hartford, CT 06106, 203-249-1207.

## St. Andrew's Society of Conneticut Scottish Festival, Goshen, CT
Early Oct.
Scottish

**Help!** The status of this event? **Days:** 1. **Site:** outdoor. Goshen Agricultural Fairgrounds. **Contact:** St. Andrew's Society of Connecticut Scottish Festival, P. O. Box 63, Winchester Center, CT 06094, 203-379-2527 **or:** St. Andrew's Society of Connecticut Scottish Festival, P. O. Box 1195, Litchfield, CT 06759, 203-489-9509.

## Scotland Highland Festival, Scotland, CT
Early Oct.
Scottish

**Help!** The status of this event, or the whereabouts of its promoters? **Days:** 1. **Site:** outdoor. Waldo Homestead. **Contact:** Scotland Highland Festival, c/o Town Clerk, Scotland, CT 203-423-9634.

## Mineral Springs Foot Stomp'n Festival, Stafford Springs, CT
Early Oct.
Bluegrass

"Come and enjoy." -- Flyer. See other dates. **Days:** 1. **Hours per day:** 14. **Site:** outdoor and indoor. Mineral Springs Campground, 135 Leonard Road. **Admission:** paid. **Daily entry:** under $10, $10 to $24. **Discounts:** multiple event or day passes, group sale discounts, **Acts:** regional acts, local acts. **Sample day's lineup:** Southern Rail, Traver Hollow, Amy Gallatin and Still Waters, Bear Bridge Band, Stonewall Bluegrass, Gary Ferguson Band, Case Brothers, Grassroots, Flatlanders. **Contact:** Mineral Springs Foot Stomp'n Festival, 48 Village Hill Road, Willington, CT 06076, 203-684-2993/9647.

## Chowderfest, Mystic, CT
Early Oct. to Middle Oct.
Maritime

**Days:** 3. **Hours per day:** 12. **Site:** outdoor and indoor. Mystic Seaport Museum, 50 Greenmanville Avenue. **Admission:** paid. **Daily entry:** under $10, $10 to $24. **Secondary genre[s]:** OTHR **Acts:** local acts. **Sample lineup:** Mystic Seaport Chanteymen, others. **Audio merchandise:** "Sea Chanteys and Forecastle Songs at Mystic Seaport" (Folkways). **Contact:** Mystic Seaport Museum, P. O. Box 6000, Mystic, CT 06355-0990, 203-572-0711/5350.

## Paucatuck Pequot Harvest Moon Powwow, North Stonington, CT
Early Oct. to Middle Oct.
Native American

Since 1992. **Days:** 3. **Site:** outdoor. Highlands Orchards Resort Park, Route 49. **Contact:** Paucatuck Pequot Harvest Moon Powwow, Highlands Orchards Resort Park, Route 49, North Stonington, CT 203-684-6984.

## APPLE HARVEST FESTIVAL, Glastonbury, CT
Middle Oct.
Variety, Folk and International

Also programs a summer-long concert series of national, regional and local names. **Days:** 2. **Site:** outdoor. Town Green. **Secondary genre[s]:** BLGS, TFOL, OTHR **Acts:** regional acts, local acts. **Sample day's lineup:** Amy Gallatin and Still Waters, plus three other local acts. **Contact:** Glastonbury Chamber of Commerce, 2400 Main Street, Glastonbury, CT 06033, 203-659-3587.

## FESTIVAL AT ROSELAND COTTAGE, Woodstock, CT
Middle Oct.
Variety, General

Since 1983. **Days:** 2. **Site:** outdoor. Roseland Cottage, 556 Route 169. **Secondary genre[s]:** MJAZ, TJAZ, CRCK, MFOL, TFOL, OTHR. **Acts:** local acts. **Sample day's lineup:** Sleepy Maggy, East Woodstock Cornet Band, Rhode Island Fiddlers, others. **Contact:** Roseland Cottage, P. O. Box 186, Woodstock, CT 06281, 203-928-4074.

## FALL FOLK MUSIC WEEKEND, Falls Village, CT
Middle Oct.
Traditional Folk

See other dates and sites. **Days:** 3. **Site:** outdoor and indoor. Camp Isabella Freedman. **Admission:** paid. **Daily entry:** $50 and over. **Discounts:** other discounts **Secondary genre[s]:** MFOL, OTHR **Acts:** regional acts, local acts. **Sample day's lineup:** Steve Gillette and Cindy Mangsen, Jeter LePont, Adaya Hennis, Allen Hopkins, Sonja Savig, others. **Contact:** New York Pinewoods Folk Music Club, 31 West 95th Street, New York, NY 10025, 212-666-9605 **or:** New York Pinewoods Folk Music Club, 19 Dongan Place, #3B, New York, NY 10040, 212-942-2847.

## NOMAD: NORTHEAST MUSIC, ART AND DANCE FESTIVAL, Sandy Hook, CT
Late Oct. to Early Nov.
Variety, Folk and International

Since 1989. **Days:** 2. **Hours per day:** 12. **Site:** indoor. Newtown High School. **Admission:** paid. **Daily entry:** under $10. **Discounts:** student discounts, multiple event or day passes, **Secondary genre[s]:** TGOS, BLGS, TFOL, ZYDC, IRSH, SCOT, OTHR. **Acts:** regional acts, local acts. **Sample day's lineup:** Different Village, Atlantic Bridge, Bayou Midnight, Rich Blazej, Ted Crane, Susan Elberger, Christine Helwig, Larry Jennings, Morley Leyton, Musical Cheers, Dan Pearl, White Cockade, Ralph Sweet, others. **Contact:** NOMAD, 50 Plum Tree Lane, Trumbull, CT 06611, 203-372-3890 **or:** NOMAD, 12 Pamela Place, Westport, CT 06880, 203-426-9266. .

## COMMUNITY CAROL SING, Mystic, CT
Middle Dec.
Traditional Gospel and Sings

**Days:** 1. **Site:** outdoor and indoor. Mystic Seaport Museum, 50 Greenmanville Avenue. **Admission:** paid. **Daily entry:** under $10, $10 to $24. **Secondary genre[s]:** MARI, OTHR **Acts:** local acts. **Sample lineup:** Mystic Seaport Chanteymen, others. **Audio merchandise:** "Sea Chanteys and Forecastle Songs at Mystic Seaport" (Folkways). **Contact:** Mystic Seaport Museum, P. O. Box 6000, Mystic, CT 06355-0990, 203-572-0711/5350.

FIRST NIGHT DANBURY, Danbury, CT
Late Dec. Variety, Folk and International

**Help!** A sample lineup? **Days:** 1. **Site:** outdoor and indoor. multiple locations. **Admission:** paid. **Daily entry:** under $10. **Discounts:** advance purchase discounts, **Restrictions:** 2. **Contact:** Danbury Downtown Council, 1 Liberty Street, Danbury, CT 06810, 203-792-5095.


FIRST NIGHT HARTFORD, Hartford, CT
Late Dec.
Variety, Folk and International

"One night like no other...One night when we celebrate our differences because being different is all we have in common...One night that's just this side of your wildest dreams..." -- Brochure. **Days:** 1. **Hours per day:** 10. **Site:** outdoor and indoor. 25 locations. **Admission:** paid. **Daily entry:** under $10. **Discounts:** advance purchase discounts, **Restrictions:** 2. **Secondary genre[s]:** MJAZ, TJAZ, MRCK, CRCK, TR&B, BGOS, MC&W, MFOL, TFOL, ZYDC, IRSH, TLAT, AFRC, BRZL, OTHR **Acts:** national acts, regional acts, local acts. **Sample day's lineup:** All The Voices, American Music Theater Group, Artists Collective, Aztec Two-Step, Paul Bisaccia, Bordeline, Capitol Winds, Celebration Community Choir, Center Church Singers, CitySingers and Soni Fidelis, CMP Jazz Quartet, Confluence, CT Classical Guitar, CT Opera Express, Espada, Greater Hartford Academy of Performing Arts, Tony Harrington Plus Two, Hartford American Guild of Organists, Hartt Community Division, I Giovanni Solisti, Insurance City Chrous, Kwanzaa, Manchester Trombone Quartet, Montage, The Nields, The Nifty 50's Band, Oronoque Trio, People Of Goodwill, Please and Thank You String Band, Bruce Pratt, The Ringroses, Rondeau Consort, Samba Brasil, Sankofa Kuumba, Sol De America, Taino, Top Brass, Nancy Tucker, Vacca/Moran, Washboard Slim and The Blue Lights, Yesterday, Today and Forever, Zydeco Zombies. **Contact:** Downtown Council, 250 Constitution Plaza, Hartford, CT 203-728-3089.

# R. I. P., M. I. A. Festival Listings

The following festivals are either confirmed or suspected to be discontinued (i.e., R. I. P.); or have **Caveat** not responded to various information requests (i.e., M. I. A.). Since all festivals are subject to last-minute changes or reinstatement, however, FESTPRESS is not responsible for any festival listing information that follows. Readers are encouraged to notify FESTPRESS of any status changes they uncover.

## YIDDISHKEIT...LOST AND FOUND! A CONFERENCE AND CELEBRATION, Hartford, CT
Early Apr.
Jewish

"Festival of performances and symposia on Yiddish culture -- past and present." -- Brochure. See other dates. **Help!** One time only? Also, a sample lineup? **Days:** 1. **Site:** indoor. Charter Oak Cultural Center, 21 Charter Oak Avenue. **Contact:** Charter Oak Cultural Center, 21 Charter Oak Avenue, Hartford, CT 06106, 203-249-1207.

## MOON PIE FESTIVAL, Windsor Locks, CT
Early Apr.
Blues and Traditional R&B

"Moon Pies! RC Colas! No Easter eggs!" -- Advertisement. NRBQ's annual Easter affair, recently revived. **Help!** Still ongoing? **Days:** 2. **Site:** indoor. Windsor Court Hotel. **Admission:** paid **Secondary genre[s]:** CRCK, OTHR. **Acts:** national acts, local acts. **Sample day's lineup:** NRBQ and The Whole Wheat Horns, plus several polka bands and other "special guests." **Contact:** 106 WHCN-FM, 1039 Asylum Avenue, Hartford, CT 06105, 203-247-1060.

## CHILDREN OF CHERNOBYL RELIEF FUND BENEFIT CONCERT, West Hartford, CT
Early May
Modern Folk

Since 1990. Lost money in 1992; likely discontinued. Other folk concerts periodically held at same site. **Help!** Still ongoing? **Days:** 1. **Site:** indoor. Lincoln Theater, University of Hartford, 200 Bloomfield Avenue. **Admission:** paid **Daily entry:** $10 to $24 **Acts:** national acts. **Sample Day's Lineup:** Tom Rush, Peter Ostroushko, Martin Sexton. **Contact:** Children of Chernobyl Relief Fund, P. O. Box 340278, 961 Wethersfield Avenue, Hartford, CT 06134-0278, 203-527-5608 **or:** Children of Chernobyl Relief Fund, 12 Gretel Lane, Simsbury, CT 06070, 203-657-9670.

## CAJUN, ZYDECO, BLUEGRASS FESTIVAL, Woodbury, CT
Middle May
Bluegrass

Discontinued in 1994. **Days:** 1. **Hours per day:** 7. **Site:** outdoor. Woodbury Ski Area, Route 47. **Admission:** paid **Daily entry:** $10 to $24 **Discounts:** advance purchase discounts, **Secondary genre[s]:** ARCK, ZYDC, **Acts:** national acts, regional acts, local acts. **Sample day's lineup:** Zachary Richard, Vassar Clements, J. D. Crowe and The New South, From Good Homes. **Other merchandise:** 25 VHS recordings of past festivals -- all genres -- available via promoter. **Contact:** Woodbury Ski Area, Route 47, Woodbury, CT 06798, 203-263-2203.

WARNER THEATER COUNTRY FAMILY FESTIVAL, Torrington, CT
> Late May
> Modern Country

Since 1994. One time only. **Days:** 1. **Hours per day:** 3. **Site:** outdoor. Fuessenich Park. **Acts:** national acts. **Sample day's lineup:** Crystal Gayle, Diamond Rio, Sawyer Brown. **Contact:** Warner Theater, Torrington, CT 203-489-7180.

CONNECTICUT COUNTRY FEST, New London, CT
> Late Jun.
> Modern Country

Since 1994. One time only. See other dates. **Days:** 3. **Site:** outdoor. Ocean Beach Park. **Acts:** regional acts, local acts. **Sample lineup:** John Lincoln Wright and The Sour Mash Boys, Square One, The Cartwrights, The Ranch Band, Walker Marshall, O. K. Chorale, Liz Bordeau and Borderline, Prudence And The Plowboys, Robin Brown and The 5 and 10 Band, The Gin Mill Band. **Contact:** Ocean Beach Park, 1225 Ocean Avenue, New London, CT 06320, 203-447-3031.

TORRINGTON ROCK AND ARTS FESTIVAL, Torrington, CT
> Early Jul.
> Modern Rock and Pop

Since 1993. Benefits Torrington Mayor's Committee on Youth. **Help!** One time only? **Days:** 1. **Site:** outdoor. Fuessenich Park, South Main Street. **Admission:** paid **Daily entry:** under $10 **Secondary genre[s]:** HRCK, **Acts:** local acts. **Sample day's lineup:** Necktie Party, Gutterpunks, Crystal Witch, Iron Horse. **Contact:** Mach I Music, 19 Water Street, Torrington, CT 203-496-1193.

INTERNATIONAL PERFORMING ARTS FESTIVAL, Hartford, CT
> Early Jul. to Middle Jul.
> Variety, Folk and International

Discontinued in 1993, a victim of state budget cuts. **Days:** 2. **Site:** outdoor. Bushnell Park. **Contact:** 203-240-8400.

SUMMER JAM, Middletown, CT
> Middle Jul.
> Classic Rock and Oldies

Since 1993. Discontinued in 1995. **Days:** 1. **Site:** outdoor. Portland Fairgrounds. **Admission:** paid **Daily entry:** $10 to $24 **Secondary genre[s]:** MJAZ, TR&B, **Acts:** local acts. **Sample day's lineup:** Michael Cleary Band, Locomotion, Zero Tolerance, Dave and Charlie. **Contact:** Greater Middletown Jaycee's, Middletown, CT 203-344-9467.

BENEFIT EAGLE ROCK CONCERT, Middlefield, CT
> Late Jul.
> Modern Rock and Pop

Since 1994. Benefits Eagle 1 Search and Rescue Helicopter Service. **Help!** The status of this event, or the whereabouts of its promoters? **Days:** 1. **Site:** outdoor. Powder Ridge Ski Area, Powder Hill Road. **Admission:** paid **Daily entry:** $10 to $24 **Discounts:** advance purchase discounts, **Secondary genre[s]:** TR&B, **Acts:** regional acts, local acts. **Sample day's lineup:** Joan Osborne Band, The Savage Brothers, UHF, The Michael Cleary Band. **Contact:** Powder Ridge Ski Area, Powder Ridge Road, Middlefield, CT 06457, 203-349-3454.

## CAMP CREEK PLANETARY POWER JAM, Woodstock, CT
Late Jul.
Classic Rock and Oldies

Since 1993. One time only. **Days:** 2. **Hours per day:** 9. **Site:** outdoor. Woodstock Valley Lodge, 73A Bungay Hill Road. **Admission:** paid **Daily entry:** $10 to $24 **Discounts:** advance purchase discounts, **Secondary genre[s]:** ZYDC, **Acts:** regional acts, local acts. **Sample day's lineup:** Max Creek, Bill Walach and Dave Howard, Zydeco Zombies. **Contact:** Municipal Cafe, 485 Main Street, Hartford, CT 06103, 203-527-5044/974-1040.

## TWELVE BEST LOCAL BANDS LIVE, Stamford, CT
Middle Aug. to Late Aug.
Alternative and College Rock

Since 1992. Discontinued at this venue. **Help!** Still ongoing at another venue? **Days:** 2. **Site:** indoor. Terrace Club. **Secondary genre[s]:** MJAZ, RAP, MR&B, RGGE, **Acts:** local acts. **Sample day's lineup:** Red Stripe, Tongue In Groove, Blue In The Face, When I Woke, Bejobe, Payback. **Contact:** Terrace Club, 1938 West Main Street, Stamford, CT 203-961-9770.

## IRISH FEST, New London, CT
Late Aug.
Irish

**Help!** The status of this event, and a sample lineup? **Days:** 1. **Site:** outdoor. Ocean Beach Park. **Contact:** Ocean Beach Park, 1225 Ocean Avenue, New London, CT 06320, 203-447-3031.

## BUDWEISER CHARITY REGGAE MUSIC FESTIVAL, Bridgeport, CT
Late Aug.
Reggae, Ska and Caribbean

Since 1992. One time only, and the biggest rip-off I've ever had the misfortune of attending. **Days:** 2. **Hours per day:** 12. **Site:** outdoor. Seaside Park. **Admission:** paid. **Daily entry:** $10 to $24 **Acts:** national acts, regional acts, local acts. **Contact:** Ujama Performing Arts Company, 203-336-3359.

## CHILI COOKOFF, Somers, CT
Early Sep.
Modern Country

Benefits Leukemia Society of America. **Help!** Still ongoing? **Days:** 3. **Hours per day:** 6. **Site:** indoor. Shallowbrook Equestrian Center, 147 Hall Hill Road. **Admission:** paid **Daily entry:** under $10 **Discounts:** other discounts **Acts:** local acts. **Contact:** Leukemia Society of America, 102 King's Highway East, Fairfield, CT 06430, 203-579-1628/359-4761.

## GALA BENEFIT, Westport, CT
Early Sep.
Modern Jazz

Reduced to one national act, Buckwheat Zydeco, in 1995. See other dates. **Days:** 1. **Site:** outdoor. Levitt Pavilion for the Performing Arts, Jesup Road. **Admission:** paid **Restrictions:** 2. **Secondary genre[s]:** MLAT, **Acts:** national acts, regional acts, local acts. **Sample day's lineup:** Tito Puente and His Orchestra, Kit McClure Band, others. **Contact:** Levitt Pavilion for the Performing Arts, Town Hall, Westport, CT 06880, 203-226-7600.

BRAZILIAN FESTIVAL DAY, Danbury, CT
> Early Sep.
> Brazilian and South American

**Help!** The status of this event, or the whereabouts of its promoters? **Days:** 1. **Hours per day:** 18. **Site:** outdoor. Hatter's Park, Hayestown Road. **Admission:** paid **Daily entry:** $10 to $24. **Contact:** Brazilian Cultural Group of Danbury, Danbury CT 203-792-9608.

12 X 12 X 12, South Norwalk, CT
> Middle Sep.
> Variety, Folk and International

Since 1993. "Named 12 x 12 for dozens of reasons, this benefit [for WPKN-FM] features acts as eclectic as the station it's going to help." -- Band Box, The Weekly. **Help!** One time only? **Days:** 1. **Hours per day:** 12. **Site:** indoor. Shenanigan's. **Admission:** paid **Daily entry:** under $10 **Secondary genre[s]:** MRCK, TR&B, BLGS, MFOL, BRZL, RGGE, **Acts:** regional acts, local acts. **Sample day's lineup:** Alison Farrell, Primitivo, Sirius Coyote, The Nields, The Redding Brothers, Ben Andrews, Jesse Austin Blues Band, K Man Band, Cathy Kreger, Tongue In Groove, others. **Contact:** CRIS-WPKN, University of Bridgeport, Bridgeport, CT 203-332-0606.

COUNTRY AND WESTERN COMES TO MYSTIC, Mystic, CT
> Middle Oct.
> Modern Country

Since 1993. Discontinued in 1994. **Days:** 1. **Contact:** Mystic Chamber of Commerce, Bank Square, Mystic, CT 06355, 203-536-8550.

WATERBURY TRADITIONAL MUSIC FESTIVAL, Waterbury, CT
> Nov.
> Traditional Folk

Experimenting in 1995 with concert-series format highlighting local ethnic musics, instead. Stay tuned. **Site:** indoor. Mattatuck Museum, 144 West Main Street. **Contact:** Mattatuck Museum, 144 West Main Street, Waterbury, CT 06702, 203-753-0381/672-6092.

~   ~   ~

*Marc Ribot Quartet, RAW Jazz Festival.*

# New York

*Swingin', Stanfordville Music and Dance Festival.*

# Artist Sightings, I: Oscar Brand

**Nassau Community College Folk Festival**, Uniondale, NY
> Late March
> Folk, Variety and International
> ***Attended***

**International Jewish Arts Festival of Long Island**, Commack, NY
> Late May
> Jewish
> ***Attended***

Spring break for many collegians means Fort Lauderdale, Daytona Beach, Padre Island and an **Introduction** ever-expanding fraternity of hedonist flings.

For the students at diminutive Nassau Community College [NCC], however, it's the culmination of a hard semester's efforts where the party starts right in their own backyard — in this case, their College Union abutting the crumbling blacktops of historic Mitchel Field (the "Cradle of Aviation" from where Lindberg launched the first trans-Atlantic flight). Since '72 NCC's concert board has elected to expend their extra-curricular efforts and student-activity fees on producing what remains a real sleeper on the indoor circuit.

Their **Nassau Community College Folk Festival** [FolkFest] boasts: three nights; 15 acts, with all but one or two being significant names; and 10 genres or more, including several that'll rock the house. It features such a wide berth of musical styles that I'm tempted to move its classification into my broader "Variety, General." Best of all, this mid-week assembly is free to you and me!

Open the program booklet and you won't be greeted by words from longtime Faculty Advisor, Phyllis Kurland. Nor by her partner, "Artistic Coordinator and Genuine Godsend," Paula Ballan. Nor by the two folk-radio heavy-hitters from New York City's WXRK-FM who act as MC's — Vin Scelsa or Pete Fornatale. Nor even by the event's founder, folk icon and NCC Adjunct Professor, Oscar Brand, who's performed at every one since.

Instead you read these kinds of sentiments from FolkFest student chairpeople:

- "The best thing about FolkFest is...we book international acts that will entertain the entire student population and our surrounding communities, too. FolkFest involves multiculturalism, world history, a hope for peace and great, great entertainment! The second best thing I like about FolkFest is the incredible excitement I feel when the lights go out on the first night!" (Jason Farber.)

- "For me FolkFest is that major project...[that] once you have finished, you get an unparalleled sense of fulfillment knowing you didn't have a complete nervous breakdown! Well, I'm still in one piece, my head feels good, I'm having a terrific time and I hope you do, too!" (Chris Antonacci.)

- "[FolkFest] has given me the best kind of experience I could have asked for." (Jackie Cohen.)

A committee of roughly 20 student put on a helluva' show for roughly 2,500 of us who patiently snake through the doors, past the hippie/rasta crafts displays, onto the couches occupying the waiting room, then into the cafeteria where plastic chairs are pushed aside for dancing when the evening's closing bands hit their strides.

It's been funny to see the audience rotation. Parents/grandparents come early for Brand's folkies while the students come late for the party-hearty acts. This all-ages quality makes each evening feel something like a homecoming, which it is for many of us "Lawn Guylanders" who consider FOLKFEST the first hint of spring to follow.

 Let's peg the lineup.

First, the legendary Brand does one set, then invites some of his contemporaries from "The Great Folk Scare" for successive nights. In '93 this meant vets Richie Havens and Tom Paxton plus the younger David Massengill.

Second, you can predict esteemed jumpin' jivers, the eight-piece Harlem Blues and Jazz Band. Although you might not recognize any names among the band roster of these pre-war traditionalists, you can be assured of authenticity and quality from their impressive credits: Ellington, Basie, Holliday, Fitzgerald, Vaughn, Cole, etc.

Third, the students, themselves, recruit a college/alternative edge with acts like "acoustic grrl," Ani DiFranco, and Austin-based thrash-grassers Killbilly.

Fourth comes a sweep of ethnic genres: Celtic (Maire Ni Chathasaigh and Chris Newman), French (Pierre Bensusan), Indian (Jai Uttai), Serbian/Croatian (Sviraj), and others.

Fifth brings a blues act or two. In '93 this was funky street duo, Satan and Adam, although Jorma Kaukonen's been a constant in previous years. (Since Kaukonen's always the FOLKFEST's top draw, make sure to get there at least an hour early the night he's booked.)

For the dancing finale, count on one night being a world-beat blow-out. The incendiary Malathini and The Mahotella Queens were '93's culprits. The other two nights that year were topped respectively by local funkers, The Authority, and Queen-Latifah-produced rappers, Bigga Sistahs.

Tally it up and you've earned yourself a first-rate musical education you won't need a student loan to enjoy. Spring break never sounded so good!

**Artist Mini-Reviews**   Here's a typical night from a recent year.

Walt Michael and Company. Four acoustic pieces doing old-timey standards in pleasant tempos with occasional nods to the present. Leader Michael proved a good tutor. Not only does he patiently explain the genesis of his various Appalachian medleys, but he also exhibits full command of one of its precursors — the jigs, reels and aires of the Shetland Isles. Relaxed, sincere, and nothing flashy, with the exception of Michael's hyper-driven hammer dulcimer solo on "Dem Golden Slippers."

Judy Small. The Australian Christine Lavin? Well, Small doesn't nearly possess Lavin's spontaneous wackiness, but shares a similarly wry sensibility and desire to coax left-handed insights from everyday detritus. I enjoyed her even-toned sentiments from a heart-warming narrative of a "cocky" (a poor Australian farmer) and his wife; and an accappella ruing the loss of Charlesworth Bay's natural splendor from the days of her youth.

Tom Paxton. Hank Williams once joked that he had just two kinds of songs, "fast and slow." That simplification might almost apply to longtime troubadour and L. I. resident, Tom Paxton. Half his set-list comprised nostalgic, melodic sing-alongs, often with a ecological/sociological bent, such as "Ramblin' Boy," "Factory Whistle Blowin'," and "Whose Garden Is This."

But serve up Paxton with pompous targets, and nobody else cuts 'em down with sharper, funnier strokes. The Reagan era provided fertile ground for his ticklish broadsides, as Paxton lampooned the sexual ambitions of Gary Hart ("The Politics Game"), the material ambitions of "Yupper West Siders" ("Yuppies in the Sky"), and the procreating ambitions of our brethren of the bar ("One Million Lawyers"). Introduced as "an election year special," Paxton was a crowd-pleaser for hometown fans.

Holmes Brothers. Boy, it's been great to see my heroes from one of New York City's seediest blues dives, Dan Lynch's, hit it big. Thirty years of long, smoky sets have put a pretty rough edge on the lead vocals of guitarist Wendell Holmes, and the harmony vocals of his brother, bassist Sherman. However, drummer Popsy Dixon miraculously retains his piercing falsetto, which lends their vocal mix its otherworldly urgency. (I once saw Dixon lift his head off Dan Lynch's bartop from what I'll charitably assume was a dead nap, shuffle over to his drum kit, and launch straight into an accappella wail that would've given Aaron Neville a run for his money!)

This night they performed as a trio with pedal-steel whiz, Gib Wharton, taking a breather. Their set-list was nothing special, notable only for the way it interchanged blues and gospel chestnuts with a country closer. Ah, but the feel! These three have it absolutely right, knowing when to tighten-up, when to loosen-up, and when to free-lance. Wendell's voice was so raw it almost hurt to hear him, yet when all three grimaced through their parts with eyes clenched tight, you could just feel the passion welling. Inspiring, as on their uniquely soulful interpretation of "Amazing Grace."

<u>Arrow</u>. I have a hard time remembering ever being rocked so relentlessly, perhaps even surpassing C. J. Chenier's and Nathan Williams' respective late-night marathons one year at the CAJUN AND BLUEGRASS MUSIC-DANCE-FOOD FESTIVAL (Escoheag, RI — see chapter). Lead singer/dancer/pied-piper Arrow introduced his seven-piece band as "a multinational force from Montserrat," then promised, "We're gonna' party 'till you sweat!" Mission accomplished. Arrow's crew put on a choreographed show virtually uninterrupted for well over two hours. Students were soaked and limp from dancing so hard for so long, on stage and off.

Soca might be described as turbocharged reggae with lightly-dancing guitars and busy horn charts supplying the syncopated stick shift. Saucy lyrics pervade. Calypso purists, I'm told, object to soca's modernism, perhaps in the same way that R&B purists objected to '70s disco. Arrow underscored the point by interspersing Kool & The Gang's "Party," along with a few other Western references.

O. K., so call me a tourist. No cultural-correctness was gonna' intimidate me when Arrow kicked off an extended jam on what he called "the soca national anthem, 'Hot, Hot, Hot'" — recently covered by David Johansen's Buster Poindexter character. I kept to a Latin dance-step, but that was my only proper concession for Arrow's charismatic libidinousness. Party service with a smile!

**See Also** In '92, I was able to hit the equally-wonderful PHILADELPHIA FOLK SONG SOCIETY SPRING FESTIVAL (see Swarthmore, PA, Late April) on the same weekend. In fact, I caught The Holmes Brothers at both gigs. Erratic scheduling blew these two events far apart in '93, yet it pays to keep alert for similar opportunities to extend the FOLKFEST's mid-week festivities.

Those looking to add to their Oscar Brand sightings would do well to check out the INTERNATIONAL JEWISH ARTS FESTIVAL OF LONG ISLAND, where Brand is a virtual regular. The United Jewish Y's of Long Island have produced this ethnic popourri annually since '81. They set down no fewer than five performing areas upon a huge grassy expanse and proffer an exceptionally wide berth of entertainment, from the sublime (David Amram conducting The United Jewish Arts Festival Orchestra in a program of Gottschalk, Copland, Bernstein, Kern, Gould and Amran, himself) to the ridiculous (any number of "Borsch Belt" comics dishing out groaners all day long). There was even a Yiddish version of Gilbert and Sullivan's "H. M. S. Pinafore" one year that I found accomplished and quite amusing. Count on a relaxed family affair with many genuine musical attractions, Brand included.

~     ~     ~

# Fox Hollow's Folk Traditions

OLD SONGS SAMPLER CONCERT, Guilderland, NY
> Late January
> Traditional Folk

**GOTTAGETGON FOLK FESTIVAL: THE PICK'N AND SINGIN' GATHERIN'**, Ballston Spa, NY
> Late May
> Traditional Folk
> ***Attended***

**OLD SONGS FESTIVAL OF TRADITIONAL MUSIC AND DANCE**, Altamont, NY
> Late June
> Variety, Folk and International
> ***Attended***

FOX HOLLOW REUNION FOLK CONCERT, Troy, NY
> Middle October
> Traditional Folk

**Introduction** Traditional folk music has two saving graces. First, it preserves musical formulas that have survived for a simple reason — they work, often from having been distilled over centuries:

- Melodies — strong enough to be passed down orally by commoners who typically couldn't read music if they could read at all;

- Lyrics — effectively speaking to everyday lives and springing from shared emotions;

- Rhythms — whether born of the plow, rail, or sail, or birthed for the dance floor — that feel natural in the fingers and feet of their participants.

You'll find these to be common threads among many ethnic sub-genres such that if you can get a handle on one, you can rotate your interest readily to another, then another. What seems eclectic to folk festival outsiders thus feels less so to the properly initiated.

These formulas are more universal than not, even extending into the commercial world. It's no accident that during modern folk music's last popular resurgence, "The Great Folk Scare" of the '60s, nearly all of its leading artists were profoundly influenced by traditional purveyors. I've heard numerous stars from that period continue to say so from the bandstand. I wonder if they're not subtly instructing any aspiring folk singer-songwriters in the audience whose work would invariably benefit from such study.

Second, traditional folk music has always been a communal experience, not something engineered in a lonely studio or cooked up in a corporate boardroom. It was made to be played, to be sung, to be danced, to be joined. "All-hands-in" was the rule within folk circles, which created an interesting dichotomy. One one hand, structures had to be basic enough to invite novices. There were no schools or elaborate apprentices — you learned from your mom or dad. On the other hand, they provided skilled musicians a mutual vocabulary with room for infinite variation and improvisation. Classical music's got nothing on a well-practiced band of traditional folk masters when it comes to subtlety and complexity.

When folk-music promoters embraced the festival format in the '60s, they immediately inserted this participatory nature via workshop offerings and such. Fans responded by bringing their instruments then stuck around onsite for campfire jams, singalongs, and dances. Folk festivals became big "back porches" for thousands. Three exemplars from that decade were the NEWPORT FOLK FESTIVAL (BEN & JERRY'S NEWPORT FOLK FESTIVAL, Newport — see chapter), the PHILADELPHIA FOLK FESTIVAL (see Schwenksville, PA, Late August), and the late, lamented FOX HOLLOW FESTIVAL in Petersburg, NY.

The communal pull of FOX HOLLOW' proved so strong it created two spin-offs:

- One from/for roughly 300 of its core organizers, the GOTTAGETGON FOLK FESTIVAL [GOTTAGETGONE], begun in '70;

- Another from its passing in '80, the OLD SONGS FESTIVAL OF TRADITIONAL MUSIC AND DANCE [OLD SONGS] for about 6,000 faithful "traddies."

Not only will you still feel those timeless techniques resonate within you at both gatherings, but you'll experience the music the way it's meant to be — passed down and around "just plain folks."

Ask Director Andy Spence what prompted the first OLD SONGS in '81, and she won't hesitate:     **Festival Review I**

- "Well, 15 years at FOX HOLLOW', I guess. It was run by [the late] Bob Beers, and it ended in '80. I was an integral part of that festival for years, and many of the people in this area were also. We all missed it terribly. We were always there, and so it was just that we knew a lot of the people, and they came from all over the country to go to that festival; many, many families. Lots of children grew up there. There's still great stories about FOX HOLLOW'.

    "But knowing we would be without a festival in this area, we started OLD SONGS in '78 knowing that we would probably end up with a festival because there wouldn't be one [laughs]. We started OLD SONGS, INC. as a not-for-profit, 501 C3, educational corporation dedicated to preserving traditional music and dance. By the time '81 came around, we already had a concert series, a country dancing series, and had some classes, so we just added the festival and went on from there [laughs]."

Spence's soft-spoken drawl and droll chuckle makes it all sound so natural, but there's a carefully-considered ethic for participation driving her every decision for OLD SONGS. In a nutshell? "I would say that we're more close to the festival that used to be," Spence claims, "you know, a more intimate setting, a more relaxed atmosphere, a way to get up close to a performer without being kicked in the teeth [laughs], or told you can't walk up there.

- "What I find in traditionally-based artists are that they have a great deal in common with each other, [yet] many of them don't know each other. So the festival really takes place on two levels. It takes place on the artist level, which is also meant to be a way for them to meet each other and find out about each other and share their music. And then it takes place on the consumer level where the person comes and participates in whatever way they want to. I mean, there are many choices."

"Many" is the understatement of the circuit!

OLD SONGS has nine stages organized loosely by themes or function. Two stages are for dancing; two are for workshops; one's for family performance; another's a "Potpourri" combing all functions. The remaining three stages are for concerts. Seven of these nine stages turn over every hour from 10:00 a.m. to 6:00 p.m.; one stage features shorter "Mini Concerts"; the last goes "In Depth" for 90-minute teaching sets.

There's more! Children have six performing/activity areas of their own. No less than seven of the 28 crafters onsite present formal demonstrations, while many instrument vendors maintain informal demonstrations and mini-concerts at their own booths. There's one of the largest Sacred Harp sings in the Northeast every morning at 9:30 a.m. sharp, not to mention a Main Stage evening concert at 7:00 p.m. featuring seven acts, followed by a country dance that runs until who knows when.

Believe it or not, this all serves mostly as a backdrop to fans and performers inter-weaving day and night. They drape the homey Altamont fairgrounds, craftily decorated with antique concession booths, folklore displays and salvaged remnants of Americana. My wife described the bustling scene on our '93 visit as a "patchwork quilt," visually and otherwise.

Spence programs a dinner break, plus 15 minutes of dead time before the start of every hour. These intervals allow you to collect yourself, plot your next move, cruise the crafts and food rows, hobnob, and make it to your next activity on time. Despite this unique consideration, Spence's questionnaires now reveal she may have succeeded all too well in programming choices for her 6,000 regulars. "They complain that there's too much to do and they can't do it all," Spence laughs:

- "We've made suggestions on how you plan your day. Make your circles on your schedule and go to those things and sit there and do it so you don't feel like at the end of the day that you haven't done anything. We also build that little system in where a performer may be in three different places in one day. This is because I know some patrons who follow a performer to everything they do and some who will have trouble getting to one place because of a conflict. So they go to another place and they get to see the performer.

"But it's unusual to ask the performers anymore to be at the festival for the entire 48 hours. They say, 'When is the time when I perform?' I say, 'You perform three or four times during the weekend.' And they say, 'Well, I'd like to have a job Saturday night or Friday night or whatever.' And I say, 'Well, when you sign our contract, you're committed to this 48-hour period.'

"Most of them, without fail, come on Friday and stay through 'till Sunday unless they have to meet a travel connection. What that does is it builds the artists' community — they get to know each other, they all eat together, they eat with our crew, and they're free to roam around. They're not barricaded in any way from the attendants. They hang around and talk to people and you find them everywhere. I mean, they're just part of the whole thing. They go to see some other performers [laughs].

"I guess it's now a really totally different approach. It used to be in the old days (I would say in the early '70s), that these kinds of festivals were more along the lines of what OLD SONGS is today. But over the past 15 years, I've found festivals have turned into mostly performance venues. In other words, the artist appears, plays the concert and leaves. Or the artist appears onstage two days, does two concerts and leaves, or hibernates somewhere in the trailer, or at the motel and doesn't participate in anything else.

"So it's a spectator sport. OLD SONGS is a hand-on sport, an all-involving way to bring music back into your life."

Spence sees a harbinger in this isolation trend:

- "Its hurting the camaraderie in the music field. It's dividing people away from each other. We're doing a lot of that in society today, separating people from people in their own peer group, and people who do the similar thing they do. It's not good because in all of learning, you learn from each other. So if you don't rub elbows and talk to people doing the same thing you do, you're never going to grow or change."

**Artist Mini-Review** "I have never been disappointed in the artistry, except once or twice in 15 years," Spence remarks of her largely traditional-based bookings, "and I find the artists to be of the highest caliber, the most interesting people. I give them my greatest respect because they're all self-taught, and they have all followed their hearts."

I prompted her about <u>Music from China Ensemble</u>, a ten-piece group performing ancient acoustic instruments with extraordinary facility, who were entrancing us just as we left for the NEWPORT JAZZ FESTIVAL/SARATOGA (Saratoga Springs, NY — see chapter).

"Weren't they spectacular?," Spence exclaims:

- "The festival is a wonderful format in order to introduce new things that people can either get up and leave from or become captivated by. You can take the risk at a festival far more than you would in a concert, but I really did like the Music of China'. I like the people, I like their attitude about performing at the festival, and they worked their tails off. I really scheduled them heavily and put them in many different areas where people could get up close to them.

"This is what it's all about to me," she concludes with a rueful chuckle. "If we lose the ability to see this music up close, any music, we're gonna' lose everything."

**Travel Tip**

"Maybe the Iroquois Museum, because it's a great drive from where we are, and there are some interesting old mills on the same road. The Iroquois Museum is new, but it's really nice," Spence offers. "There are apple-growing people in the area. In downtown Albany is the mall and the state museum. There are a lot of good places to eat. The bigger restaurants, the more interesting ones, are probably more over toward the airport 20 minutes away. [Citing a host of area mansions and museums], nothing is more than a half-hour in the Capital District."

~     ~     ~

**Festival Review II**

If GOTTAGETGON feels like OLD SONGS in miniature to its nearest and dearest, well, that's because it virtually is.

OLD SONGS' Andy Spence and FOX HOLLOW's Bob Beers were among GOTTAGETGON's chief founders, although it was begun under the auspices of FOX HOLLOW's chief volunteer pool, Albany's Pick'n and Singin' Gatherin'. The late Beers was that organization's President in '70 and had no difficulty running this idea up the flagpole:

- "Let's have FOX HOLLOW on a fraction of the scale for 'Gatherin' members only, kinda' like a reward for volunteering. Let's have an 'all-hands-in' weekend for us amateur players with maybe one or two sympathetic pros roaming about for the duration. Let's have some concerts, some workshops, some dances, some open mics, some acappella sings, some potlucks, and campfire songswaps and pickalongs galore. Let's have camping clustered cozily within the fairgrounds, let's make it affordable for families, and let's make it just-plain-fun!"

And so they did for a quarter-century, outlasting FOX HOLLOW in the process. GOTTAGETGON's recently opened itself to the public, though retaining its intimate scale and informal atmosphere.

If you didn't know to expect it every Memorial Day weekend, GOTTAGETGON might likely sneak right past you, it's being so sparsely publicized. Yet ask a traditional folk music pro, and you'd possibly get a nod of pleasant recognition. Check out who's been a featured guest over the years: Gordon Bok, David Bromberg, Jean Ritchie, Jean Redpath, Lorraine Lee, John McCutcheon, Robin and Linda Williams, Jay Unger, Bill Staines, Cindy Mangsen and Steve Gillette, Bob Franke, Claudia Schmidt, Ira Bernstein, Lui Collins, Anne Hills, Garnet Rogers, Michael Jerling, Peter Oshtroushko, Harvey Reid, Freyda Epstein, etc. How'd you like to hang out and jam with one of these guys among roughly 300 admirers?

One of GOTTAGETGON's longtime organizers is Howard Jack (exactly the decent, casual type I met there during my '93 visit), who actually apologizes to me for not being able to verify all the historical details since he's only been attending since '74 (!):

- "As I understand it, the idea was to kind of do something about that urge around May to sort of 'get gone' to the country and out of the city and have some music and some fun. A lot of people in the organization wanna' make music — they don't wanna' just sit around and listen to it. So that's one of the features of the weekend. We try to get performers who are gonna' camp there with us and who will hang out and play music with us 'till all hours as well."

I ask him how they've managed to attract this caliber of musical guest over the years. Jack laughs:

- "We can't pay all that well because we're really small, and it doesn't generate enough revenue for us to pay large dollars to performers so we try to show them our appreciation in other ways as well. Many performers have said that they really felt welcome and they felt like people treated them really well. That's what pleases me most. I like when we have performers come in...to feel good about having been at the festival, not like it was just a job."

With these performers contributing to pickin' aplenty, it's interesting Jack himself was not an immediate participant. "For years I was not very active," he admits:

- "I was just knocked out by all the music that I could hear, and I would go around from camp to camp and just kinda' hang back and listen and maybe stand way back and play very softly. That's how I really learned a lot was trying to play along with what people were doing. I just learned to play by ear gradually by that.

  "When I first joined the 'Gatherin' and started going to the GOTTAGETGONs, they used to kick it off with a Friday night dance. Then I think there might've been an evening concert on Saturday, but that dropped after a while. People found out that it was interfering too much with their ability to get together and make music on their own. They felt an obligation to go hear people. In fact, one of the problems we have now is that frequently it's difficult to get much of an audience to turn out for when the performers are performing because so many people are off still making music on their own in the campground."

A clever way Jack's crew solves the exposure problem is to schedule a Sampler Concert Saturday morning so that everyone can get a taste of GOTTAGETGON's five main acts. That way they'll know to check back for individual concerts to their liking, as well as whom to invite 'round for a pickin' session. This helps since styles and skills can vary widely even if the participatory spirit runs throughout like a brisk Hudson River ripple.

"It's a great festival for people who want to make music," Jacks summarizes, adding with a smile, "and who don't carry around too big an ego!"

**Artist Mini-Reviews**  Jack's two favorite performing recollections stem directly from GOTTAGETGON's unique character:

- "One of my favorites recently was <u>Peter Oshtroushko</u>. He and <u>David Surret</u> made some really great music together. David was just attending, you know. He and Peter were just pickin' out in the campgrounds and Peter invited him to come up and play some tunes with him on stage.

  "Probably back in the late '80s we [also] had <u>Jane Rothfield and Allan Carr</u>. Well, they were living in Connecticut. Jane is originally from there and Allan's from Scotland. They had performed with Martin Haddon, Silly Wizard and all — he was on a couple of their records. They had lived in Scotland for a number of years and then moved back over here. We had them at the festival and they had so much fun at the festival they decided to move here!"

  Now, that's an endorsement!

**Travel Tip**  "If they're not familiar with the area, they should plan on trying to get up to Cafe Lenna," Jacks suggests of the folk-music mecca in Saratoga Springs closing in on three decades' tenure. "It's just 10 minutes up the road. Saratoga's an historic town and there's a great little State Park there. If you can schedule some time at the baths, it's always nice to go, get a message, drift off in the spring water [laughs]."

**See Also**  For a nice mid-winter taste of this homey programming there's the OLD SONGS SAMPLER CONCERT, that features at least four acts indoors at a local high school. Bring the kids. Ditto for 1994's FOX HOLLOW REUNION FOLK CONCERT, which occupied the historic Troy Saving Bank Music Hall and will hopefully join the others, above, as a perennial.

~     ~     ~

# Stanfordville's Fais-Do-Do

**STANFORDVILLE MUSIC AND DANCE FESTIVAL**, Stanfordville, NY
> Late May and Late August
> Cajun and Zydeco
> ***Attended***

**WOODSTOCK/NEW PALTZ ARTS AND CRAFTS FAIR**, New Paltz, NY
> Late May and Early September
> Modern Folk
> ***Attended***

The STANFORDVILLE MUSIC AND DANCE FESTIVAL [STANFORDVILLE] is probably the closest you'll   **Introduction**
come "up N'awth" to a genuine Cajun family picnic. There's:

- Spice-happy Cajun cuisine steaming away in pots and pans;

- Three top Cajun dance bands from the area, often topped by a national headliner,
  such as 1993's Steve Riley and The Mamou Playboys;

- The backyard setting, in this case one snuggled in amidst the homey farms and
  bungalows which dot rural Route 82.

Don't let the fancy site name fool you. The Country Fare Antiques and Arts Center —
nothing more than a brilliant green lawn, an outdoor dance platform fronting a stage cubby, and
an indoor barn for non-stop dancing — is as intimate and down-right "down-home" as it gets.
We're talking out down the driveway, left past the garage, pay at the fence post, and stop a few
steps short of the cabbage field! You just lay out your blanket, breathe in the Cajun smells and
sounds and exhale, "Ahhhh."

In fact, if Promoter Bill Molloy didn't need another 100 or so folks to give his modest,
twice-yearly affairs here a steadier financial footing, I'd be tempted to keep 'em to myself.
"Shhhh!"

Molloy knows a bit about rustic settings. For years he managed the warmly-recalled
musical coffeehouse within the historic Beekman General Store. Troubles with the town (more cultural support differences than anything else, he believes) yielded Molloy an injunction to cease his
eclectic folk-based programming there, but not before he'd been shanghaied into the Cajun dance
scene.

"As soon as the popularity of the music 'round here started to show I immediately got
drawn into a band by accident," Molloy remembers:

- "As a matter of fact, it was with Tracy Schwartz [an original New Lost City Rambler, now
  leading a Cajun band, Swamp Opera]. I proposed that he come up and do a dance at the
  time. He said, 'Well, that particular date, I don't have anybody to back me up. Can you
  help me in that department?'"

Molloy recruited a local trio, the early core of Bayou Midnight Band, but couldn't find a
bass player:

- "Since I play guitar and banjo and little bits and pieces of other instruments, and I had just
  bought a bass on a real good deal, I said, 'I'll do it, what the heck! I'll follow the basics and
  provide the low end. That's all there is to it!' [laughs] They loved it. They said, 'Join the
  band,' and that was it. So, it's been great."

Molloy's association continues today through three recordings and a summer's slate of bookings.

It's with that same kind of "can-do" spirit that Molloy pulls off his two annual hoe-downs on such a shoestring. He contributes Bayou Midnight Band to the quadruple bill; he gets a deal on the site from booking other barn dances throughout the year; he even does much of the Cajun cooking himself. The result? A laid-back day's marathon for a small circle of friends and Cajun dance fanatics — a few hundred at most. Any cliques dissolve on the dance floor, though, as Molloy provides instructors throughout the day to assure you'll have some requisite steps for breaking the ice with strangers.

No excuses, y'all, for not "passing a good time."

Why a strict Cajun diet for what started out in '85 as a "multi-cultural, musically-cultural" event? Molloy notes he's merely been satisfying a demand that's remained steady since introducing Cajun music into '89's blend. "I think there's a lot of people who can't afford to exert all the time and energy necessary to learn ballroom dancing," he reflects:

- "You can just get a few basics on the Cajun style, then have a lot of fun with it. That's the beauty, you don't have to go every weekend to remember the basics. And I think people appreciate that, especially in today's lifestyle. It doesn't have to become a hard-core infatuation in order to enjoy it.

  "Zydeco [also] helps to really bridge or break a lot of barriers, as far as the general public is concerned. I think a lot of people are jumping in, learning with interest, because they hear zydeco first, and zydeco has rock elements to it. It's just a matter of time before those folks hear Cajun, and they tend to like it because the dance styles are similar, and the culture is linked together very closely, fortunately.

  "There seems to be an increase happening in the audience. I hope that continues, and I hope it's just not a short-term fascination or curiosity. As a producer, I'm a little skeptical. I've produced for many, many years, and I've seen certain musical forms really pop up and experience some real sensational response from the public, and then, out of the blue, 'psst,' die. Ecuadorian music is a good example; bluegrass is another example. Cajun seems to be holding its own quite well, and I think the dancing aspect of it is the reason. It's not just a listening experience."

Molloy's planning to hedge his bets, however, even as he expands his Cajun programming to a Friday night "fais do do" at the May festival and to 16 straight hours at the August festival:

- "There's room in the makings for variations. I'm even considering expanding the [August] festival to the Sunday, [making it] a two-day, and have the second half a folk music concert. There's a lot of folk musicians in this area that it would be interesting. I don't think there's any functions around here that brings 'em together out in the sun, out on a live outdoor stage."

Thus STANFORDVILLE comes full circle to it's origins.

Molloy's personal highlight pre-dates the Cajun changeover:

- "Alison Krauss [and Union Station] was a real standout for me. Even though she is very, very popular, there was something very, very special about the sets that she did up at STANFORDVILLE. And it was very, very intimate and everybody felt it. That was the first year she got nominated for a Grammy, so it wasn't like the pre-popular days, it was right in the middle of when it was happening.

  "But it was still the intimate, old-style bluegrass experience. That's what she loved about it. She related to that, and several members of her band, especially Alison Brown, the banjo player, loved that and wished they could've stayed. They wanted to; they tried to talk the other band members into hanging out longer even though they had another venue they had to run off to after a certain hour. They lingered around and hung around and were late getting in their vehicle and all this stuff. It was cool! [laughs]

It was a rare experience for them, because the old days are slowly fading away. The bluegrass festivals are typically like WINTERHAWK (Hillsdale, NY — see chapter), you know, these mammoth productions and everything. You walk off stage and you're surrounded by hundreds and hundreds of people. It's just a different experience.

"What stands out in my mind is that the intimacy has played a big role in the growth of all of these styles of music. [When] you start representing some area of ethnic culture, there's a certain intimacy which is based on how a lot of these pieces are handed down generation after generation. I think that's an important element that should be maintained."

Intimate? You bet! It took me probably all of two seconds at STANFORDVILLE to spot my Cajun-dance friends and alternate between learning their latest step, and reminiscing about our other festivals-in-common. Ah, too relaxing for humans. Beautiful weather contributed. Although if it rained, we'd have just trundled inside the barn and begun the evening dance that much earlier. **Festival Review**

No notes on the acts — I was too busy cruising the dance floor — but newcomers should know that Molloy's reference to zydeco doesn't quite apply here. Even though his band, along with the others, may intersperse zydeco in the technical sense, their's is not the high-powered gonzo of C. J. Chenier and Buckwheat Zydeco. Rather, it's more of a rustic swirling, closer to Cajun in acoustic sound and attitude. They're also more inclined toward laying back in the groove for the dancers than in stepping forward with instrumental flourishes for the listeners. That's not to say you won't hear some great playing. Riley's renowned on accordion; ditto Schwartz on fiddle. If you tune into their ensemble oriented work, you'll be impressed. As Cajun humorist, Justin Wilson, would say, "I garontee it!"

Dancers will know to bring comfortable shoes and a clothing change. You'll know to bring a hearty appetite and, if you've poured too much Tabasco on your jambalaya, a little sugar to rub quickly on your tongue for calming the burn. "I cook at my own function," Molloy chuckles. "I have my formulas with three different Cajun dishes and I'm working on a fourth. The people gobble up my food like it's their last meal!" **Attendance Tip**

The way it now stands, you'll have an off-day on Sunday for touring the storied environs of the Hudson River Valley. Molloy recommends checking your travel guide for the historic homesteads abundant within 20 minutes' driving. **See Also & Travel Tip**

I'd also point you towards the twice-yearly WOODSTOCK/NEW PALTZ ARTS AND CRAFTS FAIR. It parallels the May festival on Memorial Day weekend but occurs one week later than the August festival on Labor Day weekend. Fantastic crafts, 300 juried vendors strong, are the primary attraction, but there's also a daily folk-music tent featuring four of the locals Molloy refers to. One year my wife and I were entranced by a kindly Celtic-music type with his unique electric harp, hand-crafted out of metal. However, avoid the early-morning traffic exiting Route 299 off the New York State Thruway. Between the crafters and the rock-climbers headed to the nearby cliffs, we were stuck for a solid hour!

~     ~     ~

# Syracuse's Jazz and Blues Shuttles

Syracuse Area Music Awards [Sammies], Syracuse, NY
    Early May
    Variety, General

Syracuse Jazz Fest, Syracuse, NY
    Middle June
    Modern Jazz
    ***Attended***

New York State Budweiser Blues Festival, Syracuse, NY
    Late July
    Blues and Traditional R&B
    ***Attended***

**Introduction**  Frank Malfitano, Promoter of the Syracuse Jazz Fest, calls it "the hang." He's talking about the casual interaction — musician-to-musician; fan-to-fan; musician-to-fan — that his festival fosters, as does its baby brother, the New York State Budweiser Blues Festival, run by Austin Jimmy Murphy. Both take advantage of downtown Syracuse's proximate tightness to create mix-and-mingle spectaculars unique across the region.

Go to an urban club feast in Boston, or New York City, or Philadelphia, or Pittsburgh, or Washington, and you usually need to pack a wad for cab fare between the venues. Go to either of these two events in Syracuse, however, and all you need is a pair of walking shoes and an umbrella. No, scratch the walking shoes, since both events supply trolleys shuttling among the few square blocks of ongoing gigs. You'll undoubtedly end up the evening leaning against a towering pillar in the lobby of the restored dowager, the Hotel Syracuse, sipping a cool whatever. There, as the final sets count down well past midnight, you'll happily find yourself among big name artists on bar stools, die-hard fans from all across the country lounging in leather easy chairs, and either of the two promoters...

Hangin', just hangin'.

**Festival**  They used to claim of "Zerocuse" that you could shoot a cannon full of grapeshot down South
**Review I**  Salina Street right after rush-hour and not hit a soul. At least that's how I remember it from my college stay here in the late '70s. In fact, I only ventured off "the hill" three nights in three years: once to see the pre-Buster Poindexter incarnation of David Johanssen at some club under the interstate; and the others to catch B. B. King/Bobby "Blue" Bland and Bonnie Raitt/Mose Allison twin bills at the exquisite 1928 movie palace, the Landmark Theater.

Ah, but times have changed!

There've been a number of clubs retro-fitted within restored warehouses around Franklin Street that now teem with twenty-somethings. There have been a number of others occupying the historically rehab'd commercial structures of Armory Square that fill up with the smart set. Restaurants and such have sprung up around downtown for the older gentry. And the ol' Landmark has been given a roof repair and a financial makeover, thanks to its new Executive Director, Frank Malfitano. Most importantly, Malfitano's moved his pet project, the Syracuse Jazz Fest ['JazzFest'], into all of these venues and made jazz the common thread tying this refurbished urban fabric together for at least one week every summer.

Now you won't yet mistake Syracuse for, say, Paris, but you will join over 100,000 jazz pilgrims — approximately half from out-of-town — for one of the truly wonderful, accessible, and fully-featured jazz festivals anywhere. And it's free, no less!

The 'JAZZFEST had limped along for eight years at two different outdoor venues in the suburbs, drawing a few thousand annually and losing money. In '90 Malfitano approached Syracuse's Mayor about moving it downtown, making it free, and boosting it toward national prominence. The Mayor helped by lining up a $25,000 challenge grant from a local bank. Malfitano reciprocated by raising an additional $35,000 and programming a solid bill of national acts to compliment the local heroes he began with back in the early '80s. "Fund it and they will come," so to speak, as attendance instantly multiplied 20 times to 60,000.

"The first year downtown it was a two-day event," Malfitano cites:

- "Then it went to a three-day event the second year; the third year it went to a seven-day festival, [where] it's currently. But each year we're adding new things. This year we're adding two concert halls. We've expanded to five ballrooms in the hotel. We have a jazz mass going on. We have jazz films going on. We've gone from one brunch to four or five. We still have the two days of outdoor stages; and instead of one noontime concert series, we now have two.

  "So it's just gettin' better all the time, it really is!

  "Really, what I do is bring 'em to the festival and expose 'em to the music without them knowing they've been exposed. You know, you've got to outsmart 'em, and you've really got to present something that they enjoy. The best way to educate people is to entertain them. So we're looking for people who understand stage presence and entertainment value, who can really communicate with an audience."

What Malfitano's talking about is gathering as many different epochal representations of jazz together as possible, and letting you make the comparisons. No more debates about which style rocks harder — soul organ trios, jumpin' jive bands, hard bop quartets, "Cu-bop" ensembles, or '80's fusion quintets — just judge for yourself as you wander the streets from one top practitioner to another jammin' live and alive!

"Of course, that is completely by design, not by accident," Malfitano explains.

- "By presenting legends like Dizzy, you show people who were pioneers in the evolution of the music. By presenting contemporary artists who've reached a mainstream audience, you've got the people in now. And by presenting people who nobody's heard of, who are emerging talents, who are a little more cutting-edge, you give them the possibility of the future of the music. To present it in a current context with all of the technology that's available is really what the artist deserves. We made a commitment to quality presentation. I took all of my advertising and promotional expertise and production experience and said, 'If we're gonna' do it, were gonna' do it right!'

  "The guy who really inspired me — I had an opportunity to go to festivals all over the country many, many years ago — was John Sinclair and the [original, since revived] ANN ARBOR BLUES AND JAZZ FESTIVAL (see Ann Arbor, MI, Late September), which, to me, was the precursor of the NEW ORLEANS 'JAZZFEST' (see New Orleans, LA, Late April to Early May), the precursor of my festival, and really the grandaddy of all festivals. I don't think it's ever been done better, and I think he established a model precedent for many, many years.

  "John and I got to meet at NEW ORLEANS', and I walked up to him and said, 'You're the reason I do what I do.' He remembered me from being on stage at ANN ARBOR'. Yeah, man, it was a momentous reunion. I told him what I had done, and he was extremely proud of me like I was, you know, one of his disciples or stepchildren. That was a great blend of local and regional and national acts, and I have the posters from those festivals on the walls in my apartment — they're sitting across from me as we speak.

  "People like he and Bill Graham. I had an opportunity to go to the Fillmore West right after WOODSTOCK', and I went to WOODSTOCK', and what he did in terms of opening up with jazz and blues artists and exposing them to a rock audience — the collaborations he did on a nightly basis at the Fillmore — are unparalleled. Those were the guys who really inspired me, and I'm trying to carry on in that tradition."

Unlike the cavernous Fillmores, Malfitano's 'JAZZFEST holds court in a variety of sponta-neously intimate settings: clubs, restaurants, malls, squares, ballrooms, and that unique lobby wrap-up. You can picture yourself, for example, bopping heads in a funky basement bar to organ-ist Charles Earland as he's likely been enjoyed on the chitlin' circuit for a good thirty years.

"It's an urban art form," Malfitano remarks:

- "And it belongs in the city; it originated in the city; it emerged from the city; and it gets its energy from the city. To create some energy and to give that back to the city is a really great kind of reciprocity. There is something about the vibe that's created by having it in this kind of a setting. Now I've been in an outdoor suburban amphitheater setting, and I think that's nice, but it removes the festival from its origins, and I think the music suffers as a result. It becomes somewhat detached and sterilized, and it doesn't quite have the energy. It's a little more laid-back. When you look at the practitioners of this music, many of whom have come from the Chicagos, and the New Orleans, and the Philadelphias, and the New Yorks of the world, they feel more at home in this kind of a setting.

"The [Hotel Syracuse], which is kind of the last of the stately old downtown hotels, is a wonderful setting because what you really do is take the club — clubs are traditionally 100 to 200 seaters — and by putting it in a ballroom, you've got a club atmosphere in a 500 to 600-seat venue. So you've really recreated that ambience and expanded it into a much nicer setting."

"One of the things that I've learned is that audience-goers like the personal touch; they like the communion between artist and audience in this art form in particular. And what makes the club thing important for people (not necessarily for me because I tend to think that con-cert halls and festivals and series are the direction for this music to develop a broader base and a mass audience) is to retain that connection between artist and audience. By having 'the hang,' as we call it, or as the musicians call it...

"A lot of musicians who play festivals don't get a chance to hang with their colleagues. It's important for them; it's the only chance they get to see each other. It's the one thing that many of them told me, people like Jimmy Heath and Dizzy, you know, [that] this feels like Europe. The great thing about European festivals is we all get to hang together and spend the weekend together — that is very, very important for musicians. They want to to be able to hear other musicians and be with people who are at their level. They're deprived and denied that in many, many instances.

"Last year at the hotel is a prime example. I'm sitting there in the lobby with Spyro Gyra, Gato Barbieri and his band, and everybody's checking out Michael Franks and his band. You know, I look around and I'm saying to myself, 'These are fans just like me!' They like to see what other people are doing, too, and when they're done playing and their energy level is still high, they wanna' get some energy from somebody else. It's an inspirational thing, man, it's a groove!

"What we realized last year is that on Sunday night after everything winds down, there are a lot of out-of-town festival-goers who don't leave 'till the next day. And there are a lot of musicians who don't get out 'till the next day, so we're gonna' do a wrap-up jam session for everybody hangin' around.

"Oh listen," Malfitano exclaims, "the Cheathams hangin' out with Red Rodney, and Frank Foster bein' there, and everybody reminiscing about the old days — man, I mean, that shit was what was happening!"

**Artist Mini-Reviews** <u>Frank Moser Trio</u>. Moser's a local who hosted one of the noontime jams in the front lobby of the Galleries of Syracuse. His trio ran through standard repertoire as shoppers gathered around below and hung over the balcony railings above. Steady sax solos, chirping synths, tasteful drumming — I kept thinking this ought to be standard T. G. I. F. repertoire of every indoor mall.

<u>The Brecker Brothers</u>. Continuing proof that fusion acts, which makes your eyes glaze on disc, can "set your backfield in motion" in person. Their Clinton Square set was truncated on both ends by a typical Syracuse rain shower (another advantage of 'JAZZFEST's indoor orientation), but

the 'Bros. really got out the funk on about eight jams — aided by a slammin' rhythm section of Dennis Chambers on drums, James Genus on bass, and George Whitty on keys. The real revelation was guitarist Mike Stern, who took off on one Asian-flavored solo (complete with simulated bird chirps) in all directions at once before concluding with a rousing finish. Tough to clap with one hand holding an umbrella, but those assembled managed mightily.

Benny Green and Christian McBride. A pair of young lions (Green just celebrating his Blue Note debut) doing what I'd call inspired "parlor jazz" — technically fine, but a bit quiet considering what was to follow in the hotel lobby. Pianist Green preferred to take a back seat, though bassist McBride was quite capable of filling up the resulting spaces with style.

Jazz Forum Allstars with Donald Harrison. The 'Forum is trumpeter Mark Morganelli's assemblage with guitarist Vic Juris, bassist Harvie Swartz, and drummer Carl Allen. Morganelli also programs the delightful RIVERSIDE PARK ARTS FESTIVAL (New York, NY — see chapter), and is a regular at Sonny's Place in Seaford, Long Island. Had I known how tasteful his group was, I'd have been a regular all these years!

They held forth in the tightest, and certainly most exotic venue, the cosy Sakura Japanese restaurant. Nice contrast between guest saxophonist and fire-eater, Harrison, who blew searing solos in uninterrupted power playing, and Morganelli, whose careful phrasing focused more on strong tones and sweet notes. I especially enjoyed their interplay on a Weill uptempo, "Speak Low," as well as on a lilting Jobim tune, "Triste." Tasty.

Charles Earland Quartet. Groovemasters! I loved Earland's soul/jazz set in Georgia's, and so did the taproom faithful gathered virtually in his lap who cheered as if it were a church revival. Earland responded with his trademark grin while ripping into yet another Hammond XB2 workout, his head bobbing like a jackhammer. Earland's playing mirrored the image — a quick, choppy procession of blue notes, almost more percussive than melodic. However, he'd hit an occasional chord and hold it for, oh, about a minute or so to goad the crowd into yet another round of whoops and hollers. In a word, fun! I especially enjoyed the sax of Eric Alexander, who found the fat part of the bat on every solo, including a blistering rave on "Caravan."

Jeannie and Jimmy Cheatham and The Sweet Baby Blues Band. Nine pieces for the ages, and one of my musical highlights of the year! These West Coasters specialize in Kansas City jump blues from the '40s. While there are a few groups out there covering this utterly seductive, totally swingin' repertoire, nobody-but-nobody's doing it any better. These guys were smooth and tight as a bodybuilder's skin, with every hot horn capable of pumping it up. (I particularly enjoyed the razor-sharp drumming of John "Ironman" Harris spotting all the strong solos.)

Their arrangements flowed, pulsed, and built, built, built into these impossible rolling crescendos before letting you down into a fluffy cushion of funky stuff. The word rhythm just doesn't do the experience justice. The Cheathams had a basic set list — "How Long," "What Goes Around, Comes Around," "Come Back Baby," "Rock Me In Your Arms Tonight," "Roll 'Em Pete" — but the band was so organic and dynamic you felt like you were hearing these ol' chestnuts springing to life before you, birthing rock 'n' roll right on the spot.

The crowd wouldn't let 'em go! All I could hear among the few encores time afforded were cheers and screams; all I could see in front of me were arms and hands flailing in the air. Have mercy! Nelson Rangell had the dubious honor of trying to follow that up with his perfectly credible fusion of GRP jazz-goes-world beat, but there was absolutely no topping the Cheathams that night.

**Travel Tip** "A stone's throw away is the Thousand Islands region, or the Fingerlakes region, or wine country," Malfitano offers:

- "Also there's some great golfing on a multitude of great golf courses. There's a Robert Trent Jones course or two that are really exceptional, and also there's some nice boating and beach areas. There's a world-class museum, the Everson Museum of Art. Also, there's some tremendous dining opportunities right in the city, or very close to the city: certainly The Krebs in Skaneateles is a first-rate restaurant; Pascal's in Syracuse; Grimaldi's; Mr. G's. And the Hotel Syracuse has a festival rate [with] cheap rooms.

"There's no dress code [for 'JAZZFEST] — it's extremely informal, very casual. It's a very mellow crowd, very sophisticated, very appreciative. There is a tremendous camaraderie; we've never had a negative incident. People seem to get along well."

~     ~     ~

**Festival Review II** There are some differences with the NEW YORK STATE BUDWEISER BLUES FESTIVAL ['BLUESFEST]:

- It doesn't yet possess the high-level connections and powerhouse fundraising enjoyed by its older brother, the 'JAZZFEST;

- It tends to go to theme nights for its headliners instead of scrambling the sub-genres like the 'JAZZFEST does.

Thankfully, the similarities remain key — a handsome swarm of national and local artists buzzing among an attractive assortment of intimate local venues. Best of all, it wraps up the first night at the Hotel Syracuse. "The hang" lives on!

Credit the easy-going Austin Jimmy Murphy, the man in the black Stetson hat, who glides the hallways and makes sure everybody's happy. He'd initially formed the Central New York Blues Connection, a for-profit society dedicated to boosting local blues musicians and bringing name acts to town. Without his "no sweat" demeanor, the group's first 'BLUESFEST might never have gotten off the ground.

"We had held probably, oh, two, three, four months' worth of meetings," Murphy recalls:

- "I'm sure it was the 'JAZZFEST that triggered it, but it just dawned on me, 'Why couldn't we do the same thing with a blues festival?' Well, of course, the 'JAZZFEST has been around for probably goin' on a dozen years now. The support that Frank [Malfitano] has behind it and the financial funding is just incredible! We have nothing like that.

"The first year we had something like $2,300 in funding, [but] we had an $18,000 bill! And I never thought of it, you know? I mean, the last couple months heading up to the festival, everybody was backing out of it. Everybody was getting real antsy and scared. And I couldn't figure out what the hell was goin' on. I just took it real personally, like 'Here we'd been trying to work on a project and you people are backing out at the last minute!' And it never dawned on me until the next year that there was so much money that we had to raise.

"Fortunately, we raised it that weekend," Murphy sighs. "Yeah, incredible!"

Murphy thanks the local press, notably the *Syracuse New Times,* for getting the word out, as well his 50 volunteers and the 'Connection's musicians for keeping the faith. They've since given Murphy a base for reaching out to other upstate blues scenes. Last year saw him extend invitations to bands from Rochester and Buffalo, while this year he welcomed others from Albany.

Murphy's also broadened the 'BLUESFEST programmatically. Recent additions include his aforementioned theme nights (a "West Coast Blues Party" is targeting Mark Hummell, Mitch Woods and His Rocket 88s, and Rod Piazza and The Mighty Flyers, for example); a venue devoted exclusively to acoustic blues ("That was a real highlight last year; a lot of people really appreciated that."); and a workshop on Leadbelly involving film and video presentations. Still the overall attractions are quality, quantity, and affordability — all to an unexpectedly high degree.

"Well I'll tell ya'," Murphy drawls:

- "I think most [patrons] come to town not realizing how this festival is set up. When they hear so-and-so's playing at such-and-such a location, they don't realize that there's 20 other bands performing in town that night, and that it's just one huge party within a few square miles. I think that's quite a surprise to a lot of people.

"Certainly this is one of the most affordable festivals ever. There's so much entertainment here, and I think 90% of it is really high quality. I mean, you can go to a club for three bucks and stay there all night. The 'West Coast' thing we're trying to do with those three big names, that's going to be ten bucks! And the all-access pass, if you buy that for $13.50 [per day] or $20 [per weekend], you just can't beat it. So I think that for the amount of music that's going on that weekend and the professionalism of it, you just can't beat it anywhere."

Murphy sees the urban format shared by his 'BLUESFEST and Malfitano's 'JAZZFEST as the wave of the future, at least for the other upstate blues scenes he's been talking to:

- "I think this type of blues festival will catch on. It's perfect for every city... if you can get the clubs. A lot of times the clubs are kinda' funny. They're not too bad around here, but you'd like every club to participate. It's one weekend out of the year they're gonna' have a packed house no matter what...

  "As small as the 'BLUESFEST is at this point in time, we're going to have the Senator, Nancy Lorraine Hoffman, help us out this year in any way that she can. And I think that we're starting to get that recognition amongst the city that this is bringing in dollars on a weekend that is just a regular weekend. You've got people comin' out spendin' a hundred dollars a piece in these places.

"I think it's gonna be big," Murphy drawls with the same kind of casual "can-do" attitude that got the 'BLUESFEST started in the first place. "Whether there's a great amount of funding or not, it's still going to happen. It's certainly going to get bigger and better."

I hadn't planned on catching the 'BLUESFEST in its first year. However, I'd such a blast earlier at the 'JAZZFEST that when first evening of the GREATER HARTFORD JAZZ FESTIVAL got rained upon (Hartford, CT — see chapter), I simply made a beeline west. My notes are shaky (I was having too much fun cruising the clubs and "hangin'" the Hotel to be a diligent scribe), but hear's who I can recall:

**Artist Mini-Reviews**

Roosevelt Dean Band. Dean fronted a five-piece band on guitars and vocals and possessed the evening's strongest voice. He powered through several Chicago-style standards, sparking a number of couples to slow dance despite the tightly confined space, and getting the blue collars on barstools to turn around and admiringly nod along.

Murphy: "Well he's goin' with about an eight-piece band [now]. He's got three horns, I think. He's considered, at least we consider him, one of our Godfathers of the area."

White Boy and The Wagon Burners. This five-piece band is comprised of Native Americans from the nearby Onondaga Reservation (except for the referenced "White Boy"). This distinction helped them land a gig earlier that year at the prestigious SMITHSONIAN FESTIVAL OF AMERICAN FOLKLIFE (see Washington, DC, Early July) to help illustrate the diaspora of Native American music adaptations, which is really pretty funny because they're just basic party-hearties doing nothing but danceable uptempos and blues rumbles. Picture The Blues Brothers with the portly lead singer doing his best Belushi imitation, visually and vocally. Natural hams, they didn't take themselves too seriously and served up more than their fair share of fun. Their ribald burlesque, "What Did I Do Last Night," was a particular hoot.

Carey Bell and The Tough Lucks Blues Band. Tonight must've been "harp night" with Bell at the Hotel, and Jerry Portnoy and The Streamliners doing a simultaneous club gig a few blocks away. Since I'd already seen the delightfully sly Portnoy at the NEWPORT JAZZ FESTIVAL/SARATOGA (Saratoga Springs, NY — see chapter), I decided to check out Bell, instead. 'Glad I did!

Bell, sporting a shiny, pearl-colored suit, fronted a tight three-piece rhythm section clad in aloha shirts, and managed what few other entertainers successfully pull off — totally energizing the crowd (which, due to the low ballroom stage, was dancing virtually in his face) while performing completely within himself. Earthy, yet economical, Bell went straight for the feeling on every tune. My notes on his singing read "epileptic rasp," while his sensational harp solos went off with "controlled fury — each note held until it bled!" At one point, he even coaxed an extraordinary tone that seemed to cross an accordion with a guitar.

What's more, Bell physically animated each narrative with little jumps, head snaps, and jowl wiggles, leaving no doubt as to what he was talking about. His demonstrative delivery on a trio of sexy numbers, "She's Nineteen," "Sharp Dressed Lady," and "I Wancha' To Love Me, Honey" put more than one lugubrious couple in the mood! Straight through to set's end, Bell had the raucous throng and dirty dancers roaring with their hands clapping high over head.

**Attendance Tip**   Murphy advises:

- "I would definitely purchase an all-access pass, and I would go to see as many people as I could because one of the difficult things in a festival such as this is it's very difficult to get around and see everyone [on an individual cover charge basis]. You go into a place thinking you're just going to stay there for half an hour, and [you find] the local entertainment is really good, and you end up spending a little more time there than you wish you had. So I would purchase an all-access pass and go see everything that I could see."

**See Also**   Malfitano's SAMMIE awards features an eclectic lineup of 11 acts filling up his 3,000-seat Landmark Theater for one night in Late April. You'll get jazz, blues, and a whole lot more.

~     ~     ~

# Promoting the SYRACUSE JAZZ FEST:
# A Conversation with Frank Malfitano.

*If you're lucky enough to catch the busy Promoter of the SYRACUSE JAZZ FESTIVAL, Frank Malfitano, in a spare moment — typically late at night after a function or concert — you better be on your toes. Not that Malfitano's an intimidating sort. Quite the opposite. He comes across as a regular guy — accommodating, straightforward, appreciative.*

*Rather, it's because Malfitano's connected, first of all. He's been involved locally with the INTERNATIONAL JAZZ EDUCATORS ASSOCIATION (see Varies, VAR, Late January), and the JAZZMOBILE; regionally with the Mid-Atlantic Arts Foundation; and nationally with the JAZZ TIMES CONVENTION (New York, NY — see chapter), but to name a few.*

*It's also because Malfitano's acquired an ideal skill-set for a festival head from having done sports sponsorship, fundraising and community development, and concert promotion, as well as running his own advertising and public-relations agency. It's helped him take a mere showcase in a small city far off the musical mainstream and raise its attendance, funding, and profile many-fold within just a few years.*

*Mostly, it's because Malfitano's got strong opinions about elevating his beloved jazz genre via proper promotion, and he reels them off a-mile-a-minute in those flat "Salt-City" vowels I remember fondly from my college days there. It's an enlightening ride, so hop on board! (Aspiring promoters, as well as interested music fans, take note.)*

- "I was originally a player. I'd been playing since 4th grade in school bands, you know, little pickup bands here and there. I stopped playing actively many years ago. I thought I could do more for the art form by being a presenter. Actually, I had been doing some sports promotion and some other kinds of concert-promotional activity [when] my musician friends in the jazz community came to me and said, 'You know, we'd like a festival that could showcase us, and we'd like to do it in a nice venue.'

"My background is in advertising, promotion, marketing, public relations, media, etc., and I think there's a real dearth of that in the jazz industry. I wanted to take my expertise and apply that to jazz because I felt the art form was really lacking in terms of the way it was presented.

"So I jumped at the opportunity to put together this little mini-club festival that featured about eight acts. Then, after doing about five of those, and three or four JAZZMOBILES, we kind of graduated to the outdoors and put together our first outdoor festival in '83 at Song Mountain, which is a ski resort south of town. Then, we took a hiatus of a year and moved it to an established outdoor concert venue called Longbranch Park. We did probably seven additions there.

"When I got back to town [in '90], I met with the Mayor and said, 'You know, I'd really like to bring the 'JAZZFEST' downtown. It's an urban art form; it belongs in the city. I'd like to make it a free event and make it a regional or a national festival in terms of its scope.' And he was very supportive and helped find me a title sponsor, a bank in town that kicked in 25 grand. Once we got that, once we got the city's in-kind services committed, and once we got a title sponsor, we were really off and running. Everybody really kinda' jumped on the bandwagon.

"The attendance, when it was a paid fest the first year, I think we attracted about 1,200 — not a bad start. Then, every year after that when we were at Longbranch, we were in the 2-to-3,000 range. But we were consistently losing money, because of a lack of sponsorship; because of low attendance. As soon as we moved it downtown and made it a free event, the attendance swelled and so did the sponsorship. The first year downtown we ran about

30,000; the second year 40,000; and last year 50,000. And the sponsorship climbed from $60,000 to $80,000 to $110,000. So we saw a proportionate increase in both attendance and sponsorship — no surprise, that's the way it's supposed to work.

"The interesting thing is it's institutionalized now and the community has embraced it. We've networked to the point where we've got a tremendous cross-section of people involved with the event in terms of sponsors and community leaders, and it's just really working out well.

- "We've never lost a sponsor, I'm proud to say. We pick up new sponsors every year. All of our sponsors are satisfied.

"We now do a sponsor kickoff party, which used to be a wrap-up party, where we bring in a national act. We have great food, great entertainment, and it's a kickoff to the week [that] really gets people in the mode and in the mood. We really treat them like the royalty that we think they are. We give them V. I. P. seating and backstage passes, plus there's a hospitality tent. We mention them in all our radio, TV, and print advertising. We give them T-shirts, seating passes, everything. We really, really try to work with the sponsors. We understand that they're supportive because they like the music; they like the community involvement. We try to listen to the sponsors and understand what their needs are because it has to be a 'win-win' situation.

"We have a real rich mix and a very diverse blend of sponsors. We have put together a very good sponsorship proposal package — what the sponsor gets in terms of percs.; what the festival's all about. We make sure that the image and the packaging on this is first rate, so that they know that they're getting involved in a class event — something that they'd be proud to put their company's name on.

"This year, for the first time, we've established a fundraising committee... I was also wearing the fundraising cap [but] said, 'That's a bit much,' especially since I'm fundraising for all these other events. So I've now given them input and direction, and they're running with it on their own. They're getting inspired. Lead-source generation is the key, so the more people on the committee, the more new names to tap into. We just got a guy who's a major food broker who's now going to bring in people like Oscar Mayer, Tyson Foods, supermarkets, and people we haven't had. We've had breweries and wineries, but now we're going after grocery chains. We've had soda and beer, but now we're getting car dealerships, and civic organizations, and booster groups, and chambers of commerce. It is such a broad-based mix of support groups that we're not relying on any one in particular. And by going nationally now, we're not economically-interdependent on just this community.

[Citing the jazz audience make-up] "Black-to-white; male-to-female; yuppies-to-buppies — it's the right age demographic. It's the ideal audience that every advertiser's looking for... Clearly, we have such an excellent opportunity with this art form for sponsors and for people that are looking for advertising and promotional vehicles. It's really untapped. Again, the whole [jazz] industry is existing in a vacuum. It's not using the models that are out there.

"Presenting a jazz subscription series format in concert halls is something that all the other disciplines have been doing for between 50 and 100 years. You can buy a season ticket to theater, musical theater, ballet, opera, dance, the classics, masterworks — Christ, you can even buy a season ticket to basketball and football — but there are very few cities in the country where you can buy a season ticket to year-round jazz!

"There's another excellent, untapped sponsorship opportunity. A sponsor for a festival can own or dominate a market for a weekend or a month leading up to it, or with good-will residuals, for another month or two afterwards. But if you were to sponsor a year-round concert festival in a concert hall, they could own the market for a year! That's a nice dovetailing opportunity to have the series during the year to sustain interest in the music and to keep it visible; then hitting with the big punch in the summer!"

- "We don't have a jazz trade association, which I've been an advocate of at the national level for many years. We're not in concert halls to the extent we should be — legitimized alongside the other disciplines of the performing arts — which is something I've been an advocate of. I've been a proponent of the development of jazz subscription series in concert halls for a long time because I think clubs are a very selfish way to see this art form. And it does translate to the concert hall! There is a way to program a successful subscription series, and it's a very easy thing to do. So I've been working with my colleagues at developing that nationally and regionally and using the different arts federations and organizations to do that. The jazz trade association, I think, is very important.

  "I think a televised jazz award show is also really important. It's the only [major] discipline of the performing arts that doesn't currently have its own awards show. First, you have to have an award. We just honored Dick Clark with the Walk of Stars Award here in Syracuse. He and I talked about this because he developed the American Music Association Awards and the Country Music Awards. I said, 'Dick, we want to do a televised jazz awards show,' and he said, 'Well, you know, the first step is have an award. Put on an awards show; then televising is not a quantum leap.'

  "...That's where someone like me comes in handy, because you need administrative expertise; you need organizational expertise; you need somebody who can be objective.

  "You know, jazz musicians in particular have viewed themselves in a kind of 'hipper-than-thou' fashion. There's a certain amount of elitism that permeates the art form and a certain amount of outlaw mentality that permeates the art form. As long as you're an outsider, you're never gonna' succeed in the mainstream. And until we get mainstream media support and reinforcement from radio and TV; until we crossover to reach a mass audience in the concert halls; until there is a jazz trade association that can serve as an umbrella for all the different segments and disciplines and schools within the genre which have equal legitimacy; until presenters are less biased and more educatory in terms of presenting the art form in all of it's many schools...

  "One of the things you'll notice about my festival and the JAZZ TIMES CONVENTIONS that I've been involved with is that we attempt to program as many schools within the genre as possible. If you don't do that, it's a disservice. Because to call jazz one thing, or to put it in a time capsule, or to say, 'This is jazz,' then you get into that polemic of, 'What is jazz,' which serves no purpose.

  "I have my own philosophy about presenting — I'm essentially a jazz educator. I see the festival as a means of educating people and bringing them to the art form through something that is largely an entertainment vehicle but has an educatory component built in without being didactic about it. I don't think you have to beat people over the head with clinicians and workshops to get your point across. Nor do I think you have to stand on a soap box and say, 'We're America's classical art form.'

  "One thing that I think is extremely important is the continuum of jazz — showing where it's been, where it's come from, where it is now, and where it's going. So if you have some progressives and some moderates and some conservatives, if you will, you really give the whole spectrum to people. ...If you don't do that, I think you're doing a disservice to your audience and a disservice to the art form."

- [Explaining his inclusion of strong local artists] "I think 'local' has a very unflattering connotation — it connotes 'amateur'; it connotes 'less-than-national.' I prefer to think of them as 'resident artists,' or 'regional artists.' We treat them with the same integrity and respect that we give to national acts: the same percs., the same showcase, the same quality staging and sound, the same profile in the media. The integration is extremely important because the local artists who are based in a community are the people who have to sustain interest in the music year-round between visits of the national acts. They don't get the recognition they deserve and this is a wonderful showcase for them.

"We also initiated last year having a high-school ensemble, winners of the local I. A. J. E. statewide competition, open up on the main stage. We wanted to give the kids exposure to the festival. We think it's very important in terms of their musical and artistic development because ordinarily they're confined to playing in lousy clubs for audiences who are there for all the wrong reasons; for club owners who could give a shit. They're not given any respect, or afforded the treatment they deserve. So the festival has become a very important showcase for them.

"Interestingly enough, those artists who are fortunate enough to be selected to play in the 'JAZZFEST' really use that as a launching pad for work and get a lot of gigging opportunities as a result. It creates work opportunities for jazz musicians, [it] keeps the art form viable for the community on a year-round basis, and [it] really does sustain interest and help the local bands along. And listen, they have constituencies, and those local groups drag a lot of fans to the festival to see the national acts who wouldn't come otherwise. So, there's a real cross pollination there.

"I've been pleasantly surprised when I go to other festivals and I've seen opening acts, or emerging acts, or supporting acts. They wind up at my festival because I'm so taken by them. And I've gone to music festivals in Philadelphia, and New Orleans, and New York, and I see people, and I say, 'Hey, you gotta' come play my festival!'

"We [also] get people comin' to our festival. I had Jack Massanovich from the Alabama Jazz Federation come up and he said, 'Nancy Kelligan, where'd she come from? She was a gas!' And I have other people here, [like] Ronnie Lee, who's a local jazz vocalist, and they say, 'Holy Moses!' That's an important component of what we do.

"And again, it's going back to [the] ANN ARBOR [BLUES AND JAZZ FESTIVAL]. I saw all the local cats, and I went to [the] NEW ORLEANS [JAZZ AND HERITAGE FESTIVAL] and all the local cats who were there, and I said, 'Oh my God, nobody knows about these people!'"

~     ~     ~

# Artist Sightings, II: Pete Seeger

PEOPLE'S MUSIC NETWORK, Varied Sites, VAR
> Late January
> Modern Folk

SHADFEST, Peekskill, NY
> Middle May
> Modern Folk

STRAWBERRY FESTIVAL, Beacon, NY
> Early June
> Modern Folk

**CLEARWATER'S GREAT HUDSON RIVER REVIVAL**, Valhalla, NY
> Middle June
> Variety, Folk and International
> ***Attended***

NEW YORK CITY CLEARWATER FESTIVAL, Brooklyn, NYC
> Late July
> Modern Folk

CLEARWATER FESTIVAL, Highlands, NJ
> Late August
> Modern Folk
> ***Attended***

HARVEST MOON FESTIVAL, Kingston, NY
> Middle September
> Modern Folk

CLEARWATER PUMPKIN SAIL, Varied Sites, VAR
> Early October to Middle October
> Modern Folk

**Introduction**

I asked the softspoken Margie Rosenkrantz, Public Relations Director of CLEARWATER'S GREAT HUDSON RIVER REVIVAL [CLEARWATER'], for background information on this marvelous 25-year-old extravaganza. More specifically, I wanted to learn about its founder, Pete Seeger. Rosenkrantz, who's also involved in selecting the showcase talent for the FALCON RIDGE FOLK FESTIVAL (Hillsdale, NY — see chapter), as well as running Albany's Eight-Step Coffeehouse, suggested I pick up any one of Seeger's books. So I did.

David Dunaway's excellent biography, **How Can I Keep From Singing: Pete Seeger** (Da Capo), offers good insights into this folk-music icon, too good in many instances. Coming from a conservative, middle-class, middle-American perspective, I found much in Seeger's early and middle life to question severely. (Seeger's never really renounced his work for the Communist Party, for example, though when he first picked up the cause in the early '30s, Stalin was busy starving to death an estimated 5 to 7 million Ukrainians with the famine precipitated by his forced collectivism of their family farms. My mother-in-law survived that holocaust.) However, even through my jaundiced eyes I could still appreciate many of Seeger's heady accomplishments, two of which are embodied in CLEARWATER'.

Heady accomplishment number one... During his blacklisted period throughout much of the '50s, Seeger found his income opportunities drastically reduced. Anxious to feed his family of four, Seeger had his wife, Toshi (who's been responsible for booking CLEARWATER', along with much of its strategic direction), land him as many $25 gigs as he could handle across the country, often as many as five per day. Dunaway actually credits them both with pioneering the college circuit, which presently keeps a good many musicians of all genres on life support.

Seeger's more meaningful accomplishment here was in engaging his superb entertaining and communications skills to develop an entire canon for children. You see, he had to have as broad a repertoire as possible for the concerts at elementary schools and libraries with which Toshi would fill up his daytime itinerary. Seeger single-handedly gave folk music a differential advantage in this medium it holds to this day while indoctrinating wave upon wave of young listeners. From Joan Baez to Dar Williams, if you read how most such artists first came to folk music, they'll generally cite a Seeger concert they caught in their formative years. Subtract Seeger's influence in evangelizing the generations, and you might as well subtract the genre altogether. It'd be like picturing the state of bluegrass music without the parallel activities of Bill Monroe.

Ergo, enter the festive gates of CLEARWATER' and the first thing you see are kids — loads and loads of "Pete's children" — all scurrying every which-a-way. If they're not swinging on some streamer hanging from seemingly every limb of the leafy grounds, they're banging upon something or other occupying virtually every corner. There are jugglers and mimes and storytellers and dancers and singalongs and demonstrations and whatever — all of it skilled and inviting for all ages. Indeed, there's often little demarcation on the main stages between what's for elders and what's for youngsters, such as the relaxed set my wife and I caught from the multi-platinum Raffi, perhaps the most popular children's entertainer alive.

This is truly one of the most family friendly festivals I've witnessed. The only one in this book that gives CLEARWATER' a run for its money comes from the opposite end of the political spectrum, the contemporary Christian blow-out, KINGDOM BOUND (Darien, NY — see chapter). Credit Seeger for this welcoming character.

"Yeah, yeah, the quality was always extremely high," lauds Rosenkrantz of CLEARWATER's children's entertainment:

- "As a promoter myself in getting acquainted with the way that things are booked and such, I'm struck by that. And I would say that Toshi is quite as much a force in that direction as Pete is. I mean, they are definitely a pair. They work tirelessly toward the same ends. Toshi kind of puts their money where their mouths are, if you know what I mean. I think it was just one of the strongest children's bills I've seen.

"It's also as though childhood is a serious business," Rosenkrantz utters before chuckling at the seeming incongruity:

- "It sounds kinda' contradictory to what we're talking about, but it is that children are our most vital resource, and I think that really has been consistent over the years in what they've done. And I think that it's also very intelligent, because, as Pete said, a lot of the people who are involved with CLEARWATER' grew up with Pete's music, or are kind of in that work he's created, or [have been] on the Clearwater, itself."

Referring to one young brother-and-sister team who are second-generation CLEARWATER' volunteers, Rosenkrantz exclaims: "There's a certain sensibility that they have that is clearly CLEARWATER', that clearly they pick up by being around Pete, and his organization, and Toshi, and the ethos, and the view of the environment as being utterly important, and kind of the romanticism that has what, I think, been the glue that holds the whole community together. And there's something about looking out on the river and seeing the boat out there is quite moving."

Heady accomplishment number two... Although you'll also see every imaginable left-leaning banner hanging in the "Activist Area" ("Support Guatemalan Banana Pickers!" read one. Yeah, right.

'Couldn't find some constituency a little closer to home, huh?), CLEARWATER's primary beneficiary is it's self-named Sloop. This magnificent sailboat's maintained by a member-supported organization devoted to "hands-on" environmental education for 15,000 kids and adults annually as well as a myriad of other related advocacies.

According to Dunaway, Seeger's pioneering efforts in this ecology field actually stemmed from a retreat. Apparently, the ever-idealistic Seeger was disillusioned from having yet another of his cherished causes — in this case the protest movement of the Viet Nam war — abandon his pacifism for more militant tactics (and music, too). In the mid-'60s he retreated to his waterfront homestead in Beacon, only to become horrified at how the beloved Hudson River of his youth had turned into an open sewer.

Using his genius for symbolism and charisma for organizing, Seeger alighted upon the idea of building a 106-foot replica of the indigenous watercraft from the 18th and 19th centuries. He formed a nonprofit, the Hudson River Sloop Restoration, to make the dream come to life; helped raise $100,000 over three years; and oversaw the finished product make its maiden voyage in 1969 from Maine to New York City harbor — an event that first galvanized the national press toward the river's plight.

"Len [Chandler, who helped man that fateful launch] calls it the first major media event focused on the environment," Rosenkrantz relays, "which, indeed, I think it was. He was telling great stories about being out on the water with Ramblin' Jack Elliot [another original crew member], and they would lean over and pull old prophylactics and garbage from the water, and would make these sort of collages, and they would exhibit them at the dockside concerts they would do in the evenings. He said, 'You didn't have to look very far to support our claim that the river was a cesspool, 'cause it was right there in front of you!'"

Seeger's project was disparaged by his militant cohorts at the time as "out-of-touch" and "fanciful," but it has since proved itself a powerful symbol for grassroots activism that actually works, instead of futility ranting to hear itself ranting. For once, Seeger had a crusade with a specific locale, a measurable, incremental goal, and a tangible, material benefit that cut across political lines. (One of the humorous ironies of the Sloop's gestation was seeing Seeger forced to raise funds among the wealthy Hudson River sailors of his own patrician upbringing, and finding himself quite good at it, to the leftists' chagrin!) In this type of targeted environmentalism, he'd finally arrived at something that didn't necessarily pit one class against another but brought them all together in common cause — a "win-win" proposition, if you will.

Credit Seeger for helping to birth a movement that's outlasted all his others and now has proponents as high as the current Vice President of the U. S. And for all those who still disparage its value, I'd merely point you to the current closing from over-fishing of the George's Bank off Cape Cod as what happens from not being good to Mother Nature.

"As far as Pete as a person is concerned," Rosenkratz reflects:

- "My feeling about him now (and it's strictly, I guess, a fairly contemporary viewpoint) is that he has used whatever he has built up career-wise, etc. toward this campaign to clean up the Hudson and been totally dedicated to it. He may have come from a privileged background, but the way he has chosen to live is utterly consistent with what he has chosen to support and to seed there. And he is absolutely, utterly dedicated to the concept of community, of the music as being an integral part of the community life, and a tool, also, for education and for celebration.

"I have a great deal of admiration for him."

And Toshi, I prompt? "Oh, she's wonderful, and I've been working very closely with her this year, because she's basically stepped down from the booking and handed it to me. I trust that she's not going anywhere," Rosenkrantz laughs, "I think she's just brilliant."

Dunaway, Rosenkrantz, and I are all a bit fuzzy on the history of CLEARWATER', but there seem to have been many CLEARWATER's accompanying that maiden voyage, beginning with one on the piers in Portland, Maine. Close to $40,000 was raised on this first sail.

*Taconic Newspapers* notes CLEARWATER's most direct descendent as being the HUDSON VALLEY FOLK PICNIC. It claims the first one featured Seeger, Arlo Guthrie, Libba Cotton, Bernice Reagon and, likely, the "Clearwater Sloop Singers" — deckhands such as Chandler, Elliott, Jimmy Collier, Don McLean, Lou Killen and others whom you'll recognize, of course, as gifted folksingers, too (as musicians were all Seeger could initially get to join him; other lefties not finding this activity class-conscious enough for their tastes). More "Songfests" were held on Clearwater's bow up and down the Hudson in the years following. The crew even went so far as to sail in support of the first EARTH DAY in Washington, DC, on April 22, 1970.

Other festivals sprung up that would feature the "'Sloop Singers" and their performing friends, as originators or as invited guests:

- The CLEARWATER PUMPKIN SAIL ('71), which wandered down the length of the Hudson, making "Songfest" stops along the way before docking in Manhattan;

- The SHAD FEST in Peekskill, NY ('73);

- The STRAWBERRY FESTIVAL in Beacon, NY ('76);

- The HARVEST MOON FESTIVAL in Kingston, NY ('91) .

- The CLEARWATER FESTIVAL in Brooklyn, NYC ('94) .

Other groups took up the cause of the Sloop by organizing clubs patterned after the one Seeger formed in Beacon in '71. One such in Monmouth County, New Jersey, hosted their own first CLEARWATER' on the grounds of Sandy Hook State Park in '76. Two years later the HUDSON VALLEY FOLK PICNIC gave way to what is now formally called CLEARWATER'.

There are two characteristics I've been able to divine from my folk-festival friends of earlier versions:

First, they positively laud the original waterfront site at Croton Point State Park, before it was forced to move to Westchester Community College in '88 when a toxic waste dump was uncovered adjacent. (Boy, talk about having an appropriate prop land in your lap!) I personally admire the current facility, which has everything you'd want for a festival save overnight camping.

It seems, however, that's the one feature my friends miss most, aside from the Hudson River visuals. CLEARWATER' draws hundreds of these volunteer workers who love camping out under the stars and trading songs all night long. Laying out sleeping bags in a gym as they do now just doesn't cut it, they say. Rosenkrantz sympathizes:

- "The one problem with it is if you're a member of the folk community and you're not volunteering at the event, you don't get to camp there. And that's not terribly conducive to pulling the community together, although there are so many volunteers that we have a big chunk of the community there anyway. But it's still good for the folks who didn't sign up to work for us, and at the last minute want to come, or audience members who want to intermingle... That's something that I personally believe in very strongly.

"But it is a good site. It has the advantage of having buildings that we can use and so on.

"And it's accessible, which is important. That's been a very, very big CLEARWATER' priority. I was talking to some [festival promoter] in Boston who said when they want to know what's the thing to do about accessibility, they refer to CLEARWATER'. It's kinda' taken for granted — we always have signers, we always have wheelchairs available, we have people to make it happen, basically. You know, the children's area, the fact that you can just go there and feel part of the community immediately... It's not like, oh, NEWPORT (BEN & JERRY'S NEWPORT FOLK FESTIVAL, Newport, RI — see chapter) or somewhere where there are all these security bars and that sort of thing."

Second, CLEARWATER' used to program more famous names along the lines of, say, Bonnie Raitt. My friends tell me Toshi sought to get away from the big deals these headliners would involve and return to the informality and intimacy of earlier times. Looking at the 70-plus performers her Steering Committee selected for this year, I see maybe one act capable of filling a 1,000-seat theater: Sweet Honey In The Rock. The rest occupy a broad, broad spectrum of fames and genres, though I do note a well-chosen sampling of rising folk-music stars. By holding the performance fees down thus, Toshi's able to keep nearly all the entertainers onsite overnight, thus insuring a community of artists for the weekend, camaraderie and all.

Rosenkrantz explains that "part of the reason that it got a little bit smaller over the years in terms of the performers was to keep that flavor. So, that's a constant kind of struggle:

- "It changes from time to time in terms of the bookings, but the basic priorities are multi-culturalism, a vibrant children's area, and a representative sampling of performers. And many stages going. And antic artists are another thing that are more prominent at CLEARWATER', including jugglers and the unicyclists you'll sometimes see out there. There's some wonderful street performers... CLEARWATER' is basically political action and celebration, but the festival is a major fundraiser for the organization. And besides being a fundraiser, it's a celebration arm and community gathering, etc., etc."

Rosenkrantz goes on to to describe her preoccupation this year with CLEARWATER's silver anniversary, which included reuniting 25 years of the Sloop's Captains and crew members, coordinating post-event parties, and scrounging all the photo documentation she could find. "I have a wonderful photo of Pete," she says of the inaugural CLEARWATER'. "They had a sound system that was real primitive and they had a stage shaped like a boat. I have pictures of Pete on that stage."

Which brings us to CLEARWATER's chief asset — Seeger, himself.

For all my criticisms of Seeger's politics, one quality I respect is his leadership. Throughout his life, and nowadays at his festival, Seeger leads in the best way possible — unhesitatingly, humbly, and by example. Is children's entertainment important? The very first thing greeting my wife and I as we entered the grounds was Seeger doing an early set at the Small Boats Stage. Is participatory singing valued? Half the day it seemed, Seeger was leading the Walkabout Clearwater Chorus as it corralled passersby near the Food Court to join in singing "Midnight Special," "Goodnight Irene" and what-else-have-you. Is accessibility a priority? Even at 75 years young, Seeger was accessible everywhere on the grounds, much as his closest contemporary, Bill Monroe, is at his own BEAN BLOSSOM BLUEGRASS FESTIVAL (see Bean Blossom, IN, Early June)

Rosenkrantz can only marvel at Seeger's example: "CLEARWATER's the place to be if you want to see him in his natural habitat, so to speak."

**Festival Review**

Truth be told, CLEARWATER' faked me right out of my flip-flops. I just wasn't expecting this big a festival, this fully-featured, this well-designed, this artfully-presented, this professionally-run — all served-up with an inviting informality and festivity. My wife and I brought three other friends to Sunday's celebration, and we all had a great time throughout the day, though each of us went our separate ways. There's that much to do, hear, and consume!

The weather that year was beastly hot. Despite needing a few hours at midday to zone-out under a shade tree, though, our party still gloried in seven stages of continuous music and dance plus separate areas for food vendors, crafts vendors, an alternative marketplace, a books-and-records grove, solar power displays, a children's area, a Clearwater reunion tent, and more, more, more. Singing seemed to emanate from every corner, and as we reluctantly exited toward the parking lot at nightfall, the Clearwater Walkabout Chorus serenaded us to the shuttle busses.

Rosenkrantz observes:

- "I think one of the secrets of success there is [Toshi and Pete] pay attention to things like the 'Sloop Singers' singing folks out to the bus. Or there are even people in Grand Central Station, some in the New York City group, who help people into the train because the idea is that music belongs to the people — that's the definition of folk music. So there may be some wonderful people up on stages, but there's a concern that the big performers don't overshadow people with less name recognition who are every bit as talented, and we all know it. And that's a very big thing; it's a major priority."

Rosenkrantz proceeds to describe her own efforts outside of CLEARWATER' in showcasing young talent as well as this year's intent to devote two CLEARWATER' stages to amateur artists whose lives have been dedicated more to environmental activism than building music careers. I can't say I spent much time checking them out, I was too busy cruising the three main stages for aspiring acts I recognized. Here are two up-and-comers who left the greatest impression upon me: Ani DiFranco and The Billys.

**Artist Mini-Reviews**   Ani DiFranco. DiFranco, a twenty-something Buffalo native living in New York City, goes well beyond the standard "women's music" polemics and deeper into a sincere, complex, emotional response to the real world. The stance she's discovered is of an outsider. This communicates directly across her entire peer group and achieves, paradoxically, greater inclusion and universality than her brethren's gender sloganeering.

DiFranco's got a zillion techniques at her disposal. She's developed a furiously percussive strumming style that packs the wallop of a rock-and-roll band into a solo guitar. Michael Hedges fans will recognize a kinship. She sings over a full range, employing a striking, swallowed, throaty trill reminiscent of Judy Garland's. She's a remarkable agile, tactile, and visual writer who's capable of bringing most any scenario to life. And, of course, she's a genial entertainer and refreshing personality to boot.

What impressed me most, however, was the variety and believability of her emotional tones. On one side was the quirky, amused response in "4th of July" to an innocent Iowa youth's not being judgmental over DiFranco's admittedly extreme bohemian appearance. On the other was a chillingly-detached confession in "Out Of Range" of a prostitute who doesn't necessarily blame her victimizer but rather cooly acknowledges her own ulterior motives. Both rang true. If she can keep plumbing her heart in such honest, creative fashion, I see mega stars in DiFranco's future.

The Billys. This young folk duo from North Carolina, Bill Melanson and Billy Jonas, sing handsomely, play guitars, and bang what they describe as "found and foraged instruments" — various percussion pieces created from water jugs, pickle barrels, PVC pipes, cutlery, film cannisters, "pots and pans and coffee cans." Just seeing this veritable thrift shop up onstage prepares you for what you're gonna' get from The Billys. In a word, fun.

The two have a host of novelty tunes guaranteed to raise a smile if not an outright belly laugh. "Primordial Ooze" was one — a frantic antic about everything on their TV screens in recent months. This wacky medley skewers obsessions from lactose paranoia to breast implants (a typical rhyme: "surgical glue" and "womb with a view"), and features a singalong chorus even Lyle Lovett could enjoy. The Billys can also stretch a metaphor past the breaking point, such as a deliberately tongue-in-cheek narrative, "Bread," which marries every step of baking a loaf with a short-lived love affair.

But they do it all tastefully (pardon the pun), sincerely, and above all, tunefully. These guys make sure to alternate the pretty with the looney, exhibiting a particular gift for melodies that waft around your heart like the aroma of that ill-fated sourdough starter. There's warmth without sappiness, topicality without sanctimony, and delirious word-play that nevertheless doesn't leave grade-schoolers scratching their heads (good choruses help the cause). The Billys, clearly in touch with their inner child, might be the one act best suited for taking up Seeger's mantle as folk music's pied piper. Stay tuned!

Rosenkrantz:

- "I've had a lot of experience with Ani. This is my first with The Billys, but they were probably the hit of the festival in terms of the internal rumblings and what the crew and the community thought. Ani is a real phenomenon right now. You know, we present her up at the Eight-Step, and she was at FALCON RIDGE', and we get groups of kids coming up from New York City. She has a real, almost a cult, following. I think that we loosely define her as a folk singer for the '90s.

"I don't even call it folk music at the 'Step anymore. I call it acoustic music because it's just too narrow a definition, and it just doesn't cover what people are doing. Some of our folk performers, like Greg Greenway, have a rock background, and it just brings a certain excitement to the music. Then you see other people picking up on tempos or different kinds of lyrics, but there is a real sharing of resources here which I think has always been characteristic of the folk community. You don't get 'pickin'-and-singin'-people always at a slow tempo sitting on a stool.' It's not like that anymore. It's a much more exciting art form. I don't think I would've stayed in it this long [otherwise].

"Ani DiFranco, my instinct is she's kind of a law unto herself [laughs]. She's going to, I think, really take off. And The Billys [too]. Also, what's great about them is they perform children's and adults' sets..."

I admit, I've lost track of all the many festivals where Seeger's "'Sloop Singers" regularly decamp (see the partial list up in the heading). The Sandy Hook variant's probably the biggest, outside of CLEARWATER', with three stages going strong, but the acts there and at the other spin-offs are generally local in nature. Excepting Seeger, of course. **See Also**

The other festival besides CLEARWATER' that ties it all together is the CLEARWATER PUMPKIN SAIL. This moveable "feast-ival" begins in Early October with a concert hosted by Rosenkrantz at the Eight Step. The 'Sloop and its crew then embark down the Hudson River for 10 to 12 more shows, each hosted by another 'Sloop Club. The final one occurs in New York City, typically at the South Street Seaport.

"And Pete will come," Rosenkrantz points out:

- "But he will only come as one of the crew. He wants to be listed alphabetically and he doesn't want any big brouhaha about his being there. He will sit around in a semi-circle and direct the crew, and everybody takes a turn. There might be a new crew member on the boat and everybody's encouraging him or her to sing. There might be somebody who's been there for many years and a lot of people kinda' inbetween. To a large extent, it's truly a performing crew; a fascinating group of people, really. ...It's a lot of fun."

CLEARWATER' does maintain an office in downtown Poughkeepsie, but it appears the locus for all this activity is the monthly pot-luck held at the Sloop Club on Beacon's waterfront. Speak your piece, sing your part, and as Garrison Keillor would advise, "Bring a covered dish."

~     ~     ~

# Huntington's Variety Party

FOLK MUSIC SOCIETY OF HUNTINGTON MEMBERS CONCERT, Huntington, NY
Late May
Traditional Folk

**SUMMERSCAPE: HUNTINGTON SUMMER ARTS FESTIVAL**, Huntington, NY
Late June to Late August
Variety, General
***Attended***

FOLK MUSIC SOCIETY OF HUNTINGTON SUMMER FESTIVAL, Huntington, NY
Late July
Traditional Folk

**Introduction**  Huntington, your typical bedroom community about an hour east of The Big Apple on Long Island's suburban North Shore, enjoys the quiet notoriety of being Walt Whitman's birthplace. Across the highway also sits one of the nation's first indoor malls which bears Whitman's name. This is a good sign for the arts — after all, how many other communities name their shopping centers after poets?

Huntington's known around these parts as "The Little Apple" for its modest profusion of home-grown cultural institutions. It boasts the New Community Cinema, the IMAC Theater, and the Heckscher Museum plus various playhouses, societies, galleries, boutiques, arts shows and what-have-you. Its modest central village belies that close to 300,000 prospective culture vultures are spread throughout the township's wide boundaries. A goodly number of these have handsome property taxes to contribute to the cultural cause. Billy Joel kept a mansion residence in stately Lloyd Harbor, for example, before re-locating to the Hamptons, while the late Harry Chapin, a frequent local philanthropist, maintained digs by the shoreline.

But the real secret is centralized self-support. The professionally-staffed Huntington Arts Council [HAC] has long acted as an umbrella for its many arts organizations. Moreover, they've kept the summer showcasing in one location, Heckscher Park, instead of spreading it around like most other Long Island municipalities. The result? Synergy, stability, and a solid summer series which they've formally produced since '66 — SUMMERSCAPE: HUNTINGTON SUMMER ARTS FESTIVAL [SUMMERSCAPE'].

SUMMERSCAPE' schedules more than 50 dates over a nine-week period including a fair number of national acts called "Star Events." Check out the first three days of '93's schedule, for example: The Drifters and The Capris; Maura O'Connell; Bill Monroe and The Bluegrass Boys. One of HAC's members, the FOLK MUSIC SOCIETY OF HUNTINGTON, also takes the stage for it's annual SUMMER FESTIVAL. Its '93 evening bill consisted of Dave Van Ronk, Ginny Hawker and Kay Justice, and Magpie.

Of course, a more typical booking might be a local dance troupe, or concert band, or theater production, or storytelling festival, or Dixieland band. Even here you never can tell. I'd known one of my brother's friends, Scott McDonald, for nearly 20 years before finding out his father, Ken McDonald, was a music teacher and big-band arranger/conductor. Scott dragged me to his dad's Jazz Alliance concert at '93's SUMMERSCAPE', then kept pointing how this band member or another played for Glenn Miller, or Tommy Dorsey, or a like professional outfit. After all, New York City is just an hour away by train, and there's a lot of session and touring work to be had. Same deal for the other disciplines, as entire productions of Broadway's "Evita" and Off-Broadway's "Mama I Want To Sing" have visited SUMMERSCAPE' in recent years.

I'm not saying I'd plan an entire vacation around it, but if you're in the area, it pays to stop in. Best of all, it won't cost you one red cent!

Peg Lewis, who's been HAC's cheery Executive Director for nearly 20 years, is finally stepping down in '94 to retire, marry, and move to Bermuda. She remains optimistic about the continued prosperity of SUMMERSCAPE', even in light of arts funding cutbacks which have hindered most New York State nonprofits:

- "[SUMMERSCAPE's] gone on for so many years, and it's been built and built. If you tried to go out and just do it now, oh, heaven help you, because you have to have seeded it way back to keep the money coming and growing. And you know, we don't get any more money now from the town. If we want more money we have to go out and get it ourselves, so at least it's at a respectable level where we can do nice things. We are lucky."

Lewis credits the series' post-war beginnings to Rufus Kern:

- "He was then the Director of the bands up at Huntington High School, and he wanted to start a community band. He did that and they would play down at Hecksher Park on the steps of the [Hecksher] Museum. Their way was lighted by the headlights of the cars of the people who came to hear them. That really was the rock bottom start of it, and then it just grew.

"Modestly," she adds, noting their being restricted by a pedestrian stage until '79. "That was the year in the administration of Ken Butterfield," Lewis recalls of the former Township Supervisor.

- "He really believed that we needed this theater and could get it. Ken's a jazz musician and a very good one. His father was a professional musician, and his grandfather played with John Phillip Sousa! Ken has a great love of Dixieland jazz, and he has a group called The Isotope Stompers [a frequent SUMMERSCAPE' guest].

"He had a young gal who worked for him, and she was involved with grants. He asked her to research what we might look into, and she found something federal that was supposed to be for facilities for recreation. Well, it was a bit of a stretch for us to get a theatrical facility, but somehow with the paperwork and whatever they did, they got it through. We ended up with much better than just a recreational facility because it really is a theater. It could be built very simply, and then all of the tech stuff has been put in since.

"And we've had very, very good technical people using it, working it, recommending what we needed to get good coverage of the sound and lights so that we really could have large crowds who would enjoy themselves and not be telling us they couldn't see or couldn't hear. It's taken a lot of years, but we've been very bless'd, and the town has kept the funding coming for the talent."

Lewis arrived at HAC in '75:

- "I had worked for years for the Bell Telephone Hour on radio and television, so I was into booking and contacts and stuff like that before taking a diversionary route for about 10 years. I always missed the presenting, and when I found that they were looking for somebody for a new job at HAC, I applied for it. But I grew up in Huntington and went to Huntington High School, so I have a feeling of great belief in the community and closeness to it.

"HAC serves the arts community, as well as the residents of Huntington and the area. We're in support of each other; we're for advocacy; we're for the sharing of information; we do what we can to present them in this way. The only presenting we do is in the summer, and some groups go to it and others don't. I mean there are some groups, like some of the chamber-music groups, we don't encourage too much of in the park because they kinda' notoriously don't draw huge crowds. There's too much distraction in the park for things that are salon-like. So I've always felt that it's in our best interest to keep things light and large.

"I tell you, though, our member organizations have grown so much in the 18 years I've been doing this, and they don't make us apologize for anything — they're wonderful."

Lewis's view on her SUMMERSCAPE' legacy? "I've always tried to get the very best talent we could possibly afford," she assures. "We try to treat everybody happily. I hope that will continue because I think the mix is what's important."

**Artist Mini-Reviews**

Here are some of Lewis' comments on recent SUMMERSCAPE' concerts:

Walt Michael and Company. "Well, Walt Michael I was very hot on last year; they were wonderful musicians. I wish they had a better name draw at this point because I do think they're worthy of peoples attention."

Evangeline. How'd they go over, I asked? "Very well," replied Lewis:

- "I was worried about them! [laughs] Well, they had paperwork that scared me witless, but once we got them here they were fine. I think a lot of these artists really do have bad experiences out there, and they ask for so much that it's almost, you know, the tail wagging the dog. We just had to tell them we couldn't do it all, but we would make sure that they were fed properly, and we would make sure that they could be heard properly, and it really worked out very well. I thought it was a good concert. ...They ended with an acappella number that was just lovely!"

Long Island's Own Natural Element with Cathy Kreger and Howard Emerson. "We're going to do a Long Island artists night again. We thought that was popular last year, and Little Toby Walker's one of the people who's gonna' be presented."

Speaking of Walker, I asked Lewis about another local acoustic blues guitarist, Honest Tom Pomposello, who I'd witnessed at many SUMMERSCAPE's before he went on to sign with Zazou Records. "Oh yes, we had Tom for years," Lewis exclaimed, "and he has been so busy and into doing his stuff in New York City that he just really didn't have time [in '93]. In fact, Scott Sammis wanted very much to bring Tom back out here, and he killed himself doing it. I think one time Tom hurt himself, and couldn't come another time. It worked out, but he's really into other things now, and truly is, I think, a really successful artist."

Rosemary Clooney. "I just love her," Lewis chuckled over her fondest recollection from a decade prior:

- "Her comeback was rather new then, and she was doing very well. She has a wonderful style [and] had everybody she loves to have [backing her]. John Otto, of course, is her musical director, and he is such a good piano player! Trained at Eastman [School of Music], he just is excellent. And she had with her Warren Vache and Scott Hamilton, and you can't get much better than that. Some of the best things she's done have been with them, and it was just the most wonderful night.

"We have had other wonderful nights, I gotta' tell ya, but there was just a quality, a pin drop, you couldn't hear anything. It was just a sea of happy faces out there — a special, special evening."

**Attendance Tip**

"Just come early and enjoy it and let it kinda' happen to you," Lewis suggests. "It's a wonderful thing especially because there's no charge. How many places are lucky enough to have that?" Lewis also advises observing parking signs on nearby streets, or to look for for municipal lots behind Town Hall, or the New Community Cinema. Leave your beach chairs in the car and walk a few blocks into town afterwards for a bite.

**Travel Tip**

Heckscher Museum, Walt Whitman Birthplace State Historic Site, Vanderbilt Mansion Museum, Caumsett State Park, Target Rock National Wildlife Refuge, and just general touring and browsing comprise a good day's agenda. Check your travel guides, or Friday's *Newsday*, for details

~     ~     ~

# Chautauqua's Variety Party

CHAUTAUQUA SUMMER MUSIC PROGRAM, Chautauqua, NY
    Late June to Late August
    Variety, General
    **_Attended_**

"There's nothing like it anywhere," exclaims Marty Merkley, Music Program Director of the move-able fine-arts feast that has fulfilled the seasonal mission of the CHAUTAUQUA SUMMER MUSIC PROGRAM [CHAUTAUQUA] since the Chautauqua Institution's founding way back in 1874: **Introduction**

- "Nothing! There are a lot of summer festivals with this type of musical empathy, but there is nothing like CHAUTAUQUA that encompasses so much in variety of programs from the Lecture Platform, to the Continuing Studies in the Adult Study Courses, through the Children's School and the Boy's and Girl's Clubs, to the C. L. S. C... Just the scope of it; there is nothing quite like CHAUTAUQUA. And being a fenced community and second-home vacation destination, it's just unique."

You know what? Not only is Merkley absolutely correct, but he's also merely glossing over the highlights of what's made CHAUTAUQUA such a worldwide treasure — musically and oth-erwise — for millions of summertime pilgrims for over a century.

CHAUTAUQUA sprung from much the same idealistic zeal that inspired the Quakers, the Shakers and other religious groups to establish utopias throughout the "New World." This particular com-munity evolved somewhat later, of course, forged by the collaboration between Ohio industrialist Lewis Miller and Pennsylvania Methodist minister John H. Vincent to set up a vacation camp for Sunday school teachers. It quickly reached out to other Protestant denominations, expanding in time to become fully ecumenical.

Back in the old "school prayer" days, when religious and moral instruction were an every-day part of American public education, CHAUTAUQUA made quite a name for itself in pioneering a host of techniques. Classes for young people (remember that kids were distinctly second-class cit-izens back then), correspondence classes, and "great books" curricula were all first developed here. The oldest continuous book club in America, the Chautauqua Literary and Scientific Circle (the "C. L. S. C." Merkley spoke of), was begun in 1878. No small potatoes, it has enrolled over a million readers and once inspired up to 10,000 reading circles throughout the world.

What quickly distinguished the CHAUTAUQUA experience was how it brought the best minds from throughout the country for open discussions on all relevant topics, not just religion. Politics, economics, international relations, literature, and science were all fair game. This broad forum became known as the Chautauqua Platform and still operates at a fairly high-powered level on an almost daily basis. Nine U. S. presidents have spoken at CHAUTAUQUA lectures — President Reagan addressed the Third General Conference on U. S.-Soviet Relations here in 1987, and the Clintons and Gores paid a joint visit (no pun intended) in '92.

Perhaps the peak of CHAUTAUQUA's influence occurred in the 1920's. Scores of indepen-dent producers took variations across the country, delivering CHAUTAUQUA's unique religious/intellectual/cultural experience to an estimated 35 million attendees per year. These tent shows stopped with the Great Depression but left their impression upon America's psyche. You can find the word "chautauqua" in most dictionaries, for example.

Naturally, religious music was integral to the early offerings, though CHAUTAUQUA kept true to its open Platform by soon stirring classical and opera into the mix. "I remember reading an article about the outrage and the controversy that was caused by Bishop Vincent introducing sec-ular music to CHAUTAUQUA into a strictly religious community," Merkley recalls, "but over the years that has expanded to encompass nearly all the genres in the musical world."

After the turn of the century, CHAUTAUQUA's music began to rival its lectures in popularity. The New York Symphony resided here in 1920, while that same decade saw the founding of both the Chautauqua Symphony Orchestra and the Chautauqua Opera (which produces works sung only in English). These two organizations, along with the Chautauqua Conservatory Theater, continue to provide CHAUTAUQUA's cultural backbone even today.

But don't despair, pop-music lovers.

CHAUTAUQUA's expansion beyond classical and religious music started in the 1930's with jazz, ballet and musicals. A quick scan of '93's lineup reveals how popular offerings have grown in 60 years to occupy a third of CHAUTAUQUA's 65 days covering nearly 20 genres. You'll find everything from African to zydeco, from household names to the obscure.

Even though there are family-oriented bookings stamped with the "Good Housekeeping Seal of Approval," so to speak, there are many more proffering ethnic exposure, artistic challenge, or flat-out fun. A good example is local heroes, 10,000 Maniacs, reviewed below. Thus CHAUTAUQUA's music rises above the "lowest common denominator" which often plagues family programming. It's diverse and classy through and through.

"We try to do something for everybody," says Merkley, chuckling at the compliment.

- "We program from two-and-a-half to death — that's the age range. There are specific programs aimed at all different ages, and that takes in every conceivable kind of taste. It's a tricky balance trying to keep something for everybody, [but] I think we do pretty well.

"I am a musician by training, a pianist and singer. After my initial job out of school working for a computer corporation, I took up my avocation, my hobby, which was music, and have been in that ever since in some respect. I've worked in the opera world, and the symphony world, and the dance world, and done a lot of different things. So CHAUTAUQUA's a place where I can bring all of that together in one job because I'm responsible for all of the art forms. All of the professional performances on the grounds come out of my office.

"As you look at the calendar," Merkley says of the season's schedule, which runs seven days a week throughout July and August:

- "Tuesdays, Thursdays and Saturdays are always symphony nights. Friday night is the big night when we spend the money and bring in the [pop-music] headliners. Mondays and Wednesdays end up being the nights I budget so much money and try to find things that are different and interesting — sometimes challenging to the audience — but definitely things I think people should hear, and see, and experience. Because, again, we are a learning institution, and we have always been in the business of lifelong learning here. I think experiencing new and different kinds of entertainment and different cultures is very important, so I try and do that in all of the different evenings. We always try to get the best quality of that, what strikes me as something people would enjoy."

Judging from the numbers — 150,000 annual visitors supplementing 12,000 summer residents and 450 year-rounders — CHAUTAUQUA seems to agree. "After you establish a certain reputation," Merkley reasons, "people have a certain faith knowing that what you're gonna' do is good. People start coming to things they don't know about: 'Well, if you programmed it, it must be something we should go and experience.' That's kinda' nice."

Remarkably, Merkley makes every performance. Though he'd be the first to tell you his personal highlight is not reflective of his own musical tastes, he points to a Beatles' tribute act, Yesterday, as best typifying the community spirit celebrated when CHAUTAUQUA's day-trippers and residents come together:

- "That evening we moved the benches out of the tent and grew it into a dance night. We had all ages and everybody moved in. The floor was packed and (as much as we hate this, but it was wonderful), everybody had their cigarette lighters out and were waving them in the air. Remember like when we used to do that? Everybody's doing that, and singing the songs, and waving with their arms around each other. I mean, it was an absolutely fabulous night! Everybody had a hoot — Grandma and Grandpa out there dancing with their kids and their grandkids. It was very cross-generational as you know from 10,000 Maniacs.

Everyone comes and brings their families. Those who hate it stay five minutes and leave; those who stay enjoy it and have a wonderful time.

"So, that's very important. Family is a very important part of CHAUTAUQUA.

"Those kinds of thing are really highlights, even though they're probably not the most musically fabulous things in the world. The whole spirit of the occasion makes it really special, more special to me than [when] you get a performer who comes in and does a fabulous show where everybody sits, and they clap, and they go, 'Isn't that wonderful,' and they go home. Where people interact together, really experiencing a sense of joy, really getting off on the evening, that's what it's all about."

One feature we haven't talked about, perhaps CHAUTAUQUA's most-striking, is its extraordinary potpourri of architectural Americana. You can almost hear TV's Dick Vitale shouting as he passes through the main gates, "Hansel and Gretel Land, ba-by, Gingerbread City!" **Festival Review**

This entire 750-acre complex on the shores of Chautauqua Lake has been designated a National Historic Landmark. Picture a shaded Cape May fenced-in and squeezed together for a casually intimate gentility. Storybook cottages, all porches and pillars and spindles and rockers, pile up upon each other along a warren of walkways. It's all overhung by a canopy of ancient trees which simply beg you to grab a bench beneath and watch the summer pass you by. CHAUTAUQUA is the kind of place you'd come across in faded Victorian photographs but never imagined actually still existed, fully-preserved and operational.

CHAUTAUQUA is a self-contained municipality in all ways save an official designation. You'll find a full complement of city services, including a post office, along with charming shops, petite cafes and ubiquitous book stores. There is every possible recreational facility plus lodging opportunities ranging from modest apartment rentals to Gilded Age throwback, the Anthenaeum Hotel, which overlooks the lake in grand style. Since the entire family needs entertainment sometime during the summer, CHAUTAUQUA has a few spots onsite and nearby which serve teens and twenty-somethings, including its Youth Activities Center.

That's where 10,000 Maniacs came of age, believe-it-or-not.

These Jamestown natives united in '81 and played about the area (including CHAUTAUQUA) come summer much like young Springsteen gigging bars on the Jersey Shore. Their stylistic arrival at blending alternative/folk/rock might have first been viewed back during a 1987 concert in Chautauqua's Seaver Gym just before they were to tour Europe and open for REM throughout the 'States. Laura Buzard, Staff Writer for the *Chautauqua Daily*, describes the experience for lucky Chautauquans as "legendary," citing then breakthroughs in the 'Maniacs' material and performing style. Their subsequent album, *In My Tribe*, went platinum, and the rest is MTV history.

Merkley kept in touch on booking their first-ever gig in CHAUTAUQUA's century-old 5,000-seat Amphitheater. The 'Maniacs finally said yes to a date officially concluding their 1993 tour. "It just so happened that it was also to be the last time that Natalie [Merchant] sang with the group," Merkley notes of their intent to separate soon afterward, thus ending a 13-year run. "They wanted to do it here."

Now this might've already been one of the four-to-six Friday nights CHAUTAUQUA normally sells out in advance each year. Toss in the prospect of the 'Maniacs' first-ever Amphitheater homecoming, plus their last-ever performance together, and forget it! "S. R. O." Still, I was able to stand for free around the bricked lip of "the Amp," as it's called, admiring its antique wooden pews and overhung party lights. I enjoyed excellent acoustics for what played out as a true CHAUTAUQUA happening.

John and Mary. Guitarist John Lombardo was a founding 'Maniac and, together with vocalist/violinist Mary Ramsey, forms what what I call, "'Maniacs Lite." These two play acoustic, not electric, while Ramsey's voice is lighter than Merchant's, albeit with a similar color. Fortunately, Ramsey didn't push it where it didn't want to go, cultivating an airy, Celtic-flavored poignancy, instead. They delivered their catchy radio hit, "Red Wooden Beads," a few tunes into **Artist Mini-Reviews** their set before stretching out on an appealing variety of melodic folk/pop songs and instrumentals. I look forward to hearing them again in closer confines.

10,000 Maniacs. What a difference a venue makes! When I caught the 'Maniacs' opening set for the 'Dead at Buffalo's cavernous Rich Stadium a few years prior, I was impressed with the band's rhythm, but felt Merchant shrunk somewhat from the spotlight. This time 'round, though, she literally beamed amidst her rapturous welcome. The band sounded great, too, delivering an ultra-tight mix of power and grace honed by a summer's touring.

My notes suffered from my obscured vantage point, but I came to understand why they might be breaking up. Merchant's singing has some limitation in range but is compensated for by it's unique character and gutsy kind of soul. She's grown to really putting forth a tune with showmanship to match. Within the band Merchant was but a voice above the din (which acquired a certain sameness by night's end). Their opener, however, was a quieter blues/cabaret piece showcasing her interpretive skills. It left me wanting for more, presumably to follow.

Merkley: "We had a hard time throwing them out of the theater, because everybody was hanging around talking afterwards. It was very positive, very emotional for all of them. And of course, all of their families were there — literally a couple hundred people combined — so it was a real celebration of their music, and of their families, and of their lives, and everything that happened to them. It was sort of closing one era and opening up what's to come in the future. It was great, everybody enjoyed it."

**Attendance Tip**  If you have your eye on one of those hot Friday nights, better buy your tix by mail or phone a few weeks ahead. Otherwise, you can get 'em on a walk-up basis. I admit to being utterly confused by CHAUTAUQUA's myriad of gate-entry/concert-ticket combo passes, which range from somewhat cheap to very steep depending on how long you want to roam the grounds (from four hours to all summer long). The best deal seems like a weekend pass, I suppose, but don't ask me. Call and let them sort out the options.

**Travel Tip**  "If you like culture, there's plenty to do," claims Merkley.

- "If you don't like culture, go across the street and play golf on our fabulous 36-hole championship golf course. Go sailing on the lake, rent a sailboat, rent a windsurfer, go swimming on the beach. Go and sign up for tennis. Go rent a bike. Go to the book store, buy a good book, sit on the porch, put your feet up and have some iced tea. There's a range of opportunities for everybody.

  "One of the great things about CHAUTAUQUA is that you can always find a bench. You can sit down and have a conversation. A lot of times we don't allow ourselves that time for reflection."

  Amen!

**See Also**  To reiterate, there's only one CHAUTAUQUA. Although its musical sweep is predominantly secular, those religious-minded fans with a pop-music bent would also enjoy the contemporary-Christian musical smorgasbord of KINGDOM BOUND (Darien, NY — see chapter), just up the road at Darien Lake Amusement Park. You could time-travel between the 1890's and the 1990's with full family-oriented facilities to match each musical setting.

You 10,000 Maniacs fans (and you know who you are) might be able to catch some of the band members, along with a similar vibe, at the GREAT BLUE HERON MUSIC FESTIVAL (Sherman, NY — see chapter), the FINGERLAKES GRASSROOTS FESTIVAL OF MUSIC AND DANCE (Trumansburg, NY — see chapter), or others like them nearby. Send your folks to CHAUTAUQUA while you boogie.

~     ~     ~

# Saratoga's Jazz Blast

NEWPORT JAZZ FESTIVAL/SARATOGA, Saratoga Springs, NY
Early July
Modern Jazz
***Attended***

**Introduction**

"Jazzapalooza!" That's how I'd spell the gloriously gonzo happening that's become the NEWPORT JAZZ FESTIVAL/SARATOGA [SARATOGA]. It's a blast and a half and then some!

George Wein's Festival Productions Inc. [FPI] produces more than 30 of the world's leading jazz festivals, but if I had to rank 'em, I might start with their universally-acknowledged champ, the NEW ORLEANS JAZZ AND HERITAGE FESTIVAL (see New Orleans, LA, Late April to Early May). Then I'd place SARATOGA. Now that claim might "ruffle some feathers up on Capital Hill," as comedians Bob and Ray would intone in their radio skits. It might even unintentionally appear to contradict some of the glowing chapters in this book. Look, if you need the resonance of 40-year histories enjoyed by other FPI affairs to motivate your buying your tickets and taking your seats, fine. No argument from me.

But my bottom line is what takes place past the trestles — lineup quality and quantity, production and site values, audience participation and spirit. And this is one celebration that revs hot on all cylinders, yet accommodates everyone's comfort zones with good-natured grace. Basically, if you love great modern jazz and a great time to match, "Ya' gotta' SARATOGA!"

You might think that the gentility of this Victorian resort village would present an unlikely setting for jazz party of the year. Well, sort of.

You see, for well over a century Southern aristocracy would make two stops to escape their oppressive summer heat and assorted epidemics — first to Princeton to pick up junior from college; next to Saratoga Springs to settle in for the season. Here were all their accustomed trappings: thoroughbred and harness tracks, polo fields, casinos, and a never-ending whirl of balls, cotillions, dinner parties, tea parties, garden parties, parties, parties, parties. Most importantly, there were Saratoga's storied springs and mineral baths for healing hangovers. Dissipated Southerners could "take the cure" every morning to steel themselves for the next day's rounds.

Today the town retains much of this stylishly wanton spirit. A fair number of attractions remain for the high end, notably the tracks and polo fields. The low end is held down by Skidmore College students who help maintain "more bars per-capita than any other town in the country." (It's a dubious claim I've heard mouthed about other municipalities, too, but Off-Broadway has more than it's share of Tumble Inns.) In the middle sit sightseers of all stripes looking to hoist a few with pinkies extended. Like the festival itself, Saratoga Springs remains infinitely more tasteful than such tacky family gaggles as Lake George just to the north but more alive for us non-retirees than mothballed historic havens elsewhere.

Saratoga Spring's second leading summer draw for almost 30 years has been it's Performing Arts Center. "SPAC," as this full-featured outdoor amphitheater is pronounced, hosts the New York City Opera, the New York City Ballet, and the Philadelphia Orchestra plus a full slate of major pop concerts from June through Labor Day. It occupies space for 5,000 within the 2,200-acre, FDR-era Saratoga Spa State Park. This creates the only "shed" I know of offering its patrons two mineral baths (your pick — Lincoln or Roosevelt), plus the Gideon Putnam Hotel, golfing, swimming, picnicking, and such. It harbors a beautiful, pastoral scene with neo-classical overtones.

**Festival Review** Things change, though, come that fateful last weekend every June. Forget 5,000 seats. Twelve thousand a day crowd into SPAC's shaded confines. Every nook and cranny is packed with entire mini-cities of tents, nettings, tarps, blankets, tables, grills, coolers, hampers, chaises, chairs, flags, plaques, balloons — everything but kitchen sinks. Parties wheel in their one-day "homes-away-from-homes" on huge carts, gleefully scamper for prime seating, set up base camps, then become reacquainted with their neighbors in what's become their annual summer ritual. In fact, my friend Brian knows a fellow studio engineer who's gathered up a carload of buddies and made the road trip up from New York City every year for over a decade. This is the norm, too, not the exception!

There is covered reserved seating, but you'll as likely find it half-vacant throughout most sets during the daytime. That's because the action is outside on the lawn. At JAMBOREE IN THE HILLS (see St. Clairsville, OH, Middle July), the opposite sex meets and greets each other via squirt bottles. Here the calling card is marshmallows. Look up, and you'll spot one clique of young men pelting ladies several tarps over. Look over, and you'll see young women reciprocating in kind. It's all good clean fun for this youngish family set, split about 70/30 between whites and blacks.

FPI holds up its end by supplying a sensational lineup. I defy anyone to show me another festival that features as many acts on jazz's "A-list" occupying a single stage during a single day. (I underscore the word "acts." Some events may claim more artists, but you'll find them clustered together in jam sessions, not standing alone in their regular, generally-better-rehearsed bands performing their regular, generally-more-challenging material.) From noon 'till midnight, there's not one clunker on the bill. Ever!

Plus there are surprises even for the jazz-savvy. One memorable example I caught in '90 involved the first jazz festival ever played by Bela Fleck and The Flecktones. The roars Fleck's quartet earned early in the day prefigured his subsequent chart-topping success that appeared to come from out of left field. You could've caught him first at SARATOGA.

That's just the main stage. Personally, I head back to the gazebo, a small, circular porch so intimate you're practically lounging in the lap of a delightful festival-within-a-festival. True, its daily, five-act lineup might not have the drawing power of the main stage, but check out this sample day from my '90 visit: The Sir Charles Thompson Trio, The Chris Hollyday Quartet, The Byron Stripling Quartet, The Duke Robillard Band (although I recall Jerry Portnoy's Streamliners subbed), and The Horace Arnold Trio. Neat, huh?

Best of all, the gazebo loyalists applaud themselves for "going against the grain" by roaring at every musical highlight. Not only does this rabid response spur the gazebo artists onward, it also tosses the gauntlet over to the main-stage crowd. A virtual call-and-response ensues as each audience attempts to out-do each other all afternoon. Just another example of that SARATOGA spirit, which on a per-head basis might even best the NEW ORLEANS "JAZZFEST"!

Want some corroboration? Bob Jones is FPI's Senior V. P. in charge of the NEW ORLEANS "JAZZFEST" and also BEN AND JERRY'S NEWPORT FOLK FESTIVAL (Newport, RI — see chapter). He does technical support for SARATOGA, which enables him to catch a sideways glance. Here's what he says:

- Re: Main stage: "Like NEW ORLEANS, we really keep it close to schedule. I do the scheduling with George [Wein], but I also do some weird things. It may look weird, the way groups are positioned, but a lot of the groups that play there (especially some of the West Coast people) are coming through, and they're on their way to Europe. Sometimes they want to play earlier in the day so they can catch a plane from New York. Sometimes they want to play earlier in the day because they don't want to play 'till midnight [then] have to get up and drive to New York and things like that. So you're liable to have groups in different slots."

- Re: Gazebo: "We have this wonderful reviewer who comes over from England, Barry McRae, and he says, 'It's all well and good to know the other attractions, but who's on the gazebo?'

"I don't remember when the gazebo first came in. I distinctly decided it would be a nice thing to do, [to] spend a little money and give a diversion for the people way in the back. ...I think they had seen these little things happening in NEW ORLEANS where they'd put these groups in there. The place is pretty small. I remember somebody telling me, 'Yeah, we had this deal where we got some cases laid out on the side, and we had the guy's keyboards on the cases so he was playing off the side.'

"There's this real sort of 'can-do' atmosphere with the [gazebo] stage guys. They'll say, 'I know you [main stage] guys are puttin' on whoever it is but, us, we're really happening!' And there's this feeling of, 'We're really with the people!'"

- Re: Production: "They have an incredible system of staging and an incredible staff — the stage hands and sound crew and stuff. But the stage area itself is also a dream to work in. [There's] a zillion rolling risers and curtains that go up and down. They double-mic everything so the stuff rolls out and 'bang,' it's ready to go. The lighting is very good because it's set up for the ballet, so there's a lot of stuff up in the air, and we use whatever we can [for effects]."

However, Jones' advice to his friends on SARATOGA's behalf says it all:

- "I have people who wanna' come to festivals from where I am, in Ridgefield and Danbury, CT. I say, 'Well, don't go to NEW YORK (JVC JAZZ FESTIVAL, New York — see chapter), go to SARATOGA for the day!' They can get there in a couple of hours. I tell 'em, 'You're going to have a lot nicer time, you're going to see a lot more people, and it's a lot of fun.'"

**Artist Mini-Reviews** My wife and I scooted into '93's SARATOGA for a few hours between the OLD SONGS FESTIVAL OF TRADITIONAL MUSIC AND DANCE (Altamont, NY — see chapter) and BEN & JERRY'S ONE WORLD, ONE HEART FESTIVAL (Warren, VT — see chapter). I was less interested in noting individual acts than in quickly confirming the scene as I'd remembered it. Consider it confirmed, with the addition of one of the very best crafts displays I've encountered anywhere.

Instead, here are a few of Jones' recent highlights:

Miles Davis/Mel Torme: "I remember I had Miles Davis play followed by Mel Torme, and Mel's like, 'Whoa! Bob, you can't do this...' I said, 'Don't worry, Mel, you'll be fine out there,' which he was. He went out there and killed everybody! After Miles killed everybody! With that audience you can put anything out in front of them 'cause they just love good music! I mean, Mel never got an ovation like that in his life. He had, like, three standing ovations all through his set. I understand Mel's feelings — I was nervous myself about Mel having to follow Miles. Miles was unbelievable..."

Bela Fleck and The Flecktones: "I'm a friend of Bela's and I worked hard to do that. Yeah, and I remember [drummer] Ed Shaughnessy and [bassist] Milt Hinton were standing on the side of the stage; they were utterly fascinated by this. [The Flecktones] hung around a little bit — they were going off somewhere, I've forgotten where — [but] they said, 'You don't understand what it means to us to be involved in a festival,' because they're now talking with these guys whom they never would've dreamed a year ago that they'd be on the main stage with, talking back and forth." And the audience reaction? "Oh, they went crazy!"

Gilberto Gil: "We had Gilberto Gil there last year which was a big surprise to people. Gilberto came out and played with just another guitar player and a percussion player. I was like, 'I don't know what's gonna' happen. This guy's a very soft presentation in terms of what had gone on before and what was about to come on after.' But by the third or fourth tune he had them eating out of his hands. He was sensational."

Others: "We had Aretha [Franklin]. She was sensational, just unbelievable.... Buddy Guy was unbelievable out there, he got into that audience... A person who did not do that well [reaction-wise], but was sensational was Regina Belle. There have been odd kinds of things that have worked up there, too."

**Attendance Tip** A little advance prep goes a long way here. First, call SPAC some months ahead to find out when the reserved seats first go on sale plus when the gates open on game days. Getting reserved seats puts you front and center for your preferred acts (especially valuable at night, or if it rains), while early arrival insures proper lawn placement for listening, tanning, scoping, and marshmallow-tossing.

Reserved seats vaporize almost instantly, so keep alert. If you miss 'em, or get there too late for choice lawn space, simply head straight for the gazebo. It's looser back there amidst the flying frisbees, crafts tent, and wading pools. Also know there's no re-entry, so pack your wagon full for the long walk to/from parking, including rain gear and something for the evening's chill.

Local lodging's probably also at a premium. I'd recommend spending a few bucks far enough ahead to land a room in one of Saratoga Spring's extraordinary historic hotels and inns. Check your travel guide. For campers, New York State has a telephone reservation option. One year it helped me land a nice last-minute campsite about 30 minutes north at Moreau Lake. Don't let it go that long, though. SARATOGA's well worth taking care of business far, far ahead!

~   ~   ~

*Tarp town, Newport Jazz Festival/Saratoga.*

# Ithaca's New Old-Time Scene, I

WILLIAM SMITH AND HOBART COLLEGES FOLK FEST, Geneva, NY
   Early May
   Variety, General

ITHACA FESTIVAL, Ithaca, NY
   Early June
   Variety, General

**GREAT BLUE HERON MUSIC FESTIVAL**, Sherman, NY
   Early July
   Variety, General
   ***Attended***

**FINGERLAKES GRASSROOTS FESTIVAL OF MUSIC AND DANCE**, Trumansburg, NY
   Middle July to Late July
   Variety, General
   ***Attended***

My brother-in-law, Lou, gave me a wonderful Christmas present, **The Art of Rock Posters from Presley to Punk** by Paul D. Grushkin (Abbeville Press). This is the ultimate coffee-table book for music fans, a treasure lovingly produced. **Introduction**

I am especially fascinated the way it reveals rock music boosting itself to dominance using festival formats. Generation X-ers who think life began with LOLLAPALOOZA would be interested to see how this genre fueled its first boom in the mid-fifties through a matrix of "cavalcades" criss-crossing the country. Here's Alan Freed's running one-night stand from 1957, for example: Jerry Lee Lewis, Buddy Holly and The Crickets, Chuck Berry, Frankie Lymon and The Teenagers, Screamin' Jay Hawkins, Danny and The Juniors, The Chantels, The Diamonds, Billy Ford and The Thunderbirds, Dicky Doo and The Dont's, Larry Williams, The Pastels, Jo-Ann Campbell, Ed Townsend, etc. These tours, in turn, were merely portable versions of how concerts were often organized back then, thanks to The Grand Ol' Opry and other live radio shows.

Now, fast-forward a decade to San Francisco's Haight-Ashbury.

At the time, folk and blues genres harbored the acknowledged stars, while beat writers like Allen Ginsburg and Ken Kesey held top billing above such emerging groups as The Warlocks (The Grateful Dead) and The Allman Joys (The Allman Brothers). Possibly to compete with the copious folk festivals promoted by the city's colleges, aspiring promoters like Bill Graham imme-diately gravitated toward multiple bills of four rock acts or more. This created a happening suffi-cient to garner attention and justify these extraordinary posters Gruskin's book collects. It also proved great for the bands who all knew each other and jammed together, while the hippies got a never-ending soundtrack for tripping the night away. So simple, huh? Given the mini-festivals that began to take place at Graham's Fillmore West seemingly every weekend throughout the late-'60s, it's no mystery that the nation's best bands came Westward, why MONTEREY POP' burst forth, or how psychedelica grew to sweep the country.

Ironically, the festival format also gave Graham a means to re-introduce the folk and blues legends his rock bands had quickly eclipsed. Muddy Waters, Flatt and Scruggs, Clifton Chenier, and many others gained whole new audiences from Graham's respectful programming. ALTAMONT changed all that, of course, proving this particular scene had grown too big and too ugly to handle it's free-wheeling habits.

Rock music has since evolved into a big business of multi-media multi-nationals. Corporate bean counters now calculate just what it takes to break a band through well-entrenched channels. Add up the album production, the video production, the promotional budget, the tour support, and the advance, and a band can find itself saddled with hundreds of thousands of dollars of debt before it even hits the road. Their motives understandably switch toward profit maximization for sheer survival's sake: how big a venue can they play, how often, and how few other bands can they share the take with. Rock-music festivals have become a rarity, although a 25% decline in concert revenues over the past few years has been inching the touring packages past the requisite headliner and opener.

Into this dog-eat-dog world step our intrepid heroes from the college idyll of Ithaca, "high atop Cayuga's waters."

An accumulation of locals under the monicker Donna the Buffalo have taken their cue from festivals of yore, albeit traditional country-music precedents dating back as far as the '30s, like the OLD FIDDLER'S CONVENTION (see Galax, VA, Early August), and the OLD-TIME MUSIC AND RADIO CONFERENCE (see Mount Airy, NC, Late May). Raised together at "old-time" events by their '60's-era parents who followed such Ithaca stalwarts as The Henrie Brothers and The Highwoods Stringband on the festival circuit, they learned to play around campfires, gradually incorporating styles they were exposed to as they got older — rock, folk, Cajun, zydeco, bluegrass, country, reggae. Inspired by fellow Ithacans, The Horseflies, who landed a deal at MCA Records in the mid-'80s, they joined various bands with hopes of doing it full-time. And yet, they continued to hook up in festival parking lots as Donna the Buffalo for as many weekends as they could manage.

Donna the Buffalo's first thought in time, even before putting music to reels? "Let's do a festival!" Actually, it was first, "Let's have four bands do an AIDS Work benefit," whose '90 success immediately inspired their festival preparations for the following year. They booked four days in the nearby Trumansburg Fairgrounds in '91, then used the credibility accorded by Jamestown's 10,000 Maniacs to land a few other headliners for their charity bash. Their eclectic lineup of over 40 bands compelled enough to overcome lousy weather, and the event broke even sufficient to make the FINGERLAKES GRASSROOTS FESTIVAL OF MUSIC AND DANCE [GRASSROOTS] an annual in the true festival mode.

Just like in San Francisco, however, one festival has quickly begotten others from all sources. Fans have begun their own festivals for Donna the Buffalo and their companion bands (GREAT BLUE HERON MUSIC FESTIVAL). Like-minded music festivals in the area have invited them in (WILLIAM SMITH AND HOBART COLLEGES FOLK FEST, ROONEY BLUEGRASS FESTIVAL, MIDDLESEX MUSIC FESTIVAL). Ditto for nearby crafts festivals (CORN HILL ARTS FESTIVAL), community celebrations (ITHACA FESTIVAL), and summer "sheds" (GREAT CONNEAULT LAKE "TIE-DYE" MUSIC FESTIVAL). Mainstream music festivals have asked the 'Buffalo bands to handle the dance tent (TANGIER COUNTRY MUSIC FESTIVAL), while nonprofits have solicited their help for festival benefits (MECK MUSIC FEST). And if one 'Buffalo band lands a regular festival gig, they naturally lobby on behalf of the others for the following year.

Thanks to festivals, what's slowly happening is the Ithaca scene is slowly "happening." The 'Buffalo band network is growing, the fan base is growing, the festival itinerary is growing, and so is interest from record companies. The 'Buffalo's still unattached as of this writing, but The Heartbeats have been signed (Green Linnett), as have Rusted Root (Mercury), John and Mary (Rykodisc), Colorblind James Experience (Red House), Cornerstone (Folk Era), and several more of their festival comrades. Even though I've begun to detect traces of careerism in their voices as they've mainstreamed into "the 'biz," their dominant inspiration remains the grassroots communion of "old-time" affairs. The 'Buffalo bands also keep their expenses low to stretch out their festival summers together for as long as possible.

Best of all, you now know exactly where and when to join 'em! Here are two weekends among an increasing many.

Now it would be unfair to say you'll be stepping into music's next Haight-Ashbury. For one, this is an anti-star system, predicated more on joining in than standing out. For another, their collective sound has less loudness and raunch for crossover as, say, the H. O. R. D. E. tour (another scene, interestingly enough, that launched itself from out of the local festival mode — see the various listings of Arrowhead Ranch, Parksville, NY). It relies, instead, on gentler acoustic grooves and mid-tempo syncopation perfect for Cajun and contra dancing. Also, I've yet to hear that one songwriter (a Robert Hunter?) or instrumental virtuoso (a Jerry Garcia?) emerge who'd break them onto radio airwaves.

Instead, I'm more enthusiastic about the unified vibe the bands provide, and how good people promoting good music for good causes never goes out of style. It's a festival thing, so enjoy!

"Yeah, there's a saying about old time music that goes, 'Old-time music — better than it sounds.'" **Festival** General Coordinator Jeb Puryear's joking here that traditional country music, the historic prece- **Review I** dent for bluegrass, is more appreciated as a players' delight. You'd sooner experience its string-band instrumentals by sitting in on someone's back porch in Appalachia than by sitting down in a plush Lincoln Center chair.

Puryear, whose slow baritone still bespeaks his "hill-country" upbringing in Eastern Tennessee, was reared in the old-time music scene. It's where he first learned to play, where he first met his many playing partners, and where he saw the guiding light for their annual home-coming at the GRASSROOTS.

"The scene that's developed around [old-time music] is very cool, and I haven't seen anything else like it," Puryear explains about the genre's current relevance:

- "A lot of bands like The Heartbeats and The Horseflies and The Red Hots have spawned out of the old-time scene that we were heavily involved with. I think that's where a lot of my friends learned the spirit of their playing, or the source of their inspiration. Basically, the music and the festival sort of went hand in hand. When I was a kid, we used to hear the Highwoods String Band. I started playing the fiddle when I was about 7 and just took off from there. I had a band with Richie [Stearns], who started from The Horseflies — he lived with us."

The two roommates, along with Puryear's brother, Jordan, on bass, and drummer Shane Lamphier, formed Bubba George String Band for busking around Ithaca's streets. Stearns got too busy after The Horseflies' MCA signing, and Bubba George evolved with his departure into Donna the Buffalo. Stearns initially returned on keyboards before ceding to Joe Thrift who fiddles for The Red Hots. Other 'Buffalos include fiddler Tara Nevins — who also holds down the fid-dling/vocal chores for The Heartbeats — and her husband, Jim Miller, on electric guitar and vocals, plus whoever's around who knows them and their material well-enough to be called onstage.

"Basically, we're just a group of friends who've known each other forever," Puryear notes:

- "Jeff [Claus] and Judy [Hyman] from The Horseflies lived up the street, so they got it goin' [career-wise]. They were just a traditional old-time band for a long time. Then they start-ed gettin' more electric and gettin' weird. They're into real weird tonalities, y' know? They would tune the fiddles funny, and they'd make the music come out, and then play the same tune over the weird tuning, and they started developing that. Then they got a drum-mer and a buncha' other stuff, so they actually skipped genres! I mean, they used to get all the folk festival gigs, [but] became too 'rock-and-roll' really to keep gettin' those gigs.

  "That's basically my musical thing. A lot of the same people out of the old-time scene would just start different kinds of bands just because they're interested in music. Like, we played in a band called Zydeco Norton where we just started with basically the same group of people, plus a couple of others from the old-time scene. We went down [to Louisiana] and saw the zydeco and said, 'Oh, alright, we're gonna' start a zydeco band!' So, we just did it, you know.

  "That's what's nice about the [GRASSROOTS] festival to me is you get all this stuff together, and it gives people an outlet like to do some other stuff that you can't do at an old-time festival. ...There's kind of a roots genre sort of growing, but it would be nice to have it encompass a lot of things. I mean, I look at the format of our festival as basically, of course, just anything, but its gotta' have a certain feel.

"Like, I can't stand performers who are full of themselves too much," Puryear laughs, "so anything like that I sort of tend to shy away from."

This provides insight into Puryear's headliners, such as '92's Tim O'Brien and The O'Boys, Thomas Mapfumo and Blacks Unlimited, Walter Mouton and The Scott Playboys, Robin and Linda Williams, Preston Frank and His Zydeco Family, Les Tetes Brulees, John and Mary, Hank Roberts Band (an especially interesting find, well-received according to Puryear), and Charmaine Neville.

"The other thing about the festival," Puryear adds, citing CLEARWATER'S GREAT HUDSON RIVER REVIVAL (Valhalla, NY — see chapter), and the CAJUN AND BLUEGRASS MUSIC-DANCE-FOOD FESTIVAL (Escoheag, RI — see chapter) as inspirations, "is that I think it's got an intense variety. I think that's very important, because you just get brow-beat by the same thing when you go to most festivals; you get an overabundance of just one thing. It just gets maddening after awhile."

This variety extends Puryear's multi-cultural aims, but also helps invite and involve everyone, especially teens and twenties:

- "The young listener is so keyed-in on friends and stuff like that. [For them], we have bands that don't really fit my mold. We have some punk bands and hard-core bands, just 'cause we don't wanna' create a super folk-festival atmosphere; we want to have a little grit. I don't think our festival will ever lack for grit [laughs] — it seems good. When kids go to see one band, they go away liking a few others. Like, the first year we had 10,000 Maniacs. People come to see The 'Maniacs and a few other bands; they realize that all these bands are incredible; they end up having a great time!

"I enjoy it much better when the whole general population's there. You need to have every-body there to make it feel real. So many of the festivals I've been to seem like they're just removed, like they have their special, little place [laughs] where they can retreat to, which is cool, but it's not something that I'm necessarily interested in.

"We get lots of letters [from attendees about] just being comfortable at GRASSROOTS'; being able to party; not having it be a weird party that makes you uncomfortable. The thing that's really good is just the whole family coming. I think overall the way our society is set up is so cut off at age. ...I think the whole family needs to get on. I would go hear music when I was a little kid, and that really inspired me to do a lotta' things.

"I'm a huge country music fan, so if we had a bigger budget I would like to book some top-of-the-line country acts, just because I've been to a lot of festivals that were too just one type of person. I like to get the whole overview as far as music [being] a sort of knowledge, or inspiration, or an opening of the mind to see other things... I want everybody to go, because once you're there and the whole spirit is happenin', then I think just something happens. You're more accepting of the people around you, and so on and so forth. We sort of tried to keep it from gettin' labeled as a hippie event, y' know, which I'm sure everybody thinks it is anyway. So, it would be nice to book some country acts, like Emmylou Harris would be perfect. We came close to booking Mary Chapin Carpenter last year and that woulda' been great, but it just didn't quite work out at the last minute.

"If we had a bigger budget, you know I'd hire George Jones in a second," Puryear chuckles. "I think that would be far-out. In that way, yeah, my view is to get everybody there and to see what you can do with them."

**Artist Mini-Reviews** I stopped by for GRASSROOTS' preview party in '92, kept mostly to locals by arcane county laws which date back to '69's WOODSTOCK and '73's WATKINS GLEN festivals. Apparently, no camping permits are issued for longer than three days, prompting Puryear to push his scheduled headliners over to Friday night for the out-of-town sleep-overs.

No matter. That Thursday night went down as one of my special festival evenings as the full moon illuminated us blessed few deep into the morning dew. Donna the Buffalo's funky runs proved perfect for my Cajun-dance companions, Ilsa and Alan. We called the band "NRBQ goes old-time." Tribulations, an Amherst-based reggae band spawned from the Ithaca scene, followed with an energetic set that had even the volunteers dancing in place. Neon Baptist, one of '90's four founding bands, wrapped things up with a strong roots-rockin' sound undone by the lead singer's pseudo-preacher schtick. Alas. We still enjoyed our own peaceable party kingdom, one Ilsa and Alan felt exemplifying the spirited friendliness they carried throughout their weekend there.

**Travel Tip**

Trumansburg's Rongovian Embassy, with its Mexican-food platters, is the 'Buffalo bands home away from home. You might not have much time for its live music during GRASSROOTS', but you should make it part of your Fingerlakes travel itinerary another time. Two other dining musts are Trumansburg's fancy Taughannock Farms Inn and Ithaca's homey Moosewood Restaurant (yes, the one with the ubiquitous self-titled cookbooks). Otherwise, vineyards, apple farms, historic towns, skinny lakes, and miles of country highways snaking 'twixt the bluffs and gorges await your off-days.

~     ~     ~

**Festival Review II**

Here's the skinny on GREAT BLUE HERON MUSIC FESTIVAL ['BLUE HERON'] due west in tiny Sherman.

It started one year after GRASSROOTS'. It's smaller in size, stages (two vs. three), and acts (six to 10 per day vs. 10 to 20 per day). It's musical focus is strictly on whatever you'd call the Ithaca scene. Alternative old-time? New mountain wave? Roots-a-billy world-groove? There are none of GRASSROOTS' national headliners, although The Heartbeats' recent success and Rusted Root's major label signing might soon elevate them both to that status.

What's shared is the Cajun/zydeco tent boogie going all night long, with the addition of one of the most quietly gorgeous settings anywhere. Anywhere! But promise to keep it a secret because the promoters want to keep the vibe close and loose. You reach it down a veritable cow path and park on a lush lawn fronting a pond. If it all feels like someone's backyard, it's because it is. A dusty driveway deposits you onto a shaded knoll. You'll note a forested wicket on the right providing privacy for campers, while the crest extends you uninterrupted panoramas of seemingly all of Western New York. Ooh-ahh!

Thank 'BLUE HERON's Co-Promoter, Dave Tidquist.

Whereas Puryear is a laid-back musician type, Tidquist (who also books winter shows at Joyce's Keg Room in Jamestown) is very outgoing. This self-described "aging hippie" actually lined up 'BLUE HERON's exquisite site going door-to-door. "We'll have a barbeque; we'll have Donna the Buffalo here for the day all to ourselves,'" Tidquist recalls of his July 4th plans for his then-girlfriend:

- "So we went up and found this little piece of land up there and started talkin' to the owner. And she was goin', 'Yeah, yeah, that sounds pretty good.' We talked about it a little bit, so when my girlfriend and I were on the way home, by the time we got back to her house, it had expanded into eight bands, you know, two days. I'm figuring, 'If we're goin' two days, let's go the whole weekend!' It sprang almost full-born from that one day.

"The love affair went into the toilet," Tidquist laughs, "so now it's me and Julie, the lady that owns the land, out there doin' the whole damn thing ourselves!"

"My background is I'm just a flat-out music fan," Tidquist explains of his initial recruitment into the Ithaca scene:

- "And I went to the BEAVER VALLEY BLUEGRASS FESTIVAL (see Beaver Falls, PA, Late May). It turned out they had some old-time music there, one of which was The Horseflies in their original, old-time incarnation. And if there is any common thread through all of that, it's the old-time music. Most of the musicians that we have sprang out of the old-time scene: GALAX, VA and MT. AIRY, NC. That's who those people are, and that's what they do best, and do most of. 'Turns out they all have other bands, and they're all doing other kinds of interesting stuff.

"There's kind of an interesting history there, too. The old-time scene, of course, goes back hundreds of years down in Appalachia. Back in the early '70's, a bunch of hippies from Ithaca somehow all came together in that area playing music. The original was the Highwoods String Band. They did tours for the State Department; they played at Carnegie

Hall; they influenced a lot of people out there. Mac Benford, who has The Woodshed Allstars now, is from that.

"Some younger people — the Puryears, Tara and that whole group, Richie Stearns from The Horseflies — they sorta' got the old-time thing by osmosis, you know, and they came up with this original tuning. You can actually go to MT. AIRY, and if you're a musician, you listen to someone playing: 'Oh, that's that Ithaca tuning; that must be Tara, Jeb or Jim, or someone like that.' So they were the young hard chargers, the new blood. Jeb's a young guy still, he's 26 or 27, but Tara's up there and Jim just hit 40 and all that. There are very, very few of the next wave.

"I got caught really up in trying to preserve this! That's where my original interest came from.

"10,000 Maniacs are from Jamestown. I got the ear of Natalie Merchant, and we went and listened to some of their stuff. Pretty soon a couple of the bands were opening for The 'Maniacs. The Horseflies opened for 'em, and then The Heartbeats caught on and did a tour with 'em. Then Mary Chapin Carpenter heard them, and they caught on with her. This thing has so many tentacles that we could sit around and talk about it all weekend and there's still just more to learn."

Why old-time music for Ithaca musicians instead of, say, bluegrass? "I could tell you that in a minute," responds Tidquist, "It's political:

- "From my point of view, you find the more liberal-thinking, more back-to-the-earth, more peace-and-love type of people are in old-time. In bluegrass, you see a lot of suits, a lot of sculpted hairdos, a lot of religious-oriented music that harkens back to the old preachers and that type of thing. So it's actually a very societal line that you find, almost to the man. The people who play old-time music are very causally dressed, almost to the point of ridiculousness.

  "Another big reason that GALAX and MT. AIRY hold such a reverence aspect in their minds is that these people like to jam. They'll jam anytime, anywhere. But, it's almost impossible for them because if they try to jam at our festival, some guy will come over with a freakin' ukelele or something, you know? So they all just very politely go, 'Aaah, well, I'm gonna' move on here,' and then the whole jam breaks up. They go to MT. AIRY, or GALAX, or CLIFFTOP, they can sit around and jam. If someone comes in, he's hip to the scene and he'll join in on that kind of stuff knowing what he's doing and knowing where it comes from and that type of thing. That's the beauty of those festivals to the old-time people — they seek them out.

  "[Another] big difference is bluegrass features individual solos. You'll notice that in every bluegrass song, everybody takes a solo. In old-time, they just blend more and more, you know, 'Get that blend going.' In other words, the whole is more than the sum of its parts. I heard an old-time jam at BEAVER VALLEY' — there had to be 30 musicians in it — and all of a sudden it took on another sound. There was another resonance altogether. Oh, it was spiritual!

"There's room for more than the straight four, or five," Tidquist remarks. "Oh man, the bigger the better. It's very, very inclusive."

Inclusive also gives you a touchstone into 'BLUE HERON's audience. "We don't want to be a neo-hippie fest," cautions Tidquist, "We just don't want to be pachouli:

- "I mean, I love all those people, I really do, but we want to include the dance freaks; we want to include the old hippies, that type of thing. You know, Rusted Root sort of took it to that teenage level [but] there's a lot of adult stuff goin' on up there musically, and we don't want to have one band dominating it. Although we would've loved to have Rusted Root, there's two sides to it. We replaced them with The Horseflies this year.

  "The whole charm of it is...people from different age groups, different groups of thought, different life styles and attitudes sort of all exist at one level up there. I got a letter from a guy that almost brought me to tears. He'd been sort of separated philosophically from his kids and everything, and he talked them into going up there, and he ended up dancing with his daughter — that type of thing.

"We're trying to take the best out of those ['60s/'70s] festivals, which was just the fellowship and that whole scene, leaving behind the accent on drugs and drinking. I mean, we know a lot of people do it, and a lot of us do it, but definitely with more of an accent on the actual music itself. What knocks me out is for me to present a band to an audience and they're standing there with their jaws hanging open, rather than... It's really pointed more towards the musicians and presenting them.

"I think the thing that bothers a lot of us the most is commercial music, and there is none here. We hope it's an enlightenment to a lot of young people that there is so much to hear besides the bands that pay their way onto MTV, know-what-I-mean? I haven't bought a new album of a well-known group in five years, and my place is just loaded with music that has the qualities a lot of those wished they had if they weren't trying to conform to what the latest network-dictated trend is."

Tidquist then sums up the festival, the Ithaca scene, and the old-time philosophy in one line: "[We need] more creativity from the bottom up than from the top down."

I caught Saturday's sunset there in '93, suitably accompanied by Tidquist's eclectabillies. Fiddle wildman, John Specker, did a calypso take on Johnny Cash's "Ring of Fire" that had everyone free-stylin' along. The Heartbeats followed with a wonderful, danceable set — clunky, funky, and eclectically blended. I liked how they'd spice up a Cajun rhythm, for example, with a clawhammer banjo beat. Nice three-part harmonies, too, on an attractive "Another World." **Artist Mini-Reviews**

By contrast, Hypnotic Clambake set genres against each other in schizophrenic procession as if to say, "Which can party harder?" A woolly bluegrass tune, "Old Joe Clark," topped a manic zydeco, which one-upped a frantic blues. A hyperdriven klezmer parody, "The Feldmans," closed things out on a fever pitch. I'm not sure about their commercial potential, but these young dreads sure can play hard and fast, especially the fiddler. They had college kids bouncing off trees.

Rusted Root wrapped up the stage show to the now-clustered crowd before everyone moved hillside to the dance tent. A closer listen to their self-produced disc, "Cruel Sun," reveals not much yet to sing about, but oh how well they sing! If their record deal doesn't pan out, they can always get jobs as vocal arrangers for other folk-rock bands.

The lead singer/guitarist begins most tunes with a solo guitar line that sets the rhythm and tone, often with faux-Arabic flavor. He'll begin emoting spare verses as the two female vocalists chime in with soulful harmonies and leads, imaginatively alternated. The three-part rhythm team kicks in, adding vocal waves of their own. By this time, everyone's banging something — cow bells, shakers, rattles, tambourines — in what evolves into choral world-beat mini-symphonies you can dance to. It's a warm, rich, intoxicating mix that thoroughly juiced us all that fine night. Now (like the rest of the Ithaca scene), all it needs is some strong, heart-felt imagery to take on the world.

"Pay attention," advises Tidquist, "pay attention. There is so much going on that I think is so important that I go way up to the top of the hill where no one will go up to me and say, 'Great festival! All right, what's goin' on next?' Absorb it all [and] just try to take as much of it away with you as you can." **Attendance Tip**

"There is CHAUTAUQUA SUMMER MUSIC PROGRAM (Chautauqua, NY — see chapter) and you've gotta' keep an eye on their schedule," suggests Tidquist: **Travel Tip**

- "There's a big beautiful lake down there. Around the lake there's a lot of real nice places to eat and any place you go is gonna' be real inexpensive. You can get a motel for $25 a night — a nice, clean atmosphere. The charm of this place is sort of the isolation of it, the lack of anything. It turns to your own devices, [so] go hiking; go biking."

**See Also**  Two community celebrations booking the 'Buffalo bands are the ITHACA FESTIVAL and the CORN HILL ARTS FESTIVAL (Rochester, NY — see chapter). Each features multiple stages, along with superb crafts in prodigious quantities.

Two smaller single-day affairs are the MIDDLESEX MUSIC FESTIVAL (Middlesex, NY — see chapter) and the MECK MUSIC FEST (Mecklenberg, NY — see chapter) — both named after their respective Fingerlakes towns. MIDDLESEX' also takes place the same weekend as the ROONEY BLUEGRASS FESTIVAL (Deposit, NY — see chapter). Even though the 'Buffalo bands also "ROONEY," as they say, you'll need to read my public service announcement before taking that header, oops, I mean plunge. Start with MIDDLESEX' first. MECK' occurs the same weekend as a zillion other festivals in the area, giving you many simultaneous opportunities to trace the musical roots and offshoots inspiring the 'Buffalo bands.

Finally, my next book on the Mid-Atlantic states will point you toward a pair of Pennsylvania festivals: GREAT CONNEAULT LAKE "TIE-DYE" MUSIC FESTIVAL (see Conneault Lake, PA, Late June); HARVEST MOON FESTIVAL (see Whitehouse, PA, Early September). And if you really wanna' hang with the 'Buffalo bands in their closest indigenous environs, check out the APPALACHIAN STRING BAND MUSIC FESTIVAL (see Clifftop, WV, Early August). Bring your instrument and you just might end up onstage during the contest for ad-hoc non-traditional bands.

The 'Buffalo bands are rapidly expanding their range by recruiting friends, exchanging listings, and booking into otherwise-benign community celebrations — exactly what I'd do if I had a band. Moreover, they've added the word "annual" to their vocabularies in an alternative music world where "annual" is often a foreign word. I hope to have even more 'Buffalo citings by the time my next edition is ready!

~　　~　　~

# Catskills' Irish Traditions

PINES SCOTTISH WEEKEND, South Fallsburg, NY
> Early March and Late October
> Scottish

PINES NUMBER ONE IRISH WEEKEND, South Fallsburg, NY
> Early April and Middle November
> Irish

FLEADH: OLD MUSIC OF IRELAND FESTIVAL, Leeds, NY
> Early July
> Irish
> ***Attended***

GALA ALL-STAR IRISH CRUISE, Manhattan, NYC to The Bahamas
> Late July to Early August
> Irish

LEEDS IRISH FESTIVAL, Leeds, NY
> Early September
> Irish

IRISH MUSIC WEEKEND PARTY OF THE YEAR, Monticello, NY
> Late October
> Irish

## Introduction

Blame the musicians. *They* twisted the arm of Promoter Gertrude Byrne to inaugurate what amounted to a spirited Irish romp led by the finest traditional artists throughout the region during the July 4th weekend. *They* wore "miles of smiles" on stage as three generations of all-stars collaborated with glee. As the whole joyful mess wound down to a reluctant conclusion Monday afternoon, *they* cheerfully goaded Byrne between tunes that "We'll do it again next year, eh' Gertie?"

Not that Byrne minded when pats on the back from her patrons encouraged her to commit to future such affairs. "There are a type of people who are just diehards for this stuff," she notes in her soft-spoken brogue:

- "It's so intense for them. The 2,000 people that were there said, 'Oh, I hope you're gonna' do this again. This was great; this was fantastic; this is something we really need; this is something we really want.' They thought it was well-done... I think it's something you can build up very well, you know. It might take a few years, but the response was pretty good!"

I didn't wrangle any names out of Byrne, but I wouldn't be surprised if the superb flautist, Joannie Madden, was one of the party's leading instigators. After all, Madden's classy all-female band of traditional Irish musicians, called Cherish the Ladies, seems the common link between the more "commercial-style" Irish events Byrne produces five to six times a year and '93's departure into traditional territory.

There are a small but growing number of outstanding festivals throughout the Northeast which feature traditional Irish music — but usually on concert stages. It's "us playing to them," in effect, instead of "us playing amongst them" as you'd more likely find in a common Irish pub or parish hall. The FLEADH: OLD MUSIC OF IRELAND FESTIVAL [FLEADH'] leans hard toward the latter as its action unfolds either inside the glorified watering hole termed the "Irish Center" or outside around the 36'-by-36' dance floor under a big top erected in the bar's backyard. With another 20 hours of simultaneous workshops on a third stage, the FLEADH' quickly becomes a mix-and-mingle paradise for players, dancers, drinkers, and listeners alike.

This convivial flavor comes from Byrne's hospitality background. She and her husband, John, owned a club called Good Time Charlie's in the Bronx's Irish enclave of Kingsbridge from '70 to '78. "It roared in success while the Bronx was still good," Byrne says. In '76 they followed Irish migration patterns upwards and outwards to the Northern Catskills by purchasing the Irish Center in the whistle stop of Leeds. After two years of commuting they both relocated to Leeds full-time. In '82 the Byrnes got their feet wet with festivals by initiating a "commercial-style" blow-out for 10,000 of their fellow Bronx exiles, the LEEDS IRISH FESTIVAL, over Labor Day weekend.

"[Leeds] was sort of a sleepy little town, like the villages in Ireland," Byrne recalls:

- "It was your typical 'fleadh' scene [i.e., festival]. So we just decided, 'Heck,' we'd see if this was something that would work, and it certainly did! ...This particular festival has tremendous atmosphere and it's still as good as it was 12 years ago. It's a festival that's very well-behaved, which is a great achievement, I think. We have never had a problem in 12 years where, you know, with that type of a festival you can have lots of problems. There's a lot of security, and it seems we get the festival-goers that are very decent-type people."

Byrne describes the attendance mix for her Labor Day bash as 50% first generation and 50% second generation. This typifies the crowd for the "commercial-style" combination of sentimental troubadours, comedians, and "showbands" purveying Irish-music equivalents of "Borscht Belt" entertainment. Not that these offerings can't be fun for all, like at any ethnic wedding. However, you'd probably add a star if you weren't terribly far removed from abroad.

Now fast-forward a dozen years from such auspicious beginnings to witness the "Irish Alps" having spawned a plethora of similar "commercial-style" festivals now stepping on each other's toes competing for an ever-graying audience. Byrne surveyed the scene and decided to take a chance on this gently-resurging market for traditional Irish music — doubtlessly prompted by her musician friends who straddled both camps and sought a rare performing summit for appreciative younger attendees.

"There was a need for it up here," Byrne explains.

- "I mean, it was all 'commercial'; everywhere you went it was 'commercial.' So it was something that I felt would definitely work again. I had sort of the clout behind me, or the background, to really do research on who I thought were the right musicians to get in there. Again, I think I had a 'fleadh' in mind, almost like they have it back in Ireland, where they could sit on the side of the streets and play instruments if they wanted to. I talked to quite a few people who thought this was an ideal location."

Byrne hedged her bets in four manners:

- First, she drew performing aces from multiple markets to broadened her draw: Madden, Eileen Iver and Pat Kilbride from New York City; Daithi Sproule, Billy McComisk and Liz Carroll from Chicago; Seamus Connolly, Jack Coen and Larry Reynolds from Boston, etc;

- Second, she programmed workshops in parallel to attract amateur players, singers and set-dancers throughout the day;

- Third, she employed her usual array of crafters and vendors to entice the entire family regardless of their musical persuasions;

- Fourth, she capped each day off with a rollicking Ceili Mor dance that incorporated all the musicians.

"Oh, when they all got in together, and they did that concert piece Saturday and Sunday night," Byrne exclaimed of the latter happening, "there must have been on one stage over 20 of them together. That was brilliant! I believe Eileen Ivers said it was music like she'd never heard before. I mean, the talent that was up there was unbelievable, and they were just so in tune with one another."

And how'd the musicians enjoy themselves? Byrne remarks:

- "They thought that they were treated very, very well. I don't know what they're used to, but they thought that they had exceptional welcome in Leeds. And the thing is they all want to see it successful, which is a biggie. They were all workin' with me, not against me... The greatest thing they said to me is they were all made so very welcome, and they're lookin' forward to comin' back.

"That, to me, tells it all."

**Festival Review**

Leeds hugs a country road one mile inland from the New York State Thruway, Exit 21. At night you'd likely fly by and miss it. Fortunately, my wife and I drove up on a gloriously-sunny Monday afternoon. We still missed it, but upon backtracking were able to spot the street-side Irish Center tucked between a few farm homes, some unassuming pubs, and St. Bridget's Church.

Everything takes place within a few steps of everything else, like at a backyard family reunion or graduation party. If you run out of things to do, you can simply grab a bite or cold something-or-other, cross the street, sit on a curb, take a few nibbles or sips, and watch an occasional car whiz by. It's not fancy, but that's just the point. It's "down-home," and I'd be willing to trust Byrne that this is pretty much how it's like in any ordinary Irish village.

We suffered a misprint in the paper — promising music "Noon to 10 p.m. daily." Unfortunately, the ad meant to say "Noon to 10 p.m., Saturday and Sunday." Alas, a first-year error. We'd looked forward to a full evening's music, but arrived only in time for the final jam wrapping up that afternoon.

Any sense of disappointment quickly dissipated, however, when the musicians took stage: Joannie Madden, Jack Coen, Eileen Ivers, Liz Carroll, Brian Conway, Jimmy Kelly, Brendan Dolan, John Nolan, Billy McComisky all for one final go-round. I don't know if everyone above who was scheduled actually remained by day's end (Ivers had to depart early, I know), but folks, it doesn't get any better! A 40-year age spread prevailed, from thirty-something Madden to seventy-something Cohen, all united by a genuine love of the stuff. They fell in together with grace and affection, trading licks and keeping the groove going for several surprisingly-good dancers who just didn't want the party to end.

Asking around, the final stragglers recounted a rousing weekend — one they'd actively intended to repeat the following year. Perhaps we'll grab our dancing shoes, take a few lessons up there, and join 'em!

**Travel Tip**

"There's the Catskill Game Farm," Byrne offers among the area's family attractions. "There's the waterslide park. There's Carson City, which has these rodeo-type things. It's not Irish, but there's a lot of horseback riding. There's a lot of scenic things: Hunter Mountain, Windham Mountain. Albany, of course, has the Capitol [Mall] and a lot of shopping — it's only 45 minutes away."

I would also suggest the marvelous faux-Arabic castle of artist Frederic Edwin Church across the river in Hudson. You can enjoy the majestic valley views which inspired his painting while treating yourself to a lazy picnic upon its grassy slopes. A relaxing treat.

**See Also**

Byrne maintains a year-round orgy of Irish and Scottish festivals, though FLEADH' is the only one presently proferring traditional music. Her others are all "commercial style": the big LEEDS IRISH FESTIVAL at the same site, plus four PINES WEEKENDS that occur variably throughout the winter and spring at this popular Catskills resort. There's also a GALA ALL-STAR IRISH CRUISE that departs for The Bahamas from Manhattan, NYC.

For those who you who can't get enough "commercial style," you'll be pleased to know the Catskills are a steaming hotbed for the stuff. A few miles west of Leeds sits East Durham. This town is so thoroughly Irish that the local merchants combine to take out entire pages in the *Irish*

*Echo* seemingly every week throughout the summer. I've actually lost track of all the "commercial style" festivals that take place within its borders, and elsewhere throughout the Catskills, so check the **New York Festival Listings**.

Now back to traditional music — more my interest. If you're also a fan you absolutely won't want to miss October's IRISH MUSIC WEEKEND PARTY OF THE YEAR in Monticello, NY. 'Lest you think such a claim is too lofty, consider that the festival's sponsor is Connecticut-based Green Linnett Records, the world's leading label for traditional Irish music. Since '93 they've gathered over 60 top artists from their roster for three-day blowouts all throughout the glitzy Kutsher's Country Club. The *Irish Echo*'s Earle Hitchner proclaimed the inaugural affair as "one of the year's most memorable music events. You really get the feeling that everyone involved in this music is part of one gigantic extended family." All this fantastic family gathering is missing is you!

~     ~     ~

*Set dancing workshop, Irish Traditional Music and Dance Festival.*

# Ithaca's New Old-Time Scene, II

LILAC FESTIVAL, Rochester, NY
> Middle May to Late May
> Variety, General

CORN HILL FESTIVAL/FIDDLER'S FAIR, Rochester, NY
> Early July to Middle July
> Variety, General
> ***Attended***

BILLY LABEEF'S BASTILLE DAY, BARBEQUE, AND ROCK AND ROLL RODEO, Buffalo, NY
> Middle July
> Alternative and College Rock

**Introduction**

I can tell you honestly from having browsed many of the region's top arts and crafts extravaganzas: COLUMBUS ARTS FESTIVAL (see Columbus, OH, Early June); WATERSIDE ARTS AND BLUES FESTIVAL (see Louisville, KY, Early July); THREE RIVERS ARTS FESTIVAL (see Pittsburgh, PA, see Early June to Middle June); CENTRAL PENNSYLVANIA FESTIVAL OF THE ARTS (see State College, PA, Middle July); ALLENTOWN MAYFAIR (see Allentown, PA, Late May); ARTSCAPE (see Baltimore, MD, Late July); WOODSTOCK/NEW PALTZ ARTS AND CRAFTS FAIRS (New Paltz, NY — see chapter); MAINE ARTS FESTIVAL (Brunswick, ME — see chapter)...

I can also tell you honestly from having a B. F. A.-trained eye...

Rochester's CORN HILL FESTIVAL [CORN HILL'] is as good as it reasonably gets when it comes to classy crafts. If you can't find that artsy keepsake you've always wanted here, then maybe you never really wanted it after all. You can just hear TV's Joan Rivers goading her shopaholics over the prospect of 10 quaint streets bursting with 400 top crafts vendors and 50 food vendors: "C'mon people, it's shop 'till you drop; eat 'till you pop!" CORN HILL' attracts artisans from over 30 states, but its primary focus is local — proof of how much artistic talent dots the Northern Tier up here.

Of course, CORN HILL' offers it's 250,000 teeming patrons more than just crafts. Like the other biggies above, it's got a full gamut of music going on eight stages, everything from classical and Dixieland to reggae and rock.

But what makes CORN HILL' especially interesting is its ninth stage hosting a FIDDLER'S FAIR. Here, amidst the hay bales, is a perfect showcase of what makes the area's music so unique — its updating traditional country music with rock and other assorted genres. I mean, I've heard other scenes updating bluegrass with rock (Austin's Killbilly, Bad Livers, etc.); Celtic with rock (NYC's Black 47, Kips Bay Ceili Band, etc.); Cajun with rock (Lafayette's Wayne Toups, Zachary Richard, etc.); C&W with rock (Louisville's Cactus Brothers, Bodeco, etc.) — you name it — but never an adoption of old-time Appalachian string-band instrumentals to whichever other modern influences have happened by.

Two perspectives on this unusual regional flavor are available through interviews with the FINGERLAKES GRASSROOTS FESTIVAL OF MUSIC AND DANCE's Jeb Puryear and the GREAT BLUE HERON MUSIC FESTIVAL's Dave Tidquist (see chapter). Here's a third.

Richard Newman inaugurated the FIDDLER'S FAIR in '73. CORN HILL' was begun six years earlier by resident Wayne Frank to showcase the potential of this transitional neighborhood adjacent to downtown Rochester. Like many previously-neglected historic districts during this period, it started to become inhabited by artists like Newman drawn to its cheap housing with architectural character. (And, like its companion neighborhoods elsewhere, CORN HILL's since experienced gentrification, retro-fitting and such to where it's now fashionable, as well as funky.)

"The festival's put on by volunteers in the neighborhood," Newman explains:

- "So I guess I'm a neighbor, and I'm a banjo player. I had been a musician for many years. The guy who was the Chairman, Wayne Frank, was a friend of mine. He talked about wanting to have a FIDDLER'S FAIR. He asked me if I would do it, so I agreed. I'm a furniture maker; I was making banjos at the time, and it seemed like a good thing to do. It would be a way to promote my instruments.

  "So I did a one-day event. I think we started off with a haywagon for a stage. I had a host string band, The Henrie Brothers, who were friends. We used their sound system, and we had an open mic. Initially, we had them play, and then anybody who wanted could come up and play. It was a modest event, to say the least, but it was popular, and I was asked to do it again and given a little bigger budget. And it just grew and grew and grew and [became] very popular. I kept being asked to do it again, and I continued. I asked for more money, and got more interesting bands, and then I started bringing in bands from out of town."

Newman's out-of-towners have included Beausoleil, Mike Seeger, Jay Unger's Fiddle Fever — even Charlie Daniels once (see below) — but locals have lent the FIDDLER'S FAIR its characteristic flavor. "That's got a lot to do with the community around Ithaca, which is where these people all come from, specifically Trumansburg," observes Newman, as he recounts his initiation into the scene:

- "I went to school at Cornell [University] in the early '60's. I met Walt Coken there, actually — somebody who introduced me to playing the banjo then. He later went to California, came back, and formed The Highwoods String Band. It was the first hot string band to come out of that area and they were right at the top. They were nationally famous; travelled the world touring for the U. S. A.; went to South America and to Europe. This would've been in the early '70's. I don't know if they started it, but there was all sorts of music comin' outta' there. So I was quite lucky in having a lot of people to draw from.

  "The Henrie Brothers were [another] great string band back in the late '70's. They took first place at GALAX' (see FIDDLERS' CONVENTION, Galax, VA, Middle August), although they were never recorded. They were all brothers, very counter-cultural. Nobody ever got it together [laughs] yet they're still around. I don't know if you caught Bobby Henrie and The Goners [a rockabilly trio]. Bill Henrie plays in The New Alien String Band; Doug Henrie plays with Mac Benford and The Woodshed Allstars. So these guys are actually still out and around."

Newman's booking succeeds partly on the basis of these personal contacts dating back three decades but also on how well he treats his new recruits. What he lacks in funds, he makes up for in hospitality — even going so far as to arrange evening dates in town to close gaps in artists' fees.

"A lot of bands call and want to come because they know it's a good time," Newman notes of old-time bands recently stopping by, such as The Hicks, The Chicken Chokers, and The Wildcats:

- "We try to make it a party. Having been a musician, a lot of these people are friends. We put a hot tub behind the stage for the musicians and the dancers. We feed them and try to make it fun."

As for the current generation of Ithacans busy mixing what-have-you into their old-time stew? "I like the music that's evolved," he explains:

- "I really like it when somebody takes a traditional form and kinda' makes a personal contribution to it. It's [also] a very different group of people, and I like the old-time people a lot. It's not uncommon to have Ph.D.'s, and just all kinds of weirdos in there. The individuals are very interesting, I find, much more so in the old-time groups than in the bluegrass groups. It's a different kind of bunch."

Speaking of different, a striking feature of Newman's FIDDLER'S FAIR, as well as of CORN HILL'S remaining eight stages, is how close the musical setting is. This is despite over one hundred thousand people jamming the streets each day, stalking crafts and eats galore. Basically, Newman and crew plop the bands down on lawns, sidewalks, driveways, corners, whatever. Microphones are placed at street level with no elevated platforms or retaining barriers cordoning performers off. There's almost no separation from passersby, lending the entire neighborhood a unique sensation of music bubbling up organically from all around the crafts booths.

Call the effect "shop and bop."

I'm afraid my travel itinerary required me to stop bopping and split quickly for a pair of New Jersey festivals later that night, including the BRANDYWINE MOUNTAIN MUSIC CONVENTION (see Woodstown, NJ, Middle August). I did catch an 11:00 a.m. set from Donna the Buffalo, but these hardy troupers still seemed to be suffering the effects of just two hours' sleep after a distant gig the prior night. Worse yet, fiddler/vocalist Tara Nevins, the 'Buffalo's chief attraction, had to do double-duty on another stage for The Heartbeats' 11:30 slot. Alas.

Instead, here's a few of Newman's highlights from recent years:

Beausoleil. "We had Beausoleil and they were stunning! We had them right when they were at their best, I think. That was seven or eight years ago, right after they came out with *Allons a' Lafayette* (Rounder). That band was my favorite Beausoleil band and they were just great!"

Fiddle Fever. "We had Fiddle Fever several times. We had Fiddle Fever once, I believe, and Jay Unger and Molly playing as a swing band. That was wonderful!"

John Mooney. "In the old days we used to have The John Mooney Blues Band. They were wonderful. We had 'em for years and years and years before he finally moved down to Louisiana. John was a highpoint."

Charlie Daniels. "There was one year we had some interesting drama when Charlie Daniels was playing somewhere in town and somebody contacted [him.] He came to make an appearance and played with The Henrie Brothers, actually. He and Bill Henrie traded fiddle riffs on 'The Devil Went Down to Georgia.' It was really interesting to see a big white limo pull up and out comes Charlie Daniels. It was pretty neat because we got a big crowd for it; they made a lot of noise about it."

"Well, I certainly think I'd take 'em down to [Niagara's] High Falls, which is pretty interesting, pretty dramatic stuff." Newman advises area travelers:

- "I would probably be inclined to go down to the Fingerlakes for a day trip — the Fingerlakes area is fairly pretty. [Locally], the Eastman House is quite worthwhile. East Avenue is interesting — you go off of East Avenue on East Boulevard and there's a Frank Lloyd Wright house. The countryside of Rochester is interesting; Letchworth Falls is dramatic. If I was coming from New York City, I'd meander up through Ithaca, go up through the reservoir system through the Catskills, taking an offbeat path."

Later that week in Buffalo is BILLY LABEEF'S BASTILLE DAY, BARBEQUE, AND ROCK AND ROLL RODEO. LaBeef is one of the original founders of Jamestown's 10,000 Maniacs before striking out on his own. According to the *Buffalo News*:

- "LaBeef stuck to a punk rock sound and eventually turned to rockabilly. LaBeef's career was about to explode when...he was paralyzed in a driving accident [in '88]. LaBeef, in a wheelchair, went back to college, earned a communications degree, and maintains a passionate interest in music and radio. Every year on July 14th, he holds BILLY LABEEF'S BASTILLE DAY, a combination of local and national bands, Texas-style barbeque, and good times. The event is always one of Buffalo's best rock 'n' roll parties."

I can't guarantee 'Maniacs personnel will play the party, but I did note them selling LaBeef's festival T-shirt at their final CHAUTAUQUA' gig (CHAUTAUQUA SUMMER MUSIC PROGRAM, Chautauqua, NY — see chapter).

Otherwise, an arts bonanza similar in scale to Corn Hill' is Rochester's Lilac Festival two months prior. Not only will you browze one of the biggest clothesline displays in the Northeast occupying Highland Park, you'll also glory in live music all about town, including individual blues, New Orleans and C&W festival days at the Downtown Festival Tent. These three afternoons boast packed lineups of national acts, while hardy "regionals" and "locals" blossom elsewhere throughout the 10-day schedule.

~     ~     ~

*Street stage, Corn Hill Festival/Fiddlers Fair.*

# Hillsdale's
# Acoustic Roots Spectaculars

**WINTERHAWK BLUEGRASS FAMILY FESTIVAL**, Ancramdale, NY
> Middle July
> Bluegrass
> ***Attended***

**FALCON RIDGE FOLK FESTIVAL**, Hillsdale, NY
> Late July
> Modern Folk
> *Attended*

Hillsdale is a sleepy little blinking yellow light ("Nice town we're coming to, wasn't it?"), gener- **Introduction**
ally more noted for its five-star French restaurant conveniently situated for wealthy antique-ers
headed to browse the Berkshires. But for two consecutive weekends in the middle of every July,
Hillsdale transforms itself into contemporary roots-music Heaven. Period. Exclamation point.

The moveable feast begins the third weekend with the renown WINTERHAWK BLUEGRASS
FESTIVAL [WINTERHAWK'] perched atop a foothill on Rothvoss Farm, which provides its 20,000
happy campers with a panoramic sweep of the Hudson River Valley. If not also for the sensational lineup of progressive stars, intimate workshops, excellent concessions (well, for a bluegrass festival, anyway), superb production, winning spirit, and round-the-clock picking orgies, the lordly
view might be Winterhawk's chief attraction.

Contemporary singer-songwriters, along with their folk-dance counterparts, take over a
second farm the following weekend for the upstart FALCON RIDGE FOLK FESTIVAL [FALCON RIDGE'].
The view here is more pastoral — a bare ridge cradles the grounds before sloping down to the
highway and the marshy meadows beyond. However, the lineup of modern folkies is no less
packed for its genre, while the song-swapping among the 3,000 enthusiasts is, likewise, at a fever
pitch extending deep, deep into the evening.

There is an elite among progressive bluegrass festivals that can be summoned up in singular **Festival**
words: Merle, Winfield, Telluride, Yosemite... More than mere place names, they're all calls to **Review I**
action for the pickin' faithful to pack the campers, trek long stretches, weather rough camping and
whatever the elements heap upon them for the blessed glory of endless jam sessions christening
the wee, wee hours. Star-studded lineups set the bait, but fans become hooked on the camaraderie
and keep coming back for their annual communion.

Add to that cherished roster the name of WINTERHAWK'. It's the one among them with its
own theme song, "Winterhawk," which Taylor Armerding of Northern Lights penned to com-
memorate the band's extraordinary experiences there throughout the years. It graced their debut
album and quickly rose to the Top 10 on the bluegrass radio charts. (More about that later.)

"We call WINTERHAWK' the 'Bluegrass Family Festival,'" Promoter Mary Doub explains to
me:

- "And it's a sort of double entendre. We think that we have the bluegrass family there, and
  we think we're a family festival, so we really try to get that across. It's extremely important — we've got to appeal to the whole family! We've got to get some of these younger
  people coming into the music, or once again, we won't have much music. But you've probably noticed the crowd at WINTERHAWK' is a much younger crowd; it just seems to me to
  be much more open to everything."

There'd been bluegrass festivals on the site in various incarnations since the mid-'70s. Originally, a Boston-based bluegrass society presented The Berkshire Mountains Bluegrass Music Festival here. They passed the baton to Revonah Records who renamed it after their small bluegrass label. Howard Randall and a few partners took it over in '83. They gave it its present title before giving way to Doub in '85. (Randall went onto create FALCON RIDGE' and retains a financial interest in WINTERHAWK'.)

Doub, a Virginia school worker who has since risen to Chair the International Bluegrass Music Association, is a gently passionate person with a way of making you feel like an instant best friend. Yet she's also blessed with a steely will that has helped see WINTERHAWK' through such trials as The Great Mud Bath of '88, and the encroachments of its vindictive rival, the PEACEFUL VALLEY BLUEGRASS FESTIVAL (see Shinhopple, NY, Middle July). In fact, one of Doub's cherished memories was when she asked an aide to help John Hartford with some task and Hartford countered with feigned innocence, "Oh Mary, please, will you do it because you exude an aura of authority!"

Doub laughs:

- "I think it's just that I'm the oldest child, and I like to tell people what to do! But I decided when I did this that what I really needed was to communicate the feelings and ideas I had with a really good communicator. And I looked around, and I thought, 'Ron Thomason [leader of The Dry Branch Fire Squad] is the best communicator I have ever known.' He's a wonderful interviewer; he's a renaissance man, he really is...

  "I called him up (I'd met him a couple of times before, but I hadn't really known him; I just met him), and I said that I was thinking about doing this festival, and I really would like him to host it. I knew that he needed time to think about this, but I felt strongly about it, and I thought it would be a good fit. And he said, 'I've thought about it, and I want to do it!'"

The Dry Branch Fire Squad served as WINTERHAWK's host band that year and every year since.

Thomason's band is straight traditionalists with a reputation for kicking festivals off Sunday mornings with gospel sets — no mean feat since they've likely been up picking with fellow headliners until daybreak. Co-conspirators always appreciate the band giving them a few spare hours extra of sleep before their own sets. However, they're also well-networked among leading progressives and acoustic session aces. Thomason's fence-straddling presence helps WINTERHAWK' recruit its appealing mix of older and younger styles. Doub also credits the band's label head, Ken Irwin of Rounder Records, for clueing her into rising talent on the national scene, while her festival's own Bluegrass Band Competition contributes the best of the regional groups. Recent contest winners have included the highly promising Cornerstone, The Fox Family, Blue Mule, and Bluegrass Supply Company.

For all the main stage fireworks WINTERHAWK' provides, I still feel the daytime workshops are its most unique attraction. Yes, other bluegrass and folk festivals also feature workshops, but not with such high-powered names. John Hartford on songwriting? David Grisman and Tim O'Brien on mandolin? Alison Krauss and The Cox Family on harmony singing? Jerry Douglas on dobro? Pete Wernick and Bill Keith on banjo? Folks, this is as good as it gets down Nashville-way, and you'll be sharing them with clusters of fewer than 100 fans at a time. I'm not even a musician, yet I've been enraptured hour after hour by the incredible pick-up performances and high level insights I've experienced under this cozy tent (a bonus on a hot day). Not to diminish the main stage spectaculars, but this kind of intimacy is simply not available in the regular concert world at any price!

"I'm so happy to hear you say that about the workshops," Doub remarks to me:

- "Because they've been something that I think about [six months in advance] in trying to talk different artists into doing different combinations. The other thing that I think is so important is to try and get people to actually participate. Like, on Friday, we had a Beginners Jam Workshop for people to bring their instruments and sort of learn about jamming — how to get into a jam, and kind of jam etiquette. We're gonna' do that again; that was a big success.

"On Saturday, for the first time, we're gonna' have WINTERHAWK's Bluegrass Karoake Workshop. We're gonna' have a band called Foxfire, a West Coast band [who] just are tremendously good with people. We're gonna' have, maybe, 10 bluegrass songs, and we're gonna' have the words all out and everything. Then people can get up there and maybe do a little arrangement or a duet, or they might just want to sing one just by themselves. But they'll have this band backing them up, and so they can see how much fun it is to get up there and actually sing a bluegrass song."

The workshop tent sits right behind the bustling backstage area, which is certainly convenient for everybody. Artists can conduct all their business without straying too far from their legendary 18-hour picking, while enlightened fans can simply move their chairs a few feet from the daytime workshops, to the main stage finales, to the fence partition to listen in post-midnight.

"We try and make the backstage the real center of the fest," Doub explains. "I mean, we feed all of our artists, and each of them can have a guest. We feed all of them; we feed our whole staff of 300 people. A lot of these younger bands certainly aren't makin' much money. Whatever you can do to make them as comfortable as possible, I try and do. I've even, for the last three to four, had some masseuses backstage to work on some of these artists." Hospitality pays handsome dividends here.

Doub's personal highlight always comes with Saturday night's closing set, which brings the backstage jam up to the main stage:

- "We did it for a long time with Peter Rowan, and now Jerry Douglas is producing and running the jam. It was, like, getting Alison [Krauss] and Mollie O'Brien together doin' something together and it was interesting because here was Mollie singing lead and Alison backup. You know, it's that kind of thing. People do things that they don't normally do. There'll probably be some really great banjo players, the best dobro player in the world, with Tim O'Brien, I think, one of the top mandolin players. That's the kind of thing I like to see, just sort of jammin'...."

Apparently the fans concur. "One year, '88, we had what we fondly call 'The Mud Year,'" Doub recalls.

- "It rained and rained and rained. On Saturday it dawned absolutely magnificently! And I thought that the worst was over, [but] I have a close friend who's a pilot and he called the weather. He came back to me, looked, and said, 'It's comin' back on.' It was just absolutely unbelievable — we had tractors; we had everything pulling people out.

  "And there was an article about it. The thing that I really prided myself was that this reporter sat down at the bottom, and he was interviewing people as they came out. He said they were covered with mud, you know, but there were big smiles on their faces. [They] said it's the greatest thing; it was the greatest festival they had ever been to. The fact that the spirit of this festival could rise above that really meant a lot to me."

To avoid future "tractor-pulls," Doub would like to find a few hundred acres in Columbia County on which to construct permanent festival grounds, including an expanded stage for bigger acts and a summer-long concert series. She also envisions more comfortable camping with lower operating costs. It's not cheap, for example, hauling facilities and services for a small bluegrass city up and down a mountain side every year. Finder's fees, real estate searches, even airplane reconnaissances have all gone for naught to date.

"The area really loves us," Doub sighs in counterpoint:

- "They bend over backwards for us, and they make us feel tremendously at home here. I think that I could make the festival grow if I did move it, but would I want to, really? You know, that's the thing. I said that once to Jerry Douglass — this was about three years ago when we were standing backstage — and he puts his arm around me, turns me to the hill and said, 'Mary, what's wrong with this? This is wonderful!'"

**Artist**
**Mini-Reviews**

<u>Dry Branch Fire Squad</u>. Like with Garrison Keillor, it's always great fun to see Ron Thomason throw all kinds of topical spaghetti on the wall before tying it together. His homespun sermonette somehow touched upon nude beaches, Robber Barons, and The Great Society before relating them all to folk music's mission. Musical highpoints included: the band's "I'm Gonna' Walk The Streets Of Glory One Of These Days," with Thomason adding extra "yips" to the joyful noise; Thomason's solo acappella "Black Wing" — mournful to the max; and "Give Me That Old-Time Religion" with the band showing off impressive five-part harmonies.

<u>Austin Lounge Lizards</u>. Bluegrass music's smart alecks. How could you not love a band whose Nashville tribute suggests, "Let's Throw The Oak Ridge Boys In The Slammer." Or whose birthplace paean refrains: "It always draws me back wherever I may roam, to that God-forsaken hellhole I call home." Basically, when the lead vocalist/guitarist straightens his Aloha shirt collar, adjusts his "Lizardvison" sunglasses and smirks, you know something's up. Of course, the band can also pick pretty well, as their lightening-quick renditions of "Stony Creek" and "Up On The Blue Ridge" attest.

<u>Hot Rize</u>. Given a standing o' before they hit their first note, these Colorado-based stalwarts and longtime WINTERHAWK' faves seemed almost sheepish about the adulation. Actually, it was lead singer/mandolinist Tim O'Brien who seemed so, since this was to be one of the band's last appearances together (O'Brien having left the year prior to pursue his solo performing and songwriting career). Still, no one in the audience seemed to harbor a grudge against one of the acknowledged "nice guys" in the field as they maintained their love fest unabated.

O'Brien began by noting of the home-tapers how, "with all those mics, [it] looks like a Ross Perot press conference." I rushed over to catch Hartford's songwriting clinic, but not before enjoying a plaintiff ballad, "Colleen Malone," their updating of the prison song genre, "Ninety-Nine Years and One Dark Day," and a winning gospel arrangement of "See What The Lord Has Done," which scrambled group harmony and individual vocal lines before bringing it together for the final chorus line. They'll be missed.

<u>Northern Lights with Vassar Clements</u>. "The band that asks the question, 'Where is Vassar?" So Northern Lights introduced themselves before fiddle legend Clements was summoned from some backstage jam. He stepped up to join lead singer/mandolinist Taylor Armerding for a nice vocal duet on "Carolina Kinfolk." Clements' singing was quiet and quaint, but his playing was strong with style, snap and expressiveness. The band then provided Clement's bow work with many excellent settings to shine, notably a melodic instrumental, "September's End," with every member taking expert turns, a driving take of The Eagle's "Heartache Tonight," and their own soaring closer, "Northern Rail." Caught the mood perfectly!

About Armerding's homage to the festival? "I couldn't believe it when I first heard it," Doub exclaims of the first time she'd even caught the band, let along the song:

- "We'd had some problem, I've forgotten what it was. One of the bands couldn't get there for that first set, and I took Northern Lights and put 'em on at 10:30 or 11:00. Linda Bolton [the band's manager] had really gotten to me and said, 'Mary, please be out there and listen to this song.' And I went out and, I mean, I was exhausted... I listened to that song, 'Winterhawk,' and I loved it so much I went back to our stage manager and said, 'Look, I wanna' put this on tonight!' So we did. We put them out there, and Alison played fiddle for them, and it was great!"

~     ~     ~

**Festival**
**Review II**

The key to understanding the success of the more diminutive FALCON RIDGE' is in those little surveys that get passed around and conscientiously completed. "We go through those surveys very carefully," exclaims the outgoing Co-Promoter, Anne Saunders, "because they're a very astute audience. They know what they want to hear; they know what they've heard before. And when they don't know, they actually indicate that, too, by telling us: 'We'd like to hear some Celtic music, or some bluegrass.' That indicates to you that they don't know the names of the bands, so we should search a little bit. As far as singer-songwriters [though], they know."

It's a snowy day in February — the time much of this information gets reviewed and implemented — when Saunders and her husband and Co-Promoter, Howard Randall, describe how addressing survey responses helped them grow FALCON RIDGE' over six years from a one-stage concert into a fully-stocked, four-stage extravaganza, including a folk-dance-a-thon with 10 bands! Indeed, it's almost a miracle how much music occurs on FALCON RIDGE's grounds, considering how modest the crowd size really is.

Randall, more the quiet listener of the two, recalls:

- "[After WINTERHAWK'], I always wanted to do another festival by myself without a partner, so my wife at that time, Lynn, and I decided that we were gonna' do it. We found Bill Morrissey who helped us book (at that time they were the lesser-known acts, but now they're better-known) acts, like Shawn Colvin, and John Gorka, and people like that. We booked people like Holly Near, and Tom Paxton, and Taj Mahal, and Buffy Ste. Marie.

  "We did the first festival at Catamount [Ski Area in '88]. Then in '89, we did the second festival. In '90, my wife died of cancer. Anne had been a volunteer and I had met her. We did a festival in '90, and we didn't do a festival in '91, I believe. Then we went back to it in '92.

  "We got married, I guess, in '91. I consider Anne a nut, excuse my expression, on music. I mean, she's got all these records, she listens to all the people, and she can remember people's names. I can remember everybody's face, but put a name to it? Unh-huh! So it worked out really well because she knew who was back in the '60s, and I don't remember."

(As the joke goes: "If you can remember the '60s, you weren't there!")

Saunders adds:

- "We did a coffeehouse first. The times were bad. Artistically, it was very good. We had many people remember it — it was in Stamford, CT — but we just had too many overhead expenses. We didn't have our own space; we were paying a lot of rent; we were paying a lot of money for insurance; paying a lot of money for renting a sound system, etc.

  "After three years we decided we needed to concentrate on the festival because now were gonna' move it to a place where people can camp. What a lot of people said in '88 to '89 was, 'This is a great show, but it's not a festival. It's an outdoor concert because you don't have the things that festivals have, which is other stages, things for families. You don't have crafts; you don't have anything. You've just got this stage and a little bit of food, but it's a ski resort, so there's no place for us to take a walk or anything.' They were very good to us at the ski resort, and we really loved them, but there wasn't anything else to do, and you couldn't camp."

Enter Long View Farm, which Saunders describes as "one of the most beautiful farms in the Berkshires."

By this time FALCON RIDGE' had acquired a reputation for showcasing ascending acts. Sanders recites:

- "In '89 we had two really great people: Eddie Adcock and Talk of the Town, and Alison Krauss and Union Station. We've had three Grammy winners here at FALCON RIDGE' long before they thought they might get to win a Grammy. And we had lots of Grammy nominees as well, [such as] Bill [Morrissey] and Greg [Brown] this past year.

  "We had Shawn Colvin for three years in a row, '88 to '90. We've had John Gorka every year. [Randall] always like to say that John started out as the least known, and also lowest man on the pay scale, back in '88, and he's our headliner now! I mean, this is what people came to see. He was with us from the very beginning when we did our first show at the Catamount Ski Area, and I think very few people there knew who he was. I have a great picture of him and Shawn Colvin performing inside the cafeteria on a table top because it was raining. I wrote something about him in our program [that] he's still that same guy. It's like, 'Oh, you know, the crowd wants to hear me and it's raining; I'll stand on this table and entertain the folks spontaneously while the mics get set up.' He's just really a great guy, you know?"

Aside from Gorka's annual return, FALCON RIDGE's two defining characteristics — showcasing rising stars and acknowledging survey responses — come together with a four-hour Artist Showcase. Roughly, 10 percent of 300 demo tape submitters are chosen by committee to perform two songs each on a side stage Friday afternoon. The audience then notes on their ubiquitous surveys which showcasing artists they consider "Most Wanted," with the top three to five selected either to do a song swap on the main stage, or to fill-in between set changes.

"One of the reasons why we wanted to start that showcase," confides Saunders, "was because there are so many people, so much unsolicited material that we get, and we realize we can't really hire very many of these people for the main stage. In fact, we can't really hire almost any of them at all, [maybe] one or two that we can, like, cultivate a little bit each year. ...But at a festival, there's a lot more people that can sit and listen than at a coffeehouse or at a few coffeehouses. So we thought [with] this showcase some of this material could be used there.

- "We just didn't know how it would work out. But the people who are the committee have venues, so it was an opportunity for these people to be seen by someone who books Cafe Lena [Barbara Harris], and someone who books the Eight Step Coffeehouse [Margie Rosenkrantz], and, of course, [demo-tape screener] Sonny Ochs who does the Phil Ochs Song Night and has a small coffeehouse in her community as well. And, actually, all three of them have booked some of these people as openers.

"[In '92] we noticed, 'Well, when we look at our surveys, a few of these people have really been singled out by the audience; I mean, really, really singled out!' For instance, Donna Martin got put on the stage, and I think that perhaps her name was not mentioned by the M. C. (or anyway it went by a large number of people in the audience), so they didn't know this person's name. [Still], we got all these surveys saying, 'The girl with the red guitar and medium-brown hair who played on Saturday night between da-da-da and da-da-da.' We got so many surveys like that it was like, 'Who is this?!' [laughs]

"She made it the next year into the 'Most Wanted' thing, and that's something that gets picked by the audience. We just keep the surveys and read 'em very carefully. We don't let anyone else actually tabulate them for us — we actually sit here and read them ourselves, and then we just go with who the people like. It's not exactly a contest — there's no winner — but the few people that will be mentioned by the audience come back the next year.

"That showcase at FALCON RIDGE' has really burgeoned into something that's extremely popular," Saunders concludes, "and people come just to see it."

**Artist Mini-Reviews** For all my building it up, '93's Artist Showcase was a mild disappointment. Yes, there were unequivocal "diamonds-in-the-rough" on display (I was impressed by Catie Curtis, Greg Greenway, Wendy Beckerman, and Erica Wheeler, for example). But there were also too many journeymen/women, along with a smattering of Gong Show candidates. Instead of featuring *la creme de la creme* suitable for inviting A&R contacts, it merely delivered a cross-section of the New England coffeehouse circuit, interesting in itself, but clearly a missed opportunity to elevate the genre's next best much beyond the festival gates and the three venues of the committee. Still, the showcase remains a great idea in theory that I'd like to see more festivals adopt.

I had to scoot down that evening for LINCOLN CENTER's SERIOUS FUN (Manhattan, NYC — see chapter), but can still clearly recall three main-stage performances from '90:

John Gorka. Gorka had just released his Windham Hill debut, so there was a palpable buzz of recognition for his sunset gig. He appeared clearly relaxed and among friends as he took the stage wearing nothing more than a white sleeveless ribbed T-shirt and jeans. No shoes or socks. He more than satisfied the crowd's expectations, though, with confident stage presence, handsome singing, and accessible songs full of surprises, yet delivering real feelings and believable situations. Nothing overly cutesy or condescending. I sought out his disc immediately upon returning home.

Shawn Colvin. A bit of a letdown. A few months prior at the late, lamented GREAT WOODS FOLK FESTIVAL, Colvin accomplished one of the most impressive festival feats I've ever witnessed. She took on a disparate amphitheater crowd that'd just been rocked silly — first by Wayne Toups and Zydecajun, then by Malathini and The Mahotella Queens — and wielding nothing more than an acoustic guitar and that remarkable voice of her's, positively lassoed them and held them so tight you could hear them breathing. Colvin's exquisite imagery, intense emotions, percussive strumming, and searing phrasing wailed all over Joe Ely and Rickie Lee Jones who followed in succession. If not for the equally revelatory Lyle Lovett and His Large Band, I'd say Colvin stole the whole show like a brazen bandit!

Following Gorka this particular evening, though, Colvin's GREAT WOODS crispness and intensity gave way to a more meandering, self-absorbed set. Every song seemed drawn out, but with no additional insights. She seemed distracted.

Livingston Taylor. By contrast, Taylor was a pleasant surprise the following afternoon. Previously, I'd bought an album cut-out of his but found this recorded material intolerably saccharine and slick. Live, however, Taylor proved a terrific solo entertainer. I was especially impressed by his command of blues and jazz idioms, and he seemed equally at ease digging deep or swinging lithely. I gotta' find the disc where this version of Taylor resides!

Saunders most pleasant surprise? "Last year, for the first time, we presented a band that was pretty much unknown to us — we really do have a lot of good advisors — and unknown to our crowd, and that was The Kips Bay Ceili Band. And they just rocked the house; they were just unbelievable. [They play] Celtic rock [with] roots that go back to the 7th century, but they're also incorporating elements of rap and almost everything. So they were really a great surprise."

**Attendance Tip**

The funny thing about farmers' fields is they always look so smooth from a distance but are actually quite choppy when you try to lay down your blanket or set up your tent. A hay clump always seems to find the small of your back. All patrons should bring folding chairs for seating, while tent campers should consider folding cots or thick air mattresses for sleeping. Plus, if you're someone who needs your sleep, ear plugs are a must to cushion against post-midnight musical exchanges.

You should also be forewarned, too, that both events have oh-so-cold showers (although WINTERHAWK's '94 brochure promised "hot showers" for the first time). This is a key consideration with WINTERHAWK's notorious dust and/or mud and FALCON RIDGE's sweaty dance tent. Tent campers may wish to book nearby lodgings far ahead for at least one of the days to freshen themselves up in comfort.

**Travel Tip**

"Taconic State Park is divided into two parts. Bish Bash Falls and the Red Pond area are two really, really nice places," Saunders offers, while also recommending "a drive over the Massachusetts border into Great Barrington where there's some really great restaurants. There's also some really nice classical music venues.

- "For anyone who is a first-time goer to a festival and they're not sure if they can deal with camping, on our ticket form, you can send for our database of hotels, motels, and campgrounds. There's over 100 [lodgings listed] going up to 25 miles away.

"One other place that's really off the beaten track, but it's maybe half an hour from us [is] the place where we get our food, the Hawthorne Valley Farm Store. It's a living community [with] a Steiner Learning Center and they take you on tours of their completely organic farm. It's a really nice place; the store is open, and they have some ongoing things and activities on the weekends and [during] the summer."

~     ~     ~

*Hot Rize, Winterhawk Bluegrass Family Festival.*

# Hunter Mountain's Country Marathon

AMERICAN PATRIOT FESTIVAL, Hunter, NY
> Early July
> Variety, General

COUNTRY MUSIC FESTIVALS, Hunter, NY
> Middle July to Late July; Early August to Late August
> Modern Country
> ***Attended***

ROCKSTALGIA, Hunter, NY
> Early August
> Classic Rock and Oldies

INTERNATIONAL CELTIC FESTIVAL, Hunter, NY
> Middle August to Late August
> Irish

MOUNTAIN EAGLE INDIAN FESTIVAL, Hunter, NY
> Early September
> Native American

CELTIC FAIR, Hunter, NY
> Late September
> Irish

**Introduction**

The HUNTER MOUNTAIN FESTIVALS combine for what has to be the most extensive festival programming of any ski resort in the country. It even rivals the summertime schedules of most municipalities.

Yet, Hunter's prime musical showcases — the one most likely to attract serious listeners — are its two COUNTRY MUSIC FESTIVALS [HUNTER COUNTRY]. These events total 15 days, surpassing in length any other country-music festival or state fair that I know of. What's more, HUNTER COUNTRY features more than 30 big names across an entire gamut of styles, ages, and career stages. This ranges from established superstars like Tanya Tucker and Ronnie Milsap, to hot bands like Diamond Rio and Blackhawk, to the "smart set" like Rodney Crowell and Kathy Mattea, to "nostalgia" acts like Jeannie C. Riley and Johnny Rodriguez.

I've always been most impressed, though, by HUNTER COUNTRY's profusion of rising stars. Some new faces debuted to its audiences in recent years include Lorrie Morgan ('85), Sweethearts of the Rodeo ('87, '90), Mary Chapin Carpenter ('91), Neal McCoy ('91, '92), Mark Chesnutt ('92), and Pat Garrett ('92). Not only are these up-and-comers peppered throughout the schedule, but they're often accorded their own evenings, as well. In '93, one night showcased Doug Stone, Stacy Dean Campbell, Tracy Lawrence, and Paula Frazier together.

In fact, if country radio were as willing to take chances on young talent, well, I wouldn't have as many problems with country radio!

I complimented the resort's owner, Orville Slutsky, on staying one ski boot ahead of the pack. Slutsky responds in a fast, gravelly patter which bespeaks the energy of someone who's always the first one in, the last one out, and who only takes one day off a year — Yom Kippur:

- "We did the same thing with Trisha Yearwood last year and we were a year too early. She was a [financial] dud last year, but this year she's up there. I picked another young lady this year, Faith Hill. You may not even have heard of her. She's comin' on strong, but I picked her last September!

  "We've tried to select people ahead of time that we think are going to be tremendous and go places. I remember when we brought Garth Brooks in, everybody said, 'Garth who?' Hey, we got him for probably around $25,000 to $30,000; now you can't touch him for one-hundred-and-a-half! I do watch quite a bit of [TNN's] 'Nashville Now.' Yeah, I picked guys like Neal McCoy, Aaron Tippin, Joe Diffie. Now they've really gone on up!

  "I'm tone deaf, too, but I can see them," Slutsky exclaims. "I can see the way they perform and how they appeal."

Tone deaf or not, Skutsky's ear has proven financial music to the summer trade of the northern Catskills where Hunter Mountain Ski Resort is situated. "Thirty-five years ago I got involved in it," he explains, "and it was bringing business to an area that was an Appalachia. In '52, this was a distressed area, and so we rejuvenated a lot of the area. It was a tremendous tourism country from 1800 to 1920; then after that it started fading away."

Slutsky's summertime contribution began with the GERMAN ALPS FESTIVAL:

- "Don Conover, who came from down in the Pennsylvania Dutch country around the Kutztown/Allentown area, and Deiter Steinman, who was the sole importer of Dinkel Acker beer, teamed up together. They brought the festival from Barnsville and opened up in Green County at the Bavarian Manor in Pearling. There they were four miles off the beaten path on a narrow town-and-county road in the fields. It was a rainy summer then; they were bogged down in mud. The Department of Health suggested they look over Hunter Mountain because, at that time, we already had a building that had 50,000 square feet in the base lodge, plus paved parkways and lifts and so forth. And so in '75 (they started in '73 and '74 elsewhere), we got together and brought it here.

  "In those days, he put on a GERMAN ALPS FESTIVAL [for] 10 or 11 days. After he did it for two summers, I said to him, 'Don, you can't keep going this way. There's no way you can do enough business in 10 or 11 days to keep you going the year 'round.' ...I talked him into extending it two more days, bringing on other festivals. So the second year he brought on a POLKA FESTIVAL. The third year I talked him into [HUNTER COUNTRY]. We only did that for three days and then got into other festivals: the [INTERNATIONAL CELTIC FESTIVAL], the [MOUNTAIN EAGLE INDIAN FESTIVAL], and a number of other festivals.

  "So we have 10 weeks instead of just 10-to-11 days. That's where we've grown to. But since the GERMAN ALPS FESTIVAL started here, and the POLKA FESTIVAL, an awful lot of these festivals have sprung up around the area and diluted the market. And with the D. W. I. laws and changing of the drinking age from 18 to 21, we don't sell 2,000 kegs of beer in 40 days of operation. Plus the fact that [with] the GERMAN ALPS FESTIVAL, it's 19 years now, and it's a changing scene. At that time it was pretty much first-generation immigration people here. Now you've got second and third [generations]. You've got a lot of other ethnic groups that come to these, and the crowds are nowheres near what they used to be, nor is the atmosphere the same as it was then."

Perhaps they should take a cue from Slutsky's HUNTER COUNTRY, which has thrived from cultivating younger acts to a broader base. Hunter's other ethnic festivals tend to program "commercial-style" artists — their equivalents of "Borscht-Belt" entertainers geared to an ever-graying, ever-narrowing constituency. No such problem with HUNTER COUNTRY, which will likely grow with its new C&W faces to 60,000 revelers in '94.

Another feature boosting HUNTER COUNTRY is Slutsky's tendency to program sympathetic bills of like-minded artists. This differs from other area C&W venues, such as Long Island's Westbury Music Fair, which schedules contrasting artists in hopes of attracting multiple constituencies. They believe that pairing Roy Clark with, say, Asleep at the Wheel, broadens their attendance pool and mitigates their risk when all it's ever done, in my case, is to frighten me away from one act or the other. At HUNTER COUNTRY, however, you can indulge your preferences knowing you're not going to get stuck some night with someone who'll set your teeth to grinding. In '94 this means Faith Hill mated with Sammy Kershaw; Kathy Mattea with Hal Ketchum; Tanya Tucker with Steve Wariner, and so forth.

Slutsky's favorite such pairing? "[Vince Gill's] been here twice," he confides," and [here's] what I pulled on him the first year we got him. I was aware that one of the girls from Sweethearts of the Rodeo was his wife, [Janice Gill]. Unbeknown to either one of them, we scheduled them on the same day, and they just couldn't believe it when they got here! And then we did a repeat performance last year — he did his own show, and then he came out and played the guitar during their evening show, the whole show."

After the sun's set over the last lift, Slutsky prides himself on HUNTER COUNTRY's family atmosphere: "They complement me on the personnel that we have around the area, or how clean the area is, or how the pricing is, or things of that nature. [I like] to bring out families, bring out patrons, and see how they are satisfied in what we do to make it a wonderful day for them."

Let me underscore Slutsky's last word, "day." Despite what the print ads and mailers say (which **Festival** merely highlight the evening's headliners), he's got music programmed at HUNTER COUNTRY 13 **Review** hours a day, every day, on two covered stages, plus a dance tent proffering free lessons! Regional acts, too, not just a bunch of local fluff. Had I known the evening I went in '93, I would've come by earlier for the following:

- A Nashville newcomer, Maura Fogarty, who was also showcased on "Club Night" for Radio City Music Hall's week-long COUNTRY TAKES MANHATTAN earlier that year;

- A pair of reasonably solid bar bands, including one, Six Gun, I've often boogied to at Long Island's Matty T's Nashville USA;

- A "JAMBOREE" vet from out of Wheeling, WV, Terry Gorka (see JAMBOREE IN THE HILLS, St. Clairsville, OH, Middle July);

- A respected "folk traddie" and multi-instrumentalist, Jay Smar.

Since I've been spreading the word among my musician pals, I imagine the daytime will only get better.

Half the fun is getting there. The Catskills are far from the world's most imposing mountains, but they share a feature with Texas' Big Bend National Park in being clustered together amidst relatively placid surroundings. You mosey up the storied Hudson River Valley and — boom — there they are! There are no major highways to the summits, so you snake your way through the rural valleys and up the leafy creek bends to the ski bowl where Hunter sits. Once you've crested the horizon, you'll feel like you've entered Shangra-La amidst the "Irish Alps."

Slutsky's erected two contiguous big tops that shield the main stage and dance floor from inclement weather. He's also installed two big crafts tents, a "Clown Town" for the kids, a miniature golf course, a festive food alley, and a number of bustling outdoor beer kiosks for the festival faithful. Here's gotta' be the only major C&W affair where you can buy imported beer in enormous plastic mugs, maybe an ounce or two shy of a pitcher. It's a Hansel-and-Gretel holiday, all right, paved and swept for your convenience.

The crowd appeared C&W savvy, dressed to the nines in full Western regalia. I spied a number of festival T's — FARM AID; FORKS OF THE RIVER in Newport, TN; GREAT AMERICAN MUSIC FESTIVAL in Copper Mountain, CO — though the shirt of choice seemed to be Alan Jackson's, who'd played here earlier in the week. I enjoyed watching one excellent dancer with a "Boneanza" logo emblazoned across his chest and blinking Christmas lights weaved into his cowboy hat.

**Artist Mini-Reviews**

<u>Jimmy Sturr Orchestra</u>. A polka band at a C&W bash? Hey, Grammy-winner Sturr and his huge ensemble made my night! They put on a wild and woolly show whose schtick and frantic instrumentation issued a veritable summons to get up and dance! I only caught their last half-set but got swept up in a scene that had one of their members doing Cossack kicks while blazing away on a mad solo. Sturr and crew had co-headlined New York City's Lone Star Cafe earlier that week with The Texas Tornados, and I'll be sure to "roll out the barrel" when they swing themselves back into town. A blast!

<u>Suzy Bogguss</u>. Sweet and upbeat, Bogguss thanked the venue for booking her "when she wasn't working anywhere else." She began with John Hiatt's "Drive South" in a set remarkable for it's versatility: rockers, ballads, songwriter specials, nice cabarets, one Mariachi-flavored number she labelled "fiesta time," even a slow yodeller perfect for the Alpine kitsch which smattered Route 23A to the concert. I liked Bogguss best on her quieter numbers that showcased her earnest vocals to best advantage. Altogether, an appealing performance capped by the Nanci Griffith/Tom Russell uptempo, "Outbound Plane."

<u>Dwight Yoakam</u>. My musician friends complain of Yoakam's band, which they describe as "too rigid — not swinging or breathing or reacting." I complain that his vocal phrasing often seems affected, or how his writing always stops a bit sort of an introspective or emotive breakthrough. On the other hand, I've always liked Yoakam's "way cool" style, however contrived, and admired the consistent quality and tastefulness in his work. Here's one C&W star who's yet to make a grievous artistic mistake.

Yet, I couldn't really appreciate Yoakam until this night, seeing him live. He presented a really thoughtful and measured set — one that strived for variations on a lonesome mood; one that underscored any personal significance to his songs; one that put the spotlight on his extraordinary voice and its interpretative powers. In other words, it wasn't a slick run-through of his album hits. I had to leave midway, but I left impressed!

A pair of twangy rockers kicked off his set, including my fave, "Guitars, Cadillacs, Etc." — maybe the closest he's come to a biographical narrative, regrettably hampered by its metronome beat. But then, he dipped into "Lil' Sister," done perfectly as a slow burn instead of as a rave-up. This gave Yoakam an ideal vehicle to extract its pain of reluctant seduction and impending rejection. (Of course, it didn't stop him from flashin' ass to the ladies. "Hup, hup!")

Yoakam continued with a number of poignant ballads off his recent disc, artistically reminiscent of Bonnie Raitt's "Nick of Time." He sung "This Time Is the Last Time" drenched in Buck Owens, then slowed down their album collaboration, "A Town South of Bakersfield," to let the frustrated hurt of its outsider sentiments sink in. The band cooperated with an understated polka featuring some nice accordion flavoring. An especially melancholy "You're the One" followed up.

And so it went 'till the break — more adjustments, slower tempos, greater focus, stronger interpretations, and higher sincerity. It continually revealed Yoakam being ready, willing, and able to take it to the next emotional level. Can't wait for future albums!

**Attendance Tip**

"The main thing is they should familiarize themselves with what we have to offer," Slutsky recommends:

- "Everything doesn't go on under the big tent; we've got a lot to see in the base lodge. We have probably one of the largest collections of Hummel ware [porcelain figurines] anywhere in the country, and the Gerbels collectors' items. We've got one room, 7,500 square feet, that's filled up with Gerbel collections. You walk into the room, it's like walking into Macy's Department Store! It's all set up. And we have the artists there who show how the Gerbel products are made right from the design to before the design, and how they're selected, and how they're followed through, and how they're created, and how they try to keep the market from getting flooded, and things of that nature."

The remaining festivals listed above are somewhat self-explanatory. ROCKSTALGIA is Wolfman   **See Also**
Jack's touring oldies package featuring strong names from the '50's and '60's, while the
INTERNATIONAL CELTIC FESTIVAL basically combines a Scottish Highland games with an Irish fleadg-
gh. There were no names I recognized among the many "commercial-style showbands" on last
year's bill, except for Vermont's folksy Woods Tea Company.

The AMERICAN PATRIOT FESTIVAL is Slutsky's first attempt to compete with other July 4th
offerings, such as occurs on Albany's State Capitol Mall. There's the inevitable fireworks, but
there's also a nice family-oriented mix of music ranging from Sturr's Orchestra, to folkie Tom
Chapin, to The Sammy Kaye Orchestra, to Skip Parsons' River Boat Jazz Band.

I can't say I know a single name from the lineups of two more festivals Slutsky hosts —
the GERMAN ALPS FESTIVAL (Early July to Middle July) or the POLKA FESTIVAL (Late August) —
which is precisely the reason why I've chosen not to cover these categories for the time being.
Until I can tell the difference between a Grammy-winner and a wedding band, I can't pretend to
offer a meaningful guidebook to these genres. Perhaps in future editions...

~     ~     ~

# Gold Coast Jazz

RIVERHEAD JAZZ FESTIVAL, Riverhead, NY
> Late June
> Modern Jazz

LONG ISLAND JAZZ FESTIVAL, Oyster Bay, NY
> Late July
> Modern Jazz
> ***Attended***

ISLIP JAZZ FESTIVAL, Islip, NY
> Late August
> Modern Jazz
> ***Attended***

**Introduction**  Surely Long Island is one place that can support three jazz festivals!

By now most of you probably know it as home to Joey Buttafuocco, Amy Fisher, Howard Stern, Jessica Hahn, et al.....and you'd be right. Actually, during my last stint of living and working there throughout the '80s, I'd been loudly proclaiming it "Wrong Island" to all who'd listen, decrying a goodly chunk as a wasteland of big hair, name chains, pinkie rings, mall crawls, and Camaros run amok. "Who axed you," my neighbors and colleagues would taunt back, but I just knew the tabloids would finally vindicate me.

Putting a musical face on this cross-cultural phenomena would probably lead you to, well, such natives as Hicksville's Billy Joel or Merrick's Debbie Gibson. But that would be an unfair impression of this hidden corner of America with its many diverse enclaves all migrating toward one common characteristic — relative affluence. Nassau County routinely ranks among the nation's highest in per-capita income, joined not far behind by neighboring Suffolk County. It's 2.4 million combined residents possess the perfect demographics for the occasional jazz festival.

One more consideration.

There are probably more leading jazz artists living between L. I. and New York City's outer boroughs than virtually anywhere else in the world. More family-oriented than you'd suspect, with "white-picket-fence" dreams no different than the rest of us, these artists find the proximity ideal. Not only can they send their kids to good schools in safe neighborhoods, but they're also in commuting distance to Manhattan's clubs, as well as to Queens' two international airports for their big-paying European gigs. It'd be a longshot to be sure, but where else would you be as likely to find your next-door neighbor playing a hot tenor sax?

Even if L. I. is too spread-out to support many jazz venues beyond Sonny's Place in Nassau's Seaford and the IMAC in Suffolk's Huntington, there's no shortage of resident jazz talent to stock its three events. The International Art of Jazz [IAJ], the nation's oldest jazz nonprofit, has been anchoring this scene with monthly winter concerts since '65. (They print a partial list of 600 artists who've performed at IAJ concerts that would blow you away.) Since '82 they'd also presented what had been known as the ISLIP JAZZ FESTIVAL in Suffolk's Islip. Regretfully, IAJ's funding fell victim to local governmental cutbacks in '93, causing their two-day event's sudden cancellation.

Into this void stepped Friends of the Arts [FOA], who themselves had been presenting their LONG ISLAND SUMMER FESTIVAL concert series of big-name classical, jazz, pop, and folk acts in Nassau's Oyster Bay since '74. In '93, they chose to expand what had always been their weekly concert series finale into three full days, calling it the LONG ISLAND JAZZ FESTIVAL. Apparently

FOA's ambition paid off because their classy affair continues for '94 and beyond.

Meanwhile, IAJ found its festival funding restored for '94. Whether to reclaim their virtual birthright from FOA, or to embarrass Islip Township for its indiscretion, they changed their festival's name to the ORIGINAL LONG ISLAND JAZZ FESTIVAL (though they've since returned the festival's name back to the former monicker). What do we care, as long as they keet their event's unpretentious character and jam session-only format.

Quietly apart from this fray, Suffolk's East End Arts Council [EEAC] took their first festival steps in '90 with the RIVERHEAD JAZZ FESTIVAL. Though boasting a comparable lineup quality, EEAC's single-day gathering has a few differences besides its smaller size. It:

- Occurs in-town instead of on parkland;

- Often features a non-jazz act (e.g., Port Jefferson resident and jazz/blues pianist, Mose Allison; Greenpoint resident and Grammy-winning C&W songwriter, Hugh Prestwood);

- Offers July 4th fireworks to cap the evening;

- Serves the best spread, including a wine bar sampling the North Fork's renowned vintners.

They've had their financial ups-and-downs, too. Rain washed out '92's ill-fated expansion to two days, leaving the EEAC $20 grand in the hole. Among others, Montauk Point resident Paul Simon helped bail them out with proceeds from his charity fundraiser (BACK AT THE RANCH FESTIVAL, Montauk Point, NY — see chapter). Chastened, EEAC moved '93's event back a week in hopes of attracting a holiday crowd while avoiding going head-to-head with the JVC JAZZ FESTIVAL (New York, NY — see chapter). These decisions seem to have done the trick.

It now looks like L. I.'s got jazz festivals up and running on all three cylinders. So rev up the station wagon, throw your beach gear in the back, and prepare to bask in first-rate jazz! Oh, and for a little local color, tune into "Howierd" in the morning. Maybe he'll have "Jo-wee" on the line.

"Theodora Bookman." Even the Promoter's name bespeaks the Gatsby-era ambience of the LONG ISLAND JAZZ FESTIVAL. Yet her first request over the phone was "Call me Teddy." Thus the warm, gracious, and ever-enthusiastic Bookman distanced herself and her festival as much as humanly possible from the Amy Fisher crowd.       **Festival Review I**

Bookman's FOA just celebrated 20 years of presenting national acts for its seasonal series. At roughly 10 dates spanning classical, jazz, pop, and folk, their LONG ISLAND SUMMER FESTIVAL certainly doesn't compete in volume with such outdoor "sheds" as found 30 minutes south at Jones Beach. But its high-caliber bookings put it on the same conservative circuit as Tanglewood (TANGLEWOOD JAZZ FESTIVAL/FESTIVAL OF CONTEMPORARY MUSIC, Lenox, MA — see chapter), SPAC (NEWPORT JAZZ FESTIVAL/SARATOGA, Saratoga, NY — see chapter), ArtPark (see ARTPARK JAZZ/FOLK FESTIVALS, Lewiston, NY, Late August) and others like 'em. A white wedding tent hoisted above the stage covers priority seating, while general-admission patrons spread out designer blankets and well-stocked wicker baskets upon the lawn.

And, ah, what a lawn!

The Planting Fields Arboretum was one of many Gold-Coast estates turned over to government for charity when L. I.'s soaring property taxes outstripped the trust funds that maintained them. In this case, it was the 65-room Tudor mansion and 500 landscaped acres of William Robertson Coe who donated them both to New York State in '49. Coe had a knack for gardening, thus the designation of Arboretum to prepare you for its vast greenhouse displays, soaring trees, voluminous shrubs and sweeping lawns. Forget the concerts, you'd pay the modest admission fee any of 365 days a year just to breathe in its peaceful inspiration "far from the madding crowd."

When you lay down for a show, you'll likely find yourself gazing upon a century-old English garden, rose bushes and all. Or up at a 150-foot-high elm tree, one of few remaining. I found myself too mesmerized by the twinkling stars to take many notes on Dorothy Donegan,

George Wein's Newport All Stars, and Illinois Jacquet's Big Band come Sunday night. When I picked up *Newsday* to read the ordinarily-astute Wayne Robbins (who I pattern my approach after), I found it funny how he'd similarly succumbed for the prior eve's pairing of Ray Charles and Ruth Brown: "...I was lying upon my blanket looking at the sky on a night so clear that stars from possibly uncharted galaxies were visible...while that shiny moon seemed so close you could almost touch it." Misplaced your notepad too, eh?

This anecdote evokes an amused sigh from Bookman: "In a way the ambiance is the star, which is too bad." She's got ambitions, however, in wedding it to a diverse lineup of jazz stars sufficient for attracting a national and international crowd. Luring monied tourists is her ultimate objective, so much so that she hadn't even focused on the many L. I. connections of her musical bill.

"Without aiming for it, it happened because so many great musicians live on L. I. — one tells another," Bookman explains, citing Buddy Tate's being one of many locals recruited by Jacquet for his own Sunday-night tribute. This familiarity tends to bring backstage affections up front, something Bookman is consciously committed to:

- "I must say we treat all our artists with tremendous respect and we try to make them feel as comfortable as possible. There's a friendliness, there's a real rapport that starts almost immediately. We had wonderful lunches and dinners with musicians and their friends. People who are in the business could come and join them and say, 'Hello.'

  "There was just a spirit behind stage that pervaded the whole festival of a big family reunion where everybody liked each other! It was people like George Wein saying, 'Teddy, you've really got something going here. It reminds me of NEWPORT when it first started (JVC JAZZ FESTIVAL/NEWPORT, Newport, RI — see chapter), and I really feel you're gonna make it!'"

Bookman's positive feedback stems from careful attention to her artists, sure, but in more ways than just hospitality. First, she's loyal to her nearest and dearest. Clark Terry's appearance, for one, honored his being FOA's first jazz act 16 years prior. Second, she's adamant in according her jazz concerts the same status as her classical concerts. (I personally can't understand their collective chip-on-the-shoulder over what's basically a dead art form, but jazz artists take the issue quite seriously. "America's classical music," they'll insist.) Bookman's an outspoken champion on the issue, especially for her beloved "jazz legacy" types.

Third, and most importantly from my perspective, Bookman fails to take the safe route oh-so-easy in her position, but strives to embrace all her potential musical constituencies, including:

- <u>Cutting edge</u> (Saturday afternoon featuring three generations of experimenters: David Murray Trio, Don Byron Quintet, and Dewey Redmen Quartet): "I did want the young people in; I wanted that contrast; I wanted the emerging artists, the new sounds of jazz, to appear."

- <u>Crossover</u> (Friday night's spotlighting The Rippingtons following Michel Camilo Trio and Arturo Sandoval Quintet): "Let's face it, there's a whole younger generation, and if we don't target them between the ages of 25 and 45 who are the 'CD101' listeners... Although the old jazz artists don't consider that jazz, it's a way of getting them in. It's a hook."

Nor is Bookman complacent with her current reach. "I never like to stand still," she exclaims, "I want to grow!

- "This coming summer we're starting a Choral Jazz Institute involving 60 kids from junior and senior high. They'll be performing in the jazz festival. There'll be three professional administrators of this program. Part of it is, I believe in the educational aspect of it. It's a way of reaching youth. I'm gonna' target those disadvantaged areas, and I want it to really foster better understanding, camaraderie, hopefully breaking down some racial barriers. And what better way to do it than with a common denominator of jazz and voice. We'll invite the families and they'll come.

"I also want to do some gospel. There are on L. I. some of the best gospel groups. I was down at NEW ORLEANS (see NEW ORLEANS JAZZ AND HERITAGE FESTIVAL, New Orleans, LA, Late April to Early May), I mean, I love that gospel tent! That brings in a whole new denomination."

Bookman still needs to clear gospel's religious content with State Park administrators, but her educational outreach is already in full swing.

It all fosters her desire to overcome L. I.'s various stigmas, including Buttafoucco:

- "That's why I'm changing the names now to the LONG ISLAND SUMMER FESTIVAL and the LONG ISLAND JAZZ FESTIVAL, to give L. I. the needed lift and association with something that people can feel good about. It's gotta' overcome a lot of stuff and have an identity of its own. We can certainly compete with New York and its environs because you can go to a jazz concert in the city in the summertime, but it ain't the same as being out in this beautiful surrounding an hour away.

  "In the back of my mind for a long time has been the idea of creating a LONG ISLAND JAZZ FESTIVAL. The location, the beauty of this particular place was a perfect marriage. And to have it culminate in one weekend when I only had less than a year to put it together was so rewarding [when reviewing] the quality of what the audience told me and what the critics told me."

**Artist Mini-Reviews**

I confess, I dogged it under the stars Sunday evening! I've few notes besides the copious gourmet picnics nibbled by the upper-middle-class crowd, evenly combining white and black families. Apparently, it's "whoever eats best, wins."

Dorothy Donegan was her usual wacky self — her schizophrenic piano medleys nimbly followed by Ray Mosca's drums. Caution: irreverent genius at work. One such collage segued from a cat-and-mouse "Misty," to a rollicking boogie-woogie, to a minuet treatment of "Glory, Glory Hallelujah," back to the boogie-woogie, over to "What'd I Say," into a little dancing interlude by Donegan, and onto more minuet before finishing with a rhumba-flavored "Bye, Bye Blackbird." Whew! Jacquet came out to join her for a closing vocal duet of "Sunny Side of the Street."

George Wein then showed off a wonderfully diverse group of his Newport All Stars from septuagenarian trumpet plunger, Al Grey, down to thirtyish Howard Alden on keys. I liked how the intensity of the younger players, notably Warren Vache's aggressive trumpet, played against the older cats to pep up their jazz standards. Wein, himself, debuted some surprisingly effect vocal growlings. The highlight came when Alden and tenor-sax legend, Flip Phillips, performed a duet on a Django Reinhardt ballad delivering an impossible-to-describe combination of smoothness and syncopation, melancholy and sly knowing. A bewitching moment accompanied only by the crickets.

For Illinois Jacquet's Big Band, I felt guilty departing midway through to catch up on some much-needed sleep, especially since this tenor-sax titan was the one being honored. Apparently, Jacquet's 16-piece unit ran through one set (including "Twinkle Toes," a deliciously-paced "Moten Swing," and "Blue and Sentimental") before the awards were presented. Grover Washington Jr., who Jacquet had met earlier in the year when they performed together at President Clinton's Inaugural Ball, then sat in for a closing jam.

Jacquet's soloed with more passion elsewhere (see below), but I've never seen him in a more expansive mood between songs. I could readily picture his past teaching gig at Harvard as he shared terrific reminiscences on his musical journey and the underlying love of the music's heritage driving him and all his heroes. Nevermind Jacquet's superb musicianship, just hire him to speak and inspire!

Bookman:

- "It was kismet, I swear. I met Illinois and told him about what I had in mind. He loved it, saying, 'Sure I'll help you!' When it came to working out the Sunday night, we went out to lunch several times and went to his house in St. Albans, Queens to discuss it all. I knew I wanted somebody of the younger generation. I knew I needed a name, because Illinois is not a household name, but Grover is. And I said, 'What about Grover,' because they had just done that White House jazz presentation. He said, 'Well, Grover and I really hit it off. We both feel the same way about jazz.'

"Of course, they have disdain for some of the new sounds of jazz and I understand where they're coming from. It's not something that comes from that spirit that all of them seem to have, that takes them to that higher level. He said, 'Grover really has my philosophy,' and told me to get in touch with him. I couldn't afford to have his whole band, explaining, 'This is a tribute to Illinois.' I put it that way, and we worked out a price for him to come as a guest artist.

"Grover loved it, and that's what created that spirit. This is really where Grover's heart is at. It happened only indirectly through me, but I really did love that ending with the jam session."

~     ~     ~

**Festival Review II**   By contrast, L. I.'s other beloved jazz doyen, IAJ Executive Director Ann Sneed, goes for local flavor in full measure. Her nonprofit has been stoking the home fires for a remarkable 30 years, so when it comes time for IAJ's two-day ISLIP JAZZ FESTIVAL, Sneed has a heavy Rolodex of local names (or rather a Rolodex of heavy local names) to call upon.

Sponsored primarily by State University at Stony Brook's Center for Excellence and Innovation in Education, IAJ has been strongly active in schools at all levels. Their over-riding mission has been to use jazz as "a communications vehicle to improve multi-cultural awareness and appreciation" decades before such sentiments became vogue. Moreover, IAJ perceives jazz musicians as "role models who stress the importance of self-esteem, self-expression, and self-discipline." No stone goes unturned as Steed integrates them fully into the classroom experience with "Performance/Demonstrations" that might just as easily be in English and Social Studies classes where musicians relate their international travel experiences, as in Music Class workshops and auditorium performances. IAJ also develops curriculum aids through its Teacher's Resource Unit and has maintained a scholarship program now bearing fruit, as numerous recipient musicians are so introduced onstage at IAJ affairs. Awards have followed IAJ in droves.

The bottom line is that everybody gains, especially the jazz artists. Factor in three decades of good vibes, and IAJ loyalty mushrooms like an H-bomb. You'll hear it up on stage, particularly when it comes time for Sneed to honor each night's headliner. They won't just accept and continue playing, but stop and give extended acceptances loaded with anecdotes and rendered straight from the heart.

In fact, I often wonder if Sneed didn't institute her festival's relatively unique jam-session format as a means of accommodating as many musician friends as possible over the course of an evening. (I've since discovered traditional jazz festivals being structured so, but never a mainstream jazz festival.) Regardless, it lends the weekend a palpable intimacy: musician-to-promoter; musician-to-musician; musician-to-fan; fan-to-fan. If not for the superb playing, you'd almost forget there was a festival going on!

Getting there is swift. The Southern State Parkway dead-ends right into Hecksher State Park. This cluster of grassy expanses rimmed by scrub pines yields superb acoustics. Apparently, you can swim beyond the trees — even camp on the grounds. I've never known anyone to do other than picnic there, with the big crowds usually petering out by the time the music starts. This leaves you alone on your beach chair with an easy-going assembly of 5,000 suburbanite jazz buffs with their kids.

The festivities generally commence at five p.m. Township pols (who will hopefully be too ashamed to show their faces after last year's funding hiatus) take a few minutes out between grandstanding to kick off the proceedings in their thick L. I. accents. For the first three hours this means set changes every 25 minutes. As the succeeding artists grow in stature, their sets will grow in length until the headliner closes it out with an hour-plus performance.

Even though it's free, you won't want to just come and go, but rather budget the entire evening.

Surprises come in three varieties, often boasting a L. I. flavor. First, there's the rising talent you might not have heard of yet but may well soon (e.g., Lynne Arriale, Ifeachor Okeke, Rebecca Coupe Franks, Ron Jackson). Second, there's the top session players you might not recognize by name, but certainly will by their impressive credits (e.g., Danilo Perez, Lynn Seaton, Mark Elf, David Randall). They'll be jamming with the rising stars or fronting their own session. Third, there's always the unexpected sit-ins prompted, I imagine, by Sneed backstage.

It's all a brisk flurry of names and instruments being whisked about the portable stage, but Sneed recruits a pair of knowledgeable radio personalities to help sort 'em out and keep 'em moving. Thanks to this casual freewheeling, the ISLIP JAZZ FESTIVAL amply supplies what IAJ describes as its classroom experiences: "discoveries that excite!"

Two headlining sets still stand out among my ten most memorable ever, both from 1989.

**Artist Mini-Reviews**

As I recall, <u>Illinois Jacquet</u> was debuting his Big Band with Buddy Tate guesting on tenor sax and there to receive Sneed's award. Even though he and Tate both grew up in Texas, they'd spent so many years living locally that Jacquet described the gig as "hometown" to *Newsday* reporter Will Friedwald. The reviews had been raves during recent weeks, yet Jacquet was leaving nothing to chance. He basically took center stage and wailed — I mean wailed! — on solo after solo for a solid hour. I've never been so impressed with the sheer authority of someone's playing, as his dynamic star-turn would've left most rockers panting in his wake. Impressive, with impressive backing, too!

<u>Ruth Brown</u> wasn't quite that strong the next night. She'd been maintaining a seven-shows-per-week schedule for her Tony-Award-winning role on Broadway's "Black and Blue." This pace had taken a temporary toll on her voice, which I've since had a chance to hear in its full glory at THE BIG GIG (see Richmond, VA, Middle July to Late July). And it's a remarkable voice — one of the few alongside Ray Charles', Delbert McClinton's and precious others — which combines a C&W tear with an R&B vocabulary for an unmatched versatility of emotional interpretation.

No, what was very special was Sneed's "Ruth Brown Day" presentation. Brown recounted in tears how her own IAJ involvement sustained her through two decades of welfare motherhood in nearby Huntington and driving a bus for a Deer Park church.

As you know, Brown now occupies the Rock and Roll Hall of Fame for her extraordinary run of R&B hits during the '50s. Atlantic Records became known then as "The House That Ruth Built." Unfortunately, Brown's questioning the disappearance of her earnings led to a virtual banishment from the music industry. She slowly climbed back in 20 years to the Broadway revue which re-launched her recording career, but her determination to right these royalty wrongs led her to team with Charles in forming the Rhythm and Blues Foundation. Together, they've been instrumental in wrangling payments owed from record companies and in providing for destitute former R&B stars.

That night, though, the struggle almost seemed worth it all. Brown took her roses, looked out in the audience, and began naming kids she'd taught over the years. She talked at length about her many years spent in poverty, and of the sustaining faith and community support which kept her going. When Sneed embraced her, it was as if the entire audience joined in — a truly uplifting moment no sound bite could ever capture!

**Travel Tip**

The three most important travel tips for L. I.'s summertime visitors are: beaches, beaches, beaches. An oversimplification, but it's hard to ignore Robert Moses State Park/Fire Island National Seashore that offers some of the best swimming and sunbathing on the entire East Coast. And wait'll you see what the Amy Fishers wear!

Otherwise there are innumerable converted estates, several of which house fine arts museums, including Roslyn's Nassau County Fine Arts Museum and Southampton's Guild Hall. Historic towns dating back to the 1640's also dot the map.

As far as live music goes, L. I. is one of those rare markets where the daily newspaper, *Newsday*, generally out-covers the various weeklies, especially with concerts and festivals. Check the Friday edition for listings. Of course, New York City is commuting distance by car or rail, but your best strategy is to go against the grain of its brutal rush-hours. This applies not only to daytripping, but to vacation planning in general. Visit the tony Hamptons during the week when everyone's in the city, and vice-versa.

**See Also** Despite its role as Suffolk County's government seat, tiny Riverhead is very unassuming. Don't expect any Hamptons glitz and glamor. Of course, that's what I like about it. I can sit down in a local diner for some chowder while I read the paper or stroll up the street to Spicy's Barbeque for some of the best ribs and chicken north of South Carolina (seriously, ask around). Or I can drop into the RIVERHEAD JAZZ FESTIVAL on July 4th weekend.

The EEAC throws it down on the small lawn behind its reclaimed fisherman's cottage. They present two national acts daily along with a handful of solid locals. You can tune into the music, nosh among the ethnic food booths, imbibe from a copious wine bar stocked from among the area's vintners, or let your gaze drift among the reeds and rushes as the adjoining Peconic River flows lazily on out to the bay. Again, very unassuming, but very relaxing, too.

~ ~ ~

# Ithaca's New Old-Time Scene, III

ROONEY MOUNTAIN BLUEGRASS FESTIVAL, Deposit, NY
> Late July to Early August
> Bluegrass
> ***Attended***

MIDDLESEX MUSIC FESTIVAL, Middlesex, NY
> Late July
> Alternative and College Rock

**Introduction**

I first found out about this unique festival experience, known simply as "ROONEY" (slur it out in repeated hollers, like "Sooo-ey!"), from the thrash-grass band, Killbilly. They'd staggered into '92's SCENIC RIVER DAYS (see Reading, PA, Late July) the afternoon after their post-midnight ROONEY wrap-up and followed a Southern gospel act, no less, for a surrealistic segue-way.

They just couldn't stop muttering woozy praises on stage to the nuclear party they'd helped fuel the night before by firing up a frenzied bluegrass version of Hendrix's "Little Wing." The lead singer marvelled how every piece of the band's equipment and every stitch of their clothing had been slathered with mud, and how he planned to tote a pair of waders for next year's return engagement. Between sets, Louis Meyers, who was subbing for the band's regular banjo player, admiringly summarized the gig as "100% anarchy, 100% alcohol, 100% of the time." He cited bikers pounding back cases at a clip, hippies taking headers into knee-deep slop, and hundreds of women obliging the sign above the stage requesting them to "lift their shirts," shall we say. The best piece of advice offered to Myers was not to drink anything handed to him at the risk of tripping into Christmas. Fortunately, he steered clear enough to be awed by the fiddling of Vassar Clements who'd preceded him.

I immediately penciled it into my date book for next year.

A few months prior to my date with destiny, I phoned Linda Bolton who manages progressive bluegrassers, Northern Lights. She told me she'd scheduled the band there. It appears that Promoter Mary Doub wanted to give them a breather from repeated bookings at the WINTERHAWK BLUEGRASS FESTIVAL (Hillsdale, NY — see chapter). Bolton asked me if I knew anything about ROONEY.

I had to laugh! Musically, Northern Lights isn't too far off from ROONEY's mix of old-timey updates and bluegrass/rock crossovers drawn from throughout the Ithaca scene. After all, Clements guested on one of Northern Lights' albums. Personality-wise, however, putting this classy, clean-living family band into the midst of the mayhem Myers relayed was like pouring milk into moonshine.

I went back into my date book and red-pencilled it.

**Festival Review**

I couldn't "ROONEY" very long Saturday night having caught the superb POCONOS BLUES FESTIVAL (see Big Boulder Lake, PA, Late July to Early August) earlier in the day and being due back in New York City later that night. This precluded me from staying for Killbilly's now-traditional closing set, I'm sorry to say, but even the hour-plus I spent alternately chuckling at and pitying Northern Lights' plight was plenty.

The festival occupies a tall hill hanging back behind a quiet Catskills railstop, equal parts preserved and neglected. Picture a typical Appalachian hill village. You follow Main Street out beyond the cow pastures to Beebe Hill Road located by the flashing lights from the patrol car hovering near the entrance like a vulture awaiting its prey. Afternoon showers turned the single-lane cow path into a stream as cars chose to park at the road's base rather than risk the slippery ride to the top. I bailed out, too, and began the long trudge upwards in the dusk.

Normally you can hear the music before you see it. This time, though, I could hear the crowd's roar well before the first frantic strains of a fiddle. The roar got louder and louder the closer I got. I hit Checkpoint Charlie and had to foist my entry fee upon the giddily shell-shocked ticket-takers. One wore a puke-green festival T-shirt but had no advice on where I could pick one up for my collection. "Where's the stage," I hesitated. "Oh," she intoned absently, "just keep going up...there."

I felt like Captain Kurtz heading up-country in Coppolla's film, *Apocalypse Now*. ("The horror, the horror!") Past pickups and "winter rats" strewn every which-a-way. Past packs of stringy, soaked twenty-somethings whizzing by with "Genny grenades" in each hand. At last I made it — pay dirt!

As I quickly suspected, and a horrified Bolton later confirmed, they'd watered down the stage vicinity to create a mucky, foot-deep landing pad to cushion the falls from the hundreds of wobbly patrons who were maybe just a few more beers short of flopping over and out. She claimed they'd even let a greased pig loose to christen it. I'm at a loss to fully describe the gonzo scene any further than to repeat the battle cry from the attending legions who all desperately needed more blood in their alcohol systems: "Roooooooooooooo-ney!"

**Attendance Tip**  Whether or not you choose to "Rooney" depends on to whom you feel closer akin:

- Long-haired, grunge-clad Meyers who also runs the South by Southwest Conference (see Austin, TX, Late March) for thousands of rowdy roots-rockers;

- Or clean-cut Bolton, a proper vegetarian with two grown kids who's positioning her band towards performing arts centers.

I fit somewhere in the middle with a wide latitude toward either extreme. That's why I prefer the Fingerlakes Grassroots Festival of Music and Dance (Trumansburg, NY — see chapter) and it's many companion festivals. It's got the better of Rooney's bands plus its free-wheeling, communal vibe without the menace. Lucky for you, one of these companions happens the same weekend as Rooney, the Middlesex Music Festival on pretty Canandaigua Lake. Tie it together with 'Fingerlakes' the prior weekend and you can make it a vacation week to remember!

However, if you're leaning more towards Meyers (and you know who you are you naughty creatures of the malt, hops, barley, leaf, grape, and grain), you should beware that Rooney is still miles beyond anything I've experienced — even New Orleans on 20 Dixies a day. In the brief time I was there, admittedly in the eye of the hurricane, I managed to side-step three fights.

I guess that's my caution.

Promoter Dave Baskerville doesn't court publicity and declined all my attempts at interviews. Meyers told me he wants to keep Rooney to about 5,000 friends to avoid it becoming a "Sturgis" (i.e., the notorious annual rendezvous in South Dakota for hundreds of thousands of Harley riders). I wouldn't necessarily feel any more comfortable at a biker blast, but I suspect they'd be better able to handle their drugs of choice than the hyper Deadheads and rough-edged townies who populated Rooney. After all, you don't take up to 75 cocaine hits a night, as one New York City Hell's Angel testified in a recent drug trial, without building up a certain level of bodily tolerance.

Bolton remembered that one derelict tried to heist an entire camper off the back of a pickup behind them. When its owner arrived, he pounded the aspiring thief all the way down to the waiting ambulance. There is a potentially ugly side here, so be careful, set up your tent on the fringes, and ease back if it gets more than you can handle. And watch for the cops who hover the town for anyone going one smidgen faster than the posted 30 m.p.h. limit.

**See Also**  You can pretty much turn your corner of most any festival into a personal "party out of bounds." One year, I remember our civilized site at Winterhawk' adjoining eight frat boys who'd stacked their van with 50 cases of beer for the weekend. That's right, five-oh! I peeked out my tent flap around three a.m. to see them all half-naked, wrapped in plastic, whoopin' and sliding down the hill smack into the bushes.

And that's fine, because even though 99% of festival experiences are good clean fun for the whole family, their over-riding attraction is the freedom they offer — freedom from high prices and sterile auditoriums and assigned seats and programmed productions and boring concessions and every other Pavlovian stimulus that characterizes the typical concert experience. When was the last time you had a campfire jam or song swap at a concert hall, for example? Festivals let you imbibe what you feel like, musically or otherwise, whenever you feel like it. That's their beauty as long as you don't impose your lifestyle on your neighbors without their permission.

However, if you really wanna' let loose amidst lots of company -- to "Rooney" in its various permutations -- here are my other "party-hearty" recommendations from around the region:

- Hard Rock and Heavy Metal: LOUD MUSIC FESTIVAL, Northampton, MA, Early April;

- Modern Jazz: NEWPORT JAZZ FESTIVAL/SARATOGA, Saratoga Springs, NY, Early July;

- Traditional Jazz and Dixieland: ELKHART JAZZ FESTIVAL, Elkhart, IN, Late June;

- Blues and Traditional R&B: LEVITTOWN R&B PICNIC, Levittown, PA, Middle July;

- Modern Country: JAMBOREE IN THE HILLS, St. Clairsville, OH, Middle July;

- Fiddle and Banjo Events: OLD FIDDLERS' CONVENTION, Galax, VA, Early August (on the concluding weekend, that is; mid-week is much saner);

- Irish: ROCKAWAY BEACH IRISH FESTIVAL, Queens, NYC, Late July;

- Modern Latin: PUERTO RICAN DAY PARADE, Manhattan, NYC, Middle June;

- Brazilian and South American: BRAZILIAN STREET FESTIVAL, Manhattan, NYC, Early September;

- Reggae, Ska and Caribbean: WEST-INDIAN-AMERICAN DAY CARNIVAL AND FESTIVAL, Brooklyn, NYC, Early September;

- Gay and Lesbian: WIGSTOCK, Manhattan, NYC, Early September.

There are others on my list (KENTUCKY DERBY FESTIVAL, Louisville, KY, Early April; ROCKABILLY WEEKEND, Marion, IN, Early August; THUNDER ON THE BEACH, Virginia Beach, VA, Early July), but I have to visit — or should I say "survive" — them first to confirm their addition. Enjoy!

~        ~        ~

# Artist Sightings, III: Paul Simon

GREAT MIRACLE PRAYER FESTIVAL, Manhattan, NYC
    Late February
    Modern Rock and Pop

RAINFOREST BENEFIT CONCERT, Manhattan, NYC
    Middle April
    Modern Rock and Pop

**BACK AT THE RANCH FESTIVAL**, Montauk Point, NY
    Early August
    Modern Rock and Pop
    ***Attended***

**Introduction**    The BACK AT THE RANCH FESTIVAL ['RANCH'] owns the unique distinction of being simultaneously the least publicized music festival in the entire country, as well as the most publicized.

A paradox, you say? Well, here's the deal.

Understand that Montauk is where Paul Simon lives. He's walking a tightrope between hosting an event to raise significant funds for the area's charities, yet avoiding turning the private retreat of his wealthy, often testy, neighbors into the circus you can well-imagine it becoming. This translates into confining advance notice to a few neighborhood weeklies — the equivalent of advertising a Broadway opening in the neighborhood *Pennysaver* — thus reserving the first 11,000 tickets for locals who pick up on the whispers. (An additional 1,000 tickets are usually released sometime later.) It's probably the only major music festival where the local Chamber of Commerce has the scoop.

But immediately proceeding its stealth occurrence, the media floodgates open wide. No other music festival consistently garners as much national coverage. You can usually count on a big spread in *Rolling Stone*, similar coverage in New York City's four dailies, a paragraph in those personality sections that occupy, say, the fourth page or so in every other daily across the country, and whatever else the national print and television magazines have to report. I've often imagined setting up my writing career for life merely by hanging backstage among the profusion of media bigs.

Why all the fuss? First, it's Paul Simon playing anywhere from a few tunes to a full set for his adopted hometown fans. Second, it's a few of Simon's musical pals: some billed ('93's Allman Brothers, Mary Chapin Carpenter); some walk-ons ('92's G. E. Smith and High Plains Drifters, Toots Thielemans). I've yet to see Simon's wife, Edie Brickell, with anything other than a camcorder in her hands, but I expect her regular cameo sometime after their babies grow older.

Third, it's the historic village of Montauk Point on the nation's oldest cattle ranch dating back to 1661. That's no misprint. The Indian River Ranch remains a fully-operational spread more than three centuries old that gave us the country's very first cowboys. It's also accomplished Simon's balancing act flawlessly in handling a major-league rock concert that raises nearly half-a-million dollars a year, while keeping the prickly homefires quiet.

That homefires thing is no small potatoes. The same year the 'RANCH' kicked off in '90, Paul Simon's brother, Eddie, who owns radio station WWHB-FM in Hampton Bays, attempted the EVIAN MUSIC FESTIVAL down the road in Southampton. He sought to program intimate concerts by musical legends, supplemented by master classes. The three shows were by Miles Davis; The New York Rock and Soul Review with Donald Fagen and Bill Withers; and Ray Charles on Cooper Beach before a mere 1,200! The three "Advanced Musician Seminars" were with Taj Mahal, Jorma

Kaukonen and brother Paul in Amagansett's renown hole-in-the-wall, The Stephen Talkhouse.

Eddie Simon's goal was to select only musicians who'd stood the test of time and to create spontaneous environments where the audience could literally "interview" the artists and come away with "life-lasting" musical insights. Fabulous, huh? Well, not to Southampton's snooty dowagers who agitated that Charles' beach-side gig disturbed their precious tea parties. They prevailed and squashed the festival's re-occurrence.

Now, consider that Montauk's multi-millionaires summer here to peaceably escape Southampton's millionaires. There's only one thin blacktop connecting Montauk to the mainland for nearly 30 miles, which is why this narrow tip offered such a convenient shoot for herding cattle off their grasslands and into their pens. Open it up loud and proud, like with Paul Simon's free celebration that drew 750,000 to Central Park, and you'd still be unclogging traffic bottlenecks today, not to mention stirring up a bee's nest of angry dwellers with enough clout to make your life miserable.

Enter Rusty Lever, owner of Indian Field Ranch and Producer of its annual homecoming for Simon.

He'd given his neighbors confidence that his grazing pastures could handle crowds from having hosted a rodeo onsite for a number of years. Simon agreed and met with Lever over coffee in '89 to discuss a possible benefit. Lever and The Nature Conservancy had just teamed up regarding preserving Indian Field Ranch's open spaces and restoring Montauk Point's grasslands of yore. (How about that, ranchers and environmentalists working together!) Lever mentioned his then-recent cause; Simon the need of the Montauk Historical Society to restore its fabled, 19th-century lighthouse. Together they drew up a quick menu of deserving recipients. Simon would phone some performing friends, but Lever had to work out the arcane logistics of making the 'RANCH's big production seem breathlessly small.

"I think that's one of the keys to our success is that it's been a borderline military operation from the first year that we did this," Lever recounts:

- "We were so paranoid at the Ranch ourselves about having an event that would be welcomed by the community. And, of course, there was an awesome responsibility of having Paul Simon appear here. I certainly wanted to do him justice. The first year we just developed a strategy we thought that addressed most of the major issues and the potential problems and the way we sold the tickets. We felt we'd done everything we could.

  "It's a hometown event — that was [Simon's] idea. Even though we've escalated to nearly 12,000 people now, I still try to maintain that hometown feeling. [Among] the reasons, I think, the site is a great aesthetic environment for the event, but also we only sell the tickets in a way that makes it hard for people to even get ahold of them unless you're part of the community. Had we made the tickets available through TicketMaster or TicketTron, you'd have a whole different blend of folks here — not that that would be bad, it would just mean you'd have everybody from further up the Island just traipsing through everybody's back yard here. Then I think that's how you build up the resentment. In the way we do it, it's as if everybody understands locally that they get first licks and last licks at all the tickets.

  "Also I think you know we've done this enough and there's a lot of money left over at the end. It's not like one of these events where everybody says, 'Hey, great! We're going to this benefit and they give out $50,000.' Last year we gave out net $400,000 from a one-day event, so that's something we're all pretty proud of!"

So, how does Lever raise that kind of cash? There's $30-plus tickets and proceeds from a first-rate concession stand. There's also steeply-priced T-shirts, which are nevertheless artfully designed and coveted as an insider statement of East End chic. A big chunk, interestingly enough, comes from a glossy full-sized, full-color program booklet that runs 90 pages. Lever rounds up his "Friends of the 'RANCH' Committee," and has them rout out advertising from their high-powered friends. Check out a few of these names from its 90-member panel: Jayni and Chevy Chase, Bette-Ann and Charles Gwathmey, Mr. and Mrs. Percy Heath, Kelly and Calvin Klein, Mr. and Mrs.

Ronald S. Lauder, Alice and Lorne Michaels — you get the picture. They get every other Hamptonite into the act, including Dick Cavett who conducts the booklet's interviews and does the day's M. C. chores.

All this fund-raising wrangles a good share of Lever's attention:

- "I start probably in November for the event that goes off in August. We're sort of heads-down and just full-ahead workin' on all the aspects that will make a successful event and make a lot of net profit. Our concert journal probably nets us about $100,000, alone. We're all so focused on that, we don't even think about the music that much — it's gonna' be taken care of by Paul and by the other artists.

  "However, at that moment when they hit the stage, I always get chills. I always think 'Wow, this is really cool, you know. This is really pretty neat.' We've had Don Henley here, Billy Joel, Paul Simon, some of the greatest talent in the country, most of whom are legends in the industry at this point. I mean, to have the whole Highwaymen on there, of course, was a real rush."

Lever's Billy Joel reference was to the East End resident deciding for the 'Ranch's second year that it was his turn and recruiting Henley, Marc Cohn, Joe Ely, Crystal Taliefero, Ric Ocasek, Foreigner, and Carly Simon to support his two-day headlining gig. The Highwaymen's '92 appearance owes to Simon playing Willie Nelson's annual birthday picnic down Austin-way, then having Nelson and friends return the favor.

This underscores what has since become the 'Ranch's most interesting musical feature — a C&W presence still all too rare in the mainstream festival world. "I think [Simon's] what helps us draw some of the real serious country artists, especially the ones like Mary Chapin Carpenter," Lever reveals:

- "She's a writer more than anything. I mean, she's a great performer, but she's [also] a great writer, and I think great writers tend to respect each other's work. When I spoke to Mary Chapin's people and tried to set it up, I mentioned that I do this as an annual event with Paul Simon. And there's just something that appealed to Mary Chapin right away as writer-to-writer [about] the idea of performing with somebody that has that talent.

  "And, of course, the other thing that helps is Paul is always very gracious and willing to perform with other artists. Any of these country people seem to immediately say, 'Sure, I'd love to! I'd like to do a Paul Simon song with Paul Simon.' I know Mary Chapin felt the same way last year. Paul Simon's just got such great musical chops that the serious musicians, the serious country-western writers, say, 'Paul Simon? Sure, we'd love to be there!'

  "It also helps me when I speak to these country-western folks about playing at this venue. It doesn't hurt that I mention it's America's oldest cattle ranch." Indeed.

"We're just happy to be doing it," Lever reflects:

- "We're honored to be associated with Paul Simon which appears to be the way it is gonna' go each year. Paul Simon's people assist us in some of the production and they've done a great job. So we have this great team of not only people who are professionals in the rock-and-roll business, but our people at the Ranch are now seasoned, rock-and-roll productions people. Then the local community has been tremendously supportive — the police department and the fire department. Everybody knows their positions, and their jobs, and just what to do. It's actually gotten a little easier each year. At this point we've raised $1.4 million in net proceeds."

And for Montauk's privileged music fans? "It's definitely an opportunity for world-class talent to be seen in a different atmosphere," Lever adds, "a little rougher edges."

**Festival Review** Lever's "rougher edges" comment might appear incongruous at first, until you reach the front gates to the 'Ranch'. Before you spreads a rough field rimmed by scrub oaks. Lever's put the stage just before the cattle pens, and parked the artists' tour buses inside the small rodeo circle. He's also scattered hay bales about to delineate the aisles. There's no beach view, but the site's definitely rustic — perfect for a little "country and eastern."

There were three seating areas: "well to-do," "to-do," and "do-do." I entered the latter, plopped myself down amidst deeply-tanned middle-agers, catalogued some egregious "Lawn Guyland" accents, and prepared for a near-perfect musical afternoon. Here are my notes from '92.

Toots Thielemans. Jazz harmonica maestro Thielemans came out for just one song, an original **Artist** composition written for the day, "On Montauk." Guitarist Dennis Phelps handled the vocals, **Mini-Reviews** while bassist Percy Heath and drummer Dave Weckl backed 'em up. This nice mood-maker invited a whole set. Alas.

G. E. Smith and High Plains Drifters. Smith's six songs mostly served to speed the lines to the refreshment tent. There was none of the intriguingly funky, off-center eclecticism that characterizes his TV bits. Instead, Smith's four-piece outfit grappled with a nondescript roots-rock that awkwardly straddled "songwriter-ish" and "instrumental-ism." Smith's own guitar leads, best imagined as "sweet-spot grunge," were it's strongest feature.

The Highwaymen. Man, what a treat! Part of the fun was simply hearing these four legends together. I mean, here were the three festival "C's" — contrasts, comparisons and collaborations — being played out at the very highest level all at once!

The other part was checking out the welling response from this otherwise pro-Simon throng, which may have been hearing their first C&W live. (I believe The Highwaymen assumed so, too. At one point Johnny Cash gave a lengthy introduction to his former bandmate backstage, Marty Stuart, that assumed the crowd didn't know who Stuart was. They didn't. Stuart walked onstage, bowed to the tepid response, then sheepishly strode back. Cash hoped Stuart would play a tune, it appears, but this lack of recognition seemed to frighten Stuart off.) No personality-cult lockstep common with country crowds, just an honest reaction to four strong characters that grew as their even stronger songs accumulated.

With the pressure off, all save Willie Nelson bantered plenty.

- Kris Kristofferson to crowd: "I think a bunch of y'all are lookin' at us and saying, 'I bet them's older than that; I'll bet a few of 'em are dead!' But, we ain't!"

- Waylon Jennings to crowd, introducing his then new "I'm Too Dumb for NYC, Too Ugly for LA": "My first trip here almost stunted my growth."

- Cash to Kristofferson: "We're all crazy here, but you're the craziest!"

- Jennings to crowd, mostly about Kristofferson: "There's a lot of brain damage around up here!"

This fab foursome combined on a 20-tune orgy of greatest hits even this audience could recognize: Nelson's "Mama, Don't Let Your Babies Grown Up to Be Cowboys," Kristofferson's "Sunday Mornin' Comin' Down," Cash's "Ring of Fire," Guy Clark's "Desperadoes Waiting for a Train," Nelson's "Always on My Mind," and on and on, before ending with Jennings' "Let's Go Back to Luckenbach, Texas" and Nelson's "On the Road Again."

Kristofferson was the loosest cannon, though. When introducing "Slouching to the Millennium," he castigated the military for it's recent attack on Iraq as "cold-blooded, low-vision S. O. B.'s who wanna' go across the world and bomb a bunch of people." A more typically light-hearted action was his egging Jennings on to high "la la la's" on their four-part harmonies during a sensational "Me and Bobby McGee." Mission accomplished, Kristofferson planted a big kiss on Jenning's cheek at song's end.

Cash's distinctive bass was the strongest voice of the four, and his landmark songs resonated a depth to match his presence. Cash's own "Folsom Prison Blues" gained from Nelson's high pickin'. By the time he'd done intoning his last "freight train roll," backed by harmonies from the other three, you could count 12,000 C&W converts on their feet and roaring!

Paul Simon. "Un-bee-lee-va-bull!" That's how my section-mates rated Simon's two-and-a-half hour set, and I simply had to shake my head and concur. What made it all the more amazing was how he persevered, despite how the year-plus "Born at the Right Time Tour" had left his voice little more than a ragged rasp.

Simon had the tour's full African/American band to back him up for a good half-dozen numbers from his "Graceland" and "Rhythm of The Saints" albums before sneaking in gems from prior eras. Meaty bass, romping organs, sassy horns, tinkling guitars, bubbling accordions — all were delivered an intoxicating world-party mix that seemed to grant absolution on the crowd's bouncing heads, glowing yellow from the setting sun. Well-mic'd, too, it allowed you to hone in on Simon's lyrical snippets.

Highlights? Almost too many to mention (literally, since I don't know the song titles from his last two discs):

- The circular moodiness of a Brazilian-inflected "I Feel Good," my favorite song off his latest release;

- A spirited spin through a Latin-flavored "Me and Julio," delivered with wailing timbales and big smiles from Simon who seemed to acknowledge his satisfaction with closing a musical circle begun a quarter-century earlier;

- "Cinematographer's Party," given a biting merengue beat, with Simon leaning hard into the sarcasm of the lyrics;

- "Bridge Over Troubled Waters," initially done sotto voce, then with piano and choir backing before Richard Tee's funky organ took it on home.

"You Can Call Me Al" was so strong Simon's crew pounded it out twice! And let's not forget the cameos: Thielemans reprising his lyrical harmonica solo on "I Do It For You Love"; Nelson stepping out to duet his up-tempo take on "Graceland" as the crowd stood and rhythmically clapped.

My personal highlight came at the end of the band set just before Simon did an unaccompanied reprise of his early melancholia. He led a gospel-driven "Loves Me Like a Rock" before sequeing into a deliciously slow "Diamonds on the Soles of Her Shoes," done similarly. As the choir faded out their acappella "na-na-na's," I chimed in with a celebratory smile on my soul.

**Attendance Tip** You'll have to do what I did and sacrifice a day's drive to pick up your tickets, although it's such a beautiful trip it'll hardly seem like a chore. Call the Southampton or Montauk Chambers of Commerce — 516-283-0402 and 516-668-2428, respectively — sometime in May to confirm the 'RANCH's dates and when tickets go on sale (typically the week before Memorial Day). Then visit one of the designated retail outlets (typically Southampton's Long Island Sound) within a month after they get released. No telephone charges, alas. Even though there have been 1,000 extra passes issued pre-concert, locals will learn about them before you will.

Game day varies mid-week, which makes it a tad easier to score local lodgings, but just a tad. Rooms rent across the Hamptons months in advance of summertime, and you can plan on spending big bucks as well as having to confirm multiple-night reservations. Don't despair, though, because you can stay for less on the North Fork or further west approaching Riverhead. Both Chambers of Commerce above should also have listings less pricey and less likely found within the standard travel guides. There is sensational beach camping at Hither Hills State Park, but sites get booked solid via New York State's toll-free reservation line often six months ahead for minimum one-week stays. Still, it never hurts to call Hither Hills direct at 516-668-2461.

It's best to arrive well ahead to avoid the inevitable traffic lines. High-back chairs are not permitted, so bring low-back beach chairs or blankets. Coolers are welcome, but alcohol is not in deference to a family atmosphere.

**Travel Tip** There's no shortage of sights to see along one of the most picturesque and pricey stretches in America. Just drop the top and ride!

There's no shortage of dining and nightlife, either, even in Montauk. Check *Dan's Papers* for local listings. One must is The Stephen Talkhouse just up the road in Amagansett. You'll pay a heavy cover, but you and maybe 100 other patrons will party to roots rock's "A-list." It's an intimate treat, and a likely spot to catch a 'RANCH' act later that night, or that week (i.e., Kris

Kristofferson and G. E. Smith in '92).

Also, don't forget horseback riding at Indian Field Ranch. "We basically do it by reservation," Lever explains. "We have an hour and a half ride, which is the most popular. We take people through the thousands of acres of trails and then we also take them on the beach. It really fulfills a fantasy that a lot of people have about riding horseback on the beach. It's just a real pretty ride."

Another Simon sighting has been at the annual benefit for Manhattan's Tibet House, called the GREAT MIRACLE PRAYER FESTIVAL. Last year's other participants included Edie Brickell (see, I knew she'd soon come forward), Phillip Glass, Natalie Merchant, Richie Havens, The Roches, monologuist Spaulding Gray, and poet Allen Ginsburg.

One further Simon sighting has been at the annual RAINFOREST BENEFIT CONCERT — one of the few such superstars showcases that's rivalled the 'RANCH' in national publicity. Simon joined in this year with Sting, James Taylor, Elton John, Bruce Springsteen, Jon Bon Jovi and opera diva Jessye Norman. Wanna' bet that backstage hobnobbing will deliver at least one of these artists to this year's 'RANCH'?

**See Also**

~   ~   ~

# Western New York's End-of-Summer, I: Modern Christian

PRAISE, Darien, NY
    Late May
    Modern Christian

**KINGDOM BOUND**, Darien, NY
    Late August
    Modern Christian
    ***Attended***

NIAGARA: THE STUDENT AND ADULT LEADERSHIP CONFERENCE ON EVANGELISM,
Niagara Falls, NY
    Late December
    Modern Christian

**Introduction**   Matt Groening, creator of TV's "The Simpsons," should give the last laugh to his born-again character, Ned Flanders, by having him take his next-door neighbors to **KINGDOM BOUND**. Picture the possibilities!

To set the plot properly, Groening has the Flanders and the Simpsons first venture to a typical family festival at Marge Simpson's earnest insistence. (She recruits her husband Homer by promising funnel cakes.) The Mayor welcomes everyone to "...this fine celebration of the strong family values that made this country great! It shall remain 'God-free' in accordance with Springfield's Penal Code: sec. 9, ord. 13. Violators will be prosecuted." Young Bart Simpson cringes at the milquetoast entertainers — jugglers, stilt walkers, mimes — and rebels by having his face painted as death-rock star Alice Cooper. Bart's sister, Lisa, encounters folk-revivalists ("Kumbaya, my *Lord*...oops, scratch that.") and intellectualizes them in her trademark combination of wide-eyed reverence and all-too-knowing banality.

All throughout the Flanders kids are thoroughly nonplussed, even during the folkies' singalong for "Michael Row Your Boat Ashore, Hal and Julia." "Slurps," they continuously deride with bored sighs (to the confusion of the Indian Quickie Mart owner, Abu). "Why 'Slurps?,'" query Bart and Lisa in puzzlement. "Because our dad won't let us say 'Sucks,'" they whisper, clasping their hands skyward in atonement.

Fast-forward to **KINGDOM BOUND** where the Simpsons tentatively accompany the Flanders, fearful of being recruited into some cult and forced against their will to pay charity visits to comfort Springfield's elderly. "The horror!" (Again, Marge assures Homer of funnel cakes.) Once through the gates of Darien Lake Theme Park and Camping Resort, however, heck-all breaks loose:

- Bart bounces all night from Christian metal, to Christian acappella, to Christian hard rock, to Christian country, to Christian rap, to Christian folk, to Christian dance/pop, even to Christian blues. Trying to catch his breath before the Midnite Hip-Hop-A-Thon with Michael Peace and Friends, he gasps of the Flanders kids, "So, dudes, when's bedtime?" They blithely reply, "Hey, Jesus never sleeps."

- Lisa gravitates to the Seminar Pavilions, immediately finding a teen soulmate who shares her deep and abiding respect for Billy Graham, TV minister to America's Presidents. They hold hands while a speaker ponders, "Co-Dependency or God-Dependency?"

- The Flanders kids make a bee-line to the Sports Experience featuring Fellowship of Christian Athletes members: Buffalo Bills All-Pro receiver J. D. Hill, lineman Pete Metzelaars, and back-up quarterback Frank Reich. Flanders kids to Reich: "You're our hero!" Reich: "Oh, you like how I rallied the Bills from over 30 points down against the Houston Oilers in the '93 playoffs?" Flanders kids: "You mean you play football?"

- Marge becomes enthralled with the lustrous eyes and smoldering charm of Christian pop star, Carmen, who seems to be singing only for her.

- On a sugar high, Homer hallucinates Six Funnel Cakes Over Western New York and gleefully partakes among Darien Lake's copious amusements: the funnel-coaster, the funnel-copter, funnel cars and boats, the funnel-wheel, the funnel-flume, funnel golf and skeet. ("Yippie, Marge, it's 'funnel-wonderful!'")

As the last lights flicker from KINGDOM BOUND's Christian laser show, Ned and sons ring out, "Okeley-dokeley!" Homer, Marge, and Lisa all sigh contentedly, while Bart draws a cross on his skateboard and breathlessly proclaims, "Cooler than thou!"

Of course, I'm teasing ("T-E-A-S-I-N-G!"), but I hope to underscore three substantial points.

First, even without Darien Lake, KINGDOM BOUND probably has more offerings than most other family festivals can even imagine. In addition to those mentioned above, we're talking participatory sports, exhibits, concessions, displays, musicals, activities and entertainment for both children and teens, workshops, prayer tents, religious services, exercise classes ("Moving with the Spirit"), dances, swimming, camping, late-night jams, and on and on. The only obvious omission I can identify is a talent show, and that will be introduced as a separate activity come Spring '94.

Second, KINGDOM BOUND's music embraces the entire family, especially teens. Indeed, its brethren may be the only festivals outside the Lollapalooza tour to routinely incorporate the totality of pop music teens encounter daily on MTV. No more arguments about which which pop style is stronger live or which is more danceable. Simply hear for yourself as you rotate from among KINGDOM BOUND's three stages. Moreover, they're the only ones consistently taking a chance on rap, albeit of the Christian variety.

Third — and here's the real surprise for the uninitiated — contemporary Christian music is really getting good! True, it yet maintains few innovators capable of improving upon their respective genres (an exception might be Take 6 who are nothing less than the country's finest pop vocal group, wowing critics in both jazz and R&B camps). But there's an impressive sweep of Christian artists who've closed the quality gaps sufficiently to where you're hard-pressed to tell the difference. I'd consider Bruce Carroll alongside many major folkies; Steven Curtis Chapman next to most rising C&W stars; The Newsboys side-by-side any mainstream dance/pop band; King's X above most hard rockers. And those are just the few major acts I've witnessed, no pun intended. If Charlie Daniels can declare himself a Christian artist, can others be far behind?

"A lot of people got the impression that church music is (and for a long time it was) substandard; it wasn't up to par. But it really has progressed," explains KINGDOM BOUND's Promoter, Fred Caserta, whose bubbly enthusiasm belies a business sense born of years in secular music. "Right now, you see mostly all your Christian record companies have all been bought by major mainstream labels. They see the potential in it. And you gotta' remember, you try to book the best when your havin' the festival. You go for the bigger names."

I'm far from the expert on this category, but a few of the bigger names I recognized from '93's three-day blow-out included Chapman, The Newsboys, Rick Cua, DC Talk, 4 Him, Angelo and Veronica, Acappella, and White Heart. Caserta's excited at booking Bebe and Cece Winans for '94, which is as big as it gets in black gospel. It all promises musical excitement for the entire Christian family.

The circumstances prompting Caserta's launching of **KINGDOM BOUND** in '87 are both fateful and inspiring. Here's his testimony:

- "I was not just a local agent, I was trying to have some of my groups make it. I had a metal band that toured the country on an independent label and just cost me a lot of money in speculation, because we didn't have tour support. Based on that, I was hoping and praying that I would get my money back once I got a record contract for them. I did get a record contract for 'em, but unfortunately the label lost their distribution, so I had 40 grand coming in sunk money which I never received. Therefore I was stuck with $40,000 in back debts, home with a fractured knee and hip and couldn't work, just sitting there taking phone calls from bill collectors.

  "I just cried out to the Lord and said, 'Just use me, Lord. If I could just have an opportunity to be able to do what I do for You...'"

Preceding that, Caserta had been familiar with Christian singer Rick Cua from Cua's days in a Syracuse band playing the Northern Tier. Cua once called Caserta for help in booking a routing date back from a Toronto concert.

"I was just really a baby, a baby Christian," says Caserta:

- "So I called these people who were involved in music in our church, and he actually played there! Rick turned around and called me again about six months later when I was sitting home with this injury and literally crying out to the Lord that I didn't want to go back in the secular music business... Rick wanted to do a concert date, 'cause he was putting his tour together, and I said to him, 'Why are you calling me? Why don't you have an agent?' He said, 'Well I do have an agent, but he's not doin' a great job.' And I said, 'Rick, man, I wanna' be your agent!' He said, 'Let me pray about this.' So he prayed about it, came to visit me around Christmas time, and I began to book him."

Caserta then became Cua's regular scheduler, eventually fulfilling his own debts from other means. "We didn't make any money," Caserta notes of the association, "but it was a wonderful opportunity for me to experience what was goin' on in the contemporary Christian music scene around the country. I gained a lot of experience and met a lot of nice people.

- "One thing led to another. The guy who was running Darien Lakes at that particular time found out that I was saved because I wasn't workin' there anymore at my office. He called my former office and asked the fellow who was running it, 'Is this true that this Caserta is a Christian?' And he said, 'Yeah,' and that guy said, 'Well, you tell him to call me in September.'

  "In the interim that guy died in a car accident, and the fella' who took his position over (somebody that I knew) was checking his notes and said, 'Why did he want to call you?' I said to him, 'I dunno', because he wanted me to talk to him about Christian music?' He says, 'Let's get together and talk.' He made a presentation thinking that we would be interested in putting together an event, a Christian day at the park. He said, 'What do you know about this stuff?' And I said, 'Well, I'm helpin' this Rick Cua guy with his ministry and I'm talking to all the different promoters. I know a little bit about this.'

  "At that time, there was a group of us meeting on a week-to-week basis, just getting together for lunch, talking about contemporary Christian music and trying to figure out what we could do. We said, 'We don't have any money; we don't have a name; we don't have anything.' So the guy from Darien Lakes, Kevin Ketcham, said to me, 'Can you put together a proposal for an event at the theme park?' I said, 'Well, how many days?' He said, 'How many days do these things normally run?' And I said, 'Well, they usually run two or three days.'

  "I went and got all the information together. I talked to Bob Pheister [a Florida promoter], and I talked to Tim Landis [a Pennsylvania promoter]. Tim helped me tremendously — it was a pleasure to see that a brother would reach out to somebody. So I put together a proposal and gave it to them. We did it in October. It was supposed to be Indian summer [but] it was 38 degrees and it snowed!"

KINGDOM BOUND lost money that year, along with the next two, but Darien Lakes stuck with it as it turned the financial corner in 1991. From an initial attendance of 6,000 shivering faithful, it's grown in seven years to 45,000! It's also been moved to a warmer last weekend in August.

"God has really been good to us," Caserta remarks:

- "We have a wonderful arrangement with Darien Lakes, a wonderful partnership... Because of that event, we have been able to develop a ministry where we have three full-time people on staff. Throughout the year we do other things too, but the festival has grown from that idea.

  "[Darien Lakes] has made us look good because they are a quality organization and the facility is gorgeous. They're concerned about the family, and they are very cooperative and sensitive to our values. Normally on the midway there's beer trucks and all that kind of stuff. They are totally struck and moved out. There's no booze on the premises except in the restaurants. We get the opportunity before the event to walk the midway and anything that we feel is objectionable and does not fit in the Christian lifestyle, we pull it out."

Caserta's overriding aim is two-fold: (a) to achieve the breadth necessary to involve the entire family, musically and otherwise; and (b) to bring the huge production down to a personal level. How? "The Worship Tent is a major factor in our event," Caserta states. "It goes on 14 hours a day, and we have different artists. Let's say, for instance, Acappella plays on the main stage; they'll come over to the Worship Tent and maybe do an acoustic thing, just sing some old hymns.

- "Another one of the reasons why I believe our event has been successful is because the artists at the event are accessible. Every year I book certain people, and I bring in new ones who are there for the whole three days. They're there; they're walking around the grounds; they're in the amusement park with the people. It's mainly a real personal thing. Again, that was not by design, that was just the Lord."

With all his attention to musical details, you'd think performances would comprise Caserta's most satisfying remembrances. Instead, it's more the spirit gracing the Worship Tent:

- "I think people really feel the presence of God there, and the fact that the whole family's being ministered to in a different way than it would be in church. Those are the kind of compliments that excite me more than anything. I'm not impressed by the fact that we had x many people. People's lives have been changed by coming to the event. It works out in seminars. We had a guy last year who did divorce workshops; he had 25 marriages that were saved that were ready to be dissolved.

  "The Worship Tent, that's the highlight for me, seeing 2-to-3,000 people coming onto this island at 8:30 in the morning just to start the day off in praising and worshiping God. That's where God meets here, and it's just an incredible, incredible experience for me. That's what gets my juices flowing and wanting to get to work on next year's event!"

**Festival Review**

Call me Bart as I ricocheted Thursday night from stage-to-stage, back-and-forth through the midway. Caserta plans to eliminate music at the Laser Amphitheater but maintain the Midway Stage located right beside the merry-go-round. He likes how younger performers there can really integrate with their audience, getting up close and personal. And there's the Main Stage outdoors, which ordinarily fields such major pop/rock acts as Van Halen, Spin Doctors and Billy Ray Cyrus. Accordingly, the production values are excellent — another leg-up enjoyed by Christian artists here.

The crowd was teen-heavy, a constituency often missing from music festivals but brought here by the church bus load. They seemed to mix and mingle aplenty, aided by sparkling weather. When not cheering their musical heroes, teens could be found cruising the impressive exhibit tents and gobbling up various T-shirt concessions and band gear every bit as graphically-hip as their secular-music counterparts. "Lemme' tell ya'," rock conferences have nothing on contemporary Christian festivals when it comes to merchandising!

I missed the one artist I would've been most intrigued to catch, Christian bluesman Larry Howard. Oh, well. The other acts appealed to varying degrees, but The Newsboys earned two thumbs up!

**Artist Mini-Review**  <u>The Newsboys</u>. These young guys took the stage and shined! Combining current dance/rock rhythms and pop tunefulness with a bit more lyric depth than you'd normally find in this genre, The Newsboys rocked the house for teens and parents alike without condescending to either constituency. I particularly appreciated how their lead singer personalized his song intros in a genuine, unaffected manner. Sincere performers, strong showmen, very promising.

Caserta: "Yeah, they're entertaining, and they're very, very smart. They started at our festival — we started them on our Midway Stage. The first year they came here they played for free, and they have [since] become a headliner. They're becoming a major group around the country; they're gonna be a big band."

**Attendance Tip**  Although KINGDOM BOUND is officially ecumenical among Christians (there was even a Jews for Jesus exhibitor), its religious orientation is clearly fundamentalist Protestant. That's not to say Catholics and other denominations won't feel comfortable, they'll just have to account for born-again testimony and some orientations more uncommon to practicing their faiths. Hopefully, the seminar and worship hosts will be reciprocally respectful of their guests as per the recent accord announced between the Pope and evangelicals to work together in cooperation, not competition.

All practitioners, however, will appreciate an affirmative, instructive, spiritual, and family-centered emphasis running throughout all activities.

Personally, I'm more cautious on behalf of first-time patrons of Christian music who may be put off by heavy preaching from Christian performers between songs. True, you like artists to reveal themselves for creating a more personal dialog with their listeners. However, I get the impression as an outsider that too many here either over-dramatize their life stories to score "born-again" points or simply don't have the religious training to flesh-out their scriptural citations. Some are perfect, such as Nancy Honeytree whom I caught at CREATION (see Mount Union, PA, Middle June). She calmly and effectively discussed issues terribly pertinent for teen listeners as informed by her own personal experiences. Still, I wish some other Christian artists would leave their preaching to the preachers.

As for how to get the most out of KINGDOM BOUND's formidable schedule, Caserta advises: "I would definitely tell them to plan and think out their day. I would make sure that they read the topics and whatever's goin' on in their life that pertains to that particular topic, be sure that they sit and listen to that particular seminar or workshop. They can benefit from that."

Caserta highly recommends the Worship Tent but adds:

- "They should take the opportunity to fellowship and meet. There's such a spirit of people just willing and wanting to talk to one another; take an opportunity to just get acquainted with people that they don't even know around their campsite, or around the area. That's a wonderful experience, an awesome experience, of taking advantage of meeting people from different areas. Twenty-five percent of our festival is from Southern Ontario and Canada, so it's two countries that come together, and that's exciting!"

**Travel Tip**  "They'd have to go to Niagara Falls — that's one of the seven wonders one the world," exclaims Caserta of one local highlight. Of another, "They need to go to the Anchor Bar and get [the original Buffalo] chicken wings. That's a good place to go."

**See Also**  PRAISE, which runs at Darien Lake over Memorial Day Weekend, is less about music and more about worship via workshops and seminars. "Basically, there's no preaching whatsoever, except on Sunday morning," relays Caserta. However, he does maintain a 10-piece band to back up various speakers and vocalists. "We know that God, without a doubt, has called us to do this event." Ditto for NIAGARA: THE STUDENT AND ADULT LEADERSHIP CONFERENCE ON EVANGELISM, which ran at the Radisson Hotel in Niagara Falls right after Christmas in 1993, and will hopefully re-occur annually.

~     ~     ~

# Western New York's End-of-Summer, II: Acoustic Roots

**BUFFALO IRISH FESTIVAL**, Lancaster, NY
> Late August
> Irish
> ***Attended***

**BLUEGRASS FESTIVAL**, Rochester, NY
> Late August
> Bluegrass

**TURTLE HILL MUSIC FESTIVAL**, Spencerport, NY
> Late August
> Modern Folk

**MECK MUSIC FESTIVAL**, Mecklenberg, NY
> Late August
> Variety, General

**FINGERLAKES DIXIELAND JAZZ FESTIVAL**, Hector, NY
> Late August
> Traditional Jazz and Ragtime

**BUFFALO BEER FEST**, Buffalo, NY
> Middle November
> Variety, General

**Introduction**

"Mercy!" There's something about the last weekend in August that sprouts festivals like mushrooms throughout the entire Northwest corner of New York State. The six events above, each feeding different roots-music constituencies within a triangle bounded by Buffalo, Rochester, and Ithaca, are just the appetizers. We're not even talking the massive KINGDOM BOUND FESTIVAL (Darien, NY — see chapter), the tasty ARTPARK FOLK FESTIVAL (see Lewiston, NY), the season's wrap up of the classy CHAUTAUQUA INSTITUTION (Chautauqua, NY — see chapter), or three concurrent rock affairs, each a meal unto itself, which highlight the area's musical feast over the same few days.

Oh, and did I mention the NEW YORK STATE FAIR (see Syracuse, NY, Late August to Early September) or a few more festivals closer in along the Southern Tier?

For you festival gluttons it's either a dream or a nightmare depending on how broad your musical appetites are and how badly your conscience nags you if you pass up one for the other. It's been bugging me all winter that I had to race back to New York City that same weekend for a full plate of reggae, gospel, and jazz affairs. Grrr! Here's the one among them I managed to sample Friday night before the whole scene came to a boil.

"Well, I tell ya' one thing," exclaims Aby Marks, one of the Buffalo Irish Festival's three founders, about all the happenings that weekend, "you will certainly keep your toe tapping." Good sport that he is, Marks would have you take in some others during the day before closing your evening out under the big top at Willow Grove.

His three-day affair sprung eleven years ago from the shared sentiments of Marks, who hosts "Echoes of Erin" on radio station WHLD (1270 AM), Kevin Townsell, a local hotel and pub owner, and Tom O'Carroll, a Boston-based Irish entertainer.

"[We] were commenting on St. Patrick's Day, how nice it would be to have some kind of a festivity or get-together in the summer where everyone could get together," Marks recites in a voice still bearing husky traces of his native Dublin, "because on St. Patrick's Day, there's a big parade and everyone goes about their business and back to their own clubs and their own neighborhoods and parties the same day. But then you never see them again! It would be nice to all get together under one banner and really have a good time."

This grand plan almost got nipped in the bud.

"We had a terrible time the first year," Marks recalls:

- "We were hit by a tornado the first night! It was a freak thing. There was a tornado, and it hit Lancaster, and it hit Niagara Falls, and nowhere else. It knocked the tent down [laughs] and everything else. Believe it or not, after that tent came down, they kept playing. People brought their cars and formed a circle, put their lights on, and the party kept goin'. They wouldn't move! Of course, they were havin' a great time.

  "We worked all night to get the tent back. By noon the next day you wouldn't know what had happened to that place. We contacted all the radio stations, and the newspapers, and what have you and said, 'The festival will go on, etc., etc.,' and that was it. That brought more people out, you know. It was very good, they really enjoyed it and it was the first time there was really a festival here in the area that got everyone together.

  "Then the people asked, 'Are we gonna' have it again?' But before we got into it, we organized all the Irish groups there in town, went around to them all and said, 'Look, we're going to organize a festival and we want you guys to be part of it. We come in all under one banner and raise funds for all the different organizations.

  "And that's about basically how it started."

Today, Marks is witnessing the second generation of attendees bringing their young children. He also sees their parents planning annual vacations around the weekend. They include many descendants of the original Irish workers on the Erie Canal who settled in its terminus in nearby Lockport. ("Every second name is Irish there," Marks exclaims.) Others come from Rochester, Toronto, ON, and Erie, PA, while retirees drive up from wherever they'd retired.

The tornado mishap, as well as Buffalo's notoriously-fickle weather, has moved the whole affair under a warren of circus tents and pavilions. These shield a fairly classy row of crafters and importers as well as a conspicuous "wheelbarrow of cheer" (not to mention a bar serving six beers by the pitcher). It also keeps dry schools of young step-dancers — gaggles of Irish jumping jacks who are almost more the event's focus than the music. The kids then go on to an international "feis" held over in Ireland where, according to Marks, "they compete pretty heavily against the children in Ireland.

"You know what's happening," Marks observes, "is we are going more into traditional Irish music here. In Ireland it's not that they're getting away from it, but you're more likely to come across Country-Western and rock and everything else as you can see from some of the big bands, the recognizable bands in the U. S. U2, for instance, they're the number one music group in the U. S.! You have Enya; you have numerous names who've come over from Ireland and are doing very well here in modern music. So they're going one way; [laughs] we're trying to go the other way."

Marks' greatest satisfaction looking back? "We've never had an ounce of problems," he marvels.

- "People are so nice to each other on that weekend it's unbelievable. And they're the same every year — that's what kind of keeps it going. Everyone who has been there who liked the music couldn't get over the friendliness of the people. It's a happening! To the Irish, it's kind of like the Mardi Gras at the end of the season instead of at the beginning of it."

As I'll emphasize, and Marks will confirm, the BUFFALO IRISH FESTIVAL is nowhere close to the big blowouts covered elsewhere in this book. It's humble, but it's been around for over a decade, and they know pretty much just how to entertain their middle-aged, middle-and-working-class crowd of maybe a few thousand or so. It manages in a nice way. **Festival Review**

Willow Grove is a compact swatch of semi-suburban grassland on Bowen Road right off Route 20. The plot gets its name from two or three ancient willow trees that tower over everything and lend the site a comforting, pastoral quality. Since it's all separated from the main road, kids can freely run around the grounds.

The musical bill "splits the middle" between the authenticity of traditional music and the glitz of "commercial" showbands. The net result is acoustic but broadly entertaining for the general listener. "By doing that," Marks explains, "you kinda' please everybody. You get your folk singers and you have your traditional music. They can blend pretty well together without going to any extremes."

I literally popped in just to say, "Hi," before gearing up for a long night's drive back to New York City. I've no notes on the few acts I caught other than to confirm their generational orientation. "We generally have three or four or five from out of town," says Marks, citing recruits from New Bedford, MA, Washington, DC, Toronto, ON, and New York, NY, "but we employ mostly locals and build it up from there." Two I recognized from the Fiddler's Fair at the CORN HILL ARTS FESTIVAL (Rochester, NY — see chapter) are The Dady Brothers. "They do a heck of a job," Marks nods.

"For first-time visitors from out of town," Marks chuckles, "it is highly recommended that they get a hotel room months in advance because the other festivals do book out the hotels, there's no doubt about it." Fortunately, they've negotiated a very reasonable room rate at the Ramada Inn on Transit Road, Exit 49 off the new York State Thruway. **Travel Tip**

"But if I was coming up here and I wanted to stick with the entertainment," Marks hints:

- "I would book into the hotel where the musicians are. Bring your instrument if you wish, but to wind down the festival Saturday and Sunday night, when the guys go back, there's a jam session in the bar. The vendors are there; the participants in the festival mostly stay in the same hotel; and the party is very good. They're re-opening [Townsell's] Shannon Pub in the Lord Amherst Hotel. All through the year there's musicians there, too. That would be the ideal place to stay this coming year."

Simply read 'em up top and weep — or feast! Your move. You should know, furthermore, that in 1995 Townsell turned his festival acumen toward producing the first BUFFALO BEER FEST at the Erie County Fairgrounds, featuring many of the same Irish artists he books at the BUFFALO IRISH FESTIVAL. Hopefully, this event will become an annual imbibing as well. **See Also**

~     ~     ~

# Schenectady's Blues Variety Party

BLUES BAR-B-QUE, Schenectady, NY
    Early August
    Blues and Traditional R&B

PARK JAM, Schenectady, NY
    Early August
    Alternative and College Rock

LAKE GEORGE JAZZ WEEKEND, Lake George, NY
    Middle September
    Modern Jazz

TAKIN' IT TO THE STREETS: THE ELECTRIC CITY MUSIC CELEBRATION, Schenectady, NY
    Middle September
    Variety, General
    ***Attended***

**Introduction**   "Damn right I've got the blues!" That's gotta' be the motto for Don Wilcock, media renaissance man who covers the musical waterfront for the Capital region. (How's this for being plugged-in. Wilcox: (a) writes for three publications; (b) hosts three regular shows on two different radio stations; (c) produces three music events drawing over 100,000 combined attendance; (d) writes liner notes, bios and press releases for area bands and independent labels; (e) and founded the Northeast Blues Society with its newsletter, regular blues jam, and ultimate goal of producing a straight blues festival... Whew!)

It also happens to be the title of his critically-acclaimed biography of legendary blues guitarist, Buddy Guy, paralleling Guy's award-winning CD release. And it's likely the theme for his TAKIN' IT TO THE STREETS: THE ELECTRIC CITY MUSIC CELEBRATION ['STREETS].

True, 'STREETS is more than just blues. Pop into Schenectady's rambling Central Park the second Sunday in September and on each free stage scattered amidst those darkly foreboding Adirondack pines you'll find a different music genre. There's jazz and rock in the red shed facing the pond. There's C&W fronting the swings. Even on the blues stage adjacent to the tennis courts, there's gospel early in the day. Plus, Wilcock reserves "the right to make left turns," having featured oldies in past years and anticipating some world-beat in the future.

Yet blues is "the straw that stirs the drink" in the immortal words of Yankee Hall-of-Famer Reggie Jackson. It supplies the day's national headliners (i.e., Eddie Shaw and The Wolf Gang), its fastest-rising stars (i.e., Joan Osborne Band, Heavy Metal Horns), and the strongest of the local acts being showcased (i.e., Ernie Williams and The Wildcats). "That's my prejudice," admits Wilcock, who hopes the audiences for the other genres get exposed to his favored blues crews.

"What I'm trying to do here is present a wide variety of music to people who otherwise wouldn't get to hear it," Wilcock reasons:

- "The commercial establishments, the record industry, and the radio stations today have put music into boxes with labels on them. This festival categorically denies labels! The way we label is we'll put the country acts all on one stage so that the country radio station feels comfortable in promoting the show. But as far as the way we book the show, we book in terms of acts that turn us on. It has nothing to do with what kind of music it is. I can tell you as a critic that I get more enjoyment out of music that's available free to people in this market area than out of music that's costing them $25 a ticket."

The "we" Wilcock refers to is himself and his booking partner, Mona Golub, who runs one of the local labels he does publicity for. Their main booking source for headlining "up-and-comers" involves Wilcock's scouring the big blues festivals across the country. "I try to see these acts in their indigenous environment," he confirms, "and I always find it interesting to see how they transplant. Some of 'em do and some of 'em don't."

Any programming models from his travels?

"Well, I was inspired by the NEW ORLEANS JAZZ AND HERITAGE FESTIVAL (see New Orleans, LA, Late April to Early May) and the eclecticism of it," says Wilcock, who made his first pilgrimage in '88 and wrote it up for *Living Blues*. "In our area we have several cliques of people and musicians who are real energetic. There's a real positive energy in the folk community, in the blues community, in the rock community, in the alternative community, and to bring all of those various energies together in one park is an amazing high!"

One of the historic strengths of the NEW ORLEANS "JAZZFEST" has been discovering talent. I observe how 'STREETS similarly showcases blues acts who are not headliners "yet." "Ah, that's the key word," Wilcock laughs. "I take that as a compliment without your even making it. Well, you say acts that are 'on their way up' — some of these acts have already been 'up' and are considered 'down and out.' So really, it's what turns us on personally.

- "Like this Eddie Shaw and The Wolf Gang. I never expected to see the kind of energy that I saw from him in Chicago. It came as a total surprise! Here was a guy who had worked with Howlin' Wolf more than 25 years ago, and I thought this guy would be going through the usual jive set that you'd expect from someone who's been around that long. I saw him at the CHICAGO BLUES FESTIVAL (see Chicago, IL, Early June) last year and couldn't believe what I saw. So I went and saw him again at [Buddy Guy's club] Legends two nights later, and he did it again! I said, 'O. K., that's all I need to see [laughs].'"

  "I'm interested in putting on acts that are 'on their way up,' but what's more exciting to me is to put on acts that people locally here have never heard of and by the time they leave the park, they can't f___ing believe what they have just seen and heard! I like to think of myself as like a pied piper in that the acts I bring in just blow people away.

  "The year before, as another example, we brought in Marva Wright from New Orleans. We had to pay far more than that act would ever consider to be worth to any promoter in his right mind. But I'd seen her in New Orleans and said, 'I don't give a shit; I know what she can do [laughs]! And I want Schenectady to see this [because] Schenectady will never see an act like that any other way unless we bring her in.' So we devoted a large chunk of our budget towards presenting this lady with her seven-piece band out in the field in Central Park.

  "And it did, it blew people away!"

**Festival Review**

I must say, there abounded an unpretentious easiness modestly reminiscent of The Big Easy, itself. Crisp sunshine, cool shade, no humidity, perfect weather for this glorified neighborhood picnic. Best of all, there was almost no separation between artists and audience. I managed to have a nice chat with Joan Osborne as she hung out behind the performing tent, something I've yet to achieve during her many New York City club dates.

Wilcock was a benevolent presence everywhere pressing the flesh with his many acquaintances. Folks responded in kind, smiled plenty, laughed at the artists' jokes, and danced on cue — a good family crowd. Here are my notes.

**Artist Mini-Reviews**

Doctor Rouse and Her Gospel Singers. A family gospel group, way far from the most accomplished I've experienced, yet sincere and authentic.

Wilcock: "Another inspiration to me from the NEW ORLEANS 'JAZZFEST' was the gospel tent. We put on a local gospel group led by Rev. Rouse from the Christian Faith Church. Joan Osborne was so taken with Rev. Rouse that she came up about three weeks ago, spent three hours with her making music and has invited her down to the City to do some recording next week. What will become of that I don't know, but it's a real heart-tugging story because shortly after that concert Rev. Rouse's husband died."

Eddie Shaw and The Wolf Gang. I'd seen Shaw the year before at TOLEDO'S ROCK, RHYTHM AND BLUES (see Toldeo, OH, Late May). His son, Eddie Jr., managed to heat up a freezing afternoon by blazing one guitar solo after another, usually while sitting on the lip of the stage.

This time 'round Junior hung back and let Senior take the lead on sax and vocals. Shaw seemed energized (Wilcock explained he'd been moved by the passing of old bluesman, Lefty Diz, and hopped the next flight back to Chicago for the funeral). His singing boosted a bunch of tired, Chicago-style standards with energy and conviction. "Call My Job," "Lil' Red Rooster," and a nice original, "Blues Is Good News," all revved the people into dancing on the blacktop.

Nobody's Girls. I liked this quasi-roots band, especially their full-throttle vocals alternating leads and harmonies. Soulful and tuneful, if a bit heavy-handed, on a ripping tribute anthem, "Things Are Bound To Change."

Wilcock: "Unfortunately, they have just gotten into an internal argument and the three women who were the head of that group [have disbanded]. One of them has split off and started her own band. Her name is Jeanne French. Actually, she's recorded with Harry Chapin and written songs for Loretta Lynn and Dolly Parton. She's also recorded with a bunch of other acts including The Five Satins and Van Morrison, I think. She's quite a bit older than the other two and she's going in a heavy R&B direction [while] the younger women are going more into alternative rock/grunge. Anyway, she's in the process of putting a band together called 'Blue Jeanne Blue.'"

Joan Osborne Band. Vocalist Osborne was the act I really came for, seeing as she'd just inked a lucrative deal with Mercury Records. I'd heard rumors of her departure from progressive blues and was eager to check 'er out anew.

Osborne's been another surprise smash from the New York City blues scene, joining The Holmes Brothers, Bobby Radcliff, Michael Hill, and Popa Chubby in recently breaking out. Since moving from her native Bowling Green, KY, in the late '80s with no prior singing experience (!!), she quickly gathered a band from open mics and wowed critics as the second coming of Janis Joplin — albeit sober, smiling, and in control (she formed her own record label, Womanly Hips, for example). They wrote her up as a powerful and original stylist who put a healthy spin on female sensuality. I heartily agreed, however, I felt she rode a nasal inflection a bit too heavily.

This time was a whole new ballgame with the only commonality being Osborne's radiant stage manner. After easing into an aching Ann Peebles cover, "I Can't Stand The Rain," her four-piece band lit into a series of extended song jams that felt like '60s acid rock, albeit blues-based with '90s dissonances. Osborne's wardrobe underscored this retro intent: hip-hugging purple corduroy bell-bottoms, sandals, red paisley shirt, a tambourine, and Joplin-esque circular shades.

After a few numbers I concluded, "Hey, maybe it works!" The looser structures give Osborne plenty of space to either dig into the groove or stretch out and riff, while the trippy imagery still allows for hard-edged interpretation. Mood dominates, happily with a purer vocal tone. I enjoyed an atmospheric "All Night" plus a menacing cover of Captain Beefheart's "Blue Million Miles." I don't know if Osborne can carry her blues following into this alternative-rock territory, but her new sound commands my attention.

**Travel Tip**   "If you're gonna' go into downtown Schenectady," Wilcock advises:

- "You wanna' hit Jay Street, which is our one Greenwich Village-type street. It's closed to traffic and has a lot of little boutiques and shops in it. On that same street there's a very fast-rising coffeehouse called Caffe Dolce. It serves international coffees, is open to all ages and frequently has entertainment.

  "You might wanna' also check out the Van Dyke [Restaurant]. That's in the Stockade area, the old section of Schenectady that dates back to the original settlement of the city. Right now, and for the last 30 years, they've been known for doing jazz jams on Thursday nights. Then usually they'll have a jazz pianist, or sometimes somebody with international fame like Marian McPartland, comes in on a Friday and Saturday night."

As of this writing, the straight blues festival envisioned by Wilcock's Northeast Blues Society is    **See Also**
still in the exploratory stages, although Austin Jimmy Murphy told me Wilcock discussed pat-
terning it after Murphy's own NYS BUDWEISER BLUES FESTIVAL (Syracuse, NY — see chapter). Stay
tuned.

Meanwhile there's Wilcock's other Central Park blowout, the PARK JAM (for which he acts
as stage manager). This gathering of local alternative and roots rockers, scheduled the first
Tuesday in August, culminates a weekly summer concert series. Wilcock remarks:

- "The event really draws people. Initially it was a family event for people to get together to
  play baseball and see fireworks and have a cookout... Now this PARK JAM is an added element. The bands really love it because last year we drew 55,000 people! They reach an
  audience that they never would even get close to in the club scene."

To prime the pump, Wilcock books the Northeast Blues Society's annual BLUES BAR-B-QUE at the
Washington Park Playhouse a few days prior.

Wilcock is considering moving 'STREETS up one week to Labor Day in '94 so as not to compete with the Schenectady Air Show. If it stays where it's been for the past four years, however,
you could make it a full weekend of music by patronizing the LAKE GEORGE JAZZ WEEKEND
Saturday afternoon. This Shepard Park affair typically presents three acts daily of well-regarded,
if under-exposed, jazz artists from throughout the region (mainly New York City). Consider it, in
this regard, the jazz equivalent of 'STREETS.

~     ~     ~

*Toshi Reagon, Clearwater's Great Hudson River Revival.*

# New York Festival Listings

Although the vast majority are festivals are reliable and predictable, all are subject to last-minute **Caveat** changes or cancellations. Accordingly, FESTPRESS is not responsible for any festival listing information that follows. Readers are well advised to contact festivals at least twice before preparing a festival vist: (a) once at least one or two months ahead of time; and (b) once more during the week of your visit for confirmation. Ask for a festival flyer or brochure to be mailed to you. Festival promoters usually are willing to comply, and the resulting literature may answer any questions you still have.

Restrictions:                                                                                        **Key Codes**

| | | | | | |
|---|---|---|---|---|---|
| • Food and drink... | 1; | • Cameras... | 6; | • Motorcycles... | 11; |
| • Alcohol... | 2; | • Audio recording... | 7; | • Re-entry... | 12; |
| • Cans... | 3; | • Video recording... | 8; | • Other restrictions... | 13. |
| • Bottles... | 4; | • Children... | 9; | | |
| • Coolers... | 5; | • Pets... | 10; | | |

Secondary Genre[s]:

| | | | |
|---|---|---|---|
| • Variety, General... | VRGL; | • Bluegrass... | BLGS; |
| • Variety, Jazz & Blues... | VRJB; | • Modern Folk... | MFOL; |
| • Variety, Country & Bluegrass | VRCB; | • Traditional Folk... | TFOL; |
| • Variety, Folk & International | VRFI; | • Fiddle and Banjo Events... | FDDL; |
| • Modern Jazz... | MJAZ; | • Maritime... | MARI; |
| • Traditional Jazz & Ragtime... | TJAZ; | • Cajun and Zydeco... | ZYDC; |
| • Alternative Jazz... | AJAZ; | • Irish... | IRSH; |
| • Modern Rock and Pop... | MRCK; | • Jewish... | JWSH; |
| • Classic Rock and Oldies... | CRCK; | • Native American... | NATV; |
| • Alternative & College Rock | ARCK; | • Scottish... | SCOT; |
| • Hard Rock & Heavy Metal | HRCK; | • Modern Latin... | MLAT; |
| • Rap... | RAP; | • Traditional Latin... | TLAT; |
| • Modern R&B... | MR&B; | • African American... | AFRM; |
| • Blues and Traditional R&B... | TR&B; | • African... | AFRC; |
| • Acappella and Doo Wop... | ACAP; | • Brazilian & So. American... | BRZL; |
| • Modern Christian... | CHRS; | • Reggae, Ska & Caribbean... | RGGE; |
| • Black Gospel... | BGOS; | • Avant Garde & New Music... | AVNT; |
| • Southern & Bluegrass Gospel | SGOS; | • Cabaret... | CBRT; |
| • Traditional Gospel & Sings... | TGOS; | • Gay and Lesbian... | GYLS; |
| • Modern Country... | MC&W; | • Drum Corps & March. Bands | DRUM; |
| • Traditional Country... | TC&W; | • Fairs... | FAIR; |
| • Alt. Country & Rockabilly... | AC&W; | • Other Genres... | OTHR. |

Wherever "**Help!**" appears readers are invited to answer the proceeding questions and/or pro- **Note** vide updates. New festival listings that meet the criteria of this book certainly are welcome too! Please mail any current festival information you obtain — especially flyers or brochures — to FESTPRESS, P. O. Box 147, Glen Ridge, NJ 07028. *Thanks!*

WINTER BOOGIE, Monticello, NY
  Early Jan.
  Modern Jazz

"Swing, Latin and Ballroom Dance Weekend." -- Brochure. See other dates and sites. **Days:** 3. **Site:** indoor. Kutscher's Country Club. **Admission:** paid. **Daily entry:** $25 to $49, **Discounts:** group sale discounts, **Secondary genre[s]:** MLAT, **Acts:** regional acts. **Sample lineup:** Georgie Gee Orchestra, Cruz Control, others. **Contact:** Boogie Dance Productions, 119 East 15th Street, New York, NY 10003, 800-64-SWING **or:** Fallsview Hotel, Ellenville, NY 12428, 914-822-8439.

OLD SONGS SAMPLER CONCERT, Guilderland, NY
  Late Jan.
  Traditional Folk

**Days:** 1. **Site:** indoor. Guilderland High School, off Route 146. **Secondary genre[s]:** MFOL, **Acts:** regional acts, local acts. **Sample day's lineup:** Steve Gillette and Cindy Mangsen, Bill Spence and Fennig's Allstars, Chris Shaw, Bridget Ball, others. **Contact:** Old Songs, Inc., P. O. Box 399, Guilderland, NY 12084, 518-765-2815.

WINTER FOLK MUSIC WEEKEND, Saugerties, NY
  Early Feb.
  Traditional Folk

See other dates and sites. **Days:** 3. **Site:** indoor. Solway House. **Admission:** paid. **Daily entry:** $50 and over. **Discounts:** other discounts. **Secondary genre[s]:** MFOL, OTHR. **Acts:** regional acts, local acts. **Sample day's lineup:** Steve Gillette and Cindy Mangsen, Jeter LePont, Adaya Hennis, Allen Hopkins, Sonja Savig, others. **Contact:** New York Pinewoods Folk Music Club, 31 West 95th Street, New York, NY 10025, 212-666-9605 **or:** New York Pinewoods Folk Music Club, 817 Broadway, 6th Floor, New York, NY 10003-4763, 212-213-7458.

CELEBRATIONS AND EXPRESSIONS OF OUR AFRICAN AMERICAN HERITAGE, Hempstead, NY
  Early Feb.
  African American

See other dates. **Help!** A sample lineup? **Days:** 2. **Hours per day:** 3. **Site:** indoor. African American Museum, 110 North Franklin Street. **Secondary genre[s]:** BGOS, **Acts:** local acts. **Contact:** African American Museum, 110 North Franklin Street, Hempstead, NY, 516-572-0730.

## DANCE FLURRY, Guilderland, NY
### Middle Feb.
### Variety, Folk and International

Since 1988. "NEFFA-like." -- Dance Gypsy. **Days:** 3. **Hours per day:** 14. **Site:** indoor. Farnsworth Middle School, off Route 155. **Admission:** paid. **Daily entry:** $10 to $24, **Discounts:** multiple event or day passes, **Secondary genre[s]:** TJAZ, CRCK, TC&W, TFOL, FDDL, ZYDC, JWSH, NATV, SCOT, TLAT, AFRC, OTHR **Acts:** regional acts, local acts. **Sample lineup:** Jane Ainslie, Amidons, Atlantic Bridge, Karen Axelrod, BLT, Mark Bagdon, Joe Baker, David Barnert, Brea Barthel, Mike Benedict, Bog People, Bill Borgida, Teresa Broadwell, Cynthia Butcher, Cambridge Dance Orchestra, John Chambers, Carol Connolly, Omoye, Kofi and Kwabena Cooper, Silvia Cornell, Creole Dog, Joyce Crouch, Dave Davies, Andy Davis, Peter Davis, Lena Degeneff, Der Kleine Klezmer orchestra, Ruthie Dornfield, Wendy Ernst, Flying Tomatoes, Brad Foster, Larry Fountain, Larry Fountain, Earl Gaddis, Lou Gardner, Pamela Goddard, Ken Grau, Tim Grant, Green Mountain Volunteers, Laura Hagen, Laurie Hart, Joe Hetko, Andrea Hoag, Eric Hollman, Forrest and Nancy Holroyd, Dave Howard, Morty Isaacson, Ivy Vine Players, Jerry Jenkins, Larry Jennings, Liz Jones, Pete Jung, Kitty Kagay, Selma Kaplan, David Kaynor, Van Kaynor, Stuart Kenney, John Kirk, Chuck Kistler, Henry Lamont, Sonia and George Long, Ken Lovelett, Martin and Linda Lyden, Molly Mason, Barbara McLean, Don McLean, Pat MacPherson, Barbara McAllester, Alan McClintock, Pat Melita, Trish Miller, Maria Morato, Mountain Laurel, Joan Mullen, Lois New, Mike Novakowski, Mike Otis, Cindy Overstreet, Tony Parkes, Bob Pasquarello, Peacemaker's Drum, Kristin Pearson, Peyote Coyote, Phiny The Phidler, John Pisa, Pokingbrook Morris, Polanski, Stokoe and Dean, Queen Anne's Lace, Paul Rosenberg, Pat Rust, Please And Thank You String Band, Michael Ryan, Paula Ryan, Peter Salm, Sambarama, Joan Savitt, Bob Schulz, Elizabeth Shapiro, Spare Parts, Nancy Spero, St. Regis String Band, Suzurama, Ralph Sweet, Deb Tankard, Emmy Thomee, Alan Thompson, Pete Toigo, Bill Tomczak, Don Treble, Debbie Trimm, Judy Trupin, Ted Turner, Jay Ungar, Vermont Children's Band, Tom Wadsworth, Kathy and Jeff Walker, Kathryn Wedderburn, Rich Wiebe, George Wilson, Cathy Winter, Yankee Ingenuity, Nancy Yule, Zillionaires, others. **Contact:** Hudson Mohawk Country Dancers, 97 Second Avenue, Troy, NY 12180, 518-237-9520/438-3035.

## ELECTRONIC MUSIC AT STONY BROOK, Stony Brook, NY
### Late Feb.
### Avant Garde and New Music

Part of a season-long classical music series. See other dates. **Help!** A sample lineup? **Days:** 1. **Site:** indoor. Recital Hall, SUNY at Stony Brook. **Admission:** free. **Acts:** local acts. **Contact:** Department of Music, SUNY at Stony Brook, Stony Brook, NY 11794-5475, 516-632-7330/7230.

## MOUNTAIN DULCIMER MUSIC FESTIVAL, Albany, NY
### Late Feb.
### Traditional Folk

Since 1989. **Days:** 2. **Hours per day:** 9. **Site:** indoor. McKownville United Methodist Church, 1565 Western Avenue. **Acts:** local acts. **Sample day's lineup:** Susan Trump, Carrie Crompton, others. **Contact:** Dulcimer Association of Albany, 1565 Western Avenue, Albany, NY, 518-439-3699/766-2619.

## IN WOMEN'S HANDS: THE BEAT OF THE DRUM, Albany, NY
### Early Mar.
### Variety, Folk and International

Since 1993. **Days:** 3. **Site:** indoor. U/Albany's Women's Building (workshops, etc.), Performing Arts Center (concert). **Admission:** free and paid. **Secondary genre[s]:** NATV, MLAT, AFRC, RGGE, OTHR **Acts:** local acts. **Sample day's lineup:** Edwinna Lee Tyler, Harpbeat, O'Buk Chum, ASE, Kay Oland-Rotzler, others. **Contact:** Multicultural Committee, U/Albany, Women's Building, 79 Central Avenue, Albany, NY 12206, 518-465-1597.

### DICK FOX'S SPRING DOO-WOPP EXTRAVAGANZA, Westbury, NY
Early Mar.
A Cappella and Doo Wop

See other dates and sites. **Days:** 1. **Site:** indoor. Westbury Music Fair, Brush Hollow Road. **Admission:** paid. **Daily entry:** $25 to $49, **Discounts:** group sale discounts, **Secondary genre[s]:** CRCK, **Acts:** national acts, regional acts, local acts. **Sample day's lineup:** Johnny Maestro and The Brooklyn Bridge, The Tokens, Earl Lewis and The Channels, The Elegants, The Jive Five, Reparata and The Del Rons, Younger Dayz. **Contact:** Westbury Music Fair, Brush Hollow Road, Westbury, NY, 516-334-0800 **or:** Dick Fox's Doo-Wopp Extravaganza, 1650 Broadway, Suite 503, New York, NY 10019, 212-582-9074.

### PENNY ASSOCIATION MIDWINTER BLUEGRASS FESTIVAL, Vestal, NY
Early Mar.
Bluegrass

See other dates and sites. **Days:** 1. **Hours per day:** 10. **Site:** indoor. American Legion Hall. **Secondary genre[s]:** SGOS, TC&W, BLGS, **Acts:** regional acts, local acts. **Sample day's lineup:** Dyer Switch, Classic Country, Wrench's Wranglers, Fish-N-Friends, Billie and The Boys, Endless Mountain Bluegrass, others. **Contact:** Penny Association Midwinter Bluegrass Festival, 578 Laurel Lake Road, Deposit, NY 13754, 607-467-3954 **or:** Penny Association Midwinter Bluegrass Festival, P. O. Box 385, Herkimer, NY 13350, 315-797-4791.

### PINES SCOTTISH WEEKEND, South Fallsburg, NY
Early Mar.
Scottish

"It's like a cruise on land!" -- Flyer. See other dates. **Days:** 3. **Site:** indoor. Pines Resort Hotel. **Admission:** paid. **Daily entry:** $50 and over. **Discounts:** group sale discounts, **Acts:** regional acts, local acts. **Sample lineup:** Kenneth McKellar, Alex Beaton, Brigadoons, Highland-Aires, Ronnie Stewart, Joe Gordon, Sally Logan, Sandy Haine and The Clansmen, others. **Contact:** Pines Scottish Weekend, Pines Resort Hotel, South Fallsburg, NY 12779, 800-36-PINES **or:** Gertrude Byrne Promotions, P. O. Box 6, Leeds, NY 12451, 518-943-3736.

### ST. PATRICK'S DAY CELEBRATIONS, Elmsford, NY
Early Mar. to Middle Mar.
Irish

"Great Irish entertainment with Ireland's own." -- Advertisement. **Days:** 4. **Site:** indoor. Westchester Broadway Theater, 1 Broadway Plaza. **Admission:** paid. **Daily entry:** $25 to $49, $50 and over. **Acts:** national acts, regional acts. **Sample series lineup:** Day One: The Clancy Brothers and Robbie O'Connell; Day Two: Tony Kenny and guests; Day Three: The Wolfe Tones. **Contact:** Westchester Broadway Theater, 1 Broadway Plaza, Elmsford, NY 10523, 914-592-2222/8730.

### RICHARD NADER'S LET THE GOOD TIMES ROLL, Kiamesha Lake, NY
Early Mar. to Middle Mar.
A Cappella and Doo Wop

See other dates. **Days:** 2. **Site:** indoor. Concord Resort Hotel. **Admission:** paid. **Daily entry:** $50 and over. **Secondary genre[s]:** CRCK, **Acts:** national acts, local acts. **Sample day's lineup:** The Duprees, Reparata and The Del Rons, Little Anthony and The Imperials. **Contact:** Concord Resort Hotel, Kiamesha Lake, NY 12751, 800-CONCORD.

## WATERTOWN GOES GREEN IRISH FESTIVAL, Watertown, NY
Middle Mar.
Irish

**Days:** 3. **Site:** indoor. Dulles State Office Building. **Secondary genre[s]:** BLGS, FDDL, **Acts:** regional acts, local acts. **Sample day's lineup:** Chesnut Grove, others. **Contact:** Watertown Goes Green Irish Festival, Carthage-Herrings Road, Carthage, NY 13619, 315-493-1174.

## IRISH CELEBRATION, Westbury, NY
Middle Mar.
Irish

Same lineups also appear at company's twin theater-in-the-round, Valley Forge Music Fair, in Valley Forge, PA. See other dates. **Days:** 3. **Site:** indoor. Westbury Music Fair, Brush Hollow Road. **Admission:** paid. **Daily entry:** $10 to $24, $25 to $49, **Discounts:** group sale discounts, **Acts:** national acts, local acts. **Sample series lineup:** Day One: Roger Whittaker; Day Two: Hal Roach, Clancy Family Singers; Day Three: The Clancy Brothers, Northeast Winds. **Contact:** Westbury Music Fair, Brush Hollow Road, Westbury, NY, 516-334-0800.

## PINES HOTEL BLUEGRASS FESTIVAL, South Fallsburg, NY
Middle Mar.
Bluegrass

Since 1988. "Bluegrass with class." -- Brochure. See other sites and dates. **Days:** 4. **Site:** indoor. Pines Resort Hotel. **Admission:** paid. **Daily entry:** $50 and over. **Discounts:** multiple event or day passes, advance purchase discounts, group sale discounts, **Acts:** national acts, regional acts. **Sample lineup:** Del McCoury Band, California, Stevens Family, Raymond Fairchild and The Maggie Valley Boys, Jim and Jesse and The Virginia Boys, Southern Rail, Mike Stevens, Tony Rice Unit, Red Wing, Sally Mountain Show, Nashville Bluegrass Band, Tim O'Brien, Boys From Indiana, 111rd Tyme Out, Seldom Scene. **Contact:** Peaceful Valley Promotions, Inc., HC 89, Box 56, Downsville, NY 13755, 800-367-4637.

## WOMEN IN MUSIC CELEBRATION, Colonie, NY
Middle Mar.
Modern Folk

Since 1994. "Pay[ing] tribute to the richness of woman's involvement in music history." -- Advertisement. **Days:** 1. **Hours per day:** 5. **Site:** indoor. Barnes and Nobles Booksellers, 20 Wolf Road. **Acts:** local acts. **Sample day's lineup:** Veena Chandra, Joan Crane, Bridget Ball, Peg Delaney, Peggy Eyres, Amy Abdou. **Contact:** Women in Music Celebration, Barnes and Nobles Booksellers, 20 Wolf Road, Colonie, NY, 518-459-8183.

## NASSAU COMMUNITY COLLEGE FOLK FESTIVAL, Garden City, NY
Late Mar.
Variety, General

Since 1972. **Days:** 3. **Site:** indoor. College Union. **Admission:** free. **Secondary genre[s]:** MJAZ, CRCK, RAP, TR&B, BGOS, AC&W, BLGS, MFOL, TFOL, ZYDC, IRSH, MLAT, AFRC, BRZL, RGGE, OTHR. **Acts:** national acts, local acts. **Sample day's lineup:** Arrow, Tom Paxton, The Holmes Brothers, Walt Michael, Judy Small. **Contact:** Nassau Community College Folk Festival, Nassau Community College, Garden City, NY 11530, 516-222-7148.

ADIRONDACK FOLK NIGHT, Troy, NY
    Late Mar.
    Traditional Folk

"An evening of song, stories and dance." -- Advertisement. See other dates. **Help!** One time only? **Days:** 1. **Site:** indoor. Troy Saving Bank Music Hall, Second and State Streets. **Admission:** paid. **Daily entry:** $10 to $24, **Secondary genre[s]:** MFOL, **Acts:** regional acts, local acts. **Sample day's lineup:** Bill Smith, Dan Berggren, Susan Trump, Newton Street Irregulars, Peggy Eyres, Trish Miller and John Kirk, others. **Contact:** Troy Savings Bank Music Hall, 84 4th Street, Troy, NY, 518-273-0038.

COLLEGE OF SAINT ROSE HIGH SCHOOL JAZZ FESTIVAL, Albany, NY
    Late Mar.
    Modern Jazz

Since 1994. See other dates and sites. **Days:** 1. **Site:** indoor. St. Joseph Hall Auditorium, 985 Madison Avenue. **Acts:** national acts, local acts. **Sample day's lineup:** Marvin Stamm, Saint Rose Jazz Ensemble, Empire State Jazz Ensemble. **Contact:** College of Saint Rose, 423 Western Avenue, Albany, NY 12203, 518-454-5195/5193.

PYX ROCK AND ROLL EXPO, Albany, NY
    Late Mar.
    Alternative and College Rock

Since 1992. See other dates and sites. **Days:** 1. **Hours per day:** 7. **Site:** indoor. Armory, New Scotland Avenue. **Admission:** free. **Secondary genre[s]:** MRCK, TR&B, MC&W, **Acts:** national acts, local acts. **Sample day's lineup:** Buffalo Tom, Billy Falcon and His Band, Stick, Matt Smith Band, Nobody's Girls. **Contact:** WPYX-FM 106, 1054 Troy-Schenectady Road, Latham, NY 12110, 518-785-9800.

EMERALD WEEKEND, Kiamesha Lake, NY
    Early Apr.
    Irish

**Help!** Still ongoing at this site? **Days:** 3. **Site:** indoor. Concord Resort Hotel. **Admission:** paid. **Daily entry:** $25 to $49, **Acts:** regional acts, local acts. **Sample lineup:** Paddy Noonan, Andy Cooney, Pat Roper, Deirdre Reilly, Sonny Knowles, Marie Frances, Paddy McGinty, John Trotter, Joe Hayes, Michael Jesse Owens Band, Mike McCormack, others. **Contact:** Emerald Weekend, Concort Resort Hotel, Kiamesha Lake, NY 12751, 914-794-4000.

BARNABY'S BATTLE OF THE BANDS, Centereach, NY
    Early Apr.
    Hard Rock and Heavy Metal

Since 1994. "Quest for the best." -- Advertisement. **Help!** One time only? **Days:** 1. **Hours per day:** 4. **Site:** indoor. Barnaby's II, 1795 Middle Country Road. **Secondary genre[s]:** MRCK, ARCK, **Acts:** local acts. **Sample day's lineup:** Synergy, Edna's Goldfish, Fat Alice, Jam Sandwich. **Contact:** Barnaby's II, 1795 Middle Country Road, Centereach, NY, 516-467-9722/348-7718.

COUNTRY CLASSIC IN THE CATSKILLS, South Fallsburg, NY
    Early Apr.
    Modern Country

Since 1992. "Often imitated, never duplicated!" -- Brochure. See other dates. **Days:** 3. **Site:** indoor. Pines Resort Hotel. **Admission:** paid. **Daily entry:** $50 and over. **Discounts:** group sale discounts, **Acts:** regional acts, local acts. **Sample lineup:** High Sierra, The Possee, Southbound, Sage, Thunder Rose, Tim Gillis, Jan Slow and The Vanishing Cowboys, others. **Contact:** Country Dance Music Weekend, Pines Resort Hotel, South Fallsburg, NY 12779, 800-36-PINES **or:** Country Dance Music Weekend, P. O. Box 144, Baldwin, NY 11510, 516-379-4564.

## PINES NUMBER ONE IRISH WEEKEND, South Fallsburg, NY
Early Apr.
Irish

"The perfect getaway weekend!" -- Flyer. See other dates. **Days:** 3. **Site:** indoor. Pines Resort Hotel. **Admission:** paid. **Daily entry:** $50 and over. **Discounts:** group sale discounts, **Acts:** national acts, regional acts, local acts. **Sample lineup:** Joannie Madden, Sean O'Neil Band, New York Show-Band, Johnny Carroll, Dave Coady and His Irish Express, Jimmy Hughes Show-Band, Jimmy McPhail, Erin's Pride, Glen Curtin, Ann Breen, others. **Contact:** Pines Irish Weekend, Pines Resort Hotel, South Fallsburg, NY 12779, 800-36-PINES **or:** Gertrude Byrne Promotions, P. O. Box 6, Leeds, NY 12451, 518-943-3736.

## AL MASTREN MEMORIAL SCHOLARSHIP CONCERT, Cohoes, NY
Early Apr.
Modern Jazz

**Help!** A sample lineup? **Days:** 1. **Site:** indoor. Cohoes High School, Elm Street. **Acts:** local acts. **Contact:** Al Mastren Memorial Scholarship Concert, Cohoes High School, Elm Street, Cohoes, NY, 518-235-4493/482-3839.

## EMERALD PRODUCTIONS GETAWAY, Callicoon, NY
Middle Apr.
Irish

"Treat yourself!" -- Advertisement. See other dates. **Days:** 3. **Site:** indoor. Villa Roma Resort Hotel. **Admission:** paid. **Daily entry:** $50 and over. **Acts:** national acts, regional acts, local acts. **Sample lineup:** Clancy Brothers and Robbie O'Connell, Brendan Grace, Paddy Noonan Revue, The Healys and John Tabb, Cleo Meaney, Vince McCormack, Fran Raftery, Mike McCormack, Joe Hayes, Willie Lynch, others. **Contact:** Emerald Productions Getaway, Villa Roma Resort Hotel, Callicoon, NY, 800-533-6767.

## SPRINGFEST, Oceanside, NY
Middle Apr.
Modern Rock and Pop

Since 1993. See other dates. **Days:** 2. **Site:** indoor. Christopher's Sport Rock Cafe, 3297 Long Beach Road. **Admission:** paid. **Daily entry:** under $10, **Secondary genre[s]:** HRCK, **Acts:** local acts. **Sample day's lineup:** Wind, Bonnie Troy, Zen Tricksters, American Dreamer, Bobby Charles and Blue Rules, Play of Soul, Primo, Blue Ruin, Larry Mitchell, Blues Dog, Friedman and Schafer, Rotgut, Hack Squad, No Justice. **Contact:** Christophers's, 3297 Long Beach Road, Oceanside, NY 11572, 516-766-9822.

## SONGWRITER SHOWCASE, Deer Park, NY
Middle Apr.
Modern Country

"Come meet the people behind the songs that made the stars famous." -- Flyer. Dates vary widely, so call ahead. **Days:** 1. **Site:** indoor. Matty T's Nashville U. S. A., 356 Commack Road. **Admission:** paid. **Daily entry:** under $10, **Acts:** national acts, local acts. **Sample day's lineup:** Hugh Prestwood, Dr. Joe Waldbaum, A. J. Gundell, George Wurzbach, Arlene Gold, Marshall Stern, Four In The Morning. **Contact:** Matty T's Nashville U. S. A., 356 Commack Road, Deer Park, NY 11729, 516-667-6868 **or:** Nashville Songwriters Association International, 1025 16th Avenue South, Suite 200, Nashville, TN 37212 .

SWING SPRING, Troy, NY
> Late Apr.
> Modern Jazz

"Here's where we are." -- Advertisement. Benefits nonprofit host venue. See other dates. **Help!** One time only? **Days:** 1. **Site:** indoor. Troy Saving Bank Music Hall, Second and State Streets. **Admission:** paid. **Daily entry:** $10 to $24, **Secondary genre[s]:** TR&B, **Acts:** national acts, local acts. **Sample day's lineup:** Laurel Masse, Doc Scanlon's Rhythm Boys, Marlowe and Co. Big Band. **Contact:** Troy Savings Bank Music Hall, 84 4th Street, Troy, NY, 518-273-0038.

LONG ISLAND GUITAR FESTIVAL, Brookville, NY
> Late Apr.
> Modern Jazz

Since 1993. See other dates. **Days:** 2. **Site:** indoor. Interfaith Chapel, Long Island University, C. W. Post Campus, Route 25A **Admission:** paid. **Daily entry:** $10 to $24, $25 to $49, **Discounts:** multiple event or day passes, **Secondary genre[s]:** OTHR. **Acts:** national acts, local acts. **Sample day's lineup:** John "Bucky" Pizzarelli, Eliot Fisk. **Contact:** School of Visual and Performing Arts, Long Island University, C. W. Post Campus, Brookville, NY 11548, 516-299-2474/2332.

GRAND INTERNATIONAL RAGTIME/JASSTIME FOUNDATION SPRING FESTIVAL, Alexandria Bay, NY
> Late Apr.
> Traditional Jazz and Ragtime

See other dates. **Days:** 3. **Site:** indoor. Edgewood Resort. **Secondary genre[s]:** TGOS, **Acts:** regional acts, local acts. **Sample lineup:** Mimi Blais, Rich Berry, Don Burns, Jack Cuff, Bob Darch, Neville Dickie, Virginia Tichenor Gilseth, Tim Sandor, Kjell Waltman, Borgy Borgerson Trio, Et Cetera String Band, Sister Jean The Ragtime Queen and Laundry Fat, Ralph Gruegel's Eagle Jazz Band, Bob Milne's Sweet Violets Jazz Band, Brian Tower's Hot 5 Jazzmakers. **Contact:** Grand International Ragtime/Jasstime Foundation, P. O. Box 92022, 2900 Warden Avenue, Scarborough, ON M1W 3Y9, 416-494-7631.

COLLEGE OF SAINT ROSE COLLEGIATE JAZZ FESTIVAL, Albany, NY
> Late Apr.
> Modern Jazz

Since 1994. See other dates and sites. **Days:** 1. **Site:** indoor. The Empire Center at The Egg. **Admission:** paid. **Daily entry:** $10 to $24, **Discounts:** advance purchase discounts, **Acts:** national acts, regional acts, local acts. **Sample day's lineup:** Doug Sertl Big Band, Ed Shaughnessy, Nick Brignola, others. **Contact:** College of Saint Rose, 423 Western Avenue, Albany, NY 12203, 518-454-5195/5193.

NEW YORK STATE INTERCOLLEGIATE JAZZ FESTIVAL, Morrisville, NY
> Late Apr.
> Modern Jazz

Since 1974. **Days:** 1. **Site:** indoor. Student Activities Building, SUNY at Morrisville. **Admission:** paid. **Daily entry:** under $10, **Acts:** national acts, local acts. **Sample day's lineup:** New York Voices, Chris Vidala, others. **Contact:** Music Department, SUNY at Morrisville, Morrisville, NY 13664, 315-684-6058/6116.

## SPRING BLUES FESTIVAL, Westbury, NY
Late Apr.
Blues and Traditional R&B

Same lineups also appear at company's twin theater-in-the-round, Valley Forge Music Fair, in Valley Forge, PA. See other dates. **Days:** 1. **Site:** indoor. Westbury Music Fair, Brush Hollow Road. **Admission:** paid. **Daily entry:** $25 to $49, **Discounts:** group sale discounts, **Acts:** national acts. **Sample day's lineup:** B. B. King, The Manhattans, Gerald Alston and Blue Lovett, Bobby "Blue" Bland. **Contact:** Westbury Music Fair, Brush Hollow Road, Westbury, NY, 516-334-0800.

## WEQX PARTY IN THE PARK, Albany, NY
Late Apr.
Alternative and College Rock

See other dates and sites. **Days:** 1. **Site:** outdoor. Lincoln Park. **Secondary genre[s]:** TR&B, **Acts:** national acts, local acts. **Sample day's lineup:** Samples, Bloom, Ernie Williams and The Wildcats, Perfect Thyroid, Smokehouse Prophets. **Contact:** WEQX-FM, Elm Street, Manchester, VT, 802-362-4800.

## SPRING BLOSSOM FIDDLE JAMBOREE, Long Lake, NY
Late Apr.
Fiddle and Banjo Events

Since 1992. "All fiddlers welcome to participate." -- Flyer. Part of Music in the Mountains traditional music series. See other dates and sites. **Days:** 1. **Hours per day:** 4. **Site:** indoor. Long Lake Town Hall, off Route 30. **Admission:** paid. **Daily entry:** under $10, **Secondary genre[s]:** TC&W, BLGS, TFOL, **Acts:** local acts. **Contact:** Long Lake Parks, Recreation and Tourism, P. O. Box 496, Long Lake, NY 12847, 518-624-3077.

## SYRACUSE AREA MUSIC AWARDS (SAMMIES), Syracuse, NY
Early May
Variety, General

11 local acts showcasing. **Help!** A sample lineup? **Days:** 1. **Site:** indoor. Landmark Theater, South Salina Street. **Secondary genre[s]:** MLAT, **Acts:** local acts. **Contact:** Syracuse Area Music Awards (Sammies), 362 South Salina Street, P. O. Box 1400, Syracuse, NY 13201, 315-475-7979.

## FOLK MUSIC SOCIETY OF HUNTINGTON MEMBERS CONCERT, Huntington, NY
Early May
Traditional Folk

See other dates and sites. **Days:** 1. **Hours per day:** 3. **Site:** indoor. Finley Junior High School, Greenlawn Road. **Secondary genre[s]:** TJAZ, TR&B, MFOL, **Acts:** local acts. **Sample day's lineup:** Richard Barnhardt, Bill Lauter, Scott MacDonald, John Kuhn, Charlie and Maureen Mooney, Larry Moser, Colleen Donahue, Debbie Nuse, Steve Brauch, Steve Sariego, others. **Contact:** Folk Music Society of Huntington, 411 Cooper Road, North Babylon, NY 11703, 516-321-1582/549-9677.

## TURK MURPHY MEMORIAL FESTIVAL, Buffalo, NY
Early May
Traditional Jazz and Ragtime

See other dates and sites. **Days:** 1. **Site:** indoor. The Marquee at The Tralf. **Acts:** regional acts, local acts. **Sample day's lineup:** Bar-Room Buzzards, Eli Konikoff's Dixie Band, Lazy River Jazz Band, Morgan Street Stompers, Nickel City Clippers, Tin Roof Jazz Band. **Contact:** Queen City Jass and Ragtime Society, Inc., P. O. Box 269, Clarence, NY 14031, 905-685-0175 **or:** Queen City Jass and Ragtime Society, Inc., 4570 Harris Hill Road, Williamsville, NY 14221-6212, 905-634-1863.

WESTCHESTER COMMUNITY COLLEGE JAZZ FESTIVAL, White Plains, NY
   Early May
   Modern Jazz

Since 1994. **Days:** 1. **Hours per day:** 10. **Site:** indoor. Academic Arts Building. **Admission:** paid. **Daily entry:** under $10, $10 to $24, **Discounts:** student discounts, **Secondary genre[s]:** TR&B, **Acts:** national acts, regional acts, local acts. **Sample day's lineup:** David Amram's Quartet, Dave Samuels Group, Mark Morganelli's Jazz Forum Allstars, Tanareid, Houston Person and Etta Jones, Vic Juris, Ray Drummond, Jimmy Cobb, Phil Woods Quintet, others. **Audio merchandise:** 38 productions for Candid Records, including several live festival recordings. **Contact:** Jazz Forum Arts, P. O. Box 1917 Cathedral Station, New York, NY 10025, 914-785-6567/674-2005 **or:** Jazz Forum Arts, c/o Tarrtown Music Hall, 81 Grandview Avenue, Dobbs Ferry, NY 10522.


INDIAN POW WOW, Niagara Falls, NY
   Early May
   Native American

**Days:** 2. **Site:** indoor. Native American Center. **Acts:** local acts. **Contact:** Native American Center, M. P. O. Box 945, Niagara Falls, NY 14302-0945, 716-284-2427.


PINKSTERFEST/ALBANY TULIP FESTIVAL, Albany, NY
   Early May
   Variety, General

Since 1949. Combined festivals; Pinksterfest features live music. See other dates and sites. **Days:** 3. **Hours per day:** 5. **Site:** outdoor. Washington Park. **Secondary genre[s]:** MJAZ, MRCK, ARCK, TC&W, AC&W, MFOL, TFOL, GYLS, OTHR **Acts:** national acts, regional acts, local acts. **Sample day's lineup:** Material Issue, Jeffrey Gaines, Jazz Voices, Danielle Brisebois, others. **Contact:** City of Albany Mayor's Office of Special Events, 60 Orange Street, Albany, NY 12210, 518-434-2032.


WILLIAM SMITH AND HOBART COLLEGES FOLK FEST, Geneva, NY
   Early May
   Variety, Folk and International

Since 1976. Benefits Ontario Daycare Center, Community Unified. **Days:** 3. **Hours per day:** 12. **Site:** outdoor. Quad, Routes 5, 20 and 14, off Seneca Lake. **Admission:** free. **Restrictions:** 2, **Secondary genre[s]:** MJAZ, TJAZ, ARCK, BGOS, BLGS, MFOL, AFRC, OTHR. **Acts:** national acts, regional acts, local acts. **Sample day's lineup:** Rusted Root, Conehead Buddha, Christine Lavin, The Burns Sisters, Matt Stamell and Friends, others. **Contact:** William Smith and Hobart Colleges Folk Fest, William Smith and Hobart Colleges, Geneva, NY 14456-3397, 315-781-3512.


UNCLE SAM'S BLUES JAM, Troy, NY
   Early May
   Blues and Traditional R&B

Since 1993. Pub crawl via "Blues Bus" culminating in jam. **Days:** 1. **Hours per day:** 6. **Site:** indoor. 8 locations. **Admission:** paid. **Daily entry:** under $10, **Discounts:** multiple event or day passes, **Acts:** regional acts, local acts. **Sample day's lineup:** Ernie Williams and The Wildcats, Rhythm Riders, Matt Smith Blues Band, Blues Alley, Bad-Go-Getter, City Lights, Blue Jeanne Blue. **Contact:** Uncle Sam's Blues Jam, Positively 3rd Street Records, 3rd Street, Troy, NY, 518-270-9389.

## Two Rivers Ethnic Festival, Binghamton, NY
### Early May
### Variety, Folk and International

**Help!** A sample lineup? **Days:** 2. **Site:** indoor. Broome County Arena. **Acts:** local acts. **Contact:** American Civic Association, 131 Front Street, Binghamton, NY 13905, 607-785-8540/723-9419.

## WXLE Acoustic Music Festival, Clifton Park, NY
### Early May to Late May
### Modern Folk

**Days:** 3. **Site:** indoor. Village Plaza, Shopper's World. **Acts:** local acts. **Sample day's lineup:** No Man's Land, The McKrells, Ben Murray, Siobhan Quinn, others. **Contact:** WXLE-FM, 940 Route 146, Clifton Park, NY, 518-383-1063.

## Band Box Anniversary Love-Fest/Wife-Swap, Port Chester, NY
### Middle May
### Alternative and College Rock

Since 1993. "Overall, I'd say the night went four-for-four...Let's hope we can do it again next year." -- Band Box, The Weekly. **Days:** 1. **Site:** indoor. The Beat. **Acts:** regional acts, local acts. **Sample day's lineup:** The Monitors, Philistines Jr., Zambonis, Those Melvins. **Contact:** The Weekly, 180 Post Road East, Suite 8, Westport, CT 06880, 203-226-4242.

## I. A. C. A.'s International Festival of the Adirondacks, Queensbury, NY
### Middle May
### Variety, Folk and International

**Help!** One time only? Also, a sample lineup? **Days:** 2. **Hours per day:** 7. **Site:** outdoor and indoor. Adirondack Community College, Bay Road. **Admission:** paid. **Daily entry:** under $10, $10 to $24, **Discounts:** group sale discounts, **Acts:** local acts. **Contact:** I. A. C. A.'s International Festival of the Adirondacks, c/o Adirondack Community College, Bay Road, Queensbury, NY, 518-793-2773.

## Hurdy Gurdy Strings and Sings Spring Fling, Accord, NY
### Middle May
### Modern Folk

"Music, music, music...Don't forget your instruments and singing voices." -- Flyer. **Days:** 3. **Site:** indoor. Su Casa. **Admission:** paid. **Discounts:** advance purchase discounts, **Secondary genre[s]:** TFOL, **Acts:** national acts, local acts. **Sample day's lineup:** Happy and Artie Traum and The Hurdy Gurdy All-Stars, others. **Contact:** Hurdy Gurdy Folk Music Club, 191 Johnson Avenue, Dumont, NJ 07628, 201-836-4696 **or:** Hurdy Gurdy Folk Music Club, 686 Kent Avenue, Teaneck, NJ 07666.

## Lilac Festival, Rochester, NY
### Middle May to Late May
### Variety, General

**Days:** 10. **Site:** outdoor. Highland Park. **Admission:** free. **Secondary genre[s]:** MJAZ, CRCK, ARCK, TR&B, ACAP, BGOS, MC&W, ZYDC, RGGE, GYLS, OTHR **Acts:** national acts, regional acts, local acts. **Sample day's lineup:** John Mooney and Bluesiana, Mighty Sam Mclain, Saffire, Popa Chubby, Coupe De Villes, MCC Jazz Ensemble, MCC Noon Flyte, MCC Guitar Ensemble, Da Igrammo Folk Ensemble, Jive Five-O, Atlas, The Sattalites, Folclorista Italiana, Bill Welch with Gene Rogalski, The Dinner Dogs, Musical Dinosaurs, Just Foolin' Around, others. **Contact:** Greater Rochester Visitors Association, Inc., 126 Andrews Street, Rochester, NY 14604-7282, 716-546-3070.

IRISH TRADITIONAL DANCE FESTIVAL, Mineola, NY
Middle May
Irish

Since 1990. See other sites and dates. **Days:** 1. **Hours per day:** 12. **Site:** indoor. Irish American Center, 297 Willis Avenue. **Admission:** paid. **Daily entry:** $10 to $24, **Discounts:** advance purchase discounts, other discounts **Acts:** national acts, regional acts, local acts. **Sample day's lineup:** Jack Coen, Brian Conway, John Cronin, Felix Dolan, Andy McGann, John Nolan, Mike Preston. **Contact:** Irish Arts Center, 553 West 51st Street, New York, NY 10019, 212-757-3318.

SHADFEST, Peekskill, NY
Middle May
Modern Folk

Since 1991. **Days:** 1. **Hours per day:** 6. **Site:** outdoor. Riverfront Green. **Admission:** free. **Discounts:** multiple event or day passes, advance purchase discounts, **Secondary genre[s]:** TFOL, MARI, **Acts:** national acts, regional acts, local acts. **Sample day's lineup:** Cathy Winter, Margo Hennebach, Kathy and Bob Zentz, Pete Seeger, Clearwater Sloop Singers. **Contact:** Riverlovers, Inc., P. O. Box 521, Crugers, NY 10521, 914-271-8163 **or:** Hudson Sloop Clearwater, Inc., 112 Market Street, Poughkeepsie, NY 12601, 914-454-7673.

JAZZ FOR THE ARTS/SUPER JAZZ JAM BLOWOUT, Albany, NY
Middle May
Modern Jazz

Since 1993. "Featuring the region's top talent." -- Advertisement. Concludes Jazz for the Arts concert series. See other dates. **Help!** A sample lineup? **Days:** 1. **Site:** indoor. daytime workshop: College of Saint Rose, Music Building, 423 Western Avenue; evening concert: The Empire Center at The Egg. **Admission:** paid. **Daily entry:** $10 to $24, **Discounts:** student discounts, advance purchase discounts, **Acts:** regional acts, local acts. **Contact:** Jazz for the Arts, The Empire Center at the Egg, Empire State Plaza, Albany, NY, 518-473-1845.

BENEFIT FOR THE FIGHT AGAINST LEUKEMIA, Deer Park, NY
Late May
Modern Country

Since 1986. See other date. **Days:** 1. **Site:** indoor. Matty T's Nashville U. S. A., 356 Commack Road. **Admission:** paid. **Daily entry:** under $10, **Acts:** regional acts, local acts. **Sample day's lineup:** Thunder Rose, Southern Heart, Southbound, Eastern Spur, others. **Contact:** Matty T's Nashville U. S. A., 356 Commack Road, Deer Park, NY 11729, 516-667-6868.

GREAT LAWN IRISH FAIR, Brookville, NY
Late May
Irish

Since 1993. See other dates. **Days:** 1. **Hours per day:** 7. **Site:** outdoor. Long Island University, C. W. Post Campus, Route 25A. **Daily entry:** $25 to $49, **Discounts:** multiple event or day passes, **Acts:** national acts, local acts. **Sample day's lineup:** Anne Marie Maloney, Eileen Ivers, Joannie Madden, Gabriel Donohue, Kimati Dinizulu, Dermot Henry Band, Sheila Ryan, others. **Contact:** Irish Cultural Society, Long Island University, C. W. Post Campus, Brookville, NY 11548, 516-299-2332.

WESTCHESTER ARTS FESTIVAL, White Plains, NY
Late May
Variety, General

See other dates and sites. **Days:** 1. **Hours per day:** 6. **Site:** outdoor. Westchester County Center, Bronx River Parkway at Central Avenue. **Admission:** free. **Secondary genre[s]:** MJAZ, SGOS, BLGS, IRSH, RGGE, OTHR **Acts:** regional acts, local acts. **Sample day's lineup:** Golden Chordsmen, Mark Morganelli and The Jazz Forum Allstars with Andy Laverne, Youth Theater Interactions Steel Drum Band, Westchester Philharmonic, others. **Contact:** Westchester County Department of Parks and Recreation, 19 Bradhurst Avenue, Hawthorne, NY 10532, 914-593-PARK.

ISRAELI FESTIVAL, Oceanside, NY
Late May
Jewish

**Help!** One time only? **Days:** 1. **Hours per day:** 5. **Site:** outdoor. South Shore Y Jewish Community Center, 25 Castleton Court. **Admission:** free. **Daily entry:** under $10, **Secondary genre[s]:** MFOL, OTHR **Acts:** national acts, local acts. **Sample day's lineup:** Oscar Brand, Tom Chapin, David Jack, Magic Bob Infantino, Suffolk Y Chamber Ensemble, others. **Contact:** South Shore Y Jewish Community Center, 25 Castleton Court, Oceanside, NY, 516-766-4341.

PENNY ASSOCIATION MEMORIAL DAY BLUEGRASS AND COUNTRY MUSIC FESTIVAL, Coventryville, NY
Late May
Bluegrass

See other dates and sites. **Days:** 3. **Hours per day:** 10. **Site:** outdoor. Wrench Ranch, Route 206. **Secondary genre[s]:** SGOS, TC&W, BLGS, **Acts:** regional acts, local acts. **Sample day's lineup:** Dyer Switch, Classic Country, Wrench's Wranglers, Fish-N-Friends, Billie and The Boys, Endless Mountain Bluegrass, others. **Contact:** Penny Association Memorial Day Bluegrass Festival, RD 1, Box 47, Bainbridge, NY 13733, 607-639-1371 **or:** Penny Association Memorial Day Bluegrass Festival, P. O. Box 385, Herkimer, NY 13350, 315-797-4791.

PRAISE, Darien Lake, NY
Late May
Modern Christian

**Days:** 3. **Hours per day:** 15. **Site:** outdoor. Darien Lake Theme Park and Camping Resort, Route 77. **Admission:** paid. **Daily entry:** $10 to $24, $25 to $49, **Discounts:** multiple event or day passes, advance purchase discounts, group sale discounts, **Secondary genre[s]:** MRCK, HRCK, RAP, MR&B, TR&B, ACAP, BGOS, MC&W, MFOL, **Acts:** national acts, regional acts, local acts. **Sample day's lineup:** Randy Rothwell, Alvin Slaughter, Marty Nystrom, Lenny LeBlanc, Mylon LeFevre, others. **Contact:** Kingdom Bound Ministries, 8550 Sheridan Drive, P. O. Box 1622, Williamsville, NY 14231-1622, 716-633-1117.

MEMORIAL DAY WEEKEND FESTIVAL, Parksville, NY
Late May
Hard Rock and Heavy Metal

"800 acres of a wild rocker's dream!" -- Advertisement. Events and lineups highly variable, so call ahead. See other dates. **Help!** One time only? **Days:** 3. **Hours per day:** 14. **Site:** outdoor. Arrowhead Ranch, 548 Cooley Road, off Route 17W. **Admission:** paid. **Daily entry:** under $10, **Restrictions:** 4, 10, **Acts:** local acts. **Sample lineup:** After Dark, Apostates, Major Domo, Mixed Breed, My World, Pud, Spiders and Pigs, Steel Reign, Trash Can Baby, Vienna, Voodoo Storm, Zale. **Contact:** Arrowhead Ranch, R. D. 1, Box 87, Parksville, NY 12768, 914-292-6273.

BEARSVILLE THEATER MEMORIAL DAY MUSIC FESTIVAL, Bearsville, NY
Late May
Variety, General

"Three outstanding concerts!" -- Flyer. **Days:** 3. **Site:** indoor. Bearsville Theater. **Admission:** paid. **Daily entry:** $10 to $24, **Secondary genre[s]:** MRCK, TR&B, BLGS, ZYDC, **Acts:** national acts, local acts. **Sample series lineup:** Day One: Jeffrey Gaines, Chris Kowanko; Day Two: Boozoo Chavis and The Magic Sounds; Day Three: The Holmes Brothers. **Contact:** Bearsville Theater, Route 212, Bearsville, NY, 914-679-4406.

IRISH FESTIVAL, East Durham, NY
Late May
Irish

Since 1978. "Welcome to three days of Ireland in America." -- Advertisement. See other dates. **Days:** 3. **Hours per day:** 12. **Site:** outdoor. Irish Cultural and Sports Center, Route 145. **Admission:** paid. **Daily entry:** $10 to $24, **Secondary genre[s]:** MC&W, **Acts:** national acts, regional acts, local acts. **Sample lineup:** Cherish The Ladies, Tommy Flynn's New York Showband, Dermot Henry, Erin's Pride, The Porters, Sean Fleming Band, Jimmy McPhail and The Regals, Bandolero, Paula Frazier and Montana, Ralph Bargar and Peaceful Country, Tweed, Paddy Noonan's Band with Carl Corcoran, Johnny Murphy and The Clubmen, Aine, John Connors and The Irish Express, Peter Street Band, Jimmy Walsh Band, Columbia District Pipe Band, Albany Police Department Pipe Band, Middle Fort Pipe Band, Hobart Fire Dept. Pipe and Drums. **Contact:** East Durham Vacationland Association, P. O. Box 67, East Durham, NY 12423, 518-634-2286.

GOTTAGETGON FOLK FESTIVAL: THE PICK'N AND SINGIN' GATHERIN', Ballston Spa, NY
Late May
Modern Folk

Since 1970. **Days:** 4. **Hours per day:** 12. **Site:** outdoor and indoor. Saratoga County Fairgrounds, Prospect Street. **Admission:** paid. **Daily entry:** under $10, $10 to $24, **Discounts:** student discounts, multiple event or day passes, **Secondary genre[s]:** TR&B, TGOS, TC&W, BLGS, TFOL, IRSH, SCOT, **Acts:** national acts, regional acts, local acts. **Sample day's lineup:** Johnnie Collins, Cindy Mangsen and Steve Gillette, Freyda Epstein and The Atta Boys, Dan Berggren, Cathy Winter. **Contact:** GottaGetGon Folk Festival, 32 Euclid Avenue, Elsmere, NY 12054, 518-439-5501 **or:** GottaGetGon Folk Festival, 27B Beach Avenue, Albany, NY 12203, 518-355-9633.

STANFORDVILLE MUSIC AND DANCE FESTIVAL, Stanfordville, NY
Late May
Cajun and Zydeco

Since 1986. **Days:** 1. **Hours per day:** 13. **Site:** outdoor and indoor. Country Fare Antiques and Art Center, Route 82. **Admission:** paid. **Daily entry:** $10 to $24, **Discounts:** advance purchase discounts, **Acts:** national acts, regional acts, local acts. **Sample day's lineup:** Steve Riley and The Mamou Playboys, Dirty Rice Cajun Band, The Voodoobillies, Bayou Midnight. **Contact:** Beekman General Store, 578 Beekman Road, Hopewell Junction, NY 12533, 914-226-2585.

INTERNATIONAL JEWISH ARTS FESTIVAL OF LONG ISLAND, Commack, NY
Late May
Jewish

Since 1983. Has also been held Labor Day weekend; call for current dates. **Days:** 2. **Hours per day:** 8. **Site:** outdoor. Suffolk Y Jewish Community Center, 74 Hauppauge Road. **Admission:** paid. **Daily entry:** $10 to $24, **Secondary genre[s]:** MJAZ, MFOL, OTHR **Acts:** national acts, local acts. **Sample day's lineup:** Adrienne Cooper, Lillian Lux, Carol Freeman Ensemble, David Amram and The International Jewish Arts Festival Orchestra, Shimrit Carmi, Oscar Brand, Lyle Cogen, Gilbert and Sullivan Light Opera, Marilyn Michaels, Claudia Jacobs, others. **Contact:** Suffolk Jewish Community Center, 74 Hauppauge Road, Commack, NY 11725, 516-462-9800/665-1140.

## IROQUOIS ARTS SHOWCASE I, Howes Cave, NY
Late May
Native American

See other dates. **Days:** 2. **Hours per day:** 8. **Site:** outdoor and indoor. Iroquois Indian Museum, Caverns Road. **Admission:** paid. **Daily entry:** under $10, **Acts:** local acts. **Contact:** Iroquois Indian Festival, P. O. Box 7, Howes Cave, NY 12092, 518-296-8949.

## WOODSTOCK/NEW PALTZ ART AND CRAFTS FAIR, New Paltz, NY
Late May
Modern Folk

Since 1982. See other dates. **Days:** 3. **Hours per day:** 6. **Site:** outdoor. Ulster County Fairgrounds. **Admission:** paid. **Daily entry:** under $10, **Discounts: Restrictions:** 10, **Secondary genre[s]:** TJAZ, **Acts:** regional acts, local acts. **Sample day's lineup:** Kurt Henry, Pat Humphries, Jay Mankita. **Contact:** Quail Hollow Events, P. O. Box 25, Woodstock, NY 12498, 914-679-8087/246-3414.

## PEOPLE'S MUSIC NETWORK SUMMER GATHERING, Pine Bush, NY
Early Jun.
Modern Folk

**Days:** 2. **Site:** outdoor and indoor. Camp Thoreau. **Admission:** paid. **Acts:** national acts, local acts. **Sample day's lineup:** Pete Seeger, others. **Contact:** People's Music Network, P. O. Box 295, Norwich, VT 05055-0295.

## ITHACA FESTIVAL, Ithaca, NY
Early Jun.
Variety, General

**Help!** A sample lineup? **Days:** 3. **Site:** outdoor. Ithaca Commons, Dewitt Park, Stewart Park. **Admission:** free. **Acts:** regional acts, local acts. **Sample lineup:** 500 performers. **Contact:** Ithaca Festival, 215 North Cayuga Street, Ithaca, NY 14850, 607-273-3646.

## OTSININGO POW WOW AND INDIAN CRAFT FAIR, Apalachin, NY
Early Jun.
Native American

Since 1980. **Days:** 3. **Site:** outdoor and indoor. Waterman Conservation Education Center, Hilton Road. **Contact:** Waterman Conservation Education Center, P. O. Box 288, Apalachin, NY, 607-625-2221.

## LARK STREET BLUES FESTIVAL, Albany, NY
Early Jun.
Blues and Traditional R&B

Since 1994. **Days:** 1. **Hours per day:** 6. **Site:** outdoor and indoor. 9 venues. **Admission:** paid. **Daily entry:** under $10, **Acts:** local acts. **Sample day's lineup:** The Nite Owls, Jim Herlihy, Mark Patton, Collin Aberdeen and The Westcott Jug Suckers, Tom Griffin Winslow, Luke McNamee, Norm Frederick, Jim E. Velvet, Bob Messano and The New Blues Orchestra, Night Kings, Andy Follette and The Bluecasters, Uncloe Ben and The Blues Professor, Matt Smith Band, Tom Healy and Joe Hetko, Glenn Weiser, Aaron Chamberlain, Peggy Eyres. **Contact:** Lionheart Blues Cafe, 258 Lark Street, Albany, NY 12210, 518-436-9530.

CULTURAL STREET FESTIVAL, Hempstead, NY
    Early Jun.
    African American

See other dates. **Help!** A sample lineup? **Days:** 1. **Hours per day:** 3. **Site:** outdoor and indoor. African American Museum, 110 North Franklin Street. **Secondary genre[s]:** BGOS, **Acts:** local acts. **Contact:** African American Museum, 110 North Franklin Street, Hempstead, NY, 516-572-0730.


GLORY, Valley Falls, NY
    Early Jun.
    Modern Christian

**Help!** One time only? Also, a sample lineup? **Days:** 1. **Site:** outdoor. **Contact:** Larsong Productions, RD 1, Box 152, Valley Falls, NY 12185, 518-753-0975.


GLORY, Lake George, NY
    Early Jun.
    Modern Christian

**Help!** One time only? Also, a sample lineup? **Days:** 1. **Site:** outdoor. Great Escape Theme Park. **Contact:** WNGN, Kings Road, Box 152, Buskirk, NY 12028, 518-686-0975.


IRISH FESTIVAL, Hampton Bays, NY
    Early Jun.
    Irish

Benefits United Cerebral Palsy of Greater Suffolk. **Days:** 1. **Hours per day:** 6. **Site:** outdoor and indoor. Canoe Place Inn. **Admission:** paid. **Daily entry:** $10 to $24, **Acts:** local acts. **Sample day's lineup:** Tommy Doyle Band, Dennis Murray and Flashback, Spirits of Gilbride. **Contact:** Irish Festival, Canoe Place Inn, Hampton Bays, NY, 516-232-0015.


BLUEGRASS ROUNDUP, Galway, NY
    Early Jun.
    Bluegrass

"Lots of music...field picking...food and fun." -- Flyer. **Days:** 2. **Site:** outdoor. McConchie's Heritage Acres, Route 67. **Admission:** paid. **Daily entry:** under $10, **Discounts:** other discounts **Secondary genre[s]:** TC&W, TFOL, **Acts:** regional acts, local acts. **Sample day's lineup:** Cedar Ridge, Burnt Hills Bluegrass, Bluegrass Upstarts, Back Porch Pickers, Sapbush Hollow, Alice Johnson, Bluegrass Remnants, The Parlor Boys, Bear Bridge band, Dyer Switch, Dooley, Joan Crane, Ray Sears, Summit, Todd Mountain, Olin and Addie Boyle, The Banjo Boys, others. **Contact:** Adirondack Bluegrass League, 830 Pinewood Avenue, Schenectady, NY 12309, 518-377-7131 **or:** Adirondack Bluegrass League, 19 Joseph Lane, Ganesvort, NY 12831, 518-583-2356.


OLD TIME FIDDLER'S CONTEST AND JAM SESSION, Blue Mountain Lake, NY
    Early Jun.
    Fiddle and Banjo Events

Since 1983. **Days:** 1. **Site:** indoor. Adirondack Lake Center for the Arts. **Admission:** paid. **Daily entry:** under $10, **Discounts:** other discounts **Secondary genre[s]:** TC&W, BLGS, TFOL, **Acts:** local acts. **Contact:** Adirondack Lake Center for the Arts, P. O. Box 205, Blue Mountain Lake, NY 12812, 518-352-7715.

STREET FAIR, Plainview, NY
> Early Jun.
> Jewish

"Open to the community." -- Advertisement. **Help!** A sample lineup? **Days:** 1. **Hours per day:** 5. **Site:** outdoor. Mid Island Y Jewish Community Center, 45 Manetto Hill Road. **Contact:** Mid Island Y Jewish Community Center, 45 Manetto Hill Road, Plainview, NY, 516-822-3535.


WORLD OF JEWISH CULTURE, Bay Shore, NY
> Early Jun.
> Jewish

See other dates and sites. **Help!** One time only? **Days:** 1. **Site:** indoor. Jewish Center of Bay Shore, 34 North Clinton Avenue. **Admission:** paid. **Daily entry:** $10 to $24, **Acts:** local acts. **Sample day's lineup:** Laura Wetzler with Robin Bordulis, Joe Elias Ladino Trio, others. **Contact:** Suffolk Jewish Community Center, 74 Hauppauge Road, Commack, NY 11725, 516-462-9800/665-1140.


HEMPSPLASH, Parksville, NY
> Early Jun.
> Hard Rock and Heavy Metal

Since 1992. "800 acres of a wild rocker's dream!" -- Advertisement. Events and lineups highly variable, so call ahead. See other dates. **Help!** One time only? **Days:** 3. **Hours per day:** 14. **Site:** outdoor. Arrowhead Ranch, 548 Cooley Road, off Route 17W. **Admission:** paid. **Daily entry:** under $10, **Restrictions:** 4, 10, **Secondary genre[s]:** RGGE, **Acts:** national acts, local acts. **Sample lineup:** Cypress Hill, Dharma Bums, Rastarafiki, Lifeforce, The Hour, Gravity, Blind Man's Holiday, Burning Incense, others. **Contact:** Arrowhead Ranch, R. D. 1, Box 87, Parksville, NY 12768, 914-292-6273.


BLUESHOUNDS BENEFIT, Albany, NY
> Early Jun.
> Blues and Traditional R&B

Benefits the Sonny Boy Williamson Blues Museum, Helena, AR. **Help!** One time only? **Days:** 1. **Hours per day:** 8. **Site:** indoor. Pauly's Hotel, 337 Central Avenue. **Acts:** regional acts, local acts. **Sample day's lineup:** Bobby Messano and The New Blues Orchestra, Ernie Williams and The Wildcats, Smokestack Lightning, Bluesmatics, Glenn Weiser, Scotty Mac and The Night Owls. **Contact:** Blueshounds Benefit, c/o Pauly's Hotel, 337 Central Avenue, Albany, NY, 518-426-0828.


ALBION STRAWBERRY FESTIVAL, Albion, NY
> Early Jun.
> Variety, General

**Help!** A sample lineup? **Days:** 2. **Site:** outdoor. Court House Square. **Secondary genre[s]:** TJAZ, CRCK, GYLS, OTHR **Acts:** local acts. **Contact:** Greater Albion Chamber of Commerce, 101 North Main Street, P. O. Box 28, Albion, NY 14411, 716-589-7727.


THOUSAND ISLANDS BLUEGRASS FESTIVAL, Clayton, NY
> Early Jun. to Middle Jun.
> Bluegrass

**Days:** 3. **Site:** outdoor. Captain Clayton Campground, Route 12. **Acts:** national acts, local acts. **Sample lineup:** Stevens Family, Gillis Brothers, Hazel River, Grass Creek, Country Current, Cedar Ridge, Catalogue Parlor. **Contact:** Thousand Island Bluegrass Association, P. O. Box 195, Clayton, NY 13624, 315-686-5385/3771/5900 **or:** Thousand Island Bluegrass Association, 510 Riverside Drive, Clayton, NY 13624.

## BLUEGRASS ON THE GREEN, Homer, NY
Early Jun.
Bluegrass

**Help!** A sample lineup? **Days:** 1. **Site:** outdoor. Village Green, Main Street. **Contact:** Bluegrass on the Green, 4340 Alexandria Drive, Cortland, NY 13045, 607-756-9330.

## DICK FOX'S SUMMER DOO-WOPP EXTRAVAGANZA, Westbury, NY
Early Jun.
A Cappella and Doo Wop

See other dates and sites. **Days:** 1. **Site:** indoor. Westbury Music Fair, Brush Hollow Road. **Admission:** paid. **Daily entry:** $25 to $49, **Discounts:** group sale discounts, **Secondary genre[s]:** CRCK, **Acts:** national acts, regional acts, local acts. **Sample day's lineup:** The Drifters, The Duprees, The Angels, The Del Vikings, The Dimensions, Randy and The Rainbows, The Eternals, The Traditions, Frankie Ford. **Contact:** Westbury Music Fair, Brush Hollow Road, Westbury, NY, 516-334-0800 **or:** Dick Fox's Doo-Wopp Extravaganza, 1650 Broadway, Suite 503, New York, NY 10019, 212-582-9074.

## STRAWBERRY FESTIVAL, Beacon, NY
Early Jun.
Traditional Folk

Since 1976. **Days:** 1. **Hours per day:** 6. **Site:** outdoor. Beacon Waterfront Park. **Admission:** free. **Discounts:** multiple event or day passes, advance purchase discounts, **Secondary genre[s]:** MFOL, MARI, **Acts:** national acts, regional acts, local acts. **Sample day's lineup:** Kim and Reggie Harris, Quallah Battou, Stone Soup, Gravichord Duo, Pete Seeger, Clearwater Sloop Singers. **Contact:** Beacon Sloop Club, P. O. Box 527, Beacon, NY 12508, 914-534-3219 **or:** Hudson Sloop Clearwater, Inc., 112 Market Street, Poughkeepsie, NY 12601, 914-454-7673.

## ROCHESTER IRISH FESTIVAL, Gates, NY
Early Jun. to Middle Jun.
Irish

Since 1995. "The first Irish festival in the Rochester area in about 10 years...This will be an annual undertaking -- and judging by the reaction we've received so far, a very popular one." -- Correspondence. **Days:** 2. **Hours per day:** 9. **Site:** outdoor. Festival Grounds, off Lydell Road. **Admission:** paid. **Daily entry:** under $10, **Discounts:** group sale discounts, **Acts:** regional acts, local acts. **Sample day's lineup:** The Dady Brothers, Dave North Trio, Liam Magee, Cuisle Mo Chroi, Blackthorn Ceilidh Band, Comhaltas Ceoltoiri Eireann, Rutherford Family Band, Mulligan, Dolan and Parnell, The Harps Band, Mary Lester, Gerry Forde and Friends, others. **Contact:** Rochester Irish Festival, Inc., P. O. Box 90387, Rochester, NY 14609-0387, 716-482-2843.

## ALBANY RIVERFEST / ALL-AMERICA CITY FAIR, Albany, NY
Early Jun. to Middle Jun.
Variety, General

Since 1985. Combined festivals, along with Empire State Regatta. "[This event] has become one of the northeast's biggest and best-loved outdoor events." -- Program. See other dates and sites. **Days:** 10. **Hours per day:** 5. **Site:** outdoor. Riverfest (two days): Corning Preserve; City Fair (10 days): Port of Albany. **Admission:** free. **Secondary genre[s]:** MRCK, ARCK, TR&B, MC&W, **Acts:** regional acts, local acts. **Sample day's lineup:** Ernie Williams and The Wildcats, Strange Arrangement, The Staziaks, T. S. Ensemble, The Heaters, others. **Contact:** City of Albany Mayor's Office of Special Events, 60 Orange Street, Albany, NY 12210, 518-434-2032/454-5694.

FUNDRAISER, West Shokan, NY
    Middle Jun.
    Modern Country

Benefits the Coalition of Watershed Towns. **Help!** One time only? **Days:** 1. **Hours per day:** 10. **Site:** outdoor. Davis Park. **Admission:** free. **Daily entry:** under $10, **Discounts: Acts:** local acts. **Sample day's lineup:** Bob "Big Dog" Gorsiline, Frank Holdridge, Thunder Ridge, Greg Dinger, Paul Luke Band, The Suttons, Janice Santora, others. **Contact:** Phoenicia Fish and Game Association, 5419 Route 28, Mount Tremper, NY 12457, 914-688-2508.

MAYHEM ON THE MOUNTAIN, Mariaville, NY
    Middle Jun.
    Blues and Traditional R&B

"Outdoor concert of the summer." -- Advertisement. **Days:** 1. **Site:** outdoor. Ma Ria Mountain Golf Course. **Admission:** paid. **Daily entry:** $10 to $24, **Restrictions:** 3, 4, 5, **Acts:** local acts. **Sample day's lineup:** Matt Smith Band, Out of Control R&B Band, Joe Roy Jackson. **Contact:** Mayhem on the Mountain, Ma Ria Mountain Golf Course, Mariaville, NY, 518-864-5124.

ONE WITH NATURE FESTIVAL, Garrison, NY
    Middle Jun.
    Modern Folk

**Help!** One time only? **Days:** 1. **Hours per day:** 5. **Site:** outdoor. Manitoga, Route 9D. **Admission:** paid. **Daily entry:** under $10, **Discounts:** other discounts **Secondary genre[s]:** TFOL, **Acts:** regional acts, local acts. **Sample day's lineup:** Peggy Eyres, Jeff Wilkinson, Hudson River Sloop Singers, Jeff Wilkinson, Ann Marie Sacramone. **Contact:** One With Nature Festival, c/o Manitoga, Route 9D, Garrison, NY, 914-424-3812.

PSYCHOFEST, Kingston, NY
    Middle Jun.
    Classic Rock and Oldies

See other dates. **Help!** One time only? **Days:** 1. **Site:** outdoor. Brickyard, 200 North Street. **Secondary genre[s]:** MRCK, **Contact:** The Brickyard, 200 North Street, Kingston, NY, 914-339-0093.

WCBS-FM 101 DAY, Rye, NY
    Middle Jun.
    A Cappella and Doo Wop

Since 1990. **Days:** 1. **Hours per day:** 11. **Site:** outdoor. Playland Park, Rye Beach. **Secondary genre[s]:** CRCK, **Acts:** national acts, regional acts, local acts. **Sample day's lineup:** Gary U. S. Bonds, Freddy Cannon, The Teenagers, Larry Chance and The Earls, Little Isidore and The Inquisitors. **Audio merchandise:** "WCBS-FM 101 History of Rock, The Doo-Wop Era, Parts 1, 2"; "...The 50's, Parts 1, 2"; "...The 60's, Parts 1-5"; "...For Lovers Only" (all on Collectables). **Contact:** WCBS-FM 101, 51 West 52nd Street, New York, NY 10019, 914-967-2040.

BATTLE OF THE ACAPPELLA GROUPS, Poughkeepsie, NY
    Middle Jun.
    A Cappella and Doo Wop

Since 1992. Benefits United Negro Scholarship Fund. **Days:** 1. **Site:** indoor. Bardavon Opera House, 35 Market Street. **Admission:** paid. **Daily entry:** $10 to $24, **Discounts:** student discounts, **Secondary genre[s]:** CRCK, **Acts:** local acts. **Sample day's lineup:** The Cordials, Times Square, Flashback, The Tamaneers, The Shallows. **Contact:** Knights Social Club, c/o Bardavon Opera House, 35 Market Street, Poughkeepsie, NY, 914-473-2072.

FIDDLING CELEBRATION, Cross River, NY
> Early Jul.
> Traditional Folk

Since 1976. See other dates and sites. **Days:** 1. **Hours per day:** 6. **Site:** outdoor. Ward Pound Ridge Reservation. **Admission:** free. **Secondary genre[s]:** TC&W, BLGS, ZYDC, IRSH, OTHR. **Acts:** national acts, regional acts, local acts. **Sample day's lineup:** Northern Lights, Walt Michael and Company, Matt Glaser, Evening Edition, Roger Sprung and The Progressive Bluegrassers, Bud Snow Revue, Clancy Family, Bayou Midnight, Please And Thank You String Band, Damian Boucher Band, Jeff Main. **Contact:** Westchester County Department of Parks and Recreation, 19 Bradhurst Avenue, Hawthorne, NY 10532, 914-593-PARK.

INTERGENERATIONAL INTERNATIONAL FESTIVAL, Garden City, NY
> Middle Jun.
> Variety, Folk and International

**Help!** One time only? **Days:** 1. **Site:** indoor. Ethical Humanist Society of Long Island, 38 Old Country Road. **Admission:** paid. **Daily entry:** $10 to $24, **Secondary genre[s]:** MFOL, IRSH, OTHR **Acts:** local acts. **Sample day's lineup:** Cathy Kreger, James O'Malley, Dennis Cleasby, others. **Contact:** Ethical Humanist Society of Long Island, 38 Old Country Road, Garden City, NY, 516-791-6808.

LOCAL MOTION MUSICFEST, Middletown, NY
> Middle Jun.
> Blues and Traditional R&B

Since 1992. Benefits Occupations, Inc. See other dates. **Days:** 1. **Hours per day:** 5. **Site:** outdoor. Horse Ring, Fancher-Davidge Park. **Admission:** paid. **Daily entry:** under $10, **Acts:** regional acts, local acts. **Sample day's lineup:** Bo Diddley Jr., Delta Star, Females In Control. **Contact:** AAA Productions, 35 Harrison Street, Middletown, NY 10940, 914-342-1552.

BALLSTON SPA VILLAGE WIDE GARAGE SALE AND FAMILY FESTIVAL, Ballston Spa, NY
> Middle Jun.
> Variety, General

**Days:** 2. **Hours per day:** 9. **Site:** outdoor. **Secondary genre[s]:** TJAZ, TR&B, MC&W, MFOL, **Acts:** local acts. **Sample day's lineup:** Micky T. Guild and The Storm, Bandolero with Donna Phillips, Whoopee Jazz, Blues Alley. **Contact:** Ballston Spa Village Wide Garage Sale and Family Festival, 115 Malta Avenue, Ballston Spa, NY 12020, 518-885-8393/4240.

L. A. R. A. C. ARTS AND CRAFTS FESTIVAL, Glen Falls, NY
> Middle Jun.
> Variety, General

Since 1973. **Days:** 2. **Hours per day:** 7. **Site:** outdoor. City Park. **Secondary genre[s]:** TJAZ, MFOL, TFOL, OTHR. **Acts:** local acts. **Sample day's lineup:** Donner's Pass, Two Guys Who Play Trombone, Dave Foley, Society For Creative Anachronism, Marty Brandon, Lazy Mercedes, Kristine Mallette, St. Regis String Band, others. **Contact:** Lower Adirondack Regional Arts Council, P. O. Box 659, Glens Falls, NY 12801, 518-798-1144.

MILLER LITE BALLOONFEST / ART ON THE RISE, Jamesville, NY
        Middle Jun.
        Variety, General

Benefits Good Camp Days, Special Times. See other sites and dates. **Days:** 3. **Site:** outdoor. Jamesville Beach Park. **Admission:** paid. **Daily entry:** under $10, **Secondary genre[s]:** MJAZ, TJAZ, MRCK, CRCK, MR&B, TR&B, BLGS, IRSH, OTHR. **Acts:** national acts, regional acts, local acts. **Sample day's lineup:** Outfield, Mitch Molloy, Wendy Maharry, Atlas, Back Alley Boys, John Russbach, Phil Markert, others. **Contact:** Onondaga County Parks, P. O. Box 146, Liverpool, NY 13088, 315-451-PARK / 469-0880.

SYRACUSE JAZZ FEST, Syracuse, NY
        Middle Jun.
        Modern Jazz

Since 1983. **Days:** 7. **Hours per day:** 14. **Site:** outdoor and indoor. multiple locations downtown. **Admission:** free. **Secondary genre[s]:** MR&B, TR&B, MLAT, **Acts:** national acts, regional acts, local acts. **Sample day's lineup:** Jeannie and Jimmy Cheatham and The Sweet Baby Blues Band, Kenia, Mark Morganelli and The Jazz Forum Allstars with Donald Harrison, Charles Earland Quartet, Red Rodney Quintet, Benny Green and Christian McBride, Nelson Rangell, Greg Barone Trio, Tommy Bridges, Joe and Tony Riposi Quartet, Nuance. **Contact:** Syracuse Jazz Fest, 362 South Salina Street, P. O. Box 1400, Syracuse, NY 13201, 315-475-7979.

NASSAU COLISEUM FAIR, Uniondale, NY
        Middle Jun. to Late Jun.
        Fairs

**Days:** 12. **Site:** outdoor and indoor. Nassau Veteran's Memorial Coliseum. **Admission:** paid. **Daily entry:** under $10, **Secondary genre[s]:** CRCK, MR&B, OTHR **Acts:** national acts. **Sample series lineup:** Day One: Whitney Houston; Day Two: Lynyrd Skynyrd, Bad Company. **Contact:** Nassau Coliseum Fair, Nassau Veteran's Memorial Coliseum, Uniondale, NY, 516-794-9300.

EAST END MUSIC FESTIVAL, East Hampton, NY
        Middle Jun.
        Modern Folk

"Evening of folk and roots music featuring the premier songwriters indigenous to the East End of Long Island." -- Press release. Culmination of weekly show at Buckley's Restaurant, Job's Lane, Southampton. **Days:** 1. **Hours per day:** 4. **Site:** indoor. Guild Hall, 158 Main Street **Admission:** paid. **Daily entry:** under $10, **Discounts:** other discounts **Secondary genre[s]:** ZYDC, **Acts:** local acts. **Sample day's lineup:** Gene Casey, Ginny O'Shea, Richard Rosch, Melinda Novack and Sue Case, Bruce McDonald, Michael Hennessey, Ned McDonald, Alfredo Merat and Carl Obrig, Dejavoodoo. **Contact:** East End Performing Songwriters, 4 Lowell Road, Hampton Bays, NY 11946, 516-728-5476.

JUNE JAZZ, White Plains, NY
        Middle Jun.
        Modern Jazz

**Help!** One time only? **Days:** 1. **Site:** indoor. Westchester Conservatory of Music, 20 Soundview Avenue. **Admission:** paid. **Daily entry:** $10 to $24, **Acts:** national acts, local acts. **Sample day's lineup:** Doc Cheatam, Johnny Morris Quintet, Carmen Leggio. **Contact:** Westchester Conservatory of Music, 20 Soundview Avenue, White Plains, NY, 914-761-3715.

LAING FAMILY BLUEGRASS FESTIVAL, Bainbridge, NY
        Middle Jun.
        Bluegrass

Since 1984. **Days:** 3. **Site:** outdoor. General Clinton Park, Route 7. **Admission:** paid. **Daily entry:** $10 to $24, **Discounts:** multiple event or day passes, advance purchase discounts, **Acts:** national acts, local acts. **Sample day's lineup:** Bill Harrell and The Virginians, The Osborne Brothers, Lost and Found, Paul Adkins and The Borderline Band, The Norman Wright and Kevin Church Band, The Traditional Grass, Redwing, The Fox Family, The Laing Brothers. **Contact:** Galin Productions, Inc., P. O. Box 217, Bainbridge, NY 13733, 607-967-3093 **or:** Galin Productions, Inc., 926 Mystery House Road, Davenport, FL 33837, 813-421-2934.

ALL-STAR IRISH CONCERT AND DANCE, Yonkers, NY
        Middle Jun.
        Irish

Benefits Stephen Dynes Fund, Dynamite Youth Center. **Days:** 1. **Site:** outdoor and indoor. Yonkers Raceway. **Acts:** national acts, regional acts, local acts. **Sample day's lineup:** Cherish The Ladies, Dermot Henry Band, James Keane and Jerry O'Sullivan, Joe Madden Ceili Band, Eileen Ivers, Jack Coen and Friends, Celtic Cross, Makem Brothers and Brian Sullivan, 8 other bands. **Contact:** All-Star Irish Concert and Dance, c/o Green Linnett Records, 43 Beaver Brook Road, Danbury, CT 06810, 914-763-6757.

GOSPEL EXTRAVAGANZA, Kingston, NY
        Middle Jun.
        Black Gospel

Since 1986.**Days:** 1. **Site:** indoor. Ulster Performing Arts Center, 601 Broadway. **Admission:** paid. **Daily entry:** $25 to $49, **Discounts:** student discounts, group sale discounts, **Acts:** national acts, local acts. **Sample day's lineup:** Chicago Mass Choir, United Voices Choir, others. **Contact:** Riverview Missionary Baptist Church, 240 Catherine Street, Kingston, NY 12401, 914-338-4650/6084.

LAKE GEORGE HOT JAZZ PARTY AND CRUISE, Lake George, NY
        Middle Jun.
        Traditional Jazz and Ragtime

Since 1979. "Join us!" -- Advertisement. **Days:** 1. **Hours per day:** 3. **Site:** outdoor and indoor. SS Lac Du St. Sacrement. **Admission:** paid. **Daily entry:** $25 to $49, **Discounts:** advance purchase discounts, **Acts:** local acts. **Sample day's lineup:** Skip Parsons' Riverboat Jazz Band, Ralph's Moldy Figs, Don LaVoie Quintet, Nick Palumbo's Dixieland Update. **Contact:** Lake George Hot Jazz Party and Cruise, P. O. Box 9013, Albany, NY 12209, 518-439-2310 **or:** Skippy's Music, 253 Delaware Avenue, Delmar, NY 12054.

CLEARWATER'S GREAT HUDSON RIVER REVIVAL, Valhalla, NY
        Middle Jun.
        Variety, Folk and International

Since 1978. **Days:** 2. **Hours per day:** 10. **Site:** outdoor. Westchester Community College. **Admission:** paid. **Daily entry:** $10 to $24, **Discounts:** multiple event or day passes, advance purchase discounts, **Secondary genre[s]:** MJAZ, ARCK, TR&B, BGOS, TGOS, TC&W, BLGS, MFOL, TFOL, MARI, ZYDC, IRSH, NATV, TLAT, **Acts:** national acts, regional acts, local acts. **Sample day's lineup:** Balfa Toujours, Toshi Reagon, Algia Mae Hinton and Lightnin' Wells, The L-7's, Impacto Vallenando, Evelyn Blakely, Bill and Lillian Vanaver, Jay Ungar and Molly Mason, The Billys, Judy Small, Bill Harley, Sweet Honey In The Rock, Raffi, Georgia Higgs and Scott Ainslie, Walkabout Clearwater Chorus, Second Opinion, Rick Nestler, Louis Killen and Andy Wallace, Tsaye M. Barnwell, Peter Amidon, Tom Paxton, Ani DiFranco, Len Chandler, Pat Humphries, David Parker, Derek Burrows and Heather Forrest, James Bay Cree Drummers, Travis Jeffrey and Al Nejmeh, Nancy Bernstein, Sue Schmidt, Sarah Underhill, Fred Starner, Allan Aunapu, Jimmy Collier, Peter Seeger, others. **Contact:** Hudson Sloop Clearwater, Inc., 112 Market Street, Poughkeepsie, NY 12601, 914-454-7673 **or:** Clearwater's Great Hudson River Revival, 27 Midline Road, Ballston Lake, NY 12019, 518-399-4242.

## DISTANT DRUMS NATIVE AMERICAN FESTIVAL, White Plains, NY
Middle Jun.
Native American

Since 1994. **Days:** 2. **Hours per day:** 8. **Site:** outdoor and indoor. Westchester County Center, Central Avenue and Tarrytown Road. **Admission:** paid. **Daily entry:** under $10, **Contact:** Westchester County Center, Central Avenue and Tarrytown Road, White Plains, NY, 914-949-8900.

## NATIVE AMERICAN POW WOW, Bethany, NY
Middle Jun.
Native American

"We try to show the public we're not the 'Hollywood' Indian...no plastic 'Hong Kong' stuff." -- Ron Scott. **Days:** 2. **Hours per day:** 11. **Site:** outdoor. Carriage Village, adj. Gennessee County Park. **Admission:** paid. **Daily entry:** under $10, **Secondary genre[s]:** MC&W, **Contact:** Native American Pow Wow, 318 South Jackson Street, Batavia, NY 14020, 716-343-5986.

## NO BUMMER SUMMER PARTY JAM, Parksville, NY
Middle Jun.
Hard Rock and Heavy Metal

Since 1993. "800 acres of a wild rocker's dream!" -- Advertisement. Events and lineups highly variable, so call ahead. See other dates. **Help!** One time only? **Days:** 3. **Hours per day:** 14. **Site:** outdoor. Arrowhead Ranch, 548 Cooley Road, off Route 17W. **Admission:** paid. **Daily entry:** under $10, **Restrictions:** 4, 10, **Acts:** local acts. **Sample lineup:** Mr. Reality, Heavens To Murgatroid, Mark Berger and The Head Cleaners, 40 Winks, Transatlantic, Mutley's Rocket, plus 5 other bands. **Contact:** Arrowhead Ranch, R. D. 1, Box 87, Parksville, NY 12768, 914-292-6273.

## COUNTRY WESTERN FESTIVAL, Cambridge, NY
Middle Jun.
Modern Country

Since 1992. **Help!** A sample lineup? **Days:** 1. **Hours per day:** 10. **Site:** outdoor. Snuffy's Inn and Campgrounds, Route 22. **Admission:** paid. **Daily entry:** $10 to $24, **Discounts:** multiple event or day passes, advance purchase discounts, **Secondary genre[s]:** TC&W, **Acts:** local acts. **Contact:** Snuffy's Inn and Campgrounds, Route 22, Cambridge, NY, 518-677-8091.

## IRISH FESTIVAL, Patterson, NY
Middle Jun.
Irish

Since 1993. See other dates. **Help!** Formerly Rockin' The Catskills, East Durham, NY? **Days:** 1. **Site:** outdoor. Big Birch Concert Pavillion. **Admission:** paid. **Daily entry:** $10 to $24, **Secondary genre[s]:** ARCK, **Acts:** national acts, regional acts, local acts. **Sample day's lineup:** Black 47, Bagatelle, The Rogues, Speir Mor, The Mahones, Cliffs of Dooneen, Dignam and Goff, The Chanting House, others. **Contact:** Big Birch Concert Pavillion, Big Birch Music Center, Patterson, NY, 914-878-3181.

## JUNETEENTH FESTIVAL, Buffalo, NY
Middle Jun.
African American

Celebrating the anniversary of the announcement abolishing slavery, June 19, 1865. "Let freedom ring!" -- Listing. **Help!** A sample lineup? **Days:** 2. **Site:** outdoor. Martin Luther King Jr. Park. **Secondary genre[s]:** MJAZ, BGOS, AFRC, RGGE, **Acts:** local acts. **Contact:** Juneteenth Festival, 154 Hughes Avenue, Buffalo, NY 14208, 716-886-5095/876-6458.

REGGAE ON THE HUDSON, Kingston, NY
>Middle Jun.
>Reggae, Ska and Caribbean

See other dates. **Help!** One time only? **Days:** 1. **Hours per day:** 6. **Site:** outdoor. Brickyard, 200 North Street. **Restrictions:** 5, **Acts:** national acts, local acts. **Sample day's lineup:**Sister Carol, Shelley Thunder, Black Sheep. **Contact:** The Brickyard, 200 North Street, Kingston, NY, 914-339-0093.


MADRID BLUEGRASS FESTIVAL, Madrid, NY
>Late Jun.
>Bluegrass

Since 1992. "Biggest bluegrass festival by a dam site...right on a beautiful river." -- Don Rupert. **Days:** 3. **Hours per day:** 10. **Site:** outdoor. Madrid Municipal Park. **Admission:** free. **Daily entry:** under $10, **Discounts:** multiple event or day passes, **Secondary genre[s]:** SGOS, MC&W, BLGS, FDDL, **Acts:** regional acts, local acts. **Sample day's lineup:** Catalogue Parlor, The Delaney Brothers, Tom Wilson, Border's Bluegrass, Grass Creek, Merlin Childs and The Goodtimers, The Reed Family, Goodnought, others. **Contact:** Madrid Bluegrass Festival, 1961 State Highway 310, Madrid, NY 13660, 315-322-5679.


MOHONK'S MUSIC WEEK, New Paltz, NY
>Late Jun.
>Variety, General

"Enjoy relaxing outdoors at Mohonk while the sounds of music trumpet through the air." -- Brochure. **Days:** 6. **Site:** outdoor and indoor. Mohonk Mountain House. **Admission:** paid. **Daily entry:** $50 and over. **Secondary genre[s]:** TJAZ, OTHR. **Acts:** national acts, local acts. **Sample lineup:** Roger Thorpe, others. **Contact:** Mohonk's Music Week, Mohonk Mountain House, New Paltz, NY 12561, 914-255-4500.


FLY92 SUMMER JAM, Latham, NY
>Late Jun.
>Modern Rock and Pop

**Days:** 1. **Site:** outdoor. Starlite Theater "VIP" parking lot. **Admission:** paid. **Daily entry:** under $10, **Secondary genre[s]:** ARCK, MR&B, TR&B, **Acts:** national acts, regional acts, local acts. **Sample day's lineup:** Deborah Harry, Joan Jett and The Black Hearts, Ernie Williams and The Wildcats, Sagat, Collage, Lighter Shade of Brown, Ovis, Rosco Martinez, Chantay Savage, Laura Branigan, Atlantic Starr. **Contact:** WFLY 92.3 FM, 4243 Albany Street, Albany, NY 12205, 518-456-1144.


JONES BEACH GREEKFEST WEEKEND, Babylon, NY
>Late Jun.
>African American

"A stepshow competition between black fraternities and sororities and tons of musical talent will be featured." -- Long Island Newsday. "A huge event...pretty much every [major] record label gets involved." -- Jerry Graves. **Days:** 1. **Hours per day:** 8. **Site:** outdoor. Jones Beach State Park, West End 2. **Admission:** paid. **Daily entry:** under $10, **Secondary genre[s]:** ARCK, RAP, MR&B, **Acts:** national acts, regional acts. **Sample day's lineup:** Naughty By Nature, Notorious B. I. G., X-Scape, Heavy D and The Boyz, Wu-Tang Clan, Diana King, The Fugees, plus 20-to-30 other acts. **Contact:** Jones Beach Greekfest Weekend, 280 St. John's Place, Brooklyn, NY 11238, 718-230-3965 **or:** New York State Office of Parks, Historic Preservation and Recreation, Long Island Region, P. O. Box 247, Babylon, NY 11702-0247, 516-785-1600.

## SQUAREDANCE AND BLUEGRASS FESTIVAL, Hartford, NY
> Late Jun.
> Bluegrass

**Help!** A sample lineup? **Days:** 2. **Contact:** Squaredance and Bluegrass Festival, 4755 McConchie Road, Galway, NY 12074, 518-882-6140.


## SUMMERSCAPE: HUNTINGTON SUMMER ARTS FESTIVAL, Huntington, NY
> Late Jun. to Late Aug.
> Variety, General

Since 1964. **Days:** 51. **Hours per day:** 3. **Site:** outdoor. Chapin Rainbow Stage, Heckscher Park, Prime Avenue and Route 25A. **Admission:** free. **Secondary genre[s]:** MJAZ, TJAZ, MRCK, TR&B, BGOS, BLGS, MFOL, TFOL, ZYDC, TLAT, AFRC, AVNT, OTHR. **Acts:** national acts, regional acts, local acts. **Sample series lineup:** Day One: Queen Ida and Bontemps Zydeco; Day Two: Jon Faddis Quartet; Day Three: Putumayo World Dance Party. **Contact:** Huntington Arts Council, 213 Main Street, Huntington, NY 11743, 516-271-8442/8423.


## NEW YORK STATE CHAMPIONSHIP CHILI COOKOFF, New Paltz, NY
> Late Jun.
> Modern Country

Benefits Unison Arts and Learning Center. **Help!** A sample lineup? **Days:** 2. **Site:** outdoor and indoor. Rivendell Winery, 714 Albany Post Road. **Admission:** paid. **Daily entry:** under $10, **Acts:** local acts. **Contact:** Rivendell Winery, 714 Albany Post Road, New Paltz, NY, 914-255-0892.


## LAKE GEORGE SUMMERFEST, Lake George, NY
> Late Jun.
> Variety, General

Also programs a weekly summer concert series with regional acts. **Days:** 3. **Hours per day:** 5. **Site:** outdoor. Shepard Park. **Secondary genre[s]:** TR&B, MC&W, MFOL, RGGE, **Acts:** local acts. **Sample day's lineup:** Fritz Henry, Peyote Coyote, Crispy Critter, Big Smoothies, others. **Contact:** Lake George Arts Project, Canada Street, Lake George, NY 12845, 518-668-5755/2616.


## NORTHEAST DULCIMER SYMPOSIUM, Blue Mountain Lake, NY
> Late Jun.
> Traditional Folk

**Days:** 3. **Site:** indoor. Adirondack Lake Center for the Arts. **Admission:** paid. **Discounts:** other discounts **Acts:** regional acts, local acts. **Sample day's lineup:** R. P. Hale, Jerry Rockwell, Leo Kretzner, Ken Lovelett, Sam Moffett, Barbara Truex, others. **Contact:** Northeast Dulcimer Symposium, 434 Preble Street, South Portland, ME 04106, 207-799-6899 **or:** Adirondack Lake Center for the Arts, P. O. Box 205, Blue Mountain Lake, NY 12812, 518-352-7715.

### OLD SONGS FESTIVAL OF TRADITIONAL MUSIC AND DANCE, Altamont, NY
Late Jun.
Variety, Folk and International

Since 1981. **Days:** 3. **Hours per day:** 16. **Site:** outdoor and indoor. Altamont Fairgrounds, Route 146. **Admission:** paid. **Daily entry:** $10 to $24, **Discounts:** multiple event or day passes, advance purchase discounts, **Restrictions:** 7, 8, 10, **Secondary genre[s]:** TR&B, TGOS, TC&W, MFOL, TFOL, ZYDC, IRSH, SCOT, TLAT, AFRM, AFRC, BRZL, OTHR. **Acts:** national acts, regional acts, local acts. **Sample day's lineup:** Steve Gillette and Cindy Mangsen, Natalie MacMaster, Scartaglen, Anne Dodson, Bill Spence and Fennig's Allstars, Si Kahn, Masterson and Blackburn, Nego Gato African-Brazilian Music and Dance Ensemble, Bill and Livia Vanaver, Uncle Gizmo, Vic Kibler and Paul Van Arsdale, Crumtown Ramblers, George Ward, Eddie Lejuene, Mill Run Dulcimer Band, Peter Amidon, Music From China Ensemble, Roger Llandis, Woody Padgett, Double Decker Stringband, Green Mountain Volunteers, Craig Johnson, Michael Dugger, George Wilson, Dan O'Connell, George Kloppel, Helen Yee, Lou and Peter Berryman, Joe Hickerson, Carla Sciaky, Gordon Mooney, Alan Jones, Sparky Rucker, Connie Dover, Veena Chandra, Jay Mankita, Pat Humphries, Michael Jerling, others. **Contact:** Old Songs, Inc., P. O. Box 399, Guilderland, NY 12084, 518-765-2815.

### EARL'S SUNSHINE FESTIVAL, Chaffee, NY
Late Jun. to Middle Sep.
Traditional Country

Since 1956. "Food for the body, music for the soul." -- Poster. **Days:** 5. **Site:** outdoor. Earl's Sunshine Music Park, Olean Road, Routes 16 and 39. **Admission:** paid. **Daily entry:** $10 to $24, **Restrictions:** 2, 8, 13, **Secondary genre[s]:** SGOS, BLGS, **Acts:** national acts, local acts. **Sample day's lineup:** Mac Wiseman, Speedy Krise, Stevens Family, Bill Harrell and The Virginians. **Contact:** Earl's Sunshine Music Park, Olean Road, Chaffee, NY 14030, 716-496-5125.

### AFRICAN-AMERICAN HERITAGE CELEBRATION, Valhalla, NY
Late Jun.
African American

African Cultural Diversity : Time for UMOJA (Unity)." -- Theme. See other dates and sites. Also programs Ethnic Celebrations: Slavic, Arab, Polish, Italian, Ukrainian. **Days:** 1. **Hours per day:** 6. **Site:** outdoor. Kenisco Dam Plaza, Bronx River Parkway. **Admission:** free. **Secondary genre[s]:** MJAZ, OTHR. **Acts:** local acts. **Sample day's lineup:** Dave Hubbard Quartet, others. **Contact:** Westchester County Department of Parks and Recreation, 19 Bradhurst Avenue, Hawthorne, NY 10532, 914-593-PARK.

### Inwood World Music Festival, Inwood, NY
Late Jun.
Variety, Folk and International

**Help!** One time only? **Days:** 1. **Secondary genre[s]:** AFRC, BRZL, OTHR. **Acts:** local acts. **Sample day's lineup:** Limania, Markahuasi, Our Lady of Good Counsel Band, Sylvain Leroux and The Maintenance Crew. **Contact:** Inwood World Music Festival, P. O. Box 574, Inwood, NY 11696, 516-239-2036.

### CHAUTAUQUA SUMMER MUSIC PROGRAM, Chautauqua, NY
Late Jun. to Late Aug.
Variety, General

Since 1929. **Days:** 64. **Hours per day:** 13. **Site:** outdoor. Chautauqua Institution, multiple locations. **Admission:** paid. **Daily entry:** $10 to $24, **Secondary genre[s]:** MJAZ, TJAZ, MRCK, CRCK, ARCK, MR&B, ACAP, BGOS, TGOS, MC&W, AC&W, BLGS, MFOL, TFOL, ZYDC, AFRC, RGGE, CBRT, OTHR. **Acts:** national acts, regional acts, local acts. **Sample series lineup:** Day One: Lou Rawls with Paul Ferrette's Caribbean Extravaganza; Day Two: Louisiana Repertory Jazz Ensemble, Jack Pearson; Day Three: Mary Chapin Carpenter. **Contact:** Chautauqua Institution, Chautauqua, NY 14722, 800-836-ARTS.

FRIENDSHIP FESTIVAL, Buffalo, NY
> Late Jun. Early Jul.
> Variety, General

Since 1987. "Celebrating more than 180 years of peace between the U. S. and Canada." -- Buffalo Sunday News. **Days:** 7. **Site:** outdoor. multiple locations: LaSalle Park, Buffalo (local acts); Fort Erie, Ontario (national acts), plus other sites. **Admission:** free. **Secondary genre[s]:** MRCK, ARCK, TR&B, MFOL, OTHR. **Acts:** national acts, local acts. **Sample series lineup:** Day One (Buffalo): McCarthyism, Win, Lose or Draw, Unity Band, Plaster Sandals, Willie and The Reinharts, Dave Constantino, Pursuit of Happiness, American Legion Band of the Tonawandas; Day Two (Fort Erie): Billy Bragg, Barenaked Ladies, 10,000 Maniacs, The Caulfields, Susan Werner, many others. **Contact:** Friendship Festival, Eventworks, Main Place Tower, Suite 200, Buffalo, NY 14202, 716-852-0511 **or:** Friendship Festival, Fort Erie, 121 Garrison Road, Fort Erie, ON L2A 6G6, 905-871-6454.

ELLICOTTVILLE'S SUMMER FESTIVAL OF THE ARTS, Ellicottville, NY
> Late Jun. to Early Jul.
> Variety, General

**Days:** 3. **Hours per day:** 8. **Site:** outdoor. multiple locations. **Secondary genre[s]:** TJAZ, ACAP, OTHR. **Acts:** regional acts, local acts. **Sample day's lineup:**Buffalo Swing Band, Buffalo Philharmonic Orchestra, Championship Jamestown Harmony Express, E. C. S. Stage Band. **Contact:** Ellicottville Chamber of Commerce, 9 West Washinton Street, Ellicottville, NY, 716-699-5046.

PENNY ASSOCIATION OLDE TYME COUNTRY MUSIC FESTIVAL, Coventryville, NY
> Late Jun. to Early Jul.
> Bluegrass

See other dates and sites. **Days:** 3. **Hours per day:** 10. **Site:** outdoor. Wrench Ranch, Route 206. **Secondary genre[s]:** SGOS, TC&W, BLGS, **Acts:** local acts. **Sample day's lineup:** Classic Country, Spare Parts Country, Country Lads, John Woods, Prairie Ramblers. **Contact:** Penny Association Olde Tyme Country Music Festival, 321 Orchard Street, Vestal, NY 13850, 607-754-3355 **or:** Penny Association Olde Tyme Country Music Festival, P. O. Box 385, Herkimer, NY 13350, 315-797-4791.

WGNA COUNTRY FEST, Altamont, NY
> Early Jul.
> Modern Country

**Days:** 1. **Hours per day:** 8. **Site:** outdoor. Altamont Fairgrounds. **Admission:** paid. **Daily entry:** $10 to $24, **Discounts:** advance purchase discounts, **Acts:** national acts. **Sample day's lineup:** Travis Tritt, Joe Diffie, Lee Roy Parnell, Victoria Shaw, Davis Daniel, David Ball. **Contact:** WGNA-FM, 800 New Loudon Road, Latham, NY 12110, 518-782-1474/0700.

NEWPORT JAZZ FESTIVAL/SARATOGA, Saratoga Springs, NY
> Early Jul.
> Modern Jazz

**Days:** 2. **Hours per day:** 12. **Site:** outdoor and indoor. Saratoga Performing Arts Center (SPAC). **Admission:** paid. **Daily entry:** $10 to $24, $25 to $49, **Discounts:** advance purchase discounts, **Secondary genre[s]:** TJAZ, MRCK, MR&B, TR&B, MLAT, BRZL, **Acts:** national acts, regional acts. **Sample day's lineup:** Al Jarreau, Little Richard, The Brecker Brothers, Buddy Guy, Terence Blanchard, Thelonious Monk Jr., Carol Sloane, Tania Maria, Newport Jazz Festival 40th Anniversary Band, Heavy Metal Horns, Eric Reed Trio, Peter Delano Quartet, James Carter, 5 Guitars Play Mingus. **Contact:** Saratoga Performing Arts Center, P. O. Box 826, Saratoga Springs, NY 12866-0826, 518-587-3330.

### GREAT BLUE HERON MUSIC FESTIVAL, Sherman, NY
    Early Jul.
    Alternative and College Rock

Since 1992. **Days:** 3. **Hours per day:** 12. **Site:** outdoor and indoor. Corner's Road. **Admission:** paid. **Daily entry:** $10 to $24, **Discounts:** multiple event or day passes, advance purchase discounts, **Secondary genre[s]:** TC&W, AC&W, MFOL, TFOL, ZYDC, RGGE, **Acts:** national acts, regional acts, local acts. **Sample day's line-up:** Rusted Root, Jamie Notarthomas, The Heartbeats, John Specker, Colorblind James, Rasta Rafiki, Hypnotic Clambake, The Hicks, Ploughman's Lunch, Bubba George, Zydeco Norton. **Contact:** Great Blue Heron Music Festival, P. O. Box 791, Jamestown, NY 14701, 716-487-1781/761-6184.

### AMERICAN PATRIOT FESTIVAL, Hunter, NY
    Early Jul.
    Variety, General

See other dates. **Days:** 4. **Hours per day:** 12. **Site:** outdoor and indoor. Hunter Mountain Ski Bowl, Route 23A. **Admission:** paid. **Daily entry:** under $10, **Secondary genre[s]:** MJAZ, TJAZ, GYLS, OTHR **Acts:** national acts, regional acts, local acts. **Sample series lineup:** Day One: Skip Parson's Riverboat Jazz Band, The Patriot Band, others; Day Two: Sammy Kaye Orchestra, The Patriot Band, others; Day Three: Jimmy Sturr Orchestra, The Patriot Band, others. **Contact:** Hunter Mountain Festivals, Ltd., P. O. Box 295, Hunter, NY 12442, 518-263-3800.

### CATSKILL FOURTH OF JULY CELEBRATION, Catskill, NY
    Early Jul.
    Variety, General

**Days:** 1. **Hours per day:** 12. **Site:** outdoor. Dutchman's Landing Park, Main Street. **Admission:** free. **Secondary genre[s]:** CRCK, **Acts:** national acts, local acts. **Sample day's lineup:** The Shirelles (evening); other locals (daytime). **Contact:** Catskill Police Benevolent Association, P. O. Box 133, Catskill, NY 14214, 518-943-4733.

### OPUS 40 ACOUSTIC SUMMIT: BRING IT ON HOME, Saugerties, NY
    Early Jul.
    Modern Folk

Since 1994. "A Woodstock holiday celebration." -- Advertisement. Celebrating release of live recordings from "groundbreaking" 1980's radio series hosted by Happy and Artie Traum. See other dates. **Days:** 1. **Site:** outdoor. Opus 40, 7480 Fite Road. **Admission:** paid. **Daily entry:** $10 to $24, $25 to $49, **Discounts:** advance purchase discounts, other discounts **Secondary genre[s]:** TR&B, BLGS, **Acts:** national acts, regional acts, local acts. **Sample day's lineup:** Happy and Artie Traum, Rory Block, Jorma Kaukonen, Livingston Taylor, Amy Fradon and Leslie Ritter, Diane Ziegler, Josh Colow, Bill Keith, Al Mamlet, Scott Petito and The "Bring It On Home" All-Stars. **Audio merchandise:** "Bring It On Home, Vols. 1, 2" (SONY/Legacy). **Contact:** Opus 40 Sunset Concerts, 7480 Fite Road, Saugerties, NY, 914-246-3400/8584.

### CALICO DANCERS GOOD TIME POW WOW, South Glens Falls, NY
    Early Jul.
    Native American

"Southern Plains-style." -- Listing. **Days:** 2. **Site:** outdoor. Moreau Town Recreation Park, Route 32. **Acts:** local acts. **Contact:** Calico Dancers Good Time Pow Wow, 10 Fairview Street, South Glens Falls, NY 12803, 518-793-5273.

## INDEPENDENCE CELEBRATION AND DOUBLE R CHAMPIONSHIP RODEO, Rhinebeck, NY
Early Jul.
Modern Country

**Days:** 2. **Hours per day:** 11. **Site:** outdoor. Dutchess County Fairgrounds, Route 9. **Admission:** paid. **Daily entry:** under $10, **Acts:** local acts. **Sample day's lineup:** True Value/Jimmy Dean Country Showdown with 20 acts. **Contact:** Dutchess County Fairgrounds, Route 9, Rhinebeck, RI, 914-876-4001.


## SUMMERFEST, Poughkeepsie, NY
Early Jul.
Variety, General

Since 1994. Benefits United Way of Dutchess County. **Days:** 2. **Hours per day:** 12. **Site:** outdoor. DeLaval site on the Hudson River. **Admission:** paid. **Daily entry:** under $10, $10 to $24, **Secondary genre[s]:** MJAZ, CRCK, RAP, TR&B, MC&W, MFOL, RGGE, **Acts:** national acts, local acts. **Sample day's lineup:** Chuck Berry, Andy Follette and The Bluescasters, Tommy Rox, The Steve Garvino Project, Format, Don Lewis Band. **Contact:** HITS, 13 Closs Drive, Rhinebeck, NY 12572, 914-876-3666.


## AMERICAN INDIAN HERITAGE AND CRAFT FESTIVAL, Albany, NY
Early Jul.
Native American

**Days:** 3. **Hours per day:** 7. **Site:** indoor. New York State Museum, Empire State Plaza. **Admission:** paid. **Daily entry:** under $10, $10 to $24, **Discounts:** other discounts. **Contact:** New York State Museum, 3073 Cultural Education Center, Albany, NY 12230, 518-474-5801.


## FAIR HAVEN FIELD DAYS, Fair Haven, NY
Early Jul.
Variety, General

**Help!** A sample lineup? **Days:** 3. **Site:** outdoor. Fair Haven Bay. **Admission:** free. **Secondary genre[s]:** MRCK, MC&W, **Acts:** local acts. **Contact:** Fair Haven Chamber of Commerce, P. O. Box 317, Fair Haven, NY 13064, 315-947-6037.


## CAIRO APPRECIATION DAY FAIR, Cairo, NY
Early Jul.
Modern Country

Since 1990. "The panoramic view is breathtaking all by itself...affordable fun for families." -- Judith Cavanaugh. **Days:** 1. **Hours per day:** 12. **Site:** outdoor. Angelo Canna Cairo Town Park, Mountain Avenue. **Admission:** free. **Secondary genre[s]:** MRCK, **Acts:** local acts. **Sample day's lineup:** Roger Maben and Musical Combo, Hired Guns, others. **Contact:** Cairo Appreciation Day Fair, P. O. Box 712, Cairo, NY 12413, 518-622-2969.


## FOURTH OF JULY CELEBRATION, Mayville, NY
Early Jul.
Variety, General

**Days:** 1. **Site:** outdoor. Lakeside Park. **Secondary genre[s]:** MRCK, MC&W, OTHR **Acts:** local acts. **Sample day's lineup:** Mike Eck Band, Miami, Harmony Express, Dutch Meisters. **Contact:** 4th of July Celebration, P. O. Box 229, Mayville, NY 14757-0229, 716-753-2280.

MATT'S MATINEE, Lake Placid, NY
    Early Jul.
    Traditional Folk

Since 1993. Kick-off to the Lake Placid Center for the Arts' summer season. "Adirondack pickers, singers and songwriters." -- Flyer. See other dates. **Help!** One time only? **Days:** 1. **Site:** outdoor and indoor. Village Band Shell (afternoon); Lake Placid Center for the Arts (evening). **Admission:** paid. **Daily entry:** $10 to $24, **Secondary genre[s]:** TR&B, BLGS, MFOL, **Acts:** regional acts, local acts. **Sample day's lineup:** Matt McCabe, Peggy Eyres, Joan Crane, Junior Barber, The Gibson Brothers. **Audio merchandise:** "Adirondack Songwriters Live"; "Music from the Adirondacks" (Essex County Arts Council, P. O. Box 805, Elizabethtown, NY 12932, 518-873-9124). **Contact:** Starving Arts, P. O. Box 332, Elizabethtown, NY 12932, 518-873-9860/523-2512.

STAR SPANGLED SPECTACULAR, Montgomery, NY
    Early Jul.
    Variety, General

**Days:** 1. **Hours per day:** 9. **Site:** outdoor. Thomas Bull Memorial Park. **Admission:** free. **Secondary genre[s]:** TFOL, OTHR **Acts:** national acts, local acts. **Sample day's lineup:** Pete Seeger, U. S. Military Academy Concert Band, others. **Contact:** Star Spangled Spectacular, c/o Times-Herald Record, 40 Mulberry Street, Middletown, NY 10940, 914-341-1100 x1190.

SUMMER JAM, Glens Falls, NY
    Early Jul.
    Modern Rock and Pop

**Days:** 1. **Site:** outdoor. West Mountain Ski Area. **Admission:** free. **Restrictions:** 3, 4, 5, **Acts:** local acts. **Sample day's lineup:** Mark Lindsay, Tony DeSare Trio, Steve Van Zandt, Bobby Dick and The Sundowners. **Contact:** WCKM-FM, 128 Glen Street, Glens Falls, NY 12801, 518-761-9890.

IRISH SALUTE TO THE U. S. A., East Durham, NY
    Early Jul.
    Irish

Since 1978. "On her birthday." -- Advertisement. See other dates. **Help!** One time only? **Days:** 2. **Hours per day:** 9. **Site:** outdoor. Irish Cultural and Sports Center, Route 145. **Admission:** paid. **Daily entry:** under $10, **Acts:** regional acts, local acts. **Sample lineup:** Erin's Pride, Celtic Cross, Aine, Peter Street Band, Gus Hayes, Dermot Henry, Pat Keogh Band, others. **Contact:** East Durham Vacationland Association, P. O. Box 67, East Durham, NY 12423, 518-634-2286.

IROQUOIS ARTS SHOWCASE II, Howes Cave, NY
    Early Jul.
    Native American

See other dates. **Days:** 2. **Hours per day:** 8. **Site:** outdoor and indoor. Iroquois Indian Museum, Caverns Road. **Admission:** paid. **Daily entry:** under $10, **Acts:** local acts. **Contact:** Iroquois Indian Festival, P. O. Box 7, Howes Cave, NY 12092, 518-296-8949.

## FLEADH: OLD MUSIC OF IRELAND FESTIVAL, Leeds, NY
Early Jul.
Irish

Since 1993. "Ireland in the Catskills." -- Advertisement. See other dates. **Days:** 3. **Hours per day:** 12. **Site:** outdoor and indoor. Irish Center. **Admission:** paid. **Daily entry:** $10 to $24, **Discounts:** group sale discounts, **Acts:** national acts, regional acts, local acts. **Sample lineup:** Billy McComiskey, Daithi Sproule, Liz Carroll, Mick Maloney, Kips Bay Celi Band, Pat Kilbride, John Whelan, Richard Lindsay, Steve Missal, John McGann, Tony DeMarco, Rev. Charlie Coen, Jack Coen, Joannie Madden, Eileen Ivers, Larry Reynolds, John Nolan, Brendan Dolan, Jimmie Kelly, John Cronin, Buddy Connelly, Joe Burke, Eugene O'Donnell, Seamus Egan, others. **Contact:** Gertrude Byrne Promotions, P. O. Box 6, Leeds, NY 12451, 518-943-3736.

## GRUNTSTOCK, Parksville, NY
Early Jul.
Hard Rock and Heavy Metal

Since 1992. "800 acres of a wild rocker's dream!" -- Advertisement. Events and lineups highly variable, so call ahead. See other dates. **Help!** One time only? **Days:** 3. **Hours per day:** 14. **Site:** outdoor. Arrowhead Ranch, 548 Cooley Road, off Route 17W. **Admission:** paid. **Daily entry:** under $10, **Restrictions:** 4, 10, **Acts:** local acts. **Sample lineup:** After Dark, Apostates, Major Domo, Mixed Breed, My World, Pud, Spiders and Pigs, Steel Reign, Trash Can Baby, Vienna, Voodoo Storm, Zale, plus 5 other bands. **Contact:** Arrowhead Ranch, R. D. 1, Box 87, Parksville, NY 12768, 914-292-6273.

## SUMMER BOOGIE, Ellenville, NY
Early Jul. to Middle Jul.
Modern Jazz

"Swing, Latin and Ballroom Dance Weekend." -- Brochure. See other dates and sites. **Days:** 7. **Site:** indoor. Fallsview Hotel. **Admission:** paid. **Daily entry:** $25 to $49, **Discounts:** group sale discounts, **Secondary genre[s]:** MLAT, **Acts:** regional acts. **Sample lineup:** Georgie Gee Orchestra, Cruz Control, others. **Contact:** Boogie Dance Productions, 119 East 15th Street, New York, NY 10003, 800-64-SWING **or:** Fallsview Hotel, Ellenville, NY 12428, 914-822-8439. .

## ADIRONDACK FESTIVAL OF AMERICAN MUSIC, Saranac Lake, NY
Early Jul. to Late Jul.
Avant Garde and New Music

Since 1974. "The resident chorus...is the internationally acclaimed professional choral ensemble, the Gregg Smith Singers -- winners of three Grammy Awards and described by Time as 'The best in America.'" -- Program. **Days:** 19. **Site:** outdoor and indoor. multiple locations, including Lake Placid, Long Lake, Plattsburg. **Admission:** free and paid. **Secondary genre[s]:** CBRT, OTHR **Acts:** national acts, local acts. **Sample day's lineup:** Gregg Smith Singers perform works of Monteverdi, Bruckner, Hawley, Henderson, Raminish. **Contact:** Adirondack Festival of American Music, P. O. Box 562, Saranac Lake, NY 12983, 518-891-1057/1011 **or:** Adirondack Festival of American Music, 171 West 71st Street, New York, NY 10023, 212-874-2990.

## FABULOUS FOURTH FESTIVITIES, Albany, NY
Early Jul.
Variety, Jazz and Blues

"Music: Made In America!" -- Program. See other dates. **Days:** 1. **Hours per day:** 8. **Site:** outdoor. Empire State Plaza. **Admission:** free. **Secondary genre[s]:** MJAZ, TJAZ, TR&B, ACAP, OTHR. **Acts:** national acts, local acts. **Sample day's lineup:** Nick Brignola, Lil' Ed and The Blues Imperials, Paragon Ragtime Orchestra, Serendipity Singers, U. S. Army 10th Mountain Division Band. **Contact:** N. Y. S. Office of General Services, Promotion and Public Affairs, 41st Floor, Erastus Corning II Tower, Empire State Plaza, Albany, NY 12242, 518-473-0559.

RIVERHEAD JAZZ FESTIVAL, Riverhead, NY
> Early Jul.
> Variety, General

**Days:** 1. **Hours per day:** 8. **Site:** outdoor. 133 East Main Street. **Admission:** paid. **Daily entry:** $10 to $24, $50 and over. **Discounts:** advance purchase discounts, **Secondary genre[s]:** MJAZ, MC&W, MFOL, **Acts:** national acts, local acts. **Sample day's lineup:** Benny Goodman Band, Joel Cooke Band, Richie Havens, Mark Gatz. **Contact:** East End Arts Council, 133 East Main Street, Riverhead, NY 11901, 516-727-0900.


LUNCHTIME CONCERTS, Albany, NY
> Early Jul. to Late Aug.
> Variety, General

See other dates. **Days:** 32. **Hours per day:** 2. **Site:** outdoor. West Capital Park. **Admission:** free. **Secondary genre[s]:** TJAZ, MRCK, CRCK, ARCK, TR&B, MC&W, TC&W, BLGS, MFOL, BRZL, RGGE, **Acts:** national acts, local acts. **Sample series lineup:** Day One: Nick Brignola and Endangered Species; Day Two: Bandolero; Day Three: Tropical Beat Band. **Contact:** N. Y. S. Office of General Services, Promotion and Public Affairs, 41st Floor, Erastus Corning II Tower, Empire State Plaza, Albany, NY 12242, 518-473-0559.


POW WOW, Barryville, NY
> Early Jul.
> Native American

See other dates. **Days:** 1. **Site:** outdoor. off Route 55. **Acts:** local acts. **Contact:** Indian League of the Americas, Inc., P. O. Box 613, Port Jervis, NY 12771, 914-858-8309.


IRISH FESTIVAL OF CHEMUNG COUNTY, Elmira Heights, NY
> Early Jul.
> Irish

**Days:** 2. **Hours per day:** 12. **Site:** outdoor. Ukrainian Park, McCauley Avenue. **Admission:** paid. **Daily entry:** under $10, **Discounts: Acts:** local acts. **Sample day's lineup:** Pat Kane, The Hylands, The New Folk Trio, West O'Clare, others. **Contact:** Ancient Order of Hibernians, 701 Kinyon Street, Elmira, NY 14904, 607-733-3056.


TASTE OF BUFFALO, Buffalo, NY
> Early Jul.
> Variety, General

Since 1984. We WILL entertain you." -- Listing. **Days:** 2. **Site:** outdoor. Buffalo Place, Main Street. **Admission:** free. **Secondary genre[s]:** MJAZ, TJAZ, MRCK, CRCK, MR&B, MC&W, TC&W, IRSH, RGGE, OTHR **Acts:** national acts, local acts. **Sample day's lineup:** CeCe Penniston, Outer Circle Orchestra, Stone Country, Keith Allen and The Cross Country Express, Mike Hill and The New Sound of Blue Country, WNY Fiddlers Association, Variety Club Orchestra, Joyride, Wunderland, Brandy Lies, Flipside, Buffalo Jazz Allstars, Barroom Buzzards, Pappy Martin Ensemble, Malestrom Percussion, Mint Condition, Sugar and Jazz, Jerry Raven, others. **Contact:** Kaleidoscope Events, 512 Woodstock Avenue, Tonawanda, NY 14150, 716-835-0643/856-3150.

## WATERFRONT EXTRAVAGANZA, Syracuse, NY
### Early Jul. to Middle Jul.
### Variety, General

"It's Central New York's biggest splash of the summer, a tremendous combination of land, water and aerial entertainment...It's the shore thing!" -- Press Release. See other sites and dates. **Help!** Still ongoing? **Days:** 4. **Site:** outdoor. Willow Bay section, Onondaga Lake Park. **Secondary genre[s]:** MJAZ, TJAZ, MRCK, CRCK, MR&B, TR&B, MFOL, OTHR **Acts:** national acts, regional acts, local acts. **Sample day's lineup:** Little Charlie and The Night Cats, Boss Street Band, Target, Todd Hobin, Sweet Adelines, Water Street Boys, Kennedy and Spindler, Steve Chirello, Phil Market and Eddie Fagan, S. P. E. B. S. Q. A., Lowdown Alligator band, Eddie Wyznowski's Dixie Marching BandMimi's Music Makers, Dennis Friscia. **Contact:** Onondaga County Parks, P. O. Box 146, Liverpool, NY 13088, 315-451-PARK.

## INVITATIONAL PIPING CHAMPIONSHIP/MEMORIAL MILITARY TATTOO, Ticonderoga, NY
### Early Jul.
### Drum Corp and Marching Bands

See other dates. **Days:** 1. **Site:** outdoor and indoor. Fort Ticonderoga, off Route 22. **Admission:** paid. **Daily entry:** under $10, **Discounts:** group sale discounts, **Secondary genre[s]:** SCOT, **Acts:** regional acts, local acts. **Sample day's lineup:** Royal Regiment of Canada, Canadian Forces Pipe Band, Fort Ticonderoga Corps of Drums. **Contact:** Fort Ticonderoga, P. O. Box 390, Ticonderoga, NY 12883, 518-585-2821.

## SUNDAY BY THE BAY, Bellport, NY
### Early Jul.
### Modern Rock and Pop

Benefits Stopping AIDS Together. "This spectacular outdoor affair never fails to attract a glittery crowd, and boats a dazzling fashion show, live and silent auctions, exceptional food, drink and entertainment." -- Liz Smith, New York Newsday. **Days:** 1. **Hours per day:** 6. **Site:** outdoor. Great South Bay, 99 South Howells Point Road. **Admission:** paid. **Daily entry:** $50 and over. **Secondary genre[s]:** CRCK, MC&W, CBRT, **Acts:** national acts, local acts. **Sample day's lineup:** Wilson Pickett, Robin S., others. **Contact:** Stopping AIDS Together, Grey Dunes Estate, 5 Cedar Bluff Road, Bellport, NY, 516-286-1020.

## DEL-SE-NANGO FIDDLERS FESTIVAL, Bainbridge, NY
### Early Jul.
### Modern Country

Since 1984. See other dates and sites. **Days:** 2. **Hours per day:** 12. **Site:** outdoor. General Clinton Park, Route 7. **Admission:** paid. **Daily entry:** $10 to $24, **Discounts:** multiple event or day passes, advance purchase discounts, **Secondary genre[s]:** BLGS, TFOL, **Acts:** regional acts, local acts. **Sample day's lineup:** Wildwood Girls, Wayne Swartz, Stump Jumpers, Judy Carrier and Rens Vreesburg, Billy Bob and Friends, Del-Se-Nango Fiddlers, Real Country, Laura Kortwright, Ghost Riders, Lee and Shirley Eaton. **Contact:** Del-Se-Nango Olde Tyme Fiddlers, R. F. D. 3, Box 233, New Berlin, NY 13411, 607-847-8501 **or:** Del-Se-Nango Olde Tyme Fiddlers, RD #2, Alton, NY 13730, 607-639-2502.

## MAPLE RIDGE BLUEGRASS FESTIVAL, Duanesburg, NY
### Early Jul. to Middle Jul.
### Bluegrass

Since 1993. **Days:** 3. **Hours per day:** 16. **Site:** outdoor and indoor. Indian Lookout Country Club, Batter Road. **Admission:** paid. **Daily entry:** $10 to $24, **Discounts:** multiple event or day passes, advance purchase discounts, **Secondary genre[s]:** SGOS, TC&W, BLGS, **Acts:** national acts, regional acts, local acts. **Sample day's lineup:** New Coon Creek Girls, Lynn Morris Band, Smokey Greene and The Boys, Gifford Hollow Boys, Bear Bridge band, Cedar Ridge, Stonewall Bluegrass, Grass Roots, John Rossbacj and Chestnut Grove, Blades of Grass, River Bottom, Blistered Fingers. **Contact:** Gifford Hollow Promotions, P. O. Box 45, Berne, NY 12023, 800-242-5754.

### PANAMA ROCKS FOLK ARTS FAIR, Panama, NY
Early Jul. to Middle Jul.
Bluegrass

**Days:** 3. **Site:** outdoor. Panama Rocks Scenic Park, 1 Rock Hill Road. **Admission:** free. **Acts:** local acts. **Sample day's lineup:** Dempsey Station, Generic Grass, others. **Contact:** Panama Rocks Scenic Park, 1 Rock Hill Road, Panama, NY, 716-782-2845.

### BLUES IN THE NIGHT, Rochester, NY
Early Jul.
Blues and Traditional R&B

See other dates. **Days:** 1. **Site:** outdoor. Manhattan Square Park, Chestnut and Court Streets. **Admission:** free. **Acts:** national acts, local acts. **Sample day's lineup:** Clarence "Gatemouth" Brown, Saffire, Joe Beard. **Contact:** City of Rochester Events Network, City Hall, 30 Church Street, Room 222B, Rochester, NY 14614, 716-428-6690/6697.

### TUSCARORA FIELD DAY AND PICNIC, Lewiston, NY
Early Jul.
Native American

Since 1846. "People from outside the reservation enjoy coming here...because there are no high-rises, nothing is disturbed, and the land holds all that Mother Earth has to offer." -- Chief Leo Henry, Buffalo News. **Days:** 1. **Hours per day:** 12. **Site:** outdoor. grove behind Tuscarora Indian School, Walmore and Mount Hope Streets. **Secondary genre[s]:** MRCK, MC&W, **Acts:** local acts. **Sample day's lineup:** Craig Wilkins and The Western New Yorkers, Lee Beno Quartet, Joe Malfound and The Trigger Finger Band, others. **Contact:** Tuscarora Field Day and Picnic, 1387 Upper Mountain Road, Lewiston, NY 14092, 716-297-4907 **or:** Tuscarora Field Day and Picnic, 2121 Mount Hope Road, Sanborn, NY 14132 .

### CORN HILL ARTS FESTIVAL/FIDDLER'S FAIR, Rochester, NY
Early Jul. to Middle Jul.
Variety, General

Since 1970. **Days:** 2. **Site:** outdoor. multiple stages, Corn Hill neighborhood, off I-490. **Admission:** free. **Secondary genre[s]:** MJAZ, TJAZ, TR&B, ACAP, MC&W, TC&W, AC&W, BLGS, MFOL, TFOL, FDDL, ZYDC, IRSH, SCOT, RGGE, OTHR **Acts:** national acts, regional acts, local acts. **Sample day's lineup:** The Horseflies, The Heartbeats, The Dady Brothers, Variety In Motion, R Gang, Jim Ferris Quartet, New Evidence, Blue Sky, Colorblind James Experience, Gary Murphee and The Kids Koncert Band, Pallini and Pappert, Still Kickin', Culvert and Swale, Annie Wells, Luann Arena, Baroque Chamber Trio, The Showvinettes, John Wurtenberg, Foclorista Italiana, Will Shaw, Adams Street Dance Patrol, others. **Contact:** Corn Hill Neighbors Association, 140 Troup Street, Rochester, NY 14608, 716-262-3142.

### NATIVE AMERICAN POW WOW, East Durham, NY
Early Jul. to Middle Jul.
Native American

**Days:** 2. **Hours per day:** 7. **Site:** indoor. Durham Center Museum, Route 145. **Acts:** local acts. **Contact:** Durham Center Museum, Route 145, East Durham, NY, 518-239-4313.

## GOOD OLD SUMMERTIME, Utica, NY
Early Jul. to Middle Jul.
Variety, General

**Days:** 6. **Hours per day:** 11. **Site:** outdoor. Munson-Williams-Proctor Institute. **Admission:** free. **Secondary genre[s]:** MJAZ, MRCK, MC&W, RGGE, OTHR **Acts:** local acts. **Sample day's lineup:** Michael Damion, TK Band, Ivory Tower, Good Vibrations, Rattlebasket, others. **Contact:** Good Old Summertime, 207 Genesee Street, Utica, NY 13501, 315-733-6976.

## REAL WOODSTOCK FESTIVAL, Woodstock, NY
Middle Jul.
Classic Rock and Oldies

Since 1994. **Help!** One time only? **Days:** 2. **Site:** indoor. Byrdcliffe Barn, Upper Byrdcliffe Road. **Acts:** national acts, local acts. **Sample day's lineup:** The Fugs, Allen Ginsberg, others. **Contact:** The Woodstock Guild, 34 Tinker Street, Woodstock, NY 12498, 914-679-2079.

## PEACEFUL VALLEY BLUEGRASS FESTIVAL, Shinhopple, NY
Middle Jul.
Bluegrass

Since 1983. See other sites and dates. **Days:** 4. **Site:** outdoor. Peaceful Valley Campsite, Route 30. **Admission:** paid. **Daily entry:** $10 to $24, **Discounts:** multiple event or day passes, advance purchase discounts, **Acts:** national acts, regional acts. **Sample day's lineup:** Del McCoury Band, California, Ronnie Reno, Stevens Family, Lynn Morris Band, Chubby Wise, Raymond Fairchild and The Maggie Valley Boys, Jim and Jesse and The Virginia Boys, Southern Rail, Mike Stevens, Lou Reed, Terry Balcolm and Carolina. **Contact:** Peaceful Valley Promotions, Inc., HC 89, Box 56, Downsville, NY 13755, 800-844-2703.

## WINTERHAWK BLUEGRASS FAMILY FESTIVAL, Ancramdale, NY
Middle Jul.
Bluegrass

**Days:** 4. **Hours per day:** 13. **Site:** outdoor. Rothvoss Farm, Route 22. **Admission:** paid. **Daily entry:** $10 to $24, $25 to $49, **Discounts:** multiple event or day passes, advance purchase discounts, **Restrictions:** 10, **Secondary genre[s]:** SGOS, AC&W, BLGS, FDDL, **Acts:** national acts, regional acts, local acts. **Sample day's lineup:** Buck White and The Down Home Folks with Jerry Douglas, Tim and Mollie O'Brien, Sam Bush, Peter Rowan and The Rowan Brothers, Nashville Bluegrass Band, Josh Graves and Kenny Baker, Lonseome River Band, Peter Wernick, Fiddlestyx, Front Range, John Kirk and Trish Miller, Foxfire, Bill Keith, Youth Allstars, Laurel Canyon Ramblers, Michael Munford, Breakaway, Dry Branch Fire Squad, others. **Contact:** Winterhawk Bluegrass Family Festival, P. O. Box 161, Tremont City, OH 45372, 513-390-6211.

## BILL LABEEF'S BASTILLE DAY, BARBEQUE AND ROCK AND ROLL RODEO, Rochester, NY
Middle Jul.
Alternative and College Rock

**Help!** A contact? **Days:** 1. **Site:** indoor. Calumet Arts Cafe, 56 West Chippewa Street (location varies). **Admission:** paid. **Daily entry:** under $10, **Secondary genre[s]:** AC&W, OTHR **Acts:** national acts, local acts. **Sample day's lineup:** John and Mary, Ploughman's Lunch, The Matt and Terry Show, Native Soil Cello, Scott carpenter, others. **Contact:** Bill LaBeef's Bastille Day, c/o Neche's, Allen Street, Buffalo, NY, 716-886-8539/855-2220.

CARIBBEAN EXTRAVAGANZA, Catile, NY
    Middle Jul.
    Reggae, Ska and Caribbean

Part of Letchworth Performing Art Series. See other dates. **Help!** A sample lineup? **Days:** 1. **Hours per day:** 4. **Site:** outdoor. Highbanks Recreation Area, Letchworth State Park. **Admission:** free. **Acts:** local acts. **Contact:** Caribbean Extravaganza, c/o Recreation Department, Letchworth State Park, Castile, NY 14427, 716-493-3600.

GAELIC DAY, Vails Gate, NY
    Middle Jul.
    Scottish

Cut down from a full day's music to an evening concert, By the Gloaming, due to rising expense of hiring bands. See other dates. **Days:** 1. **Hours per day:** 2. **Site:** outdoor. New Windsor Cantonment, Route 300. **Secondary genre[s]:** IRSH, **Acts:** regional acts, local acts. **Sample day's lineup:** McLeod's Bagpipes of Scotland, others. **Contact:** New Windsor Cantonment State Historic Site, P. O. Box 207, Vales Gate, NY 12584, 914-561-1765.

RUSHMORE FESTIVAL, Woodbury, NY
    Middle Jul.
    Avant Garde and New Music

**Days:** 3. **Site:** outdoor. Rushmore Estate. **Admission:** paid. **Daily entry:** $10 to $24, $25 to $49, **Acts:** national acts, . **Sample day's lineup:** Lukas Foss and friends perform works of Hindemith. **Contact:** Rushmore Festival, Rushmore Estate, Woodbury, NY, 212-207-8334.

SYRACUSE ARTS AND CRAFTS FESTIVAL, Syracuse, NY
    Middle Jul.
    Variety, General

Since 1971. **Days:** 3. **Hours per day:** 9. **Site:** outdoor. Columbus Circle, Montgomery Street. **Secondary genre[s]:** MJAZ, CRCK, ARCK, RAP, TR&B, ACAP, MC&W, BLGS, MFOL, TFOL, IRSH, SCOT, MLAT, **Acts:** local acts. **Sample day's lineup:** Austin Jimmy Murphy and The Blues Kings, Shade V, New Times Banned, Jamie Notarthomas, Begonia, Scottish Highlandres, Dan Duggin, Don Laird. **Contact:** Downtown Committee of Syracuse, Inc., 1900 State Tower Building, Syracuse, NY 13202, 315-422-8284/635-6495.

AFRICAN-AMERICAN HERITAGE CELEBRATION, Yonkers, NY
    Middle Jul.
    African American

Since 1988. **Days:** 2. **Site:** outdoor. Cerrato Park, Trevor Park, off Riverdale Avenue. **Admission:** free. **Secondary genre[s]:** RAP, TR&B, BGOS, AFRC, RGGE, **Acts:** national acts, local acts. **Sample day's lineup:** Force MD's, One Nation Under God, Fishers Of Men, Nu-Lite Steel Band, Vi-Da, BensAsWin, Bokandeye. **Contact:** African-American Heritage Celebration Committee, YMCA, 87 South Broadway, Yonkers, NY 10701, 914-963-0640/965-0203.

AVERILL PARK SUMMER BLUES FEST, Averill Park, NY
    Middle Jul.
    Blues and Traditional R&B

Since 1993. **Days:** 1. **Site:** outdoor and indoor. Lakeview Inn, Route 43. **Admission:** paid. **Daily entry:** under $10, $10 to $24, **Restrictions:** 5, **Acts:** regional acts, local acts. **Sample day's lineup:** Ernie Williams and The Wildcats, Smokehouse Prophets, The Sharks, The Night Kings, Begonia, Tropical Hotdogs. **Contact:** Lakeview Inn, Route 43, Averill Park, NY 12018, 518-674-8954/3363.

## MUSIC AND THE MOUNTAIN SKY/FOLK CONCERT, Highmount, NY
    Middle Jul.
    Traditional Folk

Since 1992. Part of Music and the Mountain Sky, a bi-weekly summer concert series featuring national and local acts across various genres. See other dates. **Days:** 1. **Site:** outdoor. Belleayre Conservatory, Belleayre Ski Center. **Secondary genre[s]:** TJAZ, MFOL, NATV, **Acts:** national acts, local acts. **Sample day's lineup:** Pete Seeger, Tao Rodriguez Seeger, Kim and Reggie Harris, Gretchen Reed, Jody Gill, Powatan Swift Eagle, Matoaka Little Eagle. **Contact:** Belleayre Conservatory, P. O. Box 198, Highmount, NY 12441, 914-586-2611.

## RHYTHM AND BLUES BEACH PARTY, Caroga Lake, NY
    Middle Jul.
    Blues and Traditional R&B

**Help!** One time only? **Days:** 1. **Hours per day:** 7. **Site:** outdoor and indoor. Sherman's Yellow Rose, Route 29A. **Admission:** paid. **Daily entry:** $10 to $24, **Restrictions:** 5, **Acts:** regional acts, local acts. **Sample day's lineup:** Matt Smith, Bobby Messano, Ernie Williams and The Wildcats. **Contact:** Sherman's Yellow Rose, Route 29A, Caroga Lake, NY, 518-843-5735/835-2600.

## WOODSTOCK BEAT WORLD PERCUSSION CONCERT, Woodstock, NY
    Middle Jul.
    African

Since 1992. Benefits the Woodstock Guild. **Days:** 1. **Site:** indoor. Maverick Concert Hall, Maverick Road. **Admission:** paid. **Daily entry:** $10 to $24, **Secondary genre[s]:** MLAT, BRZL, RGGE, AVNT, **Acts:** national acts, local acts. **Sample day's lineup:** Garry Kvistad, Russell Hartenberger, Stacey Bower, Bob Becker, Steve Gorn, Thomas Workman. **Contact:** The Woodstock Guild, 34 Tinker Street, Woodstock, NY 12498, 914-679-2079.

## FIDDLE WEEKEND, Cambridge, NY
    Middle Jul.
    Fiddle and Banjo Events

Since 1980. "Combines the intimacy of a small hall with the dynamics of a festival at which the performers have as much fun playing for and with one another as they do with the audience." -- Program **Days:** 2. **Hours per day:** 11. **Site:** indoor. Hubbard Hall, 25 East Main Street. **Admission:** paid. **Daily entry:** under $10, $10 to $24, **Discounts:** other discounts **Secondary genre[s]:** TC&W, TFOL, ZYDC, TLAT, OTHR **Acts:** national acts, regional acts, local acts. **Sample day's lineup:** David Kaynor, Jay Ungar and Molly Mason, Jodie Scalise, Lyn Hardy, Susan Conger, Stewart Kenney, Selma Kaplan, The Whippersnappers. **Contact:** Hubbard Hall, 25 East Main Street, Cambridge, NY 12816, 518-677-2495.

## LONG ISLAND MUSIC FESTIVAL, Varies, NY
    Middle Jul. to Early Sep.
    Modern Rock and Pop

Since 1993. Incorporates two Legends of Long Island Rock Series concerts, plus a local band contest spread over six nights. Also programs a Long Island Music Conference (seminars only, no showcases) in Early Dec. **Days:** 8. **Site:** outdoor and indoor. Legends of Long Island Rock Series: Roxy Music, Eisenhower Park; contest: 72 bands in 24 clubs. **Admission:** free and paid. **Daily entry:** under $10, **Secondary genre[s]:** CRCK, ARCK, HRCK, OTHR **Acts:** regional acts, local acts. **Sample day's lineup:** Dark White, Groupe Therapy, Under Construction, Knockout Drops, Toast, Point Of You, Ricky and The Roaches, Gossamer, Stonehenge. **Contact:** Good Times Magazine, P. O. Box 33, Westbury, NY 11590, 516-334-9650 **or:** H. O. P. E., 237 North Virginia Avenue, North Massapequa, NY 11758-1127, 516-293-5376.

## IRISH HERITAGE CELEBRATION, Hartsdale, NY
Middle Jul.
Irish

See other dates and sites. Also programs Ethnic Celebrations: Slavic, Arab, Polish, Italian, Ukrainian. **Days:** 1. **Hours per day:** 7. **Site:** outdoor. Ridge Road Park. **Admission:** free. **Secondary genre[s]:** OTHR **Acts:** local acts. **Sample day's lineup:** Guss Hayes Band, Tim Harte, Frank O'Brien, Irish Dragoons, Keltoi, Marie McVicker, Westchester County Emerald Society Pipes and Drums, others. **Contact:** Westchester County Department of Parks and Recreation, 19 Bradhurst Avenue, Hawthorne, NY 10532, 914-593-PARK/793-4312.

## MULTICULTURAL FEST, Niagara Falls, NY
Middle Jul.
African American

Discontinued in 1994, but expected to resume. **Days:** 1. **Site:** outdoor. Whirlpool State Park. **Secondary genre[s]:** MJAZ, BGOS, RGGE, **Acts:** local acts. **Sample day's lineup:** Spider and Pappy Martin Love Supreme Jazz Ensemble, Joe Madison, others. **Contact:** Underground Railroad, Committee of the Niagara Frontier, P. O. Box 176, Niagara Falls, NY 14305, 716-278-1719.

## EMPIRE STATE BLACK ARTS AND CULTURAL FESTIVAL, Albany, NY
Middle Jul.
African American

Since 1983. "The African-American family: sustained by faith, encouraged by tomorrow." -- Program. See other dates. **Days:** 2. **Hours per day:** 7. **Site:** outdoor. multiple locations, Empire State Plaza. **Admission:** free. **Secondary genre[s]:** MJAZ, MR&B, BGOS, MLAT, RGGE, OTHR **Acts:** regional acts, local acts. **Sample day's lineup:** Sherry Winston, TC Gospel Ensemble, Danny Tucker, Plus 24, Alex Torres and The Latin Kings, others. **Contact:** Empire State Black Arts and Cultural Festival, P. O. Box 2292, Albany, NY 12220, 518-464-6230/271-5136.

## KEEPER OF THE WESTERN DOOR POW-WOW, Salamanca, NY
Middle Jul.
Native American

Presented by the Seneca Nation of Indians. **Days:** 2. **Site:** outdoor. Veteran's Memorial Park. **Acts:** national acts, regional acts, local acts. **Sample day's lineup:** Blu Spring Singers, Assiniboine Junior Singers, Whitefish Bay Singers, Iron Water Singers, Young Nation Singers, others. **Contact:** Keeper of the Western Door Pow-Wow, 3702 Center Road, Salamanca, NY 14779, 716-945-4834.

## OLD TIME MUSIC FESTIVAL AND BARBEQUE, Stone Mills, NY
Middle Jul.
Traditional Country

**Help!** A sample lineup? **Days:** 1. **Site:** outdoor. Northern New York Agricultural Museum. **Secondary genre[s]:** SGOS, MC&W, BLGS, **Acts:** local acts. **Contact:** Northern New York Agricultural Museum, Stone Mills, NY, 315-788-2882/658-4494.

## MOHONK'S FESTIVAL OF THE ARTS/INTERNATIONAL WEEK, New Paltz, NY
Middle Jul. to Late Jul.
Variety, Folk and International

Since 1990. Part of Mohonk's Festival of the Arts, Early Jul. to Mid Aug. **Help!** A sample lineup? **Days:** 6. **Site:** outdoor and indoor. Mohonk Mountain House. **Admission:** paid. **Acts:** national acts, local acts. **Contact:** Mohonk's Festival of the Arts/International Week, Mohonk Mountain House, New Paltz, NY 12561, 914-255-4500.

CANAL FEST, Tonawanda, NY
Middle Jul. to Late Jul.
Variety, General

Since 1983. "All on the banks of the historic Erie Canal!" -- Advertisement. **Days:** 8. **Hours per day:** 13. **Site:** outdoor. multiple locations. **Secondary genre[s]:** MJAZ, MRCK, TFOL, OTHR **Acts:** local acts. **Sample series lineup:** Day One: Sugar and Jazz, others; **Contact:** Tonawandas Chamber of Commerce, 20 Main Street, Tonawanda, NY 14150, 800-338-7890.

WATERFRONT FESTIVAL FREE SUMMER CONCERT SERIES/GOSPEL IN THE PARK, Buffalo, NY
Middle Jul.
Black Gospel

Gospel in the Park, with 10 local acts, is part of the Waterfront Festival, which features national and regional acts each week. See other dates. **Help!** A sample lineup? **Days:** 1. **Site:** outdoor. LaSalle Park, Porter Avenue. **Admission:** free. **Acts:** local acts. **Contact:** Junior League of Buffalo, 45 Elmwood Avenue, Buffalo, NY 14201, 716-884-8865.

HERITAGE HOEDOWN AND EMPIRE STATE FIDDLE CONTEST, Darien, NY
Middle Jul. to Late Jul.
Fiddle and Banjo Events

**Help!** Still ongoing? **Days:** 3. . **Secondary genre[s]:** TC&W, BLGS, TFOL, **Acts:** national acts, regional acts, local acts. **Sample Day's Lineup:** Chubby Wise, Paul Van Arsdale, Alice Clemens, George Harriger, Keith Ross, others. **Contact:** Western New York Old Time Fiddlers' Association, P. O. Box 529, Hamburg, NY 14075, 716-648-3981.

FINGERLAKES GRASSROOTS FESTIVAL OF MUSIC AND DANCE, Trumansburg, NY
Middle Jul. to Late Jul.
Variety, General

Since 1990. **Days:** 4. **Hours per day:** 15. **Site:** outdoor and indoor. Trumansburg Fairgrounds. **Admission:** paid. **Daily entry:** under $10, $10 to $24, **Discounts:** advance purchase discounts, **Secondary genre[s]:** AJAZ, ARCK, TR&B, ACAP, MC&W, TC&W, AC&W, BLGS, MFOL, ZYDC, NATV, AFRC, RGGE, **Acts:** national acts, regional acts, local acts. **Sample lineup:** Jimmie Dale Gilmore, The Horseflies, Preston Frank and His Zydeco Family Band, The Flirtations, Donna The Buffalo, Walter Mouton and The Scott Playboys, Ulali, Colorblind James experience, The Low Road, The Heartbeats, The Red Hots, Tin Roof, Hypnotic Clambake, John Specker, Hank Roberts, Eqypt Iowa, Perfect Thyroid, Bubba George Stringband. **Audio merchandise:** "Donna the Buffalo" (Lavakoo Records). **Contact:** Fingerlakes Grassroots Festival of Music and Dance, P. O. Box 941, Trumansburg, NY 14886, 607-387-5098 **or:** Fingerlakes Grassroots Festival of Music and Dance, 201 B Elm Street, Ithaca, NY 14850, 607-277-5638. .

COUNTRY MUSIC FESTIVAL, Hunter, NY
Middle Jul. to Late Jul.
Modern Country

Since 1978. **Days:** 10. **Hours per day:** 12. **Site:** outdoor and indoor. Hunter Mountain Ski Bowl, Route 23A. **Admission:** paid. **Daily entry:** $10 to $24, **Discounts: Secondary genre[s]:** TC&W, BLGS, MFOL, TFOL, OTHR **Acts:** national acts, regional acts, local acts. **Sample day's lineup:** Emmylou Harris, Ricky Skaggs, Robin Brown and The 5 and 10 Band, Jay Smar, Gary Nichols Band, Elwood Bunn, Maura Fogerty, Terry Gorka, The Crawfords. **Contact:** Hunter Mountain Festivals, Ltd., P. O. Box 295, Hunter, NY 12442, 518-263-3800.

## FALCON RIDGE FOLK FESTIVAL, Hillsdale, NY
Late Jul.
Variety, Folk and International

**Days:** 3. **Hours per day:** 14. **Site:** outdoor. Long Hill Farm, Route 23. **Admission:** paid. **Daily entry:** $10 to $24, $25 to $49, **Discounts:** student discounts, multiple event or day passes, advance purchase discounts, **Secondary genre[s]:** TR&B, ACAP, AC&W, BLGS, MFOL, TFOL, ZYDC, IRSH, BRZL, RGGE, **Acts:** national acts, regional acts, local acts. **Sample day's lineup:** Alan Thompson and The Little Big Band, The Clayfoot Strutters, David Kaynor and The Greenfield Dance band, George Marshall with Wild Asparagus, Mary Desrosiers, Nego Gato, Paul Rosenberg, Pat Melita, Ralph Sweet with Wild Asparagus, Steve Riley and The mamou Playboys, Amy Fradon and Leslie Ritter, Andes manta, Ani DiFranco, Camille West, Dar Williams, Donna Martin, Ellis Paul, Garnet Rigers, Greg Brown, Greg Greenway band, Hugh Blumenfeld, John Gorka, Madwoman In The Attick, Mike Casey and David DiGiuseppe, The Nields, Pete and Maura Kennedy, Peter Mulvey, Raelinda Woad, Richard Shindell, Rick Fielding, Steve Charney, others. **Contact:** Falcon Ridge Folk Festival, 74 Modley Road, Sharon, CT 06069, 203-364-0366 **or:** Falcon Ridge Folk Festival, RD 1, Box 411B, Middleburgh, NY 12122 .

## RICK AND CAROL'S COUNTRY SIDE INN BLUEGRASS FESTIVAL, Fort Ann, NY
Late Jul.
Bluegrass

Since 1986. "The Adirondack Mountains come alive with the sounds of music!" -- Flyer. **Days:** 3. **Hours per day:** 10. **Site:** outdoor and indoor. Country Side Inn, Patten Mills Road, off Route 149. **Admission:** paid. **Daily entry:** $10 to $24, **Discounts:** multiple event or day passes, advance purchase discounts, **Restrictions:** 1, **Secondary genre[s]:** SGOS, TC&W, BLGS, **Acts:** regional acts, local acts. **Sample day's lineup:** Smokey Greene and The Boys, East Country Band, Rose City Bluegrass Band, Hank and Irene Clothier, Lyle Saunders and Broder Ride, Jimmie Hamblin, Fred Pike, Sam Tidwell and The Kennebec Valley Boys. **Contact:** Country Side Inn, RR 1, Box 1273, Fort Ann, NY 12827, 518-793-8987.

## McDONALD'S GOSPELFEST, Buffalo, NY
Late Jul.
Black Gospel

"Lift every voice and sing!" -- Program. **Days:** 1. **Hours per day:** 8. **Site:** outdoor. War Memorial Stadium, Best and Jefferson Streets. **Admission:** free. **Secondary genre[s]:** RAP, **Acts:** national acts, local acts. **Sample day's lineup:** Williams Brothers of Mississippi, Voices of Methodism, Jordan Grove, U. B. Gospel Chorus, Basic, King Solomon Holiness Church Choir, Vision, Bethesda Full Gospel Church Choir, Cedar Grove Baptist Church Choir, Varsons Community Choir, Faith Bible Tabernacle Choir, The Young Sisters, Love Alive Children's Choir, Children of Inspiration, Union, Refuge Temple of Christ Choir, Mount Ararat Baptist Church Choir, Performing Arts Collection, Heavenly Voices, Salt Connection, Lighthouse Interdenominational Choir, United Church of Faith Choir, Friendship Baptist Church Choir, Oldies But Goodies Gospel Singers, Greater Works Choir, New Beginning Choral Ensemble, St. John The Baptist Church Radio Choir, The Northington Singers, St. Martin De Porre, Shelby Banks-Lewis, Calvary Baptist Church Choir, DeWayne Martin Gospel Rap, The Heavenaires, Emmanuel Temple S. D. A. Youth Choir, Memorial Baptist Chuch Choir, White Rock Baptist Church Choir, Free Spirit Baptist Church Choir, Loguen Memorial Church Choir, Restoration, Buffalo Community Partnership, New Christian Fellowship A. and S. Choir, Zion Baptist Church Choir. **Contact:** McDonald's Gospelfest, 585 North Oak Street, Buffalo, NY 14203, 716-855-1569.

## POW WOW, Barryville, NY
Late Jul.
Native American

See other dates. **Days:** 1. **Site:** outdoor. off Route 55. **Acts:** local acts. **Contact:** Indian League of the Americas, Inc., P. O. Box 613, Port Jervis, NY 12771, 914-858-8309.

## HATS OFF TO SARATOGA FESTIVAL, Saratoga Springs, NY
Late Jul.
Variety, General

See other dates. **Help!** A sample lineup? **Days:** 2. **Hours per day:** 4. **Site:** outdoor. 14 locations, Broadway. **Admission:** free. **Secondary genre[s]:** TJAZ, IRSH, OTHR **Acts:** local acts. **Contact:** Saratoga County Chamber of Commerce, 494 Broadway, Suite 212, Saratoga Springs, NY 12866, 518-584-3255.

## OPUS 40 NEW ORLEANS PARTY WEEKEND, Saugerties, NY
Late Jul.
Blues and Traditional R&B

Since 1995. "A real New Orleans party with brass bands, funeral celebration marches, and the whole festive gumbo of New Orleans music." -- Program. See other dates. **Days:** 2. **Site:** outdoor. Opus 40, 7480 Fite Road. **Admission:** paid. **Daily entry:** $10 to $24, $25 to $49, **Discounts:** advance purchase discounts, other discounts **Secondary genre[s]:** MJAZ, ZYDC, **Acts:** national acts, regional acts. **Sample lineup:** Irma Thomas, Johnny Adams, Rockin' Sidney, Rosie Ledet, The Wild Magnolias, Wardell Quezergue Band. **Audio merchandise:** "Bring It On Home, Vols. 1, 2" (SONY/Legacy). **Contact:** Opus 40 Sunset Concerts, 7480 Fite Road, Saugerties, NY, 914-246-3400/8584.

## OSWEGO HARBORFEST, Oswego, NY
Middle Jul.
Variety, General

Since 1988. "People of all ages gather in a great little city by a great big lake to celebrate summer...Music flows across the city." -- Brochure. **Days:** 4. **Hours per day:** 12. **Site:** outdoor. multiple locations downtown. **Restrictions:** 5, **Secondary genre[s]:** MJAZ, TJAZ, CRCK, TR&B, ACAP, BGOS, MC&W, BLGS, MFOL, TFOL, ZYDC, IRSH, SCOT, MLAT, TLAT, RGGE, OTHR **Acts:** national acts, regional acts, local acts. **Sample day's lineup:** Tracy Lawrence, Gruppo Folk Di Morolo, Mohawk Valley Frasers Pipeband, Rabbit In A Log, Bill Miller, Dan Duggan, Don Laird, Chenille Sisters, The Monarchs, Midlife Crisis, Lewis Banta Band, Gypsy Guerilla Band, Ken Lonnquist, Oswego Dixieland Band, Ninety-One, Midnight Snack with Rocco Barbeto, Ronnie Leigh, Jacque Washington, Danny Gatton, Adrea Miceli and Moss, Oswego Valley Barbershop Singers with Classic Touch Quartet, Nickel City Clippers, Rochester Philharmonic Brass Quintet, Linda Russell, others. **Contact:** Harbor Festivals, Inc., 41 Lake Street, Oswego, NY 13126, 315-343-FREE/6858/3040.

## ORANGE COUNTY FAIR, Middletown, NY
Late Jul.
Fairs

Since 1841. "Funtastic." -- Advertisement. **Days:** 8. **Site:** outdoor. Orange County Fairgrounds. **Secondary genre[s]:** MC&W, **Acts:** national acts, regional acts. **Sample series lineup:** Day One: Butch Baker; Day Two: Ronnie Milsap; Day Three: Conway Twitty. **Contact:** Orange County Fair, Orange County Fairgrounds, Middletown, NY, 914-343-3134/4826.

## JAZZ/REGGAE FESTIVAL, Syracuse, NY
Late Jul.
Modern Jazz

"Your student fee at work celebrating great music." -- Poster. **Days:** 1. **Hours per day:** 5. **Site:** outdoor. Syracuse University Quad. **Admission:** free. **Secondary genre[s]:** RGGE, **Acts:** local acts. **Sample day's lineup:** Ronnie Leigh Quintet, Ronnie France Project, Big Roots. **Contact:** Division of Summer Sessions and Student Activities, Syracuse University, Syracuse, NY, 315-443-5294/4181.

LOW BRIDGE FESTIVAL, Lyons, NY
> Late Jul.
> Bluegrass

**Days:** 1. **Site:** outdoor. **Acts:** regional acts, local acts. **Sample day's lineup:** Cornerstone, Fox Family, John Rossbach, Bristol Mountain Bluegrass, Tony Pearl. **Contact:** E. R. I. E. Group, 336 Pleasant Valley Road, Lyons, NY 14489, 315-946-4092/9445.

CRANBERRY DULCIMER GATHERING, Binghamton, NY
> Late Jul.
> Traditional Folk

Since 1977. "Gathering of musicians (from beginners to ol' pros) who come together for the joy of making music." -- Flyer. **Days:** 3. **Site:** outdoor and indoor. Unitarian Universalist Church, 183 Riverside Drive. **Admission:** paid. **Daily entry:** under $10, $10 to $24, **Discounts:** multiple event or day passes, advance purchase discounts, **Secondary genre[s]:** TGOS, **Acts:** local acts. **Sample day's lineup:** Carrie Crompton, Maddie MacNeil, John and Kathie Hollandsworth, Thomasina, Lee Vacarro, Tom Baehr, Dancing Strings, Sue Carpenter, Eileen Kosloff-Abrams, Randy Kochel, K. Bann and L. Keddell, B. C. Childress, Jacki Romano, Charlene Thompson, Linda Sigismondi, Ivan Stiles, Paulette Dickerson, Steve Schneider, T. J. Osborne, Drew Smith, Bernd Krause, Sally McKnight, Mark Fowler. **Contact:** Cranberry Dulcimer Gathering, 1259 Fowler Place, Binghamton, NY 13903, 607-669-4653 **or:** Cranberry Dulcimer Gathering, Unitarian Universalist Church, 183 Riverside Drive, Binghamton, NY 13905, 607-729-1899.

INTERNATIONAL FUN FEST, Monroe, NY
> Late Jul.
> Variety, Folk and International

Since 1993. **Help!** Still ongoing? **Days:** 3. **Site:** outdoor and indoor. Grove Mansion Inn, Route 208. **Secondary genre[s]:** MJAZ, IRSH, TLAT, OTHR **Acts:** regional acts, local acts. **Sample day's lineup:** Jimmy Sturr and Orchestra, Willie Lynch and His Band, others. **Contact:** International Fun Fest, Grove Mansion Inn, Route 208, Monroe, NY, 914-783-1633.

EVENING OF ADIRONDACK MUSIC, Lake Placid, NY
> Late Jul.
> Traditional Folk

Benefits Essex County Arts Council. Also programs Lake Placid Chamber Music Festival. See other dates. **Help!** One time only? **Days:** 1. **Site:** outdoor and indoor. Lake Placid Center for the Arts, Saranac Avenue. **Admission:** paid. **Daily entry:** under $10, **Secondary genre[s]:** TR&B, **Acts:** regional acts, local acts. **Sample day's lineup:** Jugless Jug Band, Bridget Ball, The Fred, Frank and Dan Band. **Audio merchandise:** "Adirondack Songwriters Live"; "Music from the Adirondacks" (Essex County Arts Council, P. O. Box 805, Elizabethown, NY 12932, 518-873-9124). **Contact:** Lake Placid Center for the Arts, Saranac Avenue, Lake Placid, NY 12946, 518-523-2512.

FIFE AND DRUM CORPS MUSTER, Ticonderoga, NY
> Late Jul.
> Drum Corp and Marching Bands

See other dates. **Help!** A sample lineup? **Days:** 1. **Site:** outdoor and indoor. Fort Ticonderoga, off Route 22. **Admission:** paid. **Daily entry:** under $10, **Discounts:** group sale discounts, **Secondary genre[s]:** SCOT, **Acts:** regional acts, local acts. **Contact:** Fort Ticonderoga, P. O. Box 390, Ticonderoga, NY 12883, 518-585-2821.

## FOLK MUSIC SOCIETY OF HUNTINGTON SUMMER FESTIVAL, Huntington, NY
Late Jul.
Traditional Folk

Since 1969. Part of Summerscape. See other dates. **Days:** 1. **Hours per day:** 3. **Site:** outdoor. Chapin Rainbow Stage, Heckscher Park, Prime Avenue and Route 25A. **Admission:** free. **Secondary genre[s]:** TR&B, MFOL, MARI, AFRC, **Acts:** national acts, regional acts, local acts. **Sample day's lineup:** Ginny Hawker and Kay Justice, Dave Van Ronk, Magpie. **Contact:** Huntington Arts Council, 213 Main Street, Huntington, NY 11743, 516-271-8442/8423 **or:** Folk Music Society of Huntington, 411 Cooper Road, North Babylon, NY 11703, 516-321-1582.

## ROUND LAKE COUNTRY MUSIC FESTIVAL, Round Lake, NY
Late Jul.
Modern Country

Benefits Round Lake Auditorium Restoration. **Days:** 1. **Hours per day:** 10. **Site:** indoor. Round Lake Auditorium. **Admission:** paid. **Daily entry:** $10 to $24, **Discounts: Secondary genre[s]:** SGOS, BLGS, **Acts:** national acts, regional acts, local acts. **Sample day's lineup:** Mark McCord and Band, Marty Wendell and His Tour Band, Micky T. Guild and The Storm, Peaceful Country, The County Line Rebels, Country Express, Concrete Cowboy, Sierra, Two Lane Highway, T. C. Rider, Lyn and Lee Thomas. **Contact:** Round Lake Country Music Festival, P. O. Box 22, Round Lake, NY 12151-0022, 518-899-2130.

## CREEK BEND MUSIC FESTIVAL, Akron, NY
Late Jul.
Bluegrass

Since 1992. **Days:** 1. **Hours per day:** 12. **Site:** outdoor. Sleepy Hollow Family Campground, Siehl Road. **Admission:** paid. **Daily entry:** $10 to $24, **Discounts:** advance purchase discounts, **Acts:** regional acts, local acts. **Sample day's lineup:** Creek Bend, Fox Family, Blue Mule, Rosewood, Lambert and Yeomans, others. **Contact:** Creek Bend Music Festival, 8522 Versailles Plank Road, Angola, NY 14006, 716-549-6017/694-3806.

## ROCKLAND COUNTY A. O. H. FEIS AND FIELD GAMES, West Haverstraw, NY
Late Jul.
Irish

Since 1974. See other dates. **Days:** 1. **Hours per day:** 11. **Site:** outdoor. Marian Shrine, Filors Lane. **Acts:** regional acts, local acts. **Sample day's lineup:** Celtic Cross, pipe bands, others. **Contact:** Rockland County A. O. H. Feis and Field Games, P. O. Box 31, Garnerville, NY 10923, 914-942-2358.

## SOUNDS ON THE SUSQUEHANNA, Endicott, NY
Late Jul.
Drum Corps and Marching Bands

Since 1988. **Help!** A sample lineup? **Days:** 1. **Site:** outdoor and indoor. Union Endicott High School. **Admission:** paid. **Daily entry:** under $10, **Contact:** Union Endicott High School, 1200 East Main Street, Endicott, NY 13760, 607-754-4165/757-2181.

## RALLY IN THE ALLEY, Buffalo, NY
Late Jul.
Modern Rock and Pop

Since 1982. "Largest one-day charity event in Western N. Y." -- Volunteer. **Days:** 1. **Site:** outdoor. **Acts:** national acts, local acts. **Sample day's lineup:** Rick Derringer, others. **Contact:** Rally in the Alley, P. O. Box 118, Buffalo, NY 14209, 716-881-2222.

### LONG ISLAND JAZZ FESTIVAL, Oyster Bay, NY
Late Jul.
Modern Jazz

Since 1993. **Days:** 3. **Hours per day:** 9. **Site:** outdoor and indoor. Planting Fields Arboretum State Historic Park. **Admission:** paid. **Daily entry:** $10 to $24, $25 to $49, **Secondary genre[s]:** AJAZ, MLAT, **Acts:** national acts. **Sample day's lineup:** Sonny Rollins, Milt Jackson Quartet, Ernestine Anderson, Terrence Blanchard Quartet, Jeanie Bryson, T. S. Monk Sextet, Mark Whitfield Trio, Chris Potter Trio. **Contact:** Friends of the Arts, P. O. Box 702, Locust Valley, NY 11560, 516-922-0061.

### PENNY ASSOCIATION BLUEGRASS AND COUNTRY MUSIC FESTIVAL, Tioga Center, NY
Late Jul.
Bluegrass

Since 1986. See other dates and sites. **Days:** 3. **Hours per day:** 10. **Site:** outdoor. Ransom Memorial Park, Route 17C. **Secondary genre[s]:** SGOS, TC&W, BLGS, **Acts:** regional acts, local acts. **Sample day's lineup:** Dyer Switch, Classic Country, Wrench's Wranglers, Fish-N-Friends, Billie and The Boys, Endless Mountain Bluegrass, others. **Contact:** Penny Association Bluegrass and Country Music Festival, 910 Jeannette Road, Endicott, NY 13760, 607-748-6671 **or:** Penny Association Bluegrass and Country Music Festival, P. O. Box 385, Herkimer, NY 13350, 315-797-4791.

### RICHARD NADER'S LET THE GOOD TIMES ROLL, Kiamesha Lake, NY
Late Jul. to Middle Mar.
A Cappella and Doo Wop

See other dates. **Days:** 3. **Site:** indoor. Concord Resort Hotel. **Admission:** paid. **Daily entry:** $50 and over. **Secondary genre[s]:** CRCK, **Acts:** national acts, local acts. **Sample day's lineup:** The Duprees, Reparata and The Del Rons, Little Anthony and The Imperials. **Contact:** Concord Resort Hotel, Kiamesha Lake, NY 12751, 800-CONCORD.

### NATIVE AMERICAN WEEKEND, Monroe, NY
Late Jul.
Native American

**Days:** 2. **Hours per day:** 8. **Site:** outdoor. Museum Village, off Route 129. **Admission:** paid. **Daily entry:** under $10, **Contact:** Native American Weekend, Museum Village, 130 Museum Village Road, Monroe, NY 10950, 914-782-8247.

### COLUMBIA COUNTY JAZZ FESTIVAL, West Ghent, NY
Late Jul.
Traditional Jazz and Ragtime

Since 1990. **Days:** 3. **Hours per day:** 3. **Site:** indoor. Kozel's Restaurant, Route 9H. **Admission:** paid. **Acts:** national acts, local acts. **Sample day's lineup:** Natalie Lamb, Blue Horizon Jazz Band, Columbia Jazz Band. **Contact:** Columbia Jazz Festival, P. O. Box 751, Philmont, NY 12565, 518-672-7109.

### TRANSPORTATION HERITAGE FESTIVAL, Kingston, NY
Late Jul.
Classic Rock and Oldies

**Days:** 1. **Hours per day:** 5. **Site:** outdoor. uptown and Rondout areas. **Admission:** free. **Acts:** national acts, . **Sample day's lineup:** The Coasters, The Marvellettes, The Drifters. **Contact:** Kingston Urban Cultural Park, 20 Broadway, Kingston, NY 12401, 914-331-7517.

## INTERNATIONAL DIXELAND JAZZ AND RAGTIME FESTIVAL, Buffalo, NY
Late Jul.
Traditional Jazz and Ragtime

Since 1987. See other dates and sites. **Days:** 2. **Hours per day:** 11. **Site:** outdoor and indoor. 5 locations in Theater District. **Admission:** paid. **Daily entry:** $10 to $24, **Discounts:** multiple event or day passes, advance purchase discounts, **Secondary genre[s]:** TGOS, OTHR **Acts:** regional acts, local acts. **Sample day's lineup:** Bearcats, Bill Stevens' Dixielanders, Dr. McJazz, Golden Grill Jazz Band, Hot 5 Jazzmakers, Lazy River Jazz Band, Lowdown Alligator Jassband, Morgan Street Stompers, Nickel City Clippers, The Tarnished Six, Tin Roof Jazz Band, Andrew Fielding, Bartz and Snider, Bob Darch, Colm O'Brien, Don Burns, Mimi Blais, Terry Waldo, Allstars Barbershop Quartet. **Contact:** Queen City Jass and Ragtime Society, Inc., P. O. Box 269, Clarence, NY 14031, 905-685-0175 **or:** Queen City Jass and Ragtime Society, Inc., 4570 Harris Hill Road, Williamsville, NY 14221-6212, 905-634-1863.

## NEW YORK STATE BUDWEISER BLUES FESTIVAL, Syracuse, NY
Late Jul.
Blues and Traditional R&B

Since 1992. **Days:** 2. **Hours per day:** 13. **Site:** indoor. multiple locations downtown. **Admission:** paid. **Daily entry:** under $10, $10 to $24, **Discounts:** multiple event or day passes, advance purchase discounts, **Restrictions:** 2, 5, 6, 7, **Secondary genre[s]:** TJAZ, **Acts:** national acts, local acts. **Sample day's lineup:** Paul Geremia, Rodney King Band, Miserable Tim and The Blue Shadows, Tom Olson, Big Time Sara, Tom Townsley and The Backsliders, The Lone Sharks, Built For Comfort, Johnny Shoes Blues Band, Westcott Jug Suckers, Steady Rollin' Bob Margolin, Austin Jimmy Murphy and The Blues Kings, Magic Slim and The Teardrops, Roosevelt Dean, Carey Bell and The Tough Luck Blues Band, others. **Contact:** Central New York Blues Connection, Inc., P. O. Box 271, Nedrow, NY 13120, 315-488-8804.

## PUTNAM COUNTY 4-H FAIR, Carmel, NY
Late Jul. to Early Aug.
Variety, Folk and International

**Days:** 3. **Hours per day:** 9. **Site:** outdoor. Fairgrounds, Gipsy Trail Road. **Secondary genre[s]:** BLGS, ZYDC, BRZL, RGGE, AVNT, **Acts:** national acts, local acts. **Sample day's lineup:** David Amram Ensemble, Casselbury-Dupree, Lydia Adams Davis, others. **Contact:** Putnam County 4-H Fair, Gipsy Trail Road, Carmel, NY, 914-278-6738.

## ROONEY MOUNTAIN BLUEGRASS FESTIVAL, Deposit, NY
Late Jul. to Early Aug.
Bluegrass

Since 1977. **Days:** 3. **Hours per day:** 16. **Site:** outdoor. Beebee Hill Road. **Admission:** paid. **Daily entry:** under $10, $10 to $24, **Discounts:** multiple event or day passes, **Restrictions:** 4, **Secondary genre[s]:** TC&W, AC&W, ZYDC, **Acts:** national acts, regional acts, local acts. **Sample day's lineup:** Northern Lights, Killbilly, Susquehanna Hat Co., Creek Bend, Stewed Mulligan, The Red Hots, Pavlov's Dogs, Rooney String Band. **Contact:** Rooney Mountain Bluegrass Festival, HCR, Box 16, Beebee Hill Road, Deposit, NY 13754, 607-467-2656/3283.

THOMAS HOMESTEAD FESTIVAL, Savona, NY
> Late Jul. to Early Aug.
> Traditional Folk

Since 1982. "The greatest music weekend all summer!" -- Flyer. See other dates. **Days:** 3. **Hours per day:** 14. **Site:** outdoor and indoor. Thomas Homestead, Route 17. **Admission:** paid. **Daily entry:** under $10, $10 to $24, **Discounts:** multiple event or day passes, advance purchase discounts, **Secondary genre[s]:** TR&B, TGOS, BLGS, IRSH, NATV, **Acts:** national acts, regional acts, local acts. **Sample day's lineup:** Odetta, Cobbler's Apron, Claudia Schmidt, Bill Brown and Friends, Connie Deming, Common Grounds Coffee House Band. **Contact:** Thomas Homestead Festival, R. D. 1, Box 406, Campbell, NY 14821, 607-583-2179.

JEFFERSONVILLE JAMBOREE, Jeffersonville, NY
> Late Jul.
> Modern Country

Since 1992. **Days:** 1. **Hours per day:** 6. **Site:** outdoor. Lion's Field, off Route 52. **Secondary genre[s]:** MFOL, **Acts:** local acts. **Sample day's lineup:** Country Cutups, Jimmy Geiger Band, Steve Jacobi, others. **Contact:** Jeffersonville Chamber of Commerce, Legion Avenue, Jeffersonville, NY, 914-794-3000 x5010.

MIDDLESEX MUSIC FEST, Middlesex, NY
> Late Jul.
> Alternative and College Rock

Since 1980. **Help!** A contact address? **Days:** 1. **Hours per day:** 9. **Site:** outdoor. Middlesex Airport. **Admission:** paid. **Daily entry:** under $10, $10 to $24, **Discounts:** advance purchase discounts, **Restrictions:** 10, **Secondary genre[s]:** TR&B, TC&W, ZYDC, **Acts:** regional acts, local acts. **Sample day's lineup:** Donna The Buffalo, Rusted Root, New Alien String Band, Dan Schmidt and The Shadows, Journeying With Drums.. **Contact:** Middlesex Music Fest, c/o Middlesex Airport, Middlesex, NY, 716-554-6029.

ROCH-A-PALOOZA, Rochester, NY
> Late Jul.
> Alternative and College Rock

Since 1993. "Rochester's first alternative music festival." -- Advertisement. See other dates. **Help!** One time only? **Days:** 1. **Site:** outdoor. Downtown Festival Tent. **Admission:** paid. **Daily entry:** under $10, **Discounts:** advance purchase discounts, **Secondary genre[s]:** HRCK, **Acts:** local acts. **Sample day's lineup:** Nerve Circus, Exploding Boy, Daisy Chain, Officer Friendly, Zezozose, others. **Audio merchandise:** "Roch-A-Palooza '93" (self-produced and distributed). **Contact:** Pilato Entertainment Group, P. O. Box 17775, Rochester, NY 14608, 716-671-2206.

DEAN MOUNTAIN BLUEGRASS FESTIVAL, Hadley, NY
> Late Jul. to Early Aug.
> Bluegrass

Since 1992. **Days:** 2. **Site:** outdoor. Dean Mountain Road. **Admission:** paid. **Daily entry:** $10 to $24, **Discounts:** multiple event or day passes, advance purchase discounts, **Restrictions:** 10, **Secondary genre[s]:** SGOS, BLGS, **Acts:** regional acts, local acts. **Sample day's lineup:** Sassygrass, Bluegrass Patriots, Chestnut Grove, Gibson Brothers, Burnt Hills Bluegrass, Cedar Ridge, Dyer Switch, Back Porch Pickers. **Contact:** Dean Mountain Bluegrass Festival, P. O. Box 205, Corinth, NY 12822, 518-654-6679/696-3128.

NATIVE AMERICAN DANCE FESTIVAL, Victor, NY
> Late Jul. to Early Aug.
> Native American

"Celebrate the anniversary of Ganondagan." -- Listing. Part of the Indigenous Music of the Americas series. **Days:** 2. **Hours per day:** 7. **Site:** outdoor. Ganondagan State Historic Site, 1488 Victor-Holcomb Road. **Acts:** regional acts, local acts. **Contact:** Friends of the Ganondagan, 1488 Victor-Holcomb Road, Victor, NY 15464, 716-924-5848/342-5772.


PARK AVENUE FESTIVAL, Rochester, NY
> Late Jul. to Early Aug.
> Variety, General

**Help!** A sample lineup? **Days:** 2. **Site:** outdoor. Park Avenue. **Secondary genre[s]:** MJAZ, MRCK, TR&B, MFOL, BRZL, RGGE, **Acts:** regional acts, local acts. **Contact:** Jerry Wolf Enterprises, 355 Canterbury Road, Rochester, NY 14607, 716-473-2525.


BACK AT THE RANCH FESTIVAL, Montauk Point, NY
> Early Aug.
> Variety, General

Since 1990. **Days:** 1. **Site:** outdoor. Indian Field Ranch. **Admission:** paid. **Daily entry:** $25 to $49, $50 and over. **Restrictions:** 13, **Secondary genre[s]:** MJAZ, MRCK, MC&W, AC&W, **Acts:** national acts. **Sample day's lineup:** Paul Simon, The Highwaymen, G. E. Smith and High Plains Drifters, Toots Thielsmans Quartet. **Contact:** Indian Field Productions, P. O. Box 835, Montauk Point, NY 11954, 516-668-3901.


BLUES BAR-B-QUE, Schenectady, NY
> Early Aug.
> Blues and Traditional R&B

**Days:** 1. **Site:** outdoor. Washington Park Playhouse. **Admission:** paid. **Daily entry:** under $10, **Discounts:** **Acts:** national acts, local acts. **Sample day's lineup:** John Mooney Band, Fruteland Jackson, others. **Contact:** Northeast Blues Society, 4 Amsterdam Avenue, Scotia, NY 12302, 518-347-1751 **or:** Second Wind Productions, 55 Loudonwood East, Suite 1, Loudonville, NY 12211, 518-463-5222. .


THOUSAND ISLANDS JAZZ FESTIVAL, Alexandria Bay, NY
> Early Aug.
> Traditional Jazz and Ragtime

"The best in traditional jazz!" -- Poster. **Days:** 1. **Site:** outdoor. Pine Tree Point Resort, Anthony Street. **Admission:** paid. **Daily entry:** under $10, **Acts:** regional acts, local acts. **Sample day's lineup:** Bar Room Buzzards, North Country Preservation Band, I Love Jazz Band, Lowdown Alligator Jazz Band, Mimi Blais. **Contact:** Pine Tree Point Resort, P. O. Box 68, Alexandria Bay, NY 13607, 800-ALEX-BAY.


DEL-SE-NANGO FIDDLERS FESTIVAL AND BLUEGRASS SUNDAY, Bainbridge, NY
> Early Aug.
> Modern Country

Since 1984. See other dates and sites. **Days:** 2. **Hours per day:** 12. **Site:** outdoor. General Clinton Park, Route 7. **Admission:** paid. **Daily entry:** $10 to $24, **Discounts:** multiple event or day passes, advance purchase discounts, **Secondary genre[s]:** BLGS, TFOL, **Acts:** regional acts, local acts. **Sample day's lineup:** Wildwood Girls, Wayne Swartz, Stump Jumpers, Judy Carrier and Rens Vreesburg, Billy Bob and Friends, Del-Se-Nango Fiddlers, Real Country, Laura Kortwright, Ghost Riders, Lee and Shirley Eaton. **Contact:** Del-Se-Nango Olde Tyme Fiddlers, R. F. D. 3, Box 233, New Berlin, NY 13411, 607-847-8501/639-2502.

PARK JAM, Schenectady, NY
> Early Aug.
> Alternative and College Rock

Part of Washington Park Concert Series, which hosts national and local acts across various genres on Monday evenings. **Help!** A sample lineup? **Days:** 1. **Site:** outdoor. Central Park. **Admission:** free. **Acts:** regional acts, local acts. **Contact:** Northeast Blues Society, 4 Amsterdam Avenue, Scotia, NY 12302, 518-347-1751 **or:** Second Wind Productions, 55 Loudonwood East, Suite 1, Loudonville, NY 12211, 518-463-5222.


BILL KNOWLTON'S BLUEGRASS RAMBLE PICNIC, Sandy Creek, NY
> Early Aug.
> Bluegrass

Since 1973. **Days:** 3. **Site:** outdoor. Oswego County Fairgrounds. **Admission:** paid. **Daily entry:** under $10, $10 to $24, **Discounts:** multiple event or day passes, **Secondary genre[s]:** TC&W, **Acts:** regional acts, local acts. **Sample day's lineup:** Spare Parts, Rosewood, Fox Family, Cornerstone, Hardwood, Salmon River Boys, Southern Rail, Delaney Brothers, Diana Gardiner. **Contact:** Bill Knowlton's Bluegrass Ramble Picnic, 125 Meyers Lane, Liverpool, NY 13088, 315-457-6100 **or:** Bill Knowlton's Bluegrass Ramble Picnic, c/o WCNY-FM, P. O. Box 2400, Syracuse, NY 13220-2400 .


TWIN RIVERS JAMBOREE, Tuscarora, NY
> Early Aug.
> Variety, Country and Bluegrass

**Days:** 3. **Site:** outdoor. County Route 5. **Admission:** paid. **Secondary genre[s]:** MC&W, BLGS, **Acts:** national acts, local acts. **Sample day's lineup:** Pirates of The Mississippi, Chely Wright, others. **Contact:** Twin River Country-Bluegrass Club, Catherine Creek Road, Addison, NY 14801, 607-359-2101.


ULSTER COUNTY FAIR, New Paltz, NY
> Early Aug.
> Fairs

Since 1888. "Where the Catsills meet the Hudson." -- Advertisement. **Days:** 5. **Site:** outdoor. Fairgrounds, Libertyville Road. **Admission:** paid. **Daily entry:** under $10, **Secondary genre[s]:** MJAZ, CRCK, MC&W, **Acts:** national acts, regional acts. **Sample series lineup:** Day One: Paulette Carlson; Day Two: Sammy Kaye Orchestra; Day Three: The Coasters, The Marvelettes. **Contact:** Ulster County Public Information Office, P. O. Box 1800, Kingston, NY 12401, 800-DIAL-UCO.


JAZZFEST CARAMOOR, Katonah, NY
> Early Aug. to Middle Aug.
> Modern Jazz

Part of Caramoor International Music Festival, a classical summer series. **Days:** 4. **Site:** outdoor. Caramoor Center for Music and The Arts, Route 22, Girdle Ridge Road. **Admission:** paid. **Daily entry:** $10 to $24, $25 to $49, **Secondary genre[s]:** AJAZ, MLAT, AFRC, **Acts:** national acts. **Sample series lineup:** Day One: Vincent Herring Quintet; Day Two: Marcus Roberts Trio and Septet; Day Three: Jacky Terrasson, Danilo Perez. **Contact:** Caramoor Center for Music and The Arts, Route 22, Girdle Ridge Road, Katonah, NY, 914-232-1252.

## IRISH TRADITIONAL MUSIC FESTIVAL, North Blenheim, NY
### Early Aug.
### Irish

Since 1991. **Days:** 1. **Hours per day:** 9. **Site:** outdoor. New York Power Authority Visitors Center, Route 30. **Admission:** paid. **Daily entry:** under $10, **Acts:** national acts, regional acts, local acts. **Sample day's lineup:** Seamus Egan, Dierdre Goulding, Eileen Ivers, Jimmy Keane, Mick Maloney, Robbie O'Connell, Regan Wick, The Coen Family, The Kelly Family, Diane Becker, John Joe Callanan, Comhaltas, The Connolly Family, Felix Dolan, Fourin A Feire, The Fitzpatricks, Phil Gillsenan, Glenfolk, Willie Kelly, Joe Madden, Andy McGann, The McHales, Peter McKiernan, Middlefort Pipe Band, others. **Contact:** Schoharie County Arts Council, P. O. Box 730, Cobleskill, NY 12043, 800-434-FEST.

## ROCKSTALGIA, Hunter, NY
### Early Aug.
### Classic Rock and Oldies

**Days:** 3. **Hours per day:** 12. **Site:** outdoor and indoor. Hunter Mountain Ski Bowl, Route 23A. **Admission:** paid. **Daily entry:** $10 to $24, **Secondary genre[s]:** ACAP, **Acts:** national acts, regional acts, local acts. **Sample day's lineup:** The Grass Roots, Shangri-La's, Little Anthony, The Drifters, Gene Chandler, Lee Andrews and The Hearts, The Sensations, The Cruisers, Times Square. **Contact:** Hunter Mountain Festivals, Ltd., P. O. Box 295, Hunter, NY 12442, 518-263-3800.

## HAMILTON HILL CULTUREFEST/GOSPEL FESTIVAL, Schenectady, NY
### Early Aug.
### Black Gospel

Gospel Festival part of a weekly summer concert series, the Hamilton Hill Culturefest, featuring twin bills of national and local acts across various genres. **Help!** A sample lineup? **Days:** 1. **Site:** outdoor. Jerry Burrell Unity Park, Hamilton and Schenectady Streets. **Contact:** Hamilton Hill Art Center, P. O. Box 115, Schenectady, NY 12301, 518-346-1262.

## RIVER FEST, Fulton, NY
### Early Aug.
### Modern Country

See other sites and dates. **Days:** 3. **Site:** outdoor. **Secondary genre[s]:** NATV, **Acts:** national acts, local acts. **Sample day's lineup:** Restless Heart, others. **Contact:** Onondaga County Parks, P. O. Box 146, Liverpool, NY 13088, 315-451-PARK/349-8322.

## COLONIAL FEST, Kingston, NY
### Early Aug.
### Drum Corps and Marching Bands

"Senior drum corps contest of champions." -- Advertisement. **Days:** 1. **Site:** outdoor. Dietz Memorial Stadium. **Admission:** paid. **Daily entry:** under $10, $10 to $24, **Acts:** local acts. **Sample day's lineup:** New York Skyliners, The Bushwackers, The Hurricanes, Sunrisers, Capitol Brass Ensemble, Steel City Ambassadors. **Contact:** Kingston Urban Cultural Park, 308 Clinton Avenue, Kingston, NY, 914-338-5913 **or:** Kingston Urban Cultural Park, 20 Broadway, Kingston, NY, 914-331-9508/7517.

COXSACKIE RIVERSIDE ARTS AND CRAFTS FESTIVAL, Coxsackie, NY
  Early Aug.
  Modern Country

Since 1979. **Days:** 1. **Hours per day:** 10. **Site:** outdoor. Riverside Park. **Acts:** local acts. **Sample day's lineup:** Peaceful Country, 5 other bands. **Contact:** Coxsackie Council on the Arts, 38 Mansion, Coxsackie, NY 12051, 518-731-2666/8413.


INTERNATIONAL FOOD FESTIVAL/FRIDAY FEST, Poughkeepsie, NY
  Early Aug.
  Variety, General

Since 1989. Part of a summer-long Friday Fest concert series/farmer's market. **Days:** 1. **Hours per day:** 7. **Site:** outdoor. Main Mall, downtown. **Admission:** free. **Secondary genre[s]:** ACAP, BGOS, MC&W, MLAT, RGGE, OTHR. **Acts:** local acts. **Sample day's lineup:** Island Dead Beats, Shika Shika, The Sensational Wonders, Capricorn Moon, The Compadres, Thomson Ensemble, Sweet Adelines, Days Gone By, others. **Contact:** City of Poughkeepsie Partnership, Inc., 313 Main Mall, Poughkeepsie, NY 12601, 914-471-9424/838-0126.


IRISH MUSIC FESTIVAL, Accord, NY
  Early Aug.
  Irish

**Days:** 1. **Hours per day:** 10. **Site:** outdoor. Shellbark Farm, Route 209. **Admission:** paid. **Daily entry:** under $10, **Discounts: Acts:** local acts. **Sample day's lineup:** Pat Roper Band, Murphy Brothers Band, others. **Contact:** Irish Music Festival, Shellbark Farm, Route 209, Accord, NY, 914-647-3224/339-1706.


MICKY RAT'S CITY JAM, Buffalo, NY
  Early Aug.
  Alternative and College Rock

**Days:** 1. **Hours per day:** 9. **Site:** outdoor. Main and Minnesota Streets. **Secondary genre[s]:** TR&B, **Acts:** national acts, local acts. **Sample day's lineup:** Animal Bag, Shotgun Messiah, Hired Guns, Tweeds, Stealin', Wonderland, Elk, Doug Iceman and The Subzero Blues, The Dooleys. **Contact:** Micky Rat's, Main and Minnesota Streets, Buffalo, NY, 716-896-6666.


WATERFRONT ARTS FESTIVAL, Canandaigua, NY
  Early Aug.
  Variety, General

Since 1974. **Days:** 2. **Hours per day:** 8. **Site:** outdoor. Kershaw Park. **Admission:** paid. **Daily entry:** under $10, **Secondary genre[s]:** TJAZ, TFOL, RGGE, **Acts:** local acts. **Sample day's lineup:** North Coast Power Co., Pan Gaia, others. **Contact:** Waterfront Arts Festival, c/o Austin Harvard Gallery, 50 State Street, Pittsfield, NY 14534, 716-383-1472.


PINE GRILL JAZZ REUNION, Rochester, NY
  Early Aug.
  Modern Jazz

Since 1990. See other dates. **Days:** 1. **Hours per day:** 5. **Site:** outdoor. Martin Luther King Park. **Secondary genre[s]:** TR&B, **Acts:** national acts, local acts. **Sample day's lineup:** Bill Doggett, Jimmy Heath, Freddy Cole, Seleno Clarke, Redd Holt. **Contact:** Colored Musicians Club, 145 Broadway, Buffalo, NY, 716-884-2013/885-9893.

## WOODSTOCK NEW MUSIC FESTIVAL, Woodstock, NY
Early Aug.
Alternative and College Rock

Since 1993. Benefits Woodstock Youth Center, G. E. D. Program. **Days:** 1. **Site:** outdoor. Comeau property. **Admission:** paid. **Daily entry:** under $10, **Discounts: Acts:** local acts. **Sample day's lineup:** Moe and The Boogie Cats, Ramen's Pride, Mxyzpltz, Dripping Gloss, Alvis Angersmog's, Earshot, La Vista Hotheads, Blissfully Ignorant, Maya, Pacemaker, Oblivion Grind, Perfect Thyroid, Go Van Go. **Contact:** Woodstock New Music Festival, c/o Town Offices, 81 Tinker Street, Woodstock, NY 12498, 914-679-2015.

## BLUEGRASS FESTIVAL, Broadalbin, NY
Early Aug.
Bluegrass

**Help!** Still ongoing? **Days:** 2. **Hours per day:** 10. **Site:** outdoor. Fishouse Fish and Game Club Grounds, Hans Creek Road. **Admission:** paid. **Daily entry:** under $10, $10 to $24, **Discounts:** multiple event or day passes, advance purchase discounts, **Secondary genre[s]:** TC&W, **Acts:** regional acts, local acts. **Sample day's lineup:** Smokey Greene and The Boys, Dyer Switch, Fred Pike, Sam Tidwell and The Kennebec Valley Boys, Dooley, Andy Pawlenko and The Smokey Hollow Boys, Bear Bridge. **Contact:** Bluegrass Festival, RD 1, Broadalbin, NY 12025, 518-883-5477.

## ADIRONDACK DRUMS, Glens Falls, NY
Early Aug.
Drum Corps and Marching Bands

**Help!** A sample lineup? **Days:** 1. **Hours per day:** 4. **Site:** outdoor. East Field, Dix and Haskell Avenues. **Admission:** paid. **Daily entry:** under $10, $10 to $24, **Contact:** Adirondack Drums, 7 Thornwood Drive, Fort Edward, NY 12828, 518-747-7234.

## CORINTH BLUEGRASS FESTIVAL, Corinth, NY
Early Aug. to Middle Aug.
Bluegrass

"Keep country in country music." -- Flyer. **Days:** 4. **Hours per day:** 11. **Site:** outdoor. 635 Main Street. **Admission:** paid. **Daily entry:** $10 to $24, **Discounts:** multiple event or day passes, advance purchase discounts, **Restrictions:** 13, **Secondary genre[s]:** SGOS, BLGS, **Acts:** regional acts, local acts. **Sample day's lineup:** Smokey Greene and The Boys, White Mountain Bluegrass, Bear Acker, Billings Gap, Cedar Ridge, Bill Matteson and B Flat Band, Jimmie Hamblin, Hank and Irene Clothier, Fred Pike, Sam Tidwell and The Kennebec Valley Boys. **Contact:** Corinth Bluegrass Festival, 635 Main Street, Corinth, NY 12822, 518-654-9424.

## COUNTRY MUSIC FESTIVAL ENCORE, Hunter, NY
Early Aug. to Middle Aug.
Modern Country

Since 1978. **Days:** 4. **Hours per day:** 12. **Site:** outdoor and indoor. Hunter Mountain Ski Bowl, Route 23A. **Admission:** paid. **Daily entry:** $10 to $24, **Secondary genre[s]:** TC&W, BLGS, MFOL, TFOL, OTHR **Acts:** national acts, regional acts, local acts. **Sample day's lineup:** Rodney Crowell, Michael Martin Murphy, Restless Heart, Robin Brown and The 5 and 10 Band, Jay Smar, Gary Nichols Band, Elwood Bunn, Maura Fogerty, Terry Gorka, The Crawfords. **Contact:** Hunter Mountain Festivals, Ltd., P. O. Box 295, Hunter, NY 12442, 518-263-3800.

COBLESKILL "SUNSHINE" FAIR, Cobleskill, NY
    Early Aug. to Middle Aug.
    Fairs

**Days:** 6. **Site:** outdoor. Fairgrounds. **Admission:** paid. **Daily entry:** under $10, **Secondary genre[s]:** MC&W, **Acts:** national acts, local acts. **Sample day's lineup:** Tammy Wynette, others. **Contact:** Cobleskill Agricultural Society, Cobleskill Fairgrounds, Cobleskill, NY, 518-234-2123.

WATERFRONT FESTIVAL, Buffalo, NY
    Early Aug. to Middle Aug.
    Variety, General

See other dates. **Site:** outdoor. LaSalle Park. **Secondary genre[s]:** CRCK, TR&B, **Acts:** national acts, local acts. **Sample series lineup:** Day One: Danny Gatton, Absolut Blues; Day Two: Rare Earth, Only Human. **Contact:** Waterfront Festival, 45 Elmwood Avenue, Buffalo, NY 14201, 716-884-8865.

FOX FAMILY BLUEGRASS FESTIVAL, Old Forge, NY
    Middle Aug.
    Bluegrass

"A lovely festival." -- Mary Doub. **Days:** 3. **Hours per day:** 14. **Site:** outdoor. McCauley Mountain Ski Center. **Admission:** paid. **Daily entry:** $10 to $24, **Discounts:** multiple event or day passes, advance purchase discounts, **Restrictions:** 2, **Acts:** national acts, regional acts, local acts. **Sample day's lineup:** Del McCoury, Dry Branch Fire Squad, Gary Ferguson, Hardwood, Cornerstone, Chestnut Grove, Bob Scott and Stoneridge, Plain and Fancy, Flaky Fingers, Northwind, Fox Family, Creek Bend. **Contact:** Fox Family Bluegrass Festival, P. O. Box 125, Old Forge, NY 13420, 315-369-3729 **or:** Fox Family Bluegrass Festival, c/o Tourist Information Center, Old Forge, NY 13420, 315-369-6983.

SUPER BLUEGRASS AND GOSPEL DAY, Norwich, NY
    Middle Aug.
    Bluegrass

**Help!** A sample lineup? **Days:** 1. **Site:** outdoor. Chenango County Fairgrounds. **Secondary genre[s]:** SGOS, BLGS, **Contact:** Super Bluegrass and Gospel Day, P. O. Box 622, Norwich, NY 13815, 607-334-9198.

PAUMANAUKE POW-WOW, Copiague, NY
    Middle Aug.
    Native American

Since 1981. "Celebration of people gathered in honor of Native American culture." -- Flyer. **Days:** 2. **Hours per day:** 12. **Site:** outdoor. Tanner Park, Wilson Avenue. **Admission:** paid. **Daily entry:** under $10, **Contact:** Babylon Citizens Council on the Arts, 71 Sawyer Avenue, West Babylon, NY 11704-6622, 516-661-7558/7559.

ROYALTY OF ROCK AND ROLL, Latham, NY
    Middle Aug.
    Classic Rock and Oldies

See other dates. **Help!** A sample lineup? **Days:** 1. **Site:** outdoor. Starlite Music Theater, Route 9R. **Admission:** paid. **Acts:** national acts. **Contact:** Starlite Music Theater, Route 9R, Latham, NY, 518-783-9300.

CARIFEST, Rochester, NY
> Middle Aug.
> Reggae, Ska and Caribbean

See other dates. **Days:** 2. **Hours per day:** 12. **Site:** outdoor. Festival Tent, downtown. **Admission:** paid. **Daily entry:** under $10, **Acts:** local acts. **Sample day's lineup:** Jah Mel and The Rhythm Factory, Trinidad and Tobago Tripoli Steel Band, Hell Gate Steel Orchestra, The Targets, others. **Contact:** Rochester West Indian Festival Organziation, Inc., 36 Backus Street, Rochester, NY 14608, 716-235-7616/254-7569.


CENTRAL NEW YORK SCOTTISH GAMES AND CELTIC FESTIVAL, Syracuse, NY
> Middle Aug.
> Scottish

Since 1942. **Days:** 1. **Site:** outdoor. Long Branch Park. **Secondary genre[s]:** IRSH, **Acts:** regional acts, local acts. **Sample day's lineup:** The Brigadoons, others in pipe band competition. **Contact:** Central New York Scottish Games Association, P. O. Box 6405, Syracuse, NY 13217, 315-446-8153.


FESTIVAL OF NORTH COUNTRY FOLK LIFE, Massena, NY
> Middle Aug.
> Fiddle and Banjo Events

**Help!** A sample lineup? **Days:** 1. **Site:** outdoor. Robert Moses State Park. **Secondary genre[s]:** NATV, **Acts:** local acts. **Sample day's lineup:** Mohawk Dancers, fiddlers, others. **Contact:** Massena Chamber of Commerce, P. O. Box 387, Massena, NY 13662, 315-386-4000/769-3525.


YIDDISH HERITAGE CELEBRATION, Valhalla, NY
> Middle Aug.
> Jewish

See other dates and sites. Also programs Ethnic Celebrations: Slavic, Arab, Polish, Italian, Ukrainian. **Help!** A sample lineup? **Days:** 1. **Hours per day:** 3. **Site:** outdoor. Kenisco Dam Plaza, Bronx River Parkway. **Admission:** free. **Secondary genre[s]:** OTHR **Acts:** local acts. **Contact:** Westchester County Department of Parks and Recreation, 19 Bradhurst Avenue, Hawthorne, NY 10532, 914-593-PARK.


ERIE COUNTY FAIR, Hamburg, NY
> Middle Aug. to Late Aug.
> Fairs

"America's county fair." -- Flyer. **Days:** 11. **Site:** outdoor. Fairgrounds, 5600 McKinley Parkway. **Admission:** paid. **Daily entry:** under $10, **Secondary genre[s]:** CRCK, TR&B, CHRS, MC&W, **Acts:** national acts, local acts. **Sample day's lineup:** Lynyrd Skynyrd, Delbert McClinton, Nelson Riddle Orchestra. **Contact:** Erie County Fair, 5600 McKinley Parkway, Hamburg, NY 14075, 716-649-3900.


ANNIVERSARY CELEBRATION OF THE COLORED MUSICIANS CLUB, Rochester, NY
> Middle Aug.
> Modern Jazz

Since 1936. See other dates. **Days:** 1. **Hours per day:** 6. **Site:** outdoor. Martin Luther King Park. **Secondary genre[s]:** TR&B, **Acts:** local acts. **Sample day's lineup:** Macy Favor and His Orchestra, Art Anderson and His Modern Sound, Zeid Aleem and The Real Thing, Count Rabbit and His Bluesmen. **Contact:** Colored Musicians Club, 145 Broadway, Buffalo, NY, 716-884-2013/885-9893.

BIG BIG BANDS, Latham, NY
　　Middle Aug.
　　Modern Jazz

See other dates. **Help!** A sample lineup? **Days:** 1. **Site:** outdoor. Starlite Music Theater, Route 9R. **Admission:** paid. **Acts:** national acts. **Contact:** Starlite Music Theater, Route 9R, Latham, NY, 518-783-9300.


INTERNATIONAL FOOD FESTIVAL, Albany, NY
　　Middle Aug.
　　Variety, General

See other dates. **Days:** 1. **Hours per day:** 10. **Site:** outdoor. Empire State Plaza. **Admission:** free. **Secondary genre[s]:** TR&B, ZYDC, AFRC, BRZL, OTHR **Acts:** national acts, regional acts, local acts. **Sample day's line-up:** Queen Ida and Bontemps Zydeco, The Holmes Brothers, Ernie Williams and The Wildcats, Sophia Bilides Greek Ensemble, The MacKrells, Samite Of Uganda, Sambarama, Ted Hawkins. **Contact:** N. Y. S. Office of General Services, Promotion and Public Affairs, 41st Floor, Erastus Corning II Tower, Empire State Plaza, Albany, NY 12242, 518-473-0559.


OUTDOOR BLUES FESTIVAL, Latham, NY
　　Middle Aug.
　　Blues and Traditional R&B

See other dates. **Help!** A sample lineup? **Days:** 1. **Site:** outdoor. Starlite Music Theater, Route 9R. **Admission:** paid. **Acts:** national acts. **Contact:** Starlite Music Theater, Route 9R, Latham, NY, 518-783-9300.


SOUTHERN TIER BLUEGRASS FESTIVAL, Savona, NY
　　Middle Aug.
　　Bluegrass

Since 1973. See other dates. **Days:** 3. **Site:** outdoor and indoor. Thomas Homestead, Route 17. **Admission:** paid. **Daily entry:** under $10, $10 to $24, **Discounts:** multiple event or day passes, advance purchase discounts, **Restrictions:** 4, **Acts:** national acts, regional acts, local acts. **Sample day's lineup:** J. D. Crowe and The New South, Cody Mountain Boys, Burnt Hills Bluegrass, Steve Davy and Free Lance, Bartholomew Family, The Stevens Family. **Contact:** Southern Tier Bluegrass Festival, 3850 College Avenue, Corning, NY 14830, 607-962-1956 **or:** Southern Tier Bluegrass Festival, P. O. Box 363, Hammondsport, NY 14840, 607-569-2889. .


ST. LAWRENCE VALLEY BLUEGRASS FESTIVAL, Gouveneur, NY
　　Middle Aug.
　　Bluegrass

"The fun and pickin' festival!" -- Flyer. **Days:** 3. **Site:** outdoor. St. Lawrence County Fairgrounds. **Admission:** paid. **Daily entry:** under $10, $10 to $24, **Discounts:** multiple event or day passes, advance purchase discounts, **Acts:** regional acts, local acts. **Sample lineup:** Bluegrass Connection, Andy Pawlenko and The Smokey Mountain Boys, The Delaney Brothers, Northwind, The Case Brothers, Cedar Ridge, Grass Creek, Dempsey Station, Hardwood, The Fantastic Fiddlers and Friends, Bluegrass Junction. **Contact:** St. Lawrence Valley Bluegrass Festival, Route 3, Box 54, Ogdensburg, NY 13669, 315-393-4531.


BLUES FEST, Patterson, NY
　　Middle Aug.
　　Blues and Traditional R&B

See other dates. **Help!** One time only? **Days:** 1. **Site:** outdoor. Big Birch Concert Pavillion. **Admission:** paid. **Daily entry:** $10 to $24, **Acts:** national acts. **Sample day's lineup:** Robert Cray, Delbert McClinton, others. **Contact:** Big Birch Concert Pavillion, Big Birch Music Center, Patterson, NY, 914-878-3181.

## OPUS 40 LEGENDS OF JAZZ/FUTURE OF JAZZ, Saugerties, NY
Middle Aug.
Modern Jazz

Since 1995. "A great afternoon of mainstream jazz. Some call it America's classical music, some call it the coolest groove of all." -- Program. See other dates. **Days:** 1. **Site:** outdoor. Opus 40, 7480 Fite Road. **Admission:** paid. **Daily entry:** $10 to $24, $25 to $49, **Discounts:** advance purchase discounts, other discounts **Acts:** national acts. **SamplelLineup:** David "Fathead" Newman, Arthur Blythe, Jeanie Bryson, Charles Craig. **Audio merchandise:** "Bring It On Home, Vols. 1, 2" (SONY/Legacy). **Contact:** Opus 40 Sunset Concerts, 7480 Fite Road, Saugerties, NY, 914-246-3400/8584.

## BUFFALO CARIBBEAN FESTIVAL, Buffalo, NY
Middle Aug.
Reggae, Ska and Caribbean

Since 1988. **Days:** 2. **Hours per day:** 9. **Site:** outdoor. LaSalle Park (Saturday and Sunday), Langston Hughes Institute, 25 High Street ("Caribash," Saturday night). **Acts:** regional acts, local acts. **Sample lineup:** Tunka Abdurama, Russell Charter, Tropicano Creative Cultural Group, Metrotones Steel Band, Positive Force band, Outer Circle Orchestra, Buffalo Express Band, Bomplene Orchestra, Sir Tiger Roots, African-American Cultural Center Drummers, Double Journey, Small Acts Band, others. **Contact:** Langston Hughes Institute, Inc., 25 High Street, Buffalo, NY 14203, 716-881-3266.

## ARTPARK BLUES AND FOLK FESTIVAL, Lewiston, NY
Middle Aug. to Late Aug.
Modern Folk

Since 1993. Part of a summer-long performing series featuring national acts across many genres. See other dates. **Days:** 3. **Hours per day:** 8. **Site:** outdoor. Artpark, South 4th Street. **Admission:** free and paid. **Daily entry:** $10 to $24, **Discounts:** other discounts **Secondary genre[s]:** TR&B, BGOS, TFOL, **Acts:** national acts, regional acts, local acts. **Sample day's lineup:** Chris Smither, Paul Geremia, Diana Kirk, Dave Van Ronk, others. **Contact:** Artpark Folk and Blues Festival, P. O. Box 371, Lewiston, NY 14092-0371, 800-659-7275.

## INTERNATIONAL CELTIC FESTIVAL, Hunter, NY
Middle Aug. to Late Aug.
Irish

**Days:** 3. **Hours per day:** 12. **Site:** outdoor and indoor. Hunter Mountain Ski Bowl, Route 23A. **Admission:** paid. **Daily entry:** under $10, **Secondary genre[s]:** SCOT, **Acts:** national acts, regional acts, local acts. **Sample day's lineup:** Middlefort Pipe Band, Tim Quinn, Ian Gallagher, Mary B., Boru, Barleycorn, Erin's Pride, Malone and Hutch, others. **Contact:** Hunter Mountain Festivals, Ltd., P. O. Box 295, Hunter, NY 12442, 518-263-3800.

## SUMMER FOLK MUSIC WEEKEND, Saugerties, NY
Middle Aug. to Late Aug.
Traditional Folk

See other dates and sites. **Days:** 3. **Site:** outdoor and indoor. Solway House. **Admission:** paid. **Daily entry:** $50 and over. **Discounts:** other discounts **Secondary genre[s]:** MFOL, OTHR **Acts:** regional acts, local acts. **Sample day's lineup:** Steve Gillette and Cindy Mangsen, Jeter LePont, Adaya Hennis, Allen Hopkins, Sonja Savig, others. **Contact:** New York Pinewoods Folk Music Club, 31 West 95th Street, New York, NY 10025, 212-666-9605 **or:** New York Pinewoods Folk Music Club, 19 Dongan Place, #3B, New York, NY 10040, 212-942-2847.

LONG LAKE BLUEGRASS FESTIVAL, Long Lake, NY
Middle Aug.
Bluegrass

Since 1981. Part of Music in the Mountains traditional music series. See other dates and sites. **Days:** 1. **Hours per day:** 6. **Site:** outdoor. Mt. Sabattis hillside. **Admission:** paid. **Daily entry:** under $10, **Acts:** regional acts, local acts. **Sample day's lineup:** Al and Kathy Bain, Gibson Brothers, Dyer Switch. **Contact:** Long Lake Parks, Recreation and Tourism, P. O. Box 496, Long Lake, NY 12847, 518-624-3077.

WATERFRONT FESTIVAL FREE SUMMER CONCERT SERIES/FAMILY FUN IN THE SUN, Buffalo, NY
Middle Aug.
Variety, General

Part of the Waterfront Festival, which features national and regional acts each week. See other dates. **Help!** A sample lineup? **Days:** 1. **Site:** outdoor. LaSalle Park, Porter Avenue. **Admission:** free. **Acts:** local acts. **Contact:** Junior League of Buffalo, 45 Elmwood Avenue, Buffalo, NY 14201, 716-884-8865.

WLIX FEST, Jamesport, NY
Middle Aug.
Modern Christian

The event of the summer...celebrating our 15th year." -- Flyer. **Help!** One time only? **Days:** 1. **Hours per day:** 15. **Site:** outdoor. Barker Farm, Route 25. **Admission:** paid. **Daily entry:** $10 to $24, **Discounts:** group sale discounts, **Acts:** national acts, local acts. **Sample day's lineup:** Kathy Troccoli, Bryan Duncan, Helen Baylor, Bob Carlisle, Scott Brown. **Contact:** WLIX, 138 West Main Street, Bay Shore, NY 11706, 516-968-5400.

ADIRONDACK FOLK MUSIC FESTIVAL, Schroon Lake, NY
Middle Aug. to Late Aug.
Traditional Folk

Since 1990. Culminates a summer-long Boathouse Concert Series featuring local acts across various genres. **Days:** 2. **Site:** outdoor. Schroon Lake Boathouse Theater and Park. **Admission:** paid. **Daily entry:** $10 to $24, **Discounts:** group sale discounts, **Secondary genre[s]:** TR&B, MFOL, **Acts:** regional acts, local acts. **Sample day's lineup:** Dan Berggren, Joan Crane, Peggy Eyres, Bridget Ball, Chris Shaw, Bill Smith, Roy Hurd, Dan Duggan, Pat Donahue. **Contact:** Schroon Lake Arts Council, P. O. Box 688, Schroon Lake, NY 12870, 518-532-9384.

HISPANIC MUSIC FESTIVAL, Buffalo, NY
Late Aug.
Modern Latin

Since 1992. **Days:** 1. **Site:** outdoor. Front Park, Porter Avenue. **Acts:** local acts. **Sample day's lineup:** Orquestra Los Imperiales, La Banda Sol, Los Tres Amigos, Antonetti Y Los Fabulosos. **Contact:** Hispanic Music Festival, 577 Niagara Street, Buffalo, NY 14201, 716-882-5887.

OLD-TIME FIDDLER'S FAIR, Mumford, NY
Late Aug.
Fiddle and Banjo Events

**Days:** 2. **Site:** outdoor. Genessee Country Museum, Flint Hill Road. **Secondary genre[s]:** TFOL, **Acts:** local acts. **Contact:** Old-Time Fiddler's Fair, Genessee Country Museum, Flint Hill Road, Mumford, NY, 716-538-6822.

## OXHANN PIANO FESTIVAL, Clinton, NY
Late Aug.
Modern Jazz

**Help!** Still ongoing? **Days:** 8. **Site:** indoor. . **Admission:** paid. **Acts:** local acts. **Sample lineup:** Jack Reilly, Malissa Rothchild, Sean Murphy Ortega, Carol Lian, others. **Contact:** Oxhann School of Music, P. O. Box 150243, Brooklyn, NY 11215-5273, 315-853-5273.


## MUSIC AT THE TY FOLKLORE CONCERT, Ticonderoga, NY
Late Aug.
Traditional Folk

Since 1992. See other dates. **Days:** 1. **Site:** outdoor and indoor. Fort Ticonderoga, off Route 22. **Admission:** paid. **Daily entry:** under $10, **Discounts:** group sale discounts, **Secondary genre[s]:** SCOT, **Acts:** local acts. **Sample day's lineup:** John Gray, Marion Covell, Rollie Swinton, Margaret McArthur. **Contact:** Fort Ticonderoga, P. O. Box 390, Ticonderoga, NY 12883, 518-585-2821.


## WBNY'S BATTLE OF THE BANDS, Buffalo, NY
Late Aug.
Modern Rock and Pop

Since 1986. **Days:** 1. **Site:** outdoor. U. S. S. Littlerock, 1 Naval Park Drive. **Admission:** paid. **Secondary genre[s]:** ARCK, HRCK, **Acts:** local acts. **Sample day's lineup:** Moe, Gumshoe, A Public Hanging, Bertha Mason, Ansley Court, Lollypop, Spavid, Scary Chicken. **Contact:** WBNY, 1300 Elmwood Avenue, Buffalo, NY 14222, 716-886-6300/878-5104.


## KINGDOM BOUND, Darien Lake, NY
Late Aug.
Modern Christian

**Days:** 4. **Hours per day:** 15. **Site:** outdoor. Darien Lake Theme Park and Camping Resort, Route 77. **Admission:** paid. **Daily entry:** $10 to $24, **Discounts:** multiple event or day passes, advance purchase discounts, group sale discounts, **Secondary genre[s]:** MRCK, HRCK, RAP, MR&B, TR&B, ACAP, BGOS, MC&W, MFOL, **Acts:** national acts, regional acts, local acts. **Sample day's lineup:** Acappella, Prayer Chain, Guardian, Joey Holder, Will McFarlane, Randy Rothwell, Alvin Slaughter, Christafari, Out Of Eden, Grits, The Brothers, Lenny LeBlanc, DC Talk, others. **Contact:** Kingdom Bound Ministries, 8550 Sheridan Drive, P. O. Box 1622, Williamsville, NY 14231-1622, 716-633-1117.


## SCHNEIDER'S BLUEGRASS FESTIVAL, Elmira, NY
Late Aug.
Bluegrass

**Help!** A contact, site, lineup? **Days:** 2. **Site:** outdoor. Schnieder's Farm. **Acts:** regional acts, local acts. **Sample day's lineup:** Dyer Switch, others. **Contact:** Schnieder's Bluegrass Festival, Schnieder's Farm, Elmira, NY .


## DUTCHESS COUNTY FAIR, Rhinebeck, NY
Late Aug.
Fairs

Since 1846. See other dates. **Days:** 6. **Hours per day:** 12. **Site:** outdoor. Fairgrounds. **Admission:** paid. **Daily entry:** under $10, **Secondary genre[s]:** MC&W, IRSH, **Acts:** national acts, local acts. **Sample series lineup:** Day One: Kathy Mattea, Firko String Band; Day Two: Charlie Daniels, Sammy Kaye Orchestra; Day Three: Clancy Brothers with Robbie O'Connell. **Contact:** Dutchess County Fairgrounds, P. O. Box 389, Rhinebeck, NY 12572-0389, 914-876-4001.

## NICHOLS FAMILY BLUEGRASS FESTIVAL, Nichols, NY
Late Aug.

Bluegrass

Since 1992. "Fun for the whole family." -- Flyer. **Days:** 4. **Hours per day:** 13. **Site:** outdoor. L and L Campgrounds, Route 17, River Road. **Admission:** paid. **Daily entry:** $10 to $24, **Discounts:** multiple event or day passes, advance purchase discounts, **Restrictions:** 4, 13, **Secondary genre[s]:** SGOS, TC&W, BLGS, **Acts:** national acts, regional acts, local acts. **Sample day's lineup:** Jim and Jesse, Raymond Fairchild, Freelance, Dempsey Station, others. **Contact:** Nichols Family Bluegrass Festival, P. O. Box 242, Nichols, NY 13812, 607-699-7402/733-1003.

## PROJECT CHILDREN IRISH FESTIVAL, Endicott, NY
Late Aug.

Irish

**Days:** 1. **Hours per day:** 9. **Site:** outdoor. Grippen Park. **Acts:** local acts. **Sample day's lineup:** Pat Kane, Hylands, Marie McVicker, BC Pipers, New Folk Trio, others. **Contact:** Project Children Irish Festival, 211 Christopher Lane, Endicott, NY, 607-785-0500.

## DOWNTOWN FESTIVAL/ROCK FEST, Rochester, NY
Late Aug.

Classic Rock and Oldies

Part of Downtown Festival, a summer-long concert series with national, regional, local acts. **Days:** 2. **Site:** outdoor. Downtown Festival Tent, 30 Capron Street. **Admission:** paid. **Daily entry:** $10 to $24, **Discounts:** multiple event or day passes, **Acts:** national acts, local acts. **Sample series lineup:** Day One: REO Speedwagon, Cheap Trick, The Shakes; Day Two: .38 Special, Bad Company, The Shakes. **Contact:** City of Rochester Special Events, City Hall, 30 Church Street, Rochester, NY 14604, 716-428-7175.

## FINAL STRETCH FESTIVAL, Saratoga Springs, NY
Late Aug.

Variety, General

"To celebrate the last weekend of the track season...features 15 different types of music...from Dixieland to Irish folk to orchestra." -- Metroland. See other dates. **Help!** A sample lineup? **Days:** 2. **Hours per day:** 8. **Site:** outdoor. Broadway. **Admission:** free. **Secondary genre[s]:** TJAZ, IRSH, OTHR. **Acts:** local acts. **Contact:** Saratoga County Chamber of Commerce, 494 Broadway, Suite 212, Saratoga Springs, NY 12866, 518-584-3255.

## TURTLE HILL MUSIC FESTIVAL, Spencerport, NY
Late Aug.

Modern Folk

See other dates and sites. **Days:** 3. **Hours per day:** 14. **Site:** outdoor. Springdale Farm. **Admission:** paid. **Daily entry:** $10 to $24, **Discounts:** multiple event or day passes, advance purchase discounts, **Secondary genre[s]:** ARCK, TR&B, BLGS, ZYDC, **Acts:** regional acts, local acts. **Sample day's lineup:** Garnet Rogers, Jem and Ariane, Cornerstone, Camille West, Colorblind James, others. **Contact:** Golden Link Folksinging Society, Inc., 9 Peachtree Lane, Pittsfield, NY 14534, 716-264-9983.

## LONG ISLAND SCOTTISH GAMES, Old Westbury, NY
Late Aug.
Scottish

**Days:** 1. **Hours per day:** 9. **Site:** outdoor. Old Westbury Gardens, Old Westbury Road. **Admission:** paid. **Daily entry:** under $10, **Secondary genre[s]:** IRSH, **Acts:** local acts. **Sample day's lineup:** Clan Gordon Highlanders Pipe Band, Amityville Pipe Band, U. S. Merchant Marine Academy Band. **Contact:** Old Westbury Gardens, Old Westbury Road, Old Westbury, NY, 516-333-0048.

## PYX BIRTHDAY BLOWOUT!, Latham, NY
Late Aug.
Modern Rock and Pop

Benefits AIDS Treatment Unit of Albany Medical Center. See other dates and sites. **Days:** 1. **Hours per day:** 7. **Site:** indoor. Starlite Music Theater, back parking lot. **Admission:** paid. **Daily entry:** under $10, **Secondary genre[s]:** TR&B, MC&W, **Acts:** national acts, local acts. **Sample day's lineup:** April Wine, Henry Lee Summer, Cry Of Love, Ian Moore, Gary Hoey, The Pinheads, Rodeo Christ, The New Blues Orchestra. **Contact:** WPYX-FM 106, 1054 Troy-Schenectady Road, Latham, NY 12110, 518-785-9800.

## SALESIAN FOLK FESTIVAL, New Rochelle, NY
Late Aug.
Modern Folk

Benefits World Hunger Year. **Help!** One time only? **Days:** 1. **Site:** indoor. Salesian High School. **Acts:** regional acts, local acts. **Sample day's lineup:** Brooks Williams, Hugh Blumenfeld, Richard Meyer, others. **Contact:** Salesian Folk Festival, Salesian High School, New Rochelle, NY, 914-235-5813.

## BUFFALO IRISH FESTIVAL, Lancaster, NY
Late Aug.
Irish

Since 1983. **Days:** 3. **Hours per day:** 10. **Site:** outdoor and indoor. Willow's Grove, Bowen Road at Route 20. **Admission:** paid. **Daily entry:** under $10, **Acts:** regional acts, local acts. **Sample day's lineup:** Dave North, Dady Brothers, Blarney Bunch, Danny Justice, Fiona Malloy, Shananagans, Kevin Kennedy, Seamus Kennedy, Kindred, Tom O'Carroll, Gerry McCrudden. **Contact:** Liffey Productions, 1830 Abbott Road, Lackawanna, NY 14218, 716-824-8711.

## SKYFEST, Cedar Lake, NY
Late Aug.
Variety, General

**Days:** 3. **Site:** outdoor. The Lanterns. **Admission:** paid. **Daily entry:** under $10, **Discounts: Secondary genre[s]:** MRCK, MC&W, **Acts:** local acts. **Sample day's lineup:** Joan Angelosa, Danny Holmes, Target, Jesse Hunter. **Contact:** Skyfest, 724 Varick Street, Utica, NY 13502, 315-797-4868.

## UNIFEST, Buffalo, NY
Late Aug.
Modern Rock and Pop

Since 1992. Benefits Independent Living Center. **Days:** 3. **Hours per day:** 12. **Site:** outdoor. Main Street, from Whisper Avenue to Minnesota Avenue. **Admission:** free. **Secondary genre[s]:** MJAZ, CRCK, ARCK, TR&B, MC&W, RGGE, **Acts:** local acts. **Sample day's lineup:** Mr. Nobody, Hardigen, Wisdom of Children, Dark Marbles, Red Tears, Stevie Ray Shannon, Win Lose Or Draw, Shining Brau, Spy Vs. Spy, Sky High, Dread Beats, Fat Brat, Potters Field, Soul Surfers, Jazz-A-Bels. **Contact:** Independent Living Center, 3108 Main Street, Buffalo, NY 14214, 716-836-0822.

NEW YORK STATE FAIR, Syracuse, NY
> Late Aug. to Early Sep.
> Fairs

Since 1847. **Days:** 12. **Hours per day:** 14. **Site:** outdoor. Fairgrounds. **Admission:** paid. **Daily entry:** under $10, $10 to $24, **Secondary genre[s]:** MRCK, CRCK, RAP, MR&B, MC&W, TFOL, IRSH, JWSH, NATV, **Acts:** national acts, local acts. **Sample day's lineup:** Jefferson Starship, Cheap Trick, REO Speedwagon, Coca Cola Talent Showcase, others. **Contact:** New York State Fair, New York State Fairgrounds, Syracuse, NY 13209, 315-487-7711.

BLUEGRASS FESTIVAL, Rochester, NY
> Late Aug.
> Bluegrass

Since 1980. See other dates. **Days:** 1. **Site:** outdoor. Manhattan Square Park, Chestnut and Court Streets. **Admission:** free. **Acts:** national acts. **Sample day's lineup:** J. D. Crowe and The New South, Kukuruza, Lynn Morris Band. **Contact:** City of Rochester Events Network, City Hall, 30 Church Street, Room 222B, Rochester, NY 14614, 716-428-6690/6697.

HISPANIC HERITAGE CELEBRATION, Valhalla, NY
> Late Aug.
> Modern Latin

See other dates and sites. Also programs Ethnic Celebrations: Slavic, Arab, Polish, Italian, Ukrainian. **Help!** A sample lineup? **Days:** 1. **Hours per day:** 6. **Site:** outdoor. Kenisco Dam Plaza, Bronx River Parkway. **Admission:** free. **Secondary genre[s]:** OTHR **Acts:** local acts. **Contact:** Westchester County Department of Parks and Recreation, 19 Bradhurst Avenue, Hawthorne, NY 10532, 914-593-PARK.

MECK MUSIC FEST, Mecklenberg, NY
> Late Aug.
> Alt. Country and Rockabilly

Since 1992. Benefits the Mecklenberg Volunteer Fire Co. **Help!** Still ongoing? Also, a sample lineup? **Days:** 1. **Site:** outdoor. Fireman's field, Route 79. **Admission:** paid. **Daily entry:** $10 to $24, **Secondary genre[s]:** TC&W, ZYDC, **Acts:** regional acts, local acts. **Contact:** Meck Music Fest, Mecklenberg Volunteer Fire Co., Mecklenberg, NY, 607-387-5644.

MUSIC AND THE MOUNTAIN SKY/JAZZ CONCERT, Highmount, NY
> Late Aug.
> Modern Jazz

Since 1980. Formerly held at Fleischmanns Theater. Part of Music and the Mountain Sky, a bi-weekly summer concert series featuring national and local acts across various genres. See other dates. **Days:** 1. **Site:** outdoor. Belleayre Conservatory, Belleayre Ski Center. **Secondary genre[s]:** TJAZ, **Acts:** national acts. **Sample day's lineup:** Jack Kleinsinger, Bucky Pizzarelli, Clark Terry, Al Grey, Kenny Davern, Warren Chiasson, Sherrie Maricel, Jay Leonhart. **Contact:** Belleayre Conservatory, P. O. Box 198, Highmount, NY 12441, 914-586-2611.

GREECE SUMMER FESTIVAL, Greece, NY
> Late Aug.
> Variety, General

**Days:** 2. **Hours per day:** 10. **Site:** outdoor. Northampton Town Center, Long Pond Road. **Admission:** free. **Secondary genre[s]:** TJAZ, CRCK, IRSH, OTHR **Acts:** regional acts, local acts. **Sample day's lineup:** Greece Symphony Orchestra, Nik and The Nice Guys, Skycoasters, others. **Contact:** Greece Summer Festival, 2777 Ridgeway Avenue, Rochester, NY 14626, 716-225-3276.

ISLIP JAZZ FESTIVAL, Islip, NY
> Late Aug.
> Modern Jazz

Since 1983. **Days:** 2. **Hours per day:** 5. **Site:** outdoor. Hecksher State Park. **Admission:** free. **Secondary genre[s]:** TJAZ, TR&B, MLAT, **Acts:** national acts, regional acts, local acts. **Sample day's lineup:** Roy Haynes Quartet, Daphne Hellman and Sean Grissom, Papo Vazquez Latin Jazz Ensemble, Dennis Wilson's Roaring 20's Ensemble, Wesiberger and Farber, Frank Vignola Group, Talib Kibwe Odyssey, Bouchard's Bebop Revisited, Lynn Arriale Trio, Juanita Fleming and Friends, special guests. **Contact:** International Art of Jazz, Inc., 5 Saywood Lane, Stony Brook, NY 11790-3103, 516-474-2929/632-6590.

FINGER LAKES DIXIELAND JAZZ FESTIVAL, Hector, NY
> Late Aug.
> Traditional Jazz and Ragtime

**Days:** 1. **Site:** outdoor. Valois-Logan-Hector Fire Co., Route 414. **Admission:** paid. **Daily entry:** $10 to $24, **Discounts:** advance purchase discounts, **Acts:** local acts. **Sample day's lineup:** Dixie Five Plus, Seneca Dixielanders, Bear Cat Jass Band, Joe Cavallero's Dixieland Band, Bourbon Street Parade, Morgan Street Stompers, 3 other bands. **Contact:** Finger Lakes Dixieland Jazz Festival, P. O. Box 188, Watkins Glen, NY 14891, 607-535-4469.

ROCKLAND IRISH FESTIVAL, West Haverstraw, NY
> Late Aug.
> Irish

Since 1972. See other dates. **Days:** 1. **Hours per day:** 14. **Site:** outdoor. Marian Shrine, Filors Lane. **Admission:** paid. **Daily entry:** under $10, **Acts:** regional acts, local acts. **Sample day's lineup:** Morningstar, John Egan and The Irish Tradewinds, The Barleycorns, Pipes and Drums of the A. O. H. of Rockland County, Celtic Justice, others. **Contact:** American Ireland Educational Foundation, Inc., 54 South Liberty Drive, Suite 401, Stony Point, NY 10980, 914-947-2726/2998.

STANFORDVILLE MUSIC AND DANCE FESTIVAL, Stanfordville, NY
> Late Aug.
> Cajun and Zydeco

Since 1986. **Days:** 1. **Hours per day:** 13. **Site:** outdoor and indoor. Country Fare Antiques and Art Center, Route 82. **Admission:** paid. **Daily entry:** $10 to $24, **Discounts:** advance purchase discounts, **Acts:** national acts, regional acts, local acts. **Sample day's lineup:** Steve Riley and The Mamou Playboys, Dirty Rice Cajun Band, The Voodoobillies, Bayou Midnight. **Contact:** Beekman General Store, 578 Beekman Road, Hopewell Junction, NY 12533, 914-226-2585.

SUMMER JAZZ FESTIVAL, Elmira, NY
> Late Aug.
> Modern Jazz

Since 1993. Presented by Twin Tiers Jazz Society. **Help!** A contact? **Days:** 1. **Site:** indoor. Coldbrook Club, Lower Maple Avenue. **Admission:** paid. **Daily entry:** under $10, **Discounts:** other discounts **Restrictions:** 5, **Acts:** local acts. **Sample day's lineup:** Moment's Notice, George Reed Quartet, Ricco's Music Express, Billy Foster Trio, others. **Contact:** Twin Tiers Jazz Society, c/o Colbrook Club, Lower Maple Avenue, Elmira, NY .

SUMMER MUSIC FESTIVAL, Amherst, NY
> Late Aug.
> Gay and Lesbian

**Help!** One time only? **Days:** 1. **Site:** indoor. Unitarian Church of Amherst, 6320 Amherst. **Admission:** paid. **Daily entry:** $10 to $24, **Secondary genre[s]:** MJAZ, OTHR **Acts:** local acts. **Sample day's lineup:** Leah Zicari, Madeline Davis, Jazz-A-Bels, Yemaya, others. **Contact:** Unitarian Church of Amherst, 6320 Main Street, Amherst, NY, 716-683-7489.

BIG BAND BASH, Albany, NY
> Late Aug.
> Modern Jazz

"You are cordially invited to dance under the stars on a sultry summer evening." -- Program. See other dates. **Days:** 1. **Site:** outdoor. Empire State Plaza. **Admission:** free. **Secondary genre[s]:** TJAZ, **Acts:** local acts. **Sample day's lineup:** Al Caveleri Orchestra, La Chic n' Bones, Marlowe and Company. **Contact:** N. Y. S. Office of General Services, Promotion and Public Affairs, 41st Floor, Erastus Corning II Tower, Empire State Plaza, Albany, NY 12242, 518-473-0559.

ARTPARK JAZZ FESTIVAL, Lewiston, NY
> Early Sep.
> Modern Jazz

Since 1992. "Live entertainment that borders on the spectacular." -- Advertisement. Part of a summer-long performing series featuring national acts across many genres. See other dates. **Days:** 2. **Hours per day:** 8. **Site:** outdoor. Artpark, South 4th Street. **Admission:** paid. **Daily entry:** $10 to $24, $25 to $49, **Discounts:** multiple event or day passes, other discounts **Secondary genre[s]:** AJAZ, TR&B, MLAT, **Acts:** national acts. **Sample day's lineup:** Poncho Sanchez, Charlie Haden's Quartet West, Bobby Watson and Horizon, Clark Terry, Chico Hamilton "Trio!," Cyrus Chestnut Trio, others. **Contact:** Artpark Jazz Festival, P. O. Box 371, Lewiston, NY 14092-0371, 800-659-7275.

SOUTH SHORE MUSIC FESTIVAL, Oceanside, NY
> Early Sep.
> Modern Rock and Pop

Since 1992. See other dates. **Days:** 2. **Site:** indoor. Christopher's Sport Rock Cafe, 3297 Long Beach Road. **Admission:** paid. **Daily entry:** under $10, **Secondary genre[s]:** HRCK, TR&B, **Acts:** local acts. **Sample day's lineup:** Chauncey Nedd and The Funk Filharmonic, Red Goose Shoes, Joey Salvia and The Third Rail, Morse Code, Sandoz Thieves, The Crabs. **Contact:** Christophers's, 3297 Long Beach Road, Oceanside, NY 11572, 516-766-9822.

## WRENCH WRANCH BLUEGRASS ROUNDUP, Coventryville, NY
> Early Sep.
> Bluegrass

Since 1984. "All night field picking mandatory." -- Flyer. See other dates and sites. **Days:** 3. **Hours per day:** 10. **Site:** outdoor. Wrench Ranch, Route 206. **Secondary genre[s]:** SGOS, TC&W, BLGS, **Acts:** regional acts, local acts. **Sample day's lineup:** Dyer Switch, Classic Country, Wrench's Wranglers, Fish-N-Friends, Billie and The Boys, Endless Mountain Bluegrass, others. **Contact:** Penny Association Memorial Day Bluegrass Festival, RD 1, Box 47, Bainbridge, NY 13733, 607-639-1371 **or:** Penny Association Memorial Day Bluegrass Festival, P. O. Box 385, Herkimer, NY 13350, 315-797-4791.

## INTERNATIONAL MUSIC AND DANCE FESTIVAL, Sacketts Harbor, NY
> Early Sep.
> Variety, Folk and International

Also programs a weekly concert series, Concerts on the Waterfront, with national, regional and local acts across various genres. **Help!** A sample lineup? **Days:** 1. **Hours per day:** 6. Sacketts Harbor Battlefield, Main Street. **Admission:** free. **Secondary genre[s]:** TFOL, IRSH, SCOT, TLAT, OTHR **Acts:** local acts. **Contact:** International Music and Dance Festival, P. O. Box 389, Sacketts Harbor, NY 13685, 315-646-3000.

## MOUNTAIN EAGLE FESTIVAL, Hunter, NY
> Early Sep.
> Native American

**Days:** 3. **Hours per day:** 12. **Site:** outdoor and indoor. Hunter Mountain Ski Bowl, Route 23A. **Admission:** paid. **Daily entry:** under $10, **Acts:** national acts, regional acts, local acts. **Sample day's lineup:** Ken Edwards, Woody Richards, Lisa Railsback, Walter Calhoun, Charlie Clark, Jim and Olivia Colabaza, Arnold Richardson, Tammy Tarbell, Walter Watso, Joanne Shenandoah Oneida, Bill Crouse, others. **Contact:** Hunter Mountain Festivals, Ltd., P. O. Box 295, Hunter, NY 12442, 518-263-3800.

## CAPITAL DISTRICT'S SCOTTISH GAMES: A CELTIC FESTIVAL OF THE ARTS, Altamont, NY
> Early Sep.
> Scottish

Since 1978. **Help!** A contact address? **Days:** 1. **Hours per day:** 9. **Site:** outdoor. Altamont Fairgrounds. **Admission:** paid. **Daily entry:** under $10, **Secondary genre[s]:** IRSH, **Acts:** regional acts, local acts. **Sample day's lineup:** The Porters, Brigadoons, The Dady Brothers, Northeastern U. S. Pipe Band Championship, others. **Contact:** Capital Disctict's Scottish Games, c/o Altamont Fairgrounds, Altamont, NY, 518-785-5951/438-4297.

## LOCALPALOOZA FESTIVAL, Rochester, NY
> Early Sep.
> Alternative and College Rock

Since 1993. Benefits WFCX radio. **Help!** One time only? **Days:** 1. **Site:** outdoor. St. John Fisher College. **Admission:** paid. **Secondary genre[s]:** HRCK, **Acts:** local acts. **Sample day's lineup:** 3rd Rail, The Infants, Big Lizard, Bone China, Ghetto Prince, others. **Contact:** Screamin' Rhino Productions, P. O. Box 14119, Rochester, NY 14614, 716-266-7641.

BOLTON LANDING BARBERSHOP QUARTET FESTIVAL, Bolton Landing, NY
Early Sep.
A Cappella and Doo Wop

Since 1990. **Help!** A sample lineup? **Days:** 2. **Site:** indoor. Bolton Landing High School, Schoolhouse Road, plus strolling quartets on Main Street. **Acts:** regional acts, local acts. **Sample day's lineup:** over 50 quartets from 15 states. **Contact:** Bolton Landing Barbershop Quartet Festival, c/o Bolton Landing Chamber of Commerce, Bolton Landing, NY, 518-644-9762/3831.


INTERNATIONAL WATERFRONT FESTIVAL, Newburgh, NY
Early Sep.
Variety, Folk and International

**Help!** A sample lineup? **Days:** 3. **Hours per day:** 12. **Site:** outdoor. Waterfront. **Acts:** local acts. **Contact:** International Waterfront Festival, c/o Chamber of Commerce, Newburgh, NY, 914-565-3333/5429.


LEEDS IRISH FESTIVAL, Leeds, NY
Early Sep.
Irish

Since 1982. "Ireland in the Catskills." -- Advertisement. See other dates. **Days:** 3. **Hours per day:** 12. **Site:** outdoor and indoor. Irish Center. **Admission:** paid. **Daily entry:** $10 to $24, **Discounts:** group sale discounts, **Acts:** regional acts, local acts. **Sample lineup:** Jerry Finlay and The Cara Band, Glen Curtin, Guss Hayes and His Band, Larry Cunningham, Butch Moore Band, Joe Mac and Band, Dermot O'Brien, Pat Roper, Erin's Pride, Banjo Burke and Co., Albany Police Pipe Band, others. **Contact:** Gertrude Byrne Promotions, P. O. Box 6, Leeds, NY 12451, 518-943-3736.


SHINNECOCK NATIVE-AMERICAN POWWOW, Southampton, NY
Early Sep.
Native American

Since 1947. "More than 60 tribes from [all across North America]...making this one of the biggest powwows east of the Mississippi." -- Listing. **Days:** 3. **Hours per day:** 10. **Site:** outdoor. Sinnecock Indian Reservation, Montauk Highway. **Admission:** paid. **Daily entry:** under $10, **Restrictions:** 2, 10, **Acts:** national acts, regional acts, local acts. **Contact:** Shinnecock Indian Reservation, Montauk Highway, Southampton, NY, 516-283-6143.


WOODSTOCK/NEW PALTZ ART AND CRAFTS FAIR, New Paltz, NY
Early Sep.
Modern Folk

Since 1982. See other dates. **Days:** 3. **Hours per day:** 6. **Site:** outdoor. Ulster County Fairgrounds. **Admission:** paid. **Daily entry:** under $10, **Discounts: Restrictions:** 10, **Secondary genre[s]:** TJAZ, **Acts:** regional acts, local acts. **Sample day's lineup:** Kurt Henry, Pat Humphries, Jay Mankita. **Contact:** Quail Hollow Events, P. O. Box 25, Woodstock, NY 12498, 914-679-8087/246-3414.


COME SUNDAY, Albany, NY
Early Sep. to Middle Sep.
African American

"[Three-week] celebration of black music and dance." -- Listing. See other dates. **Days:** 3. **Site:** outdoor and indoor. Parade Grounds, Washington Park; Empire Center at The Egg, Empire State Plaza. **Admission:** free. **Secondary genre[s]:** MJAZ, BGOS, RGGE, **Acts:** regional acts, local acts. **Sample day's lineup:** Rara Machine, Greg Henderson and The Street Jazz Ensemble, Jill Hughes. **Contact:** Albany-Schenectady League of Arts, 19 Clinton Avenue, Albany, NY 12207, 518-449-5380.

## BAND JAMBOREE, Osceola, NY
### Early Sep.
### Traditional Country

Benefits New York State Old Tyme Fiddlers Association. **Help!** Still ongoing? **Days:** 2. **Hours per day:** 5. **Site:** outdoor. Cedar Pine Restaurant Campgrounds. **Admission:** paid. **Daily entry:** under $10, **Restrictions:** 1, 2, 10, **Secondary genre[s]:** FDDL, **Acts:** regional acts, local acts. **Sample day's lineup:** Blue Ribbon Mellowdears, Curly Roberts Band, Touch Of Comfort, Show Down, Phil Beyers and Pickin' Vinnie, others. **Contact:** New York State Old Tyme Fiddlers Association, RR 1, Box 23, East Lake Road, Oswego, NY 13126, 315-342-2223/599-7372.

## IROQUOIS INDIAN FESTIVAL, Howes Cave, NY
### Early Sep.
### Native American

Since 1982. **Days:** 2. **Hours per day:** 8. **Site:** outdoor and indoor. Iroquois Indian Museum, Caverns Road. **Admission:** paid. **Daily entry:** under $10, **Acts:** local acts. **Contact:** Iroquois Indian Festival, P. O. Box 7, Howes Cave, NY 12092, 518-296-8949.

## LABOR DAY WEEKEND BLOWOUT, Parksville, NY
### Early Sep.
### Classic Rock and Oldies

Since 1992. "800 acres of a wild rocker's dream!" -- Advertisement. Events and lineups highly variable, so call ahead. See other dates. **Help!** One time only? **Days:** 3. **Hours per day:** 14. **Site:** outdoor. Arrowhead Ranch, 548 Cooley Road, off Route 17W. **Admission:** paid. **Daily entry:** under $10, **Restrictions:** 4, 10, **Acts:** national acts, local acts. **Sample lineup:** New Riders of The Purple Sage, Commander Cody, Slipknot, others. **Contact:** Arrowhead Ranch, R. D. 1, Box 87, Parksville, NY 12768, 914-292-6273.

## LOCAL MOTION MUSICFEST, Middletown, NY
### Early Sep.
### Blues and Traditional R&B

Since 1992. Benefits Occupations, Inc. See other dates. **Days:** 1. **Hours per day:** 5. **Site:** outdoor. Horse Ring, Fancher-Davidge Park. **Admission:** paid. **Daily entry:** under $10, **Acts:** regional acts, local acts. **Sample day's lineup:** Bo Diddley Jr., Delta Star, Females In Control. **Contact:** AAA Productions, 35 Harrison Street, Middletown, NY 10940, 914-342-1552.

## COMMODORE JOHN BARRY A. O. H. IRISH FESTIVAL, Olean, NY
### Early Sep. to Middle Sep.
### Irish

Since 1984. **Help!** A sample lineup? **Days:** 2. **Hours per day:** 11. **Site:** outdoor. Gargoyle Park, Route 417. **Admission:** paid. **Daily entry:** under $10, **Discounts:** group sale discounts, **Acts:** local acts. **Contact:** Gargoyle Park, Route 417, Olean, NY, 716-376-5663.

## IROQUOIS INDIAN FESTIVAL, Rhinebeck, NY
### Early Sep. to Middle Sep.
### Native American

See other dates. **Days:** 2. **Site:** outdoor and indoor. Dutchess County Fairgrounds. **Contact:** Iroquois Indian Festival, RD 2, Box 303, Red Hook, NY 12571, 914-876-4001.

LAKE GEORGE JAZZ WEEKEND, Lake George, NY
Early Sep. to Middle Sep.
Modern Jazz

Since 1984. "Jazz on the lake." -- Flyer. **Days:** 2. **Hours per day:** 4. **Site:** outdoor. Shepard Park, Canada Street. **Admission:** free. **Secondary genre[s]:** TJAZ, AJAZ, **Acts:** national acts, regional acts, local acts. **Sample line-up:** Ray Anderson Quartet, Orange Then Blue, Group 5, David Leonhardt Trio, Holly Hoffman Quartet. **Contact:** Lake George Arts Project, 310 Canada Street, Lake George, NY 12845, 518-668-2616.

ROBERSON'S HOLIDAY AND ARTS FESTIVAL, Binghamton, NY
Early Sep. to Middle Sep.
Variety, Folk and International

Since 1956. **Days:** 2. **Hours per day:** 8. **Site:** outdoor and indoor. Roberson Museum and Science Center, Decker Exhibit Hall grounds, 30 Front Street. **Admission:** paid. **Daily entry:** under $10, **Discounts:** student discounts, **Acts:** local acts. **Sample day's lineup:** The Ice Cubes, Michael Uva, One Step South, Intermezzo Trio. **Contact:** Roberson Museum and Science Center, 30 Front Street, Binghamton, NY 13905-4779, 607-772-0660.

GOLDEN LINK FOLK FESTIVAL, Honeoye Falls, NY
Early Sep. to Middle Sep.
Traditional Folk

"Spend a weekend with the folks." -- Advertisement. May have given way to Turtle Hill Music Festival. See other dates and sites. **Help!** Still ongoing? **Days:** 3. **Hours per day:** 14. **Site:** outdoor. Marcus Park, Quaker Meetinghouse Road. **Admission:** paid. **Daily entry:** $10 to $24, **Discounts:** multiple event or day passes, advance purchase discounts, **Secondary genre[s]:** TGOS, TC&W, BLGS, MFOL, IRSH, **Acts:** regional acts, local acts. **Sample day's lineup:** John Roberts and Tony Barrand, Anne Lederman and Lake, Peter and Lou Berryman, Trout Fishing In America, Joan Crane, Fred Small, others. **Contact:** Golden Link Folksinging Society, Inc., 500 White Road, Brockport, NY 14420, 716-637-0994 **or:** Golden Link Folksinging Society, Inc., P. O. Box 201, Syracuse, NY 13206, 315-463-0533. .

HARVEST MOON FESTIVAL, Kingston, NY
Middle Sep.
Traditional Folk

**Days:** 1. **Hours per day:** 5. **Site:** outdoor. Hudson River Maritime Center Museum, Roundout Landing. **Acts:** regional acts, local acts. **Sample day's lineup:** Clearwater Sloop Singers, others. **Contact:** Hudson River Maritime Center Museum, Rondout Landing, Kingston, NY, 914-338-0071.

YONKERS HUDSON RIVERFEST, Yonkers, NY
Middle Sep.
Variety, General

**Days:** 1. **Hours per day:** 9. **Site:** outdoor. Yonkers Recreational Pier, River and Dock Streets. **Admission:** free. **Secondary genre[s]:** MJAZ, ACAP, MFOL, MLAT, **Acts:** national acts, local acts. **Sample day's lineup:** Tito Puente, Tom Chapin, Don McLean, Larry Coryell, Rockapella, Jeanie Bryson and Al Defemio, Annie and The Natural Wonder Band, Michael Aloi, others. **Contact:** Mayor's Office, Yonkers City Hall, Yonkers, NY 10701, 914-377-3378/6300.

GOLDEN HARVEST FESTIVAL, Baldwinsville, NY
    Middle Sep.
    Traditional Folk

**Days:** 2. **Hours per day:** 8. **Site:** outdoor. Beaver Lake Nature Center, 8477 East Mud Lake Road. **Admission:** paid. **Daily entry:** under $10, **Secondary genre[s]:** BLGS, MFOL, **Acts:** regional acts, local acts. **Sample day's lineup:** Lynden Lee and The Cherry Valley Boys, John Rossbach and Doug Yaerhling, Water Street Boys, Trad, Dennis Friscia, Dan Duggan. **Contact:** Beaver Lake Nature Center, 8477 East Mud Lake Road, Baldwinsville, NY 13027, 315-638-2519/451-7275.


SENECA INDIAN FALL FESTIVAL, Irving, NY
    Middle Sep.
    Native American

Since 1975. See other sites and dates. **Days:** 2. **Hours per day:** 8. **Site:** indoor. Saylor Community Building, Route 438. **Contact:** Clerk's Office, Seneca Nation of Indians, 1490 Route 438, Irving, NY 14081, 716-532-4900/549-1343.


JUST JAZZ, Somers, NY
    Middle Sep.
    Modern Jazz

See other dates and sites. **Days:** 1. **Hours per day:** 4. **Site:** outdoor. Lasdon Park and Arboretum. **Admission:** paid. **Daily entry:** under $10, **Acts:** regional acts, local acts. **Sample day's lineup:** Jimmy Hill Quartet, Bob Arthurs Quintet, Mark Morganelli and The Jazz Forum Allstars, others. **Contact:** Westchester County Office of Cultural Affairs, 148 Martine Avenue, Room 936, White Plains, NY 10601, 914-593-7275.


PETRIFIED SEA GARDENS FAMILY MUSIC FESTIVAL, Saratoga Springs, NY
    Middle Sep.
    Modern Folk

**Days:** 1. **Hours per day:** 6. **Site:** outdoor. Petrified Sea Gardens, Route 29. **Admission:** paid. **Daily entry:** under $10, **Acts:** regional acts, local acts. **Sample day's lineup:** Bob Warren, Michael Jerling, Marc Woodworth and Michael Hadfield, Paul Strausman. **Contact:** Petrified Sea Gardens, Route 29, Saratoga Springs, NY, 518-584-7102.


TAKIN' IT TO THE STREETS: THE ELECTRIC CITY MUSIC CELEBRATION, Schenectady, NY
    Middle Sep.
    Variety, General

**Days:** 1. **Site:** outdoor. Central Park. **Admission:** free. **Secondary genre[s]:** MJAZ, MRCK, TR&B, BGOS, MC&W, **Acts:** national acts, regional acts, local acts. **Sample day's lineup:** Eddie Shaw and The Wolf Gang, Joan Osborne, Heavy Metal Horns, Out Of Control R&B Band, Dr. Rouse and Her Gospel Singers, Bandolero, Micky T. Guild and The Storm, Dooley Austin Band, Mother Judge and The Urban Holiness Society, Nobody's Girls, El Extreme, CD3, Tina Ward and The Matter Babies. **Contact:** Northeast Blues Society, 4 Amsterdam Avenue, Scotia, NY 12302, 518-347-1751 **or:** Second Wind Productions, 55 Loudonwood East, Suite 1, Loudonville, NY 12211, 518-463-5222.

## MUSIC AT NEW PALTZ/FACULTY SAMPLER, New Paltz, NY
Middle Sep.
Variety, General

Kicks off a winter-long series of classical, jazz, folk concerts, Music at New Paltz, featuring national, regional, local acts. **Days:** 1. **Site:** indoor. SUNY of New Paltz, College Recital Hall. **Admission:** paid. **Daily entry:** under $10, **Secondary genre[s]:** MJAZ, MFOL, OTHR **Acts:** local acts. **Sample day's lineup:** Carole Cowan, Gregory Dinger, Mark Dziuba, Marica Gates, Barbara Hardgrave, Robert Krout, Susan Powell, Susan Seligman, Sylvia Suzowski, Michael West. **Contact:** Fine and Performing Arts College at New Paltz, 75 South Manheim Boulevard, New Paltz, NY 12561-2499, 914-257-3880.

## BUFFALO COUNTRY MUSIC AWARDS, Buffalo, NY
Middle Sep.
Modern Country

Since 1990. **Days:** 1. **Site:** indoor. The Pier, 325 Fuhrman Boulevard. **Admission:** paid. **Daily entry:** under $10, **Acts:** local acts. **Sample day's lineup:** J. C. Thompson Band, Stone Country, Steve Edmonds Band, Cross Country Express. **Contact:** Buffalo Country Music Awards, 2167 Genesee Street, Buffalo, NY 14211, 716-896-6666.

## LAZY RIVER BLUEGRASS FESTIVAL, Gardiner, NY
Middle Sep.
Bluegrass

Since 1992. "A true family bluegrass festival." -- Flyer. **Days:** 3. **Site:** outdoor. Lazy River Campground, 50 Bevier Road **Admission:** paid. **Daily entry:** $10 to $24, **Discounts:** multiple event or day passes, advance purchase discounts, **Secondary genre[s]:** TC&W, **Acts:** national acts, regional acts, local acts. **Sample day's lineup:** Gibson Brothers, Bill Harrell and The Virginians, River Grass Review, Smokey Greene and The Boys, Gillis Brothers, Charlie Sizemore Band, Kevin Church and Norman Wright, Carolina Rebels. **Contact:** Lazy River Bluegrass Festival, 70 Brenda Lane, Stone Ridge, NY 12484, 914-687-9781/255-5193.

## PALMYRA CANAL TOWN DAYS, Palmyra, NY
Middle Sep.
Variety, General

Since 1967. **Days:** 2. . **Secondary genre[s]:** TJAZ, ACAP, TFOL, GYLS, **Acts:** local acts. **Sample day's lineup:** C. A. Palmer Fyfe and Drum Corps, Beale Street Dixieland Bandwagon, Genesee Barbershop Chorus, others. **Contact:** Palmyra Canal Town Days, Stafford Road, Palmyra, NY 14522, 315-597-6700/2302 **or:** Palmyra Canal Town Days, P. O. Box 64, Palmyra, NY 14522, 315-946-5470.

## DICK FOX'S FALL DOO-WOPP EXTRAVAGANZA, Westbury, NY
Middle Sep.
A Cappella and Doo Wop

See other dates and sites. **Days:** 1. **Site:** indoor. Westbury Music Fair, Brush Hollow Road. **Admission:** paid. **Daily entry:** $25 to $49, **Discounts:** group sale discounts, **Secondary genre[s]:** CRCK, **Acts:** national acts, regional acts, local acts. **Sample day's lineup:** The Platters, The Penguins, The Del Roys, Stan Zizka and The Del Satins, Eugene Pitt and The Jive Five, The Impalas, Paul and Paula. **Contact:** Westbury Music Fair, Brush Hollow Road, Westbury, NY, 516-334-0800 **or:** Dick Fox's Doo-Wopp Extravaganza, 1650 Broadway, Suite 503, New York, NY 10019, 212-582-9074.

## NATIVE AMERICAN HERITAGE DAY, Castille, NY
Middle Sep.
Native American

**Days:** 1. **Hours per day:** 7. **Site:** outdoor and indoor. Trailside Lodge, Letchworth State Park. **Acts:** local acts. **Contact:** Native American Heritage Day, Letchworth State Park, Castille, NY, 716-493-2611.

## NAPLES GRAPE FESTIVAL, Naples, NY
Middle Sep.
Variety, General

**Days:** 2. **Hours per day:** 8. **Site:** outdoor. Memorial Town Hall Park, Route 21 South. **Admission:** free. **Secondary genre[s]:** MJAZ, ARCK, TR&B, TC&W, MFOL, **Acts:** regional acts, local acts. **Sample day's lineup:** Coupe De Villes, Bonnie Abrams and Allen Hopkins, Aaron Austin, Naples Central Jazz Band, Dinner Dogs. **Contact:** Naples Grape Festival, P. O. Box 70, Naples, NY 14512, 716-374-2240/5769.

## FIDDLERS FLING, Clayton, NY
Middle Sep.
Fiddle and Banjo Events

**Help!** A sample lineup? **Days:** 3. **Site:** outdoor. Clayton Recreational Park. **Secondary genre[s]:** TC&W, TFOL, **Acts:** local acts. **Contact:** Black River Fiddlers Association, Clayton Recreational Park, Clayton, NY, 315-686-4310.

## A. O. H. NASSAU COUNTY BOARD FEIS AND FESTIVAL, Uniondale, NY
Middle Sep.
Irish

Since 1973. "May the Feis be with you!" -- Sen. Alphonse D'Amato. **Days:** 1. **Site:** outdoor. Mitchel Field Athletic Complex. **Acts:** local acts. **Sample day's lineup:** The Skelligs, plus pipe and drum band competitions. **Contact:** A. O. H. Nassau County Board Feis and Festival, 2020 Lindgren Street, Merrick, NY 11566, 516-868-8941.

## AMHERST MUSEUM SCOTTISH FESTIVAL, Amherst, NY
Middle Sep.
Scottish

Since 1985. **Help!** A sample lineup? **Days:** 1. **Hours per day:** 8. **Site:** outdoor and indoor. Amherst Museum Colony Park, 3755 Tonawanda Creek Road. **Admission:** paid. **Acts:** local acts. **Contact:** Amherst Museum Colony Park, 3755 Tonawanda Creek Road, Amherst, NY 14228, 716-689-1440.

## FIELD, FOREST AND STREAM, Elizabethtown, NY
Middle Sep.
Traditional Folk

"An Adirondack folk arts festival celebrating the harvest, hunt and traditional North Country occcupations and recreations." -- Advertisement. Fiddling contest. **Days:** 1. **Hours per day:** 7. **Site:** outdoor and indoor. Adirondack Center Museum grounds. **Admission:** paid. **Daily entry:** under $10, **Secondary genre[s]:** BLGS, FDDL, IRSH, SCOT, **Acts:** local acts. **Sample day's lineup:** Chris Layer, Keith Murphy, Cold Brook Ramblers, Matha Gallagher, others. **Contact:** Field, Forest and Stream, Essex County Historical Society, Elizabethtown, NY 14932, 518-873-6466/6301.

FLY92 END OF SUMMER JAM, Latham, NY
    Middle Sep.
    Modern R&B

**Days:** 1. **Site:** outdoor. Starlite Theater "VIP" parking lot. **Admission:** paid. **Daily entry:** under $10, **Secondary genre[s]:** MRCK, ARCK, **Acts:** national acts, regional acts, local acts. **Sample day's lineup:** Sister Sledge, YBT, Remedy, Nuttin' NYCe, Ceremony, Lisa Keith, Michael Damian. **Contact:** WFLY 92.3 FM, 4243 Albany Street, Albany, NY 12205, 518-456-1144.

LONG ISLAND FIDDLE AND FOLK MUSIC FESTIVAL, Stony Brook, NY
    Middle Sep.
    Traditional Folk

Since 1985. Co-produced by the Long Island Traditional Music Association. See other sites and dates. **Days:** 1. **Hours per day:** 6. **Site:** outdoor and indoor. Museums at Stony Brook, Route 25A. **Admission:** paid. **Daily entry:** $10 to $24, **Discounts: Secondary genre[s]:** BGOS, FDDL, IRSH, **Acts:** national acts, local acts. **Sample day's lineup:** Eugene O'Donnell, Mick Maloney, Georgia Sea Island Singers, others. **Contact:** Museums at Stony Brook, 1208 Route 25A, Stony Brook, NY 11790, 516-751-0066 **or:** Long Island Traditional Music Association, P. O. Box 2706, Setauket, NY 11733, 516-751-1339.

NATIVE AMERICAN FESTIVAL, Kingston, NY
    Middle Sep.
    Native American

**Days:** 1. **Site:** outdoor. Senate House. **Contact:** Native American Festival, c/o Senate House, Kingston, NY, 914-358-2787.

AUTUMN HARVEST FESTIVAL, Cooperstown, NY
    Middle Sep.
    Modern Country

See other dates and sites. **Days:** 2. **Site:** outdoor. Farmer's Museum, Route 80, Lake Road. **Admission:** paid. **Daily entry:** under $10, **Secondary genre[s]:** BLGS, TFOL, **Acts:** regional acts, local acts. **Sample day's lineup:** Wildwood Girls, Wayne Swartz, Stump Jumpers, Judy Carrier and Rens Vreesburg, Billy Bob and Friends, Del-Se-Nango Fiddlers, Real Country, Laura Kortwright, Ghost Riders, Lee and Shirley Eaton. **Contact:** Del-Se-Nango Olde Tyme Fiddlers, R. F. D. 3, Box 233, New Berlin, NY 13411, 607-847-8501 **or:** Farmer's Museum, P. O. Box 800, Lake Road, Cooperstown, NY 13326, 607-547-2593.

BUCKWHEAT HARVEST FESTIVAL, Penn Yan, NY
    Late Sep.
    Classic Rock and Oldies

Since 1986. **Days:** 3. **Hours per day:** 13. **Site:** outdoor. multiple locations, including Yates County Fairgrounds. **Admission:** free and paid. **Daily entry:** $10 to $24, **Acts:** national acts, regional acts, local acts. **Sample series lineup:** Day One: Neal McCoy, Ken Mate; Day Two: Aaron Tippin, Ken Mate; Day Three: Sun Mountain Fiddler, Phil Dirt and The Dozers, Nik and The Nice Guys. **Contact:** The Birkett Mills, Main Street, Pen Yan, NY 14527, 315-536-3311/7434.

BOPPER'S OLDIES CONCERT, Huntington, NY
> Late Sep.
> A Cappella and Doo Wop

Since 1994. **Help!** Still ongoing? **Days:** 1. **Site:** indoor. Huntington High School, Oakwood and McKay Roads. **Admission:** paid. **Daily entry:** $10 to $24, **Secondary genre[s]:** CRCK, **Acts:** national acts, regional acts, local acts. **Sample day's lineup:** Lenny Cocco and The Chimes, Johnny Maestro and The Brooklyn Bridge, The Jive Five, Earl Lewis and The Channels, The Traditions. **Contact:** Huntington Manor Fire Department, 1650 New York Avenue, Huntington, NY, 516-427-1629/1644.


APPLE UMPKIN FESTIVAL, Wyoming, NY
> Late Sep.
> Variety, General

"We're in an OLDE FASHIONED DAZE!!" -- Press Release. **Days:** 2. **Site:** outdoor. multiple locations. **Secondary genre[s]:** MC&W, BLGS, IRSH, **Acts:** regional acts, local acts. **Sample day's lineup:** Creek Bend, Dady Brothers, others. **Contact:** Apple Umpkin Festival Committee, P. O. Box 20, Wyoming, NY 14591, 716-495-6220.


LONG ISLAND EMERALD ISLE FESTIVAL, Hempstead, NY
> Late Sep.
> Irish

Since 1992. "One glorious day of continuous Irish music, food, drink, dance, games and goods all located under our magnificent tents." -- Flyer. **Days:** 1. **Hours per day:** 12. **Site:** outdoor. Hempstead Fire Department Training Facility, Weir Street and Grand Avenue. **Admission:** paid. **Daily entry:** under $10, **Acts:** national acts, regional acts, local acts. **Sample day's lineup:** Cherish The Ladies, Ian Gallagher, Irish Mist Band, Ivers-Egan Band, Makem Brothers with Brian Sullivan, pipe band competition, others. **Contact:** Hempstead Fire Department, 75 Clinton Street, Hempstead, NY, 516-486-6822/0311.


CELTIC FAIR, Hunter, NY
> Late Sep.
> Irish

**Days:** 2. **Hours per day:** 6. **Site:** outdoor and indoor. Base Lodge, Hunter Mountain Ski Bowl, Route 23A. **Admission:** paid. **Daily entry:** under $10, **Discounts: Secondary genre[s]:** SCOT, **Acts:** national acts, regional acts, local acts. **Sample Day's Lineup:** Tim Quinn, Tipperary Knights, Al Logan, Atlantic Bridge, others. **Contact:** Hunter Mountain Festivals, Ltd., P. O. Box 295, Hunter, NY 12442, 518-263-3800.


CELTIC DAY IN THE PARK, Staatsburg, NY
> Late Sep.
> Irish

**Help!** A sample lineup? **Days:** 1. **Hours per day:** 6. **Site:** outdoor. Mills Memorial State Park, Old Post Road. **Admission:** free. **Secondary genre[s]:** SCOT, **Acts:** local acts. **Contact:** Mills Memorial State Park, Old Post Road, Staatsburg, NY, 914-889-4100.


HILTON APPLEFEST, Hilton, NY
> Late Sep. to Early Oct.
> Variety, General

Since 1981. **Help!** A sample lineup? **Days:** 2. **Site:** outdoor. Community Center, 3 stages. **Admission:** free. **Acts:** regional acts, local acts. **Contact:** Hilton Applefest, P. O. Box 1, Hilton, NY 14468, 716-392-7773/4715.

FLAMING LEAVES FIDDLE JAMBOREE, Long Lake, NY
> Early Oct.
> Fiddle and Banjo Events

Since 1992. See other dates and sites. **Help!** A sample lineup? **Days:** 1. **Hours per day:** 6. **Site:** outdoor. Mt. Sabattis Park. **Admission:** paid. **Daily entry:** under $10, **Secondary genre[s]:** TC&W, TFOL, **Acts:** local acts. **Contact:** Long Lake Parks, Recreation and Tourism, P. O. Box 496, Long Lake, NY 12847, 518-624-3077.

ALTERNATIVE SPORTS AND MUSIC FESTIVAL, Middletown, NY
> Early Oct.
> Alternative and College Rock

"Nearby and cheap." -- Advertisment. **Days:** 2. **Hours per day:** 24. **Site:** outdoor and indoor. Orange County Speedway, 239 Wisner Avenue. **Admission:** paid. **Daily entry:** $10 to $24, **Discounts:** multiple event or day passes, **Secondary genre[s]:** HRCK, RAP, **Acts:** national acts, regional acts, local acts. **Sample lineup:** The Mighty Mighty Bosstones, Bloom, Bleed Christian, Dead Susan, Dracula Jones, Fuel, The Goats, God Street Wine, Hyperactive, Letters To Cleo, From Good Homes, Mexican Mud Band, The Other Half, Perfect Thyroid, Satchell, Seed, Signs Of Life, Sinister Dane, Stabbing Westward, Stompbox, others. **Contact:** Eastern Edge Magazine, 239 Wisner Avenue, Middletown, NY 10940, 914-343-3134.

GATHERING OF IROQUOIS, Liverpool, NY
> Early Oct.
> Native American

**Days:** 2. **Site:** outdoor. Ste. Marie Among the Iroquois. **Acts:** local acts. **Contact:** Gathering of the Iroquois, Ste. Marie Among the Iroquois, Liverpool, NY, 914-451-7275.

LONG ISLAND TRADITIONAL MUSIC ASSOCIATION FALL FOLK WEEKEND, Baiting Hollow, NY
> Early Oct.
> Traditional Folk

See other sites and dates. **Days:** 3. **Site:** outdoor and indoor. Dorothy P. Flint 4-H Camp, Sound Avenue. **Admission:** paid. **Acts:** regional acts, local acts. **Sample day's lineup:** Kim and Reggie Harris, Tony Parkes and Yankee Ingenuity, others. **Contact:** Long Island Traditional Music Association, P. O. Box 2706, Setauket, NY 11733, 516-751-1339/325-1727.

APPLEFEST, Warwick, NY
> Early Oct.
> Traditional Folk

**Days:** 1. **Hours per day:** 8. **Site:** outdoor. Railroad Avenue. **Secondary genre[s]:** TJAZ, BLGS, MFOL, **Acts:** local acts. **Sample day's lineup:** Red Rogers, Gary and Mary Jo Strait, Lee Hunter, Steve and Bob Bernstein, Hudson Valley Folk Guild, Mike Baglione, Quallah Battoo, Pride, Warwick Coffeehouse Allstars. **Contact:** Mane Event Productions, P. O. Box 402, Napanoch, NY 12458, 914-647-6491.

CATSKILL HARVEST FESTIVAL, Walton, NY
> Early Oct.
> Variety, Country and Bluegrass

Since 1992. **Days:** 1. **Hours per day:** 8. **Site:** outdoor. Delaware County Fairgrounds. **Admission:** paid. **Daily entry:** under $10, **Secondary genre[s]:** MC&W, TC&W, BLGS, **Acts:** regional acts, local acts. **Sample day's lineup:** Northern Lights, Bo Harrison, others. **Contact:** American Cancer Society, P. O. Box 270, Walton, NY 13856, 607-865-6561.

## Long Beach Irish Day Parade and Festival, Long Beach, NY
### Early Oct.
### Irish

Since 1990. "Where the spirit of the Irish and its culture abound." -- Advertisement. **Days:** 1. **Site:** outdoor and indoor. multiple locations, West End. **Acts:** local acts. **Sample day's lineup:** Maura Fogarty and Kevin Smith, Jimmy Scanlon and Gerry O'Leary, Cunningham Brothers, Joe Nellaney and The Sligo Aces, Gerry Hughes, Second Generation Band, 12 pipe bands, others. **Contact:** St. Brendan's Association, P. O. Box 379, Island Park, NY 11558, 516-935-4229/623-2680.

## Swain Country Western Music Festival, Swain, NY
### Early Oct.
### Modern Country

**Help!** One time only? **Days:** 1. **Site:** outdoor. Swain Ski Center. **Admission:** paid. **Secondary genre[s]:** TC&W, **Acts:** national acts, local acts. **Sample day's lineup:** Johnny Paycheck, Jeannie C. Riley, others. **Contact:** Swain Country Western Music Festival, Swain Ski Center, Swain, NY, 716-593-5700/545-6511.

## Fiddlers!!: A Sampler of North American Fiddle Traditions, Roxbury, NY
### Early Oct.
### Variety, Folk and International

Since 1994. "An afternoon of concerts culminating in a super jam session and dance...a large turnout of friends, fiddlers and fans for good food, good fun and great fiddling." -- Press Release. **Days:** 1. **Hours per day:** 9. **Site:** outdoor and indoor. Roxbury Arts and Community Center, Vega Mountain Road, off Route 30. **Admission:** paid. **Daily entry:** under $10, **Secondary genre[s]:** TFOL, FDDL, ZYDC, IRSH, TLAT, **Acts:** national acts, regional acts, local acts. **Sample day's lineup:** Joe Cormier, Jay Ungar and Molly Mason, Beau Thomas, Hilt Kelly, others. **Contact:** Roxbury Arts Group, Vega Mountain Road, Roxbury, NY 12474, 607-326-7908.

## Opus 40 Jazz Autumn, Saugerties, NY
### Early Oct.
### Modern Jazz

Since 1995. "A great afternoon of mainstream jazz. Some call it America's classical music, some call it the coolest groove of all." -- Program. See other dates. **Days:** 1. **Site:** outdoor. Opus 40, 7480 Fite Road. **Admission:** paid. **Daily entry:** $10 to $24, $25 to $49, **Discounts:** advance purchase discounts, other discounts **Acts:** national acts. **Sample lineup:** David "Fathead" Newman, Arthur Blythe, Jeanie Bryson, Charles Craig. **Audio merchandise:** "Bring It On Home, Vols. 1, 2" (SONY/Legacy). **Contact:** Opus 40 Sunset Concerts, 7480 Fite Road, Saugerties, NY, 914-246-3400/8584.

## Dick Fox's Ultimate Doo-Wopp Fantasy Weekend, Monitcello, NY
### Early Oct.
### A Cappella and Doo Wop

See other dates and sites. **Help!** One time only? **Days:** 3. **Site:** indoor. Kutscher's Country Club. **Admission:** paid. **Daily entry:** $50 and over. **Discounts:** group sale discounts, **Secondary genre[s]:** CRCK, **Acts:** national acts, regional acts, local acts. **Sample day's lineup:** minimum of 5 name acts. **Contact:** Dick Fox's Ultimate Doo-Wopp Fantasy Weekend, 1650 Broadway, Suite 503, New York, NY 10019, 212-582-9074.

WEQX BIRTHDAY PARTY/UNIVERSITY OF ALBANY FALLFEST, Albany, NY
    Early Oct.
    Alternative and College Rock

Since 1994. University of Albany also programs Springfest, Mid Mar., usually with two national acts. Sample, 1994: A Tribe Called Quest, De La Soul. See other dates and sites. **Days:** 1. **Site:** indoor. U/Albany Recreation and Convocation Center. **Admission:** paid. **Daily entry:** $10 to $24, **Discounts:** student discounts, **Secondary genre[s]:** MRCK, **Acts:** national acts, local acts. **Sample day's lineup:** dada, Frente! Jeffrey Gaines, Single Gun Theory, The Figgs, Seed, Bloom. **Contact:** WEQX-FM, Elm Street, Manchester, VT, 802-362-4800.

LETCHWORTH ARTS AND CRAFTS SHOW AND SALE, Castile, NY
    Early Oct.
    Variety, General

Since 1977. "Enjoy the incomparable splendor of Wyoming County's georgraphical gem...Fall just wouldn't be the same without it!" -- Press Release. See other dates. **Days:** 3. **Hours per day:** 6. **Site:** outdoor. Letchworth State Park, Highbanks Recreation Area. **Restrictions:** 2, **Secondary genre[s]:** MJAZ, ACAP, MC&W, **Acts:** local acts. **Sample day's lineup:** Collage, Key Change, Mark Wright Jazz Quartet, Step 'n Denim, others. **Contact:** Arts Council of Wyoming County, 1 North Main Street, P. O. Box 249, Perry, NY 14530-0249, 716-237-3517.

COLUMBUS WEEKEND HARVEST FAIR, East Durham, NY
    Early Oct.
    Irish

Since 1989. See other dates. **Days:** 2. **Hours per day:** 9. **Site:** outdoor. Irish Cultural and Sports Center, Route 145. **Admission:** paid. **Daily entry:** under $10, **Acts:** regional acts, local acts. **Sample lineup:** Erin's Pride, Celtic Cross, Aine, Peter Street Band, Gus Hayes, Dermot Henry, Pat Keogh Band, others. **Contact:** Irish Cultural and Sports Center, P. O. Box 320, East Durham, NY 12423, 518-634-2286/2392.

MOUNTAIN MUSIC AND DANCE WEEKEND IN THE ADIRONDACKS, Raquette Lake, NY
    Early Oct. to Middle Oct.
    Traditional Folk

**Help!** One time only? **Days:** 4. **Site:** indoor. Sagamore Lodge, Sagamore Road. **Admission:** paid. **Daily entry:** $50 and over. **Acts:** local acts. **Sample day's lineup:** Dan Berggren, Dick and Carmen Gilman, Steve Warner, Dan Duggan, Rick Bunting. **Contact:** Mountain Music and Dance Weekend in the Adirondacks, Sagamore Lodge, Sagamore Road, Raquette Lake, NY, 315-354-5311.

COLUMBUS DAY TOURNAMENT OF BANDS, Binghamton, NY
    Early Oct.
    Drum Corps and Marching Bands

**Help!** A sample lineup? **Days:** 1. **Site:** outdoor. Main Street. **Admission:** free. **Acts:** local acts. **Contact:** Columbus Day Tournament of Bands, c/o Broome County Chamber of Commerce, P. O. Box 995, Binghamton, NY 13902-0995, 800-836-6740.

## NATIVE AMERICAN/INDIGENOUS PEOPLE DAY CELEBRATION, Albany, NY
    Early Oct.
    Native American

Since 1992. Sponsored by Keepers of the Circle. **Days:** 1. **Hours per day:** 10. **Site:** outdoor and indoor. U/Albany, Page Hall, 135 Western Avenue. **Admission:** free and paid. **Daily entry:** under $10, **Discounts:** **Secondary genre[s]:** MFOL, TFOL, **Acts:** national acts, local acts. **Sample day's lineup:** Powhatan, Metoaka Swift Eagle, Pete Seeger, Maurice Kenny, Joan Henry, Melanie Printup Hope, Abenaki Dawnland Singers, others. **Contact:** Native American/Indigenous People Day Celebration, U/Albany, Page Hall, 135 Western Avenue, Albany, NY, 518-489-0758.

## SUMMERTIME BLUES CHARITY CRUISE, Troy, NY
    Middle Oct.
    Blues and Traditional R&B

Culminates a summer-long series of Blues Cruises. **Help!** One time only? **Days:** 1. **Hours per day:** 3. **Site:** outdoor and indoor. departs River Front Park. **Admission:** paid. **Daily entry:** $10 to $24, **Acts:** regional acts, local acts. **Sample day's lineup:** Ernie Williams and The Wildcats, Out Of Control, Johnny Rabb, Jim E. Velvet. **Contact:** Captain J. P. Cruise Line, 278 River Street, Troy, NY, 518-270-1901.

## NEW YORK STATE SACRED HARP SINGING CONVENTION, Ithaca, NY
    Middle Oct.
    Traditional Gospel and Sings

Since 1989. "Open to the public; no previous choral experience is required." -- Flyer. **Days:** 2. **Hours per day:** 8. **Site:** indoor. St. Peter's Episcopal Church, Albany and Mill Streets. **Admission:** free. **Acts:** regional acts, local acts. **Audio merchandise:** "1992 New York State Sacred Harp Singing Convention" (self-produced and distributed). **Contact:** Ithaca Sacred Harp Singers, 66 Van Buskirk Gulf Road, Newfield, NY 14867, 607-655-9063/564-7864.

## OCTOBER OYSTER FESTIVAL, Oyster Bay, NY
    Middle Oct.
    Variety, General

**Days:** 2. **Hours per day:** 9. **Site:** outdoor. multiple locations. **Admission:** free. **Secondary genre[s]:** MJAZ, TJAZ, MRCK, CRCK, TR&B, ACAP, MC&W, BLGS, MFOL, MARI, **Acts:** local acts. **Sample day's lineup:** Back In Time, South Street Rhythm and Blues, Tom Smith, Cold Sweat, John Carr, All Folked Up, Nancy Siriani Trio, High Country, Gloria Parker and Her Riverboat Ramblers. **Contact:** Historic Oyster Bay Chamber of Commerce, P. O. Box 21, Oyster Bay, NY 11771-0021, 516-624-8082/922-6464.

## FALL COUNTRY DANCE AND PARTY WEEKEND, Kerhonkson, NY
    Middle Oct.
    Modern Country

Since 1994. **Days:** 3. **Site:** indoor. Granit Hotel. **Admission:** paid. **Daily entry:** $50 and over. **Acts:** regional acts, local acts. **Sample lineup:** Tim Gillis Band, Six Gun, Dooley Austin Band, Lady Luck. **Contact:** Tim Gillis Weekends, P. O. Box 925, Woodbridge, NJ 07095, 800-842-3836.

FOX HOLLOW REUNION FOLK CONCERT, Troy, NY
    Middle Oct.
    Traditional Folk

See other dates. **Days:** 1. **Site:** indoor. Troy Saving Bank Music Hall, Second and State Streets. **Admission:** paid. **Daily entry:** $10 to $24, $25 to $49, $50 and over. **Acts:** regional acts, local acts. **Sample day's lineup:** Michael Cooney, John Roberts aand Tony Barrand, Sandy and Caroline Patton, Megan, Dan and Gary McArthur, Bill Spence and Fennig's Allstars, others. **Contact:** Troy Savings Bank Music Hall, 84 4th Street, Troy, NY, 518-273-0038/7232 **or:** Old Songs, Inc., P. O. Box 399, Guilderland, NY 12084, 518-765-2815.


NIAGARA'S APPLE COUNTRY FESTIVAL, Lockport, NY
    Middle Oct.
    Variety, General

**Days:** 2. **Hours per day:** 8. **Site:** outdoor and indoor. Niagara County Fairgrounds, Route 78. **Secondary genre[s]:** CRCK, TFOL, OTHR **Acts:** local acts. **Sample day's lineup:** Johnny Buick and The Fabulous Dynaflows, Newton Street Irregulars, Armor and Sturdevant. **Contact:** Eastern Niagara Chamber of Commerce, Canal Terrace, 151 West Genesee Street, Lockport, NY 14094-3686, 716-433-3828.


CELEBRATION OF JEWISH LEARNING, Brighton, NY
    Middle Oct.
    Jewish

**Help!** One time only? **Days:** 1. **Hours per day:** 9. **Site:** indoor. Jewish Community Center, 1200 Edgewood Avenue. **Admission:** paid. **Daily entry:** under $10, **Discounts:** advance purchase discounts, **Acts:** local acts. **Sample day's lineup:** Bonnie Abrams, others. **Contact:** Jewish Community Center, 1200 Edgewood Avenue, Brighton, NY, 716-461-0490.


NORTH EAST COUNTRY MUSIC ASSOCIATION AWARDS SHOW, Albany, NY
    Middle Oct.
    Variety, Country and Bluegrass

**Days:** 1. **Site:** indoor. Empire Center at The Egg. **Admission:** paid. **Secondary genre[s]:** MC&W, TC&W, BLGS, **Acts:** regional acts, local acts. **Sample day's lineup:** Aged in The Hills, The Countyline Rebels, Alive and Kickin', Bandolero, Micky T. Guild and The Storm, Al and Kathy Bain, Two-Lane Highway. **Contact:** North East Country Music Association Awards Show, RR 1, Box 1084, Salem, NY 12865, 518-854-3030.


IRISH MUSIC WEEKEND PARTY OF THE YEAR, Monticello, NY
    Late Oct.
    Irish

Since 1993. "Green Linnett Records invites you to...continuous entertainment, concerts, music sessions and dancing, all day and all night!" -- Brochure. **Days:** 3. **Site:** indoor. Kutsher's Country Club, off Route 17. **Admission:** paid. **Daily entry:** $25 to $49, $50 and over. **Acts:** national acts, regional acts, local acts. **Sample lineup:** Randal Bays, Joe Burke, Kevin Bruke, Liz Carroll, Rev. Charlie Coen, Jack Coen, Anne Conroy, Brian Conway, Mary Coogan, Johnny Cunningham, Phil Cunningham, Jackie Daly, Tony DeMarco, Kimati Dinizulu, Maureen Doherty, Brendan Dolan, Felix Dolan, Gabriel Donohue, Seamus Egan, Siobhan Egan, Michael Fee, Ged Foley, Martin Hayes, Linda Hickman, Winnie Horan, Andy Irvine, Eileen Ivers, James Keane, Jimmy Keane, Paddy keenan, Pat Kilbride, Richard Lindsey, Donna Long, Joannie Madden, Joe Madden, Billy McComiskey, Andy McGann, Zan McLeod, Steve Missal, Mick Maloney, Martin Mulhaire, Brendan Mulvihill, Jerry O'Sullivan, Mke Rafferty, Cathie Ryan, John Whelan, John Williams, John Bowe, Liam Farrell, Brendan McGlinchey, Alan O'Leary, Kevin Taylor, others. **Audio merchandise:** "The Celts Rise Again"; "Flight of the Green Linnett"; "Green Fields of America"; "The Heart of the Gaels"; plus the rest of the Green Linnett catalog. **Contact:** Green Linnett Records, 43 Beaver Brook Road, Danbury, CT 06810, 800-468-6644.

COMPUTER MUSIC AT STONY BROOK, Stony Brook, NY
> Late Oct.
> Avant Garde and New Music

Since 1990. Part of a season-long classical music series. See other dates. **Help!** A sample lineup? **Days:** 1. **Site:** indoor. Recital Hall, SUNY at Stony Brook. **Admission:** free. **Acts:** local acts. **Contact:** Department of Music, SUNY at Stony Brook, Stony Brook, NY 11794-5475, 516-632-7330/7230.

GOSPEL NIGHT, Buffalo, NY
> Late Oct.
> Southern and Bluegrass Gospel

Since 1991. **Days:** 1. **Site:** indoor. Kleinhans Music Hall. **Admission:** paid. **Daily entry:** $10 to $24, **Discounts:** advance purchase discounts, **Acts:** national acts, local acts. **Sample day's lineup:** Kingsmen, Gold City, Kelly Nelon Thompson, The Nelons, Anthony Burger. **Contact:** Dean Waldron Promotions, 5849 Albion Road, Oakfield, NY 14125, 716-948-9800.

BEST OF THE BEST POW-WOW/NATIVE AMERICAN INDIAN ARTS FESTIVAL, Suffern, NY
> Late Oct.
> Native American

**Help!** A sample lineup? **Days:** 2. **Hours per day:** 10. **Site:** indoor. Rockland Community College Field House, College Road. **Admission:** paid. **Daily entry:** under $10, **Acts:** national acts, regional acts, local acts. **Contact:** Suffern Chamber of Commerce, P. O. Box 291, Suffern, NY 10901, 914-357-8424.

FALL JAMBOREE, Rochester, NY
> Late Oct.
> Modern Country

"Bring the whole family! There's fun for everyone!" -- Advertisement. **Help!** One time only? **Days:** 1. **Hours per day:** 12. **Site:** indoor. Rustler's Roost, 4853 Henrietta Road. **Admission:** paid. **Daily entry:** under $10, **Acts:** local acts. **Sample day's lineup:** Road House, Union, The Posse, Cimarron, Reel Country, Saddle Boogie, City Limits, Pay Dirt. **Contact:** Rustler's Roost, 4853 Henrietta Road, Rochester, NY, 716-334-0360.

JAZZ FOR THE ARTS/KICK OFF, Albany, NY
> Late Oct.
> Modern Jazz

Since 1993. Opens Jazz for the Arts concert series. See other dates. **Days:** 1. **Site:** indoor. The Empire Center at The Egg. **Admission:** paid. **Daily entry:** $10 to $24, **Discounts:** student discounts, advance purchase discounts, **Acts:** national acts, local acts. **Sample day's lineup:** Doug Sertl Big Band, Nick Brignola, Phil Woods. **Contact:** Jazz for the Arts, The Empire Center at the Egg, Empire State Plaza, Albany, NY, 518-473-1845.

PROJECT CHILDREN DINNER DANCE AND VARIETY SHOW, Syracuse, NY
> Late Oct.
> Irish

Since 1984. **Days:** 1. **Hours per day:** 6. **Site:** indoor. LeMoyne College Athletic Center. **Admission:** paid. **Daily entry:** $10 to $24, **Acts:** local acts. **Sample day's lineup:** John Murphy and The Clubmen, Rev, David Sanbor, Mary Cordes, Terance Doherty, Sister Act, others. **Contact:** Project Children Dinner Dance and Variety Show, 528 Boyden Street, Syracuse, NY 13206, 315-673-1365/474-2296.

APPLE HARVEST FESTIVAL, Ithaca, NY
>    Early Oct.
>    Variety, General

**Days:** 3. **Hours per day:** 6. **Site:** outdoor. multiple locations downtown. **Secondary genre[s]:** MJAZ, TJAZ, MC&W, TC&W, MFOL, TFOL, IRSH, NATV, **Acts:** local acts. **Sample day's lineup:** Dave Davies Trio, The Spoonies, Jonathon Appleby, Chris Woodward and Brian Highland, John Simon and Coconut Therapy, Cayuga Chimes. **Contact:** Commons Coordinator's Office, Room 302, City Hall, Ithaca, NY 14850, 607-274-6546.

NATIONAL ROCKABILLY BLOWOUT, Rochester, NY
>    Late Oct.
>    Alt. Country and Rockabilly

Since 1993. "Shazam...Wild rockabilly and various perversions!" -- Poster. Semi-annual. **Days:** 2. **Site:** indoor. Friday: Nietzche's, 248 Allen Street; Saturday: Milestones, 50 East Avenue. **Admission:** paid. **Acts:** regional acts, local acts. **Sample day's lineup:** Frantic Flattops, Belmont Playboys, Moondogs, Flyin' Saucers. **Contact:** Nietzche's, 248 Allen Street, Rochester, NY, 716-886-8339 **or:** Milestones, 50 East Avenue, Rochester, NY, 716-225-6490.

PINES SCOTTISH WEEKEND, South Fallsburg, NY
>    Late Oct.
>    Scottish

Since 1991. "It's like a cruise on land!" -- Flyer. See other dates. **Days:** 3. **Site:** indoor. Pines Resort Hotel. **Admission:** paid. **Daily entry:** $50 and over. **Discounts:** group sale discounts, **Acts:** regional acts, local acts. **Sample lineup:** Kenneth McKellar, Alex Beaton, Brigadoons, Highland-Aires, Ronnie Stewart, Joe Gordon, Sally Logan, Sandy Haine and The Clansmen, others. **Contact:** Pines Scottish Weekend, Pines Resort Hotel, South Fallsburg, NY 12779, 800-36-PINES **or:** Gertrude Byrne Promotions, P. O. Box 6, Leeds, NY 12451, 518-943-3736.

HALLOWEEN DANCE WEEKEND, Ashokan, NY
>    Late Oct. to Early Nov.
>    Traditional Folk

Since 1981. Culminates a summer-long series of concerts and dance camps. **Days:** 3. **Site:** indoor. . **Admission:** paid. **Daily entry:** $10 to $24, $25 to $49, **Discounts:** multiple event or day passes, **Acts:** regional acts, local acts. **Sample day's lineup:** Swingology (with Jay Ungar and Molly Mason), L-7's, Cheshire Brats, John Krumm and Steve Zakon. **Contact:** Friends of Fiddle and Dance, RD 1, Box 489, West Hurley, NY 12491, 914-338-2996.

EAR-FEST: FESTIVAL OF TAPED MUSIC, Stony Brook, NY
>    Early Nov.
>    Avant Garde and New Music

Since 1994. Part of a season-long classical music series. See other dates. **Help!** A sample lineup? **Days:** 1. **Site:** indoor. ECC Building, Studio A, SUNY at Stony Brook. **Admission:** free. **Acts:** local acts. **Contact:** Department of Music, SUNY at Stony Brook, Stony Brook, NY 11794-5475, 516-632-7330/7230.

## PINES NUMBER ONE IRISH WEEKEND, South Fallsburg, NY
Middle Nov.

Irish

"The perfect getaway weekend!" -- Flyer. See other dates. **Days:** 3. **Site:** indoor. Pines Resort Hotel. **Admission:** paid. **Daily entry:** $50 and over. **Discounts:** group sale discounts, **Acts:** national acts, regional acts, local acts. **Sample lineup:** Joannie Madden, Sean O'Neil Band, New York Show-Band, Johnny Carroll, Dave Coady and His Irish Express, Jimmy Hughes Show-Band, Jimmy McPhail, Erin's Pride, Glen Curtin, Ann Breen, others. **Contact:** Pines Irish Weekend, Pines Resort Hotel, South Fallsburg, NY 12779, 800-36-PINES **or:** Gertrude Byrne Promotions, P. O. Box 6, Leeds, NY 12451, 518-943-3736.

## BARBERSHOP SERENADE, Buffalo, NY
Middle Nov.

A Cappella and Doo Wop

Since 1944. **Days:** 1. **Site:** indoor. Kleinhans Music Hall, Symphony Circle. **Admission:** paid. **Acts:** local acts. **Sample day's lineup:** Note Wits, Vocal Motion, Queen City Chordsmen, others. **Contact:** Barbershop Serenade, c/o Kleinhans Music Hall, Symphony Circle, Buffalo, NY 14201, 716-655-4304.

## HUNGERTHON CONCERT/WINTER BLUES FEST, New City, NY
Middle Nov.

Blues and Traditional R&B

**Help!** A sample lineup? **Days:** 1. **Site:** indoor. **Acts:** regional acts, local acts. **Contact:** Rockland County Jazz and Blues Society, 159 Grandview, Wesley Hills, NY 10954, 914-354-2837/322-TIXS.

## GRAND INTERNATIONAL RAGTIME/JASSTIME FOUNDATION FALL FESTIVAL, Alexandria Bay, NY
Middle Nov.

Traditional Jazz and Ragtime

See other dates. **Days:** 3. **Site:** indoor. Edgewood Resort. **Secondary genre[s]:** TGOS, **Acts:** regional acts, local acts. **Sample lineup:** Mimi Blais, Rich Berry, Don Burns, Jack Cuff, Bob Darch, Neville Dickie, Virginia Tichenor Gilseth, Tim Sandor, Kjell Waltman, Borgy Borgerson Trio, Et Cetera String Band, Sister Jean The Ragtime Queen and Laundry Fat, Ralph Gruegel's Eagle Jazz Band, Bob Milne's Sweet Violets Jazz Band, Brian Tower's Hot 5 Jazzmakers. **Contact:** Grand International Ragtime/Jasstime Foundation, P. O. Box 92022, 2900 Warden Avenue, Scarborough, ON M1W 3Y9, 416-494-7631.

## STARDUST DANCE WEEKEND, Ellenville, NY
Middle Nov. to Late Nov.

Modern Jazz

Since 1989. "The dancingest dance weekend ever!" -- Brochure. **Days:** 3. **Site:** indoor. Nevele Country Club. **Admission:** paid. **Daily entry:** $50 and over. **Secondary genre[s]:** MLAT, **Acts:** national acts, local acts. **Sample day's lineup:** Ray Sepulveda and His Orchestra, Madera Fina Orchestra, Jeff Kroleck Orchestra. **Contact:** Stardust Dance Weekend, P. O. Box 123, Thompsonville, NY 12784, 914-434-7760.

## BUFFALO BEER FEST, Buffalo, NY
Middle Nov.

Irish

**Days:** 1. **Site:** indoor. Erie County Fairgrounds. **Acts:** regional acts, local acts. **Sample day's lineup:** Dave North, Dady Brothers, Blarney Bunch, Danny Justice, Fiona Malloy, Shananagans, Kevin Kennedy, Seamus Kennedy, Kindred, Tom O'Carroll, Gerry McCrudden. **Contact:** Buffalo Beer Fest, 5050 Main Street, Snyder, NY 14226, 716-839-0002.

FESTIVAL OF LIGHTS, Niagara Falls, NY
Middle Nov. to Early Jan.
Modern Country

Since 1981. "Niagara's Holiday Gift to the World" -- Program. **Days:** 44. **Hours per day:** 6. **Site:** indoor. Convention Center, Carborundum Center, Native American Center, Inn at the Falls, Lackey Plaza, Turtle, elsewhere. **Admission:** free and paid. **Secondary genre[s]:** MRCK, ACAP, CHRS, TC&W, FDDL, JWSH, NATV, GYLS, OTHR **Acts:** national acts, local acts. **Sample series lineup:** Day One: The Forrester Sisters, The Bellamy Brothers, Evergreen Singing Group; Day Two: Ricky Van Shelton, Saturday Night Hayride Music Show and Dances; Day Three: Mitzi Gaynor, Rainbow Singers. **Contact:** Niagara Falls Area Chamber of Commerce, The Carborundum Center, 345 3rd Street, Suite 500, Niagara Falls, NY 14303-1117, 716-285-2400/8484/9141.

ARTVOICE ORIGINAL MUSIC AWARDS, Buffalo, NY
Late Nov.
Variety, General

Since 1992. "In the spirit of nurturing creative energies in Buffalo and surrounding areas, the awards were created to assist local musicians who write and play original music by giving them practical, valuable items instead of plaques and trophies." -- Press release. **Days:** 1. **Site:** indoor. Network, Main Place Mall. **Secondary genre[s]:** MJAZ, MRCK, ARCK, MR&B, OTHR **Acts:** national acts, regional acts, local acts. **Sample day's lineup:** John and Mary, Milt, Tugboat Annie, Shaft, Phonkbutt, The Pine Dogs, The Need, McCarthyism, Michele Weber, Snufflufugus, others. **Contact:** Artvoice Original Music Awards, 500 Franklin Street, Buffalo, NY 14202, 716-881-6604.

MOHONK'S JOY OF SINGING, New Paltz, NY
Late Nov.
Traditional Folk

"Singing is a direct and effective way of connecting with deep emotions, feeling a sense of community, and simply having a good time." -- Brochure. **Days:** 3. **Site:** indoor. Mohonk Mountain House. **Admission:** paid. **Daily entry:** $50 and over. **Acts:** national acts, local acts. **Sample lineup:** Jay Ungar and Molly Mason, Peter and Mary Alice Amidon, Grian McGregor, Pete Seeger, Pamela Warwick Smith, others. **Contact:** Mohonk's Family Festival, Mohonk Mountain House, New Paltz, NY 12561, 914-255-4500.

COUNTRY MUSIC DANCE WEEKEND, South Fallsburg, NY
Early Dec.
Modern Country

Since 1990. "Often imitated, never duplicated!" -- Brochure. See other dates. **Days:** 3. **Site:** indoor. Pines Resort Hotel. **Admission:** paid. **Daily entry:** $50 and over. **Discounts:** group sale discounts, **Acts:** regional acts, local acts. **Sample lineup:** High Sierra, The Possee, Southbound, Sage, Thunder Rose, Tim Gillis, Jan Slow and The Vanishing Cowboys, others. **Contact:** Country Dance Music Weekend, Pines Resort Hotel, South Fallsburg, NY 12779, 800-36-PINES **or:** Country Dance Music Weekend, P. O. Box 144, Baldwin, NY 11510, 516-379-4564.

EMERALD PRODUCTIONS GETAWAY, Callicoon, NY
Early Dec.
Irish

"Treat yourself!" -- Advertisement. See other dates. **Days:** 3. **Site:** indoor. Villa Roma Resort Hotel. **Admission:** paid. **Daily entry:** $50 and over. **Acts:** national acts, regional acts, local acts. **Sample lineup:** Clancy Brothers and Robbie O'Connell, Brendan Grace, Paddy Noonan Revue, The Healys and John Tabb, Cleo Meaney, Vince McCormack, Fran Raftery, Mike McCormack, Joe Hayes, Willie Lynch, others. **Contact:** Emerald Productions Getaway, Villa Roma Resort Hotel, Callicoon, NY, 800-533-6767.

GREAT IRISH WEEKEND, Ellenville, NY
Early Dec. to Middle Dec.
Irish

Since 1991. "A very special holiday weekend." -- Brochure. **Days:** 3. **Site:** indoor. Fallsview Hotel. **Admission:** paid. **Daily entry:** $25 to $49, **Discounts:** group sale discounts, **Acts:** regional acts, local acts. **Sample lineup:** Pat Roper, Erin's Pride, Dermot Henry, Cahal Dunne, Peter McQ, Eileen Clohessy, Pat Kane, Morningstar, Sheila McGirl, Shaun O'Hagan, others. **Contact:** Great Irish Weekend, Fallsview Hotel, Ellenville, NY 12428, 800-822-8439.

VALENTINE'S XMAS JAM, Albany, NY
Middle Dec.
Blues and Traditional R&B

Since 1993. **Days:** 1. **Site:** indoor. Valentine's, 17 New Scotland Avenue. **Secondary genre[s]:** MRCK, **Acts:** local acts. **Sample day's lineup:** Johnny Rabb and The Jailhouse Rockers, Eddie Angel and The Whole Wheat Horns, The Sharks, Good Friday. **Contact:** Valentine's, 17 New Scotland Avenue, Albany, NY, 518-432-6572.

WEQX ACOUSTIC HOLIDAY CONCERT FOR THE HUNGRY, Latham, NY
Middle Dec.
Alternative and College Rock

Since 1994. See other dates and sites. **Days:** 1. **Site:** indoor. Saratoga Winners, Route 9. **Admission:** paid. **Daily entry:** $10 to $24, **Acts:** national acts. **Sample day's lineup:** Paul Weller, Catherine Wheel, Cowboy Junkies, Nick Hayward, Teenage Fan Club. **Contact:** WEQX-FMSaratoga Winners, Elm StreetRoute 9, ManchesterLatham, VTNY, 802-362-4800.

HOLIDAY JAM FOR JOY, Rotterdam, NY
Middle Dec.
Blues and Traditional R&B

Since 1993. Benefits Toys for Tots, Schenectady Inner City Ministry Food Pantry. **Days:** 1. **Site:** indoor. Five Corners Restaurant, 404 Provincetown Road. **Admission:** paid. **Daily entry:** under $10, **Acts:** local acts. **Sample day's lineup:** Out Of Control R&B Band, Matt Smith Band, Doc Scanlon's Rhythm Boys, Groove Assassins. **Contact:** Five Corners Restaurant, 404 Princetown Road, Rotterdam, NY, 518-355-1311/782-0577.

DICK FOX'S HOLIDAY DOO-WOPP EXTRAVAGANZA, Westbury, NY
Middle Dec.
A Cappella and Doo Wop

See other dates and sites. **Days:** 1. **Site:** indoor. Westbury Music Fair, Brush Hollow Road. **Admission:** paid. **Daily entry:** $25 to $49, **Discounts:** group sale discounts, **Secondary genre[s]:** CRCK, **Acts:** national acts, regional acts, local acts. **Sample day's lineup:** Gary Lewis and The Playboys, The Coasters, Larry Chance and The Earls, The Shangri-Las, Dickie Lee, The Classics, The Mystics, The Passions. **Contact:** Westbury Music Fair, Brush Hollow Road, Westbury, NY, 516-334-0800 **or:** Dick Fox's Doo-Wopp Extravaganza, 1650 Broadway, Suite 503, New York, NY 10019, 212-582-9074.

KLEZKAMP, Parksville, NY
Late Dec.
Jewish

**Help!** One time only? **Days:** 6. **Site:** indoor. Paramount Hotel. **Admission:** paid. **Daily entry:** $50 and over. **Acts:** national acts, regional acts, local acts. **Sample lineup:** Kapeleye, Klezmatics, Brave Old World, Klezmer Conservatory Band, Michael Wex, Irena Klepfisz, others. **Contact:** Living Traditions, 430 West 14th Street, #514, New York, NY 10014, 212-691-1272.

KWANZAA FETE, Hempstead, NY
> Late Dec.
> African American

See other dates. **Help!** A sample lineup? **Days:** 1. **Hours per day:** 3. **Site:** indoor. African American Museum, 110 North Franklin Street. **Secondary genre[s]:** BGOS, **Acts:** local acts. **Contact:** African American Museum, 110 North Franklin Street, Hempstead, NY, 516-572-0730.

NIAGARA: THE STUDENT AND ADULT LEADERSHIP CONFERENCE ON EVANGELISM, Niagara Falls, NY
> Late Dec.
> Modern Christian

Since 1993. "Experience the power!" -- Brochure. **Days:** 3. **Hours per day:** 17. **Site:** indoor. Radisson Hotel, 3rd and Old Falls Streets. **Admission:** paid. **Daily entry:** under $10, $10 to $24, **Discounts:** advance purchase discounts, **Acts:** national acts, local acts. **Sample lineup:** Michael Peace, Jerome Olds, Freddie Langston, The Brothers. **Contact:** Western New York Youth for Christ, P. O. Box 518, Lancaster, NY 14086, 716-681-9092.

FIRST NIGHT ALBANY, Albany, NY
> Late Dec.
> Variety, Folk and International

Since 1987. "What are you doing New Year's Eve?!" -- Brochure. **Days:** 1. **Hours per day:** 6. **Site:** outdoor and indoor. 52 locations. **Admission:** paid. **Daily entry:** under $10, $10 to $24, **Discounts:** advance purchase discounts, **Restrictions:** 2, **Secondary genre[s]:** MJAZ, TJAZ, MRCK, ARCK, RAP, MR&B, TR&B, BGOS, MC&W, BLGS, MFOL, ZYDC, IRSH, SCOT, MLAT, BRZL, RGGE, AVNT, OTHR **Acts:** national acts, regional acts, local acts. **Sample day's lineup:** Jim Gaudet, Dennis D'Asaro, Bayou Coyote, Lee Shaw, St. Cecilia orchestra and Jazz Ensemble, Cole Broderick Jazz Band, Perfect Thyroid, The Matterbabies, Pat Pisinello, Courtney Ralph, Tita, Ann Fisher, Riverside Rascals, Dan Hart, Bridget Ball, Chrsitopher Shaw, Out Of Control R&B Band, The Sharks, Die Hofbrau Musikanten, Phil Foote Swing Band, Ramsey Meyer, Art Treffelitti, Not Necessarily The Blues, Burnt Hills Bluegrass, Adirondack Baroque Consort, Crosswind, The Get Go, Mind Over Matter, Ernie Williams and The Wildcats, The Jazz Factor, Capital Land Big Band, Brass Consort, The Jazz Cartel, Alex Torres and The Latin Kings, The Gospel Chorus, Heavenly Echoes, Mark Rabin, Lucy McCaffrey, A Vent Garde Woodwinds, Airwaves, Bells and Motley, Tropicalia, Uptowne Cats, Charisma, Doc Scanlon's Rhythm Boys, Mendelssohn Club, Pro Musica, Rodeo Moon, Bandolero, Sambarama, Queen Anne's Lace, Comhaltas, others. **Contact:** City of Albany Mayor's Office of Special Events, 60 Orange Street, Albany, NY 12210, 518-434-2032.

FIRST NIGHT BUFFALO, Buffalo, NY
> Late Dec.
> Variety, Folk and International

Since 1989. **Days:** 1. **Hours per day:** 5. **Site:** outdoor. 28 locations. **Admission:** paid. **Daily entry:** under $10, **Discounts:** advance purchase discounts, **Restrictions:** 2, **Secondary genre[s]:** MJAZ, TJAZ, MRCK, CRCK, ARCK, TR&B, ACAP, CHRS, BGOS, MC&W, TFOL, AFRM, AFRC, OTHR **Acts:** national acts, regional acts, local acts. **Sample day's lineup:** Sweethearts of The Rodeo, Significance, 23 Skidoo, Yale Glee Club, Renegade Riders, Jim Yeomans Band, African-American Cultural Center drummers and dancers, Wondermakers, Vision, Movement, Testify, The Gayles, Varson Community Choir, Matt Nickson and The Blues Men, Marvin Patterson Quartet, Kazoom Steve Love's New York Express, Dinner Dogs, Nan Hoffman, Sweet Adelines, Party Squad, McCarthyizm, Wisdom of Children, Planet 9, The Boomers, Hit and Run, Glenn Colton, David Kane's Them Jazzbeards, Outer Circle World Orchestra, others. **Contact:** Independent Health Foundation, 777 International Drive, Buffalo, NY 14221, 716-631-5731/635-4984.

## FIRST NIGHT FREEPORT, Freeport, NY
Late Dec.
Variety, Folk and International

Since 1993. **Help!** Still ongoing? **Days:** 1. **Hours per day:** 10. **Site:** outdoor and indoor. multiple locations. **Admission:** paid. **Daily entry:** under $10, **Discounts:** advance purchase discounts, **Restrictions:** 2, **Secondary genre[s]:** MFOL, TFOL, JWSH, AFRC, OTHR **Acts:** national acts, regional acts, local acts. **Sample day's lineup:** Oscar Brand, Akyene Baako, East Bay Chamber Players, Steve Love's New York Express, New York Madrigal Singers, Tumble Bay String Band, others. **Contact:** c/o Freeport Chamber of Commerce, 429 Atlantic Avenue, Freeport, NY 11520, 516-223-8856/378-7402.

## NEW YEAR'S EARLY EVE, Rochester, NY
Late Dec.
Variety, Folk and International

See other dates. **Help!** A sample lineup? **Days:** 1. **Site:** outdoor. Manhattan Square Park, Chestnut and Court Streets. **Admission:** free. **Acts:** local acts. **Contact:** City of Rochester Events Network, City Hall, 30 Church Street, Room 222B, Rochester, NY 14614, 716-428-6690/6697.

# R. I. P., M. I. A. Festival Listings

**Caveat**  The following festivals are either confirmed or suspected to be discontinued (i.e., R. I. P.); or have not responded to various information requests (i.e., M. I. A.). Since all festivals are subject to last-minute changes or reinstatement, however, FESTPRESS is not responsible for any festival listing information that follows. Readers are encouraged to notify FESTPRESS of any status changes they uncover.


PERFORMING ARTISTS FUND 10-10-10 BENEFIT, Schenectady, NY
     Middle Jan.
     Modern Rock and Pop

Since 1994. **Help!** One time only? Also, a sample lineup? **Days:** 1. **Hours per day:** 10. **Site:** indoor. Ramada Inn, 450 Knott Street. **Admission:** paid. **Daily entry:** $10 to $24, **Secondary genre[s]:** ARCK, TR&B, **Acts:** local acts. **Contact:** Performing Artists Support Fund, c/o Ramada Inn, 450 Knott Street, Schenectady, NY 12308, 518-370-7151.


ACOUSTIC MUSIC INDOOR FESTIVAL, Tarrytown, NY
     Late Mar.
     Modern Folk

Since 1993. One time only. **Days:** 2. **Site:** indoor. Tarrytown Music Hall, Kaldenberg and Main Streets. **Admission:** paid. **Daily entry:** $10 to $24, **Discounts:** multiple event or day passes, **Acts:** national acts, . **Sample day's lineup:** Leo Kottke, the story, John McCutcheon. **Contact:** Tarrytown Music Hall, Kaldenberg and Main Streets, Tarrytown, NY, 914-332-TIXS.


DOO-WOP SHOW AND DANCE, Hempstead, NY
     Late Mar.
     A Cappella and Doo Wop

**Help!** One time only? **Days:** 1. **Hours per day:** 3. **Site:** indoor. Best Western Hotel and Convention Center, 80 Clinton Street. **Admission:** paid. **Daily entry:** $25 to $49, **Secondary genre[s]:** CRCK, **Acts:** national acts, regional acts, local acts. **Sample day's lineup:** Velours, Orioles, Harptones, Five Discs, Stormy Weather. **Contact:** Best Western Hotel and Convention Center, 80 Clinton Street, Hempstead, NY, 718-922-0833.


NIGHT OF LEGENDS, New Rochelle, NY
     Middle Apr.
     A Cappella and Doo Wop

**Help!** One time only? **Days:** 1. **Hours per day:** 3. **Site:** indoor. Palace Nite Club, 518 Main Street. **Admission:** paid. **Daily entry:** $10 to $24, $25 to $49, **Secondary genre[s]:** CRCK, **Acts:** national acts, regional acts, local acts. **Sample day's lineup:** Arlene Smith and The Chantels, Lillian Leach and The Mellows, Yesterday's News, Kenney and Warren, HBJ Trio. **Contact:** Palace Nite Club, 518 Main Street, New Rochelle, NY, 212-307-7171.

WORLD MUSIC FESTIVAL, Schenectady, NY
> Early May
> Variety, Folk and International

One time only. **Days:** 1. **Hours per day:** 8. **Site:** indoor. Proctor's Theater. **Admission:** free. **Secondary genre[s]:** IRSH, SCOT, MLAT, AFRC, OTHR **Acts:** national acts, local acts. **Sample day's lineup:** Patrick Street, Bavarian Barons, Gogova, Flor De Cana, Veena Chandra Ensemble, Anabel and Wild Rose, Kanda Bongo Man, Los Reyes Latinos, Taconic Pipe Band. **Contact:** Second Wind Productions, 55 Loudonwood East, Suite 1, Loudonville, NY 12211, 518-463-5222.

MUSIC EXPO NORTHEAST, Varies, NY
> Early Jun.
> Modern Christian

**Help!** The status of this event, or the whereabouts of its promoter? . **Acts:** regional acts, local acts. **Contact:** Music Expo Northeast, P. O. Box 218, Pine Valley, NY 14872, 607-739-8219.

ART IN ACTION FESTIVAL, Wallkill, NY
> Middle Jun.
> Variety, General

Since 1990. Cancelled for 1995. **Days:** 2. **Hours per day:** 8. **Site:** outdoor. Borden Estate, Route 208. **Admission:** paid. **Daily entry:** under $10, **Secondary genre[s]:** MFOL, OTHR **Contact:** School of Practical Philosophy, 12 East 79th Street, New York, NY 10021, 212-744-0764.

PICK'N AND GRIN'N CAMPING WEEKEND, Cambridge, NY
> Late Jun.
> Traditional Country

Since 1992. See other dates. **Days:** 3. **Hours per day:** 10. **Site:** outdoor. Snuffy's Inn and Campgrounds, Route 22. **Admission:** paid. **Daily entry:** $10 to $24, **Discounts:** multiple event or day passes, advance purchase discounts, **Secondary genre[s]:** BLGS, FDDL, **Acts:** regional acts, local acts. **Sample day's lineup:** Laurie Ingalls and Co., Smokey Greene and The Boys, Al and Kathy Bain. **Contact:** Snuffy's Inn and Campgrounds, Route 22, Cambridge, NY, 518-677-8091.

JVC JAZZ IN WESTCHESTER, Yonkers, NY
> Late Jun. to Early Jul.
> Modern Jazz

See other dates and sites. **Help!** One time only? **Days:** 5. **Hours per day:** 5. **Site:** indoor. Defemio's Restaurant, 600 Tuckahoe Road. **Secondary genre[s]:** TR&B, **Acts:** regional acts, local acts. **Sample day's lineup:** Bob Kindred, John Basile, Noel Forbes, Lynn Seaton, Al Defemio. **Contact:** Defemio's Restaurant, 600 Tuckahoe Road, Yonkers, NY, 914-337-2617.

NEWPORT JAZZ FESTIVAL, Canandaigua, NY
> Late Jun.
> Modern Jazz

Discontinued. See other dates and sites. **Days:** 2. **Hours per day:** 12. **Site:** outdoor. Finger Lakes Performing Arts Center. **Acts:** national acts. **Contact:** Finger Lakes Performing Arts Center, Canandaigua, NY, 716-454-7091.

METALRAGE, Cheektowaga, NY
> Early Jul.
> Hard Rock and Heavy Metal

Since 1993. One time only. **Days:** 1. **Site:** indoor. Blind Mellons, 207 Youngs Road. **Admission:** paid. **Acts:** local acts. **Sample day's lineup:** Manic Jasper, Cheshire Cat, Monarch, God's Children. **Contact:** Blind Mellons, 207 Youngs Road, Cheektowaga, NY, 716-634-4462.

GREAT NORTHEAST COUNTRY JAMBOREE, Batavia, NY
> Middle Jul.
> Modern Country

Since 1994. Cancelled for 1995. **Days:** 3. **Site:** outdoor. Batavia Downs. **Acts:** local acts. **Sample day's lineup:** 10 acts. **Contact:** Genesee County Chamber of Commerce, 220 East Main Street, Batavia, NY 14020, 800-622-2686.

LAKESIDE REGGAE JAM/LAKE CHAMPLAIN WORLD MUSIC FESTIVAL, Plattsburgh, NY
> Middle Jul.
> Reggae, Ska and Caribbean

"Biggest reggae show of the year!" -- Poster. **Help!** The status of this event, or the whereabouts of its promoters? **Days:** 1. **Hours per day:** 10. **Site:** outdoor. Crete Recreational Complex, on the beach. **Admission:** paid. **Daily entry:** under $10, $10 to $24, **Discounts:** advance purchase discounts, **Restrictions:** 2, 4, 10, **Acts:** national acts, local acts. **Sample day's lineup:** Dennis Brown, Lucky Dube, Supercat, Lloyd Parks and We The People Band, Mikey Dread, Lambsbread, Nardo Ranks, Worl-A-Girl, Jah Children, Kokomos, Panashe. **Contact:** Music Festivals, Inc.,, 518-563-3344.

BIG TREE COUNTRY MUSIC FEST, Geneseo, NY
> Late Jul.
> Modern Country

Since 1994. **Help!** The status of this event, or the whereabouts of its promoters? **Days:** 4. . **Acts:** national acts. **Sample day's lineup:** Marty Stuart, Restless Heart.

IRISH FESTIVAL, Tonawanda, NY
> Late Jul.
> Irish

Switching to a carnival in 1995; just one live act on Sunday. **Days:** 3. **Site:** outdoor and indoor. Cardinal O'Hara High School, 39 O'Hara Road. **Admission:** paid. **Daily entry:** under $10, **Acts:** local acts. **Sample lineup:** Danny Justice, The Colleens, The Blarney Bunch, Jerry and Claire McCrudden, Rinca Na Tiarna, others. **Contact:** Cardinal O'Hara High School, 39 O'Hara Road, Tonawanda, NY 14150, 716-695-8091.

NEW ROCHELLE HARBOR FEST, New Rochelle, NY
> Late Jul.
> Variety, General

Since 1993. One time only. **Days:** 3. **Hours per day:** 14. **Site:** outdoor. Five Islands Park. **Restrictions:** 2, **Secondary genre[s]:** MJAZ, CRCK, MR&B, ACAP, OTHR **Acts:** national acts, local acts. **Sample day's lineup:** The Brecker Brothers, Michel Camilo, Strunz and Farah, others. **Contact:** New Rochelle Parks and Recreation Department, New Rochelle, NY, 914-654-2084.

## DRUM CORPS INTERNATIONAL NORTH CHAMPIONSHIPS, Orchard Park, NY
Late Jul.
Drum Corp and Marching Bands

"Competitors...will fill the air with stirring sounds and toe-tapping rhythms guaranteed to bring you to your feet." -- Advertisement. Regionals moved to Canton, OH, but site is hosting 1995's Nationals. **Days:** 1. **Hours per day:** 9. **Site:** outdoor. Rich Stadium. **Admission:** paid. **Daily entry:** $10 to $24, **Discounts:** advance purchase discounts, **Acts:** regional acts, local acts. **Sample day's lineup:** Cavaliers, Cadets of Bergen County, Star of Indiana, Crossmen, Boston Crusaders, Bluecoats, Northern Aurora, Dutch Boy, others. **Contact:** Drum Corps International North Championships, c/o WKBW-TV, 7 Broadcast Plaza, Buffalo, NY 14202, 716-646-5718.

## ROCK-IN THE PARK LIVE MUSIC FESTIVAL, Franklin Square, NY
Late Jul.
Modern Rock and Pop

Since 1993. "Long Island's Lalapalusa." -- Advertisement. **Help!** The status of this event, or the whereabouts of its promoters? **Days:** 1. **Hours per day:** 10. **Site:** indoor. Plattduetsche Park Restaurant and Catering Hall, 1132 Hempstead Turnpike. **Admission:** paid. **Daily entry:** under $10, **Secondary genre[s]:** HRCK, **Acts:** local acts. **Sample day's lineup:** Rising Sun, Kronin, Frank's Pants, SPD, Total Sexual Freedom, Magic Garden, Lung Fish. **Contact:** Plattduetsche Park Restaurant and Catering Hall, 1132 Hempstead Turnpike, Franklin Square, NY, 516-352-5402/354-3131.

## ACOUSTIC MUSIC INDOOR FESTIVAL, Tarrytown, NY
Early Aug.
Modern Folk

Since 1993. One time only. **Days:** 1. **Site:** indoor. Tarrytown Music Hall, Kaldenberg and Main Streets. **Admission:** paid. **Daily entry:** $10 to $24, **Discounts:** multiple event or day passes, **Secondary genre[s]:** TR&B, TFOL, MARI, **Acts:** national acts, local acts. **Sample day's lineup:** Rick Nestler, Tom Chapin, Pete Seeger, Guy Davis, Joe Heukerott, Judy Gorman, Betty and The Baby Boomers, Jan Christensen, Geoff Kauffman, Rita Falbel, Dick Manley, Rik Palieri, Mary Ellen Healy, others. **Contact:** Tarrytown Music Hall, Kaldenberg and Main Streets, Tarrytown, NY, 914-332-TIXS.

## WCBS-FM MEMORIES FAIR AND EXPO, Uniondale, NY
Middle Aug.
A Cappella and Doo Wop

Since 1992. One time only. See other dates and sites. **Days:** 1. **Hours per day:** 8. **Site:** indoor. Nassau Veteran's Memorial Coliseum. **Admission:** paid. **Daily entry:** $10 to $24, **Secondary genre[s]:** CRCK, **Acts:** national acts, regional acts, local acts. **Sample day's lineup:** Jimmy Beaumont and The Skyliners, Frankie Ford, Ray Peterson, The Passions, The Capris, The Marcels, Willie Winfield and The Harptones, The Danleers, The Elegants, The Traditions. **Audio merchandise:** "WCBS-FM 101 History of Rock, The Doo-Wop Era, Parts 1, 2"; "...The 50's, Parts 1, 2"; "...The 60's, Parts 1-5"; "...For Lovers Only" (all on Collectables).. **Contact:** WCBS-FM 101, 51West 52nd Street, NewYork, NY 10019, 914-967-2040.

## ADIRONDACK FOLK/GOSPEL FESTIVAL, Hoosick, NY
Middle Aug.
Traditional Folk

**Help!** The status of this event, or a sample lineup? **Days:** 3. **Site:** indoor. Hoosac School. **Secondary genre[s]:** TGOS, **Acts:** local acts. **Contact:** Adirondack Folk/Gospel Festival, P. O. Box 24, Saratoga Springs, NY 12866, 518-587-4962.

EVIAN MUSIC FESTIVAL, Southampton, NY
> Late Aug. to Early Sep.
> Variety, Jazz and Blues

One time only. **Days:** 6. **Site:** outdoor and indoor. multiple locations. **Admission:** paid. **Daily entry:** $10 to $24, **Secondary genre[s]:** MJAZ, MRCK, TR&B, **Acts:** national acts. **Sample Series Lineup:** Day One: Paul Simon; **Contact:** Evian Music Festival, WWHB-FM 107.1, Hampton Bays, NY.

THRASH BASH, Stanfordville, NY
> Late Aug.
> Hard Rock and Heavy Metal

Since 1992. **Help!** Still ongoing? **Days:** 1. **Site:** outdoor and indoor. Live Wire Cafe. **Admission:** paid. **Daily entry:** under $10, **Acts:** local acts. **Sample day's lineup:** D. I. E., Sorrow, Morpheus, Death Ruin, Chemikill, Decomposed, Monoxide, Dissolve, Implode, Ossuary, others. **Contact:** Vicious Metal Magazine, c/o Live Wire Cafe, Stanfordville, NY, 914-462-8514.

LOCKPORT COUNTRY FEST, Lockport, NY
> Early Sep.
> Modern Country

Since 1993. One time only. **Days:** 1. **Hours per day:** 8. **Site:** indoor. Kenan Arena, Beattie Avenue. **Admission:** paid. **Daily entry:** under $10, **Acts:** local acts. **Sample day's lineup:** Country State Of Mind, Hungry Heart, Nancy Miller Band. **Contact:** Kenan Arena, Beattie Avenue, Lockport, NY, 716-626-5560.

ACOUSTIC BLUES AND HARBOR FESTIVAL, Mount Sinai, NY
> Middle Sep.
> Blues and Traditional R&B

Since 1992. **Help!** One time only? Also, a contact address? **Days:** 1. **Site:** outdoor. Cedar Beach. **Admission:** paid. **Acts:** regional acts, local acts. **Sample day's lineup:** Little Toby Walker and The Rocket, Guy Davis, Backdoor Benny, Mike Schulz Band, Get Lost Jimmy. **Contact:** Acoustic Blues and Harbor Festival, c/o Cedar Beach, Mount Sinai, NY, 516-331-9148.

EMPIRE MUSIC CONFERENCE, Rochester, NY
> Middle Oct.
> Alternative and College Rock

Since 1992. Discontinued in 1994. May resume if sponsorship materializes. **Days:** 3. **Site:** indoor. Genesee Plaza Downtown Convention Center, plus 18 showcase locations. **Admission:** paid. **Daily entry:** $25 to $49, $50 and over. **Discounts:** advance purchase discounts, **Secondary genre[s]:** MRCK, HRCK, RAP, TR&B, **Acts:** national acts, local acts. **Sample day's lineup:** Les Paul, Begonia, Dr. Smith, Daisy Chain, Nerve Circus, Dreaming Out Loud, Eggmen, Tom Acousti and The Happy Bus, Dragonflys, Kingdom Power Glory, Woody Dodge, Still Kickin', Dick Leschorn, Kama Sutra, Good Question, Medicine Man, It's Not Us, Krystal Sin, Eargasm, Bleed Christian, Scarecrow, Vicious Circle, Tommy Grasso, Imaginary Few, Joan Burton Band, Mata Hari, Attraction, Pat Simone, VJ and Friends, Doc Apple, Maximum Concept, Mafi Yo, GVC, Masterplan, Ghetto Prince, Meen Greene, Racin' Time, Saddletramp, Emerald City, Neo Neptune, Yam Cat, Rule, Doomsday, Humongous, Marked For Pain, Scepter, Monolith, Mother Down, Shattered Innocence, Red Hush, Beat Generation, Raven Ballett, Rhythm Method, Technique, Baron Pryde, Peg Leg, Critical Mass, Flashflood. **Audio merchandise:** "EMC I, II" (self-produced and distributed). **Contact:** Empire Music Conference, Ltd., 275 Lake Avenue, Rochester, NY 14608, 716-254-6200 **or:** Pilato Entertainment Group, P. O. Box 17775, Rochester, NY 14617, 716-671-2206.

DEATH BASH, Rochester, NY
      Late Oct. to Early Nov.
      Hard Rock and Heavy Metal

"Halloween Vampyre Night...They stalk the night, searching for souls to bring into the Abyss." -- Advertisement. **Help!** One time only? **Days:** 3. **Site:** indoor. Abyss, 240 South Avenue. **Admission:** paid. **Acts:** local acts. **Sample day's lineup:** Empty Grave, Blind Harvest, Jigsaw, Wethead. **Contact:** The Abyss, 240 South Avenue, Rochester, NY, 716-325-5240.


SWING DANCE AND TRADITIONAL JAZZ WEEKEND, South Fallsburg, NY
      Late Oct. to Early Nov.
      Modern Jazz

See other dates. **Help!** Still ongoing? **Days:** 3. **Site:** indoor. Pines Resort Hotel. **Admission:** paid. **Daily entry:** $50 and over. **Discounts:** group sale discounts, **Secondary genre[s]:** TJAZ, **Acts:** regional acts, local acts. **Contact:** Swing Dance and Traditional Jazz Weekend, Pines Resort Hotel, South Fallsburg, NY 12779, 800-36-PINES.

~     ~     ~

# New York City

*Iris y Franklyn, Carnival in New York.*

# Greenwich Village's Singer-Songwriters

**FAST FOLK REVUE**, Manhattan, NYC
> Late January
> Modern Folk
> ***Attended***

**FURNALD FOLK FEST**, Manhattan, NYC
> Early April
> Modern Folk
> ***Attended***

**GREENWICH VILLAGE FOLK FESTIVAL**, Manhattan, NYC
> Early October
> Modern Folk
> ***Attended***

**SHELTER: THE NEW YORK SINGER-SONGWRITER FESTIVAL**, Manhattan, NYC
> Middle October
> Modern Folk

The light on modern folk music in New York City is always threatening to flicker out. It's a cold, cruel world here, you see. Manhattan's real estate is some of the world's most expensive, which puts club owners under the gun to book bands with draws who drink. "Hey, whadduhya' think I look like," you can just imagine these grizzled vets barking to yearning aspirants at their doorsteps, guitars in hand, chins upon their chests, "a freakin' charity?!"

Without many places to play, Big Apple folkies have little to offer their out-of-town brethren from more accommodating neighboring markets in the quid-pro-quo which characterizes folk-music bookings. Nor does it help that it's damn difficult to keep a car in New York City, thus further isolating them from the regional scene at-large. All that remains is to hole-up in East Village tenements and churn out the edgier, angrier, wittier material which oft' characterizes the scene.

Ah, but still they come as they have since the days "B. D." (Before Dylan).

Why? Despite the obstacles, New York City remains the music-media capital of the country. There's always the hope for young artists of being discovered by that influential critic from the *New York Times, Village Voice, Rolling Stone, Spin, College Music Journal, Billboard*, or what-have-you. One review from these national publications just might leapfrog you past the folk music press bunkered elsewhere and into the view of major labels, which are all headquartered here as well. It's no accident that many of the recent breakthroughs in the genre have happened to such New York City-associated artists as Suzanne Vega, Shawn Colvin, John Gorka (for years, a bi-monthly commuter from Allentown), and others plugging their crossover abilities into this dynamic. Compare their combined record sales with New England's top three folkies, if you will, and you can see the potential upside.

However, you don't have to wait for the select few to "go gold" in order to hear what's percolating beneath the surface in Gotham, folk-wise.

Here are two small festivals that effectively showcase a large quantity of locals (plus several regional and national guests) representative of the scene: the FAST FOLK REVUE ['REVUE] and the GREENWICH VILLAGE FOLK FESTIVAL [GREENWICH VILLAGE']. And in the former, you'll witness a model format for how modern folk music should present itself, but doesn't — selectively programmed, broadly varied, fully produced, and crisply paced in a top venue for maximum crossover appeal. (Sigh!) I should warn you, though, that I've caught each event in good years and not-so-good years, so quality can vary depending upon the booking inspiration and talent pool available to perform gratis.

**Festival Review I**  The 'REVUE's sponsor is New York City's Fast Folk Musical Magazine, Inc., a nonprofit begun 12 years ago by longtime folksinger Jack Hardy that produces a semi-regular magazine enclosing compilation discs of new folk songs. Want a sample roster of the nearly 600 artists who've been recorded over the years? Well, here's one:

- Suzanne Vega, Shawn Colvin, John Gorka, Christine Lavin, David Massengill, Rod MacDonald, Richard Meyer, Frank Christian, Erik Frandsen, Lucy Kaplanski and Hardy, himself.

Pretty impressive, huh? Right there you're looking at two Grammies and at least as many gold records, eight label deals, gifted entertainers, creative stylists, expressive singers, a few exquisite pickers, and a bountiful crop of songwriters' songwriters.

What's even more impressive is that this is the lineup of the first 'REVUE, January 29, 1983, back when all were struggling unknowns, unrecorded (except for Fast Folk compilations) and unable to land even an opening gig at what is still considered the premier club for acoustic roots musicians in New York City, The Bottom Line. (In fact, Hardy chuckles at remembering having to convince its owner, Allan Pepper, to keep Vega on the first bill — Pepper concerned that Vega didn't even have a following in her own hometown.) Only Hardy had played the club before as an opening act.

Yet to cite the extraordinary role of Fast Folk in fostering this folk-music boom-let throughout the '80s would be to miss the point. Hardy notes, "We've done better than any A&R department in this country at spotting talent" (as a generation of stars received their first recorded exposure on Fast Folk compilations, including Michelle Shocked, Tracy Chapman, Suzy Boggus, Lyle Lovett and many, many others), but insists that star-making is someone else's job. He's more interested in nurturing the songwriting process for future stars and nonstars, alike, and in his consuming objective — stalking the good song.

Hardy, a genial host with a compadre's welcoming grin, a shock of wispy gray hair, and the lived-in wardrobe of a college professor on his day off, offers his core philosophy:

- "My definition of folk music (which you're always forced to define) is where the song is more important than the singer or more important than the style, even. The song is what is sacred. Once you choose some good songs, everything else is dressing. Then you try to put that song in the best possible light."

In that regard, Hardy's attitude is not unlike Nashville's. Indeed, he finds much of Nashville's material folk music ("country-flavored folk music with different dressing," he muses) and considers the two art forms more united than separated in being song-driven. He recalls Del Bryant, Vice President of BMI and son of the couple who wrote many hits for The Everly Brothers, coming backstage to him after the 10th Anniversary 'REVUE to comment on "...a fairly esoteric song, 'The Child,' a mythological piece of mine based upon some elaborate Bardic riddle. He raved about it and asked for a copy of it. You don't get any more Nashville than [Bryant]," Hardy observes, "but a good song is a good song."

The 'REVUE format actually owes itself to a visit Hardy and a companion paid to Nashville's Grand Ol' Opry in the early '70s. His friend was writing an article for *National Geographic*, and as a result, Hardy gained backstage access to everywhere. He was especially impressed by the 'Opry's fast-flowing format and the extraordinary professionalism on display where performers had to shine on a dime for everything: solos, duets, band numbers, even singing the commercials.

You'll find a typical 'REVUE similar in length, therefore, in presenting up to 18 performers, including a few current stars, several future stars, and some genuine novices for one song apiece. They're likewise supported by a first-class backing band and/or harmony singers, as their song requires, and introduced with affectionate insight. (Lavin, Julie Gold and Richard Meyer did an especially good job in rotation at the 10th Anniversary 'REVUE I caught.) All join together for off-beat group numbers that generally book-end each set.

Mostly, you'll hear a careful sequence of fascinating, often funny, songs targeted to move you in some fashion. Social commentary ("songs with something to say," as Hardy describes) is a particular emphasis. A few may make you wrinkle your brow, but none, nor the pacing, will make you yawn. "I like to look at it from 'What's in it for the audience,'" Hardy offers:

- "If everyone's up there for just one song, even if someone doesn't like one song, it's only there for one song, and you're onto the next one.

"The New York audience, especially the size of The Bottom Line, is a very sophisticated audience. There may be stuff that goes over real well in a little church basement coffee-house that isn't going to go over well in this type of situation. The New York audience is tougher, but it's also a good audience. They expect more and if you deliver it to them, they'll respond."

His pacing? "I usually start off with a big group number, an uptempo, usually," Hardy explains:

- "Then we might seque-way into a more political thing, which is slower. A lot of people are still getting seated. Then you pretty much have a two-to-three-song span where audience attention is heightened. That's where I try to cameo a couple of things I'm trying to put forward.

"Then you have to back off a bit — give them a little humor so you don't run them into the ground. There are a couple of other spots where, like just before intermission, you generally like to place something heavier. You try to balance it and keep it from bogging down."

Hardy particularly disparages "hootenanies" ("where everyone ends up singing 'Amazing Grace' again," he groans), as well as other "self-indulgent" formats that put the interests of the performers first. "I try to encompass all different types of songwriting in a very varied format," he counters, "to have a balance of humorous songs, of group numbers, and of political material, so there's something for everyone. You pick the song, then you pick the people to sing the song. Sometimes it's the artists themselves."

Being loyal to the song, not it's writer, is the 'REVUE's orientation. "Here's a place for that one good song," Hardy states. "It might not be a young performer. It might be someone who is an amateur, in the true sense of the word, who loves what they're doing and has no intention of doing it professionally, [but] may have written one gem of a song that would be absolutely lost if there were no place like this to put it."

Hardy's selections ("The buck stops here," he explains, "because the quickest way you can ruin something like this is to have a committee run it.") emerge from the creative cauldron which is at the core of the Fast Folk experience: their weekly songwriter's exchange, which has taken place most Thursday nights at Hardy's third-floor tenement walk-up on Houston Street for nearly 20 years. Here, 15 to 30 songwriters at all different stages in their careers converge for potluck meals and evenings of sharp-eared critique. The only rules are to bring a song you've started that week and no showboating. Colvin, Vega, Shocked, Gorka, Lavin — all spent years apprenticing here.

Given the astounding list of performers who've honed their craft at these sessions and gone onto Fast Folk recordings, 'REVUE's, and even stardom, you'd think Fast Folk would be more of a star itself. After all, Will Ackerman recruited several Fast Folk veterans for his High Street imprint, utilized a few of the same techniques (e.g., compilation discs, group shows, etc.), then just sold his Windham Hill label to BMG for $16 million.

"I don't get bogged down in the star system," Hardy responds:

- "I get much more gratification, personally, when I can hear a good song that's written by a complete nobody, or somebody who may never be ready for prime time, and cause that song to be recorded and in a show like this (maybe not with them singing it).

  "I've always looked at myself as a catalyst. I look at Fast Folk very politically — as a means to an end, not as an end in itself. Unfortunately, it's very collectable, like stamps, or fine wine, but that would be a misuse. We don't do it to be an archive of what happened. We do it to make things happen."

Hardy smiles, then cautions in his trademark, soft rasp, "I'm not ready to write any epithets."

**Artist Mini-Reviews**   'REVUE's are unique in one other aspect. Normally, memorable festival moments involve performers' entire sets. Here, however, raves follow individual songs. Hang by the bar after a show, and you'll likely hear Dave Van Ronk growling to Fred Koller about a particular lyric, or Louise Taylor exclaiming to Wendy Beckerman over someone else's composition. Usually the song and its singer are one and the same, but not always.

Here are two of my highlights from recent years.

Buddy Mondlock. I've only heard Mondlock's "Cats Of The Colosseum" once — at '94's 'REVUE — but it's reflective mood is easily summoned. Mondlock represents the type of artist I've really gravitated toward since writing for *The Performing Songwriter*. As a Nashville resident from Indiana, who's written for Garth Brooks and others, he delivers the personalization, emotion, and accessibility customary from Music Row tunesmiths. For his own performing, though, he's also capable of the sophisticated impressionism espoused by the 'REVUE crew. This selection, sung by the thin mustachioed Mondlock in a soft tenor, effectively straddled both camps.

As I recall, the song tells the tale of an amused American tourist to Rome who gets waylaid by Gypsies, pickpocketed, and left disoriented among the winding streets in the noonday sun — all the while soaking up the ancient atmosphere like another glass of table red. The smooth tone reflects the warmth of the day, while the circular structure mirrors the alcohol-induced dizziness felt by the protagonist. The oft-repeated title refrain illustrates the knowing ways of Gypsies who prey upon unwitting travelers much like cats foraging for mice amidst this antiquity. It makes a valid point about Western folly, but gently, and not at the expense of the victim's own willing culpability. Rich and evocative.

Steve Key. This stocky twenty-something, who founded the Bronx's Uptown Coffeehouse before relocating to Washington, DC, was unable to make another 'REVUE I attended in '92, so his stunt-double, Josh Joffen, delivered "Record Time."

Key's upbeat anthem is one of the few topical numbers I've heard in recent years that I can actually stand. Unlike most others from this notorious Achilles heel of folk music, it believably inhabits the emotions of a real human being, not some shallow brushstroke like the oft-cliché'd "corrupt politician" or "greedy businessman." In this case, it's the workaday protagonist who feels modern life's mercenary pace is passing by him and his traditional values. The lyric also refrains from preaching, rather choosing to build up to its central point from small details that ring true, such as the three speeds of vinyl records "...warped and scratched and out-of-date/33, 45, 78." You feel the issue because you experience it unfold visually and tactily, not because you're told to via sweeping proclamations.

My notes from that night read: "a nice song with nice hooks...dog-eared charm...a down-home winner." You may recognize "Record Time" on Kathy Mattea's subsequent album and therein lies the tale. Folksinger Richard Meyer, who produced this particular 'REVUE, recalls:

- "We were putting together the 10th Anniversary show. Just like I kept a list of songs, I also asked people each year if they knew any great songs. I asked Josh Joffen to be on the show. He said, 'Have you heard this Steve Key song?' He brought it down. We were looking for some group songs — the hardest part about the show is finding really good, melodic, uptempo group songs — and I thought it was a great song.

"Steve was only available one night, I think it was Friday. The other nights it was performed by Josh and Tom Meltzer. One of the nights Julie Gold had asked Kathy Mattea to come by as a guest because they were good friends, and Kathy had covered one of Julie's songs ['From A Distance' on *Time Passes By*]. Kathy played 'Where Have You Been' in the first set then stuck around during intermission just to talk.

"On her way out she heard Steve's song open the second set. She apparently got knocked out, called Allan Pepper at The Bottom Line the next day, and said, 'I'd love to have that song!' We arranged to get her a tape within a day or two, and she put it on her next album! If people were to listen back through the Fast Folk catalog, there are probably a hundred songs of that quality that could be covered."

~     ~     ~

I don't know if there were any similar professional connections made at '92's GREENWICH **Festival** VILLAGE', but I personally connected with a host of strong performances from many artists then **Review II** new to me:

- John Herald, one of the pioneering "citybillies" from his days jamming with fellow Greenbriar Boys in the adjacent Washington Square Park during the '50s, revved the crowd with guns-ahead strumming and a convincing high-lonesome tenor on "I'm Saved" and "Ruby";

- Frank Christian, guitarist for Nanci Griffith on that year's tour, adjusted his French cuffs, reared back his beret, and dug into a pair of tough fingerpickers (one a children's number, "Dancing In The Kitchen") that summoned the agility and intensity of Richard Thompson's technique;

- Mark Johnson, who's had songs covered by The Roches and Dave Edmunds, combined with Frankie Lee's harmony vocals for a winning pair of spirited, melodic pop tunes — "Fire" and "Real True Love";

- Danny Kalb, an original member of seminal '60s blues-rockers, The Blues Project, conducted a Delta blues clinic with an utterly soulful "So Sweet" and "Dead Letter Blues," exhibiting every bit the expressiveness on vocals and guitar as the late Son House, from whose hands he learned the latter number;

- Jackie Washington Landron, another '60s icon, was summoned down from his acting gig in Boston to impress mightily with the night's most extravagant vocal, an acrobatic blues reading of "Red Riding Hood."

Finally, I came to appreciate the buzz surrounding contemporary Boston duo, "the story." In the hubbub of various festival settings where I'd caught them previously, their lyric and harmonic subtleties had always evaded me, their artsy presentation striking me as self-conscious and somewhat limp.

Here, however, in the faded glory of historic Washington Square Church with its crisp acoustics, while surrounded by hundreds of hushed followers, this attractive pair simply came alive. Their vocals projected strongly and soulfully on "So Much Mine," a veritable symphony of bittersweet dissonances, contrapuntal dynamics, and harmonic grace notes. I found it original and literate to a fault. Their "Dog Dreams" then charmed with an amusing canine point-of-view, replete with choreography. Even from just two songs, I came away fully appreciating what all the hype had been about.

Credit longtime folksinger Rod MacDonald for their inclusion. He's the "artistic-vision guy," as he describes himself, responsible for performer invitations and relations. The technical aspects are handled by a Stealth committee of three others who choose to keep a low public profile so as not to become swamped with inquiries for what's intended more as an informal local showcase. Besides, that's MacDonald's role. Most of the roughly 35 artists on the free five-hour bill represent his individual contacts.

Artists are allotted two songs apiece of their own choosing and invited to bring whatever musical backing they desire. Since it's a charity freebie, most appear solo. That's not to say they give it anything less than their best shot since they're playing before their peers and one of the bigger crowds they'll likely experience that year in New York City (aside from the 'Revue, of course). The two-tune limit also prompts them to go for the gusto. Let's put it this way: '92's Greenwich Village' was as good as I've seen four of the above five acts perform since.

From the fan's perspective, the setting is great. Musicians occupy the stage before an ornately-carved sacristy fronting towering brass organ pipes. Visuals are spare, but exalted. Comfort certainly beats The Bottom Line, as you rest in wooden pews lined with red mohair cushions. Though variety and pacing is not quite as tightly-arranged as the 'Revue's, it's still better than most other modern folk-music festivals I've been to, that's for sure. The best part is that so many artists hang out beside the stage or back by the record concessions. This affords you opportunities to meet-and-greet — another relative rarity on the circuit.

"Well '87 was the first year," MacDonald recalls of Greenwich Village's origins. "It was just an idea I always had wanted to do."

His friend and fellow committee member, Gerry Hinson, secured a permit for a baseball field, but rain that day forced MacDonald to put-up his own money on the spot to rent Washington Square Church. "And it's been there ever since, except for a couple of years when we did it at New York University," says MacDonald. He's subsequently gotten local sponsors each year to help him break even. Any excess income he derives from sponsorships, donations, or royalties from the three live recordings made (two by Gadfly Records; one an issue of Fast Folk) have gone toward the event, now incorporated as a non-profit organization.

"I've always thought of this festival as, and I've even put it in quotes a couple of times, 'the gift to the community,'" MacDonald reflects:

- "It's kind of like the community of folksingers gets together and plays a free concert for the community audience that wants to come. We don't spend any money on advertising; we don't turn it into a hype situation. We don't pay any of the artists, so everybody who's there wants to be there. That's the point of it."

In its looseness, Greenwich Village' is positioned as an alternative to the 'Revue'. "That's a deliberate choice on our part to keep it the kind of casual community event, as opposed to turning it into a slick entertainment venture," cites MacDonald:

- "I've been in almost every ['Revue'] except the last couple because I've been out of the country a couple of times. But the philosophy of Fast Folk is that the editor and the producer of the show pick the songs and the artists to do the songs, which I think works for Fast Folk, but we didn't want to get into that.

  "What we try to do is, we're interested in giving the public a taste of the people who are actively out working on their music in the club scene, both locally and nationally. So we try to have a cross-section of that kind of stuff. In other words, we basically ask somebody to be in the show because they're playing around a lot locally. And then we just say to them, 'Do a two-song set, you know, do whatever you do,' and give them a time frame to work with, and that's the trick. We don't really think it's our job to tell them what to play."

MacDonald's most treasured acceptance was his first — from Richie Havens:

- "When I first called Richie and asked him to play, we had never done it before. This was the very first one, and I had nothing to really sell him on it. I had to say, 'Richie, would you consider appearing at this event?' You know, it's the first annual Greenwich Village'. I know there's never been one, I don't know if anybody will be there, but you're the guy I'd like to have close the show.' And he said to me, 'I'm there, man. I wouldn't miss it for the world. This is history in the making, and this is a wonderful idea, you know?'

  "When he said, 'I wouldn't miss it for the world,' that told me that from a performer's point-of-view, I wasn't alone in thinking that this was a great idea. ...That was kind of like my touchstone. At the time I was playing a lot of gigs with Richie as his opening act, and I really admire Richie, so getting that kind of feedback from him meant a lot to me. He's a great performer, he's a wonderful guy, and I'll tell you, he really loved the idea of the festival being a community-type thing.

"That felt like, to me, we're on the right track."

You've read my GREENWICH VILLAGE' highlights, above. Here are some of MacDonald's:

**Artist Mini-Reviews**

- "Oh, every year there's always, like, ten songs that blow me away. I could tell you my own personal highlights, definitely. We had Maggie Roche from The Roches performing solo one year. She did a song from their very first Columbia album called 'George' and it was extraordinary. That's certainly one of my most vivid memories.

  "We had Richie Havens a couple of times and one of the times he played a version of James Brown's song, 'Things We Used To Do Sure Don't Do No More.' Richie started jamming with himself and [had] people just kind-of hypnotized. He just started jamming with the guitar by himself, just going off as he does so well, and everybody just started kind of drifting away. It was really beautiful."

I prompt MacDonald about Peter Yarrow's dramatic take on "Day Is Done" that Fast Folk recorded from '88's GREENWICH VILLAGE'. "Yeah, that was great," he responds. "That was a real highlight. That was one of the major moments, no doubt about it.

"We've [also] had a lot of lesser known people do really beautiful stuff," MacDonald continues:

- "We had a guy named Pat Kilbride last year who played with the Kips Bay Ceili Band. He came in, and just sat down, and played his guitar, and sang. He was terrific. I thought he was the hit of the show in '93.

  "We also have had Lucy Kaplansky, who has hardly sung in public for the last few years. We had Shawn Colvin in two or three of our early shows, and she sang one song called 'Ricochet' that I don't think she's ever recorded. That was really beautiful one year. And we had Cliff Eberhardt and Shawn doing a duet one year. We had Suzanne Vega one year. We had Christine Lavin, Richie Havens, myself, and an entire cast of people singing 'Downtown' for an encore one time. We had Odetta leading us all in 'This Land Is Your Land' one year for another encore. I mean, all of that stuff is fun."

Good news! Hardy has just signed a lease at 41 North Moore Street in trendy TriBeCa to operate a Fast Folk Cafe. It will house a 74-seat performance space for national and local acoustic artists as well as office space for the musical magazine. At last, New York City folkies will have their own hang-out, hopefully recreating the ambience of the defunct Speakeasy from which Fast Folk and its 'REVUE originally sprung.

**Attendance Tip**

You say you want yet another window into the New York City folk singer-songwriter scene, this one a little smaller, a little looser, a little younger? Well, the FURNALD FOLK FEST is even more of a sleeper than its two parent festivals, above, though it features many names in common.

**See Also**

This "Wild and Sober Event," as the flyer promises, invades Columbia University each spring and is run by the same student group that produces free folk music concerts throughout the school year at the Postcrypt Coffeehouse. Located in the basement of St. Paul's Chapel, their series has been operating continuously for 30 years — one of the longest such tenures in the country. Two concerts are held most winter weekends in a stone-lined, barrel-vaulted supplies room, lending it the character of a bomb shelter. Indeed, you'll feel like you're bunkering down in WWII Britain, cozily waiting out another Nazi bombing to the strains of one gifted young artist or another.

The festival occupies a different venue, though one no less ambient or attractive. Performers set up before the fireplace in the comfortable lobby of Furnald Hall, one of those classic Ivy League-style spaces adorned with marble tile, stained glass and inlaid wood panelling. Maybe a hundred or so students cluster themselves around on the floor and prepare for two straight evenings of full sets running from 6:00 p.m. to 1:00 a.m. It's hard to imagine experiencing musicians any more intimately or informally, short of hiring them to play in your own living room.

I'm tempted to describe this year's lineup as the "Dave Seitz Festival," since many of the headliners had been produced by this Fast-Folk alumni, either for Seitz' own start-up label, 1-800-Prime-CD, or for someone else's (Shanachie, Rounder, etc.). Most of these had their moments, though there were also promising outsiders as well (including Lisa Loeb, who's gone on to sign a reputed seven-figure deal with Geffen Records). Here's one:

The Low Road. This Philadelphia-based acoustic quintet was poised, personable and tightly-arranged with much stylistic variety between and within songs. They attractively segued alternative rock, folk and jazz styles in their musical mixes, while alternating hometown sentiments with those of a more foreboding nature. 'Kept you off-guard. Los Lobos' Steve Berlin has since taken a shine to this young band, had them open a number of tour dates, and helped them land an independent label deal. Look for the 'Road coming soon to a market near you!

Finally, 1994 witnessed a promising development — SHELTER: THE FIRST NEW YORK SINGER-SONGWRITER FESTIVAL. This top-drawer benefit showcase of the national, regional and local scenes was presented by Putumyo World Music and recorded live for commercial re-issuance. It and the record label are both outgrowths of Putumyo, a "world-beat" apparel importer with over 700 outlets nationwide, as well as several of its own retail stores in Manhattan. Over the years, President Dan Storper would put his music on the store turntables, then watch how certain combinations of genres, styles, tempos and such would cause sales to rise or fall. "Hmmm," Storper mused, and, lo', a brand extension was born from his savvy tinkering.

Storper's first singer-songwriter compilation sold almost 30,000 copies — a remarkable achievement, considering 80% came via Putumyo's alternative channel of gift stores, clothing stores and boutiques. This success emboldened Storper to not only rent out Carnegie Hall for this affair, but hand-pick the lengthy lineup, as well as which songs he wanted performed and recorded. Shades of the 'REVUE! I've no word on whether SHELTER' is ongoing, but the word, "FIRST," as well as Storper's hands-on involvement and financial resources, suggest that it is.

~     ~     ~

# Manhattan's New Music Scene

**BANG ON A CAN FESTIVAL**, Manhattan, NYC
    Middle March to Early May
    Avant Garde and New Music
    ***Attended***

**ROULETTE CONCERT SERIES/LE SALON ROULETTE**, Manhattan, NYC
    Middle March
    Avant Garde and New Music

**EXPERIMENTAL INTERMEDIA FESTIVAL WITH NO FANCY NAME**, Manhattan, NYC
    Early April to Late April
    Avant Garde and New Music

**ROULETTE CONCERT SERIES/MIXOLOGY FESTIVAL**, Manhattan, NYC
    Late April to Early May
    Avant Garde and New Music
    ***Attended***

**AMERICAN FESTIVAL OF MICROTONAL MUSIC**, Manhattan, NYC
    Middle September to Early November
    Avant Garde and New Music
    ***Attended***

**EXPERIMENTAL INTERMEDIA FOUR COUNTRY FESTIVAL**, Manhattan, NYC
    Early December to Late December
    Avant Garde and New Music

**Introduction**

When I mentioned to my friend, Andy, a classically-trained composer/pianist, that I was planning to include avant-garde and new music festivals in this book — but not "classical" events — he replied, "You're crazy! You can't really understand this stuff unless you're familiar with the classical references these people are all quoting." Fair comment, though I didn't believe not being deeply schooled in new music precluded enjoying it, especially as many of its practitioners are now intersecting with more popular musical scenes (i.e., Kronos Quartet teaming up with Elvis Costello).

I first stumbled upon these 20th century explorers while a college art student. Knowing how most recognized art movements have sprung from communities of artists, I was curious to hear what musicians of different periods were doing in relation to their visual colleagues. Accordingly, I could quickly relate on that epochal level to what many composers were attempting. At least I was stretching my ears for when I returned to my popular listening interests.

I'll admit that a good many pieces I'd unearth in the listening library went down like cold cod liver oil. Twelve-toners were not my cup of tea. But once I'd found a few folks to suit my tastes — American proponents like Copland, Thompson, Bernstein, Harrison; tape manipulators like Dodge; microtonalists like Xenakis, Takemitsu; minimalists like Reilly, Reich, Glass; iconoclasts like Cage, Partch, Nancarrow — I was hooked.

My interest has remained dormant at times, but now it's amply revived from discovering these three fine, intimate, unpretentious affairs poking around my "downtown" neighborhood. It's also been stoked by wonderful conversations with their respective spokespeople, all of whom are directly accessible at their events (another bonus of new music festivals over most classical ones).

I put my friend's challenge to each spokesperson. Here's what they offered for novice listeners like me.

Bette Snapp, Publicist for the BANG ON A CAN FESTIVAL [BANG ON A CAN'], and a classically trained violinist herself:

- "We have always cultivated an audience of serious people who want to be exposed to new things. Our audience comes from theater, dance, performance art. They're probably on gallery mailing lists. They are very interested in art and what is new in the art world, and perceive the music world the same way in which the most exciting thing is going to see someone's new play, or new show! And that hasn't been the way it is in [classical] music — 'the latest' has been the thing that kept people away. These people want this kind of exposure and they don't have degrees in musicology. They don't have that kind of education, and they don't read program notes because we don't really have program notes.

  "We've never had program notes. Now that we are at Lincoln Center there is a 'Stage Bill.' We had to put something in there, and so we developed this series of conversations with a writer named Deborah Artman. She talks to the performers and the composers and asks them questions about their music, and the way they play the music that they play, and why they play it that way. You have a composer talking about how the mountains in Vermont have always been influential and so this mountain goat piece is a result of those summers in the mountains. There's not any of this kind of strict analysis. It's still the idea that you don't have to know a thing about the piece to enjoy the piece.

  "The whole idea [is] you come in, your ears are opening, your mind is clear, and you're going to listen to music for pleasure."

Johnny Reinhard, Founder of the AMERICAN FESTIVAL OF MICROTONAL MUSIC ['MICROTONAL'] and a classically trained composer for his own virtuoso bassoon playing (Newport Classics Records):

- "I don't think you're ever wasting your time pursuing information like this. You get closer and closer to the truth. These things all interrelate; they all have tendrals going into each other.

  "What's classical about my stuff is that I happened to have been trained classically. So I can put in roots that a person who is well versed in classical can listen to and find sustenance, and at the same time, I can write 'June' — another piece which could be done in a jazz club even though it's completely written out and featured on the bassoon festival as classical work. It's the categories that are most damaging. We use the word 'inter-stylistics.' My Word Perfect program still brings it up like it doesn't exist as a word."

Jim Staley, Co-Founder of the ROULETTE FESTIVALS [ROULETTE'] and a classically trained composer for his own trombone improvising (Rift, Lumina and Nonesuch Records):

- "Of course [you don't need to know all the classical references]. That's part of the difference here. There are a lot of levels to deal with music on, and while there might be references, those are incidental. There are some books you could read that you might not pick up all the references, but that doesn't mean you can't get a basic, or in-depth, understanding of what someone is talking about. Sometimes references are embellishments.

  "I think all the composers I deal with, and my attitude, is anybody can deal with what we're doing. I don't think the composers entirely understand what they are getting at and that's part of the reason for doing it. And that means everybody is on equal footing; everybody has equal chance of coming to terms with what happens.

  "All these [composers] are trying to reach out to people. They are not trying to entertain people, but trying to engage people. If people come curious and asking questions with what they hear, they can answer a lot of them themselves. But they have to come with open mind to these things, like [being] curious and concerned. They are not going to like everything, but you can learn a lot from stuff you don't like."

Staley laughs, which is its own reminder not to come uptight and expecting every piece to be a miracle, but to ease into the familial camaraderie proffered by all three events. Tomorrow's mainstream is today's cutting edge, so go hear what the 21st century might sound like. I can assure you, too, that there's humor where they're bound.

Bang On a Can' may have been the most recent of these three festivals, but it's certainly achieved the highest profile. In '93 it completed its odyssey through a variety of small spaces by ascending to the tony reaches of Lincoln Center for the Performing Arts. In '94 Bang On a Can' even went to Lenox, Massachusetts, to kick off the Tanglewood Festival of Contemporary Music (see chapter), as well as to the Meltdown Festival at the South Bank, London's equivalent of Lincoln Center. World watch out!

**Festival Review I**

Lost was some of the funky intimacy enjoyed from squeezing 100 or so people into a condemned warehouse (e.g., R. A. P. P. Arts Center one year), as was its previously concentrated week-long format in favor of a three-evening series spread over three months. Alas. But Bang On a Can's artistic character remains intact, as does the spirit and value exemplified by its trademark all-day "Marathon" from which it sprung nine years ago. What's more, all three evenings sold out! When's the last time you heard a new music series do that, or refer to itself as "unstoppable, sexy and loud?"

Bang On a Can' was begun in '87 by its three composers/curators, Michael Gordon, Julia Wolfe and David Lang. As the *Village Voice*'s Kyle Gann explains in his liner notes for the festival's first recorded anthology, *Bang On a Can Live, Volume One* (CRI), the varied "downtown" scene from which they sprung was a reaction to waning minimalism of the '70s. Of course, there'd begun tangential explorations of jazz, rock, electronics, spoken-word, performance art and what-have-you. Gann also mentions divergent new-music interests in form, dissonance, or tonality with the first festival's selections. He concludes, however, that "rhythm, not harmony, was the structural basis."

Although I wasn't conscious of this characteristic as I attended past Bang On a Can's, a rhythmic foundation helps explain why these works connected with my baby-boomer musical mentality in ways that some ascetic LPs from my college listening days didn't. They weren't all loud, certainly, but most moved — even rocked on occasion.

Still, attempting to categorize and define the music is not what Bang On a Can' is all about. It's more about experiencing new music in an unpretentious manner for those of us who were raised in blue-jean clubs, not black-tuxedo'd halls. Taking the club analogy further...

First, there's open seating and hand-stamped re-entry as you'd find in clubs. Prior to '93 there wasn't even advance sales. Next, there's work from famous mentors to which the festival pays homage, like Cage, Carter, Feldman, and Shapey. Call them "headliners," though they're often "new" to this audience, much like B. B. King and Muddy Waters were to Bill Graham's Fillmore audiences back in the '60s.

"All of us who have been to contemporary music concerts and have listened to wonderful composers like [Elliot] Carter performed, there's always this kind of reverence feeling in the concert hall," Snapp says, "but when Carter's 'Duo' was done at The Kitchen last year, this audience didn't know from reverence! I mean, they cheered, they whistled, they thought this was fabulous. They had the same kind of response for the Carter 'Duo' that they did for the 'Guitars and Poets' concert, which was really way-out, bizarre, weird."

Third, there's the bulk of work from younger composers in varying stages of career development. Call them "opening acts." Fourth, tthere's even the equivalent of "open mics" in which the three curators solicit new entries at large for showcasing. Each year the committee screens over 400 such "demo tapes," selecting several unknown composers for what most likely are their first major performances.

"It's a lot of music," Snapp remarks of the submission deluge:

- "And every one of those tapes is listened to, every single one! The artistic directors are fervent in that effort. They have incredible stamina when it comes to listening, and they do marathon listening sessions. The tapes are submitted through the American Music Center, and we have a substantial number of tapes here of pieces we want to program and just haven't had a chance to program. [But] every year there are some composers on the 'MARATHON' who we know absolutely nothing about; who are there solely from the listening sessions."

Finally, there's often the composers on-hand to explain their pieces in layman's terms -- no "live performers-dead composers" syndrome of mainstream classical concerts, nor the "academic speak" of many new music programs. Audience rapport and humor reigns, hopefully as you'd find in clubs. "Our happiest moment is when we have a concert and all the composers are there. That is great," Snapp exclaims, citing the role of 'Meet the Composer' in funding the occasions:

- "After all, that's what it's all about! Those performers wouldn't have a lot to do if there weren't composers out there writing. It's not exclusively unique to BANG ON A CAN', but I think that we definitely stand apart in terms of the way we program because we do program by composer. And managements call up and say, 'Well what about our quartet; what about this duo?' That is not the way we program. We program pieces and then would look for the performers.

"And so, having the composer there...," Snapp trails upward. Certainly, the two highlights from my recent visits — Bunita Marcus' hypnotizing, electric word-cycle, "Adam in Eve," and Bun-Ching Lam's entrancing update of millenium-old Chinese shadow puppets, "The Child God" — both gained for me by having their respective creators there in the flesh to meet, greet and personably elaborate (I believe Lam was there; I do remember congratulating Marcus).

Snapp also waxes exuberantly about the sequencing skills of the curators, as well as the ego-free collaborations of the musicians, the BANG ON A CAN' All Stars (who've just been recorded by SONY). "The quality of their musicianship and their fervor about the music is just amazing," she says.

Perhaps the only rub in the ointment has been Gann's recent criticism that BANG ON A CAN's uptown move brought with it conservative programming baggage. Snapp earnestly disagrees:

- "Does that mean that our programming is automatically 'uptown,' or opposite of what we have been? Is our sense of discovery not there anymore? The thing is we have always programmed music that we felt deserved to be heard. Basically a huge percentage of the music we program is music you're not going to hear somebody else do somewhere. I think the festival is programmed pretty much the same way that it has always been programmed, and not everyone will agree with all of our choices."

Snapp invites anyone, uptown or downtown, to "come and check us out," promising there'll still be popcorn and soda in the Walter Reade Theater, even beer when there's a benevolent underwriter, such as Grolsch Brewery for last year's Dutch composers. "I think the music and the chance to sort of hang out with people and talk about what you heard," Snapp affirms, "those things are really important and all those things are still there."

~     ~     ~

**Festival Review II** If BANG ON A CAN's structural basis is rhythmic, then 'MICROTONAL's is, well, mictrotonal; that is, the melodic/harmonic increments shorter than half-tones within the standard twelve-tone scale. Not being musically trained, I'm not exactly sure what a microtone sounds like. But if I ever needed to know, I'd sign right up for Johnny Reinhard's class.

Over the telephone, Reinhard is positively mercurial in covering a globe of topics at a flash without going over my head. He's born to teach. You can just see the smiling Reinhard holding court at the lecture podium with the same enthusiastic, humorous demeanor that he exhibits in-person, or on stage among his fellow musicians. In short, he's one of my favorite interviews with the talk never far from his beloved microtonalism in all its wordly applications. I just wish I had the space here, since his ruminations don't easily condense into soundbites.

Reinhard's 'MICROTONAL' sprung from academia. He did four years of post-graduate fellowship at Columbia University in ethnomusicology and theory, and is currently an adjunct professor of music at New York University. (These two institutions help sponsor the festival, which has occupied spaces in both places: the Romanesque St. Paul's Chapel uptown at Columbia and the more modern N. Y. U. Theater downtown. Reinhard likes the proximity and production values of the theater but is moved by the cavernous chapel's "acoustic vitality" for which he's written pieces to exploit its otherworldly sonic ambience). Reinhard's collegiate bassoon study led him toward such extended playing techniques as circular breathing and double-tongueing. "Then you add multiphonics," he explains, "then you have to come to microtonality."

Ironically, the city's transportation strike first prompted Reinhard's microtone focus:

- "It was in my second year of graduate school at Manhattan School of Music and I couldn't get anywhere. I'm on the East Side, the school is on the Upper West Side, and I would go to Central Park and play 'Mary Had a Little Lamb' a quarter tone flat. And that is how it started. Then I would do the Mozart 'Bassoon Concerto, Second Movement' a quarter tone flat."

Given the impetus, Reinhard began hearing microtones everywhere. The Oldsmobile car horn from his youth camp? "In neutral third at the time [sings]. It's exactly in between a major and minor. It's neither major or minor, and [has] that kind of pungent ring to it that they would put on a car horn." Fluorescent lights? "Yeah, that's a B quarter tone flat. And it's very important because then if you ever need a note wherever you are, you just listen to the electrical current and, especially with relative pitch as a microtonalist, you can name any pitch. It all relates to one. That's the hierarchy of tonality."

'MICROTONAL' followed Reinhard's development as a composer for his accomplished bassoon playing. "The repertoire for bassoon that you find on paper is stifling beyond belief," Reinhard remarks, "when you take into account that nobody knows what a bassoon is. I think it is the most obscure instrument in the orchestra! I would take odds on that.

- "I want to play great music and, at first, you don't have an ego necessarily as a player to compose the music which you believe is going to be exactly what you want to play. But there is a certain responsibility that a virtuoso on an instrument has to compose, no matter what he comes up with, just because he needs to move the instrument along further. Then when you get deeper and closer, and all-of-a-sudden people start liking it, and you stop writing just for your own instrument, especially that's important. You don't know how to describe your own stuff. You have no real way to describe it and other people describe it and you go, 'Wow, yeah, that's interesting.' Not that you can't explain what skill it's in, and what organs are in there.

"You know that old Schoenberg quote," he adds, "'The form of the piece of any music has to be organic — prick it anywhere and it bleeds.' I keep that in mind."

Reinhard sought one of his own compositions for the first festival to demonstrate the range of his own instrument. He also programmed works to showcase the range of other under-appreciated lead instruments, such as bass, along with the full hue of modern microtonalism. Modern composers like Koussevitsky, himself a virtuoso bassist, were featured. "On March 7, 1981," Reinhard recites from memory, 'MICROTONAL' was born.

The festival has grown in fourteen years to a four-concert series, with each evening averaging seven works or more. Some pieces are performed by a core group of musicians drawn from New York City's leading players; others by outside virtuosi and ensembles appropriate to the music's demands.

Like with BANG ON A CAN', there's no way of readily pigeon-holing 'MICROTONAL's diverse musical styles. The night I attended featured one ensemble number with two trombones (Takemitsu's "Waves"); another with bassoons dueling solo (Gubaidulina's "Duo-Sonata"); a third with just "electric" bassoon and synthesizer (Mather's "Romance"); one of Cage's "prepared" pianos ("Daughters of the Lonesome Isle"); plus two full spoken-word incorporations, including the premier of Reinhard's own "Raven."

There was also a number from New York City composer Phil Niblock in which Ulrich Kreiger's playing of an Australian didjiridoo — nothing more than a large, deeply-resonant hollowed log — was electronically delayed and multilayered. I know it doesn't sound like much on paper, but in the flesh my wife and I both found Kreiger's dense, forboding droning simply mesmerizing.

"We used to say, 'From heavy metal to Tibetan chant,'" Reinhardt jokes, but his evenings avoid the hodgepodge threat by adhering to creative, over-reaching themes. For example, he entitled that night, "New Waves," partly to explore breaking sensibilities of many young composers, partly to illustrate pattern similarities in their works' rhythmic natures, and partly to pun off the Takemitsu opener. Reinhard's themes also run across the entire series. He fears that critics have been missing the "bird's-eye view" from only catching individual concerts.

Still, Reinhard's 'MICROTONAL' has suffered no shortage of press acclaim, even with local live-music coverage shrinking. The *Village Voice*'s Karl Yan, for one, wrote him up as "the Hendrix of the bassoon." Reinhard reflects: "As people know what microtonal music means, and everybody starts enjoying and seeing it in all the reviews of the *New York Times* now, that is probably what I'm happiest about. And comments that are, like, 'Look at the influence you're having,' are probably what I enjoy most.

"We are trying to be user-friendly," Reinhard sums up about his festival's missionary efforts on behalf of musical open-mindedness, "and we are, I hope."

~     ~     ~

**Festival Review III**  Improvisation is the structural basis for ROULETTE' and it's where the new music scene interacts most regularly with the alternative jazz scene hosted by THE KNITTING FACTORY (New York, NY — see chapter). Looking at this winter's schedule, you'll see such noted jazzmen as Bobby Previte and Wayne Horvitz side-by-side with new-music stalwarts like Neely Bruce and Louis Andriessen.

But more often you'll see listings that defy categorization:

- Eugene Chadborn's "'Crude Gene Mannipulappalachian' blends traditional Appalachian folk music and other related 'folk' forms to musique concrete, live electronics, noise music, etc." (guests include respected bluegrass mandolinist Barry Mitterhoff, Bob Jordan on "homemade instruments" and Charles Rosina on "tapes");

- Davey Williams, "composer/improvisor/guitarist with a surrealist bent, will perform solo guitar, assaulted by anything from Wonderbread to implements of an erotic nature" (guests include reedman Phillip Micol, Ikue Mori on electronic percussion and Staley on trombone);

You can tell from this admittedly skewed sample of ROULETTE's 23 fall concerts that many participants don't take themselves too seriously. The series slogan is, "Yeah, but is it music?," though that's far from implying that they don't take their art seriously. On the contrary, ROULETTE's performers have usually polished these particular improvisations to a level suitable for live recording — because that's exactly what Staley and crew do.

ROULETTE' boasts an eight-track studio on premises and has taped most of its nearly 1,000 shows over the past 15 years. The "cream" of this vast output is now being assembled for release under ROULETTE's own Einstein Records label. Their first two compilations, *A Confederacy of Dances, Vols. I and II*, debuted in '92 and '93, respectively.

So comprehensive live recording is one prime distinction ROULETTE' possesses over its two brethren, above. The other is that ROULETTE's never left its "downtown" environs. Concerts still occur in Staley's cozy second-floor loft in artsy TriBeCa. To enter the sanctum, you walk up a battered industrial staircase, get buzzed inside the door, and pass through the eat-in kitchen into a large, airy living room. There, before about 100 steel folding chairs placed in rows upon the shiny polyurethaned floor, ROULETTE's serious fun is created.

Staley moved to New York City from his native Illinois in '78, officially commencing ROULETTE' two years later. "I got this space primarily to do my own work," he explains. "This is a loft. It was sort of an extension beyond myself, a way of making the space available and more interesting than for my own use [alone]; also opening it up to other people. And it just grew into a bigger thing than that." He'd installed the tape decks to record his own music, but made sure to flip the switches whenever other artists stopped by.

Staley's own trombone odyssey evolved, oddly enough, from a stint playing in Army bands in the early '70s. While stationed in Berlin he met composers in both the experimental and "free jazz" worlds, like Cornelius Cardew, who turned him onto the emerging nexus. "Then I went back to school in Illinois and pursued it even further," Staley recalls. "University of Illinois [at Champaign-Urbana] had been a very strong experimental place. Cage had been there a number of years, Harry Partch and other people had been there, so it had some history. I went back to pursue this work, finished everything, moved out here and got this loft with some people."

Staley's initial partners were fellow composers David Weinstein — who stayed in New York City and continues to co-manage ROULETTE' — plus Dan Senn and David Means, who moved elsewhere, but still come back for frequent series appearances. "Out of the first 11 concerts we saw there was such interest from composers wanting to do stuff in the room, because it was a nice room (there's a piano, etc.), that the series just took off," Staley says.

Concerts jumped from approximately 45 the first year to about 90 annually before Reagan-era funding cutbacks reduced the schedule to its present 50 or so. Unlike most new music concert series, which tend to occur on a once-weekly timetable, if not even less frequently, Staley programs ROULETTE' in festival-dense blocks. Moreover, he's inclined toward festival themes: ROULETTE PIANO FESTIVAL, ROULETTE FESTIVAL OF IMPROVISATION, ROULETTE FESTIVAL OF WOMEN IMPROVISORS, ROULETTE MIXOLOGY FESTIVAL. Of these, MIXOLOGY' continues ongoing, though Staley kicks off each season with LE SALON ROULETTE where prospective members are enticed with refreshments, series discounts and merchandise plus a performance sampler of four separate acts previewing the ensuing schedule. Sounds like fun, as well as a good deal!

This approach stems from compatriot and mentor Phil Niblock, who's Experimental Intermedia Foundation, Staley remarks, "we are strongly patterned after." The prime difference between Niblock's tiny assemblies and ROULETTE' is that Staley sees Niblock as primarily interested in works-in-process and achieving an informal dialog between fellow composers. "Our situation was a little more formal in the sense that there was a bit of a pressure to have it together," Staleys describes. "Not that it wasn't an experiment, but we were trying to get an audience that wasn't necessary just the friends and family of the composer."

ROULETTE's somewhat-more-formal presentations than E. I. F.'s are still a far cry from the dry intellectualism found in musical academia, Staley feels. Ironically, he credits his more free-swinging academic environment at his alma mater for this characteristic, namely, the multimedia happenings of Cage tailored for inciting audience experience. "I think Phillip Glass [also] really made a concerted effort toward connecting with a popularization," he adds.

However, Staley cautions that:

- "At the same time we are fighting the nature of a lot of stuff that turns art into entertainment. And I think that happens a lot, too, in this scene in a way of making stuff accessible; turning it into entertainment, which is not entirely a good thing. I think there is a distinction, and they serve different purposes in society. To keep challenging people, engaging them, but also challenging them is really the concern [here], not just to make it easy for people. 'Cause you're not really doing your job if that's what it is, and that's all that's going on.

  "So there is that sort of balance, too. And I think that thing about the academic work is that it's certainly challenging, it's just not engaging. That's the difference. I think a lot of people came out of academia with the same feeling, and that's why they wanted to make something [more engaging]. There were things that came along that really excited them, like, it was challenging, difficult work, but it wasn't dry."

Improvisation is what excited Staley, and he cites a broad, well-developed scene in New York City to draw collaborators from:

- "There are as many approaches to improvisation as there are to composition, and that's just a different process. There are some people who compose in a very concentrated, in-the-moment kind of approach that's very close to an improvisation process. Someone like Morton Feldman, the way he talks about his composition process, is actually not so different than an improvisation process. Then there are improvisers who are dealing with real time editing, which is more of a compositional type of thinking process.

"There is a full range. But in terms of work being created in the time not being held, having an ability to change given something coming in to cause it to change, I think that's an interesting thing."

Staley notes that his interest is not always about coming up with a "good moment" on tape but more about the underlying ideas and interaction capable of producing these moments: "I think improvisation is much more about how people think, and how they interact, than what specifically they think. I think improvisation shows that probably better than anything — the process of thinking and communicating."

Yet when Staley summarizes the prime audience benefits of ROULETTE', he's also speaking for the other two festivals, too:

- "People come here, and I think they come away with a really good connection with music, a connection with music they don't get in a lot of other situations. The physical situation [of the loft's intimacy] just puts them in such proximity to the composer, the performers and the sound that they don't even get even in very good acoustical situations. It's an intimacy with a work and a process that people who come here walk away with, I think."

**Artist Mini-Review**

Ken Butler. I wanted to spare my in-person accounts to help keep this chapter length under 10,000 words, but I have to say something about the kickoff concert to ROULETTE's '93 Spring Series. The featured artist was Ken Butler, a handsome thirty-something in black shirt, jeans and cowboy boots. The real star, however, was his incredible menagerie of "hybrid" instruments — fantastic sculptures in themselves — made from assemblages of found objects.

Prose descriptions can't do justice to how Butler whimsically joins household items, discarded electronics and scrap-metal parts to the chopped-up shells of traditional instruments. Picture Mad Max meets Rube Goldberg as one "hybrid guitar" festooned with meters and protractors that even produced sparks! By hooking up various electric pick-ups, he also amplifies the resulting resonances, loops them, distorts them, whatever. This yields odd sound textures that nevertheless bear some resemblance to their parent bodies. One "hybrid" reminded me of an electrocuted Japanese koto; another, a punctured National steel guitar.

Butler built up his program by first performing several instruments solo, then having 15 musicians in succession pick up an instrument to where he'd eventually gathered on stage an entire mutant orchestra (the instruments, mind you, not the musicians). Most pieces were short and evoked some ethnic genre or another. I found them fairly quirky, spacious, impressionistic, and above all, hugely entertaining, reminiscent of some of Laurie Anderson's better tangents.

The evening concluded with full work-out of "The Nasadiya," an excerpt from David Soldier's "Symphony #1, Krakatoa." The resulting premier was surprisingly disciplined with the "hybrid strings" held in line, the "hybrid percussion" supplying a steady backbeat, and the two vocalists given actual words and choruses. It had a nice, smooth, boppish feel, not unlike the early segment of a Sun Ra show. Still, you can't imagine seeing 15 skilled, poised, coiffed musicians playing upon what looked like a pack of mangy junkyard string dogs. For this image, alone, some fine arts institution like MoMA ought to pick up on Butler's outrageous creations, and soon!

**See Also**

Niblock has presented a number of one-time festivals, but his eight-day FESTIVAL WITH NO FANCY NAME has maintained ongoing since '90, while his 16-day FOUR COUNTRY FESTIVAL has kept steady three years straight. There's usually one composer booked per evening and given full benefit of the audience's attention.

~     ~     ~

# Manhattan's Cabaret Scene

BACK STAGE BISTRO AWARDS, Manhattan, NYC
Late February
Cabaret

HEARTS AND VOICES WINTER BENEFIT SERIES, Manhattan, NYC
Middle March to Late April
Cabaret
***Attended***

MANHATTAN ASSOCIATION OF CABARETS AND CLUBS AWARDS, Manhattan, NYC
Late March
Cabaret

HEARTS AND VOICES IN CONCERT, Manhattan, NYC
Middle May
Cabaret

GRAND NIGHTS FOR SINGING, Manhattan, NYC
Early July
Cabaret

CABARET SYMPOSIUM, Waterford, CT
Middle August to Late August
Cabaret

CABARET CONVENTION, Manhattan, NYC
Middle October to Late October
Cabaret
***Attended***

TEDDYCARE, Manhattan, NYC
Early December to Late December
Cabaret

**Introduction**

Most music genres suffer their images unfairly. All I have to do is toss out the terms "rock-'n-roller," "honky-tonker," "folky-strummer," "holy-roller" and such, and you can paint your own unflattering portrait of their stereotypical artists and audiences. (You've heard the one, I'm sure, about what has fifty eyes and a hundred teeth? "The first few rows of a bluegrass festival." Or what happens when you play a country record backwards? "You get your wife back, your job back, you sober up, and your dog comes back to life." See what I mean?) The more musicians I come to know, personally, the more I recognize them as fairly sincere, sober, middle-class strivers no different than you or me. The same goes for their fans, well, a goodly portion at any rate.

But no other genre is done as much injustice by its image as cabaret music. None, I tell you. What vision comes to mind? How about some oh so world-weary chanteuse, long-stemmed cigarette holder dangling from her mouth, feather boa flung disdainfully over her bare shoulder, moaning bored nothings to tuxedoed refugees from Nick and Nora Charles films. Elitist irrelevance personified.

Well, here to reveal the lies of such self-indulgent pictures are two superb festivals: the CABARET CONVENTION ['CONVENTION] and the HEARTS AND VOICES WINTER BENEFIT SERIES ['WINTER BENEFIT SERIES]. Both are designed to evangelize new audiences and deliver satisfying listening experiences that would engage most anybody regardless of their prior musical persuasions. The settings are classy, yet casual if you choose, and surprisingly affordable.

Now, I'm the last one of an expert on this field, but what's struck me about what I've heard at both events is how unerringly real much of it tends to be. It helps that it's served up in so unadorned fashion, usually just piano and voice. But the repertoire drawn largely from the American Musical Theater over the past 80 years survives because it often speaks so directly to everyday human experience. After all, Broadway scores were the pop music of their day, long before home stereos and cable TV disseminated recorded forms. Songs had to come from the heart and communicate credibly if the sheet music was to sell, little different from today's top singles. Most of all, the key to success was in being able to have patrons pick-up the tune upon first listening for humming or whistling afterward (there was no rewind or replay button), thus conveying a melodic sense lost in all but the finest modern material.

While I've become a huge booster of the cabaret songbook, mind you, I've retained skepticism about some of its lesser performers. Since today's cabaret serves as a catch-all for a number of dispossessed genres, I've found myself on occasion wincing at the starchy hootiness of a faded opera singer, or cringing from the over-the-top salesmanship of a failed chorus aspirant. That's less frequent, however. More likely you'll hear good, though not always great, voices, common singers if you will, connecting with common listeners via uncommonly honest interpretations. Basically, it's gotta' feel real for them in order to make it feel real for their listeners. Balance reigns, I'm pleased to report, while faux posturing hopefully remains in the wings.

So if you have the slightest curiosity about New York City's most uniquely indigenous music, these two happenings afford the best window into the scene in terms of quantity, quality, variety and value. Oh, and you can leave your formal attire at home...unless you'd feel naked without it.

**Festival Review I** "Well, you know, jazz thrives and continues to thrive, and in most cities you can find some jazz rooms. What you don't find is cabaret rooms, authentically-functioning cabaret rooms, and that is very upsetting."

Donald Smith, Executive Director of the Mabel Mercer Foundation and its 'CONVENTION, is bemoaning the perilous state of cabaret music beyond the confines of New York City borders. He cites lack of dedicated spaces as one of the chief bottlenecks inhibiting the profusion of top cabaret talents struggling to reach their broader potential audiences here, there and elsewhere. "What we say is," Smith exclaims, "'Look, this music — what we call the Great American Songbook — is your heritage! Everything that one could do we have done to this music. It's in our emotional bloodstreams, but a lot of it isn't going to get heard unless this kind of entertaining continues to flourish, and it's got to have homes to flourish in.'"

Smith's other obstacle is the media, specifically television, for enforcing the kinds of elitist prejudices portrayed above. After all, if it's perceived as the exclusive domain of millionaire connoisseurs, why publicize it; what financial requirements could it possibly have? "I think that [pampered perception] has done more damage to the field than anything I can think of," Smith continues:

- "I've always had to have an enormous realistic view of this fragile, awkward world that I function in; I've always had to. And I generally am very seldom overwhelmingly, like, 'It's all wonderful.' That's just not there. But what I've found lately is that there's a much larger audience for it than is getting a chance to see it."

Ergo, the 'CONVENTION, where Smith programs 125 of the genre's finest within 21 hours over seven nights. The Town Hall setting delivers Broadway plushness, but the $10.00 nightly ticket prices brings out the TKTS crowd of middle-class novices drawn partly to an obvious bargain-of-the-year, but also to the many living legends they recognize peppering the bills. Those mainstream folks — refreshingly spirited in their responses I've observed from my balcony seat

— are precisely whom Smith seeks in hopes of building a bigger audience base.

Smith is a jack-of-all-trades in boosting the genre, though paying his rent partly as free-lance publicist for gallery and hotel openings. "When I've done those things I've always been allowed to present live entertainment," he explains:

- "And so, at some point in the festivities, I called a halt to the evening. And these people that have come are what I call 'civilians' — they haven't any particular great overwhelming interest in who's going to perform. So if I say, 'And now some wonderful Deitz and Schwartz by K. T. Sullivan,' they may not know who K. T. is, and they may not even know the phrase 'Deitz and Schwartz.' The minute they start to hear the first song, they are aware that they've been familiar with those words and music for years. On the second or third song, they're cheering this performer!

  "All of a sudden the set ends, and two things happen. My dear civilians go over to them and say, well, it used to be, 'You've got a record, of course, haven't you?' (Then, many did not; today it's, 'You've got a CD, haven't you?,' or a cassette.) And the second is — and this is always the kicker — 'I don't know why you don't do television,' as if Ms. Sullivan made a choice to not appear on television.

  "Now, that isn't what they mean. What they mean is they have been pleasantly surprised at finding someone they don't know, and [who's] entertained them so royally. Since they watch so much on television, why have they never heard about this woman? And this, I feel, is at the root of the problem."

Accordingly, Smith is as likely to devote his considerable energies to developing media deals as to expanding the 'CONVENTION to other cities (next possible stops: London, Philadelphia, L. A., Boston). Two recent projects involved a 20-part radio series for BBC 2 in England and proposals to Bravo and A&E cable-TV networks. It's no accident that the seven-to-fifteen minutes he allots most singers at the 'CONVENTION, or the prevalence of themes to four of its seven nights, conforms nicely to a broadcast format. "If we get this done for TV," Smith suggests:

- "And the marriage of as intimate an art as cabaret and television should wed beautifully, but it needs to be filmed a certain way with a live audience, etc. When that happens (and I have no doubt that it will at some point), the public is going to have no problem in understanding it. They're not going to find it esoteric. They're not going to find it 'chi-chi.' What they're going to find is: 'Gee, she's good-looking and what a wonderful voice. God, he's a nice-looking guy; what a good voice. God, those songs are great.'"

Smith is wonderfully comprehensive, one of my favorite interviews. Therefore, I'll let him tell you directly how he came to cabaret music in general and to originate the 'CONVENTION in particular. (Pardon the length, but enjoy the perspective.)

- "I heard Mabel Mercer, the great cafe singer, as a young boy and something clicked. I was here on a vacation with my Uncle Edward. How he got me into those places, I never know, but he drank a lot and I seemed to be able to go into those places with him, and a lot of it I certainly didn't understand. I always likened it to the kid in Texas with his ear next to the radio listening to the Metropolitan Opera broadcast and, all of a sudden, a great love of opera grows there...

  "I lived in Massachusetts. I was a kid. By the time that I was able to come here to stay in '55, Mabel was already 55 years old. ...I would hear people say, 'Oh, we don't go to hear her anymore because we like to remember her the way she was.' I couldn't understand it because I was coming away absolutely overwhelmed by these interpretations. What had happened is, as her voice left her, these powers, that storytelling to music, became so big that you really just didn't think about the notes that weren't there. And she had become, by that time, wildly loved by a group of people that were very strong but a small group.

  "The occasions for her to perform were becoming fewer and fewer. There were some personal problems with a gentleman in her life whose health wasn't well and things like that. And I panicked about the fact, after racing to grow up as much as I could to live in New York, that this artist who had meant so much to me in my life...

"Now, she had spent most of her life in the intimate room, the small room. Never had a hit record. If you check the files, every important singer will give her some kind of rave review for having affected them: Leontyne Price, Jo Stafford, Margaret Whiting, it just goes on and on and on. It was not unusual on any night in New York to see Warren Beatty sitting there, Nureyev, Angela Lansbury. I mean, it was quite extraordinary.

"But Mabel was a very quiet person and a very discreet person, so that she'd never had a publicist. She'd never had anybody promoting her. The kind of rooms that she performed in didn't have press agents, so there was never anything in files on the woman or anything. She was passed along by people who adored her, who would say to their friends, 'Look, when you're in New York, Jenny and Fred, you've got to go see Mabel,' you know what I mean? And she stayed in places, I mean, Mabel played in some rooms for six years. Well, you could always find her. See, the secret of successful cabaret is continuity of performance. After the talent consideration, you've got to be there doing it to build your audience.

"Anyway, in those years in the '60s, I insinuated myself into her life, and as some problems developed — I mentioned this man who had been her manager became awfully ill — I just sort of took over doing everything to help her. I did not work for her, it was all a gift. It was some way to thank her for what she had done and was doing for me.

"What happened is, with my enthusiasm and some talent, she was sort of looked at again. All of a sudden the big newspaper articles began to come out and the magazine pieces, and I got her on the Today Show and things like that. By the time Mabel was into her '80s and had received the Presidential Medal of Freedom, and I had done a five-part documentary on BBC in London with her and various things, she was enjoying the kind of celebrity that she had never had in her life in her native England or in those years in Paris in the late '20s and '30s, and it was all quite fascinating.

"Mabel died in '84, and I knew that my life was never going to be the same again, because I really was losing my best friend. ...Anyway, as often happens, by that time I had spent about 22 years of my life with her, and I would run into people (and I don't think Mabel had been dead six months), and a performer or a friend who had liked her would see me in the street and say, 'Oh, I've just been interviewed by somebody by such-and-such a paper for a story on Mabel.' Some editors had all of a sudden decided that this woman, who had been young with Picasso and Cole Porter and F. Scott Fitzgerald, would make a wonderful end-of-an-era story. Of course, I'd have to be lying to you if I didn't say my nose was out of joint that nobody had come to me.

"Well, then finally someone did, and the woman was an absolute mountain of misinformation. ...When it happened about four or five times, I was really getting very upset, and I didn't know what to do.

"At the same time, the cabaret world was having one of its harder periods. I got together with some cabaret chums and some friends of mine, and with my own financing I finally went to a not-for-profit organization lawyer, and talked out to him what I wanted to do. And what we came up with was this little organization called The Mabel Mercer Foundation that had two very strong aims. ...The first was that Miss Mercer would be remembered accurately, and the size of her contribution to this field would not be forgotten. Well, a lot of that could be documented, and I certainly could play a big role in that.

"The second was that we were going to try through this new organization to give an ongoing visibility to this very threatened world of cabaret. That's been the hard part in that, by its nature, there's an aloneness to the world of cabaret. There's no organizational kind of thing to it; you're sort of out there alone.

"What we did when we finally got going at the end of '85 [was] sponsor a dinner dance on the roof of the St. Regis, which was a hotel Mabel was long associated with; she had performed off and on for years downstairs in the lounge. In that year we approached about 70 media writers about compiling a ballot of cabaret performers that we'd like to give some support to. After we got every ballot back, people had really voted for, like, favorites rather than thinking in terms of giving younger people a sort of hand. So we abandoned that project. We just didn't see a way to do it, that this favoritism didn't creep sort of into it.

"What we started after that was the formation of this dream, which was to convene — and I use the word convention in that sense — of getting together as many cabaret people that were practicing the art, and in New York presenting them in a series of concerts at a very popular-priced ticket and see what we could do.

"So in '89 we did the first 'CONVENTION that ever existed in the world. It was four days and nights. At Town Hall at 2:00 in the afternoon we had panels of performers and journalists and writers, etc., discussing the problems of cabaret and, sadly, the audience that we attracted were really basically out-of-work cabaret people. The public did not respond to that. What they did respond to was the fact that for $5.00, they could buy a ticket for four different performances [at] $5.00 a night and get up to as many as 20 singers.

"We did that and it was wildly successful, and again, going back to that reality check, I knew it would take me about two years to raise enough money to mount the next one. Well, I bit the bullet and did a whole week. And the response was growing in such a big way. We got hundreds of letters from people thanking us for doing it (totally unsolicited) where they wrote about their thoughts of whom they had heard over the years, or what the experience in New York used to be like going out at night that they couldn't re-create any longer — always going back to the real cruel economics of it.

"Well what we wanted to dispel, too, was we didn't want it to be in any sense read as elitist in the sense that every time cabaret was portrayed, it was [exclusively for] a sort of special breed of people who seem to understand this more than anybody else, in a very expensive place, living it up.

"Now I don't expect that lady who can buy two $5.00 tickets to come away and say, 'Oh, I must find a way to get to Rainbow and Stars.' Financially, she's not going to afford that kind of evening. But she might write a letter to television and say, 'At the 'CONVENTION I heard these wonderful people! Why do I never see them on anything as popular as television?' She might buy a cassette. She certainly, when she's reading the papers, is going to pay attention because she now knows there's a person called Jeff Harnar, or Dick Gallagher, or The Wise Guys, or Mary Cleere Haran, or something, you know?

"And so, here we find ourselves at the fifth 'CONVENTION this coming October!"

The cruelest economics these days are the 'CONVENTION tickets getting gobbled up so quickly. I dawdled this year. Seats went on sale Monday, a week before opening night. By the time I got to the box office four days later, only the back balcony was available (note: do TicketMaster the first available day to avoid getting shut out). "Tsk," I thought, preferring to sit closer for better note taking than I'd done previously.

**Artist Mini-Reviews**

Anyway, my lauding scribbles from '92 still hold. I was very pleasantly surprised to find:

• Many practitioners in their 30s and 40s;

• Much modern material, including several new tunes being debuted;

• Various instrumental backings, the best being an electric-guitar-and-bass duo for a samba tribute to Havana;

• Lotsa' humor and audience interaction from the singers.

"Not maudlin at all," my notes read in summing the evening's high quality, subtlety and accessibility. My own highlight involved a buoyant Annie Hughes, who decried being raised on opera lessons and "the problem, on occasion, of being a Caucasian," for the hilarious "Singing The Great White Way." The audience roared in sympathy.

Here's one of Smith's recent highlights:

- "There was a young singer named <u>Tom Andersen</u>, and I'd heard him in the clubs — a love-ly, sweet voice. Nothing much was happening for him, and I am sure that he was ques-tioning very much what was he doing, okay?

  "Now, I invited him to one of the 'CONVENTION's. He didn't have any great prospects for what was coming along for the future, and I think he was very surprised to be asked, very nervous backstage. All of a sudden he went out and on. When he swung into the chorus of his first song, you could feel the audience's feeling for him. I will never forget it. They were like his net — he just went flying. When he finished the first song, there was an ova-tion. And he went right into the second song, and the house came down.

  "And he came off stage grinning. Well, I can't really speak for him, I can only speak for how I responded to it. But he needed that kind of vindication; he needed to hear that from a public, not going into a small room as he had in the past when he got his friends in. These people didn't know who Tom Andersen was. They were responding to this man who came out and sang beautifully.

  "I was never so proud that such a thing as the 'CONVENTION existed."

As for Hughes? "Oh, she's a wonderful talent," Smith agrees:

- "What makes me so upset is that (of course, we know what the economics are) if I heard an Annie Hughes, and I was someone who wrote shows, I'd always have in my mind that sound and the great-looking gal that she is, and think, 'Boy, would I love her in a show of mine!' But again, how much original stuff is going to get done on Broadway? I'm happy to say that Annie's going to be on again this year. She's so good."

~     ~     ~

**Festival Review II**   I tell ya', the 'CONVENTION isn't the only inspiring tale of selflessness in the cabaret music com-munity; the only magnanimous evangelizing for good cause.

Take the HEARTS AND VOICES story of Nancy Sondag's.

This wonderfully cordial and generous woman came to New York City from her native Illinois in '71 and over the next 16 years pursued the prototypic "slash" career: stage actress/"slash"/TV actress/"slash"/film actress/"slash"/cabaret singer/"slash"/whatever "sur-vival" job was needed to pay the rent. Harvey Fierstein was one of her early comrades-in-arms.

The time came, however, when Sondag felt she had taken her career as far as it could go. 'Problem was, what next? All her "survival" jobs hadn't provided her any special direction. "I wanted to do something in the arts that I thought I was utilizing my talent; I didn't know quite what that was," Sondag explains.

Then her two roommates, Don and Joseph, both contracted AIDS, and she nursed the pair until they died. "Between the two of them, they were in five different hospitals," Sondag recalls:

- "So I had, like, about four years' experience in the hospitals. I got to know so many AIDS patients, and the majority of them didn't have family or friends visiting them. The days were so long and, after a while, people didn't know what to talk about any more. They really needed something to capture their imagination. Joseph was really sad because he had written some music, and it had never been produced."

She rounded up some musical friends, produced a club act of Joseph's music, then per-formed it for him and his fellow patients at the hospital. "That was great," she says, "but it was one night and one afternoon; then it was over and my focus was back on him."

After Joseph's death, Sondag went onto pursue a master's degree in theater plus consult-ing in the public school system. Still her hospital work haunted her. When a friend and fellow cabaret performer, Matt McClenahan, returned from a European tour, "I told him about this pro-gram that we did in the hospital," Sondag recalls:

- "He said, 'Well, let's get it back. We've gotta' do this!' ...So we put together a little show, took it to Terrence Cardinal Cooke [Hospital], and the patients, of course, loved it. So we made a promise to the patients that we would have a show for them every week. Matt was working at a piano bar at that time and started telling other performers. In a month's time we had a waiting list of people wanting to do shows. So [I applied my] background in education in setting up programs. We formalized it into a program and started calling up other hospitals, lining the whole thing up."

Sondag and McClenahan managed to institute programs at six hospitals in the first year of '91, but found the management requirements taking its toll. "We called it HEARTS AND VOICES," she explains, "but it was really Mom and Pop HEARTS AND VOICES." At their height of physical and financial exhaustion, Bob Harrington, who wrote reviews for *Back Stage Magazine* among others, came to the rescue and organized a benefit. The $20,000 funds raised helped Sondag and McClenahan establish HEARTS AND VOICES as a nonprofit and get some much needed clerical help.

In less than four years, HEARTS AND VOICES has since presented over 1,200 shows at eight hospitals ongoing. Fourteen more hospitals are on a waiting list. "We're still in my apartment," Sondag rues. "We're bursting at the seams, and I think our existence can best be described as hand-to-mouth, but our beneficiaries would never know that. We've never missed a show!"

So that's the good cause. Harrington's benefits, however, have taken on a life of their own, servicing the spread of the genre to novice listeners and devotees, alike. Unfortunately, Harrington has since passed away from AIDS, but his legacy remains from numerous other volunteers who contribute benefit productions all throughout the year. There's no set pattern, but you can look for at least one blow-out in April or May (HEARTS AND VOICES IN CONCERT), and the 'WINTER BENEFIT SERIES' on a weekly basis in the months prior (this year beginning in December with Ruby Rims' weekly TEDDYCARE series).

These benefits now contribute nearly half of Sondag's funding. Other income comes from private donations, corporate sponsorship, foundation grants, and licensing fees from HEARTS AND VOICES spin-offs in Denver and Los Angeles. Sondag's especially grateful for the volunteer support she receives from among New York City's cabaret-music community. "I'm just always touched that cabaret performers think of us and want to do something to help," she notes.

For Sondag, the rewards come in three's. First, there's the personal satisfaction she feels in her own new mission:

- "I feel like my whole life has led up to what I'm doing now, which is just a wonderful way to feel. When I was performing I used to joke to people that I wanted them to put on my tombstone, 'First stone left unturned.' No one was more driven than I about my career. That was fine until it wasn't any more.

  "Right now, this has brought me tremendous joy in my life, tremendous fulfillment, and I've never felt more connected to the performing arts than I do now. But, at the same time, I just feel like I'm using all my talents doing this. ...All the 'survival jobs' I did as a performer working in offices, it was good to know that I was paying attention and was learning from all those jobs as well. There's no way I'd go back."

Second, there's the payback she witnesses in the hospitals from patients and performers, alike:

- "What performers found with HEARTS AND VOICES was that was even much more intimate than anything they had done because we were in a hospital room. There was no stage, no microphone, no lights, no sound. The people were there in pajamas because they had been stripped of any mechanisms that they may hide from. They were really open for the experience and sitting there at a stage in their life where the nonsense had been stripped away. Then the performers came in to perform, and any kind of pretense in that moment really becomes ludicrous. It becomes such honest performing. It's not about how pretty the sound can be, or about how much I can impress somebody. It's really about how I can connect with somebody. The performers usually move around the room, or touch the patients, or get right into contact with people, and do their best to draw them in.

"I really watch so many performers over the last four years after they become volunteers for HEARTS AND VOICES how that has influenced their performing just in general. They just grew so as performers after they had the experience of volunteering in the hospitals."

Third, there's the gratitude she gains from club and theater patrons:

• "When people come and see the show they're genuinely moved in a lot of different ways. HEARTS AND VOICES is an organization of unconditional love and music, and I think you get that even if you come for a benefit. ...I think that when people leave one of our 'WINTER BENEFIT SERIES, they walk away feeling very warm and happy, not just from the high standard of music, but because they've been in the presence of all these loving people.

"Another thing that makes me feel good, I cannot tell you how many people, when they leave a theater, come up and say, 'You didn't charge enough.' I think that's my most frequent comment that I get from people."

**Artist Mini-Reviews** I caught one of the six evenings of '93's 'WINTER BENEFIT SERIES. It was produced for Sondag by Teri Lynn Paul and John Hoglund who did an excellent job in recruiting a dozen of the top young talents for a couple of songs apiece. I'd describe the crowd at Steve McGraw's as convivial uptown types all sporting red AIDS ribbons discretely upon their not-quite-evening wear. Their ultimate acknowledgement of a strong showing onstage was to knowingly hum their approval, "Mmmmm!" So mmm's the word for you first-timers.

Aside from one or two singers who seemed a bit excessive, I came away impressed. My notes read: "strong focus on lyrics...positive personality points...affectionate banter...attempting to sell the songs to the audience." Common stage traits (exaggerated a tad too much by the few over-the-top types) involved quivering lower lips, heavenward glances, and beckoning hand gestures. Surprisingly, these techniques worked well because most singers were sincere and stayed within themselves, vocally. Overall, I considered it a terrific song sampler at any price, and a steal at just $12.00!

Here's what Sondag had to say about two of my highlights:

Nancy LaMott: "Isn't she wonderful? *New York Magazine* this past year picked out the best in New York City. They had all these different categories, and they said Best-in-Cabaret was Nancy LaMott. She's really amazing."

Philip Officer: "Philip is considered by many as the *creme de la creme* of cabaret. He's won a lot of different awards: BISTRO awards and MACC awards. He's had a lot of critical success in the past few years. ...A lot of people think he's one of the finest interpreters that we have right now."

Sondag's own highlight? "We had a performer, Steve Gilden, [who] also was HIV-positive," she relates:

• "He'd been one of our volunteers in the hospital, then this past year his health started to fail, so he was in and out of the hospitals. When he was well enough he would volunteer, and sometimes when he was in the hospital he would get up from the audience in his pajamas and sing. So when the HEARTS AND VOICES' came along he had just finished chemotherapy, and was out of the hospital, and wanted to be in the cabaret series.

"We put him in the Broadway night, and he sang [from] *Man of La Mancha*. He said when he'd been a boy that was the first musical he had seen. When he was 10 years old he auditioned for some boys' chorus singing 'The Impossible Dream.' And now he realized the lyrics meant a lot more to him and he sang [that].

"The words took on new meaning to everyone there. ...The screen was blue with little stars up in the back. The song became [him] standing in the universe at that moment. It was very simple and very pure. It was very moving for everyone who was there.

"Steve left us on July 1st," Sondag pauses. "That was really his last public performance."

With the demise of Steve McGraw's, 88's is now the reigning venue here for the cabaret-music   **See Also**
scene, notably its younger aspirants. (TEDDYCARE moved here this year, for example.) Club owner
Erv Raible supplements its normal weekly fare with two annual showcases.

The first is an informal preview during one evening of 40-or-so singers he plans to present during the summer season. Each does one song apiece for press and interested listeners, such
as Smith — a regular scout for his own 'CONVENTION bookings. I'm not sure of the dates, so call
ahead.

The second is the nine-year-old AWARDS show of the MANHATTAN ASSOCIATION OF CABARETS
AND CLUBS [MACC], of which Raible is co-founder and president. This event bookends Cabaret
Month along with the BACK STAGE BISTRO AWARDS, presented four weeks earlier by *Back Stage
Magazine*. Raible moves his 28-artist stage show to the Copacabana; the latter takes over the
Ballroom. At either affair you'll witness the cream of the crop entertaining each other with humor
and affection.

You should also know that Smith has spread his wings this past year by producing a number of top-drawer cabaret revues. One, GRAND NIGHTS FOR SINGING, revisited Town Hall in July,
while others are described in **New York City Festival Listings**. The very next month, Smith usually joins an impressive roster of instructors for the lauded CABARET SYMPOSIUM in Waterford, CT.
Though it's primarily intended as a working "blend of boot camp and group therapy" by day for
aspiring cabaret singers, the Eugene O'Neill Theater Center opens to the public at least four concert evenings — three of which feature the national acts who comprise the faculty and their guests.
Indulge!

~     ~     ~

# Advising CABARET CONVENTION Artists: A Conversation with Donald Smith.

*Donald Smith, Executive Director of the Mabel Mercer Foundation and its CABARET CONVENTION, is one of the world's foremost gurus to cabaret singers. He's steered the careers of Micheal Feinstein, Steve Ross and Andrea Marcovicci, among others. Often, such discoveries come directly to Smith. I thought I was deluged in screening self-produced tapes for* The Performing Songwriter; *he gets my monthly allotment across his doorstep almost every week!*

*Remarkably, Smith contributes his finely-tuned ear gratis, though there is a price — he's forthright to a fault, and his advice, as delivered articulately and patiently with a faint flavoring of his Massachusetts upbringing, might not provide the reassurance you want to hear. (I just wish there was somebody with Smith's constructive candor cruising the folk-music community, for one.)*

*Smith's discussing his role as manager sans portfolio offers valuable insights into current woes of such artistic development, yet also what's needed to succeed in general. You begin to understand why certain cabaret singers ascend to the level of such festivals as Smith's, while others continue to struggle. (Aspiring artists of all genres, as well as interested fans, take note.)*

- "Now I went to see something that happens in the city every summer: a club here ['88's' — see MANHATTAN ASSOCIATION OF CABARETS AND CLUBS AWARDS] runs through about 40 people who are going to be performing from now until the end of September. They all get up and do one number, and it's to kind of introduce them to press that might have showed up that night or an audience looking for new people. It's something that Erv Raible has done for three or four seasons now. I always try to catch it because it's a good way for me to get to see people I cannot get to.

  "But I find some of those performers totally unaware that they were supposed to be singing to us and reaching us, and that threw me. Because the one thing about cabaret is, it is immediate. It is about one-on-one with that audience. And if you're not connecting with them, you might as well be doing this out in the field somewhere. And that bothered me; that really bothered me. Before we got to what they chose to sing or [how they] presented themselves, I would think if you were going to be doing a cabaret performance, that the first thing you would have addressed is the idea that, in that intimate setting, you had to click with people that close to you.

  "I think the fact that it is so immediate has great pluses and it has drawbacks. In other words, if something is very good, it can almost be perceived as genius, but if it's merely competent, it's almost a failure because of the immediacy of it.

  "Also it's all really about you. It may say, 'Gladys Kelly and Her Songs,' when you go in, and you don't know who that is. But I feel that by the time you come out, you've really got to know how Gladys Kelly thinks about what she's just done for that hour. You have to be quite aware. I mean, it's her view of what she's presented — what that music means to her — that she therefore would like to share with these people who gathered for this period. And I think the person has to have an awareness that maybe those same things that the performer liked or responded to are universal enough that they're going to appeal to other people.

  "Another thing that I found a drawback is that the majority of the music that these people chose to sing the other night were more newer songs, but not necessarily better songs, and they had a lot of phony content. They were sort of pseudo.

  "But what bothered me is that many of the people singing them, I felt, were totally convinced that these were masterpieces. Sadly, I kept hearing the woman sing what she is singing, and I think, 'Oh boy, Harold Arlen's got something that says it so much better, and you'd get a bigger break doing it than this tortured sort of thing that doesn't seem to know how to end itself, or get back to the story it's supposed to be telling.' Of course, then you've got to go back to the degree of talent, intelligence. Every good singer is not the brightest person in the world..."

- "Most of the artists I've ever worked with have always read the material first, without the music, so that the words have got to be something they could buy into and the story that that told. Then they can go ahead with the song. Now, everyone doesn't do that. What I mean is there are lots of songs out there now that I just find very tortured, that they think the story they're telling is so important and all that, and the song isn't structured well; the choice of words is not very clever.

"We get in the Mabel Mercer Foundation office, on an average week, anywhere from a dozen videos and cassettes up to as many as 50. I will tell you that I try to listen to them and view them all, I really do. But you do get to a point where after two bands, sometimes, you know that none of it's going to be any better for the next 12. They're not going to be; they're just not going to be. And you also begin to think, 'Does that woman know what that word means that she's singing?' And in many cases, you just know the thought never entered their head what the word is, from the reading that they give the word.

"[On the other hand,] I'll tell you what happens with me is I leave some place very depressed, and I think, 'What am I doing? What am I doing with all this?' And then two nights later, somebody has said, 'Can you come hear me?' And I thought, 'All right, I said I'd go.' And I go and here's this wonderful surprise. Now, that happens with frequency, so that pleases me.

"Performers call us and say, 'Can I come talk to you? I need some advice.' Whether they take it or not doesn't matter, we make the time to see and hear that person. Sometimes it makes all the difference because, as I say, there's an aloneness to this, and you just don't know sometimes. And it's like anything, when you're working upclose on something, you often aren't the best viewer of your product.

"[There's a fear] you'll start ripping it apart. We certainly don't do it that way, but we ask them to explain things. So when often somebody will sing a song because it's been a hit song, I say, 'Well, what does it say to you? What are you trying to say to the people you're going to entertain?'

"A lot of them don't work hard enough. In other words, if you want to sing Richard Rodgers, you can often find something more interesting for you than setting yourself up to sing a Richard Rodgers song that another personality automatically comes to mind when you hear the song. And if I didn't have much of a voice (and there are a lot of people in cabaret that the voice is not the primary thing), I would make an effort to find material that the public couldn't, in advance of how I present it, say, 'Well I've heard this sung more beautifully than that.' You know, why shoot yourself in the foot to start with?

"You see, I think there has to be thought put into it. And what's kind of amazing is when you start talking with them and you ask them for some explanations, if you can get them to open up, it's amazing what they will come up with. Then you can turn and say, 'Well, you know, if that's one of the fondest memories you have in your life of those vacations on your grandpa's farm or something, you want to know something, there's a song somewhere that's going to say some of that; that might fit in with the season or the time when you went. Why don't you think that way?' I really just talk about it as a dialogue that gets going where you may then find out you have other choices.

"If a performer calls us and says, 'Can you see me? I'm sort of confused,' or 'This is what I'm doing,' or 'I sent you a tape. What do you think?' — now, you leave yourself open for a lot of things because many people when they say to you, 'I want you to be brutally honest with us,' that is the last thing in the world they mean. They don't want anything else other than [a pat on the back.]

- "Do you know about the EUGENE O'NEILL CABARET SYMPOSIUM? Okay, I taught — I don't like the word 'taught,' but that's in a sense what you're doing — last season and I'm going back this year. It'll be for nine days in late August. It's really quite something to see in action. I had been a little leery of it because I kind of felt the read I've been getting is someone went off to this for nine intense days and came back a cabaret performer. No way, this is not going to happen.

  "But when I went and experienced it myself, that wasn't it at all. What it is is a workshop process of trying to make available the tools people have within themselves to help themselves [get] better in this field, and it's fabulous to watch. They have what they call 'Master Teachers,' like Julie Wilson, and Margaret Whiting, and various people, who work on a one-on-one basis with these performers.

  "Now, I went up really to speak to them about the business of cabaret because it's an area in which all these performers let down terribly, even on the simplest level. I mean, if I showed you the letters that I got that start, 'These are not my best pictures.' Now, who did you send the best ones to? Just that phrase, no one ever thought what it means.

  "Why would you mail out a photo that's not identified? Because I'll tell you one thing, if it ends on an entertainment editor's desk, and it's separated from your bio or your letter, that goes in a wastepaper basket. Nobody has the time looking around for it. Just all those kind of basic things across the board. I mean, if you're going to send somebody an expensive cassette that you've had made and ask it back, you've got to enclose a return package stamped, so that all the person getting it has to do is shove it in, seal it and mail it. You know, 'We didn't solicit the tape. Why would we spend $2.53 to mail it back?'

  "A lot of it is just not thinking; not thinking. I mean, in the last year someone asked me to come see them and she sang 12 hits so associated with other performers that there's no way you can hear the first note of the song that you don't think of Judy Garland. Or, 'Now, where in your mind would you get the idea to do a program like this?' What could you possibly offer that would interest an audience enough to say, 'Well, Jesus, I always loved Lena singing 'Stormy Weather.' What is it going to be?' But again, no one has thought.

  "I had a performer the other day, and it was at an audition that someone asked me to go to just listen to some new people, and she sang a ballad and did a very nice, simple reading of it. There would be, probably, 20 people that day through the door that would read it as nicely. But then she said, 'My second number is 'Nelson.'' Well, I happen to know that 'Nelson' is like a revue song that Jerry Herman wrote for *A Night In Hollywood, A Day In The Ukraine*, and it's a spoof of Nelson Eddy. And she sang on and on and on, and I finally said, 'Excuse me, may I stop you?' And she said, 'Yes.'

  "These people are nervous because there are people like Miss Whiting, and Miss Wilson, and the like that are sitting around. And I said, 'Are you aware that you are singing what is supposed to be a funny song, and no one in this room has reacted to anything you have sung?' She just looked at me. And I said, 'Now I want to ask you something. You do know who Nelson Eddy was?' 'Yes.' I said, 'Now, he's available on video; you can get movies with him. Have you watched any of those?' She stared at me and said, 'No.'

  "Now, my job is not to embarrass someone in front of other people. And so I just said, 'Well, thank you.' I'll bet you $5,000 that that particular woman has not watched one since that happened. And you see, that you cannot do for someone. That's like someone having intellectual curiosity. It's like someone reading and coming upon a word they don't understand. If they don't get up and look it up then in the dictionary, they're never going to do that with anything. That's just, I think, a rule of life.

"You know, it's fascinating. I mean, one guy was singing away, 'The old ennui,' and I ask him, 'Do you know what that means?' 'No.' I said, 'Well, tell me, how do you choose to sing one of Cole Porter's most famous songs, and you can't define the word in it?' He just stared at me. But why is he singing? Julie Wilson always says to me, 'Oh, you're so hard on them.' But, I'm not, I'm not, because someone should have said these things to these specific people earlier.

- 'They don't have [managers, unfortunately]. I took Michael Feinstein out of the piano bar on the strip; I gave him that career. I took Steve Ross out of a bar and worked with him for nine years; I gave him the Algonquin Oak Room for two-and-a half years, and his San Francisco debut, and his London debut. I worked with the great Viennese chanteuse the last 11 years of her life, Greta Keller. I've worked with Andrea Marcovicci now for eight. When I worked with these people, there was no agent, manager, booker, anything. What would be ten percent of someone getting $125? $12.50? Who is going to work with that person?

"So when people say to me, 'What is it you do,' I've always done it all. I've done the managing, the booking, the press, the consultant, you know, out of necessity; it's really been out of necessity. And it's tricky, it's very, very, very tricky, because I think a lot of the bad habits that I've seen, where someone should have been helping, there was no one. So they went on their instincts and they were either right or wrong. And that was it."

~     ~     ~

# Symphony Space's Variety Party

GOSPEL CELEBRATION, Brooklyn, NYC
> Early February
> Black Gospel

MARDI GRAS CARNIVAL, Manhattan, NYC
> Middle February
> Variety, Folk and International

WEST INDIAN CARNIVAL EXPLOSION, Brooklyn, NYC
> Middle March
> Reggae, Ska and Caribbean

WALL TO WALL, Manhattan, NYC
> Late March
> Cabaret
> ***Attended***

NEW YORK WINTER BLUES FESTIVAL, Manhattan, NYC
> Late March
> Blues and Traditional R&B
> ***Attended***

WORLD OF PERCUSSION, Manhattan, NYC
> Early June
> Variety, Folk and International

CAJUN/ZYDECO JAMBOREE AND HALLOWEEN DANCE, Manhattan, NYC
> Late October
> Cajun and Zydeco

**Introduction**  Whew! A million festivals under one roof! This abundance of multiple-act musical events, admittedly more like concerts in most cases, is presented chiefly by two cultural bodies sharing the same marquee at Symphony Space.

The first main body is Symphony Space itself, a veritable cultural institution on Manhattan's Upper West Side, due in part to its being, virtually, the only cultural institution on Manhattan's Upper West Side. It provides an array of "popularly priced" arts and education programs within the environs of its invitingly restored art deco theater. Altogether, it draws annual audiences of 100,000 for nearly 250 performances of music, dance, drama, film, avant-garde and children's programs. About 20% of these are Symphony Space's own productions. The combined offerings are impressive for any performing arts center, much less one that espouses a mere community orientation.

It's also well-appreciated by the neighbors for its casual feel and convenient proximity midway between the intimidating glitz of Lincoln Center and the intimidating anti-glitz of Harlem. As one member of the Harlem Cultural Council, another co-producer at the space, once said, "You know why I like Symphony Space? It's not too far downtown for the uptown crowd, and not too far uptown for the downtown crowd to be afraid of coming too far uptown."

Most of its programs are of the "high art" variety, but several times a year Symphony Space dips down into the pop music well. There's its own MARDI GRAS CELEBRATION featuring three to four regional acts of the international folk music variety (e.g., Women of the Calabash). There's Therman Ruth's GOSPEL CELEBRATION, which boasts up to six local acts in a single night, led by one additional national headliner (e.g., The Dixie Hummingbirds). There's Ronnie Italiano's uniquely eclectic, historic and just-plain-wonderful UNITED IN GROUP HARMONY HALL OF FAME AWARDS CEREMONY (see chapter) where you're lucky to witness gospel quartet legends like the Golden Gate Singers alternating with such '50s/'60s street corner types as The Jive Five.

The centerpiece festival of Symphony Space, however, is its own WALL TO WALL that devotes 12 straight hours to a single composer (e.g., Aaron Copland), songwriter (e.g., Irving Berlin), or genre ("downtown" avant-garde) as performed by all-star casts drawn from among New York City's absolutely finest artists. All for free! As you can imagine for this unparalleled value, lines snake down the block all day long to replace those who've indulged their fill. During a typical WALL-TO-WALL — broadcast live on local radio, I might add — up to 5,000 patrons will rotate through the 844-seat theater. I know of nothing else like this simply glorious affair and heartily recommend enduring the usual one-set wait if you arrive later in the day.

The second main body is the World Music Institute [WMI]. Originally a "downtown" presenter, they've moved most of their 80 to 90 concerts per year up to Symphony Space. They still utilize other venues in the outer boroughs, however, depending upon which ethnic cluster they seek to attract.

WMI's like the old British Empire — the sun never sets on their broad programming reach of mostly traditional ethnic folk musicians recruited from all around the globe. They term a good-ly share of their shows, "festivals," though typical quantities of two or three acts suggest "concert" headings more appropriately. A few of these smaller, but no less appealing, annual bills include: WEST INDIAN CARNIVAL EXPLOSION (e.g., Chalkdust), WORLD OF PERCUSSION (e.g., Nana Vasconcelos), INTERPRETATIONS (e.g., LaMonte Young), MASTERS OF INDIAN MUSIC (e.g., Zakir Hussain), CAJUN/ZYDECO JAMBOREE AND HALLOWEEN DANCE (e.g., Beausoleil), and many more of note. WMI's also hosted a number of one-time regional tours, including the BIG SQUEEZE ACCORDION FESTIVAL, the HAWAIIAN SLACK-KEY GUITAR FESTIVAL and the N. Y./PHILLY GOSPEL CARAVAN.

But in any given year, WMI hosts at least four of its own happenings that comfortably meet my minimum festival criteria of four acts per night. IRISH NIGHTS gathers the cream of the regional scene (e.g., Joannie Madden), traditionalists and progressives alike, though perhaps a tad too irregularly for inclusion here. GOSPEL CELEBRATION does the same in Brooklyn with local black gospel choirs, as headlined by someone the caliber of Timothy Wright. SOUNDS FROM AROUND THE WORLD takes a six-act diaspora of internationals and locals (e.g., Hassan Hakmoun) to Merkin Hall near Lincoln Center. And the NEW YORK WINTER BLUES FESTIVAL ['WINTER BLUES'] mixes four interesting performers of multiple styles, fames and ages down at TriBeCa's Triplex Theater. All four events strive for a rootsy camaraderie up onstage.

Whether for festivals or concerts, WMI really digs down deep for unusual and authentic artists. If you meet world music mavens from New York City who seem to have a particularly schooled edge, who continually know of evermore obscure practitioners in ever-more distant sub-genres, you can credit/blame these guys. (*New York Times* music critic Jon Pareles is one of many who has built his knowledge base here via habitual attendance.) WMI's field research puts most festivals of a like stripe to shame.

So by all means "take the A train," as the Strayhorn song goes (though the 1, 2, or 3 subways will leave you right at the doorstep), and prepare for an easy-going, high-quality "who-knows-what" at Symphony Space almost any night of the year.

"The WALL TO WALL concerts are sort of the signature event of Symphony Space...because it's unique, but also because it's how we started." So begins Isaiah Sheffer, Artistic Director of Symphony Space, upon describing the festival's role in the center's origins:     **Festival Review I**

- "My partner, Allan Miller, and I are long-time friends on various projects in which he was the music side, and I was the word side. In '77 we lived in the same apartment building. He came across the hall to my apartment and said, 'I'm looking for a place to conduct the American Symphony Orchestra in some out-of-Carnegie Hall concerts. I'm doing one down at the World Trade Center Plaza, but I want to do one up here in our neighborhood on the Upper West Side.' My wife, Ethel Sheffer, who's a community leader, said, 'What about the defunct old Symphony Movie Theater? Why don't you bring a concert there?'

  "And we all helped out with this one-day concert. We rented this place — which was exactly that, a down-and-out, rather shabby and defunct movie theater of prior elegance — for one day. The idea was Allan's to do something called WALL TO WALL BACH, which happened on January 7, 1978. And we raised some money from the local supermarkets to buy some light bulbs. We all pitched in and cleaned up the place that day.

  "The idea of WALL TO WALL BACH was that Allan would conduct the American Symphony Orchestra because they were paid for by the Musicians Performance Trust Fund. It would be free to the public, a neighborhood community event. It would last 12 hours. And the other major ingredient was you could bring your fiddle, sit next to the professional musicians and play in with them. The professional musicians would be not only the orchestra for the orchestral segment, but [for] a lot of chamber music with many top musical stars, starting with Pincus Zuckerman who lived within a few blocks of here.

  "And so we organized. It was not intended to be a 16-year adventure, [but] at 9:00 that morning, cleaning out the bathrooms, Allan and I realized [when] Zuckerman was rehearsing, that this place had great acoustics, this old dump. We rented some folding chairs. There was no stage; where you saw the stage there was just a flat floor that had been used for occasional setting up of rings for boxing and wrestling. The television came up and covered it, which was important, because they had lights and we didn't. We were on CBS, and we still have that footage as a news feature to remind us of it all.

  "Hundreds of people came with their instruments. We had five soloists and 30 professional singers for a chorus, but for the B-Minor Mass to end the whole thing, Allan brought his baton, and probably 300 other people came, and were divided into choral sections. And many, many people sat in with the orchestra and a mighty sound was produced! We sang the B-Minor Mass, and in the middle of the Gloria in Excelsis Dio, I was weeping at what a terrific day we had pulled off! And the part of me that wasn't weeping was thinking, 'We've got to take over this joint somehow.'

  "The next morning as our kids helped us sort out the nickels, dimes, dollar bills, and occasional five-dollar bills that were thrown into the hat we passed to cover some of the expenses, I made up the name 'Symphony Space,' a space in which to do events in the old Symphony Movie Theater. We resolved it would be a place — if we could organize it, and get community support for it, and get some financing, and turn ourselves into a not-for-profit corporation (all of which happened that spring) — in which we would do various kind of events of our own making, like WALL TO WALL's, or things I would want to do in theater, or other things Allan would want to do in music, or film.

  "As we got the place organized, and we started publishing a monthly calendar that fall (and have kept it up now through 16 seasons), the WALL TO WALL concerts remained our kind of gift to the community."

Quite a gift! The early ones were all classical: Schubert, Bach a few more times, Baroque, Renaissance, Mozart, Beethoven, even a Copland showcase in which I recall seeing Copland, himself, sitting there in the front row with a beaming smile on his face as the entire range of his repertoire got first-class treatments. Given Miller's Oscar-winning filmmaking collaborations with big names like Isaac Stern and Zuben Mehta, well, you can just imagine the high caliber of willing performers taking part.

A turning point came in '85 when one of Sheffer's board members, the daughter of legendary Broadway composer Richard Rodgers, suggested a WALL TO WALL of her father's work. Sheffer and Miller rounded up top stars in the classical, Broadway, jazz and cabaret worlds for "a grand day," and lo, an entirely new direction was born. Subsequent explorations in this vein involved Cole Porter, George Gershwin, and Duke Ellington.

Sheffer then engineered two dalliances with the avant-garde — WALL TO WALL CAGE ("with a lot of wild stuff happening of John's and Merce Cunningham's) and last year's OFF THE WALL TO WALL survey of younger artists. "That was the most far-out one," he chuckles, "and which occurred on the day of the blizzard of the century. Nevertheless, we had, I think it was 2,173 people, and some wag joked that if there had been no blizzard, you would have had 2,173 people, the very same people who are interested in that far-out music."

This year Sheffer responded with an especially impressive and comprehensive look at Irving Berlin's work that my wife and I attended in rapture for several hours. "As you may have read, Mr. Berlin never wanted it to happen," he confides, "but a few years after his death, trying again with the great help of his three daughters, we were able to do this last one.

"Yeah, I was proud of the WALL TO WALL BERLIN lineup. It was a monster job," Sheffer explains of gathering and copying all the far-flung orchestral scores. "And then getting singers who could sing in the keys of the existing scores. Margaret Whiting saying, 'I'd love to do that song, but I couldn't possibly sing it in B-flat,' were among the kinds of problems in front of me. You know, there was a lot of stuff we couldn't do, but I was pleased with the outcome."

He proceeds to reveal further twists in the offing: a WALL TO WALL DEBUSSY/RAVEL in '95 with Miller conducting; a WALL TO WALL WORLD in '96 co-hosted by WMI. Sheffer relates these succession of left turns to the overall appeal of Symphony Space:

- "Our critics, the people who like us, say what's great about Symphony Space is the dazzling diversity. Anybody looking to criticize us says, 'It's incoherent! What are you there? Are you a movie house? Are you doing jazz?' Some people think we're the place where Short Stories [a spoken-word series broadcast live for NPR syndication] are. Other people only know us at the place where the Gilbert and Sullivan is. For some crowds, we're only the place where the world music comes. But the best part of Symphony Space is putting it together between grass roots and super stars, between highbrow and lowbrow, between one kind of music and another kind of music, and ethnically, racially...

"When it's working best," he exclaims, "the Symphony Space monthly calendar is a dazzling mix!" WALL TO WALL, too.

~     ~     ~

The most regular contributor to the calendar's dazzlement is WMI, led by its Executive and Artistic Director, Robert Browning.

**Festival Review II**

To foster this "very special relationship" the two groups share, Sheffer details space-rental subsidies to WMI, grants-getting to upgrade the space, co-op advertising, plus holding many prime weekend dates aside for Browning's bookings. "We're much more than landlords to Robert and we've done some things cooperative with him, like a set of American Indian events, called COYOTE WALKS AROUND, a couple of seasons ago. And we may do more like that. We really think of him as a creative collaborator in that world." WALL TO WALL WORLD is one such Sheffer has in mind for 1996 .

Browning's not a bad guy to collaborate with in this field.

His modest nonprofit "dedicated to the research and presentation of the finest in traditional and contemporary music from around the world," as their brochure reads, nevertheless has some impressive resources at hand:

- It maintains files on over 1,000 performers;

- It's approaching a thousand concert presentations at a combined few dozen sites all around the city;

- It's assembled packages that've roamed the Eastern seaboard, such as its AFRICAN HERITAGE TOUR in '93 featuring Los Pleneros De La 21, The No-Name Gospel Singers, Thokoza, and Alhaji Papa Susso;

- It's got a recording distribution service for over 3,000 titles;

- It's even co-producing a 15-part radio series for NPR syndication of their own concert recordings entitled, "World of Music".

Basically, pick a spot on the planet and Browning can probably come up with a few of its leading authentic music practitioners, track 'em down, recruit 'em, present 'em appropriately, and know how to gain 'em a turn-out. He worked his magic as consultant for one memorable BENSON & HEDGES BLUES FESTIVAL concert I caught a few years back at the Studio Museum of Harlem where Browning paired Piedmont blues pickers, Cephas and Wiggins, with an African griot, and a colorful Marrakesh oud/finger-cymbal duo for a lively demonstration of the world roots of blues. The NATIONAL FOLK FESTIVAL's Joe Wilson (see chapter) essentially took a similar package this year and toured it around inner-city performing arts centers.

Ironically, world music wasn't what got Browning started in concert promotion at all, but world art. This measured, somewhat-scholarly sort, who sports a ponytail and flowing white beard, began as an artist in his native England before immigrating to the U. S. permanently in '74. He worked at an alternative gallery led by a Puerto-Rican artist, Gino Rodriguez. The two found themselves in-between grants in '75 and had to land a new space to await their next expected funding. They located an empty warehouse at 4th and Lafayette Streets (now, Tower Video) and named it the Alternative Center for International Arts (later, the Alternative Museum) with the mission of "presenting visual artists, sculptors and painters from different ethnic and national backgrounds," as Browning relates, "because we felt every nationality had not become part of the Soho kind of scene that was big in those days."

"One day," he continues:

- "We were sitting around one late afternoon figuring out what the hell to do with this space [when] this Argentine musician came in and started talking to us and said they were looking for space to do a concert. We said we'd never done concerts before, but we had this space, and you've got the artists. So we got together. They'd been doing, like, cafes in Queens, and it was a folk group representing three countries of the Andes — Argentina, Ecuador and Bolivia. They did a concert, and we borrowed chairs from the Washington Square Church (which we still use). We got 150 people, and we were pretty excited.

  "It was at the time of the 'jazz-loft' situation downtown. A lot of jazz musicians started coming by, so we presented the first concert in New York for David Murray and about two or three people came. Then Indian musicians started getting in touch with us. We started presenting little concerts. They were all unknown musicians originally. But by '77 to '78, we were already getting quite a reputation in getting audiences varying from, like, 30 to 200 every night...one or two times every weekend. We presented the first concert in New York [from] Elsa Romanian, the Indian violinist, who is now pretty well known. He's played at Lincoln Center [and is] the folk musician from Bengal who Bob Dylan had befriended in the late '60s. And people like this. So our mailing list gradually built up."

Browning and Rodriguez heeded landlord problems by moving their concerts all about Lower Manhattan. Audiences found them, however, whether they were TriBeCa hipsters or native Indians from uptown and the outer boroughs.

"By the early '80s I was kind of getting much more into the music," he explains:

- "I had been curating a lot of the [art] shows, but really, the music had taken over by then. For a start, we were starting to get concerts where we had to turn away people. ...Mostly it was becoming a big chore putting out 250 or 300 chairs and then putting them away again, worried about people rubbing against the half-million dollars' worth of insurance on the walls. So I said to my partner, "I really want to start a music place.' ...I was taking a big chance at the time because I was really worried, because we had a five year old daughter, and we were expecting another child. It was kind-of taking a big leap; starting a new enterprise."

Browning was fortunate to hit the New York State Council on the Arts just as it had commenced $1.5 million in funding, and his concert proposal was among the few applications submitted that first year. It was handsomely supported, and his WMI was officially launched in '85.

Thanks to favorable coverage from the *New York Times*, WMI quickly became a hot spot for ethnic-music insiders. Browning even focused on such American genres as Delta blues, Texan norteno, even Louisianan Cajun/zydeco, as he was the first to program what has since swept this Bayou-crazed city in such clubs as Lone Star Cafe and Tramps. "That was quite successful," Browning adds of the latter, "we had some pretty good audiences."

Browning began with an annual budget of $80,000 but has seen it grow to $1.3 million this year for 70 to 80 concerts in New York City, two packaged tours, plus "considerable outreach programs," as he calls them. By any measure, Browning stretches his programming dollars to present the maximum of this kind of music seemingly possible. He estimates at least 55,000 were entertained last year with stuff they likely couldn't get anywhere else; a good example being the Indian-music showcases in which WMI continues to excel.

Browning sees two dynamics driving New York City audiences. On one hand, there's not the division in physical proximities that separates ethnic neighborhoods elsewhere. "They have to rub shoulders," he observes, "and I think that's one of the things that's kept New York together. However bad things become at times, we have not witnessed the sort of terrible problems that some of the other cities in the U.S. have witnessed in terms of racial and ethnic violence."

On the other hand, this mutual awareness hasn't yet translated to arena seats. Concert crowds are still segregated by ethnic genre, forcing Browning to keep most of his bills, save for WORLD OF PERCUSSION and INTERPRETATIONS, to like-minded artists. Browning finds:

- "One of the big problems is that New Yorkers are very conservative, basically. We think of ourselves as being very open, but I think that New York is very conservative...much more conservative than Europeans in terms of their musical taste. They tend to come to events the *New York Times* tell them to come to. Having the *'Times* cut back on its live-music coverage hasn't helped much."

Still he thanks that newspaper for helping spur attendance for a number of WMI firsts: The Throat Singers of Tuva ("pretty exciting and very eerie") and Nusrat Fateh Ali Khan ("to see the enormous community just coming out en masse"). Browning's fondest first occurred at a recent IRISH NIGHTS show:

- "...When I put together Johnny Cunningham and Kevin Burke for the first time because they had never played together and for years I've been trying to put them together. Johnny had gone off and started playing rock-and-roll, but finally I got in touch with him again. So we put this concert together called 'Celtic Fiddles.' Herschel Freeman took him up as an agent and put him together with Christian LeMaitre up in Canada. That became a tour. The first time they played together they'd never played together on stage. It was just great to see two great fiddlers listening to each other and playing together; I mean, it had so much energy there."

Browning's particular highlights, however, are more the responses he receives from the ethnic constituencies WMI serves. He describes two heartwarming examples:

- "I have one letter from an Arab audience member [about] a concert we did last year on Lebanese folk music, just sort of saying that he couldn't understand how we could do these wonderful things; [that] this is the most extraordinary event for him and his community. It's so rarely that they're able to see their own music performed in a concert situation and not in a party. They really felt the music was appreciated both by Lebanese and Americans. This guy was really raving. He was obviously a well-educated person.

  "We get a lot of letters, actually, from people in the various communities. I got a letter last year from a woman who came to see the percussion concert and she brought a group of people from a small town in Pennsylvania. Her letter was sort-of saying how hard it is for the Sihks in a small community where nobody understands us. 'And we love to come in to your concerts because we see all different people coming from all different ethnic groups together, and enjoying things together, and beginning to understand each other.'

  "That kind of letter, more than anything else, turns me on to realize that this is not just a concert. It's not just a art event. It's not just a community event. It's really a political and social event."

**Artist Mini-Reviews**  I caught '93's seventh annual rendition of 'WINTER BLUES' at the Triplex Theater, a nice steeply sloped space with a brilliant pink screen that would've made a great backdrop for pictures had I remembered to bring my camera. The only difficulty was finding it because Manhattan Community College neglected to post signs demarcating the entrance — no problem in the summer as you'd enjoy a nice waterside stroll in nearby Battery Park, but a real inconvenience in the winter in this dark, empty, wind-swept setting. Browning relayed one story that had a foreign cabby failing to locate the site and leaving octogenarian Delta bluesman John Jackson off in the middle of the West Side Highway.

Once inside, though, the evening unfolded warmly. This show was recorded for re-broadcast on NPR's syndicated "Blues Stage," which would give me a chance to repeat my enjoyment. As my Irish friend, Jack, who joined me quipped about the show's title, "Blues Harp Summit," and his personal propensity for sippin' the barley malt, "You can never get enough Harp!" Indeed.

When Browning first started presenting roots masters like Johnson, New York City had, at best, an underground blues scene centered around seedy dives like Dan Lynch's. Like with Cajun/zydeco, however, the local club scene for blues has since blossomed to support such home-grown talent as The Holmes Brothers, Bobby Radcliff, Joan Osborne, Michael Hill, Popa Chubby, and others still ascending. Still there's only one club, Terra Blues, which presents acoustic practitioners, and even then, it's younger talent like New York City's Guy Lewis and Philadelphia's Ari Eisinger. The older Delta legends remain dispossessed.

Except for 'WINTER BLUES'. Browning continues to find heritage-type talent rarely heard around town. I thought I had a pretty good handle on area musicians, for example, but I'd never heard of the 65-year-old opener Little Sammy Davis, who'd relocated to upstate Poughkeepsie in 1955 after touring with Earl Hooker, Jimmy Uggins and Guitar Slim. Fronting a rent-a-rock-band that gained swing as their set transpired, Davis sounded fairly spry through a half-dozen Chicago-style standards. His own harp tone was of a high whine but not unpleasant or inaccessible. I liked the engaging Davis, but I liked his parting gesture even better where he bowed grandly, his hat held high in one hand, yet grasping his harp and the mic together in the lower hand for one final blow. Now, that's entertainment!

Next up was a real find for me — Charlie Sayles, breaking in a rhythm trio of his own. I'm guessing from what looked like his lived-in Salvation Army suit and a crumpled white shirt that this D. C. resident, who tours Europe predominantly, lives on the cheap and spends a good deal of time busking. He brought much of that kind of cool, loose-limbed, off-the-cuff manner to the stage and had the audience chuckling at humorous street references throughout (e.g., intro-ing one song about police officers as "sure to get you movin'!").

Sayles' originals recall Mose Allison's with their clever lyrics and easy blend of cocktail jazz and country blues. He seemed inclined to let the feeling move him in his solos. One flamed with feeling on an extraordinary tribute to Little Walter. Another dug into a groove for an audience request for "Juke." Another shuffled along tastefully with a Nat "King" Cole smoothness. It's hard to describe Sayles' unusually relaxed and somewhateccentric style, but it certainly wore well with the crowd. I know I could've hung with the young guy all night and would really like to catch his act again if I can — on the street or otherwise.

David "Honeyboy" Edwards was grit to Sayles' gravy. This 79-year-old link to the greats was dressed more like a link to the '70s with his gray flared three-piece, black "Chess" cap, and mustard-colored shirt with huge collars spread-eagled. However, his delivery was unerring...and strong! Edwards sang in a soulful, breathy rasp, almost spooky in its effect. His solo accompaniment was great for alternating solid rhythms with tough blues inflections. You didn't miss a band at all on "Down the Road I'm Goin'" and "Sweet Home Chicago" before Sugar Blue joined-in for "Linda Lou." All throughout I could hear the roots of rock-and-roll in Edwards' ancient licks, master's pacing and just-raw attitude.

Sugar Blue, on the other hand, was rock-and-roll incarnate. This young Grammy-winning New York City native (that's his solo on the Rolling Stones' "Miss You") rarely returns in between Chicago club gigs and European jaunts, but kicked out the jams as if to compensate the home-boys for his absence. Clad head-to-toe in black leather with a harp holster strung across his chest, he re-entered the back of the auditorium wailing and hit the stage in a fusillade of notes. Yet unlike, say, Blues Traveler's John Popper, who only knows how to play one kind of fast, Blue proceeded find to the groove before exhibiting an incredibly versatile range of styles and tempos. This was real virtuosity, not slick gimmicks, and he basically blew us all away away to ovations after nearly every number.

A tight, three-piece unit, with Gil Goldstein from Pat Metheney's band sitting in on accordion, held the floor with a kind of speed funk — an intense fusion of staccato rhythms designed to keep pace with Blue's fiery technique and surprisingly searing vocals. Together they gave the blues canon modern updates, as on a jumpy "Back Door Man" and a "Hoochie Coochie Man," retitled the "Gucci Gucci Man." As the genial Blue left the by-then-limp audience with a drug-free affirmation — "power is my drug of choice" — I couldn't help feeling Blue's crew were just as capable of Robert Cray's crossover success. Let's hope some major sees the light and signs 'em pronto!

So there you have it, a perfect flow of contrasts topped off by a perfectly dynamic headliner — a simply perfect showcase of blues.

Browning:

- "I knew Sugar Blue in New York when we were in the Lower East Side. He used to come in, and he accompanied 'Honeyboy' Edwards a couple of times in concerts. We did 'Honeyboy' Edwards' first concert in New York when he was, I think, 68 at the time. So he used to accompany him, and then he went to Paris and got hooked up with The Rolling Stones. He spent a few years there. But before that, he, like Charlie, were both street players, mostly busking. There used to be an old washboard player with him as well. They used to play around Washington Square. I don't know what Charlie does these days; I know Sugar Blues has regular gigs in Chicago clubs now...."

**Attendance Tip**

For first-time listeners of unfamiliar folk-music genres, especially for Indian, Pakistani and Arab musics he describes as "exciting," Browning assures that live listening is everything; how you just can't get the same feel on disc. "You can enhance the CD recording in all kinds of ways and make it technically perfect," he claims, "but it doesn't have that pizzazz and soul that comes through in a live performance. I think folk music, in particular, in every genre, whether it be blues, or gospel, or Appalachian music, or Irish music, or whatever, when the audience is there, it's something to behold!" In other words, hear it in the flesh before making up your mind.

~ ~ ~

# College Rock Get-Togethers

INDEPENDENT MUSIC FEST, Manhattan, NYC
Late March to Early April
Alternative and College Rock
***Attended***

NEW MUSIC NIGHTS/NEW MUSIC SEMINAR, Manhattan, NYC
Middle July to Late July
Alternative and College Rock
***Attended***

CMJ MUSIC MARATHON AND MUSICFEST, Manhattan, NYC
Early September
Alternative and College Rock
***Attended***

WDRE MODERN ROCK FEST, Manhattan, NYC
Early October
Alternative and College Rock
***Attended***

WDRE ACOUSTIC CHRISTMAS, Manhattan, NYC
Middle December
Alternative and College Rock

**Introduction**  Yeah, yeah, yeah. I'm sure there are quite a few pundits out there who'd attribute the current rise of alternative and college rock solely to Nirvana. Without their four-million-unit breakthrough, "Smells Like Teen Spirit," they'd say that Seattle compatriots like Pearl Jam would've never been considered for their subsequent Top 40 airplay and the entire sub-genre would've remained sub-terranean.

Success sells, certainly. But the underlying reality is that if it weren't Nirvana, it would've been someone else. The "majors" had already scarfed up most promising "indies" in prior years (not to mention having created scores of their own "indie" subsidiaries) and had rolled their heavy publicity/promotion guns into place to flack the officially-designated "next big thing." Nirvana just happened to place the first such hit into the pipeline.

The commercial rise of a '90s musical counter culture was actually a 15-year work-in-process maintained by a succession of lean-and-mean reactionaries to clogged musical arteries. Youth will out in this field, after all, but several institutions should be credited as longtime enablers:

- New media outlets, like MTV and *Spin*, which give voice and look to the emerging movement, making it cool to be someone other than an aging baby-boomer;

- Alternative commercial radio stations, like Garden City's WDRE 92.7 FM, which kept the faith even as cheesy pretenders like Duran Duran threatened to discredit the music for all but squealing teenyboppers;

- College radio stations and concert-programming boards, like New York University's [NYU], which filled the void left by rock music-averse public radio

stations and by established venues prejudiced against young bands without label
tour support or proven audience draws;

- College radio tip sheets, like the *College Music Journal* [CMJ], which alerted both
  commercial and college radio stations to the monthly "buzz bands" and got its
  market scatterings all singing from the same hymn sheet.

Basically, these four combined to create an entire nationwide channel for "indies," sufficiently viable to engage "major" investment even before Nirvana broke out.

To this quartet add the role of "indie" music conferences holding forth on all levels:
international (NEW MUSIC NIGHTS/NEW MUSIC SEMINAR), national (CMJ MUSIC MARATHON) and
regional (INDEPENDENT MUSIC FEST). You can't underestimate the cumulative effect these kinds of
gatherings have had in uniting fractional toilers for networking; in affirming their right to exist
and hopes of sustaining a full-time career; in educating them on the intricacies of the underground
"biz"; and in showcasing their performances to legions of "indie" faithful. That these conferences
have been aped by most other music genres further suggests their value.

Now the "days of sign-and-bonus" — like when 13 bands reportedly inked deals one year
after their appearances at AUSTIN's SxSW (see Austin, TX, Late March) — seem like history. The
conferences may have done their jobs almost too well as A&R reps today are out beating the bushes within even obscure regional scenes (Dayton, Ohio anyone?). Bands everywhere generally have
quicker and easier access to labels than before, while conference appearances have become more
to do with general scene making than with scoring that one fateful discovery. Yet "majors" continue to find this networking sufficiently worthwhile to foot the tabs for their recent signings.

You'll hear grumblings from unsigned bands that conferences are increasingly being
hogged by the big guys, making it cost-ineffective for the little guys. C'mon! If these things are
indeed drawing more "majors," even if they're not biting as fiercely, it simply means better exposure for those unsigned bands who've "got it." It's those who haven't "got it" (and who rarely recognize that they don't, in my experience) who typically grumble the hardest.

My advice to aspiring "biz" types is to keep your expectations in check. Do you gain at
least one industry contact, one marketing idea, and/or one musical exposure that's tangibly worth
the conference fee? Almost always, the answer becomes "yes" in time. And that's in-person meetings. The registrant lists, alone, often pay back the admission price if you've got an appropriate
product to sell direct. This advice goes for bands or for anyone else fulfilling an industry function:
agents, managers, publicists, promoters, programmers, publishers, sponsors, retailers, vendors,
manufacturers and reps of all stripes.

My advice for basic music fans, like I still consider myself, is to simply go and indulge
yourselves! The initial investment seems steep, I know, but when you add up all the benefits, conferences offer better listening value than all but the very, very best festivals.

First, they deliver unparalleled volume ('94's NEW MUSIC NIGHTS presented about 500
bands at 35 venues in just five nights, for example), as well as unrivaled opportunities to catch up-
and-comers before almost anyone else does. Even if just 10% of these acts prove to be "happening," that's still a decent return on, say, $125, the price of its recent all access pass.

Second, the trade exhibits usually let you cart away your fee's equivalent in "comp. product." You don't need a press credential to dig in (though it helps), nor should you feel any particular guilt — that CD only costs the label about a buck to make and has already been charged
against the artist's royalties. It might as well go to someone who'll listen and spread the word.

Third, if you have any business interests at all, you'll be fascinated by the seminars.
Invariably, there are useful tips for your non-music business activities (an early INDEPENDENT
MUSIC FEST seminar is where I first learned about marketing through the internet, for example) as
well as insights into why this-or-that favorite artist of your's might be "making it," while others,
regrettably, aren't. You definitely gain a better feel for the personalities and mechanisms pro-
pelling your musical passions.

Most of all, there's always that one magic moment that makes all this "meet-and-greet"
worthwhile.

At this year's NEW MUSIC NIGHTS I was sipping a cool beverage in the city's latest hot spot, the Mercury Lounge, stacked with kibitzing insiders from brick wall to brick wall. Rising tall to my right was The Ramones' Joey Ramone, there for his buddy, Syd Straw, whose droll wackiness included a near acappella reading of ACDC's "Highway to Hell." Perched quietly two rows before me was Roseanne Cash, there for her buddy, Jim Lauderdale, who perfectly channelled Buck Owens through his terse "neo-post-retro" uptempos. Chatting at a side table was They Might Be Giants' John Flansburgh, there for his buddy, Vic Chesnutt, whose wry demeanor masked a chillingly dark vision, not unlike a redneck Robert Johnson spitting chaw into the abyss. Toss in Giant Sand and June, and you've got a nice night's music for six bucks, huh? And there were over a hundred more nights like them!

Oh, I'm sorry, the magic moment. Nervously taking the stage before Chesnutt was a young alterna-country rocker, Amy Rigby. Clad in black leather hip huggers and matching halter, her pouty lips painted crimson, and her black hair dolled up in an early-'60s flip, Rigby looked like Nancy Sinatra's evil twin. She cued her bandmates, squeezed her eyes, clawed her first twangy chords, then tore through a succession of tributes to bad marriages in the finest C&W tradition — sharp, hurt, clever, tuneful digs stacked loudly upon each other. I was impressed not one whit less for Rigby's set than for CMJ MUSIC MARATHON's magic moment two years prior from a young Mavericks, currently the hottest C&W band reigning in the known universe.

We'll see if she does half as well, and that's precisely the appeal of these events. So get your registration fee in early to secure the advance payment discounts, line up your crash pad with friends or enemies, pack your ear plugs, and prepare for a hectic week of full-metal musical gonzo.

I'm almost relieved that I couldn't wrangle interviews with the chief organizers of these two huge extravaganzas that launched this whole conference category stateside: NEW MUSIC NIGHTS/NEW MUSIC SEMINAR [NMS] and CMJ MUSIC MARATHON [CMJ']. Add up the many musical highlights I've caught over the years, and this chapter might've soared to a zillion words. Interestingly, you'll almost never find historical overviews in either conference's program. Their whole attitude seems to be more about "what's happening now," rather than "what happened when" and "what's it all mean?" In this way, they're both true to the incandescent rock-and-roll spirit they celebrate.

NMS was first in the water by one year. As the *New York Times'* Jon Pareles relates: "[NMS] started as a conspiracy in 1980. It was a gathering in one rehearsal studio of 200 people from the margins of the music business, outsiders plotting to get their music heard. [Fifteen] years later, [NMS] is the biggest music business convention in the United States...an orgy of networking, dealmaking and talent scouting, like the Cannes Film Festival without topless bathing."

I don't know about the "biggest music business convention" part, but the daytime 'SEMINAR does draw 7,500 registrants, if you're counting. However, there's no denying that the evening's NEW MUSIC NIGHTS showcase, with an all-access pass available to the general public for about a third of the seminar fee, is huge! Aside from CMJ', the closest showcase affair that compares is the INTERNATIONAL COUNTRY MUSIC FAN FAIR (see Nashville, TN, Middle June), limited to the first 20,000 C&W fan club members who apply; or possibly the GOSPEL MUSICWORKSHOP OF AMERICA NATIONAL CONVENTION (Varied Sites -- see chapter) for roughly the same number of choir singers.

Apparently, NMS wielded enormous influence in its day. *New York Newsday's* Ira Robbins recalls it as "*the* launching pad for artists on their way up from the underground. In past years, NMS delivered entire musical genres — rap, techno, shoegazing, grunge — and regional scenes, jump-starting movements throughout the industry."

Sadly, this praise may be serving as NMS' epithet.

The trouble started in '92 when one of the two NMS partners, Tom Silverman of Tommy Boy Records, who wanted a more mainstream music industry approach, sold out his interest to the other partner, Mark Josephson. The alternative-oriented Josephson was left holding the financial bag for NMS as well as for his own tip sheet, *Rockpool*, which he doubtlessly started for the same kind of debt-reducing cash flow enjoyed by CMJ's *New Music Monthly*. *Rockpool* failed in early '93, however, casting NMS six figures further in the hole.

Josephson sought to crawl out by scaling down '93's **NMS**. He booked the smaller Sheraton and returned the panel focus back toward nuts-and-bolts how-to's, away from the high-minded artistic and social-consciousness themes upon which **NMS** had built its notoriety. The following year then saw **NMS** programming more American bands and fewer name acts instead of the international selections which distinguished prior years (such as a terrific lineup of young Irish acts I caught in '92, which included LiR — currently opening Acoustic Junction's tour). Alas, I saw this straying from its broad strengths as **NMS** fruitlessly chasing **CMJ**'s more tightly-targeted tail.

I'd hoped to put the query directly to Josephson post-**NMS**, but nobody answered the phones. According to the *Village Voice*'s "Rockbeat" columnist, Josephson padlocked the offices immediately afterward, leaving staffers high and dry. Same deal with the rent, though "Rockbeat" quotes Josephson's landlord as saying, "He's done this before, and he has straightened himself out, so I can't honestly say that he's going out of business because, frankly, I don't know." Stay tuned.

Meanwhile **CMJ**'s fortunes have only risen. Their monthly trade mag, complete with full-length sampler disc, has recently been streamlined for mass-market distribution. You can now buy it on the newsstand for just $4.99 per issue or get an astonishingly-low $29.95 subscription rate for 12 issues. The new slim format looks good, the writing is credible and accessible, plus there's surprising breadth in genres (country, jazz, soul, funk, blues, etc.), media (movies, comics, fanzines, etc.), and happenings (tour schedules, local scenes, etc.).

Best of all, reviews suggest additional recordings for both "Novices" and "Enthusiasts." Forget radio programming, this is a great way to build your own record collection. Certainly, whoever made the country and blues picks in the current issue knew their stuff, nicely mixing the obscure with the pop; the heritage with the hip. They even made worthy "Reading Recommendations."

Thank Robert K. "Bobby" Haber. His genius was in being among the first to spot the connection among two developing media — college radio and new-wave music circa The Ramones, Blondie, Talking Heads, and such. Working out of his parents' basement in Great Neck, Haber published his first *CMJ* in '79, which featured a radio chart patterned after *Billboard*'s. This playlist let everyone know what was happening around the country's alternative stations, making both programmers and trade take notice that this new genre wasn't solely an underground phenomenon isolated to a few hip campuses.

Haber took **NMS**' lead and launched his own seminar/showcase, the 'MUSIC MARATHON, in '81. Unsigned bands were invited to submit demo tapes with the more promising acts being featured live in Manhattan clubs to registrants and public alike. "Majors" soon caught on to these exposure possibilities and paid to introduce their "baby bands," both as headliners for the unsigned lineups and within label-only showcases of their own. I assume **CMJ** appreciated the fees, the advertising, the publicity and the draws, and as long as the music was in keeping with its stylistic preferences, encouraged these "major" relationships. One outcome of this erstwhile partnership has been to bring "majors" and college radio types closer together, thus codifying a career path (even if at the expense of programming eclecticism and spontaneity).

Again, I don't have any source material to chart **CMJ**'s development, but it has grown in 14 years to roughly **NMS**' size. There are 6,000 registrants to **NMS**' 7,500; 350 bands to **NMS**' 500; 30 venues to **NMS**' 35; four nights to **NMS**' five, and so forth. There's not yet **NMS**' artistic breadth or hall exhibitors. However, **CMJ**'s actually overtaken **NMS** in the quality of accommodations. It now occupies the gilded dowager, the Waldorf Astoria, where President Clinton stays on his U. N. forays. The hilarious scene of tattooed grungemeisters and fur-bedecked matrons commingling under the Waldorf's crystal chandeliers simply begs a screen treatment.

**CMJ**'s carved out two artistic niches distinct from **NMS** which both speak to me.

First, there's the performing-songwriter angle. In '93, **CMJ**' staffer Jim Caligiuri put together a wonderful little noontime symposium in an upstairs ballroom featuring six artists: Julee Cruise, Patty Larkin, Lisa Germano, David Gray, Kate Jacobs and Chris Kowanko. Though the program was only an hour, each got to talk some while performing two songs solo acoustic

(Cruise was accompanied by her guitarist) to a roomful of twenty-somethings. I was intrigued to see Cruise, the chanteuse from TV's "Twin Peaks," and Larkin, the progressive folkie, booked together, and happy to see Larkin strut her formidable guitar chops before Cruise's presumably bigger draw.

I was surprised, myself, by the talent of the other four newcomers, particularly (Chris) Kowanko, an Australian native of Ukrainian descent presently holed-out in Brooklyn. Beneath his self-effacing demeanor and faux-naive style lurked an exceptionally gifted lyricist, deft with imagery and left-handed statements cutting deep to the heart of his protagonists. I turned Kowanko's self-titled debut onto my colleagues at *The Performing Songwriter* who also flipped over his work. Hopefully, Kowanko will rise from the ashes of his defunct PolyGram deal to find the wider hearing he really deserves.

Second, there's the alternative country angle (which I suspect Caligiuri has a hand in, too). **CMJ'** remains the only festival I know of north of Austin that routinely features these kinds of acts. The '92 Mavericks show I spoke of also boasted Jason Ringenwald fronting a new band, Neon Frontier, four New Orleans roustabouts calling themselves Cowboy Mouth, plus a pair of local honky-skronkers, Chain Gang and The Belmont Playboys. Not bad for a few dollars, huh? Well, check out this '91 CMA-sponsored "Writers in the Round": Guy Clark, Jimmie Dale Gilmore, Rosie Flores, Radney Foster, and Jim Lauderdale. Or these '93 Lone Star Rodehouse showcases: The Kentucky Headhunters with Jimmie Johnson (Chuck Berry's keyboardist), Jimmy Hall (from Wet Willie), Dave Hole, Kieran Kane (of the O'Kanes), The Bisquits, Paul Metsa, Melissa Ferrick, and The Cactus Brothers.

Liberty Records also snuck The Cactus Brothers into another noontime showcase at a small meeting room just off the exhibit hall. Despite the chaos from trying to clear away a prior panel and set up amidst the scattered chairs in just 10 minutes, they just blew me away. These seven bad boys combined the free-wheeling, rock-and-roll attitude of their buddies, The 'Headhunters, with the homey reverence of an Appalachian string band. Chief culprit for this winning mix was scraggly David Schnaufer, merely the best dulcimer player in the world, who seemed glad to cut loose from his Nashville session shackles and have himself some fun. Lead singer-songwriter Paul Kirby, son of noted Nashville tunesmith Dave Kirby, kept the instrumental romps from turning silly by contributing a number of crisp, sincere, emotion-centered songs to channel the band's manic energy.

The whole time I kept feeling like I was stealing an intimate pleasure we paying public aren't supposed to get. You'll feel that way yourself throughout these two conferences, I promise.

**Festival Review**  Both **NMS** and **CMJ'** declare the "indie" spirit, despite having ballooned to mega proportions. The upstart INDEPENDENT MUSIC FEST [IMF] doesn't have to make that claim — it's always been "100% indie" as its program impudently states.

**IMF** is strictly student-run by a multidisciplinary team from the NYU Programming Board (which once had its own NBT record label, mind you). Some kids from the School of Education's Music Business Technology program have career aspirations; others just wanna' have fun and boost their favorite bands. What's more, unlike too many **NMS** and **CMJ'** gatekeepers, they check any self-important attitudes at the door.

Just ask **IMF**'s "Supremo Supremo Advisor", David Schnirman (a.k.a. Assistant Director for Student Activities). "We poke fun at everything we do," he confides, "but we take ourselves very seriously, professionally anyway, in the sense that I believe, and the students end up believing, that there's no difference between them and somebody who's been doing it in the field, except that the person who's been doing it in the field is getting paid for it and has been doing it for years. [The students] can do the same thing they do."

Schnirman and four Programming Board cohorts conceived the first **IMF** for '92 while "sitting around, frustrated about what was going on musically. I'm 39 years old, and you know how old the students are, and we all listen to the same stuff. I've been in the music industry as a production manager for 20 years, and I get bored of, you know, the same old radio crap, same old everything. What we realized was...we're probably the best venue to help the underdog get a word out there."

The five-some then assembled an advisory board from the "biz" and created a weekly meeting schedule for students to be trained in the art of such trade show-presenting. An immediate problem was that NYU doesn't program any concert events where alcohol is sold. "People want to go to clubs," Schnirman explains of the preferred option, "so we just went around the first year to a bunch of clubs and said, 'Listen, we've got this idea we want to propose, you know, and we're going to get these bands from here and there and there and there...'"

Schnirman flashed a list of early sign-ups that included Bob Mould ("you can't get any more independent than him"), Freedy Johnston, Syd Straw, Scott Kempener (ex-Del Lord), Melissa Ferrick, Superchunk, Cell, Alice Donut, and 36 others. Eight clubs — "five minutes' walking distance," says Schnirman — bought in and **IMF** was off and running. There was a modest trade show on the floor of the student union plus nine panels in closely confined class rooms where attendees had a better shot at asking detailed questions and/or shouting down any pretentious bullshit. There was even a keynote speech from then Presidential candidate, Jerry Brown (remember him?), who basically blew the New York State primary that week by doing counter culture gigs like this one vs. hustling disaffected working-class votes from among the outer boroughs.

Aside from its smaller scale and tight proximity, three features positioned **IMF** apart from its conference big brothers:

- Bands didn't have to enclose any fees in order to submit demo tapes for showcase consideration.

(Schnirman makes a big deal of this as a sign of band friendliness, though I don't see how the $30 charged by **NMS** is prohibitively high. What he's likely implying is a more favorable acceptance rate than **NMS'** 150 slots culled from 3,000 submissions.)

- There was also an A&R Panel, where bands registered upon arrival for private 15-minute sessions with any two participating labels they choose to.

(Now that's the band friendliness Schnirman spoke of.)

- As for patron friendliness, there was **IMF**'s affordable admission policy: just $35 for all-access badges ($20 for students with ID's), good for all conference activities.

Unreal! Considering **IMF**'s regional band roster wasn't dramatically different from **NMS'** or **CMJ**'s in parts, it felt like a dirty steal.

Schnirman credits these features and "luck, luck, luck" for **IMF**'s resulting prosperity, but good music plays a role, too. For example, I've appreciated **IMF** introducing me to such performing songwriter-oriented labels as Bar/None (see Johnston and Jacobs, above). There's a shrewd intelligence underlying the shaggy garage/pop stance of its bands, which helps engage your mind even as you're swigging brews and shaking butts. Johnston's vein-popping vocals are a tad extreme for my tastes (though there's no denying he's an exquisite lyricist), so I've found myself drawn more to the undercard on the Hoboken label's annual **IMF** showcases, such as the strum-in-cheek Swales.

As for his own musical highlights, Schnirman cites a number of the bands signed to the Go Carts label run by "Head Headache" Greg Ross, one of **IMF**'s five co-founders. Buttsteak ("amazing"), Beserk ("love them"), and others get Schnirman's kudos. "It has nothing to do with the affiliation," he claims, "they're just great bands." More non-affiliated plusses go to Gary Lucas, Noah Harrison ("real good artist"), the Swales ("terrific") — indeed, the entire Bar/None roster ("Bar/None's been great; they're just a great label") — as well as such others' belonging to Alias, Razor & Tie, Imago, Matador, and Enemy.

Even with such a strong arsenal of "indie" labels helping out, it's interesting '93's **IMF** actually helped boost at least two local performing songwriter acts — The Murmurs and Lisa Loeb — onto "major" deals this year. "We take no credit for that," demurs Schnirman of such signings. "They do it all on their own. I mean, we don't influence it in any way; we're just the conduit for that. We set it up so it can happen, and they go from there. And we like that."

"The only thing I want to say is that it is completely student run. They do everything from soup to nuts," Schnirman concludes, noting one student's breathless exhortation, "'I'm so tired, I can't breathe!' I mean, that's my favorite comment, because they work so hard on it."

**See Also**    There are no panels or exhibitors or programs or badges or promo or keynoters or the typical seminar stuff, but the WDRE MODERN ROCK FEST ['ROCK FEST] has delivered stronger same-stage/same-night bills than any of the confabs, above. Such alterna-extravaganzas usually occur on the Saturday nearest the station's FM dial numbers, 92.7 (9/27, September 27th, get it?). Their best one might've their first one in '91.

That year WDRE, a decade-old commercial affiliate broadcasting from Garden City, sought to program a big charity bash in nearby Eisenhower Park. Plans fell through at the last minute, sending Marketing Director Theresa Byers scrambling for club sites to accommodate the 20-odd bands (with 18 being major label acts, I recall) she'd booked. I hit most of the resulting week's shows scattered across Long Island and New York City — my first live exposure to this music — and was blown right away. Among my many highlights included an ominous Smashing Pumpkins, a whimsically literate Judybats, and an incendiary Wonderstuff. (Why the latter's great live show hasn't broken them out way-big, I can't imagine.)

Byers shrunk '92's fest to one-day/six-bands and moved it to Manhattan's cavernous disco-drome, The Palladium. I caught pieces of it that year before running off to the GREENWICH VILLAGE FOLK FESTIVAL (New York, NY — see chapter), but missed seeing any listings in the papers for this year. Meanwhile, a second WDRE popped up in Philadelphia, and the two affiliates both hosted a touring package last December featuring Tony Bennett, Cowboy Junkies, Teenage Fanclub, Nick Heyward, Live, and The Catherine Wheel. They called their stop-offs WDRE ACOUSTIC HOLIDAY CONCERTS.

As I opened this week's *Village Voice*, I spied a full-page ad announcing a sarcastically-titled 75TH ANNIVERSARY WDRE ACOUSTIC CHRISTMAS. This one's booked into Manhattan's ornate Beacon Theater and boasts two days with nine major names apiece. I don't know if it's also a tour, which would disqualify it for this book, but it simply looks too big to travel. Let's hope it repeats as often as its prefix!

**Postcript**    As I'm putting the finishing touches on this book in early July, 1995, it appears the NEW MUSIC NIGHTS is no more, as I feared. However, it looks like it's been replaced by the MACINTOSH NEW YORK MUSIC FESTIVAL, which has retained the prolific showcases (its ads trumpet over 300 acts at 15 clubs over six days), while adding some big internet/interactive thing in place of the seminars/exhibits. 'Wave of the future, I guess!

~     ~     ~

# Classic Acappella

UNITED-IN-GROUP-HARMONY BLACK HISTORY MONTH CELEBRATION, Manhattan, NYC
Middle February
Acappella and Doo Wop

RONNIE I.'S HARMONY HAPPENING WEEKEND, Trevose, PA
Middle March
Acappella and Doo Wop

**HARMONY SWEEPSTAKES A CAPPELLA FESTIVAL/N. Y. REGIONAL**, Manhattan, NYC
Early April
Acappella and Doo Wop
***Attended***

**UNITED-IN-GROUP-HARMONY HALL OF FAME AWARDS CEREMONY**, Manhattan, NYC
Early April
Acappella and Doo Wop
***Attended***

RICHARD NADER'S ROCK AND ROLL REVIVAL SPECTACULARS, Multiple Sites, NY, NYC, NJ
Various Dates
Acappella and Doo Wop

DICK FOX'S DOO-WOPP EXTRAVAGANZAS, Multiple Sites, NY, NYC, NJ
Various Dates
Acappella and Doo Wop
***Attended***

**Festival Review I**

Here's not one, but two, of my most moving festival moments — from a single evening of the UNITED-IN-GROUP-HARMONY HALL OF FAME AWARDS CEREMONY [UGHA 'AWARDS'], no less.

The first involved a thirtyish acappella trio from Queens, Things To Come. My wife and I had caught them the month prior at the HARMONY SWEEPSTAKES A CAPPELLA FESTIVAL/N. Y. REGIONAL [HARMONY SWEEPS']. They were far from the most progressive act there (my wife even caught them singing flat in parts), but their driving rhythm and winning spirit on such '60s chestnuts as "Gypsy Woman" carried the afternoon and swept them to regional victory.

Anyway, Things To Come were there to introduce and support their mentor, 78-year-old vocalist Harry Douglass. This founding member of The Deep River Boys, a gospel quartet tracing its roots back to Virginia's Hampton University in '36, had moved to Jamaica, Queens, where he'd tutored the trio from toddlers to present. Needless to say, the proudly smiling Things to Come didn't miss a note in supporting Douglass' star turn on such classics as "It Had To Be You," "I'm Confessin'," and "Come Rain or Come Shine."

And what a turn it was! Douglass, who'd recorded with Count Basie, Thelma Carpenter and Fats Waller during a 40-year career, positively beamed. You could tell that here was a guy renowned as much for his buoyant personality as his graceful singing style. Vocally, Douglass appeared not to have missed a step in blending equal parts fullness, soulfulness and smoothness. Things To Come then bowed out with a driving rendition of "Take The A Train" before leaving for the waiting limo to the plane for the HARMONY SWEEPS' National Finals in San Rafael, California.

Now, to introduce this pairing, there'd been a film clip from the '40s portraying "The Deeps" in their heyday, singing as handsome young coachmen in a train scene. It would've been hard to distinguish their confident, silky harmonies from the Mills Brothers' — they were that well-meshed and percolating. So after Things to Come left, Douglass flashed his broad, toothy smile and invited 82-year-old Vernon Gardiner from his seat in the crowd to join him onstage. You see, Gardiner, who sung with Douglass for 20 years, was the only other original member of The Deeps alive and well enough to travel. "Working by themselves," *New York Newsday*'s Richard Torres reported, "the two elder statesmen dedicated a plaintive, haunting 'Poor Little Lamb' to their former colleagues. Few standing ovations were better deserved."

Standing ovations? Hell, there wasn't a dry eye left in the house! Yet even this heart-tugger proved merely a tune-up for the night's headliner.

The Golden Gate Quartet was there to celebrate their 60th year singing (that's right, 60th!) and their first performance back in their native America since Christmas Day, '57. They, too, had come out of the Hampton area in '34 with 78-year-old Orlandus Wilson and 80-year-old Clyde Riddick joining the group in '36 and '40, respectively (the other two members, Clyde Wright and Paul Brembly, signing-on in '54 and '71). "The Gates" were nothing less than the finest spiritual group of their day, having pioneered a rhythmic narrative style — some say the precursor of today's rap. Among their 200 recorded standards are "Noah," "Swing Down Chariot," "Jezebel," "Shadrack," "Wade In The Water," "Joshua Fought The Battle Of Jericho," etc. They held down their end of John Hammond Sr.'s 1938 "Spirituals to Swing" concert in Carnegie Hall while performing for F. D. R.'s 1941 inaugural.

Well, like many African-American performers from that time, The Gates tired of racism in America and found easier acceptance upon relocating to France. Their tour schedule remained unabated (they had to cancel a week's worth of concerts to appear here) as they played 77 countries in the intervening 36 years. Out of protest the U. S. had not been one; therefore, this night was to be their official concert homecoming as well their anniversary celebration. And to underscore the poignancy of the occasion, preceding their appearance there was a black-and-white film clip of the foursome in their youthful prime.

As with Douglass, the years melted away when The Gates took the stage in their purple double-breasteds, snapped their fingers and began singing. There was nothing flashy in their delivery (no leads, for example), rather, they impressed with incredible ensemble tightness, like a well-oiled machine. They began their five-song set with a sultry-smooth "Down By The Riverside," and seemed to alternate vocal parts like they traded mic stands in a nice piece of showmanship. This technique-of-the-unexpected was most evident on "Motherless Child," where wispy soft high parts seemed to emanate unseen from different members in accents mournful enough to break your heart. Though The Gates closed with a snappy "When The Saints Go Marching In," virtually every gesture of their's brought thundering applause up to, and beyond, their receiving Hall of Fame plaques.

I suppose what contributed to the outpouring I witnessed, as I scanned the art-deco auditorium of Symphony Space, was a packed house of working-class guys in their 50's and 60's, equally mixed between blacks and whites. I suspected a majority were acappella types, themselves, who'd grown up singing together on street corners and listening to groups like The Deeps and The Gates, or at least the thousands of others who'd been influenced by them. 'Like The Manhattan Transfer's Tim Hauser, who stepped up impromptu to reminisce on getting started as a teenager across the river in 'Jersey and what such a vocal heritage meant. For him and them, this was their personal art form that hadn't yet received the recognition they felt it deserved. This, in sum, was their lives, too.

The emotion in the air was so thick you could've cut it with a sword!

Thank Ronnie Italiano. He's the one in the silver dinner jacket acting as imperturbable M. C. of this multi-media extravaganza. Those slides projected to the auditorium's screen of someone flipping through all the 45's of the featured groups? Those are from his extensive record collection as are the film clips that intersperse the slides. The perfectly-detailed program notes are also Italiano's, compiled most likely from the encyclopedic data of the field he carries inside his head.

As Douglas proclaimed to the audience on his first chance meeting of this genuinely sincere and enthusiastic booster: "Man, this guy seemed to know more about me than I did!"

Italiano founded UGHA in '76 as a nonprofit organization "dedicated to preservation, exposure and education of American pioneer vocal group music." Don't use the word "doo-wop" around him. Italiano decries the standard phrase as a "parody." His preferred monicker? "Classical vintage vocal group harmony" that extends to '30s/'40s gospel inspirations like The Deeps and The Gates.

In its 18 years, UGHA has grown to 3,000 dues-paying members. They convene at Italiano's bequest on an almost monthly basis. At least twice a year it'll be at Symphony Space for a more formal concert experience: the **UGHA 'Awards'**, plus a UGHA Black History Month Celebration. All three events typically feature from six to nine groups. At least once a year they'll also occupy the Trevose Ramada Hotel for Ronnie I.'s Harmony Happening Weekend, though a second extended weekend has also taken place intermittently on New Year's Eve.

The rest of the year Italiano's fellow connoisseurs gather at various sites around the metropolitan area for what he terms, "Meetings/Shows," that is, combo festivals/expos/auctions/hang-outs, etc. (Paul Simon recently intended a brief visit, Italiano points out, yet ended up spending the entire night.) Sometimes Italiano gives these events titles, but usually he'll just refer to their number. He's up to "M/S 197" and promises a special "all-day celebration" on March 25, 1995, at Schuetzen Park in North Bergen, New Jersey for his 200th.

Italiano's a collector, himself, stretching back 40 years to his youth when he was the only kid in his Italian neighborhood searching out the records of his African-American singing idols. He now owns a record store, Clifton Music, to facilitate his lifelong hobby and has branched out into running a record label, a booking agency, and concert promotion for his beloved artists. He also hosts "Ronnie I.'s R&B Party" Wednesday nights on WYNE-FM, which is how he got into founding the UGHA in the first place.

"In '76," he explains, "I just felt there was a need for it. You know, I grew up with this music, and I loved it, and there just wasn't anything around. I had gone to places like Connecticut where they would show you a little taste of it, and I just thought the New York area would be perfect to have acappella groups dig into the roots. So we formed the organization through my radio show at the time and started with 100 people in '76."

Italiano agrees with my observation about his audience's racial and income mix, adding that members are drawn from all about the country and the world, as well. California-based Hauser is a good example of someone with New York City roots eager to "keep in touch with the scene."

Why has New York City remained such a hotbed for this classic acappella rock, even though the music's heyday in the mid-'50s saw groups from all around the country emerge to score hits? "Well, it's kind of an underground culture in this area here," Italiano adds, "because you get from the cities, you get from Brooklyn, you get from the Bronx, you get from Newark. It seems to be handed down. I've got young kids coming in here and they're asking for this kind of music — what was from their fathers, their uncles, their older brothers. It doesn't die here."

I point out the numerous commercial opportunities afforded the name acappella music acts by such promoters listed in the heading above. However, Italiano's quick to caution of his competitors that:

- "Most of the groups that they do book are commercial groups who don't even sound like their records. What we try to do is show people that it's an art form, it's not just making a quick buck and putting the group on because you remember the song. I want the people to go home and play their records of the group they saw in the show and say, 'Wow, they sound the same!' That's what we're trying to do. We're trying to stress the harmony aspects of it as an art form.

  "And a lot of times, well, you know, they have to use a large name, a name that may not be good, but they'll bring people out. And people will be disappointed, but they'll come out the next time, I don't know why. But when we do a show, we don't disappoint people. We do the real McCoy."

I agree with Italiano's assessment regarding a recent DICK FOX SUMMER-NIGHT DOO-WOP EXTRAVAGANZA my wife and I caught at Long Island's Westbury Music Fair this past June. The first half of the show was fair to middling with a number of opening acts featuring only their original lead singer who, as often as not, just didn't have it any longer. However, the headliners still had it, and then some! That particular afternoon Earl "Speedo" Lewis and The Cadillacs put on one of the sprightliest stage shows I've ever witnessed, while The Duprees awed with ultra-tight harmonies, dynamics and versatility. Invariably, solid pros such as these two are shared among all the promoters, Italiano included.

Another top practitioner I was roundly impressed with at Italiano's **UGHA 'AWARDS'**, and one that's recently been recorded by Rounder Records and booked around the folk festival circuit, is The Jive Five. "You see now, here's a perfect example, the Jive Five," Italiano exclaims. "The Jive Five, they're excellent. They're just phenomenal. If you put the records on now, you wouldn't know the difference. There's very few of those so-called big marquee performing groups that can match this, and yet, [original lead singer Eugene Pitt's] not going to get the kind of money some of those other groups get, or get the work. That's where we come in."

Italiano's ultimate ambition is to build an actual Hall-of-Fame to enshrine permanently the recipients of his annual **UGHA 'AWARDS'**. "We're collecting memorabilia now, and we do have some really rare things, some rare posters. We do have Frankie Lyman's headstone. We raised money to put it on his gravesite, and then [there was] all this litigation, and we still have it. It's in my window here in the store."

He also perceives this dream facility as a performing arts center that would house a theater to present these classic groups, a smaller hall for his monthly "M/S's," rooms to house his nonprofit association, record store and memorabilia collection, and a restaurant for hob-nobbing and such. "The main goal," Italiano explains, "is just [that] the music can be treated as an art form, and have its place with jazz and folk."

It's precisely this kind of devotion from Italiano which comes forth onstage; that brings heritage acts like The Deeps and The Gates out of retirement or exile to give of themselves so freely. "They do [appreciate it]," he responds. "That's why I'm able to motivate them and work with them. They understand that, you know, it's not a commercial venture for me, it's from the heart. It's something I want to keep alive.

"It's my life."

**Artist Mini-Reviews**  Here are Italiano's comments on my two emotional highlights:

Harry Douglass: "I felt that way, too, but we've had Harry before and every time Harry is with us it's an emotional highlight. You know, we had his birthday party a couple of years ago. When I bring him back to what I call a collectors show, which we do twice a year, Harry always steals it."

Golden Gate Quartet:

• "They were really thrilled. I mean, we communicate (they fax me or call me) and there's still talk about what a wonderful trip it was. You got to remember now, they made a vow one time they're never going to come back to this country again. 'They turned their back on us.' The Smithsonian had called them to get them and they refused.

"Then, we wrote to them, and we were talking to them, a few of our members. They felt that what we were doing was sincere and warm, and they decided they wanted to do this just before they pass away. Clyde Whitaker is 80 years old — he's not as healthy — and they did come. And we feel quite honored because they saw our sincerity, and they came for us, you know? ...It was really stirring. It was great."

~     ~     ~

**Festival Review II**  If the UGHA 'AWARDS' is all about attempting to preserve "what happened when," the HARMONY SWEEPS' is more about showcasing "what's happening now!"

The liner notes for the live compilation recording from '93's 'National Finals cites the competition's goals as: "To celebrate all forms of music performed acappella and to encourage new directions and experiments in vocal music. From the gospel jazz of Take 6 to the adventurous harmonies of Zapp Mama or The Bulgarian State Women's Choir, to the chart-topping pop and R&B of Huey Lewis and The News and Boys II Men, vocal music has once again become a presence in this [music] world dominated by technology."

You'll notice these notes don't cite avant-garde practitioners like Meredith Monk, but neither do they cite the classic '50s/'60s styles prevalent in the New York City marketplace. Progressive modern pop, a la Bobby McFerrin, dominates. That's why such past winners from this region as Regency, Doo Wa Zoo and Things To Come have generally finished out of the running at the nationals, which gathers the finest from at least seven regions for a sold-out live showdown in San Rafael, California. Oh, well.

Locally, the regional finals are really fun affairs. They're held in classy, cozy clubs such as The Ballroom and Caroline's (which recently won some kind of national architectural award for interior design). At least three-quarters of the audience are nail-biting friends and family of the dozen competing groups, which lends the afternoon a rabid partisanship wonderful to behold. Still mutual appreciation prevails as all participants gather at the end for a group rendition of "the a cappella national anthem," as the program notes declare, "Good Night Sweetheart."

The first year I attended the HARMONY SWEEPS' in '93, I stumbled in from a roadtrip for the second half, but was knocked out by the quality of the acts and the spirit of the crowd. And I didn't even catch the two winners from the first half of the show, Regency and runners-up 14 Karat Soul! I said to my wife, a classical-trained vocalist herself, "You gotta' check this out next year."

So we did.

The contrasts were fun as some groups boasted impressive credits while others appeared little more than wedding bands and street-corner types dressed up for the day. Accordingly, the musical styles ranged from Easter-suited gospel ecstasy to pinkie-ring'd-and-gold-chain'd '50s serenading. Each group got about 15 minutes to shine, which lent them time for three to four numbers each. I can't say '94's talent impressed me quite as much, though there were several repeat contenders. My wife and I saw it as a toss-up between Things To Come and eventual runners-up Afterglow, a swing-era quartet who might've won with a bit more diminuendo and crescendo to their arrangements.

However, we were both bowled over whenever hosts 14 Karat Soul took the stage. Man, these five guys had the whole package: looks, rapport, charisma, skill, style, energy, you name it. Their repertoire ran from soulful to swinging on "What A Wonderful World," "It's All Right," "This Boy," and an ultra-hot medley of "Itty Bitty Pretty One," "Don't Be Cruel," and "Rockin' Robin," which shook the house to the rafters. Whoa! If locals Milo Z. have been able to parlay their funk re-treads into a PolyGram deal, then these young men from East Orange, New Jersey, have at least as much potential. Look for 'em!

**See Also**

Italiano has two main commercial competitors plying the same vicinity, though both have broader scopes than just acappella revues. Richard Nader has been booking his 'ROCK AND ROLL REVIVAL SPECTACULARS into Madison Square Garden and other big venues fairly regularly since '69. These six-star marathons just celebrated their 25th anniversary. Nader also has his own concert promotion firm and regularly programs his artists on package tours, and into resorts and festivals all around the area. You can catch his roster at WELCOME BACK TO BROOKLYN, the QUEENS FESTIVAL, the AFRICAN STREET FESTIVAL (see respective chapters), the ATLANTIC ANTIC, and a number of other big street fairs sponsored by the *New York Daily News*.

Dick Fox appears even more active than Nader on the concert side. You can count on his even bigger 'DOO-WOPP EXTRAVAGANZA's at least four times a year at Westbury Music Fair on Long Island; once at Brooklyn's Paramount Theater; once or twice at Madison Square Garden; once, possibly, at Kutcher's Country Club in Monticello, New York; once, definitely, at the Garden State Arts Center in Holmdel, New Jersey; and once, occasionally, at the TropWorld Casino and Entertainment Resort in Atlantic City. Whew! There'll be a minimum of seven acts, up to 34 for his ULTIMATE DOO-WOPP FANTASY WEEKEND at Kutcher's. The latter even boasts "the chance of a lifetime to sing and reminisce" with these stars including a photo session, numerous performances and cast parties, plus the opportunity for you and your group to perform with full musical accom-

paniment before them, the audience and a panel of judges. 'Sounds like fun!
        Both guys put on too many events for my brief heading above, so check the **New York/ New York City Festival Listings**.

~     ~     ~

*Things To Come, Harmony Sweepstakes A Cappella Festival/N. Y. Regional.*

# Downtown Jazz, I

BROOKLYN BEAT MEETS THE BLACK ROCK COALITION, Manhattan, NYC
Middle March
Rap

P. S. 122 NEW MUSIC SERIES, Manhattan, NYC
Early April or Early November
Alternative Jazz
***Attended***

FIRE WALL TOTAL ARTS FESTIVAL, Manhattan, NYC
Middle June to Late June
Alternative Jazz
***Attended***

JIMI HENDRIX BIRTHDAY PARTY, Manhattan, NYC
Late November
Alternative and College Rock

The delightfully engaging, passionate and quick-witted Diedre Murray is resisting me. **Introduction**
   I'm trying to place a label on her combination of festival events, which also includes her summer concert series, "Rooftop Concerts at Twilight," atop the 53rd Street YWCA. Or rather, I'm attempting to give potential patrons from out-of-town a feeling for the music she programs at the FIRE WALL TOTAL ARTS FESTIVAL [FIRE WALL'], and the P. S. 122 NEW MUSIC SERIES [P. S. 122'].
   I called it "M-Based," after the loose association of Brooklyn-based alternative-jazz musicians, the M-Base Collective, who until recently had all been recording for German record label, Jazz Music Today [JMT]:

- Partly because her frequent curating partner, trombonist Craig Harris, is a JMT artist;

- Partly because there's often been at least one other JMT artist in many FIRE WALL' concerts: Steve Coleman, Jean Paul Bourelly, Bob Stewart, Tim Berne, Hank Roberts, Marvin "Smitty" Smith, Michelle Rosewoman, etc.;

- But mostly to relay how I experienced the music.

   You see, I found Murray's concerts challenging and experimental, but seductive, as well, and not unlike the many JMT discs in my collection. Or, as M D. Carnegie, writing for the *Washington City Paper* described a Coleman/Greg Osby collaboration off the latest JMT anthology, *Flashback On M-Base*: "The piece reveals immediately what is so good about M-Base at its best — the ability to make theoretical explorations without sacrificing groove and emotion."
   Unlike many strident "downtown" avant-skronkers, JMT artists tastefully insinuate a variety of mainstream musical references, mostly Afro-centric; notably the funk of James Brown. (One JMT assemblage, who appeared at '92's FIRE WALL', calls itself "Cold Sweat," after the James Brown standard.) They also modulate themselves to somewhat-more-accessible volumes, tempos and changes such that you can either lean back for enjoyment or lean forward for every note of their universally acclaimed techniques.
   Either way, JMT purveys one of my favorite musical mixes of any genre. And of course my out-of-town readers could pick up any of three JMT samplers (PolyGram) and listen for them-

selves a priori.

Convenient, huh? Not so fast.

Murray, whose own background as composer and cellist includes a touring stint with Henry Threadgill and recorded collaborations with Fred Hopkins (Black Saint, Victor), is surprised at how many JMT artists I point out but says a more likely association might be the Chicago-based A. A. C. M. However, she refutes even this characterization by citing a wealth of participating artists outside any camp or clique, as well as a host of collaborators from other genres and disciplines such as dance, rap, poetry and painting.

After all, Murray informs me, "TOTAL ARTS" means exactly that — total arts involvement and interaction, not just jazz. She explains:

- "The whole idea of FIRE WALL' is to take like-minded groups of people from all disciplines and put them together. Forinstance, put an Odetta together with a Hamiett Bluett and a [dancer] Blondell Cummings — people who normally would never work together, but who have like minds. It's supposed to be multidisciplined, always."

"Let me go into the history," Murray offers.

She'd held her post as Music Curator for P. S. 122 when her long-time colleague, Harris, approached about some dates concurrent with '92's JVC JAZZ FESTIVAL (New York, NY — see chapter). Apparently, Harris had invited some other guest musicians to join his big band for a three to four day gig, people like David Murray and others who'd been having difficulty scoring bookings on JVC's notoriously conservative lineups.

Murray felt P. S. 122 would probably be unwilling to incur the costs of re-opening their funky performing arts space for a few concerts, but might be excited about a slightly more extended festival. And to gain press attention, it would be best to make it "multisited." Murray had just begun her other booking duties at the 53rd Street Y and had a cancellation there. Plus she guessed correctly that one bastion for their breed of music, the New Music Cafe, would likely lend support.

Harris rounded up the artists, Murray ran the administration, and FIRE WALL' was born. "It was run on absolutely no money and the good-will of musicians," Murray explains. "Everybody donated their time, their space and their expertise to make it happen, and the musicians played for basically no money. It was basically a foot in the door, but they knew us for a good cause. And we talked to everybody, and they said, 'Yes.'"

Buoyed by their artistic success, plus some nice reviews from the *Village Voice* and *Down Beat* Magazine, Murray and Harris went whole hog for '93's FIRE WALL' in expanding to a rock music dance hall, Irving Plaza, as well as a free jam outdoors in Thompkins Square Park to accompany a fine arts show entitled, "BEVA's Art Around the Park."

What's more, they landed a grant from the Pew Memorial Trust to recreate the scale and style of New York City's FIRE WALL' in Philadelphia the following week, incorporating artists from that city's healthy cultural scene. (Regrettably, this involved pushing New York City's FIRE WALL' back a week prior to the JVC JAZZ FESTIVAL, voiding what had been a nice middle ground between JVC' and the KNITTING FACTORY's "WHAT IS JAZZ?" FESTIVAL. Oh well.)

"We ran around with about 80, 90 artists," Murray descibes:

- "It was wild — all throughout New York City and Philly — and it was also seriously multisited. It was an enormous thing, and, basically, we had to take a rest because the staff numbers were very small, and all that stuff was done by but a few people. Let's put it this way: if the budget is $10, we did it with 50 cents. It's that kind of thing; therefore, you wear out your ability to do it really fast, so you really have to take a break. It might be something that happens every five years."

The good news is that FIRE WALL' helped raise the profile of Murray's annual curatorial exploits at P. S. 122 and gave some free reign to her collaborative fancies. "A friend of mine says I'm a Roman," Murray chuckles, "when you conquer all these countries — a little of this, a little of that. I mean, I like performance art, American Indians, salsa, jazz, acting, poetry, CD ROM, internet. To me, it all goes together."

I credit Murray with, nevertheless, making her amalgam of interests accessible to "Joe listeners" like myself. She responds:

- "One of the things about playing for a long time, being a serious and mature artist, is you find ways to express what you do in an accessible way without changing what you do. I'll never forget when I was a kid, I used to go to Harlem and see Sun Ra who was doing those crazy performances in the middle of a park in Harlem, and the people loved it! He didn't change it. He just vibed it so they would understand. They understood it as theater!

"When I got to P. S. 122, it is multimedia, and I've been very influenced by putting different people together. I have been doing a lot of work as a composer, and I have been doing a lot of work as an artist. But I really like curating because it helps me interact with my people in the field. I see myself as an artist administrator, as much as a living, working artist."

Murray also sees her curatorial role as countering the various threats modern society poses to the market for live entertainers (including herself) such as hectic lifestyles, two-career families, home entertainment, electronic media, crime in the streets, etc. A proper curator, she feels, programs the kinds of artistic events that simply aren't available on cable TV:

- "My job is not just to tell a great singer to come and sing. My job to is to make it, from a curatorial view, make sense, which is to create a genre, a point-of-view, an artistic narrative that people can come [to experience live].

"For instance, Nuyorican [Poet's Cafe, 236 East 3rd Street] does that. When you go to Nuyorican, it's a point-of-view about going there. You know what you're going to get. You're going to get poetry; you're going to get his aesthetic, Latino; you're really going to get something sideways, you know. That's the idea. The idea is not to be Carnegie Hall, and you would be surprised [at the low] fees that people are playing for the opportunity just to do what they do unencumbered!"

Cultivating audiences to "expect the unexpected" is also illustrated in Murray's own highlight, thus far:

- "My favorite moment of **Fire Wall**' was I really liked [vocalist] Andy Bey doing show tunes, [laughs] because it was so way-out, and I forced him to collaborate with [painter] Quimetta Perle. He didn't want to do that, but then when he saw her work he fell in love.

"People were amazed. All these people who're used to all kinds of other art, who had never heard classic, beautiful, authoritative jazz, who had never heard that kind of thing, flipped out! We were doing Irving Berlin. They never heard that done that way: 'Ah, that's the way it's really done!' So that was great.

**Attendance Tip**

As Murray explained above, she, Harris, and their crew took a breather from **Fire Wall**' in '94 and may further postpone future ones until they gain more financial and volunteer support (or at least until get their collective breaths back).

**P. S. 122**' is also variable. If there's a busy fall schedule of performance art and theater there, Murray's inclined toward putting her week-long concert series off until the spring. That's what happened in '94, which explains the two dates listed above in the heading. You should also know Murray renames it every year: '92's title was "Listen Up"; '93's was "The Hearings."

Murray's really psyched about her 53rd Street YMCA's summer series, "Rooftop Concerts at Twilight," which is predictably timed and also incorporates some popular music genres like C&W and salsa, as well as participatory dancing with lessons. 'Sounds like fun! For information on all her events, she recommends contacting her, or her boss, Susan Davis, through the Y at (212)-735-9725.

As for the venues, the New Music Cafe and P. S. 122 are both clean, neat, incredibly intimate, and located in funky neighborhoods (TriBeCa and East Village, respectively) with plenty of cheap ethnic eats, pastry shops and cafes around.

**See Also**   "In for a penny, in for a pound," I say. As long as I've drawn this M-Base/JMT comparison, I might as well refer you to M-Base's reflection on the pop/rock side, the Black Rock Coalition [BRC].

Perhaps the main difference between the two groups is that BRC is guitar-driven. Otherwise, I'd say their musical similarities outweigh any divergent labels. They're both Brooklyn-based with national reach; they feature many of the same seasoned musicians; they incorporate a breadth of mainstream Afro-centric genres and disciplines; and they share similar jazz leanings. These qualities are personified in BRC's Co-Founder, guitarist Vernon Reid, himself an integral member of the "downtown" alternative jazz scene before launching the hit alternative rock band, Living Color.

Like Murray's events, BRC's multiple bills occur variably. This unpredictability piques press interest, I suppose, but creates havoc for reference guides like this. Nevertheless, you can frequently catch BRC showcases at the local rock conferences (chapter); the ROCK AGAINST RACISM CONCERT (see chapter); Spike Lee's annual affairs; INTERJAMS; or the lineups of several Brooklyn-based concert series and African-American festivals taking place throughout the summer (see **New York City Festival Listings**).

Three BRC events have occurred multiple years:

- BROOKLYN BEAT MEETS THE BLACK ROCK COALITION, where two rap factions faced off in cooperative contests;

- JIMI HENDRIX BIRTHDAY PARTY, where guitarists like Reid, Bourelly, Larry Mitchell, Felicia Collins (CBS Late Night Orchestra) and Michael Hill (Alligator Records) have joined in "All-Star Jam Sessions" celebrating their primary influence (three acts, a DJ, a tribute and a speaker also contributed);

- BLACK ROCK X-MAS CONCERT, a seven-act "X-travaganza" filmed by German TV for overseas broadcast on New Year's Eve (though it may have been discontinued a few years ago, I'm afraid).

Your best bet is to get on BRC's conscientiously-maintained mailing list. Band memberships costs $75; individuals $25. And to get an advance handle on their musical range, look for the two BRC compilations in record stores (Rykodisc Records).

~     ~     ~

# Jazz Get-Togethers

INTERNATIONAL ASSOCIATION OF JAZZ EDUCATORS CONVENTION, Varies, VAR
    Middle January
    Modern Jazz

NEW YORK BRASS CONFERENCE FOR SCHOLARSHIPS, Manhattan, NYC
    Early April
    Modern Jazz
    *Attended*

JAZZTIMES CONVENTION, Manhattan, NYC
    Middle November
    Modern Jazz
    *Attended*

**Introduction**

I'm already on record for my belief that music industry conferences offer basic music fans (as I still consider myself) fuller listening experiences than all but the very, very best festivals. Sure, they may appear expensive on the surface, that is, until you start tallying the benefits.

Start with the voluminous showcases of top names and rising stars, then tell me what you'd pay to catch the same roster of artists in individual club dates. Continue with the keynote speeches, which usually yield insights into the music world that you wouldn't find in all but the most in-depth magazine articles. Besides, how often do you get to observe a magazine article in the flesh, or ask it questions direct from the mic stand?

Follow up with the various workshops and seminars, which run continuously throughout the day. You may pick up a technique or two for your own business, while developing an appreciation for why certain artists are "making it" where others aren't. A full day's attention gives you a much better sense for the behind-the-scenes support that goes into making your favorite stars shine.

Finally, there's the exhibit halls, and promo giveaways, and cocktail hours, and hallway networking, and program notes, and awards tributes, and magazine hand-outs, and ballroom receptions, and star-sightings, and just plain hanging out — all the daily accoutrements that let you feel knee-deep in the music "biz," even if you're not. Yet! If you're like me, though, you'll get so turned on that you'll soon find yourself caught up in the field in one way or another. Last I checked, the music business still needs mature, competent, ethical businesspeople, regardless of their prior persuasions. Skills appear to transfer here, so pursue your musical passions on a small scale to start and, hopefully, the money will follow.

To help get you started, here are two fine jazz-music sleepers on the music conference circuit.

The NEW YORK BRASS CONFERENCE FOR SCHOLARSHIPS [N. Y. BRASS'] is even a sleeper on the jazz circuit, if you can imagine, despite a 22-year tenure and twelve hours of showcases per day for three straight days. It may lack an advertising budget, but it sure doesn't lack for quality performances. I'm tempted to categorize the lineup as "Traditional Jazz and Ragtime," save for the outstanding interlopers who give it very modern accents in places. In '94 such stalwarts included Tito Puente, Randy Brecker, Charlie Sepulveda, Tiger Okoshi, Shorty Rogers, and Jack Walrath. Hence, my "Modern Jazz" tag, although those listeners with big band and/or classical leanings will also find themselves in particular heaven.

The decade-old JazzTimes Convention [JazzTimes'] certainly brings out the big guns among modern jazz's management ranks, thanks to its host, *JazzTimes* Magazine. There's only one official showcase per day, though I admire how that focuses participant attention, whereas most conferences diffuse it with choices, choices, choices. Their nightly 8:15 to 10:30 p.m. slot for a single leading artist draws the heavy hitters down to the hotel lounge, that's for sure. Do your networking there, then head out to hit the seven or so clubs participating in "JazzTimes' Nightimes."

But JazzTimes' real attraction is less the showcases and more the daily workshops and panels. Festival promoters, this is the one conference you wanna' make sure to catch! Nowhere else have I witnessed as many topics which address the totality of your concerns: sponsorship, fundraising, marketing, publicity, commercial and public radio strategies, community outreach and relations, clinics and residencies, art design and promotional materials, alternative booking sources, on-line technologies, the works. In fact, the number of festival tangential topics in '93 outnumbered the mainstream music "biz" ones, though there was significant overlap.

Moreover, the magazine really does it up right. The scheduling is accommodating, the panelists are high-powered, the presentations are first-rate, the audience participation is no-nonsense — everything is right on the money! Festival types of all musical persuasions will find their time more wisely spent at JazzTimes' than at any other conference I've attended. And if they end up sighting some jazz acts for their eclectic lineups in the process, hey, so much the better!

**Festival Review I**   Conference audiences are typically eclectic, but N. Y. Brass' delivers its constituencies in two main chunks.

First, there are the somewhat older musicians, themselves, who commute from the New York City area to cruise the exhibit hall to view one the most extensive brass instrument displays in the country. They'll also renew old acquaintances in the hallways, in the lobby adjoining the ballroom showcases, and in every nook and cranny of the dowager Hotel Roosevelt — all lathered layers of creamy latex surrounding plaster moldings, red-patterned carpet, and mirrors, mirrors, mirrors.

Everybody on this level seems to know everybody else, though you may not recognize all their names and faces. That's because the conference draws under-heralded brass aces from all over: Broadway shows, studio sessions, touring bands, classical ensembles, TV shows, you name it. "The meat-and-potato players," as they're termed by the admiring Alan Colin, Co-Organizer of N. Y. Brass', along with his equally appreciative wife, Liz. "It's not the superstars. That you'll hear. Of course, we like to honor [them], but it's the guys who make these guys sound great; who are loved and admired by their peers."

Second, there are jazz-band directors from colleges and high schools shepherding their young charges through what must seem like a wonderland of product, clinics (40, total), and performances (40, also). If they, too, aren't checking out this or that instrument manufacturer, they're clustered reverently in the ballroom to catch yet another insider legend who, in turn, will usually hang around with them afterwards to share some tips. It functions as an informal university-without-walls for both parties, allowing each relaxed access to the other.

"It happens this way all the time," Alan says. "There have been times when someone will be giving a lecture and in walks Gillespie, or Maynard Ferguson will come in. The atmosphere of N. Y. Brass' is a little different than many of the other conventions in that it's very loose, very informal, and everybody is in and out at all times. ...We try to make it as comfortable as possible for the performer and the audience to intermingle."

"All the guys are very approachable," agrees Liz. "Now [the late] Dizzy [Gillespie], when he was around, was at every N. Y. Brass' that I was at. And he would just walk around..."

"What is nice about it," Alan interjects, "is the professional who the student looks up to as a superstar will be trying out a horn or a mouthpiece right next to him just like any other person. It brings everyone into one central focus."

Alan and Liz have a special handle on satisfying both segments from running Charles Colin Publications, Inc., an instructional publisher strictly for brass instruments begun 50 years ago by Alan's dad, Charles. It serves both the professional and educational jazz markets with "technical books," as Alan describes them, "how-to products, how to improvise, how to play higher, how to play longer, and method books." (That the Colins have accumulated such a devoted customer base over a full half-century helps explain why **N. Y. Brass'** is so scantily advertised — just a one-inch logo in a few national trades is all it takes to swell the registrant list every year.)

In the early-'70s, Charles (since retired) and Alan were both attending another conference in Trumpet Composing hosted by the University of Colorado. Alan recalls:

- "They had come to a point where they couldn't handle it any more financially. After [Promoter Lee Burns] had announced to the public there that it was, the last one, my dad and I were walking to breakfast, and he said, 'Hey we can do this in New York! We'll bring in all our friends, not just trumpets, but all brass instruments.' And we started it right down the block there. It used to be at a YMCA — the very first time that we did it — it just kept going from there."

The two Colins added a pair of wrinkles to Burns' format. First, they created an annual Salute to one of Alan's performing "superstars" for whom they'd orchestrate some special musical tribute. Call it a brass version of "This Is Your Life." The day I attended their honoree was the late composer/arranger Shorty Rogers who seemed genuinely floored by the Manhattan School of Music Jazz Orchestra's performing an entire evening of his charts, including quite a few obscurities. They even had the goatee'd Rogers handle a few of the trumpet solos, himself, which he did with customary aplomb.

Second, they supported the jazz programs their business serves by instituting college scholarships from the proceeds. Liz explains:

- "There are a bunch of universities that advertise in our journal. We guarantee that if a student doesn't call them and enroll in the schools, we will offer two scholarship awards which they can distribute to their own students. So their advertising is free and then some.

  "Also, any **N. Y. Brass'** [student] member who wants a scholarship award, they give us a call and say, 'Gee, I'd like to go wherever.' It doesn't have to be to that university, it can be to any other university or whatever. [The awards are] not big, but they're something, and everyone's very grateful to get them. And it's very easy. We don't ask them for any financial reports or anything. They just have to be a member, they have to show us that they're enrolled at a given program. We send them a check in their name to the program. The program gives it to the student, so they're in fact there. And that's that."

"The name of the conference is THE NEW YORK BRASS CONFERENCE FOR SCHOLARSHIPS," Alan chimes in, "and we do this to raise money for scholarships — that's what this whole thing is about!"

Well, yeah, but let's not forget the three full days of live brass on three different stages, especially the Salutes which cap the full programs. One of Alan's all-time highlights happened on Puente's Salute "when Lou Soloff came in and played a solo like I've never heard. I mean, I've never heard a greater trumpet solo, just a solo, on one of Tito's tunes. And Tito was so taken by that. He was, like, 'Whoa! What happened here?'"

One of Liz' prized memories occurred at Gillespie's Salute:

- "Tom Harrell was one of the guest soloists. Now Dizzy might not have seen Tom Harrell in-person. He probably heard his music, but I don't think he had ever seen him. So Tom Harrell, we know, has this [mentions disease which effects Harrell's appearance and posture]. He comes up to the stage, his head down. I was sitting next to Dizzy, and he turns around and wanted to know, 'What gives?' There he is waiting, and then [Harrell] does his thing. Blew everybody away! I was, like, crying it was so moving. And then after his solo, Dizzy got up and embraced him, and it was — and as I think about it, I'm about ready to fall apart — the most moving thing."

Alan mentions, too, having brought a longtime family friend, tuba player Sam Pilafian, together with five fellow pit players from a Broadway play to **N. Y. Brass'** for their first ever appearance as the Empire Brass Quartet. "They came here in role costume from the show," he recalls.

However, both agree their ultimate moment took place during the Maynard Ferguson Salute. Alan remembers "when Dave Stalls was playing on stage — one of New York's leading trumpet players — and Maynard was asked if he would like to come up and play, and he says, 'No, no, let Dave Stalls...'"

"He took his hat off to Dave Stalls," Liz explains:

- "And a guy like Dave Stalls has been a key player behind all the big players. He exemplifies what N. Y. BRASS' is very much about. You have all these key players who the general public doesn't know, and then they come to the conference, they do their groups, they do some guest showing, and all this is they're in the storefront — the guys who make everybody sound great are now in the storefront playing, doing their own stuff — and it's very exciting.

  "As an example, when this guy was playing with the Maynard group, the audience, it might as well've been a rock audience, they were so absolutely charged up. The guy was blowing 'em away and everybody was all, 'Awwww!' They were screaming; it was really wild. And then Maynard came in and did his little bow for Dave, and it was very, very exciting."

**Artist Mini-Review**    <u>Jack Walrath Group Jazz Ensemble</u> (Masters of Suspense). I wouldn't call Walrath's hallway set of Mingus interpretations as exciting as all that, but it was certainly interesting and dynamic in its own way.

The fortyish Walrath, wearing a blue blazer over a Frankenstein T-shirt, had an odd look, balancing wide-eyed innocence with Charles Coburn/Dennis Hopper's ten-mile stares. This alternating between boyishness and subversiveness best described Walrath's own playing. He'd quickly veer from straight-ahead stuff with perfect facility and tone to moments of sheer gnarliness, pique and puckish humor. I liked it!

I'm not sure I felt the same way about Dean Bowman's aggro vocal technique, which mixed Pharoah Sanders-style yodelling with nasty political raps. He even did a good Tom Waits imitation on a growling "Rats and Moles." Whew! I found him a little "out there" for my taste. Guitarist David Fiuczynski, a "downtown" regular, was user-friendlier — all liquid lines slipping 'twixt jazz and rock — but looked a bit too self-absorbed for much interaction with a willing Walrath. Bassist Lindsey Horner and drummer Cecil Brooks III seemed more in tune, holding down Mingus' muscular rhythms with steady hands.

The best part was witnessing the transformation of a young African-American teen beside me. At first, he laughed in derision at what I'm sure he perceived as dated civil-rights-era sentiments on "Freedom," but gradually fell under Bowman's ranting spell and stayed for the whole set. Mission accomplished for Walrath, the Colins' and their N. Y. BRASS'!

~     ~     ~

**Festival Review II**    Strange how the New York City jazz music media works. Last year's JAZZTIMES' garnered a paragraph heading the front page of *USA Today*'s Life section and a special written welcome from then Mayor David Dinkins, but passed unnoticed among the local press. I don't recall even one listing that year, not even among the entertainment weeklies! This helped contribute to the feeling I got at both music conferences of private stolen pleasures — an all-too-rare experience in New York City's overheated club scene where this minute's hip secret becomes next minute's crowd crush.

JAZZTIMES' didn't have quite as many showcases as N. Y. BRASS' (22 vs. 40), but the quality was uniformly excellent, balanced and progressive. Michelle Rosewoman Quintet, Benny Green Trio, Thomas Chapin Trio, Kuni Mikami Little Big Band, Hiram Bullock, Toninho Horta, Roy Hargrove, Othello Molineaux Band, etc. were just the kind of slightly-off-the-beaten-track-but-coming-up-strong-in-the-passing-lane types I especially love. The seven club settings for "JAZZTIMES' NIGHTIMES" were perfect, too — quiet, classy, uncrowded, and relatively inexpensive. They offered a perfectly understated way for jazz music outsiders to get a select undercurrent of tomorrow's headliners. Best of all, this focus didn't make you feel like you were missing 20 hot acts for every one you caught.

"We get that from the CMJ MUSIC MARATHON (New York, NY — see chapter), who do that 'take-it-to-the-clubs' thing," explains Lee Mergner, *JazzTimes*' Associate Publisher and one of JAZZTIMES' chief organizers along with General Manager, Jeff Sabin. Like CMJ' does, Mergner gets inquiries from "hundreds of musicians who want to perform, and we just can't [program them all]:

- "It would be just one big performing marathon, and we would [be forced] into a presenter kind-of-thing that we're just not equipped to do. Sometimes the setting, when you have it in an industry show, can be off-putting. So, I think to have the artists play in the clubs and have people get out (when people come to New York, they want to go to clubs) just sort of makes sense. It extends our reach a little, and it's a good setting for them."

That all goes down at night for consumers; the real deal happens in the daytime for the trade. While there was no exhibit hall, JAZZTIMES' did offer, by far, the most informative and professionally-run series of workshops and panels I've yet experienced at any music conference. Here's one sample among the 20 sessions slated:

- The festival promoters' panel — "From Small-Time to Big-Time in 10,000 Easy Lessons" — was not some random gabfest, but targeted a specific, valued purpose of achieving national prominence for artist, media and sponsorship recruitment;

- There was not a huge number of presenters, where half the time spent is handing the mic down the dais, but just three seasoned pros who really knew what the hell they were doing: Dan Kossoff (JACKSONVILLE JAZZ FEST), Ken Poston (KLON/LONG BEACH JAZZ AND BLUES FESTIVALS), and John Phillips (Festival Productions, Inc. — see numerous chapters);

- There was none of rock-music's "life sucks and then you die" negativity, but positive, constructive and exquisitely-detailed advice on what worked and why;

- There was an equally-prominent moderator, Frank Malfitano (SYRACUSE JAZZ FEST, Syracuse, NY — see chapter), who followed strict orders to keep the questions moving and pertinent.

Finally, the audience of fellow festival promoters was as high-powered as the presenters and kept the discussion at an appreciably high level. There was none of the gratuitous self-plugging, or pontificating, or blah-blah-blah you hear from those typically hogging the mic stands. Even though I entered the room with a background in corporate hospitality, I still came away with several useful tips in this area (from Kossoff, especially) I hadn't known before.

The remaining workshops I caught that day on fundraising and sponsorship — two more of my professional specialties — also added to my knowledge base. Best of all, these topics, and many others besides, are exactly what festival promoters clamor for, but can't seem to get anywhere else. Kudos to JAZZTIMES'!

"Yeah, well, it's because [jazz music] is not a particularly profitable venture in some ways, although at the same time jazz festivals are one of the more commercial ventures for the jazz market," Mergner explains:

- "I think the greatest thing we find about festivals for the jazz market is that for that one time of the year — and it could be Reading, Pennsylvania, or Boston, Massachusetts — it's jazz! It sort of takes over, and it ties into the media real well. It allows them to write articles about the jazz scene. It [also] allows them to use local talent in bigger settings; they'll use them as opening acts and that kind of thing. For the next year or two those local acts will brag about being on the same bill as whatever."

Hence, the festival importance JAZZTIMES' imparts to its workshop menu.

This year Mergner even moved the dates back one month to accommodate a large contingent of international festival representatives. "I'm not talking about little festivals," Mergner exclaims, "I'm talking about MONTREAUX, NORTH SEA, you know, the major European festivals!" Their talent scouts will hole up in one hotel suite and conduct their own seminar-within-a-seminar — entertaining agents, discussing artists, negotiating bookings, routings and such — basically saving themselves from getting hosed by over-priced acts. There's a virtual auction block taking place with a secretary employed to record and transcribe the proceedings. "It's kind of unnerving, me seeing this woman, smiling, writing down the stupid thing I just said," Mergner chuckles.

Mergner credits his boss, Founder and President Ira Sabin, for making it all happen.

Sabin began his career as a jazz record retailer and created an in-store broadside for consumers, much like Tower Records with its *Tower Pulse!* Mergner describes how this newsprint publication grew more trade-oriented in the '70s with airplay charts, tip sheets, industry notes, and such: "Then [Sabin] realized that he really wanted to develop it as more of a consumer magazine. He felt that there was a real need for a magazine geared to the real stuff for jazz, so he called it *JazzTimes* and did a more aggressive newsstand promotion."

Mergner came to Sabin about three or four years ago with a freshly-minted MBA (one of those non music-industry professionals I described up top, just following his musical passion) and together with Sabin's son, Jeff, helped develop the magazine's present glossy format.

Building the trade continued to concern the elder Sabin, however, especially with jazz music being under-represented at all the other music conferences they'd attend. Finally, Sabin decided to launch his own music conference geared specifically to jazz professionals. "He wasn't being strategic," Mergner recounts of his boss' motivations, "he just wanted to get everybody together. He wanted there to be a jazz association and he wanted to have an awards thing. He wanted to bring the industry together, and, in a way, it's nice that happens." The current format solidified in '85 and touched down elsewhere in the country before settling in New York City last year.

"I think that we take a proactive stance toward the jazz industry," Mergner continues:

- "And we feel like we can't count on the rest of the music industry to address the needs of this music. We share a lot with the other music forums, and I think we should all learn from each other... [However], there are issues which are only specific to your industry that you really have to address — obviously, the core of that are the festivals — and it's really important to do so. And for us, New York is that place, even though it's incredibly expensive. It's really the center for jazz."

**Artist Mini-Review** I was too busy enjoying my Michelle Rosewoman and T. S. Monk, Jr., showcases to take many notes. The tightly-wound Monk was particularly entertaining as he started out all fashionably clad and articulate before turning breathless and sweat-soaked from his intense work out. His vest came off, his shirt came off, his beret came off, and at one point, even his glasses popped off onto the floor during an especially springy cymbal solo. Call the gifted young drummer a "bull in a china shop," plus a very credible, passionate advocate of his late father's work as well as his own.

Instead, here's one of Mergner's highlights:

- "I actually went to JAZZTIMES' when I was younger. I remember going up to a room — it was like a showcase kind of thing — and it was Joe Williams playing with Benny Carter. Betty Carter was in the audience and he brought Betty up. And here I am in this little hotel room! We're sitting there hearing Joe Williams and Betty Carter on stage just goofing around. To me, that was the kind of stuff you just can't find anywhere. I was really struck by it. There's not as much sitting-in with musicians as there used to be and kind of that warm, like, 'come on up.' They're much more of the 'professional-gig' thing and that's understandable, but it makes you nostalgic for that other thing."

**Attendance Tip** Especially with N. Y. BRASS', the best networking and "come-on-up" stuff goes on after-hours in the hotel lounges. "Let's put it this way," Alan Colin chuckles, "they do very well at the bar at the Hotel Roosevelt when we're there!" Both conferences arrange favorable rates in New York City's obscenely priced hotel scene, so I'd advise sticking with the program. Sign up early for advance purchase discounts, then hob-nob at ease to your heart's content.

Both conferences are musical pikers when compared to the INTERNATIONAL JAZZ EDUCATORS **See Also**
ASSOCIATION's annual explosion of big-name showcases, which occupies a five-day stretch in Late
January. "It's phenomenal, phenomenal," Liz Colin exclaims. "Blew my mind!" Call IAJE to learn
which city it's scheduled to take over next.

~     ~     ~

*Marilyn Crispell, Peter Brotzman, Hamid Drake, Knitting Factory's "What Is Jazz?" Festival.*

# Gospel Choir Get-Togethers

**MCDONALD'S GOSPELFEST**, Varied Sites, NYC
> Early April to Middle June
> Black Gospel
> ***Attended***

**QUEENS COLLEGE CULTURAL HERITAGE "GREAT GOSPEL" COMPETITION**, Queens, NYC
> Middle May
> Black Gospel

**GOSPEL MUSIC WORKSHOP OF AMERICA/NEW YORK STATE CHAPTER CONVENTION**, Brooklyn, NYC
> Middle June
> Black Gospel
> ***Attended***

**GOSPEL MUSIC WORKSHOP OF AMERICA NATIONAL CONVENTION**, Varied Sites, VAR
> Early August to Middle August
> Black Gospel
> ***Attended***

**Introduction**  "Black gospel" music, to use the standard industry term, might well be America's greatest hidden cultural treasure. It's the bedrock for blues, R&B, rock-and-roll — indeed, for all African-American music which functions independently, or as an influence on such other genres as bluegrass, jazz, C&W, rap, and classical. However, we're not talking some creaky, dusty museum piece, but a still living, breathing, earthquaking, soul-shaking experience. I can only take the best choirs in short bursts before my heart starts palpitating, and I need to cool down in the lobby. It gets that intense.

Regrettably, I've had fewer opportunities to catch black gospel music at festivals than any of its off-shoots. I'm not sure why, but I've got some ideas.

First, the entire gospel music community seems balkanized by genre, region, and race. Contemporary Christian and Christian country are both hot sub-genres these days, but mostly for white audiences outside the Northeast and other urban areas. Bluegrass and southern gospel musics entertain smaller, older white audiences in even more rural outposts. Black gospel music occupies its own niche. Its biggest base lies within strong African-American populations of cities east of the Mississippi. Unfortunately, up here you won't find many state/county fairs — primary venues for the other gospel categories above — nor many opportunities for white audiences to readily hear about black gospel music. Urban whites tend to keep to their neighborhoods, churches, and newspapers; African-Americans to theirs. Too bad!

Second, the nature of the music seems ill-suited to support professional careers. After all, how can you find enough sufficiently-paying gigs to keep a 50-person choir on the road full-time (though there is significant work out there for top soloists and ensembles). A few of the more traditional "quartet-style" groups, such as The Fairfield Four or The Five Blind Boys of Alabama, have hooked up with booking agents and enjoy great success playing folk-music festivals. (Once folkies hear 'em, they love 'em!) Still they're traditionally oriented; the hot young groups are too "pop" for these white roots audiences but too noncommercial or alcohol-averse for the nonchurch circuit, including clubs and bars. I'd love to see blues venues booking these groups regularly, or "gospel brunches" becoming standard Sunday fare in restaurants everywhere, but it hasn't happened yet. Too bad!

Third, the professional attitudes of its many amateur practitioners may shoulder a good-ly share of the blame. It's not that the choir directors, singers, and musicians aren't serious about their art. Quite the opposite. However, theirs seems to be a laid-back attitude about chasing book-ings. It may be due to distractions from church activities, families, and day jobs (especially with-out expectations of a full-time choral career), to an unwillingness to mix business with religion, or to ignorance of competitive music-industry practices. Too bad!

I'll give you a "for instance." Sitting in the press room at the GOSPEL MUSIC WORKSHOP OF AMERICA NATIONAL CONVENTION [G. M. W. A. NATIONAL'] in Indianapolis, Indiana, I put the query to one of its publicity assistants: "Why aren't these phenomenal choirs on more festival bills?" The guy replied that he, too, was disappointed that [presumably white] festival promoters in his area hadn't sought out black gospel groups performing, yet waiting to be invited.

"Waiting to be invited?" I shook my head, expressing how few of the festival promoters I knew had any time to seek out anybody, instead being inundated by press kits and other inquiries. "I have friends who often make 20 to 40 phone calls just to land one top festival," I exclaimed. "You have to hustle to get yourself booked!"

He seemed taken back by my perspective, then conceded it might have more to do with the "faith first, commerce second" attitude I alluded to above. And I can understand that motiva-tion, though I still believe in the ability of this music to inspire better things of anyone given a fair hearing. There's a gift to be shared and a lot of good work waiting to be done.

Now I do have one qualification to my enthusiasm. This is music of the heart, mind you, not of the academy. Singers can get carried away, abandoning technique for a flurry of emotional affectations. Audiences react to this passion, more so than to tasteful interpretations.

That said, I still prefer black gospel music to virtually any "tasteful" contemporary R&B I hear today, even from those performers who crossover from black gospel music. That's because contemporary R&B songwriting has largely sunk to crap. For example, I'll never forget leaving one recent BENSON & HEDGES BLUES AND RHYTHM FESTIVAL in Manhattan's Paramount, disgusted that every song seemed to be comprised of maybe a dozen words, five of which were the chorus line repeated 20 or 30 times ad nauseam: "Baby, I want your body/Baby, I want your body/Baby, I want your body..."

Although black gospel music also maintains terse structures, the words are rooted in, well, the Word. As a result, there's purposefulness, depth and resonance to even the simplest refrain. Plus, there's noticeably more imagery and metaphor employed throughout. It moves me in positive ways, whereas contemporary R&B lyrics leave me ice cold.

Fortunately, here are two festivals where you can get yourself plugged in and turned on to the best in black gospel music, especially the big choirs that rarely travel outside of their home markets. Both the MCDONALD'S GOSPELFEST ['GOSPELFEST] and the G. M. W. A. proffer welcom-ing, nurturing, family environments for devotees and novices, alike. Start with the two big get-togethers, get blown away by the spirit, then follow them back to their local levels. In either place, a whole new musical world awaits you.

'GOSPELFEST brings together an extraordinary confluence of participants:

**Festival
Review I**

- The private sector, represented by small business "Owner/Operators" of McDonald's franchises in African-American neighborhoods throughout the area as well as their Fortune-500 corporate parent based out of Oak Brook, Illinois (Coca Cola Co. has also gotten involved through its local bottlers as well as their Atlanta, Georgia, headquarters);

- The multidenominational assembly of churches that supplies the majority of com-peting choirs, along with the 10 annual host sites for the various 'GOSPELFEST PRELIMINARIES AND SEMI-FINALS;

- The public sector, since public schools contribute many choir contestants of their own, such as the P. S. 81's "Voices of Joy" whom I caught this past year;

- The nonprofit sector, which hosts the 'GOSPELFEST FINAL COMPETITION / CONCERT through such performing arts centers as Carnegie Hall and Lincoln Center, and whose civic organizations supply a few choral entries as well;

- The entertainment industry, including co-sponsors of the gala wrap-up — NBC-TV, WWRL-FM (see chapter), WRKS-FM and SONY's Word/Epic subsidiary.

Interesting, huh? I think this kind of friendly partnership is more what our nation's founding fathers had in mind, rather than the antagonistic segregation of church from everything else as proselytized by the ACLU and others. 'GOSPELFEST stands as eloquent testimony to how various elements of our society can come together for common spiritual cause.

This unique union began in '85.

The New York Tri-State McDonald's Owner/Operator Association sought out the churches for a "program designed to celebrate the rich tradition of gospel music." Obviously, this combined competition/showcase/happening represented an excellent p. r. opportunity for the local entrepreneurs in "giving something back to the communities in which [they] conduct business." However, it's also been a way for them to get their corporate parent involved in supporting the college aspirations of teenagers who make up the majority of their workforces. Owner/Operators targeted the United Negro College Fund as the initial proceeds beneficiary, and have seen corporate contributions accumulate to $500,000. A handsome portion has been redistributed to 'GOSPELFEST participants in the form of $1,000 Fellowship Awards.

In the decade since 'GOSPELFEST's inauguration, roughly 100 local churches have hosted events for 2,500 participating choirs. Their involvement begins in early March as the call goes out for contestants through ads placed in local newspapers. Typically, 300 entries are received each year within three categories:

- "Choir," groups having 15 or more members;

- "Ensemble," groups having less than 15 members;

- "Youth," groups whose members are 21 years of age or younger.

(Lest you think the "Youth" category is a gimme', I'll warn you that huge choirs of 80, 90 members or more from ages five on up often give their older brethren a run for their money. At this year's 'SEMI-FINALS, the Bronx's Friendly Baptist Church Junior Choir put on a show that had the whole audience in a state of frenzy. I mean, folks jumped to their feet as even lil' tykes roared through a choreographed revue: "Higher... higher... higher, higher, higher! Stronger... stronger... stronger, stronger, stronger!" They rocked as hard as any of the other 17 groups that performed!)

The first 'PRELIMINARIES commence in Brooklyn and Queens the first Saturday afternoon in April and continue throughout the month. There's a few weeks' break before the late May 'SEMI-FINALS take place in Harlem. All these early rounds are open and free to the public. (The good folks at First Corinthian Baptist Church even had a lush soul food spread for sale in their lobby. The fragrance of fried chicken and candied yams wafting up to my balcony seat made it hard for me to concentrate until I'd bought a satisfying plate full.) Tickets then go on sale for the big finale at a prestige Manhattan venue on the second Saturday night of June.

The 'FINAL COMPETITION/CONCERT commences with a "Negro National Anthem" performed by two prior winners. In '93, this was The Jenkins Brothers and The Macedonia Baptist Church Ensemble. Each of the three categories then hosts a showdown among its two finalists "judged on the basis of their vocal ability, technique and showmanship." There are also guest performances during and after the showdowns. In '94 this meant O'Landa Draper and The Winans, among others. The night concludes with an appearance from that year's 'GOSPELFEST Mass Choir (made up from the finalists, I assume), the "Announcement of Winners," and a closing "Benediction."

Having such big name performers and industry sponsors on site definitely helps springboard future stars. The Jenkins Brothers, for example, went on to recording deals (Savoy, GST Records) and national airplay from their '86 triumph as well as a spotlight appearance at '93's **G.**

**M. W. A. National'**. Last Appeal, '89's winner, is another local ensemble since poised for bigger and better.

Ron Bailey first became a McDonald's Owner/Operator in '89. This retired lieutenant from the L. A. Police Dept. was encouraged to purchase his first franchise from his brother's favorable (and lucrative) experience before him. The upbeat Bailey chose a "blank, empty, weed-infested lot" in Hunt's Point strictly on population density analysis, not knowing a thing of the South Bronx neighborhood's forbidding reputation.

"I took a vision, and faith, and self-confidence," relays Bailey, "and made my business work in spite of the business projections [we made for] the first year. When going into the second year, it took off at a 41% increase, and it was done through a lot of aggressive local store marketing, and getting to know the customer, and interfacing with the community. That has been the success of my business — dealing [with], and becoming part of, the community."

Bailey describes his involvement in various local sports programs, neighborhood centers, and local development corporations, but it's his 'Gospelfest Chairmanship which really gets him going. Possibly, it's because Bailey identifies so with gospel music's having "evolved from humble, even obscured beginnings," as he describes it:

- "Just through hard work and spiritual guidance, gospel artists have transformed gospel music into what it is today, a multi-million dollar industry. You know, gospel has its roots in early days of black America when spiritual hymns and jubilee songs played an instrumental role in the lives of the slaves. Now everyone enjoys gospel music. There's a message, and it reaches out to so many people. So I think that the community wants gospel music and they want McDonald's to be a part of gospel music as evidenced by the response we get."

While Bailey expresses how it's hard to measure 'Gospelfest's effect in numerical terms, he points to the pristine condition of his three restaurants in an otherwise "high crime area." There's never any vandalizing his extensive plantings and upgraded appointments, he claims. "I think when you bring pride into a community, pride is what you get."

Bailey takes special pride in assisting his young staff's educational outlays, from taking care of their senior prom expenses to funding their book costs throughout college. Doubtless Bailey's informal store programs helped inspire the 'Gospelfest's Fellowship Award grants debuting this year.

"I continue to give back," he explains:

- "And if you don't do it, let's face it, Uncle Sam's going to take it. So you either give it to the government in the hole, or give it to the individual neighborhood and the people who have helped get you where you are. Certainly, these people are responsible for making me successful. And you never forget that; I never will."

Musically, Bailey's drawn to the "Choir" category: "The choirs have always been intriguing to me, because [of] the discipline that's required just to know from following the director's leadership and eye contact; that each person has to focus on that director to understand when they come in. To me, that's like an orchestra."

Apparently, Bailey considered this year's final "Choir" face-off so "outstanding," so close to call, that he decided right then and there never to be a judge. Indeed Bailey's trying to eliminate the final competition altogether in favor of co-winners, especially for the two "Youth" finalists. "We always say that they're all winners," he heartily concludes, "they're sending out a message."

~     ~     ~

You think 'Gospelfest's 18 groups per day is impressive as during the 'Semi-Finals? Well, keep in mind that each group only gets five minutes — a remarkably short time to rev-up to such strong passion, I'd add — and that the afternoon will be over in about four hours. The G. M. W. A. National' keeps that kind of energy going for, oh, about 16 hours a day! **Festival Review II**

Looking at '93's eight-day schedule, things actually kicked off as early as 5:30 a.m. with an "Aerobics Class," followed by "Prayer Services" at seven. After a full morning's slate of classes and workshops, which number 65 throughout the week, the first heavenly sounds commence at noon. Then it's pretty much wall-to-wall music until the "Youth Showcase," led by noted singer James P. Kee, wraps up at 4:00 in the morning. I've yet to figure out exactly how many different choirs perform in a single day. However, the "Nightly Musicals" — the conference's primary showcases that run from 6:00 p.m. to midnight — average a minimum of 15 choirs per night.

Moreover, some of the individual choirs are virtual conferences in themselves. The National Mass Choir contains 2,000 "voices"; the Youth Department Choir, 1,200; and the Men's Chorus, 400. The National Mass Choir even gets recorded live on-site. As you can imagine, a big slice of the week's schedule is committed to gathering these choir members, rehearsing them, and proudly presenting their musical gifts on stage.

You're probably asking yourself, "When do G. M. W. A. NATIONAL' participants sleep?" Um, good question. I've observed a certain macho attitude at these things about pulling all-nighters "high on Christ," so to speak. One vendor I talked to even put the concept of downtime to rest altogether, describing G. M. W. A. NATIONAL' as "just another 24-hour affair." Certainly, the incredible music supplies its own high octane, as does this once-a-year opportunity for its participants to mutually affirm each other. Accordingly, the coffee and camaraderie both flow freely.

The G. M. W. A. NATIONAL' was founded 26 years ago by one of the the giants in the gospel music field, the late Rev. James Cleveland. Rev. Cleveland grew up in the Chicago choir of another great legend of the genre, Thomas Dorsey, writer of the most popular gospel song of all time, "Precious Lord." Rev. Cleveland's early travels took him to Baptist churches in New York City and Philadelphia before landing him in Detroit with Rev. C. L. Franklin. It was there that Rev. Cleveland tutored Rev. Franklin's young daughter, Aretha, and inspired her toward her thrilling singing career.

Rev. Cleveland enjoyed numerous career successes of his own, including the first live gospel music recording, '62's "This Sunday in Person" (Savoy), plus '63's "Peace Be Still," the first gospel LP to sell more than 50,00 copies. Before his passing in '91, six Grammies rewarded Rev. Franklin's consummate skills as vocalist, pianist, choir director, composer and arranger, including a nomination as collaborator with Quincy Jones on the soundtrack for TV's "Roots" series.

Rev. Cleveland, commonly known as "King of Gospel," fulfilled a personal dream by founding the first G. M. W. A. NATIONAL' in Detroit in '68. It differs from all subsequent music-industry conferences in two main respects. First, it attracts 20,000 participants for a week of devotion, activities, exhibits, industry functions, workshops, seminars, training, awards, tributes, fashion shows, cotillions and, of course, singing, singing, singing. By contrast, the largest secular music conference I know of, Manhattan's NEW MUSIC SEMINAR, draws 7,500 registrants.

Second, the G. M. W. A. NATIONAL' spun off its own year-round, nation-wide organization, the G. M. W. A. This "interracial, inter-denominational" association boasts 135 chapters throughout the U. S., the Bahamas and the Virgin Isles. Its net effect is three fold: disseminating the conference's musical and spiritual training to all skill levels; spinning off local chapter conferences throughout the year; and solidifying the G. M. W. A. NATIONAL's attendance base. To that end, the G. M. W. A. NATIONAL' is probably the longest and steadiest of all the annual music conferences. You never hear "if" as you often do about the following year's NEW MUSIC SEMINAR, for example; it's always "when!"

When you go, you'll notice a few other departures from typical music conferences, doubtless a reflection upon Rev. Cleveland himself.

The choirs, themselves, are polished, accomplished, and well-presented. Ditto the largely family audiences decked out all week in their Sunday finery. You may see Kente cloth and other African fabrics but not the jeans-and-sneakers thing, like I did unwittingly. So dress properly. Propriety is not the case, though, when sitting down for the "Nightly Musicals." Here peer pressure works in reverse as you're supposed to show your encouragement to deserving singers by any means necessary — clapping, standing, shouting, even singing along! It's definitely a mutual encouragement society all night long.

However, the **G. M. W. A. NATIONAL'** does follow the increasing norm in finding a place for name acts amidst the largely amateur choirs. In '93 this meant a "Memorial Scholarship Tribute" to Rev. Cleveland and Brother Frank Williams (another gospel legend departed that year), hosted by Malaco/Savoy Records. This Mississippi-based label showcased 16 of its revival-style stars, including the absolutely incendiary Mississippi Mass Choir, originally founded by Williams in '90. Their three-hour blow-out boosted Sunday's musical festivities and was open to the public for a fairly nominal donation.

Also that same Sunday were two preachers I was to experience the following June:

- Rev. Albert Jamison, who conducted the "Early Morning Services," hosted the **G. M. W. A. NEW YORK CHAPTER CONVENTION ['N. Y. S. CHAPTER']** at his Brooklyn church;

- Rev. Richard "Mr. Clean" White, who hosted the "Midnight Service," was invited by Rev. Jamison from Atlanta, Georgia, to preach Friday evening.

Nancy Skampideri, who served '93's **G. M. W. A. NATIONAL'** as a publicity assistant, invited me to attend Rev. Jamison's Pleasant Row Baptist Tabernacle for this last of "three nights of dynamic preachers and the best in gospel music," and graciously shepherded me around.

Truth be told, that order of billing best describes the four hours I witnessed. By the time I had to leave around midnight, I'd heard three preachers but only one vocal group — an impressive David Gates and The Love, Peace and Joy Singers from Long Island. I suspect, though, that this was "just another 24-hour affair," with the remaining five groups due to sing deep, deep into the evening. Amen for hot java!

That's not to say I didn't enjoy myself. Rev. White was an experience unto himself as this outrageously charismatic speaker had the entire auditorium fully revived and hopping by the time his hour-long sermon concluded. Reluctantly! As he was wont to thunder again and again with mock glowering eyes over a knowing smile: "You've got life insurance, house insurance and car insurance, but do you have 'soul' insurance?" Well, if "Mr. Clean's" selling, then I'm buying.

Queen College runs its own classy show every May with its GREAT GOSPEL weekend. Its Golden **See Also** Center for the Performing Arts hosts six black gospel music choirs winnowed from a Tri-State area pool of 30 contestants. They're all vying for $5,000 in prize money donated by NYNEX. There's a special preview concert Saturday night with a big name, like '94's Della Reese, who preceded Sunday evening's face-off. Reese returned the next day to join the judging, while the prior year's winners, Voices of Hope, topped the septuple bill.

Tickets for Sunday's showcase were a steal at $9.00 each, so bring the whole family for this concert, and for the others above!

~     ~     ~

# Lincoln Center's Variety Party

CARNEGIE HALL FOLK FESTIVAL, Manhattan, NYC
Middle April to Late April
Variety, Folk and International
**Attended**

MIDSUMMER NIGHT SWING , Manhattan, NYC
Late June to Late July
Variety, General
**Attended**

SERIOUS FUN!, Manhattan, NYC
Early July to Late July
Avant Garde and New Music
**Attended**

LINCOLN CENTER OUT-OF-DOORS/**ROOTS OF AMERICAN MUSIC FESTIVAL**, Manhattan, NYC
Early August to Late August
Variety, General
**Attended**

**Introduction**  Sure, some groups produce multiple festivals, or even festivals across multiple genres. But what other organization can claim such extraordinary diversity achieving such high quality as Lincoln Center for the Performing Arts [Lincoln Center]? From avant-garde to traditional/modern folk, to world beat, to classic/contemporary jazz, to everything else under the sun, we're talking some of the best live music programming in New York City and with MIDSUMMER NIGHT SWING, probably the "best, best, best" participatory dance series in the whole known universe!

And that's just these three festivals, above, not to mention the controversial CLASSICAL JAZZ AT LINCOLN CENTER (see chapter), or the other independent festivals that rent Lincoln Center's multiple venues: JVC JAZZ FESTIVAL, BANG ON A CAN FESTIVAL, BENDING TOWARD THE LIGHT: A JAZZ NATIVITY, MCDONALD'S GOSPELFEST, etc. (see respective chapters). All that's missing from this exquisitely eclectic roster is for the late Jimmy Durante to raise his hat, wag his head and wink, "That'ssssss a lotta' pop music, folks!"

Ask David Rivel, Vice President of Marketing and Communications, and he'll tell you that Lincoln Center tapped each popular genre on its own artistic merits, not as a ploy to appease sponsors or trick the broader populace into classical-music appreciation:

- "As much as we'd like to make sure we have an audience 50 years from now and so forth, we're an arts organization. We're driven by the arts, and what we did realize is that as much wonderful art as we were all doing and putting on the stages around the complex here, there was some stuff that was being left out that we felt was important; that was quality that belonged at Lincoln Center. Now we knew that those would all have the effect of bringing in new people. But the cause and effect is important because, I mean, if we were Pepsi Cola, we would say, 'Oh, how do we get more 22-year-olds to drink our soda and this is what we do.' We don't think like that. We think like, 'Well, what is great art that's out there that's not being represented on the stages, and let's do that.'

"And that led to us moving into jazz in a big way; led to us creating SERIOUS FUN!; and certainly led to us creating **MIDSUMMER NIGHT SWING**. Now the effect of those decisions had been to bring in new audiences, not just younger audiences, too, but also new middle-aged people. Some of these people who go to swing dance, these aren't people who come to Lincoln Center, even though demographically they might otherwise be similar to the audience that we have here. And we've moved strongly into those areas as we've continued to uphold the classical music tradition, which, of course, we're known for."

As one such convert, I can't say I've taken out a Philharmonic subscription yet, but at least I'm no longer a stranger to Lincoln Center's doorstep. Given how expertly these festivals are put together and how much flat-out fun I've had here over the years, I'm more inclined to peek inside its classical music sanctuary than I ever was before.

Their festival season begins in Late June with the six-year-old MIDSUMMER NIGHT SWING. It's the "best, best, best" series I know of in the country for participatory dancing because it's got some of the city's "best, best, best" music for listening — a key distinction among several I'll explain below.

Lincoln Center then goes indoors in Early July with its eight-year-old SERIOUS FUN! Although this month-long series is focused more on cutting-edge collaborations between dance, theater, poetry and multimedia, you can still count on challenging music coursing through most shows. Invariably, some nights are given over largely to music, such as the delightful pairing my wife and I caught two years ago between bluegrass jokesters, The Red Clay Ramblers, and two hilarious mimes, Bill Irwin and Cirque du Soleil's David Shiner (these three had us in stitches all night long.)

Last year such music heavy evenings grew to five, respectively spotlighting:

- Cabaret (Ute Lemper);

- Klezmer ("Shlemiel The First" play featuring the Klezmer Conservatory Band);

- Jazz ("Ju Ju" dance with Max Roach);

- Avant-garde and new music (Balanescu Quartet);

- C&W ("Chippy" play starring Jo Harvey Allen, Terry Allen, Joe Ely, Butch Hancock, Wayne Hancock, Robert Earl Keen, and Barry Tubb).

Pretty cool, huh?

CLASSICAL JAZZ' gathers in the first week of August, but the 24-year-old 'OUT-OF-DOORS simultaneously extends its tentacles to both plazas for the entire month. For the longest time, 'OUT-OF-DOORS was disparaged by critics as a grab bag of nondescript music, dance, arts and kids' stuff. Maybe at one time, though Rivel feels the press missed the point that 'OUT-OF-DOORS was meant to be more of a basic showcase for the broad cultural diversity found in Lincoln Center's Upper-West-Side environs. Its free admission underscored this desire for neighborhood involvement.

A funny thing's happened in recent years. Under the stewardship of Director Jenneth Webster, 'OUT-OF-DOORS has quietly ascended to the top ranks of New York City summer series. Last year, for example, it recorded a number of unique distinctions:

- The year's best day of Latin jazz and such (Eddie Palmieri, Jerry Gonzalez and The Fort Apache Band, Danilo Perez, Los Pleneros Del Coco, Inca Son);

- The year's best children's music and entertainment;

- The year's broadest gathering of the New York City jazz scene;

- The year's only importation of an entire regional scene ("The Boston Tea Party," featuring four full days of Beantown's finest acts across jazz, folk, world-beat, Celtic, gospel, klezmer, Latin, and more; last year it was a similarly superb "The Philadelphia Story").

All this was in addition to 'Out-of-Doors' normal performing arts, ethnic dance, and world-beat overdrive, including the annual "Caribbean Carnival," courtesy of the Caribbean Cultural Center (see chapter), Putumayo's "World Music and Dance Party" featuring Majek Fashek and Kotoja, and a terrific "Brazilfest" with Vinicius Cantuaria, Claudio Roditi, Leny Andrade, Lygya Baretto, and Dandara.

"We've been putting more money into the festival," Rivel confides:

- "And the overall quality has definitely gone up. I mean, just the fact that for a free outdoor performance you can have somebody like Paul Taylor [Dance Co.], or Nanci Griffith, or a big work like Carman Moore is putting on, 'The Mass for the 21st Century' [with 200 voices, the Skymusic Ensemble, Cissy Houston and Wynton Marsalis], and being able to commission that and put on the world premier. That's something that 'Out-of-Doors' wasn't doing seven or eight years ago, and that's a tribute, really, to Jenneth Webster and the people that she's worked with."

Perhaps it's time for critics to take another look!

One such festival-within-a-festival that the press has recognized is the 10-year-old Roots Of American Music Festival [Roots'], which commands two consecutive days of the schedule. It's programmed for Webster by Coleman "Spike" Barkin, who also books the four-year-old Carnegie Hall Folk Festival [Carnegie Hall']. The former is notable for being the only one in town where such heritage legends as Doc Watson and Bill Monroe routinely share the same stage with contemporary stars like Nanci Griffith and Christine Lavin. They're supported, in turn, by other roots purveyors along the lines of Junior Wells, Barry/Holly Tashian, Carol Fran/Clarence Hollimon, and Robin/Linda Williams. Solid stuff!

The latter festival accomplishes similar mixing-and-mingling at Carnegie Hall, but in the considerably-more intimate Weill Recital Hall, where a young Bob Dylan engineered his coming-out over 30 years ago. Let's begin by meeting the "Spike" that binds these two intriguing events together.

**Festival Review I**  Barkin is yet another one of George Wein's alumni, having been a Production Coordinator for Wein's Festival Productions, Inc. [FPI] from '72 to '80, before leaving to run his own festivals: the Memphis Music Heritage Festival; Jazz Charlotte, and the Watts Tower Blues, and Gospel and Jazz Festival, along with the two others above. He credits Wein with being a "great teacher...really, the father of festivals. [FPI] was really a wonderful place to sort of learn and sort of see how different things can be put together."

Barkin came to FPI with varied musical tastes of his own. "I was a huge jazz fan when I was in school," he recounts, "and also a big folk music fan, R&B, and gospel, and rockabilly, and all different kinds of music." One of Wein's concepts for the JVC Jazz Festival (see chapter) that particularly appealed to Barkin's sense of eclecticism was its New York Jazz Repertory Company where Wein would assemble casts from multiple styles, ages and such. While in Memphis during the early-'80s, Barkin first applied a similar collaborative approach to other genres:

- "I started putting together special segments for those festivals with some of the old rockabilly guys that were around there, and we did a Western swing thing with guys that had become plumbers and bankers, but they had been wonderful musicians in the '30s and '40s. Many of them were still playing but not all together.

  "So I sort of took that repertory concept that George had created and started applying it to different channels of music. The same excitement from the musicians that I saw in the New York Jazz Repertory Company applied with C&W guys, and the swing guys, and the rockabilly guys. And the same electricity was there with the audience. It was great!"

From this particular show sprang The Sun Rhythm Section, a group who still tours the country. Other subsequent collaborations of note involved a Johnny Otis R&B Reunion in L. A., The Persuasions with The Gospel Christians Singers in North Carolina, and Mingo Salvidar with a host of fellow Texans in New York City:

- "The wonderful thing about when you get people from different genres playing together, it goes beyond the event and you really can touch the creative spirit of the artists that are involved. For instance, at CARNEGIE HALL' where Mingo was on the 'Texas Music' concert, I asked him and Ronnie Dawson to do something together with Erbie Bowser and T. D. Bell at the end of the program. It was spectacular! It was really wonderful. And with quite different types of music playing a song together. What happened after that, Ronnie and Mingo went back to Texas and started doing stuff together.

"...One of the most gratifying comments that I've gotten from musicians [about their headlining collaborations/retrospectives] is when they'll say to me that this is the most wonderful thing that they've done, and it sort of helped to make their lives complete, and that it was really special for them. That really makes me feel good."

To make these get-togethers truly unique and appreciated, Barkin prides himself on field research, that is, hunting down referrals of artists not regularly heard in New York City, if at all. He'll visit churches to hear gospel groups sing, or old bluesmen in their own living rooms. In that way he'll hear these lesser knowns in an environment more comfortable for them, learn if they're interested in performing at his festivals, even coax them out of retirement if need be. Rapport is key to such discovery, Barkin explains, "and to me, that discovery is one of the most wonderful parts of what I do."

In last year's CARNEGIE HALL', Barkin outdid himself both in packaging diverse artists under common headings and bringing obscure practitioners from out of the woodwork. A good example was his "Circus Blues" night, where he resurrected legendary pitchman Ward Hall to present such artists as Guitar Gabriel, Snake Lady, and Diamond Teeth Mary. Of the latter, Barkin recalls:

- "She's really amazing. That was an odyssey. I had this concert to do artists that sang in front of tent shows and circuses to draw a crowd, and there were all different kinds. There were jazz artists and country artists; then we decided to focus it down to the blues. In traveling around and researching it, somebody came up to me in North Carolina and said, 'You should have Diamond Teeth Mary in this festival at Charlotte.' I said, 'That sounds good. Where is she?' 'I don't know. She's a blues singer.'

  "So I started [to find] Diamond Teeth Mary. And I spent two years, and no one had ever heard of her. Then I was in Florida talking to Ward Hall who was the M.C. for the program, and he told me that there was one person that he knew of in Tampa who might know about Diamond Teeth Mary. So I called this person up at three in the afternoon, and I said, 'Hi, this is who I am and Ward Hall said maybe you'd be able to help me. I'm looking for blues artists who work in front of circuses and side shows,' and she said, 'Well, the only one that I know of who's still alive is Diamond Teeth Mary.' And she was living in Florida. I got in touch with her; she played the JAZZ CHARLOTTE festival; she was absolutely spectacular.

  "A lot of things have happened, not necessarily by accident, but there's a lot of coincidence in being in the right place at the right time and asking the right questions. ...It's exhilarating when you find artists that you don't know about [who] sort of make the program so much better than it would have been without them."

Discoveries, collaborations, retrospectives, and eclecticism are all part of Barkin's programming philosophy for which festivals are a natural outlet. First, Barkin feels festivals yield longer bills and looser structures than straight concerts can afford, thus offering more opportunities for such unscripted participations. "That's not to say you can't have spontaneous music in a concert," he adds, "but the variables are so much greater at a festival. If the festival works properly you can really have some wonderful things going on. Festivals are, for me, the type of event you can really take chances at."

Second, Barkin likes to program in themes, especially with CARNEGIE HALL', and pictures how certain collaborations can highlight musical connections in ways that consecutive concert sets just can't:

- "I really try and make many of the sets different from a normal concert program. Then, of course, the sets are all planned with the entire festival in mind. People will say, 'How come you had so-and-so in the festival? They don't seem to go together.' There's a reason for that. There's like a third element that will come in to play why I think that those two artists make a really good combination for the festival in the overall scheme of things.

"For instance, on the Jazz Charlotte Festival coming up this year, I've got Marcia Ball and Herbie Mann on the festival and they're doing their own sets, but I'm hoping that they're going to do something together in our jam session."

Ball and Mann both illustrate a point Barkin wishes to make about pairing artists who can illustrate musical themes, but not at the expense of entertaining unindoctrinated audiences: "I really try and find groups that will apply both, who will be both intellectually stimulating as well as put on a great show — they're really authentic and they have something to say. Sometimes I'm more successful than others."

Third, Barkin sees it all as one big musical family to those with open ears:

- "That philosophy is also reflected in Roots' where we have sent a lot of reviewers to look at that festival. They look at the whole 'Out-of-Doors and say it's just a hodgepodge. What they don't understand, or won't permit themselves to understand, is that it's a celebration of music. Roots' is a celebration of American music from all of the immigrants.

  "It's funny because the artists that are on that festival are not confused by it. In fact, the C&W people, folk people, blues people, R&B people, gospel people, everyone of those people have come up to me from the group and said this is the most wonderful festival where you have everything; where it's not just limited to blues, it's not just limited to folk music, it's not just limited to bluegrass. This has everything and, in some cases, they work together — where you have a couple of people come on together, like Odetta came on with Nanci Griffith at the festival as part of her program. You might think that that wouldn't work, but American music works together with all different types of genres.

  "The purpose of 'Out-of-Doors and the purpose of Roots' is to celebrate these different types of music. ...It's everything for everybody."

~     ~     ~

**Festival**  Next up mining a similar musical vein, Midsummer Night Swing. "It's really caught the imagi-
**Review II**  nation of New Yorkers in a way that, frankly, surprised us," Rivel exclaims:

- "You know, it started just as an experiment. The 30th anniversary of Lincoln Center was coming up, and we were trying to think of a nifty way to celebrate it. And we thought about, 'Well, how 'bout for the 30th anniversary, 30 nights of dancing on the plaza?' It was designed to be just a one-time event, [but] it was so successful that we launched it as a permanent program — a nice success story."

No disrespect to Rivel, but calling this affair "a nice success story" is akin to terming the Rangers' recent Stanley Cup triumph, after a half-century drought, "a nice little win."

In order to fully appreciate why Midsummer Night Swing may well be the "best, best, best" of its kind, you need to know how the participatory dance community generally works. There are, actually, few such festivals operating — the New England Folk Festival, the Cajun and Bluegrass Music-Dance-Food Festival, and the Falcon Ridge Folk Festival (see respective chapters in Natick, MA, Escoheag, RI, and Hillsdale, NY) are three of the better ones that come to mind.

More likely you'll enter a dance camp where one hefty, all-inclusive fee will imprison you for an entire weekend or longer. If you're lucky, you'll hear more than one genre, though if it's a folk dance event, usually none that's charted any time in the last quarter-century. Noncommercial reigns, understand? You may hear more than one band per night, possibly even one you'll recognize, though it's doubtful they'll be full-time touring or recording acts. It's not that they're bad musicians, it's just that their job is to submerge any flashy individual skills they may possess in order to help the ensemble keep a steady beat for lengthy stretches. Dancing rules, you see? If you were to sit off to the side, take your eyes off the dancers and simply listen, you'd be bored stiff after about three of these interminable rambles.

What's more, because the genres are typically segregated, you get a pretty narrow demographic of dance fanatics. I know folkies will claim they draw all sorts, but tell me how many bayou African-Americans you'll see at these things bopping to the zydeco beat they originated for themselves. Or how many border Mexican-Americans you'll likewise count two-stepping to their own conjunto rhythms. Or how many casual listeners you'll notice having wandered-in off the street. None, bloody likely.

Now for MIDSUMMER NIGHT SWING!

Last year there were 26 acts purveying 21 different music/dance styles on 20 successive nights. This tally conservatively counts genre-blenders like Brave Combo as one style (I filed these wildmen under polka, for instance, though they actually romp all over the Texas musical map). We're not talking folk music obscurities, either, but big band swing, Haitian compas, alternative C&W, every variation of Latin music, modern R&B, Argentine tango, classic rock, Louisiana zydeco, etc. "Whatever we think people will enjoy moving to and we think is quality will be up there, no matter what the category," Rivel adds.

They put up some cool, cool groups, too — Illinois Jacquet Big Band, Big Sandy and His Fly-Rite Boys, Harold Melvin and The Blue Notes, Nathan and The Zydeco Cha-Cha's, Joey Dee and The Starlighters, Bobby Sanabria and Ascension, Evelyn "Champagne" King, a Fania All-Stars reunion, Michelle "Evil Gal" Wilson, The Tommy Dorsey Orchestra...

And that's just the nationally-touring and recording acts who comprise about a third of the schedule. The remaining locals are no pikers. I don't know if Vince Giordano and The Nighthawks have a label deal, to name one, but these guys are absolutely the swingingest traditional jazz band I've ever seen. "Oh, they're great, they're great," Rivel agrees. "They actually opened this season this past summer, and they're a lot of fun."

Sultry young chanteuse, La India, is managed by salsa's leading impresario, Ralph Mercado (NEW YORK SALSA FESTIVAL — see chapter), and is going to be huge in the Latin market, if she's not already! You may not recognize the name Roscoe Gordon, but back in the early '50s, he was a respected and successful contemporary of fellow Memphis bluesman B. B. King. Disgusted at not receiving proper royalties for his R&B hits, he retired to New York City to operate a dry cleaning business. But he's still got it on the few dates he comes out for each year, every soulful ounce!

You get the picture.

They get it going Wednesday through Sunday nights starting at 8:15 p.m. The dancing commands the center of Lincoln Center's magnificent, modernist Fountain Plaza. On one side of the nicely decorated elevated platform stand onlookers who cluster for a close glimpse of their musical heroes. On the other side sit those patrons of the Panevino Cafe who gently sip their wine or espresso while nibbling a dijonnaise salad or Italian biscotti as the colorful scene transpires before them. It's very genteel under the canvas umbrellas, mind you, and surprisingly uncrowded for such high-powered bills.

However, get there by 6:30 p.m., Wednesdays through Fridays, and you witness the true soul of MIDSUMMER NIGHT SWING. Director Rebecca Weller scouts out the city's leading dance instructors to run through some steps in their respective styles. Though nightly admission is $7.50 (sideline action is free), on these three nights you also get an hour of group instruction. "Anyway you slice it, it's still a pretty great bargain," Rivel promises, "cheaper than a movie in New York." Because these teachers often run their own studios and anticipate recruiting paying customers from among the audience, they're motivated to provide top-flight, user-friendly coaching.

"My sense of it is definitely the same as your's," says Rivel to my compliments:

- "That we really get [good] people to come. And they do it 'cause they love it. They see it's a great thing for them. I mean, we pay 'em some money too, but, you know [laughs], we're not talking about anything that's gonna' pay the rent. And the folks get out there and they learn the dances. For some of the nights, we also have professional dancers up there dancing, either during a break or with the band, for a little bit. It's a great time."

Take the "Mambo Night with Tito Puente" my wife and I caught two years back. The leaders were the tall, portly Eddie Torrez and his petite fireball of a wife, Maria. The unlikely-looking Torrez is no less than one of the nation's leading Latin dancers and choreographers. According to the *New York Daily News*' Robert Dominguez, he actually toured with Puente for five years before forming his own orchestra and dance company, The Mambo Kings. Torrez also runs a very popular school in town and had his entire dance staff on hand to guide us all through some basic steps. A separate instructor was positioned on the floor for every four couples or so, while Torrez directed them from the bandstand before the Mr. and Mrs. joined Puente for a flashy display of their own.

Folks, you just don't get this level of personal attention anywhere, not even at a folk dance camp! This means you can be a clumsy novice like myself and still learn just enough to hold your own for that night and beyond. Though it helps to have a partner to guide you, feel free to come single and get paired up at one of the most successful mixers this otherwise impersonal city has to offer. "I think that's a great point," Rivel nods at MIDSUMMER NIGHT SWING's easy sociability. "Absolutely!"

Roughly half the dance floor is given over to us "tenderfeet"; on the rest transpires an unbelievable floor show of aspiring Astairs and Rodgers who rival the musicians for attention on most nights. "There's always professional dancers who come every year to join on the dance floor and dance to the music they enjoy," Rivel says. Marveling at their abilities has helped convince me that New York City remains the participatory dance capital of the country.

Musicians often disparage this as "a disco town," but it's simply the trajectory of what's thrived here throughout the half-century. In places like the Savoy Ballroom, The Palladium, and Studio 54, whole popular dance vocabularies developed in waves that swept the country. These practitioners didn't disappear when their crazes ebbed but remained on the scene to pass along their steps to new generations in studios and venues which still preside. There's a thriving New York Swing Society, for example, that convenes twice weekly at places like The Roseland, The Cat Club, and Cafe Society. You can catch a good many of these still sprightly originators and their disciples at MIDSUMMER NIGHT SWING, especially for big band swing and Latin shows that draw the biggest crowds.

You'll also observe expert dancing when you wouldn't expect it. For example, I've got one friend, Lou, who's a championship two-stepper. He wins competitions all across the country and has recruited other winners like Dennis, formerly of the Joffrey Ballet, and Elena, who owns her own dance studio and judges local lindy contests. They're part of Lou's mailing list numbering several thousand — a portion of which turns out for "C&W Night," where you'll see uniquely flamboyant moves that make cable TV's TNN dancers look like they're standing still.

One such cowgirl is the Mayor's wife, Donna Hanover Giuliani, who came over this year to kick up her heels. "Yeah, and she was great," Rivel exclaims:

- "She really knew the steps! I was dealing with her office before the event and she was telling me what dances she wanted to do, and she knew 'em all! She got out there, and there was a whole bunch of people who really knew what they were doing. It was amazing to have these people come out of the woodwork! It's also amazing how much crossover there is in dance styles between these genres, as well. In 'C&W Night' they were doing The Electric Glide, which is actually pretty similar, if not identical, to a disco dance that's done. It's pretty interesting."

Which brings us to MIDSUMMER NIGHT SWING's crowning glory. Nowhere else have I experienced as truly diverse a festival audience, from the Mayor's wife down to welfare recipients — all incomes and occupations, all ages, all races and ethnicities, all attires, all abilities all having the absolute time of their lives. It's positively cosmopolitan in the "best, best, best" possible manner as only New York City can still seemingly be.

"You know, it's sort of like the skating rink at Rockefeller Center," Rivel reflects of a similarly beloved institution, "where you get the top quality amateur skaters out there kinda' performing for an audience. And then you have, you know, little five-year-old kids just shuffling along at the same time beside them — that good, wonderful mix of talent and amateur, high art and low art. It's just all mixed together."

~ ~ ~

# Manhattan's African American Scene

**BLACK EXPO U. S. A.**, Manhattan, NYC
> Middle May
> African American
> ***Attended***

**HARLEM WEEK/HARLEM DAY**, Manhattan, NYC
> Early August to Middle August
> African American
> ***Attended***

**KWANZAA HOLIDAY EXPO**, Manhattan, NYC
> Middle December
> African American
> ***Attended***

Normally you take the attendance estimates given by festivals and divide them by two for greater accuracy. Especially big free ones. But standing in the middle of broad 125th Street in the butterscotch-colored afternoon sunstream and preening either way over a dense ocean of bobbing heads, I could well believe the counts attributed to HARLEM WEEK overall. There must've been a good half million right there, right then. Accounting for crowd flow throughout HARLEM DAY on 135th Street as well, plus at 70 other events throughout the two-week marathon, 2.9 million total revelers didn't seem at all unlikely. **Festival Review I**

Oddly, though, you'd never know this huge confluence of humanity was even happening if you lived south of 110th Street. The four major dailies in town, and most of the other free weeklies, glossed over the full schedule instead choosing to merely mention a few highlights:

- Max Roach's multimedia freedom suite,"We Insist!," featuring Roach, Ossie Davis, Babatunde Olatunji, Cassandra Wilson, and the Max Roach Chorus and Orchestra, got a lot of press.

- The "HARLEM MUSIC FESTIVAL" with Jerry Butler, Gloria Lynne and Freddie Scott made the general listings, as did the "HARLEM MUSICAL HERITAGE FESTIVAL" starring Gladys Knight, Smokey Robinson, The Temptations and others.

But I couldn't extract any further lineups out of the papers, nor even an acknowledgement of the big wrap-up from other than *New York Newsday*. It felt like a "stealth monster jubilee."

There didn't seem to be a race issue among the mainstream press. The African American-owned *New York Amsterdam News* and *Carib News* didn't do much better that week, further contributing only the "B. E. T. ON WHEELS — UNITY IN THE COMMUNITY" tour with Gerald Alston, Vertical Hold, Intro and others to 20,000 street dancers, plus the "FROM HARLEM TO MOTOWN" concert featuring locals, The Sensations, The Premiers, All Four Fun and The New York Classics Orchestra.

Missing were rosters for the concurrent HARLEM JAZZ FESTIVAL "ROOTS OF JAZZ" club night, the HARLEM JAZZ FESTIVAL "LATIN JAZZ AND DANCE STREET FAIR," the HARLEM JAZZ FESTIVAL "GOSPEL BRUNCH SERIES," the "UPTOWN GOES DOWNTOWN CONCERT," the "HARLEM HAPPENING CONCERT," the "FASHION AND JAZZ CONCERT," "INSPIRATIONAL GOSPEL SUNDAY," the "SENIOR CITIZEN'S/ELDER'S JUBILEE," and the "UPTOWN SATURDAY NITE" concert. And that's just some of the musical events. Other omissions involved basketball tourneys, economic expos, film festivals, youth conferences, road races, health fairs, crafts bazaars and what-have-you.

Part of the dissemination "problem" might be that pulling off this herculean task is stretching Harlem Week's small staff a little too thin. I know, for example, that everyone in the dedicated core group wears multiple hats, including being producers for nearly all of these concerts and conferences. Another part may be that Harlem Week's created such a buzz among African-Americans nationwide that the festival committee doesn't need to broadcast it much to draw multitudes from far and wide.

But a big part might be simple humility. The brief two-page press release I received made no mention of the event's vast appeal, leaving it for *New York Newsday* to report the attendance figures and proclaim it "one of the largest cultural festivals in the country." Hey, y'all, say it loud and proud: "Harlem Day/Harlem Week is the biggest African-American festival in all of North America!"

I caught a few minutes with Marko Nobles, Director of Marketing and Publicity, just before kick-off — not enough time to explore the press issue, but more to learn briefly about their celebration's objectives and genesis exactly 20 years ago.

"It started really as a one-day event," he recalls:

- "At the time, the perception of Harlem, particularly in the media, was extremely negative, and it made even the residents of Harlem have a negative view of where they lived. And so Harlem Day was [begun] to create all the positive feelings for the Harlemites who really are the ambassadors for the community. So, you know, people then like Lloyd Williams, Joe Roberts, Michelle Scott, Tony Roberts, Percy Sutton, David Dinkins and a number of others were all involved in some way, shape and form in making the first Harlem Day possible."

Two features distinguish present Harlem Day and the two preceding weeks in general. First, there's a full diaspora of musical genres and ethnic cultures — African-American, African, Caribbean and Latin — given voice on stage. "Well, that really is the goal," Nobles adds:

- "Harlem is so many things to so many people. We say Harlem is not a place, it's a state of mind. So there are so many different cultures represented in the community, and people in the community from different cultures, that it's very important to us to make sure that we cover all these various genres. ...That's what it's all about. It's definitely a matter of inclusion."

Second, getting past the big name affairs at big time venues like the Apollo Theater, Aaron Davis Hall at CUNY, City Hall and elsewhere, there's a conspicuous profusion of local talent on display. This occurs most prominently on the eight stages of Harlem Day (and outdoors during the preview days of "Harlem Shorts"). Yes, there was noted blues guitarist Leon Thomas, R&B stars Caron Wheeler and Cuba Gooding Jr., plus doo-wop veterans Chuck Jackson, Arlene Smith and The Chantelles, Freddie Scott and others. But the remaining 55 musical acts were all young aspirants.

"We specifically make sure there's a mix between a name, or headline talent, and showcase artists," Nobles notes. "We try very much to showcase local talent so that they can have that shot in front of the thousands and thousands of people." My wife and I didn't pay close attention to who might be the next Bud Powell (we were too busy cruising the vendors and revelling in the spectacle of it all). Most of the few groups we heard didn't make a real strong impression upon us, though we were knocked out by an integrated gospel troup from one of Harlem's public schools (All City Mass Choir?).

For the best of its home grown artists, though, Nobles points to "Inspirational Gospel Sunday," which takes over the park setting surrounding Grant's Tomb on Riverside Drive at 122nd Street (also site of the weekly Jazzmobile concerts of Dr. Billy Taylor's, which occur every summer Wednesday from 5:50 to 8:30 p.m. accompanied by an Afro-Caribbean craft fair):

- "Yeah, thousands of people come out to picnic, bring their lawn chairs or what-have-you, and they just sit out and listen to gospel music. We have choirs from all over the city, [and] we have major performers come out. So that's a great event."

Nobles quickly sums up the burgeoning appeal of HARLEM DAY/HARLEM WEEK: "For a combination of within the community and people outside who have heard about it who want to see [it], we show the different aspects of the Harlem community and what goes on 365 days a year."

~　　~　　~

The presumed lineup announcements for another African-American megafest, Manhattan's installment of the nationwide BLACK EXPO U. S. A. ['EXPO'], also suffered press indifference. Only this time I'm not so sympathetic to the festival staff.

**Festival Review II**

In fairness, 'EXPO' is not known primarily for its musical roster. Instead, it's highly regarded as a trade and cultural showcase for 300-plus minority entrepreneurs from B. E. T. down to local crafters struggling to supplement their day jobs. Founded by Jerry Roebuck in '89, it's grown astonishingly to entertain 125,000 patrons in New York City, alone, with subsequent expansion to 15 cities nationwide. Wow! 'EXPO's scored notable successes as a springboard for such African-American start-ups as clothing manufacturer, Cross Colours. (Indeed, I've got an MBA banker buddy who religiously cruises the aisles for similar lending prospects.) So, on the twin scores of business networking and consumer shopping, I've got no complaint with 'EXPO's exhibit hall, which I found a sensational experience.

But exactly one-third of the print copy on 'EXPO's local newspaper ads highlighted the musical offerings in their big entertainment hall. In '94 this included big pictures of Jennifer Holliday, Riff, Kirk Franklin, a three-hour gospel showcase "...& MORE!" Here's what happened to me in '93.

My travel schedule that year was tight, tight, tight as I averaged a festival per day in peak months across 18 states, typically several per weekend, each separated by hundreds of driving miles. It was imperative for me (as it would be for any entertainment critic) to have an advance schedule to maximize my harried appearance. I telephoned 'EXPO's offices about five weeks ahead for the weekend's musical particulars — a reasonable request since most music festivals secure their lineups months in advance. A woman politely answered and promised to mail me an itinerary. "No problem," she said. It never came. Two weeks later I repeated my telephone request, receiving the same confident assurances from another woman. Again, it never came.

Finally, I called Thursday morning when the 'EXPO' officially opened to plead my case. I explained how pressed I was, but that I could re-arrange my plans to free-up part of the next day to catch their musical highlights. "Oh, you might not want to come Friday," I was told by yet a third woman, "there's not that much music that day." As long as there was something going on, I responded, and immediately dashed down to the EARTH DAY CONCERTS FOR THE ENVIRONMENT (see Columbia, MD).

The next day at noontime I'd staggered back to the Javits Center, preparing to be revived from my all-nighter by some good sounds. I payed my fee, passed through the turnstiles, picked up a brochure and saw... no performances scheduled! Not "not much music," as the office worker suggested, but none whatsoever! All the acts were booked for Saturday and Sunday. Furious, I re-routed myself up north for the NEW ENGLAND FOLK FESTIVAL (Natick, MA — see chapter) and several others. Still, the schedule did state there'd be an hour-long "Gospel Showcase" on Sunday beginning at 2:00, followed by another act at 3:30, a 45-minute "Fashion Showcase," and the night's headliners — Vy Higgenson, Caron Wheeler, Milara, Jacci McGhee, TCF Crew, Boss Boyz, and Arnold Scott — starting at 5:00. "O. K.," I thought, "maybe I can make it back for that."

And I did. I arrived Sunday promptly at 2:00 p. m. for a young gospel quintet of pre-teens from Kansas City, The Thomases. They were good for their ages, filling up the cavernous space with a sprightly message of uplift entitled, "It's All About Love." After a second song, however, they were gone. The two following acts were also shelved in favor of a scrappily arranged participatory dance contest for pre-teens. Gone, too, was any remaining music for the afternoon as the shaky "Fashion Show" plugged the scheduling holes. Burned twice now in one weekend, I was also gone — for good! Maybe the name acts showed, maybe they didn't, but I was no longer willing to risk waiting to find out.

But there's more. This year I sent a copy of our magazine with a cover letter explaining my book's intent to Mike Dabney, 'EXPO's Director of Entertainment, requesting an interview. He seemed like a nice-enough guy and we scheduled a telephone appointment for July 20. "Maybe things have tightened up since '93," I hoped. I called at the agreed-upon hour, but got only his answering machine. My message was never returned, nor were any of the follow-ups I left. "Things that make you go, 'Hmmm...'"

The moral of this story is to definitely go to 'EXPO for its overflowing trade and crafts show, but don't hold your breath for whatever music show it bills.

**See Also** One of HARLEM WEEK's staff members, Dillard Boone II, produces another African-American affair at the Javits Center that does publish a printed lineup in advance and sticks to it! His KWANZAA HOLIDAY EXPO is a trifle light on musical groups in favor of ethnic dance troups, but it does feature ample displays of those intoxicatingly vibrant Afro-Caribbean crafts, along with a host of fashion shows and seminars. It's a great place to do your holiday shopping! After you've filled out your gift list, look for the groovin' C. A. S. Y. M. Steel Orchestra, or the impassioned MCDONALD'S GOSPELFEST Finalists (New York, NY — see chapter), holding forth on center stage.

~     ~     ~

# Manhattan's Ska Scene

ROCK AGAINST RACISM CONCERT, Manhattan, NYC
> Late May
> Alternative and College Rock
> ***Attended***

OI!/SKAMPILATION, Manhattan, NYC
> Dates Vary (Late May, most recently)
> Reggae, Ska and Caribbean
> ***Attended***

SKAVOOVEE, Manhattan, NYC
> Late November
> Reggae, Ska and Caribbean

SKARMAGEDDON, Manhattan, NYC
> Late December
> Reggae, Ska and Caribbean

## Introduction

First there was SKAVOOVEE. Next there was SKALAPALOOZA, followed by SKARMAGEDDON. Then there was OI!/SKAMPILATION. Now I see where SKAVOOVEE's back on tour again this year. Not to mention similarly prefixed ska festivals that have recently visited such Manhattan clubs as New Music Cafe, The Grand, Tramps, Manhattan Center, and The Ritz, plus other sites and campuses throughout the area.

It's all enough to make a bloke go, "Oi!"

While there's no formal venue or dates for these skatterings of ska fests, you can usually count on something big come the off-season. The regional ska base — which I've charted from Boy O Boy in Richmond, Virginia to Bim Skala Bim in Boston, Massachusetts to Ruder Than You in State College, Pennsylvania and beyond — has few big-name headliners. Therefore, bands must usually bunch up into festival-quantity bills to command the bigger clubs mentioned above. All the better for us festival heads!

Apparently, there's a thriving underground press which alerts ska-legions to such happenings. I haven't run across any such "fanzines" in my travels, but my contacts assure me that *Pulp, Buzz, Raw Beat* and the rest are available. I'd go to a few shows first to get on the bands' sign-up sheets. Failing that, I'd contact Moon Records, whose pooled mailing lists from its 13 signed bands numbers 20,000 names. Their address is P. O. Box 1412, Cooper Station, New York, NY 10276.

Or I'd contact Derek of New York City's Radical Records. "T. C.," as he calls himself, is a really nice, positive, upbeat guy who organized last year's two-day ska marathon for a live recording. No word yet on the record-release date for such acts as Mephiskapheles, The Scofflaws, N. Y. Citizens, Ska Voovie, Bouncing Souls, Allstonians and 13 others, but I'm sure its coming soon. Or you can write Radical Records at 77 Bleecker Street, New York, NY 10010. The SKAMPILATION twin disc might be your quickest shortcut to finding out what this hyper-kinetic scene is all about.

"And what is ska," you ask?

Though I haven't any source material at hand, I understand ska began in Jamaica as a transition between '40's/'50's calypso and '70's/'80's reggae. Seminal bands like The Skatalites boosted the lilting pace of calypso by adding the heavy beat of American R&B that trickled across the airwaves to appeal to their dance club audiences. Reggae then merely brought ska's brisk tempo way down, while deepening the low end even further. Much of the social consciousness that emerged in ska developed toward a high art in reggae.

That's part of the story, where ska might have just faded back into the cane fields as another regional fad. But when such calypso giants as Lord Kitchener brought their lithe ska variants to London in the early '60s, one of those happy accidents occurred, not unlike young Elvis stumbling across Memphis bluesman, Arthur "Big Boy" Crudup. It seems that, in such working-class neighborhoods as Brixton and Brighton where Jamaican expatriates congregated, ska shows drew integrated audiences. Poor young whites would come, groove to the music, nod to the spiritual messages of racial harmony and inner striving, adopt the clothes right down to Kitchener's shiny suits, skinny ties and pork pie hats, and dance in place to the syncopated upbeat. An entire mixed culture emerged which maintains to this day.

Of course just as The Beatles and The 'Stones reacted to parallel roots migrations of American blues with their own interpretations, white ska converts put their own spins on the genre — more horns, more speed, more edge, and more overt politics. Simultaneously, though, young Brits stayed devoted to ska's form and essence. Apparently there was an angry "Oi!" movement in the early '80s that I'm not familiar with. Yet these bands, along with such English mainstreamers as Madness, General Public, and The Specials, all kept the hybrid culture close by, even as they incorporated punk influences.

The English scene migrated to the U. S. in the '80s where native bands like Bad Brains and Mighty Mighty Bosstones further upped the aggro quotient, adding hard-core, speed metal and rap to the mix. Goals of racial unity, class struggle and spiritual direction carried through, however. You may not be able to hear these sentiments amidst the furious snarls of today's music, but they're percolating just under the buzz. The community element also persists among practitioners. For example, Moon Records functions as an equal partnership with its roster, splitting all profits with them 50%-50% (astonishing for the rapacious music industry).

What's also present is much of Kitchener's attire, plus the near pogo-like group dancing. Some of the English accoutrements now seem almost quaint. Every suburbanite today wears "bovver boots" (e.g., Dr. Marten's), and ska's close-cropped scalps and tiny tattoos pale next to standard East Village attire. Yet, the dancing is infinitely better, faster and safer than in alternative rock's mosh pits, while the music yields a definitive party experience, especially among collegians where its most taken hold. There are a few poseur rowdies who bluff fights, but it's rarely much to "bovver" about.

For us "older" folks (what, is this me talking?), I find this admitted dance music needs more modulation to sustain listening interest throughout the course of an evening. There's too many gratuitous tempo changes. And unlike one counterpart, zydeco, ska's got no ballads to break the pace. There is humor, however. You've got to love it when a band's SKAMPILATION set-closer is a rave-up on the Bumblebee Tuna commercial theme, as was Mephiskapheles'.

"Rock steady, mon," therefore is my advice to twenty-somethings (actual and at heart) looking for a good workout and a great time.

**Festival Review** SKAMPILATION's organizer, T. C., proclaims ska is more than a mere musical genre: "It's more like a very intercultural ethnic movement." Citing ska scenes in Canada, Puerto Rico, Venezuela, and Japan, he continues:

- "It's more like the United Nations of Families; everybody getting together as one big family; breaking down barriers of false stereotypes that were involved with the '70s that brought the reggae and punk movement even stronger into the ska movement; that rebelled against all negativeness within, especially in the American rock music era. It took people [in] Jamaican and English movements to shake the boots, to tell the youth, 'Listen, you don't have to be followers, you can be leaders.'

  "What I've done throughout the years is more like a unity thing — trying to look out for everybody as a social consciousness. You know, instead of looking out for number one, I say we look out for number all and help each other out as a movement."

T. C. first heard ska while growing up in New York City's East Village. "I've been into ska for, like, early '79, since I was a little kid," he recalls, "and it's, like, I really love ska, reggae, soul, jazz, calypso, early punk, rap, some hard core, you know, stuff." He quickly copped the look, though being surprised by the fierce association his Dr. Marten's brought via punk-rockers: "I was wearing them, like, 12 years ago. People saw you walking down the street with them, they wouldn't walk in front of you for some reason. I'm like, 'Damn! What's the problem; what's wrong here?'"

It wasn't long before T. C. got drawn into ska's local dance scene, populated by London immigrants and Brooklyn's strong Caribbean population. "There's people who were there were very professional going to ska shows," he says. "They knew how to dance, and they did 'skanking,' or 'pogoing.' They're not hurting one another, they're just having fun — just, like, enjoying the freedom of dancing, being happy and just getting along with everybody."

T. C. learned to play bass and drums and joined several bands. Unfortunately, various co-members would get scarfed up by tours, so T. C. let go of holding his groups together in favor of "just stick[ing] to doing what I like doing most. It's just keeping the family strong, you know, trying to help everybody out." This involved free-lance promotion with his friend, John Monahan, a ska guitarist himself, on behalf of such acts as The Slackers, Agent 99, Inspector 7, Desmond Dekker, Prince Buster and others. Benefit concerts for the homeless were the most common activities for the two. Eventually, T. C. connected with Radical Records, which had added ska to its lengthy roster of rap and hard-core signings.

The idea for the SKAMPILATION compilation came from T. C.'s many ska friends seeking help with exposure. "I said, 'Yes, sure. No problem,' because I've been doing this for a long time, and I figure [with] my knowledge of the movement I'd be the perfect one," he remarks. "Plus it's not like I'm in it for the money or anything. I'm in it for the support and unity aspect of it, you know?"

T. C., who'd helped out with SKAVOOVEE the prior year, put a somewhat larger bill together at the Grand, times two nights. It featured a host of "baby bands" from throughout the region plus an additional DJ between sets. In a nice touch, he had the shows kick off at 5:00 p.m. This let him get the venue cheaper, since the 11:00 p.m. wrap-up allowed the club to book post-fest activities for New York City's night owls.

From catching the last act of Day Two, I can tell you the shows were a definite success. The Grand's otherwise-well-ventilated interior literally dripped with dancers' perspiration. Even after five hours of frantic skanking the young, mostly white crowd's reaction to a turbocharged Mephiskapheles was still over-the-top. "I think the biggest highlight was just everybody having a good time, being up there, being free," T. C. says, noting that the bands also appreciated the well-organized, well-scheduled effort.

As for the SKAMPILATION compilation? "The sound is immense," T. C. claims. "It's a double CD, and the first CD will be 'Crazy Pulse Hard Core Punk Madness' on it, and the other CD will be 'Crazy Ska Madness Rock Steady with the Beat.' It'll have a photo layout of everybody, all the bands, friends, family, the audience, everybody. And it'll be more like a unity thing, you know?"

Another multiracial "unity thing" is the one-afternoon ROCK AGAINST RACISM CONCERT [R. A. R.']. **See Also** Whereas ska fests are hit-or-miss things, R. A. R.' has gone on like clockwork for an astonishing 16 straight years. This, despite losing a Supreme Court decision upholding a city noise ordinance that forced R. A. R.' from its customary Central Park site downtown to a flat-bed trailer at the foot of Union Square. In a unique twist of fate, '94's R. A. R.' occurred the same day as SKAMPILATION, allowing you to skank straight from noon to nearly midnight!

Sometimes there are ska bands on the bill (Ska-Danks in '94), but more often it's a mix of lesser known reggae bands, young rock bands, older Black Rock Coalition bands (**Downtown Jazz, I** -- see chapter) plus a legitimate headliner. In '93 these name acts were local bluesman-made-good Chris Whitley and up-and-coming BRC funk-rockers, Faith.

I won't kid you, R. A. R.'s a modest affair. The music's reasonably good for a freebie, though the succession of older poets and rappers between sets could've gained from some editing and focus. There was too much aimless ranting and raving against "the system"; not enough tangible activities to direct the audience toward. Overall, I don't know that I'd drive down from, say, Boston, but R. A. R.'s a worthy, relaxing afternoon for locals and daytrippers with something else planned for the evening.

~     ~     ~

*Red Rodney, Riverside Arts Festival.*

# Queens' Irish Scene

**IRISH-AMERICAN FESTIVAL AND HERITAGE FEIS**, Brooklyn, NYC
> Late May
> Irish
> ***Attended***

**GATEWAY TO THE NATIONS POW WOW**, Brooklyn, NYC
> Early July
> Native American

**ROCKAWAY IRISH FESTIVAL**, Queens, NYC
> Late July
> Irish
> ***Attended***

**AFRICAN CARIBBEAN LATINO AMERICAN FESTIVAL**, Brooklyn, NYC
> Late July
> African American

**NYC BLUEGRASS BAND AND BANJO CONTEST/GATEWAY MUSIC FESTIVAL/CITY GARDENERS' HARVEST FESTIVAL**, Brooklyn, NYC
> Late August
> Variety, Folk and International

**GREAT IRISH FAIR**, Brooklyn, NYC
> Early September to Middle September
> Irish
> ***Attended***

**ROCKAWAY MUSIC AND ARTS COUNCIL FALL FESTIVAL**, Brooklyn, NYC
> Middle September
> Variety, General

**GATEWAY SUKKOS FESTIVAL**, Brooklyn, NYC
> Late September
> Jewish

**Introduction**

The great Irish exodus of the 19th century has long, long since been absorbed here and assimilated into the suburbs. It's been decades since New York City's elected an Irish mayor, for instance. Yet there are still neighborhoods within city boundaries where as many as 60% of the residents are Irish descendents, typically first and second generations from an immigration pattern that continues today. Two such neighborhoods are Woodhaven and the Rockaways along the southern reaches of Queens. They yield core audiences for a trilogy of Irish festivals that punctuate the summer — beginning, middle, and end.

The father of them all is the **GREAT IRISH FAIR** ['IRISH FAIR], which takes over Coney Island's Steeplechase Park for three days the second weekend in September. Launched by the Ancient Order of Hibernians [A. O. H.] in '81, it has grown to an alleged two million attendance from the "Tri-State Area." This makes it the largest Irish event in the entire country, even bigger than Manhattan's St. Patrick's Day Parade.

The ROCKAWAY IRISH FESTIVAL [ROCKAWAY' FESTIVAL] followed suit in '82. During the fourth weekend in July, it fills up a two-block stretch near the boardwalk where three Irish pubs hold court. The ROCKAWAY' FESTIVAL draws about one-tenth the crowds of the 'IRISH FAIR, but that probably represents a near unanimous showing of the neighboring Irish, certainly enough for a bustling block party!

In '93 Gateway National Park supplemented its increasingly diverse roster of ethnic festivals listed above with an IRISH-AMERICAN FESTIVAL AND HERITAGE FEIS [GATEWAY' FEIS] covering three days on Memorial Day weekend. The locals came over to Floyd Bennett Field to the tune of 20,000 a day, insuring a repeat engagement in '94.

This makes three "wearin' o' the greens" within hailing distance of each other.

What lends these festivals their unique musical flavor is an uncommon mixing of Irish music styles, along with a showcasing of all the exciting young talent blossoming throughout the outer boroughs. There'll be showbands and other "commercial-style" exponents for the parents and grandparents (these are primarily family affairs, after all). However, there'll also be plenty musically for teens, twenties and thirties. Indeed, the only other U. S. cities I've seen that can boast similar crossover acts are possibly Boston (e.g., Cliffs of Dooneen) and Chicago (e.g., The Drovers).

Here's a brief musical breakdown from their combined lineups:

- Rock bands (e.g., Black 47, Speir Mor);

- Progressive acoustic acts (e.g., Eileen Ivers, Seamus Egan, Susan McKeown and The Chanting House, Four to the Bar, Pierce Turner);

- Traditionally-based acoustic acts, but with crossover appeal (e.g., Cherish the Ladies, Morningstar);

- Commercially oriented acts, but with crossover appeal (e.g., Aine, Erin's Pride).

The 'IRISH FAIR has the budget to bring over a few headliners from Ireland (The Wolfe Tones and Boru in '94, for example), but home-grown talent is what to listen for across the board. Just ask Connecticut-based Green Linnett Records, the leading Irish-music label in the world. They've already signed separate deals with Ivers, Cherish the Ladies, Cherish's leader/flautist, Joannie Madden, Cherish's lead singer-songwriter, Cathie Ryan, plus they've made an offer to McKeown, I understand. The only biggie they've missed so far is Eileen's playing partner and fellow All-Ireland Champion, Egan, and that's only because Egan's signed to Shanachie Records.

So, keep an ear out for the locals, and "May the road rise to meet you..." as you hop the Belt Parkway to Jamaica Bay.

**Festival Review I** Coney Island was once Disneyland, Disneyworld, and Atlantic City all rolled into one. I don't have to tell you what kinds of crowds gathered here throughout the first half of the 20th century — you've seen the Reginald Marsh prints or the Weegee photos picturing masses of humanity crowding the broad beachfront to the point where not even a swatch of sand is visible.

But now? Coney Island's a virtual ghost town of its former self, separating a prosperous Russian/Jewish neighborhood to the east from a grim collection of housing projects to the west. Indeed, the festival site, Steeplechase Park, functions as a peaceful memorial to the skeleton of the Parachute Jump which remains, towering high by itself above the boardwalk.

That changes three times a year: for the TRINI-JAM FEST and the NEW YORK REGGAE SUMMER BEACH PARTY — both run by George Crooks (see chapter) — and the 'IRISH FAIR. "Coney Island is not known to be a good neighborhood," observes Promoter Al O'Hagan:

- "We pack the place with all smiling Irish faces. For the community it's a complete turnaround. They rediscover Coney Island because when they come to the festival, they don't stay at the festival all day; they go down to the Cyclone, or the Wonder Wheel, or Nathan's. The Chamber of Commerce tells me that they do a better business the weekend after Labor Day than they do all season long at Coney Island."

Of course the main intent of O' Hagan's A. O. H. is not to develop the neighborhood (although they have created 11 Boys and Girls Scout troups in proximity), but to create a benefit for Brooklyn Catholic Charities, promoting Irish music and culture along the way. And if an Irish act such as commercial troubadour, Richie O'Shea, or cool college rockers, Black 47, gets sprung to greater glory, well, so much the better.

Visit the grassy grounds and you'll see a very well appointed family festival where every constituency is thoughtfully provided for. That's the job of O'Hagan. Handicapped and elderly are shaded under a 100 by 80-foot tent where they're catered to by two restaurants and their own entertainment stage. Three more restaurant-sponsored tents offer food, drink and music. Kids are utterly indulged by an "Irish Freedom Train," pony rides, rides, games, parades, and such. Those ages inbetween enjoy extensive crafts and cultural displays as well as profuse music on three more stages (for seven stages in total, if you're counting.)

The music's the job of O'Hagan's daughter, Sheila McGraw. "I give her all the credit," he says. "She handles all the entertainment. She is an entertainer herself; she used to sing. She can spot the talent." O'Hagan describes his own daughter as a "tough customer," one who plies the field and pores over audio/video tapes to get exactly whom she wants. However, she's sufficiently balanced the commercial, the traditional, and the progressive over the years to where he trusts her judgement implicitly. Many of the acts in the musical breakdown above, and others besides, first gained prominence on McGraw's stages.

O'Hagan shares my compliments on booking young traditional bands, Four to the Bar ("great") and Cherish' ("fabulous"). We also agree on young commercial/country singer, Aine ("very good"), though he feels the lead singer of Erin's Pride ("an up-and-coming group") has a tad more developed style and repertoire, including plenty of Patsy Cline.

Ask O'Hagan for his own festival highlight and he'll immediately cite the legendary tenor, Frank Patterson. Ironically, this highlight comes from catching Patterson, not at O'Hagan's own 'Irish Fair, but at the '93 Gateway' Feis. You see, he wasn't sure Patterson, his personal friend, would go over well in a festival environment. No longer! After witnessing Patterson's triumph there, O'Hagan's making sure to work him into future 'Irish Fair bills.

I leave O'Hagan to prepare for his visit to a national A. O. H. convention in Louisville, Kentucky, where he's running for top office. He leaves me, however, with this summation:

- "It's a lot of work, but it's a labor of love because I grew up with the Irish music. We're promoting it. We're supporting charity; we're supporting culture, and we're helping the quality of life in the area.

  "...I don't even have to advertise that much because we're established. We're really lucky. And it's a good weekend because everybody is back for school; they're all back from vacation and they want one last fling before the summer is over. They spend it at Coney Island, and it's fine with me."

~     ~     ~

Whereas O'Hagan's affair is formally expansive, the Rockaway' Festival is a cosy, bustling tumult. "Homespun" is how Promoter Marina Callahan describes it. It takes place along an elbow-shaped intersection of Beach 108th Street lined by Irish pubs and delis. Accordingly, a fair number of pints get tipped during this particular weekend (my sneakers actually stuck to the sidewalk in parts), but it's all in good fun for this close-knit, blue-collar outpost. **Festival Review II**

Callahan's roots are tied to this street:

- "My husband's a fireman, and he owned [the former] Rain Tower Tavern. He, myself, and another fellow, Michael Tubridy, who owns Tubridy's across the way, went to the 'Irish Fair (this is the first year that they ran it), and we said, 'Wow, this is such a wonderful event! Why can't we do this in Rockaway?' The area where our pub is located was known many, many years ago as Old Irish Town, so we thought that it would be perfect to recreate Old Irish Town, generate business for the local community, and get Rockaway sort of back on the map. Also, the real main thing that we wanted to do was to support the United Irish Foundation, which is a social-service agency that helps specifically, but not exclusively, senior citizens of all denominations."

Such causes are a big part of Callahan's mission in promoting the Rockaway' Festival. "I also pride myself in getting politics into this," she adds.

- "I'm very involved in politics. I was Congressman Floyd Flake's public relations person, and I think that making people aware that there is a lot more to Irish culture than music and art; that we have to remember our roots and where we came from; that there is a lot of inhumanity towards man that still exists and we still have to remember that. I'm very proud of that; that I can still introduce that and get people aroused a little."

But if you really want to engage Callahan's passion, just start asking her about all the homegrown talent her event has to offer. Not only has Callahan booked many of the local acts who've since gone onto national prominence, she's also got a handle on many more I didn't even know about. Morningstar, The Barleycorns, Celtic Cross, Walter Ensor, Gerald Bair, John and Annie O'Hara (formerly of the influential '70s/'80s rockers, Eggs Over Easy) — all get extensive mention.

Callahan tipped me toward an energetic acoustic band, Four to the Bar, about whom she was so excited she ended up managing them for a year:

- "Four to the Bar was introduced to me by a man named Ed Chevalin. He had seen them and knows the kind of music that I specifically like. I come from a "folk-trad." background. My parents just love folk music, and that's what I was weaned on. So he said to me, 'Marina you have to come and see this band.' And I did, and I thought they were wonderful, and I hired them for the festival.

"Two of them are from Ireland [Cork and Leeds]; one is from Astoria, Queens; and one is from Piermont, New York. Keith O'Neill, who plays the fiddle, his sister has played with Cherish the Ladies. He's an All-Ireland champion fiddle player, and he is just wonderful. Then they have Tony McQuillan from Canada who sits in with them occasionally. He's a wonderful, wonderful accordion player. I really think that he brought the band [to] like a full tilt. There was something about the fiddle and the accordion together that just worked very well, and it gave it that edge."

And how'd they go over at the Rockaway' Festival?

- "I think Four to the Bar absolutely stole the show and the reason I say that is because, at that time when they were highlighted, it was a really multi-ethnic, multi-generational group, and they pleased everyone. They did. They were selling $6 tapes, and they were doing $1,000 in sales in, like, 15 minutes. It was phenomenal! People were rushing the stage to buy these tapes. David Yeates, who is the singer and the flute and bohdran player, he climbed up to the top of the stage and jumped off, much to my dismay, because I'm thinking, 'Does this insurance cover this?' I was terrified. But he just absolutely wigged these people out [laughs]. They were so psyched, and they really loved it and they didn't want them to leave.

"And that's the kind of music that, as an Irish woman, I'm very proud of. That really simplifies to me what Irish music is about rather than the "diddle-dee-dee," pop showband type thing [although] I do feature that, I have to say. You know, it's nice to sometimes get up with your dad and dance around."

Callahan laughs at the contradiction, but that's precisely her event's musical strength: being able to satisfy the gamut of ages and tastes, from young Irish rockers just off the boat, to Irish-American grandparents landed for three generations. "It's something I work very hard to achieve," Callahan explains, "because I personally believe multigenerational, multiethnic is just the way to go."

Both days start conservatively on two stages, then grow younger in spirit toward the evening's end. What's more, due to a local Irish scene Callahan describes as remarkably free of egos, you'll see any number of musical guests sitting in — Ivers and Madden to name a few.

"I really pride myself in running a tight show," Callahan concludes, "that I'm easy to work with, and that everybody comes away happy. Really, that's it. It's a good, happy, family festival. There are really no problems. All-in-all, it's been a good 13 years."

**Festival
Review III**

The GATEWAY' FEIS is the rookie of the three, having begun in '93, Callahan tells me, because one of the Park's top supervisors is Irish and wanted one of their many ethnic festivals for his own kind, thank you very much. It occupies an abandoned runway of Floyd Bennett Field, another one of those "cradles of aviation," and offers festival-goers a rare commodity in New York City — wide open spaces. In three directions all you'll see are scrub pines, sandy dunes, tidal grasslands and sea gulls, while a northeasterly glance through Flatbush Avenue's sycamores yields an unobstructed view of Wall Street's skyscrapers far off in the distance. It offers you a welcome commune with the sky on a sunny day.

My wife and I had to motor off to two more festivals the day we attended in '93. Still, we were pleasantly surprised by the opening act, a daughter of a Queens assemblyman who goes by the name of Aine (pronounced "En-ya).

**Artist
Mini-Review**

Aine. Aine didn't let her early-morning debut for us and about 50 middle-aged Irish couples under the tented stage deter her from seducing the whole lot. Attractive, active and cheery, the young singer worked the crowd with a variety of mostly traditional Irish songs, but also some Patsy Cline ballads where her heart clearly lay. We both thought Aine's singing and entertaining skills were first-rate a la early Pam Tillis and how, with some decent material before younger crowds, she could really be going places.

Callahan:

- "Last year she performed for us, and it was a very mixed crowd, and the crowd flipped for her. They loved her! First of all, she is very attractive. And she really plays to her audience — she makes direct eye contact; she just does some of these things that make a good entertainer a good entertainer, in my opinion. And it just wasn't the mothers that loved her. The young girls loved her, too, and the kids and the old people. She really gave a very good show.

  "And this year, when she played at the GATEWAY' FEIS, she was scheduled to play an hour and half and she played for two and a half hours. They wouldn't let her go! She was so wonderful, she really was."

**Attendance
Tip**

The link between all three Irish events — the Belt Parkway — is also its bane. "The Belt" is one of New York City's most notorious parking lots, and it's just as likely to be clogged on weekends, given commercial traffic from Kennedy Airport as well as day-trippers to New Jersey and Long Island beaches. It also seems perpetually under construction. Make sure to listen to the radio for traffic reports, and to carry a detailed road map for any side street escapes as are necessary.

**See Also**

Of the remaining festivals at Floyd Bennett Field listed above, the greatest musical interest is offered by the NYC BLUEGRASS BAND AND BANJO CONTEST occurring on a variable Sunday in August. It's usually run in conjunction with the two-day-long HARVEST FESTIVAL, which also booked the modest GATEWAY MUSIC FESTIVAL in '93 to occupy the open Saturday.

Longtime bluegrass-music insider, Doug Tuchman, kicked off the contest way back in '74. I've never seen a roster of entrants, but I do know of several highly-regarded bands who've entered in recent years, including Moscow-based Kukuruza (Sugar Hill Records), and New-England-based Northern Lights (Flying Fish Records). It's free, it's nice, and the handsome prizes draw a healthy roster. With the lamentable demise of the Eagle Tavern on West 14th Street (which also hosted Irish-music acts, alas), it's also the only place you can count on hearing bluegrass music in all of New York City — and this being where "citybilly" music was born in Washington Square Park during the mid-'50s!

~     ~     ~

# New York City's Ethnic Dance Traditions

**NEW YORK ETHNIC MUSIC AND DANCE FESTIVAL**, Manhattan, NYC
Late May
Variety, Folk and International
***Attended***

**BRONX ETHNIC MUSIC AND DANCE FESTIVAL**, Bronx, NYC
Middle June
Variety, Folk and International

**QUEENS FESTIVAL/NATIONS IN NEIGHBORHOODS MULTICULTURAL DANCE PARTY,**
Queens, NYC
Late June
Variety, General
***Attended***

**NEW YORK COUNTRY MUSIC FESTIVAL**, Queens, NYC
Middle August
Modern Country

**BROOKLYN ETHNIC MUSIC AND DANCE FESTIVAL**, Brooklyn, NYC
Late October
Variety, Folk and International

**Introduction** They say good things come in "small" packages. Certainly, that's the case in New York City for when its ethnic-folk-dancing communities come together.

The chief gatherings are really delightful affairs that occupy their own private niches within big public parks. This helps them attract a high number of passersby that, alone, would dwarf the attendance of similar festivals most anywhere else in the country. ...Hmmm, I guess this makes them both not-so "small," after all. But they feel "small" (i.e., intimate, welcoming, friendly), and therein lies their charm.

Their granddaddy is the late, lamented QUEENS ETHNIC MUSIC AND DANCE FESTIVAL, that took over a community hall and beer garden in the heavily Greek section of Astoria and ran for 15 years until falling victim to funding cuts from economically troubled city and state agencies. Produced by Manhattan's Ethnic Folk Arts Center, it was hugely influential throughout the ethnic-folk-dance world as possibly the first such festival to bring a fuller range of nationalities to the table where previously only "Anglo-centric" dance styles had been served.

After a two-year hiatus, it was reborn in '93 as the BROOKLYN ETHNIC MUSIC AND DANCE FESTIVAL [BROOKLYN ETHNIC'] in Brooklyn's version of Manhattan's Central Park — Prospect Park. This move south to more heavily travelled environs not only broadened its exposure, but also let it link up with a stable budgetary entity, The New York City Department of Parks and Recreation. Together they christened the annual BROOKLYN ETHNIC' as the first of an ongoing "Folk Parks" program, the second of which was installed last year in Harlem's spanking-new Riverbank State Park as the NEW YORK ETHNIC MUSIC AND DANCE FESTIVAL [NEW YORK ETHNIC']. The third, the BRONX ETHNIC MUSIC AND DANCE FESTIVAL [BRONX ETHNIC'], touched down this year in pastoral Van Cortland Park bordering Westchester County.

Their joint literature claims "Folk Parks" to be the only multi-ethnic events in New York City where the central role is participatory dance. That's not quite true, though it may become more so in 1995 depending on the status of the QUEENS FESTIVAL or, more specifically, the wonderful NATIONS IN NEIGHBORHOODS MULTICULTURAL DANCE PARTY hidden under a side tent.

Before I explain this latter event's current predicament as of this writing, permit me a bit of reportage.

'Twas a scorching, steamy Sunday when my wife and I staggered into last year's QUEENS FESTIVAL. Our initial impression, which held fast until our leaving, was of a massive, yet soul-less, lunk of urban stew. The 18-year-old event inhabited the undistinguished sprawl of Flushing Meadows/Corona Park, where the ghosts of the '64 World's Fair were still visible in the form of monuments like the "Fountain of Planets," eerily reminiscent of the final scene from "Planet of the Apes." Though billed by the *New York Daily News* as "America's largest two-day family festival" (another exaggeration), the primary constituents among its one million attendees seemed to be roving packs of disinterested teens feasting upon every greasy variation of sausage. Schlock predominated from those few vendors who actually had something to sell; most were of the civic and commercial variety content to leave a stack of brochures at their booths and split.

**Festival Review I**

There was music, but the several main stages were segregated by genre and suffered a near-total lack of accessibility and presentation values. For example, WSKQ 97.9 offered some fairly strong salsa bands in its "Latino Village," but plopped them down in the middle of a dusty soccer field and barricaded its listeners far away from the raised stage. At least they had music going on during the day. The Great Stage didn't even bring out any of its headliners — Crystal Waters, Buster Poindexter, and a host of Richard Nader's doo-wop bands — until late, late in the afternoon. Huh? The three Asian pavilions produced richly-costumed pageants, yet held them inside darkened tents with the flaps drawn for forbiddingly stuffy viewing. And so forth.

We were hastily on our way out to catch a breeze at the IRISH TRADITIONAL MUSIC AND DANCE FESTIVAL (Bronx, NYC — see chapter) when we spied something unique — a mixed cluster of folks actually close to the music and having themselves some fun! Credit Ilana Harlow. This soft-spoken Folk Arts Director for the Queens Council on the Arts had just come over to her post that year from the renowned Folk Institute at the University of Indiana, yet managed to push all the right buttons:

- First, she assembled a daily lineup of six terrific ethnic acts from around the borough — an example being Irish flautist extraordinaire, Joannie Madden, who warmed up for her hosting the IRISH TRADITIONAL MUSIC AND DANCE FESTIVAL on Sunday with an appearance for Harlow on Saturday.

- Second, she networked within the ethnic communities to insure an enthusiastic turn out for their respective bands, such as the large contingent from the Greek Folklore Society who came fully-costumed with 100-year-old outfits brought over from their homeland.

- Third, she made sure to lay down a genuine dance floor atop the pebble-strewn grass clumps that predominated elsewhere.

- Fourth, she recruited several experts on hand for every ethnic dance style to lead the crowd through some basic steps at the start of their sets — no wallflowers allowed;

Finally, she removed as many barriers to the musicians as possible, like lowering the stage to a mere six inches and moving the monitors off to the sides. This yielded the comfortable ambience of a house party, which is precisely what transpired on the dance floor, despite the sticky heat.

I was especially impressed with Jose Quesada Y Los Cincos Diablos, a hot and rustic merengue band with Dominican roots. I had never before seen this kind of Latin accordion in the slick salsa mix to which I'd become accustomed, certainly none so blazing as Quesada's. He's your basic house-a-fire and can hold his own with most any zydeco maven I've experienced. Other genres that day included Bengali folk (Subhra Goswami Ensemble), Ghanan "highlife" (Kabajo) and Bukharan Jewish (Shashmaqam), though Harlow saved her highest compliments for Los

Macondos, a Columbian "vallenato" sextet she described to me as "good, *very* good!"

All this fun stuff may be for naught.

Shoddy unwieldiness may have finally caught up with the parent QUEENS FESTIVAL, as *New York Newsday* reports that city and borough officials plan to place their emphasis, instead, on the state-funded I LOVE NEW YORK FALL FESTIVAL. They wouldn't necessarily cancel permits to hold the privately run QUEENS FESTIVAL, but they would withdraw nearly $37,000 in targeted festival grants to such arts councils as Harlow's. This doesn't mean the end of ethnic-music programming for the Queens Council that, together with the Flushing Council on Culture, produces concerts all summer long. But it might effectively terminate the NATIONS IN NEIGHBORHOODS MULTICULTURAL DANCE PARTY — the only meaningful reason to attend whatever's left of the QUEENS FESTIVAL, that's for sure. Call ahead for confirmation.

~     ~     ~

**Festival Review II**  Meanwhile, fear not, intrepid ethnic-folk dancers. The BROOKLYN ETHNIC', the NEW YORK ETHNIC' and the BRONX ETHNIC' all remain to provide the same fine bands, thoughtful instructional features and inviting neighborly vibes. For more insights, here's their chief organizer, Ethel Raim.

Raim explains that the Ethnic Folk Arts Center was founded by Martin Canin as the Balkan Arts Center back in '66, but has since expanded its focus to nearly all the immigrant communities of New York City. Margaret Mead was one of the initial patrons. Along the way, it's evolved quite an extensive series of offerings — festivals, concerts, publications, audio and video productions, and concert tours — all "designed to have a positive impact upon the constant evolution of cultural traditions within a community," as the mission statement reads.

Basically, the 'Center continues to fight the good fight for what it calls "cultural equity — affirming the value and importance of cultural diversity as an essential component of our national identity." And it won its share, notably, when Raim bid traditional Irish-music champion, Mick Maloney, to assemble a second-generation team of young female musicians for a series of concerts from which Cherish the Ladies formed. "We had to turn hundreds of people away," she recalls of these shows. "It was a beautiful community outpouring."

Raim got introduced to Canin's groundbreaking activities in Balkan dance way back in '69 while a field researcher for the Smithsonian Institution's FESTIVAL OF AMERICAN FOLKLIFE (see Washington, DC, Early July) — an immense showcase on the Capitol Mall for all the cultural arts of a few given ethnicities per year. She brought Canin into that organization's fold the following year.

The Smithsonian played a dominant role in the folk-festival community. Its founder, the late-Ralph Rinzler, also helped guide musical selections for the NEWPORT FOLK FESTIVAL (BEN AND JERRY'S NEWPORT FOLK FESTIVAL, Newport, RI — see chapter). At both landmark events, Rain relays, "the communities presented and the music presented were pretty much African-American and Anglo." She cites rare exceptions, like Rinzler's bringing Cajun fiddler Dewey Balfa to Newport in '64, yet describes the prevailing view of traditional folk music as "Appalachian tradition, fiddling, and ballad tradition, but most of it English language."

Raim felt an inner nagging. At one festival evaluation she remembers "commenting that none of the people that I grew up [with], which were all the hyphenated [names] and people with real heavy foreign accents like my own parents...were presented at the festival. I was immediately given $3,000 to go out and really do research on other communities; to find those traditions and bring them to the festival." Social context was the aim of these forays so that listeners then could receive an authentic presentation of how the music was meant to be played and experienced. And, of course, participatory dance was the realm in which most of it functioned (i.e., at weddings, christenings, parties, etc.).

Canin's Bulgarian dance contacts provided one of Raim's first such incorporations for the '70 festival and served as a pilot for a subsequent "Old Ways in the New World" program at the Smithsonian. Another incorporation involved showcasing the rich communal traditions of what was then Yugoslavia in '73 with traditional dance bands recruited from abroad and all around the U. S. "And it was incredible," Raim remarks, "because here was an event that had Serbs and

Croatians collaborating with each other, and cooperating with each other, and celebrating with each other!"

The turning point for Raim's career involved researching the Greek communities of Maryland and New York City for '74's festival, then heeding Canin's request to join his Ethnic Folk Arts Center the following year. One of their priorities was to produce a festival. "We were out in Queens for another program, and we stumbled into Bohemian Hall," Raim recalls:

- "And it was just such an incredible place. I mean, these beautiful old sycamore trees, and the beer garden out back, and a wonderful stage, and a wood floor on the inside — just a wonderful facility. We saw the place, and we looked out of the window at the beautiful beer garden and said, 'What a beautiful place for our festival!' So we did our festival in '76 there. That was the first time we did an outdoor festival. And that was our QUEENS ETHNIC MUSIC AND DANCE FESTIVAL that ran for 15 years until '90."

It was famous for attracting folk dancers from up and down the East Coast. They were drawn partly to the festive intimacy of the setting, partly to the dance instruction from Canin (who was now giving workshops all throughout the country) and song lessons from Raim, partly to the fine production values, but mostly to the unique opportunity to share the dance floor with those other than fellow Anglo folkies.

"It [was] a very different dynamic," Raim says. "Part of the work that we tried to do was to try to have that mix occur, and the mix being people from within the various ethnic communities...then the general public, the general audience." This mix gained from a cosy site accommodating just 1,500 — a problem income-wise when recession-oriented funding cuts eventually crimped Raim's finances and forced the festival into its two-year hiatus. "When we were finally able to bring it back," she says of its return in '93 to Prospect Park as **BROOKLYN ETHNIC**', "we redesigned it so it could be a free festival, and we could accommodate really large numbers of people."

Freer and bigger were two changes, but key qualities remained. First, musicians continued to reflect the ethnic diversity of their respective "neighborhoods" — loosely defined as a few-mile radius around the park grounds. There were no national acts, but quality from rooted "locals" didn't suffer to my ears as Andy Statman's klezmer mandolin or Tom Dougherty's Irish mellodion was musically as good as it gets. Pride reigned within their respective ethnic audiences as such obviously gifted representatives carried their flags so well onstage.

Echoing the opinions of Bob Rizzo (PROVIDENCE WATERFRONT FESTIVAL, Providence RI — see chapter) on the value of presenting the finest acts available when doing multicultural programming, Raim adds:

- "There's a kind of external affirmation that helps you to re-evaluate, and re-accept, and re-embrace your own culture. I mean, there's such a pressure on children in the community to leave it behind in order to feel that they can mainstream and feel part of being American. There's also so much shame that people have about their cultures, and the pressure to be like everybody else, and 'if you leave it behind you can get ahead,' and all that stuff. I think it leaves people totally culturally impoverished. Many people return to it afterwards and say, 'My God, what richness, and I just turned my back on it!' [For] the communities that are going through the adjustment of becoming American, it's just so important to be able to hold on to those traditions and make them relevant for their new context."

Second, audiences still flocked in a spirit of eclectic enjoyment of one-another's culture, encouraged by the wide-open dance workshops lassoing all who wandered by. I'll tell you, too, as I witnessed young Dominicans fixated on the virtuoso playing of Statman, as well as middle-aged Irish couples boogie-ing to the calypso beat of Antilles, you don't often see this kind of hands-on intermingling of ages, races and classes around town. "Absolutely," agrees Raim. "It's like an utopian vision of New York that rarely comes through."

Raim's greatest satisfaction comes from being able to strengthen these kinds of cultural links, not just on the pages of folkloric academia, but in the flesh for immigrant New Yorkers and their successors wherever they've roamed. "I remember a woman coming up to us in Ohio, or wherever," she notes of one from her travels:

- "We took some of the musicians, and we went on tour. And this woman just stopped us dead in the road and said, 'You people are doing really great stuff! You know, for me, this is real. This isn't the hokey stuff I see on TV, this is real! What you're doing is real!'

"She got it."

**Artist Mini-Reviews**    My wife and I revelled in the NEW YORK ETHNIC' last year. It graced a sunny Memorial Day in Harlem's Riverbank State Park, recently built atop a vast waste treatment plant to appease the surrounding community. Don't worry, there was no sewage smell, more the damp aroma of freshly-cleaned clothes being carried from the washing machine. What there was was a shiny-bright, fully-featured facility (fresh grass in Manhattan!), a glorious panorama of the Hudson River and New Jersey's Palisades, plus a multiracial crowd buzzing the grounds in excitement over their brand new neighbor.

Raim had two performance areas going. The main stage occupied the plaza, while the dance workshops — more like loose mini-concerts in close quarters — filled the gym. The day's eight acts each comprised a different genre, while four of these came inside to accompany their respective workshops. This gave you options. You could stay inside and dance, stay outside to listen (and dance), or follow your faves inside and outside. Tough call, especially for Jose Quesada Y Los Cinco Diablos (see above) or Los Pleneros De La 21, a sensationally loose and soulful Puerto Rican "bomba" band who positively rocked their workshop, while the dancers combusted into limbo-like face-offs. Joyous!

Raim: "They were wonderful and their workshop was gorgeous."

Andy Statman was the day's highlight, though. I knew of his prowess as a bluegrass session ace, but found his sprightly klezmer romps uplifting and enlightening. In pulling tunes from throughout the Eastern European Jewish diaspora, he subtly traced the kinds of melodies that migrated to the states and took root in Tin Pan Alley. This let you hear, in effect, where pop tunesmiths like Irving Berlin came from, musically. One traditional number even reprised Berlin's coda from "Over There".

Statman's hypnotic runs on mandolin and clarinet had the crowd mesmerized for a solid hour as he transformed what I'd always heard as "screech music" into something playful, soulful, and tuneful. A Russian waltz, an Hassidic march, a Turkish rondo — Statman's trio delivered each with flair and kept the rhythmic intensity high enough to bring a number of zaftig women forward to dance with arms flying wildly. They and the whole mixed crowd all sustained applause when Statman finally signed off: "It's been a plea-zhuh."

Raim: "He was superb... He is [also] an extraordinary bluegrass mandolinist... He's a brilliant musician and you can only respect him."

**Attendance Tip**    As with any participatory dance festival, wear comfortable dancing shoes, preferably ones with smooth leather soles for slidin' and glidin', as well as a change of top for a perspiration-free ride back home. Make sure to drink plenty of liquids, which are thankfully there in abundance. Also, don't stay home if you're single — dancers are used to rotating fresh partners, especially during the instructional workshops. These are great mixers in this otherwise impersonal city.

**See Also**    Among the Queens Council on the Art's other summer concerts this year, one expanded into a mini-festival — the NEW YORK COUNTRY MUSIC FESTIVAL, which featured three local bands on one day. This modest hoe-down, co-sponsored by the New York Metropolitan Country Music Association, held the boardwalk in Far Rockaway. Their companion arts council, Flushing Council on Culture, used to produce a QUEENS JAZZ FESTIVAL in Early August boasting top acts, but has since turned its focus toward maintaining the same caliber names in a concert series format at historic Flushing Town Hall.

Finally, participatory dancers of any persuasion must, must, must investigate MIDSUMMER NIGHT SWING (Manhattan, NYC — see chapter) for a sensational approach to the format. I simply won't take "no" for an answer!

~    ~    ~

# Downtown Jazz, II

JULIUS WATKINS FRENCH HORN FESTIVAL, Manhattan, NYC
> Middle March
> Alternative Jazz
> ***Attended***

CORNER STORE SYNDICATE NEW JAZZ FESTIVAL, Manhattan, NYC
> Late April
> Alternative Jazz
> ***Attended***

SUN RA FESTIVAL, Manhattan, NYC
> Middle May to Late May
> Alternative Jazz

BROOKLYN WOODSTOCK, Brooklyn, NYC
> Early June
> Alternative and College Rock
> ***Attended***

KNITTING FACTORY'S "WHAT IS JAZZ?" FESTIVAL, Manhattan, NYC
> Middle June to Early July
> Alternative Jazz
> ***Attended***

KNITTING FACTORY AT MERKIN HALL, Manhattan, NYC
> Early October
> Alternative Jazz

"To me," remarks Michael Dorf, Founder of the Knitting Factory, about the KNITTING FACTORY'S **Festival**
"WHAT IS JAZZ?" FESTIVAL ["WHAT IS JAZZ?"]: **Review I**

- "It was always an obvious marketing or packaging concept where, in some sense, the music is no different than we would have any other time. It just happens that we call it a festival; put some great larger bills together — four acts instead of two, or five instead of one, or what have you — and then simply put out a program and call it a festival! It just seemed like a very obvious thing to do."

Well, not so obvious for most clubs, but then the Knitting Factory is not most clubs. In its own scruffy way it aspires, I imagine, to the role of the legendary Minton's uptown — where bop was born a half century before — as an incubator for jazz' next wave. Within a month of opening eight years ago (and somewhat by accident at first), it ventured to unearth the previously underground "downtown" scene. It's since given a nightly forum to what previously could only be heard surreptitiously in lofts or basements.

In the process, it's given birth to a virtual genre of its own — "knitting music" — where adventurous improvising between extremes of jazz, rock and what-have-you is "knitted" together in unfettered combinations. Sometimes the results are strident, sometimes they're sublime; usually they're stitched somewhere in-between. They're never predictable, however, and that's the root charm of the place to this day.

According to his wonderfully self-effacing account of the Knitting Factory's first five years, **Knitting Music** (Knitting Factory Works), Dorf got sucked into the music business in '85 by agreeing to manage a rock band of his hometown friends from Madison, Wisconsin, calling themselves Swamp Thing. He first undertook "a road trip to New York to make the band a success and, to be honest, to stay with my girlfriend in Queens." As you might imagine, all of Dorf's subsequent efforts at developing the band's markets involved forsaking their Madison base for points east.

Dorf moved to New York City for good in '86 and created a small record company out of his apartment for the band's paltry affairs. Forever losing what little money he had, or had borrowed from relatives, Dorf signed a few more bands and eventually self-published his booking/promotion database under the title, **A Guide to Gigging in North America** (now Writer's Digest Books). All for naught. Desperate for income, Dorf sought out a lease on a dilapidated storage space at 47 East Houston Street with plans to piece together a funky performance space/art gallery/coffeehouse. That he could roll out his futon on the floor — saving himself apartment costs elsewhere — didn't hurt either.

February, '87, debuted Dorf's low-key concept, named for the title of one of Swamp Thing's albums, *Mr. Blutstein's Knitting Factory*. The band, naturally, christened the basement space to 20 of its faithful. Yet seeking as much of the "Jack Kerouac smoky-jazz-club experience as possible," Dorf responded to an ad appearing in March's *Village Voice* promising: "Jazz band available." This notice was placed by pianist Wayne Horvitz, whom Dorf promptly booked on a $75 guarantee for Thursday nights. The first night drew just eight patrons, but Horvitz's subsequent Thursday night bookings of his fellow musician friends began filling the narrow room, to Dorf's delight.

Now Horvitz's experimental jazz cohorts might've seemed like a mismatch, but the more rock-oriented Dorf nevertheless found the music "very cool." More importantly, he could relate to their disenfranchised professional status from his own struggles with Swamp Thing. He foresaw publicity advantages from promoting a scene instead of mere individual gigs, and promptly applied his indie-rock "D. I. Y." skills to the task. Posters plastered lampposts all throughout Greenwich Village, and a loose counter-culture vibe took over inside.

The press quickly picked up on Dorf's buzz and lent the Knitting Factory a cache which continues to this day. Here's my favorite excerpt from the *New York Times*' Peter Watrous, then writing for the *Village Voice*:

- "So these three guys from Wisconsin blow into town. Nobody tells them you can't start a club in New York, or that the scene is dead, that black and white improvised music don't belong together. What do these corn-biters go and do? Start a club. Three months later they *are* the scene, with performances daily, like it's no big deal."

By June, Dorf's marketing acumen led him to book his first festival sponsored by Bigelow Tea, "TEA & COMPROVISATIONS." The lineup was representative of what had now grown to an every-night endeavor:

- Wayne Horvitz, Don Cherry, John Zorn, Zeena Parkins, Paul Hoskin, Chris Cochrane, Greg Osby, Don Byron, Charles Gayle, Yakashi Kazamaki, Ned Rothenberg, Downtown Ensemble, Tim Berne, Hank Roberts, Vincent Chauncey, J. D. Parran, Bill Horvitz, Elliot Sharp, Ushio Toraki, Charles Noyes, Kamikaze Ground Crew, David Weinstein, Anthony Coleman, Jim Pugliese, Cinni Cole, David Garland, Ikue Mori, David Shea, Kiku Wada, Kevin Norton, Jim Staley, John Zorn, Marty Erlich, Anthony Cox, Jason Hwang, Bora Bergman, Bill Frisell, Kermit Driscoll, Joe Morris, Sebastian Steinberg, Jerry Dupree.

(The large portion of Japanese artists on the five-night bill came from Zorn's performing interests and quickly pointed Dorf toward international opportunities. It's led him in time to book annual festival tours of these acts in Europe, even opening up a combined office/way station in Amsterdam to house them in their travels.)

"It's amazing," Dorf remarks:

- "If you look at [that] schedule from '87 and our schedule today, the improvisors, the people considered "the downtown scene" — John Zorn, Elliot Sharp, Fred Frith, Bill Frisell, Wayne Horvitz, whomever — those haven't changed. They're consistent. ...I've stuck with them and they've stuck with me. And of course, Wayne or Zorn has presented 15 different kinds of projects within that time. So they're all very prolific artists who have a lot of different projects, and we were just a match that worked."

As fast as all that happened, Dorf kept the pace going over the next two years with a dizzying array of activities:

- A syndicated radio show eventually underwritten by TDK Tapes, which began with a handful of stations agreeing to pay Dorf $5.00 per week to cover his tape duplicating and mailing costs;

- A record label, Knitting Factory Works, which began as an imprint of A&M Records before they were acquired by PolyGram, forcing Dorf to buy back the rights;

- Festival tours in Europe to a blizzard of press notice;

- Festival concepts stateside, seemingly on a monthly basis.

None of this frenzy seemed to make Dorf any money, but it did significantly raise his profile in a very short time, along with that of the musicians he promoted. Now finding himself an advocate for a number of intersecting scenes — ascetic composers and improvisors from "TEA & COMPROVISATIONS," the funky M-Base Collective from Brooklyn, rootsy AACM-ers from Chicago, guitar heros from Brooklyn's Black Rock Coalition, "free jazz" exemplars from the '60s, and so forth — Dorf pondered ways of mainstreaming them further into public consciousness.

In '88 he chose to piggyback the ultimate mainstream event, Manhattan's JVC JAZZ FESTIVAL (see chapter), by counter-programming 18 nights of twin bills under the heading, "KNITTING FACTORY JAZZ FESTIVAL," a precursor to "WHAT IS JAZZ?" It proved to be a critical, if not commercial, success leading Dorf to pitch JVC's George Wein to incorporate this programming the following year as "The Knitting Factory Goes Uptown." Wein agreed for '89 and '90, though the five nights of twin bills at Alice Tully Hall also followed suit critically but, alas, commercially, too. "WHAT IS JAZZ?" returned downtown to the club's humble confines for '91 where, with the exception of a fifth-year anniversary concert at Town Hall, it has prospered ever since. "WHAT IS JAZZ?" still maintains its legion of devotees among the jazz press, which will often assign writers to catch every single set over the 11-day span!

Three features distinguish the "WHAT IS JAZZ?" experience from JVC's, aside from the experimental nature and fringe status of the artists, themselves. First, "WHAT IS JAZZ?" evening bills, which have grown in '94 to as many as six sets per night, tend toward the eclectic vs. JVC's rigidly segmented double-headers. "The idea was to mix up the bills a lot, so as to mix and match different audiences every night," as Watrous quotes Dorf. "Dewey Redman, the great tenor saxophonist who played with Ornette Coleman, will share a bill with Steve Coleman, one of the young New York jazz musicians who are reinventing the language. Each has a distinct audience, but there's an overlap between the two, and hopefully each audience will find something exciting in the other."

Second, "WHAT IS JAZZ?" shows are relatively cheap — typically $10 to $12 compared to JVC's $17.50 to $40 swing — with re-entry permitted and open seating within 20 rows of the stage. Third, they run to midnight and beyond, which extends a welcome extension to adventuresome JVC patrons once their 8:00 p.m. concerts conclude. It's one of those things where Dorf's working on a shoestring works to the festival-goer's advantage.

"I had no interest to compete with JVC in a certain sense. I didn't want to take George Wein's job," cautions Dorf, but it's clear he's disappointed by Wein's artistic and financial conservatism:

- "JVC gives [Wein's] Festival Productions $700,000 for the New York City eight days... It's mind boggling. For $100,000, we could put on a festival that would be five times as big, twice as long and 100 times more enjoyable [with] as many free events if not more, and keep the ticket prices all at $10 or $12. So it drives me crazy to know how much money goes into the infrastructure of that festival and how much doesn't seem to come back. But New York could have the most amazing festival week, month, however you want to limit it, the same time as JVC if there was some other support. And part of the problem is the stranglehold that George has on it.

  "So there's a certain amount of frustration. Yes, I would love to just have daisies in my hair and [be] dancing around going, 'Well it's no problem. We'll get Bigelow Tea to give us some money.' But knowing what the [JVC] budget is, we should work together and put this thing out...

  "Going downtown to jazz clubs after [JVC concerts] is perfectly reasonable. Why not? Of course do that! It's just so obvious; it's just not encouraged. I had to do that myself when we did the 'Knitting Factory Goes Uptown' for two years with JVC. We let anyone in that night for half-price to see the show with their stubs from uptown, and it worked! People were comin' down and they liked it. So, it makes sense. It's not that difficult to do, and there's a talent pool and enough clubs to do it. And if some of those jazz clubs don't want to do it, there's enough others who would be up for booking jazz for a week if they knew there would be an audience.

  "The whole concept of making New York City the biggest jazz festival in the world to me is the most simple, obvious thing."

Again, not so obvious to most promoters, but then Dorf is not most promoters. Stay tuned.

Meanwhile Dorf pledges "WHAT IS JAZZ?" will continue to fight the good fight (indeed, he's preparing to move the Knitting Factory into bigger, more fully-featured space in TriBeCa as we talk). His advice to Knitting Factory first-timers?

- "Expect the unexpected. Don't go in thinking you're gonna' necessarily like the music. Hopefully, you will, but part of the experience of new music is to understand that this is the cutting edge of the art of music, and you're in the environment of, like, a musical laboratory watching some experimentation in various stages. Sometimes it's in that first stage when you're mixing two chemicals and you get an explosion, and sometimes you're in a stage right before you make a record would be made, and it's a discovery for cancer. So you have both extremes, and you don't have any idea of what it is.

  "You might be seeing the next Bob Dylan, or maybe you're not."

**Artist Mini-Reviws** Fair warning. The people I talk to who are often the most enthusiastic about Knitting Factory fare are musicians who can appreciate the technical proficiency and musical references underpining this experimentation. They talk glowingly in terms of "warp-speed arpeggios," "timbral jigsaws," and "heroic ostinatos," as I pulled from one review. The rest of us make do with gut reactions, but I can tell you from hitting five different Knitting Factory festivals to prepare yourself every night for at least one of Dorf's harsh, discordant "explosions" [read: bombs]. Yet there are invariably entrancing "cancer discoveries" [read: cures] any music lover would enjoy. Either way, it's all about stretching your ears.

Take the night I hit "WHAT IS JAZZ?" in '92.

Headlining was a frantic trio of <u>Peter Brotzman</u>, playing what looked like some kind of oboe, pianist <u>Marilyn Crispell</u>, and percussionist <u>Hamid Drake</u>. My notes read: "Aggro chamber jazz." Actually, I enjoyed the conga/bodhran of rastaman Drake, a picture of serenity amidst the sonic storm, whose prior work for such world-beaters as Mandingo Griot Society and Foday Musa Suso shown through with delicate, pulsing colors. This left Crispell with more of the percussionist's role, which she dove into with a molester's glee. Clad in a black Danskin, hunched over, bangs flailing, she's skittering across the lower keys like a manic crab, at one point reaching inside the baby grand to yank the strings in quick, dark succession. Crispell's bass rumblings were fine by me, even fun in spurts.

But Brotzman was another story. Looking like an avant-Hindenberg with close-cropped hair, bushy beard, and flowing moustache, his playing recalled Hitchock's birds with the film sped up — all piercing menace and fury. Eyes twitching, hands a blur, cheeks beat red, Brotzman reveled in interminable staccato screams. Toward set's end, he did play along with a softer Marrakesh-flavored modulation by imitating the effect of a snake charmer, but quickly nuked the mood with more ear-splitting arabesques. Ouch!

The program lauded Brotzman's "explosive and apocalyptic style [as] unquestionably one of the most influential...in the world today," but I couldn't ascertain any redeeming value for us unindoctrinated listeners. As the doorman confided to me when I fled, "The problem when you start out over-the-top is there's nowhere left to go."

However, the opening set of pianist/pennywhistler Steve Cohn with dual stand-up bassists, Fred Hopkins and William Parker, proved an unexpected treat, particularly the rhythm section. With one man bowing and the other plucking, the two combined for unusually dense, prickly hues. Neither one sacrificed the groove, and both were sensitive to whatever ideas the other was working out.

Cohn, thankfully humble in contrast to Brotzman's pretense, left plenty of space to savor the rhythmic flavor. His solos likewise illustrated the flow, being edgy without obnoxiousness. My notes read: "Nice, approaching tunefulness." I felt the trio would not have been out-of-place at the far reach of a Bobby McFerrin concert, and I'd look forward to hearing their next experiment.

~     ~     ~

How'd you like to exchange Houston Street grunge for the clean outdoors, but still enjoy Knitting Factory's rock fare with the same intimate, unpretentious, neighborly vibe?

**Festival Review II**

Well you're in for a hidden treat with **BROOKLYN WOODSTOCK**. The feel for this annual happening-in-miniature is of a backyard birthday party because that's precisely where it takes place and how it's adorned. You'll step off the subway right into an Ozzie-and-Harriet oasis of trimmed lawns, clipped hedges, broad porches and towering trees. You'd never know you were within city limits. The only thing missing from this image of TV suburbia is the forlorn Maytag repairman sharing a cup of coffee with busybody Mrs. Folgers.

Yet, beside the party favors and bundt cake on the shaky folding table and upon the back stairs strung with streamers there's one of the best local indie-rock lineups of the summer, playing all afternoon. Up from among the water-squirters one recent year stepped the following to take the mic: Freedy Johnston, Lenny Kaye, Babe the Blue Ox, The Aquanettas, Antietam, Carbon with Elliott Sharp, No Safety, Love Camp 7, and Kenny and The Eggplants. All for a few hundred lucky strap hangers. In fact, I'd almost thought of keeping this listing to myself if it weren't for such a sincere cause.

The organizer is Gil Schuster. The house and yard are his dad's. The decorations are his mom's. The bands are mostly his friends, including the one he plays in, Kenny and The Eggplants, and the one he co-owns the 24-track Excello Studios,with, Love Camp 7. And the cause — AmFAR and the Robert Mapplethorpe Foundation for AIDS Research — is his brother's. You see, Jonathon Schuster died of AIDS in '88, prompting Gil to organize his first **BROOKLYN WOODSTOCK** in memoriam shortly thereafter.

He explains:

- "It's a little like a New Orleans funeral. The reason why I started it and what it's trying to do is rooted in sadness, but it's also a celebration of life. Because one thing it definitely is, it's a really fun day, and a really relaxed and enjoyable day... [Although] you're there for a sad reason, everyone is having a great time.

  "As far as the bands, I guess it's a nice combination of local up-and-coming bands like Love Camp 7, the Eggplants, of course, and Life In A Blender. There's a mix of that and sort-of bigger names like Yo Lo Tengo and King Missle and Arto Lindsay and Jad Fair. The bands have been amazing, like, they've all without hesitation agreed to play. The neighbors [have been] too, obviously. My folks are unbelievable for putting up with it.

"The whole thing is dedicated to my brother's memory and the idea that we'll hopefully keep doing them until there's a cure for AIDS found. It's nice, because a lot of musicians and a lot of the bands, they're not hooked-up into, like, the fundraising scene, and they can't afford $1,000 for a dinner, like a lot of the AMFAR events. Other events are just so expensive, and it's such a different world. So it's nice just to be able to do something on a grassroots level."

Sounds like Schuster and Dorf should get together!

**See Also**   As for festivals the Knitting Factory does collaborate on, some have proven one-timers; others have perpetuated. Here's a partial update on those I've attended and/or clipped from recent newspapers:

- JULIUS WATKINS FRENCH HORN FESTIVAL, Middle March ('93 to '94). This polite one-night, four-set tribute has maintained ongoing. Lee Konitz even guested when I was there. As the *Village Voice*'s Gary Giddens joked one year, "A foxhunt begins at dawn."

- TOKYO/NEW YORK NOISE FESTIVAL, Middle March ('92, '94). Downtown Music Gallery presented one night in '92; HIPS Roads presented three nights in '94. The *Village Voice*'s Richard Gehr promised, "Loads of the finest honking, skronking, bleating, screaming and instrument mangling around." No word on whether it'll maintain ongoing.

- FESTIVAL OF RADICAL JEWISH CULTURE, Early April to Middle April ('93). Curated by John Zorn, this delightfully diverse, creative, accessible, and often humorous five-nighter — my favorite among all the Knitting Factory fests I've attended — moved in a slightly different form to CB's Gallery in '94. No word on whether it'll maintain ongoing.

- CORNER STORE SYNDICATE NEW JAZZ FESTIVAL, Late April ('90 to '94). Co-produced by Phil Haynes with the artists presented, this interesting three-nighter has maintained ongoing.

- DOWNTOWN MUSIC GALLERY'S ANNIVERSARY CELEBRATION, Middle June ('92 to '94). Dates have varied, but Kramer's Shimmy Disc record label has maintained its one-night showcase ongoing for three years. "Downtown Music Gallery really knows how to throw a party," praised the *New York Press'* J. R. Taylor. No word, however, on whether the evening, or its sponsor, will survive Kramer's current legal difficulties.

- DEWAR'S BAGPIPE FESTIVAL, Late November to Early December ('92 only). This terrific affair evolved into a five-city tour a year later. As the *New York Press'* J. R. Taylor opined, "You may have your favorite place to find guys who wear skirts and blow things, but this two-day event really isn't the joke it seems." James Doohan, "Scotty" from TV's "Star Trek," even MC'ed! Sadly, Dewars didn't maintain its sponsorship for subsequent evenings or tours.

- POST-ROCK, NEO-MOSH FESTIVAL, Early December ('93 only?). I seem to recall this six-nighter of alternative rockers occurring other years on other dates as well, but I can't find the ongoing press listings in my files.

- KLEZMER FESTIVAL, Early December to Middle December ('93 only) Seven quality nights, from roots to outer reaches. Bigger names included Andy Statman, Shirim Klezmer Orchestra, Klezmatics, and John Zorn's Massada. No word on whether it'll hopefully return.

There may be more I've missed (e.g., HAND-MADE MUSIC FESTIVAL, JOHN ZORN FESTIVAL, IMPROVISATIONS FESTIVAL, etc.), though you can also count on the Knitting Factory's multi-act, multi-night participation in all the college rock confabs (see chapter). Your best bet is to get on its mailing list. Themes, dates and lineups are subject to change wildly, but the Knitting Factory's capacity for surprise should certainly rock steady.

~     ~     ~

# Central Park's Variety Party

CENTRAL PARK SUMMERSTAGE, Manhattan, NYC
> Middle June to Early August
> Variety, General
> ***Attended***

"Where do we rank," asks Erica Ruben, the effervescent Producer of CENTRAL PARK SUMMERSTAGE ['SUMMERSTAGE]? "Right up there with the coolest of the cool," I respond, approvingly. "No way," she counters with one of her many ready laughs. "Number one?" **Introduction**

I explain that, if 'SUMMERSTAGE concerts were all bunched up into one weekend, definitely. In lieu of such scheduling density, however, I'd still have to give the nod to such other concentrated affairs as the NEW ORLEANS JAZZ AND HERITAGE FESTIVAL (see New Orleans, LA, Late April to Early May]. For now! But Ruben's programming is definitely knocking on the door of music festivals' elite and is purveying a purposeful eclecticism with a hip pop edge that nobody else can lay a hand on. It's truly the best of New York City — showcasing its real-world musical tastes to each other and the world.

It's funny, though. As I said that, I considered the consequences if 'SUMMERSTAGE did happen all at once. First, you'd probably have to move it over to the Great Lawn and prepare for the kinds of crowds that came for Paul Simon's freebie there in '91. Possibly 700,000? Or more? You'd lose 'SUMMERSTAGE's treasured vibe — relaxed, unstructured, friendly, intimate, appreciative (adjectives generally alien to New York City dwellers).

Second, you'd have less time to anticipate and savor Ruben's musical pairings; to see how her performers play off against each other; to experience how the diverse crowds interact. It would be like settling in for five lush courses at a five-star restaurant, then having it served all at once. You'd miss too much in the rush (a predicament all-too-familiar to New York City dwellers). So maybe it's just as well.

It stands to reason that Ruben came to 'SUMMERSTAGE after working as a Talent Associate for NBC's "Night Music with David Sanborne." Those who recall the show's provocative musical collaborations, or the similarly creative recorded anthologies from its Musical Producer, Hal Wilner, will recognize a close kinship with 'SUMMERSTAGE's aesthetic.

With that program's lamentable demise, Ruben found herself an unemployed free-lancer with time on her hands to habituate Central Park and dream of getting involved. "For a year or two," she says, "I used to fantasize about, 'God, it would be so cool working at 'SUMMERSTAGE!'" Ruben eventually worked up her nerve and tracked down 'SUMMERSTAGE's illusive founder, Joe Killian, for a position. She joined the small cast as Stage Manager in '90, and hired on in a succession of roles before finally ascending to lead upon Killian's departure for Radio City Music Hall in '93.

Ruben has successfully adopted Killian's noted gift for diverse community outreach, but she's also maintained the unique flavor of his artist pairings. You see, 'SUMMERSTAGE's weekend twin bills split the middle between two norms of urban outdoor music programming. Typically, you're forced to choose between:

- Concert series featuring various ethnic musics, yet generally selecting more obscure "roots" purveyors — those artists (frequently locals) who might be known within tight ethnic circles or by informed connoisseurs, but offer limited interest to mainstream listeners.

- Concert series bypassing ethnic fringes to program more popular acts — the obvious "biggies" who may guarantee mainstream draws, but offer scant challenge to sophisticated listeners.

The latter kinds serve as little more, in effect, than yet one more stop on the crowded amphitheater circuit for standard tours. Why even bother?

By contrast, here's Ruben programming philosophy that effectively splits the middle:

- "Frankly, I'm not interested in just producing who's the most popular artist. I'm interested in who's going to have a draw — of course we want people to come — but we also want to have someone whose doing something interesting with their genre, or who are the leaders. For instance, Johnny Ventura, the guy who's known as the 'Father of Merengue.' That's the kind of thing we are interested in.

  "There are a lot of different factors which I consider when I'm booking a band: will it work outside; will it be accessible; will it get people interested in that particular genre. For example, going back to Johnny Ventura, if you were to go in and not know a thing about merengue, you would be, like, 'Whoa, what is this? Who is this guy? This is great! Let me get some more. Let me go and buy the album.'

  "That's what I love, when people send me letters and say, 'I didn't have any idea who this artist was. My God, it's my new favorite artist, and I'm going to find out more about this artist and this genre.

"That's absolutely the best thing I can hear," Ruben laughs, "that aside from, 'I met my newest boyfriend at the festival.'"

Absolutely, the best thing you can hear interspersed throughout the schedule is 'SUMMERSTAGE's classy sample of alternative rock acts (10,000 Maniacs, Elvis Costello, Crash Test Dummies, They Might Be Giants, Pere Ubu, Juliana Hatfield Three, The Mekons, Yo Lo Tengo, etc.) — generally the scourge of festival programmers. Ruben books them as performers as well as in spoken word capacities. Lou Reed, Nick Cave and Patti Smith (for her first public appearance of any kind in 14 years) have joined such recent speakers as Lawrence Ferlinghetti, Joyce Carol Oates, Russell Banks, Terry McMillan, William Gibson, T. Coraghessan Boyle, Ann Beatie, William Kennedy and Ken Kesey. Folks, that's as good as such readings get — and that's just the Thursday night fare!

Ruben's centerpiece for the summer is her annual July 4th concert, easily the region's most original. This year's featured War and Wild Magnolias; last year's offered Don Byron and Black 47; the year before's had Sonic Youth and Sun Ra. "July 4th is always a fun bill," Ruben adds, "because we really try to make a statement about what is America. And whereas a lot of people just assume, 'Oh, it's July 4th. We need to have a Dixieland band,' I'm, like, 'No, we are really going to look at the real American music and all these incredible cultures that are just completely feeding American music.' So I love the July 4th bill."

The War set in particular yielded one of Ruben's musical highpoints. "It was phenomenal," she remarks. "It was one of these things where everyone had just the biggest grins on their faces.

- "I like the shows [like that] where you feel that just everyone out there is euphoric because that is such a rare vibe to get in New York City. It's like that when the real 'SUMMERSTAGE magic is working, and I hate to sound all goofy and mushy, but it's true. Unless someone comes out and experiences it, there is nothing I can say. Everyone around them is feeling great, and it's a great show, and everyone is being great and respectful and peaceful and friendly to each other; being just like normal people and not being horrible New Yorkers and stuff. It reminds you that you can still have that small-town feeling in such a large, impersonal city.

  "And what I love is just creating the feeling of, 'Oh yeah, come over and hang out with us for a while.' I like that."

For its many devotees, 'SUMMERSTAGE weekend afternoons are simply a given. You're there! It's always free and unencumbered, letting you feel like you're stumbling upon something wonderful and scooping the rest of Manhattan in the act.

Rumsey Playfield sits atop a modest dirt nob, fenced-in and shaded by towering sycamores. There are rows of benches fronting the stage and shaded bleachers rimming the rear, but for a hot act the crowd clusters and dances with little regard for holding their places. You can attend without strategy — another rarity in Manhattan.

Although I've caught many memorable sets here over the years (The Neville Brothers and Poi Dog Pondering, Lucinda Williams, Toots and The Maytals, Joe Louis Walker and Walter "Wolfman" Washington), I told Ruben beforehand I anticipated one '94 twin bill in particular: Junior Brown opening for Morphine.

"I'm so glad to hear it," Ruben exclaims:

- "Because some people on my staff don't like that bill, and I love it. It was my idea [laughs]. They're like, 'We don't get this!' I'm like, 'Trust me. When it gets up there and when you realize that I'm playing all this great Sun Records stuff, all this old rock-and-roll from Memphis, you are going to hear about the roots of rock-and-roll.'

"It's why I wanted to have Junior Brown and Morphine. I really think the alternative rock crowd that's going to come out and see Morphine is really, really going to love Junior Brown. When they hear how honky-tonk it is, I mean, they are going to love that sound. I wanted that audience to hear Junior, because it's so quirky and so alternative."

<u>Junior Brown</u>. The diminutive Brown was clad in gray slacks, white shirt, a moss-green sports coat and impossibly upswept straw cowboy hat, looking for all the world like a Texas golf announcer, or a '50s-era used car huckster. His trio looked equally unlikely — a middle-aged, cleaned-and-pressed family band straight off the Pat Robertson hour. Yet, they went about their business with calm precision, serving up Brown to a fault.

The easy-going Brown proved a revelation. I considered him better than a triple threat. He's written some terrific C&W songs, parched by his trademark dry humor, but brimming with personality, empathy and imagery (e.g., "You're Wanted By The Police And My Wife Thinks You're Dead"). He's also got a great voice, a resonant baritone even more expressive than fellow Texan and former bandmate, Asleep At The Wheel's Ray Benson. Brown's certainly renown for his unbelievable Danny Gatton-caliber fingering on his "guit-steel" — an instrument of his own design perched on a metal pole in which an electric guitar features a second neck designed to be played as a lap steel (not that he even needs it).

But the thing that really impressed me was how Brown was one from the old school — a rodehouse-trained entertainer bound to grab the audience by the lapels until they hollered "Uncle!" If it took interspersing stratospheric flights of "Secret Agent Man" or "Wipe Out" to get the initially-indifferent crowd whooping, well, that's just what he was gonna' do! Brown's whole set was wonderfully varied, paced and practiced, communicating perfectly on every level. He left me a cheering convert, as he did with most everyone else.

<u>Morphine</u>. I liked Morphine, as I liked their prior incarnation as a spare, urbane blues quartet, Treat Her Right. This time around, they'd shedded one member, replacing lead and rhythm guitars with a baritone sax. This left them a harder, deeper, more textural groove, something like Link Ray-goes-alternative with some beat-style rappings tossed in.

While there where some nice similarities with Brown, namely, droll lyrics and a stripped-down roots sensibility, Morphine fell a bit short in the entertainment department. Specifically (like with most rock music these days), it was all about sound and attitude and too little about variety and communication. Too much otherwise solid writing was lost in the too similar musical mix. Needless to say, the band members also lacked the kind of virtuoso focus Brown's slippery picking delivered. I liked Morphine, as I said, but I felt ol' Junior kicked their butts without breaking a sweat.

**See Also**  How's this for a music weekend available most anytime throughout June or July! Start off early Friday evening at Lincoln Center's MIDSUMMER NIGHT SWING (see chapter) before hitting Manhattan's club cornucopia. Carry on Saturday afternoon at 'SUMMERSTAGE; then truck on over to the CELEBRATE BROOKLYN PERFORMING ARTS FESTIVAL (see chapter) preceding a second night of club hopping. Finally, redeem your indulgences Sunday morning at one of a number of gospel brunches around town before hitting 'SUMMERSTAGE once more. And that's what's available without even considering any of the other area festivals described within these pages!

~     ~     ~

*Junior Brown, Central Park Summerstage.*

# Outreach
# at CENTRAL PARK SUMMERSTAGE:
# A Conversation With Erica Ruben.

*Erica Ruben, Producer of* CENTRAL PARK SUMMERSTAGE *['SUMMERSTAGE], is one of the few people I've met in the music industry whose field research is as frenetically paced as mine. During her "off-season" (which runs every month 'SUMMERSTAGE is not in production), she's hitting clubs throughout New York City to the tune of one to three acts per night. Every night! Mind you, this is in addition to fielding calls from a legion of booking agents and record labels, screening tapes, scouring the trades, haunting the record stores, and soliciting tips from her international network of friends and contacts — plus her heavy administrative duties of publicity, politics and fund raising.*

*Ruben's my soulmate in overload.*

*It all pays off come summertime. Her selections strike a unique balance between roots authenticity, popular appeal, and New York City cool — acclaimed by local and national critics, alike. More importantly, they draw a wide range of New Yorkers to Central Park, including diverse ethnic constituencies from the outer boroughs to a place they'd likely rarely come. Nor do Ruben's outreach efforts stop with the printed lineup or newspaper listing; she's just as likely to return to "beat the bushes," making sure these communities know who's playing for them and when. It all adds up to the "gorgeous mosaic" of former Mayor David Dinkins, while sacrificing nothing to quality, edge, or turn-out.*

*Here are a few examples of how the cheery Ruben does what she does so well. (Aspiring promoters, as well as interested music fans, take note.)*

- "There are two people whom I've hired and one is [Managing Director] Bill Bragin, who used to work at Festival Productions, and another guy, [Assistant Director] Jeffrey Gaskill, who had his own concert promotion company up in the Northeast. They both come to me their own histories and their own aesthetics.

    "Basically, the way we choose bands is a variety of ways. We get a lot of tapes, but just like any other A&R person will tell you, it's who gives you the tips about what bands. So we do the usual things. We go and see a lot of shows during the winter time. I'll see between one and three shows every single night...

    "I started establishing contacts in a number of different kinds of communities. For example, I started to really get to know people in the whole Caribbean community and go out to Queens to different calypso shows. Definitely the Latin community [also]; I go to a number of Latin clubs out in Brooklyn, Queens and Harlem. We do go out to the communities to really see what is going on out there, to see the clubs and who's performing, and stuff like that. Somehow it comes together, especially with the Indian pop show.

    "Just to give you an example of how I came across this entire genre, I went to the CALYPSO AWARDS (see **New York City Festival Listings**) and they had a thing called the 'chutney soca.' And I was, 'What is this thing?'; I'd never heard of this genre before. I just started doing more research and the next thing I knew I was learning all about 'bhangra.' We just started asking around and this whole world of Indian pop music opened up in front of us! And I was, like, 'Whoa, now that's one community we had not served, or really presented.'

    "So we put together this show where it's not just straightforward Indian classical music, but something I think our audience (who're definitely pretty open-minded music fans), and people who are just coming to the park, might want to hear. It's got a really fun sensibility to it, which is O. K. With bhangra music, it's combining traditional 'Punjabi' sounds with club sounds from the U. K. With chutney soca, it's combining traditional Indian music from the same region, which is northern India, with the sounds of Trinidad and soca. Then we've got Nadja, who's performing 'ghazals,' which are basically another form of traditional Indian music, but mixed with some jazz reflections in the music.

"It's a way of introducing audiences to this whole world of Indian pop. Certainly, once we can see how well it goes, and [whether] our audience is conditioned, then maybe next year we'll just do a chutney soca show; maybe we'll just do a bhangra show. Right now we just want to see how it all works. There is enough of a connection that they're all drawing upon traditional Indian sounds, but they are taking the music of whatever culture that they are currently living in. It's all music of the Indian diaspora, really, and that's the theme of this concert. We are going to be presenting these bands who are at the points of departure.

"It was a lot of fun to discover this. I had to have a friend of mine from Birmingham, England, send me lots of bhangra CDs because it's not readily available over here. But since then we've gotten in touch with this major bhangra DJ in the country, and he's been taking us to parties that he mixes at and different private functions for the Indian and Pakistanian community. And we are saying, 'O. K., these people are way in-the-know about bhangra, but that the rest of us don't have access to that kind of music.'

"What I'm trying to do is just open up the doors."

- [Citing a 1994 twin bill featuring Okinawan folk hero, Shoukichi Kina, joined by guitarist Ry Cooder, with ska-rockers, The Toasters] "It was a real gamble because it was our first major Asian pop concert, and we really worked hard. We did a lot of bilingual stuff and working with the Japanese communities because we wanted them to be there as much as everybody else. It was a community that we really haven't touched into, so we did a lot of work to make sure they knew about this event. We went out to the shopping mall in New Jersey where all the Japanese shop. We contacted Japanese papers, the embassy and the whole thing and let them know to spread the word.

"And it worked because we definitely had a nice percentage of Okinawans and Japanese out for the day. That audience definitely added to the true character of the show. It was great.

"We try to create double bills [for] juxtapositions of artists so that they do play to each other but also to mix-and-match audiences. That is very, very much a key component of our mission. I've stretched it a lot further this year than previous seasons, especially with something like a Morphine and Junior Brown, or a Toasters and Shoukichi Kina. But I think it's not just a haphazard kind of thing. There really is a reason that we put certain artists together, be it a theme, or trying to draw a comparison between certain genres.

"If you saw The Toasters and Shoukichi Kina, there were a lot of parallels between the bands in terms of their presentations. The other thing is Shoukichi Kina's mentor is Bob Marley. Plus the way both of those bands interact with the audience — they wanted dancing, and they both jumped out into the moshing pit, and they were both trying to get the audience into their music. There really was a parallel between the energy levels as well. Also that they both draw upon reggae traditions, but that was extremely subtle, of course. One could barely detect that, but we were able to see that, and it worked very nicely.

"I think The Toasters crowd really dug Shoukichi Kina, and the other way around. I think it worked."

- "We try to keep things real laid-back — as laid-back as we possibly can — so people feel that they can just mingle, and see each other, and see the other groups that are there. They get a chance to witness some of the other cultures. You come on Sunday, you are going to see 10 or 15 or 20,000 Africans, and you are going to see a side of New York that maybe you won't really see. Or maybe for Johnny Ventura, 10,000 Dominicans; or [for Jorge Ben], 8,000 Brazilians. And it's a great chance to see each of these cultures really at their best, because they're all having a good time.

"So that's important for us. We journey, and we talk to people in these different communities.

"Basically, the communities are served, and it also reflects the city. We have really built this up to be the festival that is really the true New York festival, the one that really speaks to the real New Yorkers — native New Yorkers and immigrants and tourists. All those people are being served through our festival; through avant-garde to conservatives; through folk to alternative rock; through Japanese party music to gay literature. Whatever it is, it's serving communities.

"And it's not just lip service to these communities. I mean, these are the best artists from the different communities. One of our basic philosophies is that we are trying to take the best of each community and present them. And even though the Indian community may not know who Junior Brown is, definitely the alternative country crowd does. Johnny Ventura maybe isn't known by the country people, but he's still the father of merengue.

"That's why it really is a New York festival, and we are not just trying to be quirky for quirky's sake. We're really looking at: who are we trying to reach, who to speak to, and what are we trying to tell New Yorkers about other New Yorkers?"

~ ~ ~

# Bronx's Irish Traditions

IRISH TRADITIONAL DANCE FESTIVAL, Mineola, NY
Middle May
Irish

**IRISH TRADITIONAL MUSIC AND DANCE FESTIVAL**, Bronx, NYC
Middle June
Irish
***Attended***

**Introduction**  "Cherish the Ladies," all right, making sure to hold Joannie Madden among the dear. This flautist for the above-named Irish traditional music ensemble, leader of her own trio to boot, daughter of noted accordionist Joe Madden, woman about town and all-around "good guy" in the genre got tagged as Artistic Director for the Irish Art Center's [IAC] 13th annual IRISH TRADITIONAL MUSIC AND DANCE FESTIVAL [IRISH FESTIVAL'], and helped breathe new life into an event I felt had begun to run out of gas.

The IAC had conducted their yearly affair until '92 at the Snug Harbor Cultural Center on Staten Island, a marvelous grounds formerly housing an old retirement home for soldiers and sailors. It boasts expansive lawns, tall trees, an impressive collection of 19th-century institutional architecture, northerly views of New York City harbor — everything but a musical celebration with a discernable pulse.

Apparently, in the pre-Reagan glory days of arts funding, the IAC spent big bucks to fly in all kinds of leading musical lights from Ireland. By the time I drove a pair of folk dance fanatics to the '91 version, however, this stream had slowed to a trickle. My friends looked around and said, "Where's the dancing?" I looked around and said, 'Where's the music, the audience, the workshops, the food, the vendors?" My mind is fuzzy on the particulars, but I don't remember any special presentation of the acts on either of two stages, nor that anybody in the "audience" was around to pay attention. Most of the patrons were elsewhere — casually strolling the grounds and perusing the sparse crafts and food tables. (I realize that Irish cuisine doesn't necessarily rank among the world's greatest, but only hamburgers, hotdogs, scones and jam? C'mon!)

I asked around about why this festival was so, so, so laid back. One of the few partaking in the music replied to the effect of, "Well, this is how it is over in Ireland." "Yeah, but this is the U. S. of A.," I thought to myself, "and we're used to some show biz here," especially knowing of so many other superb festivals going on simultaneously throughout the region. We three split the site without even waiting for the evening concert wrap-up, all the while kicking ourselves for not hitting CLEARWATER'S GREAT HUDSON RIVER REVIVAL (Valhalla, NY — see chapter) instead.

Fast-forward three years. By now, I'd begun to make it around to all the other happenings of that same weekend. Since my field research had taken a year longer than I'd planned, this excess time afforded me the luxury of tying up loose ends, including my first CLEARWATER' on Saturday and the QUEENS FESTIVAL (New York, NY — see chapter) on Sunday. Unfortunately, it was one of those 90 degrees/90-percent humidity summer swelters in New York City where even your bare skin feels like a wool suit with the collar turned up. Midway through the QUEENS FESTIVAL, I turned to my gasping wife and said, "Let's drag ourselves over to the IRISH FESTIVAL'. It's up in Riverdale this year so at least there'll be some trees and a breeze."

Around 5:00 p.m., we passed through the gates of bucolic College of Mount Saint Vincent on this residential northwestern tip of the Bronx (where one of my great aunts had taught mathematics her whole life), parked the car, strolled down the shaded walkway, poised at the rope serving as a festival gate, and beheld another world!

Number one: the site possessed everything Staten Island did, aesthetically, times ten! When you got to the main stage area, you could gaze from one end to the other and not know you were in a city at all, much less in New York City (the ultimate compliment, I might add). Before us were only stately evergreens and weeping willows, clipped hedges, manicured lawns, sun-sparkled ripples from off the Hudson River, and the treed heights of The Palisades beyond. Peace and tranquility personified.

Number two: there was actually a festival going on this time!

To the shaded right of a delightful castle-in-miniature, which serves as the college's library, there was a Gazebo Stage where intimate workshops and mini-concerts took place all day long. Now, we're not talkin' just any old workshops, but rather top-flight practitioners holding forth in unrivaled intimacy; folks like Pat Kilbride, John Whelan, Rev. Charlie Coen and Mick Maloney. To the castle's left was a pastoral glen called the Meadow Stage, replete with more musical workshops and dance instruction besides. We happened upon Joan McNiff Cass' ceili dancing class, complete with a trio of musicians proffering live accompaniment.

Finally, down by the water at the end of a rectangular field stood the main stage. Three improvements immediately caught my eye. First, there was only one stage this time backing a dance floor big enough to hold 40 sets (260 people), which greatly stimulated visual focus. Second, there was nearly continuous music from noon 'till nine, separated only by 10-minute set changes. Third, there was Madden as the day's M. C., serving up the handsome, all-ages lineup with self-deprecating humor and irresistible enthusiasm. The net result was the assembly of Irish-American families (still laid back, mind you) actually gathered around and paying attention!

My wife and I plopped down and absolutely mellowed to a sunset-drenched musical feast: "Sligo Fiddling" with Andy McGann, Brian Conway, Pat Keogh, Tony DeMarco and Felix Dolan; Cherish the Ladies running through a half-hour set; and all the musicians up for an enormous spirited jam supporting a huge ceili with dozens of gracefully swirling teams. We carried our smiles with us the whole drive back to our steamy East Village apartment.

I caught up with Madden just as she was preparing to take Cherish' over to the L'AURIEL CELTIC FESTIVAL in Brittany, France (according to Madden the largest Celtic event in the world, drawing over 11 million people in nine days). She described the IRISH FESTIVAL' as her first attempt at directing, but how, despite time demands from the band's active tour schedule and such, "I think it turned out to be a very nice day."

Funding was still tight for '94's festival. Rather than blowing the budget on importing select talent from abroad, however, Madden used her contacts to round up a larger contingent of the finest local players. "Everybody kinda' gave a little bit of themselves, too, to do this," she said.

Madden observes of this ready performing pool:

• "The one thing about New York, I think more so than any other state in the country, is that we have an unbelievable wealth of talent — old and new. Some of the greatest people that ever played [Irish] music live right here in the Tri-State area. It's unbelievable the talent that's here. No other state can put on a festival with just local talent, but we could and still be hearing living legends and some of the best groups that play music that's going. I try to get some more of them out of the closet, the older ones that don't go out too often, that are just as good as anyone, if not better."

Madden, herself, grew up in the Woodlawn section of the Bronx, absorbing Irish music from her father and his playing partner, flautist Jack Coen, a recent National Heritage Fellow recipient. "I guess I've been listening to it all my life," she recalls, "so the tunes came very easy to me. It was kind of like speaking your language. You have it back there in the back of your head and, finally, you're looking for a way to get it out of you." Madden began on violin, then piano, then tin whistle, before graduating to a flute when she had enough hot air to fill it, she laughs.

As Madden blossomed into an accomplished performer, another mentor, Mick Maloney, solicited grants in '83 to present a series of concerts featuring women artists. "Mick called me up and asked me to come and M. C. the concerts and help him organize it," she remembers. "And he said that we need a name. I just kinda' said, 'Well what are you going to call it, Cherish the Ladies, or something,' as a joke. Cherish the Ladies is an old, old jig and I just said that as a joke. He said,

'That's great, that's great; we'll call it that." The concert series sold out, the group of women artists coalesced into a working band, and their resulting recording was inducted into the Library of Congress as one of the outstanding folk albums of '85.

Nearly a decade later, and with a few personnel changes, Cherish' has grown to one of the most ubiquitous presences on the Irish festival scene. Booked by Columbia Artists Management, they're actually one of the few traditionally based bands who've successfully crossed over to the "commercial" circuit. Madden credits their universal appeal from being strongly audience-driven:

- "We based our music around arrangements, not just sitting around [playing] slow. We change tempos to keep peoples' interest. We change from, maybe, a jig to a reel where you wouldn't do that, really, when you're sitting around in a session. We've changed paces and we added the excitement of four step dancers, which people love, because it's the visual aspect, as well. Plus we have a fine singer with Cathie Ryan, a songwriter doing original stuff and writing her own music coming from an Irish-American influence of different kinds of music that we grew up with. We come from all different backgrounds so we have all different feels of where the music should sound when we play."

Madden is excited about the crossover potential for traditional Irish music, given its complexity and variety to the ear (key changes and such), the conviviality of its ensemble nature, and the booming interest, here and abroad, in ceili and set-dancing. She welcomes the uninitiated to join in. "Who would've heard of Cajun [music] 20 years ago, or 10 years ago even," Madden suggests in comparison, "and I think we're going to be the next find."

**Attendance Tip** The only rub in the ointment is the food at the IRISH FESTIVAL' still hasn't improved much (I think the selection of beers outnumbered the selection of entrees). I'd advise packing your own hamper or dining at any of the nearby eateries advertised in the program booklet .

**See Also** "I've run a set-dancing night now for the last three years at Flannery's on 14th Street and 7th Avenue," Madden offers. "I have 100 people there a week, dancing. It's on every Wednesday night. It gets a bit quiet in the summer, but come September it's [hopping]. People are very open and friendly, and they're willing to teach anybody and willing to get everybody and anybody into it." You might look for Madden's recent solo release, *A Whistle In The Wind* (Green Linnett), to help put you in the mood.

It's also worth mentioning that the IAC, located at 553 West 51 Street in Manhattan, maintains a year-round program. (The IRISH TRADITIONAL DANCE FESTIVAL in Long Island's Nassau County, functions as an annual benefit for the cause.) Their recent newsletter lists a one-man show starring MTV's Colin Quinn, entitled, "Sanctifying Grace," along with other events plus classes in Irish music, dance, language and history.

~     ~     ~

# Brooklyn's Variety Party

WELCOME BACK TO BROOKLYN, Brooklyn, NYC
    Middle June
    Variety, General

NEW YORK CITY'S GOSPEL FESTIVAL, Brooklyn, NYC
    Middle June
    Black Gospel

CELEBRATE BROOKLYN PERFORMING ARTS FESTIVAL, Brooklyn, NYC
    Late June to Middle August
    Variety, General
    ***Attended***

MIDWOOD CONCERTS AT SEASIDE, Brooklyn, NYC
    Middle July to Late August
    Variety, General
    ***Attended***

MARTIN LUTHER KING JR. CONCERT SERIES, Brooklyn, NYC
    Middle July to Late August
    African American
    ***Attended***

AFRICA MONDO FESTIVAL, Brooklyn, NYC
    Middle July
    African

BROOKLYN'S SUMMER GOSPELFEST!, Brooklyn, NYC
    Early September
    Black Gospel

NEW YORK BEER FEST, Brooklyn, NYC
    Middle September
    Variety, General

**Introduction**

For most metro markets in America, the "melting pot" is a misnomer. Perhaps a more accurate cooking metaphor might be the "fry grill." You take a few major ethnic groups — the equivalent of the burger, the cheese, the bacon and the onions — and you cook 'em and stack 'em on the same bun. Some melt in, some don't, but it's a pretty plain meal on the plate.

Brooklyn, though, is the real deal — an enormous cauldron of four million souls and seemingly as many ethnic groups. Yes, there are huge individual constituencies, such as the estimated 500,000 Caribbeans who live within a mile of Eastern Parkway, the route for Labor Day's WEST INDIAN-AMERICAN DAY CARNIVAL AND PARADE (see chapter). There are also neighborhoods which retain their near-segregated flavor, such as the Lubbavitcher enclave of Crown Heights. But, for the most part, the borough's many, many ethnic communities combine for a uniquely piquant stew where you can pick out individual spices, or savor the blend as well.

This intermingling plays out in public all summer long, thanks to terrific music programming from the borough's top three concert series:

- The CELEBRATE BROOKLYN PERFORMING ARTS FESTIVAL [CELEBRATE BROOKLYN'], produced by the Fund for the Borough of Brooklyn (which also does the four-stage extravaganza, WELCOME BACK TO BROOKLYN, as well as the one-day NEW YORK BEER FEST under the Brooklyn Bridge);

- The two presented by State Senator Marty Markowitz — MARTIN LUTHER KING JR. CONCERT SERIES [MLK'] and MIDWOOD CONCERTS AT SEASIDE [SEASIDE'] .

For the outsider like myself, it's an unequaled musical/cultural education. You learn to find the folds in blanket "Latin" programming, for example: Puerto Rican, Cuban, Dominican, Venezuelan, Columbian, Mexican or something else — each country with its own stars and hits (local as well as international), its own musical styles, and its own dances. What's more, you get to see each particular audience turn out in the flesh, and how they interact with the music and each other.

I'll never forget taking in the annual "Latino Night" (mostly Puerto Rican this time) at SEASIDE', for instance. Even though the music ranged from salsa (Tito Nieves) to jazz (Tito Puente and His Orchestra) with a stop in between (Eddie Palmieri and His Orchestra), the crowd reaction was uniquely and uniformly the same: clapping 1—3,4—6,7; 1—3,4—6,7! Impatient for the first act to commence? 1—3,4—6,7; 1—3,4—6,7! Booing the opening comic, George Lopez, off the stage? 1—3,4—6,7; 1—3,4—6,7! Cheering the burly pop troubadour, Nieves, as he ignored security's objections and carried his big crooning self off the stage, onto the grounds, and up the center aisle? 1—3,4—6,7; 1—3,4—6,7. Accompanying the many expert salsa dancers rimming the crowd? 1—3,4—6,7; 1—3,4—6,7!

It proved to me I better get with the program and learn that clave beat!

And the same goes for other genres, which run the gamut from African to zydeco, from bossa nova to boogie-woogie. (There's even a healthy contingent of alternative C&W acts along the lines of Tom Russell, Greg Trooper, 5 Chinese Brothers, The Health and Happiness Show, and all the "rig-rockers" of Diesel Only Records.) Where else could you witness someone who would otherwise be categorized as all-purpose world beat, Senegal's Youssou N'Dour, and have a community of approximately 7,000 Senegalese to draw from and cheer him on as it's supposed to be done abroad?

All three concert series feature national headliners nightly, though CELEBRATE BROOKLYN' leans toward Brooklyn-based musicians, especially with its openers. MLK'/SEASIDE' tend to program greater quantity in their evening bills. But CELEBRATE BROOKLYN' gets more press, since it books more evenings and enjoys a location closer to Manhattan-based newspapers.

However you stir the pot, Brooklyn's got a hearty simmering of music, audiences and settings at the perfect price — free! "Yo," as they'd say to welcome out-of-towners back, "you can't beat it with a stick!"

**Festival Review I**

Man, I've so many stories to tell about CELEBRATE BROOKLYN':

- There's the night I finally converted all my "N' Yawker" friends to zydeco with a double bill of a klezmer band — attended by half an auditorium of elderly Jewish couples — combined with Terrence Simien and The Mallet Playboys. Simien's red-hot set got truncated by a sudden storm (the same one, I recall, that blew a stack of lights onto Curtis Mayfield at MLK', sadly paralyzing him for life), but not before I'd confirmed about a dozen "JAZZFEST" bookings on the spot.

- Then, when introducing my wife and her friends to Bela Fleck and The Flecktones on one of this band's earliest local gigs, I spied the last of my business school professors I ever expected to see at a concert — an elderly gent with hearing aids in both ears. "What brought you here tonight," I asked? "Oh," he casually replied, tuning one hearing aid to my query, "[Flecktones harmonica wizard] Howard

Levy is my son."

The first anecdote demonstrates that you're gonna' catch some imaginative programming that may not make sense, sometimes, until you arrive and experience it directly. The second one hints at the wealth of musical connections with Brooklyn, through which an estimated one out of every four U. S. residents can trace their lineage.

But the best anecdote I've got illustrates the wealth of musical talent here, and how today's opener on CELEBRATE BROOKLYN' bills can often be tomorrow's headliner.

One of CELEBRATE BROOKLYN's unique features prior to the sponsor's withdrawal in '94 was its Brooklyn Lager Bandsearch, in which local acts from three categories — roots-rock, jazz-blues and world-beat — competed in run-offs at Manhattan clubs for opening slots on a CELEBRATE BROOKLYN' night. (Opening acts remain a strength here, though now they're not so formally organized.)

Back in 1990, my friend, Brian, an independent producer/engineer, teamed up with Felix Hernandez (Producer of N. P. R. syndications, "Blues Stage" and "Rythm Revue") and Quad Studios to produce a "Blues Stage" segment which would feature the winner in the Bandsearch jazz-blues category. As part of the Grand Prize, the winning band would receive several hours of free studio time for their own use, and would be recorded before a live audience in the studio for later broadcast on "Blues Stage."

This year the victors were Michael Hill's Blues Mob. Young was so impressed with what he heard that he approached Hill about producing a demo, which eventually led to contract with the nation's leading blues label, Alligator Records. Hill's debut disc finally came out in 1994 to critical raves, and is giving the blues genre a multicultural spin, Brooklyn-style!

So you see? And I could've just as easily talked about Greg Trooper, who's since been signed by the management of Lyle Lovett and Roseanne Cash, who's co-written with Don Henry and Steve Earle, and who's had songs covered by Vince Gill and Maura O'Connell.

Rachel Chanoff began as CELEBRATE BROOKLYN's Co-Producer this year, after a stint programming the performing arts center at SUNY/Purchase and as the Sundance Film Festival's New York City representative. Her local talent highlight involves booking dance-hall reggae trio, Worl-A-Girl, to precede Judy Mowatt, then seeing the three women catch fire in the press, including a profile in *Rolling Stone*.

"It's true," Chanoff adds, "and when we booked them it was way before their album came out. We didn't realize that they were going to be such a 'breaking band,' as they say. Right now, they're getting a tremendous amount of press. They were truly wonderful. It works out great when the opener is so hot, because it just pumps up the headliner."

Her Co-Producer, Jack Walsh, has been with CELEBRATE BROOKLYN' since its inception 12 years ago. In his spare time he leads a band, Memphis Train and The Box Car Horns, which helps explain the connection with Brooklyn's musical pipeline. Walsh's local talent highlight?

- "I remember one show in '83 where we had booked a whole batch of Caribbean singers and had one local band, the Caribbean Express, as the backup. This one performer, in the period between when we booked him in April and when we did the show in August, had a huge hit on Jamaican radio. The guy was about 16. His name was Tristan Palmer, I think. The turn-out for the show was just incredibly huge. I remember it being the kind of thing where the young Caribbean girls who turned out for the show were, really, like it was Michael Jackson on the stage. There was screaming, fainting and, you know."

To gain these kinds of reactions, Walsh credits strong production values ("that you would expect to pay $25 for"), the Bandshell's inviting park setting under the stars, and a "very hip, diversified, funky audience" that's open to supporting its own — something rare among New York City's self-consciously rootless cosmopolitanism.

It all comes together, Walsh feels, whenever he programs his headliners with the Brooklyn Philharmonic Orchestra conducted by David Amram. Typically, Walsh commissions several of the headliner's works to be scored for the 40-piece orchestra. "I would actually like to develop that idea into a situation where we digitally record the performance and do some releases," Walsh mentions.

Latin percussionist Ray Baretto and jazz vocalist Betty Carter stand out recently among BPO collaborators, but Walsh reserves special mention for this year's guest star, Brazilian vocalist, Leny Andrade:

- "She came off the stage and finished her encore with thanking the audience [and] the entire tech crew by name. She thought this was the greatest. She just moved to New York from Rio and wasn't sure how well she would be received in this kind of setting, a free concert in the park, and how many people knew about her music. And she was thrilled about the turnout. The audience actually loved her. She said she looked up at the stars and the moon and down at the audience, and the feeling was like nothing that she had ever experienced.

"To me, that is really the best kind of compliment we could have," Walsh concludes. "It typifies what is great about the festival."

~     ~     ~

**Festival Review II**  Half the fun of **MLK'**/Seaside' is the frantic antics of its producer and M. C., State Senator Marty Markowitz. He's pictured in the brochure wearing a white dinner jacket and matching bowtie (which is often how he appears onstage), and he keeps the pace briskly moving along with a stage patter combining Yiddishisms, local references galore, exhortations to applaud, an occasional scolding, Borscht Belt jokes, and an endless stream of thanks to his sponsors. There are actually a few evenings where Markowitz's shtick fits in perfectly, such as Seaside's annual Russian and Jewish Music Fest for Brighton Beach's numerous emigres, or the many other nostalgia evenings he programs there.

Yet, even among **MLK's** dominant African-American audiences, nobody complains because Markowitz delivers. For 11 years he's been bringing them the best packaged tours from the circuit of inner-city venues that includes New York City's Apollo Theater, Washington's Carter Barron Amphitheater, and Detroit's Chene Park. It might be **MLK's** "The Main Event" starring The O'Jays and The Whispers. It might be **MLK's** annual Gospel Night with Al Green and The Winans. It might be **MLK's** annual Caribbean Music Carnival, featuring local hero, The Mighty Sparrow, plus a zillion other acts.

**Artist Mini-Reviews**  I caught **MLK's** annual Ladies of the Blues, <u>Ruth Brown</u>, <u>Koko Taylor</u> and <u>Denise LaSalle</u>, which brings us to the other half of the fun — catching African-American musicians playing to their "own." For outsider like me, there are often surprises! Take this night. I would've assumed the deep growlings, churning beats and gutsy roots of Taylor's band would've carried the crowd.

Wrong. Although Taylor sang her heart out, she didn't gain nearly the reaction of the other two women. It seems the audience preferred LaSalle's stylish R&B uptempos, breezy rapport and flat-out bawdiness before, during, and after each song. They howled with delight at each bit of risque, beginning with one racy monologue on "Freak In The Bedroom," where LaSalle complained loudly about her man's size, staying power, and cheatin' ways. Look out!

LaSalle kept the momentum up with a virtual anthology of sexy cheatin' songs: "You've Been Steppin' Out," "Hey Lady, Your Husband Is Cheatin' On Us," "Don't Jump On My Pony If You Can't Ride," "Drop That Zero, Get Yourself A Hero," and the sauciest, "Don't Mess With My Toot-Toot," where she left absolutely no doubt as to what a "toot-toot" is!

Although I couldn't stay for headliner Ruth, I'm sure she was watching off-stage and kept right up where LaSalle left off. Both got invited back for next year's blues feast.

**Attendance Tip**  Subway or car are the transportation methods of choice for Celebrate Brooklyn' and Seaside', though you're best advised to travel with friends rather than alone. I'd also recommend doing your area strolls by daylight. After dark, stick to the northwest side of Celebrate Brooklyn's Prospect Park, and within Seaside's Asser Levy Park in Brighton Beach, avoiding Coney Island to the west, except to catch the subway.

While those two proximities are quite scenic and fairly mild, **MLK's** Wingate Field is located in a marginal area within East Flatbush. I'd only drive, taking care to park within one block of the site. Once you're through the chain-linked fence and onto the rubbled field, however, there's no problem. As you can imagine, for multiple national acts hosted by a State Senator, police are omnipresent. During festival hours, it's probably the safest place to be in all New York City.

"WELCOME BACK TO BROOKLYN may be eight or nine years old," Walsh believes: **See Also**

- "It's a homecoming festival — that's the key word. They have a homecoming king or queen. Generally, it's a celebrity with roots in Brooklyn. This past year we did Neil Sedaka; in the past we've had Connie Stevens. It's a nostalgia kind of thing. There's a lot of doo-wop music and Dodger Hall of Famers, and things like that. I think they get 250,000 people."

Three other stages with more contemporary expressions of Brooklyn's multicultural scene also grace the day.

Though there are seemingly innumerable festivals which also occupy Prospect Park, three of the more durable, and musically exciting, have been the AFRICA MONDO FESTIVAL, and two companion gospel festivals: NEW YORK CITY'S GOSPEL FESTIVAL and BROOKLYN'S SUMMER GOSPELFEST! All three are produced by outsiders, but you can confirm their dates merely by checking the CELEBRATE BROOKLYN' calendar. Convenient, huh?

~     ~     ~

# Uptown Jazz

**JVC Jazz Festival/Bryant Park Jazz Festival**, Manhattan, NYC
Late June to Early July
Modern Jazz
***Attended***

**JVC Jazz Festival/Newport**, Newport, RI
Middle August
Modern Jazz
***Attended***

**QE2: Newport Jazz Festival at Sea**, Manhattan, NYC to Nova Scotia
Middle September to Late September
Modern Jazz

**Introduction**  My aesthetics teacher used to claim that while some jokes were merely funny, a few were profound, funny or not. I can think of one from my youth, a *Mad Magazine* comic with two contrasting panels. The first showed a cutaway of a huge flower blossoming above ground, yet teetering on tiny roots below. It was captioned, "Youth." The second showed the inverse: a small shriveled flower propped up by an extensive network of underground roots. It was captioned, "Old Age."

This diptych had profoundly illustrated the passage through its first 40 years of the former Newport Jazz Festival ('54 to '71) and its chronological successor from '72 to the present, the **JVC Jazz Festival/Bryant Park Jazz Festival [JVC NYC]**. Prior to just recently, I would've suggested it was time to plant this festival over, along with its predecessor's rich legacy, as the first truly modern festival in America. **JVC NYC** had actually become the antithesis of everything I look for in a festival; of everything this book celebrates.

Nor was I alone in feeling so. The *New York Times*' Peter Watrous summed up the then-consensus of jazz critics everywhere:

- "Over the past several years, the **JVC Jazz Festival** has been anything but festive. Instead, it has mostly been a series of high-priced concerts, featuring a dwindling stock of big-name jazz musicians, in New York's most formal concert halls. It has been desultory, and every year the musician's save it, pulling out great performances from the mouth of a tired lion."

**JVC NYC**'s ancillary events, the Newport Jazz Festival/Saratoga (Saratoga Springs, NY — see chapter) and the back-to-back jazz picnics at Waterloo Village in Stanhope, New Jersey, had long outstripped their parent festival in terms of daily quantity, breadth, contrast, discovery, setting, amenities, audience spirit and, especially, value. Things had gotten so stale, so sparse, so pricey with **JVC NYC** that I was clipping local listings for (horrors!) an analysis of how you'd be better off spending less money on club gigs instead.

Ah, but as of this year, its 41st, "I've come to praise George," paraphrasing Shakespeare of **JVC NYC**'s legendary Founder and Producer, George Wein, "not to bury him." What happened? Well, it seems **JVC NYC**'s erosion of the past half decade or so finally up and hit Wein in the one spot it hurt most — the pocketbook. "I used to sell out ten, twelve concerts a year," as *New York Newsday*'s Gene Seymour quotes Wein. "Last year, I didn't sell out one."

All of '94's welcome changes came in direct response to '93's financial slippage, including:

- The concert focus — at last! — on more of the local festival scene, notably "Tribute to Rev. John Gensel" (All Nite Soul — see chapter), "The Musical Life of Dick Hyman" (Jazz in July — see chapter) and "A Historic First Meeting" between

Carnegie Hall Jazz Band and Lincoln Center Jazz Orchestra (Classical Jazz at Lincoln Center — see chapter), joining customary productions by Mark Morganelli (Riverside Park Arts Festival — see chapter) and Ralph Mercado (New York Salsa Festival — see chapter);

- The embracing — finally! — of the local club scene through **JVC NYC**'s officially designated "Midnight Jam at S. O. B.'s";

- The introduction — hallelujah! — of a praiseworthy festival-within-a-festival, the **Bryant Park Jazz Festival [Bryant Park']**.

The latter delivered four days of nearly 20 free outdoor concerts featuring many of the cutting-edge artists ("tightrope walkers," as the program aptly called them) critics have been screaming at **JVC NYC** for. Frankly, I found the **Bryant Park'**, like the Gazebo Stage at the Newport Jazz Festival/Saratoga, to be one of the better jazz experiences in the region all by itself. It spoke to me as a younger, more eclectic, adventuresome, ravenous, budget conscious and sun-worshipping listener for the first time here in a good long time!

Mind you, **JVC NYC** is not all the way back to what it was when it first took Manhattan by storm over 20 years ago. It still lacks many of the features which enamored critics and fans alike, then and since, such as:

- Dixieland bands on the Staten Island ferry;

- Midnight jams in Radio City Music Hall;

- Reduced-priced Jazz Piano Recitals at the commuter-friendly hour of 5:00 p.m.;

- Concert times staggered among 7:00 p.m., 8:00 p.m. and later so you could hit more than one show per evening;

- At least one multiple-act theme night per year, such as the "Jazz Meets Blues: A Blues and Jazz Jam" or "Jazz For the Fun Of It";

- Other concerts with more than two acts, especially bills not cut from the exact same musical cloth.

It still could use some of what makes Wein-produced festivals covered elsewhere in this book so noteworthy: (a) some kind of dance party; (b) more variable venues, including a few that don't require assigned seating; (c) a greater push into the outer boroughs; (d) plus other musical representations of the Gotham jazz diaspora, particularly its many ethnic scenes. And while we're at it, how 'bout discounts for multiple ticket purchases, or some kind of reduced-price all-festival pass?

However, I like to think **JVC NYC**'s now in better hands to rediscover its roots. Associate Producer John Phillips is loathe to take any special credit apart from the committee consisting of Bob Jones (Ben & Jerry's Newport Folk Festival — see chapter), Darlene Chan and Art Edelstein. Phillips replaced the departed John Schreiber and brought with him several facets enjoyed by the superb Benson & Hedges Blues Festival, which he ran successfully during it's brief tenure in New York City. I credit Phillips for at least part of this year's recognition that New York City's formidable production obstacles needn't stifle artistic creativity altogether.

Before I get to Phillips, however, let me dwell a little on his boss and the man who helped launch a thousand festivals alongside **JVC NYC**.

George Wein, now nearing 70, began his remarkable career as pianist for a local swing band in the late '40s. Wein soon discovered his unique talent was not so much playing as getting his group their gigs. This led in the early '50s to his booking Storyville, a Boston jazz club named for the infamous New Orleans neighborhood where jazz was born.

Wein often vacationed in Newport, Rhode Island with his friends, the Lorillards of cigarette wealth. One year Mrs. Lorillard wondered aloud if Wein could work some of his Storyville magic in Newport. She supplied the seed money, Wein applied his expertise, and lo, the NEWPORT JAZZ FESTIVAL [NEWPORT'] was born in 1954. It was held outdoors at the Newport Casino and in all kinds of impromptu spots around and about town — lawns, street corners, you name it. Wein's concept proved such a smash that "America's first resort" was unable to lodge the crush, and a good many patrons spent the weekend sleeping in their cars.

Now, NEWPORT' was not the first music festival. Among others, the NEW ENGLAND FOLK FESTIVAL (Natick, MA — see chapter) predated it by one decade; the OLD FIDDLERS' CONVENTION (see Galax, VA, Early August) by nearly two. It was not even jazz's first festival-quantity bill. Fellow impresario Norman Grantz had organized his famed Jazz at the Philharmonic concerts and tours 10 years earlier, leading him to found Verve Records with many of the same artists. But NEWPORT' did come at an auspicious time predating the thunderous rise of rock and roll when many jazz giants were in their unchallenged prime. "The Duke," "The Count," "The Prez," "Lady Day" and scores of others enjoyed name recognition but had too rarely been experienced outside small, smoky clubs. Newport's idyllic outdoor setting proved the perfect draw for this confluence of devotees and dilettantes and did as much to raise the profile of the genre as anything from Grantz to the present.

Wein's historic contributions were chiefly two-fold. First, he was a jazz musician himself. Not only did Wein enjoy inside knowledge of who-was-who and who-knew-who, but he also had an instinctive feel for their root nature of playing. Rather than program formal set-pieces, like you'd get from stuffy classical music concerts, Wein brought forth the loose-limbed feel of jazz club dates. Even better, he dragged after-hours jam sessions, largely hidden from public view, into daylight for mass consumption. Everyone gloried in the swinging interchange of it all.

Second, Wein lined up a major corporate sponsor, the Joseph Schlitz Brewing Co., to underwrite much of his production costs. Wein sensed from his own booking struggles that for jazz to command the bigger stages (and respect) of classical music, it would have to be similarly supported from outside sources. Although corporate sponsorship was not unknown then to popular music genres — witness National Life Insurance's supporting C&W's Grand Ol' Opry from 1924 onward — Wein can genuinely be credited with carrying this funding technique up to today's current level (with all of the accompanying pros and cons).

Being the only annually occuring jazz event of such prominence, Wein's NEWPORT' also hosted its share of historical notes, such as Miles Davis' return from four years' of heroin addiction to debut his "cool" stylings in '55, or Paul Gonsalves' remarkable 27-bar solo on Duke Ellington's "Diminuendo and Crescendo in Blue" in '56. Even NEWPORT's detractors made news, such as when Charlie Mingus organized a "salon des refuses" with his unauthorized Cliffwalk Manor concerts beginning in '60. The more enduring jazz history, however, was Wein's festival itself.

NEWPORT's "goldrush" caused Wein to leave club booking forever to form Festival Productions Inc. [FPI]. His company launched the former NEWPORT FOLK FESTIVAL in '57, along with a series of international festivals that have grown to number 30, including the universally acknowledged "world's best," the NEW ORLEANS JAZZ AND HERITAGE FESTIVAL (see New Orleans, LA, Late April to Early May). FPI now promotes more than a thousand concert events per year, including amphitheater tours named "NEWPORT JAZZ FESTIVAL" and "FESTIVAL NEW ORLEANS." FPI personnel have graduated to head top festivals the country over, while Wein has reaped his share of financial rewards. (He resides for much of the year, for example, in a multimillion-dollar villa in Nice, France.) You can catch this short, smiling, gravelly-voiced icon leading his Newport All-Stars in yet another FPI concert tour or on one of their frequent recording projects. "Go, George!"

Phillips is one of Wein's young production lions whose extensive experience here and abroad belies his modest age (having just turned 40). He came to FPI straight out of college in '78 and immediately set to work on **JVC NYC**, then onto JVC JAZZ FESTIVAL/NEWPORT, when it returned to its birthplace in '81. Like all FPI producers, Phillips' tasks vary from festival to festival: booking, production, sponsorship raising, television production, etc. "Basically, it's been the only school that I've ever been to for this type of thing," he remarks of his FPI tenure, "so I'd have to say that everything that I know in this business has either been learned through experience or from George."

In my brief interview, I alternated between congratulating Phillips for this year's **JVC NYC** turnaround and probing gently about why other characteristics remain. The following excerpts may help the interested listener appreciate some of the constraints New York City festival producers operate under. Although there's still some resistance to things I'd like to see return, I'm encouraged by Phillips' acknowledging the feature mix as "cyclical," and his willingness to keep the door open to interested parties.

On **JVC NYC**'s beginnings in '72:

- "I can tell you they were doing some interesting things, like closing down 52nd Street for outdoor stuff during the daytime. They did these famous Midnight Jams at Radio City. They were using the Staten Island Ferry for New Orleans-type boat rides. Some of it was at Carnegie Hall, and Avery Fisher [Hall], and Lincoln Center, and so, yeah, it was a very, very wide-ranging, a multivenue, day-and-night, very-much-all-over-the-place type of thing."

On my praising the BRYANT PARK JAZZ FESTIVAL seeking to recapture some of that earlier vibe:

- "Oh yeah, that was a great response. For one, it's free. For another, it's right in the center of the city. Between those two things and the time of day, which is the late afternoon, you're getting an audience that... People who want to hear it can come and hear it without too much hassle. But also, you're getting a lot of people who might just be passing by and who get caught up in the moment. And so, it's nice.

"It's kind of like a way of proselytizing for the music, on top of which you're not under pressure to fill a concert hall and make a 'nut,' you know what I mean? You can present really high-quality music that doesn't necessarily relate to immediate reimbursement of expenses — somebody like a Dave Liebman, who's a great, great musician, but might not be able to fill Carnegie Hall, out there playing to the people.

"It was a great success. I think it was Peter [Watrous] who wrote it up in the *'Times* and made those BRYANT PARK concerts the centerpiece of the festival."

On the prevalence at **JVC NYC** of double bills among remaining evening concerts:

- "Well, double bills are pretty standard because, first of all you're trying to get two major names. Usually, there's two well-known acts. You have a limited amount of time that you can play in those halls. You can't go from 7:00 to midnight; you can't do it. It's exorbitantly expensive with the unions and the rent situations, whereas if you do a two or three-hour show, then you're within the bounds of financial practability.

"Plus, I don't think people really come to those shows to sit through four or five hours of music. People start to get restless after two hours, two-and-a-half, three hours. So to give your two headliners the time they deserve, which is 55, 60 minutes, plus an intermission, you're somewhat limited.

"But actually, we've done a lot of triple bills over the years. That's not uncommon. There's probably at least, 20, 25 percent of the shows over the years that've been a triple bill, or there've been special guests, or what-have-you."

On my noting how most **JVC NYC** double bills tend to be two like-minded artists; how there's less audience mixing than at other festivals:

- "You know, so many people do so many things in **JVC NYC**, but I think we're always looking for that magic formula which is like a 'one-plus-one-equals-three' situation. If you've been noticing more compatibility with more stylistic similarities between the artists in **JVC NYC** as opposed to the artists in other festivals, it may be true. I don't know, I haven't looked at it from that perspective."

On my asking about smaller venues for **JVC NYC**, like with its former Jazz Piano Recital series:

- "Yeah, for many years that piano series was at Carnegie Recital Hall, actually. You know, things do tend to come and go in waves. For many years there weren't any large free out-door things; now there are. Maybe these small, intimate piano and other types of concerts didn't prove to be, well, in their latter years were not drawing the people that they had pre-viously. So I think their elimination was a reflection of the demand for that kind of concert, but it could be that that will come around again. I see very much a cyclical type of presen-tation."

On **JVC NYC**'s not really reaching out to the outer boroughs, unlike FPI's own Benson and Hedges Blues Festival:

- "We could definitely see that down the road. ...You know, every festival has its own stylis-tic face, but that's not to say some of the things you would like to see, like stretching out to the outer boroughs and various neighborhoods, won't happen with **JVC NYC**. It cer-tainly could. There's no policy not to, let's put it that way. I mean, various times, we've tied in with Jazzmobile. We're out in Waterloo Village, which is certainly kind of different than midtown Manhattan. We're down at the World Financial Center for many years. And, like I said, the Staten Island Ferry was going for many years, and Prospect Park we tied into many times. I think that over the years that there has been a pretty wide diversity, but I understand what you're saying. I was one of the producers of those Benson and Hedges Blues Festival's. ...Certainly, that possibility exists."

On my lauding more local color at this year's **JVC NYC**:

- "I think it was accidental, and I think that it reflects the strengthening of the jazz commu-nity here because the Carnegie Hall Jazz Band and the L. C. J. O. didn't exist five years ago, you know?

  "The other thing you run into here is that since it is such an important art center, again, you're fighting a year-round saturation of the clubs with artists, a lot of whom are New York artists. And so, it's not always easy to create something that's quintessential to New York, number one.

  "Number two, a lot of the major headliners are living right here. You put somebody on and you might not think of them as a New York artist, and yet they're living and performing [here]. So I think that those are some of the things that may have disguised a little bit the New York nature of the festival and, on the other hand, a lot has happened over the last few years that has strengthened New York and made it more apparent in the presentation of the festival."

On my appreciation how this year's "Midnight Jam at S. O. B.'s" embraced the club scene and kept the festival vibe alive after the conclusion of **JVC NYC**'s evening concerts:

- "Yeah, I agree with you. That was not my move, and it just came about through a collabo-ration between S. O. B.'s and us. I mean, we've tied in with various clubs over the years. When I first started working here, as a matter of fact, there were tie-ins which basically list-ed all the clubs and what they were doing in our brochures, and stuff like that. That's fall-en off a little bit, and it's not through competition I don't think. I think with S. O. B.'s there's a good symbiosis, but when you're including all the clubs, it's harder to do. And that becomes a festival in and of itself, like the [Panasonic Greenwich Village Jazz Festival — see **New York City Festival Listings**]."

On my desire for staggered concert starting times as in past **JVC NYC**'s, instead of the current 8:00 p.m. lock-step; how you sometimes find yourself conflicted in which concert to attend:

- "Well, 8:00 is a standard time for these concerts. And usually — I'm not saying always — the concerts are noncompeting. Hopefully, they appeal to different audiences. There are occasional nights when people are hitting themselves in the head and saying, 'I can't get to both of these shows!' But usually the programming is such that it's, like, a Lena Horne vs. a Spyro Gyra, or something like that, where the audiences are pretty different, you know what I mean? For someone who's got a really omnivorous, eclectic taste to the music, it can be problematic, but for the general public, I mean, we haven't been awash in criticisms of that sort."

On how this year's **JVC NYC** lacked a multi-act theme night, such as "The Jazz Singers" or "The Jazz Connection: The Jewish and African-American Relationship":

- "I mean, if somebody comes up with a good idea with a show like that, it's embraced. If not, if nobody's pushing it, then it doesn't happen. It all depends on the topicality and current interest for a given idea. Yeah, if somebody has a really good idea they can send a fax. Just say: 'Here's a good idea, and I'd like to get involved in workin' this out with you.' Have them call George directly."

Finally, on his recent **JVC NYC** highlights:

- "Structurally, the BRYANT PARK thing was extremely successful. I'm very impressed with the site. It's like you're in the middle of everything, so I loved that. That was impressive. Show-wise, the tribute to Jim Hall a couple years back at Town Hall ['Jim Hall Invitational' with Hall, Pat Metheny, John Abercrombie, Gary Burton, Ron Carter, Gerry Mulligan, John Scofield, Don Thompson, etc.] I think was really nice. Metheny did something on that show; I think Bob Brookmeyer, too. ...It was really a remarkable, remarkable evening [with] a lot of different musicians. [Also] the two big bands last year was a pretty interesting evening."

**Artist Mini-Reviews**

Here, I was also going to recreate a wonderful show I caught in '92 — "A Night of Chesky Records Jazz" (a label-showcase trend thankfully continued by Candid and Columbia Records in the respective years since). However, the two brothers Chesky were kind enough to record this marvelous evening at Town Hall for commercial issuance. You can go to the record store, pick up a copy, and hear for yourself how I'd prefer a typical **JVC NYC** night to be more like in terms of quantity, variety and value.

**Attendance Tip**

If there's one **JVC NYC** evening concert that you simply must catch, no questions asked, I'd recommend calling the venue at least a month ahead, maybe further. Prior to '93, particular "superstar" tributes and twin bills, such as Tito Puente's annual homecoming, always sold out far in advance.

**See Also**

NEWPORT' moved to New York City following the riots of '71. Newport's city council had cancelled Wein's permits but conceded over time that he was not to blame for the unruly hippies who stormed the gates that year before trashing the town. He was invited back in '81 and has maintained what's become a three-day, single-stage festival at two sites: Friday night at Newport Casino (a delightful, long-black-dress, long-stemmed-champagne-glass-and-strawberries affair with two top acts -- recommended!); then Saturday and Sunday afternoons at the gorgeous waterside promenade of Fort Adams State Park.

The current JVC JAZZ FESTIVAL/NEWPORT is not a bad festival by any means, though the prime attraction seems to be more the stunning site and less the lineup. Artistically, it enjoys neither the free-swinging adventuring of its much-beloved predecessor, nor the unique musical niche of its companion revival the week prior, the BEN & JERRY'S NEWPORT FOLK FESTIVAL. The new 'NEWPORT often suffers the same kind of "play-it-safe" programming, especially on the pop-music side, which dogged the old **JVC NYC**. For every musical coup, such as Nina Simone or Sonny Rollins, there's at least one questionable middle-of-the-roader, like Lou Rawls, or Tower of Power, or Frankie Beverly and Maze, or some other '70s retread. Here it hurts especially, since there's no supplemental stage to escape to.

At least the periodic jazz cruises Wein books out of New York City (e.g., the QE2: NEWPORT JAZZ FESTIVAL AT SEA) suffer no such musical equivocating. The lineup is straight-ahead swing, clearly Wein's personal preference, and I think we'd all rather have that done well than pop-music overtures to the undiscriminating over-50 crowd done unimaginatively.

~     ~     ~

# Brooklyn's African American Scene

AFRICAN STREET FESTIVAL, Brooklyn, NYC
Early July
African American
***Attended***

**Introduction** The AFRICAN STREET FESTIVAL [AFRICAN'] is a world-class spectacular just waiting to be discovered. (Indeed, if this book does nothing more than expose this fabulous happening, along with its significant other, the Caribbean Cultural Center's CARNIVAL IN NEW YORK — see chapter — it will have served its purpose.)

What makes AFRICAN' world class? For one, when you go to Brooklyn, exclaims its Co-Founder and Program Director, K. Mensah Wali, "you've got the world!" The relaxed Wali lets out a chuckle at what likely seems obvious to most Brooklynites familiar with the borough's remarkable tapestry of ethnicities. If you're not so enlightened, all you have to do is pass through the gates at Boys and Girls High School in the Bedford-Stuyvesant section of town during the five days encompassing July 4th weekend and gaze around the infield.

Wali accumulates an astonishing marketplace of vendors from all around this country and others — over 300 in all — sufficient to permit careful screening for quality and originality. He aligns these merchants into wedges around the big oval track, grouping like nationalities together. If you could possibly pull yourself away from this explosion of brilliantly-hued fabrics, tunics, tonics, bands, braids, beads, wraps, caps, scents, books, prints and such, you'd stroll through a succession of mini-villages — Sudanese, Kenyans, Ethiopians, Moroccans, Namibians, Haitians, Jamaicans, Trinidadians, etc. — each hawking their colorful wares. To serve their locally-based countrymen (there are nearly 7,000 Senegalese immigrants living nearby, for example), as well as to show off to others, every country puts its prideful best on display. Accordingly, I've never experienced festival vendors so friendly, so eager to show you what they've got.

Same deal when you complete the crafts gauntlet and enter the food court. You can just imagine the Tunisians bragging to the Antiguans, "You've got six entrees at your booth? Well, we've got eight and they're tastier!" They'll do everything short of giving you free samples just to prove their point. And so it goes as each constituency attempts to "up the ante" on the next.

The best time to experience this friendly, but spirited, competition is whenever one of the headliners takes AFRICAN's centrally-placed main stage. If it's Afro-jazz trumpeter Hugh Masakela blowing hard, the wedge of his fellow South Africans will rise as one and roar throughout the entire set. Likewise, for Zin and the compas band's Haitian compatriots. Or for jazz pianist Ifeachor Okeke and her Nigerian nationals. Or even for rising gospel star and recent Grammy winner Hezekiah Walker and his own Brooklyn brethren. They all try to outdo each other whenever somebody special is holding court.

Needless to say, this makes for a way-festive environment!

Which brings us to AFRICAN's other world-class trait. Before you make your shopping circle, you'll be handed the day's schedule for all four stages. "Barring acts of nature," Wali notes, the music proceeds as posted. No inferior substitutions, no agonizing delays, no mysterious no-shows, no taped tracks, no unexplained flip-flops. In short, no nonsense.

Though I've seen African-American festivals with greater musical quantity, AFRICAN's programming strikes a perfect quality balance. There's usually one to three name acts per day who straddle ethnic genres to appeal to as many different wedges as possible. "That's how I try to do it," Wali explains, "I try to keep a blend of world music." They'll also have some strong connection to the borough or the festival or both, thus achieving a deeper resonance with the audience. A good example is Afro-jazz alto ace Gary Bartz who kicked off AFRICAN's precursor back in '70 and has been a regular ever since.

The remaining openers are not just "filler" either, but strong locals culled from AFRICAN's extensive Talent Search and cultivated through multiple appearances. The winners, for example, will have survived a multi-borough preliminary the prior month, plus a run-off each afternoon on the main stage, then a later placement on the Apollo Theater's own notoriously-brutal Talent Search. They'll be brought back the following year to headline the AFRICAN's Talent Search, then the year after that for a paying "professional" gig. To hold their own over that long a stretch means young acts, like this year's Nubian Blues Band, are solid, y'all.

That so many openers and headliners have chosen to return so often further proves that Wali's doing them right. "Well, this goes back to '70 when I started doing this," he confides with knowing smile. "I always maintain that whatever you put out, you know, you gotta' make a show of it, and you gotta' pay the bills no matter what happens! No one can ever walk away from the festival and say they didn't get paid."

Wali's own musical preference is jazz, which predominated early AFRICAN's and still percolates within today's more eclectic orientation:

- "I've had to adapt the festival presentation to the total environment that we have here in that we have a large population from the Caribbean; we have a large population from Africa. You know, Caribbeans like reggae and calypso, steel bands, Latin music. We've got all these flavors that we've got to deal with as far as the African diaspora is concerned. So I can't just focus in on the jazz aspect like I used to, but I try to keep it in the blend. You know, I can't go a day without it."

Wali came into the jazz world through his sister. In '56, as a 12-year-old, he immigrated to Brooklyn from his native Panama and took to the music almost immediately. "Consequently, due to a friendship of my sister's (who's down in Washington) with Wynton Kelly, I got to know a lot of these people personally," he recites. "And over the years I was on 'the jazz scene,' so to speak, as a young person."

In the summer of '69, Wali's friends, a pair of teachers from the Ocean Hill/Brownsville district of Brooklyn, decided to start an alternative school for African-American youngsters. They called it Uhuru Sasa. Everybody had day jobs (Wali's was as a fashion model), but the teachers and parents managed to occupy a barn on Claver Place to get their school going.

"Because they needed some income to keep this thing going in terms of just starting the school up, I suggested that we have the music section, because I knew how to get in touch with these guys," Wali says. "So, we started off with a party on New Year's Eve '70, with Leon Thomas and some other guys." The music continued as a series Friday and Saturday nights throughout the new year, contributing an "East Cultural Center" to supplement the school's daytime activities.

Come graduation day in June, Uhuru Sasa's parents wanted to develop a ceremony to appropriately thank the children for their efforts. Many contributed art, crafts, instruments, and such; Wali supplied the live music. "Everyone was inspired by the results of that and decided, 'Well, we should do this on a regular basis.' The organization decided that we would start, what we called then the AFRICAN STREET CARNIVAL, the following year," he recalls. "So that's how this thing got off the ground."

To say there's been growth since that fateful day would be a grievous understatement. In '77 AFRICAN' moved from Claver Place to its present location, at first occupying the mere under-hang where Stage 2 now sits. In '87 it took over the full infield, then the macadams surrounding the infield. In '93 it branched out into the street from which it came. AFRICAN' now draws over 125,000 revelers, including a good 25% from beyond the immediate New York City Tri-State Area who come in by the tour-bus load. Give it another 23 years, and it might take over the entire neighborhood!

AFRICAN's growth has not let go of its family, community, educational and cultural origins, however. You'll find a highly active children's stage that incorporates top-notch musicians with storytellers, magicians, dancers, puppets, folklorists and sports. There's also a fashion show, a parade, an Ankh Awards Ceremony, and a symposium. AFRICAN' always fields a heavy roster of nonprofit exhibitors who use the gathering as a prime evangelizer and fundraiser of their own.

You'll also observe that every year Wali's crew metaphorically visits one country for a theme. He explains how:

- "Basically, it's just a teaching mechanism that Africa's a very large continent with many, many languages. I mean, one country may have 70 different languages. They have different ways of expressing things — some through symbolism, some through phrasing, [some] through proverbs. We try to use the festival to project some of these bits and pieces of African wisdom and knowledge, so the theme is usually something that's going to attempt to inspire some individual.

  "Whatever country that we go to, we try to find some communication...that will speak to the experience here that people can also incorporate into their experience. Like, last year with the violence in the area and all of that, Senegal was the area for the theme. 'Jam Ak Jam' was a phrase meaning, 'Peace and more peace.' So, we definitely felt that the whole community could benefit by that.

  "Similar this year when we went to Nigeria for the theme and came up with 'Ayeraye' — 'You will live forever' — for praise. In each native tongue that we go to, I'm sure there is something we can explore and pass on. I run into people who definitely use it in their household with their children, in their classrooms. It's part of our learning experience; it's a way of communicating something about Africa that may not have been known by the masses."

To harbor AFRICAN's family initiatives, Wali stresses his event's unblemished security record. He claims "the police captain over here declared to the community board that this is the safest, most organized event he's ever worked. So that's definitely the kind of praise that we want people who are strangers to the area to hear and know. The image that 'Bed-Stuy' may conjure up in somebody's mind may be that of a mugger, [but] we don't have any history of that."

Wali credits numerous plainclothes professionals — his "unseen security" — for keeping on top of any potential trouble, "so it gets snuffed before it even occurs. It's not that they don't try," he laughs, "it's just that they don't succeed." This wise eye assures a welcoming environment for all ages and races.

Wali recalls this year how:

- "An elderly lady — I would put her in her 70s — came up. I was standing there talking to Marta Vega from the Caribbean Cultural Center, and she just walked up and said, 'Now I'm ready! I've got my charge for the next year! I can go!' [laughs] And I said, 'Yeah, that's what we do this for, [so] you can get your charge and go!' That, for me, is the most inspiring. That makes all of this underlying work worthwhile."

**Festival Review**  As for the music, forget detailed Artist Mini-Reviews — it took me a full five hours just to make it around the crafts track! I did get to catch one of the last appearances from experimental jazz pianist <u>Sun Ra</u> (who passed away not too long afterward) and was surprised to find his Arkestra pumping out smooth, strong, accomplished charts, not out of line for a big-band dance. Now there's a departure for these legendary avant-gardeners, though the band members' wide smiles suggested they knew they were amply capable of this mainstream stuff all along.

Sun Ra's been another one of AFRICAN's perennials and gave Wali his fondest festival memory. "I mean, this goes back, now," he recalls:

- "At one point we couldn't even pay Sun Ra a thousand dollars because we just didn't have it. We weren't using the field, right? And the fee might've been a dollar for the entrance. Sun Ra may have been the top billing for the whole festival, so we may have been paying him, maybe, $700 or $800.

  "And he came from Germany! He flew in his whole band; it was, like, 25 of them there! You know? I was never so flabbergasted in my life [laughs]. I mean, they came off the airplane to the festival; it was just like that — no break. And needless to say, the performance was, like, super-magnificient, incredible, absolutely incredible [laughs].

"...Oh, yeah. We've gotten all the variations of Sun Ra [laughs]. I've been dealing with Sun Ra since '65. I've seen him in all different phases, and he's blessed us with a lot."

There are two main ways of traveling to AFRICAN' (short of a limo, of course, for the well-heeled). Wali recommends riding Duke Ellington's "A Train," sitting in the front cars for exiting at Utica Avenue right to the site. Police guard the station festival nights until 2:00 a.m., making late stays secure. **Attendance Tip**

I took my car but got stuck for an hour in Fulton Street's perpetual congestion. Take Atlantic Avenue instead, and park on the street close by the school. Remember to leave nothing of value in your car — not even in the trunk. However, you may need a big duffle bag to carry your shopping spoils around with you. "Jam Ak Jam!"

Wali's formed a joint production company with the Caribbean Cultural Center to co-present its CARNIVAL IN NEW YORK in Early August There are fewer crafts and less jazz here; otherwise, these two fine affairs are virtual mirror images of each other, including their classy family crowds. Both festivals are perfect for out-of-towners looking for a grand introduction to New York City's copious Afro-Latin-Caribbean diaspora. **See Also**

~     ~     ~

# Classic Jazz, I

LYRICS AND LYRICISTS/BOYS NIGHT OUT, Manhattan, NYC
    Late February
    Cabaret
    ***Attended***

FOLKSONGS PLUS, Manhattan, NYC
    Middle May
    Modern Folk

LYRICS AND LYRICISTS/THE NEW BREED, Manhattan, NYC
    Middle June
    Cabaret

JAZZ IN JULY, Manhattan, NYC
    Late July
    Traditional Jazz and Ragtime
    ***Attended***

**Introduction**    "I guess imitation is the best kind of flattery," sighs Hadassah Markson, Director of the 92nd Street Y's Tisch School of the Arts, "but Lincoln Center came up with their CLASSICAL JAZZ' after us (see chapter). And, of course, they had so much more money to put behind it because Lincoln Center is a little different from the 92nd Street Y. [laughs] But I think that where Dick [Hyman] has it over Wynton Marsalis is that Dick is a man of very wide experience in everything in so many areas. He knows the past so well. He's not saying that only people who are 20 years old can play in my band."

Markson is the co-founder of the 92nd Street Y's 10-year-old JAZZ IN JULY festival as well as its 25-year-old LYRICS AND LYRICISTS series. You can get a whiff, here, of the resentment that Marsalis' various stances are causing locally. Yet this is the only issue clouding Markson's otherwise eubillent disposition from which her high-spirited, high quality affair is a natural expression.

You can also see how much Markson admires her Artistic Director and Co-Founder, the keyboardist extraordinaire, Dick Hyman. As a classically trained pianist herself, Markson always had great respect for Hyman's playing, whether it be his accompanying the Y's various cabaret concerts, or the jazz piano recitals he'd often conduct at her bequest. In '85 Markson invited Hyman to fill a lull in her summer schedule by recruiting such fellow jazz "classicists" as Milt Hinton, Butch Miles, Flip Phillips, Dick Sudhalter, Warren Vache, Howard Alden and the like to present two weeks' worth of Hyman's own theme shows. "Because his name was so important and the things that we offered were so good," Markson explains, "it was successful, really, right from the beginning."

Markson credits three features for JAZZ IN JULY's continuing prosperity:

- First, there's the draw of Hyman, himself: "He is a very, very serious musician. Before a concert he plays Chopin's "Seven Etudes" at ninety miles an hour. His piano technique is absolutely flawless, and classical artists come to hear him not so much even because he improvises so well and all the different things that he does, but [because] his technique is so fantastic."

- Second, there's Hyman's industry contacts and rapport with musicians, which Markson supports by her own hospitality efforts: "Dick is so respected amongst artists that they would do anything for him. It's never hard for us to get people to perform. We don't pay tremendous amounts of money, although we are fair. The minute they know who we are and who's asking them to perform, it's always, 'Yes.'

"There is something very special at the Y; that we are a very welcoming place; that artists love to work at the Y. We are a wonderful team and people like to be there. The auditorium is extremely beautiful, the acoustics are marvelous, and we take extremely good care of everybody. All this makes a big difference when an artist comes into a place, rather than being shuffled around."

- Third, there's the creativity of Hyman's themes, which are invariably spiked by his wry humor and comic showmanship: "One night they were doing something that was Caribbean, and he came out in a white hat and a flowered shirt, you know, as loud as can be. And everybody else did — they had their sleeves rolled up with red suspenders. He will think of these things.

"We had Terry Burrell on the show, and she is a Caribbean, very toned, extremely beautiful and very sexy. And she sang. Then at one point she wrapped herself around [bookish-looking] Dick who was playing the piano, and the whole audience absolutely shrieked because they thought, "This is the last thing in the world..." And he had this very abashed look on his face. I asked him about two or three months later: 'Tell me, were you very surprised when Terry did that?' He said, 'No, not at all. In fact, we rehearsed it!'"

In that regard, Hyman's events convey the looseness and conviviality more typical of "trad. jazz" festivals happening across the country.

Hyman's nightly themes are noteworthy. The year I attended in '92 he conducted an academic exploration ("Chicago Jazz") plus an artist spotlight ("Marian McPartland's Piano Jazz"). But Hyman also attempted some artistic departures from the tradition, such as "Changes and Transformations," where his septet interacted with The Beaux Arts String Quartet, as well as "Make Believe Ballroom" that recreated traditional vehicles and environments by which some pre-war audiences experienced the genre. Several shows featured guest commentaries to illustrate the topics.

Then, of course, there was the one I caught — "I'm Hip: The Songs of Dave Frishberg and Other Hipsters" — that made a pretense of exploring a subtext of jazz "hipness" throughout the '50s, but was really an excuse to showcase the droll Frishberg and have some fun with the band. Props for this show involved (you guessed it) wrap-around shades, berets, pork-pie hats, black ties loosened and sleeves rolled up over dark suits — a combined beatnik/post-war-Sinatra look. Needless to say, the middle-aged crowd of fellow Upper East Side "hipsters" howled.

This humor, combined with an ensemble orientation where many of Hyman's crew repeat from theme-to-theme and year-to-year, creates a warmth and familiarity all too rare in New York City these days. Patrons are appreciative, as Markson describes one habitue who flies in every year from Japan for all six shows. "The fact that we have developed an audience that is so loyal, that people have been coming back for ten years," Markson reflects, "I guess is the best compliment you can get that you must be doing something very right." That, and imitation, too.

**Festival Review**

Entering the 92nd Street Y from the street was like opening up a series of Chinese boxes — each revealing a smaller one inside. You pass through a bustling marble-clad lobby, proceeding through doors inside doors until you reach the ticket takers and the performance space beyond. En route was a nice exhibit in the Weill Art Gallery of jazz-related art. The auditorium was basically a square box but handsomely appointed with burnished wood panels engraved in gold leaf with the names of Lincoln, Moses, Jefferson, David, Shakespeare, Isaiah, Beethoven, etc.

Hyman's seven-piece ensemble took the stage in their "hipster" regalia to introduce the evening's theme (see above). They even posed a "hipster" stage right at a bistro-sized table — checkered tablecloth and empty beer bottle serving as a candleholder — whose sole duty was to stroke his goatee with appropriate coolness at each solo.

**Artist Mini-Review**

<u>Dave Frishberg</u>. The band ran through three standards from the era, including "Yardbird Suite," before Frishberg took the stage for a solo set, accompanying himself on piano. Both he and Hyman could've dubbed as Woody Allen's cousins in looks, demeanor, and self-deprecating wit. "It's only appropriate," Frishberg confided of his appearance here, "because I've always tried to be hip... I'm up to 1948!"

Frishberg's originals — somewhat spoken ("shaken, not stirred") — proved a revelation. Few other writers today similarly balance such sophistication with accessibility and entertainment value; nobody else achieves his unique emotional tone of gently whimsy balancing resigned melancholia. Even his funny romps, such as my fave, "My Attorney Bernie" ("Bernie always lays it on the line/When he says sue, we sue/When he says sign, we sign"), contain a counterpoint of sadness, of innocence lost, of feeling his soul slip away under his sleazy pal's exuberant counsel.

Interestingly, Frishberg leaned toward outspoken social commentaries as his program wore on: "Quality Time," about the struggles of a dual-career couple where "romance is the bottom line"; "Report From The Planet Earth," commissioned by CBS for the Winter Olympics; "My Country Used To Be," an ominous lament on the recession; concluding with an angry, "Blizzard Of Lies," where he found poetry in audacity, namely, famous last words and the cliches of scams. Frishberg's one-liners, New Yorker references, and Yiddishisms may have played the older crowd like a violin, initially, but his procession of topics and emotions connected with their lives on a deeper level by set's end.

The band returned for a assortment of serious fun: the frantically dueling pianos of Hyman and Derek Smith on "Lullaby In Birdland"; Milton Hinton's great lead bass on "Fascinating Rhythms"; trumpeter Spanky Davis' reading from the 242 "choruses" of Kerouac's "Mexico City Blues," which Davis explained was written to be taken as a series of jazz solos. Frishberg's songs stayed with me, however, and I hope I can find his records in the stores to savor at length.

Markson: "That was a wonderful evening. He was very funny."

**Attendance Tip**

Warning: certain shows sell out even with their mid-week scheduling. Make sure you get any hot tickets (i.e., whenever clarinetest Kenny Davern is booked) a week or two ahead.

**See Also**

Thanks to Markson's Lyrics and Lyricists series, which features a number of cabaret music's leading lights interpreting one writer's output per evening, the Y has acquired a solid reputation in cabaret circles. This extends to a concert showcasing rising writers, The New Breed, plus still another spotlighting four male singers, Boys Night Out. (Dick Staller's full-throated vocal range, exquisite control and disarming demeanor proved a revelation for my wife and me at the latter affair.)

Markson remembers how they all started:

- "The Billy Rose Foundation came to me and asked if I would do something about lyricists. And I didn't know too much about lyricists, so I called up Maurice Levine, my friend, who conducted our orchestra at the Y and who had been a Broadway conductor. I said, 'Listen, we are getting $5,000 from the Billy Rose Foundation. We have to do something with that $5,000.' He said, 'That's crazy. No one is interested in lyricists!' 'I know,' I said, 'but we've got to do it anyway.'

  "So we got Gib Harper interested — he wrote 'Finian's Rainbow' and 'Brother, Can You Spare a Dime.' Once we got a hook he agreed to do a show. Then Stephen Sondheim agreed, and Jerry Herman, and Johnny Mercer, and everybody. We're going for 25 years now. It's the biggest success in New York [laughs].

  "You know, we just did a program at the Y which was very successful called, The New Breed, where we had a lot of cabaret writers. We did this in conjunction with ASCAP. It was brilliant! Andrea Marcovicci was our host, and Margaret Whiting was on that show, and just everybody who was anybody in that business was there. It was so successful that we actually made money on it! We're going to do it again next year.

"'THE NEW BREED' are people who are very much alive and young: Craig Cardelia, Francesca Blumenthal, David Friedman, Abby Green, and Brad Ross. We had a combination of them performing and top performers as well. It was marvelous, just marvelous."

But wait, there's more! Back in the '50s, the Y was on the cutting edge of the nascent folk-music revival which was to boom in the early '60s. Recently, it's brought a healthy number of its then champions back together at once for pricey benefits, FOLKSONGS PLUS. So far, there've been two such evenings in consecutive years with promises of more to follow.

Otherwise, Markson's humble Y (its marketing slogan is, "New York's most entertaining secret") is really a well-respected performing arts center regionally, as well as a leading community/educational establishment locally. Lectures, forums, storytellings and readings abound as does a wealth of classical music and theater programming. Avail yourself!

~     ~     ~

# Classic Jazz, II

CLASSICAL JAZZ AT LINCOLN CENTER, Manhattan, NYC
   Early August
   Traditional Jazz and Ragtime
   ***Attended***

**Introduction**    Hoo-boy! You know the controversy's gotten out of hand when the ever-acrimonious *Village Voice* actually strikes a pose of moderation in its cover story summation of the Jazz at Lincoln Center [JLC] brouhaha: "A Rage Supreme: The Feud That's Shaking Up Lincoln Center," by Richard B. Woodward, August 9, 1994.

JLC began in '87 with a week-long festival, CLASSICAL JAZZ AT LINCOLN CENTER [CLASSICAL JAZZ'], that remains during the first week in August. In '91, this event expanded into a year-round full-time department dedicated to "producing first-class programming of the highest caliber and showcasing the rich canon of jazz masterworks that exist in hopes of making people more aware of this great American art form," to quote JLC's official mission statement. How did such a noble objective by JLC's Artistic Director, Wynton Marsalis, and Artistic Consultant, Stanley Crouch, stir up such a hornet's nest within the jazz establishment?

Using Woodward's thorough and reasonable article as our guide, let's examine the main points, one at a time.

- Point one: the infamous letter dated May 31, 1993, and signed by Director, Rob Gibson, effectively terminating all members of the Lincoln Center Jazz Orchestra over the age of 30.

Apparently, the musicians in question threatened an age discrimination suit, as Woodward implies, and the letter was retracted. At best, this represents bad human resources management by JLC; at worst, it reveals at least one possible prejudice among many undermining the artistic credibility of its programming. (How can you espouse "classic jazz," for example, by releasing the musicians who helped make it "classic?")

Since the firings were prevented, however, it's a moot point. Besides, although the affair was handled ungracefully, the ultimate purpose was to promote young musicians and create their familiarity with and perpetuation of "the canon." Normally, you'd earn points for that intent.

- Point two: tightly strained relations between Marsalis, Crouch and the jazz music press.

This has no bearing onstage. Besides, I often wonder if Marsalis hasn't been shrewd in turning this firestorm to JLC's advantage. You see, there's a "Madonna" factor at work here where: if you treat the press badly, they ignore you, but if you treat the press really, really badly, they seem to come flocking. Marsalis came to town in '87 respected as a musician, but still unproven as a spokesman and promoter. Yet he's managed over the last year in this most cynical and crowded of all media markets to garner more attention for his event than even the 40-year-old JVC JAZZ FESTIVAL (see chapter), which has its own share of controversies. Hmmm...

- Point three: cronyism, that a majority of JLC commissions have gone to Marsalis, or other close associates.

I actually like festival promoters, who are also professional musicians, to appear on their own bills. It helps personalize the festival experience and summarize the promoter's aesthetic for fans, while suitably rewarding the promoter for his efforts. No one criticizes Paul Simon when he makes his regular cameo at his own BACK AT THE RANCH FESTIVAL (Montauk Point, NY — see chapter). Indeed, that's the main attraction! Why, then, should Marsalis be criticized for granting himself an annual commission, especially when even his harshest critics acknowledge the quality and appropriateness of his original work within JLC's format.

- Point four: conservatism, that JLC's programming ignores a range of relatively more recent, more experimental, more crossover, more rootsy, or more ethnic offshoots.

I find this criticism particularly ironic. It confounds me how regularly I hear jazz musicians insist that "jazz is America's classical music," complaining they don't get the same "respect" as classical musicians. Well guys and gals, here's exactly what you've been crying for: a premier classical-music institution treating jazz precisely the way it treats its own genre — conservatively!

The American classical-music establishment (ever aping Europe), basically entombed the genre somewhere prior to WWII, virtually severing the link with its ongoing development and yielding the norm of "live musicians playing dead composers." You'll hear similar terms as are applied to JLC — "first-class... highest caliber.... masterworks" — but you could just as readily substitute the words, "elitist... risk-averse... irrelevant." I suspect it has largely to do with not wanting to rock the boat for its "Masterpiece Theater" audience.

By contrast, jazz music is a living, breathing American art form of the 20th century. It has a much closer connection between its composers and practitioners — the two more likely being one and the same, even with the recent passing of many jazz-music giants. It has a far broader and more intimate range of venues in which programmers, composers, practitioners and fans all come together. It has a much more happening audience demographic in terms of age, race, sex, income, education, etc. Jazz musicians wanting to trade places with classical musicians strikes me like the man wanting to exchange a flowering plant in a plastic pot with a wilted plant in a gilded bowl just because he thinks the gilding carries more status. "Hey buddy, that plant's history! Give it up!"

Besides, complaints of conservatism ignore some of the uniqueness of JLC's explorations and reclamations. Tell me, for example, when was the last time that a traditional jazz festival here focused on the compositions of Johnny Dodds? Or that a modern jazz festival here highlighted the playing of Art Farmer? If those selections don't "quiver the livers" of progressive jazz music fans and/or JLC critics, though, they don't have to go home disgruntled; afterward, they can simply catch a cab downtown and go club-hopping like I do! They have options even if classical music fans don't.

- Point five: reverse racism, that JLC has ignored the spotlighting of white jazz composers/musicians.

Ah, but here's a charge that sticks, and sticks hard. (One festival promoter suggested to me a corollary of anti-Semitism, while a female musician responding by letter to Woodward's article added sexism, as well.) Eight years, nearly 150 concerts and not one white jazz composer/musician spotlighted? Not one? Not even one!

Woodward quotes *New York Times* jazz critic, Peter Watrous:

- "I don't think the people who run Jazz at Lincoln Center are racist, but I think the programming is racist. They say they have to put on all the important figures before they get to the lesser knowns, and there happen to be more important figures who are black. That's complete bullshit. I'd like to know what Dewey Redman or Gonzalo Rubalca [both subjects of of recent JLC concerts] have contributed to jazz. They've had plenty of white musicians on stage, but they have yet to have a white headliner. That is racially biased programming."

In a "Jazz Talk" debate from the most recent CLASSICAL JAZZ', entitled, "Opposing Views: Wynton Marsalis vs. Author James Lincoln Collier" (proof to me that Marsalis is milking it all marvelously; see Point two), Collier challenged Marsalis directly on why the works of such white jazz composers/musicians as Bix Beiderbecke and Bill Evans haven't yet been featured. As noted by *New York Newsday* jazz critic, Gene Seymour in "Hard Words, Great Music: Jaw Session Precedes Lincoln Center Jam Session," August 9, 1994: "Marsalis said while Beiderbecke and Evans weren't in his own personal pantheon, he was not 'excluding' them because of race. 'I'm not going to do a Bix Beiderbecke tribute,' he said, 'when we haven't done Armstrong yet.'"

Personal pantheon? Marsalis might as well have put on Al Campanis' L. A. Dodgers cap and opined that white jazz composers/musicians "don't have the necessities." Moreover, despite a racial breakdown of JLC musicians Marsalis cited as being 178 black, 98 white, and 41 Latin, his rationalizing JLC's holding spotlights of any white jazz composer/musician hostage to a Louis Armstrong tribute is pretty hard to swallow.

If Marsalis and Crouch has labelled their perspective, "African-American Classical Jazz," such truth-in-advertising might've mitigated the furor somewhat. The pity of it all, however, is that jazz music boasts a 90-year history as perhaps the most racially-harmonious activity in all of American society. Decades before integration occurred on the baseball field, in the armed forces, in civil service, in schools and universities, or anywhere, it was happening on the jazz bandstand. The fact that jazz music operates on such a high artistic level only strengthens the virtue of this positioning. It proclaims, in effect, "See what glory results when races work together," as the Olympic Dream Teams did for American basketball. Nor does the inclusion of white jazz composers/musicians of high caliber, much like the presence of Messrs. Bird, Stockton and Mullen on Dream Team I, in any way diminish the primacy of African-American contributions.

I have a hard time seeing any corporate sponsor refusing to support this positioning (i.e., "jazz is America's finest racial harmony"), and even envision a coordinated trade effort along these lines. JLC's blatant reverse racism — especially coming from such a presumably high-minded, high-profiled, and highly funded perch — seriously undermines this kind of commercial potential, not to mention jazz music's extraordinary multiracial legacy. "Ugly with a capital 'ugh!'"

**Festival Review I**   O. K., O. K., I'll get down from my soapbox and talk about what actually does take place when you walk through the doors, which absolutely nobody knocks. (Even Collier praised Marsalis' musicianship and the artistry of JLC's shows during their debate.) Despite their bunker mentality in the press room, Marsalis and friends are positively loose and swinging on stage. Mary Fiance, Assistant to the Director, explains:

- "One of the things that makes us a different program from the Village Vanguard and any of the clubs or anything, is that when [jazz musicians] play the Village Vanguard, they maybe have one day of rehearsal and then play six shows. We do it the reverse. We have six rehearsals for one show. And that is something that Wynton really prides his program on. I mean, people are paying not a little price for a ticket; they want to get the best quality, and he wants to present the best quality. So by the time they get out there, they know what they're doing. They can have fun with it on stage because they know the music. And they can do improvisations all the time with each other, kidding around or whatever."

It's been a few years since I've been there, but I can still recall the interior of Alice Tully Hall where CLASSICAL JAZZ' occurs. It's a high rectangular box on the inside, which weds modernist austerity with modern plushness — tastefully. Picture a cross between an ascetic cathedral and the interior of a millionaire's pleasure cruiser. The ceiling fans out into art-deco-shaped baffles, like ripples from the boat's wake. Fabric seats, thick carpets, velvet trim, polished rails, lacquered wood and the high copper pipes of the stage organ all blend into a soothing bath of earth tones and hushed sounds.

To play in wonderful spaces like this, I can almost justify jazz musicians selling out to classical-music establishments.

**Artist Mini-Review**   I caught a '92 show entitled, "Blue Clarinet Stomp: The Music of [Jelly Roll] Morton and [Johnny] Dodds." I've always enjoyed my records of composer/pianist Morton's Spanish-tinged melancholia (indeed, I can't understand why Marvin Hamlisch couldn't work the more chronologically-correct Morton into his film score for "The Sting"), but knew nothing about trumpeter Dodds. The thematic orientation was primarily to show Morton's use of rhythm — his own compositions evolving from the early substitution of instruments for drums; and Dodds' use of phrasing — his own playing evolving from the early substitution of instruments for voice. It's a nice parallel, one well-explained by Crouch in his liner notes and Music Director, Dr. Michael White, in his musical selections.

A key feature was to remind us that these musical developments evolved from the streets and dancehalls, there being no formal academy for learning jazz music in the '20s. Accordingly, the finely tuned 11-piece LCJO adopted a stance of sass and informality, ribbing each other and Marsalis, especially, who took it good naturedly and responded by blowing all that much harder.

The program kicked off with "Sidewalk Blues," complete with dialogue and car-horn blasts. Next up was "Pearls," one of my faves, where the horns really hammed it up to capture that N' Awlins street feel. They blatted, splurted and splatted — the musical equivalent of mugging for the camera. "Smokehouse Blues" featured a pair of sensationally brash solos from Fred Lonzo on trombone and White on clarinet. "Wolverine Blues" was jaunty and unabashedly melodic. Marcus Roberts took an interesting solo piano turn on "The Cream," as if accompanying silent film. He added some avant flourishes, such as mimicking the effects of a piano roll fast-forwarding or being scratched. The full band took over for "Mr. Jelly Lord," a lead into early Ellingtonia, with a wonderfully sinister and gluttonous beat, big and fat.

And so it went for a long, satisfying and crowd-pleasing bill of seventeen numbers plus an encore, "Lagniappe." Highlights included Marsalis' outrageous solo antics on "Wildman Blues," plus White's soulful stylings on "Blue Clarinet Stomp," with the band foot-stomping along en route to a rousing conclusion.

Two years later Fiance remembered that night as a standout, as well, adding: "That's primarily due to Wynton's dedication to making sure that it's rehearsed... I think the programming really stands on its own. You know, we're just going to keep putting it out there, hoping that people enjoy what we're presenting and learn something while they're listening."

If you go you should know there's more than just music. In addition to "Jazz Talks," there's also **Attendance** "Jazz On Film" screenings to round out a handsome educational perspective. Throughout the year **Tip** Marsalis also hosts three "Jazz For Young People" concerts, modelled after those from the late Leonard Bernstein.

If you miss the August festival, you can still catch one of the many JLC concerts during the year. **See Also** Or the LCJO on one of it's frequent tours across the country. Or Marsalis' syndicated radio program on NPR. Or JLC's live TV broadcasts on PBS. Or you can purchase any or all of a planned series of five JLC discs on SONY. That's outreach (not to mention bucks)! I can't think of another festival that offers you so many different means to sample the merchandise beforehand.

~      ~      ~

*The Moondogs, Rockaway Irish Festival.*

# Lower Manhattan's Carnival

MOTHER'S DAY CARIBBEAN ALL-STARS FESTIVAL, Manhattan, NYC
> Early May
> Reggae, Ska and Caribbean
> ***Attended***

TRIBUTE TO AFRICAN DIASPORA WOMEN, Manhattan, NYC
> Middle May
> African American
> ***Attended***

CARNIVAL IN NEW YORK, Manhattan, NYC
> Early August
> Reggae, Ska and Caribbean
> ***Attended***

UPRISE AND SHINE YOUTH CONCERT, Brooklyn, NYC
> Late August
> Rap

EXPRESSIONS INTERNATIONAL FESTIVAL, Manhattan, NYC
> Late September to Late October
> Variety, General

CHANGO CELEBRATION, Manhattan, NYC
> Early December
> Traditional Latin
> ***Attended***

**Introduction**

There are innumerable features meriting praise from among the seemingly innumerable festivals produced by the Caribbean Cultural Center. But the one feature that's always impressed me most has been the quality of their audiences in attendance. Discard whatever preconceived images you may hold of wasted white collegians flailing their tie-dyed gladrags, or roving packs of unchaperoned black teens posturing like "gangsta's." These are family crowds, classy family crowds, drawn from among the 500,000 native Caribbeans currently residing within New York City borders. It's a welcoming environment where you'll typically see:

- Entire broods, from grannies to toddlers.

- Most everyone well-dressed, Caribbean style, in coordinated casual wear featuring vibrant patterns and fabrics, all pressed and creased.

- The full range of participation, from quiet concentration to exuberant dancing, but always under control and conscious both of artists and fellow revelers.

I'll never forget one young father at last year's CARNIVAL IN NEW YORK [CARNIVAL'], for example, gathering his three elementary school-aged children around to pay attention to legendary Cuban percussion/dance troupe, Los Munequitos de Matanzas. "Listen up," he bid them, "Here's the roots."

Indeed, it's this pride in their cultural origins and in their accomplishments surviving this tough, tough town that drives Caribbean participation in these celebrations. *New York Newsday*'s Jonathon Mandell, in his recent feature article, "Caribbean Leaves It's Mark on City: Dreams, Hard Work Pay Off," summarizes the latest census data that "the percentage of Caribbean-born families in New York [City] who earned middle-class (and upper middle-class) incomes more than doubled in 10 years... More specifically, half the black households whose members were born in the West Indies earned between $25,000 and $75,000 in 1990." Similar success was recorded for those of West-Indian descent born in the U. S.

Mandell then quotes John Mollenkopf, Director of the Center for Urban Research at the City University of New York Graduate Center, to explain this industrious and, frequently, entre-. preneurial orientation: "West Indians are more likely to have two or three people working in their households. Both parents are working and maybe one of their kids, too. It's part of the West-Indian culture that people shouldn't go on welfare, that everybody in the household should work."

In other words, the West-Indian family that works together, stays together. And that's basically what you're experiencing as you comfortably make your way around the wonderful pot-pourri of CARNIVAL' and its many companion festivals. Families are together; folks are together as the diverse musical cultures of the entire Caribbean come together, individually and collectively. Respectful inclusion reigns on most every level, and you'll certainly want to include yourself and your family among these ascending celebrants!

The architect of this cultural embrace is Marta Vega. This articulate spokesperson for all things Caribbean founded the Caribbean Cultural Center, known formally as the Franklin H. Williams Caribbean Cultural Center African Diaspora Institute, in '76. She'd been an academic scholar and was continually chagrined to find so little study in American universities pertaining to her Puerto Rican upbringing. Push came to shove during one of her research fellowships in which Vega identified museum collections of the Caribbean visual arts that were under-utilized, poorly documented, improperly stored and generally inaccessible to the public, not to mention to "communities of color," as she terms them. Vega subsequently launched the Center — the first of its kind anywhere — to further this particular mission.

Yet one important mission quickly begat another and Vega soon found herself documenting the impact of African cultural traditions en toto on global cultures. This broader view evolved because she sees the 2,000-mile arc of Caribbean islands as sharing one common root — African ancestry. Accordingly, her Center's many activities seek to spotlight the entire sweep of such influence. It's not just Jamaican or Trinidadian or another immediately identifiable Caribbean island, but every musical and artistic form which flows from the "African Diaspora," including a strong Latin exploration. A parallel objective of such a wide vision is the Center's dedication to "foster cross-racial and cross-cultural understanding and respect. The paradigm," as their materials continue, "is cultural equity," and I appreciate how it never stoops to denigrate European or other cultures to do so, but rather elevates its own in all its fullness and glory. No polarizing PC rants here.

Given Vega's academic strengths, the Center has gone on to develop a wealth of scholastic programs — lectures, curriculum development, institutional consulting, teacher-parent workshops, in-school cultural programs and exhibitions, and so forth. Now renting a brownstone in midtown Manhattan, the Center also maintains its own art gallery, an international gift shop, and a Resource and Research Center containing books, magazines and audio-visual materials. All that, alone, would be enough to secure Vega's creation as a significant pioneer in roots study.

Vega's not content merely to document her Caribbean culture, though. She aims to celebrate it! And that's where all these marvelous festivals come in.

- First was the EXPRESSIONS INTERNATIONAL FESTIVAL, which Con Edison has sponsored since it's inception in '79. This month-long series rotates among multiple venues throughout October with an eye toward exploring particular cultural issues, but with an ear into solid enjoyment of music, dance, comedy, dance, visual arts, etc. A typical example was '93's

"Boko Lusanga: African Traditions in Hip Hop." Friday booked an afternoon "Block Party/Rally" with "up-and-coming rap artists 'on the positive tip' promoting voter registration and awareness." Saturday and Sunday afternoon hosted a conference highlighting "the significance of hip hop as an expression of African Diasporic cultures and as an important music movement." Sunday evening wrapped it up with a concert featuring KRS 1, The Jungle Brothers, Blue, Black and Brown, The Last Poets, 99, The Forces of Nature Dance Company, "and lots more." Mind you, that's just one weekend among four!

- Second was the CHANGO CELEBRATION, typically held in Aaron Davis Hall in Harlem's CUNY campus during the second weekend in December. This single-evening concert, recalling the Yoruban warrior-god of discipline and protection, takes a Latin slant by mixing folkloric stars from Cuba with modern purveyors from America. A fine sample was '93's tenth-year bill of rumba pioneers Los Munequitos de Matanzas, superb salsa percussionist Daniel Ponce with his band, Arawe, and fine local bomba-meisters, Los Pleneros de la 21. You can also count on a multimedia accompaniment — possibly a speaker, a slide show, an art exhibit, and/or a dance presentation — to further your appreciation .

- Third was CARNIVAL'. "Begun ten years ago as a street party for our community," Vega explains of '94's anniversary, "[it] was held on West 58th Street outside of the Center's brownstone. Over the years, as more and more people heard about it and culturally diverse forms of music became more popular, the event kept growing and we moved it to a park on the west side. This year, we've outgrown that park and we're delighted to hold our tenth anniversary at Battery Park City in a beautiful new park near the Hudson River."

"Beautiful" is actually an understatement for '94's location (one of the few places in Manhattan where you can actually lounge on fresh sod) and it's pristine, exalted surroundings amidst this freshly-planned mini-metropolis. Try "stunning," though CARNIVAL' has been such a gloriously friendly, colorful, entertaining and fully-featured bonanza of late that you'd have barely noticed the old park being little more than a scruffy baseball field off the West Side Highway with barely a blade of grass to its name. Come the first full weekend in August, there's always one main stage hosting eight continuous hours of ecumenical music both days, as well as a second stage devoted exclusively to children's activities. There's also a swath of 80 vendors offerings exceptional ethnic food and crafts at exceptionally affordable prices. Plus, the whole shebang's free, as if you needed any further excuse to plan a trip for your family.

- Fourth was the TRIBUTE TO AFRICAN DIASPORA WOMEN. This event, too, has been a single-evening, multimedia affair at Aaron Davis Hall since '87, leaning toward the rhythms of modern jazz and dance. In this case, homage is paid to Oshun, Yoruban goddess of love, beauty and community, and you can count on at least one high-powered female performer to do the honors. In '93 this meant rising jazz-piano sensation, Geri Allen, with a fine young local Latin vocalist, Cecelia Englehart, and her jazz group Tanaora, opening up.

- Fifth was the UPRISE AND SHINE YOUTH CONCERT, which moves to a skating rink in Brooklyn for a single-afternoon blowout in late August. Here, a minimum of six school-age "rap, reggae and Latin music performers," as the flyer describes, "bring the stay-in-school message to New York City's young people." I can't speak for all the acts, but one mainstay, the *New York Daily News*-sponsored C. A. S. Y. M. Steel Orchestra, is terrific. It's a poised group of teens and pre-teens who percolate a set-list of pop tunes with lugubrious rhythms and soulfulness.

That's just the perennial happenings!

The Center is also busy all throughout the year producing special concert tributes, hosting various music series, collaborating with many other New York City festivals, and booking periodic performance tours. In fact, it's become such an important conduit of Caribbean music for artists, venues and audiences, alike, that Vega's had it function as a booking agency at different times. Needless to say, such involvement brings the Center closely in-tune with what it takes to bring forth top-flight performances from every angle.

From my experiencing nearly half-a-dozen of its festivals, I consider the Center a model for roots-music programming. Strong production values and expert introductions, aside, here's what makes Vega's musical presentations so special.

Far too often, the Caribbean roots music that appears at many folk festivals is a token group or two that may actually be authentic (indeed, they often sound like they were happened upon during one of the producer's ecotourism forages, and airlifted from some remote village to play an American stage for the first time). However, they tend to sacrifice dynamism for such rusticity. Vega, on the other hand, books only the very, very best artists, often legends in their native lands, yet who are experts in entertaining, too. Los Munequitos de Matanzas is one such heritage act the Center's been associated with; Lazaro Ros is another. With performers of this stature and charisma, you'll leave educated, but also deeply moved and/or dancing frenetically. "Baile" is the word!

That's just for starters, though. Vega departs from folk festival norms, furthermore, by sparing nothing to integrate top Caribbean pop performers into her festival bills. Scanning last year's CARNIVAL' bill, it may be someone who's huge in their native lands, but lesser know here (e.g., acclaimed Haitian band Boukman Eksperyans); someone's who's big here, if not yet elsewhere (e.g. New York City's own charting "salsero" Tito Nieves); and/or someone who's recognized everywhere (e.g., world-renowned "Queen of Calypso," Calypso Rose).

Vega will then mix in all different musical styles enjoyed by New York City's Afro-Latin-Caribbean community, from Haitian compas, to Puerto Rican salsa, to Dominican merengue, to Mexican cumbia, to Zairean zoukous, to Brazilian capoeira, as well as whatever contemporary sounds its younger listeners are grooving to, such as Bronx-born rap (e.g., Doug E. Fresh) or Jamaican reggae dancehall (e.g., Brigadier General). Finally, she'll balance mainstream acts (e.g., Johnny Pacheco's band featuring Pete "El Conde" Rodriguez) with others more "on the edge," while inserting only the leading locals for support. It all works famously for nearly all ages, ethnicities and sensibilities, and helps create an enlightened vibe that the entire family can party to throughout the day.

Which brings us full-circle to CARNIVAL's classy crowds.

What really makes a festival notable is when you feel like you're entering the best of an entirely new world. We're talking lineup quality, ideally, but also the authentic audience for such a lineup so that you can really get to know who the music's for and how it's meant to be responded to. It may be bluegrass music among Bill Monroe's longtime faithful "pickers and grinners" (see BEAN BLOSSOM BLUEGRASS FESTIVAL, Bean Blossom, IN, Middle June), country music surrounded by 24,000 fan-club devotees (see INTERNATIONAL COUNTRY MUSIC FAN FAIR, Nashville, TN, Late June), or any number of other landmark gatherings.

Here it's truly the next ethnic generations living the American dream; indeed, much of what America increasingly will look and sound like over the next half-century. It's reassuring to see these families are essentially no different from your's and mine in their underlying makeup and aspirations. It's exciting to be experiencing such an intoxicating culture thriving within our midst, and it's impressive that, under Vega's encompassing stewardship, their culture is in such capable hands.

Now CARNIVAL' and its brethren don't pack the full-frontal assault of Brooklyn's massive WEST INDIAN-AMERICAN DAY CARNIVAL AND PARADE (see chapter). They're more modest, ranging from the few hundred attendees at the Aaron Davis Hall events to, maybe, one hundred thousand for CARNIVAL'. Especially CARNIVAL', however, yields a perfect point of departure to enter this Caribbean world stateside and its varied family of Afro-descended music. Just remember to bring your own family, some cash for the crafts, oh, and your dancing shoes, too!

**Festival Review**   For a modern space, Aaron Davis Hall, site of the TRIBUTE TO AFRICAN DIASPORA WOMEN, certainly possesses an inviting vibe. True, the brick walls of the inner auditorium rise forbiddingly high, but the remaining surfaces are all warm, soft and comfortable. The seats are cloth-covered, the lobby is sculpted and draped with banners, and the wrap-around glass entry lets the afternoon sunshine soak into all the carpeted surfaces. Earth tones prevail.

The Caribbean Cultural Center contributed its own sense of welcome by installing an exhibit of ethnic quilts on the lobby's fabric walls, and hosting a modest gathering of Caribbean food merchants and African crafts vendors upon the courtyard steps. Upon arriving, you felt more like you were stealing your way into a classy house party among cooks and artists than for anything resembling a formal concert.

The day had actually begun ten hours earlier with a conference, "21st Century Women: Looking Back, Moving On," followed by a poetry reading of her own work by Tracie Morris. I arrived in time for the concert proceedings beginning at 8:00 p.m.

First up, excerpts from a multimedia collaboration between <u>Merian Soto and Pepon Osorio</u>. **Artist** Entitled "Historias," their dance piece, augmented by slides and narration, illustrated the cause **Mini-Reviews** and effects of a longtime Puerto Rican program of sterilization as the primary state-sponsored form of birth control. It told this horrific tale from multiple points of view, but most movingly from the perspectives of victimized women. I found it chilling and heart-rending — one of the very few examples I've experienced that successfully melded politics, art and emotion without undo preaching. (Lincoln Center's highly selective SERIOUS FUN! programmed "Historias" for that year's series.)

<u>Cecelia Englehart</u> followed on a lighter, more lilting side. Backed by her group, <u>Tanaora</u> (Jamie Haddad on drums, Leo Travesa on bass, and Bill O'Connell on piano), this local jazz vocalist proved an unexpected delight with her bright personality, full-ranging attack and thoughtful, affirmative songwriting. Picture a Latina version of Flora Purim in black tights and red pumps, and you get a sense of her music's worldly parameters, as well as her cheery improvisational tone. Though I enjoyed Englehart's free-flowing originals, I felt her phrasing gained purpose from the crisper and more varied structure of her closing cover, Jobim's "Onda" ("Wave"), sung in Brazilian. Kudos to Vega on her ear for this promising young talent!

Of course, most every jazz insider already knows of pianist and Pittsburgh native, <u>Geri Allen</u> — one of the real comers among jazz's rising elite. Surprisingly, though, few area festivals have caught up enough to book her. So credit Vega, again, for being ahead of the musical curve.

Allen's concluding performance here was a treat and a half! Sporting a white silk tunic and matching headdress, she led her two-piece rhythm section through all kinds of diverse stylistic tangents — spotlighting, say, the creative angularity of Thelonious Monk, the linear melodiousness of Keith Jarrett, and the African rhythms of Randy Weston, for starters. I know all that sounds like a stretch of comparisons, but Allen managed to assimilate these qualities and more gracefully and accessibly all throughout her set.

My highlight came with her third tune, "Dreamtime," in which Allen deconstructed traditional blues during an unrelenting 10-minute solo. Artfully interspersing her own lusty modernism, she helped you hear the blues anew in current context. The crowd came alive in participation, and I only wish Allen's impressive display could have gone on all night long. Catch her if you can!

Even among those festivals the Caribbean Cultural Center doesn't handle, if it lends its name, or **See Also** is otherwise involved, you can usually count on quality. An excellent example is the nearly 20-year-old MOTHER'S DAY CARIBBEAN ALL-STARS FESTIVAL, which they endorse (though don't produce) and where they exhibit in the lobby.

This annual happening occupies Madison Square Garden's plush Felt Forum and features a veritable parade of calypso's finest backed by two rotating eight-piece bands. It's a boisterous, high-energy showcase that starts slowly, then quickly picks up momentum as each big-name entertainer seeks to best the prior one's response by inciting the crowd via outrageous lyrics and antics. Fun triumphs throughout both five-hour shows — one Saturday night, the other Sunday afternoon. Be forewarned that these popular events often sell out. You'd best buy your tickets at least two weeks ahead.

~     ~     ~

# August Jazz Freebies

WESTCHESTER COMMUNITY COLLEGE JAZZ FESTIVAL, Valhalla, NY
   Early May
   Modern Jazz

RIVERSIDE PARK ARTS FESTIVAL, Manhattan, NYC
   Early August to Late August
   Variety, Jazz and Blues
   ***Attended***

CHARLIE PARKER JAZZ FESTIVAL, Manhattan, NYC
   Late August
   Modern Jazz
   ***Attended***

**Introduction**   When you attempt to navigate New York City, it pays to go against the grain — taking vacations, negotiating traffic, landing parking, going shopping, scoring tickets, making reservations, whatever. Everything's such a mad crush that you've got to plan to be wherever everybody's not. Just as often, you'll find yourself better off with better bargains to boot.

Take outdoor jazz. All the hype whirls around the JVC JAZZ FESTIVAL (see chapter) toward the end of June. After that, most upscale Manhattanites head for the Hamptons. But the dog days of August offer several pleasant surprises: high quality lineups in low key settings. This contrary month may yield jazz fans the most unhassled listening of the year. And each event is priced right — free!

First, there's LINCOLN CENTER OUT-OF-DOORS, now into its third decade. Originally disparaged by critics as little more than a grab bag of performing arts offerings strewn across disciplines, genres and ethnicities, it's grown in recent years to encompass the most inclusive representation of local jazz. This year, not only did it feature the single best day of Latin jazz witnessed all year (Eddie Palmieri Orchestra, Jerry Gonzalez and The Fort Apache Band, and Danilo Perez, plus Los Pleneros del Coco and Inca Son), but it also ran the gamut:

- From the copious swing scene personified by Panama Francis' Savoy Sultans to such downtown avant-meisters from The Knitting Factory (**Downtown Jazz, II** — see chapter) as Roy Nathanson;

- From the mainstream stylings of Grady Tate and Jay Hoggard to cutting edge champions like Andrew Cyrille and P. S. 122's Deidre Murray (**Downtown Jazz, I** — see chapter).

In doing so, it quietly rebuked the controversially exclusive CLASSICAL JAZZ AT LINCOLN CENTER (see chapter), which kicked off the month.

Toss in everything else that goes on in Damrosch Park — music galore, dance aplenty and lotsa' kid's stuff — and LINCOLN CENTER OUT-OF-DOORS gives you several good excuses each week of the month to sneak up there for a breather. And, of course, its happy-hour kickoffs conveniently dodge the rush hour and position you nicely for early bistro tables afterward. Against the grain, you see?

Second, there are still two more festivals with even bigger acts and lower profiles: the RIVERSIDE PARK ARTS FESTIVAL [RIVERSIDE'] and the CHARLIE PARKER JAZZ FESTIVAL [CHARLIE PARKER']. Both deliver uniquely tranquil vibes in hidden corners of the city redolent with greenery and local color. Best of all, you'll likely scoop even your Manhattan friends on these two (although maybe we'd best keep them our own private secret for now).

Promoter Mark Morganelli, himself a noted jazz trumpeter and composer, as well as a prolific record producer, sums up RIVERSIDE's appeal best. **Festival Review I**

- "I think a lot of it is that people are surprised that you can hear music of such high quality in New York City for nothing! You can just come in, happen off the street and check out, like, last year the finale was Clark Terry, Slide Hampton, Jimmy Heath, Barry Harris, Buster Williams, Ben Riley and Winard Harper [laughs]. Just the fact that families feel comfortable coming there and safe. And it's an enjoyable thing — no pressure in a nice setting."

Not only does the well-networked Morganelli select from among his copious contacts and performing heros, but he gets to present them a few subway stops down from his apartment in a thoroughly delightful environment. Picture a cozy stone rotunda far from the madding crowd where you can gaze underneath the vaulted arches into the little known 79th Street Boat Basin, then onto the Hudson River and the majestic Palisades beyond. The circular space can comfortably accommodate about a thousand (though it feels more like a few hundred) for what becomes a thoroughly multiracial, multiethnic, multigenerational day in the park with a real focus on families. Morganelli's own wife and kids are frequently seen passing the donation buckets, manning the small refreshment and concession stand, or keeping little tots from wandering too far down the ramp toward the intimately proximate stage bowl.

In short, RIVERSIDE's a real agreeable treat.

The refreshingly casual and accommodating Morganelli, who'll turn 40 in '95, started playing trumpet when he was eight. This native of Glen Head, Long Island, fueled his muse while a member of the busy Bucknell University's Jazz and Rock Ensemble. His grades slid precariously with all that school band's work, but it boosted him to return to New York City in the late '70s and begin networking the big band circuit. In '79 Morganelli contributed to a burgeoning loft jazz scene by launching his own Jazz Forum in a succession of Greenwich Village spaces. Simultaneously, his various performing interests began infiltrating the neighborhood's elite clubs — the Blue Note, the Village Vanguard, Sweet Basil's, Fat Tuesday's, etc.

"Just to bring it full circle," Morganelli adds:

- "What I wound up doing at my Jazz Forum was in '82 I recorded my first album called 'Live on Broadway.' That was on my own label, Jazz Forum Records. Then in '87 went in the studio and recorded my second album called 'Five Is Bliss.' The first album featured one tune that I wrote. The second album featured six of my tunes, five standards, and I made it on all three formats. At the time that was still being done. And then my third album was done live in '90 at Birdland for Candide Records, for which I have produced 40 albums for that label."

Among his producing highlights include a number of performances recorded live at RIVERSIDE': Kenny Barron and Barry Harris' "Confirmation at Riverside Park"; Barron and John Hicks' "Rhythm-N-Ing". Also, a Red Rodney/Ira Sullivan collaboration called "Sprint," nominated for a Grammy, was recorded at Morganelli's Jazz Forum.

While Morganelli's record-producing career took off, however, his loft concerts lost their venue. Subsequent presenting at the Village Gate and the Intermedia Theater "took some financial hits," he relays, "and I said, 'Hey, later on this!'

- "And luck would have it, I met my wife at our 10th-year high school reunion out in Glen Head, and that was ten years ago. I moved into her apartment on West End [Avenue] and 102nd Street and went to a meeting of the Friends of Riverside Park, which, I guess, is the precursor to the Riverside Park Fund. 'Met Charles McKinney there, who is the Director of the park, and I said at the meeting, 'Why don't you have music at Riverside Park,' and he said, 'Why don't you do it?'

  "I took up the gantlet, and about a year later I started this thing called the FIRST ANNUAL RIVERSIDE PARK SUMMER MUSIC SERIES. I played four or five gigs [on] weekends in a row with my band featuring different musicians and different composers."

Morganelli cobbled together funding from various sources, including his own musician's union, and the series was born.

He faced two main obstacles. First, the rotunda was, like Grant's Tomb up the road and far too many other New York City park facilities, allowed to fall into decrepitude. "People tried to dissuade me from doing it down there," Morganelli recalls:

- "But the space is a really great space. It's got a lot of character, great vibe, and you're by the boats. We've really built it. There used to be, like, 40 or 50 homeless people living down there and [it] stunk of urine. We had some rough years, don't let me kid you, where every year I would say I'm giving it up."

Second, under the heading of "no good deed goes unpunished," Morganelli subsumed his small jazz series into a larger multi-discipline festival entitled the ROTUNDA ARTS FESTIVAL, and volunteered to direct that, too. "One year there I totally drove myself crazy," he exclaims:

- "It was one of those summers where it was 100 degrees every day, like this, and I had four events per week for 10 weeks! We had dance, theater, music, jazz music, ethnic music, classical music, rehearsals — it was unbelievable!

"I eventually toned the thing down, and scaled it back, and up-graded it artistically to be a much more intense, enjoyable festival. Now, consequently, we have the shortest duration this summer, but I think up there in quality with any of them."

**Artist Mini-Reviews** I asked Morganelli about his RIVERSIDE' highlights over the years. One was a concert I caught in '92 featuring the late Red Rodney:

- "It was a wonderful gig because everyone just had a ball. I think we recorded that for NPR. It was Barry Harris, Ray Drummond, Red Rodney and Ben Riley. It wound up being a real empathetic group. Everyone had a ball and played a lot of Bird tunes. It just was a great gig."

Another was a duet between Tommy Flanagan and Barry Harris:

- "The first one we did down there when we had a thunderstorm, an electrical storm, and they kept playing 'Here's That Rainy Day' as a bossa nova, modulating up by half steps. It was unbelievable! That also was recorded for NPR. I wanted to put out an album of it, but we never got that out."

His fondest memory, though, is of a Brazilian samba band, Pe-De-Boi:

- "There were literally 100 to 200 people hanging over the edge of the traffic circle dancing to samba when they where playing 'Brazil.' [sings] They had the place rocking! It was wall-to-wall people. People were inside the circle inside the fountain — right up inside the stage! It was just one of those incredible moments."

Given that endorsement, I rousted up my sister and brother-in-law and caught Pe-De-Boi (Portuguese for "foot of the bull") in '94. The crowd this time wasn't nearly as charged, though this easy-swingin' seven-member ensemble continued to smile and exhort their seated listeners to get up and dance if the spirit moved them.

They began as a five-piece marching percussion troupe, snaking their way out of the dressing room and onto the stage. Their rhythms were rich, though more in a street sense, with the lead snare acting as the traffic cop in directing the densely chooglin' crew through their paces. I wouldn't say Pe-De-Boi had the dynamic star quality of, say, a Gal Costa (but who does?), though I enjoyed the cheery lines of their vocalist and the solid spurts of their saxophonist.

That changed, however, when guest artist Steve Turre took the stage for the last three tunes. You may recognize this recorded horn man (Antilles/PLG) from his weekly appearances in TV's Saturday Night Live Band. He's the beatnik-looking guy with the flowing cookie-duster and ponytail tucked under a pork pie hat. The stocky, tunic-clad Turre grabbed his trombone and juiced the lilting flow perfectly, exhibiting a technique equal parts fluid and punchy, almost like another percussion player.

But for the second song, he reached down into his trunk, pulled out an incredible array of conch shells and proceeded to blow with the same tone, passion and facility. Even the band members' jaws dropped at Turre's agile display (including on two conches at once) as the crowd rose from their seats and roared! Novel and wonderful.

~     ~     ~

Of all my interviews, this was the one I'd been dreading most all year. CHARLIE PARKER's announcer, Phil Schapp, has got to be the world's greatest authority on Charlie Parker. This "ornithologist-in-residence" runs an hour-long show on WKCR-FM every morning devoted to "Bird" — nothing but Bird — and I've never heard his erudite commentary ever flag or repeat. His knowledge on this jazz topic, and most others, is so encyclopedic I imagine many artists call him to confirm their own bios or discographies. With my diminutive jazz study, I feared he'd skin me alive!

**Festival Review II**

Fortunately, for this humble observer, Schapp turned out to be merely a beneficent participant. I was pleased to discover that CHARLIE PARKER's actual founder comes from as modest a position as myself. Chantal Lindh is a public school teacher in my bohemian East Village neighborhood. She's always been a jazz lover and knew of Parker's former residence nearby at 151 Avenue B.

"I thought it would be good for the kids to help develop their awareness of jazz and birds by having the street named Charlie Parker Place," Lindh explains:

- "So I started that a couple of years ago, and my son and a couple of his friends helped me collect signatures. Then I went to City Council and they approved it. [Antonio] Pagan is our Councilman for this area and he supported it, so we decided to have a big celebration about the street naming. That's how we started about thinking about what kind of celebration to have."

Lindh went up to Parker's house in '93 and called upon its current owner, Judy Sneed, a photographer of jazz musicians and long-time musical booker. Lindh recalls:

- "Well, we wanted to have a festival. We had a variety of things to try and appeal to a lot of people, yet we also had people who performed with Bird. So that is really important to us to try always to have one group or two that were friends, or knew Bird, or performed or recorded with him."

Sneed, now Lindh's Artistic Director, helped put together a remarkable lineup on a shoestring, including Charlie Sepulveda and Turnaround, The Roy Haynes Quartet, The Red Rodney Quartet, and such special guests as Jackie McLean, Hank Jones, Percy Heath, Sheila Jordan, Kim Parker, Billy Higgins and others. (The backstage area looked like a veritable who's who all renewing their acquaintance with hugs and laughs.)

Lindh's four-person committee posted photocopied flyers about the area. Boosted by a preview from noted critic Gene Santoro, as well as Schapp's 24-hour broadcast the day before, they awoke to find the recently refurbished Thomkins Square Park packed to the rafters! And this in a place more known for homeless protests, drag contests and skirmishes between cops and heavy-metal heads. A superb afternoon of music followed redolent with "warm vibes," as *New York Newsday*'s Gene Seymour described.

"Everybody that I talked to had a really great time and really enjoyed it. It was really positive to me," Lindh notes. "We're having Milt Jackson this year, and Percy and Jimmy and Tootie Heath are going to be playing with him. So they all want to come back. I presume they enjoyed it, too." This year, Lindh's committee graduated from the street-naming toward having Bird's house listed on the National Register of Historic Places. A similar lineup ensued, highlighted by a performance of Butch Morris' "Conduction No. 44: Ornithology," with Arthur Blythe handling the lead.

Lindh's proud to be honoring Parker and filling a festival void in this part of the city "considering there are so many clubs down here, and so many musicians live in the area. And also from New York, too, you feel like Chicago and all these places have really incredible, creative, free festivals. We just don't have things like that here."

Her neighborly ambitions, however, don't stop with merely maintaining jazz on the last Sunday in August, laudable as that is:

- We're really intending to raise funds so we can have musicians play in the schools during the school year; to tell the kids who really do live in the neighborhood about Bird more; to continue an educational process with music. The city schools are struggling. I bring musicians that know personally to play for the kids and things like that in an informal way, but unless you're really like that it doesn't always happen all that much. The funding just isn't always there.

"That's why we want to fill that gap in the community," Lindh concludes. "We hope to keep going. We are definitely forging ahead!"

~          ~          ~

**Attendance Tip**   Lindh suggests:

- "You might want to highlight that around the park there are many different, interesting restaurants that are not too expensive, and certainly, too, it being a close proximity to [Greenwich Village] clubs. For them to come to our event that's free in the day, [they can] have an inexpensive meal and then be able to hear music at night. They can hear a lot of great music in a six-to-eight-hour period without really having to travel anywhere."

I'd add for CHARLIE PARKER' that, while there is pleasant, shaded lounging to be had back on the grass, if you want sight lines up close, you should arrive at least 30 minutes early. (I came a bit late; that's why I've no performance notes.) Same goes for getting a chair at RIVERSIDE'.

**See Also**   Morganelli's programming reach extends in two more directions. First, there's his Jazz at the Music Hall in Tarrytown winter series, which features big names at the delightfully restored turn-of-the-century theater about an hour's drive north. "It's a great hall," Morganelli exclaims! "You have to hear the music there." Second, he launched the first annual WESTCHESTER COMMUNITY COLLEGE JAZZ FESTIVAL in '94, which boasted ten continuous hours of jazz, topped off with The Phil Woods Quintet.

Morganelli's own performing interest, The Jazz Forum All-Stars, is also a ubiquitous presence at festivals and clubs throughout the region. Friends like Donald Harrison and Slide Hampton frequently sit it. Look for 'em!

Finally, further up Riverside Park at Grant's Tomb near 123rd Street is the long-running and much beloved Jazzmobile. Every summertime Wednesday evening from 5:00 to 8:00 p.m. name acts "give back" to the community on a portable stage surrounded by a crafts market of African vendors. I've not yet caught a Jazzmobile gig, but I've never heard anything other than positive things. The JVC JAZZ FESTIVAL and LINCOLN CENTER OUT-OF-DOORS, for example, both program annual benefits for this worthy cause.

~          ~          ~

# Queens' Gospel Radio Picnic

SAVE OUR PARK/WWRL RADIOTHON, Queens, NYC
> Late May
> Black Gospel

SOUTHEAST QUEENS' YOUTH SPORTS AND SPRING FESTIVAL/JUNETEENTH, Queens, NYC
> Middle June
> African American

**WWRL FAMILY DAY PICNIC AND FESTIVAL**, Queens, NYC
> Early August to Middle August
> Black Gospel
> ***Attended***

NORTHEAST NATIVE AMERICAN ASSOCIATION POW WOW, Queens, NYC
> Late September
> Native American

WWRL GOSPEL EXPLOSION, Manhattan, NYC
> Middle December
> Black Gospel

**Introduction**

Perhaps the only place other than New York City where I've experienced a similar checkerboard of affluent pockets alternating with poor pockets is in New Orleans. There, as here, you can go from upper class to lower class to middle class and back to upper class, all within a matter of blocks. Moreover, this pattern plays itself out repeatedly across both cities.

Jamaica, a large swath of eastern Queens, illustrates the situation well and demonstrates this economic patchwork is not confined to Manhattan:

- You start up top with the affluent Asian/Jewish Jamaica Estates, where St. John's University resides;

- Then descend to the commercial district/rail hub of Jamaica — once down on its heels, now looking somewhat upward with the fresh construction of York College and other retail and office buildings;

- Next move into poverty-stricken South Jamaica (with parts rivaling the destitution of the South Bronx), before coming through a transitional neighborhood of middle-class blacks bordering the working-class neighborhoods of Irish Woodhaven and Italian Ozone Park.

And that's just one section!

Roy Wilkins Park sits smack in the middle of South Jamaica, but in New York City as in New Orleans, appearances can be deceiving. The big swatch of choppy grassland seemed rough around the edges to me at the time, but it represents a spirited reclamation by the community of the former St. Albans Naval Yard, and is now in the midst of an ambitious redevelopment project. Driving around the marginal environs beforehand, I was surprised to find quite a few weed-choked lots occupied by tent revivals, and abandoned storefronts taken over by community churches. A tree of hope is growing for African-American families of South Jamaica, it seems, and it all comes together once yearly with the **WWRL FAMILY DAY PICNIC AND FESTIVAL ['PICNIC']**.

Vince Sanders speaks in deep, sonorous tones that suggest his former career as a stage actor 20 years ago. He's risen to General Manager of what's commonly acknowledged as the number one gospel music station in the country, WWRL (1600 on your AM dial). "We were the first to walk out on a 24-hour inspirational music format some 10, 11 years ago," Sanders explains. WWRL boasts a national profile, taking out a full-page ad every month in *Score*, black gospel music's leading magazine.

Although WWRL's headquartered in the Woodside section of Queens (immortalized by longtime Queens resident, Count Basie, in his "Jumpin' at the Woodside"), its 'PICNIC' didn't originate in Queens.

"I took over the station in '83," Sanders recalls, "and in '84 we did a free concert at the foot of Grant's Tomb in Central Park. The police reported that we had, between 2:00 pm and 7:00 pm on that particular day, about 60,000 people coming and going. From that I realized that there was a market for this kind of entertainment and community outreach, so we continued."

Sanders ran up against the typical bureaucratic snafus common to New York City festival promoters and bumped heads with park administrators in Manhattan and Brooklyn, respectively, before finally locating Roy Wilkins Park. "I don't recall how or what motivated me to [investigate this site]," Sanders continues, "but I struck on a great relationship with the Executive Director over there, Mr. Solomon Goodrich. ...I needed a place that I could feel comfortable doing the festival without too many encumbrances, so it led us there."

By this time Sanders had expanded the event to three days, eight hours per day, plus supplemented his strong gospel music offerings with a host of family-oriented activities: a 5K run with prizes, worship services, amusement rides, vendors, exhibitors, picnicking, celebrity guests, an awards ceremony, a fashion show, health and education pavilions, clowns, basketball, double dutch, even black cowboys. "I'm trying to deepen that penetration of family values and family entertainment and all of that," Sanders adds of his many attractions.

Perhaps, most strikingly, he's managed to corral a number of top politicians into addressing the family crowd. The year I attended featured then Mayor, David Dinkins, with a zillion of his aides. This year upped the ante with then Governor Mario Cuomo, plus a church service with Revs. Jesse Jackson and Al Sharpton. (I guess Sanders won't have to suffer low-level government pencil-pushers any longer.)

"It is our viewpoint here at the station that two few African-Americans really participate at a significant rate in the political process," Sanders notes:

- "It probably hasn't been mentioned recently, but H. Carl McCall, who is our State Comptroller [and who spoke at the '94 'PICNIC'], is also a minister; he's a preacher. And there are several leading politicians around who are preachers, you know. We think the political education is as much a part of the family requirement as anything else, so that's all part of what we do. And not only that, these people will attract other people to the festival, so it's all part of the development. There is some show business in there, and then there is some substance in there."

Sanders chuckles that '94 being an election year certainly hasn't hurt the 'PICNIC's political recruiting, which he basically delegates to the Queens Borough President, Claire Shulman.

As for the music, Sanders readily admits he doesn't keep up with it as he'd like, preferring to delegate musical matters to his program director. We talked about how New York City is not often referred to as a national gospel-music mecca in the same breath as, say, Detroit or Philadelphia, despite the station's strong presence here and the profusion of local talent on display. Sanders suggests a number of reasons, mainly that New York City's minority population is not so clearly African-American as the other markets mentioned above. This diaspora fragments the perceived images for outsiders as it splinters the musical tastes of New York City insiders.

"But the reason why the entertainers come out of New York is because all entertainers of whatever choosing come to New York to make it big," Sanders notes. "It's where the record companies and promoters are and all that sort of stuff. On the other hand, there is still a void when it

comes to a definitive description of what is gospel music that is appealing to New Yorkers."
Many local stars have, nevertheless, made an impression on Sanders:

- "We have had the support of Dorothy Norwood, as she has been sort-of our featured star
for a few years during these events. And she always goes over very well. Valerie Boyd has
worked very well with the crowd. There were other groups that worked exceptionally
well, [such as] the WWRL Community Chorale. I remembered the early years, Little Alvin
Green and the Limited...

"Our lineup will be as splendid this year, hopefully," Sanders concludes. "I'm looking forward to making this festival of all festivals. I think the theme — the restoration and preservation
of the American family as we know it and the African-American family, specifically — is so important to us all. I hope we can put some of this in the minds of all people."

**Festival Review I**

It must've been close to 100 degrees and 100% humidity the year I went, but the well-dressed,
well-behaved family crowd remained in dresses, blazers, coats and ties. O. K., maybe a few of the
men took off their suit jackets, but it was a remarkable display of self-control and respect for the
performers amidst sweltering heat.

I had to quickly dash down to the NEW YORK REGGAE FESTIVAL at Coney Island's
Steeplechase Park (see chapter). Yet I did get to hear two acts.

**Artist Mini-Reviews**

Rap Ministries Unlimited were well-meaning, but failed to connect with the mostly middle-aged
audience. Their best song, "Too Funky To Deal With," had good energy and purpose but lacked
the musicality of R&B or the fully-produced intensity of the rap you hear on the radio. Oh, well.

On the other hand, I was really impressed with Rev. Kent Rogers. Backed by the WWRL
Community Chorale, Rogers exhibited strength, style and charisma to spare in singing his hit, "All
These Years." I look forward to catching him again in a more extended set.

*New York Newsday* Staff Writer Esther Iverem spotlighted four of the 'PICNIC's headliners
in her '93 preview, "It'll Be Gospel All Weekend Long":

- Hezekiah Walker and The Love Crusade Choir, recent Grammy winner, whose
recordings, *Oh Lord We Praise You* (Sweet Rain), *Focus On Glory*, and a live album
(Benson), have all hit the Top 10 of *Billboard*'s gospel charts;

- The Jenkins Brothers, an "award-winning and best selling duo";

- Last Appeal, an acappella harmony sextet who won the '89 Regional Semifinals
of the MCDONALD'S GOSPELFEST (see chapter);

- Rev. Timothy Wright, whose "Trouble Don't Last Always" (Savoy), has been nominated for a Stellar Gospel Music Awards "Song of the Year."

All four acts she mentioned have local roots, so check 'em out at the next 'PICNIC' amongst their
hometown fans!

**See Also**

My files contain one additional concert event, the WWRL GOSPEL CONCERT EXPLOSION, which heat-
ed up Manhattan's cavernous Javits Center in '93 with a six-act bill featuring many of the 'PICNIC's
heavy-hitters. I'm not sure if this big gig occurs annually, so contact the station for confirmation.

Otherwise, you should know Roy Wilkins Park puts on an increasing number of festival
events, three more of which are listed in the heading, above. Rest assured that WWRL's presence
is never far away for the top two. Call either the park or the station for musical details.

~     ~     ~

# Brooklyn's Carnival

New York Trini-Jam Fest, Brooklyn, NYC
Early July
Reggae, Ska and Caribbean

**New York Reggae Summer Beach Party**, Brooklyn, NYC
Middle August
Reggae, Ska and Caribbean
*Attended*

**West Indian-American Day Carnival and Parade**, Brooklyn, NYC
Early September
Reggae, Ska and Caribbean
*Attended*

**Introduction** It used to be said that the biggest Polish city in the world was Chicago, owing to the Polish immigrants who settled, congregated and procreated there in greater numbers than in Warsaw.

Perhaps the same could be said of West Indians about Brooklyn. Estimates peg the West Indian population at about a half-million within the mile surrounding Eastern Parkway, route of the West Indian-American Day Carnival and Parade ['Carnival']. And that's not even including Puerto Ricans, Dominicans, Cubans and others there from throughout the Caribbean diaspora. Carlos Lezama, President and CEO of the West-Indian American Day Carnival Association, told me the mix comprises 85% of this dense urban neighborhood and forms the nucleus for a single-day 'Carnival' attendance running upwards of 2.5 million revelers. While there are no palm trees lining this stately boulevard, it just might offer you the most vivid and bountiful taste of the Islands in all of North America. On Labor Day weekend, anyway.

What's remarkable is how relatively self-contained this overwhelming happening has remained during its 27-year history. That is, until recently.

This West Indian city-within-a-city abuts a much smaller, but even-more-concentrated enclave to the west — Crown Heights, where the Lubavitcher sect of Hasidim have their world headquarters right on Eastern Parkway. Bubbling tensions flared to riots in August, '91, when an Hasidic driver, Yosef Lifsh, lost control of his car and plowed into a number of West Indians on the sidewalk, killing a 9-year-old boy, Gavin Cato. West Indians who gathered were incensed that the dazed driver made no inquiries about the boy, and how ambulance workers who arrived tended to, and transported, Lifsh and his family while ignoring Cato's body (underscoring a long-standing complaint of preferential treatment by hospitals, police and other city agencies).

Three days of fighting and bottle-throwing ensued, culminating in a mob of 16 rioters stabbing an Hasidic student from Australia, Yankel Rosenbaum, to death. The wishy-washy handling of these disturbances goaded both sides and contributed mightily to the election defeat of then-Mayor David Dinkins.

In a city of precious few heros, however, Lezama stood tall in a brave gesture of reconciliation by inviting the Hasidim to jointly lead 1991's 'Carnival' march. Apparently, this helped calm the waters and avert what many observers felt was a race war in the works.

Unfortunately, tensions resurfaced in '94. For the first time in over half-a-century, the Jewish holy day of Rosh Hashanah fell on Labor Day. Lubavitcher spokesmen had understandable concerns about their members being able to peacefully conduct their religious observances — which required them be indoors by 6:00 p.m. — as well as to freely cross the parade route to Montefiore Cemetery for visiting the grave of their recently deceased leader, the late Rebbe

Menachem Schneerson.

However, their proposal to then-Police Commissioner Raymond Kelly were so demanding that even the NYCLU found it, as the *Village Voice*'s Peter Noel reported, "'profoundly offensive' not only to West Indians, but to all New Yorkers." Amazingly, Kelly bought into nearly every request and tried to get Lezama to sign-off.

Secure, however, in the clout afforded by an event that contributes $50-to-$70 million in annual revenues; that has consistently gained permits and withstood court challenges as a legitimate cultural expression, Lezama wouldn't budge. He responded by letter published in *Everybody's Caribbean Magazine*: "This unprecedented request is seen as reflective of the blatant disrespect and utter contempt held against the people of the Caribbean-American community...[and] is in effect opening up old wounds at a time when all emphasis should be on bringing all the people together via a desperately needed healing process."

The new Mayor, Rudolph Giuliani, eventually heeded Lezama's higher ground and forged a compromise that had 'Carnival' proceed as planned, except that it would end precisely at 6:00 p.m., an hour earlier than usual. *New York Newsday* also reported there being a "clear corridor" restricting traffic access, but over a much wider area than just Crown Heights, and admitting all residents, not merely Hasidim. Lubavitchers would hire their own buses for transport. Parking would be forbidden, but only on Flatbush Avenue, an egress route funnelling exiting floats away from Crown Heights. The staging area between Ralph and Utica Avenues would close an hour earlier, plus the 14 steel bands participating in an imported cultural tradition called "Jou'vert" would end their all-night revelries at 9:00 a.m., instead of carrying on right up until parade hours. There would also be an additional 400 police there to keep the peace in case of any disturbance.

Naturally, as in '91, there was none. The TV news crews who gathered for blood were treated, instead, to 'Carnival' at its very best — extraordinary floats, outrageous costumes, funky music and festive celebrating that virtually exploded on camera. Well-run and well-behaved, the end product captured on local television yielded some overdue publicity for one of the truly outstanding cultural showcases of New York City, if not the entire country. (Believe me, Mardi Gras has got nothing on 'Carnival'.)

Bravo Lezama!

Of course, nearly lost amidst the politics (and something Lezama called to attention in his letter to Kelly) is that 'Carnival' is more than just the Labor Day parade, spectacular as that is. The official events begin four days prior. There are activities by day appealing to the strongly family-oriented West Indians, including steelband concerts, street carnivals and competitions — all for kids. For adults, there are concert blowouts by night, each proffering a different musical theme. In '94 this included:

- "Caribbean Nite" on Thursday featuring George Winston, D. Ivan, Winston SoSo, Iwer George, Lady Wonder and Lady Guymine;

- "Reggae Nite" on Friday (advertisements didn't list the lineup, but *New York Newsday* hinted at a dozen artists including Jamaica's Nicodemus and Brooklyn's Worl-A-Girl);

- "Steelband and Calypso Nite" on Saturday with Designer, Allrounder and Sugar Aloes;

- "Diamanche Gras Show" on Sunday billing Super Blue, The Mighty Sparrow, Crazy, Swallow, Chalkdust and Ras Iley.

I've never caught one of these official evenings, but if they're anything like the Mother's Day Caribbean All-Stars Festival (**Lower Manhattan's Carnival** -- see chapter), you can count on a rotating pair of professional calypso bands, each at least eight pieces, backing a procession of top flight stars flown in from all around the Islands. They'll engage the crowd nonstop for hours with comic banter (often risque), broad showboating, fine singing, and those unrelenting uptempo syncopated polyrhythms guaranteed to raise a smile and shake a waist. "Big up," as they'd say!

Now that's the official program. There are also a universe of private parties and public functions piggybacking the week.

On the private side, there's the "mas camps" — community clans that function much like Mardi Gras crewes in working months ahead to build the floats, choreograph the dances, and construct the unbelievable costumes you'll see. They take over back yards and open lots for their labors where impromptu parties often occupy their working hours in the weeks leading up to "Jou'vert." There's nothing here, I'm certain, that mirrors the formality of Mardi Gras balls. However, if you know somebody who knows somebody in a mas camp, maybe you can check in beforehand and see what's up.

On the public side, seemingly every Caribbean promoter in town gets something up and running that weekend. Their dances feature both live acts and DJs and commence after the official concerts end. Here's a sample from '93:

- "Caribbean Reggae Splash" with 21 artists;

- "Earth Ruler Trophy Night" with 17 artists;

- "Caribbean Comedy Fest" with 5 comedians;

- "End of Summer Shorts Party" with 3 DJs;

- "Trini/Vincy Animal Bacchanal" with 13 artists;

- "Pulse Dance Club Pre-Labor Day Anniversary Celebration" with 17 DJs.

Surprisingly, a good many of these boasted name acts! Any performers or DJs who haven't been so claimed are booked by other Caribbean associations for various counter-carnivals. Plus, such Manhattan clubs as S. O. B.'s get into the act with sympathetic programming of their own.

One such show that kicked off 'CARNIVAL' week was the NEW YORK REGGAE SUMMER BEACH PARTY. Promoter George Crooks chose to move his excellent, two-day festival in Coney Island's Steeplechase Park back two weeks in '94, probably to give himself a little more time to then produce the official "Reggae Night" on Friday. (Now watch other promoters flesh out the interval and turn 'CARNIVAL' into a four-week-long marathon!)

I'm not sure how you'd best get yourself "in the know" for your vacation planning, other than to scour one of the official concerts for flyers, or to look for copies of *Carib News, Caribbean Daylight, Caribbean Notes, Caribbean Life, Everybody's Caribbean Magazine, Dub Catcher, Jammin'* or any other local publications you can find. However you choose to "jump up and kick up," Lezama's got the best advice. "Play clean mas," as he's quoted in *Carib News*, "have healthy family fun, and make people sit up and take notice of Caribbean-Americans."

**Festival Review I**  Ironically, all the extra planning for '94's 'CARNIVAL' may have facilitated a happening that even boosters were admitting had gotten a little loose around the edges.

My party took pains to get to the '93 parade way early, affording the three of us time to land a scarce parking spot a few blocks away and to reserve standing space within sight of Prospect Park. This also left us a few hours to cruise the wonderful Caribbean food booths which line both sides of the 1.9-mile route, wall-to-wall.

We didn't so much see the parade approach as feel it. You could reach down and actually touch the black asphalt vibrating. We heard cheering throngs before finally seeing emerge from the heat-shimmering distance the first massive 16-wheeler stacked high with booming monitors. The tape circle kept yipping something like, "Whoa, donkey," a Caribbean-radio hit infused with those infectious dance hall rhythms. The drivers boogied, the speaker jockeys boogied (hearing loss guaranteed for these poor guys), and accompanying runners boogied and tried to get us to boogie, too. And if this wasn't seductive mayhem enough, the trucks were followed shortly by tribes of marchers in astonishing regalia that only a photograph could do justice.

Problem was, after a few hours, the parade route started to congest. First, there were cos-tumed stragglers walking against the grain of traffic to the staging area. Unfortunately, no one directed them to use the two side streets flanking the spacious boulevard. Second, costumed fin-ishers accompanied them back down the route. Third, unsolicited vendors wheeled huge barrels of beverages back and forth. Fourth, onlookers began to surge off the curb, unfettered by police. Marchers had to struggle through the crush while we had to strain above the myriad bobbing heads for a peek. The whole affair became terribly clogged as the day wore on.

From all accounts, however, the various additional preparations for this year's parade greatly eased movement and cleared access for all. Hopefully, '94's will serve as a model for future 'CARNIVAL's to come.

~ ~ ~

I didn't have the heart to badger the soft-spoken Lezama for a post-fest interview after all this **Festival** retired transit machinist had been through. However, George Crooks, Promoter of both the NEW **Review II** YORK REGGAE SUMMER BEACH PARTY [N. Y. REGGAE'] and the TRINI-JAM FEST [TRINI-JAM'], was kind enough to take a few minutes out from his pre-fest preparations.

Crooks launched the two-day N. Y. REGGAE' in '90 and the one-day TRINI-JAM' in '94. Both share a few key distinctions above the oft-shaky reggae circuit. (Indeed, Crooks had to overcome the stigma of another reggae promoter promising a big name festival at Steeplechase Park, July 4th, '93, but failing to deliver even a single act!)

First, they're both expertly run and deliver precisely the profusion of famous artists they promise (although the N. Y. REGGAE' I attended had to push a few of its scheduled acts from Saturday into Sunday). Crooks adds with justified pride on his lineups: "We are probably about the best [reggae music festival in the Northeast]. I don't think anyone can come close in terms of us. And we start on time. On time!"

You'll get as many as 15 headliners a day, backed by either of five bands. For those who fear the Musician's Union toss-togethers of a typical Chuck Berry tour, be assured that each back-ing band is a solid ensemble in its own right and ably supports their lead with no discernable fall-off in quality.

Second, both festivals transform this grassy swath off the somewhat-neglected jumble of Coney Island amusements into a genuine family asylum — friendly, casual and accommodating of all races. Crooks reflects on this rare vibe for New York City: "Yeah, it's very neat — a family crowd. That's what we promote, because for children under 12 it's free. So, you know, [it's] peace, love and kisses, and you don't have to worry about being with us for the day."

Crooks came to promote N. Y. REGGAE' in a round-about way, though not out of line with the entrepreneurial spirit inhabiting Brooklyn's Caribbean community. This native Jamaican began his career as a roadie for Bob Marley's band in the '70s before attending the University of North Florida in '80. While there, he launched the JACKSONVILLE CARIBBEAN FESTIVAL which, he believes, still takes place every May.

In '86 Crooks entered the travel industry by forming his own agency, Jamyns Travel, ded-icated to serving fellow Caribbeans in their international ventures. (He assures festival fanatics, for example, that he's able to package any travel plans to Jamaica's SUNSPLASH, SUMFEST, or any other Carnival celebration throughout the West Indies.) Last year he expanded to a second office in New Jersey, while also publishing his first travel/music magazine supplement to *Caribbean Life* called, *Jammin'*. Over 130,000 copies were printed, leading to an ongoing effort with national dis-tribution.

Festivals evolved from Crooks' personal interests and contacts maintained with the reg-gae music industry. "Being in the music business," he notes, "most of the musicians and artists prefer to travel with me. It's a lot easier for me to put together these things than most people because I already know where most of the artists are. So it's been a compliment in terms of what we are doing." He sized up how, despite New York City being the largest single market for reg-gae music in the world, there was nothing here "outdoors and beachy," in his words. Thus **N. Y.**

Reggae' was born in '90 and has maintained bigger and better ever since.

Crooks claims to be one of the first promoters to recognize the potential of local sensations, Worl-A-Girl, having booked them at his festival steadily since '91. Another consistent booking of his is Freddie MacGregor. "He has done my festival every year," Crooks says. "He's my personal favorite artist in terms of that. None better."

Crook's musical highlight, however, remains Third World's appearance in '92:

- "After they performed, then they worked a wee kid's show for about an hour and a half. Ben Vereen was in the audience. He was recovering [from an automobile accident, I believe], and they dedicated a song to Ben Vereen. Of course, at the end of it, they said it was one of the best organized festivals they had ever been to. That made my day, after they'd been in the business for about 20 years!"

As for supplying future highlights, Crooks assures: "We are dedicated to this event, and we look forward to doing it every year. And we are dedicated to putting on quality artists, quality entertainment that families can enjoy. That's basically our goal in terms of that — to see the music grow and see New York get the type of festival that it does deserve."

**Artist Mini-Reviews**    I had time for just two acts before the rains came in '93, having raced down from the WWRL Family Day Picnic and Festival (Queens, NYC — see chapter) earlier that day. Yet this short spurt was perfectly sufficient to confirm my positive impressions.

John Holt. Holt didn't sing the one song probably most familiar to mainstream audiences, "The Tide Is High" (made famous by Debbie Harry's cover in the early '80s), but he managed to keep the knowing crowd happy with a healthy run of tuneful favorites. I was impressed with his style — smooth and soulful, brimming with personality. I also liked his wardrobe, a shimmering orange/gold suit worn without a shirt.

Remarkably, Holt pulled off this festive display despite the recent deaths of his father, mother and sister! Crooks explains:

- "We told him he didn't have to perform; he could just go and take off, but he said, 'No!' He said there's not too much he could do right now, so did we want him to do this? And he went ahead and just did it, then he [broke] down afterwards. He did a good show."

Yellowman. I've never cared for Yellowman's high, nasal whine on disc, but live, my attitude rotated 180 degrees. For one, his vocals carried more depth and resonance in person. For another, Yellowman's a peerless showman. Dressed in an aqua blouse and billowing white pantaloons, he literally bounded from one end of the stage to the other for over a solid hour. I got worn out just watching him!

He delivered a host of effective songs, buffered by his nonstop banter designed to incite the women casting wary eyes. All told, a strong, charismatic set!

Crooks: "Yeah, Yellowman is good; one of the best!"

**See Also**    World music fans should also know that Labor Day weekend in New York City also offers the Brazilian Independence Day Celebration and the New York Salsa Festival (see chapter) on Sunday afternoon and Saturday evening, respectively. Quite honestly, these two events combine with 'Carnival' to yield the biggest world-music weekend anywhere on the continent. Bar none!

As for the rest of the year, certainly everything produced by the Caribbean Cultural Center (see chapter) guarantees like quality, musically and otherwise. Simply contact Jamyns Travel and book your weekends directly.

~     ~     ~

# Midtown Manhattan's Carnival

CONCIERTO DEL AMOR, Manhattan, NYC
   Middle February
   Modern Latin

FESTIVAL DE LOS SONEROS, Manhattan, NYC
   Middle May
   Modern Latin

COLUMBIA TE CANTA, Manhattan, NYC
   Late July
   Modern Latin

BRAZILIAN NATIONAL INDEPENDENCE DAY STREET FESTIVAL, Manhattan, NYC
   Early September
   Brazilian and South American
   ***Attended***

NEW YORK SALSA FESTIVAL, Manhattan, NYC
   Early September
   Modern Latin
   ***Attended***

COMBINACION PERFECTA, Manhattan, NYC
   Late October
   Modern Latin

This will be the shortest of my admittedly long-winded introductions, I promise. Simply, if you **Introduction** even remotely like music from the Caribbean/Latin/South American diaspora, and have just one weekend to grab as much as you can, then Labor Day weekend in New York City is when and where you wanna' be. End of story.

The festivities officially kick off Thursday night for the first of what's usually four successive mega concerts of reggae, dancehall and calypso stars from the WEST INDIAN-AMERICAN DAY CARNIVAL (see chapter), culminating in the outrageous Labor Day spectacle known throughout Brooklyn as the "WEST INDIAN 'PARADE." Saturday night you'll treat yourself to, roughly, eight of the biggest names in Latin music, courtesy of the NEW YORK SALSA FESTIVAL [NEW YORK SALSA']. Sunday afternoon you'll take to the streets of Manhattan for at least two continuous stages of samba, bossa-nova and Brazilian pop topped by a headliner along the lines of last year's Elba Ramalho. That's at the BRAZILIAN INDEPENDENCE DAY STREET FESTIVAL [BRAZILIAN 'STREET'], in case you're wondering.

Numbers — 2.5 million parade goers, a packed Madison Square Garden, and 500,000 street revelers for the three affairs, respectively — only tell half the story. What's truly amazing is that most New Yorkers probably don't have a clue that all this wonderful polyrhythmic madness is even going on! Call these three extravaganzas the Stealth Bacchanal. And that may be the sole distinction between them and Rio's CARNAVAL that, I understand, consumes the entire city in its frenzy.

So score your lodging reservations, saddle up the car, pack up the kids, grab your street maps, don your party clothes, and prepare yourself to "baile" (dance)...all...weekend...long!

**Festival Review I** You can't help but come away from hearing good Brazilian music without a skip in your step and a smile on your face. It's like sonic sunshine.

I'll leave it to musicologists and sociologists to explain why, but I suspect it has much to do with the beat. Festivals have yielded me a veritable Ph. D. in party rhythms: zydeco boogies, lindy swings, Cajun swirls, Dixieland syncopations, blues shuffles, funk stomps, Texas two-steps, conjunto polkas, and so forth. But the dense polyrhythms of samba can accommodate them all. It lets you do these Northern dances and the full range of Latin styles you know — merengue, mambo, rumba, cha-cha, salsa. Or you can simply do your basic rock-and-roll moves. No sweat, just get in the flowing groove and go!

At the BRAZILIAN 'STREET', most of the natives seemed to opt for the latter dance, willingly constricted, I suppose, by sexy body pressed upon sexy body. They bent their knees a bit, rocked their hips in a funky one-two, swayed their shoulders from side-to-side, raised their arms high and smiled, smiled, smiled. Smiles decorated most every face from stage players down to the last dancer in the undulating pack. It was infectious to the nth!

My wife and I only had a few hours to spare early in the day, but we were quickly caught up in the revel. It all occupies "Little Brazil," a two-block business district on 46th Street between Madison and Sixth Avenues that houses a number of Brazilian restaurants, shops and travel agencies. The consulate may even rent space here, I'm not sure. There are open flatbeds for the musicians on either end of the modest thoroughfare that is lined by booths from Brazilian sponsors, businesses, craftspeople, artisans and, above all, food vendors. Food actually may be the day's chief attraction (aside from continuous dancing, of course), as every imaginable type of Brazilian delicacy tempts you from both sides of the aisle. The crowds are so dense that you'll often find yourself squeezed in front of some food display with no other option than to sample every tasty plate.

In fact, crowding may be my only critique of BRAZILIAN 'STREET'. It's pretty-much outgrown its site and really needs to expand up an avenue, if not move altogether to somewhere spacious like Central Park. Ah, but then native Brazilians, which number approximately 250,000 throughout the New York City Tri-State area, might miss the libidinous chemistry engendered by such "back-to-back, belly-to-belly" density. After all, this is the country that gave the world "La Lambada."

I put the query to Eddie Mendez, who's organized the past 10 BRAZILIAN 'STREET's for the Brazilian-American Cultural Center. He's seen their annual centerpiece grow ten-fold from its initial 50,000 patrons and admits seeking to expand it to three blocks this year. "It's the kind of thing that promotes Brazil and [has been] doing very good for years," he adds. "It's very good exposure for Brazil."

Mendez comes to the event with a background in journalism and public relations. He's been especially successful lining up sponsorship from among the Brazilian business and travel community, though not so successful that he can afford the steep performances fees demanded by name acts residing in the U. S. "We tried to," he confides, "but those people don't understand the spirit of the festival. For example, we tried to invite some big names from America. They wanted to charge me something to appear. I can't afford it, you see?" Accordingly, both stages are stocked with local acts performing gratis leading up to the evening's headliner. (I thought the quality of locals was fairly high and, when I get a spare week or two someday, I look forward to tracking much of the lineup down in club settings.)

Mendez does manage to entice a number of celebrities up from Brazil to make appearances, such as last year's actress Sonia Bragia, soccer star Pele, and race driver Emerson Fittipaldi. "Brazilia, no problem," he adds of those personalities eager to celebrate what Mendez cites as the largest gathering of Brazilians in North America. It's remained pre-eminent, even as imitators have sprung-up since. "We did it before everybody else," Mendez explains, "so everybody tries to put together something that gives the idea of Brazil. They try to create something with the same experience and the same idea as the creation of the BRAZILIAN 'STREET'."

One thing the others rarely duplicate is the Brazilian 'Street's element of surprise. Last year, singer Gal Costa flew up from Brazil for an unannounced appearance onstage with Ramalho. That was Mendez' all-time highlight, he notes. Mendez can't guarantee these kind of musical fireworks every year, but he does promise newcomers that "this is a piece of Brazil. Enjoy and believe that we are doing our best." I believe!

~     ~     ~

New York Salsa' may be less than one-twentieth the size of Brazilian 'Street', but it sacrifices nothing in terms of spirit. If anything, it may even be more highly charged.

**Festival Review II**

Part of the credit goes to its Producer, Ralph Mercado. In salsa circles, Mercado has been "The Man" for over 30 years. The names he can draw from his "familia" of managed clients, alone, can get anyone excited, starting with legends like Tito Puente, Celia Cruz, Oscar D'Leon and Eddie Palmieri, before working its way down to many of the hottest young stars in Latin pop, such as Rey Ruiz, La India, Tito Nieves and Marc Anthony.

Part of the credit also goes to the top production talent Mercado gathers for his 19th-annual showcase. His longtime musical director, Sergio George, arranges and conducts the 12-piece Orquesta RMM — a necessity to back up the many young singers who don't yet have touring bands or the older stars flown in solo from around the world. The 18 Eddie Torres Dancers can be counted on for a superb floor show between, and often during, sets, while Mercado's video-production team broadcasts the action on two enormous screens. Lit up by big spots, it's got the flash and pacing of a Las Vegas revue, and helps insure never-a-dull-moment for shows that last as long as six straight hours!

Most of the credit, however, goes to the partisan crowd of 20,000 Latinos comprised of nearly every ethnic stripe. Apparently, salsa's tendrils extend far and wide, and Mercado brings in practitioners from Cuba (Cruz), Venezuela (D'Leon), Columbia (Joe Arroyo), Dominican Republic (Los Hermanos Rosario), and elsewhere — even as far away as Japan (Orquesta de la Luz). Each band invokes continual roars from its respective throng of countrymen bunkered down in New York City.

But the centerpiece constituency is Puerto Rican, even for those of its immigrants who may've been living in "Nueva York" for three generations or longer. Of all the Latino segments filling up the cavernous Madison Square Garden, they're the biggest numbered, feel the proudest, yell the loudest, and cart in these huge flags to be waved all throughout the night. Basically, they rock the house! They're a raucous, throat-clearin', song-singin', foot-stompin', hand-clappin' crowd, and you'd have to be stone cold not to join right in.

My wife and I didn't hit the whole show in '93, but we did remain long enough to catch the feeling and witness three of its promising openers. First-up was a handsome young Columbian with clipped hair, bobbed ponytail and checkerboard-fronted tux named Checo Acosta. He kicked things off in fine fashion with a succession of crowd pleasers, including a tribute to the late Hector "La Voz" Lavoe. This brought the crowd up out of their seats and clapping (the middle-aged couple seated next to us even clanged a cow bell). In fact, the audience functioned as an auxiliary rhythm section for Acosta's backers and all those who followed.

The Eddie Torres Dancers were another of these ever present sidelights. Torres and his wife, who lead the dancers through their extravagant routines, are an unlikely-looking pair. He's six-feet-plus and somewhat paunchy; she's five-feet-maybe and very petite. You've never seen a more facile, fiery, light-on-their-feet pair, however. Their dancing wizardry was so striking it often made it hard to concentrate on the lead singers.

Not to imply the singers weren't capable of commanding attention; quite the opposite. The males were all dressed and groomed like matinee idols, exhibited considerable audience rapport, danced smoothly to the clave beat, plus maintained extended medleys everyone knew and sung along to. As if that weren't enough, the announcer called upon each to deliver some personal words at the end of their active sets. It's not easy to do all that and keep the crease sharp in your tuxedo. My wife and I were impressed by these young entertainers aspiring to "old school" form.

To get a handle on the music being performed, I saw it in terms of its staging. It's a showy, charismatic form, so up front are the singers and their accompanying dancers. Next, it's pulsing, percussive dance music, so drummers form the second line — usually three to four playing congas, timbales, whatever. Piano and bass are considered part of the rhythm section, so they join in off to the side. Interestingly, it's not a bottom heavy music, so the bassist plays an acoustic stand-up model for subtler effect. Then, of course, a parade of horns forms the back line where it carries the melody in ringing bursts. Melody is subservient to rhythm, however, and when the horn players are brought up front, even they have to dance while they play.

Occasionally, there are sultry ballads. Acosta assumed the melodramatic pose of a romantic, coming to the lip of the stage, bowing on one knee, and issuing sinuous interpretations upon the melody that spoke one word: "passion." Mostly, though, it's "baile, baile, baile" all night long to those intoxicating polyrhythms.

Puerto Rican <u>Rey Ruiz</u> followed. Where Acosta displayed a nice tenor, the thirty-ish Ruiz was a bit shrill. However, he brought with him a driving pop band, lotsa' pop tunes, and a bit of a lilt to his sound.

My wife and I really liked the third act, Bronx-born <u>Marc Anthony</u>. More casual in appearance than his suited predecessors, he sported slacks, a white jacket, an open-collared shirt, glasses, and a frizzy ponytail which he'd self-consciously wind and unwind throughout his set. This younger look matched the looser, more spontaneous feel to his music.

The diminutive Anthony led a pared-down band and gave them more solo opportunities than the prior walls-of-sound, more modulations and more room to convey different beats and moods. By allowing for pensive moments in parts, Anthony was able to deliver emotive crescendos that, naturally, drove his legion of female admirers nuts. In fact, he really played to the seats in carefully constructed stages, artfully utilizing the breaks that showcased his soulful voice. Dramatic, sensual, nostalgic, intense — Anthony impressed us both as a bonafide star in the making!

Now, I'd love to be able to share some words about Anthony from Mercado, or his daughter, Deborah, who runs publicity. Unfortunately, all my attempts at securing an interview went for naught. When you visit Mercado's converted loft space in Lower Boadway, it's a bit easier to understand why — the place is a madhouse of phone calls incoming from all around the world. Gold records line the lobby walls, flyers of whatever many current events they're producing occupy the cocktail tables, and a frantic receptionist guards the roost. Perhaps for future editions I can gain an audience to learn more about this remarkable mogul and the music he's championed for over 30 years.

**Attendance Tip**  NEW YORK SALSA' has been known to sell-out, so I'd recommend beginning your ticket-purchasing inquiries, say, about a month ahead. That should put your seats right in the middle of this glorious salsa madness.

As for BRAZILIAN 'STREET', keep your eyes open. Enterprising sponsors lately have been piggybacking the day with nighttime concerts of their own. Last year, this included Caetano Veloso at Town Hall that weekend and Ney Matogrosso and Aquarella Carioca there the following weekend. Sounds of Brazil's [S. O. B.'s], a wonderful dance club on Varick Street, gets into the spirit by hosting a Brazilian band afterwards and invites the numerous Brazilian celebrities there for the day to drop by. Look for flyer discounts to the club being passed around the festival grounds.

**See Also**  Mercado seems to have a hand in most of the other big salsa splashes that oft' occur around New York City, typically in Manhattan's Madison Square Garden. Most seem to be one-shots, though those listed in the heading, above, have proven somewhat more durable, albeit with minor changes in dates and titles.

Mercado's most spectacular repeat is Late October's COMBINACION PERFECTA, featuring up to 20 of salsa's major names on a single Saturday evening drawn from Mercado's awesome artist roster. This "Latin Lollapalooza," as *New York Daily News*' Robert Dominguez termed it, may be bigger even than NEW YORK SALSA', if that's possible! You'll find this lineup, too, commanding a self-titled disc (RMM/SONY), though I believe it's a studio creation vs. NEW YORK SALSA's live recording.

Mercado's own flyers list his RMM hotline, along with Madison Square Garden's, for information and ticket sales. Given the trouble I had getting through to Mercado's offices, however, I'd suggest calling the 'Garden instead to learn what's going on.

~      ~      ~

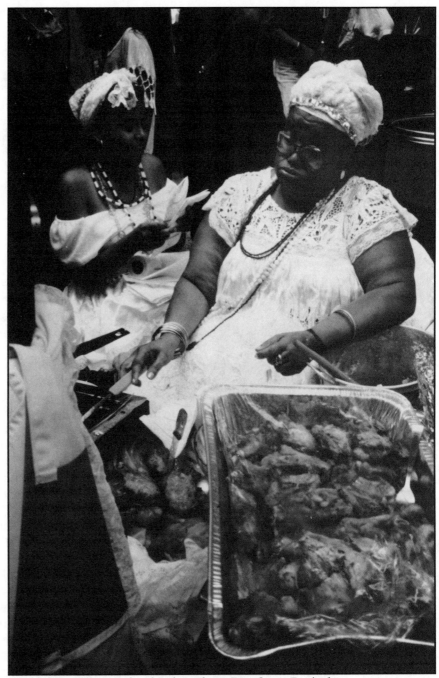

*Cookin', Brazilian National Independence Day Street Festival.*

# Queens for a Day

**WIGSTOCK**, Manhattan, NYC
    Early September
    Gay and Lesbian
    ***Attended***

**VILLAGE HALLOWEEN PARADE/ALL SOULS' HALLOWEEN BALL**, Manhattan, NYC
    Late October
    Modern Rock, Pop and Top 40
    ***Attended***

**Introduction**    Ah, **WIGSTOCK**! It was a Presidential election year, and all that summer I'd been followed around my festival route by Messrs. Bush, Clinton, Perot, even Brown who served as the keynote speaker for NYU's **INDEPENDENT MUSIC FEST** (see chapter). This foursome seemed to dog my every step. "At last," I thought as I entered Thompkins Square Park that sunny Labor Day afternoon, "here's one festival where no righteous politician will dare show his face!" Wrong. Manhattan Borough President Ruth Messinger greeted the throngs from the stage, the first in a parade of pandering civil servants, which included City Councilman Thomas Duane and City Comptroller Elizabeth Holtzman.

Why so skeptical?

Because **WIGSTOCK** is a decade-old music/dance/comedy/costume communion of, oh, about 20,000 transvestites all shimmied into a space of less than three city blocks. It's not a hundredth the size of Mardi Gras, but it's got every ounce of its hedonistic spirit and outrageousness. After all, New York City is the gay capitol of America, as well as the nation's acknowledged center of fashion, theater, arts, advertising, comedy, and so forth. There's a lot of artistic attitude to be vented and **WIGSTOCK**'ers "work it, bitch, work it" for weeks ahead on costumes that defy description. (In fact, this may be this book's shortest chapter, since mere words fail these wild displays so completely.)

The pity of it all for costume designers and other creative, festive types is that **WIGSTOCK** happens the same day as the **WEST INDIAN-AMERICAN DAY CARNIVAL AND PARADE** (see chapter) is making its similarly merry way down Brooklyn's Eastern Parkway. If you're so inclined, I'd hit the latter in the morning before hustling back to the Village.

In fairness, not every **WIGSTOCK** reveler is "trussed up" in his/her private version of the Rose Bowl Parade on high heels. I'd estimate this flashy contingent at about 25%. Another 25% were more demur, like one guy clad in an early '60s Jackie O. suit, complete with Halston pillbox hat, who sat quietly on a park bench, legs crossed, very First Lady-like. A third 25% were gay men in straight clothes feverishly cruising the park for what must've seemed like a veritable Halloween of acquaintance-making. About 5% were lesbians sporting "Support Vaginal Pride" buttons who, for solidarity's sake, dressed like men, or rather, more like men than usual. The last 20% were cops and straight gawkers, like my wife and me, cameras in hand, just taking in the whole riotous scene with smiles on our faces.

And we were absolutely welcome, I must say. Unlike at most lesbian festivals, with their exclusionary "womyn only, womyn born" admission policies, **WIGSTOCK** is open to everyone in a spirit of celebratory inclusion. "You wanna' take my picture," cross-dressers would respond to most requests, "sure, hon', lemme' strike a pose." And pose they would, whether for amateur photographers or for all the nightly news crews that routinely broadcast footage for disbelieving New Yorkers. I haven't yet caught **WIGSTOCK** pics on national feeds, but I've no doubt of eventually seeing Peter Jennings issuing a slight smirk on camera at these "queens for a day."

There is live music on the single central stage — "disco" in all its derivatives. Deee-lite, Deborah Harry, and Ru-Paul have headlined the free festivities in the past, but the real stars are the innumerable "divas" in drag who run through pretty-damn-funny revues to taped music. Everyone, on-stage or off, is a comedian/comedienne at WIGSTOCK, especially its founder and M. C., John Ingle. He's "Lady Bunny" to one and all, and his sassy "trailer trash" shtick has long-enough legs to keep the audience howling all day. As *New York Newsday*'s Frank DeCaro quotes Ingle, "The thing about Downtown drag is that it's quirky. It's not about getting up in a 'Dynasty' gown and doing a perfect Whitney Houston lip-synch. It's about doing her *pregnant*."

Ingle's creation (the festival, not the character) has actually outgrown its funky East Village origins and been forced west in '94 to Christopher Street — the equivalent of moving to gay "uptown." I've no word on how the irrepressible, cheeky WIGSTOCK did there by the piers this year, but I'm sure it went swimmingly.

If you like the WIGSTOCK experience, you'll love the VILLAGE HALLOWEEN PARADE. This extraordi- **See Also** nary event actually competes with Mardi Gras on all its terms, including size, as over one million partiers crowd the 25-block route. The costumes here are every bit as "hair-raising" as WIGSTOCK's, though the sheer scale of this spectacle gives it less of a gay identity and more one of all-purpose extravagance — an example being last year's Barbara Bush impersonator who rented a limo, dressed about a dozen accomplices as Secret Service agents, and blithely autographed "Millie" books during the entire ride.

This 21-year-old landmark is organized, remarkably, by just a handful of volunteers led by Jeanne Fleming, who works on it throughout the year at a 200-year-old, 400-acre farm upstate. This 49-year-old puppet maker by trade needs all the barn space she can get to house the larger creations she'll have leading the way. Two years ago Fleming persuaded the *Village Voice* to print its "Guide to Halloween" and was astonished to see well over 40 parallel events taking place throughout the city. This convinced her to create one of her own for this year, the ALL SOULS' HALLOWEEN BALL. The B52's headlined this charity costume bash, which occupied the Manhattan Center for Living following the parade. Let's hope this bash begats others annually.

~     ~     ~

# Manhattan's Seasonal Jazz Spirits

BEACONS IN JAZZ, Manhattan, NYC
    Late June
    Modern Jazz

ALL NITE SOUL, Manhattan, NYC
    Early October
    Modern Jazz
    ***Attended***

BENDING TOWARDS THE LIGHT...A JAZZ NATIVITY, Manhattan, NYC
    Early December
    Modern Jazz
    ***Attended***

**Introduction**  There are multiple connections between these two seasonal celebrations — ALL NITE SOUL ['SOUL] and BENDING TOWARDS THE LIGHT...A JAZZ NATIVITY ['JAZZ NATIVITY]. But the primary one is Rev. Dr. John Garcia Gensel. Known as "Pastor to the Jazz Community" among his flock of admirers, Gensel was also christened, "The Shepherd Who Watches Over The Night Flock," by the late Duke Ellington as the subject of one of his tone poems.

Here's the festival story.

Gensel came to Advent Lutheran Church 50 years ago after his ordination at the age of 26. It took him over a decade to become interested in New York City's jazz scene, but when he finally did, after taking a course at the New School for Social Research, there was no stopping him. Gensel became a regular haunt among Gotham's night spots, and jazz musicians soon drew close to him, attracted by his obvious love of the genre and his warm, nonjudgemental personality.

These fatherly traits continued when Gensel helped pioneered Jazz Vespers after moving to St. Peter's Lutheran Church in '66, marrying jazz and church for a weekly late afternoon service. His focus was more on celebrating the commonality and musicality of human existence; less on pounding scripture into people's heads. Leading musicians responded by making St. Peter's their spiritual home when in town — many going so far as to have Gensel marry them there; others, sadly, bidding Gensel to bury them in the style of a New Orleans jazz funeral (John Coltrane and Billy Strayhorn being two so remembered in this fashion).

The first 'SOUL in '70 simply was an extension of Jazz Vespers to a full 12 hours of "joyful noises" to celebrate its fifth anniversary. It continues ever since as New York City's longest running jazz festival in years as well as consecutive hours! As you can imagine, 'SOUL took on extra meaning this year for Gensel's last hurrah before retiring to his native Pennsylvania.

That installment was not '94's only recognition of this man's legacy, however. The JVC JAZZ FESTIVAL (see chapter) regaled him with one of its trademark 24-plus artist tributes, hosted by Bill Cosby — an unusual honor accorded a nonmusician such as Gensel. Not to be outdone, the New School's Jazz Program dedicated its big fundraiser, BEACONS IN JAZZ (see below), to Gensel and Max Roach with 23-plus artists of the same caliber, hosted by Ruby Dee and Ossie Davis. St. Peter's then sent Gensel off with its own big bash on New Year's Eve.

Nobody begrudged the much beloved Gensel one minute, least of all vocalist/arranger Anne Phillips and saxophonist/composer Bob Kindred. They're one of those jazz pairs married by Gensel at St. Peter's. Long before he tied the knot, however (10 years before, actually), Gensel also suggested that the couple apply their prodigious talents to Christmas lore like he, himself, had done to services via Jazz Vespers.

"Hmmm," they thought, then produced their first 'JAZZ NATIVITY benefit at St. Peter's in '85. Eventually, this original musical interpretation of that fateful night in a manger outgrew St. Peter's, bouncing to St. Bartholomew's and Stephen Wise Free Synagogue before landing at Lincoln Center's Avery Fisher Hall this year. Their parade of top-flight jazz participants followed, however, and yielded a bubbly draught of holiday rhythm that had the staid hall standing and clapping by night's end.

There you have it — two wonderful ways to "get with the spirits": 'SOUL kicking off another year of Jazz Vespers; 'JAZZ NATIVITY beckoning the holiday season. Both are ecumenical in nature. The only denomination you need to be is a fan of the finest jazz has to offer. And somewhere before a crackling retirement fire on his 90-acre Muncie farmstead, rest assured that Gensel is snapping his fingers to the imagined beat of his two inspirations.

Gensel's shoes are big ones to fill, but his successor, Rev. Dale Lind, may be the one Lutheran cleric musically suited to the task. The two actually made the jazz club rounds together in their early days. Lind, presently Assistant Pastor, came to St. Peter's directly from the same Pennsylvania seminary as Gensel in '64 and just celebrated his own 30th anniversary since ordination.

**Festival Review I**

It hasn't been a continual tenure at the "Jazz Church" for Lind, however. "I've been in and out," he notes. "I've been in the club business, too, as co-owner of The Bitter End back for eight years in '73 to '81. Then I had a place called Preachers right beside it [at] 145 Bleecker [Street], which was the old Dugout at one time. I had a lot of up-and-coming musicians playing there," including many rock-and-roll sidemen who'd make Preacher's their regular hang out when not touring.

Accordingly, Lind moved this year's 'SOUL and subsequent Jazz Vespers into musical directions it hadn't been in recent years, such as blues and Latin jazz. "We don't draw the line between 'sacred' and other types of music that a person can offer worship with," Lind explains, "other forms of music than just your traditional classical form. We have a BASICALLY BACH FESTIVAL here every year, too — a 12-hour Bach festival on Bach's birthday that weekend just before 'SOUL."

I remark how Lind's crew had better catch up on their sleep for these two contiguous marathons. "Yeah," he responds with a chuckle:

- "But the Jazz Ministry really originated with the concern for jazz musicians and their families, in particular. They really suggested having a service where they could attend because most musicians play at night 'till 4:00 or 5:00 in the morning, and 11:00 is not their cup of tea for services. So we start at 5:00 Sunday afternoons, which was found to be a good time. And they said, 'Well, let's play our music, too,' and I said, 'Why not?'"

Thus the tale of Jazz Vespers' beginnings.

This family orientation remains in three forms. First, St. Peter's makes a point of acknowledging the kin of its 'SOUL co-hosts. The year I went the program lauded Count Basie's longtime tenor saxophonist/arranger Dr. Frank Foster and his wife, Cecilia, giving both their own separate bios and crediting her extensive role in fostering (pardon the pun) his career, along with her own. Lind adds how Duke Ellington's band was similarly boosted by the musician's wives, who would maintain their own private society, tour with the band, and perform charitable works together. "There are a great many very talented women in jazz who have performed here, as well," he nods, citing the soulful Trudy C. on organ as one prime example (and one who is working with Lind to bring Jazz Vespers to churches in her native Philadelphia).

Second, 'SOUL gathers a real cross-section of the New York City jazz family — not the bigger names, but many outstanding swing-oriented locals who keep the scene percolating throughout the year when the "nationals" are out on tour. "We try to provide the opportunity for as many people to play here as is possible," Lind says of the night's revolving-door lineup. They're introduced, in turn, by the cream of the area's jazz media: Ira Gitler, Dan Morgenstern, Phil Schaap, Jack Kleinsinger and about eight others.

Third, 'SOUL even feels like a family gathering, a church potluck, except that more than 20 groups are maintaining their musical procession upon the altar beyond the modest hall's swinging doors. The ladies are serving dinner, breakfast and coffee all through the night while passersby browse the crafts and cakes for sale or peruse the photo exhibit on the walls. Indeed, it often seems there are more people relaxing on padded chairs chatting than there are people keeping vigil with the musicians. I'd be hard pressed to recall a more unpretentious festival setting than this.

Do these easy-going, middle-aged patrons all stay the distance? "Quite a few of them do," affirms Lind, "and I would say it's usually pretty full at the beginning, and 'till 1:00 in the morning the house is still pretty full — really! And many times I would say at 5:00 in the morning when we stop, there are still at least 100 people here."

~     ~     ~

**Festival Review II** I wonder if two of these remaining faithful are invariably Phillips and Kindred. This gracious, enthusiastic pair was recently married by Gensel after a decade-long romance and had originally commenced their relationship not terribly long before Gensel bid them to collaborate on their first 'JAZZ NATIVITY.

Actually, it was Phillips who was entreated to apply her writing/arranging talents to an '85 benefit for the Midtown Arts Council being held for two nights at St. Peter's. This former Brill Building regular then solicited her saxophonist love interest to serve as Musical Director. The recruiting that followed among their mutual contacts was prodigious: a full gospel choir, Kindred's regular jazz quartet supplemented by at least six pieces to complete the stage band, some dancers, some singers, designers for costumes, staging and lighting, students for videotaping, a few celebs for hosting (this year, TV's Charles Kurault and the Mayor's wife, Donna Hanover Giuliani) and a cast of biggies to play the parts, headed by Lionel Hampton, Tito Puente, Al Grey, Jimmy Slyde, Phil Woods, Jackie Cain and Roy Kral, Ursula Dudziak, and the like.

Blended smoothly and soulfully, their colorful musical narrative — one of the most uniquely rewarding holiday adaptations I've ever experienced — proved an instant success. 'JAZZ NATIVITY has maintained itself through ten years and three moves and is poised for upwards and onwards. Phillips and Kindred have been entertaining inquiries from other markets as well as from various media interests. They've even built a traveling stage in preparation for a planned tour next year. Who knows, 'JAZZ NATIVITY could be coming to a theater or cable-TV channel near you!

"I really feel (and there are a lot of people who feel) that this is the next big Christmas show," Phillips expresses:

- "There hasn't been one since Amahl and the Night Visitors. There's never been a show that communities could do or a touring company could come in and do. And this can be the one, you know? So for publishing, video, television, all of that — that's what we're trying to make happen.

  "We've done this without grants or corporate funding for eight years, just ticket sales paying the cost of the show. All the musicians in it do it for, like, a hundred and fifty bucks a performance. But everybody feels so strongly about the show that they have become this great family."

A good part of this collective inspiration comes from Phillips who designates kids as their show's chief beneficiary. In a program entitled the Jazz Nativity Children's Project, patrons are invited to sponsor as many inner-city children as they choose to have attend at a subsidized $10 rate. For most of the 4,000 recipients, this has been their first direct exposure to jazz artists of any stature, let alone the many heavy hitters making appearances here. It helps explain the excitable buzz to such features as The Three Jazz Kings (this year, Grey, Slyde and Clark Terry) entering down the aisles carrying lanterns in one hand and their instruments in the other.

"The funny thing is we didn't think of this at all as a children's show," notes Phillips.

- "But about the fourth year, I was talking afterwards to Sylvia Sims, the singer, and Sylvia had brought her godchildren to it. She just said, 'I laughed, I cried, etc., etc., etc.' Then she said, 'The kids positively screamed!' I said, 'How are we ever going to get the damn New York critics to it?' She said, 'Forget them. Aim for the kids.' That was when we started the Children's Project and it's absolutely amazing because we're introducing them to this tremendous music."

Children aren't necessarily the only ones being introduced to jazz's riches. Phillips describes the response last year to their boisterous pageant finale, a swinging collage with billowing modulations and effortless seques between different musical styles including Latin jazz:

- "At the end of that is actually 'God's Love Made Visible.' ...That's when everybody in the band gets choruses, we bring stars up from the audience, and so forth, and in 20 minutes there is the greatest lesson in what is jazz. I didn't realize it was going to be there, but that's what it's turned into. After it's over, I say, 'You just heard what jazz is!' In fact, every one of these people took the same song and brought themselves to it and played what they felt on it. It just lasts long enough so that everybody [gets to] express themselves through jazz improvisation. We walk out at the end and then march up the aisle. So I was in the lobby when people were coming out. And more people came up to me and thanked me for introducing them to jazz in a way they could understand it and they never got it before.

  "It really is amazing, and the reaction from the audience is fantastic. And what's wonderful is it's across the board. You don't have to be a jazz lover to get into this."

  Amen!

**Attendance Tip**

Though moving 'JAZZ NATIVITY to Lincoln Center alleviated the traditional crunch for tickets (typically, all five dates at St. Bartholomew's sold out), sufficient demand remained to leave me, my wife and another couple and with naught but balcony seats. Better get on the Kindred Spirits Foundation mailing list to learn of the earliest purchase availability.

**See Also**

BEACONS IN JAZZ is big bucks — $250 per plate — but a big bang, too. In addition to savoring a contingent of 20-plus all-stars playing in various configurations to fete two to three big names (such as '93's Joe Williams and Ella Fitzgerald who also get their arms twisted to perform on their own behalf), you'll get "a cocktail reception and dinner with the performers," as the ad promises. The *Village Voice*'s Gary Giddens proclaims the awards banquet/fundraiser "mainstream revelry of the highest caliber."

~     ~     ~

# New York City Travel Tips

I apologize for not getting each New York City festival promoter to supply their own travel tips. Doubtless, the combined suggestions would've proven fascinating. But this being New York City and all, they were rushed, I was rushed, and, well, you know how it goes.

Besides, it's not like there's insufficient information available on how to get the most out of your New York City festival weekend. The bookstores here boast solid racks of such travel guides covering most every imaginable angle of this city. However, there's one angle frequently overlooked — the entertainment angle, particularly on the pop music side. That's because the travel-guide market typically skews older, while the Manhattan club scene changes so rapidly.

Therefore, I recommend picking up the following on your way into town to help inform your festival off-day and nightlife picks:

- One of the two city magazines — *New Yorker* or *New York*;

- Two of the three major dailies — *New York Daily News*, *New York Times* or *New York Post* — all of which print their entertainment guides on Friday;

- One of the various alternative and entertainment weeklies — *Village Voice*, *NYPress*, *Manhattan Spirit*, etc. (*New York Press* runs a very useful club guide with colorful one-paragraph blurbs, while *Village Voice* recently responded with its own "opinionated" music previews in a pull-out section, "Voice Choices").

And if you're seeking supplemental listings for a festival with a particular racial/ethnic music slant, look for the corresponding racial/ethnic publication. Among the more prominent are: *Irish Echo*, *Irish Voice*, *Everybody's Caribbean Magazine*, *Carib News*, *Amsterdam News*, *City Sun*, *El Diaro*, *New York Latin*, etc. Most decent local news stands will carry these, plus most others above.

Now let's take a few minutes out to highlight how to tackle New York City festivals without losing your mind, or worse! My perspective? I've lived in something like 16 different U. S. cities in my adult life, as well as in and around New York City for over 25 years. Believe me, daytripping here is different from anywhere else in the country. Penalties for missteps are severe and can turn a breezy pleasure jaunt into a harrowing, threatening, and/or exorbitant nightmare (i.e., midday street parking in midtown, anyone?). That's not to say don't come...but it does take a little strategy.

After David Letterman, then, here's my own top-ten list of Gotham travel truisms:

**One:** You can't see it all in one weekend!

Maybe you can elsewhere, but trying to career from one end of New York City to the other to catch all the famous sites on your list will only leave you staring at traffic through car windows. Manhattan is simply too congested, as are the access routes to any outer-borough destination. I recall reading one recent study that found mean travel times going cross-town during business hours were actually slower than walking, less than 5 m.p.h.!

If you must take in the Statue of Liberty, or the Empire State Building, or Radio City Music Hall, or the Cloisters, or Brooklyn Heights' promenade, or whatever, try to confine yourself to maybe one such destination per day. You can do more, but only if they're gathered within walking proximity as, say, Wall Street, Fraunces Tavern, the World Trade Towers, and South Street Seaport. Take it easy! You can always return another weekend, so why stress needlessly?

**Two:** Target neighborhoods, if not those proximate to your festivals, at least others with particular interest.

Most "N' Yawkers" deal with this transportation madness by confining themselves to neighborhoods: where they work, live, or like to hang out. That's where you should join 'em.

I know most first-time visitors will be drawn to midtown Manhattan like a magnet, lured by its landmarks, tall buildings, Times Square, gaudy shops, Broadway theaters, and dense day-time crowds. Sigh! But, not unlike most central business districts, fewer locals actually live there, so there's really not that much to do, especially after dark. Yes, there are big-name plays and restaurants. Yet, let's face it, they're more for the monied over-50 crowd, not for us middle-income baby boomers with current tastes. Moreover, midtown's increasingly becoming a high-rise version of America's strip malls with chain stores replacing longstanding family businesses and the panoply of ethnic venues. The real local color is found elsewhere, roughly, above 59th Street and below 23rd Street. It's also where you'll find the densest pedestrian traffic — cause for safety-in-numbers no matter how grim the surroundings.

I advise picking one of the neighborhoods identified in your travel guides and simply checking 'em out. A good place to start would be SoHo's hubbub, followed by the more-relaxed TriBeCa or West Village. Cruise the streets, browse the stores, sample a capuccino, admire the architecture, side-step the panhandlers, check out a museum, gallery or movie theater, pick-out an alluring menu posted on restaurant windows, you name it. There are over 15,000 eateries and taverns below 96th Street — constantly changing, I'd add — with the best ambiences and values always being found right around any corner.

IBM's co-founder, Thomas Watson, coined the phrase, "Management by walking around"; I'd substitute the word "vacation" when visiting New York City.

> **Three:** Walk, use cabs or the subway when in Manhattan south of 96th Street; take your car everywhere else (the well-heeled would even do well to line up a limo service).

I mentioned New York City's traffic quagmire; however, that's generally during daytimes and weekdays. Most festivals either conclude, or occur exclusively, at night and/or on weekends. This makes taking mass transit back to your lodgings a trifle dicey, especially when returning from the outer boroughs. I feel fairly confident, but then I'm relatively inconspicuous and experienced. If you're a first-time out-of-towner, those subway platforms in Brooklyn, Queens or the Bronx can make you feel pretty damn lonely; pretty much like a target for whomever.

Nor are cabs much of an alternative. Sure, they may take you to the outer boroughs — they may — but they won't be around late at night to take you back to Manhattan or elsewhere. You might score an unlicensed "gypsy" cab, but I wouldn't if I were you. If they sniff out that you're a novice, well, who knows where you'll end up or how much you'll be charged?

I've thought long and hard about this one, but I still recommend taking your car for night-time returns from outer-borough festivals, and many in Manhattan, as well. As a bonus, you'll find weekend rates in parking garages and lots, a suspension of most metered parking on Sundays, and legal parking where posted everyday after 7:00 p.m. Plus a good many of those events on the far outskirts, such as those at Brooklyn's Floyd Bennett Field, offer guarded parking for free or a nominal charge. So take your car, but give yourself plenty of time to get there.

> **Four:** Avoid rush hour like the plague!

Aside from those sufferin' L. A. bastards, newcomers will be staggered by what New York City car commuters put up with from, approximately, 6:30 to 9:00 a.m. and 3:30 to 7:00 p.m. Can you say, "gridlock?" Plan your comings and goings to be off the highways during these hours. It used to be you could go against the grain of traffic, but no longer. I find the evening flow going into Manhattan unexpectedly worse than the reverse, abetted by the toll crossings shutting down all but a few lanes to incoming cars.

Nor is that all! New York City traffic is so continuously dense that all it takes is a small accident, or a little off-hours construction, and you can find yourself mired at anytime of day or night. Your best bets are: (a) to keep a detailed road/street map handy to plot alternate routes; (b) to listen to the radio for traffic reports (the most frequent being found on the various AM talk stations, WINS, WABC, WOR, etc.).

> **Five:** Leave absolutely nothing of value in your car, not even in your trunk!

One out of every ten cars stolen in America is taken off the streets of New York City — over 100,000 per year. Break-in's must run dozens of times that figure. It's the closest thing in town to a perfect crime with New York City police treating car vandalism as victimless: "No one gets physically hurt, the insurance companies pay up, so who gives a rat's ass? We don't want any cars in here, anyway!" A mere pittance of perpetrators are ever caught, sentenced and jailed. I've had my own car broken into too many times to count; once having gone for a midnight snack only to find a $200 window smashed to get a $5 umbrella and a $15 folder. Typical.

Do not, repeat, do not leave anything of value in your car: stereos, luggage, personal papers, anything, anywhere, anytime. A car thief only needs a few seconds and it's gone, as it certainly will be. If you need to make an extra trip back to your lodgings to deposit any of the day's shopping, do it or lose it!

**Six:** If parking on the street, make absolutely certain you understand the parking signs in question; if not, drive on!

You may imagine the city's massive bureaucracy works slow, but leave your car illegally parked anywhere for, say, 15 minutes and just see how quickly the law sweeps down. Boom! A $55 ticket. If it's one of those obscure midtown towing zones during business hours, you could be looking at a $55 ticket, a $180 towing charge, and a $15 per day storage charge. Plus you'll have to track your car down to some forbidding netherland where they'll only take cash, certified check or money order. All of a sudden your modestly-budgeted festival weekend went right out the window!

I could write a book on New York City's deliberately Byzantine parking regulations but all my advice can be summed up into one hard-earned tip: walk the length of whatever block you're considering. If you're not crystal-clear on what's posted, move along!

Lately there's been a nasty regulation in some parts of town designed to snare unwitting nightlife types: no parking from 11:00 p.m. to something a.m. This is especially devious, since typical "alternate side of the street" parking postings declare 11:00 a.m. to 2:00 p.m., so at a quick glance you assume you're legal for the night. The cops have been feasting lately on this easy misperception. Basically, it's big bucks for the city, so they enforce the living daylights out of whatever's posted. Beware!

On the plus side, those notorious "alternative side of the street" parking traps have been suspended over the last several years on Wednesdays and Saturdays for all but a few far reaches of town. Again, listen to AM talk radio for confirmation.

**Seven:** If parking in lots or garages, consider the periphery of midtown Manhattan.

I've now got most of the parking regs. down pat, but if I'd more of a budget, I wouldn't hesitate to park in a garage or lot. In fact, I often wonder if I'd have saved more money in the long run, even given Manhattan's astronomical rates.

To help spare you from garages charging something along the lines of your firstborn, it pays to drive around a bit. They're all required to post their rates in big letters that can be read while driving by. The best rates are found, naturally, on the periphery — beyond a square bordered, approximately, by 9th-to-1st Avenues and 59th-to-23rd Streets (though wealthy residential areas elsewhere, like the Upper East Side, can also be steep). Lots run less, especially those under the F. D. R. Drive. You can also find reasonable evening and weekend deals. All things considered, even top dollar beats $55 tickets.

**Eight:** If lodging in Manhattan, ask about parking availability and charges; otherwise consider staying on the outskirts.

I admit I'm less in-the-know on Manhattan lodgings, having always stayed with family and friends, if not in my own apartment. I do know that New York City's hotel tax was just reduced from its formerly usurious rate down to where it's now nearly tied for worst in the country with Chicago's. Great! Still, what's the opportunity cost for parking tickets or car thefts; what's the price of peace-of-mind? You'd probably still be better off paying these hefty rates for the convenience and enjoyment of it all. Just make sure they've made some provision for your car, plus what that's gonna' cost.

I understand there are reasonably-priced lodging alternatives. I've read where a brand-new rehab of an Upper East Side YMCA is actually quite presentable, as are several other bargain hotels. I've also read of numerous services that act as urban bed-and-breakfasts in securing lodgings in people's apartments, co-ops, condos, town homes and lofts. Check your travel guides, or even the local Yellow Pages for the latter.

On my limited funds, I'd consider crossing the river to New Jersey for their presumably lower rates and parking accommodations. I've noticed spanking new chains in two general proximities: Newark Airport and the Secaucus/East Rutherford/"Meadowlands" sports complex (Marriott Courtyards, my fave, are found in both locales). Unfortunately, you'd be dealing with traffic and such, so see tips **Three** through **Seven**, above.

**Nine:** Dress down, dress dark, look down, act casual, stay focused, and "Just say no!"

One thing I do like about Manhattan — as opposed to Boston, or Detroit, or elsewhere — is you can dress down for most everything. Attitude counts much more than appearance. My mother volunteers at MoMA, and even for their "black tie" receptions, artsy types come clothed every which-a-way. You dress how you feel, and if they don't like it, well, tough! Only the snootiest venues enforce dress codes, though you'll notice top celebs there in jeans, T's and stuff breaking the codes.

All this is to say: don't get wrapped up in this "Great White Way" nonsense. The surest way to give away that you're a tourist is to dress up. Leave the formal wear and tennis whites at home; dress down and dark, and you'll be halfway to passing for native.

As for conduct, this is not the place to do your best Mary Tyler Moore imitation, smiling wildly, spinning around, and tossing your hat in the air at the freakin' thrill of being here. Keep your eyes level, act casual, and stay focused. There are a million scammers in town, and all they need to see is your excitable countenance and you'll be put-upon left and right. The solution for all these peddlers, beggars, hustlers and such is to do like Nancy Reagan and "Just say no!" A short sharp "no" while quickly moving on gets you out of most situations. Rude? Perhaps. But I see it more as self-defense from someone who's been in every worst neighborhood in all five boroughs at every time of day and night, yet never gotten caught up in any problems.

- "Excuse me, mister, I just wanna' axe you somethin'..." — "No!"

- "Oh, ma'am, I hate to bother you, but I have to catch a bus to Scranton to see my sick mother and I only need another $1.45 to make my fare..." — "No!"

- "Hey, guy, lemme' show ya' these chains, solid gold, 14-karat..." — "No!"

Works like a charm.

**Ten:** Never let New York City's worst get to you.

Traffic, tickets, rudeness, rip-offs, whatever — don't let it spoil your weekend. Yes, I know, all these "Big Crapple" situations are irrational and unconscionable, but nobody else cares (i.e., yeah, like window workers at the Parking Violations Bureau, right?). So why should you? Short of something grievously illegal, I'd suggest letting all these indignities pass. Otherwise, you'll spend your whole time pissed-off and miss enjoying the next incredible artist to take the festival stage. As H. L. Mencken once quipped, "New York has the best of everything, including the best of the worst."

On the considerable plus side, though, scan the chapters and feast your eyes and ears on a plethora of fascinating musical scenes simply not available anywhere else. From calypso to cabaret, from jazz to jibaro, there isn't a market in the universe that features as many musical cultures operating on as high an artistic plateau as New York City. Collaborative paradise! There's also a spirit here — if even merely the spirit of survival in a hard-edged terrain — that emanates from every musician, and challenges you to take their best shot.

Because, to paraphrase Frank Sinatra, "If you can take it here, you can take it anywhere!" Musician and listener, alike.

~     ~     ~

*Cheerin', Ben and Jerry's One World, One Heart Festival.*

# New York City Festival Listings

**Caveat**

Although the vast majority are festivals are reliable and predictable, all are subject to last-minute changes or cancellations. Accordingly, FESTPRESS is not responsible for any festival listing information that follows. Readers are well advised to contact festivals at least twice before preparing a festival vist: (a) once at least one or two months ahead of time; and (b) once more during the week of your visit for confirmation. Ask for a festival flyer or brochure to be mailed to you. Festival promoters usually are willing to comply, and the resulting literature may answer any questions you still have.

## Restrictions:                                       Key Codes

| | | | | | |
|---|---|---|---|---|---|
| • Food and drink... | 1; | • Cameras... | 6; | • Motorcycles... | 11; |
| • Alcohol... | 2; | • Audio recording... | 7; | • Re-entry... | 12; |
| • Cans... | 3; | • Video recording... | 8; | • Other restrictions... | 13. |
| • Bottles... | 4; | • Children... | 9; | | |
| • Coolers... | 5; | • Pets... | 10; | | |

## Secondary Genre[s]:

| | | | |
|---|---|---|---|
| • Variety, General... | VRGL; | • Bluegrass... | BLGS; |
| • Variety, Jazz & Blues... | VRJB; | • Modern Folk... | MFOL; |
| • Variety, Country & Bluegrass | VRCB; | • Traditional Folk... | TFOL; |
| • Variety, Folk & International | VRFI; | • Fiddle and Banjo Events... | FDDL; |
| • Modern Jazz... | MJAZ; | • Maritime... | MARI; |
| • Traditional Jazz & Ragtime... | TJAZ; | • Cajun and Zydeco... | ZYDC; |
| • Alternative Jazz... | AJAZ; | • Irish... | IRSH; |
| • Modern Rock and Pop... | MRCK; | • Jewish... | JWSH; |
| • Classic Rock and Oldies... | CRCK; | • Native American... | NATV; |
| • Alternative & College Rock | ARCK; | • Scottish... | SCOT; |
| • Hard Rock & Heavy Metal | HRCK; | • Modern Latin... | MLAT; |
| • Rap... | RAP; | • Traditional Latin... | TLAT; |
| • Modern R&B... | MR&B; | • African American... | AFRM; |
| • Blues and Traditional R&B... | TR&B; | • African... | AFRC; |
| • Acappella and Doo Wop... | ACAP; | • Brazilian & So. American... | BRZL; |
| • Modern Christian... | CHRS; | • Reggae, Ska & Caribbean... | RGGE; |
| • Black Gospel... | BGOS; | • Avant Garde & New Music... | AVNT; |
| • Southern & Bluegrass Gospel | SGOS; | • Cabaret... | CBRT; |
| • Traditional Gospel & Sings... | TGOS; | • Gay and Lesbian... | GYLS; |
| • Modern Country... | MC&W; | • Drum Corps & March. Bands | DRUM; |
| • Traditional Country... | TC&W; | • Fairs... | FAIR; |
| • Alt. Country & Rockabilly... | AC&W; | • Other Genres... | OTHR. |

**Note**

Wherever "**Help!**" appears readers are invited to answer the proceeding questions and/or provide updates. New festival listings that meet the criteria of this book certainly are welcome too! Please mail any current festival information you obtain — especially flyers or brochures — to FESTPRESS, P. O. Box 147, Glen Ridge, NJ 07028. *Thanks!*

### LOU RAWLS PARADE OF STARS, Manhattan, NYC
> Early Jan.
> Modern R&B

Benefits the United Negro College Fund. **Help!** One time only? Also, a sample lineup? **Days:** 1. **Site:** indoor. Hard Rock Cafe, 221 West 57th Street. **Admission:** paid. **Daily entry:** $25 to $49, $50 and over. **Acts:** national acts, local acts. **Sample day's lineup:** Lou Rawls, others. **Contact:** Lou Rawls Parade of Stars, c/o Hard Rock Cafe, 221 West 57th Street, New York, NY, 212-326-1221.

### GRUPPEN: CHAMBER MUSIC FOR THE 21ST CENTURY, Manhattan, NYC
> Early Jan. to Middle Jan.
> Avant Garde and New Music

Since 1993. **Help!** Still ongoing? **Days:** 6. **Site:** indoor. The Kitchen, 512 West 19th Street. **Admission:** paid. **Daily entry:** under $10, $10 to $24, **Discounts:** other discounts. **Acts:** national acts, regional acts, local acts. **Sample series lineup:** Day One: Toby Twining Music, Peter Gordon; Day Two: Zusaan Kali Fasteau, Julia Heyward; Day Three: Meriden Arts Ensemble, Jon Gibson Group. **Contact:** The Kitchen, 512 West 19th Street, New York, NY 10011, 212-255-5793.

### GREAT BEER AND MUSIC FESTIVAL, Manhattan, NYC
> Middle Jan.
> Alt. Country and Rockabilly

"25 microbrews on draft." -- Advertisement. Dates have varied, though site has been consistent. **Days:** 1. **Hours per day:** 6. **Site:** indoor. Irving Plaza, 17 Irving Place. **Admission:** paid. **Daily entry:** $25 to $49, **Secondary genre[s]:** ARCK, **Acts:** national acts, regional acts, local acts. **Sample day's lineup:** G. E. Smith and High Plains Drifters, 5 Chinese Brothers, Go To Blazes, Pool, Harry. **Contact:** Great Beer and Music Festival, c/o Irving Plaza, 17 Irving Place, New York, NY, 212-777-6800/249-8870.

### PARK SLOPE NATIVE AMERICAN DANCE FESTIVAL, Brooklyn, NYC
> Middle Jan.
> Native American

Since 1994. "Meet old friends; get acquainted with new ones." -- Clint Cayou, New York Newsday. **Days:** 2. **Hours per day:** 6. **Site:** indoor. St. Francis Xavier Lyceum, 752 President Street. **Admission:** paid. **Daily entry:** under $10, **Acts:** local acts. **Contact:** Park Slope Native American Dance Festival, St. Francis Xavier Action Youth Council, 752 President Street, Brooklyn, NY .

### FOCUS!, Manhattan, NYC
> Middle Jan. to Late Jan.
> Avant Garde and New Music

**Days:** 6. **Site:** indoor. Julliard Theater, Alice Tully Hall, Lincoln Center, Broadway at 65th Street. **Admission:** free. **Acts:** local acts. **Sample day's lineup:** Julliard Orchestra, others perform works of Webern, Stockhausen, Babbitt. **Contact:** Focus!, c/o Julliard School, Broadway at 66th Street, New York, NY 10023, 212-769-7406.

### DRAMA LEAGUE'S BLACK-TIE BENEFIT, Manhattan, NYC
> Late Jan.
> Cabaret

Since 1986. Annual tribute to a noted composer. 1995's: Richard Rodgers. **Days:** 1. **Site:** indoor. Pierre Hotel, 5th Avenue and 62nd Street. **Admission:** paid. **Daily entry:** $50 and over. **Acts:** national acts, regional acts, local acts. **Sample day's lineup:** Barbara Cook, Harry Groener, Madeline Kahn, Kitty Carlisle Hart, Shirley Verrett, Mark Jacoby, Liliane Montevecchi, Margaret Whiting. **Contact:** Drama League, 165 West 46th Street, Suite 601, New York, NY 10036, 212-302-2100.

## THUNDERBIRD AMERICAN INDIAN DANCERS POW WOW AND DANCE CONCERT, Manhattan, NYC

>Late Jan. to Early Feb.
>Native American

Since 1993. "You've been to a hootenany, you've been to a hoedown, now come to a Native American pow-wow. Experience the beauty and vastness of our Native American culture." -- Advertisement. See other dates. **Days:** 6. **Site:** indoor. Theater for the New City, 155 1st Avenue at 10th Street. **Admission:** paid. **Daily entry:** $10 to $24, **Acts:** regional acts, local acts. **Sample day's lineup:** Thunderbird American Indian Dancers, others. **Contact:** Theater for the New City, 155 1st Avenue, New York, NY 10003, 212-924-0496/254-1109.

## FAST FOLK REVUE, Manhattan, NYC

>Late Jan.
>Modern Folk

Since 1983. **Days:** 1. **Hours per day:** 3. **Site:** indoor. The Bottom Line, 15 West 4th Street. **Admission:** paid. **Daily entry:** $10 to $24, **Secondary genre[s]:** TR&B, **Acts:** national acts, regional acts, local acts. **Sample day's lineup:** Ed Carey, Patrick Brayer, Wendy Beckerman, Buddy Mondlock, Camille West, Catie Curtis, Dave Van Ronk, Lisa McCormick, Jack Hardy, Chuck Brodsky, Louise Taylor, Jim Allen, David Massengill, Kitty Donohue, Richard Julian. **Audio merchandise:** "The Tenth Anniversary Fast Folk Revue" (Fast Folk Musical Magazine), plus many other live recordings in Fast Folk's catalog. **Contact:** Fast Folk Musical Magazine, Inc., P. O. Box 938 Village Station, New York, NY 10014, 212-274-1636/885-1556.

## HOT 97'S OLD SCHOOL THROWDOWN, Manhattan, NYC

>Late Jan.
>Rap

Since 1994. Occurs periodically (Late Jan., Mid. Oct. in 1994). Call for current dates. **Days:** 1. **Site:** indoor. The Paramount, Madison Square Garden, 7th Avenue at 32nd Street. **Admission:** paid. **Daily entry:** $25 to $49, **Secondary genre[s]:** CRCK, **Acts:** national acts, . **Sample day's lineup:** Run-D. M. C., Grandmaster Flash and The Furious Five with Melle Mel, Doug E. Fresh, Kurtis Blow, Rose Royce, Dazz Band, Whodini, others. **Contact:** WQHT-FM, 1372 Broadway, 16th Floor, New York, NY 10018, 212-840-0097/465-MSG1.

## GOSPEL CELEBRATION!, Brooklyn, NYC

>Early Feb.
>Black Gospel

Since 1992. Part of W. M. I.'s year-round international folk and jazz concerts featuring national, regional and local acts. Sub-series titles include Interpretations, Improvisations, World of Percussion, Irish Nights. **Days:** 1. **Site:** indoor. Whitman Hall, Brooklyn College, Campus Road, off jct. of Flatbush and Nostrand Avenues. **Admission:** paid. **Daily entry:** $10 to $24, **Discounts:** other discounts. **Acts:** national acts, regional acts, local acts. **Sample day's lineup:** Rev. Timothy Wright, Brooklyn College Gospel Choir, Spirit In Black, Wingate and Brooklyn Tech High School Choirs. **Audio merchandise:** entire W. M. I. catalog. **Contact:** World Music Institute, 49 West 27th Street, Suite 810, New York, NY 10001, 212-545-7536.

## BOB MARLEY DAY, Manhattan, NYC

>Early Feb.
>Reggae, Ska and Caribbean

"'Wake Up and Live' Birthday Concert Tribute." -- Advertisement. Date has been consistent, though site has varied. **Days:** 1. **Site:** indoor. Irving Plaza, 17 Irving Place. **Admission:** paid. **Daily entry:** $10 to $24, **Acts:** national acts, regional acts, local acts. **Sample day's lineup:** Sugar Minott, The Mighty Diamonds, Sister Carol, The City Heat Band, Worl-A-Girl. **Contact:** Bob Marley Day, c/o Irving Plaza, 17 Irving Place, New York, NY, 212-777-6800/249-8870.

WOMEN IN CABARET, Manhattan, NYC
> Early Feb. to Late Feb.
> Cabaret

"Classic and cool on the Hudson." -- Brochure. See other dates. **Help!** Still ongoing? **Days:** 6. **Site:** indoor. World Financial Center, Liberty and West Streets. **Admission:** free. **Acts:** national acts, regional acts, local acts. **Sample day's lineup:** Baby Jane Dexter, Ivy Austin, Sally Mayes. **Contact:** World Financial Center Arts and Events, 200 Liberty Street, 18th Floor, New York, NY 10281, 212-945-0505.

U. G. H. A. BLACK HISTORY MONTH CELEBRATION, Manhattan, NYC
> Middle Feb.
> A Cappella and Doo Wop

Since 1992. **Days:** 1. **Site:** indoor. Symphony Space, 2537 Broadway at 95th Street. **Admission:** paid. **Daily entry:** $25 to $49, **Discounts:** other discounts. **Secondary genre[s]:** CRCK, **Acts:** national acts, regional acts, local acts. **Sample day's lineup:** Rudy West's Five Keys, Harptones, Orioles, Solitaires, Vocaleers, Dubs, Two hearts, Students, Linda Hayes, Choice, The Sheps. **Contact:** United in Group Harmony Association, P. O. Box 185, Clifton, NJ 07011, 201-470-UGHA/365-0049.

CONCIERTO DEL AMOR, Manhattan, NYC
> Middle Feb.
> Modern Latin

Since 1994. See other sites and dates. **Days:** 1. **Site:** indoor. The Paramount, Madison Square Garden, 7th Avenue at 32nd Street. **Admission:** paid. **Daily entry:** $25 to $49, **Acts:** national acts, regional acts. **Sample day's lineup:** Tito Rojas, Luis Enrique, Rey Ruiz, La India, Edgar Joel and His Orchestra, Manny Manuel. **Contact:** RMM Productions, 568 Broadway, Suite 806, New York, NY 10012, 212-925-2828/4885.

FESTIVAL OF 20TH CENTURY MUSIC, Manhattan, NYC
> Middle Feb. to Late Feb.
> Avant Garde and New Music

Since 1985. Dates vary between Feb. and Mar., so call ahead. Also programs a classical music series in winter, plus a Manhattan Summer Jazz Workshop in conjunction with the JVC Jazz Festival. **Days:** 3. **Site:** indoor. Manhattan School of Music, John C. Borden Auditorium, Broadway at 122nd Street. **Admission:** free. **Acts:** local acts. **Sample day's lineup:** MSM Contemporary Ensemble, Charlotte Savander, Rebecca Plack, Charles Coleman perform works of Tanenbaum, Sadashige, Charvet. **Contact:** Festival of 20th Century Music, Manhattan School of Music, 120 Claremont Avenue, New York, NY 10027, 212-749-2802.

JAZZ AND POETRY MARATHON, Manhattan, NYC
> Middle Feb.
> African American

Part of the James Baldwin Literature and Music Series. See other dates. **Help!** Still ongoing? **Days:** 1. **Hours per day:** 5. **Site:** indoor. Harlem School of the Arts, 645 St. Nicholas Avenue. **Admission:** free. **Secondary genre[s]:** MJAZ, OTHR **Acts:** national acts, regional acts, local acts. **Sample day's lineup:** Amiri Baraka, Makanda Ken McIntyre Band, J. D. Parran Group, others. **Contact:** James Baldwin Literature and Music Series, Harlem School for the Arts, 645 St. Nicholas Avenue, New York, NY, 212-926-4100.

98.7 KISS-FM Gospel Celebration, Manhattan, NYC
> Middle Feb.
> Black Gospel

See other dates. **Help!** One time only? **Days:** 1. **Site:** indoor. The Paramount, Madison Square Garden, 7th Avenue at 32nd Street. **Admission:** paid. **Daily entry:** $10 to $24, $25 to $49, **Acts:** national acts, local acts. **Sample day's lineup:** John P. Kee and The New Life Community Choir, Daryl Coley and The Bronx Mass Choir, Hezekiah Walker and The Love Fellowship Crusade Choir. **Contact:** WRKS-FM, 1440 Broadway, New York, NY, 212-642-4300/465-MSG1.

Mardi Gras Carnaval, Manhattan, NYC
> Middle Feb.
> Variety, Folk and International

Since 1994. Part of W. M. I.'s year-round international folk and jazz concerts featuring national, regional and local acts. Sub-series titles include Interpretations, Improvisations, World of Percussion, Irish Nights. **Days:** 1. **Site:** indoor. Symphony Space, 2537 Broadway at 95th Street. **Admission:** paid. **Daily entry:** $10 to $24, $25 to $49, **Discounts:** other discounts. **Secondary genre[s]:** TR&B, BRZL, RGGE, OTHR **Acts:** national acts, regional acts, local acts. **Sample day's lineup:** Dirty Dozen Brass Band, Dandara, Rudy King, Silhouettes Steel Orchestra. **Audio merchandise:** entire W. M. I. catalog. **Contact:** World Music Institute, 49 West 27th Street, Suite 810, New York, NY 10001, 212-545-7536 **or:** Symphony Space, 2537 Broadway, New York, NY 10025, 212-864-5400.

Smalls Winter Festival, Manhattan, NYC
> Middle Feb.
> Modern Jazz

"New York's cutting edge jazz club." -- Advertisement. **Days:** 1. **Site:** indoor. Smalls, 183 West 10th Street. **Admission:** paid. **Daily entry:** $25 to $49, **Acts:** national acts, regional acts, local acts. **Contact:** Smalls, 183 West 10th Street, New York, NY, 212-929-7565.

Evening In Celebration of Black History Month, Brooklyn, NYC
> Late Feb.
> African American

**Help!** One time only? **Days:** 1. **Site:** indoor. Downtown Theater, 195 Cadman Park Plaza. **Admission:** paid. **Daily entry:** $10 to $24, **Acts:** regional acts, local acts. **Sample day's lineup:** Kusasa, Thuli Dumakude, Andrew Lamb Quartet, others. **Contact:** BACA/The Brooklyn Arts Council, 200 Eastern Parkway, Brooklyn, NY 11238, 718-783-4469/3077.

Music From Japan Festival, Manhattan, NYC
> Late Feb.
> Avant Garde and New Music

Since 1976. Part of a winter concert series. See other dates and sites. **Days:** 3. **Site:** indoor. Asia Society, 725 Park Avenue at 70th Street. **Admission:** paid. **Daily entry:** $10 to $24, **Discounts:** multiple event or day passes, **Acts:** national acts, regional acts. **Sample day's lineup:** Mayumi Miyata, Midori Takada perform works by Takemitsu, Hosokawa, Satoh, Cage, Takada. **Audio merchandise:** "Music From Japan, Vol. 1" (Music From Japan. **Contact:** Music from Japan, Inc., 7 East 20th Street, #6F, New York, NY 10003-1106, 212-674-4587/517-ASIA.

## LYRICS AND LYRICISTS/BOYS NIGHT OUT, Manhattan, NYC
### Late Feb.
### Cabaret

Since 1995. Part of year-round, 25-year-old Lyrics and Lyricists series, where up to eight leading singers perform works of single selected lyricist per evening. Also programs weekly Cabaret in Concert series. **Help!** One time only? **Days:** 1. **Site:** indoor. 92nd Street Y, 1395 Lexington Avenue. **Admission:** paid. **Daily entry:** $10 to $24, $25 to $49, **Secondary genre[s]:** TR&B, **Acts:** national acts, regional acts, local acts. **Sample day's lineup:** David Staller, Jeff Harner, Phillip Officer, Tom Andersen. **Contact:** Tisch Center for the Arts, 92nd Street YM-YWHA, 1395 Lexington Avenue, New York, NY 10128, 212-996-1100/415-5488.

## TROPICAL CARNIVAL/CARNIVAL FETE AND MASQUERADE JUMP-UP, Brooklyn, NYC
### Late Feb.
### Reggae, Ska and Caribbean

Since 1995. "It's a lot more than just Mardi Gras. These [combined] events showcase the styles and cultures of many different places." -- Trevor Bentley, New York Newsday. See other dates. **Days:** 1. **Hours per day:** 11. **Site:** indoor. Brooklyn Botanic Garden (free daytime Carnival), 1000 Washington Avenue; CUNY/Medgar Evers College (paid nighttime Fete). **Admission:** free and paid. **Daily entry:** $25 to $49, **Acts:** local acts. **Sample day's lineup:** C. A. S. Y. M. Steel Orchestra, Metro Steel Band, others. **Contact:** Carnival Fete and Masquerade Jump-Up, CUNY/Medgar Evers College, 1150 Carroll Street, Brooklyn, NY, 718-270-6028.

## CARNAVAL DEL MERENGUE, Manhattan, NYC
### Late Feb.
### Modern Latin

Since 1980. See other dates. **Help!** Still ongoing? **Days:** 1. **Site:** indoor. The Paramount, Madison Square Garden, 7th Avenue at 32nd Street. **Admission:** paid. **Daily entry:** $25 to $49, **Acts:** national acts, regional acts, local acts. **Sample day's lineup:** Fernandito Villalona, Sergio Vargas, Cana Brava, others. **Contact:** Carnaval Del Merengue, c/o Madison Square Garden, 4 Pennsylvania Plaza, New York, NY, 212-465-MSG1.

## EVIAN INDOOR PRO BEACH VOLLEYBALL CHAMPIONSHIPS, Manhattan, NYC
### Late Feb.
### Alternative and College Rock

Since 1980. "A winter beach fest." -- Advertisement. See other dates. **Help!** A sample lineup? **Days:** 1. **Site:** indoor. The Paramount, Madison Square Garden, 7th Avenue at 32nd Street. **Admission:** paid. **Daily entry:** $25 to $49, **Acts:** local acts. **Contact:** Evian indoor Pro Beach Volleyball Championships, c/o Madison Square Garden, 4 Pennsylvania Plaza, New York, NY, 212-465-MSG1.

## ZYDECODELIC LOUP GAROU BAL DE LA MAISON MARDI GRAS PARTY, Manhattan, NYC
### Late Feb.
### Cajun and Zydeco

Since 1994. "[Loup Garou's] last all-night 'Bal du Maison' was so successful, they're reprising it this Lundi Gras with an extensive lineup of guests." -- Village Voice. **Days:** 1. **Site:** indoor. Tramps, 51 West 21st Street, between 5th and 6th Avenues. **Admission:** paid. **Daily entry:** $10 to $24, **Discounts:** advance purchase discounts, **Secondary genre[s]:** MRCK, AC&W, **Acts:** national acts, regional acts, local acts. **Sample day's lineup:** Loup Garou, G. E. Smith and High Plains Drifters, Rob Wasserman, Eric Schenkman, Lenny Pickett, El Pantalones, Bob Gaddy, Jimmy Spruill, Babi Floyd, Bruce Martin, Marc Muller, Arnie Lawrence, Chuck Hancock, Brian O'Sullivan, Tim Ouimette, Mindy Jostyn, Shane Fontayne, others. **Contact:** Zydecodelic Loup Garou Bal de la Maison Mardi Gras Party, c/o Tramps, 51 West 21st Street, New York, NY, 212-727-7788.

## KITTY BRAZELTON'S REAL MUSIC SERIES, Manhattan, NYC
   Late Feb. to Early Apr.
   Avant Garde and New Music

See other dates. **Days:** 14. **Hours per day:** 4. **Site:** indoor. CB's Gallery, 313 Bowery. **Admission:** paid. **Daily entry:** under $10, **Discounts:** student discounts, other discounts **Acts:** local acts. **Sample day's lineup:** The Mellow Edwards, Matt Sullivan, Chris Washburne's Syotos Group, Cooper Moore. **Contact:** Kitty Brazelton's Real Music Series, c/o CB's Gallery, 313 Bowery, New York, NY, 212-677-0455.


## GREAT MIRACLE PRAYER FESTIVAL, Manhattan, NYC
   Late Feb.
   Modern Rock and Pop

Since 1992. Benefits Tibet House. See other dates. **Days:** 1. **Site:** indoor. Carnegie Hall, 57th Street at 7th Avenue. **Admission:** paid. **Daily entry:** $10 to $24, $25 to $49, $50 and over. **Secondary genre[s]:** ARCK, BGOS, AC&W, IRSH, AVNT, OTHR **Acts:** national acts, regional acts. **Sample day's lineup:** Philip Glass, Spalding Gray, Natalie Merchant, David Byrne, Ashley Macisaac, Allen Ginsberg, Gyuto Monks, Jimmie Dale Gilmore, Fontella Bass, Katell Keineg. **Contact:** Tibet House Benefit Concert, c/o Carnegie Hall, 881 7th Avenue, New York, NY 10019, 212-247-7800/696-1033.


## BACK STAGE BISTRO AWARDS, Manhattan, NYC
   Late Feb.
   Cabaret

Since 1986. **Days:** 1. **Site:** indoor. Locations vary among top clubs (The Ballroom, Cafe Carlyle, etc.). **Acts:** national acts, local acts. **Sample day's lineup:** Barbara Cook, Mathew Bennett, Erin Hill, Kevin Fox, Rick Leon, Sean McCourt, others. **Contact:** Back Stage Magazine, 1515 Broadway, 14th Floor, New York, NY 10036, 212-764-7300/536-5318.


## RHYTHM AND BLUES FOUNDATION'S PIONEER AWARDS, Manhattan, NYC
   Early Mar.
   Blues and Traditional R&B

Since 1994. **Days:** 1. **Site:** indoor. Roseland Ballroom, West 52nd Street. **Admission:** paid. **Secondary genre[s]:** CRCK, **Acts:** national acts. **Sample day's lineup:** Maceo Parker, Steve Cropper, Ry Cooder, G. E. Smith, The Shirelles, Clarence Carter, Jerry Butler, Mable John, Ben E. King, Bonnie Raitt, others. **Audio merchandise:** "Rites of Rhythm and Blues, Vols. One" (Capitol), "...Two" (Motown). **Contact:** Rhythm and Blues Foundation, Smithsonian Institution, Washington, DC 20560, 212-247-0200.


## IMPROVISORS COLLECTIVE FESTIVAL, Manhattan, NYC
   Early Mar.
   Alternative Jazz

Since 1994. "Avant garde jazz music dance poetry and art." -- Flyer. **Days:** 2. **Site:** indoor. Context, 28 Avenue A, between 2nd and 3rd Streets. **Admission:** paid. **Daily entry:** under $10, $10 to $24, **Discounts:** student discounts, **Secondary genre[s]:** AVNT, **Acts:** local acts. **Sample day's lineup:** Matthew Shipp and Yuke Otomo, Jemeel Moondoc and Mariko Tanabe, Patricia Nicholson Parker and Denis Charles, The Collective Ensemble. **Contact:** Improvisors Collective Festival, c/o Context, 28 Avenue A, New York, NY, 212-925-5256.

## CENTURY OF CHANGE/SO NICE TO COME HOME TO, Manhattan, NYC
Early Mar.
Cabaret

Since 1995. "Cabaret celebration of the USO shows and the songs of the Stage Door Canteen." -- Advertisement. Part of Town Hall's Century of Change series that focuses, musically, on one 20th Century decade per winter. **Help!** One time only? **Days:** 1. **Site:** indoor. Town Hall, 123 West 43rd Street. **Admission:** paid. **Daily entry:** $10 to $24, $25 to $49, **Acts:** national acts. **Sample day's lineup:** Julie Wilson, Margaret Whiting, K. T. Sullivan, David Staller, Liliane Montevecchi, others. **Contact:** So Nice To Come Home To, c/o Town Hall, 123 West 43rd Street, New York, NY 10036, 212-840-2824/1003.

## CARIBBEAN MUSIC AWARDS, Manhattan, NYC
Early Mar.
Reggae, Ska and Caribbean

Since 1991. Filmed for cable-TV re-broadcast, which meant interminable technical delays the year I attended. However, my friends reported improved production last year, including more live backings. See other dates. **Days:** 1. **Site:** indoor. Apollo Theater, 253 West 125th Street. **Admission:** paid. **Daily entry:** $50 and over. **Secondary genre[s]:** MR&B, MLAT, **Acts:** national acts, regional acts, local acts. **Sample day's lineup:** Roberta Flack, Third World, Baha Men, Mighty Sparrow, Mac Fingall, C. A. S. Y. M. Steel Orchestra, Nadine Sutherland, Cocoa Tea, Mega Banton, Terra Fabulous, Jigsy King, United Sisters, Ras Iley, Red Plastic Bag, Spice, Inner Circle, others. **Contact:** Inner City Theater Group, Apollo Theater, 253 West 125th Street, New York, NY, 212-222-0992/749-5838.

## FESTIVAL OF WOMEN IMPROVISORS, Manhattan, NYC
Early Mar. to Middle Mar.
Modern Jazz

Part of New Faces/New Voices/New Visions series. See other dates. **Help!** One time only? **Days:** 4. **Hours per day:** 8. **Site:** indoor. Aaron Davis Hall, West 133-to-135th Streets and Convent Avenue. **Admission:** paid. **Daily entry:** under $10, $10 to $24, **Discounts:** student discounts, other discounts **Secondary genre[s]:** NATV, **Acts:** regional acts, local acts. **Sample day's lineup:** Marlies Yearby with Pam Patrick, Jeanne Lee with Mickey Davidson. **Contact:** Festival of Women Improvisors, c/o Aaron Davis Hall, City College, West 133-to-135th Streets, New York, NY, 212-650-7100.

## WOMEN'S JAZZ FESTIVAL, Manhattan, NYC
Early Mar. to Late Mar.
Modern Jazz

Since 1978. Classy affair in a classy space. **Days:** 4. **Site:** indoor. Schomburg Center for Research in Black Culture, 515 Malcolm X Boulevard at 135th Street, Harlem. **Admission:** paid. **Daily entry:** $10 to $24, **Discounts:** multiple event or day passes, other discounts **Secondary genre[s]:** AJAZ, BGOS, AFRM, AFRC, **Acts:** national acts, local acts. **Sample series lineup:** Day One: Gerri Allen, Vinnie Knight; Day Two: Straight Ahead Spelman College Jazz Ensemble; Day Three: Bobbi Humphrey, Tuliva Donna Cumberbatch. **Contact:** Schomburg Center for Research in Black Culture, 515 Malcolm X Boulevard, New York, NY, 212-491-2206.

## BILL POPP'S BIRTHDAY TRIBUTE TO GEORGE L. POPP, Manhattan, NYC
Early Mar.
Alternative and College Rock

Since 1987. Benefits the American Heart Association. **Days:** 1. **Site:** indoor. Kenny's Castaways, 157 Bleecker Street. **Admission:** paid. **Daily entry:** under $10, **Secondary genre[s]:** MRCK, **Acts:** local acts. **Sample day's lineup:** Mark Handleman, Anne Husick, Marc Farre with Serena Jost, Carlton and Keyo, Valerie Vigoda, Bill Popp and The Tapes, Marble?, Times Square, Strange Rain. **Contact:** Bill Popp's Birthday Tribute to George L. Popp, c/o Kenny's Castaways, 157 Bleecker Street, New York, NY, 212-473-9870.

## EVENING OF ROCK AND ROLL, Manhattan, NYC
   Middle Mar.
   A Cappella and Doo Wop

Benefits the Children's Health Fund, Jeffrey Modell Foundation. **Help!** One time only? **Days:** 1. **Hours per day:** 4. **Site:** indoor. Hunter College, East 69th Street. **Admission:** paid. **Daily entry:** $25 to $49, $50 and over. **Secondary genre[s]:** CRCK, **Acts:** national acts, regional acts, local acts. **Sample day's lineup:** Johnny Maestro and The Brooklyn Bridge, The Classics, The Duprees, The Dimensions, The Tokens, The Crystals, Randy and The Rainbows, The Teenagers, The Cadillacs. **Contact:** Evening of Rock and Roll, c/o Hunter College, East 69th Street, New York, NY, 212-307-7171.

## WINNING SCORES, Manhattan, NYC
   Middle Mar.
   Avant Garde and New Music

Featuring winners of The Concordia American Composers Awards. Also programs a benefit concert in Early Jun. featuring a national classical music act. **Help!** Still ongoing? **Days:** 1. **Site:** indoor. Alice Tully Hall, Lincoln Center, Broadway at 65th Street. **Admission:** paid. **Daily entry:** $25 to $49, **Acts:** national acts, local acts. **Sample day's lineup:** Concordia Orchestra, Turtle Island String Quartet per form works of Grantham, Rouse, Tsontakis, Balakrishnan. **Contact:** The Concordia American Composers Awards, c/o Lincoln Center for the Performing Arts, 70 Lincoln Center Plaza, New York, NY 10023-6583, 212-875-5050/967-1290.

## BANG ON A CAN FESTIVAL, Manhattan, NYC
   Middle Mar. to Early May
   Avant Garde and New Music

Since 1987. **Days:** 3. **Hours per day:** 8. **Site:** indoor. Alice Tully Hall, Lincoln Center, Broadway at 65th Street, plus other locations. **Admission:** paid. **Daily entry:** $10 to $24, **Acts:** national acts, regional acts, local acts. **Sample day's lineup:** Lydian Quartet, Evan Ziporyn, Bang on a Can All-Stars, Rolfe Schulte and Martin Goldray, John Tamburello, Dora Ohrenstein, Mary Rowell, Jason Cirker, The Lark Quartet, Rova Saxophone Quartet, Elizabeth Brown, Jennie Hansen, Bill Hayes, The Cassat Quartet perform works of Ives, Wigglesworth, Glass, Bouchard, Garcia, Lang, Johnson, Feldman, Gordon, Thorne, Elliott Carter, Singleton, Wolfe, Curran, Maguire, John Carter, Brown, Marcus, Trunk, Rova Saxophone Quartet, Adams, Ochs. **Audio merchandise:** "Industry" (SONY Classical); "Bang On a Can Live, Vols. 1, 2, 3" (CRI). **Contact:** E. Snapp, Inc., 1007 Glen Cove Avenue, Glen Cove, NY 11545, 516-671-9314 **or:** Bang On a Can Festival, 222 East 5th Street, New York, NY 10003, 212-875-5050/777-8442.

## AFRICA MONDO SHOWCASE, Manhattan, NYC
   Middle Mar.
   African

See other dates. **Help!** One time only? **Days:** 1. **Site:** indoor. Sounds of Brazil, 204 Varick Street. **Admission:** paid. **Daily entry:** $10 to $24, **Discounts:** other discounts. **Acts:** regional acts, local acts. **Sample day's lineup:** Bougarabou, Mousa Kanoute, Hadja Soumano, Fode Sissoko, Djevo, Djakout, others. **Contact:** Africa Mondo Showcase, c/o S. O. B.'s, 204 Varick Street, New York, NY, 212-243-4940.

## EVENING WITH FRANK PATTERSON, Manhattan, NYC
   Early Mar.
   Irish

See other dates. **Days:** 1. **Site:** indoor. Carnegie Hall, 57th Street at 7th Avenue. **Admission:** paid. **Daily entry:** $25 to $49, **Acts:** national acts, regional acts, local acts. **Sample day's lineup:** Frank Patterson, Shaun Connors, Eily and Eanan O'Grady, The Hibernian Choir, Little Gaelic Singers and Harpists of New York, Fordham University Band, others. **Contact:** Evening with Frank Patterson, c/o Carnegie Hall, 881 7th Avenue, New York, NY 10019, 212-247-7800/696-1033.

ROULETTE CONCERT SERIES/LE SALON ROULETTE, Manhattan, NYC
Middle Mar.
Avant Garde and New Music

Since 1980. Kick-off sampler/reception to 21-evening spring concert series. **Help!** Le Salon still ongoing? **Days:** 1. **Site:** indoor. Roulette, 228 West Broadway at White Street. **Admission:** paid. **Daily entry:** $10 to $24, **Discounts:** other discounts **Acts:** national acts, regional acts, local acts. **Sample series lineup:** Day One: Pauline Oliveros and David Gamper; Day Two: Frankie Mann; Day Three: Yasunao Tone. **Audio merchandise:** "A Confederacy of Dances, Vols. 1, 2" (Einstein), plus entire Einstein catalog. **Contact:** Roulette/Einstein, 228 West Broadway, New York, NY 10013-2456, 212-219-8242.


**HEARTS AND VOICES WINTER BENEFIT SERIES**, Manhattan, NYC
Middle Mar. to Late Apr.
Cabaret

Since 1992. **Days:** 7. **Site:** indoor. Steve McGraw's, 158 West 72nd Street. **Admission:** paid. **Daily entry:** $10 to $24, **Acts:** national acts, regional acts, local acts. **Sample day's lineup:** Tom Andersen and Tim DiPasqua, Ralph Brande with Steve Marzullo, Tom Coviello, Colleen Dodson, Barbara Fasano, Linda Glick, Annie Hughes with Jason Robert Brown, Terri Klausner, Alix Korey with David Friedman, Nancy LaMott with Christopher Marlowe, Michael McAssey, Phillip Officer with Dick Gallagher. **Contact:** Hearts and Voices, 150 West 80th Street, #7D, New York, NY 10024, 212-799-4276/362-2590.


TOKYO/NEW YORK NOISE FESTIVAL, Manhattan, NYC
Middle Mar.
Alternative and College Rock

Since 1992. Also programmed the one-day Tokyo/New York Improv. Meeting with similar acts, Late Nov. **Days:** 3. **Hours per day:** 5. **Site:** indoor. Knitting Factory, 74 Leonard Street, between Broadway and Church Street. **Admission:** paid. **Daily entry:** $10 to $24, **Secondary genre[s]:** AJAZ, HRCK, **Acts:** national acts, regional acts, local acts. **Sample day's lineup:** Thurston Moore, Page Hamilton, Marc Ribot, Heino Keiji, Kofun Bokan. **Audio merchandise:** entire Knitting Factory Works catalog, including numerous festival recordings and compilations. **Other merchandise:** "Knitting Music" by Michael Dorf (Knitting Factory Works). **Contact:** Knitting Factory, 47 East Houston Street, New York, NY 10012, 212-219-3055/3006.


JULIUS WATKINS JAZZ FRENCH HORN FESTIVAL, Manhattan, NYC
Middle Mar.
Alternative Jazz

Since 1994. **Days:** 1. **Hours per day:** 5. **Site:** indoor. Knitting Factory, 74 Leonard Street, between Broadway and Church Street. **Admission:** paid. **Acts:** national acts, local acts. **Sample day's lineup:** Mark Taylor and Syzygy, Tom Varner Trio, John Clark Band, Vincent Chancey Quartet. **Audio merchandise:** entire Knitting Factory Works catalog, including numerous festival recordings and compilations. **Other merchandise:** "Knitting Music" by Michael Dorf (Knitting Factory Works). **Contact:** Knitting Factory, 47 East Houston Street, New York, NY 10012, 212-219-3055/3006.


WEST INDIAN CARNIVAL EXPLOSION, Brooklyn, NYC
Middle Mar.
Reggae, Ska and Caribbean

Since 1992. A. k. a. West Indian Steel Pan Festival. Dates, sites and length vary widely, so call ahead. **Days:** 1. **Site:** indoor. Gershwin Theater, Brooklyn College, Campus Road, off jct. of Flatbush and Nostrand Avenues. **Admission:** paid. **Daily entry:** $10 to $24, **Discounts:** other discounts **Acts:** national acts, regional acts, local acts. **Sample day's lineup:** Chalkdust, Len "Boogsie" Sharp, Merrytones Steel Orchestra. **Audio merchandise:** entire W. M. I. catalog. **Contact:** World Music Institute, 49 West 27th Street, Suite 810, New York, NY 10001, 212-545-7536.

## NATIONAL GOSPEL CHOIR COMPETITION, Manhattan, NYC
Middle Mar.
Black Gospel

Features gospel choirs from elementary schools, high schools and colleges. **Help!** One time only? **Days:** 2. **Hours per day:** 6. **Site:** indoor. Fashion Industries High School, 225 West 24th Street. **Admission:** paid. **Daily entry:** under $10, $10 to $24, **Acts:** regional acts, local acts. **Contact:** National Gospel Choir Competition, c/o Fashion Industries High School, 225 West 24th Street, New York, NY, 212-866-2474/255-1235.

## ISRAELI FOLK DANCE FESTIVAL AND FESTIVAL OF THE ARTS, Manhattan, NYC
Middle Mar.
Jewish

**Help!** A sample lineup? **Days:** 1. **Hours per day:** 6. **Site:** indoor. Martin Luther King Jr. High School, 122 Amsterdam Avenue at West 65th Street. **Admission:** paid. **Daily entry:** $10 to $24, **Acts:** local acts. **Contact:** Israeli Folk Dance Festival and Festival of the Arts, c/o Martin Luther King Jr. High School, 122 Amsterdam Avenue, New York, NY, 212-983-4806 x144.

## PARTY FOR ZOOT, Manhattan, NYC
Middle Mar.
Modern Jazz

Since 1986. Benefits New School John Haley "Zoot" Sims Scholarship Fund. See other dates. **Days:** 1. **Site:** indoor. Location varies (Zinno's, Century Cafe, etc.). **Admission:** paid. **Daily entry:** $50 and over. **Secondary genre[s]:** TJAZ, **Acts:** national acts, regional acts, local acts. **Sample day's lineup:** Clark Terry, Al Grey, others. **Contact:** Zoot's Party, New School Jazz, 66 West 12th Street, New York, NY 10011, 212-229-5898.

## THE BROOKLYN BEAT MEETS THE BLACK ROCK COALITION, Manhattan, NYC
Middle Mar.
Rap

Since 1992. See other dates and sites. **Help!** Still ongoing? **Days:** 1. **Site:** indoor. CBGB's, 315 Bowery. **Admission:** paid. **Daily entry:** under $10, $10 to $24, **Discounts:** advance purchase discounts, other discounts **Secondary genre[s]:** ARCK, HRCK, TR&B, **Acts:** regional acts, local acts. **Sample day's lineup:** Bite The Wax Godhead, The Cheese Beads, Words and Music, Cryptic Soup, Shock Council, Frank's Museum, Funkface, Jim Lapo's Band, Chemical Wedding, Acid Zone, Al Lee Wyler, Made For TV. **Audio merchandise:** "Black Rock Coalition: The History of Our Future"; "Black Rock Coalition: Blacker Than That" (both on Ryko). **Contact:** Black Rock Coalition, Inc., P. O. Box 1054 Cooper Station, New York, NY 10279, 212-713-5097.

## ST. BARNABAS IRISH VARIETY CONCERT, Bronx, NYC
Middle Mar.
Irish

**Help!** One time only? **Days:** 1. **Site:** indoor. St. Barnabas High School Auditorium, 425 East 240th Street. **Acts:** national acts, regional acts, local acts. **Sample day's lineup:** Dermot Henry Band, Eileen Ivers, others. **Contact:** St. Barnabus High School, 425 East 240th Street, Bronx, NY, 718-994-1410.

MAIN STREET U. S. A., Manhattan, NYC
Late Mar.
Variety, General

Lunchtime concerts. See other sites and dates. **Days:** 7. **Hours per day:** 2. **Site:** indoor. MetLife Building, 200 Park Avenue. **Admission:** free. **Secondary genre[s]:** CRCK, BGOS, AC&W, ZYDC, **Acts:** national acts, regional acts, local acts. **Sample series lineup:** Day One: The Marvelettes; Day Two: Loup Garou; Day Three: Ronny Dawson and High Noon. **Contact:** Grand Central Partnership, 6 East 43rd Street, New York, NY, 212-818-1777.

WALL OF SOUND, Queens, NYC
Late Mar.
A Cappella and Doo Wop

See other dates. **Days:** 1. **Site:** indoor. Golden Center for the Performing Arts, Queens College, Kissena Boulevard and Long Island Expressway, Flushing. **Admission:** paid. **Daily entry:** $10 to $24, **Secondary genre[s]:** CRCK, **Acts:** national acts, regional acts, local acts. **Sample day's lineup:** Duprees, Drifters, Larry Chance and The Earls, Capris, Classics, Yesterday's News, Younger Dayz, Skylite, Renditions. **Contact:** John Vogele Productions, Golden Center for the Performing Arts, Kissena Boulevard, Flushing, NY, 718-793-8080.

WALL TO WALL, Manhattan, NYC
Late Mar.
Cabaret

**Days:** 1. **Hours per day:** 13. **Site:** indoor. Symphony Space, 2537 Broadway at 95th Street. **Admission:** free. **Secondary genre[s]:** TJAZ, AVNT, OTHR **Acts:** national acts, regional acts, local acts. **Sample day's lineup:** Vince Giordano and The Nighthawks with Laurie Gamache, Beverly Hoch and Charles Wadsworth, Max and Kathy Morath, Lanny Myers, Lynne Vardaman and Paul Harman, Joan Morris and William Bolcom, Gay Gotham Chorus, K. T. Sullivan and James Followell, Mary Ellin Lerner, Karen Akers and Michael Abene, Emily Loesser and David Staller, Rob Fisher and The Demitasse Quintet with Mary Cleere Haran, Ivy Austin, Andrea Marcovicci and Glenn Mehrbach, Helen Stewart Marcovicci, Steve Ross, Diane Monroe and Marie Christine Delbeau, Marcy Degonge-Manfredi, Jo Sullivan Loesser and Colin Romoff, Howard McGillin, Linda Lavin and Stephen Lutvak, Petula Clark, Nora York and Jack Wilkins, Wiseguys, Melba Joyce, Loni Ackerman and Tim DiPasqua, Phillip Officer and Dick Gallagher, Betty Comden and Adolph Green, Michael Feinstein, Nancy LaMott and Chrsitopher Marlowe, Ann Hampton Calloway, The Wall-to-Wall Orchestra, Judy Kaye and Phyllis Newman, Debbie Shapiro Gravitte, Margaret Whiting, James Naughton, Nussell Nype. **Contact:** Symphony Space, 2537 Broadway, New York, NY 10025, 212-864-5400.

WPLJ-FM's 70's ROCK AND ROLL REUNION, Manhattan, NYC
Late Mar.
Classic Rock and Oldies

Formerly WPLJ-FM's Disco Dance Party. See other dates. **Days:** 1. **Site:** indoor. The Paramount, Madison Square Garden, 7th Avenue at 32nd Street. **Admission:** paid. **Daily entry:** $25 to $49, **Acts:** national acts, . **Sample day's lineup:** Three Dog Night, Looking Glass, Andrew Gold, Alan O'Day, others. **Contact:** WPLJ-FM's 70's Rock and Roll Reunion, WPLJ-FM, 2 Pennsylvania Plaza, New York, NY, 212-465-MSG1.

TAMIKA REGGAE AWARDS, Manhattan, NYC
Late Mar.
Reggae, Ska and Caribbean

Since 1987. **Days:** 1. **Site:** indoor. Town Hall, 123 West 43rd Street (though locations vary). **Admission:** paid. **Acts:** national acts, regional acts, local acts. **Sample day's lineup:** Louis Ranking, Cobra, Blacka Ranks, Rude Girl, Marcia Griffiths, Carlene Davis, Papa San, Ed Robinson, Half Pint, A-Team Band. **Contact:** Tamika Reggae Awards, c/o Town Hall, 123 West 43rd Street, New York, NY 10036, 212-840-2824/1003.

## GOSPEL EXPLOSION, Brooklyn, NYC
Late Mar.
Black Gospel

**Help!** One time only? **Days:** 1. **Site:** indoor. Boys and Girls High School, 1700 Fulton Street and Utica Avenue, Bedford-Stuyvesant. **Acts:** regional acts, local acts. **Sample day's lineup:** Dorothy Norwood, Ambassadors for Christ, Aaron Armstrong, Sandra Story, Maxine Page, Loving Brothers, others. **Contact:** Gospel Explosion, c/o Boys and Girls High School, 1700 Fulton Street, Brooklyn, NY, 718-949-9152.

## JEWISH FESTIVAL OF MUSIC, Manhattan, NYC
Late Mar.
Jewish

**Days:** 1. **Site:** indoor. Symphony Space, 2537 Broadway at 95th Street. **Admission:** paid. **Daily entry:** under $10, $10 to $24, **Discounts:** student discounts, **Acts:** regional acts, local acts. **Sample day's lineup:** Avi Hoffman, Ben Schaechter, Adrienne Cooper, West End Klezmorim. **Contact:** Symphony Space, 2537 Broadway, New York, NY 10025, 212-864-5400/662-3663.

## NEW YORK WINTER BLUES FESTIVAL, Manhattan, NYC
Late Mar.
Blues and Traditional R&B

Discontinued in 1994, but expected to return. See other dates and sites. **Days:** 1. **Hours per day:** 4. **Site:** indoor. Triplex Theater, 199 Chambers Street. **Admission:** paid. **Daily entry:** $10 to $24, $25 to $49, **Discounts:** other discounts **Acts:** national acts, regional acts, local acts. **Sample day's lineup:** Sugar Blue Band, David "Honeyboy" Edwards, Charlie Sayles, Little Sammy Davis with Midnight Slim. **Audio merchandise:** entire W. M. I. catalog. **Contact:** World Music Institute, 49 West 27th Street, Suite 810, New York, NY 10001, 212-545-7536/362-8719.

## INDEPENDENT MUSIC FEST, Manhattan, NYC
Late Mar. to Early Apr.
Alternative and College Rock

Since 1992. **Days:** 3. **Hours per day:** 18. **Site:** indoor. New York University Loeb Student Center, 566 LaGuardia Place, plus 12 local clubs. **Admission:** paid. **Daily entry:** $25 to $49, **Discounts:** student discounts, multiple event or day passes, **Secondary genre[s]:** HRCK, RAP, AC&W, MFOL, IRSH, RGGE, **Acts:** national acts, regional acts, local acts. **Sample day's lineup:** Gary Lucas, Life In A Blender, Brother Greg, Freedy Johnson, No Safety, Drink Me, The Professor and Maryann, Swales, Iconoclast, Shrieking Violets, Aquanettas, Fluffer, Gloo Girls, thrust, Sugarshock, Ruby Falls, Mothra, Gobblehoof, Small, Matt Keating, Hypnolovewheel, Archers Of Loaf, The Loud Family, Picasso Trigger, Almighty Shoehorn, Liquid Circus, Formaldehyde Blues Train, Stain, Electric World, Pinwheel, Newark, The Laurels, Friction Wheel, Cool Aid Temple, The Drovers, Pipes, Krunch, Lisa Loeb, Heather Eatman, St. Bean, One On One, Mondo Topless, Hell No, The Murmurs, Sea Monkeys, Freakbaby, The Slackers, Ruder Than You, Mephiskapheles, Paul Wilder, Choosy Mothers, Dan Roth, Shrinking Violets, Tiger Lillies, Nod, Melt, Gearhead, Random Arts festival, Bitten and Scratched, Blue House, Dirty Roots Band. **Contact:** New York University Program Board/IMF, 566 LaGuardia Place, Room 103, New York, NY 10012, 212-998-4987.

## GREAT BEER AND MUSIC FESTIVAL, Manhattan, NYC
Late Mar.
Alt. Country and Rockabilly

"25 microbrews on draft." -- Advertisement. Dates have varied, though site has been consistent. **Days:** 1. **Hours per day:** 6. **Site:** indoor. Irving Plaza, 17 Irving Place. **Admission:** paid. **Daily entry:** $25 to $49, **Secondary genre[s]:** ARCK, **Acts:** national acts, regional acts, local acts. **Sample day's lineup:** G. E. Smith and High Plains Drifters, 5 Chinese Brothers, Go To Blazes, Pool, Harry. **Contact:** Great Beer and Music Festival, c/o Irving Plaza, 17 Irving Place, New York, NY, 212-777-6800/249-8870.

### SALSA'S SOUL COMBINATION, Bronx, NYC
Early Apr.
Modern Latin

See other sites and dates. **Help!** One time only? **Days:** 1. **Site:** indoor. Lehman Center for the Performing Arts, Bedford Park Boulevard West. **Admission:** paid. **Daily entry:** $10 to $24, **Acts:** national acts, regional acts, local acts. **Sample day's lineup:** Tito Nieves, Conjunto Classico, La India, Giovanni Hildalgo. **Contact:** RMM Productions, 568 Broadway, Suite 806, New York, NY 10012, 212-925-2828/4885.

### GREAT NEW YORK MANDOLIN WEEKEND, Manhattan, NYC
Early Apr.
Bluegrass

Since 1993. "Our first [festival]...was successful beyond what anyone imagined." -- Program. See other dates and sites. **Days:** 2. **Site:** indoor. Workshops, exhibits: Warwick Suite, Warwick Hotel, 65 West 54th Street; concerts: Merkin Hall, 129 West 67th Street. **Admission:** paid. **Daily entry:** $10 to $24, **Secondary genre[s]:** MJAZ, TJAZ, CRCK, TC&W, TFOL, OTHR **Acts:** national acts, regional acts, local acts. **Sample day's lineup:** Evan Marshall, Tony Williamson, Robert Sullivan, others. **Contact:** Great New York Mandolin Weekend/Gala, P. O. Box 2770, Kensington, MD 20891, 301-530-1749 **or:** Great New York Mandolin Weekend/Gala, c/o School of Visual Arts, 141 West 21st Street, 7th Floor, New York, NY 10010-3994, 212-592-2541.

### STORK MUSIC FESTIVAL, Manhattan, NYC
Early Apr.
Alternative Jazz

Since 1994. "Over 50 musicians participated in what was very likely free jazz's finest Big Apple moment in many years." -- Chris Kelsey, Cadence. **Days:** 3. **Site:** indoor. Context, 28 Avenue A, between 2nd and 3rd Streets. **Admission:** paid. **Daily entry:** $10 to $24, **Secondary genre[s]:** AVNT, **Acts:** regional acts, local acts. **Sample day's lineup:** Collective 4-Tet, William Parker/Cooper-Moore Duo, Ellen Christi Trio, Masahiko Kono Trio, Liz Diamond, Lou Grassi Quintet, Blaise Siwula Sextet, Chris Chalfant, Jackson Krall and The Secret Music Society, others. **Contact:** Stork Music Festival, c/o Context, 28 Avenue A, New York, NY, 212-962-0842.

### HARMONY SWEEPSTAKES A CAPPELLA FESTIVAL/NEW YORK REGIONAL, Manhattan, NYC
Early Apr.
A Cappella and Doo Wop

Since 1992. Part of national competition with winners being sent to finals in San Francisco, Early May. Other regionals: Boston, Philadelphia, Chicago, Denver, Portland/Seattle, Los Angeles, San Francisco. **Days:** 1. **Site:** indoor. Locations vary (Caroline's, Synod House, The Ballroom, etc.). **Admission:** paid. **Daily entry:** $10 to $24, **Secondary genre[s]:** MJAZ, CRCK, BGOS, CBRT, **Acts:** regional acts, local acts. **Sample day's lineup:** Club Spanky, The Echelons, In Rare Form, Harmonytrix, The Accidentals, Margeaux Hayes, Remembrance, Ready, The Lords, The Notables, Doo Wa Zoo. **Audio merchandise:** "Harmony Sweepstakes A Cappella Festival '93" (self-produced and distributed). **Contact:** Harmony Sweepstakes A Cappella Festival, P. O. Box 350 Wall Street Station, New York, NY 10268-0350, 201-714-9254 **or:** Harmony Sweepstakes A Cappella Festival, P. O. Box D, San Anselmo, CA 94979, 415-455-8602.

MANHATTAN ASSOCIATION OF CABARETS AND CLUBS AWARDS, Manhattan, NYC
> Early Apr.
> Cabaret

Since 1987. **Days:** 1. **Site:** indoor. Locations vary (The Ballroom, Symphony Space, Copacabana, etc.). **Acts:** national acts, regional acts, local acts. **Sample day's lineup:** Donna McKechnie, Liliane Montevecchi, Phillip Officer, Vickie Sue Robinson, Andre DeShields, Amanda McBroom, Julie Wilson, Michael Feinstein, Barbara Cook, Margaret Whiting, others. **Contact:** Manhattan Association of Cabarets, c/o Eighty Eight's, 228 West 10th Street, New York, NY 10014, 212-924-0088.

EXPERIMENTAL INTERMEDIA FESTIVAL WITH NO FANCY NAME, Manhattan, NYC
> Early Apr. to Late Apr.
> Avant Garde and New Music

Since 1990. **Days:** 10. **Site:** indoor. Experimental Intermedia, 224 Centre Street at Grand Street. **Admission:** paid. **Daily entry:** under $10, **Acts:** regional acts, local acts. **Sample series lineup:** Day One: Jim Hi Kim; Day Two: Hans Peter Kuhn, Madelon Hooykaas and Elsa Stansfield. **Contact:** Experimental Intermedia Foundation, 224 Centre Street, New York, NY 10013, 212-431-5127.

FROM PLAINS, PUEBLOS AND TUNDRA: NATIVE AMERICAN MUSIC, DANCE AND STORYTELLING, Manhattan, NYC
> Early Apr.
> Native American

Since 1995. Part of W. M. I.'s year-round international folk and jazz concerts featuring national, regional and local acts. Sub-series titles include Interpretations, Improvisations, World of Percussion, Irish Nights. **Days:** 1. **Site:** indoor. Symphony Space, 2537 Broadway at 95th Street. **Admission:** paid. **Daily entry:** $10 to $24, **Discounts:** other discounts **Acts:** national acts, regional acts, local acts. **Sample day's lineup:** Cellicon Traditional Zuni Singers, Kevin Locke, Chuna McIntyre, Gayle Ross. **Audio merchandise:** entire W. M. I. catalog. **Contact:** World Music Institute, 49 West 27th Street, Suite 810, New York, NY 10001, 212-545-7536.

AMERICAN SWING DANCE CHAMPIONSHIPS, Manhattan, NYC
> Early Apr.
> Modern Jazz

"$20,000 in awards and prizes." -- Brochure. See other dates and sites. **Days:** 3. **Hours per day:** 18. **Site:** indoor. Irving Plaza, 17 Irving Place. **Admission:** paid. **Daily entry:** $10 to $24, **Discounts:** group sale discounts, **Secondary genre[s]:** TR&B, **Acts:** national acts, regional acts. **Sample series lineup:** Day One: Georgie Gee Orchestra; Day Two: Roomful of Blues. **Contact:** Boogie Dance Productions, 119 East 15th Street, New York, NY 10003, 800-64-SWING.

P. S. 122 MUSIC FESTIVAL, Manhattan, NYC
> Early Apr.
> Alternative Jazz

Names and dates subject to change, so call ahead. **Days:** 4. **Site:** indoor. P. S. 122, 150 1st Avenue. **Admission:** paid. **Daily entry:** under $10, **Discounts:** other discounts. **Secondary genre[s]:** MLAT, **Acts:** regional acts, local acts. **Sample series lineup:** Day One: Cruz Control; Day Two: Fred Lonberg-Holm Quartet; Day Three: Boabab 4. **Contact:** P. S. 122, 150 1st Avenue, New York, NY 10009, 212-477-5829/5288.

### U. G. H. A. HALL OF FAME AWARDS CEREMONY, Manhattan, NYC
Early Apr.
A Cappella and Doo Wop

Since 1990. **Days:** 1. **Site:** indoor. Symphony Space, 2537 Broadway at 95th Street. **Admission:** paid. **Daily entry:** $25 to $49, $50 and over. **Discounts:** other discounts. **Secondary genre[s]:** CRCK, BGOS, **Acts:** national acts, regional acts, local acts. **Sample day's lineup:** Harry Douglass, Vernon Gardner, Things To Come, The Jive Five, The Golden Gate Quartet, The Swallows, Rick and The Masters, Lar-Kings. **Contact:** United in Group Harmony Association, P. O. Box 185, Clifton, NJ 07011, 201-470-UGHA/365-0049.


### FURNALD FOLK FEST, Manhattan, NYC
Early Apr.
Modern Folk

**Days:** 2. **Hours per day:** 7. **Site:** indoor. Furnald Hall, Columbia University, 115th Street and Broadway. **Admission:** free. **Secondary genre[s]:** ARCK, AC&W, **Acts:** regional acts, local acts. **Sample day's lineup:** 5 Chinese Brothers, Dan Sullivan, Jason Rosenbury, The Low Road, Hugh Blumenfeld, Brendan, Julia and Jode, Cat-A-Tonics, Richard Shindell, Hugh Pool, Dan Ng, Brett Forman, Amy Fix and Sam Fenster, Johnson Lee, Baccantae, Jonathon Bently, Kathryn and Alexis. **Audio merchandise:** "The Postcrypt" (1-800-PRIME-CD); "Live at the Postcrypt Coffeehouse" (Fast Folk Musical Magazine). **Contact:** Postcrypt Coffeehouse, c/o Earl Hall, Columbia University, New York, NY 10027, 212-853-7116/854-1953.


### NEW YORK BRASS CONFERENCE FOR SCHOLARSHIPS, Manhattan, NYC
Early Apr.
Modern Jazz

Since 1973. **Days:** 3. **Hours per day:** 12. **Site:** indoor. Roosevelt Hotel, Madison Avenue at 45th Street. **Admission:** paid. **Daily entry:** $10 to $24, $25 to $49, **Discounts:** student discounts, multiple event or day passes, group sale discounts, other discounts. **Secondary genre[s]:** TJAZ, AJAZ, MLAT, OTHR **Acts:** national acts, regional acts, local acts. **Sample day's lineup:** Charlie Sepulveda Quintet, Doug Sertl Sextet with Randy Brecker, Tiger Okoshi Quintet, Triangle British Brass Band, Jim Pugh Quintet, Air Force Band of Liberty Symphonic Winds, Atlantic Brass Quintet, Univeristy of Oklahoma Trombone Choir, Mannes College Brass Ensemble, New School Jazz Orchestra. **Contact:** Charles Colin Publications, 315 West 53rd Street, New York, NY 10019, 212-581-1480.


### FESTIVAL OF NATIONS, Manhattan, NYC
Early Apr.
Variety, Folk and International

**Help!** A sample lineup? **Days:** 1. **Hours per day:** 7. **Site:** indoor. International House, 500 Riverside Drive. **Admission:** paid. **Daily entry:** under $10, **Acts:** local acts. **Contact:** Festival of Nations, International House, 500 Riverside Drive, New York, NY 10027, 212-316-8438.


### BETTY CARTER'S JAZZ AHEAD, Brooklyn, NYC
Early Apr.
Modern Jazz

Since 1994. Carter's annual showcase of young jazz talent (which moves to Manhattan's Apollo Theater one week later). Part of a year-round concert series featuring national, regional acts, including a weekly summer jazz concert series in Aug. See other dates. **Days:** 2. **Site:** indoor. Majestic Theater, 651 Fulton Street. **Admission:** paid. **Daily entry:** $10 to $24, **Acts:** national acts, local acts. **Sample day's lineup:** Betty Carter, 20 others. **Contact:** 651/Kings Majestic Corporation, 651 Fulton Street, Brooklyn, NY 11217, 718-636-4100.

## McDonald's Gospelfest, Varies, NYC
### Early Apr. to Middle Jun.
### Black Gospel

Since 1985. Preliminary competition rounds: Early to Late Apr., Brooklyn, Queens. Semifinals: Late May, Manhattan. Finals with national act: Mid Jun., Avery Fisher Hall, Lincoln Center, Broadway at 65th Street. **Days:** 6. **Site:** indoor. multiple locations. **Admission:** free and paid. **Daily entry:** $10 to $24, $25 to $49, **Acts:** national acts, regional acts, local acts. **Sample day's lineup:** Finals: Helen Baylor, The Jenkins Brothers, plus at least six winners across three choir categories. **Contact:** Golin/Harris Communications, Inc., 666 3rd Avenue, New York, NY 10017, 212-697-9191 **or:** McDonald's Gospelfest Committee, 95 West 95th Street, New York, NY 10025, 212-222-7725.

## Rainforest Benefit Concert, Manhattan, NYC
### Middle Apr.
### Modern Rock and Pop

Since 1990. "All-star concert rains supreme." -- New York Daily News. See other dates. **Days:** 1. **Hours per day:** 3. **Site:** indoor. Carnegie Hall, 57th Street at 7th Avenue. **Admission:** paid. **Daily entry:** $25 to $49, **Acts:** national acts. **Sample day's lineup:** Sting, James Taylor, Elton John, Paul Simon, Bruce Springsteen, Jessye Norman, Jon Bon Jovi. **Contact:** Rainforest Benefit Concert, c/o Carnegie Hall, 881 7th Avenue, New York, NY 10019, 212-247-7800/696-1033.

## International OFFestival, Manhattan, NYC
### Middle Apr. to Middle Jun.
### Avant Garde and New Music

Since 1983. "Contemporary performances from around the world. Come to be...gladdened, maddened, saddened, powerfully entertained." -- Brochure. **Days:** 22. **Site:** indoor. multiple theaters. **Admission:** paid. **Daily entry:** $10 to $24, **Discounts:** student discounts, group sale discounts, **Acts:** regional acts, local acts. **Sample day's lineup:** "'Without a Doubt': Bettina and Stefan Poetzsch's fusion of contemporary dance and music -- abstract, yet structural impulses that mirror our essential vitality, originality and warmth." -- Program. **Contact:** Fools Company, Inc., 358 West 44th Street, New York, NY 10036-5426, 212-307-6000.

## Death and Taxes, Manhattan, NYC
### Middle Apr.
### Alt. Country and Rockabilly

Since 1995. Diesel Only Records celebrates "tax day." **Help!** One time only? **Days:** 1. **Site:** indoor. Mercury Lounge, 217 East Houston Street. **Admission:** paid. **Daily entry:** under $10, **Acts:** regional acts, local acts. **Sample day's lineup:** World Famous Blue Jays, Courtney Lee Adams, Amy Allison, Eric Ambel, Bruce Bennett, Laura Cantrell, Meredith Chesney, Gideon D'Arcangelo, Brian Dewan, Laura Foulke, Robin Goldwasser, Jon Graboff, Julia Greenberg, Ryan Hedgecock, Michael McMahon, Amy Rigby, Will Rigby, Scott Schinder, Liane Smith, others. **Contact:** Death and Taxes, 85 North 3rd Street, Brooklyn, NY, 718-388-4370.

## Carnegie Hall Folk Festival, Manhattan, NYC
### Middle Apr. to Late Apr.
### Variety, Folk and International

Since 1992. **Days:** 5. **Site:** indoor. Weill Recital Hall, Carnegie Hall, 881 7th Avenue at 57th Street. **Admission:** paid. **Daily entry:** $10 to $24, $25 to $49, $50 and over. **Secondary genre[s]:** TR&B, BGOS, MC&W, TC&W, AC&W, BLGS, MFOL, TFOL, ZYDC, IRSH, NATV, TLAT, **Acts:** national acts, regional acts, local acts. **Sample day's lineup:** Ricky Skaggs, Alison Krauss, Johnson Mountain Boys, Mingo Saldivar. **Contact:** Carnegie Hall Folk Festival, Carnegie Hall, 881 7th Avenue, New York, NY 10019, 212-247-7800.

SUNNYSIDE SHOP-TILL-YOU-DROP FESTIVAL, Queens, NYC
    Middle Apr.
    Variety, General

See other dates and sites. **Days:** 1. **Hours per day:** 8. **Site:** outdoor. Greenpoint Avenue, 41st to 48th Streets, Sunnyside. **Admission:** free. **Secondary genre[s]:** MJAZ, MRCK, ARCK, TR&B, RGGE, **Acts:** local acts. **Sample day's lineup:** Zane Massey and The Foundation, Rapadoo, Joe Restivo, Son House, Dark Moon, Off Center. **Contact:** Clearview Festival Productions, 401 Lafayette Street, New York, NY 10003, 212-995-9412.

EASTER GOSPEL FESTIVAL, Manhattan, NYC
    Middle Apr.
    Black Gospel

See other dates. **Help!** Formerly New York's Gospel Explosion? **Days:** 1. **Site:** indoor. Apollo Theater, 253 West 125th Street. **Admission:** paid. **Daily entry:** $10 to $24, $25 to $49, **Acts:** local acts. **Sample day's lineup:** The Strait Gate Judah Choir, The Convent Avenue Baptist Church Male Choir, Carl Murray, Martin Robinson, others. **Contact:** Inner City Theater Group, Apollo Theater, 253 West 125th Street, New York, NY, 212-222-0992/749-5838.

GREAT NEW YORK MANDOLIN GALA, Manhattan, NYC
    Middle Apr.
    Bluegrass

Since 1993. The New York Mandolin Orchestra, conducted by Mark Ettinger with Barry Mitterhoff the concertmaster, also rehearses every Tuesday evening at the Y. M. C. A., 215 West 23rd Street, and has been holding a Spring Concert of classical music annually since 1925. Call 212-355-6715, 212-534-4440, respectively. See other dates and sites. **Days:** 1. **Site:** indoor. Washington Irving High School, Irving Place between East 16th and 17th Streets. **Admission:** paid. **Daily entry:** $10 to $24, **Secondary genre[s]:** MJAZ, TJAZ, CRCK, TC&W, TFOL, OTHR **Acts:** national acts, regional acts, local acts. **Sample day's lineup:** Duo Calace, Neil Gladd, Mair-Davis Duo, Evan Marshall, Barry Mitterhoff. **Contact:** Great New York Mandolin Weekend/Gala, P. O. Box 2770, Kensington, MD 20891, 301-530-1749 **or:** Great New York Mandolin Weekend/Gala, c/o School of Visual Arts, 141 West 21st Street, 7th Floor, New York, NY 10010-3994, 212-592-2541.

ECO-FESTIVAL, Manhattan, NYC
    Late Apr. to Early May
    Native American

Since 1992. See other dates. **Days:** 6. **Site:** indoor. Theater for the New City, 155 1st Avenue at 10th Street. **Admission:** paid. **Daily entry:** $10 to $24, **Acts:** national acts, regional acts, local acts. **Sample day's lineup:** John Trudell, Pura Fe. **Contact:** Theater for the New City, 155 1st Avenue, New York, NY 10003, 212-924-0496/254-1109.

ESSENCE AWARDS, Manhattan, NYC
    Late Apr.
    Modern R&B

Since 1988. See other dates. **Help!** A sample lineup? **Days:** 1. **Site:** indoor. The Paramount, Madison Square Garden, 7th Avenue at 32nd Street. **Admission:** paid. **Daily entry:** $25 to $49, **Acts:** national acts, . **Contact:** Essence Awards, Essence Communications, 1500 Broadway, New York, NY, 212-642-0600/465-MSG1.

## Radioactive Bodega Blacklight Prom, Brooklyn, NYC
Late Apr.
Hard Rock and Heavy Metal

See other dates and sites. **Help!** One time only? **Days:** 1. **Hours per day:** 8. **Site:** indoor. The Right Bank, 409 Kent Avenue, off Broadway, Williamsburg. **Secondary genre[s]:** ARCK, **Acts:** local acts. **Sample day's line-up:** Ff, Colored Greens, Jennifer Blowdryer, Billy Syndrome, Home, Otis, Molotov Cocktail, Wighat, Tub, intolerable monsters, The DT's. **Contact:** Radioactive Bodega, c/o The Right Bank, 409 Kent Avenue, Williamsburg, Brooklyn, NY, 718-387-7023/598-4087.

## Broadway's Easter Bonnet Competition: A Salute to 100 Years of Broadway, Manhattan, NYC
Late Apr.
Cabaret

Since 1987. Benefits Broadway Cares/Equity Fights AIDS. See other dates and sites. **Help!** The site? **Days:** 1. **Site:** indoor. **Secondary genre[s]:** CRCK, MC&W, **Acts:** national acts, . **Sample day's lineup:** Bea Arthur, Bebe Neuwirth, Gwen Verdon, K. T. Oslin, Petula Clark, John Raitt, others. **Contact:** Broadway Cares/Equity Fights AIDS, 165 West 46th Street, Suite 1300, New York, NY 10036, 212-840-0770/978-0295.

## Earth Day Celebration, Manhattan, NYC
Late Apr.
Modern Country

Events vary widely from year to year, so call ahead. **Days:** 2. **Site:** outdoor. South Street Seaport, Pier 17, Ambrose Stage. **Admission:** free. **Acts:** local acts. **Sample day's lineup:** Desiree and The Rough Riders, Stonewall, The Party Dolls, Jean Ritchie, Pierce Joyce. **Contact:** South Street Seaport Museum, 207 Front Street, New York, NY 10038, 212-669-9400/SEA-PORT.

## Corner Store Syndicate New Jazz Festival, Manhattan, NYC
Late Apr.
Alternative Jazz

Since 1990. **Days:** 3. **Hours per day:** 5. **Site:** indoor. Knitting Factory, 74 Leonard Street, between Broadway and Church Street. **Admission:** paid. **Daily entry:** $10 to $24, **Acts:** national acts, local acts. **Sample day's lineup:** Tom Varner Trio with Lee Konitz, Paul Smoker Brass Group, Marcus Rojas, Bora Bergman Tristano Legacy. **Audio merchandise:** entire Knitting Factory Works catalog, including numerous festival recordings and compilations. **Other merchandise:** "Knitting Music" by Michael Dorf (Knitting Factory Works). **Contact:** Knitting Factory, 47 East Houston Street, New York, NY 10012, 212-219-3055/3006.

## Roulette Concert Series/Roulette Mixology Festival, Manhattan, NYC
Late Apr. to Early May
Avant Garde and New Music

Since 1980. Six-evening festival a continuation of 21-evening spring concert series. **Days:** 6. **Site:** indoor. Roulette, 228 West Broadway at White Street. **Admission:** paid. **Daily entry:** under $10, **Discounts:** other discounts. **Acts:** national acts, regional acts, local acts. **Sample series lineup:** Day One: Pauline Oliveros and David Gamper; Day Two: Frankie Mann; Day Three: Ken Butler. **Audio merchandise:** "A Confederacy of Dances, Vols. 1, 2" (Einstein), plus entire Einstein catalog. **Contact:** Roulette/Einstein, 228 West Broadway, New York, NY 10013-2456, 212-219-8242.

### NATIONAL GAY AND LESBIAN BUSINESS AND CONSUMER EXPO, Manhattan, NYC
Late Apr.
Gay and Lesbian

Since 1994. **Days:** 2. **Hours per day:** 5. **Site:** indoor. Jacob Javits Center, 11th Avenue at 36th Street. **Admission:** paid. **Daily entry:** $10 to $24, **Secondary genre[s]:** VRGL, **Acts:** local acts. **Sample day's lineup:** Cheer Dallas, Bill Graber, Melinda DeMaio, Judith Sloan, Dan Martin, Sons and Lovers, Eileen Edmonds, Tom McCormack, Danny McWilliams, Sara Cytron, Nellie Olesons, Grant King, Laura Wetzler, Seraiah Carroll. **Contact:** National Gay and Lesbian Business and Consumer Expo, c/o Jacob Javits Center, 11th Avenue at 36th Street, New York, NY, 212-234-3400.

### GOSPEL COMES/RETURNS TO BROADWAY, Manhattan, NYC
Late Apr.
Black Gospel

Dates vary widely, so call ahead. Not to be confused with Gospel Festivals produced by World Music Institute here, and elsewhere. See other dates and sites. **Days:** 1. **Site:** indoor. Symphony Space, 2537 Broadway at 95th Street. **Admission:** paid. **Daily entry:** $10 to $24, $25 to $49, **Discounts:** student discounts, **Acts:** national acts, regional acts, local acts. **Sample day's lineup:** The Dixie Hummingbirds, The Harmonizing Four, Generation Singers, Charles Taylor and Singers, Samantha Holmes, State Choir 4th Ecclesiastical Jurisdiction, Charlie Storey and The All Stars. **Contact:** Symphony Space, 2537 Broadway, New York, NY 10025, 212-864-5400.

### RELIGIOUS MUSIC FESTIVAL, Brooklyn, NYC
Late Apr.
Black Gospel

**Help!** One time only? **Days:** 1. **Site:** indoor. Concord Baptist Church of Christ, 833 Dr. Gardner C. Taylor Bouelvard (Marcy Avenue). **Admission:** paid. **Daily entry:** $10 to $24, **Acts:** local acts. **Sample day's lineup:** Henry Sexton, E. Dwight Franklin and Bernice Watkins, Melodies in E. **Contact:** Concord Baptist Church of Christ, 833 Dr. Gardner C. Taylor Bouelvard (Marcy Avenue), Brooklyn, NY, 718-398-7402.

### UPPER BROADWAY SPRING CELEBRATION AND FESTIVAL, Manhattan, NYC
Late Apr.
Modern Jazz

See other sites and dates. **Days:** 1. **Hours per day:** 7. **Site:** outdoor. Broadway, 110th to 117th Streets. **Admission:** free. **Secondary genre[s]:** MFOL, **Acts:** national acts, local acts. **Sample day's lineup:** Oscar Brand, Judy Barnett, Tracy McDonough, Odetta, others. **Contact:** Upper Broadway Spring Celebration and Festival, 1501 Broadway, Suite 1808, New York, NY 10036, 212-764-6330.

### LOWER SECOND AVENUE FESTIVAL, Manhattan, NYC
Early May
Modern Jazz

See other sites and dates. **Days:** 1. **Hours per day:** 7. **Site:** outdoor. Second Avenue, 5th to 14th Streets. **Admission:** free. **Secondary genre[s]:** MFOL, **Acts:** national acts, local acts. **Sample day's lineup:** Oscar Brand, Judy Barnett, Tracy McDonough, Odetta, others. **Contact:** Lower Second Avenue Festival, 1501 Broadway, Suite 1808, New York, NY 10036, 212-764-6330.

PUSSYSTOCK, Manhattan, NYC
    Early May
    Gay and Lesbian

Since 1992. "5 nights of GRRRL CULTURE!!" -- Flyer. **Help!** Still ongoing? **Days:** 5. **Site:** indoor. Multiple locations. **Admission:** paid. **Daily entry:** under $10, **Secondary genre[s]:** ARCK, HRCK, **Acts:** regional acts, local acts. **Sample day's lineup:** Shreiking Violets, Pipsqueak, Glistening, Sex Pod, Radio One, The Wives. **Contact:** Riot Grrl N. Y. C., P. O. Box 1320 Stuyvesant Station, New York, NY 10009, 212-875-7039.

NEW YORK SHAKESPEARE FESTIVAL SPRING GALA, Manhattan, NYC
    Early May
    Variety, General

**Help!** One time only? **Days:** 1. **Site:** outdoor. Central Park, near Bethesda Fountain. **Admission:** paid. **Daily entry:** $50 and over. **Secondary genre[s]:** MJAZ, CBRT, OTHR. **Acts:** national acts. **Sample day's lineup:** Kathleen Battle, Wynton Marsalis, Mandy Patikin, Ben Vereen, others. **Contact:** New York Shakespeare Festival, Public Theater, 425 Lafayette Street, New York, NY 10003, 212-598-7100/7162.

LIBRO LATINO BOOKFEST/PATHWAYS FOR YOUTH BENEFIT, Bronx, NYC
    Middle May
    Modern Latin

Part of Libro Latino Bookfest. **Days:** 3. **Hours per day:** 9. **Site:** indoor. Hostos Community College, 450 Grand Concourse. **Admission:** free and paid. **Secondary genre[s]:** MJAZ, **Acts:** national acts, local acts. **Sample day's lineup:** Tito Puente, Dave Valentin, Marion Meadows, Joe Bataan, Bob Baldwin. **Contact:** Pathways for Youth Benefit/Libro Latino Bookfest, Hostos Community College, 450 Grand Concourse, Bronx, NY, 718-518-4195.

AREYTO FOR LIFE: HISPANIC AIDS FORUM BENEFIT GALA AND ART AUCTION, Manhattan, NYC
    Early May
    Modern Latin

Since 1993. **Days:** 1. **Hours per day:** 6. **Site:** indoor. Puck Building, 275 Lafayette Street, between Houston and Prince Streets. **Admission:** paid. **Daily entry:** $25 to $49, $50 and over. **Acts:** national acts, regional acts, . **Sample day's lineup:** Tito Nives, Rey Sepulveda, Willie Colon, others. **Contact:** Hispanic AIDS Forum, c/o The Puck Building, 275 Lafayette Street, New York, NY, 212-966-6563.

DICK FOX'S BROOKLYN PARAMOUNT REUNION, Manhattan, NYC
    Early May
    A Cappella and Doo Wop

See other dates and sites. **Days:** 1. **Site:** indoor. The Paramount, Madison Square Garden, 7th Avenue at 32nd Street. **Admission:** paid. **Daily entry:** $25 to $49, **Discounts:** group sale discounts, **Secondary genre[s]:** CRCK, **Acts:** national acts, regional acts, local acts. **Sample day's lineup:** Johnny Maestro and The Brooklyn Bridge, The Skyliners, The Duprees, The Tokens, The Shangri-La's, Buddy Holly's Original Crickets, Lewis Lymon and The Teenchords. **Contact:** Dick Fox's Brooklyn Paramount Reunion, 1650 Broadway, Suite 503, New York, NY 10019, 212-582-9074/465-MSG1.

EVERYBODY'S CALYPSO AWARDS, Brooklyn, NYC
Early May
Reggae, Ska and Caribbean

See other dates. **Days:** 1. **Site:** indoor. Farragut Manor, 1460 Flatbush Avenue. **Admission:** paid. **Daily entry:** $25 to $49, **Acts:** national acts, regional acts, local acts. **Sample day's lineup:** Errol Ince Music Makers, United Sisters of Trinidad and Tobago, Peter Humphrey, Ras Iley, Inspector, Mighty Gabby, Crazy, Super Blue, Ninja Band, Borokete, Mighty Duke. **Contact:** Everybody's Caribbean Magazine, 1630 Nostrand Avenue, Brooklyn, NY 11226, 718-941-1879.

EVERYBODY'S WORLD CALYPSO MONARCH COMPETITION, Brooklyn/Queens, NYC
Early May to Late Jul.
Reggae, Ska and Caribbean

Since 1994. Formerly programmed Everybody's Carib Fete at Brooklyn College in Late Jul., but substituted competition finals in 1994. May revert back to Fete in 1995. Call for current details. **Days:** 4. **Site:** indoor. Farragut Manor, Caribbean Dome, Calypsocity, Brooklyn College. **Admission:** paid. **Daily entry:** $25 to $49, $50 and over. **Acts:** national acts, regional acts, local acts. **Sample day's lineup:** Chalkdust, Calypso Rose, Baron, Singing Francine, Natasha Wilson, Lady Guymine, King Hurricane, Invader, Chako, Mighty Gabby, others. **Contact:** Everybody's Caribbean Magazine, 1630 Nostrand Avenue, Brooklyn, NY 11226, 718-941-1879.

ENTRE FAMILIA, Bronx, NYC
Early May
Modern Latin

See other sites and dates. **Help!** One time only? **Days:** 1. **Site:** indoor. Lehman Center for the Performing Arts, Bedford Park Boulevard West. **Admission:** paid. **Daily entry:** $10 to $24, **Acts:** national acts, regional acts, local acts. **Sample day's lineup:** Tony Vega, Marc Anthony, La India, Ray Sepulveda, Johnny Rivera, Yomo Toro, Sergio George Orchestra. **Contact:** RMM Productions, 568 Broadway, Suite 806, New York, NY 10012, 212-925-2828/4885.

IN CELEBRATION OF LIFE, Manhattan, NYC
Early May
Cabaret

Since 1992. Benefits Broadway Cares/Equity Fights AIDS. See other dates and sites. **Days:** 1. **Site:** indoor. Church of St. Paul the Apostle, Columbus Avenue between 59th and 60th Streets. **Admission:** paid. **Daily entry:** $25 to $49, $50 and over. **Acts:** national acts, regional acts, local acts. **Sample day's lineup:** Stephen Bogardus, Ann Hampton Calloway, Liz Callaway, Kim Crosby, Helen Gallagher, Jason Graae, Randy Graff, Jeff Harnar, Terri Klausner, Eddie Korbich, Alix Korey, Judy Kuhn, Nancy LaMott, Rosemary Loar, Karen Mason, Sally Mayes, Ann Morrison, Donna Murphy, Marni Nixon, Billy Porter, Lonny Price, Tony Roberts, Francis Ruivivar, The Tonics, Sal Viviano, Lillias White, Rachel York, New York City Gay Men's Chorus Chamber Choir, Phyllis Newman, others. **Contact:** Broadway Cares/Equity Fights AIDS, 165 West 46th Street, Suite 1300, New York, NY 10036, 212-840-0770/265-3495 x309.

HEART AND SOUL, Manhattan, NYC
Early May
Cabaret

Benefits People With AIDS Coalition. **Days:** 1. **Site:** indoor. Webster Hall, 119-125 East 11th Street. **Admission:** free and paid. **Daily entry:** $50 and over. **Secondary genre[s]:** CBRT, **Acts:** national acts, local acts. **Sample day's lineup:** Stockard Channing, Nell Carter, Buddy Smith, Lauren Gaffney, Siven Cotel and Jeffrey Landmen, Tammy Minoff, Michael Shulman, others. **Contact:** Heart and Soul/People With AIDS Coalition, Webster Hall, 119-125 East 11th Street, New York, NY, 212-532-0290.

## OUTMUSIC FESTIVAL, Manhattan, NYC
   Early May
   Gay and Lesbian

Since 1991. See other dates. **Help!** A sample lineup? **Days:** 1. **Hours per day:** 5. **Site:** indoor. The Center, 208 West 13th Street. **Admission:** paid. **Daily entry:** under $10, **Secondary genre[s]:** VRGL, ARCK, MR&B, MFOL, CBRT, **Acts:** local acts. **Sample day's lineup:** 25 acts. **Contact:** Outmusic Festival, c/o Spotted Dog Productions, P. O. Box 40-0041, Brooklyn, NY 11240-0041, 212-330-9197.

## SAY IT WITH LOVE NIGHT, Manhattan, NYC
   Middle May
   Classic Rock and Oldies

"A Mother's Day concert." -- Advertisement. **Help!** One time only? **Days:** 1. **Site:** indoor. Hunter College, East 68th Street. **Admission:** paid. **Secondary genre[s]:** MR&B, ACAP, **Acts:** national acts, local acts. **Sample day's lineup:** Cuba Gooding, Enchantment, Blue Magic, The Chi-Lites. **Contact:** Say It With Love Night, Hunter College, East 68th Street, New York, NY, 212-932-1935.

## HEARTS AND VOICES IN CONCERT, Manhattan, NYC
   Middle May
   Cabaret

Since 1991. **Days:** 1. **Site:** indoor. Town Hall (though locations vary). **Admission:** paid. **Daily entry:** $50 and over. **Acts:** national acts, regional acts, local acts. **Sample day's lineup:** Dorothy Loudon, Charlotte Rae, James Brennan, Len Cariou, Jo Sullivan, Nancy Dussault, Tony Randall, Karen Mason, Billy Stritch, Michael Rupert, Karen Ziemba, Connecticut Gay Men's Chorus, others. **Contact:** Hearts and Voices, 150 West 80th Street, #7D, New York, NY 10024, 212-799-4276.

## TRIBUTE TO AFRICAN DIASPORA WOMEN, Manhattan, NYC
   Middle May
   African American

Since 1987. **Days:** 3. **Site:** indoor. Aaron Davis Hall, 135th Street and Convent Avenue, Harlem. **Admission:** free and paid. **Daily entry:** under $10, $10 to $24, **Discounts:** student discounts, advance purchase discounts, other discounts **Secondary genre[s]:** AJAZ, MLAT, AFRC, **Acts:** national acts, regional acts, local acts. **Sample day's lineup:** Geri Allen, Cecilia and Tanaora, others. **Contact:** Franklin H. Williams Caribbean Cultural Center, 408 West 5th Street, New York, NY 10019, 212-307-7420.

## BLACK EXPO U. S. A., Manhattan, NYC
   Middle May
   African American

Other sites: Memphis, TN, Atlanta, GA, Philadelphia, PA, Houston, TX, Cleveland, OH, Detroit, MI, Washington, DC, Oakland, CA, Dallas, TX, Charlotte, NC, Los Angeles, CA, Fort Lauderdale, FL, Richmond, VA, Kansas City, MO. **Days:** 4. **Hours per day:** 9. **Site:** indoor. Jacob Javitz Center, 11th Avenue at 36th Street. **Admission:** paid. **Daily entry:** under $10, **Secondary genre[s]:** MJAZ, RAP, MR&B, BGOS, RGGE, **Acts:** national acts, local acts. **Sample day's lineup:** Gerald Alston, The Delfonics, Force MD's, Pieces of a Puzzle, Christopher Williams, New York Restoration Choir, Donnie McClurkin, Alumni Mass Choir, Unity Choir, others. **Contact:** Black Expo U. S. A., 206 West 137th Street, New York, NY 10030, 212-234-3400.

### MOTHER'S DAY CARIBBEAN ALL-STARS FESTIVAL, Varies, NYC
Early May
Reggae, Ska and Caribbean

Since 1978. A boisterous showcase! **Days:** 2. **Site:** indoor. The Paramount, Madison Square Garden, 7th Avenue at 32nd Street (Manhattan, Saturday); Brooklyn Center (Brooklyn, Sunday). **Admission:** paid. **Daily entry:** $25 to $49, $50 and over. **Acts:** national acts, regional acts, local acts. **Sample day's lineup:** Mighty Sparrow, Calypso Rose, Lord Kitchener, Preacher, Shadow, Imagination Brass, Crazy, Swallow, Delamo, Luta, Troubadors, King David Rudder, Ras Iley, Plastic Bag, Chalkdust, Inspector, Beckett, Pamela Maynard and Pablo G, others. **Contact:** Caribbean Arts and Cultural Association, c/o Madison Square Garden, 4 Pennsylvania Plaza, New York, NY, 212-465-MSG1.

### CAVALCADE OF STARS, Manhattan, NYC
Middle May
Cabaret

Since 1995. **Days:** 1. **Site:** indoor. Oak Room, Algonquin Hotel, 59 West 44th Street. **Admission:** paid. **Daily entry:** $25 to $49, $50 and over. **Acts:** national acts, regional acts. **Sample day's lineup:** Julie Wilson, K. T. Sullivan, Margaret Whiting, Julie Budd, Lainie Kazan, Jeff Harner, others. **Contact:** Algonquin Hotel's Oak Room, 59 West 44th Street, New York, NY, 212-840-6800.

### JAMAICA FUN RUN AND FAMILY DAY, Queens, NYC
Middle May
African American

**Help!** A sample lineup? **Days:** 1. **Site:** outdoor. multiple locations around York College, 160th Street and Liberty Avenue, Jamaica. **Admission:** free and paid. **Daily entry:** $10 to $24, $25 to $49, **Secondary genre[s]:** RAP, MR&B, TLAT, **Acts:** local acts. **Contact:** Greater Jamaica Development Corporation, 90-04 161st Street, Jamaica, NY 11432, 718-291-0282/786-8880.

### QUEENS COLLEGE CULTURAL HERITAGE GREAT GOSPEL COMPETITION, Queens, NYC
Middle May
Black Gospel

See other dates. **Site:** indoor. Golden Center for the Performing Arts, Queens College, Kissena Boulevard and Long Island Expressway, Flushing. **Admission:** paid. **Daily entry:** under $10, $10 to $24, **Discounts:** student discounts, **Secondary genre[s]:** TR&B, **Acts:** national acts, regional acts, local acts. **Sample series lineup:** Day One: Della Reese; Day Two: Voices of Hope, plus 6 choir finalists. **Contact:** Queens College Cultural Heritage Great Gospel Competition, Golden Center for the Performing Arts, Kissena Boulevard, Flushing, NY, 718-793-8080.

### BROOKLYN ROCK AWARDS, Brooklyn, NYC
Middle May
Classic Rock and Oldies

Since 1993. **Days:** 1. **Site:** indoor. Brooklyn Paramount, Flatbush Avenue and DeKalb Avenue. **Admission:** paid. **Daily entry:** $25 to $49, **Secondary genre[s]:** ACAP, **Acts:** national acts, regional acts, local acts. **Sample day's lineup:** Laverne Baker, Harptones, Cleftones, others. **Contact:** Atlantic Avenue Association Local Development Corp., 407 Atlantic Avenue, Brooklyn, NY 11217, 718-875-8993.

## Z100 May Day, Manhattan, NYC
### Middle May
### Alternative and College Rock

Since 1994. Formerly called Zoostock. Benefits Environmental Defense Fund, Coalition for Battered Women Advocates. See other dates and sites. **Days:** 1. **Site:** indoor. Roseland Ballroom, 239 West 52nd Street, between 8th Avenue and Broadway. **Admission:** paid. **Daily entry:** $25 to $49, **Secondary genre[s]:** MRCK, **Acts:** national acts. **Sample day's lineup:** The Cranberries, Mathew Sweet, Sponge, Adam Ant, Human League. **Contact:** WHTZ-FM 100.3, 767 3rd Avenue, New York, NY, 212-239-2300/249-8870.

## Brooklyn Arts Week, Brooklyn, NYC
### Middle May
### Variety, General

Since 1995. **Help!** One time only? **Days:** 5. **Hours per day:** 8. **Site:** outdoor. Cadman Park Plaza, Brooklyn Civic Center. **Admission:** free. **Secondary genre[s]:** MC&W, MFOL, AFRC, BRZL, OTHR **Acts:** national acts, regional acts, local acts. **Sample lineup:** Cumbre, Akwesi Asante, Laurie Muir, Richard Stillman, Lori Shapiro, Stonewall, Dave Goldman Trio, Kusasa, Spice of Life, Richie Havens, Dexter Daily and Jam-X, Winnie Wilson, Reggy Sonsino. **Contact:** BACA/The Brooklyn Arts Council, 200 Eastern Parkway, Brooklyn, NY 11238, 718-783-4469/3077.

## Fifth Avenue Festival, Brooklyn, NYC
### Middle May
### Variety, General

**Days:** 1. **Hours per day:** 7. **Site:** outdoor. 5th Avenue, Flatbush to Prospect Avenues, Park Slope. **Admission:** free. **Secondary genre[s]:** MRCK, TR&B, MLAT, **Acts:** regional acts, local acts. **Sample lineup:** Po' Boys Band, Luis Sanabria and Briza, Popa Chubby Band, others. **Contact:** BACA/The Brooklyn Arts Council, 200 Eastern Parkway, Brooklyn, NY 11238, 718-783-4469/3077.

## Folksongs Plus, Manhattan, NYC
### Middle May
### Traditional Folk

Since 1993. **Days:** 1. **Site:** indoor. 92nd Street Y, 1395 Lexington Avenue. **Admission:** paid. **Daily entry:** $50 and over. **Discounts:** multiple event or day passes, **Secondary genre[s]:** TR&B, MFOL, **Acts:** national acts. **Sample day's lineup:** Burl Ives, Odetta, Josh White Jr., Theodore Bikel, Tom Paxton, Oscar Brand, The Chad Mitchell Trio, others. **Contact:** Tisch Center for the Arts, 92nd Street YM-YWHA, 1395 Lexington Avenue, New York, NY 10128, 212-996-1100/415-5488.

## Union Settlement Ethnic Festival, Manhattan, NYC
### Middle May
### Variety, Folk and International

Since 1993. "Hopes to bring together the different ethnic groups that live in East Harlem, and to provide an opportunity for cultural expression." -- New York Newsday. **Days:** 1. **Hours per day:** 8. **Site:** outdoor. Union Settlement's community garden and playground, 237 East 104th Street. **Secondary genre[s]:** MJAZ, MLAT, TLAT, BRZL, **Acts:** local acts. **Contact:** Union Settlement, 237 East 4th Street, New York, NY 10029, 212-360-8800/996-3353.

MOSTLY WOMEN COMPOSERS, Manhattan, NYC
> Middle May to Late May
> Avant Garde and New Music

**Help!** One time only? **Days:** 3. **Site:** indoor. Bloomingdale House of Music, 323 West 108th Street. **Admission:** free. **Acts:** local acts. **Sample day's lineup:** Works of Gwyneth Walkers, Elizabeth Gould, Nicholas Thorne, others. **Contact:** Mostly Women Composers, Bloomingdale House of Music, 323 West 108th Street, New York, NY, 212-663-6021.

AMSTERDAM AVENUE FESTIVAL, Manhattan, NYC
> Late May
> Variety, General

Since 1985. Benefits various community programs. See other dates. **Days:** 1. **Hours per day:** 7. **Site:** outdoor. Amsterdam Avenue, 77th to 96th Streets. **Admission:** free. **Secondary genre[s]:** MJAZ, CRCK, ACAP, RGGE, **Acts:** national acts, regional acts, local acts. **Sample day's lineup:** Arlene Smith, Chuck Jackson, Cleveland Still and The Dubs, Chordettes, Passions, Cleftones, Mike Shane and The Midnight Jam, C. A. S. Y. M. Steel Orchestra, others. **Contact:** West Side Chamber of Commerce, 1841 Broadway, Suite 701, New York, NY 10023, 212-595-3333.

HEZEKIAH WALKER ANNIVERSARY SHOW, Brooklyn, NYC
> Late May
> Black Gospel

**Help!** One time only? **Days:** 1. **Site:** indoor. Friendship Baptist Church, 92 Herkimer Street. **Admission:** paid. **Daily entry:** $10 to $24, **Acts:** national acts, local acts. **Sample day's lineup:** Hezekiah Walker, Commissioned, others. **Contact:** Hezekiah Walker Anniversary Show, Friendship Baptist Church, 92 Herkimer Street, Brooklyn, NY, 718-638-2098.

SALUTE TO ISRAEL DAY PARADE AND CONCERT, Manhattan, NYC
> Late May
> Jewish

Since 1965. **Days:** 1. **Site:** outdoor. parade: 5th Avenue, from 57th to 79th Streets; concert: Central Park at 72nd Street. **Admission:** free. **Secondary genre[s]:** GYLS, **Acts:** local acts. **Sample day's lineup:** Shlomo Carlebach, Sherwood Goffin, Ira Heller, D'veykus, Kol Achai, Piamenta, Bitachon, Eli Zomick and The Neshoma Orchestra, others. **Contact:** National Council of Young Israel, 3 West 16th Street, New York, NY 10011, 212-787-7587 **or:** American Zionist Youth Foundation, 110 East 59th Street, New York, NY 10022, 212-339-6918. .

ISRAEL EXPO, Manhattan, NYC
> Late May
> Jewish

**Days:** 6. **Hours per day:** 8. **Site:** indoor. Seventh Regimental Armory, Park Avenue at East 67th Street. **Admission:** paid. **Daily entry:** under $10, $10 to $24, $50 and over. **Discounts:** multiple event or day passes, **Acts:** local acts. **Sample series lineup:** Day One: Liz Magnes; Day Two: Peter Himmelman and Chen Zimbalista; Day Three: Naomi. **Contact:** Israeli Expo, Seventh Regimental Armory, Park Avenue at East 67th Street, New York, NY, 212-244-3976.

BROADWAY COUNTY FAIR, Manhattan, NYC
> Late May
> Modern Country

Since 1993. Benefits Broadway Cares/Equity Fights AIDS. See other dates and sites. **Days:** 1. **Site:** indoor. Roseland Ballroom, 239 West 52nd Street. **Admission:** paid. **Daily entry:** $25 to $49, **Acts:** national acts, local acts. **Sample day's lineup:** Kathy Mattea, Cactus Club, others. **Contact:** Broadway Cares/Equity Fights AIDS, 165 West 46th Street, Suite 1300, New York, NY 10036, 212-840-0770.

ROCK AGAINST RACISM CONCERT, Manhattan, NYC
> Late May
> Alternative and College Rock

Since 1978. **Days:** 1. **Hours per day:** 6. **Site:** outdoor. Union Square, 14th Street and Broadway. **Admission:** free. **Secondary genre[s]:** RAP, TR&B, RGGE, **Acts:** national acts, local acts. **Sample day's lineup:** Chris Whitley, Faith, R. E. A. L., Afire, Blueprint, Freedom Land, Sha-Key, Professor Louie. **Contact:** Rock Against Racism Concert, 9 Bleecker Street, New York, NY 10012, 212-677-4899.

SUN RA FESTIVAL, Manhattan, NYC
> Middle May to Late May
> Alternative Jazz

Since 1995. **Days:** 9. **Hours per day:** 5. **Site:** indoor. Knitting Factory, 74 Leonard Street, between Broadway and Church Street. **Admission:** paid. **Secondary genre[s]:** ARCK, **Acts:** regional acts, local acts. **Sample series lineup:** Day One: Michael Ray and The Cosmic Krewe; Day Two: Anna Domino, Lazy Boy, Snakefarm; Day Three: Bayard Lancaster and His New Sounds of Africa, Dick Griffin, others. **Audio merchandise:** entire Knitting Factory Works catalog, including numerous festival recordings and compilations.. **Other merchandise:** "Knitting Music" by Michael Dorf (Knitting Factory Works). **Contact:** Knitting Factory, 47 East Houston Street, New York, NY 10012, 212-219-3055/3006.

OI!/SKAMPILATION, Manhattan, NYC
> Late May
> Reggae, Ska and Caribbean

Since 1994. Recent CD Release Party dates only; call/write for current "skactivity." **Days:** 2. **Site:** indoor. Wetlands, 161 Hudson Street. **Admission:** paid. **Secondary genre[s]:** ARCK, HRCK, **Acts:** regional acts, local acts. **Sample day's lineup:** Bouncing Souls, Wretched Ones, The Press, Oxblood, Blanks 77, Checkered Cabs, The Scofflaws, Jiker. **Audio merchandise:** "Oi!/Skampilation, Vol. 1" (Radical Records). **Contact:** Radical Records, 77 Bleecker Street, New York, NY 10012, 212-475-1111.

IRISH-AMERICAN FESTIVAL AND HERITAGE FEIS, Brooklyn, NYC
> Late May
> Irish

Since 1993. **Days:** 3. **Hours per day:** 8. **Site:** outdoor. Gateway National Recreation Area, Floyd Bennett Field, Flatbush Avenue. **Admission:** free. **Acts:** national acts, regional acts, local acts. **Sample lineup:** Frank Patterson, John Egan and The Irish Tradewind Showband, Susan McKeown and The Chanting House, Four To The Bar, Eileen Ivers and Seamus Egan, Aine, Gerry Hughes and Walter Ensor, Danny Kane and The Rockin' Rebels, The Horan Brothers, Anne-Marie Acosta with Marie Riley, others. **Contact:** National Park Service, Gateway National Recreation Area, Floyd Bennett Field, Building 69, Brooklyn, NY 11234, 718-338-3799.

52ND STREET JAZZ FESTIVAL, Manhattan, NYC
> Late May
> Modern Jazz

**Help!** A sample lineup? **Days:** 1. **Hours per day:** 7. **Site:** outdoor. 52nd Street, Lexington to 7th Avenues. **Admission:** free. **Secondary genre[s]:** RAP, MR&B, **Acts:** regional acts, local acts. **Contact:** 52nd Street Association for the Handicapped, 84 West 52nd Street, Suite 1000, New York, NY 10038, 212-809-4900.

FESTIVAL DE LOS SONEROS, Manhattan, NYC
> Middle May
> Modern Latin

Since 1994. See other sites and dates. **Days:** 1. **Site:** indoor. The Paramount, Madison Square Garden, 7th Avenue at 32nd Street. **Admission:** paid. **Daily entry:** $25 to $49, **Acts:** national acts, regional acts. **Sample day's lineup:** Tito Rojas, Oscar D'Leon, Andy Montanez, Jose Alberto, Victor Manuelle, Miles Pena, Guianko, Tony Vega, Raulin, Cano Estremera, Jose Alberto, Frankie Ruiz. **Contact:** RMM Productions, 568 Broadway, Suite 806, New York, NY 10012, 212-925-2828/4885.

MANHATTAN ETHNIC MUSIC AND DANCE FESTIVAL, Manhattan, NYC
> Late May
> Variety, Folk and International

Since 1976. **Days:** 1. **Hours per day:** 8. **Site:** outdoor. Riverbank State Park, 679 Riverside Drive at 145th Street, Harlem. **Admission:** free. **Secondary genre[s]:** RAP, IRSH, JWSH, TLAT, AFRC, RGGE, OTHR **Acts:** national acts, regional acts, local acts. **Sample day's lineup:** Inkay, Andy Statman, The Four Winds, Tom Doherty and Friends, Antilles, Los Pleneros De La 21, Spirit Ensemble, Jose Quesada and Los Cinco Diablos. **Contact:** Ethnic Folk Arts Center, 131 Varick Street, Room 907, New York, NY 10013-1493, 212-691-9510/694-3632.

MEMORIAL DAY WEEKEND CELEBRATION SCHOLARSHIP FUND RAISING DANCE, Manhattan, NYC
> Late May
> Modern Latin

**Days:** 1. **Hours per day:** 8. **Site:** indoor. Club Broadway, 2551 Broadway at 96th Street. **Admission:** paid. **Daily entry:** $10 to $24, **Acts:** regional acts, local acts. **Sample day's lineup:** Tito Nieves and His Orchestra, Santiago Ceron and His Orchestra, others. **Contact:** Grand Council of Hispanic Societies, c/o Club Broadway, 2551 Broadway, New York, NY 10025, 212-864-7600.

SAVE OUR PARK/WWRL RADIOTHON, Queens, NYC
> Late May
> African American

Since 1995. **Days:** 1. **Hours per day:** 8. **Site:** outdoor. Roy Wilkins Park, 119th Avenue and Merrick Boulevard, Jamaica. **Admission:** free. **Secondary genre[s]:** MJAZ, BGOS, RGGE, **Acts:** national acts, regional acts, local acts. **Sample day's lineup:** The Mighty Sparrow, Bill Jacobs Jazz Ensemble, others. **Contact:** WWRL-AM 1600, 41-30 58th Street, Woodside, NY 11377, 718-335-1600/276-4630.

BROADWAY ASTORIA FESTIVAL, Queens, NYC
> Late May
> Variety, General

See other dates and sites. **Days:** 1. **Hours per day:** 8. **Site:** outdoor. Crescent to 47th Street, Astoria. **Admission:** free. **Secondary genre[s]:** MJAZ, MRCK, ARCK, TR&B, RGGE, **Acts:** local acts. **Sample day's lineup:** Zane Massey and The Foundation, Rapadoo, Joe Restivo, Son House, Dark Moon, Off Center. **Contact:** Clearview Festival Productions, 401 Lafayette Street, New York, NY 10003, 212-995-9412.

## SONGWRITERS' HALL OF FAME AWARDS, Manhattan, NYC
   Late May
   Modern Rock and Pop

Since 1971. **Days:** 1. **Site:** indoor. New York Sheraton Hotel. **Admission:** paid. **Daily entry:** $50 and over. **Acts:** national acts. **Sample day's lineup:** Al Green, Taj Mahal, The Bee Gees, Carly Simon, others. **Contact:** Songwriters Hall of Fame, 600 Madison Avenue, 3rd Floor, New York, NY 10022, 212-319-1444.


## HARP AND HARMONY CONCERT, Manhattan, NYC
   Early Jun.
   Irish

Since 1993. **Help!** One time only? **Days:** 1. **Site:** indoor. Town Hall, 123 West 43rd Street. **Admission:** paid. **Daily entry:** $10 to $24, **Acts:** national acts, regional acts. **Sample day's lineup:** Tommy Makem, Cherish The Ladies, Malachy McCourt. **Contact:** Harp and Harmony Concert, c/o Town Hall, 123 West 43rd Street, New York, NY 10036, 212-840-2824/1003.


## WALL-TO-WALL RAHSAAN ROLAND KIRK, Manhattan, NYC
   Early Jun.
   Alternative Jazz

Since 1995. After Symphony Space's Wall-to-Walls. **Help!** One time only? **Days:** 2. **Site:** indoor. The Cooler, 416 West 14th Street. **Admission:** paid. **Secondary genre[s]:** ARCK, **Acts:** national acts, regional acts, local acts. **Sample day's lineup:** Lester Bowie, Rashied Ali, Amiri Bakara, Charles Gayle, Steve Turre, William Parker, William Hooker, Arthur Doyle, Wilbur Morris, Dick Griffin, Walter Perkins, Michael Marcus, Spooky, Elliott Sharp, Kelvyn Bell Trio, Damon Choice. **Contact:** Wall-to-Wall Rahsaan Roland Kirk, The Cooler, 416 West 14th Street, New York, NY, 212-229-0785.


## MURRAY HILL BLOCK PARTY AND BLUES FESTIVAL, Manhattan, NYC
   Early Jun.
   Blues and Traditional R&B

Since 1973. "With the Blues Festival [debuting in 1995], this was our most successful Block Party ever!" -- Dick Golub. Blues Festival's initiator, Eric Glatzer, may be departing, but Golub promises to keep the music aspect going strong, possibly switching to jazz in 1996. **Days:** 2. **Site:** outdoor and indoor. Block Party: East 35th Street, Madison to Lexington Avenues; plus evening club locations. **Admission:** free and paid. **Daily entry:** under $10, **Secondary genre[s]:** BGOS, **Acts:** national acts, regional acts, local acts. **Sample day's lineup:** Michael Hill's Blues Mob, Big Ed Sullivan and The Sidepockets, Bobby Radcliff, Johnny Allen, Tom Larsen Band, New York Bluesbusters, Bo Diddley Jr., Bill Sims, Irving Louis Latin, Sonny Hudson, others. **Contact:** Murray Hill Block Party and Blues Festival, 155 East 34th Street, #3R, New York, NY 10016, 212-779-7156 **or:** Murray Hill Committee, 36 East 36th Street, Box 8, New York, NY 10016, 212-243-0202. .


## PATHMARK HISPANIC ARTS FESTIVAL, Manhattan, NYC
   Early Jun.
   Modern Latin

Since 1989. Part of a sponsored metropolitan-area tour through the month. Events vary widely from year to year, so call ahead. **Days:** 3. **Hours per day:** 7. **Site:** outdoor. South Street Seaport, Pier 17, Ambrose Stage. **Admission:** free. **Secondary genre[s]:** TLAT, **Acts:** national acts, local acts. **Sample day's lineup:** Yomo Toro Band, Pathmark Latin Jazz Allstars, others. **Contact:** South Street Seaport Museum, 207 Front Street, New York, NY 10038, 212-669-9400.

## BROOKLYN WOODSTOCK, Brooklyn, NYC
Early Jun.
Alternative and College Rock

Since 1988. **Days:** 1. **Hours per day:** 10. **Site:** outdoor. 696 East 19th Street, Midwood. **Admission:** paid. **Daily entry:** $10 to $24, **Secondary genre[s]:** AJAZ, **Acts:** national acts, regional acts, local acts. **Sample day's lineup:** Antietam, The Aquanettas, B. O. X., Carbon with Elliot Sharp, Freedy Johnson, Lenny Kaye, Love Camp 7, No Safety, Kenny Young and The Eggplants, others. **Contact:** Excello Studios, 21 Powers Street, Brooklyn, NY 11211, 718-434-0171/965-9228.

## CELEBRATE 125! THE RHYTHM OF THE WORLD, Manhattan, NYC
Early Jun.
Variety, Folk and International

See other dates. **Help!** One time only? **Days:** 1. **Hours per day:** 11. **Site:** outdoor. American Museum of Natural History, Central Park West at 79th Street. **Admission:** free. **Secondary genre[s]:** MJAZ, BGOS, ZYDC, MLAT, AFRC, **Acts:** national acts, local acts. **Sample day's lineup:** O'Landa Draper, Buckwheat Zydeco, Ladysmith Black Mambazo, Willie Colon, Soh Daiko, others. **Contact:** Celebrate 125! The Rhythm of the World, American Museum of Natural History, C. P. W. at 79th Street, New York, NY, 212-769-5125.

## LESBIAN AND GAY PRIDE COMMITTEE PARADE AND FESTIVAL, Queens, NYC
Early Jun.
Gay and Lesbian

Since 1994. **Help!** A sample lineup? **Days:** 1. **Site:** outdoor. 37th Road between 73rd and 77th Streets, Jackson Heights. **Admission:** free. **Acts:** local acts. **Contact:** Lesbian and Gay Pride Committee Parade and Festival, c/o Ethical Culture Society of Queens, 61-11 220th Street, Bayside, NY 11364, 718-460-4064/229-3468.

## PLANTATHON AND MUSIC FESTIVAL, Manhattan, NYC
Early Jun.
Modern Jazz

See other sites and dates. **Days:** 1. **Hours per day:** 7. **Site:** outdoor. Broadway, 72nd to 86th Streets. **Admission:** free. **Secondary genre[s]:** MFOL, **Acts:** national acts, local acts. **Sample day's lineup:** Oscar Brand, Judy Barnett, Tracy McDonough, Odetta, others. **Contact:** Plantathon and Music Festival, 1501 Broadway, Suite 1808, New York, NY 10036, 212-764-6330.

## STARRETT AT SPRING CREEK NATIVE AMERICAN POW WOW, Brooklyn, NYC
Early Jun.
Native American

Since 1991. See other dates. **Days:** 1. **Hours per day:** 6. **Site:** outdoor. Starrett City Community Center, 1540 Van Siclen Avenue. **Admission:** free. **Acts:** regional acts, local acts. **Sample day's lineup:** Thunderbird American Dancers, Arawak Mountain Singers, Four Winds Singers, Full Circle Drum Society, others. **Contact:** Starrett at Spring Creek Native American Pow Wow, Starrett City Community Center, 1540 Van Siclen Avenue, Brooklyn, NY, 718-240-4545/642-2725.

WORLD OF PERCUSSION, Manhattan, NYC
   Early Jun.
   Variety, Folk and International

Dates and length vary slightly, so call ahead. **Days:** 1. **Site:** indoor. Symphony Space, 2537 Broadway at 95th Street. **Admission:** paid. **Daily entry:** $10 to $24, **Discounts:** other discounts **Secondary genre[s]:** MJAZ, MLAT, BRZL, RGGE, OTHR **Acts:** national acts, regional acts, local acts. **Sample day's lineup:** Babatunde Olatunji's Drums of Passion, Glen Velez Trio with Howard Levy, Big Black with Adam Rudolph, O Samba! Brazilian Dance Theater. **Audio merchandise:** entire W. M. I. catalog. **Contact:** World Music Institute, 49 West 27th Street, Suite 810, New York, NY 10001, 212-545-7536 **or:** Symphony Space, 2537 Broadway, New York, NY 10025, 212-864-5400. .

INDIAN SUMMER, Manhattan, NYC
   Early Jun. to Late Jun.
   Native American

Has also programmed a Festival of the Living Word: Voices of the African Diaspora and Indigenous America, Mid Nov. See other dates. **Days:** 13. **Site:** indoor. American Indian Community House, 404 Lafayette Street, 2nd Floor. **Admission:** paid. **Daily entry:** under $10, $10 to $24, **Acts:** regional acts, local acts. **Sample series lineup:** Day One: Coatlicue Las Colorado; Day Two: Pura Fe-Soni; Day Three: Thunderbird American Indian Dancers. **Contact:** American Indian Community House, 404 Lafayette Street, 2nd Floor, New York, NY 10003, 212-598-0100.

ISRAEL EXPO, Brooklyn, NYC
   Early Jun.
   Jewish

"A celebration of shalom...generation to generation." -- Poster. **Days:** 1. **Hours per day:** 5. **Site:** outdoor. King Bay YM-YWHA, 3495 Nostrand Avenue. **Admission:** free. **Acts:** national acts, local acts. **Sample day's lineup:** Andy Statman Klezmer Group, Shana Winoker, Kings Bay Y Choral Ensemble, Barbara Allen, others. **Contact:** Kings Bay YM-YWHA, 3495 Nostrand Avenue, Brooklyn, NY, 718-648-7703.

CROSS OVERS: MUSIC OF ASIA AMERICA, Manhattan, NYC
   Early Jun.
   Modern Jazz

Since 1995. Continuation of a winter concert series. See other dates and sites. **Days:** 3. **Site:** indoor. Sylvia and Danny Kaye Playhouse at Hunter College, 68th Street between Park and Lexington Avenues. **Admission:** paid. **Daily entry:** $10 to $24, **Discounts:** multiple event or day passes, other discounts. **Secondary genre[s]:** AVNT, **Acts:** national acts, regional acts. **Sample day's lineup:** Billy Taylor, Kenny Endo Taiko Ensemble, Jon Jang Sextet. **Contact:** Cross Overs: Music of Asia America, c/o Asia Society, 725 Park Avenue, New York, NY, 212-517-ASIA.

DISCMAKERS UNSIGNED BAND/ARTIST NEW YORK WORLD SERIES, Manhattan, NYC
   Early Jun.
   Alternative and College Rock

Since 1995. Band contest from demo submissions with finalists showcase. "This is your chance to win!" -- Advertisement. **Help!** A sample lineup? **Days:** 1. **Site:** indoor. The Lion's Den. **Acts:** local acts. **Contact:** Discmakers, 1650 Broadway, Suite 709, New York, NY 10046, 800-468-9353.

FESTIVAL OF JEWISH MUSIC, Manhattan, NYC
  Early Jun.
  Jewish

Since 1993. Benefits Housing Creation Loan Fund. **Days:** 1. **Site:** indoor. SAJ, 15 West 86th Street. **Admission:** paid. **Daily entry:** $10 to $24, **Acts:** local acts. **Sample day's lineup:** Rottenburg Chorus, Adrienne Cooper, Leonid Hambro, Harold Seletsky, Klezmorim, Marion Capriotti and Neil Rynston, Janet Leutchter. **Contact:** Coalition of West Side Synagogues, c/o S. A. J., 15 West 86th Street, New York, NY, 212-662-3663.

GOSPEL CONCERT, Brooklyn, NYC
  Early Jun.
  Black Gospel

**Days:** 1. **Site:** indoor. August Martin High School, Baisley Boulevard between 155th and 157th Streets, Jamaica. **Admission:** paid. **Daily entry:** $10 to $24, **Discounts: Acts:** national acts, local acts. **Sample day's lineup:** Five Blind Boys of Alabama, Jackson Southernaires, Soul Converters, The Angelettes of Alabama. **Contact:** August Martin High School, Baisley Boulevard, Jamaica, Queens, NY, 516-333-7660.

116TH STREET FESTIVAL IN EL BARRIO, Manhattan, NYC
  Middle Jun.
  Traditional Latin

Since 1989. In conjunction with the Puerto Rican Day Parade. **Days:** 1. **Hours per day:** 6. **Site:** outdoor. 116th Street, from 1st to Park Avenues, then down 3rd Avenue to 11th Street. **Admission:** free. **Acts:** national acts, regional acts, local acts. **Sample day's lineup:** Tito Rojas, Frankie Ruiz, Eddie Santiago, Las Chicas Del Can, plus 36 others on 7 stages. **Contact:** Nick Lugo Travel, 159 East 116th Street, New York, NY 10029, 212-348-2100.

BRONX ETHNIC MUSIC AND DANCE FESTIVAL, Bronx, NYC
  Middle Jun.
  Variety, Folk and International

Since 1976. **Days:** 1. **Hours per day:** 8. **Site:** outdoor. Van Cortland Park parade ground, Broadway and 242nd Street. **Admission:** free. **Secondary genre[s]:** RAP, IRSH, JWSH, TLAT, AFRC, RGGE, OTHR **Acts:** national acts, regional acts, local acts. **Sample day's lineup:** Inkay, Andy Statman, The Four Winds, Tom Doherty and Friends, Antilles, Los Pleneros De La 21, Spirit Ensemble, Jose Quesada and Los Cinco Diablos. **Contact:** Ethnic Folk Arts Center, 131 Varick Street, Room 907, New York, NY 10013-1493, 212-691-9510.

DOWNTOWN MUSIC GALLERY'S ANNIVERSARY CELEBRATION, Manhattan, NYC
  Middle Jun.
  Alternative and College Rock

Since 1992. Also produced Guitar Love Hell with Geoff McKay, Dave Tronzo, Leni Stern Trios at Zanzibar, 73 8th Avenue, Late Sep. **Days:** 1. **Hours per day:** 5. **Site:** indoor. Knitting Factory, 74 Leonard Street, between Broadway and Church Street. **Admission:** paid. **Secondary genre[s]:** JWSH, **Acts:** local acts. **Sample day's lineup:** Tiny Lights, Kissyfur, Azialia Snail, others. **Contact:** Downtown Music Gallery, 211 East 5th Street, New York, NY 10003, 212-473-0043.

## NEW YORK CITY'S GOSPEL FESTIVAL, Brooklyn, NYC
> Middle Jun.
> Black Gospel

Since 1990. **Days:** 1. **Hours per day:** 7. **Site:** outdoor. Prospect Park bandshell, 9th Street and Prospect Park West. **Admission:** free. **Acts:** regional acts, local acts. **Sample day's lineup:** Brooklyn Peace Chorus, Brownsville Mass Choir, Celestial Community Choir, Jeffrey Conyers and The Crusade Choir, Danny Eason and The Brooklyn Youth Choir, Eternity, Lady Peachena, New York's Youth Sunshine Choir, McDonald's Gospelfest winners, 99.7 KISS-FM's Inspirational Choir, others. **Contact:** Fund for the Borough of Brooklyn, 30 Flatbush Avenue, Brooklyn, NY 11217, 718-855-7882 x20.

## PUERTO RICAN DAY PARADE, Manhattan, NYC
> Middle Jun.
> Modern Latin

Since 1958. Salsa extravanganza with numerous "piggyback" concerts. Parade music consists of 40 bands on floats playing live and/or to taped tracks. Often, there are stages set up for national, regional and local live acts. **Days:** 1. **Hours per day:** 8. **Site:** outdoor. 5th Avenue, from 44th to 86th Streets. **Admission:** free. **Acts:** national acts, regional acts, local acts. **Contact:** Finklestein, Borah, Schwartz, Altschuler, Goldstein P. C., 377 Broadway, New York, NY 10013, 212-431-1300.

## SUPER RADIOACTIVE BODEGA BONANZA OUTDOOR FESTIVAL, Brooklyn, NYC
> Middle Jun.
> Hard Rock and Heavy Metal

See other dates and sites. **Days:** 1. **Hours per day:** 12. **Site:** indoor. Warehouse, Kent Avenue, between North 10th and 11th Streets, Williamsburg. **Admission:** free. **Secondary genre[s]:** ARCK, **Acts:** local acts. **Sample day's lineup:** Ff, The Wives, Astro Zombies, Paleface, Cracker Snatch, Thrust, Hammerbrain, Thrust, Colored Greens, others. **Contact:** Radioactive Bodega, c/o The Warehouse, Kent Avenue, Williamsburg, Brooklyn, NY, 718-387-7023/598-4087.

## WELCOME BACK TO BROOKLYN, Brooklyn, NYC
> Middle Jun.
> Variety, General

Since 1983. **Days:** 1. **Hours per day:** 5. **Site:** outdoor. Eastern Parkway, from Grand Army Plaza to the Brooklyn Museum. **Admission:** free. **Secondary genre[s]:** MJAZ, CRCK, ARCK, TR&B, ACAP, AC&W, MLAT, OTHR **Acts:** national acts, regional acts, local acts. **Sample day's lineup:** Memphis Train and The Boxcar Horns, Pucho and The Latin Soul Brothers, Melvin Sparks, Etta Jones and Houston Person, Earl Lewis and The Channels, Faith, Manny Oquendo and Libre, Neil Sedaka, others. **Contact:** Fund for the Borough of Brooklyn, 30 Flatbush Avenue, Brooklyn, NY 11217, 718-855-7882 x20.

## CITY LORE FESTIVAL, Manhattan, NYC
> Middle Jun.
> Variety, Folk and International

Previously produced Somos Boricuas: A Puerto Rican Festival. **Help!** Still ongoing? **Days:** 1. **Hours per day:** 6. **Site:** outdoor. Morris-Jumel Mansion and Park, Jumel Terrace, between 160th and 162nd Streets, Washington Heights. **Admission:** free. **Secondary genre[s]:** JWSH, TLAT, RGGE, **Acts:** regional acts, local acts. **Sample day's lineup:** Asadife, Greater Metro Klezmer Band, C. A. S. Y. M. Steel Orchestra, Los Pleneros De La 21, others. **Contact:** City Lore, 72 East 1st Street, New York, NY 10003, 212-529-1955.

LOWER EAST SIDE JEWISH FESTIVAL, Manhattan, NYC
> Middle Jun.
> Jewish

Since 1977. **Days:** 1. **Hours per day:** 7. **Site:** outdoor. East Broadway, Rutgers to Montgomery Streets. **Admission:** free. **Acts:** local acts. **Sample day's lineup:** Joanne Loewy, Malka Orchestra Klezmer Band, Yoel Sharabi, Ilan Mamber. **Contact:** Educational Alliance, 21 East 13th Street, New York, NY 10003, 212-463-8588/385-6611.

LYRICS AND LYRICISTS/THE NEW BREED, Manhattan, NYC
> Middle Jun.
> Cabaret

Since 1992. Capping year-round quarter-century-old Lyrics and Lyricists series, where up to eight leading singers perform works of single selected lyricist per evening. Also programs weekly Cabaret in Concert series. **Days:** 1. **Site:** indoor. 92nd Street Y, 1395 Lexington Avenue. **Admission:** paid. **Daily entry:** $25 to $49, **Discounts:** multiple event or day passes, **Secondary genre[s]:** TR&B, **Acts:** national acts, regional acts, local acts. **Sample day's lineup:** Andrea Marcovicci, Margaret Whiting, Craig Cardelia, Francesca Blumenthal, David Friedman, Abby Green, Brad Ross, others. **Contact:** Tisch Center for the Arts, 92nd Street YM-YWHA, 1395 Lexington Avenue, New York, NY 10128, 212-996-1100/415-5488.

FESTIVAL PLAYERO, Bronx, NYC
> Middle Jun. to Early Sep.
> Modern Latin

Festival titles, sponsors may change, but this weekend salsa series on the beach has kept steady for years. Biggest names appear Labor Day weekend. **Days:** 28. **Site:** outdoor. Orchard Beach, Orchard Beach Road. **Admission:** free. **Acts:** national acts, regional acts, local acts. **Sample day's lineup:** Oscar D'Leon, Sergio Vargas; **Contact:** Orchard Beach, 1 Orchard Beach Road, Bronx, NY 10462, 718-885-2275.

BUSKERS FARE/SUMMER FAIR, Manhattan, NYC
> Middle Jun.
> Variety, General

"Over 175 hours of circus, vaudeville, mummery and magic!" -- Advertisement. Buskers Fare, during week, preceeds Summerfaire on weekend. The latter programs local acts across various genres. **Days:** 8. **Hours per day:** 11. **Site:** outdoor. multiple locations, World Financial Center, Liberty and West Streets. **Admission:** free. **Secondary genre[s]:** TJAZ, ZYDC, OTHR **Acts:** local acts. **Sample day's lineup:** Big Nazo Puppet Band, Jambalaya Jive, Raggin' Piano Boogie, Alice Farley, Walter Thompson Marching Orchestra, others. **Contact:** World Financial Center Arts and Events, 200 Liberty Street, 18th Floor, New York, NY 10281, 212-945-0505 **or:** Lower Manhattan Cultural Council, 1 World Trade Center, Suite 1717, New York, NY 10048, 212-321-BUSK.

SUDDEN SUNSETS: HIGHLIGHTS FROM THE BENSON AIDS SERIES, Manhattan, NYC
> Middle Jun.
> Avant Garde and New Music

Since 1995. **Help!** One time only? **Days:** 1. **Site:** indoor. Alice Tully Hall, Lincoln Center, Broadway at 65th Street. **Admission:** paid. **Daily entry:** $10 to $24, $25 to $49, $50 and over. **Acts:** regional acts, local acts. **Sample day's lineup:** Savage, DeBlasio, Seyfrit, Oldham, Hampton, Chesley, Husband, Schaffner, Turner, others. **Contact:** Downtown Music Productions, 310 East 12th Street, New York, NY 10003, 212-267-8723/477-1594.

**FIRE WALL TOTAL ARTS FESTIVAL**, Manhattan, NYC
> Middle Jun. to Late Jun.
> Alternative Jazz

Since 1992. **Days:** 13. **Site:** outdoor and indoor. multiple locations in New York City, Philadelphia. **Admission:** paid. **Daily entry:** under $10, $10 to $24, **Discounts:** other discounts. **Secondary genre[s]:** MLAT, AVNT, CBRT, **Acts:** national acts, regional acts, local acts. **Sample day's lineup:** Ahmed Addullah, Chico Freeman, Oliver Lake, Elliott Sharp, Kelvyn Bell, Tony Lewis, Jamaladeen Tacuma, Craig Harris, Laurie Carlos. **Contact:** P. S. 122, 150 1st Avenue, New York, NY 10009, 212-477-5829/5288.

**CENTRAL PARK SUMMERSTAGE**, Manhattan, NYC
> Middle Jun. to Early Aug.
> Variety, General

Since 1986. **Days:** 30. **Hours per day:** 3. **Site:** outdoor. Rumsey Playfield, 72nd Street. **Admission:** free. **Secondary genre[s]:** MJAZ, AJAZ, CRCK, ARCK, RAP, MR&B, TR&B, BGOS, MC&W, AC&W, BLGS, MFOL, ZYDC, IRSH, MLAT, AFRC, BRZL, RGGE, AVNT, OTHR. **Acts:** national acts, regional acts, local acts. **Sample day's lineup:** Buckshot LeFongue with Branford Marsalis, Ali Hassan Kuban and The Nubian Band, Jessica Hagedorn with Vernon Reid, others. **Contact:** Central Park Summerstage, 830 5th Avenue, New York, NY 10021, 212-360-2756/969-0769.

**GOSPEL MUSIC WORKSHOP OF AMERICA/NEW YORK STATE CHAPTER CONVENTION**, Brooklyn, NYC
> Middle Jun.
> Black Gospel

**Days:** 4. **Site:** indoor. Pleasant Grove Baptist Tabernacle, 1927 Fulton Street at Howard Avenue, East New York. **Admission:** free and paid. **Daily entry:** under $10, $10 to $24, **Discounts:** advance purchase discounts, **Acts:** local acts. **Sample day's lineup:** Triboro, Mary Sharp and The Voices of Hope, Ronnie Felder and The Voices of Inspiration, Doreen Figueroa, David Gates and The Love, Peace and Joy Singers, Craig Hayes and The Unified Voices of Trenton. **Contact:** Pleasant Row Baptist Tabernacle, 1927 Fulton Street, Brooklyn, NY 11233, 718-773-0895.

**TWEED NEW WORKS FESTIVAL**, Manhattan, NYC
> Middle Jun. to Early Jul.
> Avant Garde and New Music

Since 1993. "Festival of international and home-grown [new] music." -- Listing. **Days:** 12. **Site:** indoor. The Vineyard's Dimson Theater, 108 East 15th Street. **Admission:** paid. **Daily entry:** $10 to $24, **Acts:** local acts. **Sample day's lineup:** Carol and Larry Lipnik, Scott Killian, Nobles of The Mystic Shrine. **Contact:** Tweed New Works Festival, The Vineyard's Dimson Theater, 108 East 15th Street, New York, NY, 212-924-0077.

**GOSPELFEST**, Brooklyn, NYC
> Middle Jun.
> Black Gospel

Since 1993. **Days:** 1. **Site:** indoor. Wayside Baptist Church, 1746-60 Broadway, between Chauncey and Rockaway. **Admission:** paid. **Daily entry:** under $10, $10 to $24, **Acts:** local acts. **Sample day's lineup:** Rev. Barbara Y. Williams II, Sisters In Blue, Wayside Mass Choir. **Contact:** New York Police Department Guardian's Association, c/o Wayside Baptist Church, 1746-60 Broadway, Brooklyn, NY, 718-963-5358.

## WPLJ-FM's 70's Dance Party, Manhattan, NYC
### Middle Jun.
### Classic Rock and Oldies

See other dates. **Days:** 1. **Site:** indoor. The Paramount, Madison Square Garden, 7th Avenue at 32nd Street. **Admission:** paid. **Daily entry:** $25 to $49, **Acts:** national acts. **Sample day's lineup:** Irene Cara, Village People, Vicki Sue Robinson, Rose Royce, Tavares, Alicia Bridges. **Contact:** WPLJ-FM's 70's Dance Party, WPLJ-FM, 2 Pennsylvania Plaza, New York, NY, 212-465-MSG1.

## Southeast Queens' Youth Sports and Spring Festival/Juneteenth, Queens, NYC
### Middle Jun.
### African American

**Days:** 3. **Hours per day:** 8. **Site:** outdoor. Roy Wilkins Park, 119th Avenue and Merrick Boulevard, Jamaica. **Admission:** free. **Secondary genre[s]:** MJAZ, MR&B, BGOS, MFOL, BRZL, RGGE, GYLS, OTHR **Acts:** national acts, regional acts, local acts. **Sample day's lineup:** Melba Moore, Richie Havens, Leontyne Watts, Nego Gato, Lariman and Jazzland, others. **Contact:** Southern Queens Park Association, 119th Avenue and Merrick Boulevard, Jamaica, NY 11434, 718-276-4630.

## Lesbian and Gay Pride Week/PrideFest, Manhattan, NYC
### Middle Jun. to Late Jun.
### Gay and Lesbian

Since 1969. **Days:** 9. **Site:** outdoor. parade: 52nd Street and 5th Avenue south to Washington Square, then west to Chrsitopher Street; PrideFest: Christopher Street, etc. **Admission:** free and paid. **Daily entry:** $10 to $24, **Discounts:** advance purchase discounts, **Secondary genre[s]:** VRGL, **Acts:** national acts, regional acts, local acts. **Sample day's lineup:** Janis Ian, Crystal Waters, BETTY, others. **Contact:** Out in New York, c/o Out Magazine, P. O. Box 1935, Marion, OH 43306-2035, 212-807-7066/7433.

## Boathouse Rock, Manhattan, NYC
### Middle Jun.
### Modern Rock and Pop

Since 1992. Benefits AmFAR. **Days:** 1. **Site:** indoor. Boathouse in Central Park, 72nd Street at 5th Avenue. **Admission:** paid. **Daily entry:** $50 and over. **Acts:** national acts. **Sample day's lineup:** Ru Paul, Mick Fleetwood, Sandra Bernhard, Taylor Dayne, Deee-Lite, Eartha Kitt, others. **Contact:** AmFar, 733 3rd Avenue, 12th Floor, New York, NY 10017, 212-682-7440 x155.

## Broadway Summer Festival, Manhattan, NYC
### Middle Jun.
### Modern Jazz

See other sites and dates. **Days:** 1. **Hours per day:** 7. **Site:** outdoor. Broadway, 86th to 96th Streets. **Admission:** free. **Secondary genre[s]:** MFOL, **Acts:** national acts, local acts. **Sample day's lineup:** Oscar Brand, Judy Barnett, Tracy McDonough, Odetta, others. **Contact:** Broadway Summer Festival, 1501 Broadway, Suite 1808, New York, NY 10036, 212-764-6330.

## IRISH TRADITIONAL MUSIC AND DANCE FESTIVAL, Bronx, NYC
Middle Jun.
Irish

Since 1981. **Days:** 1. **Hours per day:** 10. **Site:** outdoor. College of Mount St. Vincent, Riverdale Avenue at 263rd Street, Riverdale. **Admission:** paid. **Daily entry:** $10 to $24, **Discounts:** advance purchase discounts, **Acts:** national acts, regional acts, local acts. **Sample day's lineup:** Atlantic Bridge, Christy Barry, Kevin Broesler, Cara Butler, Karen Casey, Joan McNiff Cass, Cherish The Ladies, Rev. Charlie Coen, Jack Coen, Jimmy Coen, Brian Conway, Mary Coogan, Johnny Cronin, Dierdre Danaher, Tony DeMarco, Fiona Doherty, Tom Doherty, Brendan Dolan, Felix Dolan, John Doyle, Tom Dunne, Seamus Egan, Siobhan Egan, John Ford, Denis Galvin, Linda Hickman, Winifred Horan, Eileen Ivers, John Jennings, James Keane, Willy Kelly, Siobhan Kelly, Pat Kilbride, Maureen Doherty Macken, Morningstar, Mick Maloney, Martin Mulhaire, John Nolan, Patrick Ourceau, Jerry O'Sullivan, Mike Preston, Mary Rafferty, Mike Rafferty, Fred Rice, Cathy Ryan, Greg Ryan, John Whelan, others. **Contact:** Irish Arts Center, 553 West 51st Street, New York, NY 10019, 212-757-3318 **or:** Irish Traditional Music and Dance Festival, 71 Stevens Avenue, Yonkers, NY 10704, 914-776-0722.

## QUEENS BOULEVARD FESTIVAL, Queens, NYC
Middle Jun.
Variety, General

See other dates and sites. **Days:** 1. **Hours per day:** 8. **Site:** outdoor. Queens Boulevard, 70th Road to Yellowstone Boulevard, Forest Hills. **Admission:** free. **Secondary genre[s]:** MJAZ, MRCK, ARCK, TR&B, RGGE, **Acts:** local acts. **Sample day's lineup:** Zane Massey and The Foundation, Rapadoo, Joe Restivo, Son House, Dark Moon, Off Center. **Contact:** Clearview Festival Productions, 401 Lafayette Street, New York, NY 10003, 212-995-9412.

## UPPER BROADWAY SUMMER FESTIVAL, Manhattan, NYC
Middle Jun.
Modern Jazz

See other sites and dates. **Days:** 1. **Hours per day:** 7. **Site:** outdoor. Broadway, 110th to 116th Streets. **Admission:** free. **Secondary genre[s]:** MFOL, **Acts:** national acts, local acts. **Sample day's lineup:** Oscar Brand, Judy Barnett, Tracy McDonough, Odetta, others. **Contact:** Upper Broadway Summer Festival, 1501 Broadway, Suite 1808, New York, NY 10036, 212-764-6330.

## KNITTING FACTORY'S "WHAT IS JAZZ?" FESTIVAL, Manhattan, NYC
Middle Jun. to Early Jul.
Alternative Jazz

**Days:** 13. **Hours per day:** 5. **Site:** indoor. Knitting Factory, 74 Leonard Street, between Broadway and Church Street, plus other venues. **Admission:** free and paid. **Daily entry:** $10 to $24, **Acts:** national acts, regional acts, local acts. **Sample day's lineup:** Tim Hagans Trio, David Murray Big Band, Jazz Passengers, Dave Douglas Sextet, Kandalini, Zusaan Kali Fasteau, Human Feel, Walter Thompson Orchestra, Babkas. **Audio merchandise:** "Knitting Factory What is Jazz? Sampler" (Knitting Factory Works), plus entire Knitting Factory Works catalog. **Other merchandise:** "Knitting" Music by Michael Dorf (Knitting Factory Works). **Contact:** Knitting Factory, 47 East Houston Street, New York, NY 10012, 212-219-3055/3006.

## SOUNDS AT SUNSET, Manhattan, NYC
Middle Jun. to Middle Sep.
Variety, General

"Classic and cool on the Hudson." -- Brochure. See other dates. **Days:** 41. **Site:** outdoor. multiple locations, World Financial Center. **Admission:** free. **Secondary genre[s]:** MJAZ, TJAZ, MC&W, IRSH, JWSH, MLAT, CBRT, **Acts:** national acts, regional acts, local acts. **Sample series lineup:** Day One: Ray Santos and Orchestra, Pete Rodriguez and Orchestra; Day Two: Steve Ross, Judy Carmichael. **Contact:** World Financial Center Arts and Events, 200 Liberty Street, 18th Floor, New York, NY 10281, 212-945-0505.

LESBOPALOOZA, Manhattan, NYC
> Late Jul.
> Gay and Lesbian

Since 1994. **Days:** 1. **Hours per day:** 7. **Site:** indoor. Moxy, 179 Varick Street. **Admission:** paid. **Secondary genre[s]:** ARCK, HRCK, MFOL, **Acts:** regional acts, local acts. **Sample day's lineup:** Alix Dobkin, Tribe 8, Carmelita Tropicana, Cheryl Boyce Taylor, Chi Chi Valenti, Gerry Gomez Pearlberg, Kay Turner, Lisa Lerner, Melissa Ferrick, Maul Girls, Gretchen Phillips, Pamela Sneed, Rose Troche, Sexpod, Shelly Mars, others. **Contact:** Lesbopalooza, c/o Moxy, 179 Varick Street, New York, NY, 212-334-0017.

WINTER CONSORT SUMMER SOLSTICE WHOLE EARTH CELEBRATION, Manhattan, NYC
> Late Jun.
> Variety, Folk and International

See other dates. **Days:** 1. **Site:** indoor. Cathedral of St. John the Divine, 1047 Amsterdam Avenue at 112th Street. **Admission:** paid. **Daily entry:** $25 to $49, $50 and over. **Secondary genre[s]:** MJAZ, BGOS, IRSH, OTHR **Acts:** national acts, local acts. **Sample day's lineup:** Paul Winter Consort, Dimitri Pokrovsky Singers, Noirin Ni Riain, Kecia Lewis-Evans. **Contact:** Cathedral of St. John the Divine, 1047 Amsterdam Avenue, New York, NY 10025, 212-662-2133/316-7540.

MIDSUMMER NIGHT SWING, Manhattan, NYC
> Late Jun. to Late Jul.
> Variety, General

**Days:** 21. **Site:** outdoor. Fountain Plaza, Lincoln Center, Broadway at 65th Street. **Admission:** free and paid. **Daily entry:** under $10, **Discounts:** multiple event or day passes, **Secondary genre[s]:** MJAZ, TJAZ, CRCK, TR&B, MC&W, AC&W, ZYDC, MLAT, TLAT, AFRC, BRZL, **Acts:** national acts, regional acts, local acts. **Sample series lineup:** Day One: Big Sandy and His Fly-Rite Boys, Nathan and The Zydeco Cha-Cha's; Day Two: Bobby Sanabria and Ascension, Milly Y Los Vecinos; Day Three: Evelyn "Champagne" King, Harold Melvin and The Blue Notes. **Contact:** Midsummer Night Swing, Lincoln Center for the Performing Arts, Inc., 140 West 65th Street, New York, NY 10023-6583, 212-875-5446.

CELEBRATE BROOKLYN PERFORMING ARTS FESTIVAL, Brooklyn, NYC
> Late Jun. to Middle Aug.
> Variety, General

Since 1979. **Days:** 16. **Site:** outdoor. Prospect Park bandshell, 9th Street and Prospect Park West. **Admission:** free. **Secondary genre[s]:** MJAZ, TJAZ, AJAZ, CRCK, ARCK, TR&B, ACAP, BGOS, AC&W, MFOL, ZYDC, IRSH, JWSH, MLAT, TLAT, AFRC, BRZL, RGGE, OTHR **Acts:** national acts, regional acts, local acts. **Sample series lineup:** Day One: Paquito D'Rivera, Brooklyn Philharmonic Orchestra; Day Two: Randy Weston, Rodney Kendrick; Day Three: Kenny Neal, Greg Trooper. **Contact:** Fund for the Borough of Brooklyn, 30 Flatbush Avenue, Brooklyn, NY 11217, 718-855-7882 x20.

BEACONS IN JAZZ, Manhattan, NYC
> Late Jun.
> Modern Jazz

Also hosts International Association of Schools Jazz Meeting, Late Jun., in conjunction with JVC Jazz Festival. See other dates. **Days:** 1. **Site:** indoor. John L. Tishman Auditorium, New School for Social Research, 66 West 12th Street. **Admission:** paid. **Daily entry:** $50 and over. **Acts:** national acts, regional acts, local acts. **Sample day's lineup:** Max Roach, Eddie Bert, Cecil Bridgewater, Donald Byrd, Joe Chambers, Doc Cheatham, Andrew Cyrille, Jon Faddis, Frank Foster, Chico Hamilton, Barry Harris, Roy Haynes, Arnie Lawrence, Jimmy Owens, Bernard Purdie, Wallace Roney, Carrie Smith, Stanley Turrentine, Reggie Workman, The So What Brass Ensemble Quintet, others. **Contact:** Beacons In Jazz, New School Jazz, 66 Fifth Avenue, New York, NY 10011, 212-673-8717.

## JVC Jazz Festival/Bryant Park Jazz Festival, Manhattan, NYC
Late Jun. to Early Jul.
Modern Jazz

Since 1954. **Days:** 14. **Hours per day:** 8. **Site:** outdoor and indoor. multiple locations. **Admission:** free and paid. **Daily entry:** $10 to $24, $25 to $49, $50 and over. **Secondary genre[s]:** TJAZ, AJAZ, MRCK, CRCK, MR&B, TR&B, MLAT, AFRC, BRZL, CBRT, **Acts:** national acts, regional acts. **Sample day's lineup:** Al Jarreau, Zap Mama, Carnegie Hall Jazz Band, Lincoln Center Jazz Orchestra, Wessell Anderson Quartet, Carl Allen, Cyrus Chesnut Trio, James Carter Quartet, Gary Bartz Quintet, Anita O'Day, others. **Audio merchandise:** "A Night of Chesky Jazz" (Chesky), plus numerous other live recordings on various other labels. **Contact:** JVC Jazz Festival, P. O. Box 1169 Ansonia Station, New York, NY 10023, 212-787-2020 **or:** Festival Productions, Inc., 311 West 74th Street, New York, NY 10023, 212-496-9000. .

## Queens Festival/Nations in Neighborhoods Multicultural Dance Party, Queens, NYC
Late Jun.
Variety, General

Since 1977. **Days:** 2. **Hours per day:** 12. **Site:** outdoor. Flushing Meadows-Corona Park. **Admission:** free. **Secondary genre[s]:** RAP, MR&B, TR&B, ACAP, IRSH, JWSH, MLAT, TLAT, AFRC, BRZL, CBRT, OTHR **Acts:** national acts, regional acts, local acts. **Sample day's lineup:** Buster Poindexter and His Banshees of Blue, The Elegants, Jenny Burton and The Choir, The Jive Five, Four Reals, Ronny and The Rainbows, The Brats, Earl Lewis and The Channels, Brick City, Arlene Smith and The Chantels, Reparata and The Del-Rons, Subhra Goswami Ensemble, Greek American Folklore Society, Joannie Madden and The Donny Golden Ensemble, Jose Quesada and Los Cincos Diablos, Kabajo, Los Macondos, others. **Contact:** Nations in Neighborhoods Multicultural Dance Party, Queens Council on the Arts, 161-04 Jamaica Avenue, Jamaica, NYNY 11432, 718-291-1100 **or:** Queens Festival, Flushing Meadows-Corona Park, Holmsted Center, Room 53, Flushing, NY 11386, 718-760-6565.

## Underground Blues and Folk Festival, Manhattan, NYC
Late Jun.
Blues and Traditional R&B

See other dates. **Days:** 2. **Site:** indoor. Grand Central Terminal, 42nd Street and Park Avenue. **Admission:** free. **Secondary genre[s]:** MFOL, **Acts:** national acts, regional acts, local acts. **Sample day's lineup:** Carolina Slim, Ernie Williams and The Wildcats, Irving Louis Latin and His Chicago Fire, others. **Contact:** Performing in Public Spaces, 204 West 80th Street, New York, NY 10024, 212-362-3830.

## Caribbean Cultural Heritage Week Festival/Caribbean Craft and Food Fair, Brooklyn, NYC
Late Jun.
Reggae, Ska and Caribbean

Since 1985. **Help!** A sample lineup? **Days:** 1. **Hours per day:** 9. **Site:** outdoor. Prospect Park's Nethermead, Ocean Avenue and Lincoln Road. **Admission:** free. **Secondary genre[s]:** RGGE, **Acts:** local acts. **Sample day's lineup: Contact:** BACA/The Brooklyn Arts Council, 200 Eastern Parkway, Brooklyn, NY 11238, 718-783-4469/3077 **or:** Caribbean Craft and Food Fair, c/o WNWK 105.9 FM, 449 Broadway, New York, NY, 212-966-1059..

IMPROVISORS FESTIVAL, Manhattan, NYC
> Late Jun. to Early Jul.
> Alternative Jazz

Since 1994. "Avant garde jazz music dance poetry and art." -- Flyer. **Days:** 2. **Hours per day:** 5. **Site:** indoor. Context, 28 Avenue A, between 2nd and 3rd Streets. **Admission:** paid. **Daily entry:** $10 to $24, **Secondary genre[s]:** AVNT, **Acts:** local acts. **Sample day's lineup:** Jason Hwang Quartet, Mark Whitecage Ensemble, Patricia Nicholson, Cooper-Moore Ensemble. **Contact:** Improvisors Festival, c/o Context, 28 Avenue A, New York, NY, 212-343-0530.


AFRICAN STREET FESTIVAL, Brooklyn, NYC
> Late Jun. to Early Jul.
> African American

Since 1972. **Days:** 5. **Hours per day:** 14. **Site:** indoor. Boys and Girls High School, 1700 Fulton Street, between Utica and Schenectady Avenues, Bedford-Stuyvesant. **Admission:** paid. **Daily entry:** under $10, **Discounts:** student discounts, **Restrictions:** 7, 8, **Secondary genre[s]:** MJAZ, AJAZ, CRCK, RAP, MR&B, TR&B, ACAP, BGOS, MLAT, AFRC, RGGE, **Acts:** national acts, regional acts, local acts. **Sample day's lineup:** Sun Ra and His Cosmic Arkestra, David Rudder and Charlie's Roots Band, Hezekiah Walker and His Love Fellowship Crusade Choir, Harmony, Chief Bey-Libation to The Ancestors, Yekk Music, others. **Contact:** African Street Festival, 451-A Nostrand Avenue, Brooklyn, NY 11216, 718-638-6700.


NEW YORK TRINI-JAM FEST, Brooklyn, NYC
> Early Jul.
> Reggae, Ska and Caribbean

Since 1994. **Help!** A sample lineup? **Days:** 2. **Hours per day:** 8. **Site:** outdoor. Steeplechase Park, Ocean Parkway, Coney Island. **Admission:** paid. **Daily entry:** $10 to $24, $25 to $49, **Discounts:** advance purchase discounts, **Restrictions:** 4, 5, 12, **Acts:** national acts, regional acts, local acts. **Contact:** Jamyns Promotions, 32-20 Church Avenue, Brooklyn, NY 11226, 718-941-4629/372-0275.


WOODSIDE INDEPENDENCE WEEKEND FESTIVAL, Queens, NYC
> Early Jul.
> Variety, General

See other dates and sites. **Days:** 1. **Hours per day:** 8. **Site:** outdoor. Steinway Street, 28th to 35th Streets, Astoria. **Admission:** free. **Secondary genre[s]:** MJAZ, MRCK, ARCK, TR&B, RGGE, **Acts:** local acts. **Sample day's lineup:** Zane Massey and The Foundation, Rapadoo, Joe Restivo, Son House, Dark Moon, Off Center. **Contact:** Clearview Festival Productions, 401 Lafayette Street, New York, NY 10003, 212-995-9412.


PARK SLOPE 5TH AVENUE INDEPENDENCE DAY FESTIVAL, Brooklyn, NYC
> Early Jul.
> Variety, General

See other dates and sites. **Days:** 1. **Hours per day:** 8. **Site:** outdoor. 5th Avenue, 5th to 18th Streets, Park Slope. **Admission:** free. **Secondary genre[s]:** MJAZ, MRCK, ARCK, TR&B, RGGE, **Acts:** local acts. **Sample day's lineup:** Zane Massey and The Foundation, Rapadoo, Joe Restivo, Son House, Dark Moon, Off Center. **Contact:** Clearview Festival Productions, 401 Lafayette Street, New York, NY 10003, 212-995-9412.

## EL ELYON MUSIC FEST, Brooklyn, NYC
Early Jul.
Modern Christian

See other sites and dates. **Help!** A sample lineup? **Days:** 1. **Site:** outdoor. Prospect Park, West 9th Street. **Secondary genre[s]:** BGOS, MLAT, RGGE, **Acts:** local acts. **Contact:** Ministerio Internacional Musical, P. O. Box 320-158, Brooklyn, NY 11232-0003, 718-768-9459/332-7427.

## WOMEN IN JAZZ FESTIVAL, Manhattan, NYC
Early Jul.
Modern Jazz

Since 1980. Nice lunchtime concerts. **Days:** 4. **Hours per day:** 2. **Site:** outdoor. Austin Tobin Plaza, World Trade Center, Vesey and Liberty Streets. **Admission:** free. **Acts:** national acts, regional acts. **Sample series lineup:** Day One: Charmaine Neville; Day Two: Abbey Lincoln; Day Three: Ifeachor Okeke. **Contact:** Women in Jazz Festival, 1 World Trade Center, 35 West, New York, NY 10048, 212-432-0900.

## SERIOUS FUN!, Manhattan, NYC
Early Jul. to Late Jul.
Avant Garde and New Music

**Days:** 17. **Site:** indoor. Alice Tully Hall, Lincoln Center, Broadway at 65th Street. **Admission:** paid. **Daily entry:** $10 to $24, $25 to $49, $50 and over. **Acts:** national acts, regional acts. **Sample series lineup:** Day One: "Earthquake/Romance: A Story in Songs," composed by John Adama, libretto by June Jordan, directed by Peter Sellers; Day Two: "Degga," a collaboration between composer/drummer Max Roach, author Toni Morrison, dancer Bill T. Jones. **Contact:** Lincoln Center for the Performing Arts, Inc., 70 Lincoln Center Plaza, New York, NY 10023-6583, 212-875-5050.

## JULY GOSPEL EXPLOSION, Brooklyn, NYC
Early Jul.
Black Gospel

**Help!** One time only? **Days:** 1. **Site:** indoor. First A. M. E. Zion Church, 54 MacDonough Street. **Admission:** paid. **Daily entry:** $10 to $24, **Discounts:** advance purchase discounts, **Acts:** national acts, local acts. **Sample day's lineup:** Richard Smallwood Singers, O'Landra Draper and Associates, Valerie Boyd, Eric McDaniel and Pentecostal Praise, David Bratton and Spirit of Praise. **Contact:** July Gospel Explosion, c/o First A. M. E. Zion Church, 54 MacDonough Street, Brooklyn, NY, 718-636-8500.

## GATEWAY TO THE NATIONS POWWOW, Brooklyn, NYC
Early Jul.
Native American

**Days:** 2. **Hours per day:** 11. **Site:** outdoor. Gateway National Recreation Area, Floyd Bennett Field, Flatbush Avenue. **Admission:** free. **Acts:** regional acts, local acts. **Sample day's lineup:** Arawack Mountain Singers, others. **Contact:** National Park Service, Gateway National Recreation Area, Floyd Bennett Field, Building 69, Brooklyn, NY 11234, 718-338-3799/832-4884.

### 111TH STREET BOYS OLD TIMERS DAY STICKBALL FESTIVAL, Manhattan, NYC
Early Jul.
Modern Latin

Since 1969. "Salsa, finger-licking cuchifritos and back-slapping camaraderie stretch from Fifth to Lenox Avenues." -- Soledad Santiago, New York Newsday. **Days:** 1. **Site:** outdoor. 111th Street. **Admission:** free. **Acts:** national acts, regional acts, local acts. **Sample day's lineup:** Tito Puente, Tito Rodriguez, Pete Conde, many others. **Contact:** 111th Street Boys Old Timers Day Stickball Festival, 245 East 149th Street, Bronx, NY 10451, 718-402-8811.

### STEINWAY STREET FUN IN THE SUN FESTIVAL, Queens, NYC
Early Jul.
Variety, General

See other dates and sites. **Days:** 1. **Hours per day:** 8. **Site:** outdoor. Steinway Street, 28th to 35th Streets, Astoria. **Admission:** free. **Secondary genre[s]:** MJAZ, MRCK, ARCK, TR&B, RGGE, **Acts:** local acts. **Sample day's lineup:** Zane Massey and The Foundation, Rapadoo, Joe Restivo, Son House, Dark Moon, Off Center. **Contact:** Clearview Festival Productions, 401 Lafayette Street, New York, NY 10003, 212-995-9412.

### GRAND NIGHTS FOR SINGING, Manhattan, NYC
Early Jul. to Middle Jul.
Cabaret

Since 1995. **Days:** 3. **Site:** indoor. Town Hall, 123 West 43rd Street. **Admission:** paid. **Daily entry:** $10 to $24, **Acts:** national acts, local acts. **Sample day's lineup:** Maureen McGovern, Julie Wilson, Barbara Carroll, Phillip Officer, Jon Marshall Sharp, David Staller, Celeste Holm, Margaret Whiting, others. **Contact:** Mabel Mercer Foundation, 230 East 49th Street, #4D, New York, NY 10017, 212-980-3026/3109.

### B. M. I. JAZZ COMPOSER'S WORKSHOP CONCERT, Manhattan, NYC
Middle Jul.
Modern Jazz

"18-piece orchestra featuring New York's top players will premiere a dozen new works." -- Advertisement. **Days:** 1. **Site:** indoor. Location varies (Mannes College of Music, Merkin Concert Hall, etc.). **Admission:** free. **Secondary genre[s]:** AJAZ, **Acts:** regional acts, local acts. **Sample day's lineup:** Manny Albam, Roger Kellaway, Jim McNeely, others. **Contact:** B. M. I. Jazz Composer's Workshop Concert, c/o Broadcast Music, Inc., 320 West 57th Street, New York, NY 10019, 212-586-2000.

### CENTERSTAGE AT THE WORLD TRADE CENTER, Manhattan, NYC
Middle Jul. Early Sep.
Variety, General

Lunchtime concerts. **Days:** 40. **Hours per day:** 3. **Site:** outdoor. Austin Tobin Plaza, World Trade Center, Vesey and Liberty Streets. **Admission:** free. **Secondary genre[s]:** MJAZ, TJAZ, CRCK, MC&W, OTHR **Acts:** national acts, regional acts. **Sample series lineup:** Day One: Rick Trevino; Day Two: Alex Bugnon; Day Three: The Mamas and The Papas. **Contact:** Centerstage at the World Trade Center, 1 World Trade Center, 35 West, New York, NY 10048, 212-432-0900.

## NEW YORK ALL-STAR KLEZMER EXTRAVAGANZA, Manhattan, NYC
Middle Jul.
Jewish

Since 1995. **Days:** 1. **Site:** outdoor. Damrosch Park Bandshell, Lincoln Center, Amsterdam Avenue at 62nd Street. **Admission:** free. **Acts:** national acts, regional acts, local acts. **Sample day's lineup:** Kapelye, Brave Old World, Klezmer Conservatory Band, The Klezmatics, Lipovsky/Mlote/Warschauer Trio. **Contact:** Lincoln Center Out-of-Doors, Lincoln Center for the Performing Arts, Inc., 140 West 65th Street, New York, NY 10023-6583, 212-875-5400/5108.

## LIFE BEAT BENEFIT: THE MUSIC INDUSTRY FIGHTS AIDS, Manhattan, NYC
Middle Jul.
Modern Rock and Pop

Since 1994. **Days:** 1. **Site:** indoor. Beacon Theater, 74th Street and Broadway. **Admission:** paid. **Secondary genre[s]:** ARCK, MR&B, MFOL, MLAT, **Acts:** national acts. **Sample day's lineup:** Gloria Estefan, Isaac Hayes, Chris Isaak, Dave Matthews Band, Sarah McLachlan, others. **Contact:** Life Beat, 810 7th Avenue, New York, NY 10014, 212-245-3426.

## GOSPEL NITE, Manhattan, NYC
Middle Jul.
Black Gospel

Events vary widely from year to year, so call ahead. **Days:** 1. **Site:** outdoor. South Street Seaport, Pier 17, Ambrose Stage. **Admission:** free. **Acts:** local acts. **Sample day's lineup:** Heavenly Tones, The Wearyland Singers, The Pentecostal Brass Gospel Band. **Contact:** South Street Seaport Museum, 207 Front Street, New York, NY 10038, 212-669-9400/SEA-PORT.

## 360 DEGREES BLACK: NEW YORK'S HIP HOP MUSIC SEMINAR, Manhattan, NYC
Middle Jul.
Rap

"Giving and gaining respect." -- Brochure. **Help!** Still ongoing? **Days:** 3. **Site:** indoor. Embassy Suites Hotel, 1568 Broadway and 47th Street **Admission:** paid. **Daily entry:** $50 and over. **Acts:** local acts. **Sample day's lineup:** Jigmastas, B. I. G. G., Sha-Ney, Total Pack, Sam-N-The Swing, Champ M. C., +3dB, Big Kap, others. **Contact:** 360 Degrees Black, Inc., 235 West 48th Street, Suite 29B, New York, NY 10036, 212-664-0360.

## SUMMERFUN!, Staten Island, NYC
Middle Jul.
Modern Folk

"The best in folk!" -- Advertisement. Also programs the Snug Harbor Jazz Festival, a weekly concert series in Feb. featuring local acts, plus a weekly summer concert series with local acts across various genres. **Days:** 1. **Site:** outdoor. Snug Harbor Cultural Center, 1000 Richmond Terrace. **Admission:** paid. **Daily entry:** $10 to $24, **Discounts:** advance purchase discounts, **Acts:** national acts. **Sample day's lineup:** Arlo Guthrie, Richie Havens, Vance Gilbert, others. **Contact:** Snug Harbor Cultural Center, 1000 Richmond Hill Terrace, Staten Island, NY 10301, 718-448-2500.

### MIDWOOD CONCERTS AT SEASIDE, Brooklyn, NYC
Middle Jul. to Late Aug.
Variety, General

Since 1979. **Days:** 7. **Site:** outdoor. Asser Levy Seaside Park, Ocean Parkway at Seaside Avenue, Brighton Beach. **Admission:** free. **Secondary genre[s]:** CRCK, MR&B, JWSH, MLAT, **Acts:** national acts, local acts. **Sample day's lineup:** Tito Puente and His Orchestra, Eddie Palmieri and His Orchestra, Tito Nieves. **Contact:** Midwood Concerts at Seaside, 2014 Church Avenue, Brooklyn, NY 11226, 718-284-4700/469-1912.

### BACA SUMMER CELEBRATION, Brooklyn, NYC
Middle Jul.
Variety, General

**Days:** 4. **Site:** outdoor. multiple locations. **Admission:** free. **Secondary genre[s]:** TJAZ, TR&B, MLAT, RGGE, **Acts:** regional acts, local acts. **Sample Lineup:** Willi Jones and Her Band, Ellsworth, George Gee Orchestra, Al Browne Band, Bobby Rodriguez and His Band, others. **Contact:** BACA/The Brooklyn Arts Council, 200 Eastern Parkway, Brooklyn, NY 11238, 718-783-4469/3077.

### MACINTOSH NEW YORK MUSIC FESTIVAL, Manhattan, NYC
Middle Jul. to Late Jul.
Alternative and College Rock

Since 1995. "This unprecedented festival will knit the best of today's new music with the latest interactive, on-line and multi-media technology." -- Advertisement. Internet displays connect/broadcast band showcases. **Help!** Replaces New Music Nights/New Music Seminar? **Days:** 6. **Site:** indoor. 15 locations. **Admission:** paid. **Daily entry:** $10 to $24, **Discounts:** multiple event or day passes, **Secondary genre[s]:** AJAZ, MRCK, HRCK, AC&W, **Acts:** national acts, regional acts, local acts. **Sample lineup:** 16 Deluxe, Alice Donut, Laurie Anderson, Bardo Pond, Ben Folds Five, Black Velvet Flag, Boredoms, Buffalo Tom, Cardinal Woosely, Casper Brotzmann, Cake Like, The Caulfields, Cibo Matto, Chris Cochran, Congo Norvell, Contortians, Cop Shoot Cop, Dirt Merchants, Dub Narcotic Sound, System, Francis Dunnery, Gutterball, Earth 18, Heather Eatman, Engine Kidd, Jaron Lanier, Rosie Flores, Green Apple Quickstep, Innocence Mission, Katel Keinig, LaBradford, Love Battery, Low, Gary Lucas' Gods and Monsters, Makeup, Moe, Moonboot Lover, Rebecca Moore, Poe, Railroad Jerk, Vernon Reid, The Residents, Run On, Todd Rundgren, Sardina, Screaming Hedless Torsos, Skeleton Key, Space Needle, Spanky, Suck Pretty, Supergrass, Thanks To Gravity, Tribe 8, Jennifer Trynin, Ultra Bride, Yoke, Yo La Tengo, many others. **Contact:** Macintosh New York Music Festival, 285 Broadway, Suite 630, New York, NY 10013, 212-343-9290.

### AFRICA MONDO FESTIVAL, Brooklyn, NYC
Middle Jul.
African

Since 1993. **Days:** 1. **Hours per day:** 10. **Site:** outdoor. Prospect Park bandshell, 9th Street and Prospect Park West. **Admission:** free. **Secondary genre[s]:** MLAT, RGGE, **Acts:** national acts, regional acts, local acts. **Sample day's lineup:** Diblo Dibala and Matchatcha, Roots Talibe, Mendes Brothers, Lakol, Epizo. **Contact:** Fund for the Borough of Brooklyn, 30 Flatbush Avenue, Brooklyn, NY 11217, 718-855-7882 x20.

### MARTIN LUTHER KING JR. CONCERT SERIES, Brooklyn, NYC
Middle Jul. to Late Aug.
African American

Since 1983. **Days:** 7. **Site:** outdoor. Asser Levy Seaside Park, Ocean Parkway at Seaside Avenue, Brighton Beach. **Admission:** free. **Secondary genre[s]:** CRCK, MR&B, TR&B, BGOS, JWSH, RGGE, **Acts:** national acts. **Sample day's lineup:** Ruth Brown, Koko Taylor, Denise LaSalle. **Contact:** Midwood Concerts at Seaside, 2014 Church Avenue, Brooklyn, NY 11226, 718-284-4700/469-1912.

JAZZ IN JULY, Manhattan, NYC
> Late Jul.
> Traditional Jazz and Ragtime

Since 1985. **Days:** 6. **Hours per day:** 3. **Site:** indoor. 92nd Street Y, 1395 Lexington Avenue. **Admission:** paid. **Daily entry:** $25 to $49, **Discounts:** multiple event or day passes, **Secondary genre[s]:** TR&B, **Acts:** national acts, regional acts, local acts. **Sample day's lineup:** Kenny Davern, Howard Alden, Dan Barrett, Tony DiNicola, Milt Hinton, Dick Hyman, Jon-Erik Kellso, Dan Levinson, Peter Ecklund, Marty Grosz, Bob Haggart, Arnie Kinsella, Ken Peplowski. **Audio merchandise:** "The Kingdom of Swing and The Republic of Oop Bop Sh'Bam" (Classics In Jazz Musicmasters); "Piano Players and Significant Others" (Jazz Heritage), plus other Dick Hyman recordings. **Contact:** Tisch Center for the Arts, 92nd Street YM-YWHA, 1395 Lexington Avenue, New York, NY 10128, 212-996-1100.

COLUMBIA INDEPENDENCE DAY CELEBRATION, Queens, NYC
> Late Jul.
> Modern Latin

**Help!** A sample lineup? **Days:** 1. **Site:** outdoor. Flushing Meadows-Corona Park. **Admission:** free. **Acts:** local acts. **Contact:** Columbia Independence Day, Flushing Meadows-Corona Park, Holmsted Center, Room 53, Flushing, NY 11386, 718-760-6565.

COLUMBIA TE CANTA, Manhattan, NYC
> Late Jul.
> Modern Latin

Since 1993. Formerly held Late May. See other sites and dates. **Days:** 1. **Site:** indoor. The Paramount, Madison Square Garden, 7th Avenue at 32nd Street. **Admission:** paid. **Daily entry:** $25 to $49, **Acts:** national acts, regional acts. **Sample day's lineup:** Grupo Niche, Orquestra Guayacan, Orquestra Los Titanes, Binomio De Oro, Lisandro Meza and Su Conjunto, Alfredo Guiterrez and Su Orquestra, Orquestra Canela, Tino Asprilla, Carlos Valderrama. **Contact:** RMM Productions, 568 Broadway, Suite 806, New York, NY 10012, 212-925-2828/4885.

PUERTO RICAN DAY PARADE, Bronx, NYC
> Late Jul.
> Modern Latin

**Help!** A sample lineup? **Days:** 1. **Site:** outdoor. Grand Concourse. **Admission:** free. **Acts:** local acts. **Contact:** Community Board 5, c/o Bronx Borough President's Office, 851 Grand Concourse, Bronx, NY 10451, 718-364-2030/590-3500.

NEW YORK CITY CLEARWATER FESTIVAL, Brooklyn, NYC
> Late Jul.
> Traditional Folk

Since 1994. **Days:** 2. **Hours per day:** 9. **Site:** outdoor. Gateway National Recreation Area, Floyd Bennett Field, Flatbush Avenue. **Admission:** free. **Secondary genre[s]:** MFOL, NATV, **Acts:** national acts, regional acts, local acts. **Sample lineup:** Tom Chapin, Lydia Adams-Davis, D. O. O. M., Lou Del Blanco, Janice Buckner, Anna Epstein Kravis, Rande Harris, Hudson River Sloop Singers, Jerry Kidd, Bob Killian, Jonathon Kruk, Eric Levine, New York City Labor Chorus, New York City Streetsingers, Sharon Perez-Abrell, Patricia Shih, Graeme Sibirsky Jazz, Stone Soup, Dave Street Talisman, Windwolf Howie Zow, others. **Contact:** National Park Service, Gateway National Recreation Area, Floyd Bennett Field, Building 69, Brooklyn, NY 11234, 718-338-3799 **or:** New York City Friends of Clearwater, 350 East 91st Street, #4, New York, NY 10128, 212-831-5027..

## AMERICAN CABARET THEATER FESTIVAL, Manhattan, NYC
Late Jul.
Cabaret

**Days:** 8. **Site:** indoor. Merkin Hall, 129 West 67th Street. **Admission:** paid. **Acts:** national acts, regional acts, local acts. **Sample day's lineup:** Steve Ross, Judy Carmichael, Chip Zien. **Contact:** American Cabaret Theater Festival, Merkin Hall, 129 West 67th Street, New York, NY, 212-362-8060.

## BLACK FAMILY DAY, Manhattan, NYC
Late Jul.
African American

See other dates. **Days:** 1. **Site:** indoor. 369th Regiment Armory, 142nd Street and 5th Avenue, Harlem. **Admission:** paid. **Daily entry:** under $10, $10 to $24, **Discounts: Secondary genre[s]:** RAP, **Acts:** national acts, local acts. **Sample day's lineup:** Chuck D and Public Enemy, Grand Puba, Showbiz and AG, Strictly Roots, Ron G, Kam, Freddy Foxxx, Da Youngstas, Cold Crush Brothers, others. **Contact:** Muhammad's Mosque No. 7, 2033 5th Avenue, New York, NY, 718-953-2200.

## BUDWEISER SUPERFEST, Manhattan, NYC
Late Jul.
Modern R&B

Since 1980. Leg of an annual 27-city tour. **Days:** 1. **Site:** indoor. The Paramount, Madison Square Garden, 7th Avenue at 32nd Street. **Admission:** paid. **Daily entry:** $25 to $49, **Secondary genre[s]:** CRCK, RAP, **Acts:** national acts. **Sample day's lineup:** Heavy D and The Boyz, Coolio, Warren G., R. Kelly, Aaliyah. **Contact:** Budweiser Superfest, c/o Madison Square Garden, 4 Pennsylvania Plaza, New York, NY, 212-465-MSG1.

## AFRICAN CARIBBEAN LATINO AMERICAN FESTIVAL, Brooklyn, NYC
Late Jul.
African American

**Days:** 2. **Hours per day:** 10. **Site:** outdoor. Gateway National Recreation Area, Floyd Bennett Field, Flatbush Avenue. **Admission:** free. **Secondary genre[s]:** MJAZ, RAP, ACAP, MLAT, RGGE, **Acts:** national acts, regional acts, local acts. **Sample day's lineup:** The Manhattans, Sparrow, Savage, Metro Steel Band, Jam X, La Fuerza Nueva, Dakota Blue, others. **Contact:** National Park Service, Gateway National Recreation Area, Floyd Bennett Field, Building 69, Brooklyn, NY 11234, 718-338-5799/832-4884.

## ROCKAWAY IRISH FESTIVAL, Queens, NYC
Late Jul.
Irish

Since 1982. **Days:** 2. **Hours per day:** 9. **Site:** outdoor. Beach 108th and 109th Streets and Rockaway Beach Boulevard, Rockaway Beach. **Admission:** free. **Restrictions:** 5, **Secondary genre[s]:** MRCK, ARCK, **Acts:** national acts, regional acts, local acts. **Sample day's lineup:** Joannie Madden Group, Susan McKeown and The Chanting House, Four To The Bar, Gerry Hughes and Walter Ensor, New York City Police Department Emerald Society Pipe Band, Danny Kane and The Rockin' Rebels, Walter Ensor and Eileen Ivers, others. **Contact:** Rockaway Irish Festival, 176 Beach 123rd Street, Rockaway Park, NY 11694, 718-520-5911/634-8796.

## SLAMMIN' JAMMIN' SPIKE'S JOINT ANNIVERSARY BLOCK PARTY, Brooklyn, NYC
Late Jul.
Rap

**Help!** One time only? **Days:** 1. **Hours per day:** 9. **Site:** outdoor. South Elliot Place, between DeKalb and Lafayette Avenues. **Acts:** national acts. **Sample day's lineup:** Flavor Flav, Heavy D, Trends of Culture, Big Daddy Kane, others. **Contact:** Slammin' Jammin' Spike's Joint Anniversary Block Party, Spike's Joint, 1 South Elliot Place, Brooklyn, NY 11217, 718-802-1000.

## GALA ALL-STAR IRISH CRUISE, Manhattan, NYC
Late Jul. to Early Aug.
Irish

"Dream Cruise Sailing." -- Advertisement. See other dates. **Days:** 7. **Site:** indoor. Regal Empress bound to The Bahamas and back. **Admission:** paid. **Daily entry:** $50 and over. **Discounts:** group sale discounts, **Acts:** regional acts, local acts. **Sample lineup:** Jerry Finlay and The Cara Band, Christy O'Connor, Glen Curtin, Guss Hayes and His Band, Frank O'Brien, others. **Contact:** Gertrude Byrne Promotions, P. O. Box 6, Leeds, NY 12451, 518-943-3736.

## CLASSICAL JAZZ AT LINCOLN CENTER, Manhattan, NYC
Early Aug.
Modern Jazz

Since 1987. **Days:** 6. **Site:** indoor. Alice Tully Hall, Lincoln Center, Broadway at 65th Street. **Admission:** paid. **Daily entry:** $10 to $24, $25 to $49, $50 and over. **Secondary genre[s]:** TJAZ, MLAT, **Acts:** national acts, regional acts. **Sample day's lineup:** Wynton Marsalis Septet, Lincoln Center Jazz Orchestra, Roy Hargrove Quintet, Gerry Mulligan, Art Farmer, Doc Cheatham, Dr. Michael White, Marcus Roberts, Benny Golson, others. **Contact:** Jazz at Lincoln Center, 70 Lincoln Center Plaza, New York, NY 10023-6583, 212-875-5299.

## THE SOURCE AWARDS, Manhattan, NYC
Early Aug.
Rap

Since 1994. See other dates. **Days:** 1. **Site:** indoor. The Paramount, Madison Square Garden, 7th Avenue at 32nd Street. **Admission:** paid. **Daily entry:** $25 to $49, **Secondary genre[s]:** MR&B, RGGE, **Acts:** national acts, regional acts. **Sample day's lineup:** Fab 5 Freddy, Crazy Legs and Rock Steady Crew, Luke Campbell, Onyx, Tupac Shakur, A Tribe Called Quest, Mary J. Blige, Wu-Tang Clan, Grand Puba, KRS-ONE, Treach, Doug E. Fresh, MC Eiht, others. **Contact:** The Source Awards, The Source Magazine, 594 Broadway, New York, NY, 212-274-0464/465-MSG1.

## LINCOLN CENTER OUT-OF-DOORS, Manhattan, NYC
Early Aug. to Late Aug.
Variety, General

Since 1965. **Days:** 21. **Site:** outdoor. Damrosch Park Bandshell, Lincoln Center, Broadway at 65th Street. **Admission:** free. **Secondary genre[s]:** MJAZ, TJAZ, ARCK, IRSH, JWSH, NATV, SCOT, MLAT, TLAT, AFRC, BRZL, RGGE, AVNT, OTHR **Acts:** national acts, regional acts. **Sample day's lineup:** Los Munequitos De Matanzas, Phantom, D'Ivan **Contact:** Lincoln Center Out-of-Doors, Lincoln Center for the Performing Arts, Inc., 140 West 65th Street, New York, NY 10023-6583, 212-875-5400/5108.

ROCK-N-ROLL EXTRAVAGANZA, Queens, NYC
>Early Aug.
>A Cappella and Doo Wop

See other dates. **Days:** 1. **Site:** indoor. Golden Center for the Performing Arts, Queens College, Kissena Boulevard and Long Island Expressway, Flushing. **Admission:** paid. **Daily entry:** $10 to $24, **Secondary genre[s]:** CRCK, **Acts:** national acts, regional acts, local acts. **Sample day's lineup:** The Duprees, Larry Chance and The Earls, The Harptones, Lenny Coco and The Chimes, The Dubs, Younger Dayz, Traditions, Elegants. **Contact:** John Vogele Productions, Golden Center for the Performing Arts, Kissena Boulevard, Flushing, NY, 718-793-8080.

CARNIVAL IN NEW YORK, Manhattan, NYC
>Early Aug.
>Reggae, Ska and Caribbean

Since 1985. **Days:** 2. **Hours per day:** 8. **Site:** outdoor. Battery Park City, West Street between Warren and Murray Streets. **Admission:** free. **Secondary genre[s]:** RAP, MLAT, TLAT, AFRC, BRZL, **Acts:** national acts, regional acts, local acts. **Sample day's lineup:** Boukman Eksperyans, Johnny Pacheco and Pete Rodriguez, Loketo, Doug E. Fresh, Nego Gato, Los Hermanos Colon, C. A. S. Y. M. Steel Orchestra. **Contact:** Franklin H. Williams Caribbean Cultural Center, 408 West 5th Street, New York, NY 10019, 212-307-7420.

I. C. C. SONGFEST, Staten Island, NYC
>Early Aug.
>Black Gospel

Also programs a periodic concert series with national acts, plus other activities. **Days:** 1. **Hours per day:** 5. **Site:** outdoor. Parking lot, International Christian Center, 1501 Richmond Avenue. **Secondary genre[s]:** RAP, **Acts:** local acts. **Sample day's lineup:** ICC Sanctuary Choir, ICC Youth Choir, King's Kids Choir, Highland Church Choir, Highland Men's Choir, First Central Baptist Church Choir, Randy Jones. **Contact:** International Christian Center, 1501 Richmond Avenue, Staten Island, NY 10314, 718-494-LIFE.

HARLEM WEEK/HARLEM DAY, Manhattan, NYC
>Early Aug. to Middle Aug.
>African American

Since 1975. **Days:** 14. **Hours per day:** 6. **Site:** outdoor. Harlem Week: multiple sites; Harlem Day: 125th and 135th Streets, Harlem **Admission:** free and paid. **Secondary genre[s]:** MJAZ, RAP, MR&B, TR&B, ACAP, CHRS, BGOS, MC&W, AFRC, RGGE, **Acts:** national acts, local acts. **Sample day's lineup:** Ralph Dorsey Band, Sequence, Take Cover, Blues Revolution, J. W. Lance, Transit, Ras Abudah, Jaunty, Roots Alive, LaTondra Wilson, Higher Calling, The Lue Bunch, Sweet Peach, Tammy Plate, Invest, Perfect As Is, Jiggy, J. H. Starr, Denard, Ruff Skot, Dah Phyazz, Portia, Lord Give Us A Shepherd, Rude Girl, Ron East and Theresa, Anaje, All City Mass Choir, Sandra Evans, Serenity, K. C. Rogers and The New Hope Ensemble, Terry Silas, Mark Gibbs, Tim Johnson, Higher Calling, Dressed In Black, Leon Thomas, Abiding Love Ministries, 1 In A Million, Eternal Light, Karen Anderson, Kenny Tillman, John Whitehead, N Phase, TCF Crew, Caron Wheeler, NBT Doo Wop Love, Melloo-Tee, Da Youngsters, Black Madness, KISS Wake-Up Band, Doug E. Fresh, The Diplomats, Johnny and Joe, Freddie Scott, Arlene Scott and The Chantells, Chuck Jackson, Cuba Gooding, others. **Contact:** LMR Productions, 1 West 125th Street, Suite 206, New York, NY 10027, 212-427-7200/3315.

## RIVERSIDE PARK ARTS FESTIVAL, Manhattan, NYC
Early Aug. to Late Aug.
Modern Jazz

Since 1985. **Days:** 4. **Site:** outdoor. Rotunda, Riverside Park, West 79th Street at Hudson River Boat Basin. **Admission:** free. **Secondary genre[s]:** TR&B, MLAT, BRZL, **Acts:** national acts, regional acts, local acts. **Sample day's lineup:** Steve Turre, Pe-De-Boi Samba Group, The Three Masters. **Audio merchandise:** 38 productions for Candid Records, including several live festival recordings. **Contact:** Jazz Forum Arts, P. O. Box 1917 Cathedral Station, New York, NY 10025, 212914-408-0249 **or:** Jazz Forum Arts, c/o Riverside Park Administrator, 16 West 61st Street, New York, NY 10023, 212-674-2005. .

## WWRL FAMILY DAY AND PICNIC, Queens, NYC
Early Aug. to Middle Aug.
Black Gospel

Since 1990. **Days:** 5. **Hours per day:** 8. **Site:** outdoor. Roy Wilkins Park, 119th Avenue and Merrick Boulevard, Jamaica. **Admission:** free. **Secondary genre[s]:** RAP, **Acts:** national acts, regional acts, local acts. **Sample day's lineup:** WWRL Community Chorale, The Jenkins Brothers, Alvin Green and The Unlimited Sounds, Last Appeal, Bishop Billy Robinson and The Garden of Prayer Cathedral Choir, Kenton Rodgers, Rap Ministries Unlimited, Timiney Figueroa, Michelle White and The Westchester Mass Choir, Chris Jasper, Bishop Jeff Banks and Revival Temple Community Mass Choir, Rev. Milton Biggham, Bonnie Gatlin, Johnny Peoples and The Gospel Crowns, Jeffrey White, Bronx Mass Choir, Wonder Boy, Valerie Boyd and New Greater Bethel Choir, others. **Contact:** WWRL-AM 1600, 41-30 58th Street, Woodside, NY 11377, 718-335-1600/276-4630.

## NEW YORK REGGAE FESTIVAL, Brooklyn, NYC
Middle Aug.
Reggae, Ska and Caribbean

Since 1991. **Days:** 2. **Hours per day:** 8. **Site:** outdoor. Steeplechase Park, Ocean Parkway, Coney Island. **Admission:** paid. **Daily entry:** $10 to $24, $25 to $49, **Discounts:** advance purchase discounts, **Restrictions:** 4, 5, 12, **Acts:** national acts, regional acts, local acts. **Sample day's lineup:** Freddie McGregor, Beres Hammond, Third World, Junior Tucker, Tony Rebel, Worl-A-Girl, Frankie Paul, Tiger, Venus, Mr. Easy, Captain Remo, Chino Man, 809 Band, Calabash, Skool, Sagitaurus Band, Roots Talibes. **Contact:** Jamyns Promotions, 32-20 Church Avenue, Brooklyn, NY 11226, 718-941-4629/372-0275.

## 36TH AVENUE SUMMER FOOD FAIR, Queens, NYC
Middle Aug.
Variety, General

See other dates and sites. **Days:** 1. **Hours per day:** 8. **Site:** outdoor. 36th Avenue, 29th to 35th Streets, Astoria. **Admission:** free. **Secondary genre[s]:** MJAZ, MRCK, ARCK, TR&B, RGGE, **Acts:** local acts. **Sample day's lineup:** Zane Massey and The Foundation, Rapadoo, Joe Restivo, Son House, Dark Moon, Off Center. **Contact:** Clearview Festival Productions, 401 Lafayette Street, New York, NY 10003, 212-995-9412.

## NEW YORK COUNTRY MUSIC FESTIVAL, Queens, NYC
Middle Aug.
Modern Country

Since 1994. Part of Prime Time Concerts series. **Help!** One time only? **Days:** 1. **Site:** outdoor. Forest Park, Seuffert Bandshell, Woodhaven. **Admission:** free. **Acts:** local acts. **Sample day's lineup:** Gun Smoke, Stonewall, Southbound. **Contact:** New York Country Music Festival, Queens Council on the Arts, 161-04 Jamaica Avenue, Jamaica, NY 11432, 718-291-1100/647-3377.

NUYORICAN POETS CAFE BLOCK PARTY, Manhattan, NYC
Middle Aug.
Modern Latin

Since 1990. "Music, poetry and theater are all live and kickin'..." -- New York Daily News. **Days:** 1. **Hours per day:** 8. **Site:** outdoor. East 3rd Street, Avenues B to C. **Admission:** free. **Secondary genre[s]:** TLAT, **Acts:** local acts. **Sample day's lineup:** Johnny Almendra, Roland Briseno Y Los Jovenes Del Barrio, others. **Contact:** Nuyorican Poets Cafe, 236 East 3rd Street, New York, NY 10009, 212-505-8183.


PARK SLOPE FESTIVAL, Brooklyn, NYC
Middle Aug.
Variety, General

See other dates and sites. **Days:** 1. **Hours per day:** 8. **Site:** outdoor. 7th Avenue, 1st to 9th Streets, Park Slope. **Admission:** free. **Secondary genre[s]:** MJAZ, MRCK, ARCK, TR&B, RGGE, **Acts:** local acts. **Sample day's lineup:** Zane Massey and The Foundation, Rapadoo, Joe Restivo, Son House, Dark Moon, Off Center. **Contact:** Clearview Festival Productions, 401 Lafayette Street, New York, NY 10003, 212-995-9412.


MIDSUMMER'S NIGHT CABARET, Manhattan, NYC
Middle Aug.
Cabaret

Benefits Hearts and Voices, Inc. **Days:** 1. **Site:** indoor. Pegasus, 119 East 60th Street. **Admission:** paid. **Daily entry:** $10 to $24, **Acts:** national acts, regional acts, local acts. **Sample day's lineup:** Julie Wilson, Ronnie Whyte, Rohn Seykell, Mark-Alan, Mercedes Hall, Darius De Haas, Alton F. White, Tom Postillio, Tommy Femia, Jamie De Roy, Aaron Lee Battle. **Contact:** Hearts and Voices, 150 West 80th Street, #7D, New York, NY 10024, 212-799-4276/888-4702.


CARIBBEAN-AMERICAN COMMUNITY TRADE AND CULTURAL EXPO, Brooklyn, NYC
Middle Aug. to Late Aug.
Reggae, Ska and Caribbean

Since 1993. **Help!** One time only? **Days:** 6. **Site:** indoor. CUNY/Medgar Evers College, 1650 Bedford Avenue. **Acts:** national acts, regional acts, local acts. **Sample day's lineup:** Toorsman, Singing Francine, Preacher, others. **Contact:** Caribbean-American Community Trade and Cultural Expo, c/o CUNY/Medgar Evers College, 1650 Bedford Avenue, Brooklyn, NY, 718-834-4544.


PANASONIC VILLAGE JAZZ FESTIVAL, Manhattan, NYC
Middle Aug. to Late Aug.
Modern Jazz

Since 1994. "7 days in jazz heaven." -- Advertisement. Replacing former Hennessey Village Jazz Festival. **Days:** 10. **Hours per day:** 6. **Site:** outdoor and indoor. free kick-off concert in Washington Square Park; plus multiple club locations throughout Greenwich Village. **Admission:** free and paid. **Acts:** national acts, regional acts, local acts. **Sample day's lineup:** Stanley Turrentine, Eddie Harris, Cedar Walton, David Williams, Billy Higgins, David Sanchez, Nicholas Payton, Abraham Burton, Renee Rosnes, Peter Washington, Greg Hutchinson, others. **Contact:** International Music Factory, Inc., 55 Christopher Street, New York, NY 10014, 212-691-0045.

## 98.7 KISS-FM GOSPEL CELEBRATION, Manhattan, NYC
> Late Aug.
> Black Gospel

See other dates. **Help!** One time only? **Days:** 1. **Site:** indoor. The Paramount, Madison Square Garden, 7th Avenue at 32nd Street. **Admission:** paid. **Daily entry:** $10 to $24, $25 to $49, **Acts:** national acts, local acts. **Sample day's lineup:** John P. Kee and The New Life Community Choir, Donnie McClurkin and The New York Restoration Choir, Shun Pace and The Pace Sisters, 98.7 KISS-FM's Inspirations Choir. **Contact:** WRKS-FM, 1440 Broadway, New York, NY, 212-642-4300/465-MSG1.

## CITY GARDENERS' HARVEST FAIR/GATEWAY MUSIC FESTIVAL/NEW YORK CITY BLUEGRASS BAND AND BANJO FESTIVAL, Brooklyn, NYC
> Late Aug.
> Variety, Folk and International

Since 1977. Combined festivals. City Gardeners' Harvest Fair (both days); Gateway Music Festival (Saturday); New York City Bluegrass Band and Banjo Festival (since 1973, Sunday). **Help!** Still ongoing? **Days:** 2. **Hours per day:** 7. **Site:** outdoor. Gateway National Recreation Area, Floyd Bennett Field, Flatbush Avenue. **Admission:** free. **Secondary genre[s]:** BGOS, BLGS, MLAT, **Acts:** regional acts, local acts. **Sample day's lineup:** Los Pleneros De La 21, Terry Waldo and The Gotham City Band, Special Touch. **Contact:** National Park Service, Gateway National Recreation Area, Floyd Bennett Field, Building 69, Brooklyn, NY 11234, 718-338-3799 **or:** New York City Bluegrass Band and Banjo Festival, 417 East 89th Street, New York, NY 10128, 212-427-3221.

## MIDNIGHT RAVERS ANNIVERSARY PARTY, Manhattan, NYC
> Late Aug.
> African American

See other dates. **Help!** One time only? **Days:** 1. **Site:** indoor. Sounds of Brazil, 204 Varick Street. **Admission:** paid. **Daily entry:** $10 to $24, **Discounts:** other discounts **Secondary genre[s]:** RAP, AFRC, RGGE, **Acts:** regional acts, local acts. **Sample day's lineup:** Oku Onuru, Sista Bunny Brisset, Skadanks, BBC Crew, others. **Contact:** Midnight Ravers Anniversary Party, Pacifica-WBAI-FM, 505 8th Avenue, New York, NY 10018, 212-279-0707/243-4940.

## ROOTS OF AMERICAN MUSIC FESTIVAL, Manhattan, NYC
> Late Aug.
> Variety, Folk and International

Since 1985. **Days:** 2. **Hours per day:** 6. **Site:** outdoor. Damrosch Park Bandshell, Lincoln Center, Broadway at 65th Street. **Admission:** free. **Secondary genre[s]:** TR&B, BGOS, MC&W, BLGS, IRSH, SCOT, **Acts:** national acts, regional act . **Sample day's lineup:** Kris Kristofferson, Magic Slim and The Teardrops, The New Coon Creek Girls, Charlie Storey, Paul and Win Grace. **Contact:** Roots of American Music Festival, Lincoln Center for the Performing Arts, Inc., 140 West 65th Street, New York, NY 10023-6583, 212-875-5400/5108.

## BLACK FAMILY WEEKEND, Manhattan, NYC
> Late Aug.
> African American

See other dates. **Days:** 1. **Site:** indoor. 369th Regiment Armory, 142nd Street and 5th Avenue, Harlem. **Admission:** paid. **Daily entry:** under $10, $10 to $24, **Discounts: Secondary genre[s]:** RAP, **Acts:** national acts, local acts. **Sample day's lineup:** Chuck D and Public Enemy, Grand Puba, Showbiz and AG, Strictly Roots, Ron G, Kam, Freddy Foxxx, Da Youngstas, Cold Crush Brothers, others. **Contact:** Muhammad's Mosque No. 7, 2033 5th Avenue, New York, NY, 718-953-2200.

GREENWICH AVENUE SUMMER FESTIVAL, Manhattan, NYC
  Late Aug.
  Variety, General

Since 1992. See other dates and sites. **Days:** 1. **Hours per day:** 8. **Site:** outdoor. Greenwich Avenue, 7th to 8th Avenues. **Admission:** free. **Secondary genre[s]:** MJAZ, MRCK, ARCK, TR&B, RGGE, **Acts:** local acts. **Sample day's lineup:** Zane Massey and The Foundation, Rapadoo, Joe Restivo, Son House, Dark Moon, Off Center. **Contact:** Clearview Festival Productions, 401 Lafayette Street, New York, NY 10003, 212-995-9412.

UPRISE AND SHINE YOUTH CONCERT, Brooklyn, NYC
  Late Aug.
  Rap

**Days:** 1. **Hours per day:** 2. **Site:** indoor. Restoration Ice Skating Rink, 1368 Fulton Street between Brooklyn and New York Avenues. **Admission:** free. **Daily entry:** $10 to $24, **Discounts:** advance purchase discounts, **Secondary genre[s]:** MLAT, AFRC, RGGE, **Acts:** local acts. **Sample day's lineup:** Little Vicious, Off Da Head Hybrids, GQ and The Funky Republic, El Shabazz D'Jembe Orchestra, C. A. S. Y. M. Steel Orchestra, others. **Contact:** Franklin H. Williams Caribbean Cultural Center, 408 West 5th Street, New York, NY 10019, 212-307-7420.

CHARLIE PARKER JAZZ FESTIVAL, Manhattan, NYC
  Late Aug.
  Modern Jazz

Since 1993. **Days:** 1. **Hours per day:** 4. **Site:** outdoor. Tompkins Square Park, Avenue A between East 7th and 10th Streets. **Admission:** free. **Acts:** national acts. **Sample day's lineup:** The Heath Brothers with Milt Jackson, The Sheila Jordan Quartet, Lawrence "Butch" Morris with Arthur Blythe, others. **Contact:** Charlie Parker Jazz Festival Committee, P. O. Box 2105, New York, NY 10009, 212-477-0374/1395.

FIERCE PUSSY FEST, Manhattan, NYC
  Late Aug.
  Gay and Lesbian

Since 1992. "Snakes, drums...sideshow freaks...fire eaters, fire breathers...plot to take over the world, packs of crazed women...installations, spells, stilts, mud." -- Flyer. **Help!** Still ongoing? **Days:** 1. **Site:** outdoor. Thompkins Square Park, Avenue A between East 7th and 10th Streets. **Admission:** free. **Secondary genre[s]:** ARCK, HRCK, **Acts:** local acts. **Sample day's lineup:** Thrust, Summer's Eve, Shelly Mars, Bina Sharif, Cenen, Valerie Jimenez, Anna Tucker, Iternity, Carla, others. **Contact:** Riot Grrl N. Y. C., P. O. Box 1320 Stuyvesant Station, New York, NY 10009, 212-875-7039 **or:** Fierce Pussy Fest, 271 East 10th Street, #666, New York, NY 10009, 212-330-8204.

SALSA FEST, Brooklyn, NYC
  Late Aug.
  Modern Latin

See other dates. **Days:** 1. **Hours per day:** 7. **Site:** outdoor. Great Lawn at Starret City, 1540 Van Siclen Avenue. **Admission:** free. **Acts:** national acts, local acts. **Sample day's lineup:** Ray Barretto and The New World Sprit Jazz Ensemble, The Brooklyn Philharmonic Orchestra, Latin Legends with Larry Harlow, Orquestra La-Reincarnacion. **Contact:** Salsa Fest, Starrett City at Spring Creek, 1540 Van Siclen Avenue, Brooklyn, NY, 718-642-2725.

WE CARE ABOUT NEW YORK BLOCK PARTY, Manhattan, NYC
Late Aug.
Variety, General

Since 1993. "World's largest block party." -- Advertisement. **Days:** 1. **Hours per day:** 8. **Site:** outdoor. Madison Avenue, 23rd to 51st Streets. **Admission:** free. **Secondary genre[s]:** MJAZ, MRCK, CRCK, RAP, MR&B, BGOS, MC&W, MLAT, RGGE, **Acts:** national acts, regional acts, local acts. **Sample day's lineup:** Panama Francis and His Savoy Sultans, Patti Austin, Bobbi Humphrey, The Bario Boyz, 96 others. **Contact:** We Care About New York, Inc., 1 Madison Avenue, New York, NY 10010, 212-686-1001.

HEINEKEN JAZZ AND BLUES FESTIVAL, Manhattan, NYC
Late Aug.
Variety, Jazz and Blues

Since 1995. **Days:** 2. **Site:** indoor. The Paramount, Madison Square Garden, 7th Avenue at 32nd Street. **Admission:** paid. **Daily entry:** $25 to $49, **Secondary genre[s]:** MJAZ, TR&B, MLAT, **Acts:** national acts, . **Sample day's lineup:** B. B. King, Jimmie Vaughan, Etta James, Magic Dick, Jay Geils, Elvin Bishop. **Contact:** Heineken Jazz and Blues Festival, c/o Madison Square Garden, 4 Pennsylvania Plaza, New York, NY, 212-465-MSG1.

NEW YORK SALSA FESTIVAL, Manhattan, NYC
Early Sep.
Modern Latin

Since 1976. See other sites and dates. **Days:** 2. **Site:** indoor. Madison Square Garden. **Admission:** paid. **Daily entry:** $25 to $49, **Acts:** national acts, regional acts, local acts. **Sample day's lineup:** Oscar D'Leon, Joe Arroyo, Los Hermanos Rosario, Tito Nieves, Marc Anthony, Checo Acosta, Papo and Quique Lucca and La Sonora Poncena, Yolanda Rivera and Luigi Texidor, others. **Audio merchandise:** "16th New York Salsa Festival: Live from Madison Square Garden" (RMM/SONY). **Contact:** RMM Productions, 568 Broadway, Suite 806, New York, NY 10012, 212-925-2828/4885.

WEST INDIAN-AMERICAN DAY CARNIVAL AND PARADE, Brooklyn, NYC
Early Sep.
Reggae, Ska and Caribbean

Since 1968. **Days:** 5. **Site:** outdoor. Labor Day parade: Eastern Parkway from Utica Avenue to Grand Army Plaza; weekend concerts: Brooklyn Museum grounds. **Admission:** free and paid. **Acts:** national acts, regional acts, local acts. **Sample day's lineup:** "Diamanche Gras Show": Super Blue, Sparrow, Crazy, Swallow, Chalkdust, Ras Iley, several others; "Reggae Splash": Shabba Ranks, Maxi Priest, United Sisters, Mad Cobra, Richie Stephens, Trevor Sparks, Rev. Badoo, K. C. Jockey, Sister Charmaine, Daddy Screw, Shelly Thunder, Sluggy Ranks, Worl-A-Girl, Roman Stewart, Terror Fabulous, Terry Ganzy, Bounty Killer, Willow Wilson, Vinetta, Bigger Haitian, A-Team Band. **Contact:** West Indian-American Day Carnival Association, Inc., 1028 St. John's Place, Brooklyn, NY 11213, 718-774-8807/773-4052.

BRAZILIAN NATIONAL INDEPENDENCE DAY STREET FESTIVAL, Manhattan, NYC
Early Sep.
Brazilian and South American

Since 1985. **Days:** 1. **Hours per day:** 10. **Site:** outdoor. 46th Street, between Madison Avenue and 6th Avenue. **Admission:** free. **Acts:** national acts, local acts. **Sample day's lineup:** Elba Ramalho, others continuously on two stages **Contact:** Brazilian-American Cultural Center, 15 West 36th Street, New York, NY 10036, 212-382-1630.

WEST SIDE ARTS, CRAFTS, ANTIQUES FESTIVAL, Manhattan, NYC
Early Sep.
Modern Jazz

Since 1986. See other sites and dates. **Days:** 1. **Hours per day:** 7. **Site:** outdoor. Broadway, 66th to 72nd Streets. **Admission:** free. **Secondary genre[s]:** MFOL, **Acts:** national acts, local acts. **Sample day's lineup:** Oscar Brand, Judy Barnett, Tracy McDonough, Odetta, others. **Contact:** West Side Arts, Crafts, Antiques Festival, 1501 Broadway, Suite 1808, New York, NY 10036, 212-764-6330.

WEST SIDE FALL FESTIVAL, Manhattan, NYC
Early Sep.
Modern Jazz

See other sites and dates. **Days:** 1. **Hours per day:** 7. **Site:** outdoor. West End Avenue, 86th to 96th Streets. **Admission:** free. **Secondary genre[s]:** MFOL, **Acts:** national acts, local acts. **Sample day's lineup:** Oscar Brand, Judy Barnett, Tracy McDonough, Odetta, others. **Contact:** West Side Fall Festival, 1501 Broadway, Suite 1808, New York, NY 10036, 212-764-6330.

WIGSTOCK, Manhattan, NYC
Early Sep.
Gay and Lesbian

Since 1985. **Days:** 1. **Hours per day:** 8. **Site:** outdoor. Christopher Street Pier. **Admission:** free. **Secondary genre[s]:** MRCK, CBRT, **Acts:** national acts, regional acts, local acts. **Sample day's lineup:** Deee-Lite, Ru Paul, Lypsinka, Ultra Nate, Lahoma Van Zandt, Lurleen Wallace, Cookie Watkins, Michael West, Matthew Kasten's Bar Boy Beauties, Miss Guy and JoJo Americo, Miss Satellite Dish, Deaundra Peek, Princess Diandra, Sister Dimension, Sweetie, Tabboo, Larry Tee, Ffloyd, Mona Foot, French Twist, Freida Glamamore, Joey Heatherock, Dean and The Weenies, John Kelly, Joey Arias, Billy Beyond, The Channel 69 Grils, Dorian Corey, Flotilla DeBarge, Ebony Jet, Endive, Lady Bunny, others. **Contact:** Wigstock, c/o Greenwich Village Press, 319 8th Street, Brooklyn, NY 11215, 212-243-3143.

BLUEGRASS BASH, Manhattan, NYC
Early Sep.
Bluegrass

Since 1994. Replaced Seaport Folk Festival. Events vary widely from year to year, so call ahead. **Days:** 1. **Site:** outdoor. South Street Seaport, Pier 17, Ambrose Stage. **Admission:** free. **Acts:** national acts. **Sample day's lineup:** John Hartford, Nashville Bluegrass Band, Kukuruza. **Contact:** South Street Seaport Museum, 207 Front Street, New York, NY 10038, 212-669-9400/SEA-PORT.

## CMJ Music Marathon and Musicfest, Manhattan, NYC
Early Sep.
Alternative and College Rock

Since 1981. **Days:** 4. **Hours per day:** 18. **Site:** indoor. seminars: Lincoln Center; showcases: over 30 venues. **Admission:** paid. **Daily entry:** under $10, $10 to $24, $50 and over. **Discounts:** multiple event or day passes, advance purchase discounts, **Secondary genre[s]:** AJAZ, HRCK, RAP, TR&B, AC&W, MFOL, RGGE, **Acts:** national acts, regional acts, local acts. **Sample day's lineup:** Mazzy Star, Mighty Mighty Bosstones, Shootyz Groove, For Love Not Lisa, Spongehead, Where I Wake, Warm, Breakfast Music, Acid Test, Engines Of Aggression, Twisted Roots, 40 Years, Smile Orange, Last Crack, Thorn, Shove, Holly Cole Trio, Shams, Mercy Rule, Wild Carnation, Ms. Lum, Scarce, Green Magnet School, Milf, Heather Eatman, Jesse Maontague, Toshi Reagon, Lisa Loeb and 9 Stories, Christine Kelly, Julee Cruise, Lisa Germano, David Gray, Kate Jacobs, Chris Kowanko, Patty Larkin, Jasmine, Bob Sikoryak, James Adlesic with Niles Ford, Roger Manning, Huge Voodoo, Silver and the American People, Jean Smith, Boss Ton, Mike Johnson Band, Bivouac, Verlaines, The Dentists, Marizane, Thirteen, Pillbox, D Generation, Dandelion, Wives, Mercy River, David Baker, Power Of Dreams, Black Water Junction, Cubic Feet, Q-South, Redeye, S. A. M., Wighat, Therapy?, Tad, St. Johnny, Codeine, Magnapop, Polyphemus, Roller Skate Skinny, Radical Spangle, Hair and Skin Trading Co., Sun Dial, Gumme The Gun, Play Trains, Gefkens, Scott E. Moore, Oversouls, Gyration, Shepherds Of Hot Pavement, Ropers, Lorelei, Jane Pow, For Against, Chocolate USA, Screaming Headless Torsos, Faith, Sophia's Toy, Kelvynator, MeShell Ndegeocello, Red Footed Genius, Jacob's Mouse, Alice Donut, Time Is Now, Wildlife, Freedomland, Voice In Time, Altimeter, Bridget, Barnyard Slut, Envelope, Pony, Tara Key, Falstaff, World Famous Blue Jays, Blood Oranges, Donkey, Scooby Groove, Hungry Crocodiles, Authority, Uptighty, Skinky Dinx, St. Booty, Justice System, Schooly D, Sweet Lizard Illtet, Caterpillar, Fire In The Kitchen, Sleepyhead, Swirl, Paul K and The Weathermen, Karl Hendricks Trio, Buzzkill, Craw, Geezer Lake, Mama Tick, Slowworm, Heretix, Scratch, Blue Meanies, Skankin' Pickle, Royal Crescent Mob, NY Citizens, Boy O Boy, others. **Contact:** College Media, Inc., 11 Middle Neck Road, Suite 400, Great Neck, NY 11021-2301, 516-466-6000.

## MTV Music Awards, Manhattan, NYC
Early Sep.
Modern Rock and Pop

Since 1984. **Days:** 1. **Site:** indoor. Radio City Music Hall. **Admission:** paid. **Daily entry:** $50 and over. **Secondary genre[s]:** ARCK, RAP, MR&B, **Acts:** national acts. **Sample day's lineup:** Bruce Springsteen, The Rolling Stones, Snoop Doggy Dog, Aerosmith, Beastie Boys, Boyz II Men, Green Day, Salt-N-Pepa, Smashing Pumpkins, Stone Temple Pilots, Tom Petty and The Heartbreakers, others. **Audio merchandise:** "Yo! MTV Raps"; "MTV Uptown Unplugged"; "Club MTV Party to Go"; "Best of MTV 120 Minutes" (various labels).. **Contact:** MTV, 1515 Broadway, New York, NY 10036, 212-258-8000.

## Great Irish Fair, Brooklyn, NYC
Early Sep. to Middle Sep.
Irish

Since 1981. **Days:** 3. **Hours per day:** 8. **Site:** outdoor. Steeplechase Park, Ocean Parkway, Coney Island. **Admission:** paid. **Daily entry:** under $10, **Acts:** national acts, regional acts, local acts. **Sample day's lineup:** The Wolfe Tones, Peter McQ and Tony Cooper, Erin's Pride, Pat Roper, Danny Kaye, Four to the Bar, Tommy Doyle Band, Robbie Doherty, Aine, Silver Lining, Cherish The Ladies, Tony B, Richie O'Shea, others. **Contact:** Great Irish Fair, 2750 Gerritsen Avenue, Brooklyn, NY 11220, 718-891-6622/630-3822.

### BROOKLYN'S SUMMER GOSPELFEST!, Brooklyn, NYC
  Early Sep.
  Black Gospel

**Help!** One time only? **Days:** 1. **Hours per day:** 7. **Site:** outdoor. Restoration Plaza, Corner of Fulton and Marcy Avenue. **Admission:** free. **Acts:** regional acts, local acts. **Sample day's lineup:** Brooklyn Peace Chorus, Brownsville Mass Choir, Celestial Community Choir, Jeffrey Conyers and The Crusade Choir, Danny Eason and The Brooklyn Youth Choir, Eternity, Lady Peachena, New York's Youth Sunshine Choir, McDonald's Gospelfest winners, 99.7 KISS-FM's Inspirational Choir, others. **Contact:** Fund for the Borough of Brooklyn, 30 Flatbush Avenue, Brooklyn, NY 11217, 718-855-7882 x20.

### CABARET FOR A CAUSE, Manhattan, NYC
  Middle Sep. to Late Sep.
  Cabaret

Since 1994. Benefits Broadway Cares/Equity Fights AIDS. See other dates and sites. **Help!** One time only? **Days:** 3. **Site:** indoor. Eighty Eight's, 228 West 10th Street. **Admission:** paid. **Daily entry:** $10 to $24, **Acts:** regional acts, local acts. **Sample day's lineup:** Angela LaGreca, Baby Jane Dexter, Michael Marotta, Black Tie, Julie Halston, Lizz Manners. **Contact:** Broadway Cares/Equity Fights AIDS, 165 West 46th Street, Suite 1300, New York, NY 10036, 212-840-0770/265-3495 x309.

### ROCKAWAY MUSIC AND ARTS COUNCIL FALL FESTIVAL, Brooklyn, NYC
  Middle Sep.
  Variety, General

Since 1984. **Days:** 1. **Hours per day:** 9. **Site:** outdoor. Gateway National Recreation Area, Floyd Bennett Field, Flatbush Avenue. **Admission:** free. **Secondary genre[s]:** TJAZ, ACAP, BGOS, AC&W, TFOL, IRSH, GYLS, **Acts:** regional acts, local acts. **Sample day's lineup:** Twanglers, Gerry Hughes and Walter Ensor, Jump Street, Hudson River Sloop Singers, St. Camilus Marching Band. **Contact:** National Park Service, Gateway National Recreation Area, Floyd Bennett Field, Building 69, Brooklyn, NY 11234, 718-338-3799 **or:** Rockaway Music and Arts Council, Inc., 133-6 Rockaway Beach Boulevard, Belle Harbor, NY 11694, 718-474-8087. .

### WPLJ-FM'S 70'S DANCE PARTY, Manhattan, NYC
  Middle Sep.
  Classic Rock and Oldies

See other dates. **Days:** 2. **Site:** indoor. The Paramount, Madison Square Garden, 7th Avenue at 32nd Street. **Admission:** paid. **Daily entry:** $25 to $49, **Acts:** national acts, . **Sample day's lineup:** K. C. and The Sunshine Band, Gloria Gaynor, The Hues Corporation, Thelma Houston, Carol Douglas, Jean Knight, Musique, The Ritchie Family. **Contact:** WPLJ-FM's 70's Dance Party, WPLJ-FM, 2 Pennsylvania Plaza, New York, NY, 212-465-MSG1.

### AFRICAN-AMERICAN DAY PARADE, Manhattan, NYC
  Middle Sep.
  African American

Since 1970. "Largest Black Parade in America." -- Flyer. **Days:** 1. **Site:** outdoor. Adam Clayton Powell Boulevard, 111th to 142nd Street. **Admission:** free. **Secondary genre[s]:** GYLS, **Acts:** regional acts, local acts. **Sample day's lineup:** Morgan State University Band, Jackie Robinson Marching Band, Baltimore Rockers Band, Baltimore Christian Wariors, Baltimore Community Marching Bands, Nation Marching Band, Westchester Invaders, East Logan Marching Band, Hillside Dynamics, Coalition of New Jersey bands, 369th Veterans Band. **Contact:** African-American Day Parade, Inc., 1 West 125th Street, Suite 208, New York, NY 10027, 212-348-3080 **or:** African-American Day Parade, Inc., P. O. Box 501, New York, NY 10030 .

NEW YORK BEER FEST, Brooklyn, NYC
>Middle Sep.
>Variety, General

Since 1993. **Days:** 1. **Hours per day:** 7. **Site:** outdoor. Brooklyn waterfront under the Brooklyn Bridge, between River Cafe and Empire-Fulton Ferry State Park. **Admission:** paid. **Daily entry:** $10 to $24, $25 to $49, **Discounts:** advance purchase discounts, **Acts:** regional acts, local acts. **Sample day's lineup:** 5 Chinese Brothers, others. **Contact:** Fund for the Borough of Brooklyn, 30 Flatbush Avenue, Brooklyn, NY 11217, 718-855-7882 x20.


COLUMBUS AVENUE FESTIVAL, Manhattan, NYC
>Middle Sep.
>Variety, General

Since 1977. Benefits various community programs. See other dates. **Days:** 1. **Hours per day:** 7. **Site:** outdoor. Columbus Avenue, 66th to 96th Streets. **Admission:** free. **Secondary genre[s]:** MJAZ, CRCK, ACAP, RGGE, **Acts:** national acts, regional acts, local acts. **Sample day's lineup:** Arlene Smith, Chuck Jackson, Cleveland Still and The Dubs, Randy and The Rainbows, Younger Daze, DIVA, C. A. S. Y. M. Steel Orchestra, others. **Contact:** West Side Chamber of Commerce, 1841 Broadway, Suite 701, New York, NY 10023, 212-595-3333.


INTERNATIONAL FESTIVAL OF CULTURES, Staten Island, NYC
>Middle Sep.
>Variety, Folk and International

**Help!** A sample lineup? **Days:** 1. **Hours per day:** 9. **Site:** outdoor and indoor. CUNY at Staten Island, 2800 Victory Boulevard, Willowbrook. **Admission:** paid. **Daily entry:** under $10, **Acts:** local acts. **Contact:** International Festival of Cultures, CUNY at Staten Island, 2800 Victory Boulevard, Staten Island, NY, 718-982-2310.


RAFAEL HERNANDEZ/SYLVIA REXACH FESTIVAL, Manhattan, NYC
>Middle Sep.
>Traditional Latin

Since 1991. "Continues to be a big hit with the crowd, proving that there still is...an audience for truly great songs [and] genuine values of the Puerto Rican and Hispano-Antilles heritage, presented in a dignified and joyous ambience." -- Latino Village Press. **Days:** 1. **Site:** outdoor and indoor. Museum of the City of New York, 5th Avenue at 103rd Street. **Admission:** free. **Acts:** local acts. **Sample day's lineup:** Carmen Lucca, Freddie Dionysio Nunez, Louis Pasqual, Nosario, others. **Contact:** Rafael Hernandez/Sylvia Rexach Festival, c/o Museum of the City of New York, 5th Avenue and 103rd Street, New York, NY, 718-367-0780 **or:** Association for Puerto Rican-Hispanic Culture, 83 Park Terrace West, New York, NY 10034, 212-942-2338. .


QE2: NEWPORT JAZZ FESTIVAL AT SEA, Manhattan, NYC
>Middle Sep. to Late Sep.
>Modern Jazz

Since 1994. **Help!** Still ongoing? **Days:** 6. **Site:** indoor. QE2 departs Manhattan for Halifax, Nova Scotia. **Admission:** paid. **Daily entry:** $50 and over. **Secondary genre[s]:** TJAZ, MLAT, **Acts:** national acts, . **Sample day's lineup:** Tito Puente, Dave Brubeck, Newport Jazz Allstars, Dave McKenna, others. **Contact:** QE2: Newport Jazz Festival at Sea, Festival Productions, Inc., 311 West 74th Street, New York, NY 10023, 212-496-9000.

AMERICAN FESTIVAL OF MICROTONAL MUSIC, Manhattan, NYC
    Middle Sep. to Early Nov.
    Avant Garde and New Music

**Days:** 4. **Hours per day:** 4. **Site:** indoor. New York University Theater, 25 West 4th Street; St. Paul's Chapel, Columbia University, Amsterdam Avenue at 116th Street. **Admission:** paid. **Daily entry:** $10 to $24, **Discounts:** multiple event or day passes, **Acts:** regional acts, local acts. **Sample day's lineup:** Esther Lamneck, Dale Turk, Tom Goldstein, Lauarance Mahady, Chris Washburne, Gines-Didier Cano, Johnny Reinhardt, Mayumi Reinhardt, Ulrich Kreiger, Phil Niblock, Ashley Carlisle, Robert Priest, Paul Savior, Rebecca Clarey, Joshua Pierce, Guy Tyler, Don Conreaux performs works of Takemitsu, Gubaidulina, Mather, Niblock, Priest, Cage, Reinhardt. **Audio merchandise:** "Between the Keys: Microtonal Masterpieces of the 20th Century" (Newport Classic). **Contact:** American Festival of Microtonal Music, 318 East 70th Street, #5FW, New York, NY 10021, 212-517-3550.

EXPRESSIONS INTERNATIONAL FESTIVAL, Manhattan, NYC
    Late Sep. to Late Oct.
    Variety, General

Since 1979. **Days:** 16. **Site:** indoor. multiple locations. **Admission:** free and paid. **Discounts:** advance purchase discounts, **Secondary genre[s]:** AJAZ, RAP, MLAT, TLAT, AFRC, BRZL, RGGE, OTHR **Acts:** national acts, regional acts, local acts. **Sample day's lineup:** Yorubu Andabo with Merceditas Valdes, Diablos Danzates De El Quiza, Diablos Danzantes De Chuao. **Contact:** Franklin H. Williams Caribbean Cultural Center, 408 West 5th Street, New York, NY 10019, 212-307-7420.

COGNAC HENNESSY JAZZ SEARCH, Manhattan, NYC
    Late Sep.
    Modern Jazz

Since 1985. Winners of nationwide talent search submit demos, with three finalists flown in for live run-off at New York City club site. Returns in 1995 after a one-year hiatus. **Days:** 1. **Site:** indoor. Blue Note, 131 West 3rd Street (though location varies). **Acts:** regional acts, local acts. **Contact:** Schieffelin and Somerset Co., 2 Park Avenue, New York, NY 10016, 212-251-8200 **or:** Cognac Hennessy Jazz Search, 3000 West Olympic Boulevard, Suite JAZZ, Santa Monica, CA 90404 .

ECOFEST, Varies, NYC
    Late Sep.
    Modern Jazz

Since 1989. "Where ecology meets technology." -- Brochure. **Days:** 2. **Hours per day:** 7. **Site:** outdoor. Flushing Meadows-Corona Park, Queens (Sat.); Riverside Park, 83rd to 91st Streets, Manhattan (Sun.). **Admission:** free and paid. **Daily entry:** $10 to $24, $25 to $49, **Secondary genre[s]:** CRCK, MLAT, **Acts:** national acts, local acts. **Sample day's lineup:** Ray Barretto, Paul Winter Consort and Voices of Nature, Melanie, others. **Contact:** West Side Cultural Center, 136 West 70th Street, Suite 1, New York, NY 10023-4434, 212-496-2030.

GATEWAY SUKKOS FESTIVAL, Brooklyn, NYC
    Late Sep.
    Jewish

**Help!** A sample lineup? **Days:** 1. **Hours per day:** 5. **Site:** outdoor. Gateway National Recreation Area, Floyd Bennett Field, Flatbush Avenue. **Admission:** free. **Acts:** regional acts, local acts. **Contact:** National Park Service, Gateway National Recreation Area, Floyd Bennett Field, Building 69, Brooklyn, NY 11234, 718-338-3799/832-4884.

## NATIVE AMERICAN FESTIVAL, Manhattan, NYC
    Late Sep.
    Native American

Since 1983. **Days:** 1. **Site:** outdoor and indoor. Inwood Hill Park, 218th Street and Indian Road, Washington Heights. **Admission:** free. **Acts:** local acts. **Contact:** Inwood Hill Park, 218th Street and Indian Road, New York, NY, 212-427-3400.


## SEPHARDI CULTURAL FAIR, Queens, NYC
    Late Sep.
    Jewish

**Help!** A sample lineup? **Days:** 1. **Hours per day:** 8. **Site:** indoor. Moroccan Jewish Organization, 112-21 72nd Avenue, Forest Hills. **Admission:** paid. **Daily entry:** under $10, **Discounts: Acts:** local acts. **Contact:** Moroccan Jewish Organization, 112-21 72nd Avenue, Forest Hills, NY, 718-263-2021.


## 52ND STREET JAZZ FESTIVAL, Manhattan, NYC
    Late Sep.
    Modern Jazz

Since 1976. See other sites and dates. **Days:** 1. **Hours per day:** 5. **Site:** outdoor. 52nd Street, Lexington to 7th Avenue. **Admission:** free. **Acts:** national acts, local acts. **Sample day's lineup:** Milt Jackson, Charlie Persip, others. **Contact:** 52nd Street Jazz Festival, 1501 Broadway, Suite 1808, New York, NY 10036, 212-764-6330.


## DO THE RIGHT THING FESTIVAL, Brooklyn, NYC
    Late Sep.
    Variety, Folk and International

Since 1990. **Days:** 1. **Hours per day:** 8. **Site:** outdoor. Bandshell, Prospect Park, 9th Street and Prospect Park West. **Admission:** free. **Secondary genre[s]:** RAP, TFOL, IRSH, JWSH, NATV, DRUM, OTHR **Acts:** national acts, . **Sample day's lineup:** Pete Seeger, Dr. Laz and The Cure, Al-Watah, Lavendar Light, David Amram, Susan McKeown and The Chanting House, Disabled in Action Singers, Brooklyn Youth Chorus, others. **Contact:** Do the Right Thing Festival, Spike's Joint, 1 South Elliot Place, Brooklyn, NY 11217, 718-802-1000/788-1283.


## VULVAPALOOZA, Manhattan, NYC
    Late Sep.
    Gay and Lesbian

Since 1994. "Come liberate your libido." -- Village Voice. **Days:** 3. **Site:** outdoor. multiple locations. **Secondary genre[s]:** ARCK, HRCK, **Acts:** local acts. **Sample day's lineup:** Thrust, Summer's Eve, Shelly Mars, Bina Sharif, Cenen, Valerie Jimenez, Anna Tucker, Iternity, Carla, others. **Contact:** Riot Grrl N. Y. C., P. O. Box 1320 Stuyvesant Station, New York, NY 10009, 212-875-7039 **or:** Vulvapalooza, 271 East 10th Street, #666, New York, NY 10009, 212-330-8204.


## NORTHEASTERN NATIVE AMERICAN ASSOCIATION POW WOW, Queens, NYC
    Late Sep.
    Native American

Since 1992. Site may be changing; call ahead. **Days:** 1. **Hours per day:** 8. **Site:** outdoor. Roy Wilkins Park, 119th Avenue and Merrick Boulevard, Jamaica. **Admission:** free. **Secondary genre[s]:** MJAZ, MR&B, BGOS, MFOL, BRZL, RGGE, GYLS, OTHR **Acts:** national acts, regional acts, local acts. **Contact:** Southern Queens Park Association, 119th Avenue and Merrick Boulevard, Jamaica, NY 11434, 718-276-4630.

## NEW YORK STATE BIG APPLE FESTIVAL, Manhattan, NYC
Late Sep.
Variety, General

Since 1990. "Classic and cool on the Hudson." -- Brochure. See other dates. **Help!** Still ongoing? **Days:** 2. **Hours per day:** 7. **Site:** outdoor. Esplanade, World Financial Center, Liberty and West Streets. **Admission:** free. **Secondary genre[s]:** BLGS, NATV, OTHR **Acts:** regional acts, local acts. **Sample day's lineup:** Cornerstone, Akwesasne Mohawk Singers, Carnegie Hill Band, others. **Contact:** World Financial Center Arts and Events, 200 Liberty Street, 18th Floor, New York, NY 10281, 212-945-0505.

## NEXT WAVE FESTIVAL, Brooklyn, NYC
Late Sep. to Middle Dec.
Avant Garde and New Music

Since 1983. "Sixty-five thrilling performances offering a myriad of answers to the eternally intriguing question: 'What's next?'" -- Brochure. See other dates. **Days:** 65. **Site:** indoor. Brooklyn Academy of Music Opera House, 30 Lafayette Avenue. **Admission:** paid. **Daily entry:** $10 to $24, $25 to $49, **Discounts:** multiple event or day passes, **Acts:** national acts, regional acts. **Sample day's lineup:** Day One: Michael Nyman Band; Day Two: Brooklyn Philharmonic Orchestra, Gwendolyn Mok, Dennis Russell Davies perform works of Zorn, Yi, Glass. **Contact:** Brooklyn Academy of Music, 30 Lafayette Street, Brooklyn, NY 11217, 718-636-4100.

## UNDERGROUND JAZZ FESTIVAL, Manhattan, NYC
Early Oct.
Modern Jazz

See other dates. **Days:** 1. **Site:** indoor. Grand Central Terminal, 42nd Street and Park Avenue. **Admission:** free. **Acts:** national acts, regional acts, local acts. **Sample day's lineup:** Music Under New York Big Band, Roy Campbell, others. **Contact:** Performing in Public Spaces, 204 West 80th Street, New York, NY 10024, 212-362-3830.

## ACID JAZZ NIGHT, Manhattan, NYC
Early Oct.
Alternative Jazz

Since 1994. **Help!** One time only? **Days:** 1. **Hours per day:** 5. **Site:** indoor. Knitting Factory, 74 Leonard Street, between Broadway and Church Street. **Admission:** paid. **Acts:** national acts, local acts. **Sample day's lineup:** Jazzhole, Inviolate, Abstract Truth, Tuba. **Audio merchandise:** entire Knitting Factory Works catalog, including numerous festival recordings and compilations. **Other merchandise:** "Knitting" Music by Michael Dorf (Knitting Factory Works). **Contact:** Knitting Factory, 47 East Houston Street, New York, NY 10012, 212-219-3055/3006.

## ATLANTIC ANTIC, Brooklyn, NYC
Early Oct.
Variety, General

Since 1975. "Atlantic Avenue will be transformed into a unique boulevard of sight and sound, featuring a dazzling array of special attractions for the entire family." -- Brooklyn Heights Courier. **Days:** 1. **Site:** outdoor. Atlantic Avenue, 4th Avenue to East River. **Admission:** free. **Secondary genre[s]:** MJAZ, CRCK, RAP, MR&B, RGGE, GYLS, OTHR **Acts:** national acts, regional acts, local acts. **Sample day's lineup:** Cleftones, Harptones, Rob-Roys, many others on 4 stages. **Contact:** Atlantic Antic, 407 Atlantic Avenue, Brooklyn, NY, 718-875-8993.

## GAY AND LESBIAN AMERICAN MUSIC AWARDS, Manhattan, NYC
Early Oct. to Early Nov.
Gay and Lesbian

Since 1995. Kicks off Outmusic Festival. See other dates. **Help!** A sample lineup? **Days:** 1. **Site:** indoor. T. B. D. **Admission:** paid. **Secondary genre[s]:** VRGL, **Acts:** local acts. **Contact:** The GLAMA's, 267 5th Avenue, Suite 801-49, New York, NY 10016, 212-592-4455.

## CHILI PEPPER FIESTA, Brooklyn, NYC
Early Oct.
Traditional Latin

"Multicultural music, art, dance and food honoring the distinguished pepper." -- Listing. **Days:** 1. **Hours per day:** 6. **Site:** outdoor and indoor. Brooklyn Botanic Garden, 1000 Washington Avenue. **Admission:** free. **Secondary genre[s]:** BRZL, **Acts:** local acts. **Sample day's lineup:** Mariachi Zapata, Inkhay, others. **Contact:** Brooklyn Botanic Garden, 1000 Washington Avenue, Brooklyn, NY, 718-622-4433.

## WDRE MODERN ROCK FEST, Manhattan, NYC
Early Oct.
Alternative and College Rock

Since 1991. Benefit. See other dates and sites. **Days:** 1. **Site:** indoor. The Palladium, 126 East 14th Street, between 3rd and 4th Avenues. **Admission:** paid. **Daily entry:** $10 to $24, **Discounts:** advance purchase discounts, **Acts:** national acts, local acts. **Sample day's lineup:** Black 47, Terence Trent D'Arby, Buffalo Tom, Candelbox, others. **Contact:** WDRE 92.7 FM, 1600 Stewart Avenue, Garden City, NY 11590, 516-832-9400.

## OUTMUSIC FESTIVAL, Manhattan, NYC
Early Oct. to Early Nov.
Gay and Lesbian

Since 1991. See other dates. **Site:** indoor. 20 locations. **Admission:** paid. **Secondary genre[s]:** VRGL, **Acts:** national acts, local acts. **Sample day's lineup:** Lea Delaria, Loleatta Holloway, The Del Rubio Triplets, Lady Bunny. **Contact:** Outmusic Festival, c/o Spotted Dog Productions, P. O. Box 40-0041, Brooklyn, NY 11240-0041, 212-330-9197.

## GREENWICH VILLAGE FOLK FESTIVAL, Manhattan, NYC
Early Oct.
Modern Folk

Since 1987. **Days:** 1. **Hours per day:** 5. **Site:** indoor. Washington Square Church, 135 West 4th Street. **Admission:** free. **Secondary genre[s]:** TR&B, **Acts:** national acts, regional acts, local acts. **Sample day's lineup:** Dave Van Ronk, Amy Fradon and Leslie Ritter, Rod MacDonald, Frank Tedesso, Cliff Eberhardt, Lucy Kaplansky, Whirligig, Margo Hennebach, Peter Gallway, Richard Meyer, Wendy Beckerman, Hugh Blumenfeld, Jane Byaela, Frank Christian, Kate Clements, Jack Hardy, Mark Johnson, Su Polo, Ilene Weiss, others. **Audio merchandise:** "Scenes from a Scene: The Second Annual Greenwich Village Folk Festival" (Gadfly); "The 1988 Greenwich Village Folk Festival" (Fast Folk Musical Magazine). **Contact:** Greenwich Village Folk Festival, 1345 East 4th Street, Suite 3F, Brooklyn, NY 11230, 718-252-5056.

### ALL-NITE SOUL, Manhattan, NYC
Early Oct.
Modern Jazz

Since 1971. **Days:** 1. **Hours per day:** 12. **Site:** indoor. St. Peter's Lutheran Church, 54th Street at Lexington Avenue. **Admission:** paid. **Daily entry:** $10 to $24, **Secondary genre[s]:** TJAZ, TR&B, BGOS, MLAT, **Acts:** national acts, regional acts, local acts. **Sample day's lineup:** Daphne Hellman and Hellman's Angels, Harlem Blues and Jazz Band, Trudy Pitts and The Mr. C. Trio, George Gee Orchestra, Eddie Bonnemere and The JESU Choir, Jackie Arnold and The Ray Alexander Group, L. D. Frazier and Friends, Rabbi Joel Goor, Valerie Capers and John Robinson, Jack Jeffers and The New York Classics, Paul Knopf and The Washington Square United Methodist Church Jazz/Gospel/Blues Choir, Jean DuShon and Spice, Rolando Briceno Latin Ensemble, Pete Yellin Quartet, Nanci Banks Orchestra, Greg Bobulinski Quartet, Elizabeth Gerle, Bob Alexander Big Band, Eric Paulin Quartet, Patti Brown, George Tipton and Joseph Lewis, The Seong-Gwan Kim Trio, Ken Simon Quartet, Billy Taylor, Bob Stewart, Carrie Smith, Benny Powell, Harold Ousley, Christian McBride, Jane Jarvis, Warren Chiasson, others. **Contact:** St. Peter's Jazz Ministry, 619 Lexington Avenue, New York, NY 10022-4610, 212-935-2200/475-0371.

### ELEVENTH AVENUE AUTO FAIR, Manhattan, NYC
Early Oct.
Modern Jazz

See other sites and dates. **Days:** 1. **Hours per day:** 7. **Site:** outdoor. 11th Avenue, 44th to 45th Streets. **Admission:** free. **Secondary genre[s]:** MFOL, **Acts:** national acts, local acts. **Sample day's lineup:** Oscar Brand, Judy Barnett, Tracy McDonough, Odetta, others. **Contact:** Eleventh Avenue Auto Fair, 1501 Broadway, Suite 1808, New York, NY 10036, 212-764-6330.

### KNITTING FACTORY AT MERKIN HALL, Manhattan, NYC
Early Oct. to Middle Oct.
Alternative Jazz

Since 1994. **Help!** One time only? **Days:** 3. **Site:** indoor. Merkin Concert Hall, Abraham Goodman House, 129 West 67th Street. **Admission:** paid. **Daily entry:** $10 to $24, **Discounts:** multiple event or day passes, **Secondary genre[s]:** AVNT, **Acts:** national acts, regional acts. **Sample series lineup:** Day One: John Zorn's Masada; Day Two: Marilyn Crispell, Spanish Fly; Day Three: Jazz Passengers. **Audio merchandise:** entire Knitting Factory Works catalog, including numerous festival recordings and compilations. **Other merchandise:** "Knitting Music" by Michael Dorf (Knitting Factory Works). **Contact:** Knitting Factory, 47 East Houston Street, New York, NY 10012, 212-219-3055/3006.

### CHOOSE LIFE BENEFIT GOSPEL CONCERT, Manhattan, NYC
Middle Oct.
Black Gospel

Since 1991. "Don't miss this spectacular event!" -- Advertisement. **Days:** 1. **Site:** indoor. Abyssinian Baptist Church, 132 West 138th Street, Harlem. **Admission:** paid. **Daily entry:** $25 to $49, $50 and over. **Secondary genre[s]:** MJAZ, MR&B, **Acts:** national acts, local acts. **Sample day's lineup:** Tramaine Hawkins, Patti Austin, Vanessa Bell Armstrong, Unity, Hezekiah Walker and The Love Fellowship Crusade Choir, Donnie McClurkin and The New York Restoration Choir, Bronx Mass Choir, Shelton Beckton, Bonnie Gatling, Craig Crawford Players, others. **Contact:** Abyssinian Baptist Church, 132 West 138th Street, New York, NY, 212-614-0023.

## SHELTER: THE NEW YORK SINGER-SONGWRITER FESTIVAL, Manhattan, NYC
### Middle Oct.
### Modern Folk

Benefits National Coalition for the Homeless. See other dates. **Days:** 1. **Site:** indoor. Carnegie Hall, 57th Street at 7th Avenue. **Admission:** paid. **Daily entry:** $25 to $49, $50 and over. **Secondary genre[s]:** ARCK, TR&B, MC&W, AC&W, SCOT, **Acts:** national acts, regional acts, local acts. **Sample day's lineup:** Aztec Two-Step, Lori Carson, Cliff Eberhardt, Julie Gold, Kristen Hall, Laura Love, Carrie Newcomer, Pierce Pettis, Cosy Sheridan, Darden Smith, Greg Trooper, Rory Block, Catie Curtis, Sally Fingerett, Greg Greenway, Freedy Johnston, Dougie MacLean, Ellis Paul, Mike Reid, Richard Shindell, Chris Smither, David Wilcox, Rex Fowler, Carol Laura, Dana Robinson, others. **Audio merchandise:** "Shelter: The Best of Contemporary Singer-Songwriters" (Putumayo), plus entire Putumayo catalog. **Contact:** Putumayo, 627 Broadway, New York, NY 10012, 212-662-1790.

## NATIONS OF NEW YORK ARTS FESTIVAL, Manhattan, NYC
### Middle Oct. to Late Oct.
### Variety, Folk and International

Since 1993. **Help!** One time only? **Days:** 10. **Site:** outdoor and indoor. Henry Street Settlement's Abron Arts Center, 466 Grand Street. **Admission:** free and paid. **Daily entry:** $10 to $24, **Secondary genre[s]:** MJAZ, RAP, BGOS, JWSH, NATV, TLAT, AFRC, BRZL, RGGE, DRUM, OTHR. **Acts:** regional acts, local acts. **Sample day's lineup:** C. A. S. Y. M. Steel Orchestra, Inkhay, Papa Ladji Camara, La Troupe Makandal, others **Contact:** Henry Street Settlement Louis Abrons Art Center, 466 Grand Street, New York, NY 10002-4804, 212-598-0400.

## LIVE JAZZ BANDS, Queens, NYC
### Middle Oct.
### Modern Jazz

"For your shopping pleasure." -- Advertisement. **Help!** One time only? **Days:** 1. **Hours per day:** 4. **Site:** outdoor. Bell Boulevard, 39th to 43rd Avenues, Bayside. **Admission:** free. **Acts:** regional acts, local acts. **Sample day's lineup:** Bill Doggett, Sweney Rose Trio, Robert Emry Band, Steve Adelson and His Band. **Contact:** Bayside Chamber of Commerce, 39-24 Bell Boulevard, Bayside, NY 11362, 718-423-8993.

## NIGHT OF MUSICAL MAGIC, Manhattan, NYC
### Middle Oct.
### Cabaret

Benefits Lauri Strauss Leukemia Foundation. See other dates. **Help!** One time only? **Days:** 1. **Site:** indoor. Carnegie Hall, 57th Street at 7th Avenue. **Admission:** paid. **Daily entry:** $10 to $24, $25 to $49, $50 and over. **Acts:** national acts, regional acts, local acts. **Sample day's lineup:** Skitch Henderson and The New York Pops, Len Cariou, Cissy Houston, Ruth Laredo, Maureen McGovern, Robert Merrill, Jane Olivor, The Dallas Brass, Shelley Dickinson, Marcus Lovett, Karen Manson, others. **Contact:** Night of Magic, c/o Carnegie Hall, 881 7th Avenue, New York, NY 10019, 212-247-7800/696-1033.

CABARET CONVENTION, Manhattan, NYC
> Middle Oct. to Late Oct.
> Cabaret

Since 1990. **Days:** 7. **Site:** indoor. Town Hall, 123 West 43rd Street. **Admission:** paid. **Daily entry:** $10 to $24, **Acts:** national acts, regional acts, local acts. **Sample day's lineup:** Karen Akers, Tom Andersen, D. C. Andersen, Judy Argo, Tex Arnold, Yanna Avis, Helen Baldasarre, Judy Barnett, Bill Bolcom, Joyce Breach, Jason Robert Brown, Ann Hampton Calloway, Barbara Carroll, Allan Chapman and Karen Benjamin, Mary Foster Conklin, Blossom Dearie, Charles DeForest, Christopher Denny, Jamie DeRoy, Baby Jane Dexter, Gerry Diefenbach, Cleve Douglass, Michael Feinstein, Dick Gallagher, Natalie Gamsu, Eric Michael Gillett, Sammy Goldstein, Dale Gonyea, Debbie Shapiro Gravitte, Michael Greensill, David Gurland, Mercedes Hall, Mary Cleere Haran, Jeff Harnar, Shauna Hicks, Hildegarde with Bill Wright, Elizabeth Hodes, Steve Holland, Celeste Holm, Annie Hughes, Mark Hummel, Lynne Jackson and Mike Palter, Lynda Jamison, The Jesters, Judy Kaye, Alix Korey, Lina Koutrakos, Naomi Kukoff, Angela LaGreca, Nancy LaMott, Linda Lavin, Barbara Lea, Jay Leonhart, Lee Lessack, David Lewis, Andrew Lippa, Jo Sullivan Loesser, Martha Lorin, Marilyn Lovell, Meg MacKay, Lizz Manners, Andrea Marcovicci, Christopher Marlowe, Michael Marotta, Karen Mason, Evan Matthews, Sally Mayes, Wes McAfee, Amanda McBroom, Maureen McGovern, Jaymie Meyer, Liliane Montevecchi, Sharon Montgomery, Aaron Morishita, Audrey Morris, Joan Morris, Sidney Myer, Portia Nelson, Nicholas, Grover and Wray, Christian Nova, Phillip Officer, Phyllis Pastore, Forrest Perrin, Erv Raible, Angelina Reaux, Michael Renzi, Ricky Ritzel, Steve Ross, Alex Rybeck, Spider Saloff, Karen Saunders, Molly Scates, Helen Schneider, Daryl Sherman, Joel Silberman, Smitty, David Staller, Marti Stevens, Elaine Stritch, K. T. Sullivan, Billy Taylor, Paul Trueblood, Marilyn Volpe, Fran Walfish, John Wallowitch and Betram Ross, Weslia Whitfield, Margaret Whiting, Ronny Whyte, Julie Wilson, Faith Winthrop, Wiseguys, Neil Wolfe, Sara Zahn, Kristine Zbornik, Billy Barnes, Rick Jensen, Steven Lutvak, Claiborne Cary, Gerald Sterbach, Paula West. **Contact:** Mabel Mercer Foundation, 230 East 49th Street, #4D, New York, NY 10017, 212-980-3026/3109.

PETER TOSH DAY, Manhattan, NYC
> Middle Oct.
> Reggae, Ska and Caribbean

Since 1994. "Tribute to the mystic man." -- Flyer. Benefits Peter Tosh Foundation, Tosh Within, Inc. See other dates. **Days:** 1. **Site:** indoor. Sounds of Brazil, 204 Varick Street. **Admission:** paid. **Daily entry:** $10 to $24, **Discounts:** other discounts **Acts:** national acts, local acts. **Sample day's lineup:** Worl-A-Girl, Oku Onura, Laury Webb and The Tiger Bone Band, Kufire and The Bush Posse, others. **Contact:** Peter Tosh Day, c/o S. O. B.'s, 204 Varick Street, New York, NY, 212-243-4940.

HANUKKAH ARTS FESTIVAL AND JUDAICA CRAFTS FAIR/SELECTED SHORTS, Manhattan, NYC
> Middle Oct.
> Jewish

Event combined with Symphony Space's spoken-word series, Selected Shorts. **Days:** 2. **Hours per day:** 8. **Site:** indoor. festival and gala benefit: Congregation Ansche Chesed, 251 West 100th Street; reading: Symphony Space, 2537 Broadway at 95th Street. **Admission:** paid. **Daily entry:** under $10, $10 to $24, **Discounts:** student discounts, **Acts:** regional acts, local acts. **Sample day's lineup:** Avi Hoffman, Ben Schaechter, Adrienne Cooper, West End Klezmorim. **Contact:** Symphony Space, 2537 Broadway, New York, NY 10025, 212-864-5400/865-0600.

SMITHSONIAN'S NATIONAL MUSEUM OF THE AMERICAN INDIAN POWWOW, Manhattan, NYC
> Middle Oct.
> Native American

Since 1994. Celebrates museum opening. **Help!** One time only? **Days:** 2. **Hours per day:** 9. **Site:** indoor. Jacob Javits Convention Center, 11th Avenue and 36th Street. **Acts:** local acts. **Contact:** Smithsonian's National Museum of the American Indian, 1 Bowling Green, New York, NY, 212-668-6624.

## AFRICA MONDO FESTIVAL, Manhattan, NYC
Middle Oct. to Late Oct.
African

Since 1994. See other dates. **Days:** 4. **Site:** indoor. Sounds of Brazil, 204 Varick Street. **Admission:** paid. **Daily entry:** $10 to $24, **Discounts:** other discounts **Secondary genre[s]:** RGGE, **Acts:** national acts, regional acts. **Sample day's lineup:** Papa Wemba and Viva la Musica, Dominic Kanza and The African Rhythm Machine, Lucien Bokilo, Pierre Belkos, J. P. Buse. **Contact:** Africa Mondo Festival, c/o S. O. B.'s, 204 Varick Street, New York, NY, 212-243-4940.

## CALYPSO AND STEELBAND "SUNSHINE" MUSIC AWARDS, Manhattan, NYC
Late Oct.
Reggae, Ska and Caribbean

Since 1991. "Couldn't make it to the Grammies this year? Then stay in TriBeCa and party with an international array of musicians and celebrities." -- Brochure. **Days:** 1. **Site:** indoor. BMCC/CUNY TriBeCa Performing Arts Center, 199 Chambers Street (though sites vary). **Admission:** paid. **Daily entry:** $25 to $49, $50 and over. **Contact:** Calypso and Steelband "Sunshine" Music Awards, BMCC/CUNY TriBeCa Performing Arts Center, 199 Chambers Street, New York, NY 10007, 212-346-8510.

## COMBINACION PERFECTA, Manhattan, NYC
Late Oct.
Modern Latin

Since 1993. See other sites and dates. **Days:** 1. **Site:** indoor. Madison Square Garden. **Admission:** paid. **Daily entry:** $25 to $49, **Acts:** national acts, regional acts, local acts. **Sample day's lineup:** Celia Cruz, Tito Puente, Oscar D'Leon, Tony Vega, Cheo Feliciano, Tito Nieves, Jose Alberto, Luis Ortiz, Marc Anthony, Domingo Quinones, La India, Van Lester, Ray De La Paz, Ray Sepulveda, Johnny Rivera, Pete Rodriguez, Giovanni Hidalgo, Humberto Ramirez, Sergio George, Orquestra Guayacan, Los Sabrosos Del Merengue. **Audio merchandise:** "Combinacion Perfecta" (RMM/SONY). **Contact:** RMM Productions, 568 Broadway, Suite 806, New York, NY 10012, 212-925-2828/4885.

## BROOKLYN ETHNIC MUSIC AND DANCE FESTIVAL, Brooklyn, NYC
Late Oct.
Variety, Folk and International

Since 1976. **Days:** 1. **Hours per day:** 8. **Site:** outdoor. Prospect Park, Flatbush Avenue and Empire Boulevard. **Admission:** free. **Secondary genre[s]:** RAP, IRSH, JWSH, TLAT, AFRC, RGGE, OTHR **Acts:** national acts, regional acts, local acts. **Sample day's lineup:** Inkay, Andy Statman, The Four Winds, Tom Doherty and Friends, Antilles, Los Pleneros De La 21, Spirit Ensemble, Jose Quesada and Los Cinco Diablos. **Contact:** Ethnic Folk Arts Center, 131 Varick Street, Room 907, New York, NY 10013-1493, 212-691-9510.

## SONGWRITER'S EVENING, Manhattan, NYC
Late Oct.
Cabaret

Part of concert flurry typically "piggybacking" Cabaret Convention. **Help!** One time only? **Days:** 1. **Site:** indoor. The Ballroom, 253 West 28th Street. **Admission:** paid. **Daily entry:** $10 to $24, $25 to $49, $50 and over. **Acts:** national acts, local acts. **Sample day's lineup:** Andrea Marcovicci, Melissa Greene and Lincoln Mayorga, Linda Robbins, Bart Howard, Peri Lyons, Amanda McBroom, Tom Toce and David Israel, Steven Hoffman and Mark Campbell, Joel Silberman, Naomi Kukoff, Jamie Meyer, Michael Marotta, Natalie Gamsli. **Contact:** Songwriter's Evening, The Ballroom, 253 West 28th Street, New York, NY, 212-244-3005.

CULTURAL CROSSROADS' JAZZ GALA, Brooklyn, NYC
    Late Oct.
    Modern Jazz

Since 1979. **Days:** 1. **Site:** indoor. Lafayette Avenue Presbyterian Church, 85 South Oxford Street (cor. Lafayette Avenue). **Admission:** paid. **Daily entry:** $25 to $49, **Secondary genre[s]:** MLAT, **Acts:** national acts. **Sample day's lineup:** Billy Taylor Trio, Kenny Washington, Eddie Palmieri. **Contact:** Cultural Crossroads, Inc., c/o Lafayette Avenue Presbyterian Church, 85 South Oxford Street, Brooklyn, NY, 718-834-8150/625-7515.

CAJUN/ZYDECO JAMBOREE AND HALLOWEEN DANCE, Manhattan, NYC
    Late Oct.
    Cajun and Zydeco

Since 1994. Part of W. M. I.'s year-round international folk and jazz concerts featuring national, regional and local acts. Sub-series titles include Interpretations, Improvisations, World of Percussion, Irish Nights. **Days:** 2. **Site:** indoor. Symphony Space, 2537 Broadway at 95th Street; Merkin Concert Hall, 129 West 67th Street. **Admission:** paid. **Daily entry:** $10 to $24, $25 to $49, **Discounts:** other discounts **Acts:** national acts, regional acts. **Sample day's lineup:** Beausoleil, Ardoin Family, Canray Fontenot. **Audio merchandise:** entire W. M. I. catalog. **Contact:** World Music Institute, 49 West 27th Street, Suite 810, New York, NY 10001, 212-545-7536 **or:** Symphony Space, 2537 Broadway, New York, NY 10025, 212-864-5400. .

THEATER FOR THE NEW CITY VILLAGE HALOWEEN COSTUME BALL, Manhattan, NYC
    Late Oct.
    Cabaret

Since 1977. See other dates. **Days:** 1. **Site:** indoor. Theater for the New City, 155 1st Avenue at 10th Street. **Admission:** paid. **Daily entry:** $10 to $24, **Discounts: Secondary genre[s]:** TJAZ, AFRC, **Acts:** local acts. **Sample day's lineup:** Park Swing Orchestra, steve ben israel, Penny Arcade, Hot Peaches, Nightvision, Wise Guise, Illuminati, Simon Seven, Wycherly Sisters, Mark Marcante, Sparky Moskowitz, Vern Squires, Hot Kitty, Bob Dahadh, Eugenia Macer-Story, Sheila Dabney, Tuli Kupferberg, others. **Contact:** Theater for the New City, 155 1st Avenue, New York, NY 10003, 212-924-0496/254-1109.

VILLAGE HALLOWEEN PARADE/ALL SOULS' HALLOWEEN BALL, Manhattan, NYC
    Late Oct.
    Modern Rock and Pop

Since 1974. **Help!** Does anyone have a sample lineup for the Ball? Fleming discussed headliner along lines of B52's, plus other locals. **Days:** 1. **Site:** outdoor and indoor. parade: roughly 6th Avenue, from Spring to 21st Streets; ball: Manhattan Center for Living. **Admission:** free and paid. **Acts:** national acts, local acts. **Contact:** Village Halloween Parade/All Souls' Halloween Ball, The Rokeby, Barrytown, NY 12507, 914-758-5519.

CHARLIE PARKER MUSIC AND MORE AWARDS GALA, Manhattan, NYC
    Early Nov.
    Modern Jazz

**Help!** Still ongoing? **Days:** 1. **Site:** indoor. Alice Tully Hall, Lincoln Center, Broadway at 65th Street. **Admission:** paid. **Daily entry:** under $10, $10 to $24, $25 to $49, **Discounts:** student discounts, **Acts:** national acts, local acts. **Sample day's lineup:** Nancy Wilson, Israela Margalit, Martin Bookspan, Myron Walden, Indira Jaharan, Aaron Flagg, Charlie Parker Jazz Ensemble. **Contact:** Charlie Parker Music and More Awards Gala, c/o Lincoln Center for the Performing Arts, 70 Lincoln Center Plaza, New York, NY 10023-6583, 212-875-5050.

## SONIC BOOM FESTIVAL OF NEW MUSIC, Manhattan, NYC
### Early Nov. to Middle Nov.
### Avant Garde and New Music

Since 1991. "Dare to be there!" -- Brochure. **Days:** 6. **Site:** indoor. Kathryn Bache Miller Theater, Broadway at 116th Street. **Admission:** paid. **Daily entry:** $10 to $24, **Discounts:** student discounts, multiple event or day passes, **Secondary genre[s]:** AJAZ, MLAT, **Acts:** national acts, regional acts, local acts. **Sample day's lineup:** Continuum, Da Capo Chamber Players, New York New Music Ensemble, Newband perform works of Higdon, Schwartz, Drummond, Carter, Felder, Nancarrow. **Contact:** New York Consortium for New Music, 215 West 90th Street, Suite 1F, New York, NY 10024, 212-229-0128.

## NIGHT OF SHAMROCKS, Queens, NYC
### Middle Nov.
### Irish

**Help!** One time only? **Days:** 1. **Site:** indoor. Tower View Center, Roosevelt Avenue, Woodside. **Admission:** paid. **Daily entry:** $10 to $24, **Acts:** regional acts, local acts. **Sample day's lineup:** Paddy Noonan Band with Andy Cooney, Richie O'Shea, Joe Nellany Band, Tommy Mulvihill, Andrian Flannelly, Tommy Flynn and The New York Show Band, Guss Hayes band, Susan Gillespie, others. **Contact:** American Irish Musicians Society, c/o Tower View Center, Roosevelt Avenue, Woodside, NY, 212-719-1930.

## JAL JAZZ CONCERT, Manhattan, NYC
### Early Nov.
### Modern Jazz

"Together for the first time, the Japanese all-stars." -- Advertisement. There's been one such all-star jazz concert each fall for the last three years, often filmed for Japanese TV. Sites and dates vary. **Help!** One time only? **Days:** 1. **Site:** indoor. Town Hall, 123 West 43rd Street. **Admission:** paid. **Daily entry:** $25 to $49, **Acts:** national acts, regional acts. **Sample day's lineup:** Toshiko Akiyoshi, Masabumi Kikuchi, Terumasa Hino, Yoshiaki Masuo, Ryo Kawasaki, Shunzo Ono, Akira Tana, Teruo Nakamura, Helen Merrill. **Contact:** JAL Jazz Concert, c/o Town Hall, 123 West 43rd Street, New York, NY 10036, 212-997-6661.

## BUDDY RICH MEMORIAL SCHOLARSHIP CONCERT, Manhattan, NYC
### Early Nov.
### Modern Jazz

Since 1993. Part of Manny's New York City Drum Expo. **Days:** 1. **Hours per day:** 7. **Site:** indoor. Manhattan Center, 311 West 34th Street, between 8th and 9th Avenues. **Admission:** paid. **Daily entry:** $25 to $49, **Acts:** national acts. **Sample day's lineup:** Buddy Rich Band, Steve Marcus, Kenny Aronoff, Gregg Bissonette, Omar Hakim, Rod Morgenstern, Matt Sorum, Dave Weckl. **Contact:** Buddy Rich Memorial Scholarship Concert, Manny's Music, 156 West 48th Street, New York, NY, 212-819-0576.

## JUBA, JUKIN' AND JAZZIN', Manhattan, NYC
### Early Nov.
### Modern Jazz

Since 1984. **Days:** 2. **Site:** indoor. Greenwich House, 27 Barrows Street. **Admission:** paid. **Daily entry:** $10 to $24, **Acts:** local acts. **Sample day's lineup:** Wilbur Morris, Newman Baker, Debbie Williams, Imani Kahn, C. Scoby Stroman, Noel Tantambu Hall, Akwesi Munir Asante, Richard Harper, others. **Contact:** Juba, Jukin' and Jazzin', c/o Greenwich House, 27 Barrows Street, New York, NY, 718-963-2081.

## HARLEM PIANO U. S. A., Manhattan, NYC
### Middle Nov.
### Modern Jazz

Part of the James Baldwin Literature and Music Series. See other dates. **Help!** Still ongoing? **Days:** 1. **Hours per day:** 5. **Site:** indoor. Harlem School of the Arts, 645 St. Nicholas Avenue. **Admission:** free. **Secondary genre[s]:** AVNT, OTHR **Acts:** national acts, local acts. **Sample day's lineup:** Valerie Capers, Richard Alston, Gwendolyn Bynum, Barry Harris, others. **Contact:** James Baldwin Literature and Music Series, Harlem School for the Arts, 645 St. Nicholas Avenue, New York, NY, 212-926-4100.

## KITTY BRAZELTON'S REAL MUSIC SERIES/MUSIC PARTIES, Manhattan, NYC
### Early Nov. to Late Nov.
### Avant Garde and New Music

See other dates. **Days:** 2. **Hours per day:** 5. **Site:** indoor. CB's Gallery, 313 Bowery. **Admission:** paid. **Daily entry:** under $10, **Discounts:** student discounts, other discounts **Acts:** local acts. **Sample day's lineup:** Marie McAuliffe and ARK, Sandra Sprecher and Friends, Talujon Percussion Quartet, Chris Washburne's Syotos Project, Laurie Schwartz, Hildegarde of Bingen, Homer Erotic, Hamilton/Zummo Duo, P. Susser, John Myers and Blastula, others. **Contact:** Kitty Brazelton's Real Music Series, c/o CB's Gallery, 313 Bowery, New York, NY, 212-677-0455.

## FLOATING ARCHIVES' SOME KIND OF CARNIVAL, Manhattan, NYC
### Early Nov.
### Avant Garde and New Music

Since 1992. **Days:** 1. **Hours per day:** 5. **Site:** indoor. Knitting Factory, 74 Leonard Street, between Broadway and Church Street. **Admission:** paid. **Acts:** local acts. **Sample day's lineup:** N'Jie, Lori and Jim May, Will Sales, John Williams, Jasper McGruder and Henry bradley, Ben Manley, Christine Marguerite, Deborah Kayton, Heather Fenby, Yictove, Kevin Hylton, Dan Farkas, others. **Contact:** Knitting Factory, 47 East Houston Street, New York, NY 10012, 212-219-3055/3006.

## GREAT BEER AND MUSIC FESTIVAL, Manhattan, NYC
### Middle Nov.
### Alt. Country and Rockabilly

"25 microbrews on draft." -- Advertisement. Dates have varied, though site has remained consistent. **Days:** 1. **Hours per day:** 6. **Site:** indoor. Irving Plaza, 17 Irving Place. **Admission:** paid. **Daily entry:** $25 to $49, **Secondary genre[s]:** ARCK, **Acts:** national acts, regional acts, local acts. **Sample day's lineup:** G. E. Smith and High Plains Drifters, 5 Chinese Brothers, Go To Blazes, Pool, Harry. **Contact:** Great Beer and Music Festival, c/o Irving Plaza, 17 Irving Place, New York, NY, 212-777-6800/249-8870.

## RICHARD NADER'S ROCK AND ROLL REVIVAL SPECTACULAR, Manhattan, NYC
### Middle Nov.
### Classic Rock and Oldies

See other dates and sites. **Help!** One time only? **Days:** 1. **Site:** indoor. The Paramount, Madison Square Garden, 7th Avenue at 32nd Street. **Admission:** paid. **Daily entry:** $25 to $49, $50 and over. **Secondary genre[s]:** TR&B, ACAP, **Acts:** national acts. **Sample day's lineup:** Little Richard, Dion, Little Anthony and The Imperials, Bo Diddley, Jerry Lee Lewis, Leslie Gore. **Contact:** Richard Nader's Rock and Roll Revival Spectacular, c/o Madison Square Garden, 4 Pennsylvania Plaza, New York, NY, 212-465-MSG1.

## Big Band Day, Manhattan, NYC
### Middle Nov.
### Modern Jazz

Part of the James Baldwin Literature and Music Series. See other dates. **Help!** Still ongoing? **Days:** 1. **Hours per day:** 5. **Site:** indoor. Harlem School of the Arts, 645 St. Nicholas Avenue. **Admission:** free. **Secondary genre[s]:** OTHR **Acts:** local acts. **Sample day's lineup:** James Ware and The Me, We and Them Orchestra, Randolph State band with Clarence Martin, Harlem School of the Arts jazz repertory Stage Band. **Contact:** James Baldwin Literature and Music Series, Harlem School for the Arts, 645 St. Nicholas Avenue, New York, NY, 212-926-4100.

## JazzTimes Convention, Manhattan, NYC
### Middle Nov.
### Modern Jazz

Since 1985. **Days:** 4. **Hours per day:** 17. **Site:** indoor. seminar: Loew's New York Hotel (though locations vary); showcases: multiple club sites. **Admission:** paid. **Daily entry:** $25 to $49, **Discounts:** advance purchase discounts, **Secondary genre[s]:** AJAZ, MLAT, AFRC, BRZL, **Acts:** national acts, regional acts, . **Sample day's lineup:** Tiger Okoshi Band, Mike Logan Quartet, Thomas Chapin Trio, Benny Green Trio, Tana Reid Band, Michele Rosewoman Quintet, Toninho Horta Band, Othello Molineaux Band **Contact:** JazzTimes Magazine, 7961 Eastern Avenue, Suite 303, Silver Spring, MD 20910-4898, 301-588-4114.

## K-Rock's Hungerthon, Manhattan, NYC
### Middle Nov.
### Modern Rock and Pop

Concert tie-in with weekend-long charity radiothon benefitting World Hunger Year. "I think we've become sort of a holiday tradition in New York, and that's good." -- Pete Fornatale, New York Daily News. **Days:** 1. **Site:** indoor. Beacon Theater, Broadway. **Admission:** paid. **Secondary genre[s]:** CRCK, TR&B, MC&W, MFOL, **Acts:** national acts. **Sample day's lineup:** Emerson, Lake and Palmer, Southside Johnny and Bobby Bandiera, Roger McGuinn, Richie Havens, Buster Poindexter, Janis Ian, Rosanne Cash. **Contact:** WXRK-FM 92.3, 600 Madison Avenue, New York, NY 10022, 212-750-0550.

## Giving of Thanks to the First Peoples, Manhattan, NYC
### Middle Nov.
### Native American

Since 1988. See other dates. **Days:** 1. **Site:** indoor. Cathedral of St. John the Divine, 1047 Amsterdam Avenue at 112th Street. **Admission:** paid. **Daily entry:** $10 to $24, **Acts:** national acts, regional acts, local acts. **Sample day's lineup:** R. Carlos Nakai, Dennis Yerry, Ray Harrell, Joan Henry, Franc Menusan, Darryl Zephier and The Red Tail Singers, others. **Contact:** Cathedral of St. John the Divine, 1047 Amsterdam Avenue, New York, NY 10025, 212-662-2133/316-7540.

## Skavoovee, Manhattan, NYC
### Late Nov.
### Reggae, Ska and Caribbean

Since 1992. "The ultimate ska train." -- Advertisement. Dates have been consistent, though sites have varied (Mahattan Center, S. O. B.'s, Tramps, etc.). Prior years have included national acts. See other dates. **Days:** 1. **Site:** indoor. Sounds of Brazil, 204 Varick Street. **Admission:** paid. **Daily entry:** $10 to $24, **Discounts:** other discounts **Acts:** regional acts, local acts. **Sample day's lineup:** Toasters, Scofflaws, Pie Tasters, Los Pies Negros, King Chango. **Contact:** Skavoovee, c/o S. O. B.'s, 204 Varick Street, New York, NY, 212-243-4940.

AIDS DANCE-A-THON, Manhattan, NYC
> Late Nov.
> Modern Rock and Pop

Since 1990. "A five-hour fundraising dance extravaganza." -- Advertisement. Benefits Gay Men's Health Crisis. See other dates. **Days:** 1. **Hours per day:** 5. **Site:** indoor. Jacob Javitz Convention Center, 11th Avenue at 36th Street. **Admission:** paid. **Daily entry:** $50 and over. **Secondary genre[s]:** CRCK, MR&B, DRUM, **Acts:** national acts. **Sample day's lineup:** Salt-N-Pepa, The Village People, Queen Latifah, Rosie Perez, Jon Stewart and Nona Hendryx. **Contact:** Gay Men's Health Crisis, P. O. Box 10 Old Chelsea Station, New York, NY 10114-0184, 212-807-9255.

BIG BANDS AT SEA, Manhattan, NYC
> Late Nov. to Early Dec.
> Traditional Jazz and Ragtime

Since 1988. **Days:** 8. **Site:** indoor. S. S. Norway, departs Manhattan. **Admission:** paid. **Daily entry:** $50 and over. **Acts:** national acts, regional acts. **Sample day's lineup:** Glenn Miller Orchestra, Larry Elgart and His Orchestra, Sy Zentner and His Orchestra, The Bob Wilbur Tribute to Benny Goodman Orchestra. **Contact:** Big Bands at Sea, HOSS, Inc., 830 Broadway, New York, NY 10003, 212-674-0265.

RETURN OF THE BROOKLYN BRIDGE, Queens, NYC
> Late Nov.
> A Cappella and Doo Wop

See other dates. **Days:** 1. **Site:** indoor. Golden Center for the Performing Arts, Queens College, Kissena Boulevard and Long Island Expressway, Flushing. **Admission:** paid. **Daily entry:** $10 to $24, **Secondary genre[s]:** CRCK, **Acts:** national acts, regional acts, local acts. **Sample day's lineup:** Johnny Maestro and The Brooklyn Bridge, Duprees, Drifters, Younger Dayz, Traditions, Elegants. **Contact:** John Vogele Productions, Golden Center for the Performing Arts, Kissena Boulevard, Flushing, NY, 718-793-8080.

SONIDOS DE LAS AMERICAS, Varies, NYC
> Late Nov. to Early Dec.
> Modern Latin

Showcases 20th century classical compositions from South and Latin America. Venezuela and Mexico respectively featured in 1994. Winter dates vary, so call American Composers Orchestra ahead of time. **Days:** 6. **Site:** indoor. Carnegie Hall, 57th Street at 7th Avenue (Manhattan); Hostos Center for the Arts and Culture, 450 Grand Concourse (Bronx);Thalia Spanish Theater, 41-17 Greenpoint Avenue, Sunnyside (Queens). **Admission:** paid. **Daily entry:** $25 to $49, $50 and over. **Acts:** national acts, regional acts. **Sample day's lineup:** Paul Desenne, Idwer Alvarez, American Composers Orchestra perform works of Bilbao, Desenne, Mendoza. **Contact:** Sonidos de la Americas, Carnegie Hall, 881 7th Avenue, New York, NY 10019, 212-247-7800 **or:** American Composers Orchestra, 1775 Broadway, Suite 525, New York, NY 10019, 212-977-8495.

IMPROVISATIONS FESTIVAL, Manhattan, NYC
> Late Nov. to Middle Dec.
> Avant Garde and New Music

Since 1992. **Days:** 15. **Hours per day:** 13. **Site:** indoor. multiple locations. **Admission:** free and paid. **Daily entry:** under $10, $10 to $24, **Acts:** local acts. **Sample day's lineup:** Sten Rudstrom, Cassie Terman, Cathy Gatto, Francis Savage, Mark Landsman, Katrina Bangsgaard. **Contact:** Movement Research, 28 Avenue A, 3rd Floor, New York, NY, 212-929-3862.

JIMI HENDRIX BIRTHDAY PARTY, Manhattan, NYC
> Late Nov.
> Alternative and College Rock

Since 1992. See other dates and sites. **Days:** 1. **Site:** indoor. location varies (Manhattan Center, Under Acme, etc.). **Admission:** paid. **Daily entry:** under $10, $10 to $24, **Discounts:** advance purchase discounts, other discounts **Secondary genre[s]:** TR&B, **Acts:** regional acts, local acts. **Sample day's lineup:** Larry Mitchell, Bluesland, Menace, others. **Audio merchandise:** "Black Rock Coalition: The History of Our Future"; "Black Rock Coalition: Blacker Than That" (both on Ryko). **Contact:** Black Rock Coalition, Inc., P. O. Box 1054 Cooper Station, New York, NY 10279, 212-713-5097 **or:** Jimi Hendrix Birthday Party, 633 Carlton Avenue, #1, Brooklyn, NY 11238, 718-857-0173.

BENSON SERIES BENEFIT CONCERT FOR UNITED AIDS RELIEF EFFORT, Manhattan, NYC
> Early Dec.
> Avant Garde and New Music

Since 1990. See other dates and sites. **Days:** 1. **Site:** indoor. Middle Collegiate Church, 2nd Avenue and 7th Street. **Daily entry:** $10 to $24, $25 to $49, $50 and over. **Acts:** national acts, regional acts, local acts. **Sample day's lineup:** Downtown Chamber and Opera Players, Fred Hersch, Anne Hampton Calloway, Richard Barone, others perform works of Gannon, Seyfrit, Oldham, DeBlasio, Motta, others. **Contact:** Downtown Music Productions, 310 East 12th Street, New York, NY 10003, 212-477-1594.

WBLS CELEBRATION CONCERT AND SCHOLARSHIP FUND, Manhattan, NYC
> Early Dec.
> Modern R&B

Since 1975. **Help!** Still ongoing? **Days:** 1. **Site:** indoor. The Paramount, Madison Square Garden, 7th Avenue at 32nd Street. **Admission:** paid. **Daily entry:** $25 to $49, **Secondary genre[s]:** CRCK, RGGE, **Acts:** national acts, regional acts. **Sample day's lineup:** Luther Vandross, Teddy Pendergrass, Stephanie Mills, Kool and The Gang, Freddie Jackson, Howard Hewitt, Cece Penniston, Jodeci, Blackgirls, Ini Kamoze, Lieutenant Stitchie, Zhane. **Contact:** WBLS Celebration Concert and Scholarship Fund, WBLS-FM, 3 Park Avenue, New York, NY 10010, 212-447-1000/465-MSG1.

POST-ROCK, NEO-MOSH FESTIVAL, Manhattan, NYC
> Early Dec.
> Alternative and College Rock

Since 1993. **Help!** One time only? **Days:** 6. **Hours per day:** 5. **Site:** indoor. Knitting Factory, 74 Leonard Street, between Broadway and Church Street. **Admission:** paid. **Acts:** national acts, regional acts, local acts. **Sample day's lineup:** Timber, No Safety, Babe the Blue Ox. **Audio merchandise:** entire Knitting Factory Works catalog, including numerous festival recordings and compilations.. **Other merchandise:** "Knitting Music" by Michael Dorf (Knitting Factory Works). **Contact:** Knitting Factory, 47 East Houston Street, New York, NY 10012, 212-219-3055/3006.

EL ELYON MUSIC AWARDS, Manhattan, NYC
> Early Dec.
> Modern Christian

See other sites and dates. **Help!** A sample lineup, or site? **Days:** 1. **Site:** indoor. **Secondary genre[s]:** BGOS, MLAT, RGGE, **Acts:** local acts. **Contact:** Ministerio Internacional Musical, P. O. Box 320-158, Brooklyn, NY 11232-0003, 718-768-9459/332-7427.

TEDDYCARE, Manhattan, NYC
> Early Dec. to Late Dec.
> Cabaret

Since 1992. Benefits Hearts and Voices. **Days:** 4. **Site:** indoor. Don't Tell Mama, 343 West 46th Street, between 8th and 9th Avenues. **Admission:** paid. **Daily entry:** $10 to $24, **Secondary genre[s]:** DRUM, **Acts:** regional acts, local acts. **Sample day's lineup:** James Beamon, Steven Brinberg, Tommy Femia, Bryan Murphy, Jay Rogers, Clare Scandelle, Albert Walsh. **Contact:** Hearts and Voices, 150 West 80th Street, #7D, New York, NY 10024, 212-799-4276/362-2590.

LATIN JAZZ U. S. A. CONCERT AND AWARDS, Manhattan, NYC
> Early Dec.
> Modern Latin

Since 1989. **Help!** Still ongoing? **Days:** 1. **Site:** indoor. Avery Fisher Hall, Lincoln Center, Broadway at 65th Street. **Admission:** paid. **Daily entry:** $10 to $24, $25 to $49, $50 and over. **Secondary genre[s]:** MJAZ, **Acts:** national acts, regional acts. **Sample day's lineup:** Paquito D'Rivera, Ray Barretto, Dave Valentin, Hilton Ruiz, Charlie Sepulveda, Mitch Frohman, Roberto Hernandez, The Bronx Horns, others. **Contact:** Latin Jazz U. S. A. Concert and Awards, c/o Jazz at Lincoln Center, 70 Lincoln Center Plaza, New York, NY 10023-6583, 212-875-5299.

BENDING TOWARD THE LIGHT: A JAZZ NATIVITY, Manhattan, NYC
> Early Dec.
> Modern Jazz

Since 1985. **Days:** 2. **Hours per day:** 3. **Site:** indoor. Lincoln Center, Avery Fisher Hall, West 65th Street and Columbus Avenue. **Admission:** paid. **Daily entry:** $10 to $24, $25 to $49, **Discounts:** group sale discounts, **Secondary genre[s]:** BGOS, MLAT, **Acts:** national acts, regional acts, local acts. **Sample day's lineup:** Bob Kindred, Clark Terry, Al Grey, Jon Faddis, Tito Puente, Lionel Hampton, Dave Brubeck, Jackie Cain and Roy Kral, Gail Winters, New York Voices, Jon Gordon, Maeretha Stewart, Ursula Dudziak, others. **Contact:** Kindred Spirits Foundation, 170 West End Avenue, #16D, New York, NY 10023, 212-580-2349.

Z100 ACOUSTIC CHRISTMAS, Manhattan, NYC
> Early Dec.
> Alternative and College Rock

Since 1994. Benefits American Suicide Foundation, Lifebeat. See other dates and sites. **Days:** 1. **Site:** indoor. Madison Square Garden. **Admission:** paid. **Daily entry:** $25 to $49, **Secondary genre[s]:** MRCK, **Acts:** national acts. **Sample day's lineup:** Weezer, Toad The Wet Sprocket, Indigo Girls, Hole, Green Day, Sheryl Crow, Bon Jovi, Melissa Etheridge, Pansy Division, Cheer. **Contact:** WHTZ-FM 100.3, 767 3rd Avenue, New York, NY, 212-239-2300.

COLORS OF CHRISTMAS, Manhattan, NYC
> Early Dec.
> Modern R&B

"Hear these chart-topping superstars perform their greatest hits and traditional holiday favorites." -- Advertisement. See other dates. **Days:** 1. **Site:** indoor. Carnegie Hall, 57th Street at 7th Avenue (though locations vary). **Admission:** paid. **Daily entry:** $25 to $49, $50 and over. **Secondary genre[s]:** MRCK, BGOS, **Acts:** national acts. **Sample day's lineup:** Peabo Bryson, Sheena Easton, Roberta Flack, James Ingram, others. **Contact:** Colors of Christmas, c/o Carnegie Hall, 881 7th Avenue, New York, NY 10019, 212-247-7800.

WNEW-FM CHRISTMAS CONCERT, Manhattan, NYC
> Early Dec.
> Alternative and College Rock

Since 1973. Benefits United Cerebral Palsy. **Days:** 1. **Site:** indoor. Roseland Ballroom, 239 West 52nd Street. **Admission:** paid. **Daily entry:** $25 to $49, **Discounts:** advance purchase discounts, **Acts:** national acts, . **Sample day's lineup:** Big Head Todd and The Monsters, Hootie and The Blowfish, Gods Child, Pete Droge, others. **Contact:** WNEW-FM, 888 7th Avenue, New York, NY 10106, 212-489-1027.


WINTER REVELS, Manhattan, NYC
> Early Dec.
> Traditional Folk

"A Celebration of the Winter Solstice: traditional and ritual dances, processionals, carols and drama." -- Program. See other dates and sites. **Days:** 4. **Site:** indoor. Main Auditorium, American Museum of Natural History, 79th Street and Central Park West. **Admission:** paid. **Daily entry:** under $10, $10 to $24, $25 to $49, **Discounts: Secondary genre[s]:** OTHR **Acts:** local acts. **Sample day's lineup:** King Arthur's Brass, Henry Chapin, Solstice Singers, Riverside Early Music Ensemble, Peter Johnson, John Langstaff, Heather Wood, Christa Patton, others. **Audio merchandise:** "The Christmas Revels"; "Seasons for Singing"; "Blow, Ye Winds in the Morning" (all on Revels Records). **Contact:** Revels, Inc., One Kendall Square, Building 600, Cambridge, MA 02139-1562, 718-399-9282.


CHANGO CELEBRATION, Manhattan, NYC
> Early Dec.
> Traditional Latin

Since 1984. **Days:** 1. **Site:** indoor. Aaron Davis Hall, 135th Street and Convent Avenue, Harlem. **Admission:** paid. **Daily entry:** $10 to $24, **Discounts:** student discounts, advance purchase discounts, other discounts **Secondary genre[s]:** MLAT, **Acts:** national acts, regional acts. **Sample day's lineup:** Lazaros Ros, Orlando Rios and Nueva Generacion, others. **Contact:** Franklin H. Williams Caribbean Cultural Center, 408 West 5th Street, New York, NY 10019, 212-307-7420.


KWANZAA, Queens, NYC
> Early Dec.
> African American

**Days:** 1. **Hours per day:** 12. **Site:** indoor. Queens Borough Public Library's Langston Hughes Community Library and Cultural Center. **Admission:** free. **Secondary genre[s]:** MJAZ, MR&B, **Acts:** local acts. **Sample day's lineup:** Slyte Touch, Ernest Stubbs and Drummers, Carlos Garnett Quartet, others. **Contact:** Florence E. Smith Community Center, 102-19 34th Avenue, Corona, NY, 718-990-0700.


EXPERIMENTAL INTERMEDIA FOUR COUNTRY FESTIVAL, Manhattan, NYC
> Early Dec. to Late Dec.
> Avant Garde and New Music

Since 1993. **Days:** 16. **Site:** indoor. New York City: Experimental Intermedia, 224 Centre Street at Grand Street (4 concerts). Also Holland, Germany, Belgium (4 concerts each). **Admission:** paid. **Daily entry:** under $10, **Acts:** regional acts, local acts. **Sample series lineup:** Day One: Phil Niblock; Day Two: Hans Peter Kuhn; Day Three: Arne Deforce. **Contact:** Experimental Intermedia Foundation, 224 Centre Street, New York, NY 10013, 212-431-5127.

HANUKKAH FESTIVAL, Queens, NYC
> Middle Dec.
> Jewish

**Help!** A sample lineup? **Days:** 1. **Site:** outdoor and indoor. Queens Theater on the Park, Flushing Meadows Park, by the skating rink. **Admission:** paid. **Daily entry:** $10 to $24, **Discounts:** advance purchase discounts, **Contact:** Hanukkah Festival, Queens Theater on the Park, Flushing Meadows Park, Queens, NY, 718-268-5011.

WDRE ACOUSTIC CHRISTMAS, Manhattan, NYC
> Middle Dec.
> Alternative and College Rock

Since 1993. Benefit. See other dates and sites. **Days:** 2. **Site:** indoor. Beacon Theater, 74th Street and Broadway. **Admission:** paid. **Daily entry:** $25 to $49, **Discounts:** advance purchase discounts, **Acts:** national acts. **Sample day's lineup:** Big Audio Dynamite, Evan Dando, Jesus and Mary Chain, The Go-Go's, Radiohead, Love Spit Love, Frente!, Black 47, G. Love and Special Sauce. **Contact:** WDRE 92.7 FM, 1600 Stewart Avenue, Garden City, NY 11590, 516-832-9400.

WINTER CONSORT WINTER SOLSTICE WHOLE EARTH CHRISTMAS CELEBRATION, Manhattan, NYC
> Middle Dec.
> Variety, Folk and International

Since 1981. See other dates. **Days:** 3. **Site:** indoor. Cathedral of St. John the Divine, 1047 Amsterdam Avenue at 112th Street. **Admission:** paid. **Daily entry:** $25 to $49, $50 and over. **Secondary genre[s]:** MJAZ, BGOS, IRSH, OTHR **Acts:** national acts, local acts. **Sample day's lineup:** Paul Winter Consort, Dimitri Pokrovsky Singers, Noirin Ni Riain, Kecia Lewis-Evans. **Contact:** Cathedral of St. John the Divine, 1047 Amsterdam Avenue, New York, NY 10025, 212-662-2133/316-7540.

KWANZAA HOLIDAY EXPO, Manhattan, NYC
> Middle Dec.
> African American

Since 1988. **Days:** 4. **Hours per day:** 10. **Site:** indoor. Jacob Javits Convention Center, 11th Avenue at West 35th Street. **Admission:** paid. **Daily entry:** under $10, **Discounts: Secondary genre[s]:** MJAZ, MR&B, BGOS, AFRC, RGGE, **Acts:** local acts. **Sample day's lineup:** All City Jazz Band, Zahmu and His Kwanzaa Band, others. **Contact:** Kwanzaa Holiday Expo, 1000 Grand Concourse, Suite 2E, Bronx, NY 10452, 718-992-9933.

INDIAN MARKET, Manhattan, NYC
> Middle Dec. to Late Dec.
> Native American

See other dates. **Days:** 8. **Hours per day:** 8. **Site:** indoor. American Indian Community House Gallery, 708 Broadway, 2nd Floor. **Admission:** paid. **Daily entry:** under $10, **Discounts:** student discounts, **Contact:** American Indian Community House Gallery, 708 Broadway, 2nd Floor, New York, NY 10003, 212-598-0100.

SOUNDS AROUND THE WORLD, Manhattan, NYC
        Middle Dec.
        Variety, Folk and International

Since 1994. Part of W. M. I.'s year-round international folk and jazz concerts featuring national, regional and local acts. Sub-series titles include Interpretations, Improvisations, World of Percussion, Irish Nights. **Days:** 1. **Site:** indoor. Merkin Concert Hall, 129 West 67th Street. **Admission:** paid. **Daily entry:** $10 to $24, $25 to $49, **Discounts:** other discounts **Secondary genre[s]:** BRZL, RGGE, OTHR **Acts:** national acts, regional acts, local acts. **Sample day's lineup:** Djivan Gasparyan, Hassan Hakmoun, Ilyas Malayev, Inkhay, Music From China, Simon Shaheen. **Audio merchandise:** entire W. M. I. catalog. **Contact:** World Music Institute, 49 West 27th Street, Suite 810, New York, NY 10001, 212-545-7536/362-8719.

NEW YORK JAZZ TODAY!, Manhattan, NYC
        Middle Dec.
        Modern Jazz

Presented by Jazz Institute of Harlem. See other dates. **Help!** One time only? **Days:** 1. **Site:** indoor. Aaron Davis Hall, West 133-to-135th Streets and Convent Avenue. **Admission:** paid. **Daily entry:** $10 to $24, **Discounts:** group sale discounts, **Acts:** national acts, local acts. **Sample day's lineup:** Carl Allen Quintet with Vincent Herring and Nicholas Payton, Herb Harris Quartet, Tess Marsalis Quartet, Eric Reed Trio, David Sanchez Quartet with Danilo Perez, Jacky Terrasson Trio. **Contact:** New York Jazz Today!, c/o Aaron Davis Hall, City College, West 133-to-135th Streets, New York, NY, 212-650-7100.

WWRL GOSPEL EXPLOSION, Manhattan, NYC
        Middle Dec.
        Black Gospel

Since 1993. **Help!** One time only? **Days:** 1. **Site:** indoor. Jacob Javits Convention Center, 625 West 34th Street. **Admission:** paid. **Daily entry:** $10 to $24, **Discounts:** advance purchase discounts, **Acts:** national acts, regional acts, local acts. **Sample day's lineup:** Rev. Timothy Wright and The Concert Choir, Hezekiah Walker and The Love Fellowship Crusade Choir, Donald Malloy, Bronx Mass Choir, Jerrfrey White and The Soul Stirring Crusade, St. Charles Gospel Light Choir. **Contact:** WWRL-AM 1600, 41-30 58th Street, Woodside, NY 11377, 718-335-1600.

COMMUNITY HOLIDAY FESTIVAL, Manhattan, NYC
        Late Dec. to Early Jan.
        Variety, General

11 area community arts organizations, including BACA/The Brooklyn Arts Council (see below), program afternoon shows. See other dates and sites for BACA. **Days:** 11. **Site:** indoor. Alice Tully Hall, Lincoln Center, Broadway at 66th Street. **Admission:** paid. **Acts:** national acts, local acts. **Sample day's lineup:** The Persuasions, Aztec Two-Step, Rosetta Jefferson. **Contact:** BACA/The Brooklyn Arts Council, 200 Eastern Parkway, Brooklyn, NY 11238, 718-783-4469/3077.

BLACK NATIVITY, Manhattan, NYC
        Late Dec.
        African American

See other dates. **Help!** A sample lineup? **Days:** 2. **Site:** indoor. Apollo Theater, 253 West 125th Street. **Admission:** paid. **Daily entry:** $10 to $24, $25 to $49, **Secondary genre[s]:** BGOS, **Acts:** local acts. **Contact:** Inner City Theater Group, Apollo Theater, 253 West 125th Street, New York, NY, 212-222-0992/749-5838.

## S. O. B.'s KWANZAA CELEBRATION, Manhattan, NYC
Late Dec.
African American

Since 1983. "Join the longest-running Kwanzaa celebration in N. Y. C." -- Advertisement. See other dates. **Days:** 1. **Hours per day:** 6. **Site:** indoor. Sounds of Brazil, 204 Varick Street. **Admission:** paid. **Daily entry:** $10 to $24, **Discounts:** other discounts **Secondary genre[s]:** MJAZ, AFRC, **Acts:** national acts, regional acts, local acts. **Sample day's lineup:** Kimati Dinizulu and The Kotoko Society. Randy Weston, Antonio Hart, Steve Turre. **Contact:** S. O. B.'s Kwanzaa Celebration, c/o S. O. B.'s, 204 Varick Street, New York, NY, 212-243-4940.

## SKARMAGEDDON, Manhattan, NYC
Late Dec.
Reggae, Ska and Caribbean

"Don't let 1994 end without a SKA-BOOM." -- Advertisement. **Help!** One time only? **Days:** 1. **Site:** indoor. Manhattan Center, 311 West 34th Street. **Admission:** paid. **Daily entry:** $10 to $24, **Discounts:** advance purchase discounts, **Acts:** national acts, regional acts, local acts. **Sample day's lineup:** Skatalites, Scofflaws, New York City Ska Jazz Ensemble, Inspector 7, King Chango, Shaken Not Stirred. **Contact:** Skarmageddon, c/o Manhattan Center, 311 West 34th Street, New York, NY, 212-279-7740.

## CONCERT FOR PEACE, Manhattan, NYC
Late Dec.
Variety, Folk and International

Since 1990. See other dates. **Days:** 1. **Site:** indoor. Cathedral of St. John the Divine, 1047 Amsterdam Avenue at 112th Street. **Admission:** free. **Secondary genre[s]:** TR&B, BGOS, MFOL, OTHR **Acts:** national acts, local acts. **Sample day's lineup:** Brooklyn Philharmonic, Lukas Foss, Eugene Fodor, Odetta, Terry Cook, others. **Contact:** Cathedral of St. John the Divine, 1047 Amsterdam Avenue, New York, NY 10025, 212-662-2133/316-7540.

## FIRST NIGHT NEW YORK, Manhattan, NYC
Late Dec.
Variety, Folk and International

"Midtown's biggest New Year's Eve party for the whole family." -- Advertisement. **Days:** 1. **Hours per day:** 13. **Site:** indoor. multiple locations, midtown. **Admission:** paid. **Daily entry:** under $10, $10 to $24, **Discounts:** advance purchase discounts, **Secondary genre[s]:** TJAZ, TR&B, MC&W, ZYDC, JWSH, MLAT, AFRC, BRZL, OTHR. **Acts:** national acts, regional acts, local acts. **Sample day's lineup:** Loup Garou, Wayne Gorbea's Salsa Picante, Johnny Allen, Jeff Lubin Band, West End Klezmorim, Kimati Dinizulu and His Kotoko Society, The Tango Project, Tribal Legacy, Tommy Joe White Band, Beth Ann Clayton, Vince Giordano and The Nighthawks, Sean Grissom, Rachel Hennelly, Orchestra of St. Luke's, The Hi-Tops, String of Pearls, others. **Contact:** First Night New York, c/o Grand Central Partnership, 6 East 43rd Street, New York, NY, 212-745-8360 **or:** Bruce Cohen Group, 160 West 71st Street, New York, NY 10023, 212-580-9895.

# R. I. P., M. I. A. Festival Listings

The following festivals are either confirmed or suspected to be discontinued (i.e., R. I. P.); or have **Caveat** not responded to various information requests (i.e., M. I. A.). Since all festivals are subject to last-minute changes or reinstatement, however, FESTPRESS is not responsible for any festival listing information that follows. Readers are encouraged to notify FESTPRESS of any status changes they uncover.

WKCR-FM 88.9 LOFT JAZZ FESTIVAL, Manhattan, NYC
> Middle Jan.
> Alternative Jazz

**Help!** One time only? **Days:** 2. **Site:** indoor. Altschul Auditorium, Columbia University, 118th Street and Amsterdam Avenue. **Admission:** paid. **Daily entry:** $10 to $24, **Discounts:** multiple event or day passes, **Acts:** national acts, regional acts, local acts. **Sample day's lineup:** Hamiett Bluiett Trio, Tom Bruno and Rick DellaRatta. **Contact:** WKCR-FM 88.9 Loft Jazz Festival, 595 West 114th Street, New York, NY 10027, 212-854-5223/853-7708.

LANDERPALOOZA, Manhattan, NYC
> Middle Feb.
> Alternative and College Rock

Since 1994. Benefits New York City Police Foundation Goods-for-Guns Program. See other dates and sites. **Help!** One time only? **Days:** 1. **Site:** indoor. Webster Hall, 125 East 11th Street. **Admission:** paid. **Acts:** national acts. **Sample day's lineup:** Gin Blossoms, US3, Candelbox. **Contact:** WHTZ-FM 100.3, 767 3rd Avenue, New York, NY, 212-239-2300.

BLACK HISTORY MONTH CELEBRATION, Manhattan, NYC
> Late Feb.
> African American

See other dates. **Help!** Still ongoing? **Days:** 3. **Hours per day:** 4. **Site:** indoor. American Museum of Natural History, Central Park West at 79th Street. **Admission:** paid. **Daily entry:** under $10, **Discounts: Secondary genre[s]:** MJAZ, AFRC, **Acts:** regional acts, local acts. **Sample series lineup:** Day One: Mickey D. and Friends; **Contact:** Black History Month Celebration, American Museum of Natural History, C. P. W. at 79th Street, New York, NY, 212-769-5310.

TRIBUTES TO BOB MARLEY, Queens, NYC
> Late Feb.
> Reggae, Ska and Caribbean

Afternoon, evening programs. **Help!** One time only? **Days:** 1. **Hours per day:** 16. **Site:** indoor. Trafalgar Square, 91-12 144th Place, Jamaica. **Admission:** paid. **Daily entry:** under $10, $10 to $24, $25 to $49, **Discounts:** advance purchase discounts, **Secondary genre[s]:** MJAZ, **Acts:** national acts, local acts. **Sample day's lineup:** Ziggy Marley and The Melody Makers, Calypso Rose, Worl-A-Girl, Simone Gordon, others. **Contact:** Tributes to Bob Marley, Trafalgar Square, 91-12 144th Place, Jamaica, NY, 718-209-2032.

## Sista Ax: The B. R. C. Celebrates Women's Month, Manhattan, NYC
Early Mar. to Late Mar.

### Alternative and College Rock

Since 1994. One time only. See other dates and sites. **Days:** 4. **Site:** indoor. The Fez, 380 Lafayette Street at Great Jones Street. **Admission:** paid. **Daily entry:** under $10, $10 to $24, **Discounts:** advance purchase discounts, other discounts **Secondary genre[s]:** TR&B, **Acts:** regional acts, local acts. **Sample day's lineup:** Faith, Amafujo and Mood Swing, Debbe Cole, others. **Audio merchandise:** "Black Rock Coalition: The History of Our Future"; "Black Rock Coalition: Blacker Than That" (both on Ryko). **Contact:** Black Rock Coalition, Inc., P. O. Box 1054 Cooper Station, New York, NY 10279, 212-713-5097.

## Dewar's Bagpipe Festival, Manhattan, NYC
Middle Mar.
Alternative Jazz

Since 1992. Discontinued in 1994. **Days:** 3. **Hours per day:** 5. **Site:** indoor. Knitting Factory, 74 Leonard Street, between Broadway and Church Street. **Admission:** paid. **Secondary genre[s]:** ARCK, SCOT, **Acts:** national acts, regional acts, local acts. **Sample day's lineup:** Battlefied Band, Samm Bennett, Lindsey Hroner Quartet, Andy Haus/Judy McSarely Duo. **Audio merchandise:** "Dewar's Bagpipe Festival: Live at The Knitting Factory" (Knitting Factory Works), plus entire Knitting Factory Works catalog. **Other merchandise:** Knitting Music by Michael Dorf (Knitting Factory Works). **Contact:** Knitting Factory, 47 East Houston Street, New York, NY 10012, 212-219-3055/3006.

## Gospel Caravan, Manhattan, NYC
Middle Mar.
Black Gospel

**Help!** One time only? **Days:** 1. **Site:** indoor. Metropolitan Community United Methodist Church, 1975 Madison Avenue at 126th Street, Harlem. **Admission:** paid. **Daily entry:** $10 to $24, **Acts:** local acts. **Sample day's lineup:** The Buddies of the 60's, Bishop William Robinson, Marenda Perry, Melodious Voices, George E. Canton Jr., Johnny M. Brown, Ouida W. Harding, others. **Contact:** Metropolitan Community United Methodist Church, 1975 Madison Avenue, New York, NY, 212-289-6157.

## New Jewish Music Nights, Manhattan, NYC
Late Mar. to Early Apr.
Jewish

Since 1994. Formerly the Radical New Jewish Culture Festival at the Knitting Factory? **Help!** One time only? **Days:** 4. **Site:** indoor. CB's Gallery, 313 Bowery. **Admission:** paid. **Secondary genre[s]:** AJAZ, ARCK, AVNT, **Acts:** national acts, regional acts, local acts. **Sample day's lineup:** Mark Degliantoni, Arto Lindsay, The Amazing Johnny Polansky, Sim Cain and Sebastian Steinberg, Duo Masada with John Zorn and Marc Ribot. **Contact:** New Jewish Music Nights, c/o CB's Gallery, 313 Bowery, New York, NY, 212-677-0455.

## Radical New Jewish Culture Festival, Manhattan, NYC
Early Apr. to Middle Apr.
Jewish

Since 1992. Discontinued in 1994. **Help!** Moved to CB's Gallery? **Days:** 5. **Hours per day:** 5. **Site:** indoor. Knitting Factory, 74 Leonard Street, between Broadway and Church Street. **Admission:** paid. **Secondary genre[s]:** AJAZ, ARCK, HRCK, AVNT, OTHR **Acts:** national acts, local acts. **Sample day's lineup:** Marc Ribot's Shrek, Annie Gosfield, Steve Drury, Evan Lurie. **Audio merchandise:** entire Knitting Factory Works catalog, including numerous festival recordings and compilations. **Other merchandise:** Knitting Music by Michael Dorf (Knitting Factory Works). **Contact:** Knitting Factory, 47 East Houston Street, New York, NY 10012, 212-219-3055/3006.

## NEW YORK/PHILLY GOSPEL CARAVAN, Manhattan, NYC
Early Apr. to Middle Apr.
Black Gospel

Discontinued in 1993. See other dates and sites. **Days:** 2. **Site:** indoor. Symphony Space, 2537 Broadway at 95th Street. **Admission:** paid. **Daily entry:** $10 to $24, **Discounts:** other discounts **Acts:** national acts, regional acts, local acts. **Sample day's lineup:** The Dixie Hummingbirds, The Swan Silvertones, McCullough's Sons of Thunder, Angelic Gospel Singers. **Audio merchandise:** entire W. M. I. catalog. **Contact:** World Music Institute, 49 West 27th Street, Suite 810, New York, NY 10001, 212-545-7536.

## CHEESEFEST, Manhattan, NYC
Middle Apr.
Hard Rock and Heavy Metal

Since 1994. "Free cheese." -- Flyer. See other dates. **Help!** One time only? **Days:** 1. **Hours per day:** 8. **Site:** indoor. Gas Station, 26 Avenue B. **Admission:** paid. **Daily entry:** under $10, **Secondary genre[s]:** ARCK, **Acts:** local acts. **Sample day's lineup:** Thrust, Ottis, Ultra Bide, Wighat, Wives, Home, Molotov Cocktail, Disease, Ff, Rats of Unusual Size. **Contact:** Cheesefest, 150 East 2nd Street, #1A, New York, NY 10009, 212-592-3686.

## EARTH DAY WALK AND ROLL, Manhattan, NYC
Middle Apr.
Modern Jazz

**Help!** One time only? **Days:** 1. **Hours per day:** 3. **Site:** outdoor. Austin Tobin Plaza, World Trade Center, Vesey and Liberty Streets. **Admission:** free. **Acts:** national acts. **Sample day's lineup:** Larry Coryell, Ray baretto, Dave Samuels. **Contact:** Earth Day Walk and Roll, 1 World Trade Center, 35 West, New York, NY 10048, 212-432-0900.

## HEARTS AND VOICES SONGWRITERS EVENING, Manhattan, NYC
Middle Apr.
Cabaret

Since 1993. **Help!** One time only? **Days:** 1. **Site:** indoor. The Ballroom, 253 West 28th Street. **Admission:** paid. **Daily entry:** $10 to $24, $25 to $49, **Acts:** regional acts, local acts. **Sample day's lineup:** John Bucchino, Craig Carnelia, David Friedman, Julie Gold, Jake Holmes, Phillip Namanworth, others. **Contact:** Hearts and Voices, 150 West 80th Street, #7D, New York, NY 10024, 212-799-4276/244-3005.

## SPRING TIME ROCK 'N ROLL FUNDRAISER SHOW, Queens, NYC
Late Apr.
A Cappella and Doo Wop

Benefits 104th Precinct Youth Council. **Help!** One time only? **Days:** 1. **Site:** indoor. Christ the King High School, 68-02 Metropolitan Avenue, Middle Village. **Admission:** paid. **Daily entry:** $25 to $49, **Secondary genre[s]:** CRCK, **Acts:** national acts, regional acts, local acts. **Sample day's lineup:** Shirely Alston Reeves, The Drifters, The Coasters, Fred Paris and the Five Satins, Bruno and The Volkswagens. **Contact:** Spring Time Rock 'N Roll Fundraiser Show, Christ the King High School, 68-02 Metropolitan Avenue, Queens, NY, 718-326-7536/894-6976.

WORLD MUSIC FESTIVAL, Brooklyn, NYC
Early May
Variety, Folk and International

Since 1993. One time only in 1993; 100 Years of Jazz and Blues one time only in 1992. However, there's usually some event of similar quantity/quality around that time, so call ahead. See other dates. **Days:** 1. **Site:** indoor. Brooklyn Academy of Music Opera House, 30 Lafayette Avenue. **Admission:** paid. **Daily entry:** under $10, $10 to $24, **Discounts: Secondary genre[s]:** MLAT, AFRC, **Acts:** national acts, . **Sample day's lineup:** Kanda Bongo Man, Milton Cardona, Les Miserables Brass Band. **Contact:** 651/Kings Majestic Corporation, 651 Fulton Street, Brooklyn, NY 11217, 718-636-4100.

MARLBORO MUSIC FESTIVAL, Manhattan, NYC
Early May to Late May
Modern Country

Discontinued in 1992. **Days:** 12. **Site:** indoor. 12 locations. **Admission:** paid. **Daily entry:** under $10, $10 to $24, $25 to $49, **Secondary genre[s]:** AC&W, BLGS, **Acts:** national acts. **Sample day's lineup:** Guy Clark, Joe Ely, Lyle Lovett, John Hiatt. **Contact:** Marlboro Music Festival,, 800-688-6117/637-6560.

MOTHER'S DAY SOCA SUNSPLASH, Brooklyn, NYC
Early May
Reggae, Ska and Caribbean

Since 1992. See other dates. **Help!** One time only? **Days:** 1. **Site:** indoor. Brooklyn Academy of Music Opera House, 30 Lafayette Avenue. **Admission:** paid. **Daily entry:** $25 to $49, **Acts:** national acts, regional acts, local acts. **Sample day's lineup:** Calypso Rose, King Swallow, Gryner, Crazy, Princess Natasha, Chalkdust, Ronnie McIntosh, Iwer George, Poser, Soca Kid, Francine, Nap Hepburn, Trini Devo, Trevoe Eastman, United Garifuna of Belize, The Rebels. **Contact:** Brooklyn Academy of Music, 30 Lafayette Street, Brooklyn, NY 11217, 718-636-4100.

COUNTRY TAKES MANHATTAN, Manhattan, NYC
Middle May to Late May
Modern Country

Since 1994. One time only. **Days:** 8. **Site:** indoor. multiple locations. **Admission:** paid. **Daily entry:** $10 to $24, $25 to $49, **Secondary genre[s]:** AC&W, **Acts:** national acts, local acts. **Sample day's lineup:** Mary Chapin Carpenter, Rodney Crowell, Lucinda Williams, Joe Ely. **Contact:** Radio City Music Hall Productions, 1260 Avenue of the Americas, New York, NY 10020, 212-247-4777.

BEN AND JERRY'S ONE-WORLD, ONE-HEART FESTIVAL, Manhattan, NYC
Middle May
Variety, General

Since 1993. One time only. **Days:** 1. **Hours per day:** 8. **Site:** outdoor. Central Park. **Admission:** free. **Secondary genre[s]:** CRCK, MFOL, MLAT, AFRC, RGGE, **Acts:** national acts, regional acts, . **Sample day's lineup:** The Band, Steel Pulse, Peter Blegvad, Women of The Calabash, Eddie Palmieri and His Orchestra. **Contact:** Ben and Jerry's, Route 100, Box 240, Waterbury, VT 05676, 800-BJ-FESTS.

LAMBDA GALA, Manhattan, NYC
> Late May
> Gay and Lesbian

Benefits Lambda Legal Defense and Education Fund. See other dates. **Help!** One time only? **Days:** 1. **Site:** indoor. Carnegie Hall, 57th Street at 7th Avenue. **Admission:** paid. **Daily entry:** $25 to $49, $50 and over. **Acts:** national acts. **Sample day's lineup:** Janis Ian, others. **Contact:** Lambda Gala, c/o Carnegie Hall, 881 7th Avenue, New York, NY 10019, 212-247-7800.

COUNT BASIE ORCHESTRA CONCERT AND JAZZ EXTRAVAGANZA, Manhattan, NYC
> Late May
> Modern Jazz

Since 1991. Discontinued in 1993. See other dates. **Help!** Did this event resume in 1994 as planned? **Days:** 1. **Site:** indoor. Carnegie Hall, 57th Street at 7th Avenue. **Admission:** paid. **Daily entry:** $10 to $24, $25 to $49, **Acts:** national acts, local acts. **Sample day's lineup:** Count Basie Orchestra, Tara High School Jazz Ensemble, Henry Ford Community College Jazz Ensemble, University of Minnesota at Morris Jazz Ensemble. **Contact:** Count Basie Orchestra Concert and Jazz Extravaganza, c/o Carnegie Hall, 881 7th Avenue, New York, NY 10019, 212-247-7800/239-4699.

NEW YORK INTERNATIONAL FESTIVAL OF THE ARTS, Manhattan, NYC
> Early Jun. to Late Jun.
> Variety, General

Since 1988. Discontinued in 1992. **Site:** outdoor and indoor. 55 events from 23 countries at multiple locations. **Admission:** paid. **Daily entry:** $10 to $24, **Secondary genre[s]:** MJAZ, ARCK, HRCK, ACAP, IRSH, JWSH, MLAT, AFRC, BRZL, AVNT, CBRT, **Acts:** national acts, regional acts, . **Sample day's lineup:** David Bryne, Orchestra of St. Luke's, New York Voices. **Contact:** New York International Festival of the Arts, 120 5th Avenue, 6th Floor, New York, NY 10011, 212-679-5200.

CONGAMANIA, Bronx, NYC
> Early Jun.
> Modern Latin

Since 1992. This talent contest and other concerts discontinued in favor of concert co-sponsorship with Central Park Summerstage and Celebrate Brooklyn Performing Arts Festival (see respective chapters). **Days:** 1. **Site:** outdoor. Orchard Beach. **Acts:** local acts. **Contact:** WADO-FM, 666 3rd Avenue, 17th Floor, New York, NY 10017, 212-687-9236.

FESTIVAL OF THE SUN, Manhattan, NYC
> Middle Jun.
> Brazilian and South American

**Help!** One time only? **Days:** 1. **Site:** indoor. Town Hall, 123 West 43rd Street. **Admission:** paid. **Daily entry:** $10 to $24, $25 to $49, **Acts:** regional acts, local acts. **Sample day's lineup:** Inkhay, others. **Contact:** Festival of the Sun, c/o Town Hall, 123 West 43rd Street, New York, NY 10036, 212-840-2824/1003.

HEARTS AND VOICES IN CONCERT AGAIN, Manhattan, NYC
>Middle Jun.
>Cabaret

Since 1994. **Help!** One time only? **Days:** 1. **Site:** indoor. Symphony Space, Broadway at 95th Street. **Admission:** paid. **Daily entry:** $25 to $49, $50 and over. **Acts:** national acts, regional acts, local acts. **Sample day's lineup:** Liza Minelli, Eartha Kitt with Daryl Waters, Andre DeShields with Joel Shilberman, Debra Byrd and Freida Williams, Baby Jane Dexter with Ross Patterson, Steve Hayes, Billy Stritch, B. D. Wong with Wayne Barker, others. **Contact:** Hearts and Voices, 150 West 80th Street, #7D, New York, NY 10024, 212-799-4276/888-4702.

BOB DYLAN IMITATOR AWARDS, Manhattan, NYC
>Early Jul.
>Modern Folk

Since 1983. "My fantasy is to see the real Dylan enter and lose." -- Ken Kwapis, New York Newsday. **Help!** The status of this event, or the whereabouts of its promoters? **Days:** 1. **Site:** indoor. Speakeasy, 107 McDougal Street, between Bleecker and West 3rd Streets. **Acts:** local acts. **Sample day's lineup:** David Massengill, others in 5 categories. **Other merchandise:** "It Ain't Me, Babe" (16mm documentary).. **Contact:** Bob Dylan Imitator Awards, c/o The Speakeasy, 107 McDougal Street, New York, NY, 212-598-9670.

HISPANIC WORLD'S FAIR, Manhattan, NYC
>Late Jul.
>Modern Latin

**Help!** The status of this event, or the whereabouts of its promoters? **Days:** 3. **Contact:** Hispanic World's Fair,, 212-923-2020/244-3100.

Z100 PERFECT TEN BIRTHDAY BASH, Manhattan, NYC
>Late Jul.
>Alternative and College Rock

Since 1994. Benefit. See other dates and sites. **Help!** One time only? **Days:** 1. **Site:** indoor. Madison Square Garden. **Admission:** paid. **Daily entry:** $25 to $49, **Secondary genre[s]:** MRCK, **Acts:** national acts, . **Sample day's lineup:** Proclaimers, Terence Trent D'Arby, 10,000 Maniacs, Duran Duran, Bon Jovi. **Contact:** WHTZ-FM 100.3, 767 3rd Avenue, New York, NY, 212-239-2300.

THUNDERBIRD AMERICAN INDIAN POW-WOW, Queens, NYC
>Late Jul.
>Native American

**Days:** 2. **Hours per day:** 6. **Site:** outdoor. Queens County Farm Museum, Little Neck Parkway, Floral Park. **Admission:** paid. **Daily entry:** under $10, **Discounts: Acts:** regional acts, local acts. **Sample day's lineup:** Thunderbird American Indian Dancers, others. **Contact:** Flushing Council on Culture and The Arts at Town Hall, 137-35 Northern Boulevard, Flushing, NY 11354, 718-463-7700/587-9633.

QUEENS JAZZ FESTIVAL, Queens, NYC
>Early Aug.
>Modern Jazz

Discontinued in favor of weekly concert series of national, regional, local acts, Jazz Live from Flushing Town Hall. **Days:** 1. **Site:** outdoor. Cunningham Park, 196th Street and Union Turnpike, Fresh Meadows. **Admission:** free. **Secondary genre[s]:** TJAZ, MLAT, **Acts:** national acts, . **Sample day's lineup:** Doc Cheatham, Jimmy Heath, Bobby Sanabria and Ascension. **Contact:** Flushing Council on Culture and The Arts at Town Hall, 137-35 Northern Boulevard, Flushing, NY 11354, 718-463-7700.

EL FIESTON DE NUEVA YORK EN BROADWAY, Manhattan, NYC
      Early Sep.
      Modern Latin

Since 1992. "A staggering array of Latin-Caribbean music, dance and theater on four outdoor stages." -- Village Voice. One time only. **Days:** 1. **Hours per day:** 7. **Site:** outdoor. Broadway, from 42nd to 34th Streets. **Admission:** free. **Secondary genre[s]:** RGGE, **Acts:** national acts, regional acts, local acts. **Sample day's lineup:** Joese Felicano, Willie Colon, Oscar D'Leon, El General, Wilfrido Vargas, Lisa M, Ray Barretto, Luis Enrique, Johnny Ventura, Andy Montanez, many others. **Contact:** WXTV, 605 3rd Avenue, 12th Floor, New York, NY 10158, 212-455-5400.

MELT IN, Brooklyn, NYC
      Early Sep.
      Alternative and College Rock

Since 1994. **Help!** One time only? **Days:** 1. **Hours per day:** 6. **Site:** outdoor. Prospect Park bandshell, 9th Street and Prospect Park West. **Admission:** free. **Secondary genre[s]:** HRCK, **Acts:** local acts. **Sample day's lineup:** Rock Minority, Urban Nature, Gamma Rays, Spitball, Delta Nine, Itchy Trigger Finger, Crossforce. **Contact:** Fund for the Borough of Brooklyn, 30 Flatbush Avenue, Brooklyn, NY 11217, 718-855-7882 x20.

MEXICAN INDEPENDENCE DAY CONCERT, Manhattan, NYC
      Middle Sep.
      Traditional Latin

**Help!** One time only? **Days:** 1. **Site:** indoor. Town Hall, 123 West 43rd Street. **Admission:** paid. **Daily entry:** $10 to $24, $25 to $49, **Acts:** national acts, regional acts, . **Sample day's lineup:** Maria Elena Leal, Ofelia Medina, others. **Contact:** Mexican Independence Day Concert, c/o Town Hall, 123 West 43rd Street, New York, NY 10036, 212-840-2824/1003.

PICKLE FEST, Manhattan, NYC
      Middle Sep. to Early Oct.
      Hard Rock and Heavy Metal

Since 1994. "Free pickles and musical abuse." -- Flyer. See other dates. **Help!** One time only? **Days:** 2. **Hours per day:** 8. **Site:** indoor. Gas Station, 26 Avenue B. **Admission:** paid. **Daily entry:** under $10, **Secondary genre[s]:** ARCK, **Acts:** local acts. **Sample day's lineup:** Iron Prostate, Sea Monkeys, Wives, Thrust, Molotov Cocktail, Hammerbrain, Colored Greens, E-Trance, Tub, Hot Corn Girls. **Contact:** Pickle Fest, 150 East 2nd Street, #1A, New York, NY 10009, 212-979-6922/592-3686.

D. M. C./B. M. I. INTERNATIONAL DJ MIXING CHAMPIONSHIPS, Manhattan, NYC
      Late Sep.
      Rap

Finals of nation compeition, culminating run-offs in Los Angeles, Miami, New York. Finalist goes on to international finals in London, Early Nov. **Help!** Still ongoing? **Days:** 1. **Site:** indoor. Home Base. **Acts:** local acts. **Sample day's lineup:** Q-Bert, DJ Mike, DJ Apollo, others. **Contact:** D. M. C./B. M. I. International DJ Mixing Championships, c/o Broadcast Music, Inc., 320 West 57th Street, New York, NY 10019, 212-586-2000.

EL DIARIO FESTIVAL MUSICAL, Manhattan, NYC
　　　Early Oct.
　　　Modern Latin

**Help!** One time only? **Days:** 1. **Site:** indoor. The Paramount, Madison Square Garden, 7th Avenue at 32nd Street. **Admission:** paid. **Daily entry:** $25 to $49, **Secondary genre[s]:** TLAT, **Acts:** national acts. **Sample day's lineup:** Vincente Fernandez, Alejandro Fernandez, Jessica Christina. **Contact:** El Diario Festival Musicale, El Diario La Prensa, 143 Varick Street, New York, NY, 212-807-4600/465-MSG1.


INTERNATIONAL JAZZ FESTIVAL, Manhattan, NYC
　　　Middle Oct.
　　　Modern Jazz

Since 1992. One time only. **Days:** 1. **Site:** indoor. Village Gate, 160 Bleecker Street. **Admission:** paid. **Daily entry:** $10 to $24, **Acts:** national acts, local acts. **Sample day's lineup:** Sadao Wantanabe, Yoshiaki Masuo Quintet, New Sound Workshop. **Contact:** International Jazz Festival, c/o Village Gate, 160 Bleecker Street, New York, NY, 212-475-5120.


HUDSON HARVEST FESTIVAL, Manhattan, NYC
　　　Middle Oct.
　　　Modern Country

**Help!** One time only? **Days:** 1. **Hours per day:** 9. **Site:** outdoor. 8th Avenue, Bleecker to 14th Streets. **Admission:** free. **Secondary genre[s]:** AC&W, **Acts:** local acts. **Sample day's lineup:** Mike Heaphy and Infinite Heart, The Luce Amen Band, Peachfish Pie, High Sierra, Stonewall. **Contact:** Hudson Harvest Festival, c/o WYNY-FM 103.5, 1120 6th Avenue, New York, NY, 212-704-3900.


U. G. H. A.'s ACAPPELLA COMES TO BROADWAY, Manhattan, NYC
　　　Late Oct.
　　　A Cappella and Doo Wop

Since 1993. Discontinued in 1994. **Days:** 1. **Site:** indoor. Symphony Space, 2537 Broadway at 95th Street. **Admission:** paid. **Daily entry:** $10 to $24, **Discounts:** other discounts **Secondary genre[s]:** CRCK, **Acts:** regional acts, local acts. **Sample day's lineup:** Ecstacies, Elevations, Heart's Desire, Magic Moments, Sheps, The Nutmegs with Harold Jaynes. **Contact:** United in Group Harmony Association, P. O. Box 185, Clifton, NJ 07011, 201-470-UGHA/365-0049.


TANQUERAY ROCKS TALENT CONTEST, Manhattan, NYC
　　　Late Oct.
　　　Alternative and College Rock

Since 1990. Finals of a nation-wide talent contest. Discontinued in 1994. **Days:** 1. **Site:** indoor. The Grand, 76 East 13th Street. **Secondary genre[s]:** MRCK, **Acts:** regional acts, local acts. **Sample day's lineup:** Boys Named Sue, Surreal McCoys, Natural Causes, On, Valentine Smith. **Contact:** Bragman Nyman Cafarelli, 9171 Wilshire Boulevard, Penthouse Suite, Beverly Hills, CA 90210-5530, 310-274-7800.

## BENSON AND HEDGES BLUES FESTIVAL, Manhattan, NYC
### Early Nov.
### Modern R&B

Since 1990. Discontinued in New York City in 1992, alas, but rolled out across the country as Benson and Hedges Blues and Rhythm Festivals, often in conjunction with leading area festivals. See other dates and sites. **Days:** 1. **Site:** indoor. The Paramount, Madison Square Garden, 7th Avenue at 32nd Street. **Admission:** paid. **Daily entry:** $25 to $49, **Acts:** national acts, . **Sample day's lineup:** Freddie Jackson, Meli'sa Morgan, Najee, Cece Penniston. **Contact:** Benson and Hedges Blues and Rhythm Festival, P. O. Box 1169 Ansonia Station, New York, NY 10023, 800-BLUES-91 **or:** Festival Productions, Inc., 311 West 74th Street, New York, NY 10023, 212-496-9000. .

## BRAZILIAN LATIN JAZZ FESTIVAL, Manhattan, NYC
### Middle Nov.
### Modern Jazz

Also programmed a Kwaanza [sic] Jazz Fest with Roy Ayers, Spirit Ensemble, Double Trouble, Hymie Riviera's New Wave Bebop Jazz Ensemble at Indigo Blues, 221 West 46th Street, Late Dec. **Help!** One time only? **Days:** 1. **Site:** indoor. BMCC/CUNY TriBeCa Performing Arts Center, 199 Chambers Street. **Admission:** paid. **Daily entry:** $25 to $49, $50 and over. **Secondary genre[s]:** MLAT, BRZL, **Acts:** national acts, local acts. **Sample day's lineup:** Tania Maria and The Nouvelle Vogue, Jerry Gonzalez and The Fort Apache Band, New Wave BeBop, Marvin Neal. **Contact:** Brazilian Latin Jazz Festival, BMCC/CUNY TriBeCa Performing Arts Center, 199 Chambers Street, New York, NY 10007, 212-346-8510/641-3337.

## SEXI CEILI, Manhattan, NYC
### Late Nov.
### Irish

Since 1992. Benefits Irish Arts Center. **Help!** One time only? **Days:** 1. **Hours per day:** 6. **Site:** indoor. Tramps, 51 West 21st Street. **Admission:** paid. **Daily entry:** $10 to $24, **Discounts:** advance purchase discounts, other discounts **Acts:** national acts, regional acts, local acts. **Sample day's lineup:** Morningstar, The Itinerants, Tony DeMarco, Kips Bay Ceili Band, Susan McKeown and The Chanting House, others. **Contact:** Irish Arts Center, 553 West 51st Street, New York, NY 10019, 212-757-3318.

## HOWARD SILVER'S HOLIDAY SHOW SPECTACULAR, Manhattan, NYC
### Early Dec.
### Classic Rock and Oldies

**Help!** One time only? **Days:** 1. **Site:** indoor. The Paramount, Madison Square Garden, 7th Avenue at 32nd Street. **Admission:** paid. **Daily entry:** $25 to $49, $50 and over. **Secondary genre[s]:** TR&B, ACAP, **Acts:** national acts. **Sample day's lineup:** Jay Black and The Americans, The Spinners, Little Anthony and The Imperials, Johnny Maestro and The Brooklyn Bridge, Gary Puckett and The Union Gap, Martha Reeves and The Vandellas, Fred Parris and The Five Satins, Harold Melvin and The Blue Notes. **Contact:** Howard Silver's Holiday Show Spectacular, c/o Madison Square Garden, 4 Pennsylvania Plaza, New York, NY, 212-465-MSG1.

## KLEZMER FESTIVAL, Manhattan, NYC
### Early Dec. to Middle Dec.
### Jewish

Since 1993. One time only. **Days:** 7. **Hours per day:** 5. **Site:** indoor. Knitting Factory, 74 Leonard Street, between Broadway and Church Street. **Admission:** paid. **Secondary genre[s]:** AJAZ, AVNT, **Acts:** national acts, regional acts, local acts. **Sample series lineup:** Day One: Kapelye, Andy Statman Band; **Audio merchandise:** entire Knitting Factory Works catalog, including numerous festival recordings and compilations. **Other merchandise:** Knitting Music by Michael Dorf (Knitting Factory Works). **Contact:** Knitting Factory, 47 East Houston Street, New York, NY 10012, 212-219-3055/3006.

### FESTIVAL OF JEWISH WRITERS, PERFORMERS AND MUSICIANS, Manhattan, NYC
Middle Dec.

Jewish

Since 1993. **Help!** One time only? **Days:** 1. **Site:** indoor. Great Hall, Cooper Union, East 8th Street. **Admission:** paid. **Daily entry:** $10 to $24, **Discounts:** advance purchase discounts, **Secondary genre[s]:** AJAZ, MFOL, **Acts:** national acts, regional acts, local acts. **Sample day's lineup:** Phranc, Elliott Sharp, G-d is My Co-Pilot, others. **Contact:** Jews for Racial and Economic Justice, 64 Fulton Street, #605, New York, NY 10038, 212-964-9210.

### HOT 97'S HOT NIGHT NEW YORK, Manhattan, NYC
Middle Dec.

Rap

"Hip-hop party of the year." -- Advertisement. **Help!** One time only? **Days:** 1. **Site:** indoor. The Paramount, Madison Square Garden, 7th Avenue at 32nd Street. **Admission:** paid. **Daily entry:** $25 to $49, **Secondary genre[s]:** MR&B, **Acts:** national acts. **Sample day's lineup:** SWV, Zhane, Onyx, Mary J. Blige, Wu-Tang Clan, K7, others. **Contact:** WQHT-FM, 1372 Broadway, 16th Floor, New York, NY 10018, 212-840-0097/465-MSG1.

### MTV SPECIAL SHOW/CONCERT PARTY, Manhattan, NYC
Middle Dec.

Alternative and College Rock

Since 1992. "Formal funky attire." -- Advertisement. **Help!** One time only? **Days:** 1. **Site:** indoor. Roseland Ballroom, 239 West 52nd Street. **Admission:** free. **Restrictions:** 6, **Secondary genre[s]:** MRCK, RAP, MR&B, **Acts:** national acts. **Sample day's lineup:** Alice in Chains, Arrested Development, Boyz II Men, Bobby Brown, Extreme, Spin Doctors, 10,000 Maniacs. **Audio merchandise:** "Yo! MTV Raps"; "MTV Uptown Unplugged"; "Club MTV Party to Go"; "Best of MTV 120 Minutes" (various labels). **Contact:** MTV, 1515 Broadway, New York, NY 10036, 212-258-8000.

### BLACK ROCK X-MAS CONCERT, Manhattan, NYC
Middle Dec.

Alternative Jazz

Since 1991. Although this particular event may have discontinued after 1992, similar B. R. C. showcases occur periodically at the same site. See other dates and sites. **Days:** 1. **Site:** indoor. Manhattan Center, 311 West 34th Street. **Admission:** paid. **Daily entry:** $10 to $24, **Discounts:** advance purchase discounts, other discounts **Secondary genre[s]:** ARCK, RAP, TR&B, **Acts:** national acts, regional acts, local acts. **Sample day's lineup:** The Crunch, Defunkt, Jean Paul Bourelly, Kelvynator, Eric Gales Band, Sonny Sharrock, D-Nice, Melvin Gibbs, Vernon Reid, Ronnie Drayton, others. **Audio merchandise:** "Black Rock Coalition: The History of Our Future"; "Black Rock Coalition: Blacker Than That" (both on Ryko). **Contact:** Black Rock Coalition, Inc., P. O. Box 1054 Cooper Station, New York, NY 10279, 212-713-5097.

### TRADITIONAL ARTS FESTIVAL, Manhattan, NYC
Middle Dec.

Variety, Folk and International

Since 1993. One time only. **Days:** 1. **Hours per day:** 12. **Site:** indoor. Hilton Hotel, Beekman Parlor, 53rd Street and Avenue of the Americas. **Admission:** paid. **Daily entry:** $10 to $24, **Discounts:** other discounts **Secondary genre[s]:** TFOL, IRSH, BRZL, RGGE, OTHR **Acts:** national acts, regional acts, local acts. **Sample day's lineup:** Boys of The Lough, Mike and Peggy Seeger, Samite of Uganda, Obo Addy and Okropong, Sophia Bilides Greek Ensemble. **Audio merchandise:** entire W. M. I. catalog. **Contact:** World Music Institute, 49 West 27th Street, Suite 810, New York, NY 10001, 212-545-7536/364-2490.

Kwanzaa, Manhattan, NYC
      Late Dec.
      African American

See other dates. **Days:** 1. **Hours per day:** 5. **Site:** indoor. American Museum of Natural History, Central Park West at 79th Street. **Admission:** paid. **Daily entry:** under $10, **Discounts: Secondary genre[s]:** AFRC, RGGE, **Acts:** regional acts, local acts. **Sample series lineup:** Spirit Ensemble, Sesame Flyers Steel Pan Orchestra, Sister Griots, Sabar Ak Ru Afriq, others. **Contact:** Kwanzaa, American Museum of Natural History, C. P. W. at 79th Street, New York, NY, 212-769-5310.

~    ~    ~

*Posin', Wigstock.*

# Varied Sites

*John Hartford, Winterhawk Bluegrass Family Festival.*

# Varied Sites Festival Listings

**Caveat**

Although the vast majority are festivals are reliable and predictable, all are subject to last-minute changes or cancellations. Accordingly, FESTPRESS is not responsible for any festival listing information that follows. Readers are well advised to contact festivals at least twice before preparing a festival vist: (a) once at least one or two months ahead of time; and (b) once more during the week of your visit for confirmation. Ask for a festival flyer or brochure to be mailed to you. Festival promoters usually are willing to comply, and the resulting literature may answer any questions you still have.

## Restrictions:

| | | | | | |
|---|---|---|---|---|---|
| • Food and drink... | 1; | • Cameras... | 6; | • Motorcycles... | 11; |
| • Alcohol... | 2; | • Audio recording... | 7; | • Re-entry... | 12; |
| • Cans... | 3; | • Video recording... | 8; | • Other restrictions... | 13. |
| • Bottles... | 4; | • Children... | 9; | | |
| • Coolers... | 5; | • Pets... | 10; | | |

## Secondary Genre[s]:

| | | | |
|---|---|---|---|
| • Variety, General... | VRGL; | • Bluegrass... | BLGS; |
| • Variety, Jazz & Blues... | VRJB; | • Modern Folk... | MFOL; |
| • Variety, Country & Bluegrass | VRCB; | • Traditional Folk... | TFOL; |
| • Variety, Folk & International | VRFI; | • Fiddle and Banjo Events... | FDDL; |
| • Modern Jazz... | MJAZ; | • Maritime... | MARI; |
| • Traditional Jazz & Ragtime... | TJAZ; | • Cajun and Zydeco... | ZYDC; |
| • Alternative Jazz... | AJAZ; | • Irish... | IRSH; |
| • Modern Rock and Pop... | MRCK; | • Jewish... | JWSH; |
| • Classic Rock and Oldies... | CRCK; | • Native American... | NATV; |
| • Alternative & College Rock | ARCK; | • Scottish... | SCOT; |
| • Hard Rock & Heavy Metal | HRCK; | • Modern Latin... | MLAT; |
| • Rap... | RAP; | • Traditional Latin... | TLAT; |
| • Modern R&B... | MR&B; | • African American... | AFRM; |
| • Blues and Traditional R&B... | TR&B; | • African... | AFRC; |
| • Acappella and Doo Wop... | ACAP; | • Brazilian & So. American... | BRZL; |
| • Modern Christian... | CHRS; | • Reggae, Ska & Caribbean... | RGGE; |
| • Black Gospel... | BGOS; | • Avant Garde & New Music... | AVNT; |
| • Southern & Bluegrass Gospel | SGOS; | • Cabaret... | CBRT; |
| • Traditional Gospel & Sings... | TGOS; | • Gay and Lesbian... | GYLS; |
| • Modern Country... | MC&W; | • Drum Corps & March. Bands | DRUM; |
| • Traditional Country... | TC&W; | • Fairs... | FAIR; |
| • Alt. Country & Rockabilly | AC&W; | • Other Genres... | OTHR. |

**Note**

Wherever "**Help!**" appears readers are invited to answer the proceeding questions and/or provide updates. New festival listings that meet the criteria of this book certainly are welcome too! Please mail any current festival information you obtain — especially flyers or brochures — to FESTPRESS, P. O. Box 147, Glen Ridge, NJ 07028. *Thanks!*

ROCK AND ROLL HALL OF FAME INDUCTION DINNER, Varied Sites, VAR
Middle Jan.
Classic Rock and Oldies

Since 1985. **Days:** 1. **Site:** indoor. varies between Los Angeles and Manhattan, NYC (Waldorf-Astoria Hotel, Park Avenue), though it's ultimately destined for Cleveland, OH in 1997. **Admission:** paid. **Daily entry:** $50 and over **Secondary genre[s]:** TR&B, BGOS, **Acts:** national acts. **Sample day's lineup:** Al Green, Melissa Etheridge, Neil Young, The Allman Brothers, others. **Contact:** Rock and Roll Hall of Fame Museum, 50 Public Square, Cleveland OH, 216-781-7625 **or:** Rock and Roll Hall of Fame Induction Foundation, 1290 6th Avenue, New York, NY 10104, 212-484-1755.

INTERNATIONAL ASSOCIATION OF JAZZ EDUCATORS CONVENTION, Varied Sites, VAR
Middle Jan.
Modern Jazz

Since 1973. Huge number of big-name showcases. Music, workshops, seminars, exhibits galore! **Days:** 4. **Site:** indoor. large hotel, center-city. **Admission:** paid. **Discounts:** other discounts. **Acts:** national acts, regional acts, local acts. **Sample lineup:** Geri Allen, April Arabian, Buddy Baker, Ignacio Berroa, Darius Brubeck, Sigi Busch, Heinz Cazdeck, The Dolphins, Marica Dunscomb, J. B. Dyas, Madeline Eastman, Eliane Elias Trio, Werner Englert, John Fedchock Big Band, Bruce Forman, Al Foster, Urbie Green, Jeff Halsey, Antionette Handy, Billy Hart, Joe Henderson Quartet, Dave Holland, Yasutoshi Inamori, Jazz Foundation Allstars, Sheila Jordan, Geoff Keezer, Ernie Krivda, Andy Laverne, Janet Lawson, David Liebman, Mike Mainieri, Bart Marantz, Dave McMurdo Big Band, T. S. Monk, Vaughn Nark, Lewis Nash, New School Allstars, Phil Nimmons, The Real Group, Marcus Roberts, John Scofield, Bob Sinicrope, Mike Smith, Stockholm Jazz Orchestra, Rick Stone, Straight Ahead, Harvie Swartz, Billy Taylor Trio, Fred Tillis, Dennis Trini, Stanley Turrentine, Joep Van Leeuwen, Bill Warfield Big Band, James Williams, Dennis Wilson, Phil Wilson, plus 25 high school and college bands.**Contact:** International Association of Jazz Educators, P. O. Box 724, Manhattan, KS 66502, 913-776-8744.

PEOPLE'S MUSIC NETWORK WINTER GATHERING, Varied Sites, VAR
Late Jan.
Variety, Folk and International

"Musicians, music lovers, promoters, and cultural organizers dedicated to social change. We believe that the strength of song fulfills our deepest need to move, inform, and transform ourselves and our communities." -- Keith Kelly, Fast Folk Musical Magazine. **Days:** 3. **Site:** indoor. school, or other modest venue. **Admission:** paid. **Daily entry:** $10 to $24, $25 to $49. **Discounts:** multiple event or day passes, **Acts:** national acts, regional acts, local acts. **Sample day's lineup:** Pete Seeger, others. **Contact:** People's Music Network, 1539 Pine Street, Philadelphia, PA 19102. **or:** People's Music Network, P. O. Box 6664, Syracuse, NY 13217-6664.

FOLK ALLIANCE CONFERENCE, Varied Sites, VAR
> Middle Feb.
> Variety, Folk and International

Since 1989. "Enriching the folk community through multicultural diversity." -- Program. Recently, there've also been regional conferences established. Call for particulars. **Days:** 4. **Site:** indoor. mid-sized hotel, center-city. **Admission:** paid. **Secondary genre[s]:** TR&B, TGOS, TC&W, BLGS, MFOL, TFOL, MARI, ZYDC, IRSH, JWSH, NATV, SCOT, TLAT, AFRC, BRZL, RGGE, OTHR. **Acts:** national acts, regional acts, local acts. **Sample day's lineup:** Convention Showcase: Fourin A Feire, Peter Keane, Ouzo Power, Garnet Rogers, Tip Splinter, Zhentian Zhang, Flor De Cana, Ani DiFranco, The New St. George, Lynn Miles, Zlatne Uste Balkan Brass Band; Club Showcases: James Durst, Nancy Morton, Pete Kennedy and Maura Boudreau, Linda Worster, Dean Stevens, Kathy Phipps and Wendy Sobel, Geoff Bartley, Ellis Paul, Bernice Lewis, Molly Bancroft, Michael Lille, Michael McNevin, Buddy Mondlock, Dar Williams, Vicky Pratt Keating, Raymond and Amy Malkoff, Jim Infantino, The Proper Ladies, Cathy Winter, The Bawdy Ladies, Gypsy Anabel, Purly Gates, The Boogaloo Swamis, Joe Cormier, Ellen Kushner, Loose Ties, Two for The Show, She's Busy, The Nields, Tinker's Wagon, Zan McLeod and Grace Griffith, Susan Werner, Joseph Parsons, Eileen McGann, Carla Sciaky, Buckwheat Zydeco; plus innumerable "guerrilla" showcases. **Contact:** The North American Folk Music and Dance Alliance, P. O. Box 5010, Chapel Hill, NC 27514, 919-962-3397.

NORTHEAST INVITATIONAL COUNTRY MUSIC AWARDS SHOW, Varied Sites, VAR
> Middle Feb.
> Modern Country

Competition of bands from throughout New England: ME, VT, NH, MA, RI, and CT. Site rotates annually from state to state. Winner goes on to national competition hosted by CMAA. Entries welcome! **Days:** 2. **Site:** indoor. **Acts:** regional acts. **Contact:** Down East Country Music Association, RR 3, Box 1845, Wells, ME 04090, 207-646-7118.

THE CONSORTIUM, Varied Sites, VAR
> Late Feb. to Middle Apr.
> Avant Garde and New Music

Since 1995. **Help!** One time only? **Days:** 7. **Site:** indoor. MA: Paine Hall, Harvard University, Cambridge. NYC: Miller Theater, Columbia University. **Admission:p:** paid. **Daily entry:** under $10. **Discounts:** student discounts, **Acts:** national acts, regional acts. **Sample day's lineup:** New Jersey Percussion Ensemble performs works of Cowell, Pollock, Chavez, Kreiger, Olan, Varese. **Contact:** The Consortium, c/o Fritz Reiner Center for Contemporary Music, 609 Dodge Hall, Columbia University, New York, NY 10027, 212-854-7799.

NEW ENGLAND FOUNDATION FOR THE ARTS JAZZ CONFERENCE, Varied Sites, VAR
> Early Jun. to Middle Jun.
> Modern Jazz

Since 1991. "Community Jazz Connections: mobilize and unite your community through jazz." -- Brochure. In 1995, coordinated with the Discover Jazz Festival, Burlington, VT (see chapter). **Help!** A sample lineup? **Days:** 4. **Hours per day:** 9. **Site:** indoor. .**Admission:** paid. **Daily entry:** $10 to $24, $25 to $49 **Discounts:** advance purchase discounts, other discounts. **Acts:** regional acts, local acts. **Contact:** New England Foundation for the Arts, 678 Massachusetts Avenue, 8th Floor, Cambridge, MA 02139, 617-492-2194.

GOSPEL MUSIC WORKSHOP OF AMERICA NATIONAL CONVENTION, Varied Sites, VAR
Early Aug. to Middle Aug.
Black Gospel

Since 1968. "Where all God's children get together...what a time!" -- Program. **Days:** 8. **Site:** indoor. large hotel/convention center, center-city. **Admission:** paid. **Acts:** national acts, regional acts, local acts. **Sample day's lineup:** Betty Griffin-Keller, Christiannaires, Oscar Hayes and A. L. F., Rev. John P. Kee, N. L. C. C., Rev. James Moore, Williams Brothers, DFW Mass Choir, K. Dobbins and Ressurection, Hezekiah Walker and The Love Fellowship Crusade Choir, Yolanda Adams, Kelly Williams with Witness, D. J. Rogers, Doug Miller, Jessy Dixon, Albertina Walker, Rev, Timothy Wright, Ben Tankard, Rev. Kenneth Moales, Voices of Binghamton, New Jerusalem, Al Hobbs and The Indy Mass Choir, Trinity C. O. G. I. C., Robert Turner and Silver Hearts, Norman Hutchins, Kinnection, Debbie and Angie, Herman Harris, many others. **Audio merchandise:** numerous live recordings of the G. M. W. A. Mass Choir (Benson, Savoy). **Contact:** Gospel Music Workshop of America, 3908 West Warren Avenue, Detroit, MI 48208, 313-898-2340.

INTERNATIONAL DUKE ELLINGTON CONFERENCE, Varied Sites, VAR
Middle Aug.
Modern Jazz

Since 1983. **Days:** 5. **Site:** indoor. moderate-sized hotel in center-city. **Admission:** paid. **Daily entry:** $10 to $24, $25 to $49, $50 and over. **Secondary genre[s]:** TJAZ, **Acts:** national acts, regional acts. **Sample lineup:** Dick Hyman, Kenny Burrell, Rufus Reid, Louis Belleson, Barbara Lea, Ellis Larkins, Haywood Henry Quartet, Brooks Kerr, others. **Contact:** The Duke Ellington Society, Inc., P. O. Box 253 JAF Station, New York, NY 10016-0253, 800-988-7473/556-3865.

DRUM CORPS INTERNATIONAL WORLD CHAMPIONSHIPS, Varied Sites, VAR
Middle Aug.
Drum Corps and Marching Bands

Since 1971. **Help!** A sample lineup? **Days:** 5. **Site:** outdoor. Big stadium, center-city. **Acts:** regional acts, local acts. **Contact:** Drum Corps International, P. O. Box 548, Lombard, IL 60148, 708-495-9866.

NATIONAL BAPTIST CONVENTION OF AMERICA, Varied Sites, VAR
Early Sep. to Middle Sep.
Black Gospel

Needless to say, gospel music abounds wherever the convention touches down -- both in the convention program, and from area churches outdoing themselves as peripheral musical hosts. **Days:** 7. **Site:** indoor. Multiple locations, typically at city's largest convention center. **Acts:** national acts, regional acts, local acts. **Sample day's lineup:** Bahamas National Choir, many others. **Contact:** National Baptist Convention U. S. A., Inc., 1700 Baptist World Center Drive, Nashville, TN 615-228-6292.

NEW ENGLAND SACRED HARP SINGING CONVENTION, Varied Sites, VAR
Early Oct.
Traditional Gospel and Sings

Since 1974. "Sacred Harp Singing is perhaps the greatest traditional American choral music. This hearty New England sound of beautiful modal melodies, open harmonies and rhythmic, four-part "fugue-ing tunes" evolved in the 18th century as a method for teaching singers in churches without organs or other instruments...Come listen and sing!" -- Vermont News Guide. **Days:** 2. **Hours per day:** 6. **Site:** indoor. rotates annually: Burlington, VT (1995, 1998), Wellesley, MA (1996), and Middletown, CT (1997). **Admission:** free. **Restrictions:** 2. **Acts:** local acts. **Contact:** New England Sacred Harp Singing Convention, 23 Montvert Road, Middletown, VT, 802-426-3210 **or:** Norumbega Harmony, 365 Park Street, North Reading, MA 01864, 508-664-4246.

CLEARWATER'S PUMPKIN SAIL, Varied Sites, VAR
> Early Oct. to Middle Oct.
> Modern Folk

Since 1971. **Days:** 14. **Site:** outdoor. Multiple locations along Hudson River, from Albany to New York City. **Discounts:** multiple event or day passes, advance purchase discounts, **Secondary genre[s]:** TFOL, MARI, **Acts:** national acts, regional acts, local acts. **Sample day's lineup:** Cathy Winter, Margo Hennebach, Kathy and Bob Zentz, Pete Seeger, Clearwater Sloop Singers. **Contact:** Hudson Sloop Clearwater, Inc., 112 Market Street, Poughkeepsie, NY 12601, 914-454-7673.

NEW MUSIC ACROSS AMERICA, Varied Sites, VAR
> Early Oct.
> Avant Garde and New Music

Since 1983. Begun in Manhattan's The Kitchen, it has evolved into a large avant-garde showcase at different sites each year -- up to 18 cities simultaneously. Coordinates with existing institutions, festivals. **Days:** 3. **Site:** indoor. Multiple locations. **Admission:** free and paid. **Secondary genre[s]:** AJAZ, ARCK, AC&W, MLAT, AFRC, BRZL, OTHR **Acts:** national acts, regional acts, local acts. **Sample day's lineup:** La Monte Young, Lawrence Morris, The Horseflies, Cachao and Son Primero, Tiye Giraud, Sussan Deihim with Richard Horowitz, Theoung Son Group, Aster Aweke, The Ordinaires, Ned Rothenberg and Paul Dresher, Bobby Previte, World Saxophone Quartet, The Butthole Surfers, Gary Lucas, Geri Allen, Club Foot Orchestra, Frederic Rzewski, others. **Contact:** New Music Alliance, 508 Woodland Terrance, Philadelphia, PA 19104, 215-382-2521.

AMERICAN BANJO FRATERNITY'S FALL RALLY, Varied Sites, VAR
> Middle Oct. to Late Oct.
> Traditional Folk

Small gathering of "5-string" devotees. Likes of Tony Trischka have been past participants in "Special Programs." Fall sites vary (1994: Binghamton, NY; 1995: Punxatawney, PA). Spring Rallies, however, Memorial Day weekend have remained constant at Gettysburg, PA. **Days:** 3. **Secondary genre[s]:** TC&W, BLGS, **Acts:** national acts, regional acts, local acts. **Sample day's lineup:** Tony Trischka, Roger Sprung, William Ball, Clarke Buehling, Peter LeBau, Drew Frech, Geoff Freed, others. **Contact:** American Banjo Fraternity, 636 Pelis Road, Newark, NJ 14513, 315-331-6717.

~      ~      ~

# Index

*Louise Taylor, week preceeding Left Bank Cafe Country Blues Festival.*

# Festival Names
# in Chronological Order

## January

Lou Rawls Parade of Stars, Manhattan, NYC, Early Jan.
KISS 95.7 Anniversary Birthday Jam, Hartford, CT, Early Jan.
Ralph Page Legacy Weekend, Durham, NH, Early Jan.
Reggaefests, New Haven, CT, Early Jan.
Sugarloaf Ski-A-Palooza/College Weeks, Kingfield, ME, Early Jan. to Middle Jan.
Gruppen: Chamber Music for the 21st Century, Manhattan, NYC, Early Jan. to Middle Jan.
Rock and Roll Hall of Fame Induction Dinner, Varied Sites, VAR, Middle Jan.
Great Beer and Music Festival, Manhattan, NYC, Middle Jan.
International Association of Jazz Educators Convention, Varied Sites, VAR, Middle Jan.
Park Slope Native American Dance Festival, Brooklyn, NYC, Middle Jan.
CMAC's A Joyful Noise, Cambridge, MA, Middle Jan.
Songstreet Festival of Funny Songwriters, Somerville, MA, Middle Jan.
Papsaquoho Pow-Wow, Braintree, MA, Middle Jan.
Focus!, Manhattan, NYC, Middle Jan. to Late Jan.
Drama League's Black-Tie Benefit, Manhattan, NYC, Late Jan.
University of Vermont Lane Series/49th Parallel Music Festival, Burlington, VT, Late Jan.
Winter Boogie, Monticello, NY, Late Jan.
Thunderbird American Indian Dancers Pow Wow and Dance Concert, Manhattan, NYC, Late Jan. to Early Feb.
New Women's Voices, Cambridge, MA, Late Jan.
People's Music Network Winter Gathering, Varied Sites, VAR, Late Jan.
Newport Winter Festival, Newport, RI, Late Jan. to Early Feb.
Boston Blues Festival, Allston, MA, Late Jan. to Late Feb.
Fast Folk Revue, Manhattan, NYC, Late Jan.
Hot 97's Old School Throwdown, Manhattan, NYC, Late Jan.
Old Songs Sampler Concert, Guilderland, NY, Late Jan.

## February

Black History Month, Boston, MA, Early Feb. to Late Feb.
Seacoast African-American Heritage Festival, Portsmouth, NH, Early Feb. to Late Feb.
Winter Folk Music Weekend, Saugerties, NY, Early Feb.
Anthony Spinazzola Gala Festival of Food and Wine, Boston, MA, Early Feb.
Songstreet Folk and Bluegrass Fest, Cambridge, MA, Early Feb.
Gospel Celebration!, Brooklyn, NYC, Early Feb.
Seacoast Music Awards, Portsmouth, NH, Early Feb.
Celebrations and Expressions of Our African American Heritage, Hempstead, NY, Early Feb.
Bob Marley Day, Manhattan, NYC, Early Feb.
Women in Cabaret, Manhattan, NYC, Early Feb. to Late Feb.
Pride of Maine Fiddling Festival, Caribou, ME, Early Feb.
Northeast Indoor Blue Grass Festival, Boxborough, MA, Early Feb. to Middle Feb.
U. G. H. A. Black History Month Celebration, Manhattan, NYC, Middle Feb.
Pride of Maine Fiddling Festival, Machias, ME, Middle Feb.

Folk Song Society of Greater Boston's Member's Concert, Watertown, MA, Middle Feb.
Gospel Festival, Hartford, CT, Middle Feb.
Concierto Del Amor, Manhattan, NYC, Middle Feb.
Dance Flurry, Guilderland, NY, Middle Feb.
Boston Festival:  A Carnival of Cultures, Boston, MA, Middle Feb. to Late Feb.
Festival of 20th Century Music, Manhattan, NYC, Middle Feb. to Late Feb.
Greater Hartford Festival of Jazz Fundraiser, Hartford, CT, Middle Feb.
Jazz and Poetry Marathon, Manhattan, NYC, Middle Feb.
Folk Alliance Conference, Varied Sites, VAR, Middle Feb.
Cajun and Zydeco Mardi Gras Ball, Cranston, RI, Middle Feb.
Northeast Invitational Country Music Awards Show, Varied Sites, VAR, Middle Feb.
98.7 KISS-FM Gospel Celebration, Manhattan, NYC, Middle Feb.
Mardi Gras Carnaval, Manhattan, NYC, Middle Feb.
Smalls Winter Festival, Manhattan, NYC, Middle Feb.
Brazilian Festival of the Arts, Somerville, MA, Middle Feb.
Jazz Expos, New Haven, CT, Late Feb.
Electronic Music at Stony Brook, Stony Brook, NY, Late Feb.
Evening In Celebration of Black History Month, Brooklyn, NYC, Late Feb.
Music from Japan Festival, Manhattan, NYC, Late Feb.
The Consortium, Varied Sites, VAR, Late Feb. to Middle Apr.
Mardi Gras Celebration, Woonsocket, RI, Late Feb.
Lyrics and Lyricists/Boys Night Out, Manhattan, NYC, Late Feb.
Mountain Dulcimer Music Festival, Albany, NY, Late Feb.
Tropical Carnival/Carnival Fete and Masquerade Jump-Up, Brooklyn, NYC, Late Feb.
Multicultural Festival, Roxbury, MA, Late Feb.
Carnaval Del Merengue, Manhattan, NYC, Late Feb.
Evian Indoor Pro Beach Volleyball Championships, Manhattan, NYC, Late Feb.
Zydecodelic Loup Garou Bal de la Maison Mardi Gras Party, Manhattan, NYC, Late Feb.
Kitty Brazelton's Real Music Series, Manhattan, NYC, Late Feb. to Early Apr.
Great Miracle Prayer Festival, Manhattan, NYC, Late Feb.
Back Stage Bistro Awards, Manhattan, NYC, Late Feb.

## March

Rhythm and Blues Foundation's Pioneer Awards, Manhattan, NYC, Early Mar.
Improvisors Collective Festival, Manhattan, NYC, Early Mar.
Century of Change/So Nice To Come Home To, Manhattan, NYC, Early Mar.
In Women's Hands:  The Beat of the Drum, Albany, NY, Early Mar.
Harvard Winter Folk Festival, Cambridge, MA, Early Mar.
UMass Jazz Festival, North Dartmouth, MA, Early Mar.
Dick Fox's Spring Doo-Wopp Extravaganza, Westbury, NY, Early Mar.
Penny Association Midwinter Bluegrass Festival, Vestal, NY, Early Mar.
Caribbean Music Awards, Manhattan, NYC, Early Mar.
Berklee College of Music High School Jazz Festival, Boston, MA, Early Mar.
Women's Voices, Providence, RI, Early Mar.
Pines Scottish Weekend, South Fallsburg, NY, Early Mar.
Festival of Women Improvisors, Manhattan, NYC, Mar. to Middle Mar.
Gloucester Folklife Festival, Gloucester, MA, Early Mar.
Countryfest, Laconia, NH, Early Mar.
St. Patrick's Day Celebrations, Elmsford, NY, Early Mar. to Middle Mar.
Women's Jazz Festival, Manhattan, NYC, Early Mar. to Late Mar.
Bill Popp's Birthday Tribute to George L. Popp, Manhattan, NYC, Early Mar.
Richard Nader's Let the Good Times Roll, Kiamesha Lake, NY, Early Mar. to Middle Mar.
Watertown Goes Green Irish Festival, Watertown, NY, Middle Mar.

Irish Celebration, Westbury, NY, Middle Mar.
Evening of Rock and Roll, Manhattan, NYC, Middle Mar.
Winning Scores, Manhattan, NYC, Middle Mar.
Down East Country Dance Festival, South Portland, ME, Middle Mar.
Clark Terry/University of New Hampshire Jazz Festival, Durham, NH, Middle Mar.
CMAC's Gala Benefit, Cambridge, MA, Middle Mar.
Harpoon's St. Patrick's Day Bash, Boston, MA, Middle Mar.
Bang On a Can Festival, Manhattan, NYC, Middle Mar. to Early May
Africa Mondo Showcase, Manhattan, NYC, Middle Mar.
Evening with Frank Patterson, Manhattan, NYC, Early Mar.
Roulette Concert Series/Le Salon Roulette, Manhattan, NYC, Middle Mar.
Hearts and Voices Winter Benefit Series, Manhattan, NYC, Middle Mar. to Late Apr.
Tokyo/New York Noise Festival, Manhattan, NYC, Middle Mar.
Pines Hotel Bluegrass Festival, South Fallsburg, NY, Middle Mar.
Songstreet Festival of Women Songwriters, Somerville, MA, Middle Mar.
Julius Watkins Jazz French Horn Festival, Manhattan, NYC, Middle Mar.
West Indian Carnival Explosion, Brooklyn, NYC, Middle Mar.
National Gospel Choir Competition, Manhattan, NYC, Middle Mar.
River Tree Arts Country Jamboree, Kennebunk, ME, Middle Mar.
Black Expo, New Haven, CT, Middle Mar.
Women in Music Celebration, Colonie, NY, Middle Mar.
Israeli Folk Dance Festival and Festival of the Arts, Manhattan, NYC, Middle Mar.
Party for Zoot, Manhattan, NYC, Middle Mar.
The Brooklyn Beat Meets The Black Rock Coalition, Manhattan, NYC, Middle Mar.
St. Barnabas Irish Variety Concert, Bronx, NYC, Middle Mar.
Nassau Community College Folk Festival, Garden City, NY, Late Mar.
Main Street U. S. A., Manhattan, NYC, Late Mar.
Wall of Sound, Queens, NYC, Late Mar.
Wall to Wall, Manhattan, NYC, Late Mar.
WPLJ-FM's 70's Rock and Roll Reunion, Manhattan, NYC, Late Mar.
Adirondack Folk Night, Troy, NY, Late Mar.
College of Saint Rose High School Jazz Festival, Albany, NY, Late Mar.
PYX Rock and Roll Expo, Albany, NY, Late Mar.
Tamika Reggae Awards, Manhattan, NYC, Late Mar.
Gospel Explosion, Brooklyn, NYC, Late Mar.
Jewish Festival of Music, Manhattan, NYC, Late Mar.
New York Winter Blues Festival, Manhattan, NYC, Late Mar.
Hot, Hot Tropics, Boston, MA, Late Mar.
Boston Phoenix/WFNX Best Music Poll Celebration, Boston, MA, Late Mar.
Independent Music Fest, Manhattan, NYC, Late Mar. to Early Apr.
Great Beer and Music Festival, Manhattan, NYC, Late Mar.
Blistered Fingers Helping Hands of Bluegrass, Brunswick, ME, Late Mar. to Early Apr.

## April

Salsa's Soul Combination, Bronx, NYC, Early Apr.
Great New York Mandolin Weekend, Manhattan, NYC, Early Apr.
Loud Music Festival, Northampton, MA, Early Apr.
Stork Music Festival, Manhattan, NYC, Early Apr.
Cabin Fever Folklife Festival, Middlebury, VT, Early Apr.
Songstreet Cajun-Bluegrass Festival, Somerville, MA, Early Apr.
Harmony Sweepstakes A Cappella Festival/New York Regional, Manhattan, NYC, Early Apr.
World Fair at Boston University, Boston, MA, Early Apr. to Middle Apr.
Manhattan Association of Cabarets and Clubs Awards, Manhattan, NYC, Early Apr.

Emerald Weekend, Kiamesha Lake, NY, Early Apr.

American Indian Day at the Children's Museum, Boston, MA, Early Apr.

Experimental Intermedia Festival with No Fancy Name. Manhattan, NYC, Early Apr. to Late Apr.

Pepsi Boston Music Awards, Boston, MA, Early Apr.

Barnaby's Battle of the Bands, Centereach, NY, Early Apr.

From Plains, Pueblos and Tundra: Native American Music, Dance and Storytelling, Manhattan, NYC, Early Apr.

Sugarloaf Reggae Ski Bash, Kingfield, ME, Early Apr.

Country Classic in the Catskills, South Fallsburg, NY, Early Apr.

American Swing Dance Championships, Manhattan, NYC, Early Apr.

P. S. 122 Music Festival, Manhattan, NYC, Early Apr.

Native American Day at The Forum, Framingham, MA, Early Apr.

Songstreet Folk-Rock Festival, Somerville, MA, Early Apr.

U. G. H. A. Hall of Fame Awards Ceremony, Manhattan, NYC, Early Apr.

Furnald Folk Fest, Manhattan, NYC, Early Apr.

Pines Number One Irish Weekend, South Fallsburg, NY, Early Apr.

New York Brass Conference for Scholarships, Manhattan, NYC, Early Apr.

Festival of Nations, Manhattan, NYC, Early Apr.

Betty Carter's Jazz Ahead, Brooklyn, NYC, Early Apr.

McDonald's Gospelfest, Varies, NYC, Early Apr. to Middle Jun.

Connecticut Historical Society's International Spring Festival, Hartford, CT, Early Apr.

Al Mastren Memorial Scholarship Concert, Cohoes, NY, Early Apr.

Rainforest Benefit Concert, Manhattan, NYC, Middle Apr.

International OFFestival, Manhattan, NYC, Middle Apr. to Middle Jun.

Scottish Fiddle Rally, Somerville, MA, Middle Apr.

Sugarloaf Mountain Blues Festival, Kingfield, ME, Middle Apr.

Death and Taxes, Manhattan, NYC, Middle Apr.

Emerald Productions Getaway, Callicoon, NY, Middle Apr.

Carnegie Hall Folk Festival, Manhattan, NYC, Middle Apr. to Late Apr.

Sunnyside Shop-Till-You-Drop Festival, Queens, NYC, Middle Apr.

Springfest, Oceanside, NY, Middle Apr.

Olde Tyme Fiddlers Concert, Sterling, CT, Middle Apr.

Easter Gospel Festival, Manhattan, NYC, Middle Apr.

Great New York Mandolin Gala, Manhattan, NYC, Middle Apr.

Songwriter Showcase, Deer Park, NY, Middle Apr.

Eco-Festival, Manhattan, NYC, Late Apr. to Early May

WBOS-FM Earth Day Concert and Festival, Boston, MA, Late Apr.

Swing Spring, Troy, NY, Late Apr.

Essence Awards, Manhattan, NYC, Late Apr.

Radioactive Bodega Blacklight Prom, Brooklyn, NYC, Late Apr.

New England Blues Conference, Portsmouth, NH, Late Apr.

Long Island Guitar Festival, Brookville, NY, Late Apr.

Vermont Maple Festival/Fiddler's Variety Show, St. Albans, VT, Late Apr.

Grand International Ragtime/Jasstime Foundation Spring Festival, Alexandria Bay, NY, Late Apr.

Country Jamborees, New Haven, CT, Late Apr.

College of Saint Rose Collegiate Jazz Festival, Albany, NY, Late Apr.

New York State Intercollegiate Jazz Festival, Morrisville, NY, Late Apr.

Spring Blues Festival, Westbury, NY, Late Apr.

New England Folk Festival, Natick, MA, Late Apr.

Earth Day Pow-Wow, Leominster, MA, Late Apr.

Kenmore Square Rites of Spring Charity Rockfest, Boston, MA, Late Apr.

Students for Students/Human Rights Festival, Boston, MA, Late Apr.

WEQX Party in the Park, Albany, NY, Late Apr.
Broadway's Easter Bonnet Competition: A Salute to 100 Years of Broadway, Manhattan, NYC, Late Apr.
Spring Blossom Fiddle Jamboree, Long Lake, NY, Late Apr.
Earth Day Celebration, Providence, RI, Late Apr.
Earth Day Celebration, Manhattan, NYC, Late Apr.
Corner Store Syndicate New Jazz Festival, Manhattan, NYC, Late Apr.
Roulette Concert Series/Roulette Mixology Festival, Manhattan, NYC, Late Apr. to Early May
Sheep Shearing Festival, Waltham, MA, Late Apr.
National Gay and Lesbian Business and Consumer Expo, Manhattan, NYC, Late Apr.
Gospel Comes/Returns to Broadway, Manhattan, NYC, Late Apr.
Religious Music Festival, Brooklyn, NYC, Late Apr.
Upper Broadway Spring Celebration and Festival, Manhattan, NYC, Late Apr.
Arts First: A Harvard/Radcliffe Celebration, Cambridge, MA, Late Apr. to Middle May
Blacksmith House Dulcimer Festival, Cambridge, MA, Late Apr. to Early May
Abenaki Festival Days, Rutland/Burlington, VT, Late Apr. to Early May

## May

Syracuse Area Music Awards (Sammies), Syracuse, NY, Early May
Folk Music Society of Huntington Members Concert, Huntington, NY, Early May
Turk Murphy Memorial Festival, Buffalo, NY, Early May
Lower Second Avenue Festival, Manhattan, NYC, Early May
Pussystock, Manhattan, NYC, Early May
Harvard Square's May Fair, Cambridge, MA, Early May
New York Shakespeare Festival Spring Gala, Manhattan, NYC, Early May
Libro Latino Bookfest/Pathways for Youth Benefit, Bronx, NYC, Middle May
Westchester Community College Jazz Festival, White Plains, NY, Early May
Areyto for Life: Hispanic AIDS Forum Benefit Gala and Art Auction, Manhattan, NYC, Early May
Dick Fox's Brooklyn Paramount Reunion, Manhattan, NYC, Early May
Everybody's Calypso Awards, Brooklyn, NYC, Early May
Contemporary Music Festival, Concord, NH, Early May
Indian Pow Wow, Niagara Falls, NY, Early May
Pinksterfest/Albany Tulip Festival, Albany, NY, Early May
William Smith and Hobart Colleges Folk Fest, Geneva, NY, Early May
Everybody's World Calypso Monarch Competition, Brooklyn/Queens, NYC, Early May to Late Jul.
Uncle Sam's Blues Jam, Troy, NY, Early May
Entre Familia, Bronx, NYC, Early May
In Celebration of Life, Manhattan, NYC, Early May
Two Rivers Ethnic Festival, Binghamton, NY, Early May
WXLE Acoustic Music Festival, Clifton Park, NY, Early May to Late May
Irish Cultural Day, Burlington, VT, Early May
International Festival, Manchester, NH, Early May
Heart and Soul, Manhattan, NYC, Early May
Outmusic Festival, Manhattan, NYC, Early May
Say It With Love Night, Manhattan, NYC, Middle May
WBCN Rock 'n' Roll Rumble, Boston, MA, Early May to Late May
Hearts and Voices In Concert, Manhattan, NYC, Middle May
Tribute to African Diaspora Women, Manhattan, NYC, Middle May
Black Expo U. S. A., Manhattan, NYC, Middle May
Mother's Day Caribbean All-Stars Festival, Varies, NYC, Early May
Raven Wind Pow-Wow, Evansville, VT, Middle May

Nutmeg Bluegrass Get-Together, Burlington, CT, Middle May
Fiddlehead Festival, Unity, ME, Middle May
Boston Brewer's Festival, Boston, MA, Middle May
WGBH "T" Party, Boston, MA, Middle May
Legends of Folk Music, Westport, CT, Middle May
Band Box Anniversary Love-Fest/Wife-Swap, Port Chester, NY, Middle May
Cavalcade of Stars, Manhattan, NYC, Middle May
Jamaica Fun Run and Family Day, Queens, NYC, Middle May
Sigonomeg Pow-Wow, Middleboro, MA, Middle May
I. A. C. A.'s International Festival of the Adirondacks, Queensbury, NY, Middle May
Queens College Cultural Heritage Great Gospel Competition, Queens, NYC, Middle May
Maritime Arts Festival, Newport, RI, Middle May
Hurdy Gurdy Strings and Sings Spring Fling, Accord, NY, Middle May
Lilac Festival, Rochester, NY, Middle May to Late May
Acoustic Underground Concerts and CD Release Parties, Varies, MA, Middle May
Jambalaya on the River:  Spring Riverboat Festival, Hartford, CT, Middle May to Late May
Boston Kite Festival, Boston, MA, Middle May
Irish Traditional Dance Festival, Mineola, NY, Middle May
Brooklyn Rock Awards, Brooklyn, NYC, Middle May
Z100 May Day, Manhattan, NYC, Middle May
Brooklyn Arts Week, Brooklyn, NYC, Middle May
Art Newbury Street, Boston, MA, Middle May
Make-a-Wish-Foundation Country Jamboree, Ipswich, MA, Middle May
Taste of Summer, Middletown, CT, Middle May
Shadfest, Peekskill, NY, Middle May
Fifth Avenue Festival, Brooklyn, NYC, Middle May
Folksongs Plus, Manhattan, NYC, Middle May
Dartmouth Festival of New Musics, Hanover, NH, Middle May
Bennington Folk Festival, Bennington, VT, Middle May
Pride of Maine Fiddling Festival, Waldo, ME, Middle May
Jazz for the Arts/Super Jazz Jam Blowout , Albany, NY, Middle May
Union Settlement Ethnic Festival, Manhattan, NYC, Middle May
Mostly Women Composers, Manhattan, NYC, Middle May to Late May
Homefolks Concert, Boston, MA, Late May
Alternative Skateboard Festival, Woodbury, CT, Late May
Honey, Hide the Banjo!  It's the Folk Next Door, West Hartford, CT, Late May
Amsterdam Avenue Festival, Manhattan, NYC, Late May
Hezekiah Walker Anniversary Show, Brooklyn, NYC, Late May
Salute to Israel Day Parade and Concert, Manhattan, NYC, Late May
Israel Expo, Manhattan, NYC, Late May
Folk Festival/Flea Market and Craft Show, Braintree, MA, Late May
Benefit for the Fight Against Leukemia, Deer Park, NY, Late May
Great Lawn Irish Fair, Brookville, NY, Late May
Westchester Arts Festival, White Plains, NY, Late May
Broadway County Fair, Manhattan, NYC, Late May
Rock Against Racism Concert, Manhattan, NYC, Late May
Sun Ra Festival, Manhattan, NYC, Middle May to Late May
Indian Ranch Country Music Festival and Chicken Barbeque, Webster, MA, Late May
Native American Days, Westerly, RI, Late May
Blue Sky Music Fest, Wallingford, CT, Late May
Israeli Festival, Oceanside, NY, Late May
Street Performers Festival, Boston, MA, Late May
Hartford Advocate's Best of the Bands Bash, New Britain, CT, Late May
Hebron Pines Bluegrass Festival, Hebron, ME, Late May

Penny Association Memorial Day Bluegrass and Country Music Festival, Coventryville, NY,
    Late May
Oi!/Skampilation, Manhattan, NYC, Late May
Salem Seaport Festival, Salem, MA, Late May
Praise, Darien Lake, NY, Late May
Irish-American Festival and Heritage Feis, Brooklyn, NYC, Late May
Spring Folk Music Weekend, Falls Village, CT, Late May
Memorial Day Weekend Festival, Parksville, NY, Late May
Bluegrass Festival, Woodstock, CT, Late May
52nd Street Jazz Festival, Manhattan, NYC, Late May
Festival De Los Soneros, Manhattan, NYC, Middle May
Manhattan Ethnic Music and Dance Festival, Manhattan, NYC, Late May
Memorial Day Weekend Celebration Scholarship Fund Raising Dance, Manhattan, NYC, Late
    May
Save Our Park/WWRL Radiothon, Queens, NYC, Late May
New Hampshire's Lilac Time Festival, Lisbon, NH, Late May
Planting Moon Pow-Wow, Topsfield, MA, Late May
Bearsville Theater Memorial Day Music Festival, Bearsville, NY, Late May
Irish Festival, East Durham, NY, Late May
GottaGetGon Folk Festival: The Pick'n and Singin' Gatherin', Ballston Spa, NY, Late May
Indian Pow Wow, Charlemont, MA, Late May
Stanfordville Music and Dance Festival, Stanfordville, NY, Late May
International Jewish Arts Festival of Long Island, Commack, NY, Late May
Iroquois Arts Showcase I, Howes Cave, NY, Late May
Lobster Fest, Mystic, CT, Late May
Woodstock/New Paltz Art and Crafts Fair, New Paltz, NY, Late May
Lamplight Service and Hymn Sing, North Danville, VT, Late May to Late Aug.
Bluegrass Festival, Washington, MA, Late May
Maritime Music Festival, Salem, MA, Late Mar.
Broadway Astoria Festival, Queens, NYC, Late May
Country Music Festival to Benefit American Heart Association, Webster, MA, Late May
Songwriters' Hall of Fame Awards, Manhattan, NYC, Late May

## June

People's Music Network Summer Gathering, Pine Bush, NY, Early Jun.
Harp and Harmony Concert, Manhattan, NYC, Early Jun.
Fair Haven Festival, New Haven, CT, Early Jun.
Wall-to-Wall Rahsaan Roland Kirk, Manhattan, NYC, Early Jun.
Lake Champlain Balloon Festival, Essex Junction, VT, Early Jun.
Strawberry Park Bluegrass Festival, Preston, CT, Early Jun.
Ithaca Festival, Ithaca, NY, Early Jun.
Otsiningo Pow Wow and Indian Craft Fair, Apalachin, NY, Early Jun.
American Pit Masters Bar-B-Q Round-Up, Boston, MA, Middle Jun.
Kaleidoscope Family Arts Festival, Augusta, ME, Early Jun.
Boston Festival of Bands, Boston, MA, Early Jun.
Different Tastes Outdoor Crawfish and Alligator Feast, Hartford, CT, Early Jun.
Lark Street Blues Festival, Albany, NY, Early Jun.
Murray Hill Block Party and Blues Festival, Manhattan, NYC, Early Jun.
Pathmark Hispanic Arts Festival, Manhattan, NYC, Early Jun.
Vermont Dairy Festival, Enosburg Falls, VT, Early Jun.
Taste of Chicopee, Chicopee, MA, Early Jun.
La Festa, North Adams, MA, Early Jun. to Late Jun.
KISS-108 FM Concert, Mansfield, MA, Early Jun.

City Fest Arts Jubilee, Middletown, CT, Early Jun.
Cultural Street Festival, Hempstead, NY, Early Jun.
Glory, Valley Falls, NY, Early Jun.
Glory, Lake George, NY, Early Jun.
Irish Festival, Hampton Bays, NY, Early Jun.
Brooklyn Woodstock, Brooklyn, NYC, Early Jun.
Celebrate 125! The Rhythm of the World, Manhattan, NYC, Early Jun.
Lesbian and Gay Pride Committee Parade and Festival, Queens, NYC, Early Jun.
Plantathon and Music Festival, Manhattan, NYC, Early Jun.
Starrett at Spring Creek Native American Pow Wow, Brooklyn, NYC, Early Jun.
World of Percussion, Manhattan, NYC, Early Jun.
Summer Arts Fest Chair Fair, West Kingston, RI, Early Jun.
Bluegrass Roundup, Galway, NY, Early Jun.
Indian Summer, Manhattan, NYC, Early Jun. to Late Jun.
Old Port Festival, Portland, ME, Early Jun.
Jamaica Plain Folk Festival, Jamaica Plain, MA, Early Jun.
Bloomfield Festival, Bloomfield, CT, Early Jun.
Riversplash, Simsbury, CT, Early Jun.
Old Time Fiddler's Contest and Jam Session, Blue Mountain Lake, NY, Early Jun.
Street Fair, Plainview, NY, Early Jun.
World of Jewish Culture, Bay Shore, NY, Early Jun.
Israel Expo, Brooklyn, NYC, Early Jun.
Hyannis Harbor Festival, Hyannis, MA, Early Jun.
Pow-Wow, Rutland, MA, Early Jun.
Hempsplash, Parksville, NY, Early Jun.
Blueshounds Benefit, Albany, NY, Early Jun.
Festival of Traditional Sea Music, Bath, ME, Early Jun.
Cross Overs: Music of Asia America, Manhattan, NYC, Early Jun.
Arcady Music Festival/Ragtime Evening Benefit, Bangor, ME, Early Jun.
Discover Jazz Festival, Burlington, VT, Early Jun. to Middle Jun.
Discmakers Unsigned Band/Artist New York World Series, Manhattan, NYC, Early Jun.
New England Foundation for the Arts Jazz Conference, Varied Sites, VAR, Early Jun. to Middle
    Jun.
Festival of Jewish Music, Manhattan, NYC, Early Jun.
Albion Strawberry Festival, Albion, NY, Early Jun.
Sterling Park Campground Bluegrass Festival, Sterling, CT, Early Jun. to Middle Jun.
Thousand Islands Bluegrass Festival, Clayton, NY, Early Jun. to Middle Jun.
Taste of Hartford, Hartford, CT, Early Jun. to Middle Jun.
Native American Intertribal Festival/Cape Heritage, Mashpee, MA, Early Jun.
Main Street U. S. A., New Britain, CT, Early Jun.
Bluegrass on the Green, Homer, NY, Early Jun.
Dick Fox's Summer Doo-Wopp Extravaganza, Westbury, NY, Early Jun.
Strawberry Festival, Beacon, NY, Early Jun.
Gospel Concert, Brooklyn, NYC, Early Jun.
Citibank Taste of Stamford, Stamford, CT, Early Jun. to Middle Jun.
Rochester Irish Festival, Gates, NY, Early Jun. to Middle Jun.
Market Square Day, Portsmouth, NH, Early Jun. to Middle Jun.
Harpoon's Brewstock, Boston, MA, Late Jun.
Albany Riverfest/All-America City Fair, Albany, NY, Early Jun. to Middle Jun.
Family Fun Fair, Portland, ME, Middle Jun.
Rattling Brook Bluegrass Festival, Belvidere, VT, Middle Jun.
Riverfest, Buckland, MA, Middle Jun.
Rock 'N Roll Block Party, Holyoke, MA, Middle Jun.
Schwepes Chowder Cook-Off, Newport, RI, Middle Jun.

Brass Valley Ethnic Music Festival, Waterbury, CT, Middle Jun.

Mad Murphy's Cajun, Zydeco Music and Art Festival, East Haddam, CT, Middle Jun.

Manchester Association of Pipe Bands Festival, Manchester, CT, Middle Jun.

Fundraiser, West Shokan, NY, Middle Jun.

Mayhem on the Mountain, Mariaville, NY, Middle Jun.

One With Nature Festival, Garrison, NY, Middle Jun.

Psychofest, Kingston, NY, Middle Jun.

WCBS-FM 101 Day, Rye, NY, Middle Jun.

116th Street Festival in El Barrio, Manhattan, NYC, Middle Jun.

Bronx Ethnic Music and Dance Festival, Bronx, NYC, Middle Jun.

Downtown Music Gallery's Anniversary Celebration, Manhattan, NYC, Middle Jun.

New York City's Gospel Festival, Brooklyn, NYC, Middle Jun.

Puerto Rican Day Parade, Manhattan, NYC, Middle Jun.

Super Radioactive Bodega Bonanza Outdoor Festival, Brooklyn, NYC, Middle Jun.

Welcome Back to Brooklyn, Brooklyn, NYC, Middle Jun.

Celebrate! West Hartford, West Hartford, CT, Middle Jun.

Irish Cultural Center's Festival, North Easton, MA, Middle Jun.

Sea Music Festival, Mystic, CT, Middle Jun.

Taste of Fairfield, Fairfield, CT, Middle Jun.

Back Cove Family Day, Portland, ME, Middle Jun.

New Hampshire Women's Music Festival, Northfield, NH, Middle Jun.

Cambridge International Fair, Cambridge, MA, Middle Jun.

Cambridge Public Library Jazz Festival, Cambridge, MA, Middle Jun.

Old Home Day, Middlefield, CT, Middle Jun.

Battle of the Acappella Groups, Poughkeepsie, NY, Middle Jun.

Fiddling Celebration, Cross River, NY, Early Jul.

Intergenerational International Festival, Garden City, NY, Middle Jun.

Local Motion MusicFest, Middletown, NY, Middle Jun.

City Lore Festival, Manhattan, NYC, Middle Jun.

Lower East Side Jewish Festival, Manhattan, NYC, Middle Jun.

Lyrics and Lyricists/The New Breed, Manhattan, NYC, Middle Jun.

Happy Horseshoe Blue Grass Festival, North New Portland, ME, Middle Jun.

New England Bluegrass Festival, Laconia, NH, Middle Jun.

Boston Waterfront Festival, Boston, MA, Middle Jun.

Fall River Festival, Fall River, MA, Middle Jun.

Pridefest, Boston, MA, Middle Jun.

Wollomonuppoag Indian Council Inter-Tribal Pow Wow, Attleboro, MA, Middle Jul.

Ballston Spa Village Wide Garage Sale and Family Festival, Ballston Spa, NY, Middle Jun.

L. A. R. A. C. Arts and Crafts Festival, Glen Falls, NY, Middle Jun.

Miller Lite Balloonfest/Art on the Rise, Jamesville, NY, Middle Jun.

Boston Globe Jazz Festival, Boston, MA, Middle Jun.

Festival Playero, Bronx, NYC, Middle Jun. to Early Sep.

Race Unity Day, Boston, MA, Middle Jun.

Harlem Renaissance Garden Party, Cranston, RI, Middle Jun.

Syracuse Jazz Fest, Syracuse, NY, Middle Jun.

Buskers Fare/Summer Fair, Manhattan, NYC, Middle Jun.

Local Bands on the Downtown Green, New Haven, CT, Middle Jun. to Late Aug.

Sudden Sunsets: Highlights from the Benson AIDS Series, Manhattan, NYC, Middle Jun.

Peter Pan Taste of Springfield, Springfield, MA, Middle Jun.

Fire Wall Total Arts Festival, Manhattan, NYC, Middle Jun. to Late Jun.

Central Park Summerstage, Manhattan, NYC, Middle Jun. to Early Aug.

Blistered Fingers Family Bluegrass Music Festival, Sidney, ME, Middle Jun.

Gospel Music Workshop of America/New York State Chapter Convention, Brooklyn, NYC, Middle Jun.

Nassau Coliseum Fair, Uniondale, NY, Middle Jun. to Late Jun.
Tweed New Works Festival, Manhattan, NYC, Middle Jun. to Early Jul.
Gospelfest, Brooklyn, NYC, Middle Jun.
WPLJ-FM's 70's Dance Party, Manhattan, NYC, Middle Jun.
Pink Tent Festival of the Arts, Stamford, CT, Middle Jun.
East End Music Festival, East Hampton, NY, Middle Jun.
June Jazz, White Plains, NY, Middle Jun.
Midsummer Revels, Lincoln, MA, Middle Jun. to Late Dec.
Quechee Hot Air Balloon Festival, Quechee, VT, Middle Jun.
Fairfield County Irish Festival, Fairfield, CT, Middle Jun.
Laing Family Bluegrass Festival, Bainbridge, NY, Middle Jun.
Southeast Queens' Youth Sports and Spring Festival/Juneteenth, Queens, NYC, Middle Jun.
Boston Pops, Boston, MA, Middle Jun. to Early Jul.
Somersworth International Children's Festival, Somersworth, NH, Middle Jun.
Summerfest, Great Barrington, MA, Middle Jun.
Blues Blockbusters, New Haven, CT, Middle Jun.
All-Star Irish Concert and Dance, Yonkers, NY, Middle Jun.
Gospel Extravaganza, Kingston, NY, Middle Jun.
Lake George Hot Jazz Party and Cruise, Lake George, NY, Middle Jun.
Boston Book Fair, Boston, MA, Middle Jun.
Clearwater's Great Hudson River Revival, Valhalla, NY, Middle Jun.
Distant Drums Native American Festival, White Plains, NY, Middle Jun.
Native American Pow Wow, Bethany, NY, Middle Jun.
High Hopes Hot Air Balloon Festival, Milford, NH, Middle Jun.
No Bummer Summer Party Jam, Parksville, NY, Middle Jun.
Lesbian and Gay Pride Week/PrideFest, Manhattan, NYC, Middle Jun. to Late Jun.
Fiddling Competition and Contra Dance, Damariscotta, ME, Middle Jun.
Oak Bluffs Harbor Day, Oak Bluffs, MA, Middle Jun.
Praise and Harmony, Lowell, MA, Middle Jun.
West Fest/Taste of Westville, Westville, CT, Middle Jun.
Country Western Festival, Cambridge, NY, Middle Jun.
Irish Festival, Patterson, NY, Middle Jun.
Boathouse Rock, Manhattan, NYC, Middle Jun.
Broadway Summer Festival, Manhattan, NYC, Middle Jun.
Irish Traditional Music and Dance Festival, Bronx, NYC, Middle Jun.
Queens Boulevard Festival, Queens, NYC, Middle Jun.
Upper Broadway Summer Festival, Manhattan, NYC, Middle Jun.
Pow-Wow, Sterling, MA, Late Jun.
Mother of Waters, Rocky Hill, CT, Middle Jun.
Juneteenth Festival, Buffalo, NY, Middle Jun.
Knitting Factory's "What is Jazz?" Festival, Manhattan, NYC, Middle Jun. to Early Jul.
Country Music Shows, Escoheag, RI, Middle Jun. to Early Aug.
Sounds at Sunset, Manhattan, NYC, Middle Jun. to Middle Sep.
Barnum Festival/Gospel Festival, Bridgeport, CT, Middle Jun.
Reggae on the Hudson, Kingston, NY, Middle Jun.
Pequot and Narragansett Indian Nations Pow Wow, Westerly, RI, Middle Jun. to Late Jun.
Summer Series, Westport, CT, Middle Jun. to Middle Aug.
Lesbopalooza, Manhattan, NYC, Late Jun.
Winter Consort Summer Solstice Whole Earth Celebration, Manhattan, NYC, Late Jun.
Red Cross Waterfront Festival, Greenwich, CT, Middle Jun.
Midsummer Night Swing, Manhattan, NYC, Late Jun. to Late Jul.
Celebrate Brooklyn Performing Arts Festival, Brooklyn, NYC, Late Jun. to Middle Aug.
Jazz Showcase, Portsmouth, NH, Late Jun.
Beacons In Jazz, Manhattan, NYC, Late Jun.

Louisiana Cookin' and Cajun Music Festival, Norwich, CT, Late Jun.
Madrid Bluegrass Festival, Madrid, NY, Late Jun.
Portsmouth Jazz Festival, Portsmouth, NH, Late Jun.
Mohonk's Music Week, New Paltz, NY, Late Jun.
JVC Jazz Festival/Bryant Park Jazz Festival, Manhattan, NYC, Late Jun. to Early Jul.
FLY92 Summer Jam, Latham, NY, Late Jun.
Jones Beach Greekfest Weekend, Babylon, NY, Late Jun.
Big Easy Bash, Escoheag, RI, Late Jun.
Strawberry Moon Pow-Wow, Somers, CT, Late Jun.
Squaredance and Bluegrass Festival, Hartford, NY, Late Jun.
Queens Festival/Nations in Neighborhoods Multicultural Dance Party, Queens, NYC, Late Jun.
Underground Blues and Folk Festival, Manhattan, NYC, Late Jun.
Katahdin Family Bluegrass Music Festival, Medway, ME, Late Jun.
LaKermesse Franco-Americaine Festival, Biddeford, ME, Late Jun.
Green Mountain Chew Chew/Vermont Food Fest, Burlington, VT, Late Jun.
Fun Summer Concerts, Wellfleet, MA, Late Jun.
Hot Steamed Music Festival, Essex, CT, Late Jun.
Amesbury Days Festival, Amesbury, MA, Late Jun. to Early Jul.
Newburyport Yankee Homecoming, Newburyport, MA, Late Jun. to Early Jul.
Summerscape: Huntington Summer Arts Festival, Huntington, NY, Late Jun. to Late Aug.
Blues Festival, North Yarmouth, ME, Late Jun.
Portland Waterfront Festival, Portland, ME, Late Jun.
Rutland Region Ethnic Festival, Rutland, VT, Late Jun.
Joe Val Memorial Bluegrass Festival, Waltham, MA, Late Jun.
Pickin' in the Pines Bluegrass Day, Northampton, MA, Late Jun.
Reggae Festival, Woodbury, CT, Late Jun.
Caribbean Cultural Heritage Week Festival/Caribbean Craft and Food Fair, Brooklyn, NYC, Late
     Jun.
Strawberry Festival, South Berwick, ME, Late Jun.
Ben and Jerry's One World, One Heart Festival, Warren, VT, Late Jun.
Connecticut Irish Festival, New Haven, CT, Late Jun.
Great American Music Fest, Goshen, CT, Late Jun.
New York State Championship Chili Cookoff, New Paltz, NY, Late Jun.
American Pit Masters Bar-B-Q Roundup, Providence, RI, Late Jun.
Lake George Summerfest, Lake George, NY, Late Jun.
Northeast Dulcimer Symposium, Blue Mountain Lake, NY, Late Jun.
Old Songs Festival of Traditional Music and Dance, Altamont, NY, Late Jun.
Great Whatever Week and Race, Augusta, ME, Late Jun. to Early Jul.
Earl's Sunshine Festival, Chaffee, NY, Late Jun. to Middle Sep.
Classic Rock Festival, Plymouth, NH, Late Jun.
Fiddler's Contest, Lincoln, NH, Late Jun.
Stark Old Time Fiddlers' Contest, Stark, NH, Late Jun.
Vermont Lesbian Gay Bisexual Pride Day, Burlington, VT, Late Jun.
Chilifest, Boston, MA, Late Jun.
Massachusetts Highland Games, Waltham, MA, Late Jun.
Pan-African Cultural Festival, Boston, MA, Late Jun.
WBCS Boston Country Sunday, Mansfield, MA, Late Jun.
Yankee Music Festival Big Band Jazz Invitational, Salem, MA, Late Jun.
Afternoon of Jazz, Norwalk, CT, Late Jun.
Barnum Festival/Champions on Parade, Bridgeport, CT, Late Jun.
Blues at the Ives, Danbury, CT, Late Jun.
Lake Wangumbaug Folk Festival, Coventry, CT, Late Jun.
African-American Heritage Celebration, Valhalla, NY, Late Jun.
Inwood World Music Festival, Inwood, NY, Late Jun.

Plymouth Summer Blastoff, Plymouth, MA, Late Jun.
Grand Riviere Festival, Van Buren, ME, Late Jun. to Middle Aug.
Chautauqua Summer Music Program, Chautauqua, NY, Late Jun. to Late Aug.
Cambridge Street Performer's Festival, Cambridge, MA, Late Jun.
Marblehead Festival of the Arts, Marblehead, MA, Late Jun. to Early Jul.
Windjammer Days, Boothbay Harbor, ME, Late Jun.
Acadian Festival Celebration, Madawaska, ME, Late Jun. to Early Jul.
Old Home Week and Independence Day, Eastport, ME, Late Jun. to Early Jul.
Friendship Festival, Buffalo, NY, Late Jun. to Early Jul.
Trumbull Day, Trumbull, CT, Late Jun.
Improvisors Festival, Manhattan, NYC, Late Jun. to Early Jul.
Mineral Springs Foot Stomp'n Festival, Stafford Springs, CT, Late Jun. to Early Jul.
Ellicottville's Summer Festival of the Arts, Ellicottville, NY, Late Jun. to Early Jul.
Penny Association Olde Tyme Country Music Festival, Coventryville, NY, Late Jun. to Early Jul.
African Street Festival, Brooklyn, NYC, Late Jun. to Early Jul.
Boston Harborfest, Boston, MA, Late Jun.
Battle of the Blues Bands, Allston, MA, Late Jun. to Early Jul.

## July

WGNA Country Fest, Altamont, NY, Early Jul.
4th of July Celebration, Enfield, CT, Early Jul.
All AmericanFest, Lincoln, NH, Early Jul.
Newport Jazz Festival/Saratoga, Saratoga Springs, NY, Early Jul.
New York Trini-Jam Fest, Brooklyn, NYC, Early Jul.
Great Blue Heron Music Festival, Sherman, NY, Early Jul.
Bath Heritage Days, Bath, ME, Early Jul.
American Patriot Festival, Hunter, NY, Early Jul.
Blue Hill Pops, Blue Hill, ME, Early Jul.
Cape Verdean Heritage Festival, Providence, RI, Early Jul.
Riverfest, Hartford, CT, Early Jul.
Catskill Fourth of July Celebration, Catskill, NY, Early Jul.
Opus 40 Acoustic Summit: Bring It On Home, Saugerties, NY, Early Jul.
Woodside Independence Weekend Festival, Queens, NYC, Early Jul.
Calico Dancers Good Time Pow Wow, South Glens Falls, NY, Early Jul.
Independence Celebration and Double R Championship Rodeo, Rhinebeck, NY, Early Jul.
Summerfest, Poughkeepsie, NY, Early Jul.
American Indian Heritage and Craft Festival, Albany, NY, Early Jul.
Fair Haven Field Days, Fair Haven, NY, Early Jul.
American Pit Masters Bar-B-Q Round-Up, Manchester, NH, Early Jul.
Battle of the Bands, Westport, CT, Early Jul. to Middle Aug.
WERU 89.9FM Full Circle Summer Fair, Union, ME, Early Jul.
Burlington Independence Day Waterfront Celebration, Burlington, VT, Early Jul.
Mountain Jam, Killington, VT, Early Jul.
Funkfest, New Haven, CT, Early Jul.
Round Hill Scottish Games, Norwalk, CT, Early Jul.
WPLR July 4th Celebration, New Haven, CT, Early Jul.
Cairo Appreciation Day Fair, Cairo, NY, Early Jul.
Fourth of July Celebration, Mayville, NY, Early Jul.
Matt's Matinee, Lake Placid, NY, Early Jul.
Star Spangled Spectacular, Montgomery, NY, Early Jul.
Summer Jam, Glens Falls, NY, Early Jul.
Park Slope 5th Avenue Independence Day Festival, Brooklyn, NYC, Early Jul.
Boarding House Park Concert Series Kickoff, Lowell, MA, Early Jul.

New Vineyard Mountains Bluegrass Festival, North Anson, ME, Early Jul.
Your Hometown America Parade, Pittsfield, MA, Early Jul.
Irish Salute to the U. S. A., East Durham, NY, Early Jul.
Iroquois Arts Showcase II, Howes Cave, NY, Early Jul.
Mashpee Wampanoag Powwow, Mashpee, MA, Early Jul.
Subfest, Groton, CT, Early Jul.
Fleadh: Old Music of Ireland Festival, Leeds, NY, Early Jul.
Gruntstock, Parksville, NY, Early Jul.
Summer Boogie, Ellenville, NY, Early Jul. to Middle Jul.
New Haven Jazz Festival, New Haven, CT, Early Jul. to Late Jul.
Adirondack Festival of American Music, Saranac Lake, NY, Early Jul. to Late Jul.
Coor's Lite Music Festival, Brewer, ME, Early Jul.
Rock 'N' Roll Bar-B-Q, Old Orchard Beach, ME, Early Jul.
Thomaston Independence Day Celebration, Thomaston, ME, Early Jul.
Cape Verdean Festival, Boston, MA, Early Jul.
Monson's Summerfest, Monson, MA, Early Jul.
Summer Celebration, Dayville, CT, Early Jul.
Fabulous Fourth Festivities, Albany, NY, Early Jul.
Riverhead Jazz Festival, Riverhead, NY, Early Jul.
El Elyon Music Fest, Brooklyn, NYC, Early Jul.
Women in Jazz Festival, Manhattan, NYC, Early Jul.
Lunchtime Concerts, Albany, NY, Early Jul. to Late Aug.
Pow Wow, Barryville, NY, Early Jul.
Serious Fun!, Manhattan, NYC, Early Jul. to Late Jul.
Irish Festival of Chemung County, Elmira Heights, NY, Early Jul.
Breakneck Mountain Bluegrass Festival, Crawford, ME, Early Jul.
Basin Bluegrass Festival, Brandon, VT, Early Jul.
Lupo's Birthday Party, Providence, RI, Early Jul.
Blandford Mountain Bluegrass Festival, Blandford, MA, Early Jul.
Taste of Buffalo, Buffalo, NY, Early Jul.
Downeast Dulcimer and Harp Festival, Bar Harbor, ME, Early Jul.
Festival de la Bastille, Augusta, ME, Early Jul.
Schooner Days, Rockland, ME, Early Jul.
Warebrook Contemporary Music Festival, Irasburg, VT, Early Jul.
Puerto Rican Cultural Festival, Springfield, MA, Early Jul. to Middle Jul.
Waterfront Extravaganza, Syracuse, NY, Early Jul. to Middle Jul.
Seaside Festival, Kittery, ME, Early Jul.
Twin Mountain Country Western Jamboree, Bretton Woods, NH, Early Jul.
City of Presidents Blues Festival, Quincy, MA, Early Jul.
Latin American Festival, Lowell, MA, Late Jun.
Global Blues Fest, Norwalk, CT, Early Jul.
Invitational Piping Championship/Memorial Military Tattoo, Ticonderoga, NY, Early Jul.
Sunday By the Bay, Bellport, NY, Early Jul.
July Gospel Explosion, Brooklyn, NYC, Early Jul.
Midsummer Festival of Vermont Art and Music, Montpelier, VT, Early Jul.
Del-Se-Nango Fiddlers Festival, Bainbridge, NY, Early Jul.
Gateway to the Nations Powwow, Brooklyn, NYC, Early Jul.
Rotary Oyster Festival, Damariscotta, ME, Early Jul. to Middle Jul.
Whaling City Festival, New Bedford, MA, Early Jul. to Middle Jul.
New London Sail Festival/Connecticut Maritime Festival, New London, CT, Early Jul. to Middle
    Jul.
Maple Ridge Bluegrass Festival, Duanesburg, NY, Early Jul. to Middle Jul.
Panama Rocks Folk Arts Fair, Panama, NY, Early Jul. to Middle Jul.
Celebrate Gorham, Gorham, ME, Early Jul.

Native American Festival, Bar Harbor, ME, Early Jul.
North Atlantic Blues Festival, Rockland, ME, Early Jul.
Families Outdoor Festival, Ferrisburgh, VT, Middle Jul.
Blues in the Night, Rochester, NY, Early Jul.
Tuscarora Field Day and Picnic, Lewiston, NY, Early Jul.
111th Street Boys Old Timers Day Stickball Festival, Manhattan, NYC, Early Jul.
Steinway Street Fun in the Sun Festival, Queens, NYC, Early Jul.
Oxfam America WorldFest, Boston, MA, Early Jul. to Middle Jul.
Connecticut Convention of the Sacred Harp, Middletown, CT, Early Jul. to Middle Jul.
High Ridge Folk Festival, Stamford, CT, Early Jul. to Middle Jul.
Corn Hill Arts Festival/Fiddler's Fair, Rochester, NY, Early Jul. to Middle Jul.
Native American Pow Wow, East Durham, NY, Early Jul. to Middle Jul.
Motahkmikuk Indian Day Celebration, Princeton, ME, Middle Jul. to Middle Jul.
Grand Nights for Singing, Manhattan, NYC, Early Jul. to Middle Jul.
Good Old Summertime , Utica, NY, Early Jul. to Middle Jul.
Middlebury Summer Festival-on-the-Green, Middlebury, VT, Middle Jul.
Maine Potato Blossom Festival/Crown of Maine Balloon Festival, Fort Fairfield, ME, Early Jul.
    to Middle Jul.
WXCT Family Festival, New Haven, CT, Middle Jul.
B. M. I. Jazz Composer's Workshop Concert, Manhattan, NYC, Middle Jul.
Left Bank Cafe Country Blues Festival, Blue Hill, ME, Middle Jul.
Centerstage at the World Trade Center, Manhattan, NYC, Middle Jul. to Early Sep.
New York All-Star Klezmer Extravaganza, Manhattan, NYC, Middle Jul.
Belfast Bay Festival, Belfast, ME, Middle Jul.
Life Beat Benefit:  The Music Industry Fights AIDS, Manhattan, NYC, Middle Jul.
Real Woodstock Festival, Woodstock, NY, Middle Jul.
Peaceful Valley Bluegrass Festival, Shinhopple, NY, Middle Jul.
Winterhawk Bluegrass Family Festival, Ancramdale, NY, Middle Jul.
Bill LaBeef's Bastille Day, Barbeque and Rock and Roll Rodeo, Rochester, NY, Middle Jul.
Caribbean Extravaganza, Catile, NY, Middle Jul.
Gaelic Day, Vails Gate, NY, Middle Jul.
Street Fair, Keene, NH, Middle Jul.
Rushmore Festival, Woodbury, NY, Middle Jul.
Syracuse Arts and Crafts Festival, Syracuse, NY, Middle Jul.
Bright Moments Festival, Amherst, MA, Middle Jul. to Late Jul.
Gilmanton Bluegrass Festival, Gilmanton, NH, Middle Jul.
Hartland Folk Festival, East Hartland, CT, Middle Jul.
Roxbury Pickin' N Fiddlin' Contest, Roxbury, CT, Middle Jul.
Gospel Nite, Manhattan, NYC, Middle Jul.
Hayseed Music Fest, Franconia, NH, Middle Jul.
Southern Vermont Highland Games, Mount Snow, VT, Middle Jul.
African-American Heritage Celebration, Yonkers, NY, Middle Jul.
Yarmouth Clam Festival, Yarmouth, ME, Middle Jul.
Native American Show, Littleton, NH, Middle Jul.
Afro-Latin-Caribbean Festival, Waterbury, CT, Middle Jul.
360 Degrees Black:  New York's Hip Hop Music Seminar, Manhattan, NYC, Middle Jul.
Celebration of the Arts, Kennebunk, ME, Middle Jul. to Late Jul.
Celebrate Vermont Arts and Crafts Show, Rochester, VT, Middle Jul.
Vermont Reggae Fest, Johnson, VT, Middle Jul.
Great American Blues Festival, Woodstock, CT, Middle Jul.
World Music Festival, Woodbury, CT, Middle Jul.
Averill Park Summer Blues Fest, Averill Park, NY, Middle Jul.
Music and The Mountain Sky/Folk Concert, Highmount, NY, Middle Jul.
Rhythm and Blues Beach Party, Caroga Lake, NY, Middle Jul.

Woodstock Beat World Percussion Concert, Woodstock, NY, Middle Jul.

Summerfun! , Staten Island, NYC, Middle Jul.

Mollyockett Day, Bethel, ME, Middle Jul.

Old Hallowell Day, Hallowell, ME, Middle Jul.

Towwakeeswush Pow-Wow, Marshfield, MA, Middle Jun.

UpCountry Hot Air Balloon Fair, Greenfield, MA, Middle Jul.

Deep River Ancient Fife and Drum Corps Muster and Parade, Deep River, CT, Middle Jul.

Fiddle Weekend, Cambridge, NY, Middle Jul.

Aquafest, Newport, VT, Middle Jul.

Irish Festival in the Park, Tewksbury, MA, Middle Jul.

Richmond Days, Richmond, ME, Middle Jul. to Late Jul.

Midwood Concerts at Seaside, Brooklyn, NYC, Middle Jul. to Late Aug.

Waterville Valley Summer Music Festival, Waterville Valley, NH, Middle Jul. to Early Sep.

Long Island Music Festival, Varies, NY, Middle Jul. to Early Sep.

Rangeley's Old-Time Fiddlers' Contest, Rangeley, ME, Middle Jul.

Irish Heritage Celebration, Hartsdale, NY, Middle Jul.

Multicultural Fest, Niagara Falls, NY, Middle Jul.

Empire State Black Arts and Cultural Festival, Albany, NY, Middle Jul.

Keeper of the Western Door Pow-Wow, Salamanca, NY, Middle Jul.

BACA Summer Celebration, Brooklyn, NYC, Middle Jul.

Macintosh New York Music Festival, Manhattan, NYC, Middle Jul. to Late Jul.

Hanover Street-Fest, Hanover, NH, Middle Jul.

Multicultural Family Festival, Roxbury, MA, Middle Jul.

Stamford A. O. H. Feis, Stamford, CT, Middle Jul.

Summer Sizzler, East Hartford, CT, Middle Jul.

Old Time Music Festival and Barbeque, Stone Mills, NY, Middle Jul.

Mohonk's Festival of the Arts/International Week, New Paltz, NY, Middle Jul. to Late Jul.

Deering Oaks Family Festival, Portland, ME, Middle Jul. to Late Jul.

Canal Fest, Tonawanda, NY, Middle Jul. to Late Jul.

Central Maine Egg Festival, Pittsfield, ME, Middle Jul. to Late Jul.

Waterfront Festival Free Summer Concert Series/Gospel in the Park, Buffalo, NY, Middle Jul.

Africa Mondo Festival, Brooklyn, NYC, Middle Jul.

Provincetown Waterfront Festival, Provincetown, MA, Middle Jul. to Late Jul.

Heritage Hoedown and Empire State Fiddle Contest, Darien, NY, Middle Jul. to Late Jul.

Fingerlakes Grassroots Festival of Music and Dance, Trumansburg, NY, Middle Jul. to Late Jul.

Country Music Festival , Hunter, NY, Middle Jul. to Late Jul.

Martin Luther King Jr. Concert Series, Brooklyn, NYC, Middle Jul. to Late Aug.

Rock 'N' Blues AIDS Benefit, East Hartford, CT, Late Jul.

Falcon Ridge Folk Festival, Hillsdale, NY, Late Jul.

Rick and Carol's Country Side Inn Bluegrass Festival, Fort Ann, NY, Late Jul.

Puerto Rican Festival, Boston, MA, Late Jul.

Jazz in July, Manhattan, NYC, Late Jul.

Glasgow Lands Scottish Festival, Blandford, MA, Late Jul.

Folk Music Showcase, Westport, CT, Late Jul.

McDonald's Gospelfest, Buffalo, NY, Late Jul.

Pow Wow, Barryville, NY, Late Jul.

Loon MountainPark BrewFest, Lincoln, NH, Late Jul.

Hats Off to Saratoga Festival, Saratoga Springs, NY, Late Jul.

Opus 40 New Orleans Party Weekend, Saugerties, NY, Late Jul.

Oswego Harborfest, Oswego, NY, Middle Jul.

Orange County Fair, Middletown, NY, Late Jul.

WPVQ Music Day, Greenfield, MA, Late Jul.

BASH: Bradley Airport Summer Happening, Windsor Locks, CT, Late Jul.

Jazz/Reggae Festival, Syracuse, NY, Late Jul.

Low Bridge Festival, Lyons, NY, Late Jul.
Columbia Independence Day Celebration, Queens, NYC, Late Jul.
Columbia Te Canta, Manhattan, NYC, Late Jul.
Puerto Rican Day Parade, Bronx, NYC, Late Jul.
Pico Mountain Jazz Festival, Sherburne, VT, Late Jul.
Great New England Brewers' Festival, Northampton, MA, Late Jul.
R. A. W. Jazz Festival, Hartford, CT, Late Jul.
New York City Clearwater Festival, Brooklyn, NYC, Late Jul.
Lowell Folk Festival, Lowell, MA, Middle Jul.
Cranberry Dulcimer Gathering, Binghamton, NY, Late Jul.
International Fun Fest, Monroe, NY, Late Jul.
American Cabaret Theater Festival, Manhattan, NYC, Late Jul.
York Days, York, ME, Late Jul. to Early Aug.
Quaboag Scottish Festival, Warren, MA, Late Jul.
Evening of Adirondack Music, Lake Placid, NY, Late Jul.
Fife and Drum Corps Muster, Ticonderoga, NY, Late Jul.
Folk Music Society of Huntington Summer Festival, Huntington, NY, Late Jul.
Round Lake Country Music Festival, Round Lake, NY, Late Jul.
Black Family Day, Manhattan, NYC, Late Jul.
New England Reggae Festival, Escoheag, RI, Late Jul.
Native American Fair and Pow Wow, Grafton, MA, Late Jul.
Barbershop Quartet Benefit Concert, Block Island, RI, Late Jul.
Rockfest, East Hartford, CT, Late Jul.
Creek Bend Music Festival, Akron, NY, Late Jul.
Rockland County A. O. H. Feis and Field Games, West Haverstraw, NY, Late Jul.
Sounds on the Susquehanna, Endicott, NY, Late Jul.
Sugarloaf Country Music Festival, Kingfield, ME, Late Jul. to Late Aug.
Rally in the Alley, Buffalo, NY, Late Jul.
Connecticut Agricultural Fair, Goshen, CT, Late Jul.
Greater Hartford Irish Festival, Glastonbury, CT, Late Jul.
Long Island Jazz Festival, Oyster Bay, NY, Late Jul.
Penny Association Bluegrass and Country Music Festival, Tioga Center, NY, Late Jul.
Richard Nader's Let the Good Times Roll, Kiamesha Lake, NY, Late Jul. to Middle Mar.
Gamper Festival of Contemporary Music, Brunswick, ME, Late Jul.
Greater Hartford Festival of Jazz/Hartford Mega! Weekend, Hartford, CT, Late Jul. to Early
     Aug.
Bar Harbor Festival/New Composers Concert, Bar Harbor, ME, Late Jul.
Crackerbarrel Fiddlers Contest, Newbury, VT, Late Jul.
WCLB Country Club Festival, Foxboro, MA, Late Jul.
Newport Rhythm and Blues Festival, Newport, RI, Late Jul.
Budweiser Superfest, Manhattan, NYC, Late Jul.
World Music Fest, Groton, CT, Late Jul.
Native American Weekend, Monroe, NY, Late Jul.
African Caribbean Latino American Festival, Brooklyn, NYC, Late Jul.
Rockaway Irish Festival, Queens, NYC, Late Jul.
East Providence Heritage Festival, East Providence, RI, Late Jul.
Columbia County Jazz Festival, West Ghent, NY, Late Jul.
Bangor State Fair, Bangor, ME, Late Jul. to Early Aug.
Transportation Heritage Festival, Kingston, NY, Late Jul.
Apsge Pow-Wow, Westford, MA, Late Jul.
International Dixeland Jazz and Ragtime Festival, Buffalo, NY, Late Jul.
New York State Budweiser Blues Festival, Syracuse, NY, Late Jul.
Homecoming, Grand Isle, ME, Late Jul. to Early Aug.
Putnam County 4-H Fair, Carmel, NY, Late Jul. to Early Aug.

Rooney Mountain Bluegrass Festival, Deposit, NY, Late Jul. to Early Aug.
Thomas Homestead Festival , Savona, NY, Late Jul. to Early Aug.
International Festival, Calais, ME, Late Jul. to Early Aug.
East Benton Fiddlers' Convention and Contest, East Benton, ME, Late Jul.
Ole Time Fiddlers Contest, Hardwick, VT, Late Jul.
Vermont Women's Celebration, Burlington, VT, Late Jul.
ARTBEAT, Somerville, MA, Late Jul.
Positively Pomfret Day, Putnam, CT, Late Jul.
Rock and Roll Hall of Fame Revue, Danbury, CT, Late Jul.
Jeffersonville Jamboree, Jeffersonville, NY, Late Jul.
Middlesex Music Fest, Middlesex, NY, Late Jul.
Roch-A-Palooza , Rochester, NY, Late Jul.
Slammin' Jammin' Spike's Joint Anniversary Block Party, Brooklyn, NYC, Late Jul.
Rhode Island Indian Council Pow Wow:  Temple to Music, Providence, RI, Late Jul. to Early
     Aug.
Connecticut Family Folk Festival, Hartford, CT, Late Jul. to Early Aug.
Dean Mountain Bluegrass Festival, Hadley, NY, Late Jul. to Early Aug.
Native American Dance Festival, Victor, NY, Late Jul. to Early Aug.
Park Avenue Festival, Rochester, NY, Late Jul. to Early Aug.
Gala All-Star Irish Cruise, Manhattan, NYC, Late Jul. to Early Aug.
Tanglewood Festival of Contemporary Music, Lenox, MA, Late Jul. to Late Aug.

## August

Boston Jazz Society Barbeque and Festival, Milton, MA, Early Aug.
Charlestown Chamber of Commerce Seafood Festival, Charlestown, RI, Early Aug.
Back at the Ranch Festival, Montauk Point, NY, Early Aug.
Blues Bar-B-Que, Schenectady, NY, Early Aug.
Thousand Islands Jazz Festival, Alexandria Bay, NY, Early Aug.
Del-Se-Nango Fiddlers Festival and Bluegrass Sunday, Bainbridge, NY, Early Aug.
Harmony Ridge Brass Center Summer Festival, Poultney, VT, Early Aug.
West Indian Independence Celebration Week/Hartford Mega! Weekend, Hartford, CT, Early
     Aug.
H. O. M. E. Craft and Farm Fair, Orland, ME, Early Aug.
Classical Jazz at Lincoln Center, Manhattan, NYC, Early Aug.
Park Jam, Schenectady, NY, Early Aug.
The Source Awards, Manhattan, NYC, Early Aug.
Maine Lobster Festival, Rockland, ME, Early Aug.
Summer in the Parks, Portland, ME, Early Aug. to Middle Aug.
Pemi Valley Bluegrass Festival, Campton, NH, Early Aug.
SoNo Arts Celebration, South Norwalk, CT, Early Aug.
Bill Knowlton's Bluegrass Ramble Picnic, Sandy Creek, NY, Early Aug.
Twin Rivers Jamboree, Tuscarora, NY, Early Aug.
Maine Festival of the Arts, Brunswick, ME, Early Aug.
Sweet Chariot Music Festival and Schooner Gam, Swans Island, ME, Early Aug.
Ulster County Fair, New Paltz, NY, Early Aug.
Jazzfest Caramoor, Katonah, NY, Early Aug. to Middle Aug.
Irish Traditional Music Festival, North Blenheim, NY, Early Aug.
Loon MountainPark IrishFest, Lincoln, NH, Early Aug.
Knights of Columbus Festival de Joie, Lewiston, ME, Early Aug.
Champlain Valley Festival, Burlington, VT, Early Aug.
Great Connecticut Traditional Jazz Festival, East Haddam, CT, Early Aug.
Rockstalgia, Hunter, NY, Early Aug.
Taste of History, Mystic, CT, Early Aug.

Cumberlandfest, Cumberland, RI, Early Aug.
Lincoln Center Out-of-Doors, Manhattan, NYC, Early Aug. to Late Aug.
National Fife and Drum Muster, Waterbury, VT, Early Aug.
Hamilton Hill Culturefest/Gospel Festival, Schenectady, NY, Early Aug.
Rock-N-Roll Extravaganza, Queens, NYC, Early Aug.
American Indian Honor-the-Earth Pow Wow, Northampton, MA, Early Aug.
American Indian Federation of Rhode Island Pow Wow, Escoheag, RI, Early Aug.
Ben and Jerry's Newport Folk Festival, Newport, RI, Early Aug.
Carnival in New York, Manhattan, NYC, Early Aug.
Kent Summer Days, Kent, CT, Early Aug.
River Fest, Fulton, NY, Early Aug.
Fat Tire Polo Tournament and Music Bash, Farmington, ME, Early Aug.
Tam O'Shanter Scottish Highland Games and Festival, Easton, MA, Early Aug.
Verano Explosivo Festival, West Hartford, CT, Early Aug.
Colonial Fest, Kingston, NY, Early Aug.
Coxsackie Riverside Arts and Crafts Festival, Coxsackie, NY, Early Aug.
International Food Festival/Friday Fest, Poughkeepsie, NY, Early Aug.
Irish Music Festival, Accord, NY, Early Aug.
Micky Rat's City Jam, Buffalo, NY, Early Aug.
I. C. C. Songfest, Staten Island, NYC, Early Aug.
Native American Awareness Pow-Wow, Peabody, MA, Early Aug.
Taste of the South Shore, Quincy, MA, Early Aug.
Waterfront Arts Festival, Canandaigua, NY, Early Aug.
Harlem Week/Harlem Day, Manhattan, NYC, Early Aug. to Middle Aug.
Riverside Park Arts Festival, Manhattan, NYC, Early Aug. to Late Aug.
Dominican Festival, Boston, MA, Early Aug.
Pine Grill Jazz Reunion, Rochester, NY, Early Aug.
Woodstock New Music Festival, Woodstock, NY, Early Aug.
Bluegrass Festival, Broadalbin, NY, Early Aug.
Gospel Music Workshop of America National Convention, Varied Sites, VAR, Early Aug. to
    Middle Aug.
Musicfest, Exeter, NH, Early Aug.
Adirondack Drums, Glens Falls, NY, Early Aug.
WWRL Family Day and Picnic, Queens, NYC, Early Aug. to Middle Aug.
Corinth Bluegrass Festival, Corinth, NY, Early Aug. to Middle Aug.
Country Music Festival Encore, Hunter, NY, Early Aug. to Middle Aug.
Cobleskill "Sunshine" Fair, Cobleskill, NY, Early Aug. to Middle Aug.
Waterfront Festival, Buffalo, NY, Early Aug. to Middle Aug.
Green Mountain Dulcimer Daze and Rendezvous, West Dover, VT, Middle Aug.
Connecticut River Valley Bluegrass Festival, East Haddam, CT, Middle Aug.
Fox Family Bluegrass Festival, Old Forge, NY, Middle Aug.
Taste of Northampton, Northampton, MA, Middle Aug.
International Duke Ellington Conference, Varied Sites, VAR, Middle Aug.
Skowhegan State Fair, Skowhegan, ME, Middle Aug.
Titcom Mountain Fiddling and Bluegrass Festival, Farmington, ME, Middle Aug.
Irish Night, Manchester, CT, Middle Aug.
Super Bluegrass and Gospel Day, Norwich, NY, Middle Aug.
Paumanauke Pow-Wow, Copiague, NY, Middle Aug.
New York Reggae Festival, Brooklyn, NYC, Middle Aug.
Passamaquoddy Traditional Indian Festival, Perry, ME, Middle Aug.
Bennington Battle Day Weekend, Bennington, VT, Middle Aug.
JVC Jazz Festival/Newport, Newport, RI, Middle Aug.
Sudbury Canada Days, Bethel, ME, Middle Aug.
Hyannis Seaport Festival, Hyannis, MA, Middle Aug.

Washington County Fair, Richmond, RI, Middle Aug.

Summertime Street Festival, New Haven, CT, Middle Aug.

Massachusetts Rock and Reggae for the Homeless, Great Barrington, MA, Middle Aug.

Morris Bluegrass Festival, Morris, CT, Middle Aug.

Royalty of Rock and Roll, Latham, NY, Middle Aug.

36th Avenue Summer Food Fair, Queens, NYC, Middle Aug.

New York Country Music Festival, Queens, NYC, Middle Aug.

Hot Country Music Festival, Burlington, VT, Middle Aug.

Carifest, Rochester, NY, Middle Aug.

Coors Country Chili Fest, Stratton Mountain, VT, Late Aug.

Fall River Celebrates America , Fall River, MA, Middle Aug.

Duracell Jazz Festival, Danbury, CT, Middle Aug.

Central New York Scottish Games and Celtic Festival, Syracuse, NY, Middle Aug.

Festival of North Country Folk Life, Massena, NY, Middle Aug.

Yiddish Heritage Celebration, Valhalla, NY, Middle Aug.

Nuyorican Poets Cafe Block Party, Manhattan, NYC, Middle Aug.

Park Slope Festival, Brooklyn, NYC, Middle Aug.

Summertime Blues Weekend, Lowell, MA, Middle Aug.

Pow Wow, Charlestown, RI, Middle Aug.

Erie County Fair, Hamburg, NY, Middle Aug. to Late Aug.

Precision and Pageantry Drum and Bugle Corps Competition, Pittsfield, MA, Middle Aug.

Newcomers of Country, Wallingford, CT, Middle Aug.

Anniversary Celebration of the Colored Musicians Club, Rochester, NY, Middle Aug.

Midsummer's Night Cabaret, Manhattan, NYC, Middle Aug.

Buttermilk Hill Old Time Music Show, Belgrade Lakes, ME, Middle Aug.

Drum Corps International World Championships, Varied Sites, VAR, Middle Aug.

Big Big Bands, Latham, NY, Middle Aug.

International Food Festival, Albany, NY, Middle Aug.

Carlos Fest, Brookline, MA, Middle Aug.

Harvey Robbins' Royalty of Rock 'n Roll/Cape Cod Melody Tent, Hyannis, MA, Middle Aug.

Outdoor Blues Festival, Latham, NY, Middle Aug.

Oxford County Bluegrass Festival, Norway/Oxford, ME, Middle Aug.

Lobsterfest/Celebrate Canton, Canton, CT, Middle Aug.

Southern Tier Bluegrass Festival, Savona, NY, Middle Aug.

St. Lawrence Valley Bluegrass Festival, Gouveneur, NY, Middle Aug.

Caribbean-American Community Trade and Cultural Expo, Brooklyn, NYC, Middle Aug. to
    Late Aug.

Shake-a-Leg Benefit Concert, Newport, RI, Middle Aug.

Blues Fest, Patterson, NY, Middle Aug.

Opus 40 Legends of Jazz/Future of Jazz, Saugerties, NY, Middle Aug.

Loon MountainPark CajunFest, Lincoln, NH, Middle Aug.

Gloucester Waterfront Festival, Gloucester, MA, Middle Aug.

Buffalo Caribbean Festival, Buffalo, NY, Middle Aug.

Martha's Vineyard Agricultural Fair Fiddle Contest: A Festival of Traditional Music, Vineyard
    Haven, MA, Middle Aug. to Late Aug.

Artpark Blues and Folk Festival, Lewiston, NY, Middle Aug. to Late Aug.

International Celtic Festival, Hunter, NY, Middle Aug. to Late Aug.

Boston Seaport Festival, Charlestown, MA, Middle Aug. to Late Aug.

Cabaret Symposium, Waterford, CT, Middle Aug. to Late Aug.

Panasonic Village Jazz Festival, Manhattan, NYC, Middle Aug. to Late Aug.

Summer Folk Music Weekend, Saugerties, NY, Middle Aug. to Late Aug.

Maine Highland Games , Brunswick, ME, Middle Aug.

Sankofa Street Festival, Belfast, ME, Middle Aug.

Spring Point Festival, South Portland, ME, Middle Aug.

Arts Jubilee/Country in the Valley, North Conway, NH, Late Aug.

Scituate Music Fest, Scituate, RI, Middle Aug.

Earth Jam, Woodstock, CT, Middle Aug.

Southern Fried Festival, Woodbury, CT, Middle Aug.

Long Lake Bluegrass Festival, Long Lake, NY, Middle Aug.

Waterfront Festival Free Summer Concert Series/Family Fun in the Sun, Buffalo, NY, Middle Aug.

WLIX Fest, Jamesport, NY, Middle Aug.

Adirondack Folk Music Festival, Schroon Lake, NY, Middle Aug. to Late Aug.

Native American Abenaki Pow-Wow, Evansville, VT, Late Aug.

Quinnehukqut Rendezvous and Native American Festival, Haddam, CT, Middle Aug. to Late Aug.

Caribbean Carnival, Boston, MA, Middle Aug. to Late Aug.

Down East Jazz Festival, Camden, ME, Late Aug.

Music Fest, Danielson, CT, Late Aug.

Hispanic Music Festival, Buffalo, NY, Late Aug.

98.7 KISS-FM Gospel Celebration, Manhattan, NYC, Late Aug.

Old-Time Fiddler's Fair, Mumford, NY, Late Aug.

City Gardeners' Harvest Fair/Gateway Music Festival/New York City Bluegrass Band and Banjo Festival, Brooklyn, NYC, Late Aug.

Oxhann Piano Festival, Clinton, NY, Late Aug.

Prescott Parks Arts Festival/Celebration of Jazz, Portsmouth, NH, Late Aug.

Music at The Ty Folklore Concert, Ticonderoga, NY, Late Aug.

WBNY's Battle of the Bands, Buffalo, NY, Late Aug.

Blues Bash for Homeless People, Smithfield, RI, Late Aug.

Midnight Ravers Anniversary Party, Manhattan, NYC, Late Aug.

Kingdom Bound, Darien Lake, NY, Late Aug.

Schneider's Bluegrass Festival, Elmira, NY, Late Aug.

Dutchess County Fair, Rhinebeck, NY, Late Aug.

Nichols Family Bluegrass Festival, Nichols, NY, Late Aug.

Dominican Festival, Providence, RI, Late Aug.

Project Children Irish Festival, Endicott, NY, Late Aug.

Downtown Festival/Rock Fest , Rochester, NY, Late Aug.

Final Stretch Festival, Saratoga Springs, NY, Late Aug.

Roots of American Music Festival, Manhattan, NYC, Late Aug.

New England Salty Dog Bluegrass Festival, Cambridge, ME, Late Aug.

Great Yankee Rib Cook-Off, Boston, MA, Late Aug.

Turtle Hill Music Festival, Spencerport, NY, Late Aug.

Western New England Bluegrass and Old-Time Championships and Steak Fry, Sheffield, MA, Late Aug.

Chopmist Hill Inn Summer Festival, North Scituate, RI, Late Aug.

Long Island Scottish Games, Old Westbury, NY, Late Aug.

PYX Birthday Blowout!, Latham, NY, Late Aug.

Salesian Folk Festival, New Rochelle, NY, Late Aug.

Black Family Weekend, Manhattan, NYC, Late Aug.

Greenwich Avenue Summer Festival, Manhattan, NYC, Late Aug.

Uprise and Shine Youth Concert, Brooklyn, NYC, Late Aug.

Taste Buds Festival, Hartford, CT, Late Aug.

Westbrook Drum Corps Muster, Westbrook, CT, Late Aug.

North American Northumbrian Piper's Convention, North Hero, VT, Late Aug.

Connecticut River Pow-Wow, Farmington, CT, Late Aug.

HAFOS:  Festival Hispano-Americano de Stamford, Stamford, CT, Late Aug.

Buffalo Irish Festival, Lancaster, NY, Late Aug.

Skyfest, Cedar Lake, NY, Late Aug.

Unifest, Buffalo, NY, Late Aug.
New York State Fair, Syracuse, NY, Late Aug. to Early Sep.
Circle of Sound Benefit Concert, Bath, ME, Late Aug.
Quechee Scottish Festival, Quechee, VT, Late Aug.
Bluegrass Festival, Rochester, NY, Late Aug.
Hispanic Heritage Celebration, Valhalla, NY, Late Aug.
Meck Music Fest, Mecklenberg, NY, Late Aug.
Music and The Mountain Sky/Jazz Concert, Highmount, NY, Late Aug.
Charlie Parker Jazz Festival, Manhattan, NYC, Late Aug.
Fierce Pussy Fest, Manhattan, NYC, Late Aug.
Salsa Fest, Brooklyn, NYC, Late Aug.
Vulvapalooza, Manhattan, NYC, Late Aug.
We Care About New York Block Party, Manhattan, NYC, Late Aug.
Greece Summer Festival, Greece, NY, Late Aug.
Islip Jazz Festival, Islip, NY, Late Aug.
Malden Irish Festival, Malden, MA, Late Aug.
Harbor Day, Norwich, CT, Late Aug.
Finger Lakes Dixieland Jazz Festival, Hector, NY, Late Aug.
Rockland Irish Festival, West Haverstraw, NY, Late Aug.
Stanfordville Music and Dance Festival, Stanfordville, NY, Late Aug.
Summer Jazz Festival, Elmira, NY, Late Aug.
Summer Music Festival, Amherst, NY, Late Aug.
Heineken Jazz and Blues Festival, Manhattan, NYC, Late Aug.
Champlain Valley Exposition, Essex Junction, VT, Late Aug. to Early Sep.
Big Band Bash, Albany, NY, Late Aug.

## September

Newsound Festival, Merrimac, MA, Early Sep.
Cajun and Bluegrass Music-Dance-Food Festival, Escoheag, RI, Early Sep.
Tanglewood Jazz Festival, Lenox, MA, Early Sep.
Blandford Fair Old Time Fiddle Contest, Blandford, MA, Early Sep.
Artpark Jazz Festival, Lewiston, NY, Early Sep.
South Shore Music Festival, Oceanside, NY, Early Sep.
New York Salsa Festival, Manhattan, NYC, Early Sep.
Thomas Point Beach Bluegrass Festival, Brunswick, ME, Early Sep.
Newburyport Waterfront Festival, Newburyport, MA, Early Sep.
Wrench Wranch Bluegrass Roundup, Coventryville, NY, Early Sep.
Maine Healing Arts Festival, Freedom, ME, Early Sep.
West Indian-American Day Carnival and Parade, Brooklyn, NYC, Early Sep.
White Mountain Jazz and Blues CraftsFestival, Bartlett, NH, Early Sep.
International Music and Dance Festival, Sacketts Harbor, NY, Early Sep.
Chandler's New World Festival, Randolph, VT, Early Sep.
Blues Festival, Portsmouth, NH, Early Sep.
Mountain Eagle Festival, Hunter, NY, Early Sep.
Old Time Country Music Festival, Hebron, ME, Early Sep.
Celtic Festival at the Hatch Shell, Boston, MA, Early Sep.
Reggae Festival, Washington, MA, Early Sep.
Labor and Ethnic Heritage Festival, Pawtucket, RI, Early Sep.
Eli Whitney Folk Festival, New Haven, CT, Early Sep.
WPLR Labor Day Celebration, New Haven, CT, Early Sep.
Capital District's Scottish Games: A Celtic Festival of the Arts, Altamont, NY, Early Sep.
Localpalooza Festival, Rochester, NY, Early Sep.
Brazilian National Independence Day Street Festival, Manhattan, NYC, Early Sep.

West Side Arts, Crafts, Antiques Festival, Manhattan, NYC, Early Sep.
West Side Fall Festival, Manhattan, NYC, Early Sep.
Wigstock, Manhattan, NYC, Early Sep.
Bolton Landing Barbershop Quartet Festival, Bolton Landing, NY, Early Sep.
International Waterfront Festival, Newburgh, NY, Early Sep.
Leeds Irish Festival, Leeds, NY, Early Sep.
Shinnecock Native-American Powwow, Southampton, NY, Early Sep.
Woodstock/New Paltz Art and Crafts Fair, New Paltz, NY, Early Sep.
Labor Day Weekend Music Festival, Conway, NH, Early Sep.
Sober in the Sun Labor Day Weekend Experience, Spencer, MA, Early Sep.
Vermont State Fair, Rutland, VT, Early Sep. to Middle Sep.
Come Sunday, Albany, NY, Early Sep. to Middle Sep.
Southbury Jazz Festival, Southbury, CT, Early Sep.
Bluegrass Bash, Manhattan, NYC, Early Sep.
Band Jamboree, Osceola, NY, Early Sep.
Iroquois Indian Festival, Howes Cave, NY, Late Sep.
Native American Days, Westerly, RI, Early Sep.
Labor Day Weekend Blowout, Parksville, NY, Early Sep.
Bread and Roses Labor Day Heritage Heritage Festival, Lawrence, MA, Early Sep.
DeCordova Labor Day Jazz Festival, Lincoln, MA, Early Sep.
New England Country Jamboree, Webster, MA, Middle Sep.
Local Motion MusicFest, Middletown, NY, Early Sep.
CMJ Music Marathon and Musicfest, Manhattan, NYC, Early Sep.
National Baptist Convention of America, Varied Sites, VAR, Early Sep. to Middle Sep.
Welcome Back to School Show: The Beginning of the End, New Haven, CT, Early Sep.
MTV Music Awards, Manhattan, NYC, Early Sep.
Simsbury Septemberfest, Simsbury, CT, Early Sep.
Lowell Riverfest, Lowell, MA, Early Sep. to Middle Sep.
Great Irish Fair, Brooklyn, NYC, Early Sep. to Middle Sep.
River Tree Arts Fiddle Contest and Old Time Country Music Show, Kennebunk, ME, Early Sep.
Banjo and Fiddle Contest, Lowell, MA, Middle Sep.
Pedal Steel Guitar Anniversary Bash, Lee, MA, Early Sep.
Brooklyn's Summer Gospelfest!, Brooklyn, NYC, Early Sep.
Chief Red Blanket Memorial Pow-Wow, Haverill, MA, Early Sep. to Middle Sep.
Martha's Vineyard Singer-Songwriters' Retreat, Vineyard Haven, MA, Early Sep. to Middle Sep.
Commodore John Barry A. O. H. Irish Festival, Olean, NY, Early Sep. to Middle Sep.
Iroquois Indian Festival, Rhinebeck, NY, Early Sep. to Middle Sep.
Lake George Jazz Weekend, Lake George, NY, Early Sep. to Middle Sep.
Roberson's Holiday and Arts Festival, Binghamton, NY, Early Sep. to Middle Sep.
Riverfest: Manchester Celebrating Itself, Manchester, NH, Early Sep. to Middle Sep.
Bourne Scallop Fest, Buzzards Bay, MA, Early Sep. to Middle Sep.
Oyster Festival, South Norwalk, CT, Early Sep. to Middle Sep.
Taste of Connecticut Food Festival, Mystic, CT, Early Sep. to Middle Sep.
Golden Link Folk Festival, Honeoye Falls, NY, Early Sep. to Middle Sep.
Salmon Sunday, Eastport, ME, Middle Sep.
Cambridge River Festival, Cambridge, MA, Middle Sep.
Day at the Lake, Worcester, MA, Middle Sep.
Septemberfest, Groton, MA, Middle Sep.
Apple Valley Family Folk Festival, Southington, CT, Middle Sep.
Taste of Greater Danbury, Danbury, CT, Middle Sep.
Harvest Moon Festival, Kingston, NY, Middle Sep.
Yonkers Hudson Riverfest, Yonkers, NY, Middle Sep.
Native American Appreciation Day, Cumberland, ME, Middle Sep.
Seafood Festival and Sidewalk Sale Days, Hampton Beach, NH, Middle Sep.

Vermont Brewers Festival, Various, VT, Middle Sep.
Chief Red Blanket Memorial Pow-Wow, Haverill, MA, Middle Sep.
Nipmuck Pow Wow, Oxford, MA, Middle Sep.
Providence Waterfront Festival/Waterfront Jazz Festival, Providence, RI, Middle Sep.
Sterling Park Campground Bluegrass Festival, Sterling, CT, Middle Sep.
Golden Harvest Festival, Baldwinsville, NY, Middle Sep.
Seneca Indian Fall Festival, Irving, NY, Middle Sep.
Cabaret for a Cause, Manhattan, NYC, Middle Sep. to Late Sep.
Fall Festival, Attleboro Falls, MA, Middle Sep.
Irish Fall Festival, Lincoln, RI, Middle Sep.
Just Jazz, Somers, NY, Middle Sep.
Petrified Sea Gardens Family Music Festival, Saratoga Springs, NY, Middle Sep.
Takin' It to the Streets:  The Electric City Music Celebration, Schenectady, NY, Middle Sep.
Music at New Paltz/Faculty Sampler, New Paltz, NY, Middle Sep.
Buffalo Country Music Awards, Buffalo, NY, Middle Sep.
Lazy River Bluegrass Festival , Gardiner, NY, Middle Sep.
New Hampshire Highland Games, Lincoln, NH, Middle Sep.
Schemitzun:  Feast of Green Corn, Hartford, CT, Middle Sep.
Eastern States Exposition -- The Big E!, West Springfield, MA, Middle Sep. to Late Sep.
Codman Farm Festival, Lincoln, MA, Middle Sep.
Rockaway Music and Arts Council Fall Festival, Brooklyn, NYC, Middle Sep.
Rockport Folk Festival, Rockport, ME, Middle Sep.
Palmyra Canal Town Days, Palmyra, NY, Middle Sep.
WPLJ-FM's 70's Dance Party, Manhattan, NYC, Middle Sep.
Folk Song Society of Greater Boston Fall Getaway Weekend, Hillsboro, NH, Middle Sep.
Gloucester Seafood Festival, Gloucester, MA, Middle Sep.
Housatonic Dulcimer Celebration, New Milford, CT, Middle Sep.
Shelburne Farms Harvest Festival, Shelburne, VT, Middle Sep.
Great Awakening Fest, Granby, MA, Middle Sep.
Barbershop Harmony Day, Mystic, CT, Middle Sep.
Dick Fox's Fall Doo-Wopp Extravaganza, Westbury, NY, Middle Sep.
Native American Heritage Day, Castille, NY, Middle Sep.
African-American Day Parade, Manhattan, NYC, Middle Sep.
New York Beer Fest, Brooklyn, NYC, Middle Sep.
Duke Ellington Festival, Portland, ME, Middle Sep.
Naples Grape Festival, Naples, NY, Middle Sep.
Northeast Squeeze-In, Washington, MA, Middle Sep.
Fiddlers Fling, Clayton, NY, Middle Sep.
Maine Invitational Country Music Semi-Finals Show, West Buxton, ME, Middle Sep. to Late Sep.
Old Time Country Jamboree, Waterville, ME, Middle Sep.
AutumnFest, Middlebury, VT, Middle Sep.
Banjo Contest, Craftsbury, VT, Middle Sep.
Bud Rocks the Block Party, Lowell, MA, Middle Sep.
Chowderfest, Charlestown, MA, Middle Sep.
John Penny Liver Foundation Jamboree, Webster, MA, Middle Sep.
Hartford Jazz Society Riverboat Cruise, Middletown, CT, Middle Sep.
A. O. H. Nassau County Board Feis and Festival, Uniondale, NY, Middle Sep.
Amherst Museum Scottish Festival, Amherst, NY, Middle Sep.
Field, Forest and Stream, Elizabethtown, NY, Middle Sep.
FLY92 End of Summer Jam, Latham, NY, Middle Sep.
Long Island Fiddle and Folk Music Festival, Stony Brook, NY, Middle Sep.
Native American Festival, Kingston, NY, Middle Sep.
Columbus Avenue Festival, Manhattan, NYC, Middle Sep.
International Festival of Cultures, Staten Island, NYC, Middle Sep.

Rafael Hernandez/Sylvia Rexach Festival, Manhattan, NYC, Middle Sep.
Sugarbush Brewers Festival, Warren, VT, Middle Sep.
Autumn Harvest Festival, Cooperstown, NY, Middle Sep.
Art Newbury Street, Boston, MA, Middle Sep.
Folk Heritage Festival, Lexington, MA, Middle Sep.
Rhode Island's Heritage Day, Providence, RI, Middle Sep.
Trumbull Arts Festival, Trumbull, CT, Middle Sep.
QE2: Newport Jazz Festival at Sea, Manhattan, NYC, Middle Sep. to Late Sep.
American Festival of Microtonal Music, Manhattan, NYC, Middle Sep. to Early Nov.
Expressions International Festival, Manhattan, NYC, Late Sep. to Late Oct.
Cognac Hennessy Jazz Search, Manhattan, NYC, Late Sep.
Durham Agricultural Fair, Durham, CT, Late Sep.
Buckwheat Harvest Festival, Penn Yan, NY, Late Sep.
Eisteddfod Festival of Traditional Music and Dance, North Dartmouth, MA, Late Sep.
New England Ragtime Festival, East Lyme, CT, Late Sep.
Bopper's Oldies Concert, Huntington, NY, Late Sep.
Settlers' Day, Lincoln, RI, Late Sep.
Taste of Rhode Island, Newport, RI, Late Sep.
Westport Blues Festival, Westport, CT, Late Sep.
Apple Umpkin Festival, Wyoming, NY, Late Sep.
Ecofest, Varies, NYC, Late Sep.
Common Ground Country Fair, Windsor, ME, Late Sep.
Star Hampshire Traditional Music/Dance Retreat, Portsmouth, NH, Late Sep.
Autumn Hills Dulcimer Festival, Great Barrington, MA, Late Sep.
Strawberry Park Country Western Jamboree, Preston, CT, Late Sep.
Country Fest, Webster, MA, Middle Sep.
Long Island Emerald Isle Festival, Hempstead, NY, Late Sep.
Gateway Sukkos Festival, Brooklyn, NYC, Late Sep.
Native American Festival, Manhattan, NYC, Late Sep.
Sephardi Cultural Fair, Queens, NYC, Late Sep.
National Traditional Old Time Fiddlers' and Step Dancing Contest, Barre, VT, Late Sep.
Swamp Yankee Days, Charlestown, RI, Late Sep.
Eagle Wing Press Powwow, Watertown, CT, Late Sep.
Celtic Fair, Hunter, NY, Late Sep.
Celtic Day in the Park, Staatsburg, NY, Late Sep.
52nd Street Jazz Festival, Manhattan, NYC, Late Sep.
Do the Right Thing Festival, Brooklyn, NYC, Late Sep.
Northeastern Native American Association Pow Wow, Queens, NYC, Late Sep.
New York State Big Apple Festival, Manhattan, NYC, Late Sep.
M. C. M. A. A. Awards Show, Randolph, MA, Late Sep.
Next Wave Festival, Brooklyn, NYC, Late Sep. to Middle Dec.
Hilton Applefest, Hilton, NY, Late Sep. to Early Oct.

## October

New England Sacred Harp Singing Convention, Varied Sites, VAR, Early Oct.
Underground Jazz Festival, Manhattan, NYC, Early Oct.
Flaming Leaves Fiddle Jamboree, Long Lake, NY, Early Oct.
Acid Jazz Night, Manhattan, NYC, Early Oct.
Atlantic Antic, Brooklyn, NYC, Early Oct.
Gay and Lesbian American Music Awards, Manhattan, NYC, Early Oct. to Early Nov.
New England Sacred Harp Singing Convention, Wellesley, MA, Early Oct.
Pow Wow, Charlestown, RI, Early Oct.
Alternative Sports and Music Festival, Middletown, NY, Early Oct.

Gathering of Iroquois, Liverpool, NY, Early Oct.

Long Island Traditional Music Association Fall Folk Weekend, Baiting Hollow, NY, Early Oct.

Clearwater's Pumpkin Sail, Varied Sites, VAR, Early Oct. to Middle Oct.

John Coltrane Memorial Concert, Boston, MA, Early Oct.

Roots and Fruits Fiddle and Dance Festival, Hartford, CT, Early Oct.

Applefest, Warwick, NY, Early Oct.

Catskill Harvest Festival, Walton, NY, Early Oct.

Long Beach Irish Day Parade and Festival, Long Beach, NY, Early Oct.

Swain Country Western Music Festival, Swain, NY, Early Oct.

Chili Pepper Fiesta, Brooklyn, NYC, Early Oct.

WDRE Modern Rock Fest, Manhattan, NYC, Early Oct.

Norman Bird Sanctuary Harvest Fair, Middletown, RI, Early Oct.

New Music Across America, Varied Sites, VAR, Early Oct.

Outmusic Festival, Manhattan, NYC, Early Oct. to Early Nov.

St. Andrew's Society of Conneticut Scottish Festival, Goshen, CT, Early Oct.

Scotland Highland Festival, Scotland, CT, Early Oct.

Acoustic Underground:  Boston's National Acoustic Music Showcase, Boston, MA, Early Oct. to
    Early Nov.

Mineral Springs Foot Stomp'n Festival, Stafford Springs, CT, Early Oct.

Fiddlers!!:  A Sampler of North American Fiddle Traditions, Roxbury, NY, Early Oct.

Opus 40 Jazz Autumn, Saugerties, NY, Early Oct.

Dick Fox's Ultimate Doo-Wopp Fantasy Weekend, Monitcello, NY, Early Oct.

WEQX Birthday Party/University of Albany Fallfest, Albany, NY, Early Oct.

Greenwich Village Folk Festival, Manhattan, NYC, Early Oct.

Scottish Performing Arts Weekend and Workshop, Bar Harbor, ME, Middle Oct.

Gaelic Roots:  The Music, Song and Dance of Ireland, Chestnut Hill, MA, Early Oct.

Autumnfest, Woonsocket, RI, Early Oct.

Scituate Arts Festival, North Scituate, RI, Early Oct.

Letchworth Arts and Crafts Show and Sale, Castile, NY, Early Oct.

All-Nite Soul, Manhattan, NYC, Early Oct.

Eleventh Avenue Auto Fair, Manhattan, NYC, Early Oct.

Mix 98.5 Fall Fest, Boston, MA, Early Oct.

Columbus Weekend Harvest Fair, East Durham, NY, Early Oct.

Chowderfest, Mystic, CT, Early Oct. to Middle Oct.

Paucatuck Pequot Harvest Moon Powwow, North Stonington, CT, Early Oct. to Middle Oct.

Mountain Music and Dance Weekend in the Adirondacks, Raquette Lake, NY, Early Oct. to
    Middle Oct.

Knitting Factory at Merkin Hall, Manhattan, NYC, Early Oct. to Middle Oct.

Whaling City Jazz Festival, New Bedford, MA, Early Oct.

Columbus Day Tournament of Bands, Binghamton, NY, Early Oct.

Native American/Indigenous People Day Celebration, Albany, NY, Early Oct.

Summertime Blues Charity Cruise, Troy, NY, Middle Oct.

Vermont Apple Festival and Crafts Show, Springfield, VT, Middle Oct.

Westport Harvest Festival, Westport, MA, Early Oct. to Middle Oct.

French Heritage Festival, Barre, VT, Late Oct.

New York State Sacred Harp Singing Convention, Ithaca, NY, Middle Oct.

Choose Life Benefit Gospel Concert, Manhattan, NYC, Middle Oct.

Shelter:  The New York Singer-Songwriter Festival, Manhattan, NYC, Middle Oct.

Apple Harvest Festival, Glastonbury, CT, Middle Oct.

Festival at Roseland Cottage, Woodstock, CT, Middle Oct.

October Oyster Festival, Oyster Bay, NY, Middle Oct.

Fall Folk Music Weekend, Falls Village, CT, Middle Oct.

Fall Country Dance and Party Weekend, Kerhonkson, NY, Middle Oct.

Nations of New York Arts Festival, Manhattan, NYC, Middle Oct. to Late Oct.

Irish Variety Show, Braintree, MA, Middle Oct.
Fox Hollow Reunion Folk Concert, Troy, NY, Middle Oct.
Live Jazz Bands, Queens, NYC, Middle Oct.
Bowen's Wharf Waterfront Seafood Festival, Newport, RI, Middle Oct.
Niagara's Apple Country Festival, Lockport, NY, Middle Oct.
Chilifest, Charlestown, MA, Middle Oct.
Irish Music Festival, Boston, MA, Middle Oct.
Celebration of Jewish Learning, Brighton, NY, Middle Oct.
North East Country Music Association Awards Show, Albany, NY, Middle Oct.
Night of Musical Magic, Manhattan, NYC, Middle Oct.
Cabaret Convention, Manhattan, NYC, Middle Oct. to Late Oct.
Peter Tosh Day, Manhattan, NYC, Middle Oct.
Hanukkah Arts Festival and Judaica Crafts Fair/Selected Shorts, Manhattan, NYC, Middle Oct.
Smithsonian's National Museum of the American Indian Powwow, Manhattan, NYC, Middle
      Oct.
American Banjo Fraternity's Fall Rally, Varied Sites, VAR, Middle Oct. to Late Oct.
Africa Mondo Festival, Manhattan, NYC, Middle Oct. to Late Oct.
Calypso and Steelband "Sunshine" Music Awards, Manhattan, NYC, Late Oct.
Irish Music Weekend Party of the Year, Monticello, NY, Late Oct.
Combinacion Perfecta, Manhattan, NYC, Late Oct.
Blue Hill Festival of Music/Singer-Songwriter Marathon, Blue Hill, ME, Late Oct.
Computer Music at Stony Brook, Stony Brook, NY, Late Oct.
Gospel Night, Buffalo, NY, Late Oct.
Brooklyn Ethnic Music and Dance Festival, Brooklyn, NYC, Late Oct.
Best of the Best Pow-Wow/Native American Indian Arts Festival, Suffern, NY, Late Oct.
FolkTree Jamboree, Boston, MA, Late Oct.
Fall Jamboree, Rochester, NY, Late Oct.
Songwriter's Evening, Manhattan, NYC, Late Oct.
Jazz for the Arts/Kick Off, Albany, NY, Late Oct.
Cultural Crossroads' Jazz Gala, Brooklyn, NYC, Late Oct.
Cajun/Zydeco Jamboree and Halloween Dance, Manhattan, NYC, Late Oct.
Fall MusicFest, Portland, ME, Late Oct. to Early Nov.
WBCN Rock of Boston Concert, Boston, MA, Late Oct.
Project Children Dinner Dance and Variety Show, Syracuse, NY, Late Oct.
Apple Harvest Festival, Ithaca, NY, Early Oct.
National Rockabilly Blowout, Rochester, NY, Late Oct.
Pines Scottish Weekend, South Fallsburg, NY, Late Oct.
Halloween Dance Weekend, Ashokan, NY, Late Oct. to Early Nov.
Theater for the New City Village Haloween Costume Ball, Manhattan, NYC, Late Oct.
Village Halloween Parade/All Souls' Halloween Ball, Manhattan, NYC, Late Oct.
NOMAD:  Northeast Music, Art and Dance Festival, Sandy Hook, CT, Late Oct. to Early Nov.
Boston International Festival, Dorcester, MA, Late Oct. to Late Nov.

## November

WFNX Birthday Party, Boston, MA, Early Nov.
Charlie Parker Music and More Awards Gala, Manhattan, NYC, Early Nov.
Battle of the Bands, Burlington, VT, Early Nov.
Sonic Boom Festival of New Music, Manhattan, NYC, Early Nov. to Middle Nov.
Night of Shamrocks, Queens, NYC, Middle Nov.
Maine Invitational Country Music Finals Show, West Buxton, ME, Early Nov.
JAL Jazz Concert, Manhattan, NYC, Early Nov.
CMAC's Boston Rhythm, Cambridge, MA, Early Nov.
Buddy Rich Memorial Scholarship Concert, Manhattan, NYC, Early Nov.

Juba, Jukin' and Jazzin', Manhattan, NYC, Early Nov.
Phil Ochs Song Night, Cambridge, MA, Early Nov.
Harlem Piano U. S. A., Manhattan, NYC, Middle Nov.
Kitty Brazelton's Real Music Series/Music Parties, Manhattan, NYC, Early Nov. to Late Nov.
Ear-Fest: Festival of Taped Music, Stony Brook, NY, Early Nov.
Floating Archives' Some Kind of Carnival, Manhattan, NYC, Early Nov.
Great Beer and Music Festival, Manhattan, NYC, Middle Nov.
Pines Number One Irish Weekend, South Fallsburg, NY, Middle Nov.
Richard Nader's Rock and Roll Revival Spectacular, Manhattan, NYC, Middle Nov.
Blacksmith House Folk Festival/Folk Arts Conference, Cambridge, MA, Middle Nov.
Barbershop Serenade, Buffalo, NY, Middle Nov.
Big Band Day, Manhattan, NYC, Middle Nov.
JazzTimes Convention, Manhattan, NYC, Middle Nov.
K-Rock's Hungerthon, Manhattan, NYC, Middle Nov.
Hungerthon Concert/Winter Blues Fest, New City, NY, Middle Nov.
Grand International Ragtime/Jasstime Foundation Fall Festival, Alexandria Bay, NY, Middle
    Nov.
National Native American Heritage Day Pow-Wow, Concord, MA, Middle Nov.
Songstreet Folk-Rock Festival, Somerville, MA, Middle Nov.
Stardust Dance Weekend, Ellenville, NY, Middle Nov. to Late Nov.
CMAC's Fall Benefit, Cambridge, MA, Middle Nov.
Buffalo Beer Fest, Buffalo, NY, Middle Nov.
Giving of Thanks to the First Peoples, Manhattan, NYC, Middle Nov.
Festival of Lights, Niagara Falls, NY, Middle Nov. to Early Jan.
Artvoice Original Music Awards, Buffalo, NY, Late Nov.
Mohonk's Joy of Singing, New Paltz, NY, Late Nov.
Skavoovee, Manhattan, NYC, Late Nov.
AIDS Dance-A-Thon, Manhattan, NYC, Late Nov.
Big Bands at Sea, Manhattan, NYC, Late Nov. to Early Dec.
Return of The Brooklyn Bridge, Queens, NYC, Late Nov.
Sonidos de las Americas, Varies, NYC, Late Nov. to Early Dec.
Improvisations Festival, Manhattan, NYC, Late Nov. to Middle Dec.
Jimi Hendrix Birthday Party, Manhattan, NYC, Late Nov.
Strathspey and Reel Society of New Hampshire's Scottish Gala Concert, Concord, NH, Late Nov.

## December

Benson Series Benefit Concert for United AIDS Relief Effort, Manhattan, NYC, Early Dec.
WBLS Celebration Concert and Scholarship Fund, Manhattan, NYC, Early Dec.
Post-Rock, Neo-Mosh Festival, Manhattan, NYC, Early Dec.
El Elyon Music Awards, Manhattan, NYC, Early Dec.
Country Music Dance Weekend, South Fallsburg, NY, Early Dec.
TeddyCare, Manhattan, NYC, Early Dec. to Late Dec.
Emerald Productions Getaway, Callicoon, NY, Early Dec.
Latin Jazz U. S. A. Concert and Awards, Manhattan, NYC, Early Dec.
Bending Toward the Light: A Jazz Nativity, Manhattan, NYC, Early Dec.
Z100 Acoustic Christmas, Manhattan, NYC, Early Dec.
Colors of Christmas, Manhattan, NYC, Early Dec.
WNEW-FM Christmas Concert, Manhattan, NYC, Early Dec.
Winter Revels, Manhattan, NYC, Early Dec.
Chango Celebration, Manhattan, NYC, Early Dec.
Kwanzaa, Queens, NYC, Early Dec.
Festival of Light and Song, Jamaica Plain, MA, Middle Dec.
Great Irish Weekend, Ellenville, NY, Early Dec. to Middle Dec.

Experimental Intermedia Four Country Festival, Manhattan, NYC, Early Dec. to Late Dec.
Valentine's XMas Jam, Albany, NY, Middle Dec.
Hanukkah Festival, Queens, NYC, Middle Dec.
Irish and Cape Breton Christmas Concert and Ceili, Chestnut Hill, MA, Middle Dec.
WDRE Acoustic Christmas, Manhattan, NYC, Middle Dec.
WEQX Acoustic Holiday Concert for the Hungry, Latham, NY, Middle Dec.
Winter Consort Winter Solstice Whole Earth Christmas Celebration, Manhattan, NYC, Middle
     Dec.
Holiday Jam for Joy, Rotterdam, NY, Middle Dec.
Kwanzaa Holiday Expo, Manhattan, NYC, Middle Dec.
Indian Market, Manhattan, NYC, Middle Dec. to Late Dec.
Dick Fox's Holiday Doo-Wopp Extravaganza, Westbury, NY, Middle Dec.
Sounds Around the World, Manhattan, NYC, Middle Dec.
Christmas Revels, Hanover, NH, Middle Dec.
Christmas Revels, Cambridge, MA, Middle Dec. to Late Dec.
New York Jazz Today!, Manhattan, NYC, Middle Dec.
Community Carol Sing, Mystic, CT, Middle Dec.
WWRL Gospel Explosion, Manhattan, NYC, Middle Dec.
Klezkamp, Parksville, NY, Late Dec.
Community Holiday Festival, Manhattan, NYC, Late Dec. to Early Jan.
Kwanzaa Fete, Hempstead, NY, Late Dec.
Niagara: The Student and Adult Leadership Conference on Evangelism, Niagara Falls, NY, Late
     Dec.
Black Nativity, Manhattan, NYC, Late Dec.
S. O. B.'s Kwanzaa Celebration, Manhattan, NYC, Late Dec.
Skarmageddon, Manhattan, NYC, Late Dec.
New Year's Eve Portland, Portland, ME, Late Dec.
First Night Keene, Keene, NH, Late Dec.
First Night New Hampshire, Concord, NH, Late Dec.
First Night Portsmouth, Portsmouth, NH, Late Dec.
First Night Burlington, Burlington, VT, Late Dec.
First Night Rutland, Rutland, VT, Late Dec.
First Night St. Johnsbury, St. Johnsbury, VT, Late Dec.
First Night Boston, Boston, MA, Late Dec.
First Night Brockton, Brockton, MA, Late Dec.
First Night Chatham, Chatham, MA, Late Dec.
First Night in Hyannis, Falmouth, MA, Late Dec.
First Night New Bedford, New Bedford, MA, Late Dec.
First Night Newburyport, Newburyport, MA, Late Dec.
First Night Northampton, Northampton, MA, Late Dec.
First Night Pittsfield, Pittsfield, MA, Late Dec.
First Night Quincy, Quincy, MA, Late Dec.
First Night Worcester, Worcester, MA, Late Dec.
Lowell Family First Night, Lowell, MA, Late Dec.
Opening Night, Salem, Salem, MA, Late Dec.
First Night Providence, Providence, RI, Late Dec.
Opening Night, Newport, RI, Late Dec.
First Night Danbury, Danbury, CT, Late Dec.
First Night Hartford, Hartford, CT, Late Dec.
First Night Albany, Albany, NY, Late Dec.
First Night Buffalo, Buffalo, NY, Late Dec.
First Night Freeport, Freeport, NY, Late Dec.
New Year's Early Eve, Rochester, NY, Late Dec.
Concert for Peace, Manhattan, NYC, Late Dec.

First Night New York, Manhattan, NYC, Late Dec.

~     ~     ~

*Frogboy, Hartford Advocate's Best of the Local Music Bash.*

# Festival Names in Alphabetical Order

## Maine

Acadian Festival Celebration, Madawaska, ME, Late Jun. to Early Jul.
Arcady Music Festival/Ragtime Evening Benefit, Bangor, ME, Early Jun.
Back Cove Family Day, Portland, ME, Middle Jun.
Bangor State Fair, Bangor, ME, Late Jul. to Early Aug.
Bar Harbor Festival/New Composers Concert, Bar Harbor, ME, Late Jul.
Bath Heritage Days, Bath, ME, Early Jul.
Belfast Bay Festival, Belfast, ME, Middle Jul.
Blistered Fingers Family Bluegrass Music Festival, Sidney, ME, Middle Jun.
Blistered Fingers Helping Hands of Bluegrass, Brunswick, ME, Late Mar. to Early Apr.
Blue Hill Festival of Music/Singer-Songwriter Marathon, Blue Hill, ME, Late Oct.
Blue Hill Pops, Blue Hill, ME, Early Jul.
Blues Festival, North Yarmouth, ME, Late Jun.
Breakneck Mountain Bluegrass Festival, Crawford, ME, Early Jul.
Buttermilk Hill Old Time Music Show, Belgrade Lakes, ME, Middle Aug.
Celebrate Gorham, Gorham, ME, Early Jul.
Celebration of the Arts, Kennebunk, ME, Middle Jul. to Late Jul.
Central Maine Egg Festival, Pittsfield, ME, Middle Jul. to Late Jul.
Circle of Sound Benefit Concert, Bath, ME, Late Aug.
Common Ground Country Fair, Windsor, ME, Late Sep.
Coor's Lite Music Festival, Brewer, ME, Early Jul.
Deering Oaks Family Festival, Portland, ME, Middle Jul. to Late Jul.
Down East Country Dance Festival, South Portland, ME, Middle Mar.
Down East Jazz Festival, Camden, ME, Late Aug.
Downeast Dulcimer and Harp Festival, Bar Harbor, ME, Early Jul.
Duke Ellington Festival, Portland, ME, Middle Sep.
East Benton Fiddlers' Convention and Contest, East Benton, ME, Late Jul.
Fall MusicFest, Portland, ME, Late Oct. to Early Nov.
Family Fun Fair, Portland, ME, Middle Jun.
Fat Tire Polo Tournament and Music Bash, Farmington, ME, Early Aug.
Festival de la Bastille, Augusta, ME, Early Jul.
Festival of Traditional Sea Music, Bath, ME, Early Jun.
Fiddlehead Festival, Unity, ME, Middle May
Fiddling Competition and Contra Dance, Damariscotta, ME, Middle Jun.
Gamper Festival of Contemporary Music, Brunswick, ME, Late Jul.
Grand Riviere Festival, Van Buren, ME, Late Jun. to Middle Aug.
Great Whatever Week and Race, Augusta, ME, Late Jun. to Early Jul.
H. O. M. E. Craft and Farm Fair, Orland, ME, Early Aug.
Happy Horseshoe Blue Grass Festival, North New Portland, ME, Middle Jun.
Hebron Pines Bluegrass Festival, Hebron, ME, Late May
Homecoming, Grand Isle, ME, Late Jul. to Early Aug.
International Festival, Calais, ME, Late Jul. to Early Aug.
Kaleidoscope Family Arts Festival, Augusta, ME, Early Jun.
Katahdin Family Bluegrass Music Festival, Medway, ME, Late Jun.
Knights of Columbus Festival de Joie, Lewiston, ME, Early Aug.
LaKermesse Franco-Americaine Festival, Biddeford, ME, Late Jun.
Left Bank Cafe Country Blues Festival, Blue Hill, ME, Middle Jul.

Maine Festival of the Arts, Brunswick, ME, Early Aug.
Maine Healing Arts Festival, Freedom, ME, Early Sep.
Maine Highland Games , Brunswick, ME, Middle Aug.
Maine Invitational Country Music Finals Show, West Buxton, ME, Early Nov.
Maine Invitational Country Music Semi-Finals Show, West Buxton, ME, Middle Sep. to Late Sep.
Maine Lobster Festival, Rockland, ME, Early Aug.
Maine Potato Blossom Festival/Crown of Maine Balloon Festival, Fort Fairfield, ME, Early Jul.
    to Middle Jul.
Mollyockett Day, Bethel, ME, Middle Jul.
Motahkmikuk Indian Day Celebration, Princeton, ME, Middle Jul. to Middle Jul.
Native American Appreciation Day, Cumberland, ME, Middle Sep.
Native American Festival, Bar Harbor, ME, Early Jul.
New England Salty Dog Bluegrass Festival, Cambridge, ME, Late Aug.
New Vineyard Mountains Bluegrass Festival, North Anson, ME, Early Jul.
New Year's Eve Portland, Portland, ME, Late Dec.
North Atlantic Blues Festival, Rockland, ME, Early Jul.
Old Hallowell Day, Hallowell, ME, Middle Jul.
Old Home Week and Independence Day, Eastport, ME, Late Jun. to Early Jul.
Old Port Festival, Portland, ME, Early Jun.
Old Time Country Jamboree, Waterville, ME, Middle Sep.
Old Time Country Music Festival, Hebron, ME, Early Sep.
Oxford County Bluegrass Festival, Norway/Oxford, ME, Middle Aug.
Passamaquoddy Traditional Indian Festival, Perry, ME, Middle Aug.
Portland Waterfront Festival, Portland, ME, Late Jun.
Pride of Maine Fiddling Festival, Waldo, ME, Middle May
Pride of Maine Fiddling Festival, Caribou, ME, Early Feb.
Pride of Maine Fiddling Festival, Machias, ME, Middle Feb.
Rangeley's Old-Time Fiddlers' Contest, Rangeley, ME, Middle Jul.
Richmond Days, Richmond, ME, Middle Jul. to Late Jul.
River Tree Arts Country Jamboree, Kennebunk, ME, Middle Mar.
River Tree Arts Fiddle Contest and Old Time Country Music Show, Kennebunk, ME, Early Sep.
Rock 'N' Roll Bar-B-Q, Old Orchard Beach, ME, Early Jul.
Rockport Folk Festival, Rockport, ME, Middle Sep.
Rotary Oyster Festival, Damariscotta, ME, Early Jul. to Middle Jul.
Salmon Sunday, Eastport, ME, Middle Sep.
Sankofa Street Festival, Belfast, ME, Middle Aug.
Schooner Days, Rockland, ME, Early Jul.
Scottish Performing Arts Weekend and Workshop, Bar Harbor, ME, Middle Oct.
Seaside Festival, Kittery, ME, Early Jul.
Skowhegan State Fair, Skowhegan, ME, Middle Aug.
Spring Point Festival, South Portland, ME, Middle Aug.
Strawberry Festival, South Berwick, ME, Late Jun.
Sudbury Canada Days, Bethel, ME, Middle Aug.
Sugarloaf Country Music Festival, Kingfield, ME, Late Jun. to Late Aug.
Sugarloaf Mountain Blues Festival, Kingfield, ME, Middle Apr.
Sugarloaf Reggae Ski Bash, Kingfield, ME, Early Apr.
Sugarloaf Ski-A-Palooza/College Weeks, Kingfield, ME, Early Jan. to Middle Jan.
Summer in the Parks, Portland, ME, Early Aug. to Middle Aug.
Sweet Chariot Music Festival and Schooner Gam, Swans Island, ME, Early Aug.
Thomas Point Beach Bluegrass Festival, Brunswick, ME, Early Sep.
Thomaston Independence Day Celebration, Thomaston, ME, Early Jul.
Titcom Mountain Fiddling and Bluegrass Festival, Farmington, ME, Middle Aug.
WERU 89.9FM Full Circle Summer Fair, Union, ME, Early Jul.
Windjammer Days, Boothbay Harbor, ME, Late Jun.

Yarmouth Clam Festival, Yarmouth, ME, Middle Jul.
York Days, York, ME, Late Jul. to Early Aug.

## New Hampshire

All AmericanFest, Lincoln, NH, Early Jul.
American Pit Masters Bar-B-Q Round-Up, Manchester, NH, Early Jul.
Arts Jubilee/Country in the Valley, North Conway, NH, Late Aug.
Blues Festival, Portsmouth, NH, Early Sep.
Christmas Revels, Hanover, NH, Middle Dec.
Clark Terry/University of New Hampshire Jazz Festival, Durham, NH, Middle Mar.
Classic Rock Festival, Plymouth, NH, Late Jun.
Contemporary Music Festival, Concord, NH, Early May
Countryfest, Laconia, NH, Early Mar.
Dartmouth Festival of New Musics, Hanover, NH, Middle May
Fiddler's Contest, Lincoln, NH, Late Jun.
First Night Keene, Keene, NH, Late Dec.
First Night New Hampshire, Concord, NH, Late Dec.
First Night Portsmouth, Portsmouth, NH, Late Dec.
Folk Song Society of Greater Boston Fall Getaway Weekend, Hillsboro, NH, Middle Sep.
Gilmanton Bluegrass Festival, Gilmanton, NH, Middle Jul.
Hanover Street-Fest, Hanover, NH, Middle Jul.
Hayseed Music Fest, Franconia, NH, Middle Jul.
High Hopes Hot Air Balloon Festival, Milford, NH, Middle Jun.
International Festival, Manchester, NH, Early May
Jazz Showcase, Portsmouth, NH, Late Jun.
Labor Day Weekend Music Festival, Conway, NH, Early Sep.
Loon MountainPark BrewFest, Lincoln, NH, Late Jul.
Loon MountainPark CajunFest, Lincoln, NH, Middle Aug.
Loon MountainPark IrishFest, Lincoln, NH, Early Aug.
Market Square Day, Portsmouth, NH, Early Jun. to Middle Jun.
Musicfest, Exeter, NH, Early Aug.
Native American Show, Littleton, NH, Middle Jul.
New England Bluegrass Festival, Laconia, NH, Middle Jun.
New England Blues Conference, Portsmouth, NH, Late Apr.
New Hampshire Highland Games, Lincoln, NH, Middle Sep.
New Hampshire Women's Music Festival, Northfield, NH, Middle Jun.
New Hampshire's Lilac Time Festival, Lisbon, NH, Late May
Pemi Valley Bluegrass Festival, Campton, NH, Early Aug.
Portsmouth Jazz Festival, Portsmouth, NH, Late Jun.
Prescott Parks Arts Festival/Celebration of Jazz, Portsmouth, NH, Late Aug.
Ralph Page Legacy Weekend, Durham, NH, Early Jan.
Riverfest: Manchester Celebrating Itself, Manchester, NH, Early Sep. to Middle Sep.
Seacoast African-American Heritage Festival, Portsmouth, NH, Early Feb. to Late Feb.
Seacoast Music Awards, Portsmouth, NH, Early Feb.
Seafood Festival and Sidewalk Sale Days, Hampton Beach, NH, Middle Sep.
Somersworth International Children's Festival, Somersworth, NH, Middle Jun.
Star Hampshire Traditional Music/Dance Retreat, Portsmouth, NH, Late Sep.
Stark Old Time Fiddlers' Contest, Stark, NH, Late Jun.
Strathspey and Reel Society of New Hampshire's Scottish Gala Concert, Concord, NH, Late Nov.
Street Fair, Keene, NH, Middle Jul.
Twin Mountain Country Western Jamboree, Bretton Woods, NH, Early Jul.
Waterville Valley Summer Music Festival, Waterville Valley, NH, Middle Jul. to Early Sep.
White Mountain Jazz and Blues CraftsFestival, Bartlett, NH, Early Sep.

## Vermont

Abenaki Festival Days, Rutland/Burlington, VT, Late Apr. to Early May
Aquafest, Newport, VT, Middle Jul.
AutumnFest, Middlebury, VT, Middle Sep.
Banjo Contest, Craftsbury, VT, Middle Sep.
Basin Bluegrass Festival, Brandon, VT, Early Jul.
Battle of the Bands, Burlington, VT, Early Nov.
Ben and Jerry's One World, One Heart Festival, Warren, VT, Late Jun.
Bennington Battle Day Weekend, Bennington, VT, Middle Aug.
Bennington Folk Festival, Bennington, VT, Middle May
Burlington Independence Day Waterfront Celebration, Burlington, VT, Early Jul.
Cabin Fever Folklife Festival, Middlebury, VT, Early Apr.
Celebrate Vermont Arts and Crafts Show, Rochester, VT, Middle Jul.
Champlain Valley Exposition, Essex Junction, VT, Late Aug. to Early Sep.
Champlain Valley Festival, Burlington, VT, Early Aug.
Chandler's New World Festival, Randolph, VT, Early Sep.
Coors Country Chili Fest, Stratton Mountain, VT, Late Aug.
Crackerbarrel Fiddlers Contest, Newbury, VT, Late Jul.
Discover Jazz Festival, Burlington, VT, Early Jun. to Middle Jun.
Families Outdoor Festival, Ferrisburgh, VT, Middle Jul.
First Night Burlington, Burlington, VT, Late Dec.
First Night Rutland, Rutland, VT, Late Dec.
First Night St. Johnsbury, St. Johnsbury, VT, Late Dec.
French Heritage Festival, Barre, VT, Late Oct.
Green Mountain Chew Chew/Vermont Food Fest, Burlington, VT, Late Jun.
Green Mountain Dulcimer Daze and Rendezvous, West Dover, VT, Middle Aug.
Harmony Ridge Brass Center Summer Festival, Poultney, VT, Early Aug.
Hot Country Music Festival, Burlington, VT, Middle Aug.
Irish Cultural Day, Burlington, VT, Early May
Lake Champlain Balloon Festival, Essex Junction, VT, Early Jun.
Lamplight Service and Hymn Sing, North Danville, VT, Late May to Late Aug.
Middlebury Summer Festival-on-the-Green, Middlebury, VT, Middle Jul.
Midsummer Festival of Vermont Art and Music, Montpelier, VT, Early Jul.
Mountain Jam, Killington, VT, Early Jul.
National Fife and Drum Muster, Waterbury, VT, Early Aug.
National Traditional Old Time Fiddlers' and Step Dancing Contest, Barre, VT, Late Sep.
Native American Abenaki Pow-Wow, Evansville, VT, Late Aug.
North American Northumbrian Piper's Convention, North Hero, VT, Late Aug.
Ole Time Fiddlers Contest, Hardwick, VT, Late Jul.
Pico Mountain Jazz Festival, Sherburne, VT, Late Jul.
Quechee Hot Air Balloon Festival, Quechee, VT, Middle Jun.
Quechee Scottish Festival, Quechee, VT, Late Aug.
Rattling Brook Bluegrass Festival, Belvidere, VT, Middle Jun.
Raven Wind Pow-Wow, Evansville, VT, Middle May
Rutland Region Ethnic Festival, Rutland, VT, Late Jun.
Shelburne Farms Harvest Festival, Shelburne, VT, Middle Sep.
Southern Vermont Highland Games, Mount Snow, VT, Middle Jul.
Sugarbush Brewers Festival, Warren, VT, Middle Sep.
University of Vermont Lane Series/49th Parallel Music Festival, Burlington, VT, Late Jan.
Vermont Apple Festival and Crafts Show, Springfield, VT, Middle Oct.
Vermont Brewers Festival, Various, VT, Middle Sep.
Vermont Dairy Festival, Enosburg Falls, VT, Early Jun.
Vermont Lesbian Gay Bisexual Pride Day, Burlington, VT, Late Jun.

Vermont Maple Festival/Fiddler's Variety Show, St. Albans, VT, Late Apr.
Vermont Reggae Fest, Johnson, VT, Middle Jul.
Vermont State Fair, Rutland, VT, Early Sep. to Middle Sep.
Vermont Women's Celebration, Burlington, VT, Late Jul.
Warebrook Contemporary Music Festival, Irasburg, VT, Early Jul.

## Massachusetts

Acoustic Underground: Boston's National Acoustic Music Showcase, Boston, MA, Early Oct. to
     Early Nov.
Acoustic Underground Concerts and CD Release Parties, Varies, MA, Middle May
American Indian Day at the Children's Museum, Boston, MA, Early Apr.
American Indian Honor-the-Earth Pow Wow, Northampton, MA, Early Aug.
American Pit Masters Bar-B-Q Round-Up, Boston, MA, Middle Jun.
Amesbury Days Festival, Amesbury, MA, Late Jun. to Early Jul.
Anthony Spinazzola Gala Festival of Food and Wine, Boston, MA, Early Feb.
Apsge Pow-Wow, Westford, MA, Late Jul.
Art Newbury Street, Boston, MA, Middle Sep.
Art Newbury Street, Boston, MA, Middle May
ARTBEAT, Somerville, MA, Late Jul.
Arts First: A Harvard/Radcliffe Celebration, Cambridge, MA, Late Apr. to Middle May
Autumn Hills Dulcimer Festival, Great Barrington, MA, Late Sep.
Banjo and Fiddle Contest, Lowell, MA, Middle Sep.
Battle of the Blues Bands, Allston, MA, Late Jun. to Early Jul.
Berklee College of Music High School Jazz Festival, Boston, MA, Early Mar.
Black History Month, Boston, MA, Early Feb. to Late Feb.
Blacksmith House Dulcimer Festival, Cambridge, MA, Late Apr. to Early May
Blacksmith House Folk Festival/Folk Arts Conference, Cambridge, MA, Middle Nov.
Blandford Fair Old Time Fiddle Contest, Blandford, MA, Early Sep.
Blandford Mountain Bluegrass Festival, Blandford, MA, Early Jul.
Bluegrass Festival, Washington, MA, Late May
Boarding House Park Concert Series Kickoff, Lowell, MA, Early Jul.
Boston Blues Festival, Allston, MA, Late Jan. to Late Feb.
Boston Book Fair, Boston, MA, Middle Jun.
Boston Brewer's Festival, Boston, MA, Middle May
Boston Festival: A Carnival of Cultures, Boston, MA, Middle Feb. to Late Feb.
Boston Festival of Bands, Boston, MA, Early Jun.
Boston Globe Jazz Festival, Boston, MA, Middle Jun.
Boston Harborfest, Boston, MA, Late Jun.
Boston International Festival, Dorcester, MA, Late Oct. to Late Nov.
Boston Jazz Society Barbeque and Festival, Milton, MA, Early Aug.
Boston Kite Festival, Boston, MA, Middle May
Boston Phoenix/WFNX Best Music Poll Celebration, Boston, MA, Late Mar.
Boston Pops, Boston, MA, Middle Jun. to Early Jul.
Boston Seaport Festival, Charlestown, MA, Middle Aug. to Late Aug.
Boston Waterfront Festival, Boston, MA, Middle Jun.
Bourne Scallop Fest, Buzzards Bay, MA, Early Sep. to Middle Sep.
Brazilian Festival of the Arts, Somerville, MA, Middle Feb.
Bread and Roses Labor Day Heritage Heritage Festival, Lawrence, MA, Early Sep.
Bright Moments Festival, Amherst, MA, Middle Jul. to Late Jul.
Bud Rocks the Block Party, Lowell, MA, Middle Sep.
Cambridge International Fair, Cambridge, MA, Middle Jun.
Cambridge Public Library Jazz Festival, Cambridge, MA, Middle Jun.
Cambridge River Festival, Cambridge, MA, Middle Sep.

Cambridge Street Performer's Festival, Cambridge, MA, Late Jun.
Cape Verdean Festival, Boston, MA, Early Jul.
Caribbean Carnival, Boston, MA, Middle Aug. to Late Aug.
Carlos Fest, Brookline, MA, Middle Aug.
Celtic Festival at the Hatch Shell, Boston, MA, Early Sep.
Chief Red Blanket Memorial Pow-Wow, Haverill, MA, Middle Sep.
Chief Red Blanket Memorial Pow-Wow, Haverill, MA, Early Sep. to Middle Sep.
Chilifest, Charlestown, MA, Middle Oct.
Chilifest, Boston, MA, Middle Jun.
Chowderfest, Charlestown, MA, Middle Sep.
Christmas Revels, Cambridge, MA, Middle Dec. to Late Dec.
City of Presidents Blues Festival, Quincy, MA, Early Jul.
CMAC's A Joyful Noise, Cambridge, MA, Middle Jan.
CMAC's Boston Rhythm, Cambridge, MA, Early Nov.
CMAC's Fall Benefit, Cambridge, MA, Middle Nov.
CMAC's Gala Benefit, Cambridge, MA, Middle Mar.
Codman Farm Festival, Lincoln, MA, Middle Sep.
Country Fest, Webster, MA, Middle Sep.
Country Music Festival to Benefit American Heart Association, Webster, MA, Late May
Day at the Lake, Worcester, MA, Middle Sep.
DeCordova Labor Day Jazz Festival, Lincoln, MA, Early Sep.
Dominican Festival, Boston, MA, Early Aug.
Earth Day Pow-Wow, Leominster, MA, Late Apr.
Eastern States Exposition -- The Big E!, West Springfield, MA, Middle Sep. to Late Sep.
Eisteddfod Festival of Traditional Music and Dance, North Dartmouth, MA, Late Sep.
Fall Festival, Attleboro Falls, MA, Middle Sep.
Fall River Celebrates America , Fall River, MA, Middle Aug.
Fall River Festival, Fall River, MA, Middle Jun.
Festival of Light and Song, Jamaica Plain, MA, Middle Dec.
First Night Boston, Boston, MA, Late Dec.
First Night Brockton, Brockton, MA, Late Dec.
First Night Chatham, Chatham, MA, Late Dec.
First Night in Hyannis, Falmouth, MA, Late Dec.
First Night New Bedford, New Bedford, MA, Late Dec.
First Night Newburyport, Newburyport, MA, Late Dec.
First Night Northampton, Northampton, MA, Late Dec.
First Night Pittsfield, Pittsfield, MA, Late Dec.
First Night Quincy, Quincy, MA, Late Dec.
First Night Worcester, Worcester, MA, Late Dec.
Folk Festival/Flea Market and Craft Show, Braintree, MA, Late May
Folk Heritage Festival, Lexington, MA, Middle Sep.
Folk Song Society of Greater Boston's Member's Concert, Watertown, MA, Middle Feb.
FolkTree Jamboree, Boston, MA, Late Oct.
Fun Summer Concerts, Wellfleet, MA, Late Jun.
Gaelic Roots:  The Music, Song and Dance of Ireland, Chestnut Hill, MA, Early Oct.
Glasgow Lands Scottish Festival, Blandford, MA, Late Jul.
Gloucester Folklife Festival, Gloucester, MA, Early Mar.
Gloucester Seafood Festival, Gloucester, MA, Middle Sep.
Gloucester Waterfront Festival, Gloucester, MA, Middle Aug.
Great Awakening Fest, Granby, MA, Middle Sep.
Great New England Brewers' Festival, Northampton, MA, Late Jul.
Great Yankee Rib Cook-Off, Boston, MA, Late Aug.
Harpoon's Brewstock, Boston, MA, Late Jun.
Harpoon's St. Patrick's Day Bash, Boston, MA, Middle Mar.

Harvard Square's May Fair, Cambridge, MA, Early May
Harvard Winter Folk Festival, Cambridge, MA, Early Mar.
Harvey Robbins' Royalty of Rock 'n Roll/Cape Cod Melody Tent, Hyannis, MA, Middle Aug.
Homefolks Concert, Boston, MA, Late May
Hot, Hot Tropics, Boston, MA, Late Mar.
Hyannis Harbor Festival, Hyannis, MA, Early Jun.
Hyannis Seaport Festival, Hyannis, MA, Middle Aug.
Indian Pow Wow, Charlemont, MA, Late May
Indian Ranch Country Music Festival and Chicken Barbeque, Webster, MA, Late May
Irish and Cape Breton Christmas Concert and Ceili, Chestnut Hill, MA, Middle Dec.
Irish Cultural Center's Festival, North Easton, MA, Middle Jun.
Irish Festival in the Park, Tewksbury, MA, Middle Jul.
Irish Music Festival, Boston, MA, Middle Oct.
Irish Variety Show, Braintree, MA, Middle Oct.
Jamaica Plain Folk Festival, Jamaica Plain, MA, Early Jun.
Joe Val Memorial Bluegrass Festival, Waltham, MA, Late Jun.
John Coltrane Memorial Concert, Boston, MA, Early Oct.
John Penny Liver Foundation Jamboree, Webster, MA, Middle Sep.
Kenmore Square Rites of Spring Charity Rockfest, Boston, MA, Late Apr.
KISS-108 FM Concert, Mansfield, MA, Early Jun.
La Festa, North Adams, MA, Early Jun. to Late Jun.
Latin American Festival, Lowell, MA, Late Jun.
Loud Music Festival, Northampton, MA, Early Apr.
Lowell Family First Night, Lowell, MA, Late Dec.
Lowell Folk Festival, Lowell, MA, Middle Jul.
Lowell Riverfest, Lowell, MA, Early Sep. to Middle Sep.
M. C. M. A. A. Awards Show, Randolph, MA, Late Sep.
Make-a-Wish-Foundation Country Jamboree, Ipswich, MA, Middle May
Malden Irish Festival, Malden, MA, Late Aug.
Marblehead Festival of the Arts, Marblehead, MA, Late Jun. to Early Jul.
Maritime Music Festival, Salem, MA, Late Mar.
Martha's Vineyard Agricultural Fair Fiddle Contest: A Festival of Traditional Music, Vineyard
    Haven, MA, Middle Aug. to Late Aug.
Martha's Vineyard Singer-Songwriters' Retreat, Vineyard Haven, MA, Early Sep. to Middle Sep.
Mashpee Wampanoag Powwow, Mashpee, MA, Early Jul.
Massachusetts Highland Games, Waltham, MA, Late Jun.
Massachusetts Rock and Reggae for the Homeless, Great Barrington, MA, Middle Aug.
Midsummer Revels, Lincoln, MA, Middle Jun. to Late Dec.
Mix 98.5 Fall Fest, Boston, MA, Early Oct.
Monson's Summerfest, Monson, MA, Early Jul.
Multicultural Family Festival, Roxbury, MA, Middle Jul.
Multicultural Festival, Roxbury, MA, Late Feb.
National Native American Heritage Day Pow-Wow, Concord, MA, Middle Nov.
Native American Awareness Pow-Wow, Peabody, MA, Early Aug.
Native American Day at The Forum, Framingham, MA, Early Apr.
Native American Fair and Pow Wow, Grafton, MA, Late Jul.
Native American Intertribal Festival/Cape Heritage, Mashpee, MA, Early Jun.
New England Country Jamboree, Webster, MA, Middle Sep.
New England Folk Festival, Natick, MA, Late Apr.
New England Sacred Harp Singing Convention, Wellesley, MA, Early Oct.
New Women's Voices, Cambridge, MA, Late Jan.
Newburyport Waterfront Festival, Newburyport, MA, Early Sep.
Newburyport Yankee Homecoming, Newburyport, MA, Late Jun. to Early Jul.
Newsound Festival, Merrimac, MA, Early Sep.

Nipmuck Pow Wow, Oxford, MA, Middle Sep.
Northeast Indoor Blue Grass Festival, Boxborough, MA, Early Feb. to Middle Feb.
Northeast Squeeze-In, Washington, MA, Middle Sep.
Oak Bluffs Harbor Day, Oak Bluffs, MA, Middle Jun.
Opening Night, Salem, Salem, MA, Late Dec.
Oxfam America WorldFest, Boston, MA, Early Jul. to Middle Jul.
Pan-African Cultural Festival, Boston, MA, Late Jun.
Papsaquoho Pow-Wow, Braintree, MA, Middle Jan.
Pedal Steel Guitar Anniversary Bash, Lee, MA, Early Sep.
Pepsi Boston Music Awards, Boston, MA, Early Apr.
Peter Pan Taste of Springfield, Springfield, MA, Middle Jun.
Phil Ochs Song Night, Cambridge, MA, Early Nov.
Pickin' in the Pines Bluegrass Day, Northampton, MA, Late Jun.
Planting Moon Pow-Wow, Topsfield, MA, Late May
Plymouth Summer Blastoff, Plymouth, MA, Late Jun.
Pow-Wow, Rutland, MA, Early Jun.
Pow-Wow, Sterling, MA, Late Jun.
Praise and Harmony, Lowell, MA, Middle Jun.
Precision and Pageantry Drum and Bugle Corps Competition, Pittsfield, MA, Middle Aug.
Pridefest, Boston, MA, Middle Jun.
Provincetown Waterfront Festival, Provincetown, MA, Middle Jul. to Late Jul.
Puerto Rican Cultural Festival, Springfield, MA, Early Jul. to Middle Jul.
Puerto Rican Festival, Boston, MA, Late Jul.
Quaboag Scottish Festival, Warren, MA, Late Jul.
Race Unity Day, Boston, MA, Middle Jun.
Reggae Festival, Washington, MA, Early Sep.
Riverfest, Buckland, MA, Middle Jun.
Rock 'N Roll Block Party, Holyoke, MA, Middle Jun.
Salem Seaport Festival, Salem, MA, Late May
Scottish Fiddle Rally, Somerville, MA, Middle Apr.
Septemberfest, Groton, MA, Middle Sep.
Sheep Shearing Festival, Waltham, MA, Late Apr.
Sigonomeg Pow-Wow, Middleboro, MA, Middle May
Sober in the Sun Labor Day Weekend Experience, Spencer, MA, Early Sep.
Songstreet Cajun-Bluegrass Festival, Somerville, MA, Early Apr.
Songstreet Festival of Funny Songwriters, Somerville, MA, Middle Jan.
Songstreet Festival of Women Songwriters, Somerville, MA, Middle Mar.
Songstreet Folk and Bluegrass Fest, Cambridge, MA, Early Feb.
Songstreet Folk-Rock Festival, Somerville, MA, Early Apr.
Songstreet Folk-Rock Festival, Somerville, MA, Middle Nov.
Street Performers Festival, Boston, MA, Late May
Students for Students/Human Rights Festival, Boston, MA, Late Apr.
Summerfest, Great Barrington, MA, Middle Jun.
Summertime Blues Weekend, Lowell, MA, Middle Aug.
Tam O'Shanter Scottish Highland Games and Festival, Easton, MA, Early Aug.
Tanglewood Festival of Contemporary Music, Lenox, MA, Late Jul. to Late Aug.
Tanglewood Jazz Festival, Lenox, MA, Early Sep.
Taste of Chicopee, Chicopee, MA, Early Jun.
Taste of Northampton, Northampton, MA, Middle Aug.
Taste of the South Shore, Quincy, MA, Early Aug.
Towwakeeswush Pow-Wow, Marshfield, MA, Middle Jun.
UMass Jazz Festival, North Dartmouth, MA, Early Mar.
UpCountry Hot Air Balloon Fair, Greenfield, MA, Middle Jul.
WBCN Rock 'n' Roll Rumble, Boston, MA, Early May to Late May

WBCN Rock of Boston Concert, Boston, MA, Late Oct.
WBCS Boston Country Sunday, Mansfield, MA, Late Jun.
WBOS-FM Earth Day Concert and Festival, Boston, MA, Late Apr.
WCLB Country Club Festival, Foxboro, MA, Late Jul.
Western New England Bluegrass and Old-Time Championships and Steak Fry, Sheffield, MA,
     Late Aug.
Westport Harvest Festival, Westport, MA, Early Oct. to Middle Oct.
WFNX Birthday Party, Boston, MA, Early Nov.
WGBH "T" Party, Boston, MA, Middle May
Whaling City Festival, New Bedford, MA, Early Jul. to Middle Jul.
Whaling City Jazz Festival, New Bedford, MA, Early Oct.
Wollomonuppoag Indian Council Inter-Tribal Pow Wow, Attleboro, MA, Middle Jul.
World Fair at Boston University, Boston, MA, Early Apr. to Middle Apr.
WPVQ Music Day, Greenfield, MA, Late Jul.
Yankee Music Festival Big Band Jazz Invitational, Salem, MA, Late Jun.
Your Hometown America Parade, Pittsfield, MA, Early Jul.

## Rhode Island

American Indian Federation of Rhode Island Pow Wow, Escoheag, RI, Early Aug.
American Pit Masters Bar-B-Q Roundup, Providence, RI, Late Jun.
Autumnfest, Woonsocket, RI, Early Oct.
Barbershop Quartet Benefit Concert, Block Island, RI, Late Jul.
Ben and Jerry's Newport Folk Festival, Newport, RI, Early Aug.
Big Easy Bash, Escoheag, RI, Late Jun.
Blues Bash for Homeless People, Smithfield, RI, Late Aug.
Bowen's Wharf Waterfront Seafood Festival, Newport, RI, Middle Oct.
Cajun and Bluegrass Music-Dance-Food Festival, Escoheag, RI, Early Sep.
Cajun and Zydeco Mardi Gras Ball, Cranston, RI, Middle Feb.
Cape Verdean Heritage Festival, Providence, RI, Early Jul.
Charlestown Chamber of Commerce Seafood Festival, Charlestown, RI, Early Aug.
Chopmist Hill Inn Summer Festival, North Scituate, RI, Late Aug.
Country Music Shows, Escoheag, RI, Middle Jun. to Early Aug.
Cumberlandfest, Cumberland, RI, Early Aug.
Dominican Festival, Providence, RI, Late Aug.
Earth Day Celebration, Providence, RI, Late Apr.
East Providence Heritage Festival, East Providence, RI, Late Jul.
First Night Providence, Providence, RI, Late Dec.
Harlem Renaissance Garden Party, Cranston, RI, Middle Jun.
Irish Fall Festival, Lincoln, RI, Middle Sep.
JVC Jazz Festival/Newport, Newport, RI, Middle Aug.
Labor and Ethnic Heritage Festival, Pawtucket, RI, Early Sep.
Lupo's Birthday Party, Providence, RI, Early Jul.
Mardi Gras Celebration, Woonsocket, RI, Late Feb.
Maritime Arts Festival, Newport, RI, Middle May
Native American Days, Westerly, RI, Late May
Native American Days, Westerly, RI, Early Sep.
New England Reggae Festival, Escoheag, RI, Late Jul.
Newport Rhythm and Blues Festival, Newport, RI, Late Jul.
Newport Winter Festival, Newport, RI, Late Jan. to Early Feb.
Norman Bird Sanctuary Harvest Fair, Middletown, RI, Early Oct.
Opening Night, Newport, RI, Late Dec.
Pequot and Narragansett Indian Nations Pow Wow, Westerly, RI, Middle Jun. to Late Jun.
Pow Wow, Charlestown, RI, Middle Aug.

Pow Wow, Charlestown, RI, Early Oct.
Providence Waterfront Festival/Waterfront Jazz Festival, Providence, RI, Middle Sep.
Rhode Island Indian Council Pow Wow: Temple to Music, Providence, RI, Late Jul. to Early
    Aug.
Rhode Island's Heritage Day, Providence, RI, Middle Sep.
Schwepes Chowder Cook-Off, Newport, RI, Middle Jun.
Scituate Arts Festival, North Scituate, RI, Early Oct.
Scituate Music Fest, Scituate, RI, Middle Aug.
Settlers' Day, Lincoln, RI, Late Sep.
Shake-a-Leg Benefit Concert, Newport, RI, Middle Aug.
Summer Arts Fest Chair Fair, West Kingston, RI, Early Jun.
Swamp Yankee Days, Charlestown, RI, Late Sep.
Taste of Rhode Island, Newport, RI, Late Sep.
Washington County Fair, Richmond, RI, Middle Aug.
Women's Voices, Providence, RI, Early Mar.

## Connecticut

4th of July Celebration, Enfield, CT, Early Jul.
Afro-Latin-Caribbean Festival, Waterbury, CT, Middle Jul.
Afternoon of Jazz, Norwalk, CT, Late Jun.
Alternative Skateboard Festival, Woodbury, CT, Late May
Apple Harvest Festival, Glastonbury, CT, Middle Oct.
Apple Valley Family Folk Festival, Southington, CT, Middle Sep.
Barbershop Harmony Day, Mystic, CT, Middle Sep.
Barnum Festival/Champions on Parade, Bridgeport, CT, Late Jun.
Barnum Festival/Gospel Festival, Bridgeport, CT, Middle Jun.
BASH: Bradley Airport Summer Happening, Windsor Locks, CT, Late Jul.
Battle of the Bands, Westport, CT, Early Jul. to Middle Aug.
Black Expo, New Haven, CT, Middle Mar.
Bloomfield Festival, Bloomfield, CT, Early Jun.
Blue Sky Music Fest, Wallingford, CT, Late May
Bluegrass Festival, Woodstock, CT, Late May
Blues at the Ives, Danbury, CT, Late Jun.
Blues Blockbusters, New Haven, CT, Middle Jun.
Brass Valley Ethnic Music Festival, Waterbury, CT, Middle Jun.
Cabaret Symposium, Waterford, CT, Middle Aug. to Late Aug.
Celebrate! West Hartford, West Hartford, CT, Middle Jun.
Chowderfest, Mystic, CT, Early Oct. to Middle Oct.
Citibank Taste of Stamford, Stamford, CT, Early Jun. to Middle Jun.
City Fest Arts Jubilee, Middletown, CT, Early Jun.
Community Carol Sing, Mystic, CT, Middle Dec.
Connecticut Agricultural Fair, Goshen, CT, Late Jul.
Connecticut Convention of the Sacred Harp, Middletown, CT, Early Jul. to Middle Jul.
Connecticut Family Folk Festival, Hartford, CT, Late Jul. to Early Aug.
Connecticut Historical Society's International Spring Festival, Hartford, CT, Early Apr.
Connecticut Irish Festival, New Haven, CT, Late Jun.
Connecticut River Pow-Wow, Farmington, CT, Late Aug.
Connecticut River Valley Bluegrass Festival, East Haddam, CT, Middle Aug.
Country Jamborees, New Haven, CT, Late Apr.
Deep River Ancient Fife and Drum Corps Muster and Parade, Deep River, CT, Middle Jul.
Different Tastes Outdoor Crawfish and Alligator Feast, Hartford, CT, Early Jun.
Duracell Jazz Festival, Danbury, CT, Middle Aug.
Durham Agricultural Fair, Durham, CT, Late Sep.

Eagle Wing Press Powwow, Watertown, CT, Late Sep.

Earth Jam, Woodstock, CT, Middle Aug.

Eli Whitney Folk Festival, New Haven, CT, Early Sep.

Fair Haven Festival, New Haven, CT, Early Jun.

Fairfield County Irish Festival, Fairfield, CT, Middle Jun.

Fall Folk Music Weekend, Falls Village, CT, Middle Oct.

Festival at Roseland Cottage, Woodstock, CT, Middle Oct.

First Night Danbury, Danbury, CT, Late Dec.

First Night Hartford, Hartford, CT, Late Dec.

Folk Music Showcase, Westport, CT, Late Jul.

Funkfest, New Haven, CT, Early Jul.

Global Blues Fest, Norwalk, CT, Early Jul.

Gospel Festival, Hartford, CT, Middle Feb.

Great American Blues Festival, Woodstock, CT, Middle Jul.

Great American Music Fest, Goshen, CT, Late Jun.

Great Connecticut Traditional Jazz Festival, East Haddam, CT, Early Aug.

Greater Hartford Festival of Jazz Fundraiser, Hartford, CT, Middle Feb.

Greater Hartford Festival of Jazz/Hartford Mega! Weekend, Hartford, CT, Late Jul. to Early
    Aug.

Greater Hartford Irish Festival, Glastonbury, CT, Late Jul.

HAFOS:  Festival Hispano-Americano de Stamford, Stamford, CT, Late Aug.

Harbor Day, Norwich, CT, Late Aug.

Hartford Advocate's Best of the Bands Bash, New Britain, CT, Late May

Hartford Jazz Society Riverboat Cruise, Middletown, CT, Middle Sep.

Hartland Folk Festival, East Hartland, CT, Middle Jul.

High Ridge Folk Festival, Stamford, CT, Early Jul. to Middle Jul.

Honey, Hide the Banjo!  It's the Folk Next Door, West Hartford, CT, Late May

Hot Steamed Music Festival, Essex, CT, Late Jun.

Housatonic Dulcimer Celebration, New Milford, CT, Middle Sep.

Irish Night, Manchester, CT, Middle Aug.

Jambalaya on the River:  Spring Riverboat Festival, Hartford, CT, Middle May to Late May

Jazz Expos, New Haven, CT, Late Feb.

Kent Summer Days, Kent, CT, Early Aug.

KISS 95.7 Anniversary Birthday Jam, Hartford, CT, Early Jan.

Lake Wangumbaug Folk Festival, Coventry, CT, Late Jun.

Legends of Folk Music, Westport, CT, Middle May

Lobster Fest, Mystic, CT, Late May

Lobsterfest/Celebrate Canton, Canton, CT, Middle Aug.

Local Bands on the Downtown Green, New Haven, CT, Middle Jun. to Late Aug.

Louisiana Cookin' and Cajun Music Festival, Norwich, CT, Late Jun.

Mad Murphy's Cajun, Zydeco Music and Art Festival, East Haddam, CT, Middle Jun.

Main Street U. S. A., New Britain, CT, Early Jun.

Manchester Association of Pipe Bands Festival, Manchester, CT, Middle Jun.

Mineral Springs Foot Stomp'n Festival, Stafford Springs, CT, Late Jun. to Early Jul.

Mineral Springs Foot Stomp'n Festival, Stafford Springs, CT, Early Oct.

Morris Bluegrass Festival, Morris, CT, Middle Aug.

Mother of Waters, Rocky Hill, CT, Middle Jun.

Music Fest, Danielson, CT, Late Aug.

New England Ragtime Festival, East Lyme, CT, Late Sep.

New Haven Jazz Festival, New Haven, CT, Early Jul. to Late Jul.

New London Sail Festival/Connecticut Maritime Festival, New London, CT, Early Jul. to Middle
    Jul.

Newcomers of Country, Wallingford, CT, Middle Aug.

NOMAD:  Northeast Music, Art and Dance Festival, Sandy Hook, CT, Late Oct. to Early Nov.

Nutmeg Bluegrass Get-Together, Burlington, CT, Middle May
Old Home Day, Middlefield, CT, Middle Jun.
Olde Tyme Fiddlers Concert, Sterling, CT, Middle Apr.
Oyster Festival, South Norwalk, CT, Early Sep. to Middle Sep.
Paucatuck Pequot Harvest Moon Powwow, North Stonington, CT, Early Oct. to Middle Oct.
Pink Tent Festival of the Arts, Stamford, CT, Middle Jun.
Positively Pomfret Day, Putnam, CT, Late Jul.
Quinnehukqut Rendezvous and Native American Festival, Haddam, CT, Middle Aug. to Late
    Aug.
R. A. W. Jazz Festival, Hartford, CT, Late Jul.
Red Cross Waterfront Festival, Greenwich, CT, Middle Jun.
Reggae Festival, Woodbury, CT, Late Jun.
Reggaefests, New Haven, CT, Early Jan.
Riverfest, Hartford, CT, Early Jul.
Riversplash, Simsbury, CT, Early Jun.
Rock and Roll Hall of Fame Revue, Danbury, CT, Late Jul.
Rock 'N' Blues AIDS Benefit, East Hartford, CT, Late Jul.
Rockfest, East Hartford, CT, Late Jul.
Roots and Fruits Fiddle and Dance Festival, Hartford, CT, Early Oct.
Round Hill Scottish Games, Norwalk, CT, Early Jul.
Roxbury Pickin' N Fiddlin' Contest, Roxbury, CT, Middle Jul.
Schemitzun: Feast of Green Corn, Hartford, CT, Middle Sep.
Scotland Highland Festival, Scotland, CT, Early Oct.
Sea Music Festival, Mystic, CT, Middle Jun.
Simsbury Septemberfest, Simsbury, CT, Early Sep.
SoNo Arts Celebration, South Norwalk, CT, Early Aug.
Southbury Jazz Festival, Southbury, CT, Early Sep.
Southern Fried Festival, Woodbury, CT, Middle Aug.
Spring Folk Music Weekend, Falls Village, CT, Late May
St. Andrew's Society of Conneticut Scottish Festival, Goshen, CT, Early Oct.
Stamford A. O. H. Feis, Stamford, CT, Middle Jul.
Sterling Park Campground Bluegrass Festival, Sterling, CT, Early Jun. to Middle Jun.
Sterling Park Campground Bluegrass Festival, Sterling, CT, Middle Sep.
Strawberry Moon Pow-Wow, Somers, CT, Late Jun.
Strawberry Park Bluegrass Festival, Preston, CT, Early Jun.
Strawberry Park Country Western Jamboree, Preston, CT, Late Sep.
Subfest, Groton, CT, Early Jul.
Summer Celebration, Dayville, CT, Early Jul.
Summer Series, Westport, CT, Middle Jun. to Middle Aug.
Summer Sizzler, East Hartford, CT, Middle Jul.
Summertime Street Festival, New Haven, CT, Middle Aug.
Taste Buds Festival, Hartford, CT, Late Aug.
Taste of Connecticut Food Festival, Mystic, CT, Early Sep. to Middle Sep.
Taste of Fairfield, Fairfield, CT, Middle Jun.
Taste of Greater Danbury, Danbury, CT, Middle Sep.
Taste of Hartford, Hartford, CT, Early Jun. to Middle Jun.
Taste of History, Mystic, CT, Early Aug.
Taste of Summer, Middletown, CT, Middle May
Trumbull Arts Festival, Trumbull, CT, Middle Sep.
Trumbull Day, Trumbull, CT, Late Jun.
Verano Explosivo Festival, West Hartford, CT, Early Aug.
Welcome Back to School Show: The Beginning of the End, New Haven, CT, Early Sep.
West Fest/Taste of Westville, Westville, CT, Middle Jun.

West Indian Independence Celebration Week/Hartford Mega! Weekend, Hartford, CT, Early Aug.

Westbrook Drum Corps Muster, Westbrook, CT, Late Aug.

Westport Blues Festival, Westport, CT, Late Sep.

World Music Fest, Groton, CT, Late Jul.

World Music Festival, Woodbury, CT, Middle Jul.

WPLR July 4th Celebration, New Haven, CT, Early Jul.

WPLR Labor Day Celebration, New Haven, CT, Early Sep.

WXCT Family Festival, New Haven, CT, Middle Jul.

## New York

A. O. H. Nassau County Board Feis and Festival, Uniondale, NY, Middle Sep.

Adirondack Drums, Glens Falls, NY, Early Aug.

Adirondack Festival of American Music, Saranac Lake, NY, Early Jul. to Late Jul.

Adirondack Folk Music Festival, Schroon Lake, NY, Middle Aug. to Late Aug.

Adirondack Folk Night, Troy, NY, Late Mar.

African-American Heritage Celebration, Valhalla, NY, Late Jun.

African-American Heritage Celebration, Yonkers, NY, Middle Jul.

Al Mastren Memorial Scholarship Concert, Cohoes, NY, Early Apr.

Albany Riverfest/All-America City Fair, Albany, NY, Early Jun. to Middle Jun.

Albion Strawberry Festival, Albion, NY, Early Jun.

All-Star Irish Concert and Dance, Yonkers, NY, Middle Jun.

Alternative Sports and Music Festival, Middletown, NY, Early Oct.

American Indian Heritage and Craft Festival, Albany, NY, Early Jul.

American Patriot Festival, Hunter, NY, Early Jul.

Amherst Museum Scottish Festival, Amherst, NY, Middle Sep.

Anniversary Celebration of the Colored Musicians Club, Rochester, NY, Middle Aug.

Apple Harvest Festival, Ithaca, NY, Early Oct.

Apple Umpkin Festival, Wyoming, NY, Late Sep.

Applefest, Warwick, NY, Early Oct.

Artpark Blues and Folk Festival, Lewiston, NY, Middle Aug. to Late Aug.

Artpark Jazz Festival, Lewiston, NY, Early Sep.

Artvoice Original Music Awards, Buffalo, NY, Late Nov.

Autumn Harvest Festival, Cooperstown, NY, Middle Sep.

Averill Park Summer Blues Fest, Averill Park, NY, Middle Jul.

Back at the Ranch Festival, Montauk Point, NY, Early Aug.

Ballston Spa Village Wide Garage Sale and Family Festival, Ballston Spa, NY, Middle Jun.

Band Box Anniversary Love-Fest/Wife-Swap, Port Chester, NY, Middle May

Band Jamboree, Osceola, NY, Early Sep.

Barbershop Serenade, Buffalo, NY, Middle Nov.

Barnaby's Battle of the Bands, Centereach, NY, Early Apr.

Battle of the Acappella Groups, Poughkeepsie, NY, Middle Jun.

Bearsville Theater Memorial Day Music Festival, Bearsville, NY, Late May

Benefit for the Fight Against Leukemia, Deer Park, NY, Late May

Best of the Best Pow-Wow/Native American Indian Arts Festival, Suffern, NY, Late Oct.

Big Band Bash, Albany, NY, Late Aug.

Big Big Bands, Latham, NY, Middle Aug.

Bill Knowlton's Bluegrass Ramble Picnic, Sandy Creek, NY, Early Aug.

Bill LaBeef's Bastille Day, Barbeque and Rock and Roll Rodeo, Rochester, NY, Middle Jul.

Bluegrass Festival, Broadalbin, NY, Early Aug.

Bluegrass Festival, Rochester, NY, Late Aug.

Bluegrass on the Green, Homer, NY, Early Jun.

Bluegrass Roundup, Galway, NY, Early Jun.

Blues Bar-B-Que, Schenectady, NY, Early Aug.

Blues Fest, Patterson, NY, Middle Aug.

Blues in the Night, Rochester, NY, Early Jul.

Blueshounds Benefit, Albany, NY, Early Jun.

Bolton Landing Barbershop Quartet Festival, Bolton Landing, NY, Early Sep.

Bopper's Oldies Concert, Huntington, NY, Late Sep.

Buckwheat Harvest Festival, Penn Yan, NY, Late Sep.

Buffalo Beer Fest, Buffalo, NY, Middle Nov.

Buffalo Caribbean Festival, Buffalo, NY, Middle Aug.

Buffalo Country Music Awards, Buffalo, NY, Middle Sep.

Buffalo Irish Festival, Lancaster, NY, Late Aug.

Cairo Appreciation Day Fair, Cairo, NY, Early Jul.

Calico Dancers Good Time Pow Wow, South Glens Falls, NY, Early Jul.

Canal Fest, Tonawanda, NY, Middle Jul. to Late Jul.

Capital District's Scottish Games: A Celtic Festival of the Arts, Altamont, NY, Early Sep.

Caribbean Extravaganza, Catile, NY, Middle Jul.

Carifest, Rochester, NY, Middle Aug.

Catskill Fourth of July Celebration, Catskill, NY, Early Jul.

Catskill Harvest Festival, Walton, NY, Early Oct.

Celebration of Jewish Learning, Brighton, NY, Middle Oct.

Celebrations and Expressions of Our African American Heritage, Hempstead, NY, Early Feb.

Celtic Day in the Park, Staatsburg, NY, Late Sep.

Celtic Fair, Hunter, NY, Late Sep.

Central New York Scottish Games and Celtic Festival, Syracuse, NY, Middle Aug.

Chautauqua Summer Music Program, Chautauqua, NY, Late Jun. to Late Aug.

Clearwater's Great Hudson River Revival, Valhalla, NY, Middle Jun.

Cobleskill "Sunshine" Fair, Cobleskill, NY, Early Aug. to Middle Aug.

College of Saint Rose Collegiate Jazz Festival, Albany, NY, Late Apr.

College of Saint Rose High School Jazz Festival, Albany, NY, Late Mar.

Colonial Fest, Kingston, NY, Early Aug.

Columbia County Jazz Festival, West Ghent, NY, Late Jul.

Columbus Day Tournament of Bands, Binghamton, NY, Early Oct.

Columbus Weekend Harvest Fair, East Durham, NY, Early Oct.

Come Sunday, Albany, NY, Early Sep. to Middle Sep.

Commodore John Barry A. O. H. Irish Festival, Olean, NY, Early Sep. to Middle Sep.

Computer Music at Stony Brook, Stony Brook, NY, Late Oct.

Corinth Bluegrass Festival, Corinth, NY, Early Aug. to Middle Aug.

Corn Hill Arts Festival/Fiddler's Fair, Rochester, NY, Early Jul. to Middle Jul.

Country Classic in the Catskills, South Fallsburg, NY, Early Apr.

Country Music Dance Weekend, South Fallsburg, NY, Early Dec.

Country Music Festival , Hunter, NY, Middle Jul. to Late Jul.

Country Music Festival Encore, Hunter, NY, Early Aug. to Middle Aug.

Country Western Festival, Cambridge, NY, Middle Jun.

Coxsackie Riverside Arts and Crafts Festival, Coxsackie, NY, Early Aug.

Cranberry Dulcimer Gathering, Binghamton, NY, Late Jul.

Creek Bend Music Festival, Akron, NY, Late Jul.

Cultural Street Festival, Hempstead, NY, Early Jun.

Dance Flurry, Guilderland, NY, Middle Feb.

Dean Mountain Bluegrass Festival, Hadley, NY, Late Jul. to Early Aug.

Del-Se-Nango Fiddlers Festival, Bainbridge, NY, Early Jul.

Del-Se-Nango Fiddlers Festival and Bluegrass Sunday, Bainbridge, NY, Early Aug.

Dick Fox's Fall Doo-Wopp Extravaganza, Westbury, NY, Middle Sep.

Dick Fox's Holiday Doo-Wopp Extravaganza, Westbury, NY, Middle Dec.

Dick Fox's Spring Doo-Wopp Extravaganza, Westbury, NY, Early Mar.

Dick Fox's Summer Doo-Wopp Extravaganza, Westbury, NY, Early Jun.
Dick Fox's Ultimate Doo-Wopp Fantasy Weekend, Monitcello, NY, Early Oct.
Distant Drums Native American Festival, White Plains, NY, Middle Jun.
Downtown Festival/Rock Fest , Rochester, NY, Late Aug.
Dutchess County Fair, Rhinebeck, NY, Late Aug.
Ear-Fest:  Festival of Taped Music, Stony Brook, NY, Early Nov.
Earl's Sunshine Festival, Chaffee, NY, Late Jun. to Middle Sep.
East End Music Festival, East Hampton, NY, Middle Jun.
Electronic Music at Stony Brook, Stony Brook, NY, Late Feb.
Ellicottville's Summer Festival of the Arts, Ellicottville, NY, Late Jun. to Early Jul.
Emerald Productions Getaway, Callicoon, NY, Middle Apr.
Emerald Productions Getaway, Callicoon, NY, Early Dec.
Emerald Weekend, Kiamesha Lake, NY, Early Apr.
Empire State Black Arts and Cultural Festival, Albany, NY, Middle Jul.
Erie County Fair, Hamburg, NY, Middle Aug. to Late Aug.
Evening of Adirondack Music, Lake Placid, NY, Late Jul.
Fabulous Fourth Festivities, Albany, NY, Early Jul.
Fair Haven Field Days, Fair Haven, NY, Early Jul.
Falcon Ridge Folk Festival, Hillsdale, NY, Late Jul.
Fall Country Dance and Party Weekend, Kerhonkson, NY, Middle Oct.
Fall Jamboree, Rochester, NY, Late Oct.
Festival of Lights, Niagara Falls, NY, Middle Nov. to Early Jan.
Festival of North Country Folk Life, Massena, NY, Middle Aug.
Fiddle Weekend, Cambridge, NY, Middle Jul.
Fiddlers!!:  A Sampler of North American Fiddle Traditions, Roxbury, NY, Early Oct.
Fiddlers Fling, Clayton, NY, Middle Sep.
Fiddling Celebration, Cross River, NY, Early Jul.
Field, Forest and Stream, Elizabethtown, NY, Middle Sep.
Fife and Drum Corps Muster, Ticonderoga, NY, Late Jul.
Final Stretch Festival, Saratoga Springs, NY, Late Aug.
Finger Lakes Dixieland Jazz Festival, Hector, NY, Late Aug.
Fingerlakes Grassroots Festival of Music and Dance, Trumansburg, NY, Middle Jul. to Late Jul.
First Night Albany, Albany, NY, Late Dec.
First Night Buffalo, Buffalo, NY, Late Dec.
First Night Freeport, Freeport, NY, Late Dec.
Flaming Leaves Fiddle Jamboree, Long Lake, NY, Early Oct.
Fleadh:  Old Music of Ireland Festival, Leeds, NY, Early Jul.
FLY92 End of Summer Jam, Latham, NY, Middle Sep.
FLY92 Summer Jam, Latham, NY, Late Jun.
Folk Music Society of Huntington Members Concert, Huntington, NY, Early May
Folk Music Society of Huntington Summer Festival, Huntington, NY, Late Jul.
Fourth of July Celebration, Mayville, NY, Early Jul.
Fox Family Bluegrass Festival, Old Forge, NY, Middle Aug.
Fox Hollow Reunion Folk Concert, Troy, NY, Middle Oct.
Friendship Festival, Buffalo, NY, Late Jun. to Early Jul.
Fundraiser, West Shokan, NY, Middle Jun.
Gaelic Day, Vails Gate, NY, Middle Jul.
Gathering of Iroquois, Liverpool, NY, Early Oct.
Glory, Valley Falls, NY, Early Jun.
Glory, Lake George, NY, Early Jun.
Golden Harvest Festival, Baldwinsville, NY, Middle Sep.
Golden Link Folk Festival, Honeoye Falls, NY, Early Sep. to Middle Sep.
Good Old Summertime , Utica, NY, Early Jul. to Middle Jul.
Gospel Extravaganza, Kingston, NY, Middle Jun.

Gospel Night, Buffalo, NY, Late Oct.
GottaGetGon Folk Festival: The Pick'n and Singin' Gatherin', Ballston Spa, NY, Late May
Grand International Ragtime/Jasstime Foundation Fall Festival, Alexandria Bay, NY, Middle
    Nov.
Grand International Ragtime/Jasstime Foundation Spring Festival, Alexandria Bay, NY, Late
    Apr.
Great Blue Heron Music Festival, Sherman, NY, Early Jul.
Great Irish Weekend, Ellenville, NY, Early Dec. to Middle Dec.
Great Lawn Irish Fair, Brookville, NY, Late May
Greece Summer Festival, Greece, NY, Late Aug.
Gruntstock, Parksville, NY, Early Jul.
Halloween Dance Weekend, Ashokan, NY, Late Oct. to Early Nov.
Hamilton Hill Culturefest/Gospel Festival, Schenectady, NY, Early Aug.
Harvest Moon Festival, Kingston, NY, Middle Sep.
Hats Off to Saratoga Festival, Saratoga Springs, NY, Late Jul.
Hempsplash, Parksville, NY, Early Jun.
Heritage Hoedown and Empire State Fiddle Contest, Darien, NY, Middle Jul. to Late Jul.
Hilton Applefest, Hilton, NY, Late Sep. to Early Oct.
Hispanic Heritage Celebration, Valhalla, NY, Late Aug.
Hispanic Music Festival, Buffalo, NY, Late Aug.
Holiday Jam for Joy, Rotterdam, NY, Middle Dec.
Hungerthon Concert/Winter Blues Fest, New City, NY, Middle Nov.
Hurdy Gurdy Strings and Sings Spring Fling, Accord, NY, Middle May
I. A. C. A.'s International Festival of the Adirondacks, Queensbury, NY, Middle May
In Women's Hands: The Beat of the Drum, Albany, NY, Early Mar.
Independence Celebration and Double R Championship Rodeo, Rhinebeck, NY, Early Jul.
Indian Pow Wow, Niagara Falls, NY, Early May
Intergenerational International Festival, Garden City, NY, Middle Jun.
International Celtic Festival, Hunter, NY, Middle Aug. to Late Aug.
International Dixeland Jazz and Ragtime Festival, Buffalo, NY, Late Jul.
International Food Festival, Albany, NY, Middle Aug.
International Food Festival/Friday Fest, Poughkeepsie, NY, Early Aug.
International Fun Fest, Monroe, NY, Late Jul.
International Jewish Arts Festival of Long Island, Commack, NY, Late May
International Music and Dance Festival, Sacketts Harbor, NY, Early Sep.
International Waterfront Festival, Newburgh, NY, Early Sep.
Invitational Piping Championship/Memorial Military Tattoo, Ticonderoga, NY, Early Jul.
Inwood World Music Festival, Inwood, NY, Late Jun.
Irish Celebration, Westbury, NY, Middle Mar.
Irish Festival, Patterson, NY, Middle Jun.
Irish Festival, Hampton Bays, NY, Early Jun.
Irish Festival, East Durham, NY, Late May
Irish Festival of Chemung County, Elmira Heights, NY, Early Jul.
Irish Heritage Celebration, Hartsdale, NY, Middle Jul.
Irish Music Festival, Accord, NY, Early Aug.
Irish Music Weekend Party of the Year, Monticello, NY, Late Oct.
Irish Salute to the U. S. A., East Durham, NY, Early Jul.
Irish Traditional Dance Festival, Mineola, NY, Middle May
Irish Traditional Music Festival, North Blenheim, NY, Early Aug.
Iroquois Arts Showcase I, Howes Cave, NY, Late May
Iroquois Arts Showcase II, Howes Cave, NY, Early Jul.
Iroquois Indian Festival, Rhinebeck, NY, Early Sep. to Middle Sep.
Iroquois Indian Festival, Howes Cave, NY, Late Sep.
Islip Jazz Festival, Islip, NY, Late Aug.

Israeli Festival, Oceanside, NY, Late May

Ithaca Festival, Ithaca, NY, Early Jun.

Jazz for the Arts/Kick Off, Albany, NY, Late Oct.

Jazz for the Arts/Super Jazz Jam Blowout , Albany, NY, Middle May

Jazz/Reggae Festival, Syracuse, NY, Late Jul.

Jazzfest Caramoor, Katonah, NY, Early Aug. to Middle Aug.

Jeffersonville Jamboree, Jeffersonville, NY, Late Jul.

Jones Beach Greekfest Weekend, Babylon, NY, Late Jun.

June Jazz, White Plains, NY, Middle Jun.

Juneteenth Festival, Buffalo, NY, Middle Jun.

Just Jazz, Somers, NY, Middle Sep.

Keeper of the Western Door Pow-Wow, Salamanca, NY, Middle Jul.

Kingdom Bound, Darien Lake, NY, Late Aug.

Klezkamp, Parksville, NY, Late Dec.

Kwanzaa Fete, Hempstead, NY, Late Dec.

L. A. R. A. C. Arts and Crafts Festival, Glen Falls, NY, Middle Jun.

Labor Day Weekend Blowout, Parksville, NY, Early Sep.

Laing Family Bluegrass Festival, Bainbridge, NY, Middle Jun.

Lake George Hot Jazz Party and Cruise, Lake George, NY, Middle Jun.

Lake George Jazz Weekend, Lake George, NY, Early Sep. to Middle Sep.

Lake George Summerfest, Lake George, NY, Late Jun.

Lark Street Blues Festival, Albany, NY, Early Jun.

Lazy River Bluegrass Festival , Gardiner, NY, Middle Sep.

Leeds Irish Festival, Leeds, NY, Early Sep.

Letchworth Arts and Crafts Show and Sale, Castile, NY, Early Oct.

Lilac Festival, Rochester, NY, Middle May to Late May

Local Motion MusicFest, Middletown, NY, Middle Jun.

Local Motion MusicFest, Middletown, NY, Early Sep.

Localpalooza Festival, Rochester, NY, Early Sep.

Long Beach Irish Day Parade and Festival, Long Beach, NY, Early Oct.

Long Island Emerald Isle Festival, Hempstead, NY, Late Sep.

Long Island Fiddle and Folk Music Festival, Stony Brook, NY, Middle Sep.

Long Island Guitar Festival, Brookville, NY, Late Apr.

Long Island Jazz Festival, Oyster Bay, NY, Late Jul.

Long Island Music Festival, Varies, NY, Middle Jul. to Early Sep.

Long Island Scottish Games, Old Westbury, NY, Late Aug.

Long Island Traditional Music Association Fall Folk Weekend, Baiting Hollow, NY, Early Oct.

Long Lake Bluegrass Festival, Long Lake, NY, Middle Aug.

Low Bridge Festival, Lyons, NY, Late Jul.

Lunchtime Concerts, Albany, NY, Early Jul. to Late Aug.

Madrid Bluegrass Festival, Madrid, NY, Late Jun.

Maple Ridge Bluegrass Festival, Duanesburg, NY, Early Jul. to Middle Jul.

Matt's Matinee, Lake Placid, NY, Early Jul.

Mayhem on the Mountain, Mariaville, NY, Middle Jun.

McDonald's Gospelfest, Buffalo, NY, Late Jul.

Meck Music Fest, Mecklenberg, NY, Late Aug.

Memorial Day Weekend Festival, Parksville, NY, Late May

Micky Rat's City Jam, Buffalo, NY, Early Aug.

Middlesex Music Fest, Middlesex, NY, Late Jul.

Miller Lite Balloonfest/Art on the Rise, Jamesville, NY, Middle Jun.

Mohonk's Festival of the Arts/International Week, New Paltz, NY, Middle Jul. to Late Jul.

Mohonk's Joy of Singing, New Paltz, NY, Late Nov.

Mohonk's Music Week, New Paltz, NY, Late Jun.

Mountain Dulcimer Music Festival, Albany, NY, Late Feb.

Mountain Eagle Festival, Hunter, NY, Early Sep.

Mountain Music and Dance Weekend in the Adirondacks, Raquette Lake, NY, Early Oct. to Middle Oct.

Multicultural Fest, Niagara Falls, NY, Middle Jul.

Music and The Mountain Sky/Folk Concert, Highmount, NY, Middle Jul.

Music and The Mountain Sky/Jazz Concert, Highmount, NY, Late Aug.

Music at New Paltz/Faculty Sampler, New Paltz, NY, Middle Sep.

Music at The Ty Folklore Concert, Ticonderoga, NY, Late Aug.

Naples Grape Festival, Naples, NY, Middle Sep.

Nassau Coliseum Fair, Uniondale, NY, Middle Jun. to Late Jun.

Nassau Community College Folk Festival, Garden City, NY, Late Mar.

National Rockabilly Blowout, Rochester, NY, Late Oct.

Native American Dance Festival, Victor, NY, Late Jul. to Early Aug.

Native American Festival, Kingston, NY, Middle Sep.

Native American Heritage Day, Castille, NY, Middle Sep.

Native American Pow Wow, Bethany, NY, Middle Jun.

Native American Pow Wow, East Durham, NY, Early Jul. to Middle Jul.

Native American Weekend, Monroe, NY, Late Jul.

Native American/Indigenous People Day Celebration, Albany, NY, Early Oct.

New Year's Early Eve, Rochester, NY, Late Dec.

New York State Budweiser Blues Festival, Syracuse, NY, Late Jul.

New York State Championship Chili Cookoff, New Paltz, NY, Late Jun.

New York State Fair, Syracuse, NY, Late Aug. to Early Sep.

New York State Intercollegiate Jazz Festival, Morrisville, NY, Late Apr.

New York State Sacred Harp Singing Convention, Ithaca, NY, Middle Oct.

Newport Jazz Festival/Saratoga, Saratoga Springs, NY, Early Jul.

Niagara: The Student and Adult Leadership Conference on Evangelism, Niagara Falls, NY, Late Dec.

Niagara's Apple Country Festival, Lockport, NY, Middle Oct.

Nichols Family Bluegrass Festival, Nichols, NY, Late Aug.

No Bummer Summer Party Jam, Parksville, NY, Middle Jun.

North East Country Music Association Awards Show, Albany, NY, Middle Oct.

Northeast Dulcimer Symposium, Blue Mountain Lake, NY, Late Jun.

October Oyster Festival, Oyster Bay, NY, Middle Oct.

Old Songs Festival of Traditional Music and Dance, Altamont, NY, Late Jun.

Old Songs Sampler Concert, Guilderland, NY, Late Jan.

Old Time Fiddler's Contest and Jam Session, Blue Mountain Lake, NY, Early Jun.

Old Time Music Festival and Barbeque, Stone Mills, NY, Middle Jul.

Old-Time Fiddler's Fair, Mumford, NY, Late Aug.

One With Nature Festival, Garrison, NY, Middle Jun.

Opus 40 Acoustic Summit: Bring It On Home, Saugerties, NY, Early Jul.

Opus 40 Jazz Autumn, Saugerties, NY, Early Oct.

Opus 40 Legends of Jazz/Future of Jazz, Saugerties, NY, Middle Aug.

Opus 40 New Orleans Party Weekend, Saugerties, NY, Late Jul.

Orange County Fair, Middletown, NY, Late Jul.

Oswego Harborfest, Oswego, NY, Middle Jul.

Otsiningo Pow Wow and Indian Craft Fair, Apalachin, NY, Early Jun.

Outdoor Blues Festival, Latham, NY, Middle Aug.

Oxhann Piano Festival, Clinton, NY, Late Aug.

Palmyra Canal Town Days, Palmyra, NY, Middle Sep.

Panama Rocks Folk Arts Fair, Panama, NY, Early Jul. to Middle Jul.

Park Avenue Festival, Rochester, NY, Late Jul. to Early Aug.

Park Jam, Schenectady, NY, Early Aug.

Paumanauke Pow-Wow, Copiague, NY, Middle Aug.

Peaceful Valley Bluegrass Festival, Shinhopple, NY, Middle Jul.
Penny Association Bluegrass and Country Music Festival, Tioga Center, NY, Late Jul.
Penny Association Memorial Day Bluegrass and Country Music Festival, Coventryville, NY,
    Late May
Penny Association Midwinter Bluegrass Festival, Vestal, NY, Early Mar.
Penny Association Olde Tyme Country Music Festival, Coventryville, NY, Late Jun. to Early Jul.
People's Music Network Summer Gathering, Pine Bush, NY, Early Jun.
Petrified Sea Gardens Family Music Festival, Saratoga Springs, NY, Middle Sep.
Pine Grill Jazz Reunion, Rochester, NY, Early Aug.
Pines Hotel Bluegrass Festival, South Fallsburg, NY, Middle Mar.
Pines Number One Irish Weekend, South Fallsburg, NY, Early Apr.
Pines Number One Irish Weekend, South Fallsburg, NY, Middle Nov.
Pines Scottish Weekend, South Fallsburg, NY, Late Oct.
Pines Scottish Weekend, South Fallsburg, NY, Early Mar.
Pinksterfest/Albany Tulip Festival, Albany, NY, Early May
Pow Wow, Barryville, NY, Early Jul.
Pow Wow, Barryville, NY, Late Jul.
Praise, Darien Lake, NY, Late May
Project Children Dinner Dance and Variety Show, Syracuse, NY, Late Oct.
Project Children Irish Festival, Endicott, NY, Late Aug.
Psychofest, Kingston, NY, Middle Jun.
Putnam County 4-H Fair, Carmel, NY, Late Jul. to Early Aug.
PYX Birthday Blowout!, Latham, NY, Late Aug.
PYX Rock and Roll Expo, Albany, NY, Late Mar.
Rally in the Alley, Buffalo, NY, Late Jul.
Real Woodstock Festival, Woodstock, NY, Middle Jul.
Reggae on the Hudson, Kingston, NY, Middle Jun.
Rhythm and Blues Beach Party, Caroga Lake, NY, Middle Jul.
Richard Nader's Let the Good Times Roll, Kiamesha Lake, NY, Early Mar. to Middle Mar.
Richard Nader's Let the Good Times Roll, Kiamesha Lake, NY, Late Jul. to Middle Mar.
Rick and Carol's Country Side Inn Bluegrass Festival, Fort Ann, NY, Late Jul.
River Fest, Fulton, NY, Early Aug.
Riverhead Jazz Festival, Riverhead, NY, Early Jul.
Roberson's Holiday and Arts Festival, Binghamton, NY, Early Sep. to Middle Sep.
Roch-A-Palooza , Rochester, NY, Late Jul.
Rochester Irish Festival, Gates, NY, Early Jun. to Middle Jun.
Rockland County A. O. H. Feis and Field Games, West Haverstraw, NY, Late Jul.
Rockland Irish Festival, West Haverstraw, NY, Late Aug.
Rockstalgia, Hunter, NY, Early Aug.
Rooney Mountain Bluegrass Festival, Deposit, NY, Late Jul. to Early Aug.
Round Lake Country Music Festival, Round Lake, NY, Late Jul.
Royalty of Rock and Roll, Latham, NY, Middle Aug.
Rushmore Festival, Woodbury, NY, Middle Jul.
Salesian Folk Festival, New Rochelle, NY, Late Aug.
Schneider's Bluegrass Festival, Elmira, NY, Late Aug.
Seneca Indian Fall Festival, Irving, NY, Middle Sep.
Shadfest, Peekskill, NY, Middle May
Shinnecock Native-American Powwow, Southampton, NY, Early Sep.
Skyfest, Cedar Lake, NY, Late Aug.
Songwriter Showcase, Deer Park, NY, Middle Apr.
Sounds on the Susquehanna, Endicott, NY, Late Jul.
South Shore Music Festival, Oceanside, NY, Early Sep.
Southern Tier Bluegrass Festival, Savona, NY, Middle Aug.
Spring Blossom Fiddle Jamboree, Long Lake, NY, Late Apr.

Spring Blues Festival, Westbury, NY, Late Apr.
Springfest, Oceanside, NY, Middle Apr.
Squaredance and Bluegrass Festival, Hartford, NY, Late Jun.
St. Lawrence Valley Bluegrass Festival, Gouveneur, NY, Middle Aug.
St. Patrick's Day Celebrations, Elmsford, NY, Early Mar. to Middle Mar.
Stanfordville Music and Dance Festival, Stanfordville, NY, Late May
Stanfordville Music and Dance Festival, Stanfordville, NY, Late Aug.
Star Spangled Spectacular, Montgomery, NY, Early Jul.
Stardust Dance Weekend, Ellenville, NY, Middle Nov. to Late Nov.
Strawberry Festival, Beacon, NY, Early Jun.
Street Fair, Plainview, NY, Early Jun.
Summer Boogie, Ellenville, NY, Early Jul. to Middle Jul.
Summer Folk Music Weekend, Saugerties, NY, Middle Aug. to Late Aug.
Summer Jam, Glens Falls, NY, Early Jul.
Summer Jazz Festival, Elmira, NY, Late Aug.
Summer Music Festival, Amherst, NY, Late Aug.
Summerfest, Poughkeepsie, NY, Early Jul.
Summerscape: Huntington Summer Arts Festival, Huntington, NY, Late Jun. to Late Aug.
Summertime Blues Charity Cruise, Troy, NY, Middle Oct.
Sunday By the Bay, Bellport, NY, Early Jul.
Super Bluegrass and Gospel Day, Norwich, NY, Middle Aug.
Swain Country Western Music Festival, Swain, NY, Early Oct.
Swing Spring, Troy, NY, Late Apr.
Syracuse Area Music Awards (Sammies), Syracuse, NY, Early May
Syracuse Arts and Crafts Festival, Syracuse, NY, Middle Jul.
Syracuse Jazz Fest, Syracuse, NY, Middle Jun.
Takin' It to the Streets: The Electric City Music Celebration, Schenectady, NY, Middle Sep.
Taste of Buffalo, Buffalo, NY, Early Jul.
Thomas Homestead Festival , Savona, NY, Late Jul. to Early Aug.
Thousand Islands Bluegrass Festival, Clayton, NY, Early Jun. to Middle Jun.
Thousand Islands Jazz Festival, Alexandria Bay, NY, Early Aug.
Transportation Heritage Festival, Kingston, NY, Late Jul.
Turk Murphy Memorial Festival, Buffalo, NY, Early May
Turtle Hill Music Festival, Spencerport, NY, Late Aug.
Tuscarora Field Day and Picnic, Lewiston, NY, Early Jul.
Twin Rivers Jamboree, Tuscarora, NY, Early Aug.
Two Rivers Ethnic Festival, Binghamton, NY, Early May
Ulster County Fair, New Paltz, NY, Early Aug.
Uncle Sam's Blues Jam, Troy, NY, Early May
Unifest, Buffalo, NY, Late Aug.
Valentine's XMas Jam, Albany, NY, Middle Dec.
Waterfront Arts Festival, Canandaigua, NY, Early Aug.
Waterfront Extravaganza, Syracuse, NY, Early Jul. to Middle Jul.
Waterfront Festival, Buffalo, NY, Early Aug. to Middle Aug.
Waterfront Festival Free Summer Concert Series/Family Fun in the Sun, Buffalo, NY, Middle Aug.
Waterfront Festival Free Summer Concert Series/Gospel in the Park, Buffalo, NY, Middle Jul.
Watertown Goes Green Irish Festival, Watertown, NY, Middle Mar.
WBNY's Battle of the Bands, Buffalo, NY, Late Aug.
WCBS-FM 101 Day, Rye, NY, Middle Jun.
WEQX Acoustic Holiday Concert for the Hungry, Latham, NY, Middle Dec.
WEQX Birthday Party/University of Albany Fallfest, Albany, NY, Early Oct.
WEQX Party in the Park, Albany, NY, Late Apr.
Westchester Arts Festival, White Plains, NY, Late May

Westchester Community College Jazz Festival, White Plains, NY, Early May
WGNA Country Fest, Altamont, NY, Early Jul.
William Smith and Hobart Colleges Folk Fest, Geneva, NY, Early May
Winter Boogie, Monticello, NY, Late Jan.
Winter Folk Music Weekend, Saugerties, NY, Early Feb.
Winterhawk Bluegrass Family Festival, Ancramdale, NY, Middle Jul.
WLIX Fest, Jamesport, NY, Middle Aug.
Women in Music Celebration, Colonie, NY, Middle Mar.
Woodstock Beat World Percussion Concert, Woodstock, NY, Middle Jul.
Woodstock New Music Festival, Woodstock, NY, Early Aug.
Woodstock/New Paltz Art and Crafts Fair, New Paltz, NY, Late May
Woodstock/New Paltz Art and Crafts Fair, New Paltz, NY, Early Sep.
World of Jewish Culture, Bay Shore, NY, Early Jun.
Wrench Wranch Bluegrass Roundup, Coventryville, NY, Early Sep.
WXLE Acoustic Music Festival, Clifton Park, NY, Early May to Late May
Yiddish Heritage Celebration, Valhalla, NY, Middle Aug.
Yonkers Hudson Riverfest, Yonkers, NY, Middle Sep.

## New York City

111th Street Boys Old Timers Day Stickball Festival, Manhattan, NYC, Early Jul.
116th Street Festival in El Barrio, Manhattan, NYC, Middle Jun.
360 Degrees Black:  New York's Hip Hop Music Seminar, Manhattan, NYC, Middle Jul.
36th Avenue Summer Food Fair, Queens, NYC, Middle Aug.
52nd Street Jazz Festival, Manhattan, NYC, Late May
52nd Street Jazz Festival, Manhattan, NYC, Late Sep.
98.7 KISS-FM Gospel Celebration, Manhattan, NYC, Middle Feb.
98.7 KISS-FM Gospel Celebration, Manhattan, NYC, Late Aug.
Acid Jazz Night, Manhattan, NYC, Early Oct.
Africa Mondo Festival, Manhattan, NYC, Middle Oct. to Late Oct.
Africa Mondo Festival, Brooklyn, NYC, Middle Jul.
Africa Mondo Showcase, Manhattan, NYC, Middle Mar.
African Caribbean Latino American Festival, Brooklyn, NYC, Late Jul.
African Street Festival, Brooklyn, NYC, Late Jun. to Early Jul.
African-American Day Parade, Manhattan, NYC, Middle Sep.
AIDS Dance-A-Thon, Manhattan, NYC, Late Nov.
All-Nite Soul, Manhattan, NYC, Early Oct.
American Cabaret Theater Festival, Manhattan, NYC, Late Jul.
American Festival of Microtonal Music, Manhattan, NYC, Middle Sep. to Early Nov.
American Swing Dance Championships, Manhattan, NYC, Early Apr.
Amsterdam Avenue Festival, Manhattan, NYC, Late May
Areyto for Life:  Hispanic AIDS Forum Benefit Gala and Art Auction, Manhattan, NYC, Early
    May
Atlantic Antic, Brooklyn, NYC, Early Oct.
B. M. I. Jazz Composer's Workshop Concert, Manhattan, NYC, Middle Jul.
BACA Summer Celebration, Brooklyn, NYC, Middle Jul.
Back Stage Bistro Awards, Manhattan, NYC, Late Feb.
Bang On a Can Festival, Manhattan, NYC, Middle Mar. to Early May
Beacons In Jazz, Manhattan, NYC, Late Jun.
Bending Toward the Light:  A Jazz Nativity, Manhattan, NYC, Early Dec.
Benson Series Benefit Concert for United AIDS Relief Effort, Manhattan, NYC, Early Dec.
Betty Carter's Jazz Ahead, Brooklyn, NYC, Early Apr.
Big Band Day, Manhattan, NYC, Middle Nov.
Big Bands at Sea, Manhattan, NYC, Late Nov. to Early Dec.

Bill Popp's Birthday Tribute to George L. Popp, Manhattan, NYC, Early Mar.

Black Expo U. S. A., Manhattan, NYC, Middle May

Black Family Day, Manhattan, NYC, Late Jul.

Black Family Weekend, Manhattan, NYC, Late Aug.

Black Nativity, Manhattan, NYC, Late Dec.

Bluegrass Bash, Manhattan, NYC, Early Sep.

Boathouse Rock, Manhattan, NYC, Middle Jun.

Bob Marley Day, Manhattan, NYC, Early Feb.

Brazilian National Independence Day Street Festival, Manhattan, NYC, Early Sep.

Broadway Astoria Festival, Queens, NYC, Late May

Broadway County Fair, Manhattan, NYC, Late May

Broadway Summer Festival, Manhattan, NYC, Middle Jun.

Broadway's Easter Bonnet Competition:  A Salute to 100 Years of Broadway, Manhattan, NYC, Late Apr.

Bronx Ethnic Music and Dance Festival, Bronx, NYC, Middle Jun.

Brooklyn Arts Week, Brooklyn, NYC, Middle May

Brooklyn Ethnic Music and Dance Festival, Brooklyn, NYC, Late Oct.

Brooklyn Rock Awards, Brooklyn, NYC, Middle May

Brooklyn Woodstock, Brooklyn, NYC, Early Jun.

Brooklyn's Summer Gospelfest!, Brooklyn, NYC, Early Sep.

Buddy Rich Memorial Scholarship Concert, Manhattan, NYC, Early Nov.

Budweiser Superfest, Manhattan, NYC, Late Jul.

Buskers Fare/Summer Fair, Manhattan, NYC, Middle Jun.

Cabaret Convention, Manhattan, NYC, Middle Oct. to Late Oct.

Cabaret for a Cause, Manhattan, NYC, Middle Sep. to Late Sep.

Cajun/Zydeco Jamboree and Halloween Dance, Manhattan, NYC, Late Oct.

Calypso and Steelband "Sunshine" Music Awards, Manhattan, NYC, Late Oct.

Caribbean Cultural Heritage Week Festival/Caribbean Craft and Food Fair, Brooklyn, NYC, Late Jun.

Caribbean Music Awards, Manhattan, NYC, Early Mar.

Caribbean-American Community Trade and Cultural Expo, Brooklyn, NYC, Middle Aug. to Late Aug.

Carnaval Del Merengue, Manhattan, NYC, Late Feb.

Carnegie Hall Folk Festival, Manhattan, NYC, Middle Apr. to Late Apr.

Carnival in New York, Manhattan, NYC, Early Aug.

Cavalcade of Stars, Manhattan, NYC, Middle May

Celebrate 125!  The Rhythm of the World, Manhattan, NYC, Early Jun.

Celebrate Brooklyn Performing Arts Festival, Brooklyn, NYC, Late Jun. to Middle Aug.

Centerstage at the World Trade Center, Manhattan, NYC, Middle Jul. to Early Sep.

Central Park Summerstage, Manhattan, NYC, Middle Jun. to Early Aug.

Century of Change/So Nice To Come Home To, Manhattan, NYC, Early Mar.

Chango Celebration, Manhattan, NYC, Early Dec.

Charlie Parker Jazz Festival, Manhattan, NYC, Late Aug.

Charlie Parker Music and More Awards Gala, Manhattan, NYC, Early Nov.

Chili Pepper Fiesta, Brooklyn, NYC, Early Oct.

Choose Life Benefit Gospel Concert, Manhattan, NYC, Middle Oct.

City Gardeners' Harvest Fair/Gateway Music Festival/New York City Bluegrass Band and Banjo Festival, Brooklyn, NYC, Late Aug.

City Lore Festival, Manhattan, NYC, Middle Jun.

Classical Jazz at Lincoln Center, Manhattan, NYC, Early Aug.

CMJ Music Marathon and Musicfest, Manhattan, NYC, Early Sep.

Cognac Hennessy Jazz Search, Manhattan, NYC, Late Sep.

Colors of Christmas, Manhattan, NYC, Early Dec.

Columbia Independence Day Celebration, Queens, NYC, Late Jul.

Columbia Te Canta, Manhattan, NYC, Late Jul.
Columbus Avenue Festival, Manhattan, NYC, Middle Sep.
Combinacion Perfecta, Manhattan, NYC, Late Oct.
Community Holiday Festival, Manhattan, NYC, Late Dec. to Early Jan.
Concert for Peace, Manhattan, NYC, Late Dec.
Concierto Del Amor, Manhattan, NYC, Middle Feb.
Corner Store Syndicate New Jazz Festival, Manhattan, NYC, Late Apr.
Cross Overs: Music of Asia America, Manhattan, NYC, Early Jun.
Cultural Crossroads' Jazz Gala, Brooklyn, NYC, Late Oct.
Death and Taxes, Manhattan, NYC, Middle Apr.
Dick Fox's Brooklyn Paramount Reunion, Manhattan, NYC, Early May
Discmakers Unsigned Band/Artist New York World Series, Manhattan, NYC, Early Jun.
Do the Right Thing Festival, Brooklyn, NYC, Late Sep.
Downtown Music Gallery's Anniversary Celebration, Manhattan, NYC, Middle Jun.
Drama League's Black-Tie Benefit, Manhattan, NYC, Late Jan.
Earth Day Celebration, Manhattan, NYC, Late Apr.
Easter Gospel Festival, Manhattan, NYC, Middle Apr.
Eco-Festival, Manhattan, NYC, Late Apr. to Early May
Ecofest, Varies, NYC, Late Sep.
El Elyon Music Awards, Manhattan, NYC, Early Dec.
El Elyon Music Fest, Brooklyn, NYC, Early Jul.
Eleventh Avenue Auto Fair, Manhattan, NYC, Early Oct.
Entre Familia, Bronx, NYC, Early May
Essence Awards, Manhattan, NYC, Late Apr.
Evening In Celebration of Black History Month, Brooklyn, NYC, Late Feb.
Evening of Rock and Roll, Manhattan, NYC, Middle Mar.
Evening with Frank Patterson, Manhattan, NYC, Early Mar.
Everybody's Calypso Awards, Brooklyn, NYC, Early May
Everybody's World Calypso Monarch Competition, Brooklyn/Queens, NYC, Early May to Late
    Jul.
Evian Indoor Pro Beach Volleyball Championships, Manhattan, NYC, Late Feb.
Experimental Intermedia Festival with No Fancy Name, Manhattan, NYC, Early Apr. to Late
    Apr.
Experimental Intermedia Four Country Festival, Manhattan, NYC, Early Dec. to Late Dec.
Expressions International Festival, Manhattan, NYC, Late Sep. to Late Oct.
Fast Folk Revue, Manhattan, NYC, Late Jan.
Festival De Los Soneros, Manhattan, NYC, Middle May
Festival of 20th Century Music, Manhattan, NYC, Middle Feb. to Late Feb.
Festival of Jewish Music, Manhattan, NYC, Early Jun.
Festival of Nations, Manhattan, NYC, Early Apr.
Festival of Women Improvisors, Manhattan, NYC, Early Mar. to Middle Mar.
Festival Playero, Bronx, NYC, Middle Jun. to Early Sep.
Fierce Pussy Fest, Manhattan, NYC, Late Aug.
Fifth Avenue Festival, Brooklyn, NYC, Middle May
Fire Wall Total Arts Festival, Manhattan, NYC, Middle Jun. to Late Jun.
First Night New York, Manhattan, NYC, Late Dec.
Floating Archives' Some Kind of Carnival, Manhattan, NYC, Early Nov.
Focus!, Manhattan, NYC, Middle Jan. to Late Jan.
Folksongs Plus, Manhattan, NYC, Middle May
From Plains, Pueblos and Tundra: Native American Music, Dance and Storytelling, Manhattan,
    NYC, Early Apr.
Furnald Folk Fest, Manhattan, NYC, Early Apr.
Gala All-Star Irish Cruise, Manhattan, NYC, Late Jul. to Early Aug.
Gateway Sukkos Festival, Brooklyn, NYC, Late Sep.

Gateway to the Nations Powwow, Brooklyn, NYC, Early Jul.
Gay and Lesbian American Music Awards, Manhattan, NYC, Early Oct. to Early Nov.
Giving of Thanks to the First Peoples, Manhattan, NYC, Middle Nov.
Gospel Celebration!, Brooklyn, NYC, Early Feb.
Gospel Comes/Returns to Broadway, Manhattan, NYC, Late Apr.
Gospel Concert, Brooklyn, NYC, Early Jun.
Gospel Explosion, Brooklyn, NYC, Late Mar.
Gospel Music Workshop of America/New York State Chapter Convention, Brooklyn, NYC,
    Middle Jun.
Gospel Nite, Manhattan, NYC, Middle Jul.
Gospelfest, Brooklyn, NYC, Middle Jun.
Grand Nights for Singing, Manhattan, NYC, Early Jul. to Middle Jul.
Great Beer and Music Festival, Manhattan, NYC, Middle Jan.
Great Beer and Music Festival, Manhattan, NYC, Late Mar.
Great Beer and Music Festival, Manhattan, NYC, Middle Nov.
Great Irish Fair, Brooklyn, NYC, Early Sep. to Middle Sep.
Great Miracle Prayer Festival, Manhattan, NYC, Late Feb.
Great New York Mandolin Gala, Manhattan, NYC, Middle Apr.
Great New York Mandolin Weekend, Manhattan, NYC, Early Apr.
Greenwich Avenue Summer Festival, Manhattan, NYC, Late Aug.
Greenwich Village Folk Festival, Manhattan, NYC, Early Oct.
Gruppen: Chamber Music for the 21st Century, Manhattan, NYC, Early Jan. to Middle Jan.
Hanukkah Arts Festival and Judaica Crafts Fair/Selected Shorts, Manhattan, NYC, Middle Oct.
Hanukkah Festival, Queens, NYC, Middle Dec.
Harlem Piano U. S. A., Manhattan, NYC, Middle Nov.
Harlem Week/Harlem Day, Manhattan, NYC, Early Aug. to Middle Aug.
Harmony Sweepstakes A Cappella Festival/New York Regional, Manhattan, NYC, Early Apr.
Harp and Harmony Concert, Manhattan, NYC, Early Jun.
Heart and Soul, Manhattan, NYC, Early May
Hearts and Voices In Concert, Manhattan, NYC, Middle May
Hearts and Voices Winter Benefit Series, Manhattan, NYC, Middle Mar. to Late Apr.
Heineken Jazz and Blues Festival, Manhattan, NYC, Late Aug.
Hezekiah Walker Anniversary Show, Brooklyn, NYC, Late May
Hot 97's Old School Throwdown, Manhattan, NYC, Late Jan.
I. C. C. Songfest, Staten Island, NYC, Early Aug.
Improvisations Festival, Manhattan, NYC, Late Nov. to Middle Dec.
Improvisors Collective Festival, Manhattan, NYC, Early Mar.
Improvisors Festival, Manhattan, NYC, Late Jun. to Early Jul.
In Celebration of Life, Manhattan, NYC, Early May
Independent Music Fest, Manhattan, NYC, Late Mar. to Early Apr.
Indian Market, Manhattan, NYC, Middle Dec. to Late Dec.
Indian Summer, Manhattan, NYC, Early Jun. to Late Jun.
International Festival of Cultures, Staten Island, NYC, Middle Sep.
International OFFestival, Manhattan, NYC, Middle Apr. to Middle Jun.
Irish Traditional Music and Dance Festival, Bronx, NYC, Middle Jun.
Irish-American Festival and Heritage Feis, Brooklyn, NYC, Late May
Israel Expo, Manhattan, NYC, Late May
Israel Expo, Brooklyn, NYC, Early Jun.
Israeli Folk Dance Festival and Festival of the Arts, Manhattan, NYC, Middle Mar.
JAL Jazz Concert, Manhattan, NYC, Early Nov.
Jamaica Fun Run and Family Day, Queens, NYC, Middle May
Jazz and Poetry Marathon, Manhattan, NYC, Middle Feb.
Jazz in July, Manhattan, NYC, Late Jul.
JazzTimes Convention, Manhattan, NYC, Middle Nov.

Jewish Festival of Music, Manhattan, NYC, Late Mar.
Jimi Hendrix Birthday Party, Manhattan, NYC, Late Nov.
Juba, Jukin' and Jazzin', Manhattan, NYC, Early Nov.
Julius Watkins Jazz French Horn Festival, Manhattan, NYC, Middle Mar.
July Gospel Explosion, Brooklyn, NYC, Early Jul.
JVC Jazz Festival/Bryant Park Jazz Festival, Manhattan, NYC, Late Jun. to Early Jul.
K-Rock's Hungerthon, Manhattan, NYC, Middle Nov.
Kitty Brazelton's Real Music Series, Manhattan, NYC, Late Feb. to Early Apr.
Kitty Brazelton's Real Music Series/Music Parties, Manhattan, NYC, Early Nov. to Late Nov.
Knitting Factory at Merkin Hall, Manhattan, NYC, Early Oct. to Middle Oct.
Knitting Factory's "What is Jazz?" Festival, Manhattan, NYC, Middle Jun. to Early Jul.
Kwanzaa, Queens, NYC, Early Dec.
Kwanzaa Holiday Expo, Manhattan, NYC, Middle Dec.
Latin Jazz U. S. A. Concert and Awards, Manhattan, NYC, Early Dec.
Lesbian and Gay Pride Committee Parade and Festival, Queens, NYC, Early Jun.
Lesbian and Gay Pride Week/PrideFest, Manhattan, NYC, Middle Jun. to Late Jun.
Lesbopalooza, Manhattan, NYC, Late Jun.
Libro Latino Bookfest/Pathways for Youth Benefit, Bronx, NYC, Middle May
Life Beat Benefit:  The Music Industry Fights AIDS, Manhattan, NYC, Middle Jul.
Lincoln Center Out-of-Doors, Manhattan, NYC, Early Aug. to Late Aug.
Live Jazz Bands, Queens, NYC, Middle Oct.
Lou Rawls Parade of Stars, Manhattan, NYC, Early Jan.
Lower East Side Jewish Festival, Manhattan, NYC, Middle Jun.
Lower Second Avenue Festival, Manhattan, NYC, Early May
Lyrics and Lyricists/Boys Night Out, Manhattan, NYC, Late Feb.
Lyrics and Lyricists/The New Breed, Manhattan, NYC, Middle Jun.
Macintosh New York Music Festival, Manhattan, NYC, Middle Jul. to Late Jul.
Main Street U. S. A., Manhattan, NYC, Late Mar.
Manhattan Association of Cabarets and Clubs Awards, Manhattan, NYC, Early Apr.
Manhattan Ethnic Music and Dance Festival, Manhattan, NYC, Late May
Mardi Gras Carnaval, Manhattan, NYC, Middle Feb.
Martin Luther King Jr. Concert Series, Brooklyn, NYC, Middle Jul. to Late Aug.
McDonald's Gospelfest, Varies, NYC, Early Apr. to Middle Jun.
Memorial Day Weekend Celebration Scholarship Fund Raising Dance, Manhattan, NYC, Late
    May
Midnight Ravers Anniversary Party, Manhattan, NYC, Late Aug.
Midsummer Night Swing, Manhattan, NYC, Late Jun. to Late Jul.
Midsummer's Night Cabaret, Manhattan, NYC, Middle Aug.
Midwood Concerts at Seaside, Brooklyn, NYC, Middle Jul. to Late Aug.
Mostly Women Composers, Manhattan, NYC, Middle May to Late May
Mother's Day Caribbean All-Stars Festival, Varies, NYC, Middle May
MTV Music Awards, Manhattan, NYC, Early Sep.
Murray Hill Block Party and Blues Festival, Manhattan, NYC, Early Jun.
Music from Japan Festival, Manhattan, NYC, Late Feb.
National Gay and Lesbian Business and Consumer Expo, Manhattan, NYC, Late Apr.
National Gospel Choir Competition, Manhattan, NYC, Middle Mar.
Nations of New York Arts Festival, Manhattan, NYC, Middle Oct. to Late Oct.
Native American Festival, Manhattan, NYC, Late Sep.
New York All-Star Klezmer Extravaganza, Manhattan, NYC, Middle Jul.
New York Beer Fest, Brooklyn, NYC, Middle Sep.
New York Brass Conference for Scholarships, Manhattan, NYC, Early Apr.
New York City Clearwater Festival, Brooklyn, NYC, Late Jul.
New York City's Gospel Festival, Brooklyn, NYC, Middle Jun.
New York Country Music Festival, Queens, NYC, Middle Aug.

New York Jazz Today!, Manhattan, NYC, Middle Dec.
New York Reggae Festival, Brooklyn, NYC, Middle Aug.
New York Salsa Festival, Manhattan, NYC, Early Sep.
New York Shakespeare Festival Spring Gala, Manhattan, NYC, Early May
New York State Big Apple Festival, Manhattan, NYC, Late Sep.
New York Trini-Jam Fest, Brooklyn, NYC, Early Jul.
New York Winter Blues Festival, Manhattan, NYC, Late Mar.
Next Wave Festival, Brooklyn, NYC, Late Sep. to Middle Dec.
Night of Musical Magic, Manhattan, NYC, Middle Oct.
Night of Shamrocks, Queens, NYC, Middle Nov.
Northeastern Native American Association Pow Wow, Queens, NYC, Late Sep.
Nuyorican Poets Cafe Block Party, Manhattan, NYC, Middle Aug.
Oi!/Skampilation, Manhattan, NYC, Late May
Outmusic Festival, Manhattan, NYC, Early Oct. to Early Nov.
Outmusic Festival, Manhattan, NYC, Early May
P. S. 122 Music Festival, Manhattan, NYC, Early Apr.
Panasonic Village Jazz Festival, Manhattan, NYC, Middle Aug. to Late Aug.
Park Slope 5th Avenue Independence Day Festival, Brooklyn, NYC, Early Jul.
Park Slope Festival, Brooklyn, NYC, Middle Aug.
Park Slope Native American Dance Festival, Brooklyn, NYC, Middle Jan.
Party for Zoot, Manhattan, NYC, Middle Mar.
Pathmark Hispanic Arts Festival, Manhattan, NYC, Early Jun.
Peter Tosh Day, Manhattan, NYC, Middle Oct.
Plantathon and Music Festival, Manhattan, NYC, Early Jun.
Post-Rock, Neo-Mosh Festival, Manhattan, NYC, Early Dec.
Puerto Rican Day Parade, Manhattan, NYC, Middle Jun.
Puerto Rican Day Parade, Bronx, NYC, Late Jul.
Pussystock, Manhattan, NYC, Early May
QE2: Newport Jazz Festival at Sea, Manhattan, NYC, Middle Sep. to Late Sep.
Queens Boulevard Festival, Queens, NYC, Middle Jun.
Queens College Cultural Heritage Great Gospel Competition, Queens, NYC, Middle May
Queens Festival/Nations in Neighborhoods Multicultural Dance Party, Queens, NYC, Late Jun.
Radioactive Bodega Blacklight Prom, Brooklyn, NYC, Late Apr.
Rafael Hernandez/Sylvia Rexach Festival, Manhattan, NYC, Middle Sep.
Rainforest Benefit Concert, Manhattan, NYC, Middle Apr.
Religious Music Festival, Brooklyn, NYC, Late Apr.
Return of The Brooklyn Bridge, Queens, NYC, Late Nov.
Rhythm and Blues Foundation's Pioneer Awards, Manhattan, NYC, Early Mar.
Richard Nader's Rock and Roll Revival Spectacular, Manhattan, NYC, Middle Nov.
Riverside Park Arts Festival, Manhattan, NYC, Early Aug. to Late Aug.
Rock Against Racism Concert, Manhattan, NYC, Late May
Rock-N-Roll Extravaganza, Queens, NYC, Early Aug.
Rockaway Irish Festival, Queens, NYC, Late Jul.
Rockaway Music and Arts Council Fall Festival, Brooklyn, NYC, Middle Sep.
Roots of American Music Festival, Manhattan, NYC, Late Aug.
Roulette Concert Series/Le Salon Roulette, Manhattan, NYC, Middle Mar.
Roulette Concert Series/Roulette Mixology Festival, Manhattan, NYC, Late Apr. to Early May
S. O. B.'s Kwanzaa Celebration, Manhattan, NYC, Late Dec.
Salsa Fest, Brooklyn, NYC, Late Aug.
Salsa's Soul Combination, Bronx, NYC, Early Apr.
Salute to Israel Day Parade and Concert, Manhattan, NYC, Late May
Save Our Park/WWRL Radiothon, Queens, NYC, Late May
Say It With Love Night, Manhattan, NYC, Middle May
Sephardi Cultural Fair, Queens, NYC, Late Sep.

Serious Fun!, Manhattan, NYC, Early Jul. to Late Jul.

Shelter: The New York Singer-Songwriter Festival, Manhattan, NYC, Middle Oct.

Skarmageddon, Manhattan, NYC, Late Dec.

Skavoovee, Manhattan, NYC, Late Nov.

Slammin' Jammin' Spike's Joint Anniversary Block Party, Brooklyn, NYC, Late Jul.

Smalls Winter Festival, Manhattan, NYC, Middle Feb.

Smithsonian's National Museum of the American Indian Powwow, Manhattan, NYC, Middle Oct.

Songwriter's Evening, Manhattan, NYC, Late Oct.

Songwriters' Hall of Fame Awards, Manhattan, NYC, Late May

Sonic Boom Festival of New Music, Manhattan, NYC, Early Nov. to Middle Nov.

Sonidos de las Americas, Varies, NYC, Late Nov. to Early Dec.

Sounds Around the World, Manhattan, NYC, Middle Dec.

Sounds at Sunset, Manhattan, NYC, Middle Jun. to Middle Sep.

Southeast Queens' Youth Sports and Spring Festival/Juneteenth, Queens, NYC, Middle Jun.

St. Barnabas Irish Variety Concert, Bronx, NYC, Middle Mar.

Starrett at Spring Creek Native American Pow Wow, Brooklyn, NYC, Early Jun.

Steinway Street Fun in the Sun Festival, Queens, NYC, Early Jul.

Stork Music Festival, Manhattan, NYC, Early Apr.

Sudden Sunsets: Highlights from the Benson AIDS Series, Manhattan, NYC, Middle Jun.

Summerfun! , Staten Island, NYC, Middle Jul.

Sun Ra Festival, Manhattan, NYC, Middle May to Late May

Sunnyside Shop-Till-You-Drop Festival, Queens, NYC, Middle Apr.

Super Radioactive Bodega Bonanza Outdoor Festival, Brooklyn, NYC, Middle Jun.

Tamika Reggae Awards, Manhattan, NYC, Late Mar.

TeddyCare, Manhattan, NYC, Early Dec. to Late Dec.

The Brooklyn Beat Meets The Black Rock Coalition, Manhattan, NYC, Middle Mar.

The Source Awards, Manhattan, NYC, Early Aug.

Theater for the New City Village Haloween Costume Ball, Manhattan, NYC, Late Oct.

Thunderbird American Indian Dancers Pow Wow and Dance Concert, Manhattan, NYC, Late Jan. to Early Feb.

Tokyo/New York Noise Festival, Manhattan, NYC, Middle Mar.

Tribute to African Diaspora Women, Manhattan, NYC, Middle May

Tropical Carnival/Carnival Fete and Masquerade Jump-Up, Brooklyn, NYC, Late Feb.

Tweed New Works Festival, Manhattan, NYC, Middle Jun. to Early Jul.

U. G. H. A. Black History Month Celebration, Manhattan, NYC, Middle Feb.

U. G. H. A. Hall of Fame Awards Ceremony, Manhattan, NYC, Early Apr.

Underground Blues and Folk Festival, Manhattan, NYC, Late Jun.

Underground Jazz Festival, Manhattan, NYC, Early Oct.

Union Settlement Ethnic Festival, Manhattan, NYC, Middle May

Upper Broadway Spring Celebration and Festival, Manhattan, NYC, Late Apr.

Upper Broadway Summer Festival, Manhattan, NYC, Middle Jun.

Uprise and Shine Youth Concert, Brooklyn, NYC, Late Aug.

Village Halloween Parade/All Souls' Halloween Ball, Manhattan, NYC, Late Oct.

Vulvapalooza, Manhattan, NYC, Late Aug.

Wall of Sound, Queens, NYC, Late Mar.

Wall to Wall, Manhattan, NYC, Late Mar.

Wall-to-Wall Rahsaan Roland Kirk, Manhattan, NYC, Early Jun.

WBLS Celebration Concert and Scholarship Fund, Manhattan, NYC, Early Dec.

WDRE Acoustic Christmas, Manhattan, NYC, Middle Dec.

WDRE Modern Rock Fest, Manhattan, NYC, Early Oct.

We Care About New York Block Party, Manhattan, NYC, Late Aug.

Welcome Back to Brooklyn, Brooklyn, NYC, Middle Jun.

West Indian Carnival Explosion, Brooklyn, NYC, Middle Mar.

West Indian-American Day Carnival and Parade, Brooklyn, NYC, Early Sep.
West Side Arts, Crafts, Antiques Festival, Manhattan, NYC, Early Sep.
West Side Fall Festival, Manhattan, NYC, Early Sep.
Wigstock, Manhattan, NYC, Early Sep.
Winning Scores, Manhattan, NYC, Middle Mar.
Winter Consort Summer Solstice Whole Earth Celebration, Manhattan, NYC, Late Jun.
Winter Consort Winter Solstice Whole Earth Christmas Celebration, Manhattan, NYC, Middle
    Dec.
Winter Revels, Manhattan, NYC, Early Dec.
WNEW-FM Christmas Concert, Manhattan, NYC, Early Dec.
Women in Cabaret, Manhattan, NYC, Early Feb. to Late Feb.
Women in Jazz Festival, Manhattan, NYC, Early Jul.
Women's Jazz Festival, Manhattan, NYC, Early Mar. to Late Mar.
Woodside Independence Weekend Festival, Queens, NYC, Early Jul.
World of Percussion, Manhattan, NYC, Early Jun.
WPLJ-FM's 70's Dance Party, Manhattan, NYC, Middle Sep.
WPLJ-FM's 70's Dance Party, Manhattan, NYC, Middle Jun.
WPLJ-FM's 70's Rock and Roll Reunion, Manhattan, NYC, Late Mar.
WWRL Family Day and Picnic, Queens, NYC, Early Aug. to Middle Aug.
WWRL Gospel Explosion, Manhattan, NYC, Middle Dec.
Z100 Acoustic Christmas, Manhattan, NYC, Early Dec.
Z100 May Day, Manhattan, NYC, Middle May
Zydecodelic Loup Garou Bal de la Maison Mardi Gras Party, Manhattan, NYC, Late Feb.

## Varied Sites

American Banjo Fraternity's Fall Rally, Varied Sites, VAR, Middle Oct. to Late Oct.
Clearwater's Pumpkin Sail, Varied Sites, VAR, Early Oct. to Middle Oct.
Drum Corps International World Championships, Varied Sites, VAR, Middle Aug.
Folk Alliance Conference, Varied Sites, VAR, Middle Feb.
Gospel Music Workshop of America National Convention, Varied Sites, VAR, Early Aug. to
    Middle Aug.
International Association of Jazz Educators Convention, Varied Sites, VAR, Middle Jan.
International Duke Ellington Conference, Varied Sites, VAR, Middle Aug.
National Baptist Convention of America, Varied Sites, VAR, Early Sep. to Middle Sep.
New England Foundation for the Arts Jazz Conference, Varied Sites, VAR, Early Jun. to Middle
    Jun.
New England Sacred Harp Singing Convention, Varied Sites, VAR, Early Oct.
New Music Across America, Varied Sites, VAR, Early Oct.
Northeast Invitational Country Music Awards Show, Varied Sites, VAR, Middle Feb.
People's Music Network Winter Gathering, Varied Sites, VAR, Late Jan.
Rock and Roll Hall of Fame Induction Dinner, Varied Sites, VAR, Middle Jan.
The Consortium, Varied Sites, VAR, Late Feb. to Middle Apr.

~     ~     ~

# Festival Cities in Alphabetical Order

## Maine

Augusta, ME, Kaleidoscope Family Arts Festival, Early Jun.
Augusta, ME, Great Whatever Week and Race, Late Jun. to Early Jul.
Augusta, ME, Festival de la Bastille, Early Jul.
Bangor, ME, Arcady Music Festival/Ragtime Evening Benefit, Early Jun.
Bangor, ME, Bangor State Fair, Late Jul. to Early Aug.
Bar Harbor, ME, Downeast Dulcimer and Harp Festival, Early Jul.
Bar Harbor, ME, Native American Festival, Early Jul.
Bar Harbor, ME, Bar Harbor Festival/New Composers Concert, Late Jul.
Bar Harbor, ME, Scottish Performing Arts Weekend and Workshop, Middle Oct.
Bath, ME, Festival of Traditional Sea Music, Early Jun.
Bath, ME, Bath Heritage Days, Early Jul.
Bath, ME, Circle of Sound Benefit Concert, Late Aug.
Belfast, ME, Belfast Bay Festival, Middle Jul.
Belfast, ME, Sankofa Street Festival, Middle Aug.
Belgrade Lakes, ME, Buttermilk Hill Old Time Music Show, Middle Aug.
Bethel, ME, Mollyockett Day, Middle Jul.
Bethel, ME, Sudbury Canada Days, Middle Aug.
Biddeford, ME, LaKermesse Franco-Americaine Festival, Late Jun.
Blue Hill, ME, Blue Hill Pops, Early Jul.
Blue Hill, ME, Left Bank Cafe Country Blues Festival, Middle Jul.
Blue Hill, ME, Blue Hill Festival of Music/Singer-Songwriter Marathon, Late Oct.
Boothbay Harbor, ME, Windjammer Days, Late Jun.
Brewer, ME, Coor's Lite Music Festival, Early Jul.
Brunswick, ME, Blistered Fingers Helping Hands of Bluegrass, Late Mar. to Early Apr.
Brunswick, ME, Gamper Festival of Contemporary Music, Late Jul.
Brunswick, ME, Maine Festival of the Arts, Early Aug.
Brunswick, ME, Maine Highland Games , Middle Aug.
Brunswick, ME, Thomas Point Beach Bluegrass Festival, Early Sep.
Calais, ME, International Festival, Late Jul. to Early Aug.
Cambridge, ME, New England Salty Dog Bluegrass Festival, Late Aug.
Camden, ME, Down East Jazz Festival, Late Aug.
Caribou, ME, Pride of Maine Fiddling Festival, Early Feb.
Crawford, ME, Breakneck Mountain Bluegrass Festival, Early Jul.
Cumberland, ME, Native American Appreciation Day, Middle Sep.
Damariscotta, ME, Fiddling Competition and Contra Dance, Middle Jun.
Damariscotta, ME, Rotary Oyster Festival, Early Jul. to Middle Jul.
East Benton, ME, East Benton Fiddlers' Convention and Contest, Late Jul.
Eastport, ME, Old Home Week and Independence Day, Late Jun. to Early Jul.
Eastport, ME, Salmon Sunday, Middle Sep.
Farmington, ME, Fat Tire Polo Tournament and Music Bash, Early Aug.
Farmington, ME, Titcom Mountain Fiddling and Bluegrass Festival, Middle Aug.
Fort Fairfield, ME, Maine Potato Blossom Festival/Crown of Maine Balloon Festival, Early Jul.
    to Middle Jul.
Freedom, ME, Maine Healing Arts Festival, Early Sep.
Gorham, ME, Celebrate Gorham, Early Jul.
Grand Isle, ME, Homecoming, Late Jul. to Early Aug.

Hallowell, ME, Old Hallowell Day, Middle Jul.
Hebron, ME, Hebron Pines Bluegrass Festival, Late May
Hebron, ME, Old Time Country Music Festival, Early Sep.
Kennebunk, ME, River Tree Arts Country Jamboree, Middle Mar.
Kennebunk, ME, Celebration of the Arts, Middle Jul. to Late Jul.
Kennebunk, ME, River Tree Arts Fiddle Contest and Old Time Country Music Show, Early Sep.
Kingfield, ME, Sugarloaf Ski-A-Palooza/College Weeks, Early Jan. to Middle Jan.
Kingfield, ME, Sugarloaf Reggae Ski Bash, Early Apr.
Kingfield, ME, Sugarloaf Mountain Blues Festival, Middle Apr.
Kingfield, ME, Sugarloaf Country Music Festival, Late Jun. to Late Aug.
Kittery, ME, Seaside Festival, Early Jul.
Lewiston, ME, Knights of Columbus Festival de Joie, Early Aug.
Machias, ME, Pride of Maine Fiddling Festival, Middle Feb.
Madawaska, ME, Acadian Festival Celebration, Late Jun. to Early Jul.
Medway, ME, Katahdin Family Bluegrass Music Festival, Late Jun.
North Anson, ME, New Vineyard Mountains Bluegrass Festival, Early Jul.
North New Portland, ME, Happy Horseshoe Blue Grass Festival, Middle Jun.
North Yarmouth, ME, Blues Festival, Late Jun.
Norway/Oxford, ME, Oxford County Bluegrass Festival, Middle Aug.
Old Orchard Beach, ME, Rock 'N' Roll Bar-B-Q, Early Jul.
Orland, ME, H. O. M. E. Craft and Farm Fair, Early Aug.
Perry, ME, Passamaquoddy Traditional Indian Festival, Middle Aug.
Pittsfield, ME, Central Maine Egg Festival, Middle Jul. to Late Jul.
Portland, ME, Old Port Festival, Early Jun.
Portland, ME, Family Fun Fair, Middle Jun.
Portland, ME, Back Cove Family Day, Middle Jun.
Portland, ME, Portland Waterfront Festival, Late Jun.
Portland, ME, Deering Oaks Family Festival, Middle Jul. to Late Jul.
Portland, ME, Summer in the Parks, Early Aug. to Middle Aug.
Portland, ME, Duke Ellington Festival, Middle Sep.
Portland, ME, Fall MusicFest, Late Oct. to Early Nov.
Portland, ME, New Year's Eve Portland, Late Dec.
Princeton, ME, Motahkmikuk Indian Day Celebration, Middle Jul. to Middle Jul.
Rangeley, ME, Rangeley's Old-Time Fiddlers' Contest, Middle Jul.
Richmond, ME, Richmond Days, Middle Jul. to Late Jul.
Rockland, ME, Schooner Days, Early Jul.
Rockland, ME, North Atlantic Blues Festival, Early Jul.
Rockland, ME, Maine Lobster Festival, Early Aug.
Rockport, ME, Rockport Folk Festival, Middle Sep.
Sidney, ME, Blistered Fingers Family Bluegrass Music Festival, Middle Jun.
Skowhegan, ME, Skowhegan State Fair, Middle Aug.
South Berwick, ME, Strawberry Festival, Late Jun.
South Portland, ME, Down East Country Dance Festival, Middle Mar.
South Portland, ME, Spring Point Festival, Middle Aug.
Swans Island, ME, Sweet Chariot Music Festival and Schooner Gam, Early Aug.
Thomaston, ME, Thomaston Independence Day Celebration, Early Jul.
Union, ME, WERU 89.9FM Full Circle Summer Fair, Early Jul.
Unity, ME, Fiddlehead Festival, Middle May
Van Buren, ME, Grand Riviere Festival, Late Jun. to Middle Aug.
Waldo, ME, Pride of Maine Fiddling Festival, Middle May
Waterville, ME, Old Time Country Jamboree, Middle Sep.
West Buxton, ME, Maine Invitational Country Music Semi-Finals Show, Middle Sep. to Late Sep.
West Buxton, ME, Maine Invitational Country Music Finals Show, Early Nov.
Windsor, ME, Common Ground Country Fair, Late Sep.

Yarmouth, ME, Yarmouth Clam Festival, Middle Jul.
York, ME, York Days, Late Jul. to Early Aug.

## New Hampshire

Bartlett, NH, White Mountain Jazz and Blues CraftsFestival, Early Sep.
Bretton Woods, NH, Twin Mountain Country Western Jamboree, Early Jul.
Campton, NH, Pemi Valley Bluegrass Festival, Early Aug.
Concord, NH, Contemporary Music Festival, Early May
Concord, NH, Strathspey and Reel Society of New Hampshire's Scottish Gala Concert, Late Nov.
Concord, NH, First Night New Hampshire, Late Dec.
Conway, NH, Labor Day Weekend Music Festival, Early Sep.
Durham, NH, Ralph Page Legacy Weekend, Early Jan.
Durham, NH, Clark Terry/University of New Hampshire Jazz Festival, Middle Mar.
Exeter, NH, Musicfest, Early Aug.
Franconia, NH, Hayseed Music Fest, Middle Jul.
Gilmanton, NH, Gilmanton Bluegrass Festival, Middle Jul.
Hampton Beach, NH, Seafood Festival and Sidewalk Sale Days, Middle Sep.
Hanover, NH, Dartmouth Festival of New Musics, Middle May
Hanover, NH, Hanover Street-Fest, Middle Jul.
Hanover, NH, Christmas Revels, Middle Dec.
Hillsboro, NH, Folk Song Society of Greater Boston Fall Getaway Weekend, Middle Sep.
Keene, NH, Street Fair, Middle Jul.
Keene, NH, First Night Keene, Late Dec.
Laconia, NH, Countryfest, Early Mar.
Laconia, NH, New England Bluegrass Festival, Middle Jun.
Lincoln, NH, Fiddler's Contest, Late Jun.
Lincoln, NH, All AmericanFest, Early Jul.
Lincoln, NH, Loon MountainPark BrewFest, Late Jul.
Lincoln, NH, Loon MountainPark IrishFest, Early Aug.
Lincoln, NH, Loon MountainPark CajunFest, Middle Aug.
Lincoln, NH, New Hampshire Highland Games, Middle Sep.
Lisbon, NH, New Hampshire's Lilac Time Festival, Late May
Littleton, NH, Native American Show, Middle Jul.
Manchester, NH, International Festival, Early May
Manchester, NH, American Pit Masters Bar-B-Q Round-Up, Early Jul.
Manchester, NH, Riverfest: Manchester Celebrating Itself, Early Sep. to Middle Sep.
Milford, NH, High Hopes Hot Air Balloon Festival, Middle Jun.
North Conway, NH, Arts Jubilee/Country in the Valley, Late Aug.
Northfield, NH, New Hampshire Women's Music Festival, Middle Jun.
Plymouth, NH, Classic Rock Festival, Late Jun.
Portsmouth, NH, Seacoast African-American Heritage Festival, Early Feb. to Late Feb.
Portsmouth, NH, Seacoast Music Awards, Early Feb.
Portsmouth, NH, New England Blues Conference, Late Apr.
Portsmouth, NH, Market Square Day, Early Jun. to Middle Jun.
Portsmouth, NH, Jazz Showcase, Late Jun.
Portsmouth, NH, Portsmouth Jazz Festival, Late Jun.
Portsmouth, NH, Prescott Parks Arts Festival/Celebration of Jazz, Late Aug.
Portsmouth, NH, Blues Festival, Early Sep.
Portsmouth, NH, Star Hampshire Traditional Music/Dance Retreat, Late Sep.
Portsmouth, NH, First Night Portsmouth, Late Dec.
Somersworth, NH, Somersworth International Children's Festival, Middle Jun.
Stark, NH, Stark Old Time Fiddlers' Contest, Late Jun.
Waterville Valley, NH, Waterville Valley Summer Music Festival, Middle Jul. to Early Sep.

Barre, VT, National Traditional Old Time Fiddlers' and Step Dancing Contest, Late Sep.
Barre, VT, French Heritage Festival, Late Oct.
Belvidere, VT, Rattling Brook Bluegrass Festival, Middle Jun.
Bennington, VT, Bennington Folk Festival, Middle May
Bennington, VT, Bennington Battle Day Weekend, Middle Aug.
Brandon, VT, Basin Bluegrass Festival, Early Jul.
Burlington, VT, University of Vermont Lane Series/49th Parallel Music Festival, Late Jan.
Burlington, VT, Irish Cultural Day, Early May
Burlington, VT, Discover Jazz Festival, Early Jun. to Middle Jun.
Burlington, VT, Green Mountain Chew Chew/Vermont Food Fest, Late Jun.
Burlington, VT, Vermont Lesbian Gay Bisexual Pride Day, Late Jun.
Burlington, VT, Burlington Independence Day Waterfront Celebration, Early Jul.
Burlington, VT, Vermont Women's Celebration, Late Jul.
Burlington, VT, Champlain Valley Festival, Early Aug.
Burlington, VT, Hot Country Music Festival, Middle Aug.
Burlington, VT, Battle of the Bands, Early Nov.
Burlington, VT, First Night Burlington, Late Dec.
Craftsbury, VT, Banjo Contest, Middle Sep.
Enosburg Falls, VT, Vermont Dairy Festival, Early Jun.
Essex Junction, VT, Lake Champlain Balloon Festival, Early Jun.
Essex Junction, VT, Champlain Valley Exposition, Late Aug. to Early Sep.
Evansville, VT, Raven Wind Pow-Wow, Middle May
Evansville, VT, Native American Abenaki Pow-Wow, Late Aug.
Ferrisburgh, VT, Families Outdoor Festival, Middle Jul.
Hardwick, VT, Ole Time Fiddlers Contest, Late Jul.
Irasburg, VT, Warebrook Contemporary Music Festival, Early Jul.
Johnson, VT, Vermont Reggae Fest, Middle Jul.
Killington, VT, Mountain Jam, Early Jul.
Middlebury, VT, Cabin Fever Folklife Festival, Early Apr.
Middlebury, VT, Middlebury Summer Festival-on-the-Green, Middle Jul.
Middlebury, VT, AutumnFest, Middle Sep.
Montpelier, VT, Midsummer Festival of Vermont Art and Music, Early Jul.
Mount Snow, VT, Southern Vermont Highland Games, Middle Jul.
Newbury, VT, Crackerbarrel Fiddlers Contest, Late Jul.
Newport, VT, Aquafest, Middle Jul.
North Danville, VT, Lamplight Service and Hymn Sing, Late May to Late Aug.
North Hero, VT, North American Northumbrian Piper's Convention, Late Aug.
Poultney, VT, Harmony Ridge Brass Center Summer Festival, Early Aug.
Quechee, VT, Quechee Hot Air Balloon Festival, Middle Jun.
Quechee, VT, Quechee Scottish Festival, Late Aug.
Randolph, VT, Chandler's New World Festival, Early Sep.
Rochester, VT, Celebrate Vermont Arts and Crafts Show, Middle Jul.
Rutland, VT, Rutland Region Ethnic Festival, Late Jun.
Rutland, VT, Vermont State Fair, Early Sep. to Middle Sep.
Rutland, VT, First Night Rutland, Late Dec.
Rutland/Burlington, VT, Abenaki Festival Days, Late Apr. to Early May
Shelburne, VT, Shelburne Farms Harvest Festival, Middle Sep.
Sherburne, VT, Pico Mountain Jazz Festival, Late Jul.
Springfield, VT, Vermont Apple Festival and Crafts Show, Middle Oct.
St. Albans, VT, Vermont Maple Festival/Fiddler's Variety Show, Late Apr.
St. Johnsbury, VT, First Night St. Johnsbury, Late Dec.
Stratton Mountain, VT, Coors Country Chili Fest, Late Aug.
Various, VT, Vermont Brewers Festival, Middle Sep.
Warren, VT, Ben and Jerry's One World, One Heart Festival, Late Jun.

Warren, VT, Sugarbush Brewers Festival, Middle Sep.
Waterbury, VT, National Fife and Drum Muster, Early Aug.
West Dover, VT, Green Mountain Dulcimer Daze and Rendezvous, Middle Aug.

## Massachusetts

Allston, MA, Boston Blues Festival, Late Jan. to Late Feb.
Allston, MA, Battle of the Blues Bands, Late Jun. to Early Jul.
Amesbury, MA, Amesbury Days Festival, Late Jun. to Early Jul.
Amherst, MA, Bright Moments Festival, Middle Jul. to Late Jul.
Attleboro, MA, Wollomonuppoag Indian Council Inter-Tribal Pow Wow, Middle Jul.
Attleboro Falls, MA, Fall Festival, Middle Sep.
Blandford, MA, Blandford Mountain Bluegrass Festival, Early Jul.
Blandford, MA, Glasgow Lands Scottish Festival, Late Jul.
Blandford, MA, Blandford Fair Old Time Fiddle Contest, Early Sep.
Boston, MA, Black History Month, Early Feb. to Late Feb.
Boston, MA, Anthony Spinazzola Gala Festival of Food and Wine, Early Feb.
Boston, MA, Boston Festival:  A Carnival of Cultures, Middle Feb. to Late Feb.
Boston, MA, Berklee College of Music High School Jazz Festival, Early Mar.
Boston, MA, Harpoon's St. Patrick's Day Bash, Middle Mar.
Boston, MA, Hot, Hot Tropics, Late Mar.
Boston, MA, Boston Phoenix/WFNX Best Music Poll Celebration, Late Mar.
Boston, MA, World Fair at Boston University, Early Apr. to Middle Apr.
Boston, MA, American Indian Day at the Children's Museum, Early Apr.
Boston, MA, Pepsi Boston Music Awards, Early Apr.
Boston, MA, WBOS-FM Earth Day Concert and Festival, Late Apr.
Boston, MA, Kenmore Square Rites of Spring Charity Rockfest, Late Apr.
Boston, MA, Students for Students/Human Rights Festival, Late Apr.
Boston, MA, WBCN Rock 'n' Roll Rumble, Early May to Late May
Boston, MA, Boston Brewer's Festival, Middle May
Boston, MA, WGBH "T" Party, Middle May
Boston, MA, Boston Kite Festival, Middle May
Boston, MA, Art Newbury Street, Middle May
Boston, MA, Homefolks Concert, Late May
Boston, MA, Street Performers Festival, Late May
Boston, MA, American Pit Masters Bar-B-Q Round-Up, Middle Jun.
Boston, MA, Boston Festival of Bands, Early Jun.
Boston, MA, Harpoon's Brewstock, Late Jun.
Boston, MA, Boston Waterfront Festival, Middle Jun.
Boston, MA, Pridefest, Middle Jun.
Boston, MA, Boston Globe Jazz Festival, Middle Jun.
Boston, MA, Race Unity Day, Middle Jun.
Boston, MA, Boston Pops, Middle Jun. to Early Jul.
Boston, MA, Boston Book Fair, Middle Jun.
Boston, MA, Chilifest, Middle Jun.
Boston, MA, Pan-African Cultural Festival, Late Jun.
Boston, MA, Boston Harborfest, Late Jun.
Boston, MA, Cape Verdean Festival, Early Jul.
Boston, MA, Oxfam America WorldFest, Early Jul. to Middle Jul.
Boston, MA, Puerto Rican Festival, Late Jul.
Boston, MA, Dominican Festival, Early Aug.
Boston, MA, Caribbean Carnival, Middle Aug. to Late Aug.
Boston, MA, Great Yankee Rib Cook-Off, Late Aug.
Boston, MA, Celtic Festival at the Hatch Shell, Early Sep.

Boston, MA, Art Newbury Street, Middle Sep.

Boston, MA, John Coltrane Memorial Concert, Early Oct.

Boston, MA, Acoustic Underground: Boston's National Acoustic Music Showcase, Early Oct. to
     Early Nov.

Boston, MA, Mix 98.5 Fall Fest, Early Oct.

Boston, MA, Irish Music Festival, Middle Oct.

Boston, MA, FolkTree Jamboree, Late Oct.

Boston, MA, WBCN Rock of Boston Concert, Late Oct.

Boston, MA, WFNX Birthday Party, Early Nov.

Boston, MA, First Night Boston, Late Dec.

Boxborough, MA, Northeast Indoor Blue Grass Festival, Early Feb. to Middle Feb.

Braintree, MA, Papsaquoho Pow-Wow, Middle Jan.

Braintree, MA, Folk Festival/Flea Market and Craft Show, Late May

Braintree, MA, Irish Variety Show, Middle Oct.

Brockton, MA, First Night Brockton, Late Dec.

Brookline, MA, Carlos Fest, Middle Aug.

Buckland, MA, Riverfest, Middle Jun.

Buzzards Bay, MA, Bourne Scallop Fest, Early Sep. to Middle Sep.

Cambridge, MA, CMAC's A Joyful Noise, Middle Jan.

Cambridge, MA, New Women's Voices, Late Jan.

Cambridge, MA, Songstreet Folk and Bluegrass Fest, Early Feb.

Cambridge, MA, Harvard Winter Folk Festival, Early Mar.

Cambridge, MA, CMAC's Gala Benefit, Middle Mar.

Cambridge, MA, Arts First: A Harvard/Radcliffe Celebration, Late Apr. to Middle May

Cambridge, MA, Blacksmith House Dulcimer Festival, Late Apr. to Early May

Cambridge, MA, Harvard Square's May Fair, Early May

Cambridge, MA, Cambridge International Fair, Middle Jun.

Cambridge, MA, Cambridge Public Library Jazz Festival, Middle Jun.

Cambridge, MA, Cambridge Street Performer's Festival, Late Jun.

Cambridge, MA, Cambridge River Festival, Middle Sep.

Cambridge, MA, CMAC's Boston Rhythm, Early Nov.

Cambridge, MA, Phil Ochs Song Night, Early Nov.

Cambridge, MA, Blacksmith House Folk Festival/Folk Arts Conference, Middle Nov.

Cambridge, MA, CMAC's Fall Benefit, Middle Nov.

Cambridge, MA, Christmas Revels, Middle Dec. to Late Dec.

Charlemont, MA, Indian Pow Wow, Late May

Charlestown, MA, Boston Seaport Festival, Middle Aug. to Late Aug.

Charlestown, MA, Chowderfest, Middle Sep.

Charlestown, MA, Chilifest, Middle Oct.

Chatham, MA, First Night Chatham, Late Dec.

Chestnut Hill, MA, Gaelic Roots: The Music, Song and Dance of Ireland, Early Oct.

Chestnut Hill, MA, Irish and Cape Breton Christmas Concert and Ceili, Middle Dec.

Chicopee, MA, Taste of Chicopee, Early Jun.

Concord, MA, National Native American Heritage Day Pow-Wow, Middle Nov.

Dorcester, MA, Boston International Festival, Late Oct. to Late Nov.

Easton, MA, Tam O'Shanter Scottish Highland Games and Festival, Early Aug.

Fall River, MA, Fall River Festival, Middle Jun.

Fall River, MA, Fall River Celebrates America , Middle Aug.

Falmouth, MA, First Night in Hyannis, Late Dec.

Foxboro, MA, WCLB Country Club Festival, Late Jul.

Framingham, MA, Native American Day at The Forum, Early Apr.

Gloucester, MA, Gloucester Folklife Festival, Early Mar.

Gloucester, MA, Gloucester Waterfront Festival, Middle Aug.

Gloucester, MA, Gloucester Seafood Festival, Middle Sep.

Grafton, MA, Native American Fair and Pow Wow, Late Jul.
Granby, MA, Great Awakening Fest, Middle Sep.
Great Barrington, MA, Summerfest, Middle Jun.
Great Barrington, MA, Massachusetts Rock and Reggae for the Homeless, Middle Aug.
Great Barrington, MA, Autumn Hills Dulcimer Festival, Late Sep.
Greenfield, MA, UpCountry Hot Air Balloon Fair, Middle Jul.
Greenfield, MA, WPVQ Music Day, Late Jul.
Groton, MA, Septemberfest, Middle Sep.
Haverill, MA, Chief Red Blanket Memorial Pow-Wow, Early Sep. to Middle Sep.
Haverill, MA, Chief Red Blanket Memorial Pow-Wow, Middle Sep.
Holyoke, MA, Rock 'N Roll Block Party, Middle Jun.
Hyannis, MA, Hyannis Harbor Festival, Early Jun.
Hyannis, MA, Hyannis Seaport Festival, Middle Aug.
Hyannis, MA, Harvey Robbins' Royalty of Rock 'n Roll/Cape Cod Melody Tent, Middle Aug.
Ipswich, MA, Make-a-Wish-Foundation Country Jamboree, Middle May
Jamaica Plain, MA, Jamaica Plain Folk Festival, Early Jun.
Jamaica Plain, MA, Festival of Light and Song, Middle Dec.
Lawrence, MA, Bread and Roses Labor Day Heritage Heritage Festival, Early Sep.
Lee, MA, Pedal Steel Guitar Anniversary Bash, Early Sep.
Lenox, MA, Tanglewood Festival of Contemporary Music, Late Jul. to Late Aug.
Lenox, MA, Tanglewood Jazz Festival, Early Sep.
Leominster, MA, Earth Day Pow-Wow, Late Apr.
Lexington, MA, Folk Heritage Festival, Middle Sep.
Lincoln, MA, Midsummer Revels, Middle Jun. to Late Dec.
Lincoln, MA, DeCordova Labor Day Jazz Festival, Early Sep.
Lincoln, MA, Codman Farm Festival, Middle Sep.
Lowell, MA, Praise and Harmony, Middle Jun.
Lowell, MA, Boarding House Park Concert Series Kickoff, Early Jul.
Lowell, MA, Latin American Festival, Late Jun.
Lowell, MA, Lowell Folk Festival, Middle Jul.
Lowell, MA, Summertime Blues Weekend, Middle Aug.
Lowell, MA, Lowell Riverfest, Early Sep. to Middle Sep.
Lowell, MA, Banjo and Fiddle Contest, Middle Sep.
Lowell, MA, Bud Rocks the Block Party, Middle Sep.
Lowell, MA, Lowell Family First Night, Late Dec.
Malden, MA, Malden Irish Festival, Late Aug.
Mansfield, MA, KISS-108 FM Concert, Early Jun.
Mansfield, MA, WBCS Boston Country Sunday, Late Jun.
Marblehead, MA, Marblehead Festival of the Arts, Late Jun. to Early Jul.
Marshfield, MA, Towwakeeswush Pow-Wow, Middle Jun.
Mashpee, MA, Native American Intertribal Festival/Cape Heritage, Early Jun.
Mashpee, MA, Mashpee Wampanoag Powwow, Early Jul.
Merrimac, MA, Newsound Festival, Early Sep.
Middleboro, MA, Sigonomeg Pow-Wow, Middle May
Milton, MA, Boston Jazz Society Barbeque and Festival, Early Aug.
Monson, MA, Monson's Summerfest, Early Jul.
Natick, MA, New England Folk Festival, Late Apr.
New Bedford, MA, Whaling City Festival, Early Jul. to Middle Jul.
New Bedford, MA, Whaling City Jazz Festival, Early Oct.
New Bedford, MA, First Night New Bedford, Late Dec.
Newburyport, MA, Newburyport Yankee Homecoming, Late Jun. to Early Jul.
Newburyport, MA, Newburyport Waterfront Festival, Early Sep.
Newburyport, MA, First Night Newburyport, Late Dec.
North Adams, MA, La Festa, Early Jun. to Late Jun.

North Dartmouth, MA, UMass Jazz Festival, Early Mar.

North Dartmouth, MA, Eisteddfod Festival of Traditional Music and Dance, Late Sep.

North Easton, MA, Irish Cultural Center's Festival, Middle Jun.

Northampton, MA, Loud Music Festival, Early Apr.

Northampton, MA, Pickin' in the Pines Bluegrass Day, Late Jun.

Northampton, MA, Great New England Brewers' Festival, Late Jul.

Northampton, MA, American Indian Honor-the-Earth Pow Wow, Early Aug.

Northampton, MA, Taste of Northampton, Middle Aug.

Northampton, MA, First Night Northampton, Late Dec.

Oak Bluffs, MA, Oak Bluffs Harbor Day, Middle Jun.

Oxford, MA, Nipmuck Pow Wow, Middle Sep.

Peabody, MA, Native American Awareness Pow-Wow, Early Aug.

Pittsfield, MA, Your Hometown America Parade, Early Jul.

Pittsfield, MA, Precision and Pageantry Drum and Bugle Corps Competition, Middle Aug.

Pittsfield, MA, First Night Pittsfield, Late Dec.

Plymouth, MA, Plymouth Summer Blastoff, Late Jun.

Provincetown, MA, Provincetown Waterfront Festival, Middle Jul. to Late Jul.

Quincy, MA, City of Presidents Blues Festival, Early Jul.

Quincy, MA, Taste of the South Shore, Early Aug.

Quincy, MA, First Night Quincy, Late Dec.

Randolph, MA, M. C. M. A. A. Awards Show, Late Sep.

Roxbury, MA, Multicultural Festival, Late Feb.

Roxbury, MA, Multicultural Family Festival, Middle Jul.

Rutland, MA, Pow-Wow, Early Jun.

Salem, MA, Salem Seaport Festival, Late May

Salem, MA, Maritime Music Festival, Late Mar.

Salem, MA, Yankee Music Festival Big Band Jazz Invitational, Late Jun.

Salem, MA, Opening Night, Salem, Late Dec.

Sheffield, MA, Western New England Bluegrass and Old-Time Championships and Steak Fry, Late Aug.

Somerville, MA, Songstreet Festival of Funny Songwriters, Middle Jan.

Somerville, MA, Brazilian Festival of the Arts, Middle Feb.

Somerville, MA, Songstreet Festival of Women Songwriters, Middle Mar.

Somerville, MA, Songstreet Cajun-Bluegrass Festival, Early Apr.

Somerville, MA, Songstreet Folk-Rock Festival, Early Apr.

Somerville, MA, Scottish Fiddle Rally, Middle Apr.

Somerville, MA, ARTBEAT, Late Jul.

Somerville, MA, Songstreet Folk-Rock Festival, Middle Nov.

Spencer, MA, Sober in the Sun Labor Day Weekend Experience, Early Sep.

Springfield, MA, Peter Pan Taste of Springfield, Middle Jun.

Springfield, MA, Puerto Rican Cultural Festival, Early Jul. to Middle Jul.

Sterling, MA, Pow-Wow, Late Jun.

Tewksbury, MA, Irish Festival in the Park, Middle Jul.

Topsfield, MA, Planting Moon Pow-Wow, Late May

Varies, MA, Acoustic Underground Concerts and CD Release Parties, Middle May

Vineyard Haven, MA, Martha's Vineyard Agricultural Fair Fiddle Contest: A Festival of Traditional Music, Middle Aug. to Late Aug.

Vineyard Haven, MA, Martha's Vineyard Singer-Songwriters' Retreat, Early Sep. to Middle Sep.

Waltham, MA, Sheep Shearing Festival, Late Apr.

Waltham, MA, Joe Val Memorial Bluegrass Festival, Late Jun.

Waltham, MA, Massachusetts Highland Games, Late Jun.

Warren, MA, Quaboag Scottish Festival, Late Jul.

Washington, MA, Bluegrass Festival, Late May

Washington, MA, Reggae Festival, Early Sep.

Washington, MA, Northeast Squeeze-In, Middle Sep.
Watertown, MA, Folk Song Society of Greater Boston's Member's Concert, Middle Feb.
Webster, MA, Indian Ranch Country Music Festival and Chicken Barbeque, Late May
Webster, MA, Country Music Festival to Benefit American Heart Association, Late May
Webster, MA, New England Country Jamboree, Middle Sep.
Webster, MA, John Penny Liver Foundation Jamboree, Middle Sep.
Webster, MA, Country Fest, Middle Sep.
Wellesley, MA, New England Sacred Harp Singing Convention, Early Oct.
Wellfleet, MA, Fun Summer Concerts, Late Jun.
West Springfield, MA, Eastern States Exposition -- The Big E!, Middle Sep. to Late Sep.
Westford, MA, Apsge Pow-Wow, Late Jul.
Westport, MA, Westport Harvest Festival, Early Oct. to Middle Oct.
Worcester, MA, Day at the Lake, Middle Sep.
Worcester, MA, First Night Worcester, Late Dec.

## Rhode Island

Block Island, RI, Barbershop Quartet Benefit Concert, Late Jul.
Charlestown, RI, Charlestown Chamber of Commerce Seafood Festival, Early Aug.
Charlestown, RI, Pow Wow, Middle Aug.
Charlestown, RI, Swamp Yankee Days, Late Sep.
Charlestown, RI, Pow Wow, Early Oct.
Cranston, RI, Cajun and Zydeco Mardi Gras Ball, Middle Feb.
Cranston, RI, Harlem Renaissance Garden Party, Middle Jun.
Cumberland, RI, Cumberlandfest, Early Aug.
East Providence, RI, East Providence Heritage Festival, Late Jul.
Escoheag, RI, Country Music Shows, Middle Jun. to Early Aug.
Escoheag, RI, Big Easy Bash, Late Jun.
Escoheag, RI, New England Reggae Festival, Late Jul.
Escoheag, RI, American Indian Federation of Rhode Island Pow Wow, Early Aug.
Escoheag, RI, Cajun and Bluegrass Music-Dance-Food Festival, Early Sep.
Lincoln, RI, Irish Fall Festival, Middle Sep.
Lincoln, RI, Settlers' Day, Late Sep.
Middletown, RI, Norman Bird Sanctuary Harvest Fair, Early Oct.
Newport, RI, Newport Winter Festival, Late Jan. to Early Feb.
Newport, RI, Maritime Arts Festival, Middle May
Newport, RI, Schwepes Chowder Cook-Off, Middle Jun.
Newport, RI, Newport Rhythm and Blues Festival, Late Jul.
Newport, RI, Ben and Jerry's Newport Folk Festival, Early Aug.
Newport, RI, JVC Jazz Festival/Newport, Middle Aug.
Newport, RI, Shake-a-Leg Benefit Concert, Middle Aug.
Newport, RI, Taste of Rhode Island, Late Sep.
Newport, RI, Bowen's Wharf Waterfront Seafood Festival, Middle Oct.
Newport, RI, Opening Night, Late Dec.
North Scituate, RI, Chopmist Hill Inn Summer Festival, Late Aug.
North Scituate, RI, Scituate Arts Festival, Early Oct.
Pawtucket, RI, Labor and Ethnic Heritage Festival, Early Sep.
Providence, RI, Women's Voices, Early Mar.
Providence, RI, Earth Day Celebration, Late Apr.
Providence, RI, American Pit Masters Bar-B-Q Roundup, Late Jun.
Providence, RI, Cape Verdean Heritage Festival, Early Jul.
Providence, RI, Lupo's Birthday Party, Early Jul.
Providence, RI, Rhode Island Indian Council Pow Wow: Temple to Music, Late Jul. to Early
    Aug.

Providence, RI, Dominican Festival, Late Aug.
Providence, RI, Providence Waterfront Festival/Waterfront Jazz Festival, Middle Sep.
Providence, RI, Rhode Island's Heritage Day, Middle Sep.
Providence, RI, First Night Providence, Late Dec.
Richmond, RI, Washington County Fair, Middle Aug.
Scituate, RI, Scituate Music Fest, Middle Aug.
Smithfield, RI, Blues Bash for Homeless People, Late Aug.
West Kingston, RI, Summer Arts Fest Chair Fair, Early Jun.
Westerly, RI, Native American Days, Late May
Westerly, RI, Pequot and Narragansett Indian Nations Pow Wow, Middle Jun. to Late Jun.
Westerly, RI, Native American Days, Early Sep.
Woonsocket, RI, Mardi Gras Celebration, Late Feb.
Woonsocket, RI, Autumnfest, Early Oct.

## Connecticut

Bloomfield, CT, Bloomfield Festival, Early Jun.
Bridgeport, CT, Barnum Festival/Gospel Festival, Middle Jun.
Bridgeport, CT, Barnum Festival/Champions on Parade, Late Jun.
Burlington, CT, Nutmeg Bluegrass Get-Together, Middle May
Canton, CT, Lobsterfest/Celebrate Canton, Middle Aug.
Coventry, CT, Lake Wangumbaug Folk Festival, Late Jun.
Danbury, CT, Blues at the Ives, Late Jun.
Danbury, CT, Rock and Roll Hall of Fame Revue, Late Jul.
Danbury, CT, Duracell Jazz Festival, Middle Aug.
Danbury, CT, Taste of Greater Danbury, Middle Sep.
Danbury, CT, First Night Danbury, Late Dec.
Danielson, CT, Music Fest, Late Aug.
Dayville, CT, Summer Celebration, Early Jul.
Deep River, CT, Deep River Ancient Fife and Drum Corps Muster and Parade, Middle Jul.
Durham, CT, Durham Agricultural Fair, Late Sep.
East Haddam, CT, Mad Murphy's Cajun, Zydeco Music and Art Festival, Middle Jun.
East Haddam, CT, Great Connecticut Traditional Jazz Festival, Early Aug.
East Haddam, CT, Connecticut River Valley Bluegrass Festival, Middle Aug.
East Hartford, CT, Summer Sizzler, Middle Jul.
East Hartford, CT, Rock 'N' Blues AIDS Benefit, Late Jul.
East Hartford, CT, Rockfest, Late Jul.
East Hartland, CT, Hartland Folk Festival, Middle Jul.
East Lyme, CT, New England Ragtime Festival, Late Sep.
Enfield, CT, 4th of July Celebration, Early Jul.
Essex, CT, Hot Steamed Music Festival, Late Jun.
Fairfield, CT, Taste of Fairfield, Middle Jun.
Fairfield, CT, Fairfield County Irish Festival, Middle Jun.
Falls Village, CT, Spring Folk Music Weekend, Late May
Falls Village, CT, Fall Folk Music Weekend, Middle Oct.
Farmington, CT, Connecticut River Pow-Wow, Late Aug.
Glastonbury, CT, Greater Hartford Irish Festival, Late Jul.
Glastonbury, CT, Apple Harvest Festival, Middle Oct.
Goshen, CT, Great American Music Fest, Late Jun.
Goshen, CT, Connecticut Agricultural Fair, Late Jul.
Goshen, CT, St. Andrew's Society of Conneticut Scottish Festival, Early Oct.
Greenwich, CT, Red Cross Waterfront Festival, Middle Jun.
Groton, CT, Subfest, Early Jul.
Groton, CT, World Music Fest, Late Jul.

Haddam, CT, Quinnehukqut Rendezvous and Native American Festival, Middle Aug. to Late Aug.

Hartford, CT, KISS 95.7 Anniversary Birthday Jam, Early Jan.

Hartford, CT, Gospel Festival, Middle Feb.

Hartford, CT, Greater Hartford Festival of Jazz Fundraiser, Middle Feb.

Hartford, CT, Connecticut Historical Society's International Spring Festival, Early Apr.

Hartford, CT, Jambalaya on the River: Spring Riverboat Festival, Middle May to Late May

Hartford, CT, Different Tastes Outdoor Crawfish and Alligator Feast, Early Jun.

Hartford, CT, Taste of Hartford, Early Jun. to Middle Jun.

Hartford, CT, Riverfest, Early Jul.

Hartford, CT, R. A. W. Jazz Festival, Late Jul.

Hartford, CT, Greater Hartford Festival of Jazz/Hartford Mega! Weekend, Late Jul. to Early Aug.

Hartford, CT, Connecticut Family Folk Festival, Late Jul. to Early Aug.

Hartford, CT, West Indian Independence Celebration Week/Hartford Mega! Weekend, Early Aug.

Hartford, CT, Taste Buds Festival, Late Aug.

Hartford, CT, Schemitzun: Feast of Green Corn, Middle Sep.

Hartford, CT, Roots and Fruits Fiddle and Dance Festival, Early Oct.

Hartford, CT, First Night Hartford, Late Dec.

Kent, CT, Kent Summer Days, Early Aug.

Manchester, CT, Manchester Association of Pipe Bands Festival, Middle Jun.

Manchester, CT, Irish Night, Middle Aug.

Middlefield, CT, Old Home Day, Middle Jun.

Middletown, CT, Taste of Summer, Middle May

Middletown, CT, City Fest Arts Jubilee, Early Jun.

Middletown, CT, Connecticut Convention of the Sacred Harp, Early Jul. to Middle Jul.

Middletown, CT, Hartford Jazz Society Riverboat Cruise, Middle Sep.

Morris, CT, Morris Bluegrass Festival, Middle Aug.

Mystic, CT, Lobster Fest, Late May

Mystic, CT, Sea Music Festival, Middle Jun.

Mystic, CT, Taste of History, Early Aug.

Mystic, CT, Taste of Connecticut Food Festival, Early Sep. to Middle Sep.

Mystic, CT, Barbershop Harmony Day, Middle Sep.

Mystic, CT, Chowderfest, Early Oct. to Middle Oct.

Mystic, CT, Community Carol Sing, Middle Dec.

New Britain, CT, Hartford Advocate's Best of the Bands Bash, Late May

New Britain, CT, Main Street U. S. A., Early Jun.

New Haven, CT, Reggaefests, Early Jan.

New Haven, CT, Jazz Expos, Late Feb.

New Haven, CT, Black Expo, Middle Mar.

New Haven, CT, Country Jamborees, Late Apr.

New Haven, CT, Fair Haven Festival, Early Jun.

New Haven, CT, Local Bands on the Downtown Green, Middle Jun. to Late Aug.

New Haven, CT, Blues Blockbusters, Middle Jun.

New Haven, CT, Connecticut Irish Festival, Late Jun.

New Haven, CT, Funkfest, Early Jul.

New Haven, CT, WPLR July 4th Celebration, Early Jul.

New Haven, CT, New Haven Jazz Festival, Early Jul. to Late Jul.

New Haven, CT, WXCT Family Festival, Middle Jul.

New Haven, CT, Summertime Street Festival, Middle Aug.

New Haven, CT, Eli Whitney Folk Festival, Early Sep.

New Haven, CT, WPLR Labor Day Celebration, Early Sep.

New Haven, CT, Welcome Back to School Show: The Beginning of the End, Early Sep.

New London, CT, New London Sail Festival/Connecticut Maritime Festival, Early Jul. to Middle Jul.

New Milford, CT, Housatonic Dulcimer Celebration, Middle Sep.

North Stonington, CT, Paucatuck Pequot Harvest Moon Powwow, Early Oct. to Middle Oct.

Norwalk, CT, Afternoon of Jazz, Late Jun.

Norwalk, CT, Round Hill Scottish Games, Early Jul.

Norwalk, CT, Global Blues Fest, Early Jul.

Norwich, CT, Louisiana Cookin' and Cajun Music Festival, Late Jun.

Norwich, CT, Harbor Day, Late Aug.

Preston, CT, Strawberry Park Bluegrass Festival, Early Jun.

Preston, CT, Strawberry Park Country Western Jamboree, Late Sep.

Putnam, CT, Positively Pomfret Day, Late Jul.

Rocky Hill, CT, Mother of Waters, Middle Jun.

Roxbury, CT, Roxbury Pickin' N Fiddlin' Contest, Middle Jul.

Sandy Hook, CT, NOMAD: Northeast Music, Art and Dance Festival, Late Oct. to Early Nov.

Scotland, CT, Scotland Highland Festival, Early Oct.

Simsbury, CT, Riversplash, Early Jun.

Simsbury, CT, Simsbury Septemberfest, Early Sep.

Somers, CT, Strawberry Moon Pow-Wow, Late Jun.

South Norwalk, CT, SoNo Arts Celebration, Early Aug.

South Norwalk, CT, Oyster Festival, Early Sep. to Middle Sep.

Southbury, CT, Southbury Jazz Festival, Early Sep.

Southington, CT, Apple Valley Family Folk Festival, Middle Sep.

Stafford Springs, CT, Mineral Springs Foot Stomp'n Festival, Late Jun. to Early Jul.

Stafford Springs, CT, Mineral Springs Foot Stomp'n Festival, Early Oct.

Stamford, CT, Citibank Taste of Stamford, Early Jun. to Middle Jun.

Stamford, CT, Pink Tent Festival of the Arts, Middle Jun.

Stamford, CT, High Ridge Folk Festival, Early Jul. to Middle Jul.

Stamford, CT, Stamford A. O. H. Feis, Middle Jul.

Stamford, CT, HAFOS: Festival Hispano-Americano de Stamford, Late Aug.

Sterling, CT, Olde Tyme Fiddlers Concert, Middle Apr.

Sterling, CT, Sterling Park Campground Bluegrass Festival, Early Jun. to Middle Jun.

Sterling, CT, Sterling Park Campground Bluegrass Festival, Middle Sep.

Trumbull, CT, Trumbull Day, Late Jun.

Trumbull, CT, Trumbull Arts Festival, Middle Sep.

Wallingford, CT, Blue Sky Music Fest, Late May

Wallingford, CT, Newcomers of Country, Middle Aug.

Waterbury, CT, Brass Valley Ethnic Music Festival, Middle Jun.

Waterbury, CT, Afro-Latin-Caribbean Festival, Middle Jul.

Waterford, CT, Cabaret Symposium, Middle Aug. to Late Aug.

Watertown, CT, Eagle Wing Press Powwow, Late Sep.

West Hartford, CT, Honey, Hide the Banjo! It's the Folk Next Door, Late May

West Hartford, CT, Celebrate! West Hartford, Middle Jun.

West Hartford, CT, Verano Explosivo Festival, Early Aug.

Westbrook, CT, Westbrook Drum Corps Muster, Late Aug.

Westport, CT, Legends of Folk Music, Middle May

Westport, CT, Summer Series, Middle Jun. to Middle Aug.

Westport, CT, Battle of the Bands, Early Jul. to Middle Aug.

Westport, CT, Folk Music Showcase, Late Jul.

Westport, CT, Westport Blues Festival, Late Sep.

Westville, CT, West Fest/Taste of Westville, Middle Jun.

Windsor Locks, CT, BASH: Bradley Airport Summer Happening, Late Jul.

Woodbury, CT, Alternative Skateboard Festival, Late May

Woodbury, CT, Reggae Festival, Late Jun.

Woodbury, CT, World Music Festival, Middle Jul.
Woodbury, CT, Southern Fried Festival, Middle Aug.
Woodstock, CT, Bluegrass Festival, Late May
Woodstock, CT, Great American Blues Festival, Middle Jul.
Woodstock, CT, Earth Jam, Middle Aug.
Woodstock, CT, Festival at Roseland Cottage, Middle Oct.

## New York

Accord, NY, Hurdy Gurdy Strings and Sings Spring Fling, Middle May
Accord, NY, Irish Music Festival, Early Aug.
Akron, NY, Creek Bend Music Festival, Late Jul.
Albany, NY, Mountain Dulcimer Music Festival, Late Feb.
Albany, NY, In Women's Hands: The Beat of the Drum, Early Mar.
Albany, NY, College of Saint Rose High School Jazz Festival, Late Mar.
Albany, NY, PYX Rock and Roll Expo, Late Mar.
Albany, NY, College of Saint Rose Collegiate Jazz Festival, Late Apr.
Albany, NY, WEQX Party in the Park, Late Apr.
Albany, NY, Pinksterfest/Albany Tulip Festival, Early May
Albany, NY, Jazz for the Arts/Super Jazz Jam Blowout , Middle May
Albany, NY, Lark Street Blues Festival, Early Jun.
Albany, NY, Blueshounds Benefit, Early Jun.
Albany, NY, Albany Riverfest/All-America City Fair, Early Jun. to Middle Jun.
Albany, NY, American Indian Heritage and Craft Festival, Early Jul.
Albany, NY, Fabulous Fourth Festivities, Early Jul.
Albany, NY, Lunchtime Concerts, Early Jul. to Late Aug.
Albany, NY, Empire State Black Arts and Cultural Festival, Middle Jul.
Albany, NY, International Food Festival, Middle Aug.
Albany, NY, Big Band Bash, Late Aug.
Albany, NY, Come Sunday, Early Sep. to Middle Sep.
Albany, NY, WEQX Birthday Party/University of Albany Fallfest, Early Oct.
Albany, NY, Native American/Indigenous People Day Celebration, Early Oct.
Albany, NY, North East Country Music Association Awards Show, Middle Oct.
Albany, NY, Jazz for the Arts/Kick Off, Late Oct.
Albany, NY, Valentine's XMas Jam, Middle Dec.
Albany, NY, First Night Albany, Late Dec.
Albion, NY, Albion Strawberry Festival, Early Jun.
Alexandria Bay, NY, Grand International Ragtime/Jasstime Foundation Spring Festival, Late Apr.
Alexandria Bay, NY, Thousand Islands Jazz Festival, Early Aug.
Alexandria Bay, NY, Grand International Ragtime/Jasstime Foundation Fall Festival, Middle Nov.
Altamont, NY, Old Songs Festival of Traditional Music and Dance, Late Jun.
Altamont, NY, WGNA Country Fest, Early Jul.
Altamont, NY, Capital District's Scottish Games: A Celtic Festival of the Arts, Early Sep.
Amherst, NY, Summer Music Festival, Late Aug.
Amherst, NY, Amherst Museum Scottish Festival, Middle Sep.
Ancramdale, NY, Winterhawk Bluegrass Family Festival, Middle Jul.
Apalachin, NY, Otsiningo Pow Wow and Indian Craft Fair, Early Jun.
Ashokan, NY, Halloween Dance Weekend, Late Oct. to Early Nov.
Averill Park, NY, Averill Park Summer Blues Fest, Middle Jul.
Babylon, NY, Jones Beach Greekfest Weekend, Late Jun.
Bainbridge, NY, Laing Family Bluegrass Festival, Middle Jun.
Bainbridge, NY, Del-Se-Nango Fiddlers Festival, Early Jul.

Bainbridge, NY, Del-Se-Nango Fiddlers Festival and Bluegrass Sunday, Early Aug.
Baiting Hollow, NY, Long Island Traditional Music Association Fall Folk Weekend, Early Oct.
Baldwinsville, NY, Golden Harvest Festival, Middle Sep.
Ballston Spa, NY, GottaGetGon Folk Festival: The Pick'n and Singin' Gatherin', Late May
Ballston Spa, NY, Ballston Spa Village Wide Garage Sale and Family Festival, Middle Jun.
Barryville, NY, Pow Wow, Early Jul.
Barryville, NY, Pow Wow, Late Jul.
Bay Shore, NY, World of Jewish Culture, Early Jun.
Beacon, NY, Strawberry Festival, Early Jun.
Bearsville, NY, Bearsville Theater Memorial Day Music Festival, Late May
Bellport, NY, Sunday By the Bay, Early Jul.
Bethany, NY, Native American Pow Wow, Middle Jun.
Binghamton, NY, Two Rivers Ethnic Festival, Early May
Binghamton, NY, Cranberry Dulcimer Gathering, Late Jul.
Binghamton, NY, Roberson's Holiday and Arts Festival, Early Sep. to Middle Sep.
Binghamton, NY, Columbus Day Tournament of Bands, Early Oct.
Blue Mountain Lake, NY, Old Time Fiddler's Contest and Jam Session, Early Jun.
Blue Mountain Lake, NY, Northeast Dulcimer Symposium, Late Jun.
Bolton Landing, NY, Bolton Landing Barbershop Quartet Festival, Early Sep.
Brighton, NY, Celebration of Jewish Learning, Middle Oct.
Broadalbin, NY, Bluegrass Festival, Early Aug.
Brookville, NY, Long Island Guitar Festival, Late Apr.
Brookville, NY, Great Lawn Irish Fair, Late May
Buffalo, NY, Turk Murphy Memorial Festival, Early May
Buffalo, NY, Juneteenth Festival, Middle Jun.
Buffalo, NY, Friendship Festival, Late Jun. to Early Jul.
Buffalo, NY, Taste of Buffalo, Early Jul.
Buffalo, NY, Waterfront Festival Free Summer Concert Series/Gospel in the Park, Middle Jul.
Buffalo, NY, McDonald's Gospelfest, Late Jul.
Buffalo, NY, Rally in the Alley, Late Jul.
Buffalo, NY, International Dixeland Jazz and Ragtime Festival, Late Jul.
Buffalo, NY, Micky Rat's City Jam, Early Aug.
Buffalo, NY, Waterfront Festival, Early Aug. to Middle Aug.
Buffalo, NY, Buffalo Caribbean Festival, Middle Aug.
Buffalo, NY, Waterfront Festival Free Summer Concert Series/Family Fun in the Sun, Middle Aug.
Buffalo, NY, Hispanic Music Festival, Late Aug.
Buffalo, NY, WBNY's Battle of the Bands, Late Aug.
Buffalo, NY, Unifest, Late Aug.
Buffalo, NY, Buffalo Country Music Awards, Middle Sep.
Buffalo, NY, Gospel Night, Late Oct.
Buffalo, NY, Barbershop Serenade, Middle Nov.
Buffalo, NY, Buffalo Beer Fest, Middle Nov.
Buffalo, NY, Artvoice Original Music Awards, Late Nov.
Buffalo, NY, First Night Buffalo, Late Dec.
Cairo, NY, Cairo Appreciation Day Fair, Early Jul.
Callicoon, NY, Emerald Productions Getaway, Middle Apr.
Callicoon, NY, Emerald Productions Getaway, Early Dec.
Cambridge, NY, Country Western Festival, Middle Jun.
Cambridge, NY, Fiddle Weekend, Middle Jul.
Canandaigua, NY, Waterfront Arts Festival, Early Aug.
Carmel, NY, Putnam County 4-H Fair, Late Jul. to Early Aug.
Caroga Lake, NY, Rhythm and Blues Beach Party, Middle Jul.
Castile, NY, Letchworth Arts and Crafts Show and Sale, Early Oct.

Castille, NY, Native American Heritage Day, Middle Sep.
Catile, NY, Caribbean Extravaganza, Middle Jul.
Catskill, NY, Catskill Fourth of July Celebration, Early Jul.
Cedar Lake, NY, Skyfest, Late Aug.
Centereach, NY, Barnaby's Battle of the Bands, Early Apr.
Chaffee, NY, Earl's Sunshine Festival, Late Jun. to Middle Sep.
Chautauqua, NY, Chautauqua Summer Music Program, Late Jun. to Late Aug.
Clayton, NY, Thousand Islands Bluegrass Festival, Early Jun. to Middle Jun.
Clayton, NY, Fiddlers Fling, Middle Sep.
Clifton Park, NY, WXLE Acoustic Music Festival, Early May to Late May
Clinton, NY, Oxhann Piano Festival, Late Aug.
Cobleskill, NY, Cobleskill "Sunshine" Fair, Early Aug. to Middle Aug.
Cohoes, NY, Al Mastren Memorial Scholarship Concert, Early Apr.
Colonie, NY, Women in Music Celebration, Middle Mar.
Commack, NY, International Jewish Arts Festival of Long Island, Late May
Cooperstown, NY, Autumn Harvest Festival, Middle Sep.
Copiague, NY, Paumanauke Pow-Wow, Middle Aug.
Corinth, NY, Corinth Bluegrass Festival, Early Aug. to Middle Aug.
Coventryville, NY, Penny Association Memorial Day Bluegrass and Country Music Festival,
    Late May
Coventryville, NY, Penny Association Olde Tyme Country Music Festival, Late Jun. to Early Jul.
Coventryville, NY, Wrench Wranch Bluegrass Roundup, Early Sep.
Coxsackie, NY, Coxsackie Riverside Arts and Crafts Festival, Early Aug.
Cross River, NY, Fiddling Celebration, Early Jul.
Darien, NY, Heritage Hoedown and Empire State Fiddle Contest, Middle Jul. to Late Jul.
Darien Lake, NY, Praise, Late May
Darien Lake, NY, Kingdom Bound, Late Aug.
Deer Park, NY, Songwriter Showcase, Middle Apr.
Deer Park, NY, Benefit for the Fight Against Leukemia, Late May
Deposit, NY, Rooney Mountain Bluegrass Festival, Late Jul. to Early Aug.
Duanesburg, NY, Maple Ridge Bluegrass Festival, Early Jul. to Middle Jul.
East Durham, NY, Irish Festival, Late May
East Durham, NY, Irish Salute to the U. S. A., Early Jul.
East Durham, NY, Native American Pow Wow, Early Jul. to Middle Jul.
East Durham, NY, Columbus Weekend Harvest Fair, Early Oct.
East Hampton, NY, East End Music Festival, Middle Jun.
Elizabethtown, NY, Field, Forest and Stream, Middle Sep.
Ellenville, NY, Summer Boogie, Early Jul. to Middle Jul.
Ellenville, NY, Stardust Dance Weekend, Middle Nov. to Late Nov.
Ellenville, NY, Great Irish Weekend, Early Dec. to Middle Dec.
Ellicottville, NY, Ellicottville's Summer Festival of the Arts, Late Jun. to Early Jul.
Elmira, NY, Schneider's Bluegrass Festival, Late Aug.
Elmira, NY, Summer Jazz Festival, Late Aug.
Elmira Heights, NY, Irish Festival of Chemung County, Early Jul.
Elmsford, NY, St. Patrick's Day Celebrations, Early Mar. to Middle Mar.
Endicott, NY, Sounds on the Susquehanna, Late Jul.
Endicott, NY, Project Children Irish Festival, Late Aug.
Fair Haven, NY, Fair Haven Field Days, Early Jul.
Fort Ann, NY, Rick and Carol's Country Side Inn Bluegrass Festival, Late Jul.
Freeport, NY, First Night Freeport, Late Dec.
Fulton, NY, River Fest, Early Aug.
Galway, NY, Bluegrass Roundup, Early Jun.
Garden City, NY, Nassau Community College Folk Festival, Late Mar.
Garden City, NY, Intergenerational International Festival, Middle Jun.

Gardiner, NY, Lazy River Bluegrass Festival , Middle Sep.

Garrison, NY, One With Nature Festival, Middle Jun.

Gates, NY, Rochester Irish Festival, Early Jun. to Middle Jun.

Geneva, NY, William Smith and Hobart Colleges Folk Fest, Early May

Glen Falls, NY, L. A. R. A. C. Arts and Crafts Festival, Middle Jun.

Glens Falls, NY, Summer Jam, Early Jul.

Glens Falls, NY, Adirondack Drums, Early Aug.

Gouveneur, NY, St. Lawrence Valley Bluegrass Festival, Middle Aug.

Greece, NY, Greece Summer Festival, Late Aug.

Guilderland, NY, Old Songs Sampler Concert, Late Jan.

Guilderland, NY, Dance Flurry, Middle Feb.

Hadley, NY, Dean Mountain Bluegrass Festival, Late Jul. to Early Aug.

Hamburg, NY, Erie County Fair, Middle Aug. to Late Aug.

Hampton Bays, NY, Irish Festival, Early Jun.

Hartford, NY, Squaredance and Bluegrass Festival, Late Jun.

Hartsdale, NY, Irish Heritage Celebration, Middle Jul.

Hector, NY, Finger Lakes Dixieland Jazz Festival, Late Aug.

Hempstead, NY, Celebrations and Expressions of Our African American Heritage, Early Feb.

Hempstead, NY, Cultural Street Festival, Early Jun.

Hempstead, NY, Long Island Emerald Isle Festival, Late Sep.

Hempstead, NY, Kwanzaa Fete, Late Dec.

Highmount, NY, Music and The Mountain Sky/Folk Concert, Middle Jul.

Highmount, NY, Music and The Mountain Sky/Jazz Concert, Late Aug.

Hillsdale, NY, Falcon Ridge Folk Festival, Late Jul.

Hilton, NY, Hilton Applefest, Late Sep. to Early Oct.

Homer, NY, Bluegrass on the Green, Early Jun.

Honeoye Falls, NY, Golden Link Folk Festival, Early Sep. to Middle Sep.

Howes Cave, NY, Iroquois Arts Showcase I, Late May

Howes Cave, NY, Iroquois Arts Showcase II, Early Jul.

Howes Cave, NY, Iroquois Indian Festival, Late Sep.

Hunter, NY, American Patriot Festival, Early Jul.

Hunter, NY, Country Music Festival , Middle Jul. to Late Jul.

Hunter, NY, Rockstalgia, Early Aug.

Hunter, NY, Country Music Festival Encore, Early Aug. to Middle Aug.

Hunter, NY, International Celtic Festival, Middle Aug. to Late Aug.

Hunter, NY, Mountain Eagle Festival, Early Sep.

Hunter, NY, Celtic Fair, Late Sep.

Huntington, NY, Folk Music Society of Huntington Members Concert, Early May

Huntington, NY, Summerscape: Huntington Summer Arts Festival, Late Jun. to Late Aug.

Huntington, NY, Folk Music Society of Huntington Summer Festival, Late Jul.

Huntington, NY, Bopper's Oldies Concert, Late Sep.

Inwood, NY, Inwood World Music Festival, Late Jun.

Irving, NY, Seneca Indian Fall Festival, Middle Sep.

Islip, NY, Islip Jazz Festival, Late Aug.

Ithaca, NY, Ithaca Festival, Early Jun.

Ithaca, NY, New York State Sacred Harp Singing Convention, Middle Oct.

Ithaca, NY, Apple Harvest Festival, Early Oct.

Jamesport, NY, WLIX Fest, Middle Aug.

Jamesville, NY, Miller Lite Balloonfest/Art on the Rise, Middle Jun.

Jeffersonville, NY, Jeffersonville Jamboree, Late Jul.

Katonah, NY, Jazzfest Caramoor, Early Aug. to Middle Aug.

Kerhonkson, NY, Fall Country Dance and Party Weekend, Middle Oct.

Kiamesha Lake, NY, Richard Nader's Let the Good Times Roll, Early Mar. to Middle Mar.

Kiamesha Lake, NY, Emerald Weekend, Early Apr.

Kiamesha Lake, NY, Richard Nader's Let the Good Times Roll, Late Jul. to Middle Mar.
Kingston, NY, Psychofest, Middle Jun.
Kingston, NY, Gospel Extravaganza, Middle Jun.
Kingston, NY, Reggae on the Hudson, Middle Jun.
Kingston, NY, Transportation Heritage Festival, Late Jul.
Kingston, NY, Colonial Fest, Early Aug.
Kingston, NY, Harvest Moon Festival, Middle Sep.
Kingston, NY, Native American Festival, Middle Sep.
Lake George, NY, Glory, Early Jun.
Lake George, NY, Lake George Hot Jazz Party and Cruise, Middle Jun.
Lake George, NY, Lake George Summerfest, Late Jun.
Lake George, NY, Lake George Jazz Weekend, Early Sep. to Middle Sep.
Lake Placid, NY, Matt's Matinee, Early Jul.
Lake Placid, NY, Evening of Adirondack Music, Late Jul.
Lancaster, NY, Buffalo Irish Festival, Late Aug.
Latham, NY, FLY92 Summer Jam, Late Jun.
Latham, NY, Royalty of Rock and Roll, Middle Aug.
Latham, NY, Big Big Bands, Middle Aug.
Latham, NY, Outdoor Blues Festival, Middle Aug.
Latham, NY, PYX Birthday Blowout!, Late Aug.
Latham, NY, FLY92 End of Summer Jam, Middle Sep.
Latham, NY, WEQX Acoustic Holiday Concert for the Hungry, Middle Dec.
Leeds, NY, Fleadh: Old Music of Ireland Festival, Early Jul.
Leeds, NY, Leeds Irish Festival, Early Sep.
Lewiston, NY, Tuscarora Field Day and Picnic, Early Jul.
Lewiston, NY, Artpark Blues and Folk Festival, Middle Aug. to Late Aug.
Lewiston, NY, Artpark Jazz Festival, Early Sep.
Liverpool, NY, Gathering of Iroquois, Early Oct.
Lockport, NY, Niagara's Apple Country Festival, Middle Oct.
Long Beach, NY, Long Beach Irish Day Parade and Festival, Early Oct.
Long Lake, NY, Spring Blossom Fiddle Jamboree, Late Apr.
Long Lake, NY, Long Lake Bluegrass Festival, Middle Aug.
Long Lake, NY, Flaming Leaves Fiddle Jamboree, Early Oct.
Lyons, NY, Low Bridge Festival, Late Jul.
Madrid, NY, Madrid Bluegrass Festival, Late Jun.
Mariaville, NY, Mayhem on the Mountain, Middle Jun.
Massena, NY, Festival of North Country Folk Life, Middle Aug.
Mayville, NY, Fourth of July Celebration, Early Jul.
Mecklenberg, NY, Meck Music Fest, Late Aug.
Middlesex, NY, Middlesex Music Fest, Late Jul.
Middletown, NY, Local Motion MusicFest, Middle Jun.
Middletown, NY, Orange County Fair, Late Jul.
Middletown, NY, Local Motion MusicFest, Early Sep.
Middletown, NY, Alternative Sports and Music Festival, Early Oct.
Mineola, NY, Irish Traditional Dance Festival, Middle May
Monitcello, NY, Dick Fox's Ultimate Doo-Wopp Fantasy Weekend, Early Oct.
Monroe, NY, International Fun Fest, Late Jul.
Monroe, NY, Native American Weekend, Late Jul.
Montauk Point, NY, Back at the Ranch Festival, Early Aug.
Montgomery, NY, Star Spangled Spectacular, Early Jul.
Monticello, NY, Winter Boogie, Late Jan.
Monticello, NY, Irish Music Weekend Party of the Year, Late Oct.
Morrisville, NY, New York State Intercollegiate Jazz Festival, Late Apr.
Mumford, NY, Old-Time Fiddler's Fair, Late Aug.

Naples, NY, Naples Grape Festival, Middle Sep.

New City, NY, Hungerthon Concert/Winter Blues Fest, Middle Nov.

New Paltz, NY, Woodstock/New Paltz Art and Crafts Fair, Late May

New Paltz, NY, Mohonk's Music Week, Late Jun.

New Paltz, NY, New York State Championship Chili Cookoff, Late Jun.

New Paltz, NY, Mohonk's Festival of the Arts/International Week, Middle Jul. to Late Jul.

New Paltz, NY, Ulster County Fair, Early Aug.

New Paltz, NY, Woodstock/New Paltz Art and Crafts Fair, Early Sep.

New Paltz, NY, Music at New Paltz/Faculty Sampler, Middle Sep.

New Paltz, NY, Mohonk's Joy of Singing, Late Nov.

New Rochelle, NY, Salesian Folk Festival, Late Aug.

Newburgh, NY, International Waterfront Festival, Early Sep.

Niagara Falls, NY, Indian Pow Wow, Early May

Niagara Falls, NY, Multicultural Fest, Middle Jul.

Niagara Falls, NY, Festival of Lights, Middle Nov. to Early Jan.

Niagara Falls, NY, Niagara: The Student and Adult Leadership Conference on Evangelism, Late Dec.

Nichols, NY, Nichols Family Bluegrass Festival, Late Aug.

North Blenheim, NY, Irish Traditional Music Festival, Early Aug.

Norwich, NY, Super Bluegrass and Gospel Day, Middle Aug.

Oceanside, NY, Springfest, Middle Apr.

Oceanside, NY, Israeli Festival, Late May

Oceanside, NY, South Shore Music Festival, Early Sep.

Old Forge, NY, Fox Family Bluegrass Festival, Middle Aug.

Old Westbury, NY, Long Island Scottish Games, Late Aug.

Olean, NY, Commodore John Barry A. O. H. Irish Festival, Early Sep. to Middle Sep.

Osceola, NY, Band Jamboree, Early Sep.

Oswego, NY, Oswego Harborfest, Middle Jul.

Oyster Bay, NY, Long Island Jazz Festival, Late Jul.

Oyster Bay, NY, October Oyster Festival, Middle Oct.

Palmyra, NY, Palmyra Canal Town Days, Middle Sep.

Panama, NY, Panama Rocks Folk Arts Fair, Early Jul. to Middle Jul.

Parksville, NY, Memorial Day Weekend Festival, Late May

Parksville, NY, Hempsplash, Early Jun.

Parksville, NY, No Bummer Summer Party Jam, Middle Jun.

Parksville, NY, Gruntstock, Early Jul.

Parksville, NY, Labor Day Weekend Blowout, Early Sep.

Parksville, NY, Klezkamp, Late Dec.

Patterson, NY, Irish Festival, Middle Jun.

Patterson, NY, Blues Fest, Middle Aug.

Peekskill, NY, Shadfest, Middle May

Penn Yan, NY, Buckwheat Harvest Festival, Late Sep.

Pine Bush, NY, People's Music Network Summer Gathering, Early Jun.

Plainview, NY, Street Fair, Early Jun.

Port Chester, NY, Band Box Anniversary Love-Fest/Wife-Swap, Middle May

Poughkeepsie, NY, Battle of the Acappella Groups, Middle Jun.

Poughkeepsie, NY, Summerfest, Early Jul.

Poughkeepsie, NY, International Food Festival/Friday Fest, Early Aug.

Queensbury, NY, I. A. C. A.'s International Festival of the Adirondacks, Middle May

Raquette Lake, NY, Mountain Music and Dance Weekend in the Adirondacks, Early Oct. to Middle Oct.

Rhinebeck, NY, Independence Celebration and Double R Championship Rodeo, Early Jul.

Rhinebeck, NY, Dutchess County Fair, Late Aug.

Rhinebeck, NY, Iroquois Indian Festival, Early Sep. to Middle Sep.

Riverhead, NY, Riverhead Jazz Festival, Early Jul.
Rochester, NY, Lilac Festival, Middle May to Late May
Rochester, NY, Blues in the Night, Early Jul.
Rochester, NY, Corn Hill Arts Festival/Fiddler's Fair, Early Jul. to Middle Jul.
Rochester, NY, Bill LaBeef's Bastille Day, Barbeque and Rock and Roll Rodeo, Middle Jul.
Rochester, NY, Roch-A-Palooza , Late Jul.
Rochester, NY, Park Avenue Festival, Late Jul. to Early Aug.
Rochester, NY, Pine Grill Jazz Reunion, Early Aug.
Rochester, NY, Carifest, Middle Aug.
Rochester, NY, Anniversary Celebration of the Colored Musicians Club, Middle Aug.
Rochester, NY, Downtown Festival/Rock Fest , Late Aug.
Rochester, NY, Bluegrass Festival, Late Aug.
Rochester, NY, Localpalooza Festival, Early Sep.
Rochester, NY, Fall Jamboree, Late Oct.
Rochester, NY, National Rockabilly Blowout, Late Oct.
Rochester, NY, New Year's Early Eve, Late Dec.
Rotterdam, NY, Holiday Jam for Joy, Middle Dec.
Round Lake, NY, Round Lake Country Music Festival, Late Jul.
Roxbury, NY, Fiddlers!!:  A Sampler of North American Fiddle Traditions, Early Oct.
Rye, NY, WCBS-FM 101 Day, Middle Jun.
Sacketts Harbor, NY, International Music and Dance Festival, Early Sep.
Salamanca, NY, Keeper of the Western Door Pow-Wow, Middle Jul.
Sandy Creek, NY, Bill Knowlton's Bluegrass Ramble Picnic, Early Aug.
Saranac Lake, NY, Adirondack Festival of American Music, Early Jul. to Late Jul.
Saratoga Springs, NY, Newport Jazz Festival/Saratoga, Early Jul.
Saratoga Springs, NY, Hats Off to Saratoga Festival, Late Jul.
Saratoga Springs, NY, Final Stretch Festival, Late Aug.
Saratoga Springs, NY, Petrified Sea Gardens Family Music Festival, Middle Sep.
Saugerties, NY, Winter Folk Music Weekend, Early Feb.
Saugerties, NY, Opus 40 Acoustic Summit:  Bring It On Home, Early Jul.
Saugerties, NY, Opus 40 New Orleans Party Weekend, Late Jul.
Saugerties, NY, Opus 40 Legends of Jazz/Future of Jazz, Middle Aug.
Saugerties, NY, Summer Folk Music Weekend, Middle Aug. to Late Aug.
Saugerties, NY, Opus 40 Jazz Autumn, Early Oct.
Savona, NY, Thomas Homestead Festival , Late Jul. to Early Aug.
Savona, NY, Southern Tier Bluegrass Festival, Middle Aug.
Schenectady, NY, Blues Bar-B-Que, Early Aug.
Schenectady, NY, Park Jam, Early Aug.
Schenectady, NY, Hamilton Hill Culturefest/Gospel Festival, Early Aug.
Schenectady, NY, Takin' It to the Streets:  The Electric City Music Celebration, Middle Sep.
Schroon Lake, NY, Adirondack Folk Music Festival, Middle Aug. to Late Aug.
Sherman, NY, Great Blue Heron Music Festival, Early Jul.
Shinhopple, NY, Peaceful Valley Bluegrass Festival, Middle Jul.
Somers, NY, Just Jazz, Middle Sep.
South Fallsburg, NY, Pines Scottish Weekend, Early Mar.
South Fallsburg, NY, Pines Hotel Bluegrass Festival, Middle Mar.
South Fallsburg, NY, Country Classic in the Catskills, Early Apr.
South Fallsburg, NY, Pines Number One Irish Weekend, Early Apr.
South Fallsburg, NY, Pines Scottish Weekend, Late Oct.
South Fallsburg, NY, Pines Number One Irish Weekend, Middle Nov.
South Fallsburg, NY, Country Music Dance Weekend, Early Dec.
South Glens Falls, NY, Calico Dancers Good Time Pow Wow, Early Jul.
Southampton, NY, Shinnecock Native-American Powwow, Early Sep.
Spencerport, NY, Turtle Hill Music Festival, Late Aug.

Staatsburg, NY, Celtic Day in the Park, Late Sep.

Stanfordville, NY, Stanfordville Music and Dance Festival, Late May

Stanfordville, NY, Stanfordville Music and Dance Festival, Late Aug.

Stone Mills, NY, Old Time Music Festival and Barbeque, Middle Jul.

Stony Brook, NY, Electronic Music at Stony Brook, Late Feb.

Stony Brook, NY, Long Island Fiddle and Folk Music Festival, Middle Sep.

Stony Brook, NY, Computer Music at Stony Brook, Late Oct.

Stony Brook, NY, Ear-Fest: Festival of Taped Music, Early Nov.

Suffern, NY, Best of the Best Pow-Wow/Native American Indian Arts Festival, Late Oct.

Swain, NY, Swain Country Western Music Festival, Early Oct.

Syracuse, NY, Syracuse Area Music Awards (Sammies), Early May

Syracuse, NY, Syracuse Jazz Fest, Middle Jun.

Syracuse, NY, Waterfront Extravaganza, Early Jul. to Middle Jul.

Syracuse, NY, Syracuse Arts and Crafts Festival, Middle Jul.

Syracuse, NY, Jazz/Reggae Festival, Late Jul.

Syracuse, NY, New York State Budweiser Blues Festival, Late Jul.

Syracuse, NY, Central New York Scottish Games and Celtic Festival, Middle Aug.

Syracuse, NY, New York State Fair, Late Aug. to Early Sep.

Syracuse, NY, Project Children Dinner Dance and Variety Show, Late Oct.

Ticonderoga, NY, Invitational Piping Championship/Memorial Military Tattoo, Early Jul.

Ticonderoga, NY, Fife and Drum Corps Muster, Late Jul.

Ticonderoga, NY, Music at The Ty Folklore Concert, Late Aug.

Tioga Center, NY, Penny Association Bluegrass and Country Music Festival, Late Jul.

Tonawanda, NY, Canal Fest, Middle Jul. to Late Jul.

Troy, NY, Adirondack Folk Night, Late Mar.

Troy, NY, Swing Spring, Late Apr.

Troy, NY, Uncle Sam's Blues Jam, Early May

Troy, NY, Summertime Blues Charity Cruise, Middle Oct.

Troy, NY, Fox Hollow Reunion Folk Concert, Middle Oct.

Trumansburg, NY, Fingerlakes Grassroots Festival of Music and Dance, Middle Jul. to Late Jul.

Tuscarora, NY, Twin Rivers Jamboree, Early Aug.

Uniondale, NY, Nassau Coliseum Fair, Middle Jun. to Late Jun.

Uniondale, NY, A. O. H. Nassau County Board Feis and Festival, Middle Sep.

Utica, NY, Good Old Summertime , Early Jul. to Middle Jul.

Vails Gate, NY, Gaelic Day, Middle Jul.

Valhalla, NY, Clearwater's Great Hudson River Revival, Middle Jun.

Valhalla, NY, African-American Heritage Celebration, Late Jun.

Valhalla, NY, Yiddish Heritage Celebration, Middle Aug.

Valhalla, NY, Hispanic Heritage Celebration, Late Aug.

Valley Falls, NY, Glory, Early Jun.

Varies, NY, Long Island Music Festival, Middle Jul. to Early Sep.

Vestal, NY, Penny Association Midwinter Bluegrass Festival, Early Mar.

Victor, NY, Native American Dance Festival, Late Jul. to Early Aug.

Walton, NY, Catskill Harvest Festival, Early Oct.

Warwick, NY, Applefest, Early Oct.

Watertown, NY, Watertown Goes Green Irish Festival, Middle Mar.

West Ghent, NY, Columbia County Jazz Festival, Late Jul.

West Haverstraw, NY, Rockland County A. O. H. Feis and Field Games, Late Jul.

West Haverstraw, NY, Rockland Irish Festival, Late Aug.

West Shokan, NY, Fundraiser, Middle Jun.

Westbury, NY, Dick Fox's Spring Doo-Wopp Extravaganza, Early Mar.

Westbury, NY, Irish Celebration, Middle Mar.

Westbury, NY, Spring Blues Festival, Late Apr.

Westbury, NY, Dick Fox's Summer Doo-Wopp Extravaganza, Early Jun.

Westbury, NY, Dick Fox's Fall Doo-Wopp Extravaganza, Middle Sep.
Westbury, NY, Dick Fox's Holiday Doo-Wopp Extravaganza, Middle Dec.
White Plains, NY, Westchester Community College Jazz Festival, Early May
White Plains, NY, Westchester Arts Festival, Late May
White Plains, NY, June Jazz, Middle Jun.
White Plains, NY, Distant Drums Native American Festival, Middle Jun.
Woodbury, NY, Rushmore Festival, Middle Jul.
Woodstock, NY, Real Woodstock Festival, Middle Jul.
Woodstock, NY, Woodstock Beat World Percussion Concert, Middle Jul.
Woodstock, NY, Woodstock New Music Festival, Early Aug.
Wyoming, NY, Apple Umpkin Festival, Late Sep.
Yonkers, NY, All-Star Irish Concert and Dance, Middle Jun.
Yonkers, NY, African-American Heritage Celebration, Middle Jul.
Yonkers, NY, Yonkers Hudson Riverfest, Middle Sep.

## New York City

Bronx, NYC, St. Barnabas Irish Variety Concert, Middle Mar.
Bronx, NYC, Salsa's Soul Combination, Early Apr.
Bronx, NYC, Libro Latino Bookfest/Pathways for Youth Benefit, Middle May
Bronx, NYC, Entre Familia, Early May
Bronx, NYC, Bronx Ethnic Music and Dance Festival, Middle Jun.
Bronx, NYC, Festival Playero, Middle Jun. to Early Sep.
Bronx, NYC, Irish Traditional Music and Dance Festival, Middle Jun.
Bronx, NYC, Puerto Rican Day Parade, Late Jul.
Brooklyn, NYC, Park Slope Native American Dance Festival, Middle Jan.
Brooklyn, NYC, Gospel Celebration!, Early Feb.
Brooklyn, NYC, Evening In Celebration of Black History Month, Late Feb.
Brooklyn, NYC, Tropical Carnival/Carnival Fete and Masquerade Jump-Up, Late Feb.
Brooklyn, NYC, West Indian Carnival Explosion, Middle Mar.
Brooklyn, NYC, Gospel Explosion, Late Mar.
Brooklyn, NYC, Betty Carter's Jazz Ahead, Early Apr.
Brooklyn, NYC, Radioactive Bodega Blacklight Prom, Late Apr.
Brooklyn, NYC, Religious Music Festival, Late Apr.
Brooklyn, NYC, Everybody's Calypso Awards, Early May
Brooklyn, NYC, Brooklyn Rock Awards, Middle May
Brooklyn, NYC, Brooklyn Arts Week, Middle May
Brooklyn, NYC, Fifth Avenue Festival, Middle May
Brooklyn, NYC, Hezekiah Walker Anniversary Show, Late May
Brooklyn, NYC, Irish-American Festival and Heritage Feis, Late May
Brooklyn, NYC, Brooklyn Woodstock, Early Jun.
Brooklyn, NYC, Starrett at Spring Creek Native American Pow Wow, Early Jun.
Brooklyn, NYC, Israel Expo, Early Jun.
Brooklyn, NYC, Gospel Concert, Early Jun.
Brooklyn, NYC, New York City's Gospel Festival, Middle Jun.
Brooklyn, NYC, Super Radioactive Bodega Bonanza Outdoor Festival, Middle Jun.
Brooklyn, NYC, Welcome Back to Brooklyn, Middle Jun.
Brooklyn, NYC, Gospel Music Workshop of America/New York State Chapter Convention, Middle Jun.
Brooklyn, NYC, Gospelfest, Middle Jun.
Brooklyn, NYC, Celebrate Brooklyn Performing Arts Festival, Late Jun. to Middle Aug.
Brooklyn, NYC, Caribbean Cultural Heritage Week Festival/Caribbean Craft and Food Fair, Late Jun.
Brooklyn, NYC, African Street Festival, Late Jun. to Early Jul.

Brooklyn, NYC, New York Trini-Jam Fest, Early Jul.

Brooklyn, NYC, Park Slope 5th Avenue Independence Day Festival, Early Jul.

Brooklyn, NYC, El Elyon Music Fest, Early Jul.

Brooklyn, NYC, July Gospel Explosion, Early Jul.

Brooklyn, NYC, Gateway to the Nations Powwow, Early Jul.

Brooklyn, NYC, Midwood Concerts at Seaside, Middle Jul. to Late Aug.

Brooklyn, NYC, BACA Summer Celebration, Middle Jul.

Brooklyn, NYC, Africa Mondo Festival, Middle Jul.

Brooklyn, NYC, Martin Luther King Jr. Concert Series, Middle Jul. to Late Aug.

Brooklyn, NYC, New York City Clearwater Festival, Late Jul.

Brooklyn, NYC, African Caribbean Latino American Festival, Late Jul.

Brooklyn, NYC, Slammin' Jammin' Spike's Joint Anniversary Block Party, Late Jul.

Brooklyn, NYC, New York Reggae Festival, Middle Aug.

Brooklyn, NYC, Park Slope Festival, Middle Aug.

Brooklyn, NYC, Caribbean-American Community Trade and Cultural Expo, Middle Aug. to
    Late Aug.

Brooklyn, NYC, City Gardeners' Harvest Fair/Gateway Music Festival/New York City
    Bluegrass Band and Banjo Festival, Late Aug.

Brooklyn, NYC, Uprise and Shine Youth Concert, Late Aug.

Brooklyn, NYC, Salsa Fest, Late Aug.

Brooklyn, NYC, West Indian-American Day Carnival and Parade, Early Sep.

Brooklyn, NYC, Great Irish Fair, Early Sep. to Middle Sep.

Brooklyn, NYC, Brooklyn's Summer Gospelfest!, Early Sep.

Brooklyn, NYC, Rockaway Music and Arts Council Fall Festival, Middle Sep.

Brooklyn, NYC, New York Beer Fest, Middle Sep.

Brooklyn, NYC, Gateway Sukkos Festival, Late Sep.

Brooklyn, NYC, Do the Right Thing Festival, Late Sep.

Brooklyn, NYC, Next Wave Festival, Late Sep. to Middle Dec.

Brooklyn, NYC, Atlantic Antic, Early Oct.

Brooklyn, NYC, Chili Pepper Fiesta, Early Oct.

Brooklyn, NYC, Brooklyn Ethnic Music and Dance Festival, Late Oct.

Brooklyn, NYC, Cultural Crossroads' Jazz Gala, Late Oct.

Brooklyn/Queens, NYC, Everybody's World Calypso Monarch Competition, Early May to Late
    Jul.

Manhattan, NYC, Lou Rawls Parade of Stars, Early Jan.

Manhattan, NYC, Gruppen: Chamber Music for the 21st Century, Early Jan. to Middle Jan.

Manhattan, NYC, Great Beer and Music Festival, Middle Jan.

Manhattan, NYC, Focus!, Middle Jan. to Late Jan.

Manhattan, NYC, Drama League's Black-Tie Benefit, Late Jan.

Manhattan, NYC, Thunderbird American Indian Dancers Pow Wow and Dance Concert, Late
    Jan. to Early Feb.

Manhattan, NYC, Fast Folk Revue, Late Jan.

Manhattan, NYC, Hot 97's Old School Throwdown, Late Jan.

Manhattan, NYC, Bob Marley Day, Early Feb.

Manhattan, NYC, Women in Cabaret, Early Feb. to Late Feb.

Manhattan, NYC, U. G. H. A. Black History Month Celebration, Middle Feb.

Manhattan, NYC, Concierto Del Amor, Middle Feb.

Manhattan, NYC, Festival of 20th Century Music, Middle Feb. to Late Feb.

Manhattan, NYC, Jazz and Poetry Marathon, Middle Feb.

Manhattan, NYC, 98.7 KISS-FM Gospel Celebration, Middle Feb.

Manhattan, NYC, Mardi Gras Carnaval, Middle Feb.

Manhattan, NYC, Smalls Winter Festival, Middle Feb.

Manhattan, NYC, Music from Japan Festival, Late Feb.

Manhattan, NYC, Lyrics and Lyricists/Boys Night Out, Late Feb.

Manhattan, NYC, Carnaval Del Merengue, Late Feb.
Manhattan, NYC, Evian Indoor Pro Beach Volleyball Championships, Late Feb.
Manhattan, NYC, Zydecodelic Loup Garou Bal de la Maison Mardi Gras Party, Late Feb.
Manhattan, NYC, Kitty Brazelton's Real Music Series, Late Feb. to Early Apr.
Manhattan, NYC, Great Miracle Prayer Festival, Late Feb.
Manhattan, NYC, Back Stage Bistro Awards, Late Feb.
Manhattan, NYC, Rhythm and Blues Foundation's Pioneer Awards, Early Mar.
Manhattan, NYC, Improvisors Collective Festival, Early Mar.
Manhattan, NYC, Century of Change/So Nice To Come Home To, Early Mar.
Manhattan, NYC, Caribbean Music Awards, Early Mar.
Manhattan, NYC, Festival of Women Improvisors, Early Mar. to Middle Mar.
Manhattan, NYC, Women's Jazz Festival, Early Mar. to Late Mar.
Manhattan, NYC, Bill Popp's Birthday Tribute to George L. Popp, Early Mar.
Manhattan, NYC, Evening of Rock and Roll, Middle Mar.
Manhattan, NYC, Winning Scores, Middle Mar.
Manhattan, NYC, Bang On a Can Festival, Middle Mar. to Early May
Manhattan, NYC, Africa Mondo Showcase, Middle Mar.
Manhattan, NYC, Evening with Frank Patterson, Early Mar.
Manhattan, NYC, Roulette Concert Series/Le Salon Roulette, Middle Mar.
Manhattan, NYC, Hearts and Voices Winter Benefit Series, Middle Mar. to Late Apr.
Manhattan, NYC, Tokyo/New York Noise Festival, Middle Mar.
Manhattan, NYC, Julius Watkins Jazz French Horn Festival, Middle Mar.
Manhattan, NYC, National Gospel Choir Competition, Middle Mar.
Manhattan, NYC, Israeli Folk Dance Festival and Festival of the Arts, Middle Mar.
Manhattan, NYC, Party for Zoot, Middle Mar.
Manhattan, NYC, The Brooklyn Beat Meets The Black Rock Coalition, Middle Mar.
Manhattan, NYC, Main Street U. S. A., Late Mar.
Manhattan, NYC, Wall to Wall, Late Mar.
Manhattan, NYC, WPLJ-FM's 70's Rock and Roll Reunion, Late Mar.
Manhattan, NYC, Tamika Reggae Awards, Late Mar.
Manhattan, NYC, Jewish Festival of Music, Late Mar.
Manhattan, NYC, New York Winter Blues Festival, Late Mar.
Manhattan, NYC, Independent Music Fest, Late Mar. to Early Apr.
Manhattan, NYC, Great Beer and Music Festival, Late Mar.
Manhattan, NYC, Great New York Mandolin Weekend, Early Apr.
Manhattan, NYC, Stork Music Festival, Early Apr.
Manhattan, NYC, Harmony Sweepstakes A Cappella Festival/New York Regional, Early Apr.
Manhattan, NYC, Manhattan Association of Cabarets and Clubs Awards, Early Apr.
Manhattan, NYC, Experimental Intermedia Festival with No Fancy Name, Early Apr. to Late
    Apr.
Manhattan, NYC, From Plains, Pueblos and Tundra:  Native American Music, Dance and
    Storytelling, Early Apr.
Manhattan, NYC, American Swing Dance Championships, Early Apr.
Manhattan, NYC, P. S. 122 Music Festival, Early Apr.
Manhattan, NYC, U. G. H. A. Hall of Fame Awards Ceremony, Early Apr.
Manhattan, NYC, Furnald Folk Fest, Early Apr.
Manhattan, NYC, New York Brass Conference for Scholarships, Early Apr.
Manhattan, NYC, Festival of Nations, Early Apr.
Manhattan, NYC, Rainforest Benefit Concert, Middle Apr.
Manhattan, NYC, International OFFestival, Middle Apr. to Middle Jun.
Manhattan, NYC, Death and Taxes, Middle Apr.
Manhattan, NYC, Carnegie Hall Folk Festival, Middle Apr. to Late Apr.
Manhattan, NYC, Easter Gospel Festival, Middle Apr.
Manhattan, NYC, Great New York Mandolin Gala, Middle Apr.

Manhattan, NYC, Eco-Festival, Late Apr. to Early May
Manhattan, NYC, Essence Awards, Late Apr.
Manhattan, NYC, Broadway's Easter Bonnet Competition: A Salute to 100 Years of Broadway, Late Apr.
Manhattan, NYC, Earth Day Celebration, Late Apr.
Manhattan, NYC, Corner Store Syndicate New Jazz Festival, Late Apr.
Manhattan, NYC, Roulette Concert Series/Roulette Mixology Festival, Late Apr. to Early May
Manhattan, NYC, National Gay and Lesbian Business and Consumer Expo, Late Apr.
Manhattan, NYC, Gospel Comes/Returns to Broadway, Late Apr.
Manhattan, NYC, Upper Broadway Spring Celebration and Festival, Late Apr.
Manhattan, NYC, Lower Second Avenue Festival, Early May
Manhattan, NYC, Pussystock, Early May
Manhattan, NYC, New York Shakespeare Festival Spring Gala, Early May
Manhattan, NYC, Areyto for Life: Hispanic AIDS Forum Benefit Gala and Art Auction, Early May
Manhattan, NYC, Dick Fox's Brooklyn Paramount Reunion, Early May
Manhattan, NYC, In Celebration of Life, Early May
Manhattan, NYC, Heart and Soul, Early May
Manhattan, NYC, Outmusic Festival, Early May
Manhattan, NYC, Say It With Love Night, Middle May
Manhattan, NYC, Hearts and Voices In Concert, Middle May
Manhattan, NYC, Tribute to African Diaspora Women, Middle May
Manhattan, NYC, Black Expo U. S. A., Middle May
Manhattan, NYC, Cavalcade of Stars, Middle May
Manhattan, NYC, Z100 May Day, Middle May
Manhattan, NYC, Folksongs Plus, Middle May
Manhattan, NYC, Union Settlement Ethnic Festival, Middle May
Manhattan, NYC, Mostly Women Composers, Middle May to Late May
Manhattan, NYC, Amsterdam Avenue Festival, Late May
Manhattan, NYC, Salute to Israel Day Parade and Concert, Late May
Manhattan, NYC, Israel Expo, Late May
Manhattan, NYC, Broadway County Fair, Late May
Manhattan, NYC, Rock Against Racism Concert, Late May
Manhattan, NYC, Sun Ra Festival, Middle May to Late May
Manhattan, NYC, Oi!/Skampilation, Late May
Manhattan, NYC, 52nd Street Jazz Festival, Late May
Manhattan, NYC, Festival De Los Soneros, Middle May
Manhattan, NYC, Manhattan Ethnic Music and Dance Festival, Late May
Manhattan, NYC, Memorial Day Weekend Celebration Scholarship Fund Raising Dance, Late May
Manhattan, NYC, Songwriters' Hall of Fame Awards, Late May
Manhattan, NYC, Harp and Harmony Concert, Early Jun.
Manhattan, NYC, Wall-to-Wall Rahsaan Roland Kirk, Early Jun.
Manhattan, NYC, Murray Hill Block Party and Blues Festival, Early Jun.
Manhattan, NYC, Pathmark Hispanic Arts Festival, Early Jun.
Manhattan, NYC, Celebrate 125! The Rhythm of the World, Early Jun.
Manhattan, NYC, Plantathon and Music Festival, Early Jun.
Manhattan, NYC, World of Percussion, Early Jun.
Manhattan, NYC, Indian Summer, Early Jun. to Late Jun.
Manhattan, NYC, Cross Overs: Music of Asia America, Early Jun.
Manhattan, NYC, Discmakers Unsigned Band/Artist New York World Series, Early Jun.
Manhattan, NYC, Festival of Jewish Music, Early Jun.
Manhattan, NYC, 116th Street Festival in El Barrio, Middle Jun.
Manhattan, NYC, Downtown Music Gallery's Anniversary Celebration, Middle Jun.

Manhattan, NYC, Puerto Rican Day Parade, Middle Jun.
Manhattan, NYC, City Lore Festival, Middle Jun.
Manhattan, NYC, Lower East Side Jewish Festival, Middle Jun.
Manhattan, NYC, Lyrics and Lyricists/The New Breed, Middle Jun.
Manhattan, NYC, Buskers Fare/Summer Fair, Middle Jun.
Manhattan, NYC, Sudden Sunsets: Highlights from the Benson AIDS Series, Middle Jun.
Manhattan, NYC, Fire Wall Total Arts Festival, Middle Jun. to Late Jun.
Manhattan, NYC, Central Park Summerstage, Middle Jun. to Early Aug.
Manhattan, NYC, Tweed New Works Festival, Middle Jun. to Early Jul.
Manhattan, NYC, WPLJ-FM's 70's Dance Party, Middle Jun.
Manhattan, NYC, Lesbian and Gay Pride Week/PrideFest, Middle Jun. to Late Jun.
Manhattan, NYC, Boathouse Rock, Middle Jun.
Manhattan, NYC, Broadway Summer Festival, Middle Jun.
Manhattan, NYC, Upper Broadway Summer Festival, Middle Jun.
Manhattan, NYC, Knitting Factory's "What is Jazz?" Festival, Middle Jun. to Early Jul.
Manhattan, NYC, Sounds at Sunset, Middle Jun. to Middle Sep.
Manhattan, NYC, Lesbopalooza, Late Jul.
Manhattan, NYC, Winter Consort Summer Solstice Whole Earth Celebration, Late Jun.
Manhattan, NYC, Midsummer Night Swing, Late Jun. to Late Jul.
Manhattan, NYC, Beacons In Jazz, Late Jun.
Manhattan, NYC, JVC Jazz Festival/Bryant Park Jazz Festival, Late Jun. to Early Jul.
Manhattan, NYC, Underground Blues and Folk Festival, Late Jun.
Manhattan, NYC, Improvisors Festival, Late Jun. to Early Jul.
Manhattan, NYC, Women in Jazz Festival, Early Jul.
Manhattan, NYC, Serious Fun!, Early Jul. to Late Jul.
Manhattan, NYC, 111th Street Boys Old Timers Day Stickball Festival, Early Jul.
Manhattan, NYC, Grand Nights for Singing, Early Jul. to Middle Jul.
Manhattan, NYC, B. M. I. Jazz Composer's Workshop Concert, Middle Jul.
Manhattan, NYC, Centerstage at the World Trade Center, Middle Jul. to Early Sep.
Manhattan, NYC, New York All-Star Klezmer Extravaganza, Middle Jul.
Manhattan, NYC, Life Beat Benefit: The Music Industry Fights AIDS, Middle Jul.
Manhattan, NYC, Gospel Nite, Middle Jul.
Manhattan, NYC, 360 Degrees Black: New York's Hip Hop Music Seminar, Middle Jul.
Manhattan, NYC, Macintosh New York Music Festival, Middle Jul. to Late Jul.
Manhattan, NYC, Jazz in July, Late Jul.
Manhattan, NYC, Columbia Te Canta, Late Jul.
Manhattan, NYC, American Cabaret Theater Festival, Late Jul.
Manhattan, NYC, Black Family Day, Late Jul.
Manhattan, NYC, Budweiser Superfest, Late Jul.
Manhattan, NYC, Gala All-Star Irish Cruise, Late Jul. to Early Aug.
Manhattan, NYC, Classical Jazz at Lincoln Center, Early Aug.
Manhattan, NYC, The Source Awards, Early Aug.
Manhattan, NYC, Lincoln Center Out-of-Doors, Early Aug. to Late Aug.
Manhattan, NYC, Carnival in New York, Early Aug.
Manhattan, NYC, Harlem Week/Harlem Day, Early Aug. to Middle Aug.
Manhattan, NYC, Riverside Park Arts Festival, Early Aug. to Late Aug.
Manhattan, NYC, Nuyorican Poets Cafe Block Party, Middle Aug.
Manhattan, NYC, Midsummer's Night Cabaret, Middle Aug.
Manhattan, NYC, Panasonic Village Jazz Festival, Middle Aug. to Late Aug.
Manhattan, NYC, 98.7 KISS-FM Gospel Celebration, Late Aug.
Manhattan, NYC, Midnight Ravers Anniversary Party, Late Aug.
Manhattan, NYC, Roots of American Music Festival, Late Aug.
Manhattan, NYC, Black Family Weekend, Late Aug.
Manhattan, NYC, Greenwich Avenue Summer Festival, Late Aug.

Manhattan, NYC, Charlie Parker Jazz Festival, Late Aug.
Manhattan, NYC, Fierce Pussy Fest, Late Aug.
Manhattan, NYC, Vulvapalooza, Late Sep.
Manhattan, NYC, We Care About New York Block Party, Late Aug.
Manhattan, NYC, Heineken Jazz and Blues Festival, Late Aug.
Manhattan, NYC, New York Salsa Festival, Early Sep.
Manhattan, NYC, Brazilian National Independence Day Street Festival, Early Sep.
Manhattan, NYC, West Side Arts, Crafts, Antiques Festival, Early Sep.
Manhattan, NYC, West Side Fall Festival, Early Sep.
Manhattan, NYC, Wigstock, Early Sep.
Manhattan, NYC, Bluegrass Bash, Early Sep.
Manhattan, NYC, CMJ Music Marathon and Musicfest, Early Sep.
Manhattan, NYC, MTV Music Awards, Early Sep.
Manhattan, NYC, Cabaret for a Cause, Middle Sep. to Late Sep.
Manhattan, NYC, WPLJ-FM's 70's Dance Party, Middle Sep.
Manhattan, NYC, African-American Day Parade, Middle Sep.
Manhattan, NYC, Columbus Avenue Festival, Middle Sep.
Manhattan, NYC, Rafael Hernandez/Sylvia Rexach Festival, Middle Sep.
Manhattan, NYC, QE2: Newport Jazz Festival at Sea, Middle Sep. to Late Sep.
Manhattan, NYC, American Festival of Microtonal Music, Middle Sep. to Early Nov.
Manhattan, NYC, Expressions International Festival, Late Sep. to Late Oct.
Manhattan, NYC, Cognac Hennessy Jazz Search, Late Sep.
Manhattan, NYC, Native American Festival, Late Sep.
Manhattan, NYC, 52nd Street Jazz Festival, Late Sep.
Manhattan, NYC, New York State Big Apple Festival, Late Sep.
Manhattan, NYC, Underground Jazz Festival, Early Oct.
Manhattan, NYC, Acid Jazz Night, Early Oct.
Manhattan, NYC, Gay and Lesbian American Music Awards, Early Oct. to Early Nov.
Manhattan, NYC, WDRE Modern Rock Fest, Early Oct.
Manhattan, NYC, Outmusic Festival, Early Oct. to Early Nov.
Manhattan, NYC, Greenwich Village Folk Festival, Early Oct.
Manhattan, NYC, All-Nite Soul, Early Oct.
Manhattan, NYC, Eleventh Avenue Auto Fair, Early Oct.
Manhattan, NYC, Knitting Factory at Merkin Hall, Early Oct. to Middle Oct.
Manhattan, NYC, Choose Life Benefit Gospel Concert, Middle Oct.
Manhattan, NYC, Shelter: The New York Singer-Songwriter Festival, Middle Oct.
Manhattan, NYC, Nations of New York Arts Festival, Middle Oct. to Late Oct.
Manhattan, NYC, Night of Musical Magic, Middle Oct.
Manhattan, NYC, Cabaret Convention, Middle Oct. to Late Oct.
Manhattan, NYC, Peter Tosh Day, Middle Oct.
Manhattan, NYC, Hanukkah Arts Festival and Judaica Crafts Fair/Selected Shorts, Middle Oct.
Manhattan, NYC, Smithsonian's National Museum of the American Indian Powwow, Middle
   Oct.
Manhattan, NYC, Africa Mondo Festival, Middle Oct. to Late Oct.
Manhattan, NYC, Calypso and Steelband "Sunshine" Music Awards, Late Oct.
Manhattan, NYC, Combinacion Perfecta, Late Oct.
Manhattan, NYC, Songwriter's Evening, Late Oct.
Manhattan, NYC, Cajun/Zydeco Jamboree and Halloween Dance, Late Oct.
Manhattan, NYC, Theater for the New City Village Haloween Costume Ball, Late Oct.
Manhattan, NYC, Village Halloween Parade/All Souls' Halloween Ball, Late Oct.
Manhattan, NYC, Charlie Parker Music and More Awards Gala, Early Nov.
Manhattan, NYC, Sonic Boom Festival of New Music, Early Nov. to Middle Nov.
Manhattan, NYC, JAL Jazz Concert, Early Nov.
Manhattan, NYC, Buddy Rich Memorial Scholarship Concert, Early Nov.

Manhattan, NYC, Juba, Jukin' and Jazzin', Early Nov.
Manhattan, NYC, Harlem Piano U. S. A., Middle Nov.
Manhattan, NYC, Kitty Brazelton's Real Music Series/Music Parties, Early Nov. to Late Nov.
Manhattan, NYC, Floating Archives' Some Kind of Carnival, Early Nov.
Manhattan, NYC, Great Beer and Music Festival, Middle Nov.
Manhattan, NYC, Richard Nader's Rock and Roll Revival Spectacular, Middle Nov.
Manhattan, NYC, Big Band Day, Middle Nov.
Manhattan, NYC, JazzTimes Convention, Middle Nov.
Manhattan, NYC, K-Rock's Hungerthon, Middle Nov.
Manhattan, NYC, Giving of Thanks to the First Peoples, Middle Nov.
Manhattan, NYC, Skavoovee, Late Nov.
Manhattan, NYC, AIDS Dance-A-Thon, Late Nov.
Manhattan, NYC, Big Bands at Sea, Late Nov. to Early Dec.
Manhattan, NYC, Improvisations Festival, Late Nov. to Middle Dec.
Manhattan, NYC, Jimi Hendrix Birthday Party, Late Nov.
Manhattan, NYC, Benson Series Benefit Concert for United AIDS Relief Effort, Early Dec.
Manhattan, NYC, WBLS Celebration Concert and Scholarship Fund, Early Dec.
Manhattan, NYC, Post-Rock, Neo-Mosh Festival, Early Dec.
Manhattan, NYC, El Elyon Music Awards, Early Dec.
Manhattan, NYC, TeddyCare, Early Dec. to Late Dec.
Manhattan, NYC, Latin Jazz U. S. A. Concert and Awards, Early Dec.
Manhattan, NYC, Bending Toward the Light:  A Jazz Nativity, Early Dec.
Manhattan, NYC, Z100 Acoustic Christmas, Early Dec.
Manhattan, NYC, Colors of Christmas, Early Dec.
Manhattan, NYC, WNEW-FM Christmas Concert, Early Dec.
Manhattan, NYC, Winter Revels, Early Dec.
Manhattan, NYC, Chango Celebration, Early Dec.
Manhattan, NYC, Experimental Intermedia Four Country Festival, Early Dec. to Late Dec.
Manhattan, NYC, WDRE Acoustic Christmas, Middle Dec.
Manhattan, NYC, Winter Consort Winter Solstice Whole Earth Christmas Celebration, Middle
    Dec.
Manhattan, NYC, Kwanzaa Holiday Expo, Middle Dec.
Manhattan, NYC, Indian Market,  Dec. to Late Dec.
Manhattan, NYC, Sounds Around the World, Middle Dec.
Manhattan, NYC, New York Jazz Today!, Middle Dec.
Manhattan, NYC, WWRL Gospel Explosion, Middle Dec.
Manhattan, NYC, Community Holiday Festival, Late Dec. to Early Jan.
Manhattan, NYC, Black Nativity, Late Dec.
Manhattan, NYC, S. O. B.'s Kwanzaa Celebration, Late Dec.
Manhattan, NYC, Skarmageddon, Late Dec.
Manhattan, NYC, Concert for Peace, Late Dec.
Manhattan, NYC, First Night New York, Late Dec.
Queens, NYC, Wall of Sound, Late Mar.
Queens, NYC, Sunnyside Shop-Till-You-Drop Festival, Middle Apr.
Queens, NYC, Jamaica Fun Run and Family Day, Middle May
Queens, NYC, Queens College Cultural Heritage Great Gospel Competition, Middle May
Queens, NYC, Save Our Park/WWRL Radiothon, Late May
Queens, NYC, Broadway Astoria Festival, Late May
Queens, NYC, Lesbian and Gay Pride Committee Parade and Festival, Early Jun.
Queens, NYC, Southeast Queens' Youth Sports and Spring Festival/Juneteenth, Middle Jun.
Queens, NYC, Queens Boulevard Festival, Middle Jun.
Queens, NYC, Queens Festival/Nations in Neighborhoods Multicultural Dance Party, Late Jun.
Queens, NYC, Woodside Independence Weekend Festival, Early Jul.
Queens, NYC, Steinway Street Fun in the Sun Festival, Early Jul.

Queens, NYC, Columbia Independence Day Celebration, Late Jul.
Queens, NYC, Rockaway Irish Festival, Late Jul.
Queens, NYC, Rock-N-Roll Extravaganza, Early Aug.
Queens, NYC, WWRL Family Day and Picnic, Early Aug. to Middle Aug.
Queens, NYC, 36th Avenue Summer Food Fair, Middle Aug.
Queens, NYC, New York Country Music Festival, Middle Aug.
Queens, NYC, Sephardi Cultural Fair, Late Sep.
Queens, NYC, Northeastern Native American Association Pow Wow, Late Sep.
Queens, NYC, Live Jazz Bands, Middle Oct.
Queens, NYC, Night of Shamrocks, Middle Nov.
Queens, NYC, Return of The Brooklyn Bridge, Late Nov.
Queens, NYC, Kwanzaa, Early Dec.
Queens, NYC, Hanukkah Festival, Middle Dec.
Staten Island, NYC, Summerfun! , Middle Jul.
Staten Island, NYC, I. C. C. Songfest, Early Aug.
Staten Island, NYC, International Festival of Cultures, Middle Sep.
Varies, NYC, McDonald's Gospelfest, Early Apr. to Middle Jun.
Varies, NYC, Mother's Day Caribbean All-Stars Festival, Early May
Varies, NYC, Ecofest, Late Sep.
Varies, NYC, Sonidos de las Americas, Late Nov. to Early Dec.

## Varied Sites

Varied Sites, VAR, Rock and Roll Hall of Fame Induction Dinner, Middle Jan.
Varied Sites, VAR, International Association of Jazz Educators Convention, Middle Jan.
Varied Sites, VAR, People's Music Network Winter Gathering, Late Jan.
Varied Sites, VAR, Folk Alliance Conference, Middle Feb.
Varied Sites, VAR, Northeast Invitational Country Music Awards Show, Middle Feb.
Varied Sites, VAR, The Consortium, Late Feb. to Middle Apr.
Varied Sites, VAR, New England Foundation for the Arts Jazz Conference, Early Jun. to Middle Jun.
Varied Sites, VAR, Gospel Music Workshop of America National Convention, Early Aug. to Middle Aug.
Varied Sites, VAR, International Duke Ellington Conference, Middle Aug.
Varied Sites, VAR, Drum Corps International World Championships, Middle Aug.
Varied Sites, VAR, National Baptist Convention of America, Early Sep. to Middle Sep.
Varied Sites, VAR, New England Sacred Harp Singing Convention, Early Oct.
Varied Sites, VAR, Clearwater's Pumpkin Sail, Early Oct. to Middle Oct.
Varied Sites, VAR, New Music Across America, Early Oct.
Varied Sites, VAR, American Banjo Fraternity's Fall Rally, Middle Oct. to Late Oct.

~     ~     ~

# Festival Names by Primary Genre

**Caveat**  One of the reigning glories of festivals is how they merrily combine musical genres -- often ignoring the labels arbitrary assigned by the music industry for marketing purposes -- in striving towards a more organic and stimulating listening experience for their wide audiences. Of course, all this genre-blending makes the following grouping highly problematic. How do you categorize Long Island's JONES BEACH GREEKFEST WEEKEND, for example? It's one of the largest gatherings of African-American fraternity members in the country; yet boasts one of the nation's biggest rap showcases; yet also features healthy samplings of modern R&B and alternative rock acts. I cited its Primary Genre as "African American," since that's its main intent, but I could've been persuaded otherwise (i.e., "Rap?" "Modern Rock and Pop?" "Variety, General?").

In deciding the Primary Genre of each festival, I tried to consider the "big picture" -- looking at its entire lineup, often over several years. Your best bet, if in doubt, is to return to the Festival Listings and examine its Secondary Genres, Acts (national, regional, local), and Sample Day's Lineup. Then contact the festival for current information. Readers are invited to mail any suggested corrections, revisions, updates, etc. to FESTPRESS, P. O. Box 147, Glen Ridge, NJ 07028.

## Variety, General

Kaleidoscope Family Arts Festival, Augusta, ME, Early Jun.
Old Port Festival, Portland, ME, Early Jun.
Family Fun Fair, Portland, ME, Middle Jun.
Back Cove Family Day, Portland, ME, Middle Jun.
LaKermesse Franco-Americaine Festival, Biddeford, ME, Late Jun.
Strawberry Festival, South Berwick, ME, Late Jun.
Great Whatever Week and Race, Augusta, ME, Late Jun. to Early Jul.
Grand Riviere Festival, Van Buren, ME, Late Jun. to Middle Aug.
Windjammer Days, Boothbay Harbor, ME, Late Jun.
Old Home Week and Independence Day, Eastport, ME, Late Jun. to Early Jul.
Bath Heritage Days, Bath, ME, Early Jul.
Blue Hill Pops, Blue Hill, ME, Early Jul.
WERU 89.9FM Full Circle Summer Fair, Union, ME, Early Jul.
Thomaston Independence Day Celebration, Thomaston, ME, Early Jul.
Schooner Days, Rockland, ME, Early Jul.
Seaside Festival, Kittery, ME, Early Jul.
Rotary Oyster Festival, Damariscotta, ME, Early Jul. to Middle Jul.
Celebrate Gorham, Gorham, ME, Early Jul.
Maine Potato Blossom Festival/Crown of Maine Balloon Festival, Fort Fairfield, ME, Early Jul.
    to Middle Jul.
Belfast Bay Festival, Belfast, ME, Middle Jul.
Yarmouth Clam Festival, Yarmouth, ME, Middle Jul.
Mollyockett Day, Bethel, ME, Middle Jul.
Old Hallowell Day, Hallowell, ME, Middle Jul.
Richmond Days, Richmond, ME, Middle Jul. to Late Jul.
Deering Oaks Family Festival, Portland, ME, Middle Jul. to Late Jul.
Central Maine Egg Festival, Pittsfield, ME, Middle Jul. to Late Jul.
York Days, York, ME, Late Jul. to Early Aug.
Homecoming, Grand Isle, ME, Late Jul. to Early Aug.
International Festival, Calais, ME, Late Jul. to Early Aug.
H. O. M. E. Craft and Farm Fair, Orland, ME, Early Aug.

Maine Lobster Festival, Rockland, ME, Early Aug.
Summer in the Parks, Portland, ME, Early Aug. to Middle Aug.
Fat Tire Polo Tournament and Music Bash, Farmington, ME, Early Aug.
Sankofa Street Festival, Belfast, ME, Middle Aug.
Spring Point Festival, South Portland, ME, Middle Aug.
Salmon Sunday, Eastport, ME, Middle Sep.
Duke Ellington Festival, Portland, ME, Middle Sep.
Blue Hill Festival of Music/Singer-Songwriter Marathon, Blue Hill, ME, Late Oct.
Fall MusicFest, Portland, ME, Late Oct. to Early Nov.
New Year's Eve Portland, Portland, ME, Late Dec.
Seacoast Music Awards, Portsmouth, NH, Early Feb.
New Hampshire's Lilac Time Festival, Lisbon, NH, Late May
Market Square Day, Portsmouth, NH, Early Jun. to Middle Jun.
Somersworth International Children's Festival, Somersworth, NH, Middle Jun.
High Hopes Hot Air Balloon Festival, Milford, NH, Middle Jun.
American Pit Masters Bar-B-Q Round-Up, Manchester, NH, Early Jul.
Street Fair, Keene, NH, Middle Jul.
Waterville Valley Summer Music Festival, Waterville Valley, NH, Middle Jul. to Early Sep.
Hanover Street-Fest, Hanover, NH, Middle Jul.
Musicfest, Exeter, NH, Early Aug.
Riverfest: Manchester Celebrating Itself, Manchester, NH, Early Sep. to Middle Sep.
Seafood Festival and Sidewalk Sale Days, Hampton Beach, NH, Middle Sep.
Lake Champlain Balloon Festival, Essex Junction, VT, Early Jun.
Vermont Dairy Festival, Enosburg Falls, VT, Early Jun.
Quechee Hot Air Balloon Festival, Quechee, VT, Middle Jun.
Green Mountain Chew Chew/Vermont Food Fest, Burlington, VT, Late Jun.
Ben and Jerry's One World, One Heart Festival, Warren, VT, Late Jun.
Burlington Independence Day Waterfront Celebration, Burlington, VT, Early Jul.
Celebrate Vermont Arts and Crafts Show, Rochester, VT, Middle Jul.
Aquafest, Newport, VT, Middle Jul.
Harmony Ridge Brass Center Summer Festival, Poultney, VT, Early Aug.
AutumnFest, Middlebury, VT, Middle Sep.
Sugarbush Brewers Festival, Warren, VT, Middle Sep.
Anthony Spinazzola Gala Festival of Food and Wine, Boston, MA, Early Feb.
Boston Festival: A Carnival of Cultures, Boston, MA, Middle Feb. to Late Feb.
Multicultural Festival, Roxbury, MA, Late Feb.
Hot, Hot Tropics, Boston, MA, Late Mar.
Pepsi Boston Music Awards, Boston, MA, Early Apr.
WBOS-FM Earth Day Concert and Festival, Boston, MA, Late Apr.
Arts First: A Harvard/Radcliffe Celebration, Cambridge, MA, Late Apr. to Middle May
Harvard Square's May Fair, Cambridge, MA, Early May
WGBH "T" Party, Boston, MA, Middle May
Art Newbury Street, Boston, MA, Middle May
Street Performers Festival, Boston, MA, Late May
American Pit Masters Bar-B-Q Round-Up, Boston, MA, Middle Jun.
Taste of Chicopee, Chicopee, MA, Early Jun.
La Festa, North Adams, MA, Early Jun. to Late Jun.
Hyannis Harbor Festival, Hyannis, MA, Early Jun.
Riverfest, Buckland, MA, Middle Jun.
Fall River Festival, Fall River, MA, Middle Jun.
Peter Pan Taste of Springfield, Springfield, MA, Middle Jun.
Boston Pops, Boston, MA, Middle Jun. to Early Jul.
Summerfest, Great Barrington, MA, Middle Jun.
Oak Bluffs Harbor Day, Oak Bluffs, MA, Middle Jun.

Amesbury Days Festival, Amesbury, MA, Late Jun. to Early Jul.
Chilifest, Boston, MA, Middle Jun.
Plymouth Summer Blastoff, Plymouth, MA, Late Jun.
Boston Harborfest, Boston, MA, Late Jun.
Monson's Summerfest, Monson, MA, Early Jul.
Whaling City Festival, New Bedford, MA, Early Jul. to Middle Jul.
Great New England Brewers' Festival, Northampton, MA, Late Jul.
Taste of the South Shore, Quincy, MA, Early Aug.
Taste of Northampton, Northampton, MA, Middle Aug.
Fall River Celebrates America , Fall River, MA, Middle Aug.
Boston Seaport Festival, Charlestown, MA, Middle Aug. to Late Aug.
Great Yankee Rib Cook-Off, Boston, MA, Late Aug.
Lowell Riverfest, Lowell, MA, Early Sep. to Middle Sep.
Bourne Scallop Fest, Buzzards Bay, MA, Early Sep. to Middle Sep.
Cambridge River Festival, Cambridge, MA, Middle Sep.
Day at the Lake, Worcester, MA, Middle Sep.
Fall Festival, Attleboro Falls, MA, Middle Sep.
Gloucester Seafood Festival, Gloucester, MA, Middle Sep.
Chowderfest, Charlestown, MA, Middle Sep.
Art Newbury Street, Boston, MA, Middle Sep.
Mix 98.5 Fall Fest, Boston, MA, Early Oct.
Westport Harvest Festival, Westport, MA, Early Oct. to Middle Oct.
Chilifest, Charlestown, MA, Middle Oct.
Newport Winter Festival, Newport, RI, Late Jan. to Early Feb.
Earth Day Celebration, Providence, RI, Late Apr.
Maritime Arts Festival, Newport, RI, Middle May
Summer Arts Fest Chair Fair, West Kingston, RI, Early Jun.
Schwepes Chowder Cook-Off, Newport, RI, Middle Jun.
Big Easy Bash, Escoheag, RI, Late Jun.
American Pit Masters Bar-B-Q Roundup, Providence, RI, Late Jun.
East Providence Heritage Festival, East Providence, RI, Late Jul.
Charlestown Chamber of Commerce Seafood Festival, Charlestown, RI, Early Aug.
Cumberlandfest, Cumberland, RI, Early Aug.
Scituate Music Fest, Scituate, RI, Middle Aug.
Cajun and Bluegrass Music-Dance-Food Festival, Escoheag, RI, Early Sep.
Providence Waterfront Festival/Waterfront Jazz Festival, Providence, RI, Middle Sep.
Taste of Rhode Island, Newport, RI, Late Sep.
Autumnfest, Woonsocket, RI, Early Oct.
Scituate Arts Festival, North Scituate, RI, Early Oct.
Bowen's Wharf Waterfront Seafood Festival, Newport, RI, Middle Oct.
Hartford Advocate's Best of the Bands Bash, New Britain, CT, Late May
Fair Haven Festival, New Haven, CT, Early Jun.
City Fest Arts Jubilee, Middletown, CT, Early Jun.
Bloomfield Festival, Bloomfield, CT, Early Jun.
Riversplash, Simsbury, CT, Early Jun.
Taste of Hartford, Hartford, CT, Early Jun. to Middle Jun.
Main Street U. S. A., New Britain, CT, Early Jun.
Citibank Taste of Stamford, Stamford, CT, Early Jun. to Middle Jun.
Celebrate! West Hartford, West Hartford, CT, Middle Jun.
Taste of Fairfield, Fairfield, CT, Middle Jun.
Old Home Day, Middlefield, CT, Middle Jun.
Pink Tent Festival of the Arts, Stamford, CT, Middle Jun.
West Fest/Taste of Westville, Westville, CT, Middle Jun.
Summer Series, Westport, CT, Middle Jun. to Middle Aug.

Red Cross Waterfront Festival, Greenwich, CT, Middle Jun.

Trumbull Day, Trumbull, CT, Late Jun.

4th of July Celebration, Enfield, CT, Early Jul.

Riverfest, Hartford, CT, Early Jul.

Subfest, Groton, CT, Early Jul.

Summer Celebration, Dayville, CT, Early Jul.

New London Sail Festival/Connecticut Maritime Festival, New London, CT, Early Jul. to Middle Jul.

Greater Hartford Festival of Jazz/Hartford Mega! Weekend, Hartford, CT, Late Jul. to Early Aug.

SoNo Arts Celebration, South Norwalk, CT, Early Aug.

Kent Summer Days, Kent, CT, Early Aug.

Summertime Street Festival, New Haven, CT, Middle Aug.

Taste Buds Festival, Hartford, CT, Late Aug.

Harbor Day, Norwich, CT, Late Aug.

Simsbury Septemberfest, Simsbury, CT, Early Sep.

Oyster Festival, South Norwalk, CT, Early Sep. to Middle Sep.

Taste of Connecticut Food Festival, Mystic, CT, Early Sep. to Middle Sep.

Taste of Greater Danbury, Danbury, CT, Middle Sep.

Festival at Roseland Cottage, Woodstock, CT, Middle Oct.

Nassau Community College Folk Festival, Garden City, NY, Late Mar.

Syracuse Area Music Awards (Sammies), Syracuse, NY, Early May

Pinksterfest/Albany Tulip Festival, Albany, NY, Early May

Lilac Festival, Rochester, NY, Middle May to Late May

Westchester Arts Festival, White Plains, NY, Late May

Bearsville Theater Memorial Day Music Festival, Bearsville, NY, Late May

Ithaca Festival, Ithaca, NY, Early Jun.

Albion Strawberry Festival, Albion, NY, Early Jun.

Albany Riverfest/All-America City Fair, Albany, NY, Early Jun. to Middle Jun.

Ballston Spa Village Wide Garage Sale and Family Festival, Ballston Spa, NY, Middle Jun.

L. A. R. A. C. Arts and Crafts Festival, Glen Falls, NY, Middle Jun.

Miller Lite Balloonfest/Art on the Rise, Jamesville, NY, Middle Jun.

Mohonk's Music Week, New Paltz, NY, Late Jun.

Summerscape: Huntington Summer Arts Festival, Huntington, NY, Late Jun. to Late Aug.

Lake George Summerfest, Lake George, NY, Late Jun.

Chautauqua Summer Music Program, Chautauqua, NY, Late Jun. to Late Aug.

Friendship Festival, Buffalo, NY, Late Jun. to Early Jul.

Ellicottville's Summer Festival of the Arts, Ellicottville, NY, Late Jun. to Early Jul.

American Patriot Festival, Hunter, NY, Early Jul.

Catskill Fourth of July Celebration, Catskill, NY, Early Jul.

Summerfest, Poughkeepsie, NY, Early Jul.

Fair Haven Field Days, Fair Haven, NY, Early Jul.

Fourth of July Celebration, Mayville, NY, Early Jul.

Star Spangled Spectacular, Montgomery, NY, Early Jul.

Riverhead Jazz Festival, Riverhead, NY, Early Jul.

Lunchtime Concerts, Albany, NY, Early Jul. to Late Aug.

Taste of Buffalo, Buffalo, NY, Early Jul.

Waterfront Extravaganza, Syracuse, NY, Early Jul. to Middle Jul.

Corn Hill Arts Festival/Fiddler's Fair, Rochester, NY, Early Jul. to Middle Jul.

Good Old Summertime , Utica, NY, Early Jul. to Middle Jul.

Syracuse Arts and Crafts Festival, Syracuse, NY, Middle Jul.

Canal Fest, Tonawanda, NY, Middle Jul. to Late Jul.

Fingerlakes Grassroots Festival of Music and Dance, Trumansburg, NY, Middle Jul. to Late Jul.

Hats Off to Saratoga Festival, Saratoga Springs, NY, Late Jul.

Oswego Harborfest, Oswego, NY, Middle Jul.
Park Avenue Festival, Rochester, NY, Late Jul. to Early Aug.
Back at the Ranch Festival, Montauk Point, NY, Early Aug.
International Food Festival/Friday Fest, Poughkeepsie, NY, Early Aug.
Waterfront Arts Festival, Canandaigua, NY, Early Aug.
Waterfront Festival, Buffalo, NY, Early Aug. to Middle Aug.
International Food Festival, Albany, NY, Middle Aug.
Waterfront Festival Free Summer Concert Series/Family Fun in the Sun, Buffalo, NY, Middle
    Aug.
Final Stretch Festival, Saratoga Springs, NY, Late Aug.
Skyfest, Cedar Lake, NY, Late Aug.
Greece Summer Festival, Greece, NY, Late Aug.
Yonkers Hudson Riverfest, Yonkers, NY, Middle Sep.
Takin' It to the Streets: The Electric City Music Celebration, Schenectady, NY, Middle Sep.
Music at New Paltz/Faculty Sampler, New Paltz, NY, Middle Sep.
Palmyra Canal Town Days, Palmyra, NY, Middle Sep.
Naples Grape Festival, Naples, NY, Middle Sep.
Apple Umpkin Festival, Wyoming, NY, Late Sep.
Hilton Applefest, Hilton, NY, Late Sep. to Early Oct.
Letchworth Arts and Crafts Show and Sale, Castile, NY, Early Oct.
October Oyster Festival, Oyster Bay, NY, Middle Oct.
Niagara's Apple Country Festival, Lockport, NY, Middle Oct.
Apple Harvest Festival, Ithaca, NY, Early Oct.
Artvoice Original Music Awards, Buffalo, NY, Late Nov.
Main Street U. S. A., Manhattan, NYC, Late Mar.
Sunnyside Shop-Till-You-Drop Festival, Queens, NYC, Middle Apr.
New York Shakespeare Festival Spring Gala, Manhattan, NYC, Early May
Brooklyn Arts Week, Brooklyn, NYC, Middle May
Fifth Avenue Festival, Brooklyn, NYC, Middle May
Amsterdam Avenue Festival, Manhattan, NYC, Late May
Broadway Astoria Festival, Queens, NYC, Late May
Welcome Back to Brooklyn, Brooklyn, NYC, Middle Jun.
Buskers Fare/Summer Fair, Manhattan, NYC, Middle Jun.
Central Park Summerstage, Manhattan, NYC, Middle Jun. to Early Aug.
Queens Boulevard Festival, Queens, NYC, Middle Jun.
Sounds at Sunset, Manhattan, NYC, Middle Jun. to Middle Sep.
Midsummer Night Swing, Manhattan, NYC, Late Jun. to Late Jul.
Celebrate Brooklyn Performing Arts Festival, Brooklyn, NYC, Late Jun. to Middle Aug.
Queens Festival/Nations in Neighborhoods Multicultural Dance Party, Queens, NYC, Late Jun.
Woodside Independence Weekend Festival, Queens, NYC, Early Jul.
Park Slope 5th Avenue Independence Day Festival, Brooklyn, NYC, Early Jul.
Steinway Street Fun in the Sun Festival, Queens, NYC, Early Jul.
Centerstage at the World Trade Center, Manhattan, NYC, Middle Jul. to Early Sep.
Midwood Concerts at Seaside, Brooklyn, NYC, Middle Jul. to Late Aug.
BACA Summer Celebration, Brooklyn, NYC, Middle Jul.
Lincoln Center Out-of-Doors, Manhattan, NYC, Early Aug. to Late Aug.
36th Avenue Summer Food Fair, Queens, NYC, Middle Aug.
Park Slope Festival, Brooklyn, NYC, Middle Aug.
Greenwich Avenue Summer Festival, Manhattan, NYC, Late Aug.
We Care About New York Block Party, Manhattan, NYC, Late Aug.
Rockaway Music and Arts Council Fall Festival, Brooklyn, NYC, Middle Sep.
New York Beer Fest, Brooklyn, NYC, Middle Sep.
Columbus Avenue Festival, Manhattan, NYC, Middle Sep.
Expressions International Festival, Manhattan, NYC, Late Sep. to Late Oct.

New York State Big Apple Festival, Manhattan, NYC, Late Sep.
Atlantic Antic, Brooklyn, NYC, Early Oct.
Community Holiday Festival, Manhattan, NYC, Late Dec. to Early Jan.

## Variety, Jazz and Blues

Portsmouth Jazz Festival, Portsmouth, NH, Late Jun.
White Mountain Jazz and Blues CraftsFestival, Bartlett, NH, Early Sep.
Discover Jazz Festival, Burlington, VT, Early Jun. to Middle Jun.
Bright Moments Festival, Amherst, MA, Middle Jul. to Late Jul.
Fabulous Fourth Festivities, Albany, NY, Early Jul.
Heineken Jazz and Blues Festival, Manhattan, NYC, Late Aug.

## Modern Jazz

Clark Terry/University of New Hampshire Jazz Festival, Durham, NH, Middle Mar.
Jazz Showcase, Portsmouth, NH, Late Jun.
Pico Mountain Jazz Festival, Sherburne, VT, Late Jul.
UMass Jazz Festival, North Dartmouth, MA, Early Mar.
Berklee College of Music High School Jazz Festival, Boston, MA, Early Mar.
Cambridge Public Library Jazz Festival, Cambridge, MA, Middle Jun.
Boston Globe Jazz Festival, Boston, MA, Middle Jun.
Boston Book Fair, Boston, MA, Middle Jun.
Yankee Music Festival Big Band Jazz Invitational, Salem, MA, Late Jun.
Boston Jazz Society Barbeque and Festival, Milton, MA, Early Aug.
Tanglewood Jazz Festival, Lenox, MA, Early Sep.
DeCordova Labor Day Jazz Festival, Lincoln, MA, Early Sep.
John Coltrane Memorial Concert, Boston, MA, Early Oct.
Whaling City Jazz Festival, New Bedford, MA, Early Oct.
Harlem Renaissance Garden Party, Cranston, RI, Middle Jun.
JVC Jazz Festival/Newport, Newport, RI, Middle Aug.
Greater Hartford Festival of Jazz Fundraiser, Hartford, CT, Middle Feb.
Jazz Expos, New Haven, CT, Late Feb.
Afternoon of Jazz, Norwalk, CT, Late Jun.
New Haven Jazz Festival, New Haven, CT, Early Jul. to Late Jul.
Duracell Jazz Festival, Danbury, CT, Middle Aug.
Hartford Jazz Society Riverboat Cruise, Middletown, CT, Middle Sep.
Winter Boogie, Monticello, NY, Late Jan.
College of Saint Rose High School Jazz Festival, Albany, NY, Late Mar.
Al Mastren Memorial Scholarship Concert, Cohoes, NY, Early Apr.
Swing Spring, Troy, NY, Late Apr.
Long Island Guitar Festival, Brookville, NY, Late Apr.
College of Saint Rose Collegiate Jazz Festival, Albany, NY, Late Apr.
New York State Intercollegiate Jazz Festival, Morrisville, NY, Late Apr.
Westchester Community College Jazz Festival, White Plains, NY, Early May
Jazz for the Arts/Super Jazz Jam Blowout , Albany, NY, Middle May
Syracuse Jazz Fest, Syracuse, NY, Middle Jun.
June Jazz, White Plains, NY, Middle Jun.
Newport Jazz Festival/Saratoga, Saratoga Springs, NY, Early Jul.
Summer Boogie, Ellenville, NY, Early Jul. to Middle Jul.
Jazz/Reggae Festival, Syracuse, NY, Late Jul.
Long Island Jazz Festival, Oyster Bay, NY, Late Jul.
Jazzfest Caramoor, Katonah, NY, Early Aug. to Middle Aug.

Pine Grill Jazz Reunion, Rochester, NY, Early Aug.
Anniversary Celebration of the Colored Musicians Club, Rochester, NY, Middle Aug.
Big Big Bands, Latham, NY, Middle Aug.
Opus 40 Legends of Jazz/Future of Jazz, Saugerties, NY, Middle Aug.
Oxhann Piano Festival, Clinton, NY, Late Aug.
Music and The Mountain Sky/Jazz Concert, Highmount, NY, Late Aug.
Islip Jazz Festival, Islip, NY, Late Aug.
Summer Jazz Festival, Elmira, NY, Late Aug.
Big Band Bash, Albany, NY, Late Aug.
Artpark Jazz Festival, Lewiston, NY, Early Sep.
Lake George Jazz Weekend, Lake George, NY, Early Sep. to Middle Sep.
Just Jazz, Somers, NY, Middle Sep.
Opus 40 Jazz Autumn, Saugerties, NY, Early Oct.
Jazz for the Arts/Kick Off, Albany, NY, Late Oct.
Stardust Dance Weekend, Ellenville, NY, Middle Nov. to Late Nov.
Smalls Winter Festival, Manhattan, NYC, Middle Feb.
Festival of Women Improvisors, Manhattan, NYC, Early Mar. to Middle Mar.
Women's Jazz Festival, Manhattan, NYC, Early Mar. to Late Mar.
Party for Zoot, Manhattan, NYC, Middle Mar.
American Swing Dance Championships, Manhattan, NYC, Early Apr.
New York Brass Conference for Scholarships, Manhattan, NYC, Early Apr.
Betty Carter's Jazz Ahead, Brooklyn, NYC, Early Apr.
Upper Broadway Spring Celebration and Festival, Manhattan, NYC, Late Apr.
Lower Second Avenue Festival, Manhattan, NYC, Early May
52nd Street Jazz Festival, Manhattan, NYC, Late May
Plantathon and Music Festival, Manhattan, NYC, Early Jun.
Cross Overs: Music of Asia America, Manhattan, NYC, Early Jun.
Broadway Summer Festival, Manhattan, NYC, Middle Jun.
Upper Broadway Summer Festival, Manhattan, NYC, Middle Jun.
Beacons In Jazz, Manhattan, NYC, Late Jun.
JVC Jazz Festival/Bryant Park Jazz Festival, Manhattan, NYC, Late Jun. to Early Jul.
Women in Jazz Festival, Manhattan, NYC, Early Jul.
B. M. I. Jazz Composer's Workshop Concert, Manhattan, NYC, Middle Jul.
Classical Jazz at Lincoln Center, Manhattan, NYC, Early Aug.
Riverside Park Arts Festival, Manhattan, NYC, Early Aug. to Late Aug.
Panasonic Village Jazz Festival, Manhattan, NYC, Middle Aug. to Late Aug.
Charlie Parker Jazz Festival, Manhattan, NYC, Late Aug.
West Side Arts, Crafts, Antiques Festival, Manhattan, NYC, Early Sep.
West Side Fall Festival, Manhattan, NYC, Early Sep.
QE2: Newport Jazz Festival at Sea, Manhattan, NYC, Middle Sep. to Late Sep.
Ecofest, Varies, NYC, Late Sep.
52nd Street Jazz Festival, Manhattan, NYC, Late Sep.
Cognac Hennessy Jazz Search, Manhattan, NYC, Late Sep.
Underground Jazz Festival, Manhattan, NYC, Early Oct.
All-Nite Soul, Manhattan, NYC, Early Oct.
Eleventh Avenue Auto Fair, Manhattan, NYC, Early Oct.
Live Jazz Bands, Queens, NYC, Middle Oct.
Cultural Crossroads' Jazz Gala, Brooklyn, NYC, Late Oct.
Charlie Parker Music and More Awards Gala, Manhattan, NYC, Early Nov.
JAL Jazz Concert, Manhattan, NYC, Early Nov.
Buddy Rich Memorial Scholarship Concert, Manhattan, NYC, Early Nov.
Juba, Jukin' and Jazzin', Manhattan, NYC, Early Nov.
Harlem Piano U. S. A., Manhattan, NYC, Middle Nov.
Big Band Day, Manhattan, NYC, Middle Nov.

JazzTimes Convention, Manhattan, NYC, Middle Nov.
Bending Toward the Light: A Jazz Nativity, Manhattan, NYC, Early Dec.
New York Jazz Today!, Manhattan, NYC, Middle Dec.
International Association of Jazz Educators Convention, Varied Sites, VAR, Middle Jan.
New England Foundation for the Arts Jazz Conference, Varied Sites, VAR, Early Jun. to Middle Jun.
International Duke Ellington Conference, Varied Sites, VAR, Middle Aug.

## Traditional Jazz and Ragtime

Arcady Music Festival/Ragtime Evening Benefit, Bangor, ME, Early Jun.
Down East Jazz Festival, Camden, ME, Late Aug.
Prescott Parks Arts Festival/Celebration of Jazz, Portsmouth, NH, Late Aug.
Hot Steamed Music Festival, Essex, CT, Late Jun.
Great Connecticut Traditional Jazz Festival, East Haddam, CT, Early Aug.
Southbury Jazz Festival, Southbury, CT, Early Sep.
New England Ragtime Festival, East Lyme, CT, Late Sep.
Grand International Ragtime/Jasstime Foundation Spring Festival, Alexandria Bay, NY, Late Apr.
Turk Murphy Memorial Festival, Buffalo, NY, Early May
Lake George Hot Jazz Party and Cruise, Lake George, NY, Middle Jun.
Columbia County Jazz Festival, West Ghent, NY, Late Jul.
International Dixeland Jazz and Ragtime Festival, Buffalo, NY, Late Jul.
Thousand Islands Jazz Festival, Alexandria Bay, NY, Early Aug.
Finger Lakes Dixieland Jazz Festival, Hector, NY, Late Aug.
Grand International Ragtime/Jasstime Foundation Fall Festival, Alexandria Bay, NY, Middle Nov.
Jazz in July, Manhattan, NYC, Late Jul.
Big Bands at Sea, Manhattan, NYC, Late Nov. to Early Dec.

## Alternative Jazz

R. A. W. Jazz Festival, Hartford, CT, Late Jul.
Improvisors Collective Festival, Manhattan, NYC, Early Mar.
Julius Watkins Jazz French Horn Festival, Manhattan, NYC, Middle Mar.
Stork Music Festival, Manhattan, NYC, Early Apr.
P. S. 122 Music Festival, Manhattan, NYC, Early Apr.
Corner Store Syndicate New Jazz Festival, Manhattan, NYC, Late Apr.
Sun Ra Festival, Manhattan, NYC, Middle May to Late May
Wall-to-Wall Rahsaan Roland Kirk, Manhattan, NYC, Early Jun.
Fire Wall Total Arts Festival, Manhattan, NYC, Middle Jun. to Late Jun.
Knitting Factory's "What is Jazz?" Festival, Manhattan, NYC, Middle Jun. to Early Jul.
Improvisors Festival, Manhattan, NYC, Late Jun. to Early Jul.
Acid Jazz Night, Manhattan, NYC, Early Oct.
Knitting Factory at Merkin Hall, Manhattan, NYC, Early Oct. to Middle Oct.

## Modern Rock and Pop

Coor's Lite Music Festival, Brewer, ME, Early Jul.
KISS-108 FM Concert, Mansfield, MA, Early Jun.
Rock 'N Roll Block Party, Holyoke, MA, Middle Jun.
WBCN Rock of Boston Concert, Boston, MA, Late Oct.
KISS 95.7 Anniversary Birthday Jam, Hartford, CT, Early Jan.

Taste of Summer, Middletown, CT, Middle May
Battle of the Bands, Westport, CT, Early Jul. to Middle Aug.
Rockfest, East Hartford, CT, Late Jul.
Springfest, Oceanside, NY, Middle Apr.
FLY92 Summer Jam, Latham, NY, Late Jun.
Summer Jam, Glens Falls, NY, Early Jul.
Sunday By the Bay, Bellport, NY, Early Jul.
Long Island Music Festival, Varies, NY, Middle Jul. to Early Sep.
Rally in the Alley, Buffalo, NY, Late Jul.
WBNY's Battle of the Bands, Buffalo, NY, Late Aug.
PYX Birthday Blowout!, Latham, NY, Late Aug.
Unifest, Buffalo, NY, Late Aug.
South Shore Music Festival, Oceanside, NY, Early Sep.
Great Miracle Prayer Festival, Manhattan, NYC, Late Feb.
Rainforest Benefit Concert, Manhattan, NYC, Middle Apr.
Songwriters' Hall of Fame Awards, Manhattan, NYC, Late May
Boathouse Rock, Manhattan, NYC, Middle Jun.
Life Beat Benefit:  The Music Industry Fights AIDS, Manhattan, NYC, Middle Jul.
MTV Music Awards, Manhattan, NYC, Early Sep.
Village Halloween Parade/All Souls' Halloween Ball, Manhattan, NYC, Late Oct.
K-Rock's Hungerthon, Manhattan, NYC, Middle Nov.
AIDS Dance-A-Thon, Manhattan, NYC, Late Nov.

## Classic Rock and Oldies

Rock 'N' Roll Bar-B-Q, Old Orchard Beach, ME, Early Jul.
Classic Rock Festival, Plymouth, NH, Late Jun.
Harvey Robbins' Royalty of Rock 'n Roll/Cape Cod Melody Tent, Hyannis, MA, Middle Aug.
Summer Sizzler, East Hartford, CT, Middle Jul.
Rock and Roll Hall of Fame Revue, Danbury, CT, Late Jul.
Psychofest, Kingston, NY, Middle Jun.
Real Woodstock Festival, Woodstock, NY, Middle Jul.
Transportation Heritage Festival, Kingston, NY, Late Jul.
Rockstalgia, Hunter, NY, Early Aug.
Royalty of Rock and Roll, Latham, NY, Middle Aug.
Downtown Festival/Rock Fest , Rochester, NY, Late Aug.
Labor Day Weekend Blowout, Parksville, NY, Early Sep.
Buckwheat Harvest Festival, Penn Yan, NY, Late Sep.
WPLJ-FM's 70's Rock and Roll Reunion, Manhattan, NYC, Late Mar.
Say It With Love Night, Manhattan, NYC, Middle May
Brooklyn Rock Awards, Brooklyn, NYC, Middle May
WPLJ-FM's 70's Dance Party, Manhattan, NYC, Middle Jun.
WPLJ-FM's 70's Dance Party, Manhattan, NYC, Middle Sep.
Richard Nader's Rock and Roll Revival Spectacular, Manhattan, NYC, Middle Nov.
Rock and Roll Hall of Fame Induction Dinner, Varied Sites, VAR, Middle Jan.

## Alternative and College Rock

Sugarloaf Ski-A-Palooza/College Weeks, Kingfield, ME, Early Jan. to Middle Jan.
Loon MountainPark BrewFest, Lincoln, NH, Late Jul.
Mountain Jam, Killington, VT, Early Jul.
Battle of the Bands, Burlington, VT, Early Nov.
Boston Phoenix/WFNX Best Music Poll Celebration, Boston, MA, Late Mar.

Loud Music Festival, Northampton, MA, Early Apr.
Kenmore Square Rites of Spring Charity Rockfest, Boston, MA, Late Apr.
Students for Students/Human Rights Festival, Boston, MA, Late Apr.
Harpoon's Brewstock, Boston, MA, Late Jun.
Fun Summer Concerts, Wellfleet, MA, Late Jun.
Carlos Fest, Brookline, MA, Middle Aug.
Bud Rocks the Block Party, Lowell, MA, Middle Sep.
WFNX Birthday Party, Boston, MA, Early Nov.
Lupo's Birthday Party, Providence, RI, Early Jul.
Shake-a-Leg Benefit Concert, Newport, RI, Middle Aug.
Alternative Skateboard Festival, Woodbury, CT, Late May
Local Bands on the Downtown Green, New Haven, CT, Middle Jun. to Late Aug.
WPLR July 4th Celebration, New Haven, CT, Early Jul.
Earth Jam, Woodstock, CT, Middle Aug.
WPLR Labor Day Celebration, New Haven, CT, Early Sep.
Welcome Back to School Show: The Beginning of the End, New Haven, CT, Early Sep.
PYX Rock and Roll Expo, Albany, NY, Late Mar.
WEQX Party in the Park, Albany, NY, Late Apr.
Band Box Anniversary Love-Fest/Wife-Swap, Port Chester, NY, Middle May
Great Blue Heron Music Festival, Sherman, NY, Early Jul.
Bill LaBeef's Bastille Day, Barbeque and Rock and Roll Rodeo, Rochester, NY, Middle Jul.
Middlesex Music Fest, Middlesex, NY, Late Jul.
Roch-A-Palooza , Rochester, NY, Late Jul.
Park Jam, Schenectady, NY, Early Aug.
Micky Rat's City Jam, Buffalo, NY, Early Aug.
Woodstock New Music Festival, Woodstock, NY, Early Aug.
Localpalooza Festival, Rochester, NY, Early Sep.
Alternative Sports and Music Festival, Middletown, NY, Early Oct.
WEQX Birthday Party/University of Albany Fallfest, Albany, NY, Early Oct.
WEQX Acoustic Holiday Concert for the Hungry, Latham, NY, Middle Dec.
Evian Indoor Pro Beach Volleyball Championships, Manhattan, NYC, Late Feb.
Bill Popp's Birthday Tribute to George L. Popp, Manhattan, NYC, Early Mar.
Tokyo/New York Noise Festival, Manhattan, NYC, Middle Mar.
Independent Music Fest, Manhattan, NYC, Late Mar. to Early Apr.
Z100 May Day, Manhattan, NYC, Middle May
Rock Against Racism Concert, Manhattan, NYC, Late May
Brooklyn Woodstock, Brooklyn, NYC, Early Jun.
Discmakers Unsigned Band/Artist New York World Series, Manhattan, NYC, Early Jun.
Downtown Music Gallery's Anniversary Celebration, Manhattan, NYC, Middle Jun.
Macintosh New York Music Festival, Manhattan, NYC, Middle Jul. to Late Jul.
CMJ Music Marathon and Musicfest, Manhattan, NYC, Early Sep.
WDRE Modern Rock Fest, Manhattan, NYC, Early Oct.
Jimi Hendrix Birthday Party, Manhattan, NYC, Late Nov.
Post-Rock, Neo-Mosh Festival, Manhattan, NYC, Early Dec.
Z100 Acoustic Christmas, Manhattan, NYC, Early Dec.
WNEW-FM Christmas Concert, Manhattan, NYC, Early Dec.
WDRE Acoustic Christmas, Manhattan, NYC, Middle Dec.

## Hard Rock and Heavy Metal

WBCN Rock 'n' Roll Rumble, Boston, MA, Early May to Late May
Barnaby's Battle of the Bands, Centereach, NY, Early Apr.
Memorial Day Weekend Festival, Parksville, NY, Late May
Hempsplash, Parksville, NY, Early Jun.

No Bummer Summer Party Jam, Parksville, NY, Middle Jun.
Gruntstock, Parksville, NY, Early Jul.
Radioactive Bodega Blacklight Prom, Brooklyn, NYC, Late Apr.
Super Radioactive Bodega Bonanza Outdoor Festival, Brooklyn, NYC, Middle Jun.

### Rap

Hot 97's Old School Throwdown, Manhattan, NYC, Late Jan.
The Brooklyn Beat Meets The Black Rock Coalition, Manhattan, NYC, Middle Mar.
360 Degrees Black: New York's Hip Hop Music Seminar, Manhattan, NYC, Middle Jul.
Slammin' Jammin' Spike's Joint Anniversary Block Party, Brooklyn, NYC, Late Jul.
The Source Awards, Manhattan, NYC, Early Aug.
Uprise and Shine Youth Concert, Brooklyn, NYC, Late Aug.

### Modern R&B

Boston Kite Festival, Boston, MA, Middle May
Funkfest, New Haven, CT, Early Jul.
FLY92 End of Summer Jam, Latham, NY, Middle Sep.
Lou Rawls Parade of Stars, Manhattan, NYC, Early Jan.
Essence Awards, Manhattan, NYC, Late Apr.
Budweiser Superfest, Manhattan, NYC, Late Jul.
WBLS Celebration Concert and Scholarship Fund, Manhattan, NYC, Early Dec.
Colors of Christmas, Manhattan, NYC, Early Dec.

### Blues and Traditional R&B

Sugarloaf Mountain Blues Festival, Kingfield, ME, Middle Apr.
Blues Festival, North Yarmouth, ME, Late Jun.
North Atlantic Blues Festival, Rockland, ME, Early Jul.
Left Bank Cafe Country Blues Festival, Blue Hill, ME, Middle Jul.
New England Blues Conference, Portsmouth, NH, Late Apr.
Blues Festival, Portsmouth, NH, Early Sep.
Boston Blues Festival, Allston, MA, Late Jan. to Late Feb.
Boston Brewer's Festival, Boston, MA, Middle May
Battle of the Blues Bands, Allston, MA, Late Jun. to Early Jul.
City of Presidents Blues Festival, Quincy, MA, Early Jul.
Summertime Blues Weekend, Lowell, MA, Middle Aug.
Newport Rhythm and Blues Festival, Newport, RI, Late Jul.
Blues Bash for Homeless People, Smithfield, RI, Late Aug.
Blues Blockbusters, New Haven, CT, Middle Jun.
Blues at the Ives, Danbury, CT, Late Jun.
Global Blues Fest, Norwalk, CT, Early Jul.
Great American Blues Festival, Woodstock, CT, Middle Jul.
Rock 'N' Blues AIDS Benefit, East Hartford, CT, Late Jul.
Southern Fried Festival, Woodbury, CT, Middle Aug.
Westport Blues Festival, Westport, CT, Late Sep.
Spring Blues Festival, Westbury, NY, Late Apr.
Uncle Sam's Blues Jam, Troy, NY, Early May
Lark Street Blues Festival, Albany, NY, Early Jun.
Blueshounds Benefit, Albany, NY, Early Jun.
Mayhem on the Mountain, Mariaville, NY, Middle Jun.
Local Motion MusicFest, Middletown, NY, Middle Jun.

Blues in the Night, Rochester, NY, Early Jul.
Averill Park Summer Blues Fest, Averill Park, NY, Middle Jul.
Rhythm and Blues Beach Party, Caroga Lake, NY, Middle Jul.
Opus 40 New Orleans Party Weekend, Saugerties, NY, Late Jul.
New York State Budweiser Blues Festival, Syracuse, NY, Late Jul.
Blues Bar-B-Que, Schenectady, NY, Early Aug.
Outdoor Blues Festival, Latham, NY, Middle Aug.
Blues Fest, Patterson, NY, Middle Aug.
Local Motion MusicFest, Middletown, NY, Early Sep.
Summertime Blues Charity Cruise, Troy, NY, Middle Oct.
Hungerthon Concert/Winter Blues Fest, New City, NY, Middle Nov.
Valentine's XMas Jam, Albany, NY, Middle Dec.
Holiday Jam for Joy, Rotterdam, NY, Middle Dec.
Rhythm and Blues Foundation's Pioneer Awards, Manhattan, NYC, Early Mar.
New York Winter Blues Festival, Manhattan, NYC, Late Mar.
Murray Hill Block Party and Blues Festival, Manhattan, NYC, Early Jun.
Underground Blues and Folk Festival, Manhattan, NYC, Late Jun.

## Acappella and Doo-Wop

Barbershop Quartet Benefit Concert, Block Island, RI, Late Jul.
Barbershop Harmony Day, Mystic, CT, Middle Sep.
Dick Fox's Spring Doo-Wopp Extravaganza, Westbury, NY, Early Mar.
Richard Nader's Let the Good Times Roll, Kiamesha Lake, NY, Early Mar. to Middle Mar.
Dick Fox's Summer Doo-Wopp Extravaganza, Westbury, NY, Early Jun.
WCBS-FM 101 Day, Rye, NY, Middle Jun.
Battle of the Acappella Groups, Poughkeepsie, NY, Middle Jun.
Richard Nader's Let the Good Times Roll, Kiamesha Lake, NY, Late Jul. to Middle Mar.
Bolton Landing Barbershop Quartet Festival, Bolton Landing, NY, Early Sep.
Dick Fox's Fall Doo-Wopp Extravaganza, Westbury, NY, Middle Sep.
Bopper's Oldies Concert, Huntington, NY, Late Sep.
Dick Fox's Ultimate Doo-Wopp Fantasy Weekend, Monitcello, NY, Early Oct.
Barbershop Serenade, Buffalo, NY, Middle Nov.
Dick Fox's Holiday Doo-Wopp Extravaganza, Westbury, NY, Middle Dec.
U. G. H. A. Black History Month Celebration, Manhattan, NYC, Middle Feb.
Evening of Rock and Roll, Manhattan, NYC, Middle Mar.
Wall of Sound, Queens, NYC, Late Mar.
Harmony Sweepstakes A Cappella Festival/New York Regional, Manhattan, NYC, Early Apr.
U. G. H. A. Hall of Fame Awards Ceremony, Manhattan, NYC, Early Apr.
Dick Fox's Brooklyn Paramount Reunion, Manhattan, NYC, Early May
Rock-N-Roll Extravaganza, Queens, NYC, Early Aug.
Return of The Brooklyn Bridge, Queens, NYC, Late Nov.

## Modern Christian

Newsound Festival, Merrimac, MA, Early Sep.
Praise, Darien Lake, NY, Late May
Glory, Valley Falls, NY, Early Jun.
Glory, Lake George, NY, Early Jun.
WLIX Fest, Jamesport, NY, Middle Aug.
Kingdom Bound, Darien Lake, NY, Late Aug.
Niagara: The Student and Adult Leadership Conference on Evangelism, Niagara Falls, NY, Late
    Dec.

El Elyon Music Fest, Brooklyn, NYC, Early Jul.
El Elyon Music Awards, Manhattan, NYC, Early Dec.

## Black Gospel

CMAC's A Joyful Noise, Cambridge, MA, Middle Jan.
Praise and Harmony, Lowell, MA, Middle Jun.
Gospel Festival, Hartford, CT, Middle Feb.
Barnum Festival/Gospel Festival, Bridgeport, CT, Middle Jun.
Gospel Extravaganza, Kingston, NY, Middle Jun.
Waterfront Festival Free Summer Concert Series/Gospel in the Park, Buffalo, NY, Middle Jul.
McDonald's Gospelfest, Buffalo, NY, Late Jul.
Hamilton Hill Culturefest/Gospel Festival, Schenectady, NY, Early Aug.
Gospel Celebration!, Brooklyn, NYC, Early Feb.
98.7 KISS-FM Gospel Celebration, Manhattan, NYC, Middle Feb.
National Gospel Choir Competition, Manhattan, NYC, Middle Mar.
Gospel Explosion, Brooklyn, NYC, Late Mar.
McDonald's Gospelfest, Varies, NYC, Early Apr. to Middle Jun.
Easter Gospel Festival, Manhattan, NYC, Middle Apr.
Gospel Comes/Returns to Broadway, Manhattan, NYC, Late Apr.
Religious Music Festival, Brooklyn, NYC, Late Apr.
Queens College Cultural Heritage Great Gospel Competition, Queens, NYC, Middle May
Hezekiah Walker Anniversary Show, Brooklyn, NYC, Late May
Gospel Concert, Brooklyn, NYC, Early Jun.
New York City's Gospel Festival, Brooklyn, NYC, Middle Jun.
Gospel Music Workshop of America/New York State Chapter Convention, Brooklyn, NYC, Middle Jun.
Gospelfest, Brooklyn, NYC, Middle Jun.
July Gospel Explosion, Brooklyn, NYC, Early Jul.
Gospel Nite, Manhattan, NYC, Middle Jul.
I. C. C. Songfest, Staten Island, NYC, Early Aug.
WWRL Family Day and Picnic, Queens, NYC, Early Aug. to Middle Aug.
98.7 KISS-FM Gospel Celebration, Manhattan, NYC, Late Aug.
Brooklyn's Summer Gospelfest!, Brooklyn, NYC, Early Sep.
Choose Life Benefit Gospel Concert, Manhattan, NYC, Middle Oct.
WWRL Gospel Explosion, Manhattan, NYC, Middle Dec.
Gospel Music Workshop of America National Convention, Varied Sites, VAR, Early Aug. to Middle Aug.
National Baptist Convention of America, Varied Sites, VAR, Early Sep. to Middle Sep.

## Southern and Bluegrass Gospel

Great Awakening Fest, Granby, MA, Middle Sep.
Gospel Night, Buffalo, NY, Late Oct.

## Traditional Gospel and Sings

Sudbury Canada Days, Bethel, ME, Middle Aug.
Lamplight Service and Hymn Sing, North Danville, VT, Late May to Late Aug.
New England Sacred Harp Singing Convention, Wellesley, MA, Early Oct.
Connecticut Convention of the Sacred Harp, Middletown, CT, Early Jul. to Middle Jul.
Community Carol Sing, Mystic, CT, Middle Dec.
New York State Sacred Harp Singing Convention, Ithaca, NY, Middle Oct.

New England Sacred Harp Singing Convention, Varied Sites, VAR, Early Oct.

## Variety, Country and Bluegrass

All AmericanFest, Lincoln, NH, Early Jul.
Bluegrass Festival, Washington, MA, Late May
Chopmist Hill Inn Summer Festival, North Scituate, RI, Late Aug.
Swamp Yankee Days, Charlestown, RI, Late Sep.
Twin Rivers Jamboree, Tuscarora, NY, Early Aug.
Catskill Harvest Festival, Walton, NY, Early Oct.
North East Country Music Association Awards Show, Albany, NY, Middle Oct.

## Modern Country

Sugarloaf Country Music Festival, Kingfield, ME, Late Jun. to Late Aug.
Maine Invitational Country Music Semi-Finals Show, West Buxton, ME, Middle Sep. to Late Sep.
Maine Invitational Country Music Finals Show, West Buxton, ME, Early Nov.
Countryfest, Laconia, NH, Early Mar.
Twin Mountain Country Western Jamboree, Bretton Woods, NH, Early Jul.
Arts Jubilee/Country in the Valley, North Conway, NH, Late Aug.
Hot Country Music Festival, Burlington, VT, Middle Aug.
Coors Country Chili Fest, Stratton Mountain, VT, Late Aug.
Vermont Brewers Festival, Various, VT, Middle Sep.
Make-a-Wish-Foundation Country Jamboree, Ipswich, MA, Middle May
Indian Ranch Country Music Festival and Chicken Barbeque, Webster, MA, Late May
Country Music Festival to Benefit American Heart Association, Webster, MA, Late May
WBCS Boston Country Sunday, Mansfield, MA, Late Jun.
WPVQ Music Day, Greenfield, MA, Late Jul.
WCLB Country Club Festival, Foxboro, MA, Late Jul.
New England Country Jamboree, Webster, MA, Middle Sep.
Pedal Steel Guitar Anniversary Bash, Lee, MA, Early Sep.
John Penny Liver Foundation Jamboree, Webster, MA, Middle Sep.
Country Fest, Webster, MA, Middle Sep.
M. C. M. A. A. Awards Show, Randolph, MA, Late Sep.
Country Music Shows, Escoheag, RI, Middle Jun. to Early Aug.
Country Jamborees, New Haven, CT, Late Apr.
Great American Music Fest, Goshen, CT, Late Jun.
BASH: Bradley Airport Summer Happening, Windsor Locks, CT, Late Jul.
Newcomers of Country, Wallingford, CT, Middle Aug.
Lobsterfest/Celebrate Canton, Canton, CT, Middle Aug.
Strawberry Park Country Western Jamboree, Preston, CT, Late Sep.
Country Classic in the Catskills, South Fallsburg, NY, Early Apr.
Songwriter Showcase, Deer Park, NY, Middle Apr.
Benefit for the Fight Against Leukemia, Deer Park, NY, Late May
Fundraiser, West Shokan, NY, Middle Jun.
Country Western Festival, Cambridge, NY, Middle Jun.
New York State Championship Chili Cookoff, New Paltz, NY, Late Jun.
WGNA Country Fest, Altamont, NY, Early Jul.
Independence Celebration and Double R Championship Rodeo, Rhinebeck, NY, Early Jul.
Cairo Appreciation Day Fair, Cairo, NY, Early Jul.
Del-Se-Nango Fiddlers Festival, Bainbridge, NY, Early Jul.
Country Music Festival , Hunter, NY, Middle Jul. to Late Jul.
Round Lake Country Music Festival, Round Lake, NY, Late Jul.

Jeffersonville Jamboree, Jeffersonville, NY, Late Jul.
Del-Se-Nango Fiddlers Festival and Bluegrass Sunday, Bainbridge, NY, Early Aug.
River Fest, Fulton, NY, Early Aug.
Coxsackie Riverside Arts and Crafts Festival, Coxsackie, NY, Early Aug.
Country Music Festival Encore, Hunter, NY, Early Aug. to Middle Aug.
Buffalo Country Music Awards, Buffalo, NY, Middle Sep.
Autumn Harvest Festival, Cooperstown, NY, Middle Sep.
Swain Country Western Music Festival, Swain, NY, Early Oct.
Fall Country Dance and Party Weekend, Kerhonkson, NY, Middle Oct.
Fall Jamboree, Rochester, NY, Late Oct.
Festival of Lights, Niagara Falls, NY, Middle Nov. to Early Jan.
Country Music Dance Weekend, South Fallsburg, NY, Early Dec.
Earth Day Celebration, Manhattan, NYC, Late Apr.
Broadway County Fair, Manhattan, NYC, Late May
New York Country Music Festival, Queens, NYC, Middle Aug.
Northeast Invitational Country Music Awards Show, Varied Sites, VAR, Middle Feb.

### Traditional Country

River Tree Arts Country Jamboree, Kennebunk, ME, Middle Mar.
Buttermilk Hill Old Time Music Show, Belgrade Lakes, ME, Middle Aug.
Old Time Country Music Festival, Hebron, ME, Early Sep.
Old Time Country Jamboree, Waterville, ME, Middle Sep.
Earl's Sunshine Festival, Chaffee, NY, Late Jun. to Middle Sep.
Old Time Music Festival and Barbeque, Stone Mills, NY, Middle Jul.
Band Jamboree, Osceola, NY, Early Sep.

### Alternative Country and Rockabilly

Meck Music Fest, Mecklenberg, NY, Late Aug.
National Rockabilly Blowout, Rochester, NY, Late Oct.
Great Beer and Music Festival, Manhattan, NYC, Middle Jan.
Great Beer and Music Festival, Manhattan, NYC, Late Mar.
Death and Taxes, Manhattan, NYC, Middle Apr.
Great Beer and Music Festival, Manhattan, NYC, Middle Nov.

### Bluegrass

Blistered Fingers Helping Hands of Bluegrass, Brunswick, ME, Late Mar. to Early Apr.
Fiddlehead Festival, Unity, ME, Middle May
Hebron Pines Bluegrass Festival, Hebron, ME, Late May
Happy Horseshoe Blue Grass Festival, North New Portland, ME, Middle Jun.
Blistered Fingers Family Bluegrass Music Festival, Sidney, ME, Middle Jun.
Katahdin Family Bluegrass Music Festival, Medway, ME, Late Jun.
New Vineyard Mountains Bluegrass Festival, North Anson, ME, Early Jul.
Breakneck Mountain Bluegrass Festival, Crawford, ME, Early Jul.
Oxford County Bluegrass Festival, Norway/Oxford, ME, Middle Aug.
New England Salty Dog Bluegrass Festival, Cambridge, ME, Late Aug.
Thomas Point Beach Bluegrass Festival, Brunswick, ME, Early Sep.
New England Bluegrass Festival, Laconia, NH, Middle Jun.
Gilmanton Bluegrass Festival, Gilmanton, NH, Middle Jul.
Hayseed Music Fest, Franconia, NH, Middle Jul.
Pemi Valley Bluegrass Festival, Campton, NH, Early Aug.

Rattling Brook Bluegrass Festival, Belvidere, VT, Middle Jun.
Basin Bluegrass Festival, Brandon, VT, Early Jul.
Northeast Indoor Blue Grass Festival, Boxborough, MA, Early Feb. to Middle Feb.
Joe Val Memorial Bluegrass Festival, Waltham, MA, Late Jun.
Pickin' in the Pines Bluegrass Day, Northampton, MA, Late Jun.
Blandford Mountain Bluegrass Festival, Blandford, MA, Early Jul.
Nutmeg Bluegrass Get-Together, Burlington, CT, Middle May
Bluegrass Festival, Woodstock, CT, Late May
Strawberry Park Bluegrass Festival, Preston, CT, Early Jun.
Sterling Park Campground Bluegrass Festival, Sterling, CT, Early Jun. to Middle Jun.
Mineral Springs Foot Stomp'n Festival, Stafford Springs, CT, Late Jun. to Early Jul.
Connecticut River Valley Bluegrass Festival, East Haddam, CT, Middle Aug.
Sterling Park Campground Bluegrass Festival, Sterling, CT, Middle Sep.
Mineral Springs Foot Stomp'n Festival, Stafford Springs, CT, Early Oct.
Penny Association Midwinter Bluegrass Festival, Vestal, NY, Early Mar.
Pines Hotel Bluegrass Festival, South Fallsburg, NY, Middle Mar.
Penny Association Memorial Day Bluegrass and Country Music Festival, Coventryville, NY,
    Late May
Bluegrass Roundup, Galway, NY, Early Jun.
Thousand Islands Bluegrass Festival, Clayton, NY, Early Jun. to Middle Jun.
Bluegrass on the Green, Homer, NY, Early Jun.
Laing Family Bluegrass Festival, Bainbridge, NY, Middle Jun.
Madrid Bluegrass Festival, Madrid, NY, Late Jun.
Squaredance and Bluegrass Festival, Hartford, NY, Late Jun.
Penny Association Olde Tyme Country Music Festival, Coventryville, NY, Late Jun. to Early Jul.
Maple Ridge Bluegrass Festival, Duanesburg, NY, Early Jul. to Middle Jul.
Panama Rocks Folk Arts Fair, Panama, NY, Early Jul. to Middle Jul.
Peaceful Valley Bluegrass Festival, Shinhopple, NY, Middle Jul.
Winterhawk Bluegrass Family Festival, Ancramdale, NY, Middle Jul.
Rick and Carol's Country Side Inn Bluegrass Festival, Fort Ann, NY, Late Jul.
Low Bridge Festival, Lyons, NY, Late Jul.
Creek Bend Music Festival, Akron, NY, Late Jul.
Penny Association Bluegrass and Country Music Festival, Tioga Center, NY, Late Jul.
Rooney Mountain Bluegrass Festival, Deposit, NY, Late Jul. to Early Aug.
Dean Mountain Bluegrass Festival, Hadley, NY, Late Jul. to Early Aug.
Bill Knowlton's Bluegrass Ramble Picnic, Sandy Creek, NY, Early Aug.
Bluegrass Festival, Broadalbin, NY, Early Aug.
Corinth Bluegrass Festival, Corinth, NY, Early Aug. to Middle Aug.
Fox Family Bluegrass Festival, Old Forge, NY, Middle Aug.
Super Bluegrass and Gospel Day, Norwich, NY, Middle Aug.
Southern Tier Bluegrass Festival, Savona, NY, Middle Aug.
St. Lawrence Valley Bluegrass Festival, Gouveneur, NY, Middle Aug.
Long Lake Bluegrass Festival, Long Lake, NY, Middle Aug.
Schneider's Bluegrass Festival, Elmira, NY, Late Aug.
Nichols Family Bluegrass Festival, Nichols, NY, Late Aug.
Bluegrass Festival, Rochester, NY, Late Aug.
Wrench Wranch Bluegrass Roundup, Coventryville, NY, Early Sep.
Lazy River Bluegrass Festival , Gardiner, NY, Middle Sep.
Great New York Mandolin Weekend, Manhattan, NYC, Early Apr.
Great New York Mandolin Gala, Manhattan, NYC, Middle Apr.
Bluegrass Bash, Manhattan, NYC, Early Sep.

## Variety, Folk and International

Acadian Festival Celebration, Madawaska, ME, Late Jun. to Early Jul.
Festival de la Bastille, Augusta, ME, Early Jul.
Maine Festival of the Arts, Brunswick, ME, Early Aug.
Sweet Chariot Music Festival and Schooner Gam, Swans Island, ME, Early Aug.
Knights of Columbus Festival de Joie, Lewiston, ME, Early Aug.
International Festival, Manchester, NH, Early May
Star Hampshire Traditional Music/Dance Retreat, Portsmouth, NH, Late Sep.
First Night Keene, Keene, NH, Late Dec.
First Night New Hampshire, Concord, NH, Late Dec.
First Night Portsmouth, Portsmouth, NH, Late Dec.
Rutland Region Ethnic Festival, Rutland, VT, Late Jun.
Midsummer Festival of Vermont Art and Music, Montpelier, VT, Early Jul.
Families Outdoor Festival, Ferrisburgh, VT, Middle Jul.
Middlebury Summer Festival-on-the-Green, Middlebury, VT, Middle Jul.
Champlain Valley Festival, Burlington, VT, Early Aug.
Chandler's New World Festival, Randolph, VT, Early Sep.
Shelburne Farms Harvest Festival, Shelburne, VT, Middle Sep.
Vermont Apple Festival and Crafts Show, Springfield, VT, Middle Oct.
French Heritage Festival, Barre, VT, Late Oct.
First Night Burlington, Burlington, VT, Late Dec.
First Night Rutland, Rutland, VT, Late Dec.
First Night St. Johnsbury, St. Johnsbury, VT, Late Dec.
Songstreet Folk and Bluegrass Fest, Cambridge, MA, Early Feb.
Gloucester Folklife Festival, Gloucester, MA, Early Mar.
Songstreet Cajun-Bluegrass Festival, Somerville, MA, Early Apr.
World Fair at Boston University, Boston, MA, Early Apr. to Middle Apr.
New England Folk Festival, Natick, MA, Late Apr.
Salem Seaport Festival, Salem, MA, Late May
Jamaica Plain Folk Festival, Jamaica Plain, MA, Early Jun.
Cambridge International Fair, Cambridge, MA, Middle Jun.
Boston Waterfront Festival, Boston, MA, Middle Jun.
Cambridge Street Performer's Festival, Cambridge, MA, Late Jun.
Marblehead Festival of the Arts, Marblehead, MA, Late Jun. to Early Jul.
Boarding House Park Concert Series Kickoff, Lowell, MA, Early Jul.
Oxfam America WorldFest, Boston, MA, Early Jul. to Middle Jul.
Multicultural Family Festival, Roxbury, MA, Middle Jul.
Provincetown Waterfront Festival, Provincetown, MA, Middle Jul. to Late Jul.
Lowell Folk Festival, Lowell, MA, Middle Jul.
ARTBEAT, Somerville, MA, Late Jul.
Gloucester Waterfront Festival, Gloucester, MA, Middle Aug.
Newburyport Waterfront Festival, Newburyport, MA, Early Sep.
Bread and Roses Labor Day Heritage Heritage Festival, Lawrence, MA, Early Sep.
Septemberfest, Groton, MA, Middle Sep.
Codman Farm Festival, Lincoln, MA, Middle Sep.
Boston International Festival, Dorchester, MA, Late Oct. to Late Nov.
First Night Boston, Boston, MA, Late Dec.
First Night Brockton, Brockton, MA, Late Dec.
First Night Chatham, Chatham, MA, Late Dec.
First Night in Hyannis, Falmouth, MA, Late Dec.
First Night New Bedford, New Bedford, MA, Late Dec.
First Night Newburyport, Newburyport, MA, Late Dec.
First Night Northampton, Northampton, MA, Late Dec.

First Night Pittsfield, Pittsfield, MA, Late Dec.

First Night Quincy, Quincy, MA, Late Dec.

First Night Worcester, Worcester, MA, Late Dec.

Opening Night, Salem, Salem, MA, Late Dec.

Labor and Ethnic Heritage Festival, Pawtucket, RI, Early Sep.

Rhode Island's Heritage Day, Providence, RI, Middle Sep.

Norman Bird Sanctuary Harvest Fair, Middletown, RI, Early Oct.

First Night Providence, Providence, RI, Late Dec.

Opening Night, Newport, RI, Late Dec.

Connecticut Historical Society's International Spring Festival, Hartford, CT, Early Apr.

Brass Valley Ethnic Music Festival, Waterbury, CT, Middle Jun.

World Music Fest, Groton, CT, Late Jul.

Positively Pomfret Day, Putnam, CT, Late Jul.

Trumbull Arts Festival, Trumbull, CT, Middle Sep.

Apple Harvest Festival, Glastonbury, CT, Middle Oct.

NOMAD: Northeast Music, Art and Dance Festival, Sandy Hook, CT, Late Oct. to Early Nov.

First Night Danbury, Danbury, CT, Late Dec.

First Night Hartford, Hartford, CT, Late Dec.

Dance Flurry, Guilderland, NY, Middle Feb.

In Women's Hands: The Beat of the Drum, Albany, NY, Early Mar.

William Smith and Hobart Colleges Folk Fest, Geneva, NY, Early May

Two Rivers Ethnic Festival, Binghamton, NY, Early May

I. A. C. A.'s International Festival of the Adirondacks, Queensbury, NY, Middle May

Intergenerational International Festival, Garden City, NY, Middle Jun.

Clearwater's Great Hudson River Revival, Valhalla, NY, Middle Jun.

Old Songs Festival of Traditional Music and Dance, Altamont, NY, Late Jun.

Inwood World Music Festival, Inwood, NY, Late Jun.

Mohonk's Festival of the Arts/International Week, New Paltz, NY, Middle Jul. to Late Jul.

Falcon Ridge Folk Festival, Hillsdale, NY, Late Jul.

International Fun Fest, Monroe, NY, Late Jul.

Putnam County 4-H Fair, Carmel, NY, Late Jul. to Early Aug.

International Music and Dance Festival, Sacketts Harbor, NY, Early Sep.

International Waterfront Festival, Newburgh, NY, Early Sep.

Roberson's Holiday and Arts Festival, Binghamton, NY, Early Sep. to Middle Sep.

Fiddlers!!: A Sampler of North American Fiddle Traditions, Roxbury, NY, Early Oct.

First Night Albany, Albany, NY, Late Dec.

First Night Buffalo, Buffalo, NY, Late Dec.

First Night Freeport, Freeport, NY, Late Dec.

New Year's Early Eve, Rochester, NY, Late Dec.

Mardi Gras Carnaval, Manhattan, NYC, Middle Feb.

Festival of Nations, Manhattan, NYC, Early Apr.

Carnegie Hall Folk Festival, Manhattan, NYC, Middle Apr. to Late Apr.

Union Settlement Ethnic Festival, Manhattan, NYC, Middle May

Manhattan Ethnic Music and Dance Festival, Manhattan, NYC, Late May

Celebrate 125! The Rhythm of the World, Manhattan, NYC, Early Jun.

World of Percussion, Manhattan, NYC, Early Jun.

Bronx Ethnic Music and Dance Festival, Bronx, NYC, Middle Jun.

City Lore Festival, Manhattan, NYC, Middle Jun.

Winter Consort Summer Solstice Whole Earth Celebration, Manhattan, NYC, Late Jun.

City Gardeners' Harvest Fair/Gateway Music Festival/New York City Bluegrass Band and
    Banjo Festival, Brooklyn, NYC, Late Aug.

Roots of American Music Festival, Manhattan, NYC, Late Aug.

International Festival of Cultures, Staten Island, NYC, Middle Sep.

Do the Right Thing Festival, Brooklyn, NYC, Late Sep.

Nations of New York Arts Festival, Manhattan, NYC, Middle Oct. to Late Oct.
Brooklyn Ethnic Music and Dance Festival, Brooklyn, NYC, Late Oct.
Winter Consort Winter Solstice Whole Earth Christmas Celebration, Manhattan, NYC, Middle Dec.
Sounds Around the World, Manhattan, NYC, Middle Dec.
Concert for Peace, Manhattan, NYC, Late Dec.
First Night New York, Manhattan, NYC, Late Dec.
People's Music Network Winter Gathering, Varied Sites, VAR, Late Jan.
Folk Alliance Conference, Varied Sites, VAR, Middle Feb.

## Modern Folk

Portland Waterfront Festival, Portland, ME, Late Jun.
Celebration of the Arts, Kennebunk, ME, Middle Jul. to Late Jul.
Circle of Sound Benefit Concert, Bath, ME, Late Aug.
Maine Healing Arts Festival, Freedom, ME, Early Sep.
Rockport Folk Festival, Rockport, ME, Middle Sep.
New Hampshire Women's Music Festival, Northfield, NH, Middle Jun.
Labor Day Weekend Music Festival, Conway, NH, Early Sep.
Cabin Fever Folklife Festival, Middlebury, VT, Early Apr.
Bennington Folk Festival, Bennington, VT, Middle May
Vermont Women's Celebration, Burlington, VT, Late Jul.
Green Mountain Dulcimer Daze and Rendezvous, West Dover, VT, Middle Aug.
Songstreet Festival of Funny Songwriters, Somerville, MA, Middle Jan.
New Women's Voices, Cambridge, MA, Late Jan.
Harvard Winter Folk Festival, Cambridge, MA, Early Mar.
Songstreet Festival of Women Songwriters, Somerville, MA, Middle Mar.
Songstreet Folk-Rock Festival, Somerville, MA, Early Apr.
Acoustic Underground Concerts and CD Release Parties, Varies, MA, Middle May
Homefolks Concert, Boston, MA, Late May
Newburyport Yankee Homecoming, Newburyport, MA, Late Jun. to Early Jul.
UpCountry Hot Air Balloon Fair, Greenfield, MA, Middle Jul.
Hyannis Seaport Festival, Hyannis, MA, Middle Aug.
Sober in the Sun Labor Day Weekend Experience, Spencer, MA, Early Sep.
Martha's Vineyard Singer-Songwriters' Retreat, Vineyard Haven, MA, Early Sep. to Middle Sep.
Acoustic Underground: Boston's National Acoustic Music Showcase, Boston, MA, Early Oct. to Early Nov.
FolkTree Jamboree, Boston, MA, Late Oct.
Phil Ochs Song Night, Cambridge, MA, Early Nov.
Blacksmith House Folk Festival/Folk Arts Conference, Cambridge, MA, Middle Nov.
Songstreet Folk-Rock Festival, Somerville, MA, Middle Nov.
Festival of Light and Song, Jamaica Plain, MA, Middle Dec.
Lowell Family First Night, Lowell, MA, Late Dec.
Women's Voices, Providence, RI, Early Mar.
Ben and Jerry's Newport Folk Festival, Newport, RI, Early Aug.
Legends of Folk Music, Westport, CT, Middle May
Honey, Hide the Banjo! It's the Folk Next Door, West Hartford, CT, Late May
Blue Sky Music Fest, Wallingford, CT, Late May
Lake Wangumbaug Folk Festival, Coventry, CT, Late Jun.
Hartland Folk Festival, East Hartland, CT, Middle Jul.
Folk Music Showcase, Westport, CT, Late Jul.
Music Fest, Danielson, CT, Late Aug.
Eli Whitney Folk Festival, New Haven, CT, Early Sep.
Apple Valley Family Folk Festival, Southington, CT, Middle Sep.

Women in Music Celebration, Colonie, NY, Middle Mar.
WXLE Acoustic Music Festival, Clifton Park, NY, Early May to Late May
Hurdy Gurdy Strings and Sings Spring Fling, Accord, NY, Middle May
Shadfest, Peekskill, NY, Middle May
GottaGetGon Folk Festival: The Pick'n and Singin' Gatherin', Ballston Spa, NY, Late May
Woodstock/New Paltz Art and Crafts Fair, New Paltz, NY, Late May
People's Music Network Summer Gathering, Pine Bush, NY, Early Jun.
One With Nature Festival, Garrison, NY, Middle Jun.
East End Music Festival, East Hampton, NY, Middle Jun.
Opus 40 Acoustic Summit: Bring It On Home, Saugerties, NY, Early Jul.
Artpark Blues and Folk Festival, Lewiston, NY, Middle Aug. to Late Aug.
Turtle Hill Music Festival, Spencerport, NY, Late Aug.
Salesian Folk Festival, New Rochelle, NY, Late Aug.
Woodstock/New Paltz Art and Crafts Fair, New Paltz, NY, Early Sep.
Petrified Sea Gardens Family Music Festival, Saratoga Springs, NY, Middle Sep.
Fast Folk Revue, Manhattan, NYC, Late Jan.
Furnald Folk Fest, Manhattan, NYC, Early Apr.
Summerfun! , Staten Island, NYC, Middle Jul.
Greenwich Village Folk Festival, Manhattan, NYC, Early Oct.
Shelter: The New York Singer-Songwriter Festival, Manhattan, NYC, Middle Oct.
Clearwater's Pumpkin Sail, Varied Sites, VAR, Early Oct. to Middle Oct.

## Traditional Folk

Down East Country Dance Festival, South Portland, ME, Middle Mar.
Downeast Dulcimer and Harp Festival, Bar Harbor, ME, Early Jul.
Common Ground Country Fair, Windsor, ME, Late Sep.
Ralph Page Legacy Weekend, Durham, NH, Early Jan.
Folk Song Society of Greater Boston Fall Getaway Weekend, Hillsboro, NH, Middle Sep.
Christmas Revels, Hanover, NH, Middle Dec.
Folk Song Society of Greater Boston's Member's Concert, Watertown, MA, Middle Feb.
Sheep Shearing Festival, Waltham, MA, Late Apr.
Blacksmith House Dulcimer Festival, Cambridge, MA, Late Apr. to Early May
Folk Festival/Flea Market and Craft Show, Braintree, MA, Late May
Midsummer Revels, Lincoln, MA, Middle Jun. to Late Dec.
Northeast Squeeze-In, Washington, MA, Middle Sep.
Folk Heritage Festival, Lexington, MA, Middle Sep.
Eisteddfod Festival of Traditional Music and Dance, North Dartmouth, MA, Late Sep.
Autumn Hills Dulcimer Festival, Great Barrington, MA, Late Sep.
Christmas Revels, Cambridge, MA, Middle Dec. to Late Dec.
Settlers' Day, Lincoln, RI, Late Sep.
Spring Folk Music Weekend, Falls Village, CT, Late May
High Ridge Folk Festival, Stamford, CT, Early Jul. to Middle Jul.
Connecticut Family Folk Festival, Hartford, CT, Late Jul. to Early Aug.
Housatonic Dulcimer Celebration, New Milford, CT, Middle Sep.
Roots and Fruits Fiddle and Dance Festival, Hartford, CT, Early Oct.
Fall Folk Music Weekend, Falls Village, CT, Middle Oct.
Old Songs Sampler Concert, Guilderland, NY, Late Jan.
Winter Folk Music Weekend, Saugerties, NY, Early Feb.
Mountain Dulcimer Music Festival, Albany, NY, Late Feb.
Adirondack Folk Night, Troy, NY, Late Mar.
Folk Music Society of Huntington Members Concert, Huntington, NY, Early May
Strawberry Festival, Beacon, NY, Early Jun.
Fiddling Celebration, Cross River, NY, Early Jul.

Northeast Dulcimer Symposium, Blue Mountain Lake, NY, Late Jun.
Matt's Matinee, Lake Placid, NY, Early Jul.
Music and The Mountain Sky/Folk Concert, Highmount, NY, Middle Jul.
Cranberry Dulcimer Gathering, Binghamton, NY, Late Jul.
Evening of Adirondack Music, Lake Placid, NY, Late Jul.
Folk Music Society of Huntington Summer Festival, Huntington, NY, Late Jul.
Thomas Homestead Festival , Savona, NY, Late Jul. to Early Aug.
Summer Folk Music Weekend, Saugerties, NY, Middle Aug. to Late Aug.
Adirondack Folk Music Festival, Schroon Lake, NY, Middle Aug. to Late Aug.
Music at The Ty Folklore Concert, Ticonderoga, NY, Late Aug.
Golden Link Folk Festival, Honeoye Falls, NY, Early Sep. to Middle Sep.
Harvest Moon Festival, Kingston, NY, Middle Sep.
Golden Harvest Festival, Baldwinsville, NY, Middle Sep.
Field, Forest and Stream, Elizabethtown, NY, Middle Sep.
Long Island Fiddle and Folk Music Festival, Stony Brook, NY, Middle Sep.
Long Island Traditional Music Association Fall Folk Weekend, Baiting Hollow, NY, Early Oct.
Applefest, Warwick, NY, Early Oct.
Mountain Music and Dance Weekend in the Adirondacks, Raquette Lake, NY, Early Oct. to
    Middle Oct.
Fox Hollow Reunion Folk Concert, Troy, NY, Middle Oct.
Halloween Dance Weekend, Ashokan, NY, Late Oct. to Early Nov.
Mohonk's Joy of Singing, New Paltz, NY, Late Nov.
Folksongs Plus, Manhattan, NYC, Middle May
New York City Clearwater Festival, Brooklyn, NYC, Late Jul.
Winter Revels, Manhattan, NYC, Early Dec.
American Banjo Fraternity's Fall Rally, Varied Sites, VAR, Middle Oct. to Late Oct.

## Fiddle and Banjo Events

Pride of Maine Fiddling Festival, Caribou, ME, Early Feb.
Pride of Maine Fiddling Festival, Machias, ME, Middle Feb.
Pride of Maine Fiddling Festival, Waldo, ME, Middle May
Fiddling Competition and Contra Dance, Damariscotta, ME, Middle Jun.
Rangeley's Old-Time Fiddlers' Contest, Rangeley, ME, Middle Jul.
East Benton Fiddlers' Convention and Contest, East Benton, ME, Late Jul.
Titcom Mountain Fiddling and Bluegrass Festival, Farmington, ME, Middle Aug.
River Tree Arts Fiddle Contest and Old Time Country Music Show, Kennebunk, ME, Early Sep.
Fiddler's Contest, Lincoln, NH, Late Jun.
Stark Old Time Fiddlers' Contest, Stark, NH, Late Jun.
Vermont Maple Festival/Fiddler's Variety Show, St. Albans, VT, Late Apr.
Crackerbarrel Fiddlers Contest, Newbury, VT, Late Jul.
Ole Time Fiddlers Contest, Hardwick, VT, Late Jul.
Banjo Contest, Craftsbury, VT, Middle Sep.
National Traditional Old Time Fiddlers' and Step Dancing Contest, Barre, VT, Late Sep.
Martha's Vineyard Agricultural Fair Fiddle Contest: A Festival of Traditional Music, Vineyard
    Haven, MA, Middle Aug. to Late Aug.
Western New England Bluegrass and Old-Time Championships and Steak Fry, Sheffield, MA,
    Late Aug.
Blandford Fair Old Time Fiddle Contest, Blandford, MA, Early Sep.
Banjo and Fiddle Contest, Lowell, MA, Middle Sep.
Olde Tyme Fiddlers Concert, Sterling, CT, Middle Apr.
Roxbury Pickin' N Fiddlin' Contest, Roxbury, CT, Middle Jul.
Morris Bluegrass Festival, Morris, CT, Middle Aug.
Spring Blossom Fiddle Jamboree, Long Lake, NY, Late Apr.

Old Time Fiddler's Contest and Jam Session, Blue Mountain Lake, NY, Early Jun.
Fiddle Weekend, Cambridge, NY, Middle Jul.
Heritage Hoedown and Empire State Fiddle Contest, Darien, NY, Middle Jul. to Late Jul.
Festival of North Country Folk Life, Massena, NY, Middle Aug.
Old-Time Fiddler's Fair, Mumford, NY, Late Aug.
Fiddlers Fling, Clayton, NY, Middle Sep.
Flaming Leaves Fiddle Jamboree, Long Lake, NY, Early Oct.

## Maritime

Festival of Traditional Sea Music, Bath, ME, Early Jun.
Maritime Music Festival, Salem, MA, Late Mar.
Lobster Fest, Mystic, CT, Late May
Sea Music Festival, Mystic, CT, Middle Jun.
Taste of History, Mystic, CT, Early Aug.
Chowderfest, Mystic, CT, Early Oct. to Middle Oct.

## Cajun and Zydeco

Loon MountainPark CajunFest, Lincoln, NH, Middle Aug.
Cajun and Zydeco Mardi Gras Ball, Cranston, RI, Middle Feb.
Mardi Gras Celebration, Woonsocket, RI, Late Feb.
Jambalaya on the River: Spring Riverboat Festival, Hartford, CT, Middle May to Late May
Different Tastes Outdoor Crawfish and Alligator Feast, Hartford, CT, Early Jun.
Mad Murphy's Cajun, Zydeco Music and Art Festival, East Haddam, CT, Middle Jun.
Louisiana Cookin' and Cajun Music Festival, Norwich, CT, Late Jun.
Stanfordville Music and Dance Festival, Stanfordville, NY, Late May
Stanfordville Music and Dance Festival, Stanfordville, NY, Late Aug.
Zydecodelic Loup Garou Bal de la Maison Mardi Gras Party, Manhattan, NYC, Late Feb.
Cajun/Zydeco Jamboree and Halloween Dance, Manhattan, NYC, Late Oct.

## Irish

Loon MountainPark IrishFest, Lincoln, NH, Early Aug.
Irish Cultural Day, Burlington, VT, Early May
Harpoon's St. Patrick's Day Bash, Boston, MA, Middle Mar.
Irish Cultural Center's Festival, North Easton, MA, Middle Jun.
Irish Festival in the Park, Tewksbury, MA, Middle Jul.
Malden Irish Festival, Malden, MA, Late Aug.
Gaelic Roots: The Music, Song and Dance of Ireland, Chestnut Hill, MA, Early Oct.
Irish Variety Show, Braintree, MA, Middle Oct.
Irish Music Festival, Boston, MA, Middle Oct.
Irish and Cape Breton Christmas Concert and Ceili, Chestnut Hill, MA, Middle Dec.
Irish Fall Festival, Lincoln, RI, Middle Sep.
Fairfield County Irish Festival, Fairfield, CT, Middle Jun.
Connecticut Irish Festival, New Haven, CT, Late Jun.
Stamford A. O. H. Feis, Stamford, CT, Middle Jul.
Greater Hartford Irish Festival, Glastonbury, CT, Late Jul.
Irish Night, Manchester, CT, Middle Aug.
St. Patrick's Day Celebrations, Elmsford, NY, Early Mar. to Middle Mar.
Watertown Goes Green Irish Festival, Watertown, NY, Middle Mar.
Irish Celebration, Westbury, NY, Middle Mar.
Emerald Weekend, Kiamesha Lake, NY, Early Apr.

Pines Number One Irish Weekend, South Fallsburg, NY, Early Apr.
Emerald Productions Getaway, Callicoon, NY, Middle Apr.
Irish Traditional Dance Festival, Mineola, NY, Middle May
Great Lawn Irish Fair, Brookville, NY, Late May
Irish Festival, East Durham, NY, Late May
Irish Festival, Hampton Bays, NY, Early Jun.
Rochester Irish Festival, Gates, NY, Early Jun. to Middle Jun.
All-Star Irish Concert and Dance, Yonkers, NY, Middle Jun.
Irish Festival, Patterson, NY, Middle Jun.
Irish Salute to the U. S. A., East Durham, NY, Early Jul.
Fleadh: Old Music of Ireland Festival, Leeds, NY, Early Jul.
Irish Festival of Chemung County, Elmira Heights, NY, Early Jul.
Irish Heritage Celebration, Hartsdale, NY, Middle Jul.
Rockland County A. O. H. Feis and Field Games, West Haverstraw, NY, Late Jul.
Irish Traditional Music Festival, North Blenheim, NY, Early Aug.
Irish Music Festival, Accord, NY, Early Aug.
International Celtic Festival, Hunter, NY, Middle Aug. to Late Aug.
Project Children Irish Festival, Endicott, NY, Late Aug.
Buffalo Irish Festival, Lancaster, NY, Late Aug.
Rockland Irish Festival, West Haverstraw, NY, Late Aug.
Leeds Irish Festival, Leeds, NY, Early Sep.
Commodore John Barry A. O. H. Irish Festival, Olean, NY, Early Sep. to Middle Sep.
A. O. H. Nassau County Board Feis and Festival, Uniondale, NY, Middle Sep.
Long Island Emerald Isle Festival, Hempstead, NY, Late Sep.
Celtic Fair, Hunter, NY, Late Sep.
Celtic Day in the Park, Staatsburg, NY, Late Sep.
Long Beach Irish Day Parade and Festival, Long Beach, NY, Early Oct.
Columbus Weekend Harvest Fair, East Durham, NY, Early Oct.
Irish Music Weekend Party of the Year, Monticello, NY, Late Oct.
Project Children Dinner Dance and Variety Show, Syracuse, NY, Late Oct.
Pines Number One Irish Weekend, South Fallsburg, NY, Middle Nov.
Buffalo Beer Fest, Buffalo, NY, Middle Nov.
Emerald Productions Getaway, Callicoon, NY, Early Dec.
Great Irish Weekend, Ellenville, NY, Early Dec. to Middle Dec.
Evening with Frank Patterson, Manhattan, NYC, Early Mar.
St. Barnabas Irish Variety Concert, Bronx, NYC, Middle Mar.
Irish-American Festival and Heritage Feis, Brooklyn, NYC, Late May
Harp and Harmony Concert, Manhattan, NYC, Early Jun.
Irish Traditional Music and Dance Festival, Bronx, NYC, Middle Jun.
Rockaway Irish Festival, Queens, NYC, Late Jul.
Gala All-Star Irish Cruise, Manhattan, NYC, Late Jul. to Early Aug.
Great Irish Fair, Brooklyn, NYC, Early Sep. to Middle Sep.
Night of Shamrocks, Queens, NYC, Middle Nov.

### Jewish

Israeli Festival, Oceanside, NY, Late May
International Jewish Arts Festival of Long Island, Commack, NY, Late May
Street Fair, Plainview, NY, Early Jun.
World of Jewish Culture, Bay Shore, NY, Early Jun.
Yiddish Heritage Celebration, Valhalla, NY, Middle Aug.
Celebration of Jewish Learning, Brighton, NY, Middle Oct.
Klezkamp, Parksville, NY, Late Dec.
Israeli Folk Dance Festival and Festival of the Arts, Manhattan, NYC, Middle Mar.

Jewish Festival of Music, Manhattan, NYC, Late Mar.
Salute to Israel Day Parade and Concert, Manhattan, NYC, Late May
Israel Expo, Manhattan, NYC, Late May
Israel Expo, Brooklyn, NYC, Early Jun.
Festival of Jewish Music, Manhattan, NYC, Early Jun.
Lower East Side Jewish Festival, Manhattan, NYC, Middle Jun.
New York All-Star Klezmer Extravaganza, Manhattan, NYC, Middle Jul.
Gateway Sukkos Festival, Brooklyn, NYC, Late Sep.
Sephardi Cultural Fair, Queens, NYC, Late Sep.
Hanukkah Arts Festival and Judaica Crafts Fair/Selected Shorts, Manhattan, NYC, Middle Oct.
Hanukkah Festival, Queens, NYC, Middle Dec.

## Native American

Native American Festival, Bar Harbor, ME, Early Jul.
Motahkmikuk Indian Day Celebration, Princeton, ME, Middle Jul. to Middle Jul.
Passamaquoddy Traditional Indian Festival, Perry, ME, Middle Aug.
Native American Appreciation Day, Cumberland, ME, Middle Sep.
Native American Show, Littleton, NH, Middle Jul.
Abenaki Festival Days, Rutland/Burlington, VT, Late Apr. to Early May
Raven Wind Pow-Wow, Evansville, VT, Middle May
Native American Abenaki Pow-Wow, Evansville, VT, Late Aug.
Papsaquoho Pow-Wow, Braintree, MA, Middle Jan.
American Indian Day at the Children's Museum, Boston, MA, Early Apr.
Native American Day at The Forum, Framingham, MA, Early Apr.
Earth Day Pow-Wow, Leominster, MA, Late Apr.
Sigonomeg Pow-Wow, Middleboro, MA, Middle May
Planting Moon Pow-Wow, Topsfield, MA, Late May
Indian Pow Wow, Charlemont, MA, Late May
Pow-Wow, Rutland, MA, Early Jun.
Native American Intertribal Festival/Cape Heritage, Mashpee, MA, Early Jun.
Wollomonuppoag Indian Council Inter-Tribal Pow Wow, Attleboro, MA, Middle Jul.
Pow-Wow, Sterling, MA, Late Jun.
Mashpee Wampanoag Powwow, Mashpee, MA, Early Jul.
Towwakeeswush Pow-Wow, Marshfield, MA, Middle Jun.
Native American Fair and Pow Wow, Grafton, MA, Late Jul.
Apsge Pow-Wow, Westford, MA, Late Jul.
American Indian Honor-the-Earth Pow Wow, Northampton, MA, Early Aug.
Native American Awareness Pow-Wow, Peabody, MA, Early Aug.
Chief Red Blanket Memorial Pow-Wow, Haverill, MA, Early Sep. to Middle Sep.
Chief Red Blanket Memorial Pow-Wow, Haverill, MA, Middle Sep.
Nipmuck Pow Wow, Oxford, MA, Middle Sep.
National Native American Heritage Day Pow-Wow, Concord, MA, Middle Nov.
Native American Days, Westerly, RI, Late May
Pequot and Narragansett Indian Nations Pow Wow, Westerly, RI, Middle Jun. to Late Jun.
Rhode Island Indian Council Pow Wow: Temple to Music, Providence, RI, Late Jul. to Early
     Aug.
American Indian Federation of Rhode Island Pow Wow, Escoheag, RI, Early Aug.
Pow Wow, Charlestown, RI, Middle Aug.
Native American Days, Westerly, RI, Early Sep.
Pow Wow, Charlestown, RI, Early Oct.
Mother of Waters, Rocky Hill, CT, Middle Jun.
Strawberry Moon Pow-Wow, Somers, CT, Late Jun.

Quinnehukqut Rendezvous and Native American Festival, Haddam, CT, Middle Aug. to Late Aug.
Connecticut River Pow-Wow, Farmington, CT, Late Aug.
Schemitzun: Feast of Green Corn, Hartford, CT, Middle Sep.
Eagle Wing Press Powwow, Watertown, CT, Late Sep.
Paucatuck Pequot Harvest Moon Powwow, North Stonington, CT, Early Oct. to Middle Oct.
Indian Pow Wow, Niagara Falls, NY, Early May
Iroquois Arts Showcase I, Howes Cave, NY, Late May
Otsiningo Pow Wow and Indian Craft Fair, Apalachin, NY, Early Jun.
Distant Drums Native American Festival, White Plains, NY, Middle Jun.
Native American Pow Wow, Bethany, NY, Middle Jun.
Calico Dancers Good Time Pow Wow, South Glens Falls, NY, Early Jul.
American Indian Heritage and Craft Festival, Albany, NY, Early Jul.
Iroquois Arts Showcase II, Howes Cave, NY, Early Jul.
Pow Wow, Barryville, NY, Early Jul.
Tuscarora Field Day and Picnic, Lewiston, NY, Early Jul.
Native American Pow Wow, East Durham, NY, Early Jul. to Middle Jul.
Keeper of the Western Door Pow-Wow, Salamanca, NY, Middle Jul.
Pow Wow, Barryville, NY, Late Jul.
Native American Weekend, Monroe, NY, Late Jul.
Native American Dance Festival, Victor, NY, Late Jul. to Early Aug.
Paumanauke Pow-Wow, Copiague, NY, Middle Aug.
Mountain Eagle Festival, Hunter, NY, Early Sep.
Shinnecock Native-American Powwow, Southampton, NY, Early Sep.
Iroquois Indian Festival, Howes Cave, NY, Late Sep.
Iroquois Indian Festival, Rhinebeck, NY, Early Sep. to Middle Sep.
Seneca Indian Fall Festival, Irving, NY, Middle Sep.
Native American Heritage Day, Castille, NY, Middle Sep.
Native American Festival, Kingston, NY, Middle Sep.
Gathering of Iroquois, Liverpool, NY, Early Oct.
Native American/Indigenous People Day Celebration, Albany, NY, Early Oct.
Best of the Best Pow-Wow/Native American Indian Arts Festival, Suffern, NY, Late Oct.
Park Slope Native American Dance Festival, Brooklyn, NYC, Middle Jan.
Thunderbird American Indian Dancers Pow Wow and Dance Concert, Manhattan, NYC, Late Jan. to Early Feb.
From Plains, Pueblos and Tundra: Native American Music, Dance and Storytelling, Manhattan, NYC, Early Apr.
Eco-Festival, Manhattan, NYC, Late Apr. to Early May
Starrett at Spring Creek Native American Pow Wow, Brooklyn, NYC, Early Jun.
Indian Summer, Manhattan, NYC, Early Jun. to Late Jun.
Gateway to the Nations Powwow, Brooklyn, NYC, Early Jul.
Native American Festival, Manhattan, NYC, Late Sep.
Smithsonian's National Museum of the American Indian Powwow, Manhattan, NYC, Middle Oct.
Giving of Thanks to the First Peoples, Manhattan, NYC, Middle Nov.
Indian Market, Manhattan, NYC, Dec. to Late Dec.

## Scottish

Maine Highland Games , Brunswick, ME, Middle Aug.
Scottish Performing Arts Weekend and Workshop, Bar Harbor, ME, Middle Oct.
New Hampshire Highland Games, Lincoln, NH, Middle Sep.
Strathspey and Reel Society of New Hampshire's Scottish Gala Concert, Concord, NH, Late Nov.
Southern Vermont Highland Games, Mount Snow, VT, Middle Jul.

North American Northumbrian Piper's Convention, North Hero, VT, Late Aug.
Quechee Scottish Festival, Quechee, VT, Late Aug.
Scottish Fiddle Rally, Somerville, MA, Middle Apr.
Massachusetts Highland Games, Waltham, MA, Late Jun.
Glasgow Lands Scottish Festival, Blandford, MA, Late Jul.
Quaboag Scottish Festival, Warren, MA, Late Jul.
Tam O'Shanter Scottish Highland Games and Festival, Easton, MA, Early Aug.
Celtic Festival at the Hatch Shell, Boston, MA, Early Sep.
Manchester Association of Pipe Bands Festival, Manchester, CT, Middle Jun.
Round Hill Scottish Games, Norwalk, CT, Early Jul.
St. Andrew's Society of Conneticut Scottish Festival, Goshen, CT, Early Oct.
Scotland Highland Festival, Scotland, CT, Early Oct.
Pines Scottish Weekend, South Fallsburg, NY, Early Mar.
Gaelic Day, Vails Gate, NY, Middle Jul.
Central New York Scottish Games and Celtic Festival, Syracuse, NY, Middle Aug.
Long Island Scottish Games, Old Westbury, NY, Late Aug.
Capital District's Scottish Games:  A Celtic Festival of the Arts, Altamont, NY, Early Sep.
Amherst Museum Scottish Festival, Amherst, NY, Middle Sep.
Pines Scottish Weekend, South Fallsburg, NY, Late Oct.

## Modern Latin

Cape Verdean Festival, Boston, MA, Early Jul.
Puerto Rican Cultural Festival, Springfield, MA, Early Jul. to Middle Jul.
Puerto Rican Festival, Boston, MA, Late Jul.
Dominican Festival, Boston, MA, Early Aug.
Cape Verdean Heritage Festival, Providence, RI, Early Jul.
Dominican Festival, Providence, RI, Late Aug.
WXCT Family Festival, New Haven, CT, Middle Jul.
Verano Explosivo Festival, West Hartford, CT, Early Aug.
Hispanic Music Festival, Buffalo, NY, Late Aug.
Hispanic Heritage Celebration, Valhalla, NY, Late Aug.
Concierto Del Amor, Manhattan, NYC, Middle Feb.
Carnaval Del Merengue, Manhattan, NYC, Late Feb.
Salsa's Soul Combination, Bronx, NYC, Early Apr.
Libro Latino Bookfest/Pathways for Youth Benefit, Bronx, NYC, Middle May
Areyto for Life:  Hispanic AIDS Forum Benefit Gala and Art Auction, Manhattan, NYC, Early
    May
Entre Familia, Bronx, NYC, Early May
Festival De Los Soneros, Manhattan, NYC, Middle May
Memorial Day Weekend Celebration Scholarship Fund Raising Dance, Manhattan, NYC, Late
    May
Pathmark Hispanic Arts Festival, Manhattan, NYC, Early Jun.
Puerto Rican Day Parade, Manhattan, NYC, Middle Jun.
Festival Playero, Bronx, NYC, Middle Jun. to Early Sep.
111th Street Boys Old Timers Day Stickball Festival, Manhattan, NYC, Early Jul.
Columbia Independence Day Celebration, Queens, NYC, Late Jul.
Columbia Te Canta, Manhattan, NYC, Late Jul.
Puerto Rican Day Parade, Bronx, NYC, Late Jul.
Nuyorican Poets Cafe Block Party, Manhattan, NYC, Middle Aug.
Salsa Fest, Brooklyn, NYC, Late Aug.
New York Salsa Festival, Manhattan, NYC, Early Sep.
Combinacion Perfecta, Manhattan, NYC, Late Oct.
Sonidos de las Americas, Varies, NYC, Late Nov. to Early Dec.

Latin Jazz U. S. A. Concert and Awards, Manhattan, NYC, Early Dec.

## Traditional Latin

Latin American Festival, Lowell, MA, Late Jun.
HAFOS: Festival Hispano-Americano de Stamford, Stamford, CT, Late Aug.
116th Street Festival in El Barrio, Manhattan, NYC, Middle Jun.
Rafael Hernandez/Sylvia Rexach Festival, Manhattan, NYC, Middle Sep.
Chili Pepper Fiesta, Brooklyn, NYC, Early Oct.
Chango Celebration, Manhattan, NYC, Early Dec.

## African American

Seacoast African-American Heritage Festival, Portsmouth, NH, Early Feb. to Late Feb.
Black History Month, Boston, MA, Early Feb. to Late Feb.
CMAC's Gala Benefit, Cambridge, MA, Middle Mar.
Race Unity Day, Boston, MA, Middle Jun.
CMAC's Boston Rhythm, Cambridge, MA, Early Nov.
CMAC's Fall Benefit, Cambridge, MA, Middle Nov.
Black Expo, New Haven, CT, Middle Mar.
Afro-Latin-Caribbean Festival, Waterbury, CT, Middle Jul.
Celebrations and Expressions of Our African American Heritage, Hempstead, NY, Early Feb.
Cultural Street Festival, Hempstead, NY, Early Jun.
Juneteenth Festival, Buffalo, NY, Middle Jun.
Jones Beach Greekfest Weekend, Babylon, NY, Late Jun.
African-American Heritage Celebration, Valhalla, NY, Late Jun.
African-American Heritage Celebration, Yonkers, NY, Middle Jul.
Multicultural Fest, Niagara Falls, NY, Middle Jul.
Empire State Black Arts and Cultural Festival, Albany, NY, Middle Jul.
Come Sunday, Albany, NY, Early Sep. to Middle Sep.
Kwanzaa Fete, Hempstead, NY, Late Dec.
Jazz and Poetry Marathon, Manhattan, NYC, Middle Feb.
Evening In Celebration of Black History Month, Brooklyn, NYC, Late Feb.
Tribute to African Diaspora Women, Manhattan, NYC, Middle May
Black Expo U. S. A., Manhattan, NYC, Middle May
Jamaica Fun Run and Family Day, Queens, NYC, Middle May
Save Our Park/WWRL Radiothon, Queens, NYC, Late May
Southeast Queens' Youth Sports and Spring Festival/Juneteenth, Queens, NYC, Middle Jun.
African Street Festival, Brooklyn, NYC, Late Jun. to Early Jul.
Martin Luther King Jr. Concert Series, Brooklyn, NYC, Middle Jul. to Late Aug.
Black Family Day, Manhattan, NYC, Late Jul.
African Caribbean Latino American Festival, Brooklyn, NYC, Late Jul.
Harlem Week/Harlem Day, Manhattan, NYC, Early Aug. to Middle Aug.
Midnight Ravers Anniversary Party, Manhattan, NYC, Late Aug.
Black Family Weekend, Manhattan, NYC, Late Aug.
African-American Day Parade, Manhattan, NYC, Middle Sep.
Northeastern Native American Association Pow Wow, Queens, NYC, Late Sep.
Kwanzaa, Queens, NYC, Early Dec.
Kwanzaa Holiday Expo, Manhattan, NYC, Middle Dec.
Black Nativity, Manhattan, NYC, Late Dec.
S. O. B.'s Kwanzaa Celebration, Manhattan, NYC, Late Dec.

## African

Pan-African Cultural Festival, Boston, MA, Late Jun.
Woodstock Beat World Percussion Concert, Woodstock, NY, Middle Jul.
Africa Mondo Showcase, Manhattan, NYC, Middle Mar.
Africa Mondo Festival, Brooklyn, NYC, Middle Jul.
Africa Mondo Festival, Manhattan, NYC, Middle Oct. to Late Oct.

## Brazilian and South American

Brazilian Festival of the Arts, Somerville, MA, Middle Feb.
Brazilian National Independence Day Street Festival, Manhattan, NYC, Early Sep.

## Reggae, Ska and Caribbean

Sugarloaf Reggae Ski Bash, Kingfield, ME, Early Apr.
Vermont Reggae Fest, Johnson, VT, Middle Jul.
Massachusetts Rock and Reggae for the Homeless, Great Barrington, MA, Middle Aug.
Caribbean Carnival, Boston, MA, Middle Aug. to Late Aug.
Reggae Festival, Washington, MA, Early Sep.
New England Reggae Festival, Escoheag, RI, Late Jul.
Reggaefests, New Haven, CT, Early Jan.
Reggae Festival, Woodbury, CT, Late Jun.
World Music Festival, Woodbury, CT, Middle Jul.
West Indian Independence Celebration Week/Hartford Mega! Weekend, Hartford, CT, Early
    Aug.
Reggae on the Hudson, Kingston, NY, Middle Jun.
Caribbean Extravaganza, Catile, NY, Middle Jul.
Carifest, Rochester, NY, Middle Aug.
Buffalo Caribbean Festival, Buffalo, NY, Middle Aug.
Bob Marley Day, Manhattan, NYC, Early Feb.
Tropical Carnival/Carnival Fete and Masquerade Jump-Up, Brooklyn, NYC, Late Feb.
Caribbean Music Awards, Manhattan, NYC, Early Mar.
West Indian Carnival Explosion, Brooklyn, NYC, Middle Mar.
Tamika Reggae Awards, Manhattan, NYC, Late Mar.
Everybody's Calypso Awards, Brooklyn, NYC, Early May
Everybody's World Calypso Monarch Competition, Brooklyn/Queens, NYC, Early May to Late
    Jul.
Mother's Day Caribbean All-Stars Festival, Varies, NYC, Early May
Oi!/Skampilation, Manhattan, NYC, Late May
Caribbean Cultural Heritage Week Festival/Caribbean Craft and Food Fair, Brooklyn, NYC, Late
    Jun.
New York Trini-Jam Fest, Brooklyn, NYC, Early Jul.
Carnival in New York, Manhattan, NYC, Early Aug.
New York Reggae Festival, Brooklyn, NYC, Middle Aug.
Caribbean-American Community Trade and Cultural Expo, Brooklyn, NYC, Middle Aug. to
    Late Aug.
West Indian-American Day Carnival and Parade, Brooklyn, NYC, Early Sep.
Peter Tosh Day, Manhattan, NYC, Middle Oct.
Calypso and Steelband "Sunshine" Music Awards, Manhattan, NYC, Late Oct.
Skavoovee, Manhattan, NYC, Late Nov.
Skarmageddon, Manhattan, NYC, Late Dec.

## Avant Garde and New Music

Gamper Festival of Contemporary Music, Brunswick, ME, Late Jul.
Bar Harbor Festival/New Composers Concert, Bar Harbor, ME, Late Jul.
Contemporary Music Festival, Concord, NH, Early May
Dartmouth Festival of New Musics, Hanover, NH, Middle May
University of Vermont Lane Series/49th Parallel Music Festival, Burlington, VT, Late Jan.
Warebrook Contemporary Music Festival, Irasburg, VT, Early Jul.
Tanglewood Festival of Contemporary Music, Lenox, MA, Late Jul. to Late Aug.
Electronic Music at Stony Brook, Stony Brook, NY, Late Feb.
Adirondack Festival of American Music, Saranac Lake, NY, Early Jul. to Late Jul.
Rushmore Festival, Woodbury, NY, Middle Jul.
Computer Music at Stony Brook, Stony Brook, NY, Late Oct.
Ear-Fest: Festival of Taped Music, Stony Brook, NY, Early Nov.
Gruppen: Chamber Music for the 21st Century, Manhattan, NYC, Early Jan. to Middle Jan.
Focus!, Manhattan, NYC, Middle Jan. to Late Jan.
Festival of 20th Century Music, Manhattan, NYC, Middle Feb. to Late Feb.
Music from Japan Festival, Manhattan, NYC, Late Feb.
Kitty Brazelton's Real Music Series, Manhattan, NYC, Late Feb. to Early Apr.
Winning Scores, Manhattan, NYC, Middle Mar.
Bang On a Can Festival, Manhattan, NYC, Middle Mar. to Early May
Roulette Concert Series/Le Salon Roulette, Manhattan, NYC, Middle Mar.
Experimental Intermedia Festival with No Fancy Name, Manhattan, NYC, Early Apr. to Late
    Apr.
International OFFestival, Manhattan, NYC, Middle Apr. to Middle Jun.
Roulette Concert Series/Roulette Mixology Festival, Manhattan, NYC, Late Apr. to Early May
Mostly Women Composers, Manhattan, NYC, Middle May to Late May
Sudden Sunsets: Highlights from the Benson AIDS Series, Manhattan, NYC, Middle Jun.
Tweed New Works Festival, Manhattan, NYC, Middle Jun. to Early Jul.
Serious Fun!, Manhattan, NYC, Early Jul. to Late Jul.
American Festival of Microtonal Music, Manhattan, NYC, Middle Sep. to Early Nov.
Next Wave Festival, Brooklyn, NYC, Late Sep. to Middle Dec.
Sonic Boom Festival of New Music, Manhattan, NYC, Early Nov. to Middle Nov.
Kitty Brazelton's Real Music Series/Music Parties, Manhattan, NYC, Early Nov. to Late Nov.
Floating Archives' Some Kind of Carnival, Manhattan, NYC, Early Nov.
Improvisations Festival, Manhattan, NYC, Late Nov. to Middle Dec.
Benson Series Benefit Concert for United AIDS Relief Effort, Manhattan, NYC, Early Dec.
Experimental Intermedia Four Country Festival, Manhattan, NYC, Early Dec. to Late Dec.
The Consortium, Varied Sites, VAR, Late Feb. to Middle Apr.
New Music Across America, Varied Sites, VAR, Early Oct.

## Cabaret

Cabaret Symposium, Waterford, CT, Middle Aug. to Late Aug.
Drama League's Black-Tie Benefit, Manhattan, NYC, Late Jan.
Women in Cabaret, Manhattan, NYC, Early Feb. to Late Feb.
Lyrics and Lyricists/Boys Night Out, Manhattan, NYC, Late Feb.
Back Stage Bistro Awards, Manhattan, NYC, Late Feb.
Century of Change/So Nice To Come Home To, Manhattan, NYC, Early Mar.
Hearts and Voices Winter Benefit Series, Manhattan, NYC, Middle Mar. to Late Apr.
Wall to Wall, Manhattan, NYC, Late Mar.
Manhattan Association of Cabarets and Clubs Awards, Manhattan, NYC, Early Apr.
Broadway's Easter Bonnet Competition: A Salute to 100 Years of Broadway, Manhattan, NYC,
    Late Apr.

Heart and Soul, Manhattan, NYC, Early May
In Celebration of Life, Manhattan, NYC, Early May
Hearts and Voices In Concert, Manhattan, NYC, Middle May
Cavalcade of Stars, Manhattan, NYC, Middle May
Lyrics and Lyricists/The New Breed, Manhattan, NYC, Middle Jun.
Grand Nights for Singing, Manhattan, NYC, Early Jul. to Middle Jul.
American Cabaret Theater Festival, Manhattan, NYC, Late Jul.
Midsummer's Night Cabaret, Manhattan, NYC, Middle Aug.
Cabaret for a Cause, Manhattan, NYC, Middle Sep. to Late Sep.
Night of Musical Magic, Manhattan, NYC, Middle Oct.
Cabaret Convention, Manhattan, NYC, Middle Oct. to Late Oct.
Songwriter's Evening, Manhattan, NYC, Late Oct.
Theater for the New City Village Haloween Costume Ball, Manhattan, NYC, Late Oct.
TeddyCare, Manhattan, NYC, Early Dec. to Late Dec.

## Drum Corps and Marching Bands

National Fife and Drum Muster, Waterbury, VT, Early Aug.
Bennington Battle Day Weekend, Bennington, VT, Middle Aug.
Boston Festival of Bands, Boston, MA, Early Jun.
Your Hometown America Parade, Pittsfield, MA, Early Jul.
Precision and Pageantry Drum and Bugle Corps Competition, Pittsfield, MA, Middle Aug.
Barnum Festival/Champions on Parade, Bridgeport, CT, Late Jun.
Deep River Ancient Fife and Drum Corps Muster and Parade, Deep River, CT, Middle Jul.
Westbrook Drum Corps Muster, Westbrook, CT, Late Aug.
Invitational Piping Championship/Memorial Military Tattoo, Ticonderoga, NY, Early Jul.
Fife and Drum Corps Muster, Ticonderoga, NY, Late Jul.
Sounds on the Susquehanna, Endicott, NY, Late Jul.
Colonial Fest, Kingston, NY, Early Aug.
Adirondack Drums, Glens Falls, NY, Early Aug.
Columbus Day Tournament of Bands, Binghamton, NY, Early Oct.
Drum Corps International World Championships, Varied Sites, VAR, Middle Aug.

## Gay and Lesbian

Vermont Lesbian Gay Bisexual Pride Day, Burlington, VT, Late Jun.
Pridefest, Boston, MA, Middle Jun.
Summer Music Festival, Amherst, NY, Late Aug.
National Gay and Lesbian Business and Consumer Expo, Manhattan, NYC, Late Apr.
Pussystock, Manhattan, NYC, Early May
Outmusic Festival, Manhattan, NYC, Early May
Lesbian and Gay Pride Committee Parade and Festival, Queens, NYC, Early Jun.
Lesbian and Gay Pride Week/PrideFest, Manhattan, NYC, Middle Jun. to Late Jun.
Lesbopalooza, Manhattan, NYC, Late Jun.
Fierce Pussy Fest, Manhattan, NYC, Late Aug.
Vulvapalooza, Manhattan, NYC, Late Sep.
Wigstock, Manhattan, NYC, Early Sep.
Gay and Lesbian American Music Awards, Manhattan, NYC, Early Oct. to Early Nov.
Outmusic Festival, Manhattan, NYC, Early Oct. to Early Nov.

### Fairs

Bangor State Fair, Bangor, ME, Late Jul. to Early Aug.
Skowhegan State Fair, Skowhegan, ME, Middle Aug.
Champlain Valley Exposition, Essex Junction, VT, Late Aug. to Early Sep.
Vermont State Fair, Rutland, VT, Early Sep. to Middle Sep.
Eastern States Exposition -- The Big E!, West Springfield, MA, Middle Sep. to Late Sep.
Washington County Fair, Richmond, RI, Middle Aug.
Connecticut Agricultural Fair, Goshen, CT, Late Jul.
Durham Agricultural Fair, Durham, CT, Late Sep.
Nassau Coliseum Fair, Uniondale, NY, Middle Jun. to Late Jun.
Orange County Fair, Middletown, NY, Late Jul.
Ulster County Fair, New Paltz, NY, Early Aug.
Cobleskill "Sunshine" Fair, Cobleskill, NY, Early Aug. to Middle Aug.
Erie County Fair, Hamburg, NY, Middle Aug. to Late Aug.
Dutchess County Fair, Rhinebeck, NY, Late Aug.
New York State Fair, Syracuse, NY, Late Aug. to Early Sep.

~     ~     ~

*"Ugly from the front,"* Old Songs Festival of Traditional Music and Dance.

# How to Order:

To order your copies of *Festival Fever: The Ultimate Guide to Musical Celebrations in the Northeast*™, please make your check or money order for $49.95 each ($74.95 each for foreign shipments) payable to *FestPress*, and mail it to:

- **FESTPRESS**
  **P. O. BOX 147**
  **GLEN RIDGE, NJ 07028**

Prices include shipping (though New Jersey adressees must add 6% sales tax, or $3.00, per copy). Orders prepaid in U. S. funds only. Please allow approximately four-to-six weeks for delivery.

Be sure to note the number of copies of *Festival Fever* you are ordering, and to include your complete name and mailing address as follows:

Salutation: Mr. \_\_\_\_ Ms. \_\_\_\_ Dr. \_\_\_\_ Rev. \_\_\_\_ Other: _____

First Name: _____

Last Name: _____

Title (if applicable): _____

Organization (if applicable): _____

Address: _____

City: _____

State: _____ Zip: _____

Country: _____

Area Code: _____ Phone: _____

Retailers, vendors, promoters, organizations, suppliers, distributors, or anyone interested in reselling *Festival Fever*: attractive terms are available for this one-of-a-kind book in high demand among interested pop-music fans and professionals. To receive a wholesale price list and order forms, please contact **FestPress** at the above address or phone (201) 743-5939.     . . . Thank you!

# How to Order:

To order your copies of *Festival Fever: The Ultimate Guide to Musical Celebrations in the Northeast*™, please make your check or money order for $49.95 each ($74.95 each for foreign shipments) payable to *FestPress*, and mail it to:

- **FESTPRESS**
  **P. O. BOX 147**
  **GLEN RIDGE, NJ 07028**

Prices include shipping (though New Jersey adressees must add 6% sales tax, or $3.00, per copy). Orders prepaid in U. S. funds only. Please allow approximately four-to-six weeks for delivery.

Be sure to note the number of copies of *Festival Fever* you are ordering, and to include your complete name and mailing address as follows:

---

Salutation: Mr. _____ Ms. _____ Dr. _____ Rev. _____ Other: _____

First Name: _____

Last Name: _____

Title (if applicable): _____

Organization (if applicable): _____

Address: _____

City: _____

State: _____ Zip: _____

Country: _____

Area Code: _____ Phone: _____

---

Retailers, vendors, promoters, organizations, suppliers, distributors, or anyone interested in reselling *Festival Fever*: attractive terms are available for this one-of-a-kind book in high demand among interested pop-music fans and professionals. To receive a wholesale price list and order forms, please contact **FestPress** at the above address or phone (201) 743-5939.   . . . Thank you!

# How to Order:

To order your copies of *Festival Fever: The Ultimate Guide to Musical Celebrations in the Northeast*™, please make your check or money order for $49.95 each ($74.95 each for foreign shipments) payable to *FestPress*, and mail it to:

- **FESTPRESS**
  **P. O. BOX 147**
  **GLEN RIDGE, NJ 07028**

Prices include shipping (though New Jersey adressees must add 6% sales tax, or $3.00, per copy). Orders prepaid in U. S. funds only. Please allow approximately four-to-six weeks for delivery.

Be sure to note the number of copies of *Festival Fever* you are ordering, and to include your complete name and mailing address as follows:

Salutation: Mr. _____ Ms. _____ Dr. _____ Rev. _____ Other: _____

First Name: _____

Last Name: _____

Title (if applicable): _____

Organization (if applicable): _____

Address: _____

City: _____

State: _____ Zip: _____

Country: _____

Area Code: _____ Phone: _____

Retailers, vendors, promoters, organizations, suppliers, distributors, or anyone interested in reselling *Festival Fever*: attractive terms are available for this one-of-a-kind book in high demand among interested pop-music fans and professionals. To receive a wholesale price list and order forms, please contact **FestPress** at the above address or phone (201) 743-5939.    . . . Thank you!